The Wiley Blackwell Handbook of the Psychology of Recruitment, Selection and Employee Retention

T0342440

The Wiley Blackwell Handbook of the Psychology of Recruitment, Selection and Employee Retention

Edited by Harold W. Goldstein, Elaine D. Pulakos,
Jonathan Passmore and Carla Semedo

WILEY Blackwell

Registered Offices
John Wiley & Sons, Inc., 111 River Street, Hoboken, NJ 07030, USA
John Wiley & Sons Ltd, The Atrium, Southern Gate, Chichester, West Sussex, PO19 8SQ, UK

Editorial Office
111 River Street, Hoboken, NJ 07030, USA

For details of our global editorial offices, customer services, and more information about Wiley products visit us at www.wiley.com.

Wiley also publishes its books in a variety of electronic formats and by print-on-demand. Some content that appears in standard print versions of this book may not be available in other formats.

Library of Congress Cataloging-in-Publication Data

Names: Goldstein, Harold William, 1965– editor. | Pulakos, Elaine Diane, 1959– editor. | Passmore, Jonathan, editor | Semedo, Carla, 1973– editor.
Title: The Wiley Blackwell handbook of the psychology of recruitment, selection and employee retention / edited by Harold W. Goldstein, Elaine D. Pulakos, Jonathan Passmore and Carla Semedo.
Description: Hoboken : Wiley, 2017. | Series: Wiley blackwell handbooks in organizational psychology | Includes bibliographical references and index.
Identifiers: LCCN 2016046164 (print) | LCCN 2016058044 (ebook) | ISBN 9781118972694 (cloth) | ISBN 9781119673644 (paperback)| ISBN 9781118972687 (pdf) | ISBN 9781118972601 (epub)
Subjects: LCSH: Employee selection. | Employee retention. | Psychology, Industrial.
Classification: LCC HF5549.5.S38 W55 2017 (print) | LCC HF5549.5.S38 (ebook) | DDC 658.3/1019–dc23
LC record available at https://lccn.loc.gov/2016046164

A catalogue record for this book is available from the British Library.

Cover Design: Wiley
Cover Image: © busypix/Gettyimages

Set in 9.5/11pt Galliard by SPi Global, Pondicherry, India

Printed and bound by CPI Group (UK) Ltd, Croydon, CR0 4YY.

10 9 8 7 6 5 4 3 2 1

Dedicated in loving memory of Irwin L. Goldstein, a luminary of our field who dedicated his life to education and taught so many so much. Most importantly he taught me what it meant to be a loving father. To paraphrase the dedication he wrote to our family in his own book so many years ago: you knew what support was and specialized in love. Thanks Dad.

Contents

Notes on Editors

Harold W. Goldstein is Professor of Industrial/Organizational Psychology at Baruch College, the City University of New York, USA. He is a recognized expert in the management of human capital with over twenty years of independent consulting experience. His research focuses on the development and implementation of staffing systems that result in hiring a talented diverse work force. His research has been published in top journals and books and has received awards for innovation and outstanding applied research contributions to the field.

Elaine D. Pulakos is CEO of PDRI and an internationally recognized contributor to the field of industrial and organizational psychology. In 2010 she received the Distinguished Professional Contributions Award from SIOP, where she has also served as President. She has published numerous articles on performance management, staffing and human resources best practices, and is the author of five books, including *Performance Management Transformation: Lessons Learned and Next Steps*.

Jonathan Passmore (Series Editor) is the Professor of Coaching and Behavioural Change at Henley Business School, University of Reading and a professor of psychology at the University of Evora, Portugal. He is a chartered psychologist, holds five degrees, and has an international reputation for his work in coaching and leadership, including being listed by Thinkers50 as one of the top 10 coaches in the world. He has published widely books on the themes of leadership, personal development and change, and served as editor for the *Association for Coaching* book series. He speaks widely at conferences across the world and has published over 100 journal papers and book chapters.

Carla Semedo is Assistant Professor in the Department of Psychology at the University of Évora, Portugal, where she leads on occupational health psychology. She also works as a consultant in the field of organizational psychology in evaluation and intervention at health services. She is responsible for teaching psychology at undergraduate, masters, and doctoral level, and for coordinating the occupational health psychology research line. She worked for more than 10 years as HR consultant, mainly in recruitment and selection.

Notes on Contributors

Juliet R. Aiken PhD   Juliet is a clinical assistant professor of industrial-organizational psychology and program director of the master's in industrial-organizational psychology at the University of Maryland. Her work focuses on employee selection, diversity in organizations and statistics/measurement. Juliet received her PhD from the University of Maryland in 2011.

Dave Bartram PhD   Dave was chief psychologist for CEB's Talent Management Labs prior to his retirement in 2016. He is a past-President of the ITC and Extraordinary Professor in the Department of Human Resource Management at the University of Pretoria. He has published widely in the area of Psychological testing in scientific research and in relation to professional issues.

Mark Batey PhD   Mark is senior lecturer in organizational-psychology and Head of Global Open Programmes at Alliance Manchester Business School at the University of Manchester. He is also academic lead of the Manchester Leadership Programme. His research interests are in creativity, innovation and leadership. He has extensive executive education and consulting experience across industries worldwide, having worked with organizations such as Bank of America, Rolls-Royce, Sony and Zurich.

Talya N. Bauer PhD   Talya is the Cameron professor of management at Portland State University. She conducts research on relationships at work throughout the employee life-cycle from recruitment to departure. She is a Fellow of SIOP, APA and APS, and is an associate editor of the *Journal of Applied Psychology*.

Brian L. Bellenger PhD   Brian received his doctoral doctorate in industrial-organizational psychology from Auburn University, Alabama and currently manages the Employment Testing Department with the Personnel Board of Jefferson County, Birmingham, Alabama. He is also a partner with Centrus Personnel Solutions, LLC. Brian has extensive experience in the field of employee selection, specifically in developing valid, non-discriminatory selection tools under legal scrutiny.

Melinda Blackman PhD   Melinda is Distinguished Professor of Psychology at California State University, Fullerton. She received her BA in psychology from Stanford University and a PhD in psychology from the University of California, Riverside. She was honoured in 2013 with the Western Psychological Association Outstanding Teaching Award.

James A. Breaugh PhD   James is a professor of management at the University of Missouri–St. Louis. He has conducted research in recruitment, selection, the work–family balance and turnover. His research contributions have resulted in his being voted a Fellow of the Society for Industrial and Organizational Psychology.

Carla Cabo-Leitão   Carla is a work and organizational psychologist, currently working as a Talent Management Expert. She has worked in headhunting, recruitment and HR development, and has completed the Management Acceleration programme at Nova School of Business and Economics. Her research interests include decent work, contributive uniqueness, cooperation and organizational recognition.

Anthony W. Caputo   Anthony is a Consultant at Mercer/Sirota, where he made many contributions to the firm's Research and Development efforts. He holds a MA in social-organizational psychology from Teachers College at Columbia University and a BA from Seton Hall University, where he serves as an adjunct professor of industrial-organizational psychology.

Jeanette N. Cleveland PhD   Jeanette is a full professor in industrial-organizational psychology at Colorado State University. Her research focuses on age and gender diversity and work–life outcomes. Her interests are in how context factors can mitigate the negative effects of stereotyping and bias and enhance work productivity and well-being.

Stephen M. Colarelli PhD   Stephen is professor of psychology at Central Michigan University. His research focuses on the intersection between evolutionary and organizational psychology. His most recent book (with Richard Arvey) is *The Biological Foundations of Organizational Behavior*.

Jan Corstjens   Jan is a PhD candidate at the Department of Personnel Management and Work and Organizational Psychology, Ghent University. He obtained his BA in cognitive psychology in 2011 and an MA in work and organizational psychology in 2012 from Maastricht University, The Netherlands. His research interests are in the field of selection and assessment.

Michael M. DeNunzio   Michael is a doctoral student in industrial-organizational psychology at the Graduate Center, City University of New York. His research focuses on work engagement, motivation and personnel selection. His research has been published in the *Encyclopedia of Industrial and Organizational Psychology* and the *Encyclopedia of the History of Psychological Theories*.

Marcus W. Dickson PhD   Marcus is a professor of industrial-organizational psychology at Wayne State University, Detroit. His research focuses on leadership, especially cross-cultural leadership, and he served as co-principal investigator on Project GLOBE. His work has been published in the *Journal of Applied Psychology, Leadership Quarterly, Advances in Global Leadership* and *AP:AIR*, among others.

Nuno Rebelo dos Santos PhD   Nuno Rebelo is a professor of work and organizational psychology at the University of Evora, Portugal. His work involves teaching PhD and MA courses, as well as executive training and development, areas where he has long experience. His research interests include ethics, leadership, cooperation, coaching in organizations and decent work.

Geeta D'Souza PhD   Geeta is an assistant professor in Human Resources & Behavioral Sciences at Narsee Monjee Institute of Management Studies, Mumbai, India. She received her PhD from Central Michigan University. Her research interests include virtual teams, selection and conflict.

Mark G. Ehrhart PhD   Mark is a professor in the Department of Psychology at San Diego State University. His current research interests include organizational climate and culture, organizational citizenship behaviour, leadership and work stress, and the application of these fields across levels of analysis, and in service and health and mental health settings.

Michael Fetzer PhD   Michael was awarded a PhD in industrial-organizational psychology, and has since gained 15 years' experience in developing and implementing talent measurement and talent management products and services. As Vice President and Managing Principal at CultureFactors, he designs and executes client engagements, focusing on organizational culture and leadership.

Jacob W. Forsman   Jacob is a senior associate at KPMG. He has experience in employee and leadership development techniques, selection and assessment methodologies, psychometric analyses, competence modelling, career paths and training evaluations. He completed his MA in industrial-organizational psychology at Minnesota State University, Mankato.

Adrian Furnham PhD   Adrian studied at the London School of Economics, where he obtained a distinction in an MSc Econ, and at Oxford University where he completed a DPhil in 1981. He subsequently earned a DSc in 1991 and DLitt in 1995. Formerly a lecturer in psychology at Pembroke College, Oxford, he has been professor of psychology at University College London since 1992.

Alexa M. Garcia   Alexa is a doctoral candidate studying industrial-organizational psychology at Portland State University. Her research spans a variety of topics, including applicant perceptions of the hiring process, diversity in the workplace, workplace aggression prevention and occupational health and safety.

Jennifer L. Geimer PhD   Jennifer is a managing research scientist at CEB. In this role she leads the development of innovative multimedia simulations. Prior to joining CEB, Jennifer directed job analyses and assessment centres and developed rich-media virtual role-play simulations. She earned her PhD in industrial-organizational psychology at Bowling Green State University, Ohio.

Angela R. Grotto PhD   Angela is the Gabriel Hauge Assistant Professor of Management at Manhattan College. She received her doctorate in industrial-organizational psychology from Baruch College & The Graduate Center, CUNY. Angela's research focuses on employee work-life management. She has published in the *American Sociological Review, Gender in Management*, and *Journal of Vocational Behavior*.

Stanley M. Gully PhD   Stanley is a professor of human resource management in the School of Labor and Employment Relations, Pennsylvania State University and a Fellow of SIOP. He has served on the editorial boards of leading journals. His research has been published in top outlets and his research interests focus on recruitment, leadership and team effectiveness, motivation, training and learning.

Paul J. Hanges PhD   Paul is a professor of industrial-organizational psychology at the University of Maryland. His work focuses on developing human resource practices (selection, promotion, training systems) and aligning organizational policies, practices and procedures to improve organizations. Paul received his PhD from the University of Akron, Ohio in 1987.

Jason L. Huang PhD   Jason is an assistant professor at the School of Human Resources and Labor Relations, Michigan State University. His research focuses on individuals' adaptation to their work experience, specifically as it relates to personality, training transfer and cultural influences. He was awarded a PhD in organizational psychology at Michigan State University.

David J. Hughes PhD   David is a lecturer in organizational psychology at the Alliance Manchester Business School at the University of Manchester. His research interests centre on individual differences in three areas: theory and measurement of individual differences; the role of individual differences in workplace performance and deviance; and individual differences in everyday and unethical financial behaviour.

Patrick K. Hyland PhD   Patrick is Director of Research & Development at Mercer/Sirota. He has over 15 years of experience in organizational research and consulting. He received his doctorate in social-organizational psychology from Teachers College, Columbia University, and his BA in English from the University of Pennsylvania.

Mary Ignagni PhD   Mary is a lecturer of psychology at Sacred Heart University, Fairfield, CT. Her research focuses on how self-identification impacts employees' experience in the workplace, intelligence testing, biculturalism and gender and diversity issues in the workplace.

Joshua A. Isaacson PhD   Joshua is a senior consultant and business development manager at PDRI, a CEB Company. In this role he leads product development and marketing initiatives and helps organizations improve their approach to hiring, employee engagement, workforce analytics, performance management, and leader development. He earned his doctorate in industrial-organizational psychology from the Florida Institute of Technology.

Eric A. Knudsen   Eric is a doctoral candidate studying industrial-organizational psychology at the Graduate Center, CUNY. His primary interests include goal-setting, technology and work–life topics. His research has been presented at annual meetings of the Society for Industrial and Organizational Psychology and the Association for Psychological Science and published in the *Encyclopedia of Industrial and Organizational Psychology*.

Stefan Krumm PhD   Stefan is a full professor of psychological assessment and personality psychology in the Department of Education and Psychology, Freie Universität Berlin. Prior to that, he was a postdoctoral researcher and worked as a business consultant specializing in personnel selection. His research interests include personnel selection methods and individual differences in basic cognitive abilities. His research has been published in the *Journal of Applied Psychology*, *Journal of Organizational Behavior* and the *European Journal of Work and Organizational Psychology*.

Maribeth Kuenzi PhD   Maribeth is an associate professor in the department of management and organizations at Southern Methodist University, Dallas. Her research focus is in organizational climate and culture, and how these affect employee behaviours, attitudes and organizational performance. She also studies ethical leadership and ethical decision making in organizations.

Claus Langfred PhD   Claus is an associate professor of management and academic director of executive MBA programmes at George Mason University, Fairfax, VA. He teaches leadership to executive students as well as to corporate and government clients. He received his PhD in organizational behaviour from Northwestern University, Evanson, IL.

Elliott C. Larson   Elliott is a doctoral candidate in industrial-organizational psychology at the Graduate Center and Baruch College, CUNY. His research interests include predicting performance in high-stakes testing and investigating the predictors of constructive and destructive reactions to envy in the workplace.

Filip Lievens PhD   Fillip is currently a full professor at Ghent University, Belgium. His research interests focus on organizational attractiveness and alternative selection procedures. He has published widely, including in the *Annual Review of Psychology*, *Journal of Applied Psychology* and *Personnel Psychology*. He has received a number of awards, including the Distinguished Early Career Award of the Society for Industrial and Organizational Psychology in 2006 and the Laureate of the Royal Flemish Academy of Sciences and Arts in 2008.

Mengqiao Liu MA   Mengqiao is a doctoral candidate of industrial-organizational psychology at Wayne State University, Detroit. Her research focuses on psychological measurement, personality in the workplace and occupational health psychology.

Jennifer McNamara   Jennifer is vice president of serious games and strategic partnerships at BreakAway Games and director of the non-profit Serious Games Showcase and Challenge, an international competition and exhibition for learning and assessment games. She holds an MEd from Pennsylvania State University and a BS in cognitive psychology from Drexel University, Philadelphia.

Jaclyn Menendez   Jaclyn is a doctoral candidate in industrial-organizational psychology at Colorado State University. Her research interests include assessment, selection and minority outreach. Her dissertation topic is on recruitment and selection strategies to increase disclosure rates among applicants with disabilities.

Neta Moye PhD   Neta is a clinical professor of management at the Robert H. Smith School of Business, University of Maryland, where she specializes in leadership development for MBA students, executives and both corporate and government clients. Previously, she was faculty director at Owen Graduate School of Management Leadership Development, Vanderbilt University.

Rose Mueller-Hanson PhD   Rose is director of the Performance Impact Solutions Group at CEB. In this role she helps organizations improve their approach to performance management and employee and leader development. She is a Fellow of the Society for Industrial and Organizational Psychology and received her PhD in industrial and organizational psychology from Colorado State University.

Ryan S. O'Leary PhD   Ryan is a Director for Talent Management Solutions at PDRI, a CEB Company where he leads teams of consultants developing human capital systems, including selection systems and simulation assessments, for public and private sector clients. He is a Fellow of the Society for Industrial and Organizational Psychology and earned his PhD in industrial-organizational psychology from Auburn University.

Justina Oliveira PhD   Justina is an assistant professor of psychology at Southern New Hampshire University, Hooksett, NH. Her research focuses on understanding the role of culture on perceptions of work and work teams, organizational survey ethics and cognitive ability testing. Her work has been published in the *Journal of Organizational Change Management* and *Industrial and Organizational Psychology: Perspectives on Science and Practice*.

Leonor Pais PhD   Leonor is a professor at the University of Coimbra, Portugal where she teaches pre-graduate and postgraduate courses in work and organizational psychology. She is the Portuguese coordinator of the European WOP-P master's course sponsored by the European Commission (Erasmus + Programme). Leonor is also supervisor of several PhD and master's theses. Her research interests include knowledge management, human resource management and decent work.

Kat Palaiou   Kat is an organizational-business psychologist specializing in the dark side of personality and its effects at work in a broad spectrum, from performance and organizational attitudes to recruitment and promotion. She is currently completing her doctoral thesis at University College, London. During her studies she has been awarded a scholarship from Onassis Foundation, New York and provided consultancy to various international firms, including M&G Investments, PHD Media, Serco and Unilever.

Jean M. Phillips PhD   Jean is a professor of human resource management in the School of Labor and Employment Relations, Penn State University. She has published in leading journals and served on the editorial boards of top journals in the field. She is a Cummings Scholar Award recipient and a Fellow of SIOP. Her research interests focus on recruitment and staffing, teams and leadership, and the processes that lead to employee and organizational success.

Matthew S. Prewett PhD   Matthew is an assistant professor of industrial-organizational psychology at Central Michigan University. His research focuses on teamwork processes and the assessment of multi-level phenomena, including team personality composition, group dynamics and team virtuality. His research has been published in *Human Performance, Computers in Human Behavior, Journal of Applied Social Psychology* and other titles in the areas of industrial-organizational psychology and human factors. He received his PhD from the University of South Florida, Tampa.

Jesús F. Salgado PhD   Jesús is a professor of work psychology and human resources at the University of Santiago de Compostela, Spain, where he received a PhD in psychology. He has published five books and more than 100 chapters and articles. He is the editor of the *Journal of Work and Organizational Psychology* and is a Fellow of the Society of Industrial and Organizational Psychology.

Charles A. Scherbaum PhD Charles is an associate professor of psychology at Baruch College, CUNY. His research focuses on personnel selection, cognitive ability testing and applied psychometrics. His research has been published in *Personnel Psychology*, *Organizational Research Methods* and the *Journal of Business and Psychology*.

Kristen M. Shockley PhD Kristen is an assistant professor of psychology at the University of Georgia. Her main area of research focuses on understanding the intersection of employees' work and family lives. Her work has been published in several journals and edited volumes.

Christine R. Smith Christine is currently a doctoral candidate in industrial-organizational psychology at the Graduate Center, CUNY. Her research includes work–life issues, person–environment fit, mentorship and diversity.

Jim Stewart PhD Jim is professor of human resource development at Coventry University. He previously held similar positions at Leeds Beckett and Nottingham Trent Universities. Jim is the author and co-editor of more than 20 books and numerous chapters and articles on all aspects of human resource development. He is executive secretary and former chair of the University Forum for Human Resource Development.

Nancy Tippins PhD Nancy has worked in the field of selection and assessment throughout her career. She is active in professional affairs and has participated in the development of standards for tests and assessments. She is the author of numerous articles and presentations on psychological testing.

Donald M. Truxillo PhD Donald is a professor in the Department of Psychology, Portland State University. His research examines applicant perceptions of the hiring process, age diversity in work organizations and occupational health and safety. He is a Fellow of SIOP, APA and APS, and serves on several journal editorial boards.

Lauren Wallace Lauren is a doctoral candidate in industrial-organizational psychology at Colorado State University. Her research focuses on selection and employment law. Recently she has studied perceptions of the employability of ex-offenders with and without knowledge of the likelihood of recidivism and the use of information from online professional networking in selection.

Kenneth P. Yusko PhD Kenneth is a professor of management and human resources in the School of Business Administration at Marymount University, and co-principal of Siena Consulting, a human capital consulting firm. Ken also serves as director of the Marymount University Big Data Institute. He earned his doctorate in industrial-organizational psychology at the University of Maryland. Ken is an expert in the design of personnel selection, development and performance management systems.

Crystal Zhang PhD Crystal is a principal lecturer of human resource management and organizational behaviour at Coventry University. Crystal is the author and co-editor of CIPD's *International Human Resource Management* and has published extensively in the area of international human resource management and human resource development. She is also a regular reviewer and track leader for the *University Forum for Human Resource Development* and EuroMed conferences.

Foreword

As I write this, the *Journal of Applied Psychology*, the flagship for the field of industrial and organizational psychology, is completing its 100th year of publication. In the first empirical article in the first issue of the journal of 1917, Lewis Terman and colleagues presented a study they labelled 'perhaps the first of its kind to be made in this, or any, country.' It involved administering a set of psychological tests to a group of job candidates and analysing whether their test scores were related to occupational attainment. Here we see the introduction of the scientific method to personnel selection. Hiring has a long history of being done subjectively, based on hunches and intuition, but Terman suggested empirically testing theories which attributes predict future job success.

For the last century the systematic evaluation of selection and other employment practices has become a central activity of the field of industrial and organizational psychology. Viewed through a modern lens, Terman's work now seems quaint and naïve. His sample included only 30 individuals; but since then we have learned much about the need for much larger samples in order to produce credible results. He studied a narrow range of tests; we have since broadened our focus to include a wide range of individual attributes relevant to work behaviour. He examined a single outcome variable, namely, salary; we have broadened our focus to encompass a wide range of work outcomes, including task performance, organizational citizenship, counterproductive work behaviour and attrition, to name just a few. Nevertheless, the animating sprit of scientific inquiry behind Terman's effort drives the field to this day.

I have spent the last 40 years or so immersed studying these issues. Along with a large number of scientist-practitioners we have built a large base of theoretical and empirical work addressing what attracts people to organizations, the attributes that contribute to individuals' effectiveness in a given organization, and what causes some to stay with the organization and others to leave. Often these are compartmentalized as different fields of study and we see free-standing works on recruitment, selection and attrition. This handbook is animated by the interrelationship among these domains, as laid out in Benjamin Schneider's seminal Attraction-Selection-Attribution framework, and thus is an integrative approach.

I had the privilege of receiving advance copies of all of the chapters. I am impressed with the breadth of coverage, the inclusion of cutting-edge topics and the thoughtful selection of contributors to represent a truly global perspective on the field. I trust you will find it as useful as I have.

Paul Sackett
University of Minnesota

Series Preface

Welcome to this seventh book in the Wiley Blackwell Industrial and Organizational Psychology series. This title focuses on recruitment, selection and retention, and builds on the previous six titles in the series on leadership and change, coaching and mentoring, training and development, health and safety, positive psychology and teams and collaborative processes

Attracting the best talent, selecting those who will fit the culture and retaining the best performers are challenges every business faces, whether it's a global, billion-dollar manufacturer or a local shop in the mall. In a competitive world, the best organizations, who aim to compete on quality, service or design, need to secure the very best in their industry. This volume examines the latest research on employee recruitment, selection and retention and provides an insight into this continuing developing area of psychological practice for researchers and science practitioners.

This volume is, however, just one of eight books in this series totalling over 2 million words on industrial and organizational psychology. We believe this series differs in four ways from other titles in the field:

First, the focus is aimed at the academic researcher and student, as opposed to the practitioner, although scholar practitioners may also find this an interesting read. The aim of this book is to offer comprehensive coverage of the main topics of inquiry within the domain, and in each of these to offer a comprehensive, critical literature review of the main topic areas. Each chapter is an attempt to gather together the key papers, book chapters and ideas, and to present these as a starting point for research in the key topics of I-O psychology. Therefore, the book aims to operate as a focused, 10,000 word starting point for any in-depth inquiry into the field.

Second, while many books take a UK/European or a US/North American approach with contributors drawn predominantly from one continent or the other, in this series we have made strenuous efforts to create an international approach. For each title in the series we have drawn contributors from across the globe and encouraged them to take an international, as opposed to national or regional, focus. Such an approach creates challenges in terms of language and spelling, but also in the way ideas and concepts are applied in each country or region. We have encouraged our contributors to highlight such differences and we encourage you as the reader to reflect on these to better understand how and why these differences have emerged and what implications there are for your research and our deeper understanding of the psychological constructs that underpin these ideas.

Third, the chapters avoid a single perspective based on the ideas of a single contributor. Instead, we have invited leading writers in the field to critically review the literature in their areas of expertise. The chapters thus offer a unique insight into the literature in each of these areas, with leading scholars sharing their interpretation of the literature in their area.

Finally, as series editor I have invited contributors and editors to donate their royalties to a charity. Given the international feel for the title we selected an international charity – The Railway Children – which supports run-away and abandoned children across the world. This means up to 10% of the cover price has been donated to charity. In this way we collectively are making a small contribution to making the world a slightly better place.

With any publication of this kind there are errors, and as editors we apologies in advance for these.

Jonathan Passmore
Series Editor, I-O Psychology

Railway Children

Railway Children supports children alone and at risk on the streets of India, East Africa and in the Unitd Kingdom. Children migrate to the streets for many reasons, but once there they experience physical and sexual abuse, exploitation, drugs and even death. We focus on early intervention, getting to the street kids before the street gets to them; where possible we reunite them with their families and communities.

In addressing the issue we work through our three-step change agenda to

- Meet the immediate needs of children on the streets – we work with local organizations to provide shelter, education or vocational training, counselling, and if possible, reintegration in family life.
- Shift perception in the local context – we work with local stakeholders to ensure that street children are not viewed as commodities to be abused and exploited, but as children in need of care and protection.
- Hold governments to account – if we are to see a long-term, sustainable change for the children with whom we work, we must influence key decision makers, ensuring that provisions for safeguarding children are made within their policies and budgets.

In 2013 we reached over 27,000 children. Of these 14,690 were in India where we reunited 2,820 with their families. In the UK we launched our research, 'Off the Radar' which revealed the experiences of over 100 of the most detached children. Many of these children received no intervention either before leaving home or once they were on the streets. We have made recommendations that include emergency refuge for under 16s and a wrap-round of other services, such as Misper schemes, local helplines, outreach and family liaison to allow children and young people to access interventions in a variety of ways.

To find out more about our work or to help us support more vulnerable children, please go to www.railwaychildren.org.uk or call 00 44 1270 757596.

Section I
Recruitment

Section I

Instrument

1

The Psychology of Employee Recruitment, Selection and Retention

Harold W. Goldstein, Elaine D. Pulakos, Jonathan Passmore and Carla Semedo

Introduction

The people make the place. With this simple, direct statement, Professor Benjamin Schneider opened his presidential address to the Society of Industrial and Organizational at the annual meeting in 1985. These words, which also served as the title of his landmark article published in *Personnel Psychology*, capture the very nature of organizations and the central role that people play in how they form, behave and perform (Schneider, 1987). In other words, an organization is a reflection of its people and the success of the organization depends on the quality of the talent employed by the organization.

At the time of his speech this was a dramatic shift in how organizations were conceptualized. Typically, organizations focused on strategy, structure and process without much consideration for the people needed to execute the strategy, fill the structure and operate the process. However, a change was occurring in which organizations recognized the importance of people in the equation and that the human resources of an organization could be conceptualized as a critical, competitive advantage for an organization. By the 1990s, organizations were placing greater emphasis on personnel, and even the language was changing as people were referred to as *human capital* – with the term 'capital' signifying something of value to the organization.

In the late 1990s a landmark study conducted by McKinsey and Company entitled *The War for Talent* focused on personnel talent as the most important corporate resource for organizations (Michaels, Hadfield-Jones & Axelrod, 2001). As noted by researchers Jermoe Rosow and John Hickey,

> most other major components of competitiveness are universally available: natural resources can be bought, capital can be borrowed, and technology can be copied. Only the people in the workforce, with their skills and commitment, and how they are organized, are left to make the difference between economic success and failure. (1994: 1)

The Wiley Blackwell Handbook of the Psychology of Recruitment, Selection and Employee Retention, First Edition. Edited by Harold W. Goldstein, Elaine D. Pulakos, Jonathan Passmore and Carla Semedo.

As organizations now place a premium on human capital, a critical question centres on how people become part of an organization. That is, what causes an organization to have the personnel talent that it has? Schneider's Attraction-Selection-Attrition (ASA) theory pinpoints three primary forces that determine the people that make up an organization. His theory describes how three interrelated, dynamic processes determine the kinds of people in an organization and consequently defines the nature of the organization and how it behaves and performs. The first force – Attraction – notes that of the total range of possible organizations that exist, individuals only select certain organizations to which they apply for employment. That is, people find organizations differentially attractive, based on numerous factors; and their perceived congruence or fit with that organization determines whether or not they apply for employment. The second force – Selection – notes that an organization determines who they want to hire for employment, based on an assessment of the characteristics and capabilities of the people who apply. That is, organizations select whom to employ based on a perceived fit between the makeup of the person and the needs of the organization. The third force – Attrition – notes that people will choose to leave an organization if they do not fit. That is, an organization will retain people who are congruent with its characteristics and makeup while people who do not mesh with the qualities of the organization will turn over. Thus, according to the model, the forces of attraction, selection and attrition greatly contribute to the people that makeup an organization.

These three forces serve as the fundamental pillars on which this book focuses, with each force aligning with a primary section of this work. The first section covering recruitment discusses how people are attracted to an organization; the next, on selection, examines how people are selected for employment by an organization; and the final section, on retention, explores how people are retained to work in an organization.

The goal of this handbook is to summarize the current psychological research and findings pertaining to these central forces of recruitment, selection and retention so that we better understand the people that make the place the way it is and impact how the organization behaves and performs. The handbook takes an international perspective by examining research that has been conducted around the world in order to provide a global view of this literature. In addition, authors representing many parts of the world have been recruited to contribute to this volume in order to provide a more diverse perspective on this area of science. While the handbook has sections to reflect the three key areas of focus – recruitment, selection and retention – it is worth noting that some chapters span multiple areas given the interrelated nature of some topics. Thus, Chapter 4 on applicant reactions is in the recruitment section but reviews literature that is also pertinent to the selection section; while Chapter 6 on ethics is in the recruitment section but also discusses issues relevant to selection and retention. All the contributors focus on providing a review of the latest theoretical and empirical research in a given area while also discussing practical applications, as would be expected given the scientist-practitioner model of this field of inquiry. We now provide an overview of the sections and summarize each chapter to give the reader an idea of what the handbook will cover.

Section 1: Recruitment

Section 1 focuses on the recruitment of people to work in an organization. Recruitment in general was an area characterized by a lighter level of scientific psychological research when compared to areas of inquiry like selection. However, as highlighted in the depth and breadth of the chapters in this handbook, the level of rigour when studying recruiting has grown over time in concert with technological advances in communicating with and tracking potential hires as well as the shift from a local to a global recruiting model. All these changes have made the area of recruiting highly dynamic in terms of psychological research, something that is captured by the wide range of chapters on the topic presented in this handbook.

In Chapter 2, James A. Breaugh leads the recruitment section of the handbook exactly where all personnel processes should begin: the job analysis. While job analysis is often the starting point when discussing the design of selection systems, Breaugh points out the importance of job analysis for gathering the critical information required for developing a strong recruitment process. Instead of focusing on typical details regarding the job analysis process, which have been covered in many volumes over the years, he pinpoints how to structure a job analysis to obtain the specific information needed for recruitment. Breaugh discusses how a typical job analysis will be deficient when it comes to gathering the information needed for recruiting and then specifies how to supplement the job analysis so it successfully yields the required information. He specifically guides the reader on how to conduct a job analysis that will answer critical questions of the recruitment process, such as whom to target and how to properly convey the recruitment message.

In Chapter 3, Jean M. Phillips and Stanley M. Gully discuss global recruiting, which aligns closely with the international perspective of this handbook. The authors focus on how talent management practices are evolving to meet the challenges of recruiting human capital for global organizations and how this area has shifted from a local to a global perspective. They discuss how to transform the basic recruiting model to tackle the global nature of organizations. This includes how to identify individuals that fit the organization's global strategic priorities as well as how to recruit individuals who will be successful in various national contexts. The authors provide an in-depth review of the literature covering a wide range of topics, including issues impacting both the internal and external sourcing of talent in a global organization and the implications of using newer techniques, such as offshoring, to place individuals in jobs.

In Chapter 4, Donald M. Truxillo, Talya N. Bauer and Alexa M. Garcia focus on candidate reactions to hiring procedures and the implications of applicants' opinions on the staffing process for the organization. As these authors note, the reactions of candidates to selection systems was initially largely neglected in the literature but as recognition emerged regarding the importance of this factor and as technological advances that foster communication between the applicant and the organization have emerged, this area of research has greatly expanded. The authors discuss core theoretical models of the impact that candidate reactions have on both the applicant and the organization. The authors also delve into the literature to explore research findings on important antecedents and outcomes of job applicant reactions to characteristics of the staffing system.

In Chapter 5, Adrian Furnham and Kat Palaiou explore the heart of the attraction process by examining the forces that impact organization and job choice. The authors summarize both the organizational characteristics and the candidates' individual differences that have been found to impact the attraction process. The authors draw from the traditional vocational job choice perspective to form a foundation for their review and then expand to newer concepts of employer branding in order to gain a fuller understanding of what attracts talent to a particular job as well as to a specific organization.

In Chapter 6, the final chapter of this section, Nuno Rebelo dos Santos and colleagues examine the role of ethics in the hiring process. The authors cover a wide range of issues which demonstrate the fundamental role that ethics plays in recruiting and selecting individuals to work in an organization. The chapter examines topics such as the use of values and their accompanying ethical dimensions in the recruitment and selection of candidates, the ethical and fair treatment of candidates applying for jobs and the ethical implications of using various types of techniques when recruiting individuals. The authors conclude by touching on the evolving complexity of these ethical issues as technology expands and changes the way we interact, the data we have access to and the differential access that various groups have to the technology.

Section 2: Selection

Section 2 focuses on selection, an area with a rich history of rigorous scientific research. People possess a wide array of characteristics and capabilities – often referred to as individual differences – which have a direct impact on their job performance in organizations. These individual differences include a large taxonomy of cognitive, interpersonal and physical competences. Organizations select the 'right' people to hire, place and promote by measuring these job-relevant individual differences.

While this area of selection has a long history, it is still evolving in exciting ways as measurement, statistical and technological advances drive the field forward. We have seen the great progress and expansion in this area of research, which is reflected in the range and number of topics covered in this section of the handbook. The first six chapters focus on well-established techniques used to assess people for selection and promotion. The techniques covered include standardized tests (intelligence, ability, personality, biodata and situational judgment tests [SJTs]), as well as more interactive, higher fidelity approaches, such as interviews and simulations. This is followed by two chapters that look at modern technological advances and their impact on selection, covering online testing and gamification approaches to assessment. Next, the section turns to new challenges in designing selection systems, such as their use for selecting individuals to regular as well as virtual teams. There is also a chapter on using selection to facilitate leadership development. The section ends by touching on diversity, a central topic in the study of selection, and includes chapters on gender findings, race, ethnicity, national culture findings and legal issues in general.

In Chapter 7, Jesús F. Salgado begins by focusing on the selection method with the longest research history: ability testing. The roots of ability testing can be found in the study of intelligence, which can be traced to the end of the nineteenth century. The author discusses the history of general and specific cognitive ability testing, covering topics that include construct definitions and structures as well as various models of intelligence. Salgado goes on to discuss validity evidence in terms of the use of ability tests in predicting job performance and furthermore touches on important topics such as validity generalization. The author examines this research by surveying a wide range of predicted outcomes, including task, non-task and training performance. Salgado also discusses the implications for subgroup differences and applicant reactions to these types of measures.

In Chapter 8, David J. Hughes and Mark Batey focus on the other side of the coin from ability testing: personality assessment. While the origin of personality assessment can be found in clinical psychology and the study of dysfunction, this chapter concentrates on identifying job-relevant facets of personality to use for predicting performance at work. Their chapter explores the validity evidence for personality assessments used in selection systems and examines research on the various structural models of personality and their efficacy for predicting in job settings. The authors delve into research on topics such as the incremental validity of personality assessments, whether broad or specific factors are more predictive and the challenges of response distortion when collecting personality data. The authors conclude by summarizing how and when personality assessments can best be used and also suggest further areas of study that can help us improve personality testing for selection systems.

In **Chapter 9, Melinda Blackman** tackles the interview which arguably has a longer history of use than either ability or personality testing, but not as long a history when it comes to scientific study. Employment interviews have long remained the most commonly used selection instrument, but have often been informal and less rigorously developed. Blackman reviews the evolution of interviewing over time and the scientific progress that has led to the development of different types of interview, procedural advances and formats of use. The author reviews the latest research on the wide range of options and approaches that can be used when interviewing so that a highly reliable and valid interview process can be put in place.

In **Chapter 10, Adrian Furnham** reviews a wide range of alternative selection instruments and screens that have been used by organizations to assess job candidates. Furnham discusses the use of these instruments in assessing an array of key outcomes, including the candidate's ability, motivation and preference for certain type of activities and roles. This chapter covers an assortment of approaches for collecting this information, including self-report, observational and personal history methodologies. The chapter discusses the many techniques that fall under these categories, such as biodata, résumés, references and even graphology. Furnham delves into the research on these techniques and compares and contrasts the findings regarding the reliability and validity of these selection methods. The chapter examines the psychological issues that impact the validity of these approaches, such as self-insight and distortion, as well as how to properly design these instruments to maximize their validity and utility in work settings.

In **Chapter 11, Jan Corstjens, Filip Lievens and Stefan Krumm** examine the literature on situational judgment tests (SJTs), a relatively new technique that focuses on providing scenarios for candidates to react to as a means of assessing their judgement and decision-making capabilities. The authors start by presenting the traditional SJT approach, which focuses on decision making in context, then segue to a new perspective which focuses on removing context in order to capture a candidate's generalized knowledge. The chapter closely examines key research on both perspectives, including findings on reliability, validity, subgroup differences and applicant reactions, and concludes by discussing future directions for research about these two perspectives.

In **Chapter 12, Ryan S. O'Leary, Jacob W. Forsman and Joshua A. Isaacson** conclude discussion of the main techniques for selection by focusing on the role of simulations in assessing talent. Simulations are assessments that measure candidates' abilities by having them perform work-relevant tasks. That is, by having candidates perform activities that resemble what they are required to do on the job, it is believed they can readily be assessed for their ability to succeed in that job. In the chapter, the authors present a taxonomy of the wide array of simulation types used in selection and go on to discuss key psychometric outcomes, including validity evidence and impact in terms of subgroup differences. The authors also tackle key underlying psychological issues, such as the influence of fidelity and the implications of construct validity when it comes to using simulations. They conclude by discussing a host of other important topics relating to simulations, including applicant reactions, cross-cultural considerations and the role of simulations in recruiting and organizational branding.

Chapter 13, by Dave Bartram and Nancy Tippins, begins an examination of the direct impact of technology on selection systems by focusing on the implications of using online testing for selecting individuals for jobs. Much as was seen in performance management with the proliferation of processes like 360-degree feedback as the technology permitted, we have seen a parallel growth in the development and implementation of online selection testing thanks to advances in technology. The authors focus on the globalization of selection systems as enabled by online tools and the implications for validity. The chapter covers the research findings for online testing as well as critical associated issues, such as the security and cheating concerns that emerge when testing candidates online.

In Chapter 14, Michael Fetzer, Jennifer McNamara and Jennifer L. Geimer discuss the exciting advances in gaming and the use of these evolving, technologically-based processes to scientifically make accurate selection decisions. The authors discuss the nature of gaming-derived assessment instruments and why such approaches are expected to yield strong validity results. They present the current findings from this field of research and discuss future directions for study. The chapter also explores the challenges faced in utilizing gaming-based selection devices. The authors go on to provide practical guidelines for successfully implementing these types of systems in work organizations.

The section next shifts to exploring how selection systems can be used to handle teams rather than individuals as the key level of analysis in work organizations. That is, with a shift in many organizations to team-based processes and structures, the next two chapters consider the implications of this shift for putting in place successful selection systems.

In Chapter 15 Mengqiao Liu, Jason L. Huang and Marcus W. Dickson specifically focus on how to assess and select individuals to teams in a manner that leads to successful team performance. To explore this topic, the authors examine the nature of teams and the individual capabilities required for effective team work. From this foundation, the chapter goes on to identify various assessment tools that can measure these capabilities for selection purposes. The chapter concludes by highlighting key areas for future research on this evolving topic.

In Chapter 16, Geeta D'Souza, Matthew S. Prewett and Stephen M. Colarelli take a different perspective on teams by focusing on the growing phenomenon of virtual teams and how selection processes can be leveraged to facilitate their success. They note how the increase in the number of virtual teams as a product of globalization and rapid improvement in communication technologies has raised the question of how to select individuals who will be successful in this novel setting. The chapter begins by defining virtual teams and exploring the nature of this context and how it differs from typical normal settings. After fully conceptualizing the context, the authors go on to extrapolate which individual capabilities are required to be successful in this setting and review a variety of selection tools that can be useful in measuring these target competencies. Their review includes discussing the strengths and limitations of these selection tools with regard to their validity when used to select for virtual teams.

In Chapter 17, Neta Moye, Rose Mueller-Hanson and Claus Langfred examine a different use of assessment and selection systems. Based on the premium placed on having successful leaders to drive organizational success, the focus of this chapter is on using assessment to foster leadership development. The authors begin by discussing how the purpose of the assessment, which in this case is development, has implications for the design of the assessment process. They explore the unique challenges of the leadership development context and provide both research-based and best practice lessons on how to implement effective leadership development systems based on assessment. In particular, the chapter comprehensively examines the key attributes of a leader that should be assessed for developmental purposes and the type of assessment instruments that can be used to measure these targeted competencies.

The final part of the selection section of the handbook focuses on diversity. With selection systems acting as an important gateway to success in work organizations, societal concerns regarding potential racial, ethnic and gender differences have greatly influenced work in the area of staffing.

In Chapter 18, Jeannette N. Cleveland, Jaclyn Melendez and Lauren Wallace focus specifically on gender differences relating to selection processes. As they note, most research shows that men and women do not substantially differ in terms of their performance at work, however differences have been observed on selection systems that have led to differential outcomes based on gender. The chapter examines the historical entry of large numbers of women into the workforce since the 1960s and the impact this has had on organizations when it comes to recruitment, selection and retention. The chapter closely examines a number of topics that have emerged from gender research, including the occupational segregation of jobs based on gender, limiting beliefs and perceptions held by both men and women that have impacted the success of women in the workplace, the uneven playing field for women found outside the workplace and the impact on women of the organizations' narrow criteria for success.

In Chapter 19, Charles A. Scherbaum and his colleagues explore the controversial finding of significant racial, ethnic and national culture differences on common selection tests and assessments. The contributors closely examine the body of research conducted in this area in order to understand the differences that have been found and, even more importantly, what possible explanations there are to account for these differences. While many chapters have been written that examine this issue, Scherbaum and his colleagues take the novel approach of systematically integrating findings regarding cultural differences with the well-known work done on racial and ethnic differences. In addition, they explore more recent explanations for these differences that challenge long-standing positions advocated by researchers in this area in order to drive our thinking forward when designing valid and fair selection systems.

In Chapter 20, Kenneth P. Yusko and colleagues conclude this section by discussing legal issues and their role and impact on the design of selection systems. The authors focus on how to design valid employee selection systems that comply with current legal hiring requirements and standards. While laws and legal guidelines are constantly changing and vary greatly around the globe, this chapter is important for understanding the critical impact that legal issues have when designing a valid and fair selection systems. The chapter initially focuses on the United States and then shifts to examine legal issues in many other parts of the world in keeping with the broader global perspective of this handbook. The authors provide both a historical review of key legal developments and events that have impacted selection system design and an examination of the professional standards that provide a foundation for building psychometrically sound and legal selection systems.

Section 3: Retention

The final section focuses on retention. This topic has been raised the most in the study of turnover in work organizations. While this section has the fewest chapters, we hope by including a focus on it here that it will spur more thinking and scientific research on retention, a topic that organizations constantly wrestle with as a practical problem that they strive to solve.

In Chapter 21, Angela R. Grotto, Patrick K. Hyland, Anthony W. Caputo and Carla Semedo focus on the general topic of employee turnover and strategies to drive retention. The authors examine the wealth of research conducted on the factors that impact retention and work to synthesize and integrate the various models and findings from this research in order to better understand the key levers that drive turnover in organizations. The chapter is a comprehensive review of the literature and contributes to a unifying framework for this important area of research so that we can gain a better understanding of the psychology that underlies employees' decisions to remain with or leave an organization.

In Chapter 22, Crystal Zhang and Jim Stewart turn to talent management systems in organizations and how they impact retention. The authors provide an overview of talent management systems and their role in promoting retention. They focus on discussing how organizations can attract and retain talent despite the strong demand for those who are highly skilled. To examine this issue in depth, the authors explore specific retention strategies, including employer branding, organizational attractiveness and talent engagement, to determine their impact on talent retention. The authors conclude by describing future trends in talent management, such as people analytics and the implications of these changes for retention of employees.

In Chapter 23, Mark G. Ehrhart and Maribeth Kuenzi discuss the organizational climate and culture and how these broad constructs impact employee retention. The authors explore the cues that employees derive from the culture and climate of their work organization and the impact these cues have on employee attitudes and behaviours that lead to turnover. The chapter begins by examining the nature of culture and climate and how these constructs on the one hand can make an organization more desirable and attractive to employees, while on the other hand can drive them to leave. The authors explore the types of cultures that drive turnover and also examine the notion of cultural fit between the employee and organization and the extent to which this leads to the desire to stay or leave. The authors also focus on the climate literature to describe findings that pertain to turnover. Their review discusses the effects of general climate as well as the impact of a variety of specific, focused climates on turnover (e.g., climate for safety, justice, service, diversity).

Finally, **in Chapter 24, Kristen M. Shockley, Christine R. Smith and Eric A. Knudsen** complete the retention section by discussing the relationship between work–life balance and employee retention. As the authors note, many organizations have come to recognize the importance of attending to employees' work–life balance and research has shown that it has become an even stronger imperative for younger generations of workers. This chapter examines research findings that link the work–life balance to retention-related outcomes. The authors discuss the role of both formal and informal work–family support policies in impacting retention and also offer practical ideas for improving the work–life culture based on research findings from the literature.

Conclusion

In conclusion, if an organization is truly a reflection of its people as posited by Schneider (1987), this makes the case for the central role that psychology plays in understanding organizational behaviour. That is, the organization behaves and performs in the way it does in part because of the people that staff it and their psychological makeup. This perspective embodies the psychological link between the people of the organization and organizational behaviour. This handbook embraces this perspective and delves into three primary forces that determine who is in an organization: recruitment, selection and retention. The handbook focuses on exploring the wealth of rigorous psychological research on these forces in order to further synthesize and integrate our knowledge in the hope that this will both inform readers and spur future research in this important and fundamental area of inquiry in the field of business and organizational psychology.

References

Michaels, E., Handfield-Jones, H., & Axelrod, B. (2001). *The War for Talent*. Boston, MA: Harvard Business School Press.

Rosow, J., & Hickey, J. (1994). *Strategic Partners For High Performance, Part 1: The Partnership Paradigm for Competitive Advantage*. Scarsdale, NY: Work in America Institute.

Schneider, B. (1987). The people make the place. *Personnel Psychology, 40*, 437–453.

2

The Contribution of Job Analysis to Recruitment

James A. Breaugh

Introduction

It is generally accepted that an organization's success depends on the quality of its work-force. Because the way an employer recruits influences the type of individuals that are hired, the importance of the recruitment process is widely recognized (Darnold & Rynes, 2013). This chapter describes how an employer attempting to fill a job opening needs to have certain types of information concerning the position (e.g., skills needed, job rewards) in order to intelligently answer three important recruitment questions: 'Whom should we target for recruitment?' 'What should we convey in a recruitment message?' and 'How can we design a recruitment website?' In many cases, not all the information needed is readily available (e.g., obtained from an existing job description). Therefore, many organizations will need to supplement the information they do possess on a job with information gathered from a job analysis conducted for recruitment purposes. In order to understand how to conduct such a job analysis and why the results of a traditional job analysis are likely to be deficient for recruitment purposes, I begin this chapter by providing an overview of the topic of job analysis. Following this, I discuss the topic of job analysis from a recruitment perspective. Next, I address each of the three recruitment questions. The chapter concludes by noting several issues that merit future research.

The Job Analysis Process

Although researchers define the term 'job analysis' slightly differently, the definition provided by Brannick, Cadle and Levine (2012) captures common usage of the term: 'job analysis refers to a broad array of activities designed to discover and document the essential nature of work' (2012, p. 119). In other words, a job analysis is a process for understanding a job (though some authors, such as Morgeson & Dierdorff, 2011, use the term

The Wiley Blackwell Handbook of the Psychology of Recruitment, Selection and Employee Retention,
First Edition. Edited by Harold W. Goldstein, Elaine D. Pulakos, Jonathan Passmore and Carla Semedo.
© 2017 John Wiley & Sons Ltd. Published 2020 by John Wiley & Sons Ltd.

'work analysis' to reflect the fact that jobs today are often less rigidly defined than in the past). The two major outcomes of a job analysis are a job description and a list of job specifications. A job description is a statement of the tasks, duties and responsibilities that a position entails. It also may provide information about the work environment (e.g., an unheated warehouse). Unlike a job description, which focuses on work activities, job specifications involve worker attributes. Job specifications describe the knowledge, skills, abilities and other characteristics (KSAOs) that an employee should possess to successfully perform a job.

Space limitations here do not allow for in-depth coverage of the topic of job analysis and readers interested in greater detail are referred to Brannick, Levine and Morgeson (2007) and Wilson, Bennett, Gibson and Alliger (2012). However, a cursory review of four key topics – uses of job analysis data, methods of data collection, sources of information and information accuracy – is necessary in order to understand how a certain type of job analysis can generate data that contribute to an effective employee recruitment process.

Employers conduct a job analysis for a variety of reasons. Three of the most common ones involve the human resource functions of employee selection, training and compensation. With regard to selecting employees, having information concerning the KSAOs that a recruit should possess is essential (Pearlman & Sanchez, 2010). In terms of training, information concerning tasks a job involves that an individual is not expected to have mastered prior to hiring is needed to develop a training programme to facilitate mastery of these tasks (Aguinas & Kraiger, 2009). Finally, information about KSAOs and working conditions derived from a job analysis can be useful for making compensation decisions, such as determining a starting salary (Gerhart & Rynes, 2003).

In terms of collecting job analysis information, Voskuijl (2005) discussed several methods. Among these are observation, an interview and a job analysis questionnaire. These methods can involve data gathering from various sources. In particular, job incumbents, their supervisors and professional job analysts, such as a personnel from a consulting firm, have been relied on to provide information (Pearlman & Sanchez, 2010). As examples of job analysis practice: 1) job incumbents may be interviewed about the tasks they are expected to do and how frequently they do them; 2) supervisors may complete a questionnaire rating the importance of job duties; and 3) job analysts may observe employees as they work in order to assess the worker attributes required to do a job and the working conditions involved. An employer also may find useful information about a job (e.g., a generic job description) is available from an organization such as the Society for Human Resource Management or O*NET Online (Morgeson & Dierdorff, 2011). To develop a thorough understanding of a job, Voskuijl (2005) advocated the use of multiple job analysis methods, with data gathered from numerous sources.

The final issue that merits attention is the accuracy of the information gathered. Regardless of how it is to be used, accurate information about the tasks required, the necessary KSAOs and working conditions is imperative. Yet it is difficult to evaluate the accuracy of job analysis data because there is no 'true score' to use as a quality standard (Voskuijl, 2005). In place of a direct assessment of information accuracy, some researchers (e.g., Dierdorff & Wilson, 2003) have used a high level of rater reliability (e.g., are the ratings of the importance of job tasks given by supervisors quite similar?) as a proxy. Other researchers (e.g., Morgeson, Delanie-Klinger, Mayfield, Ferrara & Campion, 2004) focus on biases (e.g., self–presentation, conformity) that may contaminate job analysis data and how to reduce them. Given the complexity of the topic, it must suffice to state that steps should be taken to ensure the quality of the information gathered. These steps could include: 1) conducting individual (rather than group) interviews to reduce conformity pressure; 2) observing employees doing the job over a period of time to increase the likelihood of capturing that job in full; 3) the use of several job experts to complete a job analysis questionnaire to control for idiosyncratic views of a job; and 4) having supervisors or other job experts edit job incumbent data in order to reduce the risk of exaggeration.

The use of job analysis information for recruitment purposes has received scant attention. For example, in Yu and Cable's *The Oxford Handbook of Recruitment* (2013), none of the 28 chapters focuses on job analysis. In Brannick and colleagues' (2007) book on job analysis, less than one page addresses the topic in the context of recruitment. This lack of attention is surprising given that the way a job analysis is conducted should be closely tied to how the information will be used (Sackett, Walmsley & Laczo, 2013).

As previously noted, the emphasis in most job analyses is on describing work activities (tasks) and worker attributes (skills). Information concerning both these variables is important for recruitment purposes. For example, presenting information during the recruitment process concerning work activities helps a potential applicant evaluate an advertised position (e.g., is it too physically demanding?). Providing information concerning KSAOs needed (e.g., fluency in speaking a foreign language) allows individuals to judge whether they are likely to receive a job offer.

Although information from a job analysis conducted for other purposes is useful for recruitment purposes, it is generally insufficient in terms of its breadth. For example, a typical job description provides little detail if any about the advantages of a particular job with an employer (e.g., whether the employer pays for insurance). Yet presenting information on potential advantages and disadvantages of a particular position helps an individual make an informed decision about whether to apply for a position, whether to maintain interest in it during the selection process and whether to accept a job offer if one is made.

Although space does not permit a detailed discussion of job attributes that tend to be viewed favourably or unfavourably by job applicants (Harold, Uggerslev & Kraichy, 2013 provide a good review of research from the applicant's perspective), a brief treatment of the issue of job attribute desirability is important to establish a foundation from which to address key recruitment questions, such as what information to convey in a recruitment message. With regard to the potential benefits of working in a specific job for an employer, they can be intrinsic to the job itself (e.g., performing tasks that require a variety of skills) or derived from having the job (e.g., good compensation). Two aspects of a job that applicants commonly view as important (Breaugh, 2014) involve the supervisor an applicant will report to if hired (e.g., how does the supervisor treat employees?) and the co-workers the new hire will work with (e.g., do they work cooperatively?). In addition to focusing on job-related rewards in conducting a recruitment-oriented job analysis, attention should be given to rewards that are linked to working for the employer. For example, researchers (e.g., Highhouse, Thornbury & Little, 2007) have found that an organization's reputation (e.g., its ethical standards) and culture (e.g., egalitarianism) can influence individuals' decisions about whether to apply for a job.

A recruitment-oriented job analysis should not only focus on positive outcomes linked to a job. Potential negative outcomes should also be investigated. These can be intrinsic to the job (e.g., dealing with dissatisfied customers), tied to the job (e.g., having to wear formal business attire) or tied to the employer (e.g., the organization's poor reputation). Although researching negative job-related attributes may seem unwise, with the result that some employers tone down the undesirable features of a job, in so far as the attributes are real, new employees will soon become aware of them. The view taken in this chapter is that it is better for an employer to be aware of the pros and cons of a job so that informed decisions can be made. Ideally, such an awareness may result in undesirable attributes being rectified. When this is not possible, being aware of such information may allow an organization to target individuals for recruitment who will be less adversely affected by these attributes. Alternatively, an employer may decide to be forthcoming concerning these attributes during the recruitment process so that applicants can withdraw (self-select out) from job consideration.

A final factor that should receive attention in conducting a job analysis for recruitment purposes is the community (its political climate, ethnic diversity) in which a person who accepts a job offer will live. Research on recruitment (e.g., Turban, Campion & Eyring, 1995) has shown location can have a major impact on whether a job offer is accepted. A poor fit between important community-related variables (e.g., a suitable religious community) and a new hire could result in voluntary turnover. Providing information on community-related variables during the recruitment process is particularly important if an employer is recruiting individuals unfamiliar with the location in which they will work.

The goal of most job analyses is to gather descriptive information about a job, such as the weight of objects lifted, the type of equipment used. Although descriptive information may be sufficient for some purposes, such as when designing a selection system, descriptive information alone can be limiting in designing a recruitment strategy. For example, consider informing a recruit that a position requires 'entering data on a computer eight hours a day' or 'working rotating shifts'. At a basic level, an applicant may understand the information provided. However, a 'visceral' understanding may be absent (Breaugh, 2010). In other words, descriptive information alone does not provide a sense of how one is likely to react to the conditions described (e.g., intensive computer use can result in headaches; working a rotating shift can cause digestive problems). Yet visceral reactions can have important consequences (e.g., ill-health). This being the case, an employer should consider gathering information on such reactions (Sanchez & Levine, 2012), addressed in the context of a job analysis. Two further points should be noted. First, although a job analysis may provide information about how most job incumbents interviewed react to an objective job attribute such as standing all day, this does not mean a given individual will react in the same way. Second, visceral reactions can be positive as well as negative. For example, a hospice nurse I interviewed stressed how she could not have imagined the satisfaction she would experience from her job until she was working.

In terms of methods used to gather recruitment-oriented job analysis information, the same ones discussed for other job analysis purposes should be effective. With regard to sources of recruitment information, job incumbents and supervisors can supply much of the needed information. Particular attention should be given to new employees' reports (e.g., what was there about the job that surprised them?), especially those who resigned: why did they leave? To supplement information gathered from job incumbents and supervisors, an employer could reach out to individuals it was trying to recruit but who failed to submit a job application (e.g., a person who attended a job fair), who withdrew from the applicant pool after submitting an application or who declined a job offer, in order to understand why. Other potential sources of information include people who worked in the position who have been promoted who could comment on advancement opportunity and career paths – important issues for many recruits. The web may be useful for gathering data on community variables, such as the presence of a particular religious congregation.

In this section, I have provided a general sense of the different content an employer may wish to generate from a recruitment-oriented job analysis. Of necessity, my treatment of several issues has been brief. In the sections that follow, I expand on many of the issues raised.

Whom to Target for Recruitment

The decision an employer makes concerning whom to target for recruitment (e.g., a competitor's employees, military veterans) is critical. Focusing on the wrong type of individuals can result in job applicants who lack the KSAOs necessary to do the job or who are unlikely to accept a job offer. To understand the importance of the decision made concerning the type of individuals to target, consideration of common recruitment goals is helpful.

Although an organization can have numerous goals when recruiting (e.g., developing a diverse applicant pool), the primary focus of many employers is filling a job opening with a person who will perform effectively and remain in the position for a satisfactory length of time (Breaugh, 2013b). To fulfil these two objectives, an employer needs to bring a job opening to the attention of viable prospective candidates (those with the KSAOs needed) who are likely to be attracted to the position because they want what the employer is offering.

With regard to targeting individuals who are likely to be attracted to a position, Devendorf and Highhouse (2008) are informative. They examined whether individuals were more attracted to an organization where prospective co-workers have personality characteristics similar to their own. Devendorf and Highhouse (2008) found support for a similarity–attraction relationship. In discussing their findings, they note that this relationship could be the result of individuals feeling more comfortable working with others who are similar to themselves and/or because they believe they are more likely to receive a job offer if an organization has previously hired individuals like them. In terms of position attractiveness, research supports the benefits of focusing recruitment efforts on individuals who will not need to relocate. Becker, Connolly and Slaughter (2010) found that applicants who did not have to relocate were more likely to accept a job offer. An employer also may be able to develop an applicant pool that is attracted to an opening by targeting persons who have fewer opportunities. In this regard, Barthold (2004) noted that persons with physical impairments frequently have fewer job options, as may individuals who are located in areas experiencing high rates of unemployment (Zimmerman, 2006). Rau and Adams (2013) reviewed research that shows that older workers are attracted to jobs that allow a flexible work schedule, including working part-time. If an employer can offer such hours, seniors may be a good group to target.

In terms of targeted recruitment impacting the KSAOs applicants possess, little research is available to draw on. One relevant study (Rynes, Orlitsky & Bretz, 1997) investigated how firms decide whether to recruit new college graduates or more experienced individuals. They reported that new graduates were perceived as being more willing to learn, whereas more experienced individuals were seen as having greater technical skills and a stronger work ethic.

Although only tangentially related to targeting, research examining differences among employee referrals (i.e., persons made aware of a job opening by a current employee of the hiring organization) and persons recruited by other means merits consideration. Fernandez and Weinberg (1997) found that, compared to other groups of applicants, referrals were superior for computer skills, language skills, education and work experience (important KSAOs for the job studied). These differences appear to have resulted from employee referrals being pre-screened by the employees who referred them. Yakubovich and Lup (2006) also found that employee referrals were superior in terms of KSAOs (i.e., scoring higher on objective selection measures) than individuals recruited from other sources. It is, therefore, not surprising that Castilla (2005) found employee referrals to be superior to that of new hires generated by other means. Taken as a whole, it appears that organizations should encourage their workers to publicize job openings and give preference to individuals recruited via employee referrals when making hiring decisions.

It is common for recruits to lack a good understanding of what a job opening involves (Landis, Earnest & Allen, 2013). New hires also often lack such an understanding (Breaugh, 2010) in part because employers typically exaggerate the positives of an advertised position during the recruitment process, so that new hires often have inflated job expectations. This may result in job dissatisfaction and turnover. Research suggests that appropriate targeting of groups can result in hiring individuals who have a better understanding of an advertised position. Williams, Labig and Stone (1993) found that nurses who had previously worked at a hospital reported having more knowledge about what working there involved than those lacking such experience (rehires also had a lower turnover rate). Another group that should have a better understanding of what working for an employer entails are those with relatives working there. Ryan, Horvath and Kriska (2005) found that new employees who had a family member working for a local municipality reported greater person–organizational fit compared to new hires lacking a family connection. It is likely that such fit resulted from individuals with a family connection having greater pre-hire knowledge concerning a job opening and applying or accepting a job offer only if they perceived a good fit.

In terms of recruits possessing accurate job and organizational expectations, Breaugh, Macan and Grambow (2008) presented a theoretical rationale for why targeting former employees, former interns, those with family members working for an employer, persons who had worked in jobs similar to the job vacancy and individuals who had worked for organizations similar to the hiring organization is beneficial. The fundamental argument was that members of these groups should have more accurate and richer information about a particular job given their sources of information (e.g., direct work experience, a credible family source). Such information should, in turn, help applicants from these groups make better job choice decisions and not accept a job offer for a position that is not a good fit.

In addition, recruits sometimes lack insight concerning their talents and what they want in a job. Brooks, Cornelius, Greenfeld and Joseph (1995) suggested that having an internship gave students greater insight compared to students who did not. Breaugh and colleagues' (2008) view also applies to self-insight. For example, having previously worked for an organization should result in individuals having a good sense of whether the employer represents a good fit in terms of satisfying their wants and needs. Although less impactful, having worked for a similar organization or in a similar job (e.g., one that requires working a rotating shift schedule) should help an individual evaluate whether an advertised position will satisfy what the person is looking for in a position.

The experience of RightNow Technologies (Spors, 2007) provides a good example of effectively targeting individuals. This Bozeman, Montana-based firm needed to fill a number of openings including for a software engineer. As there was an insufficient supply of local talent, RightNow placed job advertisements in major cities in the western United States. Due to the lack of response, it concluded that many people did not view Bozeman as an attractive location. Reconsidering its recruitment strategy, RightNow decided to attempt to attract former Montana residents to return home. In order to reach such individuals, it purchased a list of Montana State University alumni. This proved to be so effective that other employers in the area have started using lists of Montana State graduates to fill job openings.

The U.S. Army provides an example of a different type of targeting. Based on an analysis of its past recruitment efforts, the Army determined that it made sense to focus on recruiting at high schools in which most of the students do not go on to college

(Breaugh, 2013b) as students from such schools were more likely to enlist or re-enlist. These positive outcomes are thought to be because students from less affluent schools are more attracted to the enlistment bonus, have fewer options (i.e., relatively speaking, the Army is an attractive employer) and are more likely to understand what Army life is like as many know others, such as former classmates or siblings, who had previously enlisted.

In summary, the decision an organization makes about the type of individuals to target for recruitment is important because: it can affect the attractiveness of a position; applicants' likelihood of possessing the KSAOs needed to successfully perform the job; the accuracy of their job expectations, including a visceral understanding of the likely effects of a job on them; and how much self-insight they possess. However, it should be emphasized that these beneficial outcomes are only likely to occur if a recruitment-oriented job analysis has resulted in an organization having accurate job-related information on which to base its decision about whom to target (e.g., an organization knows that the job and organizational attributes it offers are attractive to the targeted individuals).

What to Convey in a Recruitment Message

Having decided on the type of individuals it wishes to recruit, an employer needs to design a recruitment message that is suitable for this audience. A recruitment message can be viewed from a micro- or macro-perspective. A micro-perspective considers each communication with a prospective employee (e.g., a job advertisement, comments by a recruiter) as a separate message. A macro-perspective views a recruitment message as the totality of the information exchanges an employer has with an applicant over the course of the recruitment process. In this section, I focus primarily on specific communications. However, in planning a recruitment campaign, an employer should consider whether the sum of these communications conveys its overall message.

Before discussing research on the recruitment message, four general points are noted in order to provide a context for the topic. First, it is assumed that an employer wants to provide accurate information. Failure to do so is unethical (Buckley, Fedor, Carraher, Frink & Marvin, 1997) and can result in undesirable outcomes (e.g., employee turnover). Second, the recruitment message should be tailored to the group targeted (e.g., providing information concerning the local community may be important for recruits from outside the area but unnecessary if only members of the local community are recruited). Albers (2003) addressed how to conduct an 'audience analysis'. Third, an employer should be aware that the message it sends is not always the message received. As noted by political consultant Frank Luntz (Colbert Report, 16 August 2011), 'It's not what you say; it's what they hear.' In terms of increasing the connection between a 'sent' and a 'received' message, pilot testing can be important (e.g., do message recipients truly grasp the positives and negatives of a position?). Fourth, it is not possible to present much of the theory that underlies the research discussed. Readers interested in a detailed treatment of relevant theory are referred to Breaugh (2013a).

With regard to the recruitment message, researchers have studied the effects of the amount of information communicated, its specificity, its realism and how it is framed. In terms of the amount of information, research has shown that providing more information results in: a job opening being viewed as more attractive (Allen, Maho & Otondo, 2007); the message being perceived as more credible (Allen, Van Scotter & Otondo, 2004); a greater probability of individuals applying for a job (Gatewood, Gowan & Lautenschlager, 1993); and a higher probability of a job offer being accepted (Barber & Roehling, 1993).

It is not sufficient for a recruitment message to be lengthy; the information presented should be specific (Walker & Hinojosa, 2013). Communicating more detailed information has been shown to cause more attention being paid to the recruitment message (Barber & Roehling, 1993) and to generate a higher level of interest in a job opening (Garcia, Posthuma & Quiñones, 2010). Providing specific information about the KSAOs the employer is looking for can facilitate self-selection by prospective recruits. Mason and Belt (1986) found that conveying specific information in a job advertisement about the personal attributes (e.g., education, experience) sought reduced the percentage of unqualified applicants. Stevens and Szmerekovsky (2010) also suggest that greater specificity in a recruitment message concerning the KSAOs desired – in this case, personality attributes – can facilitate self-selection, resulting in a better quality applicant pool.

The realism of the information presented in a recruitment message has received considerable attention. Much of the research has focused on the use of a realistic job preview (RJP), which involves 'the presentation by an organization of both favourable and unfavourable job-related information to job candidates' (Phillips, 1998, p. 673). Providing realistic information about a job opening during the recruitment process can have several benefits (Earnest, Allen & Landis, 2011; Phillips, 1998). For example, RJPs have been shown to: reduce the inflated job expectations that many recruits have; allow applicants who do not perceive good person–job/organizational fit to withdraw; help new employees to cope with job demands because they were forewarned of job challenges; and result in RJP recipients perceiving the hiring organization as trustworthy.

A realistic recruitment message, however, can have a drawback. Bretz and Judge (1998) found that presenting accurate but negative information about a job can result in desirable candidates withdrawing from the recruitment process. In this regard, I would argue that such withdrawal is preferable to workers quitting shortly after being hired when they discover what the job is really like. Maio and Haddock (2007) show that presenting negative information can make a message more credible. In a study dealing with 'dirty work' (e.g., sanitation workers), Ashforth, Kreiner, Clark and Fugate (2007) found that even jobs that are perceived as undesirable can be described accurately but in such a way as to make them appear less unattractive (individuals being recruited to fill unattractive jobs often have few better options and have lower expectations concerning position attractiveness).

New York City's Administration for Children's Services department provides an excellent example of an employer being realistic in a job announcement. Their ad read: 'Wanted: men and women willing to walk into strange buildings in dangerous neighborhoods, be screamed at by unhinged individuals – perhaps in a language you do not understand – and, on occasion, forcibly remove a child from the custody of a parent because the alternative could be tragic consequences' (Santora, 2008, p. B3). The ad was the result of the problems that Children's Services was having with employee turnover on the part of its new hires. In an attempt to reduce this, the department decided to convey how challenging the job of caseworker could be (steps also are being taken to improve the caseworker job).

Some researchers have examined the effects of the way in which a recruitment message is framed. Highhouse, Beadle, Gallo and Miller (1998) investigated whether describing job openings as being few in number would affect ratings of job and organizational attributes. They reported a number of scarcity effects. For example, their job opening scarcity manipulation resulted in pay being estimated as $1.70 higher than in the non-scarcity condition. This suggests that individuals may infer certain information from the wording of an ad (e.g., if an employer has several openings, it must not pay well).

A recruitment goal for some employers is generating a diverse pool of job applicants. It is not surprising then that considerable research has examined how a recruitment communication may affect applicant diversity. Some of this research provides a good example of how the framing of a recruitment message does not necessarily involve the wording. Instead, pictorial representations can be important. Avery, Hernandez and Hebl (2004) discovered that including pictures of minorities increased how attracted Latinos and Blacks were to an employer, but did not affect how attracted non-minorities were. In a related study, Avery (2003) demonstrated that pictures had a greater influence on minorities if some of the minorities in the photos were in supervisory positions. The results of these studies suggest that employers may have discouraged minorities from pursuing a job by failing to include photos of them or using pictures in which minorities were represented in lower-level jobs. Although research is lacking, the same issue may apply to females and/or older individuals.

Gaucher, Friesen and Kay (2011) also have demonstrated the effects of the framing of a recruitment message. In their first study, they analysed actual job advertisements using an established list of masculine and feminine words. They found that masculine words more commonly appeared in ads for male-dominated jobs (e.g., engineer), but feminine words were equally likely to appear in ads for male-dominated and female-dominated (e.g., nurse) jobs. Similar results were found for Gaucher and colleagues' second study, which involved job postings at a university. In their third study, students read job ads that were constructed to be masculine- or feminine-worded. For male-dominated, female-dominated and gender-neutral jobs, male and female students perceived there were fewer women within the occupations advertised with more masculine wording. In their fourth study, Gaucher and colleagues examined whether masculine wording in an ad resulted in women having less interest in a job because such wording suggested they do not belong. Masculine wording resulted in both less interest and perceptions of not belonging in the job. Gaucher and colleagues' final study replicated these results and extended them by showing that masculine wording in ads did not affect women's perceptions of their having the skill needed to perform the job. Taken as a whole, the results of these studies suggest that gendered wording is commonly found in advertisements and can result in women believing they do not belong in a job, but not because they lack the necessary skill. These results also suggest that employers who do not mean to discourage female applicants may nevertheless be doing so because of the way their advertisement is worded.

A recruitment message includes more than just written words and photographs. Spoken words should be considered a recruitment message. In this regard, research has shown that individuals respond favourably to informative recruiters (Chapman, Uggerslev, Carroll, Piasentin & Jones, 2005). Research (Boswell, Roehling, LePine & Moynihan, 2003; Rynes, Bretz & Gerhart, 1991) also has shown that poor communication on the part of a recruiter (e.g., not responding in a professional manner) can result in a job candidate withdrawing from the recruitment process.

In conclusion, three points should be stressed. First, it should be apparent that a recruitment-oriented job analysis provides essential raw material for crafting a recruitment message. Without detailed knowledge of what a job involves – its tasks, KSAOs, working conditions, job rewards – and typical employee reactions to the job – their visceral reactions to such things as repetitive tasks, a lack of co-worker interaction and/or long hours – an employer may present a 'vanilla' description of a job opening, one that results in a recruit accepting a job that is a poor fit. Second, when attempting to convey an accurate picture of an open position, three aspects – the supervisor, co-workers and advancement opportunity/career paths – should not be overlooked. With regard to the supervisor and co-workers, presenting specific information is a challenge as these people will be tied to a specific job opening. For this reason, the recruitment message concerning a supervisor or co-workers needs to be tailored to a specific job opening. Personal interactions (e.g., a face-to-face conversation with a prospective co-worker) may be necessary to convey information such as that concerning the supervisor's management style. Recruitment interaction intended to convey such content is best saved for later in the recruitment process (Breaugh, 2012). A third point to highlight is the value of an organization evaluating its communication process (Carlson & Mecham, 2013). For example, an employer might follow up with new employees to investigate whether certain aspects of a job were not addressed or were addressed in a way that failed to characterize the true state of affairs. During such data gathering an organization could seek advice on how to better convey what a position involves and how new hires can be expected to react to various aspects of the position. Failure to conduct such an evaluation may result in an organization assuming it is doing a good job of communicating during the recruitment process when it is not.

How to Design a Recruitment Website

Having decided on the type of individuals to recruit and recruitment message to convey, an employer needs to decide how to bring a job opening to the attention of targeted individuals. There are several recruitment methods an employer can use (e.g., job fairs, college placement offices, professional job boards) to publicize a job vacancy. Research (e.g., SHRM Staffing Research, 2008) has shown the use of an employer's website is among the most commonly used methods. This is not surprising as an organization's website has the potential to generate a large number of job applicants at relatively low cost, especially for organizations that are well known and have a good reputation (Dineen & Soltis, 2011). In this section, I focus on the use of an employer's website; readers interested in a broader discussion of recruitment methods are referred to Yu and Cable (2013).

Although a relatively new means of recruiting employees, considerable research on the use of websites has been conducted in the last decade. This research has involved the analysis of both actual company websites and the creation of simulated websites in which various site characteristics were manipulated. Cober, Brown and Levy's (2004) study is representative of the first type of study. They focused on the aesthetic features of a website (e.g., effective use of colour, fonts used), how easily a website was to navigate and the positivity of the information conveyed. All three factors were found to be important to potential recruits. Braddy, Meade and Kroustalis (2006) also documented the importance of corporate website design. They found that presenting information about awards the employer has won had a positive influence on impressions of the organization. This is probably due to awards being seen as reflecting the judgement of an impartial third party, which adds credibility to the information presented.

Because some research (e.g., Cable & Yu, 2006) has found that employer websites are viewed as deficient in terms of providing useful and credible information, researchers have explored ways to increase website effectiveness. Walker, Feild, Giles, Armenakis and Bernerth (2009) used a simulation study involving students to manipulate two aspects of a website: the absence/presence of employee testimonials and the richness of the media used to present a testimonial (picture with text vs. video with audio). They reported that the inclusion of employee testimonials increased the amount of time a student spent on a website, information credibility and employer attractiveness. Using a richer medium resulted in increased information credibility and employer attractiveness. Braddy, Meade, Michael and Fleenor (2009) also investigated ways to improve the effectiveness of a website for recruiting. In their study, four website attributes were manipulated – awards received, employee testimonials, pictures of employees and organizational policies – and their effect on perceptions of organizational culture examined. Braddy and colleagues concluded that all four attributes had an effect on how culture was viewed.

The use of an employer's website for recruiting can have several advantages (Breaugh, 2013b). Among these are: an employer can convey unlimited information on a wide range of job-related topics; if employee testimonials are provided and awards an employer has won are publicized, the information conveyed may have greater credibility than that conveyed by other commonly used methods; a website allows a site browser to control what information is assessed and how much time is spent reviewing it. Such control enables individuals to access the information that is of greatest importance to them; it is possible to utilize multiple media; and in many cases the cost of developing and maintaining a website is modest when compared to visiting college campuses or hiring a search firm. However, the use of a website is not without drawbacks, two of which are seemingly contradictory: generating too few or too many applicants. Too few applicants may be the result of an employer not being well known by the individuals targeted for recruitment. It also can occur if the individuals targeted for recruitment are not actively looking for a new job. In cases such as these, an employer may need to use other recruitment methods (e.g., employee referrals, radio advertisements) to attract the attention of the targeted individuals and bring them to its website. In contrast, for many employers (e.g., those with stellar reputations), a drawback of using its website to recruit is being inundated with applications, many from people who lack the attributes the employer desires.

As a possible means for dealing with the receipt of a large number of applications, Dineen, Ash and Noe (2002) and Dineen, Ling, Ash and Del Vecchio (2007) investigated the benefits of providing job applicants with information concerning person–organization fit (i.e., a score that reflected the degree of similarity between what an organization was like and what the person wanted in an employer was provided). The results of these studies demonstrated the benefits of providing fit information. For example, individuals receiving information that person–organization fit was high spent more time viewing the website, were better able to recall the information reviewed and were more attracted to the organization.

The majority of studies of websites have used students. Therefore, the results of two recent studies that did not use students merit attention. Selden and Orenstein (2011) studied the websites used by state government agencies for recruiting. Their findings are consistent with many of the results of the studies conducted with students. For example, they found that websites that were easy to navigate generated more applicants. They also reported that sites with higher-quality content (e.g., more detailed job information) received fewer applications, which they interpreted to mean that providing detailed content allowed individuals to screen themselves out if they did not perceive a good fit with the job and/or the employer. Van Hoye and Lievens (2009), in a study involving individuals visiting the website of the Belgium military, reported that receiving negative information had little effect on job attractiveness. This parallels the finding of studies conducted with students.

Most of the research on websites has focused on the main effect of variables such as the impact of including employee testimonials. However, a few researchers have investigated the possibility of interaction effects between website characteristics and site visitor attributes. In this regard, three studies conducted by Walker and colleagues are noteworthy. Walker, Feild, Giles and Bernerth (2008) examined whether website effects were contingent on a person's work and job-hunting experience. They manipulated website content (e.g., information being presented about the training provided) and characteristics (e.g., physical attractiveness of the individuals portrayed). They found that in rating organizational attractiveness less experienced individuals were more affected by peripheral website attributes, while more experienced individuals were affected by site content. Walker, Feild, Giles, Bernerth and Short (2011) were interested in whether the effects of website characteristics depended on a person's familiarity with an organization. They examined whether the technological sophistication of a website (e.g., including video testimonials from employees) had a greater impact on individuals who were less familiar with the organization. They found this to be the case and suggested that this may be due to those who are less familiar with an employer drawing inferences about unknown job and organizational characteristics from website attributes. One aspect of Walker and colleagues' (2009) study that was not discussed in reviewing this study earlier sheds light on the possible interactions between website attributes and site visitor characteristics. In this study, not only did these researchers examine the impact of including employee testimonials, they also manipulated the ratio of racial minorities to non-minorities portrayed in the testimonials (one of four, two of four or three of four). They found different results for the minority and non-minority participants in their study. As the proportion of minorities portrayed increased, minority student perceptions of information credibility and organizational attractiveness also increased, but non-minority student perceptions of both variables decreased.

Future Research

In this section, I highlight four themes that merit future research attention. Two of these – factors underlying why recruitment targeting should matter, and the use of third-party information as a way to increase the credibility of an employer's recruitment message – are directly relevant to the three recruitment questions addressed in this chapter. The other two themes – the need for more nuanced research, and for theory-driven research – transcend most recruitment topics. Readers interested in exploring a wider range of issues that experts in the field have suggested deserve future investigation (e.g., the use of social media, recruiting in different cultural contexts) are referred to Yu and Cable's (2013) edited handbook.

Although targeting particular groups for recruitment (e.g., family members of current employees, individuals who have already worked in similar jobs) may be advantageous for an employer, as previously noted there is little research to draw on. In the future, it is important for researchers to investigate whether particular types of individuals make better employees in terms of superior performance and less turnover and whether this is due to greater self-insight, more realistic job expectations, better skills or their being more receptive to job offers.

For an employer's recruitment campaign to be effective, its recruitment message in a macro-sense must be seen as credible by those targeted for recruitment. In this regard, a quick scan of a few corporate websites shows that many employers tend to emphasize the positives of working for their company with little attention given to the negatives. Providing a somewhat glossy view of a job can result in its overall recruitment message being viewed as lacking credibility. Although the use of employee testimonials and publicizing awards an employer has received can increase message credibility, third-party information can be a powerful source for buttressing the credibility of an organization's communications. One type of third-party source is a website (e.g., Vault.com, Glassdoor.com) that is not affiliated to the organization. Another third-party source is word-of-mouth information (information about an employer that is independent of its recruitment efforts). Word-of-mouth information can derive from friends, alumni of one's college or neighbours who work for the employer. Research on the use of third-party sources (e.g., Jaidi, Van Hooft & Arends, 2011; Van Hoye & Lievens, 2009) suggests the information they provide has a high level of credibility. Future research on how an employer might make use of such third-party sources is recommended.

Regardless of the recruitment issue being investigated, I would echo the theme of other writers (e.g., Dineen & Soltis, 2011). Future research needs to be more nuanced. In this regard, I have noted how researchers have only recently begun to look at how the effects of recruitment variables (e.g., the nature of the message communicated) may depend on certain characteristics (e.g., knowledge of the organization) of the individual considering a job opening. Although studies investigating interactions of recruitment variables and individual difference variables are needed, research involving interactions of different recruitment variables is also called for. For example, in an earlier paper (Breaugh, 2012), I suggested that the effects of providing a realistic job preview may be minimal if a person was referred by a current employee of the hiring firm. A study by Bäker (2015) is an example of the type of research suggested. Bäker examined the effects of stressing the need for teamwork skills as a KSAO in a job advertisement. Bäker found that including team-work skills had the intended effect of increasing the probability of potential employees with such skills applying for a position. However, she also found that emphasizing the need for teamwork skills had the unintended effect of potential employees with higher task-related skills being less likely to apply for a position. Clearly, such results need to be replicated. However, they suggest that, by highlighting the need for certain KSAOs, an employer may reduce the likelihood that it will receive applications from individuals who possess other valuable skills (this may occur when the possession of one skill is inversely related to the possession of another skill).

As Rynes, Reeves and Darnold (2013) discuss, much of the research conducted on recruitment-related topics has been somewhat atheoretical. This is disappointing given theorizing from a variety of fields, especially social psychology, has great relevance for what goes on during the recruitment process. Dunning (2007) reviewed research sug-gesting that individuals often have an inflated opinion of their abilities and why this is likely to occur. As accurate self-insight is fundamental to an individual being able to make an intelligent self-selection decision after receiving realistic information from an employer, the theoretical ideas offered by social psychology for why self-awareness may be lacking could be incorporated into future recruitment research. As another example of the potential value of incorporating ideas drawn from psychological theory into research on recruitment issues, consider attitude change (for a detailed discussion of this issue, see Breaugh, 2013a). A number of organizations attempt to change attitudes held by prospective job candidates about the desirability of working for them during the recruitment process by highlighting awards they have received, for example. Although such a strategy may be beneficial, theory on attitude change suggests three rea-sons – selective exposure, confirmation bias and biased information processing – why it might make more sense for an organization to target for recruitment individuals who already have a positive attitude to the organization or who have yet to form an opinion. Simply stated, selective attention refers to the tendency to avoid attitude-incongruent information (this has been shown to be more pronounced with more strongly held atti-tudes). Confirmation bias reflects the fact that individuals try to confirm pre-existing beliefs by seeking attitude-consistent information. In addition to the tendency to avoid attitude-discrepant information and seek attitude-supportive information, the way information is processed also contributes to attitude stability. More specifically, research has shown that individuals tend to process information in a biased way to overcome cognitive inconsistency.

Conclusion

This chapter began by focusing on the critical role that a recruitment-oriented job analysis can play in providing an employer with information needed for addressing three central recruitment questions: whom to target for recruitment; what to convey in a recruitment message; and how to design a recruitment website. Next, I reviewed research that has been conducted that is relevant to each of these issues. Following this, I highlighted some important points that merit attention from future researchers. Throughout the chapter, I cited key references that interested readers could investigate (e.g., on the timing of recruitment actions) that were beyond the scope of this chapter so that they could delve more deeply into research that has been conducted relevant to the three questions addressed.

Readers should now have an appreciation of the multitude of factors that have to be considered before beginning the recruitment process. They also should understand that subtle factors (e.g., gendered wording of a job advertisement; the type of photographs presented) can have an unintended effect on prospective job candidates. To sum up the underlying theme of this chapter: done well, the recruitment process provides an employer with a pool of job applicants who possess knowledge, skills, abilities, interests, experience, values, motivation and self-insight so that it can get maximum value from its selection system. Done poorly, the recruitment process can create a pool of applicants who are rejected by the organization's selection system, who reject job offers that are extended, who perform poorly if hired and/or are likely to leave quickly if hired.

References

Aguinas, H., & Kraiger, K. (2009). Benefits of training and development for individuals, teams, organizations, and society. *Annual Review of Psychology, 60*, 451–474.

Albers, M. J. (2003). Multidimensional audience analysis for dynamic information. *Journal of Technical Writing and Communication, 33*(3), 263–279.

Allen, D. G., Maho, R. V., & Otondo, R. F. (2007). Web-based recruitment: Effects of information, organizational brand, and attitudes toward a web site on applicant attraction. *Journal of Applied Psychology, 92*, 1696–1708.

Allen, D. G., Van Scotter, J. R., & Otondo, R. F. (2004). Recruitment communication media: Impact on prehire outcomes. *Personnel Psychology, 57*, 143–171.

Ashforth, B. E., Kreiner, G. E., Clark, M. A., & Fugate, M. (2007). Normalizing dirty work: Managerial tactics for countering occupational taint. *Academy of Management Journal, 50*, 149–174.

Avery, D. R. (2003). Reactions to diversity in recruitment advertising – Are differences black and white? *Journal of Applied Psychology, 88*, 672–679.

Avery, D. R., Hernandez, M., & Hebl, M. R. (2004). Who's watching the race? Racial salience in recruitment advertising. *Journal of Applied Social Psychology, 34*, 146–161.

Bäker, A. (2015). The downside of looking for team players in job advertisements. *Journal of Business Economics, 85*(20), 157–179.

Barber, A. E., & Roehling, M. V. (1993). Job postings and the decision to interview: A verbal protocol analysis. *Journal of Applied Psychology, 78*, 845–856.

Barthold, J. (2004, April). Waiting in the wings. *HR Magazine, 49*, 89–95.

Becker, W. J., Connolly, T., & Slaughter, J. E. (2010). The effect of job offer timing on offer acceptance, performance, and turnover. *Personnel Psychology, 63*, 223–241.

Boswell, W. R., Roehling, M. V., LePine, M. A., & Moynihan, L. M. (2003). Individual job- choice decisions and the impact of job attributes and recruitment practices: A longitudinal field study. *Human Resource Management, 42*, 23–37.

Braddy, P. W., Meade, A. W., & Kroustalis, C. M. (2006). Organizational recruitment website effects on viewers' perceptions of organizational culture. *Journal of Business and Psychology, 20*, 525–543.

Braddy, P. W., Meade, A, W., Michael, J. J., & Fleenor, J. W. (2009). Internet recruiting: Effects of website content features on viewers' perceptions of organizational culture. *International Journal of Selection and Assessment, 17*, 19–34.

Brannick, M. T., Cadle, A., & Levine, E. L. (2012). Job analysis for knowledge, skills, abilities, and other characteristics, predictor measures, and performance outcomes. *In* N. Schmitt (Ed.), *The Oxford Handbook of Personnel Assessment and Selection* (pp. 119–146). New York: Oxford University Press.

Brannick, M. T., Levine, E. L., & Morgeson, F. P. (2007). *Job and Work Analysis: Methods, Research, and Applications for Human Resource Management.* Los Angeles: Sage.

Breaugh, J. A. (2010). Improving employee retention through the use of realistic job previews. *In* R. Watkins & D. Leigh (Eds.), *Handbook of Performance Interventions* (pp. 203–220). San Francisco: Wiley-Jossey/Bass.

Breaugh, J. A. (2012). Employee recruitment: Current knowledge and suggestions for future research. *In* N. Schmitt (Ed.), *The Oxford Handbook of Personnel Assessment and Selection* (pp. 68–87). New York: Oxford University Press.

Breaugh, J. A. (2013a). Employee recruitment. *Annual Review of Psychology, 64*, 389–416.

Breaugh, J. A. (2013b). Setting recruitment objectives and recruitment strategy development. *In* K. Y. Yu & D. M. Cable (Eds.), *The Oxford Handbook of Recruitment* (pp. 361–381). New York: Oxford University Press.

Breaugh, J. A. (2014). Employee recruitment: A communication perspective. *In* V. D. Miller & M. E. Gordon (Eds.), *Meeting the Challenges of Human Resource Management: A Communication Perspective* (pp. 29–39). New York: Routledge.

Breaugh, J. A., Macan, T. H., & Grambow, D. M. (2008). Employee recruitment: Current knowledge and directions for future research. *In* G. P. Hodgkinson & J. K. Ford, (Eds.), *International Review of Industrial and Organizational Psychology* (Vol. 23, pp. 45–82). Hoboken, NJ: John Wiley & Sons.

Bretz, R. D., & Judge, T. A. (1998). Realistic job previews: A test of the adverse self-selection hypothesis. *Journal of Applied Psychology, 83*, 330–337.

Brooks, L., Cornelius, A., Greenfeld, E., & Joseph, R. (1995). The relation of career-related work or internship experiences to the development of college seniors. *Journal of Vocational Behavior, 46*, 332–349.

Buckley, M. R., Fedor, D. B., Carraher, S. M., Frink, D. D., & Marvin, D. (1997). The ethical imperative to provide recruits realistic job previews. *Journal of Managerial Psychology, 9*, 468–484.

Cable, D., & Yu, K. Y. (2006). Managing job seekers' organizational image beliefs: The role of media richness and media credibility. *Journal of Applied Psychology, 91*, 828–840.

Carlson, K. D., & Mecham, R. L. (2013). Research design in evaluating recruitment effectiveness: Past, present, and future. *In* K. Y. Yu & D. M. Cable (Eds.), *The Oxford Handbook of Recruitment* (pp. 184–214). New York: Oxford University Press.

Castilla, E. J. (2005). Social networks and employee performance in a call center. *American Journal of Sociology, 110*, 1243–1283.

Chapman, D. S., Uggerslev, K. L., Carroll, S. A., Piasentin, K. A., & Jones, D. A. (2005). Applicant attraction to organizations and job choice: A meta-analytic review of the correlates of recruiting outcomes. *Journal of Applied Psychology, 90*, 928–944.

Cober, R. T., Brown, D. J., & Levy, P. E. (2004). Form, content, and function: An evaluative methodology for corporate employment web sites. *Human Resource Management, 43*, 201–218.

Darnold, T. D., & Rynes, S. L. (2013). Recruitment and job choice research: Same as it ever was? *In* N. Schmitt & S. Highhouse. (Eds.), *Handbook of Psychology: Industrial and Organizational Psychology* (Vol. 12, pp. 104–142). Hoboken, NJ: John Wiley & Sons.

Devendorf, S. A., & Highhouse, S. (2008). Applicant–employee similarity and attraction to an employer. *Journal of Occupational and Organizational Psychology, 81*, 607–617.

Dierdorff, E. C., & Wilson, M. A. (2003). A meta-analysis of job analysis reliability. *Journal of Applied Psychology, 88*, 635–646.

Dineen, B. R., Ash, S. R., & Noe, R. A. (2002). A web of applicant attraction: Person–organization fit in the context of web-based recruitment. *Journal of Applied Psychology, 87,* 723–734.

Dineen, B. R., Ling, J., Ash, S. R., & Del Vecchio, D. (2007). Aesthetic properties and message customization: Navigating the dark side of web recruitment. *Journal of Applied Psychology, 92,* 356–372.

Dineen, B. R., & Soltis, S. M. (2011). Recruitment: A review of research and emerging directions. *In* S. Zedeck (Ed.), *APA Handbook of Industrial and Organizational Psychology* (Vol. 2, pp. 43–66). Washington, DC: American Psychological Association.

Dunning, D. (2007). Prediction: The inside view. *In* A. W. Kruglanski & E. T. Higgins (Eds.), *Social Psychology: A Handbook* (pp. 69–90). New York: Guilford Press.

Earnest, D. R., Allen, D. G., & Landis, R. S. (2011). Mechanisms linking realistic job previews with turnover: A meta-analytic path analysis. *Personnel Psychology, 64,* 865–897.

Fernandez, R. M., & Weinberg, N. (1997). Sifting and sorting: Personal contacts and hiring in a retail bank. *American Sociological Review, 62,* 883–903.

Garcia, M. F., Posthuma, R. A., & Quiñones, M. (2010). How benefit and demographic information influence employee recruiting in Mexico. *Journal of Business and Psychology, 25,* 523–531.

Gatewood, R. D., Gowan, M. A., & Lautenschlager, G. J. (1993). Corporate image, recruitment image and initial job choice decisions. *The Academy of Management Journal, 36,* 414–427.

Gaucher, D., Friesen J., & Kay, A. C. (2011). Evidence that gendered wording in job advertisements exists and sustains gender inequality. *Journal of Personality and Social Psychology, 101,* 109–128.

Gerhart, B., & Rynes, S. L. (2003). *Compensation: Theory, Evidence, and Strategic Implications.* Thousand Oaks, CA: Sage.

Harold, C., Uggerslev, K. L., & Kraichy, D. (2013). Recruitment and job choice. *In* K. Y. Yu & D. M. Cable (Eds.), *The Oxford Handbook of Employee Recruitment.* New York: Oxford University Press.

Highhouse, S., Beadle, D., Gallo, A., & Miller, L. (1998). Get 'em while they last: Effects of scarcity information in job advertisements. *Journal of Applied Social Psychology, 28,* 779–795.

Highhouse, S., Thornbury, E., & Little, I. S. (2007). Social-identity functions of attraction to organizations. *Organizational Behavior and Human Decision Processes, 103,* 134–146.

Jaidi, Y., Van Hooft, E. A., & Arends, L. R. (2011). Recruiting highly educated graduates: A study on the relationship between recruitment information sources, the theory of planned behavior, and actual job pursuit. *Human Performance, 24,* 135–157.

Landis, R. S., Earnest, D. R., & Allen, D. G. (2013). Realistic job previews: Past, present, and future. *In* K. Y. Yu & D. M. Cable (Eds.), *The Oxford Handbook of Recruitment* (pp. 423–436). New York: Oxford University Press.

Luntz, F. (2011). *Colbert Report,* 16 August.

Maio, G. R., & Haddock, G. (2007). Attitude change. *In* A. W. Kruglanski & E. T. Higgins (Eds.). *Social Psychology: Handbook of Basic Principles* (pp. 565–586). New York: Guilford Press.

Mason, N. A., & Belt, J. A. (1986). The effectiveness of specificity in recruitment advertising. *Journal of Management, 12,* 425–432.

Morgeson, F. P., Delanie-Klinger, K. A., Mayfield, M. S., Ferrara, P., & Campion, M. A. (2004). Self-presentation in job analysis: A field experiment investigating inflation in abilities, tasks, and competencies. *Journal of Applied Psychology, 89,* 674–686.

Morgeson, F. P., & Dierdorff, E. C. (2011). Work analysis: From technique to theory. *In* S. Zedeck (Ed.), *APA Handbook of Industrial and Organizational Psychology* (Vol. 2, pp. 3–41). Washington, DC: American Psychological Association.

Pearlman, K., & Sanchez, J. I. (2010). Work analysis. *In* J. L. Farr & N. T. Tippins (Eds.), *Handbook of Employee Selection* (pp. 73–94). New York: Routledge.

Phillips, J. M. (1998). Effects of realistic job previews on multiple organizational outcomes: A meta-analysis. *Academy of Management Journal, 41,* 673–690.

Rau, B. L., & Adams, G. A. (2013). Recruiting older workers: Realities and needs of the future workforce. *In* K. Y. Yu & D. M. Cable (Eds.), *The Oxford Handbook of Recruitment* (pp. 88–109). New York: Oxford University Press.

Ryan, A. M., Horvath, M., & Kriska, D. (2005). The role of recruiting informativeness and organizational perceptions in decisions to apply. *International Journal of Selection and Assessment, 4,* 235–249.

Rynes, S. L., Bretz, R. D., Jr., & Gerhart, B. (1991). The importance of recruitment in job choice: A different way of looking. *Personnel Psychology, 44,* 487–521.

Rynes, S. L., Orlitzky, M. O., & Bretz, R. D. (1997). Experienced hiring versus college recruiting: Practices and emerging trends. *Personnel Psychology, 50,* 487–521.

Rynes, S. L., Reeves, C. J., & Darnold, T. C. (2013). The history of recruitment research. *In* K. Y. Yu & D. M. Cable (Eds.), *The Oxford Handbook of Employee Recruitment* (pp. 335–360). New York: Oxford University Press.

Sackett, P. R., Walmsley, P. T., & Laczo, R. M. (2013). Job and work analysis. *In* N. Schmitt & S. Highhouse (Eds.), *Handbook of Psychology: Industrial and Organizational Psychology* (Vol. 12, pp. 61–80). Hoboken, NJ: John Wiley & Sons.

Sanchez, J. I., & Levine, E. L. (2012). The rise and fall of job analysis and the future of work analysis. *Annual Review of Psychology,* 397–425.

Santora, M. (2008). To recruit caseworkers, a dose of reality. *New York Times,* 3 March, p. B3.

Selden, S., & Orenstein, J. (2011). Government e-recruiting web sites: The influence of e-recruitment content and usability on recruiting and hiring outcomes in US state governments. *International Journal of Selection and Assessment, 19,* 31–40.

SHRM Staffing Research (2008). *Online Technologies and Their Impact on Recruitment Strategies, July–September.* Alexandria, VA: Society for Human Resource Management.

Spors, K. R. (2007). For company in remote location, ex-residents offer promising pool. *Wall Street Journal,* 4 June, p. B4.

Stevens, C. D., & Szmerekovsky, J. G. (2010). Attraction to employment advertisements: Advertisement wording and personality characteristics. *Journal of Managerial Issues, 22,* 107–126.

Turban, D. B., Campion, J. E., & Eyring, A. R. (1995). Factors related to job acceptance decisions of college recruits. *Journal of Vocational Behavior, 47,* 193–213.

Van Hoye, G., & Lievens, F. (2009). Tapping the grapevine: A closer look at word-of-mouth as a recruiting source. *Journal of Applied Psychology, 94,* 341–352.

Voskuijl, O. (2005). Job analysis: Current and future perspectives. *In* A. Evers, N. Anderson & O. Voskuijl (Eds.), *Handbook of Personnel Selection* (pp. 27–46). Malden, MA: Blackwell.

Walker, H. J., Feild, H. S., Giles, W. F., Armenakis, A. A., & Bernerth, J. B. (2009). Displaying employee testimonials on recruitment web sites: Effects of communication media, employee race, and job seeker race on organizational attraction and information credibility. *Journal of Applied Psychology, 94,* 1354–1364.

Walker, H. J., Field, H. S., Giles, W. F., & Bernerth, J. B. (2008). The interactive effects of job advertisement characteristics and applicant experience on reactions to recruitment messages. *Journal of Occupational and Organizational Psychology, 81,* 619–638.

Walker, H. J., Feild, H. S., Giles, W. F., Bernerth, J. B., & Short, J. C. (2011). So what do you think of the organization? A contextual priming explanation for recruitment web site characteristics as antecedents of job seekers' organizational image perceptions. *Organizational Behavior and Human Decision Process, 114,* 165–178.

Walker, H. J., & Hinojosa, A. (2013). Recruitment: The role of job advertisements. *In* K. Y. Yu & D. M. Cable (Eds.), *The Oxford Handbook of Recruitment* (pp. 269–283). New York: Oxford University Press.

Williams, C. R., Labig, C. E., & Stone, T. H. (1993). Recruitment sources and posthire outcomes for job applicants and new hires: A test of two hypotheses. *Journal of Applied Psychology, 42,* 163–172.

Wilson, M. A., Bennett, W., Gibson, S. G., & Alliger, G. M. (2012). *The Handbook of Work Analysis: Methods, Systems, and Science of Work Measurement in Organizations.* New York: Routledge.

Yakubovich, V., & Lup, D. (2006). Stages of the recruitment process and the referrer's performance effect. *Organizational Science, 17,* 710–723.

Yu, K. Y., & Cable, D. M. (2013). *The Oxford Handbook of Employee Recruitment.* New York: Oxford University Press.

Zimmerman, E. (2006). New strategies for police recruiters. *New York Times,* 17 September, section 10, p. 3.

3

Global Recruiting

Jean M. Phillips and Stanley M. Gully

Introduction

Global talent management strategies and activities, including recruiting, are influenced by a complex web of challenges resulting from the interaction of industry and organizational factors with institutional and cultural forces (Farndale, Paauwe, Morris, Stahl, Stiles, Trevor & Wright, 2010; Scullion & Collings, 2011). Emerging global talent management approaches have adopted more strategic, innovative and cooperative methods of finding, recruiting and developing talent (Beechler & Woodward, 2009). Because it influences the number and types of applicants ultimately available for hire, global recruiting is critical to global talent management and strategic human resource management (Gully, Phillips & Kim, 2014).

We define global recruiting as organizational activities that identify, attract, acquire or reassign sufficient numbers of successful employees, accounting for both the organization's global strategic priorities and differences in how talent should be managed in different national contexts (adapted from Scullion & Collings, 2011). Research has shown that the level of international expansion, cultural distance, required capabilities and organizational interdependence can influence the use of global talent (Bonache, Brewster, Suutari & De Saá, 2010). Additionally, economic forces such as recession can influence global talent management strategies, including the attraction of talent (Beechler & Woodward, 2009; Garavan, 2012).

This chapter focuses on reviewing global recruiting research in three main areas. After providing background information on global recruitment, we first focus on organizations' internal recruiting efforts and review the literature on expatriates, alternative international assignments and inpatriates. Second, we review research on external recruiting, including the recruitment of self-initiated expatriates, host country nationals and skilled migrants who are willing to relocate globally. Research on sourcing or identifying high potential talent, desired characteristics to target and external recruiting strategies for attracting

The Wiley Blackwell Handbook of the Psychology of Recruitment, Selection and Employee Retention,
First Edition. Edited by Harold W. Goldstein, Elaine D. Pulakos, Jonathan Passmore and Carla Semedo.
© 2017 John Wiley & Sons Ltd. Published 2020 by John Wiley & Sons Ltd.

internationally mobile talent, is considered. Third, we review the literature on recruiting talent by globally relocating the jobs to be filled to be closer to the targeted recruits, or offshoring. Offshoring has raised many practical as well as ethical issues which have received both research and popular press attention. We conclude with a discussion of opportunities for future research.

Global Recruiting

More than 100,000 parent transnational corporations (TNCs) and nearly 900,000 foreign affiliates are estimated to exist around the world (UNCTAD, 2011). In 2013, these TNCs and affiliates globally accounted for more than $34.5 trillion in sales and $7.7 trillion in exports (UNCTAD, 2014a). Additionally, there were over 8,600 cross-border mergers and acquisitions and nearly 14,000 greenfield projects resulting from foreign direct investment across a wide range of industries (UNCTAD, 2014b, 2014c). As a result, organizations are conducting an increasing proportion of their operations in a global context, resulting in increased pressure to address global recruitment needs (Phillips, Gully, McCarthy, Castellano & Kim, 2014). Because the implementation of global strategies can be constrained by global talent shortages (Collings, Scullion & Dowling, 2009), TNCs must attend to global recruitment and selection practices to ensure a sufficient supply of quality talent is available (Tahvanainen, Welch & Worm, 2005).

Millar and Salt (2006) highlight a number of factors that have increased demand for new forms of international mobility, including the need for skilled expatriates to help build new international markets (Findlay, Li, Jowett & Skeldon, 1996) and temporary and short-term access to specialized talent to assist the execution of overseas projects (Minbaeva & Michailova, 2004; Hocking, Brown & Harzing, 2004). Dickmann and Doherty (2010) also note that organizations use international assignments to fill skills gaps, launch new initiatives, transfer technology or knowledge, establish managerial control, build culture and create expertise.

Manpower's 2012 Talent Shortage Survey of 40,000 employers in 41 countries found that 34% of employers globally experience difficulties filling job openings (Manpower, 2012). Demographic trends have created labour supply declines in some countries, a worldwide shortage of globally competent managerial talent and an increasing recognition that acquiring sufficient quantities of successful talent for key organizational roles now and in the future requires a global perspective and strategy (Farndale, Scullion & Sparrow, 2010; Scullion & Collings, 2011; Scullion, Collings & Caligiuri, 2010). These challenges have increased interest in better understanding the global acquisition and management of talent (Björkman & Lervik, 2007; Boudreau & Ramstad, 2007; Taylor, 2005).

As summarized by Sparrow (2007), global recruiting includes a variety of fragmented groups, including permanent global managers (Suutari, 2003); contract expatriates (Baruch & Altman, 2002); assignees on short- or intermediate-term foreign postings (Mayerhofer, Hartmann & Herbert, 2004; Morley & Heraty, 2004); international commuters (Economist, 2006; Shaffer, Kraimer, Chen & Bolino, 2012); employees on long-term business trips (Mayerhofer, Hartmann, Michelitsch-Riedl & Kollinger, 2004); international transferees who move from one subsidiary to another (Millar & Salt, 2006); global expatriate managers who return to their host country (Thite, Srinivasan, Harvey & Valk, 2009); virtual international employees assigned to cross-border project teams (Janssens & Brett, 2006); skilled individuals working in geographically remote centres of excellence serving global operations (Sparrow, 2005); self-initiated movers who live in a third country but are willing to work for a multinational (Tharenou, 2013); host country nationals

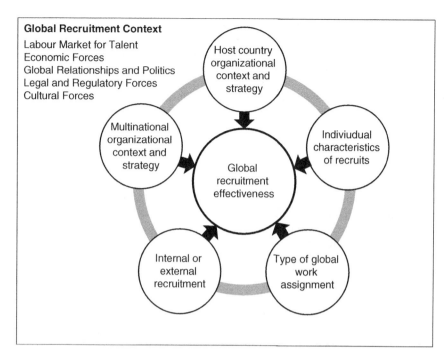

Figure 3.1 Factors influencing global recruitment effectiveness.

wanting to work for global multinational organizations (Froese, Vo & Garrett, 2010); and immigrants attracted to a national labour market (Millar & Salt, 2006). Some of the attributes that distinguish these different forms of global recruitment include global assignment stability and length, migration direction and the assignment's initiator. Although length limitations prevent us from addressing the full range of global workers, we discuss those most used by multinational organizations and researched in the global recruiting literature. Nonetheless, it is important to note that recruitment research is scarce on a number of the aforementioned types of global assignments not covered in this chapter. Figure 3.1 illustrates the primary factors influencing global recruitment effectiveness.

Internal Recruiting

One of the primary means by which multinational organizations coordinate and control their foreign operations is through various types of international assignees (Collings & Scullion, 2008; Harzing, 2004). International assignments are important for individual career development (Cerdin & Brewster, 2014) as well as organizational development because internationally mobile employees play a key role in transferring knowledge to company locations around the world. Global managers face some unique challenges, including creating a global and shared mind-set among team members, coordinating with others at a distance, adapting to rapid, cross-cultural transitions and balancing work and life demands (Cappellen & Janssens, 2010). Despite considerable research on international assignments, which has provided much useful information on this topic however, we still have a very incomplete picture of how to identify and recruit people for these important roles. By reviewing the global recruiting literature we hope to enable researchers to continue to work in this promising and important area.

We first turn our attention to the literature on internal recruiting, or the recruiting and reassigning of talent that the organization already employs to some form of globally-based work. Research suggests managers' willingness to accept traditional longer-term assignments as well as short-term and travelling assignments is influenced by individual characteristics, destination country characteristics, family concerns, rewards and career fit (Konopaske, Robie & Ivancevich, 2009).

Expatriates

Expatriates are employees supported by their organizations to move and work abroad (Doherty & Dickmann, 2013). The most common recruiting source of expatriates has historically been for a company to identify high-performing and high-potential employees from within their domestic or foreign operations to whom to give international assignments. When a company reassigns employees to locations in other countries these are called company-initiated or assigned expatriates (Scullion & Collings, 2006). Research on company-initiated expatriate recruitment has focused on assessing and developing high-potential employees' ability to perform successfully in a global environment (Collings, Scullion & Morley, 2007). Collings and Mellahi (2009) appropriately note the talent required to operate successfully in other countries exists and should be recognized as an important resource at lower levels as well as at the upper echelons of the organization. To date, however, research on company-initiated expatriates has primarily focused on higher-level positions.

Most work on expatriate assignments has focused on selection processes and outcomes rather than recruitment. However, research on expatriates shows that self-selection works in terms of enhancing expatriate success (Caligiuri & Phillips, 2003; Caligiuri, Tarique & Jacobs, 2009). Accordingly, selection and recruitment processes for expatriates may be intertwined and thus may require stages. First, an organization must identify potentially effective expatriates. Second, the organization must recruit the identified high-potential employees to consider the expatriate assignment. Third, the organization can present realistic job previews to allow the self-selection process to unfold (Caligiuri & Phillips, 2003; Phillips, 1998). Finally, the organization can assist in transition to the new location and assess expatriate assignment effectiveness, as well as enhance and assess repatriation adjustment outcomes (Cerdin & Brewster, 2014). Research has demonstrated that international assignees who are more extroverted, emotionally stable, conscientious, agreeable, more receptive and flexible to learning about new cultures and interacting with host nationals are more likely to be successful (Caligiuri, Tarique & Jacobs, 2009). Recruitment efforts thus should focus on enhancing the presence of these and related competences or personality characteristics in the talent pool. However, other than self-selection, there is limited research on how to attract such talent.

Research on calculating the return on investment (ROI) of expatriate assignments has identified a common difficulty; a failure to plan for the measurement of expatriate performance and its contribution to unit or organizational performance (Scullion & Collings, 2006). Also, a lack of reliable data allowing for accurate ROI calculations has impeded assessment of expatriate recruiting effectiveness (Collings, 2014). The inability to calculate the ROI of such assignments extends to recruitment efforts as well. Research has also investigated the systems organizations use to recruit assigned expatriates. Managers exhibit variability in their willingness to send employees on global assignments. Managers who are higher in the organizational hierarchy and managers who have had international or global experiences are more likely to assign a global role to others (Benson, Pérez-Nordtvedt & Datta, 2009). These findings suggest that managerial recruiting practice may vary based on such factors, but to our knowledge research has not explored the determinants of managerial recruitment practices.

Research on internal recruiting has also tried to identify the best internal sourcing or talent identification systems and processes. As McDonnell, Lamare, Gunnigle and Lavelle (2010) note, however, although some multinational employers have formal systems in place to strategically identify and develop their talent, an ad hoc or haphazard approach is much more common. McDonnell and colleagues (2010) found that less than half of all multinational enterprises (MNEs) had both global succession planning and formal management development programmes for their high-potentials. It is likely that talent identification and recruitment processes vary across subsidiaries and by region for MNEs, but much work is needed to understand how and why this might happen, if it happens, and the potential impact on talent flow. This is clearly an area for future research to help inform HR practice as it provides the foundation for internal talent identification and recruitment for international assignments.

Alternative international assignments

Research on alternative (non-expatriate) international assignments has found that 'commuter', 'short-term', 'frequent flyer' and 'flexpatriate' assignments have become increasingly common (Collings, Scullion & Morley, 2007; Mayerhofer, Hartmann, Michelitsch-Riedl & Kollinger, 2004; Shaffer, Kraimer, Chen & Bolino, 2012). The use of international frequent flyers and short-term assignments in the context of higher education has even been investigated (McDonnell & Boyle, 2012). Although research in this area is still scarce, what has been done suggests that relative to domestic recruiting practices, global recruiting practices need to change to adjust to the differing dynamics of alternative international assignments (Meyskens, Von Glinow, Werther & Clarke, 2009). It should be noted that there are unique stressors associated with short-term assignments such as managing work–family conflicts during frequent absences and adjusting to frequent changes in cultural context (Shaffer, Kraimer, Chen & Bolino, 2012). Determining the nature of the most frequently encountered stressors, as well as identifying individual characteristics that enable coping with such stressors, would enable organizations to recruit more effectively for such positions. Research suggests that organizations overestimate the role of financial motives and underestimate the importance of career, work–life balance and development considerations in the acceptance of international assignments (Dickmann, Doherty, Mills & Brewster, 2008). These factors should influence both the practice and outcomes of any global recruitment effort targeted at alternative international assignments.

Inpatriates

As noted by Collings, McDonnell, Gunnigle and Lavelle (2010), although research on expatriates is fairly substantial, much less is known about the flow of subsidiary employees to other subsidiaries as third country nationals and to corporate headquarters as inpatriates. Collings and colleagues (2010) built on insights from the resource-based view and neo-institutional theory to develop and test a theoretical model to explain staffing flows from subsidiaries in Ireland to either the parent country or to third country operations. They found that almost half of all foreign MNEs use some form of outward staffing flows from their Irish operations and that headquarters, subsidiary, structural and HR systems factors emerge as strong predictors of such staffing flows. Collings and colleagues (2010) also found that the impact of specific variables in explaining inter-organization variation differs between the utilization of inpatriate and third country national assignments.

As noted by Kim (2013), inpatriates clearly form a heterogeneous group and differ from expatriates in their positions, strengths and roles. Reiche (2011) and Harvey, Novicevic, Buckley and Fung (2005) have discussed the factors that facilitate inpatriation as a means of knowledge transfer in multinational corporations. Scholars suggest that migration trends from subsidiaries to parent countries rather than from parent countries to subsidiaries can convert brain drain into talent flow (Beechler & Woodward, 2009; Carr, Inkson & Thorn, 2005). Harvey, Reiche and Moeller (2011) discussed the importance of inpatriates' trust-building in global organizations to their success, suggesting that individual differences in the ability to build trust may predict inpatriates' success. Reiche, Kraimer and Harzing (2011) also found that inpatriates' trust ties with headquarters' staff and their fit with the headquarters positively predict firm-specific learning and their perceived prospects, which is positively related to 2- and 4-year retention. These findings indicate that inpatriation recruitment can be influenced by the purpose of the assignment, the degree of trust and both subsidiary and headquarter characteristics.

Importantly for recruiting, research has begun to address the paths through which employees evolve into global staff (Holt & Seki, 2012; McPhail, Fisher, Harvey & Moeller, 2012). To the extent that we can understand the career paths of internationally mobile talent, multinational organizations can better identify ways to source and recruit potential global talent early in their careers. The barriers to the corporate advancement of employees located in subsidiaries and the barriers to the promotion of talent already employed by the MNE to be part of the top management team have also attracted some research attention (Mellahi & Collings, 2010; Vaiman, Scullion & Collings, 2012). Future research must address both attraction and barriers to recruiting in-house talent for a variety of global roles and job assignments. Perceptions about post-assignment adjustment and support are likely to be important for recruiting replacement talent for such assignments. This line of research is important to enhancing our understanding of the global talent supply chain and maximizing the efficiency of the recruitment and career development of future global workers.

External Recruiting

External recruiting addresses the identification and attraction of talent that does not currently work for the organization. Globalization and lower immigration and emigration barriers have increased the mobility of people across cultural and geographical boundaries (Beechler & Woodward, 2009; Tung & Lazarova, 2006) and changed the nature of global recruiting. The increasing mobility of talent also means that companies must compete internationally for the best recruits (Farndale, Scullion & Sparrow, 2010). We now turn our attention to the literature on the external recruiting of internationally mobile talent.

Self-initiated expatriates

In addition to company-assigned expatriates, self-initiated expatriates (SIE) voluntarily move to another country to find work (Haslberger & Vaiman, 2013). As summarized by Doherty (2013), SIE research has included the work-related experiences and characteristics of successful SIEs, comparative studies of assigned versus self-initiated expatriation and SIEs as global talent flow. Research has found that cultural adjustment is related to expatriate performance (Bhaskar-Shrinivas, Harrison, Shaffer & Luk, 2005) and that this adjustment and cultural assimilation are a highly personal process resulting from the impact of cognitions and emotions on behavioural effectiveness (Haslberger, 2008). Again, these findings suggest that recruiting outcomes can be optimized by attending to individual characteristics and competences found to be related to greater cultural assimilation and adjustment.

As mentioned earlier, alternative forms of international work, including SIE, have been growing in popularity (Andresen, Bergdolt, Margenfeld & Dickmann, 2014; Demel & Mayrhofer, 2010; Tahvanainen, Welch & Worm, 2005). Multinational organizations have been moving away from assigning traditional parent-country expatriates towards relying more on third-country nationals instead (Tungli & Peiperl, 2009). Research on the repatriation difficulties of returning expatriates suggests that inter-organizational mobility tends to be high among expatriates due to timing issues and the changing nature of work situations (Banai & Harry, 2004; Cerdin & Brewster, 2014). This reduces barriers to their recruitment by other companies and potentially forms the basis for migration or immigration by SIE. Indeed, SIE and traditional expatriates share many of the values for lifestyle, internationalism, challenge and autonomy, although significant differences are found (Cerdin & Le Pargneux, 2010). Recruitment efforts can take into consideration that SIEs often seek global opportunities for the purposes of personal and professional career development (Cerdin & Le Pargneux, 2010; Richardson & McKenna, 2003), although it should be noted that SIE from developing countries often face unique structural barriers to career development (Al Ariss & Özbilgin, 2010).

Tharenou (2013) concluded that SIEs are likely not a suitable alternative to company-assigned expatriates for roles requiring firm-specific competences, including running the foreign operation and management development. Tharenou concluded that SIEs are most suited to roles requiring cross-cultural and host location-specific competences, including filling technical and lower and middle management positions requiring more generic, specialist competences. Additionally, research on SIEs has had a tendency to ignore highly skilled immigrants arriving from developing countries (as opposed to developed countries) even though such talent pools offer organizations alternatives in a global talent environment (Al Ariss & Özbilgin, 2010). This suggests that global recruiting practices need to account for differences in the nature of the roles being filled, the migration direction from one country to another and the motivations of SIEs to pursue such opportunities.

Emerging markets remain one of the biggest global recruiting challenges. Rodriguez and Scurry (2014) called for more research exploring the characteristics of successful SIEs and how they navigate contextual constraints, such as localization policies in emerging markets, including the Middle East (Sidani & Al Ariss, 2014). Individuals' willingness to be globally mobile, especially in emerging markets, and the organizational capability needed to manage this talent must be better understood (Farndale, Scullion & Sparrow, 2010). The most effective recruiting methods, talent profiles and sourcing processes for high-potential employees from developing countries are not yet well understood.

Host Country Nationals

The high cost of expatriates has led to many MNEs turning to host country nationals to meet international subsidiary staffing needs (Tarique, Schuler & Gong, 2006). In addition, multinational companies typically staff their subsidiaries below the highest management level with host country nationals (HCNs). These localization strategies also involve recruiting and developing HCN managers for future senior management positions from within their local subsidiaries. Finding, developing and retaining this high-potential local talent is often challenging for multinationals, particularly where there is a scarcity of managerial talent such as in emerging markets (Sparrow, Brewster & Harris, 2015). Paik and Ando (2011) found staffing in foreign affiliates with HCNs versus parent company nationals was dependent on the strategic orientation of the firm. Sidani and Al Arriss (2014) found that although localization policies (replacing foreign workers with local ones) altered the ratio of host to parent country nationals employed in MNEs, the effect was uneven and could alter perceptions about the quality of local talent that is hired. Additionally, the effect of strategic orientation and localization policies on the global recruitment process is understudied. Another area in need of further research is how recruitment takes place when expatriates return to a country to become an HCN. Thite, Srinivasan, Harvey and Valk (2009) found that expatriates returning home to manage host-company operations were more willing to accept such assignments than expatriates from the parent company, but research has not yet built on this work to better understand these dynamics.

The recruitment of host-country managers is also made more difficult by a weak or lacking employer image, a deficiency of local labour market and local education system knowledge, language and cultural problems at interviews, trying to transfer recruitment methods which work well in the home country to foreign countries and trying to recruit to a formal set of criteria when flexibility is required (Scullion, 1994; Scullion & Brewster, 2001). Recruiting HCNs also requires awareness and understanding of how MNE origination country images as well as images about the MNE itself influence employer brand perceptions among HCNs (Froese, Vo & Garrett, 2010).

We know little about the effectiveness of recruitment practices across cultures (Ma & Allen, 2009). Culture seminars targeting cognitive, affective and behavioural competence development (Waxin & Panaccio, 2005) and mentoring systems (Howe-Walsh & Schyns, 2010) have been found to improve SIEs' cultural assimilation and adjustment and improve recruiting outcomes. Host country nationals have also been found to play an important role as socializing agents (Toh & DeNisi, 2007), suggesting that recruiting the right host country nationals to work with global talent can improve the effectiveness of international assignments. Unfortunately, little research has been done in this area.

Many international firms have neglected the training and development needs of their host country managers and focused virtually all of their management development efforts on their parent country national managers (Scullion, 1994). However, research suggests that a reputation for training and skill development can enhance recruitment, particularly in emerging markets (Holtbrügge, Friedmann & Puck, 2010). It is has also been suggested that when seeking to recruit high-potential managers, international firms should emphasize their localization strategy and link their plans for localization to the career prospects of local managers (Evans, Pucik & Barsoux, 2002).

In general, we do not know much about the determinants of effective recruitment of HCNs. It is likely that HCN recruitment and attraction to firms is influenced by characteristics of the local subsidiary, parent company, originating country of the parent company, as well as local culture, laws, regulations and talent market. Additionally, managers at different host company locations are likely to recruit differently as a function of local norms, cultures, laws, and so forth. Thus, there are likely to be important determinants of recruitment outcomes of HCNs, but most of these issues remain to be identified and studied.

Skilled migrants

The recruitment of skilled migrants is increasing in many countries (Forde & MacKenzie, 2009; Moriarty, Wickham, Kings, Salamonska & Bobek, 2012). Migrants are attractive employees in many countries because they increase the recruiting country's pool of highly trained workers, bring new skills and often reduce cost (Moriarty et al., 2012). Sidani and Al Arriss (2014) found that although companies in the Arab Gulf region were willing to hire foreign nationals if they arrived with the training and skills to make an immediate contribution, they were more willing to spend time and money developing local talent.

Due to the low birth rates and ageing populations of most economically developed countries, recruiting younger migrant workers helps to maintain the number of working-age adults necessary to support the growing pool of retired elderly (Ziguras & Law, 2006). However, research shows college graduates are becoming more reluctant to move and that quality of life and lifestyle issues can be more important than gaining international experience (Sparrow, 1999; Scullion, 1994). Work by Almeida and colleagues suggests that migrants to a new country may also face challenges in being recruited by organizations even though the organizations may be seeking people with their specific skills (Almeida, Fernando & Sheridan, 2012). Research has begun to study the simultaneous pressure to address both organizational goals to place talent internationally and individual, self-initiated expatriation goals and address how these goals might be balanced to the benefit of both parties (Farndale, Pai, Sparrow & Scullion, 2014).

Chaloff and Lemaître (2009) discuss the importance of engaging in active recruitment for skilled migrants rather than merely facilitating work permits for immigrant applicants. Although highly skilled migrants may find countries with widely spoken languages and high wages attractive regardless of the employment obstacles that may exist, a country with lower wages and a unique language will need to do more than just lower administrative barriers to recruit and attract skilled migrants (Chaloff & Lemaître, 2009). What makes different locations and employment opportunities more or less attractive to different types of skilled migrants is not yet well understood.

Sourcing Talent

Research has begun to address the question of how organizations source talent internally and externally for global assignments. Mäkelä, Björkman and Ehrnrooth (2010) identify cultural and institutional distance between the locations of a potential global talent pool member and the decision makers, homophily between the decision makers and the potential global talent pool member, the network position of the person in question and performance appraisal evaluations as important factors in being labelled 'global talent' in a multinational corporation. There is evidence that organizations from developed countries may under-recruit or exclude strong yet untapped sources of talent from subsidiaries, developing countries or countries with problematic images or histories due to structural, perceptual and cultural factors (Almeida, Fernando & Sheridan, 2012; Felker, 2012; Forstenlechner, Madi, Selim & Rutledge, 2012; Mellahi & Collings, 2010).

The different impacts of social network-based recruiting methods across cultures have also received some research attention. Strong social ties based on trust, affection and reciprocity are important in collectivistic cultures but may be less important in individualistic cultures (Miller & Guo, 2014). For example, due to the importance of *guanxi*, Warner (2009) recommends that recruitment strategies in China capitalize on affective ties rather than bureaucratic procedures. This is likely to be important when sourcing talent, either internally or externally. One way to target employees' social networks in global recruiting is to ensure that current employees are kept aware of current job openings and have up-to-date and accurate company and job information to share with prospective external applicants within their personal networks (Han & Han, 2009; Huang, 2008; Warner, 2009).

Which competences and characteristics to recruit?

Research has continued to identify the competences and characteristics on which recruiting should focus to enable effective employee functioning in a global environment, including the ability to deal with complexity and the presence of proficient social and networking skills (Bird & Osland, 2004; Jokinen, 2005). Caligiuri (2006) found that openness to experiences, self-awareness, curiosity, empathy and optimism are important to success in the global context. Cultural intelligence has also been found to be important in explaining effectiveness in cross-cultural interactions (Thomas, Elron et al., 2008).

Research continues to explore the role of an employee's family situation, including issues with parents or extended family in the country of origin (Collings & Scullion, 2008). Better understanding the individual differences that influence success on global assignments will improve our ability to effectively source candidates who are likely to succeed. Research has also found that realistic job previews are related to higher self-efficacy for global assignment success as well as a greater perceived ability to make an informed decision about accepting the global assignment (Caligiuri & Phillips, 2003).

Chapman, Uggerslev, Carroll, Piasentin and Jones (2005) found that perceived fit was one of the best predictors of applicant attraction to organizations. As discussed by Caligiuri and Tarique (2006), both research and practice recommend providing information to candidates and their families during the recruitment process to enable them to make accurate decisions on their fit with a global assignment to improve recruiting and staffing outcomes.

External Recruiting Strategies and Methods

The effectiveness of different types of recruiting methods and strategies has also received research attention over the past decade. Recruitment strategies and outcomes may be influenced by a variety of global factors, including culture, brand importance and reputational effects. For example, word-of-mouth recruitment may be more important in collectivistic cultures than in individualistic cultures because collectivistic cultures may rely on strong ties as sources of information (Ma & Allen, 2009). Research on the role of job advertisement wording in recruiting effectiveness, employer brand image, cross-national advertising and how the internet is being used to recruit internationally mobile talent is discussed next.

Job advertisement wording

Including information on important competences and characteristics related to success in international assignments in job advertisements has the potential to influence the quality and quantity of job applicants for positions requiring international travel. The wording of job advertisements has been found to interact with the individual difference of global openness to influence recruiting outcomes. Phillips and colleagues (2014) found that people with a very high level of global openness and flexibility were more likely to perceive job or organizational fit when a global organizational presence was mentioned in a job ad. However, people with a very low level of global openness were less likely to perceive strong job or organizational fit when a global organizational presence was communicated in the advertisement. Research has also found that individual values (work-centrism, money orientation and collectivism) exert both direct and indirect effects on job seekers' attraction to Japanese companies (Kim, Froese & Cox, 2012). It has also been suggested that the degree to which information on hierarchical relationships and individual versus team rewards is communicated in job advertisements will differentially influence attraction and recruitment outcomes in various types of cultural contexts (Ma & Allen, 2009).

Brand image

To attract and recruit internationally mobile employees, researchers have suggested that companies differentiate themselves through a unique and attractive employer image or brand (Christiaans & Buettgen, 2014; Knox & Freeman, 2006; Lewis & Heckman, 2006). Job seekers' application decisions depend in part on the employer's brand image, which is often measured according to job seekers' attitudes and perceived job and organizational attributes and fit (Collins & Stevens, 2002; Lievens, van Hoye, & Anseel, 2007; Phillips et al., 2014). Research has found a strong influence of employer image on perceived employer attractiveness and job seekers' application intentions (Chapman et al., 2005; Knox & Freeman, 2006; Lemmink, Schuijf & Streukens, 2003; Lievens, van Hoye & Schreurs, 2005; Phillips et al., 2014). Martin, Gollan and Grigg (2011) discuss the possibility that employer branding's potential effects will be better understood in the context of multinational organizations when theory and practice better connect the internal application of marketing and branding to the key reputational and innovation agendas of MNEs.

National differences have been acknowledged as potentially important when developing international employer brands (Froese et al., 2010; Stahl, Björkman, Farndale, Morris, Paauwe, Stiles, Trevor & Wright, 2012). Similarly, the effectiveness of recruitment practices may vary as a function of cultural values (Ma & Allen, 2009). If international work location preferences differ due to national culture or other national differences, the employer's brand positioning should be adapted rather than standardized (Berthon, Ewing & Hah, 2005; Martin & Hetrick, 2009). Research has found that some facets of organizational image (e.g., task attractiveness) vary across countries, while other facets (e.g., work atmosphere and perceived career opportunities) are more stable in their influence on application intentions (Baum & Kabst, 2013).

Caligiuri, Colakoglu, Cerdin and Kim (2010) found that cross-cultural and individual differences influence the role of employer reputation in organizational attraction and recruiting effectiveness. Caligiuri and colleagues (2010) found that, at the cultural level, collectivism, and at the individual level, the need for power and achievement, were related to the importance of employer reputation in organizational attraction. Caligiuri and colleagues suggest that companies consider crafting their recruitment messages to fit the cultural norms of the country in which they are recruiting and also to encourage recruiters to tailor their messages to fit the candidates they are targeting. In developing countries, foreign companies may have a brand advantage simply by virtue of being foreign, as foreign companies are often perceived as offering better pay, opportunities and working conditions (Froese et al., 2010; Newburry, Gardberg & Belkin, 2006). Despite increasing awareness of the important role of employer branding in global recruitment, however, we lack sufficient information about how international companies should adapt their employer branding strategies to different cultural or individual environments or rely on global brand positioning (Caligiuri, 2010).

Cross-national advertising

Despite the potential cost of mistakes in global advertising campaigns, multinational organizations are increasingly using this recruiting method to attract managers and professionals (Scullion & Brewster, 2001). Advertising agencies frequently operate as part of an international network, and although advertising trends vary across sectors, print advertising has decreased in popularity as companies turn to more creative alternatives, including targeted outdoor billboards, airport lounges and airline magazines (Scullion & Brewster, 2001).

As more international managers come into the organization from a variety of countries it becomes more important for the recruitment and selection technology which is used to be globally fair and, even more importantly, to be seen as globally fair by job seekers and employees (Scullion & Collings, 2006). International advertising agencies increasingly need to ensure that recruitment campaigns are culturally sensitive in the local markets and attend to the softer cultural issues, such as the wording of advertisements and the design of recruiting brochures and other marketing material (Harris, Brewster & Sparrow, 2003).

Internet recruitment

The internet has increasingly become a significant source of recruitment for international managers (Harris, Brewster & Sparrow, 2003). Research has begun to explore the role of companies' website presentations and wording of international mobility and global careers in recruiting success. Puck, Mohr and Holtbrügge (2006) found that the use of corporate websites for recruitment varied across countries. Organizations from countries that show a high level of individualism tend to make more intensive use of recruitment through corporate websites than organizations from more collectivist societies. Additionally, companies from cultures with a high level of uncertainty avoidance tend to use corporate website recruitment less intensively.

Point and Dickman (2012) found that most websites mentioning international work focused on operational issues regarding international experience and expatriation rather than on global careers. The internet has become one of the fastest growing methods of recruitment for filling senior international senior manager and technical positions and it is likely that it will become more popular in the future as the internet spreads to more countries in the less developed world (Harris et al., 2003). Research is still somewhat scarce on the best uses of the internet for global recruiting and on its limitations.

Globally Relocating Jobs

In addition to acquiring internationally mobile talent internally or externally, organizations can often accomplish their recruiting goals by moving the work to be closer to the targeted talent pool. Offshoring company activities can be done internally through company-owned and controlled subsidiaries or centres in foreign countries (Bunyaratavej, Hahn & Doh, 2007) or externally by outsourcing business functions to foreign service providers (Hahn & Bunyaratavej, 2010; Kedia & Mukherjee, 2009). Organizations that engage more extensively in benchmarking activities appear to be more likely to outsource HR activities such as training and recruitment (Tremblay, Patry & Lanoie, 2008). However, global firms often encounter challenges when trying to replicate HR practices among culturally and geographically dispersed subsidiaries (Morris et al., 2009).

Anner (2011) shows that to the extent that labour costs comprise a large portion of total production costs organizations are more motivated to relocate jobs globally to capitalize on low labour costs. Although labour cost control is often cited as a primary reason for offshoring, research has found that organizations are increasingly offshoring innovation projects, not for labour arbitrage, but merely to access the qualified talent unavailable in the home country (Doh, Lewin, Massini, Hahn & Bunyaratavej, 2010; Kedia & Lahiri, 2007; Lewin, Massini & Peeters, 2009). Although labour cost is often an important factor, as offshoring is frequently motivated by the opportunity to benefit from lower wage standards in foreign countries (Stringfellow, Teagarden & Nie, 2008), the abundance and quality of human capital (Doh, 2005), and access to talent (Couto, Mani, Lewin & Peeters, 2006; Lewin et al., 2009) are increasingly driving offshoring decisions. The global sourcing and recruiting of science and engineering talent through offshoring have increased as the availability of this talent has decreased in advanced economies while increasing in emerging economies (Manning, Massini & Lewin, 2008). Unfortunately, we know little about how recruitment takes place when jobs are offshored and determinants of attraction to positions and opportunities that are the result of offshoring efforts.

Although significant variability has been found with regard to the performance associated with offshoring projects (Elia, Caniato, Luzzini & Piscitello, 2014), the ramifications of offshoring have been found to go well beyond immediate cost reduction (Doh, Lewin, Massini, Hahn & Bunyaratavej, 2010; Ellram, Tate & Billington, 2008; Mudambi & Venzin, 2010). The impact of offshoring also includes negative job impacts in developed countries (Amiti & Wei, 2009; Farrell, 2005; Farrell, Laboissiere & Rosenfeld, 2006), and often service quality declines (Ren & Zhou, 2008). Additionally, offshoring activities can have significant consequences for organizational image and branding, which can then influence recruitment outcomes, both domestically and globally.

When offshoring fails to attain desired objectives or when the offshoring process itself increases labour costs, reduces productivity or quality, increases customer dissatisfaction or detrimentally increases transportation costs, then reshoring (also known as onshoring, inshoring or backshoring) or returning jobs to the original country, often with increased automation of the work, can take place (Gray, Skowronski, Esenduran & Rungtusanatham, 2013; Jensen, Kirkegaard & Laugesen, 2009; Kinkel & Maloca, 2009). However, the conditions in which this can take place and the manner in which organizations can effectively recruit people to reshore projects and activities are completely unknown. As an illustration, we do not know if effective recruitment processes for offshoring operations are the same as reshoring operations. If people have experienced temporary job loss as a result of global relocation of operations, then if the job opportunity opens up during a return of operations, will recruitment processes unfold identically? Most likely not, but we know nothing about such effects.

Also, nothing is known about the possible spillover effects to a company's employer image or reputation or its recruiting effectiveness from offshoring or reshoring decisions or treatment of offshore employees. If an organization moves jobs to a less developed economy to benefit from labour arbitrage, what are the consequences? Does an organization's treatment of offshore workers have any spillover effects? What are the effects on the remaining employees in the company and on the organization's ability to recruit quality talent in the future of deciding to move some jobs to another country? Additional research is needed to explore these important questions.

Future Research

Despite the considerable body of research on global recruiting that has been published over the past decade, much work remains to be done in this important area. Inpatriate and third country national assignments have received relatively little research attention in comparison to assigned expatriates. As noted by Collings, Scullion and Vaiman (2011), much of our understanding of talent management is premised on research undertaken in the North American context. How global recruiting might differ in other contexts is ripe for future study.

As Sparrow (2007) notes, globalization has brought a number of changes to the practice of international human resource management, including global recruiting. In particular, the choice between globally standardized, optimized or localized HR processes is critical but not well understood as our theoretical understanding of the issues involved is still driven by concepts based on the management of small cadres of international managers, particularly expatriates. Collings and Scullion (2008) also raise the excellent point that globally standardized recruitment criteria, including educational background, skills and work preferences, likely vary dramatically between domestic job seekers and self-initiated expatriates, often leading to overlooking high-potential candidates. Flexible recruiting and selection criteria would allow a more holistic assessment of candidates against longer-term strategic and operational international objectives (Doherty & Dickmann, 2013). Research on the tradeoffs made when using different recruitment criteria and methods would help to inform this important topic.

McDonnell, Hickey and Gunnigle (2011) discuss the popularity and challenges of talent pool segmentation as a means of identifying and managing global talent. Some organizations recruit the best talent and then assign them to positions rather than recruiting and hiring specific people for specific jobs (Seigel, 2008). The implications of globally recruiting for a talent profile as opposed to recruiting for specific job requirements is wide open for future study.

Another direction for future research concerns the importance of recruiting host country nationals who possess the characteristics and competences necessary to maximize expatriates' performance and knowledge transfer. As Vance, Vaiman and Andersen (2009) discuss, host country nationals play many roles in local knowledge management and knowledge transfer, including cultural interpreter, information resource broker and change partner. Bonache and Zárraga-Oberty (2008) identify the abilities and motivation of local employees, and the relationship between local and international staff as two of the three human-related factors that influence knowledge transfer success. Foreign–local relationships were also highlighted by Toh, DeNisi and Leonardelli (2012) as being critical to expatriate socialization. If the wrong people are recruited and placed in these important roles, even the highest potential expatriates will experience difficulty being successful, yet the international business and management literature has paid scant attention to these critical employees (Caprar, 2011; Takeuchi, 2010; Toh & DeNisi, 2005). Future research is sorely needed to identify not only the expatriate characteristics related to expatriate success (Varma, Pichler, Budhwar & Biswas, 2009; Varma, Toh & Budhwar, 2006), but also the characteristics of local staff, including perhaps attitudinal and behavioural openness (Caligiuri, Jacobs & Farr, 2000; Phillips et al., 2014), that create an environment maximally receptive to expatriates and most conducive to two-way knowledge transfer.

Stepping back to survey the landscape of global recruitment research, we see endless possibilities for building theory and conducting research that better informs practice. As Figure 3.1 shows, a number of key factors influence global recruitment outcomes, but the ways in which these factors combine to influence effectiveness remain understudied. We know little about what drives different recruitment activities as well as the underlying process mechanisms that connect recruitment activities to global recruitment outcomes. Below, we highlight some examples of possible research directions that can be derived from Figure 3.1 which span multiple levels of analyses.

Economic forces and local and global labour markets can influence recruitment processes. However, we do not know if HCN recruits are attracted to firms for different reasons from recruits from parent country headquarters, and if so, whether this changes as a function of labour market conditions or the general economic context. Similarly, we do not know if recruiters look for and interact differently with HCN recruits versus recruits from operations in the parent country, and if so, whether this varies by the economic environment. As shown in Figure 3.1, characteristics of the recruit (experience, cultural values, ability and self-efficacy) are likely to influence how recruits respond to the recruitment context, particularly in economic downturns or expansions.

There is evidence that regulations, such as localization policies, influence recruitment activities, but the impact of such regulations on recruiter or job seeker perceptions (e.g., fairness) about the recruitment process are relatively unknown. Do regulations influence how recruiters perceive local talent and if so, do these perceptions change over time? Do regulations and localization policies have different effects on recruitment processes and outcomes depending on the country, region and culture? Do organizations with different talent management strategies react differently to regulations and policies, and if so, in what way and when?

Figure 3.1 also highlights that the type of work assignment can influence recruitment for both host country and parent country operations. However, we do not know if recruitment activities are differentially effective for different types of assignments (e.g., short-term, business traveller, expatriate, inpatriate and third country national assignments). Additionally, we do not know if recruitment activities work similarly when seeking talent for parent company operations versus host country or subsidiary operations. There is evidence that culture matters, but much more research is needed to better understand the role of culture as well as other aspects of the recruitment context (e.g., parent country images and stereotypes; organizational talent strategy) on global recruitment effectiveness. All of these issues are likely to be moderated by characteristics the recruit possesses, such as career orientation, global openness, willingness to travel and the need for work–life balance.

Research is needed to better understand how international interests and global career paths develop. Do expatriates acquire an interest in such assignments through exposure to diverse cultures and by gaining international experience through work? Better understanding how organizations can generate interest in global assignments and cultivate high-quality, talented global managers through a global talent management system would be helpful to managers and executives. Another possibility is that global interests are stable individual differences that manifest themselves many years earlier to become the driver of expatriate interest and global orientation later during the career cycle. If this is true, then the focus is as much on selecting people with a global orientation as it is on recruiting and cultivating such interests through career development.

If global talent is recruited and developed through specific career experiences, then this opens the door to many new types of global recruiting and talent management investigations and practices. As an illustration, international internships and global mentoring are neither commonly practised nor well investigated. One can imagine that firms that offer international internships in which the global employee is paired with an international mentor will have global employees who are more likely to perform effectively on subsequent assignments and will be more attracted to such assignments. Thus, recruitment practices can become blended with other talent management strategies such as intern placement, mentoring partnerships and career pathing.

As Figure 3.1 shows, the type of work assignment will influence which recruitment activities take place, the timing of those activities and their effectiveness when put in place. Phillips and colleagues (2014) found individual differences of global openness and willingness to travel influence receptiveness to jobs requiring short-term global travel assignments. It is possible that such individual differences will be more or less important for other types of global assignments, and other individual differences may appear in the foreground or background as being important, depending on the nature of the global assignment.

The direction of migration for global assignments is likely to shape recruitment activities and effectiveness. Different recruitment processes may be needed when recruiting from parent country headquarters to work in subsidiaries than when the direction of migration is reversed; or perhaps they will work in the same way. We simply do not know how well recruitment efforts translate from the parent country context to the context for subsidiaries or host country operations. Similarly, migration from one subsidiary to another may require recruits with a different value system compared to migration from parent country operations to host country subsidiaries.

The connection between repatriation processes, post-global assignment adjustment and recruitment effectiveness is not well understood. Global recruiting must not only attend to success on a given assignment, but must also consider long-term retention of global talent if an organization is going to benefit from the skills, talents and experiences of managers who have returned from global assignments. Here, inpatriation and repatriation processes must be considered part of the recruitment process. Accordingly, resocialization and transition processes become critical for improving post-assignment adjustment and outcomes. Failure to do so will almost certainly diminish the effectiveness of future global recruitment efforts.

If other global managers see that repatriation or inpatriation is handled poorly, then they may be less willing to accept such assignments themselves. Or if incoming or returning managers fail to be given career opportunities as a result of their enhanced global experience and skills, or if they are poorly treated, then the rewards for accepting such assignments are ambiguous at best. In contrast, if repatriation and inpatriation processes are deftly handled, with the incoming or returning manager being well integrated with current or future projects through new opportunities and rewards, then two factors will enhance subsequent recruitment effectiveness. First, the global opportunities themselves will be appealing because they demonstrate a clear instrumentality for future career success and rewards. Second, by better integrating repatriates and inpatriates within the workforce, an organization will foster interactions with others who have had global experiences. As people become familiar with others from a variety of global backgrounds and global experiences, they themselves are likely to feel more comfortable with and interested in such assignments. In this way, global recruiting efforts must necessarily be tied to other activities in the human resource management system.

A key issue is that any recruitment effort, including a global one, does not take place in a vacuum. Recruitment activities must be aligned vertically with the economic environment, national context, organizational strategy, operational needs and strategies, and the values and needs of the individual recruit (Gully et al., 2014; Phillips & Gully, 2015). Likewise, recruitment activities must be aligned horizontally with other human resource functions from career development to compensation to training to performance management. Recruitment inputs, processes and outcomes at a given level (e.g., organization, subsidiary, individual) must be aligned to yield positive recruitment outcomes (Phillips & Gully, 2015). These points demonstrate that global recruitment activities are embedded in a complex mesh of processes and structures that are challenging to align, and thus are rare to see properly aligned. However, when properly aligned, these systems are highly valuable as they provide the foundation for a consistent pipeline of future global talent within the firm. Additionally, because they are difficult to create and must be tailored to the country, firm, subsidiary and overall strategy of the organization, they can neither be easily substituted nor easily imitated by other organizations. As such, according to the resource-based view, effective and well-aligned global recruitment systems form the basis for sustainable competitive advantage (Barney & Wright, 1998).

Conclusion

We have reviewed and explored theory and research most relevant to understanding the determinants of global recruitment effectiveness by considering three main areas of global talent management. These areas are internal global recruitment, external global recruitment and global relocation. We consider how different types of global assignments, various recruitment activities, individual differences and parent, host and third country factors influence global recruitment outcomes. We find that although there is substantial research interest in global talent management, much less work has focused specifically on global recruitment practices. We highlight that global recruitment systems and associated outcomes are influenced by a variety of factors that span multiple levels of analysis and propose ideas for future research directions. Our feeling is that global recruitment is at the dawn of an increasingly important era of research and practice because it is a foundation for global talent management strategies. The prospects for creating important theoretical advances and for conducting impactful research in global recruitment are both wide and deep, with an open ocean of opportunity in front of us.

References

Almeida, S., Fernando, M., & Sheridan, A. (2012). Revealing the screening: Organisational factors influencing the recruitment of immigrant professionals. *International Journal of Human Resource Management, 23*(9), 1950–1965. doi: 10.1080/09585192.2011.616527.

Amiti, M., & Wei, S. J. (2009). Service offshoring and productivity: Evidence from the U.S. *World Economy, 32*, 203–220.

Andresen, M., Bergdolt, F., Margenfeld, J., & Dickmann, M. (2014). Addressing international mobility confusion – Developing definitions and differentiations for self-initiated and assigned expatriates as well as migrants. *The International Journal of Human Resource Management, 25*, 2295–2318.

Anner, M. S. (2011). The impact of international outsourcing on unionization and wages: Evidence from the apparel export sector in Central America. *Industrial & Labor Relations Review, 64*, 305–322.

Al Ariss, A., & Özbilgin, M. (2010). Understanding self-initiated expatriates: Career experiences of Lebanese self-initiated expatriates in France. *Thunderbird International Business Review, 52*(4), 275–285.

Banai, M., & Harry, W. (2004). Boundaryless global careers: The international itinerants. *International Studies of Management & Organization, 34*, 96–120.

Barney, J. B., & Wright, P. M. (1998). On becoming a strategic partner: The role of human resource in gaining competitive advantage. *Human Resource Management, 37*, 31–46.

Baruch, Y., & Altman, Y. (2002). Expatriation and repatriation in MNCs: A taxonomy. *Human Resource Management, 41*, 239–259.

Baum, M., & Kabst, R. (2013). How to attract applicants in the Atlantic versus the Asia-Pacific region? A cross-national analysis on China, India, Germany, and Hungary. *Journal of World Business, 48*, 175–185.

Beechler, S., & Woodward, I. C. (2009). The global 'war for talent'. *Journal of International Management, 15*(3), 273–285.

Benson, G. S., Pérez-Nordtvedt, L., & Datta, D. K. (2009). Managerial characteristics and willingness to send employees on expatriate assignments. *Human Resource Management, 48*(6), 849–869.

Berthon, P., Ewing, M., & Hah, L. L. (2005). Captivating company: Dimensions of attractiveness in employer branding. *International Journal of Advertising, 24*, 151–172.

Bhaskar-Shrinivas, P., Harrison, D. A., Shaffer, M. A., & Luk, D. M. (2005). Input-based and time-based models of international adjustment: Meta-analytic evidence and theoretical extensions. *Academy of Management Journal, 48*, 257–281.

Bird, A., & Osland, J. S. (2004). Global competencies: An introduction. *In* H. Lane, M. Maznarkis, M. E. Mendenhall & J. McNett (Eds.), *The Blackwell Handbook of Global Management: A Guide to Managing Complexity* (pp. 57–80). London: Blackwell.

Björkman, I., & Lervik, J. F. (2007). Transferring HR practices within multinational corporations. *Human Resource Management Journal, 17,* 320–335.

Bonache, J., Brewster, C., Suutari, V., & De Saá, P. (2010). Expatriation: Traditional criticisms and international careers: Introducing the special issue. *Thunderbird International Business Review, 52*(4), 263–274.

Bonache, J., & Zárraga-Oberty, C. (2008). Determinants of the success of international assignees as knowledge transferors: A theoretical framework. *The International Journal of Human Resource Management, 19,* 1–18.

Boudreau, J. W., & Ramstad, P. M. (2007). *Beyond HR: The New Science of Human Capital.* Boston, MA: Harvard Business School Press.

Bunyaratavej, K., Hahn, E. D., & Doh, J. P. (2007). International offshoring of services: A parity study. *Journal of International Management, 13,* 7–21.

Caligiuri, P. (2010). Global talent management. *Journal of World Business, 45,* 105–108.

Caligiuri, P. M. (2006). Developing global leaders. *Human Resource Management Review, 16,* 219–228.

Caligiuri, P., Colakoglu, S., Cerdin, J. L., & Kim, M. S. (2010). Examining cross-cultural and individual differences in predicting employer reputation as a driver of employer attraction. *International Journal of Cross-Cultural Management, 10,* 137–151.

Caligiuri, P. M., Jacobs R. R., & Farr J. L. (2000). The attitudinal and behavioral openness scale: Scale development and construct validation. *International Journal of Intercultural Relations, 24,* 27–46.

Caligiuri, P. M., & Phillips, J. M. (2003). An application of self-assessment realistic job previews to expatriate assignments. *International Journal of Human Resource Management, 14,* 1102–1116.

Caligiuri, P., & Tarique, I. (2006). International assignee selection and cross-cultural training and development. *In* G. K. Stahl, I. Björkman & S. Morris (Eds.), *Handbook of Research in International Human Resource Management* (pp. 321–342). Northampton, MA: Edward Elgar.

Caligiuri, P., Tarique, I., & Jacobs, R. (2009). Selection for international assignments. *Human Resource Management Review, 19*(3), 251–262.

Cappellen, T., & Janssens, M. (2010). Characteristics of international work: Narratives of the global manager. *Thunderbird International Business Review, 52*(4), 337–348.

Caprar, D. V. (2011). Foreign locals: A cautionary tale on the culture of MNC local employees. *Journal of International Business Studies, 42,* 608–628.

Carr, S. C., Inkson, K., & Thorn, K. (2005). From global careers to talent flow: Reinterpreting 'brain drain'. *Journal of World Business, 40*(4), 386–398.

Cerdin, J. L., & Brewster, C. (2014). Talent management and expatriation: Bridging two streams of research and practice. *Journal of World Business, 49*(2), 245–252.

Cerdin, J. L., & Le Pargneux, M. (2010). Career anchors: A comparison between organization-assigned and self-initiated expatriates. *Thunderbird International Business Review, 52*(4), 287–299.

Chaloff, J., & Lemaitre, G. (2009). *Managing Highly-Skilled Labour Migration: A Comparative Analysis of Migration Policies and Challenges in OECD Countries (No. 79).* Geneva: OECD Publishing.

Chapman, D. S., Uggerslev, K. L., Carroll, S. A., Piasentin, K. A., & Jones, D. A. (2005). Applicant attraction to organizations and job choice: A meta-analytic review of the correlates of recruiting outcomes. *Journal of Applied Psychology, 90,* 928–944.

Christiaans, L., & Buettgen, M. (2014). The impact of national and individual characteristics on students' employer choice. *International Journal of Business and Social Science, 5,* 44–60.

Collings, D. G. (2014). Integrating global mobility and global talent management: Exploring the challenges and strategic opportunities. *Journal of World Business, 49,* 253–261.

Collings, D. G., McDonnell, A., Gunnigle, P., & Lavelle, J. (2010). Swimming against the tide: Outward staffing flows from multinational subsidiaries. *Human Resource Management, 49,* 575–598.

Collings, D. G., & Mellahi, K. (2009). Strategic talent management: A review and research agenda. *Human Resource Management Review, 19,* 304–313.

Collings, D. G., & Scullion, H. (2008). Resourcing international assignees. *In* C. Brewster, M. Dickmann & P. Sparrow (Eds.), *International Human Resource Management* (2nd ed., pp. 87–106). London: Routledge.

Collings, D. G., Scullion, H., & Dowling, P. J. (2009). Global staffing: A review and thematic research agenda. *International Journal of Human Resource Management, 20,* 1253–1272.

Collings, D. G., Scullion, H., & Morley, M. J. (2007). Changing patterns of global staffing in the multinational enterprise: Challenges to the conventional expatriate assignment and emerging alternatives. *Journal of World Business, 42,* 198–213.

Collings, D. G., Scullion, H., & Vaiman, V. (2011). European perspectives on talent management. *European Journal of International Management, 5,* 453–462.

Collins, C. J., & Stevens, C. K. (2002). The relationship between early recruitment-related activities and the application decisions of new labor-market entrants: A brand equity approach to recruitment. *Journal of Applied Psychology, 87,* 1121–1133.

Couto, V., Mani, M., Lewin, A. Y., & Peeters, C. (2006). *The Globalization of White-Collar Work.* Tysons Corner, VA: Booz Allen Hamilton.

Demel, B., & Mayrhofer, W. (2010). Frequent business travelers across Europe: Career aspirations and implications. *Thunderbird International Business Review, 52,* 301–311. doi: 10.1002/tie.20352.

Dickman, M., & Doherty, N. (2010). Exploring organizational and individual career goals, interactions, and outcomes of developmental international assignments. *Thunderbird International Business Review, 52*(4), 313–324.

Dickmann, M., Doherty, N., Mills, T., & Brewster, C. (2008). Why do they go? Individual and corporate perspectives on the factors influencing the decision to accept an international assignment. *International Journal of Human Resource Management, 19*(4), 731–751.

Doh, J. P. (2005). Offshore outsourcing: Implications for international business and strategic management theory and practice. *Journal of Management Studies, 42,* 695–704.

Doh, J., Lewin, A., Massini, S., Hahn, E., & Bunyaratavej, K. (2010). Conceptual issues in services offshoring research: A multidisciplinary review. *Group & Organization Management,* doi: 10.1177/1059601110390996.

Doherty, N. (2013). Understanding the self-initiated expatriate: A review and directions for future research. *International Journal of Management Reviews, 15,* 447–469. doi: 10.1111/ijmr.12005.

Doherty, N., & Dickmann, M. (2013). Self-initiated and assigned expatriates: Talent management and career considerations. *In* V. Vaiman & A. Haslberger (Eds.), *Talent Management of Self-Initiated Expatriates: A Neglected Source of Global Talent* (pp. 234–255). New York: Palgrave Macmillan.

Economist. (2006). Travelling more lightly. *The Economist, 379,* 83–99.

Elia, S., Caniato, F., Luzzini, D., & Piscitello, L. (2014). Governance choice in global sourcing of services: The impact on service quality and cost saving performance. *Global Strategy Journal, 4,* 181–199.

Ellram, L. M., Tate, W. L., & Billington, C. (2008). Offshore outsourcing of professional services: A transaction cost economics perspective. *Journal of Operations Management, 26,* 148–163.

Evans, P., Pucik, V., & Barsoux, J. L. (2002). *The Global Challenge: Frameworks for International Human Resource Management.* Chicago: McGraw-Hill Irwin.

Farndale, E., Paauwe, J., Morris, S. S., Stahl, G. K., Stiles, P., Trevor, J., & Wright, P. M. (2010). Context-bound configurations of corporate HR functions in multinational corporations. *Human Resource Management, 49*(1), 45–66.

Farndale, E., Pai, A., Sparrow, P., & Scullion, H. (2014). Balancing individual and organizational goals in global talent management: A mutual-benefits perspective. *Journal of World Business, 49,* 204–214.

Farndale, E., Scullion, H., & Sparrow, P. (2010). The role of the corporate HR function in global talent management. *Journal of World Business, 45,* 161–168.

Farrell, D. (2005). Offshoring: Value creation through economic change. *Journal of Management Studies, 42,* 675–683.

Farrell, D., Laboissière, M. A., & Rosenfeld, J. (2006). Sizing the emerging global labor market: Rational behavior from both companies and countries can help it work more efficiently. *Academy of Management Perspectives, 20,* 23–34.

Felker, J. A. (2012). EU's new member states: An untapped (and underappreciated) source of talent for MNCs? *International Journal of Human Resource Management, 23*(2), 255–277.

Findlay, A. M., Li, F. L. N., Jowett, A. J., & Skeldon, R. (1996). Skilled international migration and the global city: A study of expatriates in Hong Kong. *Transactions of the Institute of British Geographers,* 49–61.

Forde, C., & MacKenzie, R. (2009). Employers' use of low-skilled migrant workers: Assessing the implications for human resource management. *International Journal of Manpower, 30,* 437–452.

Forstenlechner, I., Madi, M. T., Selim, H. M., & Rutledge, E. J. (2012). Emiratisation: Determining the factors that influence the recruitment decisions of employers in the UAE. *International Journal of Human Resource Management, 23*(2), 406–421.

Froese, F., Vo, A., & Garrett, T. C. (2010). Organizational attractiveness of foreign-based companies: A country of origin perspective. *International Journal of Selection & Assessment, 18*(3), 271–281. doi:10.1111/j.1468-2389.2010.00510.x.

Garavan, T. N. (2012). Global talent management in science-based firms: An exploratory investigation of the pharmaceutical industry during the global downturn. *International Journal of Human Resource Management, 23*(12), 2428–2449.

Gray, J. V., Skowronski, K., Esenduran, G., & Rungtusanatham, M. J. (2013). The reshoring phenomenon: What supply chain academics ought to know and should do. *Journal of Supply Chain Management, 49*(2), 27–33.

Gully, S. M., Phillips, J. M., & Kim, M. S. (2014). Strategic recruitment: A multilevel perspective. In K. Y. T. Yu & D. M. Cable (Eds.), *The Oxford Handbook f Recruitment* (pp. 161–183). New York: Oxford University Press.

Hahn, E. D., & Bunyaratavej, K. (2010). Services cultural alignment in offshoring: The impact of cultural dimensions on offshoring location choices. *Journal of Operations Management, 28,* 186–193.

Han, J., & Han, J. (2009). Network-based recruiting and applicant attraction in China: Insights from both organizational and individual perspectives. *The International Journal of Human Resource Management, 20,* 2228–2249.

Harris, H., Brewster, C., & Sparrow, P. (2003). *International Human Resource Management.* London: Chartered Institute of Personnel and Development.

Harvey, M., Novicevic, M., Buckley, M. R., & Fung, H. (2005). Reducing inpatriate managers' 'liability of foreignness' by addressing stigmatization and stereotype threats. *Journal of World Business, 40,* 267–280.

Harvey, M., Reiche, B. S., & Moeller, M. (2011). Developing effective global relationships through staffing with inpatriate managers: The role of interpersonal trust. *Journal of International Management, 17,* 150–161.

Harzing, A. W. K. (2004). Composing an international staff. In A. W. J. Harzing & J. Van Ruysseveldt (Eds.), *International Human Resource Management.* London: Sage.

Haslberger, A. (2008). Expatriate adjustment. *International Human Resource Management: A European Perspective, 21,* 130–149.

Haslberger, A., & Vaiman, V. (2013). Self-initiated expatriates: A neglected source of global talent flow. In V. Vaiman & A. Haslberger (Eds.), *Talent Management of Self-Initiated Expatriates – A Neglected Source of Global Talent* (pp. 1–18). New York: Palgrave Macmillan.

Hocking, J. B., Brown, M., & Harzing, A. W. (2004). A knowledge transfer perspective of strategic assignment purposes and their path-dependent outcomes. *International Journal of Human Resource Management, 15,* 565–586.

Holt, K., & Seki, K. (2012). Global leadership: A developmental shift for everyone. *Industrial and Organizational Psychology, 2,* 196–215.

Holtbrügge, D., Friedmann, C. B., & Puck, J. F. (2010). Recruitment and retention in foreign firms in India: A resource-based view. *Human Resource Management, 49,* 439–455.

Howe-Walsh, L., & Schyns, B. (2010). Self-initiated expatriation: Implications for HRM. *The International Journal of Human Resource Management, 21,* 260–273.

Huang, X. (2008). Guanxi networks and job searches in China's emerging labour market: A qualitative investigation. *Work, Employment & Society, 22,* 467–484.

Janssens, M., & Brett, J. M. (2006). Cultural intelligence in global teams: A fusion model of collaboration. *Group and Organization Management, 31,* 124–153.

Jensen, P. D. Ø., Kirkegaard, J. F., & Laugesen, N. S. (2009). Beyond job losses: The net effects of offshoring and inshoring on employment in the Danish economy. *Strategic Outsourcing: An International Journal, 2*(2), 123–144.

Jokinen, T. (2005). Global leadership competencies: A review and discussion. *Journal of European Industrial Training, 29,* 199–216.

Kedia, B. L., & Lahiri, S. (2007). International outsourcing of services: A partnership model. *Journal of International Management, 13,* 22–37.

Kedia, B. L., & Mukherjee, D. (2009). Understanding offshoring: A research framework based on disintegration, location and externalization advantages. *Journal of World Business, 44,* 250–261.

Kim, H. (2013). Inpatriation: A review of three research streams. *Annals of Business Administrative Science, 12,* 327–343.

Kim, S., Froese, F. J., & Cox, A. (2012). Applicant attraction to foreign companies: The case of Japanese companies in Vietnam. *Asia Pacific Journal of Human Resources, 50,* 439–458.

Kinkel, S., & Maloca, S. (2009). Drivers and antecedents of manufacturing offshoring and backshoring – A German perspective. *Journal of Purchasing and Supply Management, 15*(3), 154–165.

Knox, S., & Freeman, C. (2006). Measuring and managing employer brand image in the service industry. *Journal of Marketing Management, 22,* 695–716.

Konopaske, R., Robie, C., & Ivancevich, J. M. (2009). Managerial willingness to assume traveling, short-term and long-term global assignments. *Management International Review, 49*(3), 359–387.

Lemmink, J., Schuijf, A., & Streukens, S. (2003). The role of corporate image and company employment image in explaining application intentions. *Journal of Economic Psychology, 24,* 1–15.

Lewin, A. Y., Massini, S., & Peeters, C. (2009). Why are companies offshoring innovation? The emerging global race for talent. *Journal of international Business Studies, 40,* 901–925.

Lewis, R., & Heckman, R. (2006). Talent management: A critical review. *Human Resource Management Review, 16,* 139–154.

Lievens, F., van Hoye, G., & Anseel, F. (2007). Organizational identity and employer image: Towards a unifying framework. *British Journal of Management, 18,* 45–59.

Lievens, F., Van Hoye, G., & Schreurs, B. (2005). Examining the relationship between employer knowledge dimensions and organizational attractiveness: An application in a military context. *Journal of Occupational and Organizational Psychology, 78*(4), 553–572.

Ma, R., & Allen, D. G. (2009). Recruiting across cultures: A value-based model of recruitment. *Human Resource Management Review, 19*(4), 334–346.

Mäkelä, K., Björkman, I., & Ehrnrooth, M. (2010). How do MNCs establish their talent pools? Influences on individuals' likelihood of being labeled as talent. *Journal of World Business, 45,* 134–142.

Manning, S., Massini, M., & Lewin, A. Y. (2008). A dynamic perspective on next-generation offshoring: The global sourcing of science and engineering talent. *Academy of Management Perspectives, 22,* 35–54.

Manpower. (2012). Manpower Group annual survey reveals U.S. talent shortages persist in skilled trades, engineers and IT staff. 10 December. press.manpower.com/press/2012/talent-shortage.

Martin, G., Gollan, P. J., & Grigg, K. (2011). Is there a bigger and better future for employer branding? Facing up to innovation, corporate reputations and wicked problems in SHRM. *The International Journal of Human Resource Management, 22,* 3618–3637.

Martin, G., & Hetrick, S. (2009). Employer branding and corporate reputation management in an international context. *In* P. Sparrow (Ed.), *Handbook of International Human Resource Management: Integrating People, Process, and Context* (pp. 293–320). Chichester: John Wiley & Sons.

Mayerhofer, H., Hartmann, L. C., & Herbert, A. (2004). Career management issues for flexpatriate international staff. *Thunderbird International Business Review, 46,* 647–666.

Mayerhofer, H., Hartmann, L.C., Michelitsch-Riedl, G., & Kollinger, I. (2004). Flexpatriate assignments: A neglected issue in global staffing. *The International Journal of Human Resource Management, 15*(8), 1371–1389.

McDonnell, A., & Boyle, B. (2012). Higher education in flight: A new direction for international assignments research. *The International Journal of Human Resource Management*, 23, 4342–4358.

McDonnell, A., Hickey, C., & Gunnigle, P. (2011). Global talent management: Exploring talent identification in the multinational enterprise. *European Journal of International Management*, 5, 174–193.

McDonnell, A., Lamare, R., Gunnigle, P., & Lavelle, J. (2010). Developing tomorrow's leaders – Evidence of global talent management in multinational enterprises. *Journal of World Business*, 45, 150–160.

McPhail, R., Fisher, R., Harvey, M., & Moeller, M. (2012). Staffing the global organization: 'Cultural nomads'. *Human Resource Development Quarterly*, 23, 259–276.

Mellahi, K., & Collings, D. G. (2010). The barriers to effective global talent management: The example of corporate elites in MNEs. *Journal of World Business*, 45, 143–149.

Meyskens, M., Von Glinow, M. A., Werther, W. B., & Clarke, L. (2009). The paradox of international talent: Alternative forms of international assignments. *The International Journal of Human Resource Management*, 20, 1439–1450.

Millar, J., & Salt, J. (2006). The mobility of expertise in transnational corporations. Migration Research Unit. Working Paper. University College London.

Miller, J. K., & Guo, G. C. (2014). Recruitment: International cross-cultural perspectives. *In* K. Y. T. Yu & D. M. Cable (Eds.), *The Oxford Handbook of Recruitment* (pp. 402–422). New York: Oxford University Press.

Minbaeva, D. B., & Michailova, S. (2004). Knowledge transfer and expatriation in multinational corporations: The role of disseminative capacity. *Employee Relations*, 26, 663–679.

Moriarty, E., Wickham, J., Krings, T., Salamonska, J., & Bobek, A. (2012). Taking on almost everyone? Migrant and employer recruitment strategies in a booming labour market. *International Journal of Human Resource Management*, 23(9), 1871–1887.

Morley, M., & Heraty, N. (2004). International assignments and global careers. *Thunderbird International Business Review*, 46, 633–646.

Morris, S. S., Wright, P. M., Trevor, J., Stiles, P., Stahl, G. K., Snell, S., Paauwe, J., & Farndale, E. (2009). Global challenges to replicating HR: The role of people, processes, and systems. *Human Resource Management*, 48, 973–995.

Mudambi, R., & Venzin, M. (2010). The strategic nexus of offshoring and outsourcing decisions. *Journal of Management Studies*, 47, 1510–1533.

Newburry, W., Gardberg, N., & Belkin, L. Y. (2006). Organizational attractiveness in the eye of the beholder: The interaction of demographic characteristics with foreignness. *Journal of International Business Studies*, 37, 666–686.

Paik, Y., & Ando, N. (2011). MNC's competitive strategies, experiences, and staffing policies for foreign affiliates. *International Journal of Human Resource Management*, 22(15), 3003–3019.

Phillips, J. M. (1998). Effects of realistic job previews on multiple organizational outcomes: A meta-analysis. *Academy of Management Journal*, 41, 673–690.

Phillips, J. M., & Gully, S. M. (2015). Multilevel and strategic recruiting: Where have we been, where can we go from here? *Journal of Management*. 41(5), 1416–1445. doi: 10.1177/0149206315582248.

Phillips, J. M., Gully, S. M., McCarthy, J. E., Castellano, W. G., & Kim, M. S. (2014). Recruiting global travelers: The role of global travel recruitment messages and individual differences in perceived fit, attraction, and job pursuit intentions. *Personnel Psychology*, 67, 153–201.

Point, S., & Dickmann, M. (2012). Branding international careers: An analysis of multinational corporations' official wording. *European Management Journal*, 30, 18–31.

Puck, J. F., Mohr, A. T., & Holtbrügge, D. (2006). Cultural convergence through web-based management techniques? The case of corporate website recruiting. *Journal of International Management*, 12(2), 181–195.

Reiche, B. S. (2011). Knowledge transfer in multinationals: The role of inpatriates' boundary spanning. *Human Resource Management*, 50, 365–389.

Reiche, B. S., Kraimer, M. L., & Harzing, A. (2011). Why do international assignees stay? An organizational embeddedness perspective. *Journal of International Business Studies*, 42, 521–544.

Ren, Z. J., & Zhou, Y. P. (2008). Call center outsourcing: Coordinating staffing level and service quality. *Management Science, 54*, 369–383.

Richardson, J., & McKenna, S. (2003). International experience and academic careers: What do academics have to say? *Personnel Review, 32*, 774–795.

Rodriguez, J. K., & Scurry, T. (2014). Career capital development of self-initiated expatriates in Qatar: Cosmopolitan globetrotters, experts and outsiders. *The International Journal of Human Resource Management, 25*, 1046–1067.

Scullion, H. (1994). Staffing policies and strategic control in multinationals. *International Studies of Management and Organisation, 3*, 86–104.

Scullion, H., & Brewster, C. (2001). The management of expatriates: messages from Europe. *Journal of World Business, 36*, 346–365.

Scullion, H., & Collings, D. G. (2006). International recruitment and selection. *In* H. Scullion & D. G. Collings, *Global Staffing* (pp. 59–83). New York: Routledge.

Scullion, H., & Collings, D. G. (2011). *Global Talent Management.* New York: Routledge.

Scullion, H., Collings, D. G., & Caligiuri, P. (2010). Global talent management. *Journal of World Business, 45*(2), 105–108.

Seigel, J. (2008). Global talent management at Novartis. Harvard Business School, Case # 9-708-486.

Shaffer, M. A., Kraimer, M. L., Chen, Y. P., & Bolino, M. C. (2012). Choices, challenges, and career consequences of global work experiences: A review and future agenda. *Journal of Management, 38*, 1282–1327.

Sidani, Y., & Al Ariss, A. (2014). Institutional and corporate drivers of global talent management: Evidence from the Arab Gulf region. *Journal of World Business, 49*(2), 215–224.

Sparrow, P. R. (2005). Global human resource management. *In* M. Shams & P. Jackson (Eds.), *Developments in Work and Organizational Psychology: Implications for International Business* (pp. 105–129). New York: Elsevier.

Sparrow, P. R. (1999). International recruitment, selection and assessment. *In* P. Joynt & B. Morton (Eds.), *The global HR manager: Creating the seamless organisation* (pp. 87–114). London: Institute of Personnel Development.

Sparrow, P. R. (2007). Globalization of HR at function level: Four UK-based case studies of the international recruitment and selection process. *The International Journal of Human Resource Management, 18*, 845–867.

Sparrow, P., Brewster, C., & Harris, H. (2015). *Globalizing Human Resource Management* (2nd ed.). New York: Routledge.

Stahl, G., Björkman, I., Farndale, E., Morris, S. S., Paauwe, J., Stiles, P., Trevor, J., & Wright, P. (2012). Six principles of effective global talent management. *Sloan Management Review, 53*(2), 25–42.

Stringfellow, A., Teagarden, M., & Nie, W. (2008). Invisible costs in offshoring services work. *Journal of Operations Management, 26*(2), 164–179.

Suutari, V. (2003). Global managers: Career orientations, career tracks, life-style implications and career commitment. *Journal of Managerial Psychology, 18*, 185–233.

Tahvanainen, M., Welch, D., & Worm, V. (2005). Implications of short-term international assignments. *European Management Journal, 23*, 663–673.

Takeuchi, R. (2010). A critical review of expatriate adjustment research through a multiple stakeholder view: Progress, emerging trends, and prospects. *Journal of Management, 36*, 1040–1064.

Tarique, I., Schuler, R., & Gong, Y. (2006). A model of multinational enterprise subsidiary staffing composition. *The International Journal of Human Resource Management, 17*, 207–224.

Taylor, A. (2005). Global growth to fall unless people work longer. *Financial Times* (London), 12.

Tharenou, P. (2013). Self-initiated expatriates: An alternative to company-assigned expatriates? *Journal of Global Mobility: The Home of Expatriate Management Research, 1*, 336–356.

Thite, M., Srinivasan, V., Harvey, M., & Valk, R. (2009). Expatriates of host-country origin: 'Coming home to test the waters'. *International Journal of Human Resource Management, 20*(2), 269–285.

Thomas, D. C., Elron, E., Stahl, G., Ekelund, B. Z., Ravlin, E. C., Cerdin, J. L., Poelmans, S., Brislin, R., Pekerti, A., Aycan, Z., Maznevski, M., Au. K., & Lazarova, M. B. (2008). Cultural intelligence domain and assessment. *International Journal of Cross-Cultural Management, 8,* 123–143.

Toh, S. M., & DeNisi, A. S. (2005). A local perspective to expatriate success. *Academy of Management Executive, 19,* 132.

Toh, S. M., & DeNisi, A. S. (2007). Host country nationals as socializing agents: A social identity approach. *Journal of Organizational Behavior, 28,* 281–301.

Toh, S. M., DeNisi, A. S., & Leonardelli, G. J. (2012). The perspective of host country nationals in socializing expatriates: The importance of foreign–local relations. *In* C. R. Wanberg (Ed.), *Oxford Handbook of Socialization* (pp. 230–249). New York: Oxford University Press.

Tremblay, M., Patry, M., & Lanoie, P. (2008). Human resources outsourcing in Canadian organizations: An empirical analysis of the role of organizational characteristics, transaction costs and risks. *International Journal of Human Resource Management, 19*(4), 683–715.

Tung, R. L., & Lazarova, M. (2006). Brain drain versus brain gain: An exploratory study of ex-host country nationals in Central and East Europe. *The International Journal of Human Resource Management, 17,* 1853–1872.

Tungli, Z., & Peiperl, M. (2009). Expatriate practices in German, Japanese, U.K. and U.S. multinational companies: A comparative survey of changes. *Human Resource Management, 48,* 153–171.

UNCTAD. (2011). United Nations conference on trade and development. *The World Investment Report 2011. Non-Equity Modes of International Production and Development. Annex Table 34, Number of Parent Corporations and Foreign Affiliates, by Region and Economy.* Geneva: United Nations. unctad.org/Sections/dite_dir/docs/WIR11_web%20tab%2034.pdf. Last accessed 5 January 2015.

UNCTAD. (2014a). United Nations conference on trade and development. *The World Investment Report 2014. Table 2. Selected Indicators of FDI and International Production, 2013 and Selected Years.* Geneva: United Nations. unctad.org/en/PublicationsLibrary/wir2014_en.pdf. Last accessed 4 January 2015.

UNCTAD. (2014b). United Nations conference on trade and development. *World Investment Report 2014: Annex Tables. Web Table 16. Number of Cross-Border M&A Purchases, by Sector/Industry, 1990–2013.* Geneva: United Nations. unctad.org/en/Pages/DIAE/World%20 Investment%20Report/Annex-Tables.aspx. Last accessed 4 January 2015.

UNCTAD. (2014c). United Nations conference on trade and development. *World Investment Report 2014: Annex Tables. Web Table 23. Number of Greenfield FDI Projects, by Sector/Industry, 2003–2013.* Geneva: United Nations. unctad.org/en/Pages/DIAE/World%20Investment%20 Report/Annex-Tables.aspx Last accessed 4 January 2015.

Vaiman, V., Scullion, H., & Collings, D. (2012). Talent management decision making. *Management Decision, 50*(5), 925–941.

Vance, C. M., Vaiman, V., & Andersen, T. (2009). The vital liaison role of host country nationals in MNC knowledge management. *Human Resource Management, 48,* 649–659.

Varma, A., Pichler, S., Budhwar, P., & Biswas, S. (2009). Chinese host country nationals' willingness to support expatriates: The role of collectivism, interpersonal affect, and guanxi. *International Journal of Cross-Cultural Management, 9,* 99–216.

Varma, A., Toh, S. M., & Budhwar, P. S. (2006). A new perspective on the female expatriate experience: The role of host country national categorization. *Journal of World Business, 41,* 112–120.

Warner, M. (2009). 'Making sense' of HRM in China: Setting the scene 1. *The International Journal of Human Resource Management, 20,* 2169–2193.

Waxin, M., & Panaccio, A. (2005). Cross-cultural training to facilitate expatriate adjustment: It works! *Personnel Review, 34,* 51–67.

Ziguras, C., & Law, S. F. (2006). Recruiting international students as skilled migrants: The global 'skills race' as viewed from Australia and Malaysia. *Globalisation, Societies and Education, 4,* 59–76.

4

Applicant Reactions to Hiring Procedures

Donald M. Truxillo, Talya N. Bauer and Alexa M. Garcia

Introduction

Over the past century the basic paradigm of personnel selection research and practice has been testing validity and validity coefficients (Ryan & Ployhart, 2014). During the twentieth century consideration of job applicants – to the extent that their viewpoint was considered at all – dealt with the concept of 'face validity' (e.g., Schmidt, Greenthal, Hunter, Berner & Seaton, 1977), the idea that tests should at least appear to be job-related to applicants. However, a deeper understanding of job applicants' opinions of selection procedures and the effects of their attitudes and behaviours towards employers and themselves were given little consideration, and certainly no systematic examination in the industrial-organizational (I-O) literature.

In some of the earliest research on applicant reactions, Gilliland (1993) argues that the study of applicant reactions should be an important aspect of research and practice for three reasons. The first is that, for business reasons, organizations should care about how applicants perceive the hiring process. Their perceptions can impact whether individuals recommend the organization to others, as well as their attitudes towards recommending or purchasing the organization's products. Gilliland's second reason is that applicant perceptions of the hiring process may have legal ramifications for organizations. Individuals who perceive the process to be unfair may ultimately pursue litigation. Finally, Gilliland argues that, for ethical reasons, we should care about applicant reactions. It is important to understand how the hiring processes that are developed and implemented impact individuals both positively and negatively.

In recent years this landscape has changed considerably, with an increased focus on job applicants' perceptions of the hiring procedures used by companies and the treatment of applicants during the selection process. With this has come the recognition that these perceptions on the part of applicants can affect a number of outcomes that organizations care about, from intentions to purchase products from the hiring organization (e.g., Macan,

The Wiley Blackwell Handbook of the Psychology of Recruitment, Selection and Employee Retention,
First Edition. Edited by Harold W. Goldstein, Elaine D. Pulakos, Jonathan Passmore and Carla Semedo.
© 2017 John Wiley & Sons Ltd. Published 2020 by John Wiley & Sons Ltd.

Avedon, Paese & Smith, 1994) to whether applicants decide to accept job offers (e.g., Harold, Holtz, Griepentrog, Brewer & Marsh, 2015). This recognition of the field of 'applicant reactions' has been accelerated by changes in the ways that hiring procedures are now be deployed in organizations, specifically, the use of technological solutions in selection that speed up the process and can even be used as a messaging tool for organizations.

The purpose of this chapter is to provide an overview of the field of applicant reactions in terms of both where the field is now and where it might go next. We begin by discussing the theoretical models that have shaped this field. Next, we briefly discuss which selection procedures applicants prefer, followed by a description of the antecedents and outcomes of job applicant reactions to selection. We conclude with a discussion of new research avenues that appear to be emerging in this field.

Theoretical Models

Organizational justice theory

Organizational justice theory was originally proposed by Greenberg (1987), who distinguished between two forms of justice: procedural and distributive. Procedural justice can be distinguished from distributive justice in that procedural justice is the fairness associated with the processes for resource allocation in the workplace. In contrast, distributive justice is the fairness associated with the actual resource allocation among employees in the workplace. Organizational justice theory is applied widely across a variety of areas of research in I-O psychology (e.g., Colquitt, Conlon, Wesson, Porter & Ng, 2001) and has been particularly foundational for much of the research in the applicant reactions field. When applied to applicant reactions research, procedural justice refers to the fairness associated with the hiring procedures and distributive justice refers to the fairness associated with the hiring decision.

The increasing academic attention that the applicant reactions research area has garnered since 1990 has been greatly enhanced by the development and publication of Gilliland's (1993) theoretical 'Model of applicants' reactions to employment selection systems'. What makes this model especially compelling is the idea that it blends the theoretical nuances of the literature on organizational justice and selection with the practical context and implications that applicants and hiring personnel face in the field.

At its highest level, the model focuses on the two key aspects of organizational justice that Greenberg (1987) identified. As previously mentioned, procedural justice refers to perceptions of the fairness of the way that individuals are treated. In other words, 'Am I being treated fairly?' Second, distributive justice refers to perceptions of fairness in one's outcomes to a given decision. In other words, 'Am I getting the outcome I deserve?' A key point of Gilliland's (1993) model is that although a fair outcome is important to applicants, as has been consistently observed in the literature (Ryan & Ployhart, 2000), the use of a fair processes matter a lot to applicants as well.

Procedural justice　The aspect of Gilliland's (1993) model which has driven a great deal of research is the notion of 10 procedural justice rules which were developed by Leventhal (1980) and had been captured in previous research on applicant reactions (e.g., Arvey & Sackett, 1993; Schuler, 1993). Categorizing and embedding each of the 10 procedural justice rules into the context of selection systems allowed future researchers to remain tied to the literature, theory and practice at the same time. Following Greenberg (1990), the three categories of procedural justice rules include formal characteristics, explanations, and interpersonal treatment.

Table 4.1   Gilliland's (1993) 10 selection procedural justice rules.

Justice Rules	*Definitions*
Formal Characteristics	
Job-relatedness	The extent to which a test is thought to measure aspects of the actual job situation.
Opportunity to perform	Giving applicants a chance to express themselves before a decision is made.
Reconsideration opportunity	The ability of applicants to challenge or modify the decision-making process.
Consistency	Ensuring consistency across all candidates for the selection procedures.
Explanations	
Feedback	Provision of both timely and useful information.
Selection information	Giving applicants a justification for a given decision.
Honesty	Truthfulness of information given to applicants during the selection process.
Interpersonal Treatment	
Interpersonal effectiveness of the administrator(s)	Respect and warmth given to applicants during the selection process.
Two-way communication	The opportunity that applicants have to offer input or to have their views considered during the selection process.
Propriety of questions	Being asked appropriate and non-prejudicial statements during the selection process.

Source: Truxillo, D. M., Bauer, T. N., & McCarthy, J. (2015). Applicant fairness reactions to the selection process. *In* R. Cropanzano & M. Ambrose (Eds.), *Oxford Handbook of Justice in the Workplace*. Oxford: Oxford University Press. Reproduced with permission.

Table 4.1 summarizes the 10 selection procedural justice rules. Under the *formal characteristics* heading are job-relatedness, opportunity to perform, reconsideration opportunity and consistency of administration. Job-relatedness refers to the extent to which a selection procedure, or set of procedures, is perceived to measure aspects of the job the applicant is applying to do. Opportunity to perform refers to the perception of applicants that they are able to express themselves and show what they can do before a final selection decision is made. Reconsideration opportunity refers to the ability of applicants to appeal a selection decision, either at a given hurdle or at the end of the process. Consistency refers to all job applicants being equally treated throughout the selection process.

Under the *explanation* heading are feedback, selection information and honesty. Feedback refers to the perception that applicants are provided with both timely and useful information about their application. Selection information refers to the perception of the reasons given for a selection decision. Finally, honesty refers to the perception that applicants are given accurate and truthful information about their application process and status.

Under the *interpersonal treatment* heading are interpersonal effectiveness of administrator, two-way communication and propriety of questions. Interpersonal effectiveness of the administrator(s) refers to the perception of the warmth and respect that those administering the selection procedure(s) show applicants. Two-way communication refers to the applicants' ability to voice concerns, perspectives or input throughout the hiring process.

And propriety of questions refers to the perception that administrators, such as interviewers, ask appropriate and non-prejudicial questions during the selection process.

Distributive justice   The distributive justice rules included in Gilliland's (1993) model are equity, equality and needs. The idea is that applicants may hold different views regarding which rules constitute 'fair' outcomes. If applicants focus on equity, then their focus is on the fact that people should receive rewards that are consistent with the inputs they contribute in a distribution situation in comparison to a reference comparison other. Equality, on the other hand, refers to the idea that everyone should receive an equal chance of receiving the outcome, regardless of their effort or inputs. Finally, needs distribution refers to the idea that rewards should be distributed based on the individuals' situation rather than solely on merit. Examples of this include affirmative action programmes or for those needing accommodations to perform the job.

Relationship between procedural and distributive justice   Another key component of Gilliland's (1993) model is the relationship between procedural and distributive justice. There are two key points here. First is the assumption that the outcomes applicants receive (distributive justice) are major components of applicant reactions, but that the fairness of procedures could have an effect on applicant reactions as well. In other words, what was new about Gilliland's model was that applicants' reactions could be affected above and beyond these outcomes by the selection process; that is, how they were treated by the selection procedures and the organizational personnel. It is for this reason that subsequent applicant reactions research has generally examined the effects of procedural justice from the applicant's perspective above and beyond the outcomes the applicants received (e.g., Ryan & Ployhart, 2000). Second, Gilliland's model notes that procedural and distributive justice may interact, such that the effects of distributive justice may be stronger when procedural justice is high. This is consistent with prior notions of organizational justice (e.g., Brockner & Wiesenfeld, 1996). For example, applicants' self-perceptions may be more negatively affected by the outcome they receive when they believe that the process was fair. Such interactive effects on self-perceptions have been generally supported by subsequent research (e.g., Bauer, Maertz, Dolen & Campion, 1998).

Critiques and updates of Gilliland's model   Since its development, Gilliland's model of applicant reactions has been critiqued by several researchers, and many of these critiques have been addressed by subsequent research, which included updated models.

In their review, Ryan and Ployhart (2000) note that a nomological network in the applicant reactions field was missing in that there was a lack of empirical evidence testing the relationships among these variables and applicant perceptions. They also argued that while the justice rules that are central to Gilliland's model have strong theoretical foundations, they may not be such strong predictors of fairness perceptions since there had been few manipulations of these rules in research up to that point. Additionally, Ryan and Ployhart argue that test-taking attitudes may be important determinants of applicant perceptions. Another critique of Gilliland's model is that there was a lack of empirical evidence linking justice perceptions to subsequent outcomes for both individuals and organizations. Finally, Ryan and Ployhart argue that the application of organizational justice theory to applicant reactions may differ from applications of justice theory to other research in I-O psychology in that in the selection context, applicants are usually external to the organization. Therefore, applications of organizational justice theory to applicants during selection may be different from how it is applied to employees internal to the organization. In order to address some of these issues, Ryan and Ployhart expanded Gilliland's model.

One of the more notable characteristics of their model is that it distinguishes between different types of applicant perceptions (perceptions of the hiring process, perceptions of the individuals' affective/cognitive state, perceptions of the hiring decision and overall perceptions of the hiring processes/procedures).

Others sought to further understand Gilliland's propositions. Bauer and colleagues (2001) empirically confirmed the existence of the 10 procedural justice rules of Gilliland's model (plus an additional rule: job-relatedness-content), and that these rules could be explained by two higher-order factors focused on the structure of the selection system and how applicants are treated. They also found that the procedural justice rules affected later applicant outcomes (e.g., intentions to take legal action against the organization) beyond the outcomes that applicants received. Building on both Gilliland's (1993) model and Ryan and Ployhart's (2000) model, Hausknecht, Day and Thomas (2004) devised another updated model of applicant reactions based on a meta-analytic examination of the literature. Hausknecht and colleagues categorized antecedents of applicant perceptions into four categories: person characteristics, perceived procedure characteristics, job characteristics and organizational context. These antecedents predict applicant perceptions (procedural justice, distributive justice, test anxiety, test motivation, attitudes towards tests and towards selection). In turn, these perceptions predict four categories of outcomes: selection procedure performance, self-perceptions, attitudes and behaviours towards the organization, and work attitudes and behaviours. Furthermore, the links between antecedents and perceptions and the links between perceptions and outcomes are moderated by variables such as job desirability and stage in the selection process. Addressing Ryan and Ployhart's concern about lack of empirical support for these relationships in applicant reactions research, Hausknecht and colleagues tested these relationships in their meta-analysis of 86 independent samples, finding support for the relationship between justice perceptions and applicant outcomes such as perceptions of the organization.

Finally, some justice rules have proved to be consistently related to applicant attitudes and behaviours. For example, research supports the view that perceived job-relatedness (i.e., whether the selection procedure seems job-related to applicants), consistent treatment of applicants and opportunity to 'show what you know' (opportunity to perform; Schleicher, Venkataramani, Morgeson & Campion, 2006) are related to applicant reactions. That said, all the justice rules have been shown to relate to applicant reactions to some degree (Bauer, Truxillo, Sanchez, Craig, Ferrara & Campion, 2001; Hausknecht et al., 2004). The continued challenge for the field is to demonstrate whether the justice rules relate to more 'hard' outcomes such as applicant behaviours for although some support in this arena (e.g., job offer acceptance; Harold et al., 2015) has been found, other behaviours proposed by Gilliland's model, such as actual litigation, have remained almost entirely unexamined.

Other theoretical approaches

In addition to Gilliland's (1993) model of applicant reactions, there are several other theoretical approaches used in this literature. Although these theories have received far less attention in terms of empirical research and support, they are still of value in the applicant reactions field and may prove useful as research and knowledge continue to develop in this area.

Social validity theory Schuler's (1993) social validity theory strongly emphasizes the applicant's perspective of the selection procedures and the extent to which they perceive they have been treated with dignity and respect. According to Schuler, social validity consists of four dimensions: *informativeness* – whether applicants are provided with meaningful and useful information; *participation* – whether applicants feel that they have sufficiently been a part of the process and to show their abilities; *transparency* – whether it is clear what procedures are being used and how; and *feedback* – whether applicants are given adequate feedback, even if they do not receive a job offer.

Interestingly, Anderson, Salgado and Hülsheger (2010) note that while much of the applicant reactions research in the United States has been grounded in Gilliland's model, most of the applicant reactions research in Europe has been grounded in Schuler's social validity theory. While there are different preferences for theories in the US versus Europe, when both Gilliland's and Schuler's models are compared, there is significant similarity between the aspects of social validity and Gilliland's procedural justice rules, suggesting that these theories function similarly in providing a basis for applicant reactions research.

Arvey and Sackett's model   Another influential model of applicant reactions was developed by Arvey and Sackett (1993). Although this model does not have a single unifying theoretical approach, in their model the fairness perceptions of applicants *and* the organization and its decision makers are considered. Overall, this model is similar to Gilliland's and conceptualizes multiple sources of antecedents of fairness. In their consideration of the organization and its decision makers, Arvey and Sackett include characteristics of selection tests and organizational context as contributing to fairness. As previously mentioned, most of the applicant reactions in the US has foundations in Gilliland's model, most likely because of its strong theoretical basis. However, it is important to note that there are still some studies that use Arvey and Sackett as their basis (e.g., Madigan & Macan, 2005; Nicolaou & Judge, 2007; Viswesvaran & Ones, 2004).

Fairness theory   A third alternative to Gilliland's model is Folger and Cropanzano's fairness theory (2001). According to their theory, applicants' reactions are impacted by their interpretation of the situation based on three counterfactuals about the situation: could, would and should. Applicants ask themselves questions such as: *Should* the organization have provided more feedback? There are two types of explanations that are used when answering counterfactuals: excuses and justifications. Excuses are used to reduce *could* counterfactuals and justifications are used to reduce *should* counterfactuals. Overall, research shows that excuses tend to be more effective than justifications (Shaw, Wild & Colquitt, 2003), although a meta-analysis of these explanations, specifically in the context of applicant reactions research, did not find that one type of explanation was more effective than the others (Truxillo, Bodner, Bertolino, Bauer & Yonce, 2009).

Applicant Attribution-Reaction theory   Ployhart and Harold's (2004) Applicant Attribution-Reaction theory (AART) postulates that individuals make attributions about the hiring process that result in applicant reaction outcomes such as fairness, motivation and test perceptions. Attributions made can be about the individual's behaviour or the behaviour of someone else (e.g., the hiring organization). Ployhart and Harold argue that these attributions are automatic and tend to occur immediately following the event. Attributions are formed when individuals compare their situation to their expectations, which Ployhart and Harold purport are shaped by the justice rules proposed by Gilliland. Although justice rules do play a part in AART, what distinguishes it from Gilliland's model is that it largely focuses on applicants' attributions largely driving applicant reactions (although justice rules do play a role in this process). Some research (Ployhart & Ryan, 1997) has established the usefulness of the attribution approach to applicant reactions, but AART has not 'grown legs' compared to other applicant reactions approaches, perhaps because of the complexity of measuring applicants' varied attributions about selection procedures.

Summary of other theoretical approaches In large part these other theoretical approaches to applicant reactions research are similar to Gilliland's (1993) model. These approaches all involve fairness of the selection procedure in one way or another. They differ, however, in terms of what determines the fairness perceptions for applicants (e.g., attributions vs. actual characteristics of selection procedures), how these fairness perceptions relate to outcomes for individuals and organizations, and their depth of theoretical underpinnings. Additionally, Gilliland's model is more comprehensive and includes a wide variety of antecedents and outcomes that should be related to applicant perceptions of the hiring process, making his model very attractive to researchers in this field. Ultimately, what may drive choice for certain theories over others for research in this field may be individual preference. For example, as previously mentioned, there is a strong preference for social validity theory in Europe, whereas researchers in the US have tended to prefer Gilliland's model (Anderson, Salgado & Hülsheger, 2010).

Effects of Different Selection Procedure Characteristics on Reactions

Gilliland's largest contribution from his model of application reactions was the 10 procedural justice rules. Since the development of this model, there have been many studies that have provided empirical support for the role that these rules play in determining applicant reactions.

Foundational for much of applicant reactions research, Gilliland's model has paved the way for other models of applicant reactions. For example, some more recent models have built on Gilliland's model by adding more antecedents (e.g., organizational characteristics like selection ratio) and moderator variables (e.g., stage in the selection process) to the framework; see Hausknech et al., 2004; Ryan & Ployhart, 2000). It is important to note that these updated applicant reactions models still include Gilliland's procedural justice rules as central components. Other research (Bauer et al., 2001) has found that Gilliland's rules can be divided into two dimensions. The first is structure fairness, which relates to the logistical components of the actual selection process (e.g., timing of feedback). The second dimension is social fairness, which taps into more interpersonal aspects of the selection process (e.g., communication with applicants).

In terms of how each of Gilliland's 10 procedural justice rules relate to applicant reactions and both individual and organizational outcomes, job-relatedness has by far received the most attention in the literature. In their meta-analysis, Hausknecht and colleagues (2004) show that job-relatedness is the most studied rule in the literature and, across studies, it tends to relate to outcomes such as product purchase intentions, offer acceptance intentions, recommendation intentions and organizational attractiveness.

Other rules that have been given some attention in the literature, although notably less than job-relatedness, include interpersonal treatment, propriety of questions and opportunity to perform (Hausknecht et al., 2004). Interestingly, Schleicher, Venkataramani, Morgeson and Campion (2006) found that after receiving negative feedback, opportunity to perform was the most important rule. For individuals who were not hired, opportunity to perform was a strong driver of fairness perceptions. Given the number of procedural justice rules that seem to be less studied in the literature, these may provide fruitful areas of research.

Which selection procedures do applicants prefer?

One question that often arises when discussing the topic of applicant reactions is: which selection procedures do applicants prefer? Given that we know that applicant reactions largely derive from the satisfaction (or dissatisfaction) of justice rules, it is easy to see how some types of selection procedures would be more likely to satisfy these rules and thus be preferable to applicants. This was the basis of many studies that have examined applicant preferences for different selection procedures and across many cultural contexts, starting with a study by Steiner and Gilliland (1996), which compared US and French students' preferences for different selection procedures. Since then, applicant reactions have been studied with a variety of samples from different countries, including Italy (e.g., Bertolino & Steiner, 2007), Vietnam (e.g., Hoang, Truxillo, Erdogan & Bauer, 2012), South Africa (e.g., De Jong & Visser, 2000), Singapore (e.g., Phillips & Gully, 2002), Germany (e.g., Marcus, 2003) and Greece (e.g., Nikolaou & Judge, 2007), to name a few.

This issue of which procedures are preferred by applicants was one of the questions that Hausknecht and colleagues (2004) addressed in their meta-analysis. In their study, there were 12 samples that asked individuals to rate the favourability (job-relatedness or fairness) of a variety of selection procedures. Rated most favourably were interviews, work samples, résumés and references. Individuals rated cognitive ability testing, personality testing and biodata as moderately favourable. Personal contacts, honesty tests and graphology were rated as the least favourable selection procedures.

In an effort to update this meta-analysis and determine whether there are cross-cultural differences in preferences, Anderson, Salgado and Hülsheger (2010) conducted a meta-analysis of 38 samples from 17 countries. Additionally, they measured preferences according to eight dimensions relating to Gilliland's justice rules: overall favourability, scientific evidence, employers' right to use, opportunity to perform, interpersonal warmth, face validity, widely used, and respectful of privacy. Overall, the results showed that preferences for selection procedures were similar to those Hausknecht and colleagues found. The most preferred methods were work samples and résumés. Favourably evaluated were cognitive ability tests, references and personality tests. The least preferred were honesty tests, personal contacts and graphology. Moreover, there were no differences across countries in these preferences.

Overall, these findings are somewhat reassuring in that applicants tend to prefer the valid selection procedures. Unfortunately, though, organizations are not always able to use the most preferred procedures in the selection process. This could be for reasons such as cost, validity and other practical constraints such as time. For example, an organization would not realistically be able to interview everyone in a pool of 2,000 applicants. Thus, organizations and HR professionals may want to consider ways to make some of the less preferable methods more favourably evaluated by applicants, for example, providing explanations about the selection procedures – an issue we discuss below.

Antecedents of applicant reactions

Perhaps the most consistent determinant of applicant reactions is outcome favourability, that is, the outcome received by an applicant from the selection process (Ryan & Ployhart, 2000). This could mean the test score the applicant received, whether or not they are asked to go on in the selection process (e.g., to a selection interview or some other hurdle) or whether they got a job. It is for that reason that most current applicant reactions research considers applicant reactions after applicants have received their outcome, as reactions can be quite different before and after a selection decision, and applicants are generally poor at guessing how well they actually performed on a selection procedure (i.e., actual and perceived test performance are not highly correlated). In addition to outcome favourability, surrogate variables for actual test performance are sometimes used in this research, such as perceptions of distributive justice or outcome fairness and measures of perceived performance.

In addition to these measures of applicant outcomes, applicant reactions models such as Gilliland's (1993) go a step further: while acknowledging that outcomes affect applicants' perceptions, the model points out that procedural justice dimensions (e.g., job-relatedness, opportunity to perform, as discussed earlier) can also affect applicant reactions. This is a core assumption of organizational justice theory more generally: although the final outcome (e.g., a performance rating) is important, the process used and the way a person is treated are important as well (e.g., Colquitt, 2001).

In addition to outcome received and procedural justice dimensions derived from the selection context, a number of other antecedents of applicant reactions have been identified (see Hausknecht et al., 2004 for a more detailed review). For example, some authors have noted that applicant reactions are not only a function of selection system characteristics, but also of individual differences. Truxillo and colleagues (2006) found that Big Five personality measured at baseline was related to fairness, self-perceptions and organizational attractiveness later in the process in conceptually logical ways, with, for instance, agreeableness related to positive reactions and neuroticism related to negative reactions. Viswesvaran and Ones (2004) found that a number of individual differences were related to the importance placed on different selection system characteristics. For instance, cognitive ability was related to applicants perceiving greater importance being placed on the content of the selection procedure. However, these authors found relatively few differences between men and women in the importance placed on selection system aspects, and only a few differences in the selection system characteristics of most importance to different ethnic groups. More recently, Honkaniemi, Feldt, Metsäpelto and Tolvanen (2013) found that certain personality profiles, such as being resilient, were related to positive applicant reactions. Taken together, these findings suggest that reactions are partly determined by applicant characteristics and not only by the selection process itself.

Effects of Applicant Reactions on Individual and Organizational Outcomes

The effects on 'soft' versus 'hard' outcomes

Truxillo, Steiner and Gilliland (2004) note that outcomes of applicant reactions can be broken down into 'soft' outcomes, that is, attitudes and behaviour proximal to the hiring procedure, and 'hard' outcomes that occur later, on the job. This classification continues to be useful, with the most consistent effects of applicant reactions on a number of 'soft' outcomes. Here we provide a general overview of the effects of applicant reactions on a range of outcomes, although we also point the reader to detailed meta-analyses and reviews (Hausknech et al., 2004; Truxillo & Bauer, 2011; Truxillo, Bauer, McCarthy, Anderson & Ahmed, in press; Truxillo, Steiner & Gilliland, 2004).

One of the early promises of applicant reactions models was that job applicants' perceptions of the selection process might affect their later attitudes and behaviour on the job if they were hired. Truxillo, Steiner and Gilliland (2004) referred to these as 'hard' outcomes. For the most part, these types of outcome have not been found to be affected by applicant reactions, at least for external job applicants (see Gilliland, 1994, for a laboratory study that suggests the relation between reactions and job performance). For example, Truxillo, Bauer, Campion and Paronto (2002) found that while providing police officer candidates with a fairness explanation did affect their fairness perceptions, it did not affect their later turnover during the training period. One of the explanations for this lack of results is that these on-the-job outcomes are too distal from the hiring process to be affected by applicant reactions. In other words, how a person is treated in the hiring process is less likely to affect their job attitudes six months after they are hired; rather, job satisfaction is likely to be affected by other factors more proximal to the actual job situation, such as characteristics of the job and treatment by the supervisor. However, it is notable that recent research (Harold et al., 2015) has found a relationship between justice perceptions and job offer acceptance (see below). Moreover, it is important to note that applicant reactions may affect these 'hard' outcomes among promotional candidates (Ambrose & Cropanzano, 2003), an issue we discuss as an avenue for future research.

In the sections that follow, we describe the effects of reactions on outcomes that are relevant to the organization versus those that are relevant to the individual applicant.

Organizational outcomes

Gilliland (1993) noted that one of the drivers of applicant reactions research comes from an organizational perspective. Organizations want to attract and hire the most qualified applicants, and especially to avoid litigation. Indeed, the research indicates that applicant reactions do have an impact on outcomes such as organizational attractiveness, recommendation intentions and litigation, for example.

Organizational attractiveness Numerous studies, including meta-analyses (e.g., Hausknecht et al., 2004) have shown that organizational attractiveness is related to perceptions of justice, both procedural and distributive. There is also evidence to indicate that the impact of fairness on organizational attractiveness persists over time (e.g., Bauer, Maertz, Dolen & Campion, 1998).

Recommendation intentions Much like the research regarding organizational attractiveness, there is support for a positive relationship between fairness and whether individuals would recommend that organization to others (e.g., Ababneh, Hackett & Schat, 2014; Bauer et al., 1998; Hausknecht et al., 2004). Unlike the relationship between organizational attractiveness and fairness, though, the relationship between fairness and recommendation intentions tends to weaken over time (Bauer et al., 1998).

Litigation As previously mentioned, an organization's litigation concerns are a primary driver for its interests in applicant reactions research. Unfortunately, researchers have not yet examined the relationship between applicant fairness perceptions and actual litigation (Truxillo & Bauer, 2011). However, there is evidence to suggest that, not surprisingly, there is a negative relationship between fairness perceptions and litigation intentions (e.g., Ababneh et al., 2014; Bauer et al., 2001; Bauer et al., 2004).

Job offer acceptance Until 2010, research had only examined the relationship between fairness and job acceptance intentions, and the findings have been mixed. Some have found a negative relationship (e.g., Hausknecht et al., 2004; Macan et al., 1994) and others have found no relationship (e.g., Ployhart & Ryan, 1997). Recent research, however, has examined the relationship between fairness perceptions and actual job offer acceptance. In a field study of military job applicants, Harold and colleagues (2015) found that procedural justice significantly predicted job offer acceptance and provided an incremental prediction over other variables such as person–organization fit. Moreover, interactional justice was also a significant predictor of job acceptance. This provides further evidence of the value of applicant reactions research to organizations.

Test performance and validity   One of the key questions is whether applicant reactions affect test performance and test validity. For example, some early research (Schmit & Ryan, 1992) found that candidate motivation could increase the validity of a cognitive ability test and decrease the validity of a personality test. However, a more recent paper by McCarthy and colleagues (2013) examined this issue for six different types of selection procedures (e.g., cognitive ability, work sample) in four studies in North America, South America and Europe. McCarthy and colleagues indeed found that candidate reactions were related to the level of test scores (which is consistent with previous research; e.g., Bauer et al., 2006; Hausknecht et al., 2004). However, in none of the samples did they find that reactions moderated the criterion-related validity of the test. Although more research may be warranted, the comprehensive nature of this study suggests that reactions have relatively few effects on test validity.

Individual outcomes

In addition to the importance of studying applicant reactions from an organizational perspective, Gilliland (1993) argued that, from an ethical perspective, we should care about the well-being of applicants and thus study their reactions to selection procedures. Research suggests that applicant reactions impact self-efficacy and self-esteem.

Self-efficacy   Some research has found that fairness perceptions are positively related to self-efficacy (e.g., Bauer et al., 1998; Truxillo et al., 2002; Truxillo, Bauer & Sanchez, 2001). This is important because applicants with higher test-taking self-efficacy tend to perform better on selection procedures. For example, McCarthy, Hrabluik and Jelley (2009) demonstrated that in four studies using six selection procedures, self-efficacy had a positive relationship with test scores on these selection procedures. Interestingly, an interaction effect between procedural justice and selection outcome has found that when individuals perceive unfairness and do not receive a job offer, self-efficacy is lowest (e.g., Ployhart & Ryan, 1997).

Self-esteem   In addition to placing importance on understanding how the selection process impacts self-efficacy, Gilliland (1993) placed value on understanding how fairness and selection outcomes might predict self-esteem. In general, research has indicated that there is a positive relationship between the two (e.g., Bauer et al., 2001; Hausknecht et al., 2004).

Future Research

Privacy concerns

One of the largest areas of new development in relation to online testing is privacy concerns. Bauer and colleagues (2006) examined these in the lab with students in a simulated employment situation and in the field at a large state agency. Consistent with their predictions, they found that procedural justice moderated the relationship between privacy concerns and important outcomes such as test-taking motivation, organizational attraction and organizational intentions. Furthermore, more internet-savvy job applicants are more satisfied with online application procedures than those who are less familiar with this technology (Sylva & Mol, 2009).

These concerns become much more specific when employers use information available on social media accounts (Stoughton, Thompson & Meade, 2015; Van Iddekinge, Lanivich, Roth & Junco, in press) or use credit score information, or both (Bernerth, Taylor, Walker & Whitman, 2012) in their selection processes. These factors are consistent with Alge's (2001) work, which shows that individual value control over their public persona when it can be damaging. Thus, there is fertile ground to further examine how the digitalization of data is influencing applicants and their perceptions of selection processes.

Social networking and applicant reactions

Relatedly, in recent years the popular press has made much about the use of social networking sites (SNSs) in personnel selection, both in recruitment and as a potential selection tool. In that time, a research literature on SNSs for these personnel uses has begun to develop, illustrating both the value and risks of using SNSs for selection. Use of SNSs for recruitment appears to have grown rapidly and research suggests that it is especially useful for attracting 'passive' job seekers, that is, those who are not actively looking for work (Nikolaou, 2014; Nikolaou, Bauer & Truxillo, 2015). In fact, SNSs such as LinkedIn are becoming part of the standard networking landscape.

However, the use of SNSs for making selection decisions is more problematic. First, the research thus far suggests that the use of SNSs may not lead to valid selection decisions. Van Iddekinge and colleagues (in press) provided recruiters with job applicants' Facebook profiles and asked them to rate the profiles. These ratings were unrelated to supervisors' job performance ratings and turnover, and provided no incremental validity beyond personality and cognitive ability tests. Moreover, they found that the ratings tended to favour White and female applicants, suggesting that there could be some adverse impact. In other words, this research suggests that ratings of SNSs may not be valid and may make an adverse impact.

However, applicant reactions are a separate issue, since applicants may not always prefer the most valid selection procedures, such as unstructured interviews. Nevertheless, the research thus far generally suggests that applicants do not react very positively to the use of SNSs for selection. In a sample of participants at a career fair for the hospitality industry, Madera (2012) found lower perceived fairness and intentions to pursue a job for organizations that used SNSs as a selection tool compared to those that did not. Stoughton, Thompson and Meade (2015) examined applicant reactions to SNS in selection across two studies. In Study 1, which involved people who applied for a research assistant position, they found that SNS screening led to applicants feeling that their privacy had been invaded and to have lower organizational attraction. In Study 2, which involved participants in a simulated hiring scenario, the use of SNSs to screen applicants led to increases in perceived invasion of privacy, decreased organizational attraction and increased intentions to litigate. Overall, these studies suggest that using SNSs is perceived negatively by job applicants and may affect important outcomes such as litigation. Indeed, Roth, Bobko, Van Iddekinge and Thatcher (in press) point out a number of potential concerns with the use of SNSs for personnel selection, including the possibility for adverse impact and the likelihood of recruiters over-relying on negative information about applicants – issues which, if known to applicants, should lead to fewer applicant reactions.

Although the use of SNSs for applicant screening is of concern at this point, one can foresee how their careful use, especially those focused specifically on professional issues such as LinkedIn, could lead to more positive applicants. Roulin (2014) found that *faux pas* postings on SNSs (i.e., showing inappropriate content) on the part of applicants is lower when candidates are informed that employers may use SNSs for hiring decisions. Thus, if the general use of SNSs in recruitment and selection continues such that all applicants use them, and if SNS content were to be in some way standardized across applicants, and if recruiters could be trained in the standardized evaluation of SNSs, much as they are with structured interviews, one could argue that SNSs could lead to acceptable validities and acceptable applicant reactions. While these may be worthy goals we are not there yet, and using SNS for making selection decisions seems risky for reasons related to legal issues, validity and applicant reasons.

Reactions of internal candidates for promotion

Perhaps one of the greatest missed opportunities in the field of applicant reactions is the issue of internal candidates. Although relatively little research has examined this area, there are three reasons that it may be a particularly fruitful avenue for research. First, although external job applicants typically do not become organizational members (except for the few that are hired), internal applicants for promotion remain with an organization. That is, they are 'rejected but still there' (Ford, Truxillo & Bauer, 2009). That is, internal candidates remain as organizational members, with potentially negative effects on outcomes such as job attitude and performance. In other words, while the research has generally not found that selection procedures used with external candidates affect their job attitudes and behaviours once they are hired, this has received little scrutiny in promotional contexts, where job attitudes and behaviours are more proximal to the selection processes. Second, because internal candidates experience social consequences if they are not promoted when they face their co-workers (Ford, Truxillo & Bauer, 2009), arguably they may face greater consequences than external candidates who can simply move on. Third, because of these high stakes in the promotional context – internal candidate have some investment in the organization and their membership of it – the effects of applicant reactions on various outcomes are likely to be amplified.

The few studies that have examined the effects of candidate reactions to promotions suggest that this is a promising area. First, fairness perceptions of promotional procedures do appear to affect important outcomes and last over time. Using a sample of academics up for tenure and promotion, Ambrose and Cropanzano (2003) found that fairness perceptions associated with the process were related to job satisfaction, organizational commitment and turnover intentions. Not surprisingly, and consistent with the demonstrated importance of outcome fairness in applicant reactions (Ryan & Ployhart, 2000), they found that the effects of the distributive justice of the promotion decision lasted over time. Second, applicant reactions appear to be amplified in the promotion context compared to the external hiring process. Truxillo and Bauer (1999) used three samples of police applicants (two external samples; one internal sample of promotional candidates) to examine applicant reactions to test score banding (Sackett & Wilk, 1994). They found that the belief that banding is associated with affirmative action interacted with race to affect applicant reactions. However, these effects in the promotional sample were approximately double those found among external candidates.

Although there have been frequent calls to examine applicant reactions to promotions, the empirical studies have been relatively scant (for exceptions see García-Izquierdo,

Moscoso & Ramos-Villagrasa, 2012; Giumetti & Sinar, 2012; McCarthy et al., 2009). However, we think that reactions to promotional decisions continue to beg further studies because of the potentially larger effect sizes, broader range of outcomes (e.g., performance, well-being, job attitudes) likely to be affected and more direct impact on the organization (due to disaffected applicants staying with the employer) compared to external selection.

Reactions in the digital age of selection

Over the years selection theory and technology have evolved. However, the last two decades have seen explosive growth in new techniques and procedures designed to process a large number of applicants using technology and automation. Because of these radical changes it is not always clear what testing and selection procedures mean in a high-tech context. For example, applicants may be pre-qualified for multiple jobs across multiple organizations through a central 'clearing house' that resides with a single organization or a consortium of hiring organizations. To our knowledge, this type of process has not yet been examined in terms of the key factors studied in application reactions to selection procedures such as fairness, security and/or privacy concerns. Other procedures, such as potential applicant self-assessments of fit based on reading about or watching videos about life within the organization, are another interesting example. Technically, these individuals have not yet applied for any jobs so there is no way of knowing how these bits of information help or hinder the selection process.

One area of practice that has seen a little more attention is that of information given to applicants during the selection process. Like Allen, Mahto and Otondo (2007), Walker and colleagues (2013) found that communication during the recruitment process has signalling value and that organizational attraction increases and decreases over time based on these signals and other factors. However, overall it is clear that there is a great deal of catching up that researchers in the area of applicant reactions have still to do, given how quickly the field of selection is evolving.

Overcoming negative applicant reactions

Although applicants' reactions may be beyond the organization's control, there are things employers can do to influence applicant reactions. As noted earlier, applicants prefer certain selection procedures to others (e.g., Anderson et al., 2010; Hausknecht et al., 2004; Steiner & Gilliland, 1996); however, the selection procedures applicants prefer may not always be the most valid (e.g., unstructured interviews) or most practical for organizations to use on a large scale (e.g., work samples). For this reason, research has also examined providing explanations to applicants to improve their reactions (e.g., Gilliland, Groth, Backer, Dew, Polly & Langdon, 2001; Truxillo et al., 2002). A meta-analysis (Truxillo et al., 2009) showed that providing explanations to applicants about selection procedures to show that they are valid appears to affect applicant fairness perceptions, self-perceptions, test-taking motivation and test performance. In other words, providing explanations to job applicants about selection procedures shows promise as a way to improve applicant reactions. Although some of these effect sizes were small ($r = 0.10$), we believe that this area shows promise for future research. As noted by Truxillo and colleagues (2009), the research on applicant explanations has included a broad range of explanations (e.g., those that focus on the job-relatedness of the test or on respectful treatment of applicants), and more research is needed to determine which explanation types are most likely to affect applicant reactions.

Conclusion

Applicant reactions research has evolved considerably since 1990, with a move away from simple considerations of face validity to more sophisticated, theory-based models. In that time, applicant reactions have been shown to relate to a number of important outcomes proximal to the selection procedure, such as attitudes to the employer and actual job acceptance decisions on the part of applicants. Recent developments in the online deployment of HR systems have opened a number of avenues for future research. For these reasons, we see this area as continuing to blossom in the coming decades.

References

Ababneh, K. I., Hackett, R. D., & Schat, A. C. (2014). The role of attributions and fairness in understanding job applicant reactions to selection procedures and decisions. *Journal of Business and Psychology, 29*, 111–129.

Alge, B. J. (2001). Effects of computer surveillance on perceptions of privacy and procedural justice. *Journal of Applied Psychology, 86*, 797–804.

Allen, D. G., Mahto, R. V., & Otondo, R. F. (2007). Web-based recruitment: Effects of information, organizational brand, and attitudes toward a web site on applicant attraction. *Journal of Applied Psychology, 92*, 1696–1708.

Ambrose, M. L., & Cropanzano, R. (2003). A longitudinal analysis of organizational fairness: An examination of reactions to tenure and promotion decisions. *Journal of Applied Psychology, 88*, 266–275.

Anderson, N., Salgado, J. F., & Hülsheger, U. R. (2010). Applicant reactions in selection: Comprehensive meta-analysis into reaction generalization versus situational specificity. *International Journal of Selection and Assessment, 18*, 291–304.

Arvey, R., & Sackett, P. (1993). Fairness in selection: Current developments and perspectives. *In* N. Schmitt & W. C. Borman (Eds.), *Personnel Selection on Organization* (pp. 171– 202). San Francisco: Jossey-Bass.

Bauer, T. N., Maertz, C. P., Dolen, M. R., & Campion, M. A. (1998). Longitudinal assessment of applicant reactions to employment testing and test outcome feedback. *Journal of Applied Psychology, 83*, 892–903.

Bauer, T. N., Truxillo, D. M., Paronto, M., Weekley, J., & Campion, M. A. (2004). Applicant reactions to different selection technology: Face-to-face, interactive voice response, and computer-assisted telephone screening interviews. *International Journal of Selection and Assessment, 12*, 135–148.

Bauer, T. N., Truxillo, D. M., Sanchez, R. J., Craig, J., Ferrara, P., & Campion, M. A. (2001). Applicant reactions to selection: Development of the selection procedural justice scale (SPJS). *Personnel Psychology, 54*, 387–419.

Bauer, T. N., Truxillo, D. M., Tucker, J. S., Weathers, V., Bertolino, M., Erdogan, B., & Campion, M. A. (2006). Selection in the information age: The impact of privacy concerns and computer experience on applicant reactions. *Journal of Management, 32*, 601–621.

Bernerth, J. B., Taylor, S. G., Walker, H. J., & Whitman, D. S. (2012). An empirical investigation of dispositional antecedents and performance-related outcomes of credit scores. *Journal of Applied Psychology, 97*, 469–478.

Bertolino, M., & Steiner, D. (2007). Fairness reactions to selection methods: An Italian study. *International Journal of Selection and Assessment, 15*, 197–205.

Brockner, J., & Wiesenfeld, B. M. (1996). An integrative framework for explaining reactions to decisions: Interactive effects of outcomes and procedures. *Psychological Bulletin, 120*, 189–208.

Colquitt, J. A. (2001). On the dimensionality of organizational justice: A construct validation of a measure. *Journal of Applied Psychology, 86*, 386–400.

Colquitt, J. A., Conlon, D. E., Wesson, M. J., Porter, C. O. L. H., & Ng, K. Y. (2001). Justice at the millennium: A meta-analytic review of 25 years of organizational justice research. *Journal of Applied Psychology, 86,* 425–445.

De Jong, A., & Visser, D. (2000). Black and White employees' fairness perceptions of personnel selection techniques. *South African Journal of Psychology, 30,* 17–24.

Folger, R., & Cropanzano, R. (2001). Fairness theory: Justice as accountability. *In* J. Greenberg & R. Cropanzano (Eds.), *Advances in Organizational Justice* (pp. 1–55). Stanford, CA: Stanford University Press.

Ford, D. K., Truxillo, D. M., & Bauer, T. N. (2009). Rejected but still there: Shifting the focus in applicant reactions to the promotional context. *International Journal of Selection and Assessment, 17,* 402–416.

García-Izquierdo, A. L., Moscoso, S., & Ramos-Villagrasa, P. J. (2012). Reactions to the fairness of promotion methods: Procedural justice and job satisfaction. *International Journal of Selection and Assessment, 20,* 394–403.

Gilliland, S. (1994). Effects of procedural and distributive justice on reactions to a selection system. *Journal of Applied Psychology, 79,* 691–701.

Gilliland, S. W. (1993). The perceived fairness of selection systems: An organizational justice perspective. *Academy of Management Review, 18,* 694–734.

Gilliland, S. W., Groth, M., Backer IV, R. C., Dew, A. F., Polly, L. M., & Langdon, J. C. (2001). Improving applicants' reactions to rejection letters: An application of fairness theory. *Personnel Psychology, 54,* 669–703.

Giumetti, G. W., & Sinar, E. F. (2012). Don't you know me well enough yet? Comparing reactions of internal and external candidates to employment testing. *International Journal of Selection and Assessment, 20,* 139–148.

Greenberg, J. (1987). A taxonomy of organizational justice theories. *Academy of Management Review, 12,* 9–22.

Greenberg, J. (1990). Organizational justice: Yesterday, today, and tomorrow. *Journal of Management, 16,* 399–432.

Harold, C. M., Holtz, B. C., Griepentrog, B. K., Brewer, L. M., & Marsh, S. M. (2015). Investigating the effects of applicant justice perceptions on job offer acceptance. Personnel Psychology. doi: 10.1111/peps.12101.

Hausknecht, J. P., Day, D. V., & Thomas, S. C. (2004). Applicant reactions to selection procedures: An updated model and meta-analysis. *Personnel Psychology, 57,* 639–683.

Hoang, T. G., Truxillo, D. M., Erdogan, B., & Bauer, T. N. (2012). Cross-cultural examination of applicant reactions to selection methods: United States and Vietnam. *International Journal of Selection and Assessment, 20,* 209–219.

Honkaniemi, L., Feldt, T., Metsäpelto, R., & Tolvanen, A. (2013). Personality types and applicant reactions in real-life selection. *International Journal of Selection and Assessment, 21,* 32–45.

Leventhal, G. S. (1980). What should be done with equity theory? *In* K. J. Gergen, M. S. Greenberg & R. H. Willis (Eds.), *Social exchange: Advances in theory and research* (pp. 27–55). New York: Plenum.

Macan, T., Avedon, M., Paese, M., & Smith, E. (1994). The effects of applicants' reactions to cognitive ability tests and an assessment center. *Personnel Psychology, 47,* 715–738.

Madera, J. M. (2012). Using social networking websites as a selection tool: The role of selection process fairness and job pursuit intentions. *International Journal of Hospitality Management, 31,* 1276–1282.

Madigan, J., & Macan, T. H. (2005). Improving candidate reactions by altering test administration. *Applied H.R.M. Research, 10,* 73–88.

Marcus, B. (2003). Attitudes towards personnel selection methods: A partial replication and extension in a German sample. *Applied Psychology, 52,* 515–532.

McCarthy, J. M., Hrabluik, C., & Jelley, R. B. (2009). Progression through the ranks: Assessing employee reactions to high-stakes employment testing. *Personnel Psychology, 62,* 793–832.

McCarthy, J. M., Van Iddekinge, C. H., Lievens, F., Kung, M. C., Sinar, E. F., & Campion, M. A. (2013). Do candidate reactions relate to job performance or affect criterion-related validity? A multistudy investigation of relations among reactions, selection test scores, and job performance. *Journal of Applied Psychology, 98,* 701.

Nikolaou, I. (2014). Social networking web sites in job search and employee recruitment. *International Journal of Selection and Assessment, 22,* 179–189.

Nikolaou, I., Bauer, T. N., & Truxillo, D. M. (2015). Applicant reactions to selection methods: An overview of recent research and suggestions for the future. *In* I. Nikolaou & J. Oostrom (Eds.), *Current Issues in Personnel Selection* (pp. 80–96). Hove: Psychology Press/Taylor and Francis.

Nikolaou, I., & Judge, T. (2007). Fairness reaction to personnel techniques in Greece: The core of self-evaluations. *International Journal of Selection and Assessment, 15,* 206–219.

Phillips, J. M., & Gully, S. M. (2002). Fairness reactions to personnel selection techniques in Singapore and the United States. *International Journal of Human Resource Management, 13,* 1186–1205.

Ployhart, R. E., & Harold, C. M. (2004). The applicant attribution-reaction theory (AART): An integrative theory of applicant attributional processing. *International Journal of Selection and Assessment, 12,* 84–98.

Ployhart, R. E., & Ryan, A. M. (1997). Toward an explanation of applicant reactions: An examination of organizational justice and attribution frameworks. *Organizational Behavior and Human Decision Processes, 72,* 308–335.

Ployhart, R. E., & Ryan, A. M. (1998). Applicants' reactions to the fairness of selection procedures: The effects of positive rule violations and time of measurement. *Journal of Applied Psychology, 83,* 3–16.

Roth, P. L., Bobko, P., Van Iddekinge, C. H., & Thatcher, J. B. (in press). Social media in employee-selection-related decisions A research agenda for uncharted territory. *Journal of Management,* online. doi: 10.1177/0149206313503018.

Roulin, N. (2014). The influence of employers' use of social networking websites in selection, online self-promotion, and personality on the likelihood of *faux pas* postings. *International Journal of Selection and Assessment, 22,* 80–87.

Ryan, A. M., & Ployhart, R. E. (2000). Candidates' perceptions of selection procedures and decisions: A critical review and agenda for the future. *Journal of Management, 26,* 565–606.

Ryan, A. M., & Ployhart, R. E. (2014). A century of selection. *Annual Review of Psychology, 65,* 693–717.

Sackett, P. R., & Wilk, S. L. (1994). Within-group norming and other forms of score adjustment in preemployment testing. *American Psychologist, 49,* 929–954.

Schleicher, D. J., Venkataramani, V., Morgeson, F. P., & Campion, M A. (2006). So you didn't get the job…*now* what do you think? Examining opportunity-to- perform fairness perceptions. *Personnel Psychology, 59,* 559–590.

Schmidt, F. L., Greenthal, A. L., Hunter, J. E., Berner, J. G., & Seaton, F. W. (1977). Job sample vs. paper-and-pencil trades and technical tests: Adverse impact and examinee attitudes. *Personnel Psychology, 30,* 187–197.

Schmit, M. J., & Ryan, A. M. (1992). Test-taking dispositions: A missing link? *Journal of Applied Psychology, 77,* 629–637.

Schuler, H. (1993). Social validity of selection situations: A concept and some empirical results. *In* J. Schuler, J. L. Farr & M. Smith (Eds.), *Personnel Selection and Assessment: Individual and Organizational Perspectives* (pp. 41–55). Hillsdale, NJ: Lawrence Erlbaum.

Shaw, J. C., Wild, E., & Colquitt, J. A. (2003). To justify or excuse? A meta-analytic review of the effects of explanations. *Journal of Applied Psychology, 88,* 444–458.

Steiner, D. D., & Gilliland, S. W. (1996). Fairness reactions to personnel selection techniques in France and the United States. *Journal of Applied Psychology, 81,* 134–141.

Stoughton, J. W., Thompson, L., & Meade, A. (2013). Examining applicant reactions to the use of social networking websites in pre-employment screening. *Journal of Business and Psychology, 28,* 1–16.

Stoughton, J. W., Thompson, L. F., & Meade, A. W. (2015). Examining applicant reactions to the use of social networking websites in pre-employment screening. *Journal of Business & Psychology, 30,* 73–88.

Sylva, H., & Mol, S. T. (2009). E-recruitment: A study into applicant perceptions of an online application system. *International Journal of Selection and Assessment, 17,* 311–323.

Truxillo, D. M., & Bauer, T. N. (1999). Applicant reactions to test scores banding in entry-level and promotional contexts. *Journal of Applied Psychology, 84,* 322–339.

Truxillo, D. M., & Bauer, T. N., (2011). Applicant reactions to organizations and selection systems. *In* S. Zedeck (Ed.), *APA Handbook of I/O Psychology* (Vol. 2, pp. 379–397). Washington, DC: American Psychological Association Press.

Truxillo, D. M., Bauer, T. N., Campion, M. A., & Paronto, M. E. (2002). Selection fairness information and applicant reactions: A longitudinal field study. *Journal of Applied Psychology, 87,* 1020–1031.

Truxillo, D. M., Bauer, T. N., Campion, M. A., & Paronto, M. E. (2006). A field study of the role of Big Five personality in applicant perceptions of selection fairness, self, and the hiring organization. *International Journal of Selection and Assessment, 14,* 269–277.

Truxillo, D., Bauer, T., McCarthy, J., Anderson, N. R., & Ahmed, S. (in press). Applicant perspectives on employee selection systems. *In* D. Ones, N. R. Anderson, C. Viswesvaran & H. K. Sinangil (Eds.), *Handbook of Industrial, Work and Organizational Psychology* (2nd ed.). London and New York: Sage.

Truxillo, D. M., Bauer, T. N., & Sanchez, R. J. (2001). Multiple dimensions of procedural justice: Longitudinal effects on selection system fairness and test-taking self-efficacy. *International Journal of Selection and Assessment, 9,* 336–349.

Truxillo, D. M., Bodner, T. B., Bertolino, M., Bauer, T. N., & Yonce, C. (2009). Effects of explanations on applicant reactions: A meta-analytic review. *International Journal of Selection and Assessment, 17,* 346–361.

Truxillo, D. M., Steiner, D., & Gilliland, S. (2004). The importance of organizational justice in personnel selection: Defining when selection fairness really matter. *International Journal of Selection and Assessment, 12,* 39–53.

Van Iddekinge, C. H., Lanivich, S. E., Roth, P. L. & Junco, E. (in press). Social media for selection? Validity and adverse impact potential of a Facebook-based assessment. *Journal of Management,* online. doi: 10.1177/0149206313515524.

Viswesvaran, C., & Ones, D. S. (2004). Importance of perceived personnel selection system fairness determinants: Relations with demographic, personality, and job characteristics. *International Journal of Selection and Assessment, 12,* 172–186.

Walker, J., Bauer, T. N., Cole, M. S., Bernerth, J. B., Feild, H. S., & Short, J. C. (2013). Is this how I will be treated? Reducing uncertainty through recruitment interactions. *Academy of Management Journal, 56,* 1325–1347.

5

Applicant Attraction to Organizations and Job Choice

Adrian Furnham and Kat Palaiou

Introduction

Human capital is arguably the most important asset that an organization can have. Consequently, recruitment offers the valuable function of attracting the necessary talent to the organization (Rynes & Cable, 2003). The future success of organizations lies in their being able to attract, as well as select and develop, high-potential people with ability, drive and talent (MacCrae & Furnham, 2014). The high-potential and talent literature seems more concerned with selection and training than the literature, mainly from vocational psychology, on what attracts people to work for an organization.

It is challenging for companies to create and change their personnel image to attract the 'right' staff, a process called *employer branding* (Edwards, 2010). The first stage of recruitment, when companies try to identify potential applicants, especially high flyers, and convince them to apply through the use of a wide array of recruitment practices, is vital to gain a better understanding of which features affect applicants' initial attraction to companies. If they are not attracted at the first stage, they will withdraw and will not be reached by later recruitment or selection activities (Collins & Stevens, 2002; Slaughter, Stanton, Mohr & Schoel, 2005).

This chapter examines the literature on the factors that attract job applicants to a particular organization. It is important to distinguish between being attracted to a *job*, with well-established and well-known characteristics and skill requirements, and an *organization* that has very different and often unknown attributes (Gomes & Neves, 2011).

There is inevitably a number of factors that play a part in that choice which differ according to the demographic and psychographic characteristics of the applicant, as well as the cultural, economic and social conditions of the time. Factors that play an important part include salary and working conditions, location and training programmes available. Organizations try to develop a reputation as a good employer and a place where people want to work. In short, they want a brand that attracts 'good' people.

The Wiley Blackwell Handbook of the Psychology of Recruitment, Selection and Employee Retention, First Edition. Edited by Harold W. Goldstein, Elaine D. Pulakos, Jonathan Passmore and Carla Semedo.
© 2017 John Wiley & Sons Ltd. Published 2020 by John Wiley & Sons Ltd.

This brand marketing may or may not be grounded in reality. That is, what they say about themselves, such as their culture and values, may be at odds with the experience of the people who actually work for the organization.

Attraction-Selection-Attrition Theory

It is probably true to say that there are no specific theories of applicant attraction, however various ideas, concepts and models have been applied to the area. Of these perhaps the best known is Attraction-Selection-Attrition (ASA) theory.

Schneider (1987) proposed a simple but popular theory based on three concepts:

- *Attraction*: People are differentially attracted to careers as a function of their own interests and personality. That is, they search out potential jobs and employers as a function of 'fit'.
- *Selection*: Organizations then select people who they think have the abilities, personality and motivation to be successful at the job in their organization. Thus, organizations end up choosing people who have many characteristics in common with them and hence become more and more homogeneous.
- *Attrition*: This occurs when people do not fit the organization and leave.

It is possible to add another stage – *socialization* – which suggests that once people have been selected they are taught 'what to think' and 'how to behave'. In other words, they become socialized in the explicit and implicit organizational culture. Thus, people come to share a common set of assumptions, values and beliefs.

The theory is simple: for all sorts of reasons people are attracted to certain jobs. They may or may not be well informed about the nature of the job or the organizations, or indeed whether their particular skills, knowledge or motivation are appropriate. Consequently, applicants may be attracted to jobs without any real knowledge of the industry or their particular abilities. After potential employees apply to a particular job or organization that they are attracted to, they go through a selection process which is aimed at hiring people who will thrive in that work. Selection processes differ considerably among organizations. The theory suggests that candidates do some sort of matching, where they consider their personal assets in terms of abilities, preference and values; and then to what extent the organization and the job require those assets. This may seem too complicated, implying very purposeful data gathering and decision making on the part of applicants.

People often spontaneously apply for several jobs at the same time according to convenience of place and time, as well as salary. Nevertheless, the theory is popular because it has validity and makes good sense. Moreover, it has been tested in a variety of contexts, such as in the context of management (Baron, Franklin & Hmieleski, 2013) showing that successful entrepreneurs will pursue their activities and the success that they experience will mitigate stress.

The literature on the topic of organizational attraction goes back many years. The latest studies concern web applications and the great difference that the web has made to the process (Dineen, Ash & Noe, 2002). Unlike traditional print media, internet-based recruitment allows for inexpensive, rapid and mass communication to large numbers of applicants. Organizational websites become the main source of information for applicants. Moreover, an organization's website can provide a positive first impression and communicate its culture to leverage person–organization (PO) fit (Cober, Brown, Levy, Cober & Keeping, 2003).

This application has proved to be particularly valuable to public sectors agencies, which had traditionally lagged behind in attracting young workers (Chetkovich, 2001).

It is also acknowledged that recruitment is no longer local or even national but international, and that recruiting globally poses particular challenges (Phillips, Gully, McCarthy, Castellano & Kim, 2014). While researchers acknowledge that a wide variety of factors play a part in the whole attraction issue, they focus on very particular issues. Thus, Hsiao, Ma and Auld (2014), researching attractiveness for working in the hotel sector in Taiwan, focused on ethnic diversity as a central issue, while other studies have looked at issues such as the desirability of flextime and flexiplace (Thompson, Payne & Taylor, 2014). Furthermore, many acknowledge that it is a dynamic process, which can change as a function of where in the process a candidate is (von Walter, Wentzel & Tomczak, 2010).

The Measurement of Attraction

The measurement of job/organizational attraction is self-report, usually by interview or questionnaire. The central issue is what question(s) to ask to gain a full understanding of an applicant's perception. Nearly all the early studies used single-item measures, but Fisher, Ilgen and Hoyer (1979) devised four-item measures, which were combined into a general company attractiveness measure. The items included attraction and intention, though some other studies asked candidates about the organization's reputation and prestige.

Highhouse, Lievens and Sinar (2003) were perhaps the first to devise a psychometrically sound, multidimensional measure which could be used in research studies to make them in some sense comparable. They developed a 12-item, 3-factor measure which assesses the general attractiveness of the organization, intentions to pursue and prestige. Their model suggests that the attractiveness and prestige of the organization together predicted the intention to get a job, which leads to organizational pursuit. It remains one of the few measures in this area. It is perhaps surprising that no one appears to have developed a multidimensional measure of organizational attractiveness.

Another research avenue concerns attempting to describe organizations in trait terms. For instance, there is a literature on symbolic, trait-based inferences about organizations in five dimensions: sincerity, excitement, competence, prestige and ruggedness (Schreurs Druart, Proost & De Witte, 2009). This enables people to match more easily their perceived own personality with that of the organization (Nolan & Harold, 2010).

What do applicants want?

The first impressions of a company as an employer have been shown to be related to initial attraction to an organization (e.g. Turban, Forret & Hendrickson, 1998). Brand image is a concept with a long history in the marketing literature (e.g. Keller, 1993; Levy, 1957). Lievens and Highhouse (2003) developed the 'instrumental-symbolic' framework (based on brand image theory) where images are composed of both instrumental and symbolic dimensions. Instrumental image dimensions describe the company in terms of objective, concrete and factual attributes that may or may not obtain (Lievens, van Hoye & Anseel, 2007). Applicants' attraction to instrumental attributes is related to more utilitarian needs, such as pay, advancement opportunities and job security (van Hoye, Saks, & Weijters, 2014). Symbolic image dimensions describe the company in terms of subjective, abstract and intangible traits. In lay terms, symbolic image dimensions concern how people understand a company and make inferences about it. Employees use these symbolic traits because they help them to maintain their self-identity, improve their self-image or express themselves (Shavitt, 1990).

Studies on this theoretical framework have shown that instrumental/symbolic image dimensions are related to the perception of organizational attractiveness, organizational identification and recommendation intentions from employees (Lievens, van Hoye & Anseel, 2007). The most important finding is that symbolic image dimensions account for more incremental variance than instrumental image dimensions predicting organizational attractiveness. Moreover, companies are better differentiated from each other based on symbolic than on instrumental attributes (Lievens & Highhouse, 2003). Van Hoye, Bas, Cromheecke and Lievens (2013), using a Turkish sample, investigated whether these findings apply in collectivistic cultures. They confirmed that both dimensions are related to companies' attractiveness as an employer (e.g., Lievens, 2007). More specifically, they found that Turkish applicants are more attracted to companies that offer better working conditions and to companies that are perceived to be more competent. However, the most important conclusion from their study is that their findings are in line with findings in Western societies, demonstrating generalization. As in Western countries, symbolic traits that applicants associate with companies account by far for more incremental variance than instrumental traits, indicating that they may be the key determinants of companies' attraction.

As noted above, the first issue for researchers in the area is to try to list the most important factors in the prediction of applicant attraction. Thereafter, research needs to concentrate on how these may be ranked and weighted, and more importantly how they interact with each other dynamically.

Many studies have attempted to list the factors. One of the first and most important meta-analysis, by Chapman, Uggerslev, Carroll, Piasentin and Jones (2005), looked at studies on applicants' attraction, job choice and reactions to selection procedures. They concluded that the best way to address this issue is to split the literature into three types of variables. *Recruitment outcomes* include:

1   *Job pursuit intentions:* These include submitting an application, visiting a site, attending an interview or generally staying in the applicant pool without committing to the job.
2   *Job/organization attraction:* This is the applicant's overall evaluation of the job and/or the organization.
3   *Acceptance intentions:* This refers to accepting intentions before and/or after a job offer is made.
4   *Job choice:* This refers to accepting or declining a job offer.

The second type of variable is *predictors* of which there are six:

1   *Job and organizational characteristics:* Those relate to the job (pay, benefits, type of work) and the organization (image, size, location).
2   *Recruiter characteristics:* Who and how the recruitment is done.
3   *Perceptions of the recruiter process:* Interpersonal treatment, timely information as well as the validity and procedural fairness of the whole process.
4   *Perceived fit:* This is the process where the applicant interprets the perceived characteristics of the job, organization and recruiter in the light of their own needs and values.
5   *Perceived alternatives:* The applicants' perceived marketability, namely the perception of viable and attractive job alternatives.
6   *Hiring expectation:* Evaluations of the likelihood of being offered a position in the organization.

The third part is the *moderator variables*, which include gender and race. Chapman and colleagues concluded that both job and organization characteristics are important parameters of the recruiting outcome, that how the recruiting is done is much more important than who does it. Third, the perception of fit is one of the strongest predictors of attraction, and can involve considerable organizational resources to achieve.

Finally, an important practical question is, what should employers do to maximize the effects of their recruiting efforts with the fewest resources? Our results suggest several answers to this question. Early in the recruitment process, recruiters demonstrating personable behaviours may persuade applicants to pursue the position. Thus, selecting recruiters for how personable they are or training them to be personable would be worthwhile. Emphasizing positive characteristics associated with the work environment and organizational image may also enhance attraction to the position. Fair and considerate treatment throughout the recruitment process appears to be important with respect to acceptance intentions. Training recruiters to enhance perceptions of fairness by providing explanations for selection procedures, keeping applicants informed and avoiding undue delays in responses are all recommended to improve recruiting effectiveness. Although it is not a marked effect, a recruiter may entice a desired applicant into accepting a job offer by letting the applicant know that a job offer is likely in an effort to raise expectations about being hired. At a minimum, recruiters using difficult selection procedures should attempt to mitigate the negative consequences of reduced expectations of being hired by informing candidates that the selection task is very difficult and that many successful applicants find it challenging. Recruiters should also be aware that if time and resources are available, additional gains may be had by focusing on the values and needs that seem most in line with the values and needs of the applicant (i.e., enhancing the applicant's perceived fit with the organization). Next, we discuss the limitations associated with this research and suggest some issues that we believe researchers should focus on in the future (Chapman et al., 2005, p. 940).

Another meta-analysis by Uggerslev, Fassina and Kraichy (2012) followed Chapman and colleagues' (2005) but reduced it to seven characteristics:

1 *Job characteristics:* The favourability of attributes associated with the job, such as the intrinsic nature of the job and the compensation package.
2 *Organizational characteristics:* These include the image of the company, work environment, familiarity with the application, location and size. It might involve whether the company is in the private or public sector or indeed whether the company is foreign owned.
3 *Recruiter behaviours:* These include perceived recruiter competence, how personable, trustworthy and informative they are, and time spent recruiting.
4 *Recruitment process characteristics:* These include the attractiveness of various recruiter activities, as well as the perception of messages being complete, credible, realistic and timely. It also includes perceptions of procedural justice and of job-relatedness, treatment, timeliness and selection testing.
5 *Perceived fit:* This includes the perceptions of person–job and person–organization fit, such as in how well their goals, ideals and values fit the organization.
6 *Perceived alternatives:* These include all perceptions of employment alternatives.
7 *Hiring expectations:* These include the perceptions of how likely they are to receive a job offer from the company.

Uggerslev and colleagues (2012) conclude:

Organizational characteristics are more heavily weighed by applicants when maintaining applicant status as compared to the stage of application, and recruitment process characteristics are weighed progressively more as the recruitment stages advance. Job characteristics accounted for the greatest unique variance in job choice decisions. Job characteristics are more predictive in field studies, whereas recruiter behaviours, recruitment process characteristics, hiring expectancies, and perceived alternatives produced larger effect sizes in the laboratory. Results are discussed in terms of their theoretical and practical implications with future research suggestions. (p. 597)

However, the application process is dynamic and changes over time. Carless (2005) noted that perceptions of person–job and person–organization fit were important at different stages in the process, with the former being more important in the early stages. Harold and Ployhart (2008) were interested in how, when and why applicant decision making changes. They argue that the weighting of items changes as they progress. For instance, the process might affect their beliefs about their market value, which is an important factor. Von Walter and colleagues (2010) have argued that the time perspective makes a difference. Individuals with a more distant time perspective seem more interested in more abstract, higher-level factors.

One issue for those interested in attracting good staff is where to advertise and what to say. There is a variety of media to choose from: print media, websites, etc. It is possible to make all sorts of distinctions: websites may be been as high-information, younger person-oriented and more flexible, while print media is low-information, older person-oriented and less flexible. It is also a matter of branding for the organization which might want to be seen as high-tech and modern or more serious and conservative. Baum and Kabst (2014) note that 'high-information rich' media-like websites are much more effective than older, 'low-information' websites. They suggest that online job boards or social media are excellent platforms for recruitment advertisements.

The Selection Process

One factor that plays a part in applicants' attraction is the organization's reputation in how it selects its personnel. Some organizations make a big issue of the selection process, while others try to keep it quiet. Some invest large sums in designing assessment centres, while others continue to rely on the gut instinct of particular individuals, some of whom are trained and others not.

There is a considerable literature on the role of trustworthiness in recruitment and selection, reviewed by Klotz, Da Motta Veiga, Buckley and Gavin (2013). Both applicants and interviewer(s) expect the other party to tell the truth about themselves and the organization. Most expect information to be accurate, complete and honest, and that promises made will be kept. This is as true of the recruitment, pre-entry period as it is of the selection process. Both parties make judgements about the benevolence, integrity and ability of the other, which has an immediate impact on the outcome of the process. Both candidates and selectors are often tempted to indulge in 'impression management', which can seriously backfire when they are exposed.

Serious candidates for any job like to feel that any assessment method is fair and accurate and that they have a full opportunity to express their opinions, but also show their strengths. It has been reported that candidates object strongly to certain selection tests or processes, resulting in an organization attract poor publicity (Furnham, 2008). There are issues of who does the selection and these include in-house managers and HR specialists, as well as consultants employed for their technical knowledge and skill. The second issue is what the selection process involves, which is often little more than the standard trio of application form, references and (unstructured) interview.

On the other hand, there is an extensive literature on job applicants' perceptions of selection methods (Rynes, 1993). This topic has gathered considerable academic interest and has attracted more than one special issue in relevant journals (Anderson, 2004; Hulsheger & Anderson, 2009). One research focus has been applicants' fairness perceptions of different selection methods (Carless, 2006; Chan & Schmitt, 2004; Truxillo, Bauer, Campion & Paronto, 2006; Truxillo, Steiner & Gilliland, 2004). These include applicant perceptions of assessment centres (Baron & Janman, 1996), cognitive ability tests (Chan, Schmitt, DeShon, Declause & Delbridge, 1997) and online selections methods (Lievens, De Corte & Brysse, 2003). It seems that applicants tend to favour, and rate as fair, work samples and interviews over paper-and pencil tests (Bertolino & Steiner, 2007; Nikolaou & Judge, 2007).

Studies have indicated that fairness perceptions of selection methods have an impact on various outcomes, including applicant self-efficacy and self-esteem (Robertson & Smith, 2001), job-acceptance intentions, motivation to pursue employment and likelihood of recommending the organization to friends (Sanchez, Truxillo & Bauer, 2000).

Some researchers have aimed to model exactly what the conditions and aspects of the selection process are that applicants react to. Gilliland (1993) proposed that fairness perceptions are based on whether the selection method is strongly job-related; if the applicant is given the opportunity to perform; whether they get feedback; and the existence of two-way communication channels. However, Gilliland's procedural and distributive justice model, as well as a large proportion of the fairness perception literature, has been criticized for not taking into consideration more individual characteristics (e.g., sex and age) which might explain variation seen in fairness perceptions of different selection methods across studies (Chan & Schmitt, 2004).

In their meta-analysis of 15 years of fairness perception literature, Ryan and Ployhart (2000) note that 'few studies have looked at individual difference correlates. Indeed few studies have looked at subjects across multiple types of procedures and we need such research to determine how malleable applicant perceptions are' (p. 590). Reeve and Lam (2007) found that intelligence (*g*) was the common antecedent for cognitive test performance, test motivation and perceived fairness of selection method, suggesting that cognitive ability can explain a significant proportion of fairness perception variations. Bernerth, Field, Giles and Cole (2006) found that agreeableness and openness were positively associated, and neuroticism negatively associated with procedural and distributive justice. Similarly, Truxillo and colleagues (2006) found that neuroticism and agreeableness were the most constant predictors of applicant perceptions. Viswesvaran and Ones (2004) investigated whether personality and cognitive ability were related to the importance attached to personnel selection system characteristics, but found that few personality variables were associated. However, it should be noted that this study investigated the 'importance placed on selection method characteristics' as the outcome measure, which is not the same as fairness perceptions per se.

One recent study explored beliefs about both fairness and accuracy in university selection. Furnham and Chamorro-Premuzic (2010) investigated students' perceptions of the accuracy and fairness of 17 assessment methods to measure eight traits/characteristics thought to be desirable in students. Results for accuracy and fairness judgements are shown in Tables 5.1 and 5.2 and were similar, with drug, general knowledge and intelligence tests being thought of as the least accurate and fair, while panel interviews and references were thought of as among the fairest. Factor analyses of the accuracy data showed that there are two underlying components: test methods and face-to-face methods. There was considerable consensus among the 322 respondents. The only individual difference variable which was shown to explain any variance in accuracy perceptions was self-assessed intelligence.

Table 5.1 Descriptive statistics and Cronbach's alphas for all
assessment methods – accuracy.

Selection method	Cronbach's alpha	M	SD
Face-to-face interview	0.79	25.69	8.65
Outward-bound leadership	0.76	26.59	9.34
References	0.89	27.43	11.70
Panel interview	0.80	27.64	8.91
Discussion	0.78	28.62	8.56
Oral presentation	0.78	30.78	9.11
Personality test	0.68	32.93	8.21
Telephone interview	0.87	33.77	10.94
Video	0.82	34.54	10.43
Essay	0.79	35.17	10.39
Situation exam	0.83	35.54	10.78
Assessment centre	0.87	36.45	10.97
Unseen course-related exam	0.84	36.45	10.31
Application form	0.86	38.46	12.89
General knowledge test	0.96	42.60	11.81
Intelligence test	.83	44.08	11.11
Drug test	0.92	52.17	15.84

N = 185–322

Table 5.2 Descriptive statistics and Cronbach's alphas for all
assessment methods – fairness.

Selection method	Cronbach's alpha	M	SD
Face-to-face interview	0.88	43.28	12.97
Outward-bound leadership	0.76	30.66	10.38
References	0.90	27.49	12.34
Panel interview	0.83	20.18	10.78
Discussion	0.81	30.65	9.84
Oral presentation	0.85	32.36	11.09
Personality test	0.87	35.30	12.03
Telephone interview	0.87	34.93	11.88
Video	0.84	35.37	11.09
Essay	0.85	35.89	11.76
Situation exam	0.88	36.86	12.63
Assessment centre	0.89	38.74	12.82
Unseen course-related exam	0.86	42.04	12.53
Application form	0.88	37.42	14.17
General knowledge test	0.90	42.94	13.99
Intelligence test	0.88	43.28	12.97
Drug test	0.93	54.08	15.89

The job interview process is an opportunity for an organization to showcase its values. It is a marketing opportunity to attract staff. If an organization gains a reputation for being perfunctory, prejudicial or outdated in their selection methods, this will have an impact on its reputation and the willingness of people to apply to it. The two factors that seem to interest applicants is the fairness of the procedure, followed by its perceived validity. It may be that people are very poorly informed about the validity of different measures as the data in Tables 5.1 and 5.2 show. That is, for whatever reason they believe there is good evidence that certain tests/procedures are highly valid when they are not (e.g., unstructured interviews) or invalid when they are (e.g., intelligence tests). This can present a problem for an organization that wishes to use proven methods in selection but where applicants believe them to be inaccurate or prejudicial.

The Public versus the Private Sector

There are many differences between jobs in the public and private sectors. Certainly, ideology plays a part in job choice. Some people declare that for socio-political reasons they would never work for a particular organization, such as an international bank, a pharmaceutical company or a fast-food manufacturer. They argue that their personal values conflict with those of the organization. While there are many inaccurate stereotypes about the differences between these different types of organizations (e.g., people in the public sector have less well paid but more secure jobs and enjoy many more fringe benefits) studies have explored differences between those working in the two sectors. The assumption is that these differences are, in part, responsible for their attraction to and choice of an organization in different sectors.

Public service motivation (PSM) is defined as 'an individual's predisposition to respond to motives grounded primarily or uniquely in public institutions and organizations' (Perry & Wise, 1990, p. 368). PSM is related to organizational commitment, job satisfaction and task performance (Hilliard, Doverspike & Carpenter, 2010). Individuals with high PSM scores tend to be female, managers and obtain higher education qualifications (Bright, 2005). A very interesting finding is that PSM is more related to the perceptions of fit with the public sector than with attraction to it. Thus, an individual's attraction to a company depends on perception of fit with the company's values and culture. They also show that PSM overlaps with agreeableness. As a consequence, people attracted to public service tend to be more compassionate, friendly, cooperative, caring and willing to make sacrifices for others.

Some have looked at personal values, while others have concentrated on personality traits and motivation (Carpenter, Doverspike & Miguel, 2012). Solomon (1986) compared 240 Israeli managers from the two sectors and found private sector managers reported greater job satisfaction. Flynn and Tannenbaum (1993), two US psychologists, found private sector managers showed higher organizational commitment, as well as a sense of autonomy and challenge, than public sector managers. Lyons, Duxbury and Higgins (2006), in their study of 549 private, public and 'para-public' knowledge workers, found that private sectors workers expressed more organizational commitment. However there were few differences between them on general or work values. Bourantas and Papalexandris (1999) compared 778 public and 139 private sector Greek managers on nine measures, including locus of control, a Protestant work ethic (PWE) and tolerance of ambiguity. All but three showed significant differences from private sector managers, with higher needs for growth and clarity, as well as a sense of competence and general activity level. In a review of 34 studies comparing managers in public and private sector jobs, Boyne (2002) examined 13 hypotheses, most of which showed no significant differences. He did, however, find that public sector managers are less materialistic and organizationally committed than their private sector counterparts. Buelens and Van den Broeck (2007) studied 3,314 Belgian private and 409 public sector employees and found the former much more extrinsically oriented than the latter. They found the choice of work–life balance the most powerful motivational difference, accounting for people choosing the sector. Also, by looking at other, potentially confounding factors such as gender, age, education and job level, they showed that most of the observed differences in motivation (intrinsic/extrinsic) were explained by differences in job content rather than sector. In a study of motivational differences of 1,220 American managers, Lee and Wilkins (2011) concluded that the difference between the two sectors creates discrete organizational cultures, which affect their ability to attract potential employees.

In a recent study, Furnham, Hyde and Trickey (2014) looked at the 'dark side' of employees in the two sectors. They found that public sector employees tend to be more cautious, socially anxious, withdrawn and acquiescent than those in the private sector. Further, public sector employees were less likely to display the same levels of persuasive, influential, self-confident and innovative behavioural styles than those in the private sector. On the other hand, people in the private sector were more likely to be cynical about others' motives and to suspect others of organizational politicking and other machinations. Private sector employees tended to be more outgoing, optimistic, charming and innovative and have enhanced communication skills. They were also more likely to involve others in work activities and have a stronger social presence than those in the public sector. The job attraction literature appears not to have taken much interest in this difference, which merits more research.

One interesting question is whether these results are replicable across countries and cultures, particularly if the country has a long history of socialism versus capitalism.

Values at work

It seems obvious that people are (partly) attracted to their work as a function of their values and interests. There is a considerable literature on this.

Holland (1973) suggests that there are only six types of jobs and six types of people who fit them. Within a person or environment, some pairs of types are more closely related than others, and that the relationship within (which yields a measure of consistency) and between (which yields a measure of congruency) personality types or environments can be ordered according to a hexagonal model as shown in Figure 5.1, in which the distance within and between the personality profiles and job codes are inversely proportional to the theoretical relationships between them. The types are ordered as follows: realistic, investigative, artistic, social, enterprising and conventional (RIASEC).

The letters are listed in rank order, so that the type listed first is the type the person most resembles. As a useful and approximate way of showing the degrees of relatedness among the six types, they are arranged at the vertices of a hexagon, such that the closest are the most similar. Thus, the investigative and artistic types are similar and hence closer, because both are concerned with intellectual pursuits, although in different ways: the investigative type is more methodological and data-oriented, the artistic type more spontaneous. By contrast, the investigative type who is relatively asocial and analytical differs most from the self-confident and persuasive enterprising type. Similarly, the spontaneous, disorganized and creative artistic type contrasts sharply with the self-controlled, conforming, unimaginative conventional type. The idea is all about fitting a round peg into a round hole, in other words, finding the most appropriate job given a person's values, preferences and attitudes.

Many researchers in this area attempt to measure motivation at work, as well as attraction to a job by values. Furnham, Eracleous and Chamorro-Premuzic (2009) used the Work Values Questionnaire (WVQ) factored into three factors: security and conditions, status and rewards, and personal development and stimulation. More recently, MacCrae and Furnham (2014)

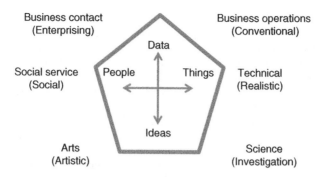

Figure 5.1   RIASEC. *Source*: Adapted from Holland (1973).

found evidence on two major factors: the intrinsic and the extrinsic. A factor analysis of the 15 extrinsic items found three factors explaining 64% of the variance: Extrinsic Facet 1: Security 21%; Extrinsic Facet 2: Compensation 24%; Extrinsic Facet 3: Comfort 19%. A factor analysis of the 15 intrinsic items found three factors explaining 60% of the variance: Intrinsic Facet 1: Autonomy 20%; Intrinsic Facet 2: Recognition 24%; Intrinsic Facet 3: Affiliation 16%.

   Indeed, one of the most fundamental distinctions made in this area is between intrinsic and extrinsic motivation. The former refers to the fundamental nature of the job. People are attracted to a job because they enjoy the tasks they are required to do; it is meaningful and fits their ability, temperament and skills. They represent a preferred activity where job demands are fully met by individual talents. Extrinsic motivation refers to the rewards for the activity rather than the activity itself. These may include salary, benefits, holidays, etc. People choose these jobs not specifically for the activity but rather the objective rewards. All jobs offer both, but it is interesting to note that job advertisements more often stress extrinsic over intrinsic rewards. However, jobs such as military service or work in the health service stress intrinsic motivation.

Individual Differences

It is clear that there are individual differences in job attraction and choice (Bipp & Demerouti, 2014). To a large extent this is the central concern of vocational psychology, though this is mainly concerned with person–job rather than person–organization fit. The central question is: which individual difference factors are relevant to person–job attraction? The following seem particularly relevant.

Perceived control

Those who believe they are in control of their own actions, and the results of those actions tend to be more proactive, seek more control and exert more effort to succeed. Perceived control describes whether they are in control of they own actions and outcomes (internal locus of control) or outside forces control their outcomes and action (external locus of control). It assumes that individuals develop general expectations regarding their ability to control their lives.

   People who believe that the events that occur in their lives are the result of their own behaviour and/or ability, personality and effort are said to have the expectation of internal control, whereas those who believe events in their lives to be a function of luck, chance, fate (i.e., God(s), powerful others or powers beyond their control), comprehension or manipulation are said to have an expectation of external control. Managers with internal locus of control tend to see threatening events at work as less stressful and cope with it better than managers with external locus of control.

Locus of control is related to desire for control, conceived as a trait reflecting the extent to which individuals are generally motivated to control events in their lives. People with a high desire for control tend to have internal control, higher aspirations, to be more persistent and respond more to challenge, and to see themselves as the source of their success (Spector, 1982).

There is also considerable evidence to suggest that personality traits and cognitive abilities are significantly and logically related to general as well as work-specific locus of control beliefs. Thus, these beliefs may moderate or mediate the relationship between traits, abilities and work-related outcomes. Those with high conscientiousness tend to have more confidence in their ability to control situations so they in turn are more likely to plan, act and succeed.

The work ethic

The concept of the Protestant work ethic (PWE) was devised by the German sociologist Max Weber (1905), who saw it in part as the explanation for the origin of capitalism. People who believe in PWE tend to be achievement- and success-oriented, stress the need for efficacy and practicality, tend to be disinclined to leisure, and are conservative and conscious about wasting time, energy and money.

Despite all the arguments and research on PWE, there are relatively few clear definitions of what it is. PWE can be summarized as follows: a universal taboo is placed on idleness, while industriousness is considered a religious ideal; waste is a vice and frugality a virtue; complacency and failure are proscribed, and ambition and success are taken as signs of God's favour; a universal sign of sin is poverty, and the crowning sign of God's favour is wealth.

At the centre of the concept is the idea that the values and beliefs underlying PWE (morality, control, delayed gratification, asceticism, hard work) lead to economic success at both an individual and national level. In this sense, PWE can be conceived as a personally held belief system that is predictive of economic success. The latest measure of PWE assesses seven beliefs:

1   *The centrality of work*: A belief in work for its own sake; the central part of one's life.
2   *Self-reliance*: The value of striving for independence and success at work.
3   *Hard work*: A belief in the virtue of hard work – long hours, intense concentration.
4   *Leisure*: A belief in productive leisure.
5   *Morality and ethics*: A strong sense of justice at work.
6   *Delayed gratification*: An orientation to the future and an ability to postpone rewards.
7   *Wasted time*: A stress on the productive use of time.

Work passion

Over a 20-year period, Vallerand (2008) worked on the psychology of passion. Vallerand defined passion as a 'strong inclination toward an activity that people like, find important and in which they invest their time and energy' (p. 1). Over time people discover that some activities rather than others seem to satisfy their needs for competence, autonomy and relatedness. These thus become passionate, self-defining and identity-determining to which people devote time and energy. Passion has powerful affective outcomes and relates strongly to persistence in various activities.

Vallerand (2008) distinguished between healthy harmonious (HP) and unhealthy obsessive passion (OP). He suggests that HP is the autonomous internalization of an activity into identity when people freely accept the activity as important for them. It is done voluntarily, and not by compunction. HP for an activity is a significant but not over-powering part of identity and harmonizes with other aspects of a person's life. On the other hand, the drivers of OP are essentially specific contingencies and include self-esteem, excitement or self-acceptance. People feel compelled to engage in certain activities because of these contingencies which then come to control them. OP has an addictive quality because it is perhaps the only source of important psychological rewards. In this sense, 'workaholism' is a sign of OP not HP.

The theory suggests that HP leads to more flexible task engagement, which in turn leads to more engagement through the process of absorption, concentration, flow and positive effect. OP, on the other hand, leads to more rigid and conflicted task performance, which reduces engagement. HP controls the activity; OP is controlled by it. The former promotes healthy adaptation, while the latter thwarts it.

The question is how organizations encourage HP rather than OP. The answer is to

> provide employees with a healthy, flexible, and secure working environment, one where their opinion is valued, will create conditions that facilitate the development of harmonious passion...organizational support seems to foster an autonomous-supportive context that allows individuals to internalise the activity in their identity in an autonomous fashion. (Vallerand, 2008, p. 193)

Need for cognition

One variable that has been shown to relate to both intelligence and personality traits is the need for cognition (NFC), introduced by Cacioppo and Petty (1982) as a stable person-ality trait relating to the tendency to engage in and enjoy effortful cognitive activity. Individuals high in NFC tend to seek information when faced with a problem. Such people also think about and reflect on issues, use more rational arguments and are more open to new ideas. Individuals low in NFC, by contrast, tend to use cognitive heuristics and rely on others for information or opinions. NFC is not an ability to think, but an intrinsic motiva-tion to think, and indeed correlates strongly with various measures of intrinsic motivation. Tanaka, Panter and Winborne (1988), for example, identified three factors in the 34-item scale, which they labelled cognitive persistence (enjoyment of engaging in cognitive tasks), cognitive confidence (confidence about engaging in cognitive activities) and cognitive complexity (preference for complex or simple information processing demands).

Typical Intellectual Engagement scale

Goff and Ackerman (1992) conceptualized the Typical Intellectual Engagement (TIE) scale as a measure of an individual's typical level of intelligence and developed a self-report scale to assess (rather than measure) an individual's level of intelligence. Higher scores indicate a stronger inclination to engage in intellectual activities. Sample items from the TIE scale are: 'You enjoy thinking out complicated problems', 'The notion of thinking abstractly is not appealing to me (reverse-scored)', and 'I read a great deal.'

The conceptual importance of TIE is advocated on the basis of possible differences in individuals' level of intellectual investment. Two individuals with the same IQ or maximal performance may differ in their level of intellectual investment or typical performance. TIE posits that an individual's level of intellectual investment will have positive developmental effects on their acquisition of skills and knowledge in adulthood. TIE implies that typical performance may be as important in determining future intellectual competence as maximal performance, or, in simple terms, that personality may explain differences in adult intellectual competence, while ability may not. TIE may refer to aspects of typical performance not encompassed by established personality traits and is therefore of potential value in expanding or understanding individual differences, in particular with regard to the dispositional or trait determinants of educational achievement.

Entrepreneurial spirit

Many but not all high flyers tend to have an entrepreneurial spirit. There are various components to this, including ideas as a need for achievement. Those who have a high need for achievement tend to:

- Exercise some control over the means of production and produce more than they consume.
- Set moderately difficult goals for themselves.
- Try to maximize the likelihood of achievement satisfaction.
- Want concrete and regular feedback on how well they are doing.
- Like assuming responsibility for problem-solving.
- Show high initiative and exploratory behaviour in their environment.
- Continually research the environment for opportunities of all sorts.
- Regard growth and expansion as the most direct signs of success.
- Continually strive to improve – the Japanese *kaizen* concept.

Entrepreneurs show a number of clear behaviour patterns. They tend to be more proactive and more opportunistic than the general population. They tend to be efficient and produce high quality work, while often being seen as personally driven and competitive. Finally, they are more likely than the general population to show deeper commitment to others and their business relationships.

The Five-Factor Model

The five-factor model (FFM; also known as the Big Five) assesses five basic personality domains: extraversion, neuroticism or emotional stability, agreeableness, conscientiousness and openness to experience (McCrae & Costa, 1990). FFM is considered one of the most valid and reliable research models on personality and leadership (Barrick & Mount, 1991; Judge, Bono, Ilies & Gerhardt, 2002; McCrae & Costa, 1997) for two main reasons. First, the five domains are extremely stable over the lifespan (McCrae & Costa, 1990; Rantanen, Metsapelto, Feldt, Pulkkinen & Kokko, 2007); and second, it consistently predicts many work-related findings (Barrick & Mount, 1991; Furnham, 2008). The FFM domains have been identified as the 'bright side' of personality (Hogan, Curphy & Hogan, 1994) because they characterize people when they are at their best (Hogan, Hogan & Kaiser, 2010).

People who score high on openness to experience are said to be artistic, curious, imaginative, insightful and original; they have a wide range of interests. They tend to value intellectual matters and can be rather unconventional, with possible 'unusual thought patterns'. Synonyms for openness include intellectance or intellectual competence and it is no surprise that, of all the trait variables, it shows the highest correlation with intelligence, in the region of $r = 0.30$. This suggests that open, curious individuals read more, explore their environment and seek answers to many questions. In doing so, they acquire a large knowledge base, which is related to crystallized intelligence. Thus, open people perform well on intelligence tests. Furthermore, this increases as they get older. Openness is associated with intellectual curiosity, a life of the mind, imagination and artistic sensitivity. It is also related to need for cognition.

Openness is also correlated with creativity. Open individuals tend to have a wide range of interests, they often tend to have unusual thought processes and they acquire a reputation for making unconventional judgements. They value intellectual matters and are questioning. Therefore, it is no surprise that the correlations between intelligence tests (both fluid and crystallized) and creativity and measures of openness are significant and positive, usually in the range $r = 0.2$–0.5. Of all the personality traits it is openness that can best serve as a proxy for intelligence, because it is so (relatively) highly correlated with it (Furnham, 2008).

Individual differences can influence applicant attraction by how they respond to stimuli (e.g., Hough, Oswald & Ployhart, 2001, show that individuals with higher scores in extraversion and emotional stability have more positive responses to situations), by behaviour patterns and by traits that would turn into positive work outcomes once hired (e.g., ability experience and conscientiousness).

Bernerth, Feild, Giles & Cole (2006) found that agreeableness and openness were positively associated, and neuroticism negatively with procedural and distributive justice. Similarly, Truxillo, Bauer, Campion and Paronto (2006) found that neuroticism and agreeableness were the most constant predictors of applicant perceptions.

Swider, Zimmerman, Charlier and Pierotti (2015) conducted a meta-analysis to investigate the relation between applicants' deep-level characteristics such as ability, personality and experience and surface-level characteristics such as race, age and gender with applicant attraction. They note: 'Based on the results of this study, applicants high in Conscientiousness, Extraversion, work experience, and Emotional Stability as well as low in ability would be wise to recognize that they are more likely to be predisposed to feeling attracted to organizations, which may prevent them from eliminating alternatives' (p. 80). Having been clearer about their real preferences such individuals may be better able to make more informed choices from a narrower set of options (Barber, Daly, Giannantonio & Phillips, 1994). The study highlighted the independent influence of the person, and that self-awareness of personal preferences can assist applicants in making better career choices rather than relying on organizations to deselect them. Swider and colleagues 2015, p. 80) also noted that organizations that seek to attract conscientious, emotionally stable, extraverted and experienced applicants benefit from a head start in engendering attraction in applicants. However, high-ability applicants are likely to be high-performers once hired and are rightfully sought by recruiting organizations (Schmidt & Hunter, 1998), and thus are in greater demand. While ability–attraction relationships had relatively modest effect sizes in terms of main effects and across moderator analyses, in the study their consistency was substantially impacted the success of selection systems, as even small changes in offer acceptance rates have a sizeable effect on recruitment plans (Murphy, 1986).

Future Research

There are many opportunities for future research in this area.

One such area is the development and use of a well-validated, multidimensional measure of job attraction. International research collaboration or cross-cultural studies using different populations and a consistent test would help in deepening our understanding.

A second area is the paucity of models or overarching theories. The development and sequent testing of such a model could provide a more comprehensive list of the factors involved; further, by testing in different national and generational populations a more sophisticated understanding of their relationship and weightings developed.

Conclusion

Choosing the right job in the right organization is important to an individual's long-term happiness and welfare, as well as that of the organization they choose to work for. Most organizations spend considerable resources on recruitment and selection. They aim to attract people with particular skills, values and motivation who will be both happy and productive in the organization. Similarly, job-seekers want accurate and reliable information about all aspects of the job and the organization before they apply. It is clear that there are individual differences in job/organizational attraction as a function of ability, personality and values.

From a recruiting perspective, in the early stages recruiters should show personable behaviours that will entice applicants to pursue the job. Recruiters should enhance the perception of fairness by explaining the selection procedures, keeping the applicants informed and minimizing delays. The recruiter has the ability to influence a desired applicant into accepting an offer. Finally, recruiters should mitigate any negative consequences of difficult selection procedures that may reduce the expectations of being hired and inform the applicants that the selection task is demanding and could be challenging for many successful applicants.

There are no powerful theories in this area, save perhaps ASA theory. Moreover, there are many studies that measure two or three factors at a time without providing a model of all the factors that are relevant to the issue of attraction.

Regarding personality, extraversion and conscientiousness seem to have the strongest positive relation in applicant attraction. Energetic, enthusiastic, talkative, assertive and gregarious individuals who are also thorough, careful, efficient, organized, self-disciplined, task-oriented and aim for achievement tend to be the most desired employees.

Emphasizing the positive elements linked with the work environment and organizational image enhances attraction to the job. Also, fair and considerate treatment through the recruitment stage plays an important role in accepting a job offer. Person–organization fit plays a critical role influencing organizational attraction. From an organization perspective, attraction is related to the instrumental-symbolic framework, where applicants differentiate between organizations based on their trait inferences (symbolic) rather than traditional job and organization characteristics (instrumental). Instrumental traits are tangible and objective, whereas symbolic traits are related to self-expression, image and brand (Lievens & Highhouse, 2003). Using this knowledge, organizations can differentiate themselves from their competitors and use their culture and identity as an advantage to attract personnel that have similar values and are more committed.

References

Anderson, N. (2004). Editorial – The dark side of the moon. *International Journal of Selection and Assessment, 12*, 1–8.

Barber, A. E., Daly, C. L., Giannantonio, C. M., & Phillips, J. M. (1994). Job search activities: An examination of changes over time. *Personnel Psychology, 47*, 739–766.

Baron, H., & Janman, K. (1996) Fairness in the assessment centre. *International Review of Industrial and Organizational Psychology, 11*, 61–114.

Baron, R. A., Franklin, R. J., & Hmieleski, K. M. (2013). Why entrepreneurs often experience low, not high, levels of stress: The joint effects of selection and psychological capital. *Journal of Management*. doi.org/10.1177/0149206313495411.

Barrick, M. R., & Mount, M. K. (1991). The Big Five personality dimensions and job performance: A meta-analysis. *Personnel Psychology, 44*, 1–26. doi: 10.1111/j.1744-6570.1991.tb00688.x.

Baum, M., & Kabst, R. (2014). The effectiveness of recruitment advertisements and recruitment websites: Indirect and interactive effects on applicant attraction. *Human Resource Management, 53*, 353–378. doi: 10.1002/hrm.21571.

Bernerth, J., Feild, H., Giles, W., & Cole, M. (2006) Perceived fairness in employee selection. *Journal of Business and Psychology, 20*, 545–563.

Bertolino, M., & Steiner, D. D. (2007). Fairness reactions to selection methods: An Italian study. *International Journal of Selection and Assessment, 15*, 197–205.

Bipp, T., & Demerouti, E. (2014). Which employees craft their jobs and how? Basic dimensions of personality and employees' job crafting behaviour. *Journal of Occupational and Organizational Psychology*. doi: 10.1111/joop.12089.

Bourantas, D., & Papalexandris, N. (1999). Personality traits discriminating between employees in public- and in private-sector organizations. *International Journal of Human Resource Management, 10*(5), 858–869.

Boyne, G. (2002). Public and private management: What's the difference? *Journal of Management Studies, 39*, 97–122.

Bright, L. (2005). Public employees with high levels of public service motivation: Who are they, where are they, and what do they want? *Review of Public Personnel Administration, 25*, 138–154.

Buelens, M., & Van den Broeck, H. (2007). An analysis of differences in work motivation between public and private sector organizations. *Public Administration Review, 67*(1), 65–74.

Cacioppo, J. T., & Petty, R. E. (1982). The need for cognition. *Journal of Personality and Social Psychology, 42*(1), 116.

Carless, A. (2006). Applicant reactions to multiple procedures for the police force. *Applied Psychology: An International Review, 55*, 145–167.

Carless, S. A. (2005). Person–job fit versus person–organization fit as predictors of organizational attraction and job acceptance intentions: A longitudinal study. *Journal of Occupational and Organizational Psychology, 78*, 411–429. doi: 10.1348/096317905X25995.

Carpenter, J., Doverspike, D., & Miguel, R. F. (2012). Public service motivation as a predictor of attraction to the public sector. *Journal of Vocational Behavior, 80*(2), 509–523.

Chan, D., & Schmitt, N. (2004). An agenda for future research on applicant reactions to selection procedures: A construct-oriented approach. *International Journal of Selection and Assessment, 12*, 9–23.

Chan, D., Schmitt, N., DeShon, R. P., Clause, C. S., & Delbridge, K. (1997). Reactions to cognitive ability tests: The relationships between race, test performance, face validity, perceptions, and test-taking motivation. *Journal of Applied Psychology, 82*, 300–310.

Chapman, D. S., Uggerslev, K. L., Carroll, S. A., Piasentin, K. A., & Jones, D. A. (2005). Applicant attraction to organizations and job choice: A meta-analytic review of the correlates of recruiting outcomes. *Journal of Applied Psychology, 90*, 928–944. doi: 10.1037/0021-9010.90.5.928.

Chetkovich, C. (2001). Winning the best and brightest: Increasing attraction to public service. In M. A. Abramson & N. W. Gardner (Eds.), *Human Capital 2002* (pp. 17–58). Boulder, CO: Rowman & Littlefield.

Cober, R. T., Brown, D. J., Levy, P. E., Cober, A. B., & Keeping, L. M. (2003). Organizational web sites: Web site content and style as determinants of organizational attraction. *International Journal of Selection and Assessment, 11*, 158–169.

Collins, C. J., & Stevens, C. K. (2002). The relationship between early recruitment related activities and the application decisions of new labor-market entrants: A brand equity approach to recruitment. *Journal of Applied Psychology, 87*, 1121–1133.

Dineen, B. R., Ash, S. R., & Noe, R. A. (2002). A web of applicant attraction: Person–organization fit in the context of web-based recruitment. *Journal of Applied Psychology, 87*(4), 723.

Edwards, M. R. (2010). An integrative review of employer branding and OB theory. *Personnel Review, 39*, 5–23.

Fisher, C. D., Ilgen, D. R., & Hoyer, W. D. (1979). Source credibility, information favorability, and job offer acceptance. *Academy of Management Journal, 22*(1), 94–103.

Flynn, D. M., & Tannenbaum, S. I. (1993). Correlates of organizational commitment: Differences in the public and private sector. *Journal of Business and Psychology, 8*(1), 103–116.

Furnham, A. (2008). *Personality and Intelligence at Work: Exploring and Explaining Individual Differences at Work*. London: Routledge.

Furnham, A., & Chamorro-Premuzic, T. (2010). Consensual beliefs about the fairness and accuracy of selection methods at university. *International Journal of Selection and Assessment, 18*, 417–424. doi: 10.1111/j.1468-2389.2010.00523.x.

Furnham, A., Eracleou, A., & Chamorro-Premuzic, T. (2009). Personality, motivation and job satisfaction: Herzberg meets the Big Five. *Journal of Managerial Psychology, 24*, 765–779.

Furnham, A., Hyde, G., & Trickey, G. (2014). Do your dark side traits fit? Dysfunctional personalities in different work sectors. *Applied Psychology, 63*(4), 589–606.

Gilliland, S. W. (1993). The perceived fairness of selection systems: An organizational justice perspective. *Academy Management Review, 18*, 694–734.

Goff, M., & Ackerman, P. L. (1992). Personality–intelligence relations: Assessment of typical intellectual engagement. *Journal of Educational Psychology, 84*(4), 537.

Gomes, D., & Neves, J. (2011). Organizational attractiveness and prospective applicants' intentions to apply. *Personnel Review, 40*, 684–699. doi: 10.1108/00483481111169634.

Harold, C. M., & Ployhart, R. E. (2008). What do applicants want? Examining changes in attribute judgments over time. *Journal of Occupational and Organizational Psychology, 81*, 191–218. doi: 10.1348/096317907X235774

Highhouse, S., Lievens, F., & Sinar, E. F. (2003). Measuring attraction to organizations. *Educational and Psychological Measurement, 63*, 986–1001. doi: 10.1177/0013164403258403.

Hilliard, A., Doverspike, D., & Carpenter, J. E. (2010). *Antecedents and outcomes of public service motivation: A meta-analytic perspective*. Unpublished manuscript. Akron, OH: University of Akron.

Hogan, R., Curphy, G. J., & Hogan, J. (1994). What we know about leadership: Effectiveness and personality. *American Psychologist, 49*, 493–504. doi: 10.1037/0003-066X.49.6.493.

Hogan, R., Hogan, J., & Kaiser, R. (2010). Management derailment: Personality assessment and mitigation. *In* S. Zedeck (Ed.), *American Psychological Association Handbook of Industrial and Organizational Psychology* (pp. 555–575). Washington, DC: American Psychological Association.

Holland, J. L. (1973). *Making Vocational Choices: A Theory of Careers*. Upper Saddle River, NJ: Prentice Hall.

Hough, L. M., Oswald, F.L., & Ployhart, R.E. (2001). Determinants, detection and amelioration of adverse impact in personnel selection procedures: Issues, evidence and lessons learned. *International Journal of Selection and Assessment, 9*, 152–194.

Hsiao, A., Ma, E., & Auld, C. (2014). Organizational attractiveness in the Taiwanese hotel sector: Perceptions of indigenous and non-indigenous employees, *Journal of Hospitality and Tourism Management, 21*, 116–126. doi: 10.1016/j.jhtm.2014.09.002.

Hulsheger, U., & Anderson, N. (2009). Applicant perspectives in selection. *International Journal of Selection and Assessment, 17*, 335–345.

Judge, T. A., Bono, J. E., Ilies, R., & Gerhardt, M. W. (2002). Personality and leadership: A qualitative and quantitative review. *Journal of Applied Psychology, 87*, 765–780. doi: 10.1037/0021-9010.87.4.765.

Keller K. L. (1993). Conceptualizing, measuring, and managing customer-based brand equity. *Journal of Marketing 57*, 1–22.

Klotz, A. C., Da Motta Veiga, S. P., Buckley, M. R., & Gavin, M. B. (2013). The role of trustworthiness in recruitment and selection: A review and guide for future research. *Journal of Organizational Behavior*, *34*, 104–119. doi: 10.1002/job.1891.

Lee, Y. J., & Wilkins, V. M. (2011). More similarities or more differences? Comparing public and nonprofit managers' job motivations. *Public Administration Review*, *71*(1), 45–56.

Levy S. J. (1957). Symbols for sales. *Harvard Business Review*, *37*, 117–124.

Lievens, F. (2007). Employer branding in the Belgian Army: The importance of instrumental and symbolic beliefs for potential applicants, actual applicants, and military employees. *Human Resource Management*, *46*, 51–69.

Lievens, F., De Corte, W., & Brysse, K. (2003). Applicant perceptions of selection procedures: The role of selection information, belief in tests, and comparative anxiety. *International Journal of Selection and Assessment*, *11*(1), 67–77.

Lievens, F., & Highhouse, S. (2003). The relation of instrumental and symbolic attributes to a company's attractiveness as an employer. *Personnel Psychology*, *56*, 75–102.

Lievens, F., Van Hoye, G., & Anseel, F. (2007). Organizational identity and employer image: Towards a unifying framework. *British Journal of Management*, *18*, 45– 59.

Lyons, S. T., Duxbury, L. E., & Higgins, C. A. (2006). A comparison of the values and commitment of private sector, public sector, and parapublic sector employees. *Public Administration Review*, 605–618.

MacCrae, I., & Furnham, A. (2014). *High Potential: How to Spot, Manage and Develop Talented People at Work*. London: Bloomsbury.

McCrae, R. R., & Costa, P. T. (1990). *Personality in Adulthood*. New York: Guilford Press.

McCrae, R. R., & Costa, P. T. (1997). Conceptions and correlates of openness to experience. *In* J. A. J. R. Hogan & S. R. Briggs (Eds.), *Handbook of Personality Psychology* (pp. 825–847). Orlando, FL: Academic Press. doi: 10.1016/B978-012134645-4/50032-9.

Murphy, K. J. (1986). Incentives, learning, and compensation: A theoretical and empirical investigation of managerial labour contracts. *The Rand Journal of Economics*, 59–76.

Nikolaou, I., & Judge, T. A. (2007). Fairness reactions to personnel selection and techniques in Greece: The role of core self-evaluations. *International Journal of Selection and Assessment*, *15*, 206–219.

Nolan, K. P., & Harold, C. M. (2010). Fit with what? The influence of multiple self-concept images on organizational attraction, *Journal of Occupational and Organizational Psychology*, *83*, 645 –663. doi: 10.1348/096317909X465452.

Perry, J. L., & Wise, L. R. (1990). The motivational bases of public service. *Public Administration*, *50*, 367–373.

Phillips, J. M., Gully, S. M., McCarthy, J. E., Castellano, W. G., & Kim, M. S. (2014). Recruiting global travelers: The role of global travel recruitment messages and individual differences in perceived fit, attraction, and job pursuit intentions. *Personnel Psychology*, *67*, 153 –201. doi: 10.1111/peps.12043.

Rantanen, J., Metsapelto, R. L., Feldt, T., Pulkkinen, L., & Kokko, K. (2007). Long-term stability in the Big Five personality facets in adulthood. *Scandinavian Journal of Psychology*, *48*, 511–518. doi: 10.1111/j.1467-9450.2007.00609.x.

Reeve, C. L., & Lam, H. (2007). Consideration of *g* as a common antecedent for cognitive ability test performance, test motivation, and perceived fairness. *Intelligence*, *35*, 347 –358.

Robertson, I. T., & Smith, M. (2001). Personnel selection. *Journal of Occupational and Organizational Psychology*, *74*, 441–473.

Ryan, A. M., & Ployhart, R. E. (2000). Applicants' perceptions of selection procedures and decisions: A critical review and agenda for the future. *Journal of Management*, *26*, 565–606.

Rynes, S. L. (1993). Who is selecting whom? Effect of selection practices on applicant attitude and behavior. *In* N. Schmitt & W. C. Barman (Eds.), *Personnel Selection in Organizations* (pp. 240 –274). San Francisco, CA: Jossey-Bass.

Rynes, S. L., & Cable, D. M. (2003). Recruitment research in the twenty-first century. *In* W. C. Borman, D. R. Ilgen & R. J. Klimoski (Eds.), *Handbook of Psychology: Industrial and Organizational Psychology* (Vol. *12*, pp. 55–76). Hoboken, NJ: John Wiley & Sons.

Sanchez, R. J., Truxillo, D. M., & Bauer, T. N. (2000). Development and examination of an expectancy-based measure of test-taking motivation. *Journal of Applied Psychology*, *85*, 739–750.

Schmidt, F. L., & Hunter, J.E. (1998). The validity and utility of selection methods in personnel psychology: Practical and theoretical implications of 85 years of research findings. *Psychological Bulletin*, *124*, 262–274.

Schneider, B. (1987). The people make the place. *Personnel Psychology*, *40*(3), 437–453.

Schreurs, B., Druart, C., Proost, K., & De Witte, K. (2009). Symbolic attributes and organizational attractiveness: The moderating effects of applicant personality. *International Journal of Selection and Assessment*, *17*, 35–46. doi: 10.1111/j.1468-2389.2009.00449.x.

Shavitt, S. (1990). The role of attitude objects in attitude functions. *Journal of Experimental Social Psychology*, *26*, 124–148.

Slaughter, J. E., Stanton, J. M., Mohr, D. C., & Schoel III, W. A. (2005). The interaction of attraction and selection: Implications for college recruitment and Schneider's ASA model. *Applied Psychology: An International Review*, *54*, 419– 441.

Solomon, E. E. (1986). Private and public sector managers: An empirical investigation of job characteristics and organizational climate. *Journal of Applied Psychology*, *71*(2), 247.

Spector, P. E. (1982). Behavior in organizations as a function of employee's locus of control. *Psychological Bulletin*, *91*(3), 482.

Swider, B. W., Zimmerman, R. D., Charlier, S.D., & Pierotti, A. J. (2015). Deep-level and surface-level individual differences and applicant attraction to organizations: A meta-analysis. *Journal of Vocational Behaviour*, *88*, 73–83.

Tanaka, J. S., Panter, A. T., & Winborne, W. C. (1988). Dimensions of the need for cognition: Subscales and gender differences. *Multivariate Behavioral Research*, *23*(1), 35–50.

Thompson, R. J., Payne, S. C., & Taylor, A. B. (2014). Applicant attraction to flexible work arrangements: Separating the influence of flextime and flexplace. *Journal of Occupational and Organizational Psychology*, 1–24. doi: 10.1111/joop.12095.

Truxillo, D. M., Bauer, T. N., Campion, M. A., & Paronto, M. E. (2006). A field study of the role of Big Five personality in applicant perceptions of selection fairness, self and the hiring organization. *International Journal of Selection and Assessment*, *14*, 269–277.

Truxillo, D. M., Steiner, D. D., & Gilliland, S. W. (2004). The importance of organizational justice in personnel selection: Defining when selection fairness really matters. *International Journal of Selection and Assessment*, *12*, 39–53.

Turban D. B., Forret M. L, & Hendrickson, C. L. (1998). Applicant attraction to firms: Influences of organization reputation, job and organizational attributes, and recruiter behaviours. *Journal of Vocational Behavior*, *52*, 24–44.

Uggerslev, K. L., Fassina, N. E., & Kraichy, D. (2012). Recruiting through the stages: A meta-analytic test of predictors of applicant attraction at different stages of the recruiting process. *Personnel Psychology*, *65*, 597–660. doi: 10.1111/j.1744-6570.2012.01254.x.

Vallerand, R. J. (2008). On the psychology of passion: In search of what makes people's lives most worth living. *Canadian Psychology/Psychologie Canadienne*, *49*(1), 1.

van Hoye, G., Bas, T., Cromheecke, S., & Lievens, F. (2013). The instrumental and symbolic dimensions of organizations' image as an employer: A large-scale field study on employer branding in Turkey. *Applied Psychology: An International Review*, *62*, 543–557.

van Hoye, G., Saks, A. M., Lievens, F., & Weijters, B. (2014). Development and test of an integrative model of job search behaviour. *European Journal of Work and Organizational Psychology* (ahead-of-print), 1–16.

Viswesvaran, C., & Ones, D. S. (2004). Importance of perceived personnel selection system fairness determinants: Relations with demographic, personality and job characteristics. *International Journal of Selection and Assessment*, *12*, 172–186.

Von Walter, B., Wentzel, D., & Tomczak, T. (2010). The effect of applicant–employee fit and temporal construal on employer attraction and pursuit intentions. *Journal of Occupational and Organizational Psychology*, *85*, 116–135. doi: 10.1348/2044-8325.002006.

Weber, M. (1905). *The Protestant Ethic and Spirit of Capitalism*. New York: Scribner's.

6

Ethics in Recruitment and Selection

Nuno Rebelo dos Santos, Leonor Pais, Carla Cabo-Leitão and Jonathan Passmore

Introduction

Ethics in recruitment and selection has two main approaches, one regarding the policies underlying decisions to recruit professionals in a specific social group to provide a community with necessary services (e.g., Xu & Zhang, 2005), the other related to the way in which the specific processes of recruitment and selection are carried out (e.g., Chidi, Ogunyomi & Badejo, 2012; Dineen, Noe & Wang, 2004). This chapter focuses on the second approach, whether it concerns relationships among the people involved, the criteria used to exclude and rank the applicants or the transparency and fairness of the processes undertaken.

In this chapter we use the term 'ethics' anchored in the business ethics field. Recruitment and selection are actions carried out in a business context and for that reason it seems appropriate to frame the concept in this context. The business ethics concept was characterized by Robin (2009) based on fairness and respect for people. Both concepts apply to the various stakeholders involved in business activity. Inspired by these ideas, we use the expression 'ethics in recruitment and selection' in a comprehensive sense, corresponding to: the procedures, attitudes and behaviours that ought to be shown by those who are co-responsible at all levels for recruitment and selection in organizations, taking into consideration fairness and respect for everyone directly or indirectly affected by those procedures, attitudes and behaviours; and the characteristics of candidates which can be seen as ethical, where used as an explicit criterion for recruitment and selection.

First, we review the literature on values as a criterion for recruiting and selecting candidates. Although values are not the same as ethics, some values have an ethical dimension. Next, we review the relationships between those responsible for carrying out the recruitment and assessment process and applicants. Those on the employer's side have the power

The Wiley Blackwell Handbook of the Psychology of Recruitment, Selection and Employee Retention,
First Edition. Edited by Harold W. Goldstein, Elaine D. Pulakos, Jonathan Passmore and Carla Semedo.
© 2017 John Wiley & Sons Ltd. Published 2020 by John Wiley & Sons Ltd.

to hire candidates for a specific position, and this asymmetric power requires special attention to the way the interaction and the relationship are put in place to guarantee fair and decent treatment. Then we turn to ethics in executive search and headhunting. These practices are based on a direct type of search for potential candidates (usually active employees) rather than using traditional methods, such as advertising a vacancy and waiting for applications. In the following section we focus on the ethical dimensions of the recruitment and selection process brought about by the exponential growth of social networks and social media. This technological tool adds complexity to recruitment and selection. As we further discuss, the integration of these tools has led to an urgent need to analyse the ethics underlying these processes in the HR field. We conclude by structuring the main conclusions, practical implications and avenues for future research.

The Emergence of Ethics in Organizational Psychology

Ethics has been a growing research topic in the organizational literature, especially since the economic and financial crisis beginning in 2008. This crisis is viewed by some as a result of disregarding ethical issues in executive education (Floyd, Xu, Atkins & Caldwell, 2013). Literature reviews published in the last 12 years illustrate this concern for ethical issues in business, in several subjects: sales (McClaren, 2013); religiosity, business and consumer ethics (Vitell, 2009); organizational ethics (Suhonen, Stolt, Virtanen & Leino-Kilpi, 2011); entrepreneurship (Hannafey, 2003), decision making (Craft, 2013; Lehnert, Park & Singh, 2015) and corruption (Fein & Weibler, 2014), to name but a few. Lindorff (2007) also points out the importance of reflecting on the ethical dimensions of business and organizational research.

In spite of this growing focus on business and organizational ethics only one literature review was found in databases related to ethics, recruitment and selection (Patterson, et al., 2015). We say 'only' as this is a preliminary review specifically focused on one aspect of the subject: values-based recruitment and selection. Although values-based recruitment and selection does not have a sharp focus on ethics, it is closely related to it.

The weak expression of concern for ethical issues in research literature focused on recruitment and selection seems surprising, for two primary reasons. First, recruitment and selection are a human resource management process with a strong link to what people think and feel about organizations (i.e., their respectability or wickedness). This is true whether we think as an employee, a customer or another stakeholder of the organization. Second, ethical aspects of the situations that individuals have to deal with are co-determinants of what they choose to do. Where behaviour is performed freely an ethical dimension is always present. Therefore, performance in organizations depends on the ethical criteria that individuals use at work. Ethical dimensions seem to be a co-determinant of work performance (Lee, Stettler & Antonakis, 2011; Schwepker & Ingram, 1996; Wahyudi, Haryono, Riyani & Harsono, 2013). In general, organizational survival and organizational performance depend largely on ethical aspects of their different stakeholders' daily lives. The values underlying organizational practices are continuously communicating the rules that are in place. As recruitment and selection practices often cause first impressions to be formed, those practices have an impact on employees' behaviours beyond the time of recruitment and selection. Furthermore, those who are excluded (i.e., not hired) may also be customers and bring to the market the impression they have formed about the organization during the recruitment and selection processes.

Values as a Criterion for Recruitment and Selection

In recent decades values were seldom used as a criterion in the selection process. However, the systematic assessment of values through validated and effective measurement is a recent effort seen in a few countries in healthcare. That orientation follows the trend of values-based practice, as observed in some countries, (e. g., Petrova, Dale & Fulford, 2006; Rankin, 2013). This approach encompasses the idea that values are related to a high-performing worker in a specific job. Healthcare is a sector where values are often viewed as a component of performance or quality. Waugh, Smith, Horsburgh and Gray (2014) found that for nurses and midwives honesty and trustworthiness were considered to be among the top seven characteristics when asked which were relevant for the profession.

Although values are always present in every decision-making process, 'when sets of values are shared, their presence may remain unnoticed' (Petrova et al., p. 2). This may explain why the explicit inclusion of values has been neglected in recruitment and selection (possibly with the exception of the value of appreciating diversity; e.g., Ma & Allen, 2009). The effort to include values in recruitment and selection, however, is found in other areas of human resource management (e.g., May, Luth & Schwoerer, 2014; Yap, 2014).

Values are not the same as ethics, but values are related to what individuals think they ought to do as a moral obligation. Using a values-based approach in recruitment and selection, at least in some jobs, can be a useful criterion alongside others for considering individuals' fit in the organization's culture and thus a factor in their subsequent performance at work.

Research on values as a criterion for recruitment and selection has been developed mainly in the healthcare sector in England. Patterson et al., (2015) reviewed 20 papers exploring the impact of values-based approaches. In their review, they identify, describe and evaluate the instruments used to assess candidates' values, based on the following criteria: 1) accuracy and effectiveness; 2) costs and efficiency; 3) practicalities and implementation; and 4) stakeholders' acceptance and feedback. Based on these criteria Patterson and colleagues argued that situational judgement tests are most effective in assessing applicants' values. Personality assessment is sometimes useful in the earlier self-assessment phase. The other tools they evaluated (personal statements and references) were shown to be ineffective (Patterson et al., 2015) for shortlisting. For the final stage of selection, Patterson's team evaluated four other instruments. Structured interviews and mini-multiple interviews and selection centres using work samples were shown to be effective, while traditional interviews and group interviews were shown to be ineffective (Patterson et al., 2015).

Following these findings, a number of studies have been published. Husbands, Rodgerson, Dowell and Patterson (2015) explored the validity of psychometric tools for selection in a values-based environment. Their work revealed that integrity-based situational judgement tests have good psychometric properties for medical school admissions. Earlier work by Patterson et al. (2012) on the situational judgement test (SJT) showed these were well suited to assessing values (e.g., integrity). Patterson, Zibarras and Ashworth (2015) published a guide to help those who want to use SJTs in recruitment and selection of applicants to medical education and training.

Others have pointed out the importance of including values as a criterion for recruiting and selecting. Miller and Bird (2014) presented a point of view on values-based recruitment and selection for the National Health Service (NHS) in the United Kingdom. They describe how the overarching values of the NHS steer the criteria used in assessing applicants to education in healthcare professions and job vacancies in this field. Miller and Bird focus their claim on a Department of Health (2014) policy document, where it is stated that 'HEE [Health Education England] will ensure that recruitment, education, training and development of the healthcare workforce contributes to patients, carers and the public reporting a positive experience of healthcare consistent with the values and behaviours identified in the NHS' (2014, p. 42). These policy guidelines state values explicitly as core aspects of the workforce to be employed by the NHS.

Miller and Bird (2014) point out the risks of using values-based recruitment to address these policy guidelines, namely the failure to identify individuals who are able to communicate their real values. To overcome this problem, they propose values-based recruitment as 'part of the selection process' instead of a stand-alone tool.

Miller (2015) returned to the approach of values-based recruitment to consider why it is important in healthcare. Miller analysed the implications of values-based recruitment for those applying to nursing courses as well as newly qualified nurses applying for their first job. According to Miller, a values-based approach to recruitment and selection processes addresses the problems in the quality of the health service provided in the UK. The adoption of the six Cs (care, compassion, competence, communication, courage and commitment) in nursing, midwifery and care staff (Commissioning Board Chief Nursing Officer and DH Chief Nursing Adviser, 2012) means that values have to be assessed when selecting applicants for a nursing course in higher education, as well as when they apply for a vacancy in the healthcare sector (Miller, 2015).

Using the same approach, Kare-Silver, Spicer, Khan and Ahluwalia (2014) describe the recruitment for general practitioner (GP) training based on values following the policy guidelines. They describe this process as an in-progress challenge and emphasize the bias that can arise with the coaching for recruitment that is offered by several corporations to GPs who want to apply to the NHS. This bias has to be overcome, they claim, otherwise the purpose of values-based recruitment and selection will be jeopardized.

Bore, Munro, Kerridge and Powis (2005) explored the use of the Mojac Scale as a tool to select medical students based on their moral orientation. This construct was proposed in place of moral reasoning, given its impact on decisions when individuals face ethical dilemmas, and the desire to reduce the 'likelihood of inappropriate ethical behaviour in medicine' (Bore et al., 2005, p. 266). The research was carried out over four years in six countries and has shown the instrument's psychometric properties to be good in assessing moral orientation between libertarian and communitarian values.

In general, the use of values-based recruitment and selection has grown in the healthcare sector since 2000, partly in response to policy guidelines that in the UK encourage the health service to ensure that its workforce is in line with its publicly stated values. However, without adequate recruitment tools, such as the psychometric, values-based approaches will fail.

Considering the crises that have emerged in recent decades, viewed as a result, in part, of the lack of ethics in executive education (Floyd et al., 2013), a wide avenue is open for spreading the practice of and research on values-based recruitment and selection to other sectors in the hope that such practices will deliver superior ethical behaviour.

Ethics in the Relationship with Applicants

In this section we focus on ethics in the relationship with applicants. This relationship is present in all the procedures associated with the recruitment and selection process that directly or indirectly involve the presence of applicants (which is not necessarily physical).

Therefore, any norm or procedure involving the collection, sharing or use of data, information or knowledge relating to the applicant concerns a 'relationship' with the application and requires that the employer's conduct is ethical. The literature in this area is scant, and those papers that do exist stress the importance of following the law in recruitment and selection processes (Wallace, Page & Lippstreu, 2006). However, if meeting legal obligations is the criterion, this does not in itself guarantee ethical behaviour in the relationship with applicants.

In the previous and following sections we refer to a set of values that guide professional practice in this domain, most of which are reflected in codes of conduct/ethical and deontological codes, and in the orientations provided by professional associations. Nevertheless, this set of values, which should be part of a professional's behaviour throughout the recruitment and selection process, does not cover all the ethical concerns that should mark the relationship with applicants. These additional ethical concerns are related to the nature of the interaction between the professional who recruits and selects and the applicant willing to participate in that process.

A review of the literature reveals some 40 articles exploring this topic. Table 6.1 presents information about the group of 27 articles retained, allowing analysis of their content. These articles were categorized in four themes reflected in their titles. The first 11 papers explored the central issues of fairness, justice and procedural justice. The second set of seven papers focused on ethics. The third set of four papers dealt with questions related to web-based procedures and the fourth contains six papers with diverse content.

In a global analysis of the 11 articles focusing on questions of fairness, justice and procedural justice, seven are empirical studies (six quantitative and one qualitative) and four are theoretical. In this set of articles three concentrated on questions relating to justice and fairness in the selection process (Arvey & Renz, 1992; Bernerth, 2005; Osca & López-Araújo, 2009); one on recruitment (Kanerva et al., 2010); two on preferential hiring (Singer & Singer, 1991; Philips, 1991); one on the employment interview, presenting an expansive view of impression management and contending that organizations can use this to make employment interviews fairer (Rosenfeld, 1997); and one on selection fairness information (Truxillo, Bauer, Campion & Paronto, 2002). Three of these articles focus on procedural justice (Ambrose & Rosse, 2003; Fodchuk & Sidebotham, 2005; Truxillo, Bauer & Sanchez, 2001). Osca and López-Araújo (2009) claim that women are more influenced by procedural justice and men by interactional justice and informational justice. These papers express the perspective of the authors. They focus on ethical content relating to the interaction behaviour with applicants through the questions of fairness/justice studied. By ensuring that questions related to fair behaviour are asked throughout the recruitment and selection process, employers can enhance the prospect of the process being experienced as fair and just.

In the set of seven papers focused specifically on ethical matters, four are theoretical and three are empirical (two qualitative and one quantitative). Focusing on these articles, one explores ethical issues in the context of the employee and executive recruitment process (Whitney, 1969), one in the scope of the selection interview, concluding that this needs clear guidelines for ethical behaviour to increase its effectiveness (Fletcher, 1992), and another, by Alder and Gilbert (2006), concerns ethics and fairness in hiring. Alder and Gilbert consider that ethical fairness underlies the law and regulations in hiring, but is not limited to them. They argue that, from an ethical and human rights perspective, applicants have the right to be treated with courtesy and respect, and not subjected to potentially invasive techniques, and to receive open and honest communication. The authors also consider that the relationship with applicants includes aspects of distributive justice (e.g., validated hiring tools), procedural justice (e.g., procedures that promote transparency)

Table 6.1 Publications on ethics in the relationship with applicants.

Author(s)	Year of publication	Publication	Type of article	Title words
Osca & López-Araújo	2009	Revista de Psicología del Trabajo y de las Organizaciones	Empirical (quantitative study)	Justice in selection and candidates' intentions
Arvey & Renz	1992	Journal of Business Ethics	Theoretical	Fairness in the selection
Bernerth	2005	International Journal of Selection and Assessment	Empirical (quantitative study)	Justice in employment selection decisions
Kanerva, Lammintakanen & Kivinen	2010	Journal of Nursing Management	Empirical (qualitative study)	Fairness of recruitment from unsuccessful applicants
Singer & Singer	1991	Journal of Business Ethics	Empirical (quantitative study)	Justice in preferential hiring
Philips	1991	Journal of Business Ethics	Theoretical	Preferential hiring and the question of competence
Rosenfeld	1997	Journal of Business Ethics	Theoretical	Impression management, fairness and employment interview
Truxillo et al.	2002	Journal of Applied Psychology	Empirical (quantitative/longitudinal study)	Selection fairness information and applicant reactions
Truxillo et al.	2001	International Journal of Selection and Assessment	Empirical (quantitative study)	Multiple dimensions of procedural justice
Ambrose & Rosse	2003	Group & Organization Management	Empirical (quantitative study)	Procedural justice and personality testing
Fodchuk & Sidebotham	2005	The Psychologist-Manager Journal	Theoretical	Procedural justice in the selection process
Beeson	2001	Management Review	Theoretical	Ethics and executive search
Lim & Chan	2001	Journal of Business Ethics	Empirical (quantitative study)	Ethical values of executive search consultants
Whitney	1969	Management of Personnel Quarterly	Theoretical	Ethics for recruiting employees and executives
Tsahuridu & Perryer	2002	Public Administration & Management: An Interactive Journal	Empirical (qualitative study)	Ethics and integrity in recruitment advertisements
Alder & Gilbert	2006	Journal of Business Ethics	Theoretical	Ethics and fairness in hiring
Fletcher	1992	Journal of Business Ethics	Theoretical	Ethical issues and selection interview

Author	Year	Journal	Type	Topic
Forde & MacKenzie	2010	*Journal of Business Ethics*	Empirical (qualitative/case studies)	Ethical agendas and migrant workers
Wallace et al.	2006	*Journal of Business and Psychology*	Empirical (quantitative study)	Applicant reactions to application blanks
Davison, Maraist & Bing	2011	*Journal of Business and Psychology*	Theoretical	The promise and pitfalls of using social networking sites
Dineen et al.	2004	*Human Resource Management*	Empirical (quantitative study)	Perceived fairness of web-based applicant screening procedures
García-Izquierdo, Aguinis & Ramos-Villagrasa	2010	*International Journal of Selection and Assessment*	Empirical (qualitative study)	Science–practice gap in e-recruitment
Ware	1984	*Sam Advanced Management Journal*	Theoretical	Managing confidentiality
van den Brink, Benschop & Jansen	2010	*Organization Studies*	Empirical (qualitative study)	Transparency in academic recruitment
Noon, Healy, Forson & Oikelome	2013	*British Journal of Management*	Empirical (qualitative study)	Effects of the 'hyper-formalization' of selection
Björklund, Bäckström & Wolgast	2012	*The Journal of Psychology*	Empirical (quantitative study)	Company norms affect which traits are preferred
Walker, Field, Giles & Bernerth	2008	*Journal of Occupational and Organizational Psychology*	Empirical (quantitative study)	Job advertisement characteristics and applicant experience

and interactional justice. This last point has particular relevance in this section since it centres precisely on questions relating to interaction. In this respect, the authors state that special care should be given to details and that rigour is essential; that applicants should be treated with dignity; that the need to use less transparent techniques should be explained clearly; that ongoing updates should be provided on the status of the search; and that rejection decisions should be explained. A fourth article deals with ethical questions in the executive search process as a whole (Beeson, 2001) and a fifth focuses on ethics and integrity in recruitment advertisements, and concludes that most organizations make little effort to communicate ethical requirements to potential employees or to consider the importance of ethics when advertising job opportunities (Tsahuridu & Perryer, 2002). Lim and Chan (2001), in the sixth article, focus on the ethical values of executive search consultants. Executive search consultants have grown in popularity as organizations see them as a response to the growing complexity of recruiting and selecting senior personnel. Lim and Chan (2001) argue that the consultants that do consider ethical aspects and that employ ethical practices contribute to their status and long-term sustainability as individual businesses. According to the authors, many executive search consultants use a code of conduct to guide their interaction with applicants, and that this allows them to make more informed choices. They also argue that a relationship marked by transparency is beneficial for the hiring organization, for the executive search consultant and for job applicants themselves. Finally, in the seventh of this group of papers, Forde and MacKenzie (2010) discuss ethical questions associated with the selection of migrant workers. These applicants have characteristics which need special attention regarding the ethical nature of the interaction established with them. In the capacity of intermediaries between applicants and hiring organizations, agencies have comprehensive ethical codes to manage the diversity and growing numbers of migrant workers. Forde and MacKenzie (2010) refer to the potential tension between: the need to place migrant workers and the strategic and competitive imperatives followed by agencies; and these agencies' commitment to provide disadvantaged groups with access to the labour market and the pressure to place those with fewer difficulties and who are more job-ready. According to the authors, these tensions draw attention to the challenge and relevance of an ethical approach on the part of agencies serving as intermediaries in the labour market. Ethical questions seem, therefore, to be central when considering the profile of consultants, the structure of each stage in the process and the process itself. Ethics also emerges in association with integrity. These questions are closely related to how the interactions with applicants take place and can have an impact on the perception the latter develop of the degree of ethics displayed.

The four articles making up the third group concern how applicants respond when confronted with web-based procedures or with questions related to these (Davison et al., 2011; Dineen et al., 2004; García-Izquierdo et al., 2010). We develop the ethical issues raised in the use of social media and social networks in recruitment and selection below. In this section we consider the specific research focused on the relationships between applicants and those who are responsible for or carry out the process in web-based recruitment and selection.

In this set of four articles, three are empirical (two quantitative and one qualitative) and one is theoretical. Dineen et al. (2004) show that five characteristics of procedural justice influence applicants' perceptions of fairness and that there is a hierarchy of the characteristics considered. Wallace et al. (2006) conclude that applicants confronted with a legal but problematic application had lower perceptions of justice than those that faced a legally sound application, especially in the case of applicants who were rejected without an explanation. These applicants also expressed higher litigation intentions.

The emergence of new forms of conducting the executive search process, particularly those that are web-based, has given rise to new questions around ensuring that interactions with applicants respect ethical principles. García-Izquierdo et al. (2010) conclude there is a science–practice gap in e-recruitment. They suggest that many companies ask for information that can be used for illegal discrimination and can potentially be perceived as unfair and invasive of applicants' privacy. Academic research infers that requesting that kind of information leads to negative applicant reactions. Furthermore, Davison et al. (2011) warn that, in this area, practice is preceding research, and research needs to catch up as a matter of urgency.

The fourth theme includes five papers with more diverse content. This set is made up of four empirical studies (two quantitative and two qualitative) and one theoretical study. Confidentiality (Ware, 1984), transparency and accountability (van den Brink et al., 2010) are aspects considered fundamentally and permanently inherent to the recruitment and selection process and contribute to establishing ethical interactions with applicants. Ensuring confidentiality represents an especially relevant ethical dimension of the relationship with applicants and is expressed in numerous ways in recruitment and selection processes. According to Ware (1984), confidentiality is reflected in the treatment applicants receive throughout the selection process (telephone and e-mail contact, for example, or in face-to-face situations such as interviews, group trials, etc.). According to Ware (1984), these ethical concerns are just as apparent when headhunting as in an advertisement or internally managed process. It is therefore important to communicate the organization's confidentiality policy and to respect it during the entire process. The impact of hyper-formalization of the selection process (Noon et al., 2013) and job advertisement characteristics (Walker et al., 2008) are also aspects with ethical dimensions which, it is argued, need to be managed. Björklund et al. (2012) reveal how recruiters` preferences could be influenced by information on company norms, and that the effect could be to increase discrimination against members of some groups.

Ethics in Executive Search and Headhunting

In this section we review executive search and headhunting practices and their growth since the 1990s, with specific reference to ethical considerations.

Executive search and headhunting

The main reasons given by several authors for the growth of the executive search profession include the confidentiality, impartial evaluation and discreet attraction of talent (Beeson, 1965; Hunter, 1989; Meyer, 1995; Taylor, 1984). Others cite the high price paid by the organization when the wrong person is selected (Taylor, 1984), the specialized skills needed to hire the right person – their solid database and depth of search service provide a more effective and efficient way of identifying the right professional for a certain position (Breaugh, 2008; Finlay & Coverdill, 2000; Jones, 1995; Lee, 1997; Taylor, 1984) – and the objectivity that is brought to the selection process by a third party. Another reason is that companies may not have the time and availability to conduct their own searches, and therefore ask headhunters to help them handle the more demanding aspects of the task (Cronin, 1981; Rutledge, 1997; Taylor, 1984). Despite these possible advantages, from the point of view of the executive's career success, headhunting seems to have unclear and inconsistent consequences (Clerkin & Lee, 2010; Hamori, 2010).

Overall, these factors have contributed to establishing headhunting as a powerful tool in many organizations, especially for global organizations and thus global talent (Lim & Chan, 2001). This practice is particularly focused on locating and recruiting elite talent, which some authors describe as workers occupying positions at the pinnacle of organizational hierarchies or specialist skilled roles (e.g., in the oil and gas industry, or the technology industry; Faulconbridge, Beaverstock, Hall & Hew, 2009).

Even with some reduction due to factors such as economic downturns (Stephen, 2002; Wells, 2003), executive recruitment continues to be one of the services most required by companies; and the higher the position in the organization's hierarchy, the higher the probability of a company asking for these specialized services (Clark, 1992, Purkiss & Edlmair, 2005).

With the phenomenal growth and awareness of the executive search service worldwide, it became a central issue among professionals and academics to analyse more deeply the ethical conduct of search consultants. In the next section we discuss this matter further.

Executive search, headhunting and ethical values

The Association of Executive Search Consultants (AESC) offers guidance to its members on their conduct (Bettleyon & Weston, 1986). Several standards of excellence have been developed in line with its code of professional practice. According to the AESC, the values aligned with executive search practices are:

1 *Integrity*: Above all, headhunters should maintain open communication, strong and mutual commitment and a transparent purpose of the assignment and inherent expectations and obligations with their clients, candidates and other interested parties.
2 *Excellence*: Headhunters should focus on providing a high-quality service and using rigorous, results-focused methodologies. Furthermore, they should have a full understanding of their client's business and industry, challenges and opportunities, and economic and cultural environment, as well as the position description and search strategy.
3 *Objectivity*: Professionals should serve as trusted advisers, exercising independent and objective judgement in identifying and evaluating the field of candidates, and communicate openly when, in their opinion, clients should consider modifying their specifications or approach.
4 *Diversity and inclusion*: Consultants should provide leadership to clients to benefit from the advantages of diversity and inclusion, and assist them in the successful integration and development of talent and help them to build a culture of inclusion.
5 *Confidentiality*: Client relationships are built on a foundation of trust; therefore, these professionals should protect confidential information concerning both clients and candidates and share any client and candidate information on a strictly need-to-know only basis.
6 *Avoiding conflicts of interest*: Headhunters have an obligation to avoid conflicts of interest with their clients and should refuse an assignment where such conflicts exist. The AESC adds that they should not accept gifts of a material nature that could influence their impartiality.

The literature presents some ethical values associated with the executive search and headhunting practice.

Off-limits guarantee Headhunters have an ethical obligation to inform their client of the off-limit constraints as long as such information is relevant for the client to decide whether to engage the headhunter (Mele & Roig, 1995). This guarantee is for a limited period only (usually 1–2 years) and the search firm is free to do business in other industries if it so desires, but this drawback should not be used as an excuse for not offering the off-limit guarantee (Lim & Chan, 2001).

Gather adequate and accurate job vacancy data It is the headhunter's responsibility to define the job vacancy accurately for the job candidate, so that the candidate has sufficient information to make a choice (Lim & Chan, 2001). The headhunter must not only provide accurate information, such as job requirements and the social and organizational environments that will affect the job candidate's performance (Jenn, 1994; Mele & Roig, 1995), but also help the candidate to examine whether the job fits their profile. However, as Lim and Chan (2001) point out, a search consultant with low ethical values may not provide sufficient information to the candidate and accept a search assignment even when the chances of success are limited (McCreary, 1997).

Information collection and provision Both the candidate and client organization have a right to receive sufficient information about the job vacancy. An unethical headhunter may, however, deceive the candidate into accepting a job by withholding critical information, such as the risks involved in the new job (Mele & Roig, 1995). Failure to inform is unethical because it is a direct violation of the principle of truthfulness, which demands that the headhunter maintains a high level of trust and accurate information regarding all the parties involved (Lim & Chan, 2001). The absence of important information may lead to costly mistakes when the candidate is unable to perform well on the job (Mele & Roig, 1995; Whitney, 1969).

Adequate evaluation of the candidate It is critical that headhunters conduct an in-depth assessment of the candidate (background and current performance) as well as evaluate the compatibility between the candidate's work style and personality and the client organization's corporate culture. Thus, an ethical headhunter will conduct a thorough search for all relevant information; failure to do so may lead to their presenting unqualified professionals to the client organizations (Lim & Chan, 2001; Mele & Roig, 1995).

Use of confidential information According to Lim and Chan (2001) the main concern with the use of confidential information is its possible unauthorized use for purposes beyond the process of recruitment. Headhunters who maintain a high ethical standard are usually able to assess the potential damage of the search and recognize that candidates have the right to choose their employer and job position (Mele & Roig, 1995).

Harm to the candidate's employer An ethical headhunter should always consider the potential harm of approaching an employee in another organization, especially if it is clear this may have have profound consequences, such as bankruptcy or a drastic drop in profitability and sales (Lim & Chan, 2001).

Despite the convergence of perspectives regarding ethical values in executive search firms, it is important to consider research that challenges the universal application of these standards. Surveys conducted in the UK show that more than one third of respondents (employers) have had bad experiences with executive search consultants, mainly when they proposed unqualified candidates and their failure to honour agreements (Nash, 1989). In the United States, many client organizations have expressed dissatisfaction with the discrepancies between what they received and what they were promised (Adshead, 1990; Smith & Sussman, 1990). Others state that recruiters have been found to be unduly opportunistic about their prospects of recruiting a candidate and less concerned with maintaining a high level of ethical conduct throughout the process (Smith & Sussman, 1990).

Lim and Chan (2001) developed a systematic research of 65 search consultant firms which agreed to participate in their study in order to understand whether the unethical headhunting practices reported in the literature were representative of the overall headhunting industry. The results show that headhunters generally adhere to most of the ethical values and were more ethically inclined than expected.

Based on this literature, we can conclude that headhunting remains popular and that standards of ethical practice may not be too dissimilar from internal organizational practices. However, further research is needed to analyse the current ethical position of headhunting in the search and selection industry, especially the direct impact of these practices on potential candidates, employees and organizations.

Clerkin and Lee (2010) conclude that when search firms initiated contacts with potential candidates these were usually closely associated with career success. On the other hand, when the contact was initiated by candidates looking for a new job opportunity, firms seemed to make a potentially negative association, as they assumed that such candidates must be unsuccessful professionals.

This bias is just one example of candidates' experiences. Bias that influences the decision-making process and relationships between professionals leading to different outcomes can be the difference between finding a successful job position and being excluded or under-evaluated. These concerns should lead us to discuss the ethics underlying these practices more thoroughly.

Ethics in Social Network Recruitment and Selection

In this section we discuss the advantages of using social media websites, such as Facebook and LinkedIn, in the recruitment and selection process. We then address some critical ethical aspects that should be taken into consideration when using those tools.

Social networks as a tool for recruitment and selection

Social networks (SNs) have become a vital part of a world in which information and resources flow constantly. They are in our everyday life and are growing. As we shall see, the business area is no exception.

Pew Research Center (2013) found that in 2005 only 8% of internet users were using SNs. By contrast, SN usage by adults in 2013 was up to 67%. As a consequence of the accelerating growth of these platforms, a growing number of organizations see online recruitment as an additional resource to take into consideration (Bartram, 2000). In fact, since the beginning of the century, as a strategy to increase the probability of finding the right candidate (Verhoeven & Williams, 2008), organizations have started to devote time to establishing a contact network through SNs, either to replace or in addition to traditional routes, such as advertising job opportunities in newspapers (Faroldi, 2007; Sameen & Cornelius, 2013).

SNs allow greater interaction between companies and candidates, facilitating the job hunting (Zhitomirsky-Geffet & Bratspiess, 2015) and selection processes (Capelli, 2001). As a result, HR professionals have come to see the rise of SNs as an opportunity to redefine recruitment and the way they find talent (Sambhi, 2009). Nonetheless, it is important to bear in mind that SNs are not a substitute for the recruitment process itself. Cappelli (2001) emphasizes that this tool should complement the recruitment process, since there are still some variables that recruiters will only be able to assess in personal contact by conducting interviews and using other validated assessment methods.

Through SNs it is now possible to have a closer relationship between companies and candidates (Mitter & Orlandini, 2005), by sharing interests, resources and information among all those involved (Boyd & Ellison, 2007). Some authors have described the advantages of this type of recruitment for companies and recruiters. These include the cost-effectiveness of the method (Breaugh, 2008; Peretti, 2007; Walsh & Kleiner, 1990); the ability of organizations to attract different candidates compared to traditional recruitment methods carrying out active and passive recruitment (Dutta, 2014; Peretti, 2007); the ability to segment candidates more finely (Dutta, 2014; Peretti, 2007) and to review different candidates' experience to more precisely find the right fit (Mitter & Orlandini, 2005).

Zall (2000) claims that hiring via SNs is less time-consuming than traditional recruitment and selection methods. Studies conducted in the US concluded that the recruitment process dropped from 32 days or more using traditional methods to 16 days using internet recruitment (Burt, 2004; Veger, 2006; Zall, 2000). Furthermore, SNs not only help job seekers but also give hiring managers and recruiters access to high-quality but passive job applicants (i.e., those who are currently employed and not searching for a new position but may switch job if the opportunity and offer are attractive; Joos, 2008). Hence, SNs provide a platform for employers to convert passive candidates into job applicants.

But recruiters are not the only ones enjoying the benefits of SNs. Advantages were also pointed out for the candidates. According to Peretti (2007), they offered candidates three benefits:

1 Their professional and personal information is available globally, 24 hours a day, 7 days a week.
2 Job seekers can look for job opportunities at any time, anywhere in the world.
3 They receive, more directly, job opportunities that best fit their profile and motivations.

Professional networking sites such as LinkedIn have started to become an important resource for job seekers, providing them the opportunity to advertise their skills and accomplishments, and promote their value in the market (McFadden, 2014).

Launched in 2003, LinkedIn has more than 300 million members worldwide (Novet, 2015). Its mission is to help career professionals succeed through networking opportunities, job listings, news and insights from other professionals in the field.

Surveys carried out by the Society for Human Resource Management, the US body for HR professionals, reveal that 77% of companies studied used SNs to recruit applicants, rising from 56% in 2011 and a mere 34% in 2008 (Segal, 2014). As we have seen in previous sections this is a particularly common practice in industries that deal with sensitive information or need a rapid response from the market, which therefore resort frequently to this type of direct recruitment.

According to the literature, we can summarize some of the advantages of using SN tools in the recruitment and selection process (Table 6.2).

Table 6.2 Advantages of using SNs in the recruitment and selection process.

Advantages	Definition
Prevents negligent hiring	Employers feel they have a responsibility to conduct online checks in order to protect themselves from negligent hiring (Clark & Roberts, 2010; Elzweig & Peeples, 2009; Slovensky & Ross, 2012).
Information verification	Information on SNs may provide more honest information than traditional cover letters and CVs, which are compiled to highlight a person's best characteristics. It has also been suggested that screening SNs may be more cost-effective in the early stages of the selection process than the cost of an extensive background check (Slovensky & Ross, 2012).
Correlation to personal characteristics	Screening an applicant's SN profile may also provide a 'big picture' of the applicant in order to determine fit with a company or job (Bottomly, 2011). Kluemper and Rosen (2009) found evidence supporting the validity of using SN information to determine personality, intelligence and global performance.
Influence on hiring decisions	Bohnert and Ross (2010) suggest that SN information does influence how an applicant is evaluated and can influence hiring decisions, such as wage offered and whether the applicant receives a job offer or not. It may also reinforce initial impressions or decisions based on other information, such as a cover letter or résumé (Elzweig & Peeples, 2009; Slovensky & Ross, 2012).

Despite the undeniable advantages of using SNs in the recruitment process, this comes with added ethical implications which are discussed in the next section.

The ethical risks of using social networks as a tool in recruitment and selection

With the emergence and increasing popularity of SN tools such as Facebook and LinkedIn in the HR field, more employers and recruiters have started to use the information available on these sites (Brown & Vaughn, 2011) in order to screen not only job applicants but also passive potential candidates.

Consequently, it became important to make a thorough analysis of potential and significant risks, especially in ethical terms. Table 6.3 presents some of the risks found in a search of the literature on SN use.

As noted, SN information is easily accessible by and visible to employers and hiring managers (Chu & Snider, 2013), however, it also carries the risk of introducing biases to the screening process. For instance, possible bias via Facebook occurs when hiring managers reject suitable applicants after looking at their profile picture, which they believe reflects the applicant's personality (Sameen & Cornelius, 2013). This reduces the likelihood of the applicant being invited for an interview (Caers & Castelyns, 2011). Empirical research indicates that hiring managers are often influenced by factors such as age (Lahey, 2008; Weiss & Maurer, 2004), gender (Riach & Rich, 2002; Swim & Hunter, 1995), sexual orientation (Drydakis, 2009; Weichselbaumer, 2003), race (Cesare, 1996; Pager, 2003), obesity (Roehling, 1999) and facial attractiveness (Tews, Stafford & Zhu, 2009) when screening candidates.

Therefore, by using information from sites such as Facebook or LinkedIn to screen applicants, employers are potentially violating privacy rights, obtaining misleading or inaccurate information about an applicant, and receiving protected information that an HR professional otherwise would not inquire about in order to conform to the employment legislation (Brown & Vaughn, 2011; Elzweig & Peeples, 2009; Slovensky & Ross, 2012).

Table 6.3 Risks of using social networks in the recruitment and selection process.

Risks	Definition
Inaccurate or incomplete information	When screening SN information, employers risk receiving inaccurate or incomplete information about a candidate (Dennis, 2011; Elzweig & Peeples, 2009; Slovensky & Ross, 2012). The profile may be falsified or created to make the applicant appear better or worse than they are, depending on the intended audience (Johnson, 2011); the information may also be outdated (Slovensky & Ross, 2012).
Misidentification of applicants	It is not always easy to determine if it was actually the applicant who posted the information on the SN profile (Dennis, 2011). Also, because of the popularity of SNs, it is possible that the profile an employer is looking at is not actually the applicant's but a profile of someone who has a similar name (Slovensky & Ross, 2012).
Fairness perceptions	An applicant who discovers their SN information was screened may feel that their privacy has been violated and thus perceive that practice as having low procedural justice (Slovensky & Ross, 2012). These perceptions can influence an applicant's decision to accept or reject a job offer (Bauer et al., 2006; Blacksmith & Peoppelman, 2014; Slovensky & Ross, 2012).
Invasion of privacy	Employers use a variety of measures to gain access to information from SN profiles, which may or may not violate the individual's right to privacy (Benraïss-Noailles & Viot, 2012; Slovensky & Ross, 2012).
Potential discrimination	Employers are able to choose whom they want to hire, fire or promote without direct limitations (Elzweig & Peeples, 2009). That can introduce a bias in the process (Blacksmith & Poeppelman, 2014).

A survey of 300 hiring professionals showed that 91% of surveyed employers use some sort of SN to evaluate applicants, and 69% have reported rejecting an applicant because of unacceptable profile content (MacLeod, 2011). To reinforce this, some studies have shown that employers usually reject candidates in the screening process if: applicants have inappropriate photographs on their SN profiles; have posted drugs- or alcohol-related information; have insulted their previous employer/colleague/friend or relative; have poor communication skills; have posted discriminatory comments regarding religion, gender or race; have stated incorrect qualifications; have shared any confidential information about a previous employer; and have links to criminality or have an unprofessional screen name (Careerbuilder, 2014).

Based on all this, some authors claim there are two important concerns about employers using these tools. The first is the potential of a claim for discrimination. In the US, Title VII of the Civil Rights Act 1964 makes it unlawful for an employer to make employment decisions based on race, religion, sex or national origin (Darragh, 2012). Similar legislation exists in the UK and most EU member states. Despite the current lack of legal guidance and legislation, employers must be vigilant in relation to discrimination that may occur when recruiting via SNs.

A second type of discrimination pointed out by some authors is when potential candidates with little or no web presence are overlooked or excluded when using SNs as the only recruitment tool (Bartram, 2000; Feldman & Klaas, 2002; Singh & Finn, 2003). Effland (2010) warns that, even though the internet is considered a public domain, laws will soon be needed to address the use of information gathered on a potential employee using SNs. For instance, ensuring there is transparency in decisions to include or exclude specific candidates (Effland, 2010).

Another ethical concern is invasion of privacy and security (Singh & Finn, 2003). Although creating a LinkedIn or Facebook profile greatly enhances users' online visibility (for better or for worse) employees may still feel their privacy has been violated when current or potential employers gather information from their profiles that could influence their chance of being recruited or employed (Davison et al., 2011). In the matter of security, Zeidner (2007) states that by resorting to online recruitment methods, some security aspects should be emphasized since with the high exchange of information (contacts, personal data), companies and candidates may run some additional risks of having confidential information accessed by or leaked to third parties.

From these studies we can conclude that, regarding SNs' presence in recruitment and selection, each advantage seems to bring with it an ethical concern. Although the fast pace and development of SNs is an obstacle in dealing with these concerns in good time, organizations need to consider these issues and publicly state how they intend to manage these dilemmas ethically.

Future Research

The ethical issues facing organizations in recruitment and selection are under-researched. That is surprising considering its importance for society, organizations and individuals alike. The recent growing interest in the ethical dimensions of organizations' actions has not yet impacted the recruitment and selection process and there are thus significant gaps in knowledge and practice. The literature found is mostly practitioner-oriented and based on reflection rather than empirical data or research.

In this chapter we have noted the limited number of empirical research studies on values-based recruitment and selection, and those that do exist are almost exclusively in the field of healthcare. A preliminary literature review shows that researchers are becoming more aware of the importance of values for organizational actions as part of the way individuals perform their duties. Further research could usefully explore the application of values within sectors outside of healthcare.

Ethics in the organizations' relationship with applicants is the focus of some, but scarce, empirical research in the third section of the chapter. The papers here are however mainly theoretical and prescriptive. Research is needed to explore the relevance of fairness and justice, from organizational perspectives, as well as from both successful and unsuccessful candidates. Further, empirical research is also needed to understand the mechanisms that organizations can be put in place to promote and develop an ethical relationship with applicants.

Ethics in executive search and headhunting has also been subject to little empirical research. Most literature is practitioner-oriented and refers to codes of conduct applicable to the field. Prescriptive literature offers advice on what should be done, but these views are based on the authors' opinions and are not informed by systematic evidence from candidates. Ethical research in other areas, such as executive education, can become a source of inspiration for new studies (e.g., Floyd et al., 2013).

We found no research literature focused on the ethical aspects of the use of social networks for recruitment and selection purposes. The main publications we did find focus on descriptive aspects of these tools and on the advantages and risks of using them. In some articles we can infer the ethical aspects, in others a short reference is made (Blacksmith & Poeppelman, 2014), but evidence is sparse. Therefore, this subject is a promising avenue for future research.

Conclusion

In this chapter we have reviewed the ethical issues facing organizations and candidates in recruitment and selection, from values to the development of new practices, such as online and SN recruitment methods. While practices are changing, the evidence suggests that research is not keeping pace, and that there is a risk that ethics will be left behind in the rush to secure the 'best' candidates.

References

Adshead, J. (1990). Headhunting without tears. *Personnel Management*, 56–57.

Alder, G. S., & Gilbert, J. (2006). Ethics and fairness in hiring. *Journal of Business Ethics, 68*, 449–464.

Ambrose, M. L., & Rosse, J. G. (2003). Procedural justice and personality testing. An examination of concern and typicality. *Group & Organization Management, 28*(4), 502–526.

Arvey, R. D., & Renz, G. L. (1992). Fairness in the selection of employees. *Journal of Business Ethics, 11*, 331–340.

Bartram, D. (2000). Internet recruitment and selection: Kissing frogs to find princes. *International Journal of Selection and Assessment, 8*(4), 261–274.

Beeson, W. B. (1965). Ethics and executive search. *Management Review, 54*(7), 59–62.

Benraïss-Noailles, L., & Viot, C. (2012). Les médias sociaux dans les stratégies de recrutement: Quelle compatibilité avec la vie privée? *Revue Française de Gestion, 224*, 125–138.

Bernerth, J. B. (2005). Perceptions of justice in employment selection decisions: The role of applicant gender. *International Journal of Selection and Assessment, 13*(3), 206–212.

Bettleyon, S., & Weston, T. (1986). Executive search firms: Are they looking for you? *Orange County Business Journal, 9*, 25.

Björklund, F., Bäckström, M., & Wolgast, S. (2012). Company norms affect which traits are preferred in job candidates and may cause employment discrimination. *The Journal of Psychology, 146*(6), 579–594.

Blacksmith, N., & Poeppelman, T. (2014). Three ways social media and technology have changed recruitment. *The Industrial Organizational Psychologist, 52*(1), 114–121.

Bohnert, D., & Ross, W. H. (2010). The influence of social networking web sites on the evaluation of job candidates. *Cyberpsychology, Behavior, and Social Network, 13*(3), 341–347. doi: 10.1089/cyber.2009.0193.

Bore, M., Munro, D., Kerridge, I., & Powis, D. (2005). Selection of medical students according to their moral orientation. *Medical Education, 39*, 266–275.

Bottomly, L. G. (2011). Social Media: New Opportunities and Headaches. *Employment Law Seminar, Atter Wynn LLP, 1–13*.

Boyd, D. M., & Ellison, N. B. (2008). Social network sites: Definition, history, and scholarship. *Journal of Computer-mediated Communication, 13*, 210–230.

Breaugh, J. A. (2008). Employee recruitment: Current knowledge and important areas for future research. *Human Resource Management Review, 18*(3), 103–118.

Brown, V. R., & Vaughn, E. D. (2011). The writing on the (Facebook) wall: The use of social networking sites in hiring decisions. *Journal of Business and Psychology, 26*, 219–225. doi: 10.1007/s10869-011-9221-x.

Burt, L. (2004). Recruitment revolution. Personnel Today, 31.

Caers, R., & Castelyns, V. (2011). LinkedIn and Facebook in Belgium: The influence and biases of social network sites in recruitment and selection procedures. *Social Science Computer Review, 29*(4), 437–448.

Cappeli, P. (2001). Making the most of on-line recruiting: The war for talent has moved to the internet. You'd better have a battle plan. *Harvard Business Review, 79*, 139–146.

CareerBuilder (2014). Number of employers passing on applicants due to social media posts continues to rise according to new *CareerBuilder* survey. *CareerBuilder, 1*. www.careerbuilder.

com/share/aboutus/pressreleasesdetail.aspx?sd=6%2F26%2F2014&id=pr829&ed=12%2F31 %2F2014. Last accessed 1 November 2015.

Cesare, S. J. (1996). Subjective judgments and the selection interview: A methodological review. *Public Personnel Management, 25,* 291–306.

Chidi, O. C., Ogunyomi, O. P., & Badejo, A. E. (2012). Promoting ethical human resource management practices in work organisations in Nigeria: Roles of HR professionals. *International Journal of Human Resource Studies, 2*(2), 116–131.

Chu, J. L., & Snider, C. E. (2013). Use of a social networking web site for recruiting Canadian youth for medical research. *Journal of Adolescent Health, 52,* 792–794.

Clark, L. A., & Roberts, S. J. (2010). Employers' use of social networking sites: A socially irresponsible practice. *Journal of Business Ethics, 95,* 507–525. doi: 10.1007/s10551-010-0436-y.

Clark, T. (1992). Management selection by executive recruitment consultancies: A survey and explanation of selection methods. *Journal of Managerial Psychology, 7*(6), 3–10.

Clerkin, T. A., & Lee, J. Y. (2010). Executive search relationships – Contacts between executives and search firm professionals: Scale development and validation. *Organization Management Journal, 7,* 208–228.

Commissioning Board Chief Nursing Officer and DH Chief Nursing Adviser. (2012). Compassion in practice: Nursing, midwifery and care staff. Our vision and strategy. tinyurl. www.england. nhs.uk/wp-content/uploads/2012/12/compassion-in-practice.pdf. Last accessed 1 November 2015.

Craft, J. L. (2013). A review of the empirical ethical decision-making literature: 2004–2011. *Journal of Business Ethics, 117,* 221–259.

Cronin, R. J. (1981). Executive recruiters: Are they necessary? *Personnel Administrator, 26*(2), 31–34.

Darragh, R. (2012). Recruiting risk: Hiring via social media channels. www.Complainceweek.com, February, 49–57.

Davison, H. K., Maraist, C., & Bing, M. N. (2011). Friend or foe? The promise and pitfalls of using social networking sites for HR decisions. *Journal of Business and Psychology. 26*(2), 153–159.

Dennis, C. M. (2011). Legal implications of employee social media use. *Massachusetts Law Review, 93*(4), 380–395. www.massbar.org/publications/massachusetts-law-review/2011/vol-93-no-4/ legal-implications-of-employee-social-media-use. Last accessed 1 November 2015.

Department of Health – SER-WS-WDS 13500. (2014). Delivering high quality, effective, compassionate care: Developing the right people with the right skills and the right values. A mandate from the Government to Health Education England: April 2014 to March 2015. www.gov.uk/ government/uploads/system/uploads/attachment_data/file/310170/DH_HEE_Mandate. pdf. Last accessed 1 November 2015.

Dineen, B. R., Noe, R. A., & Wang, C. (2004). Perceived fairness of web-based applicant screening procedures: Weighing the rules of justice and the role of individual differences. *Human Resource Management, 43*(2/3), 127–145.

Drydakis, N. (2009). Sexual orientation discrimination in the labour market. *Labour Economics, 16,* 364–372.

Dutta, D. (2014). Tweet your tune – Social media, the new pied piper in talent acquisition. *VIKALPA, 39*(3), 93–104.

Effland, M. S. (2010). Lawyer warns Facebook a risky tool for background checks. *Workforce Management.* http://www.workforce.com/section/06/feature/25/45/83/254585.html. Last accessed 1 November 2015.

Elzweig, B., & Peeples, D. K. (2009). Using social networking web sites in hiring and retention decisions. *Advanced Management Journal,* 27–35.

Faroldi, L. (2007). Redes socials y Mercado de trabajo. *Revista hispana para el análises de redes socials, 13,* 1–12.

Faulconbridge, J. R., Beaverstock, J. V., Hall, S., & Hewitson, A. (2009). The 'war for talent': The gatekeeper role of executive search firms in elite labour markets. *Geoforum, 40,* 800–808.

Fein, E., & Weibler, J. (2014). Review and shortcomings of literature on corruption in organizations in offering a multi-faceted and integrative understanding of the phenomenon. *Behavioral Development Bulletin, 19*(3), 67–77.

Feldman, D., & Klaas, B. (2002). Internet job hunting: A field study of applicant experiences with online recruiting. *Human Resource Management, 41*(2), 175–192.

Finlay, W., & Coverdill, J. E. (2000). Risk, opportunism and structural holes: How headhunters manage clients and earn fees. *Work and Occupations,* 377–405.

Fletcher, C. (1992). Ethical issues in the selection interview. *Journal of Business Ethics, 11,* 361–367.

Floyd, L. A., Xu, F., Atkins, R., & Caldwell, C. (2013). Ethical outcomes and business ethics: Toward improving business ethics education. *Journal of Business Ethics, 117,* 753–776.

Fodchuk, K. M., & Sidebotham, E. J. (2005). Procedural justice in the selection process: A review of research and suggestions for practical applications. *The Psychologist-Manager Journal, 8*(2), 105–120.

Forde, C., & MacKenzie, R. (2010). Ethical agendas towards migrant workers. *Journal of Business Ethics, 97,* 31–41.

García-Izquierdo, A. L., Aguinis H., & Ramos-Villagrasa P. J. (2010). Science–practice gap in e-recruitment'. *International Journal of Selection and Assessment, 18*(4), 432–438.

Hamori, M. (2010). Who gets headhunted – And who gets ahead? The impact of search firms on executive careers. *Academy of Management Perspectives, 24*(4), 46, 59.

Hannafey, F. T. (2003). Entrepreneurship and ethics: A literature review. *Journal of Business Ethics, 46,* 99–110.

Hunter, M. (1989). Executive safari. Headhunters: How they work, how they bill, and how to find the right one for you. *Folio: The Magazine for Magazine Management,* 116–125.

Husbands, A., Rodgerson, M. J., Dowell, J., & Patterson, F. (2015). Evaluating the validity of an integrity-based situational judgement test for medical school admissions. *BMC Medical Education, 15,* 144–152.

Jenn, N. G. (1994). *Executive Search in Asia-Pacific: Choosing and Using a Headhunter.* London: The Economist Intelligence Unit.

Johnson, E. M. (2011). *Social media and labor & employment law: Job applications & background checks, employer misconduct ethical consideration.* Paper presented at the 2011 Annual Association Law Symposium, Washington D.C.

Jones, S. (1995). *Headhunting: A Guide to Executive Search in Asia.* London: Prentice-Hall.

Joos, J. G. (2008). Social media: New frontiers in hiring and recruiting. *Employment Relations Today,* 51–59.

Kanerva, A., Lammintakanen, J., & Kivinen, T. (2010). Experiences of the fairness of recruitment from unsuccessful applicants in the field of nursing. *Journal of Nursing Management, 18,* 293–301.

Kare-Silver, N., Spicer, J., Khan, A., & Ahluwalia, S. (2014). Competency and practice: Selection of speciality GP trainees for the 21st century. *Education for Primary Care, 25,* 129–131.

Kluemper, D. H., & Rosen, P. A. (2009). Future employment selection methods: Evaluating social networking websites. *Journal of Managerial Psychology, 24,* 567–580.

Lahey, J. (2008). Age, women, and hiring: An experimental study. *Journal of Human Resources, 43,* 30–56.

Lee, M. (1997). Executive recruitment firms work in various ways. www.amcity.com/tampabay/stories/082597/smallb 5.html. Last accessed 1 November 2015.

Lee, Y., Stettler, A., & Antonakis, J. (2011). Incremental validity and indirect effect of ethical development on work performance. *Personality and Individual Differences, 50*(7), 1110–1115.

Lehnert, K., Park, Y-H., & Singh, N. (2015). Research note and review of the empirical ethical decision-making literature: Boundary conditions and extensions. *Journal of Business Ethics, 129,* 195–219.

Lim, G. S., & Chan, C. (2001). Ethical values of executive search consultants. *Journal of Business Ethics,* 213–226.

Lim, G–S., & Chan, C. (2001). Ethical values of executive search consultants. *Journal of Business Ethics, 29,* 213–226.

Lindorff, M. (2007). The ethical impact of business and organisational research: The forgotten methodological issue? *The Electronic Journal of Business Research Methods, 5*(1), 21–28. www.ejbrm.com.

Ma, R., & Allen, D. G. (2009). Recruiting across cultures: A value-based model of recruitment. *Human Resource Management Review,* doi: 10.1016/j.hrmr.2009.03.001.

MacLeod, I. (2011). 91% of employers use social media to scan applicants. *The Drum*. www. thedrum.com/news/2011/10/24/91-employers-use-socialmedia-screen-applicants. Last accessed 1 November 2015.

May, D. R., Luth, M. T., & Schwoerer, C. E. (2014). The influence of business ethics education on moral efficacy, moral meaningfulness, and moral courage: A quasi-experimental study. *Journal of Business Ethics, 124,* 67–80.

McClaren, N. (2013). The personal selling and sales management ethics research: Managerial implications and research directions from a comprehensive review of the empirical literature. *Journal of Business Ethics, 112,* 101–125.

McCreary, C. (1997). Get the most out of search firms. *Workforce,* 28–30.

McFadden, K. (2014). Why LinkedIn is so important for professionals and job-seekers. smartbusinesstrends.com/linkedin-important-professionals-job-seekers. Last accessed 1 November 2015.

Mele, D., & Roig, B. (1995), Ethical issues in executive search consultancy. *In* H. W. Hoivik & A. Follesdal (Eds.), *Ethics and Consultancy: European Perspectives* (pp. 135–148). Boston, MA: Kluwer Academic.

Meyer, J. D. (1995). Modern-day headhunters. *Directions,* 42–44.

Miller, S. L. (2015). Values-based recruitment in health care. *Nursing Standard, 29*(21), 37–41.

Miller, S., & Bird, J. (2014). Assessment of practitioners' and students' values when recruiting. *Nursing Management, 21*(5), 22–29.

Mitter, G., & Orlandini, J. (2005). Recrutamento on-line/internet. *Maringá Management: Revista de Ciências Empresariais, 2,* 19–34.

Nash, T. (1989). Up for grabs: Is poaching staff wrong? *Director, 42,* 90–96.

Noon, M., Healy, G., Forson, C., & Oikelome, F. (2013). The equality effects of the 'hyper-formalization' of selection. *British Journal of Management, 24,* 333–346.

Novet, J. (2015). LinkedIn now counts 347 M members, up from 277 M at the end of 2013. venturebeat.com/2015/02/05/linkedin-now-counts-more-than-300 m-members-up-from-277 m-at-the-end-of-2013. Last accessed 1 November 2015.

Osca, A., & López-Araújo, B. (2009). Does justice in selection predict candidate's intentions? *Revista de Psicología del Trabajo y de las Organizaciones, 25*(3), 219–229.

Pager, D. (2003). The mark of a criminal record. *American Journal of Sociology, 108,* 937–975.

Patterson, F., Ashworth, V., Zibarras, L., Coan, P., Kerrin, M., & O'Neill, P. (2012). Evaluations of situational judgement tests to assess non-academic attributes in selection. *Medical Education, 46,* 850–868.

Patterson, F., Prescott-Clements, L., Zibarras, L., Edwards, H., Kerrin, M., & Cousans, M. (2015). Recruiting for values in healthcare: A preliminary review of the evidence. *Advances in Health Sciences Education,* dx.doi.org/10.1007/s10459-014-9579-4.

Patterson, F., Zibarras, L., & Ashworth, V. (2015). Situational judgement tests in medical education and training: Research, theory and practice: AMEE Guide No. 100. *Medical Teacher,* 1–15.

Peretti, J. M. (2007). *Ressources humaines.* Paris: Vuibert.

Petrova, M., Dale, J., & Fulford, K. W. M. (2006). Values-based practice in primary care: Easing the tensions between individual values, ethical principles and best evidence. *British Journal of General Practice, 56*(530), 703–709.

Pew Research Center (2013). Instagram, Vine, and the evolution of social media. www.pewresearch. org/facttank/2013/06/20/instagram-vine-and-the-evolution-of-social-media Last accessed 1 November 2015.

Philips, M. (1991). Preferential hiring and the question of competence. *Journal of Business Ethics, 10,* 161–163.

Purkiss, J., & Edlmair, B. (2005). How to be headhunted. *In* F. Mitchell (Ed.), *How Executive Search Works* (pp. 15–29). Oxford: How to Books.

Rankin, B. (2013). Emotional intelligence: Enhancing values-based practice and compassionate care in nursing. *Journal of Advanced Nursing 69*(12), 2717–2725. doi: 10.1111/jan.12161.

Riach, P. A., & Rich, R. J. (2002). Field experiments of discrimination in the market place. *Economic Journal, 112,* 480–518.

Robin, D. (2009). Toward an applied meaning for ethics in business. *Journal of Business Ethics, 89,* 139–150.

Roehling, M. R. (1999). Weight-based discrimination in employment: Psychology and legal aspects. *Personnel Psychology, 52,* 969–1016.

Rosenfeld, P. (1997). Impression management, fairness, and the employment interview. *Journal of Business Ethics, 16,* 801–808.

Rutledge, J. (1997). Don't headhunt without a guide. *Forbes, 146.*

Sambhi, H. (2009). Social media can be used for recruitment. *Canadian HR Reporter.* 22–23.

Sameen, S., & Cornelius, S. (2013). Social networking sites and hiring: How social media profiles influence hiring decisions. *Journal of Business Studies Quarterly, 7,* 29–35.

Sameen, S., & Cornelius, S. (2013). Social networking sites and hiring: How social media profiles influence hiring decisions. *Journal of Business Studies Quarterly, 7*(1), 27–35.

Schwepker, C. H. Jr., & Ingram, T. N. (1996). Improving sales performance through ethics: The relationship between salesperson moral judgement and job performance. *Journal of Business Ethics, 15,* 1151–1160.

Segal, J. A. (2014). Social media use in hiring: Assessing the risks. *The Society of Human Resource Management,* 1 October, 59, 9.

Singer, M. S., & Singer, A. E. (1991). Justice in preferential hiring. *Journal of Business Ethics, 10,* 797–803.

Singh, P., & Finn, D. (2003). The effects of information technology on recruitment. *Journal of Labor Research, 24,* 395–408.

Slovensky, R., & Ross, W. H. (2012). Should human resource managers use social media to screen job applicants? *Managerial and Legal Issues in the USA, 14*(1), 55–69. doi: 10.1108/14636691211196941.

Smith, R. L., & Sussman, L. (1990). Conclusion: the future of collaboration. *In* J. J. Parker & R. H. Perry (Eds.), *The Executive Search Collaboration: A Guide for Human Resources Professionals and Their Search Firms* (pp. 227–232). New York: Quorum Books.

Stephen, O. (2002). Headhunters feel the pinch. *Personnel Today, 40.*

Suhonen, R., Stolt, M., Virtanen, H., & Leino-Kilpi, H. (2011). Organizational ethics: A literature review. *Nursing Ethics, 18*(3), 285–303.

Swim, J. K., & Hunter, B. A. (1995). Sexism and racism: Old-fashioned and modern prejudice. *Journal of Personality and Social Psychology, 68,* 199–214.

Taylor, A. R. (1984). *How to Select and Use an Executive Search Firm.* New York: McGraw-Hill.

Tews, M., Stafford, K., & Zhu, J. (2009). Beauty revisited: The impact of attractiveness, ability and personality in the assessment of employment suitability. *International Journal of Selection and Assessment, 17,* 92–100.

Truxillo, D. M., Bauer, T. N., Campion, M. A., & Paronto, M. E. (2002). Selection fairness information and applicant reactions: A longitudinal field study. *Journal of Applied Psychology, 87*(6), 1020–1031.

Truxillo, D. M., Bauer, T. N., & Sanchez, R. J. (2001). Multiple dimensions of procedural justice: Longitudinal effects on selection system fairness and test-taking self-efficacy. *International Journal of Selection and Assessment, 9*(4), 336–349.

Tsahuridu, E., & Perryer, C. (2002). Ethics and integrity: What Australian organizations seek and offer in recruitment advertisements. *Public Administration & Management: An Interactive Journal, 7*(4), 304–319.

van den Brink, M., Benschop, Y., & Jansen, W. (2010). Transparency in academic recruitment: A problematic tool for gender equality? *Organization Studies, 31*(12), 1–25.

Veger, M. (2006). How does internet recruitment have effect on recruitment performance? *Fourth Twente Student Conference on IT,* 30 January, Enschede, The Netherlands.

Verhoeven, H., & Williams, S. (2008). Advantages and disadvantages of internet recruitment: A UK study into employers' perceptions. *International Review of Business Research Papers, 4,* 364–373.

Vitell, S. J. (2009). The role of religiosity in business and consumer ethics: A review of the literature. *Journal of Business Ethics, 90,* 155–167.

Wahyudi, A., Haryono, T., Riyani, A. L., & Harsono, M. (2013). The impact of work ethics on performance using job satisfaction and affective commitment as mediating variables: Evidences from lecturers in Central Java. *Issues in Social and Environmental Accounting, 7*(3), 165–184.

Walker, H. J., Feild, H. S., Giles, W. F., & Bernerth, J. B. (2008). The interactive effects of job advertisement characteristics and applicant experience on reactions to recruitment messages. *Journal of Occupational and Organizational Psychology, 81*, 619–638.

Wallace, J. C., Page, E. E., & Lippstreu, M. (2006). Applicant reactions to pre-employment application blanks: A legal and procedural justice perspective. *Journal of Business and Psychology, 20*, 467–488.

Walsh, J. M., & Kleiner, B. H. (1990). New developments in recruitment and selection. *American Business Review, 8*(1), 39–42.

Ware, F. A. (1984). Managing confidentiality in an academic presidential search. *Sam Advanced Management Journal*, 30–34.

Waugh, A., Smith, D., Horsburgh, D., & Gray, M. (2014). Towards a values-based person specification for recruitment of compassionate nursing and midwifery candidates: A study of registered and student nurses' and midwives' perceptions of prerequisite attributes and key skills. *Nurse Education Today, 34*(9), 1190–1195. doi: 10.1016/j.nedt.2013.12.009.

Weichselbaumer, D. (2003). Sexual orientation discrimination in hiring. *Labour Economics, 10*, 629–642.

Weiss, E. M., & Maurer, T. J. (2004). Age discrimination in personnel decisions: A reexamination. *Journal of Applied Social Psychology, 34*, 1551–1562.

Wells, S. (2003). Slow times for executive recruiting, *HR Magazine, 48*(4), 60–68.

Whitney, K. (1969). Ethics for recruiting employees and executives. *Management of Personnel Quarterly*, Summer, 13–15.

Xu, Y., & Zhang, J. (2005). One size doesn't fit all: Ethics of international nurse recruitment from the conceptual framework of stakeholder interests. *Nursing Ethics, 12*(6), 571–581.

Yap, S. F. (2014). Beliefs, values, ethics and moral reasoning in socio-scientific education. *Issues in Educational Research, 24*(3), 299–319.

Zall, M. (2000). Internet recruiting. *Strategic Finance, 81*, 66–72.

Zeidner, R. (2007). Making online recruiting more secure. *HR Magazine, 52*, 75–77.

Zhitomirsky-Geffet, M., & Bratspiess, Y. (2015). Perceived effectiveness of social networks for job search. *Libri: International Journal of Libraries & Information Services, 65*(2), 105–118.

Section II
Selection

7

Using Ability Tests in Selection

Jesús F. Salgado

Introduction

General mental ability (GMA) and specific cognitive tests have been recognized as the most powerful predictors of overall job performance, task performance, academic performance and training proficiency (Ackerman & Heggestad, 1997; Guion, 1998; Murphy, 2002; Ones, Dilchert, Viswesvaran & Salgado, 2010; Reeve & Hackel, 2002; Salgado, 1999; Schmidt & Hunter, 1998; Schmitt, 2014; Vinchur & Koppes, 2011). Thus, cognitive ability tests occupy the most relevant place among the personnel selection procedures.

There are at least six important reasons supporting the claim that cognitive ability tests play a key role in personnel selection procedures (Scherbaum, Goldstein, Yusko, Ryan & Hanges; 2012; Schmidt & Hunter, 1998). First, GMA tests have the highest validity and lowest application cost. Second, the empirical evidence on the validity of GMA measures for predicting job performance is stronger than that for any other method. Third, GMA has been shown to be the best predictor of job-related learning. It is the best predictor of acquisition of job knowledge on the job and of performance in job training programmes. Fourth, the theoretical foundations of GMA are stronger than for any other personnel selection measure, and theories of intelligence have been developed and tested by psychologists for over 90 years. Fifth, the incremental contribution of specific abilities (defined as ability factors unrelated to the general factor, or g) to the prediction of performance or training outcomes may be minimal beyond g. Sixth, the findings on the validity of GMA and cognitive tests are the major contribution of industrial, work and organizational (IWO) psychology to the study of GMA and its use in applied settings.

This chapter reviews the literature on the use of ability tests in personnel selection, focusing on several relevant issues: 1) the definition of cognitive abilities and prevalence of use in personnel selection; 2) the main theoretical models of the psychometric structure of GMA and cognitive abilities; 3) the criterion validity and validity generalization of GMA

The Wiley Blackwell Handbook of the Psychology of Recruitment, Selection and Employee Retention,
First Edition. Edited by Harold W. Goldstein, Elaine D. Pulakos, Jonathan Passmore and Carla Semedo.
© 2017 John Wiley & Sons Ltd. Published 2020 by John Wiley & Sons Ltd.

and specific cognitive abilities, including their incremental validity over GMA validity; 4) issues of group differences, bias and fairness; 5) applicant reactions and justice perceptions; and 6) suggestions for future research.

General Mental Ability and Specific Cognitive Abilities: Definition Issues

In this chapter, the terms general mental ability (GMA), general cognitive ability (GCA), general intelligence and *g* will be used as equivalents. GMA may be defined as the capacity of an individual to learn quickly and accurately a task, a subject matter or a skill, under optimal instructional conditions (Carroll, 1993; Hunt, 2011; Jensen, 1998). Less time and more precision indicate higher GMA. In this sense, solving problems correctly, making rapid but sound decisions, judging situations accurately, being able to use abstract reasoning, to acquire knowledge and to be able to use it in new contexts are examples of a high GMA. Some researchers have suggested that adaptability should be included in the definition of intelligence (Goldstein, Scherbaum & Yusko, 2010; Scherbaum, Goldstein, Yusko, Ryan & Hanges, 2012). To this effect, in the earliest years of intelligence research, the German psychologist William Stern (1912, p. 3) defined intelligence as 'a general capacity of an individual consciously to adjust his thinking to new requirements: it is general mental adaptability to new problems and conditions of life' (see Sternberg & Detterman, 1986, for other definitions). Stern's definition appears to be even more relevant today than it was in the past for it underscores that adaptability to new problems and life conditions is one characteristic of intelligence, and new problems and changing conditions are the essence of current work tasks and situations, as Scherbaum and colleagues (2012) have pointed out. Thirty years earlier, Humphreys (1983, p. 236) expressed a similar view, and defined intelligence as 'the resultant of the processes of acquiring, storing in memory, retrieving, combining, comparing, and using in new contexts information and conceptual skills; it is abstraction'. Accordingly, cognitive tests have to be composed of numerous and content-heterogeneous items, and have only moderate levels of inter-item correlations in order to sample these behaviours adequately (Humphreys, 1983).

The prevalence of cognitive tests in personnel selection

Since the early decades of the twentieth century GMA and ability tests have been extensively used for decision making in personnel selection in virtually all countries around the world (Salgado, 2001, Salgado et al., 2010; Vinchur & Koppes-Bryan, 2012). It is well known that ability and aptitude tests have been used systematically for decades in personnel selection and currently many private companies (e.g., IBM, Microsoft), and public organizations (e.g., the U.S. Armed Forces, UK civil service, and so on) have their own GMA tests; there is, additionally, a wide array of tests commercially available for measuring GMA.

In the last 20 years surveys have been carried out to evaluate the extent to which typical instruments for selecting personnel are used. Gowing and Slivinski (1994) reported on a survey carried out in the United States, which found that 16% of companies administered cognitive ability tests and 42% administered specific aptitude tests for selection purposes. They also reported that 43% of companies in Canada used aptitude tests. In another American survey, Marsden (1994) reported that 7.4% of companies used mental ability tests for hiring decisions in non-managerial occupations, and 9.1% in managerial jobs. A survey conducted in 12 EU member states showed that the use of psychometric tests (e.g., GMA tests) by companies ranged from 6% of companies in Germany to 74% of companies in Finland

(Dany & Torchy, 1994). The average for these 12 countries was 34%. In another survey conducted in five European countries, Shackleton and Newell (1994) showed that the use of cognitive tests ranged from 20% of Italian companies to 70% of companies based in the UK. In Australia cognitive tests were used by 56.2% of companies (DiMilia, Smith & Brown, 1994). Similar results were reported for New Zealand (Taylor, Mills & O'Driscoll, 1993) and for 15 countries from all continents (Ryan, McFarland, Baron & Page, 1999). Salgado and Anderson's (2002) compilation of a large number of surveys on the use of cognitive ability tests in 16 European countries found that cognitive tests were more frequently used in Belgium, the UK, The Netherlands, Portugal and Spain, but less so in France, Germany, Greece, Ireland and Italy. They also found that ability tests were used more in graduate- and managerial-level appointments than for general selection processes.

Surveys conducted in the last 12 years show a similar picture. Taylor, Keelty and McDonnell's (2002) survey on the use of personnel selection methods in large organizations and recruitment firms in New Zealand found that cognitive tests were used in 31% of non-management positions, 47% of management positions in organization, and that 64% of recruitment firms used cognitive tests for management positions. These results were more than double the proportion used 10 years earlier (Taylor, Mills & O'Driscoll, 1993). Pereira, Primi and Cobèro (2003) found that cognitive ability tests were used by 44% of organizations in Brazil and that they were the most extensively used personnel selection procedures. In the UK, the Chartered Institute of Personnel and Development (2007) found 72% of responding companies indicated that they used general cognitive tests. In 2015, a study on the use of cognitive tests in small and medium-sized companies in Spain revealed that 28% of companies used cognitive tests for decisions on personnel (Alonso, Moscoso & Cuadrado, 2015). This finding contradicted previous reports (e.g., Salgado & Anderson, 2002) and may suggest two factors are involved. The first is that the use of cognitive tests varies according to the size of the company (i.e., the larger the company the greater the use of cognitive tests). Second, since around 2005 cognitive tests have gradually been replaced by other selection procedures (e.g., emotional intelligence tests). Thus, further research is required to assess both developments in relation to the practice of personnel selection. Finally, a 2014 survey conducted for the British-based multinational company SHL (now part of CEB), with a large sample of international companies ($N = 1,406$ throughout the world), found that 59% of companies used cognitive ability tests, 47% used specific ability tests in pre-hiring evaluations and 24% used cognitive ability tests and 25% of specific ability tests for post-hiring assessment (Kantrowitz, 2014).

In short, cognitive tests have been used extensively for personnel selection purposes, and continue to do so. Excluding interviews, they are one of the most extensively used personnel selection procedures. Nonetheless, their use appears to be determined by the type of profession (e.g., managerial vs. non-managerial occupations), the size of the company (large vs. medium or small companies) and legislation on equal opportunities, which varies widely across countries (see Myors, Livenes, Schollaert et al., 2008; Sackett, Borneman & Connelly, 2008).

The Psychometric Structure of GMA and Specific Cognitive Abilities

In IWO psychology the structure of cognitive abilities has been the focus of research for at least 80 years, following the publication of Spearman's (1904) model. As Schmitt (2014) points out, cognitive abilities are typically hierarchically represented, with a general factor at the top, several broad content abilities on a lower level and the narrowest cognitive

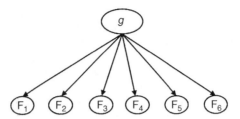

Figure 7.1a   Spearman's model of cognitive abilities.

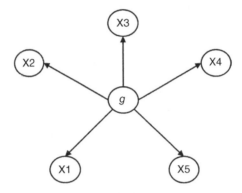

Figure 7.1b   A *g*-centric representation of Spearman's model.

abilities typically represented at the bottom of the hierarchy. Two psychometric models of the structure of cognitive ability have predominated for years: Spearman's one-general cognitive ability factor and its derivatives (e.g., Vernon's model, Carroll's model) and Cattell and Horn's two-general factor model (Cattell, 1963, 1971, 1987; Cattell & Horn, 1978; Horn, 1989). In the last 20 years, the most dominant model has been the three-strata model developed by Carroll (1993) and its derivatives (e.g., Cattell–Horn–Carroll's model). However, several alternatives have been proposed, such as Holzinger's model, Vernon's model, the Berlin model and Johnson and Bouchard's VPS model (2005), among others. In order to provide a general overview, the main models of the structure of cognitive ability will be briefly examined as well as more recent theoretical contributions, such as van der Maas and colleagues' (2006) revitalization of Thomson's model and Bartholomew, Deary and Lawn (2009).

Spearman (1904, 1927) proposed that every test consisted of a general factor (*g*), which was common to all tests, and a specific factor (*s*), which was unique to each test. For this reason, Spearman's model has often been represented as a large, central circle representing *g*, and a number of smaller circles arrayed radially, which represent the specific factors or abilities (e.g., Ree & Carretta, 1998; van der Maas et al., 2006). In this sense, Spearman's model is *g*-centric. Figures 7.1a and 7.1b represent Spearman's model. For many years, Spearman refused to accept that 'group factors' or 'specific abilities' were possible, but eventually admitted they were possible in his key book of 1927.

Spearman's model has been challenged since its inception, and several researchers have suggested that there are additional factors rather than a single general factor. The first challenge to Spearman's model was the claim made by the British psychologist Cyril Burt that not one, but several group factors are involved (Burt, 1909). Moreover, Godfrey

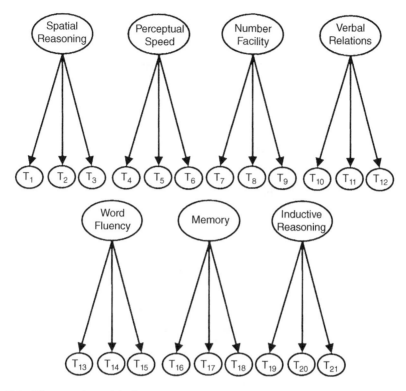

Figure 7.2 Thurstone's model of primary abilities.

Thomson (1916, 1919, 1951) proposed group factors could exist without the need for a general factor to explain the positive manifold by mathematically demonstrating that a general factor could arise randomly.

Some years later, Spearman's model was again challenged by Leon Thurstone (1938), who proposed a primary mental abilities (PMA) model, with seven orthogonal primary factors and no general factor. Figure 7.2 represents the PMA model. Initially, Thurstone refused to accept a second-order general factor, but admitted the existence of a general factor two years later (Thurstone & Thurstone, 1941). Therefore, both Spearman and Thurstone eventually agreed on the structure of cognitive abilities, although insisting on their respective emphasis on the upper or the lower level of the hierarchy.

Spearman's model was also challenged by his disciple Karl Holzinger (Holzinger & Swineford, 1937), who proposed there was both a general factor – called the basic factor by Burt – and group factors, but that there was no hierarchical order. Holzinger's contribution initiated the idea of nested models of cognitive abilities. This proposal was called a bi-factor theory because the group factors are independent of the general factor. In other words, this model assumes that all battery tests measure a common factor (i.e., GMA) but the variance of each test is influenced by an additional and smaller common factor reflected in tests tapping similar aspects of the smaller factor. Therefore, in a bi-factor model tests are free to load on a general factor and a set of group factors. It is important to appreciate that a bi-factor model is not a hierarchical model, as both the general factor and the group factors explain common variance of tests (or items) (Reise, Moore & Haviland, 2010).

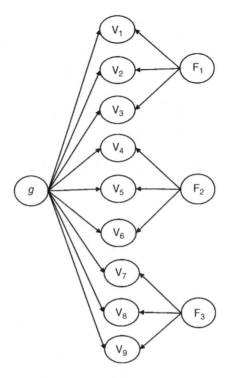

Figure 7.3 Holzinger's bi-factor model.

Research undertaken since the 1940s has lent some support to Holzinger's view (Harman, 1976; Jenrich & Bentler, 2011; Swineford, 1949). Typically, bi-factor models use confirmatory factor analysis (CFA), but Jenrich and Bentler (2011) have proposed a method for conducting exploratory bi-factor analysis. Figure 7.3 represents Holzinger's view.

Cattell (1963, 1971, 1987) hypothesized that there are two general factors of intelligence rather than one: fluid intelligence (*Gf*) and crystallized intelligence (*Gc*). According to Cattell (1971, p. 96), *Gc* arises from educational opportunities and from motivation and persistence in applying fluid intelligence to approved areas of learning. This means that *Gc* reflects scholastic and cultural knowledge acquisition, and therefore would be consolidated knowledge. *Gf* would be most highly loaded in tests like Raven's matrices, D-48 or verbal tests designed to identify the relationship between words with similar meanings. *Gc* is the most highly loaded in tests based on scholastic knowledge and tests with a cultural content. Horn (1965, 1989; Cattell & Horn, 1978; Horn and Cattell, 1966), Cattell's disciple, extended this initial model by including five broad factors (although they are narrower than *Gf* and *Gc*): visual inspection speed (*Gs*), visual–spatial reasoning (*Gv*), auditory thinking (*Ga*), quantitative reasoning (*Gq*) and fluency in recall of learned information (*Gr*). Figure 7.4 represents the Cattell–Horn model of intelligence. Subsequently, the Swedish researcher Jan-Eric Gustafsson (1988, 1992; Kvist & Gustafsson, 2008) found that a hierarchical factor analysis of a large battery of tests measuring *Gf* and *Gc* showed that, when the second-order factor is residualized, *Gf* disappears and is subsumed in GMA, and the residualized *Gc* remains as a verbal–numerical–educational factor. This last factor is very similar to the verbal–educational factor of Vernon's (1957) model of intelligence.

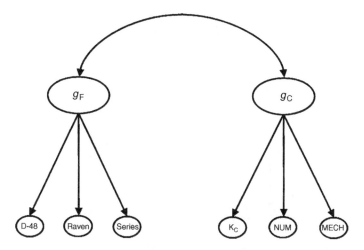

Figure 7.4 Cattell–Horn's two-factor theory of intelligence.

Vernon's (1957, 1971) model consists of three levels, with *g* at the highest level and two broad factors at the lower level. The first broad factor was termed verbal–educational and the second practical–mechanical. At the primary level, Vernon distinguished six primary abilities: verbal, numerical, abstract, mechanical, perceptual and spatial. The first three abilities can be explained by the verbal–educational factor and the other three by the mechanical–practical factor. According to Carroll (1993, p. 60), Vernon's model was the first truly hierarchical model of intelligence. Figure 7.5 represents Vernon's intelligence model.

A further contribution relevant to the structure of intelligence is the Berlin Intelligence Structure (BIS; Jäger, 1967, 1982, 1984; see also Beauducel & Kersting, 2002), which is a hierarchical model with multiple facets. A general factor of intelligence is placed at the top of the hierarchy, and below this level a content facet with three abilities: verbal, numerical and figural, with an operation facet of processing speed, memory, creativity and processing capacity. At the lowest level, there are 12 'structuples' (3 contents × 4 operations). These structuples serve to classify the task in the BIS. Beauducel and Kersting (2002) found that the BIS model included Cattell–Horn's model of *Gf–Gc*. Figure 7.6 represents the BIS model, including *Gf/Gc* distinction.

Carroll's (1993) three-strata model of cognitive abilities is worth a special mention as it is based on an impressive analysis of more than 400 datasets. Carroll (1993) found that cognitive ability can be hierarchically described using three levels or strata. At the highest level there is a general cognitive ability (also referred to as general mental ability, general intelligence, or factor *g*). At the second level, there are several specific broad cognitive abilities. According to Carroll, specific broad cognitive abilities are: 1) fluid intelligence; 2) crystallized intelligence; 3) general memory ability; 4) visual perception; 5) auditory perception; 6) retrieval ability; and 7) cognitive speed. The first stratum includes a large number of more specific and narrow cognitive abilities, which are more homogeneous than those of the second stratum. Figure 7.7 represents Carroll's model.

Over the last 15 years several researchers have suggested that Cattell–Horn's model and Carroll's model can be combined into a single model, usually denominated the Cattell–Horn–Carroll's (CHC) model (Alfonso, Flanagan & Radwan, 2005; Flanagan, McGrew & Ortiz, 2000; McGrew, 1997). The CHC model consists of 10 broad cognitive abilities

Selection

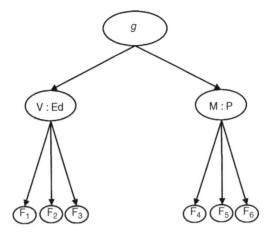

Figure 7.5   Vernon's hierarchical model of cognitive abilities.

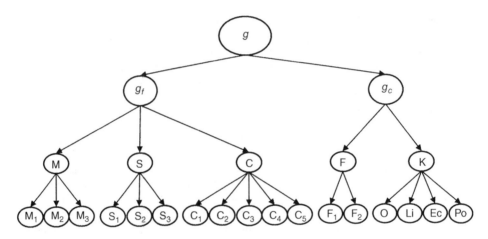

Figure 7.6   Berlin's model of intelligence structure.

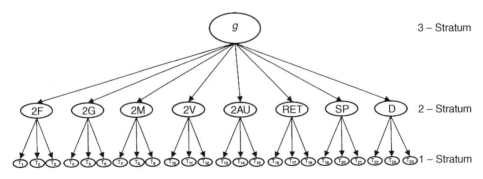

Figure 7.7   Carroll's three-strata model.

and more than 70 narrow abilities (see Alfonso, Flanagan & Radwan, 2007, for a complete list of the narrow abilities and their dependence on the broad cognitive abilities). The findings of the Berlin model (Beauducel & Kersting, 2003) and of Kvist and Gustafsson (2008) converge somewhat with the perspective of the CHC model.

Johnson and Bouchard have offered an innovative hierarchical model (Johnson & Bouchard, 2005a, 2005b, 2007, 2011; Johnson et al., 2004), which is an alternative to Carroll's (1993) three-strata model. Inspired by Vernon's (1957) model, Johnson and Bouchard's model proposes a four-strata model. The lowest level consists of primary abilities assessed by tests, such as solving anagrams or simple arithmetical calculations. The second stratum consists of broader but still narrow abilities. The third stratum consists of three factors: a verbal (V) factor, a perceptual (P) factor and an image rotation (R) factor. The factors in the third level are highly correlated, indicating the need for a fourth stratum in which Johnson and Bouchard found a general cognitive factor, which explains why Johnson and Bouchard labelled the model VPR. Figure 7.8 represents the VPR model.

van der Maas and colleagues (2006) and Bartholomew, Deary and Lawn (2009) have proposed models for explaining intelligence structure, which were inspired by Thomson's sampling theory of intelligence. van der Maas and colleagues (2006) proposed two possible structures of intelligence called the 'mutualism model' and the 'extended

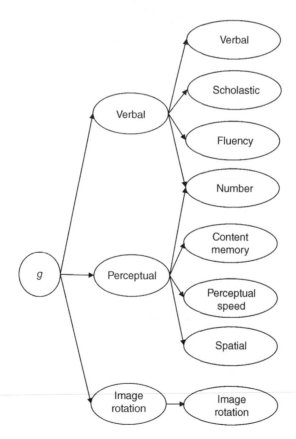

Figure 7.8 Johnson–Bouchard's VPR model of intelligence.

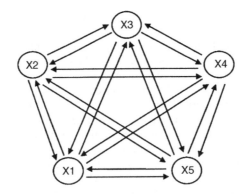

Figure 7.9 The mutualism model.

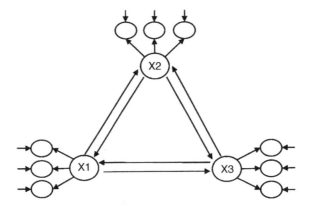

Figure 7.10 The extended mutualism model.

mutualism model', which explain the positive manifold without the need for a general factor. Figures 7.9 and 7.10 represent these two structures of intelligence.

Bartholomew and colleagues (2009), after pointing out certain limitations of van der Mass and colleagues' models, proposed a revised version of Thomson's model. This revised model supposes that the brain has N 'bonds', which can be called on when a person tries to respond to an item. If the bond i is active, then it contributes an amount e_i to the total score. This quantity e_i is a characteristic of each individual, and if the bond is selected it will contribute that quantity whatever the test items on all occasions. Because the essence of Thomson's model is to assume that a fixed proportion of bonds, p_i, are selected when the test item I is selected, then the resulting score is the sum of the es resulting from the sampled bonds. The model also assumes that each bond is selected independently with probability p_i, $I=1...$, N, where N is the number of items. Finally, the model supposes that the final score is arrived at by repeating the sampling process independently, several times.

Together the earlier models converge to the extent that they accept the existence of a general factor. Notwithstanding, whether the general factor is exactly the same or substantially the same when it is extracted from the different test batteries conceptualized and developed for specific cognitive models remains to be ascertained.

Johnson and colleagues (2009) addressed this issue by examining whether the *g* factor extracted from three test batteries is substantially the same or not. This point is important because, if GMA is not consistently found across batteries, then its theoretical and practical importance will be small (Jensen, 1998) due to its dependence on the specific battery. Johnson and Bouchard (2005a, 2005b, 2007) conducted several comparative studies using three datasets in which they compared the Cattell–Horn model, the *g*–VPR model and Vernon's model. In these three datasets, the *g*–VPR model was a better fit than the others. Another important finding was that the general factor of each battery correlated largely with the others (0.99, 0.99 and 1.00). In other words, the individual differences in GMA were identical for the three different batteries (Deary, 2012).

Woolley and colleagues (2010) have made another contribution to the cognitive ability domain, in this case from the group perspective rather than from the individual one. They claim they have found a collective intelligence factor, which explains how well a group performed tasks, and which is not the mean of the GMA of the group members. Earlier, Heylighen (1999) defined collective intelligence (CI) as the ability of a group to produce better solutions to a problem than group members can work individually. Woolley and colleagues (2010) found that CI was higher in groups where turn-taking in speaking was relatively evenly distributed among members and in groups whose members had higher mean social sensitivity. A practical suggestion from this study is that it can be useful to include CI for selecting team workers.

In short, despite the multiple sub-factors and abilities measured in the various tests and batteries, most of the variance of these measures is due to a general factor, sometimes referred to as *g*, and sometimes as general mental ability (GMA) or general cognitive ability (GCA). Although computerized and video-based versions of cognitive tests have been developed, there are no relevant differences in their predictive capacity. Thus, there is a general consensus that a general cognitive factor, or GMA, appears to be present in most ability tests and test batteries (Carroll, 1993; Deary, 2012; Hunt, 2011; Schmitt, 2014). There is less consensus regarding the number and type of the narrower abilities, although verbal, numerical, spatial, perceptual and memory abilities are typically found in factor analytic studies.

Criterion Validity and Validity Generalization

Criterion validity is defined in the *Principles for the Validation and Use of Personnel Selection Procedures* (Society for Industrial and Organizational Psychology, SIOP, 2003) as the demonstration of a useful relationship between the test (predictor) and one or more measures of job-relevant behaviour (criteria). Currently, the most useful and robust method for assessing the evidence of criterion validity of personnel selection procedures (e.g., GMA tests) is a meta-analysis (Hunter & Schmidt, 2000). In personnel selection, a meta-analysis is also used to examine whether there is evidence of validity generalization across studies (Schmidt & Hunter, 1977). In this section, the main findings on the validity of GMA for predicting different organizational criteria across the world are reviewed, as well as some relevant issues regarding differential validity and differential prediction. The section is divided into four subsections: (a) validity of GMA for predicting overall and task performance and training; (b) primary validity studies in Africa, Latin America and the Indian-Pacific Ocean countries; (c) validity of GMA for predicting non-task performance and other organizational criteria; and (d) validity and incremental validity of specific cognitive abilities.

Validity of GMA for predicting overall and task performance and training

To date, numerous meta-analyses on the validity of GMA and cognitive abilities for predicting job performance and training proficiency have been undertaken. Meta-analyses have been performed in many countries and regions, including the United States, European Union (EU), Japan and South Korea. This chapter includes a summary of the major meta-analytic findings in different countries and for various organizational criteria. These data are from major sources, including Ghiselli (1966, 1973), Hunter (1983, 1986; Hunter & Hunter, 1984), Hartigan and Wigdor (1989), Schmitt and colleagues (1984), Levine and colleagues (1996), Salgado and colleagues (2003a, 2003b), Hülsheger and colleagues (2007) and Lang and colleagues (2010), among others. Additional meta-analyses were reviewed in Ones, Diclhert and Viswesvaran (2012).

The seminal quantitative syntheses of the criterion-related validity of cognitive ability tests must be attributed to Ghiselli (1966, 1973), although they were not a proper meta-analysis. Ghiselli (1966, 1973) grouped validity coefficients from thousands of studies and found an average observed validity of 0.25 for predicting job performance ratings. Ghiselli's data were subsequently re-analyzed by Hunter and Hunter (1984).

Probably the most comprehensive meta-analyses were conducted by Hunter (1983, 1986; Hunter & Hunter, 1984), with a database consisting of 515 studies ($N = 38,620$), carried out using the GATB database of the US Employment Service (USES). Hunter presented the results for two criteria: job performance ratings and training success. He corrected the observed mean validity for criterion unreliability and range restriction. Hunter used 0.60 as an estimate of criterion reliability for a single rater, 0.80 as training reliability and 0.67 as the ratio between the standard deviation of the selected group and the standard deviation of the large group. Hunter found an average operational validity of 0.45 for job performance ratings and 0.54 for training success (see Table 7.1). Hunter and Hunter's (1984) work was subsequently replicated by the US National Research Council (Hartigan & Wigdor, 1989), but with three main differences with respect to Hunter and Hunter's meta-analysis: the number of studies was enlarged by 264 ($N = 38,521$), the estimate of job performance ratings reliability was 0.80 and they did not correct for range restriction. Under these conditions, the panel found an estimated average operational validity of 0.22 ($K = 755$; $N = 77,141$) for predicting job performance ratings. Interestingly, the analysis of the 264 additional studies showed an average observed validity of 0.20. Several studies have shown that Hunter and Hunter's estimate of job performance ratings reliability was very accurate with interrater reliability for a single rater of 0.52 (Rothstein, 1990; Salgado et al., 2003a; Salgado & Moscoso, 1996; Salgado & Tauriz, 2014; Viswesvaran, Ones & Schmidt, 1996). If Hunter and Hunter's figures are applied to the mean validity found by the panel, average operational validity are 0.38, a figure closer to Hunter and Hunter's result for job performance ratings.

Another meta-analysis was carried out by Schmitt, Gooding, Noe and Kirsch (1984), using the studies published between 1964 and 1982 in the *Journal of Applied Psychology and Personnel Psychology*. They found an average validity of 0.22 (uncorrected) for predicting job performance ratings. Correcting this last value using Hunter and Hunter's figures for criterion unreliability and the ratio of range restriction, the average operational validity was essentially the same in both studies (see Hunter & Hirsh, 1987).

Meta-analyses of the criterion-related validity of cognitive ability have also been performed for specific jobs. Pearlman, Schmidt and Hunter (1980) found that GMA was a valid predictor of job performance for clerical occupations, and its validity generalized across job families and organizations. Schmidt, Hunter and Caplan (1981) meta-analysed

Table 7.1 Average validity of general cognitive ability for predicting job performance and training in different countries.

Country	K	N	ρ	90CV
	Job Performance			
USA[a]	425	32,124	0.45	0.29
European Union[b]	93	9,554	0.62	0.37
France	26	1,445	0.64	0.48
Germany	8	701	0.68	0.35
Belgium & The Netherlands	15	1,075	0.63	0.20
Spain	11	1,182	0.64	0.45
United Kingdom	68	7,725	0.56	0.46
South Korea[c]	8	1,098	0.57	0.57
Japan[c]	126	26,095	0.20	0.04
	Training			
USA[a]	90	6,496	0.54	0.32
European Union[b]	97	16,065	0.54	0.29
France	22	5,796	0.38	0.26
Germany	26	4,645	0.63	0.42
Belgium & The Netherlands	8	706	0.65	0.48
Spain	7	712	0.61	0.41
United Kingdom	59	11,218	0.50	0.29

Source: [a] = Hunter (1986, p. 344) and Hunter & Hunter (1984, p. 81); [b] = Salgado et al. (2003); [c] = Oh, Schmidt, Shaffer & Le (2008; average of two meta-analyses); Oh, Schmidt, Shaffer & Le (2008; average of three meta-analyses).

the validities for craft jobs in the petroleum industry, and Hirsh, Northrop and Schmidt (1986) summarized the validity findings for police officers. Hunter (1986), in his review of studies conducted in the US military, estimated GMA validity was 0.63. Another relevant meta-analysis for craft jobs in the utility industry (e.g., electrical assembly, telephone technicians and mechanical jobs) was carried out by Levine, Spector, Menon, Narayanon and Canon-Bowers (1996), who found an average observed validity of 0.25 and an average operational validity of 0.43 for job performance ratings. For training success, the average observed validity was 0.38 and the average operational validity was 0.67. Applying Hunter and Hunter's estimates for criteria reliability and range restriction, the results show an operational validity of 0.47 for job performance ratings and 0.62 for training success. Both results agree with Hunter and Hunter's findings.

Two single studies conducted in the US using large samples deserve a mention. In 1990 the results of Project A, a research project carried out in the US Army, were published. McHenry, Hough, Toquam, Hanson and Ashworth (1990) reported validities of 0.63 and 0.65 for predicting ratings of core technical proficiency and general soldering proficiency. The second large-sample study was carried out by Ree and Earles (1991), who showed that a composite of GMA predicted training performance, with a corrected validity of 0.76.

In the EU, Salgado, Anderson and colleagues conducted a series of meta-analyses using primary validity studies carried out in several European countries, including Belgium, France, Germany, Spain, The Netherlands, and the UK (Bertua, Anderson & Salgado, 2005; Salgado & Anderson, 2002, 2003a, 2003b; Salgado et al., 2003a, 2003b). They found that GMA predicted both job performance and training proficiency, and generalized validity across studies and countries. Globally, they found an operational validity of 0.62 for predicting job performance and 0.54 for predicting training success.

They also found that GMA predicted both criteria in 10 occupational families: engineering, chemistry, managerial, typing and filing, information, sales, police, mechanics, electrical and driving occupations. Hülsheger and colleagues (2007) conducted another meta-analysis with German validity studies and found essentially the same results.

Japanese validity studies have been collected and analysed in three meta-analyses over the last 20 years. In 1994, Takahasi and Nishida (cited by Oh, 2010, p. 14) conducted an initial meta-analysis with 15 studies ($N=5898$) and found a corrected validity of 0.28. Nimura, Imashiro and Naito (2000) conducted a second meta-analysis of 24 validity studies of the new managerial aptitude test and found an observed validity of 0.18 and a corrected validity of 0.26 ($N=4420$). In 2010, Oh (2010) published the third meta-analysis with 65 studies ($N=14{,}777$), and found a corrected validity of 0.15. The aggregation of these three validity studies resulted in an average corrected validity of 0.20, which is remarkably lower than the validity size found in US and European validity studies. Nimura and colleagues (2000) speculated that, in Japan, organizational citizenship behaviours (OCB) are more explicitly expected and appraised, and that GMA is a better predictor of task performance than OCB. An alternative explanation is that the values of range restriction and criterion reliability were remarkably larger than those found in American and European validity studies, and that training proficiency and job performance ratings were collapsed as a single criterion in the initial meta-analyses.

Two independent meta-analyses were conducted with Korean validity studies of GMA. Lee (2005) found a corrected validity of 0.59 ($N=665$), and Oh (2010) found a corrected validity of 0.53 ($N=443$). The weighted-sample average validity of these meta-analyses was 0.56 ($N=1098$), which was a value similar to that found in the American and European meta-analyses.

An important finding in both American and European meta-analyses was that job complexity was a very significant moderator of GMA criterion validity. In the US Hunter and Hunter (1984) found that GMA validity dropped from 0.56 to 0.40 as job complexity decreased. The same pattern was found in the European studies, as GMA validity dropped from 0.64 for high complexity to 0.51 for low complexity. Tables 7.1 and 7.2 summarize the meta-analytic findings for the different countries and the moderator effects of job complexity.

Primary validity studies in Africa, Latin America and the Indian-Pacific Ocean countries

A number of primary validity studies are worth mentioning as they have been carried out in less known countries, such as South Africa, Abu Dhabi, New Zealand, Australia, Singapore, Brazil, Chile, Mexico, Peru and Argentina.

With regard to African countries, an increasing number of studies have been undertaken in South Africa in the last 15 years. Muller and Schepers (2003) carried out a study on the validity of GMA for predicting success in a training course for the South African National Defence Force. They found that a cognitive composite of four tests (Raven's matrices, conceptualization, reading comprehension and listening comprehension) predicted training proficiency ($r=0.584$, $N=96$). Kriek and Dowdeswell (2009) reported two concurrent validity studies, with validity coefficients separated for Black and White participants. In the first study, they found an average coefficient of 0.39 ($N=66$) for Black participants and 0.27 ($N=34$) for White participants. In the second study, Kriek and Dowdeswell found a validity coefficient of 0.48 ($N=47$) for Black participants and 0.36 ($N=57$) for White participants. In another South African study, Strachan (2008) examined the predicted validity of the APIL-SV (a cognitive battery assessing fluid intelligence for predicting training success) in a sample of auditing employees. Strechan found an average uncorrected validity of

Table 7.2 Moderator effects of job complexity on validity size.

Ability	K	N	ρ	90CV
Training				
USA studies[a]				
Low complexity	8	575	0.54	0.49
Medium complexity	54	3,823	0.57	0.36
High complexity	4	235	0.65	0.65
EU studies[b]				
Low complexity	29	8,152	0.73	0.60
Medium complexity	66	22,100	0.74	0.60
High complexity	4	596	0.75	0.67
Job Performance				
USA studies[a]				
Low complexity	201	14,403	0.40	0.36
Medium complexity	151	12,933	0.51	0.31
High complexity	17	1,114	0.56	0.52
EU studies[b]				
Low complexity	12	864	0.51	0.38
Medium complexity	43	4,744	0.53	0.21
High complexity	14	1,604	0.64	0.33

K = number of studies; N = sample size; ρ = operational validity; 90CV = 90% credibility value.
Source: [a] = Hunter (1986, p. 344) and Hunter and Hunter (1984, p. 81); [b] = Salgado et al. (2003); [c] = Oh, Schmidt, Shaffer & Le (2008; average of two meta-analyses); Oh, Schmidt, Shaffer & Le (2008; average of three meta-analyses).

0.38 (N=69). Fertig (2009) found that cognitive ability predicted managerial performance in a multi-ethnic sample of brand managers (average r=0.16, N=124). De Kock and Schlechter (2009) found that a battery of fluid and spatial ability tests predicted flight training (r=0.35; N=108). Nicholls, Viviers and Visser (2009) found that cognitive ability predicted supervisory performance ratings, call handling time and call quality in a sample of call centre operators (0.24, 0.28 and 0.33, respectively; N=140). In another study, Pelser, Berg and Visser (2005) found that GMA predicted supervisor job performance ratings in a sample of truck operators (r=0.24; N=104). Dale (2010) found that a test of mental alertness predicted work performance among leaners in the clothing industry (r=0.33, N=200). The correlations were meta-analysed for this chapter and the results show that, on average, cognitive abilities have an observed validity of 0.30 (K=9, N=841), and 0.44 (K=3, N=273) for predicting job performance and training, respectively. These validities corrected for indirect range restriction (using the u values found by Salgado & Anderson, 2003a), and criterion unreliability (using 0.52 for job performance and 0.56 for training) resulted in operational validities of 0.66 (90CV=0.66) and 0.81(90CV=0.76) for job performance and training, respectively.

In the Indian subcontinent and the South Pacific islands (i.e., Australia, Singapore and New Zealand) a few small-sample studies have been undertaken in the last 15 years. In New Zealand, Mann's (2011) small-sample study found that a battery of three cognitive tests predicted overall job performance (average r=0.20, N=43). Mann (2011) also found that general cognitive ability predicted task performance efficiently (r=0.30), but predicted neither contextual performance (r=0.03) nor team performance (r=−0.12). Black (2000) found that GMA predicted training performance in a sample of New Zealand police recruits (r=0.33, N=284). In Australia, Green and Macqueen (2008) reported a small-sample study (N=37) in which they found that cognitive ability predicted job performance in managers and supervisors (r=0.37). In Singapore, Chan and Schmitt (2002) found that cognitive ability predicted task performance (r=0.25), but not OCB (r=0.03) or overall job performance (r=–0.02) in a sample of civil servants (N=160), and Roberts, Harms, Caspi and Moffit (2005) found that IQ predicted occupational level (r=0.44, N=838) and showed a very small correlation with counterproductive work behaviour (r=0.08, N=838). In Abu Dhabi, Al-Ali, Gamer and Magadley (2009) found that GMA predicted both objective CWB (r=–0.14) and self-rated CWB (r=–0.20) in a sample of police officers (N=310). These studies were also meta-analysed for this chapter and the results showed that cognitive abilities had an average validity of 0.11 (K=3, N=240) for predicting job performance. This validity corrected for indirect range restriction (using the u values found by Salgado and Anderson, 2003a), and criterion unreliability (using 0.52 for job performance) resulted in an operational validity of 0.27 (90CV=0.07).

A few studies have been carried out in the last 20 years in Latin American countries. In Brazil, Baumgartl and Primi (2006) found that a cognitive ability test was a predictor of job accidents in an electrical power company (r=–0.39), Thadeu and Ferreira (2013) found that cognitive ability predicted training in a large sample of police officers (r=0.14, N=1,177), and Cobêro, Primi and Muniz (2006) found that GMA predicted supervisory job performance in a sample of heterogeneous workers (r=0.39, N=119). In Argentina, Castro-Solano and Casullo (2005) found that Raven's test predicted training in an Army sample (r=0.23, N=137). In Peru, Rosales-Lopez (2012) found that a mechanical aptitude test predicted performance in skilled workers (r=0.78; N=88). In Mexico, Moreno-Garcia (2011) found that GMA predicted job performance ratings in managers of a financial company (r=0.22, N=87). In Chile, Cuadra-Peralta (1990) found that cognitive ability, as measured by the GATB, predicted performance in a sample of 80 workers of a copper mining company (r=0.33), and Barros, Kausel, Cuadra and Diaz (2014) found observed validities of 0.16 (N=253), –0.04 (N=156) and 0.35 (N=103) in three independent studies. I carried out a small-scale meta-analysis with these studies. The present meta-analysis shows that, on average, cognitive ability predicted job performance with an observed validity of 0.26 (K=7, N=886) and training with a validity of 0.15 (K=2, N=1,314). These validities, corrected for indirect range restriction using the u values found by Salgado and colleagues (2003a) and criterion unreliability using 0.52 for job performance and 0.56 for training, resulted in operational validities of 0.53 (90CV=0.09), and 0.36 (90CV=0.36) for job performance and training, respectively.

In summary, primary validity studies in countries of Africa, the Asia-Pacific region and Latin America in the last 12 years show that GMA predicted both job performance and training criteria. Small-scale meta-analyses carried out for this chapter with these validity studies show operational validities similar to those found in the US and Europe, confirming that GMA consistently predicts performance across cultures. The results of these small-scale meta-analyses are shown in Table 7.3.

Validity of GMA for Predicting Non-Task Performance and Other Organizational Criteria

A number of recent studies, both primary and meta-analytic, consider the criterion domain to be more than overall and task performance. There is broad consensus that, in addition to task performance, job performance encompasses two additional dimensions: organizational citizenship behaviour (OCB) and counterproductive work behaviour (CWB).

Table 7.3 Average validity of general cognitive ability for predicting job performance and training in Latin America, South Africa and South Pacific countries.

Country	K	N	ρ	90CV
	Job Performance			
Latin America	7	886	0.53	0.09
South Pacific countries	3	240	0.27	0.07
South Africa	9	841	0.66	0.66
	Training			
Latin America	2	1,314	0.36	0.36
South Africa	3	273	0.81	0.76

K = number of studies; N = sample size; ρ = operational validity; 90CV = 90% credibility.

These two broad dimensions can be clearly distinguished from task performance, and are increasingly exerting an important influence on the outcomes of the organizations. For this last reason, meta-analytic studies have recently turned to obtaining estimates of the relationship of GMA with OCB and CWB.

Gonzalez-Mulé, Mount and Oh (2014) examined the validity of GMA for predicting CWB and OCB. They found that the validity of GMA for predicting overall counterproductive behaviours at work was essentially 0 ($K=35$, $\underline{N}=12,074$). However, GMA showed a small, though not generalizable, validity size ($\rho=-0.20$, $K=7$, $N=1,854$) for predicting organizational CWB, one of the sub-dimensions of CBW.

Postlethwaite (2011) examined the validity of general cognitive ability (GCA), as measured by a compound of *Gf* and *Gc* for predicting OCB, and found an operational validity of 0.18 ($K=7$, $N=871$). For their part, Gonzalez-Mulé Mount and Oh (2014) examined the validity of GMA for predicting supervisory ratings of OCB and found an operational validity of 0.24 ($K=36$, $N=10,404$). Consequently, the two estimates of GMA were predictors of OCB, though the validity size was remarkably smaller than the validity for predicting overall job performance and task performance.

An important conclusion in Gonzalez-Mulé Mount and Oh's (2014) and Postlethwaite's (2011) meta-analyses is that GMA seems to be only moderately useful for predicting OCB and CWB-O, it has very small practical utility for predicting CWB-I and it has practically 0 validity for predicting overall CWB. Nevertheless, further research is required given that the predictive validity for these criteria has been shown to be culturally determined (Nimura, Ishashiro & Naito, 2000; Al-Ali, Gamer & Magadley, 2009). A summary of these meta-analytic results is given in Tables 7.4 and 7.5.

Earlier meta-analytic efforts examined the validity of cognitive ability for predicting other non-performance criteria, such as turnover, achievement/grades, status change and work sample. Schmitt, Gooding, Noe and Kirsch (1984) performed the first meta-analysis of the relationship between cognitive ability and these criteria and found that GMA predicted turnover ($r=0.14$; $N=12,449$), achievement/grades ($r=0.44$, $N=888$), status change ($r=0.28$, $N=21,190$) and work samples ($r=0.43$, $N=1,793$). It should borne in mind that these validity estimates were not corrected for criterion unreliability and range restriction. When these corrections are done the figures are much higher. Table 7.6 reports a summary of these findings.

In brief, meta-analyses have shown that GMA predicted one of the dimensions of job performance, OCB, but not the other, CWB. Moreover, GMA appears to be a predictor of objective organizational criteria such as turnover, achievement, status change and work samples.

Table 7.4 Validity of GMA for predicting counterproductive work behaviour.

Ability	K	N	ρ	90CV
Overall CWB	35	12,074	−0.02	0.04
CWB – Organizational	7	1,854	−0.20	0.01
CWB – Interpersonal	4	1,462	−0.09	0.10

CWB = counterproductive work behaviour; K = number of studies; N = sample size;
ρ = operational validity; 90CV = 90% credibility.
Source: Gonzalez-Mulé et al. (2014, Table 1, p. 1228).

Table 7.5 Validity of GMA and GCA for predicting supervisor ratings of organizational citizenship behaviours.

Relation	K	N	ρ	90CV
GMA-overall OCB[a]	36	10,404	0.24	0.03
GCA-overall OCB[b]	7	871	0.18	0.03

OCB = organizational citizenship behaviours; K = number of studies; N = sample size;
ρ = operational validity; 90CV = 90% credibility
Source: [a] = Adapted from Gonzalez-Mulé et al. (2014, Table 2, p.1229); [b] = Adapted from Postlethwaite (2011).

Table 7.6 Validity of GMA for predicting less common organizational criteria.

Criteria	K	N	ρ
Turnover	8	12,449	0.14
Achievement/grades	5	888	0.44
Status change	9	21,190	0.28
Work sample	4	1,793	0.43

K = number of studies; N = sample size; ρ = operational validity; 90CV = 90% credibility.
Source: Schmitt et al. (1984).

Validity and Incremental Validity of Specific Cognitive Abilities

Several meta-analyses have examined the validity of specific abilities. Hunter and Hunter (1984) examined the validity of perceptual ability, as measured by the GATB, and found validity was 0.35, 0.40 and 0.35 for predicting job performance and 0.53, 0.44 and 0.26 for predicting training for the low, medium and high levels of job complexity. Salgado and colleagues (2003a) examined the validity of verbal, numerical, spatial-mechanical abilities and memory for predicting training and job performance in the EU. They found that all the specific cognitive abilities were predictors of both criteria, with a moderately large validity size, but smaller than for GMA validity. The findings of this meta-analysis can be seen in Table 7.7.

Postlethwaite (2011) meta-analysed the validity of fluid ability (*Gf*), crystallized ability (*Gc*) and general cognitive ability (CGA) as compounds of *Gf* plus *Gc*. Postlethwaite found that these three measures of cognitive ability showed large validity sizes for predicting training and job performance. In addition, Postlethwaite (2011) found that crystallized ability was a more valid predictor of the two criteria than fluid ability or the *Gf* or *Gc* compounds.

Table 7.7 Average validity of specific cognitive abilities for predicting job performance and training in different countries.

Country	K	N	ρ	90CV
	Job Performance			
EU studies				
Verbal	44	4,781	0.35	0.04
Numerical	48	5,241	0.52	0.52
Spatial-mechanical	40	3,750	0.51	0.13
Perceptual	38	3,798	0.52	0.28
Memory	14	946	0.56	0.56
	Training			
EU studies				
Verbal	58	11,123	0.44	0.20
Numerical	58	10,860	0.48	0.24
Spatial-mechanical	84	15,834	0.40	0.16
Perceptual	17	3,935	0.25	0.00
Memory	15	3,323	0.34	0.08

K = number of studies; N = sample size; ρ = operational validity; 90CV = 90% credibility.
Source: Salgado et al. (2003).

This author also found that job complexity moderated the validity of *Gf*, *Gc* and GCA for predicting job performance, but the moderator effects were very small for predicting training proficiency. Table 7.8 reports these findings.

With regard to the incremental validity of specific ability tests, Hunter and Hunter's (1984) meta-analysis found that perceptual ability did not show incremental validity beyond GMA and psychomotor ability for predicting performance. Also, several large-sample primary studies investigated whether specific cognitive abilities showed incremental validity over GMA. Ree and Earles (1991) and Ree, Earles and Teachout (1994) have shown that specific abilities did not account for any additional variance beyond GMA for job performance ratings and training success. In fact, the average increase by adding specific abilities to GMA was 0.02 across 89 training studies, and 0.02 across 7 job performance studies. A study of specific abilities showed an incremental validity over GMA of 0.08 for pilots and 0.02 for navigators (Olea & Ree, 1994). Thus, the empirical data appear to indicate that specific abilities do not predict job performance ratings and training success much more than GMA.

Nevertheless, this conclusion has been challenged by several studies. Campbell and Cat-ano (2004) found that auditory attention showed incremental validity for predicting training proficiency in Canadian military personnel. Mount, Oh and Burns (2008) found that a test of perceptual speed showed incremental validity over GMA for predicting task performance. Lang, Kersting, Hülsheger and Lang (2010) found that the incremental validity of specific abilities for predicting performance beyond GMA can be related in part to the method used to examine the contribution of the specific abilities. They found that when they conducted multiple regression analyses, the validity of specific abilities explained 20% of criterion variance, but when they used relative importance analyses (Johnson & LeBreton, 2004) the contribution of verbal ability was larger than that of GMA. However, in interpreting these last findings, it should be taken into account that there was construct redundancy as verbal ability contained GMA variance. As Tonidandel and LeBreton (2011, p. 5) point out: 'construct redundancy will have the apparent effect of reducing the overall importance of a particular variable because the overall importance of that variable will be

Table 7.8 Validity of fluid ability, crystallized ability and general cognitive ability for predicting training and job performance.

Ability	K	N	ρ	90CV
	Training			
Fluid (*Gf*)	20	3,724	0.54	0.32
Medium complexity	11	2,658	0.44	0.25
High complexity	5	569	0.67	0.42
Crystallized (*Gc*)	114	38,793	0.70	0.53
Low complexity	29	8,152	0.73	0.60
Medium complexity	66	22,100	0.74	0.60
High complexity	4	596	0.75	0.67
GCA	24	7,563	0.59	0.39
Low complexity	2	156	0.53	0.53
Medium complexity	14	2,581	0.56	0.31
High complexity	2	2,824	0.57	0.44
	Job Performance			
Fluid (*Gf*)	23	3,273	0.27	−0.07
Low complexity	2	251	−0.01	0.46
Medium complexity	10	1,677	0.26	0.02
High complexity	2	132	0.64	0.52
Crystallized (*Gc*)	199	18,619	0.49	0.31
Low complexity	108	9,307	0.45	0.30
Medium complexity	58	6,603	0.54	0.38
High complexity	27	2,214	0.59	0.38
GCA	86	8,070	0.43	0.23
Low complexity	37	3,420	0.37	0.20
Medium complexity	31	2,456	0.48	0.25
High complexity	11	861	0.60	0.38

K = number of studies; N = sample size; ρ = operational validity; 90CV = 90% credibility.
Source: Adapted from Postlethwaite (2011).

divided up among the redundant predictors thereby possibly producing a misleading result'. Salgado and colleagues (2015; see also Salgado, Moscoso & Berges, 2013) illustrated a way for residualizing variance and examining the relative contributions of primary and second-order factors.

Briefly, the empirical data indicate that specific cognitive ability are good predictors of job performance and training proficiency, but their validities are smaller than GMA validity. With regard to the incremental validity of specific abilities, there is no overall consensus on the potential value over GMA, but the findings suggest that the incremental validity is small.

Ethnic Group Differences and Biased Prediction

An important issue regarding the use of cognitive tests in personnel selection is whether they produce ethnic group differences and biased predictions. In the US it has been well documented that cognitive tests show subgroup differences, for example when African-Americans and White groups were compared. It has typically been presumed that there is

1 SD difference between African-Americans and Whites, with African-Americans scoring lower (Hough, Oswald & Ployhart, 2001; Hunter & Hunter, 1984; Sackett, Bornerman & Connelly, 2008). However, the relevant estimates should be based on applicant samples rather than on incumbent samples and take into account the complexity of the job (Bobko & Roth, 2013). These issues are described below.

Schmitt, Clause and Pulakos (1996) reviewed the subgroup differences in the more widely used personnel selection procedures, including GMA and cognitive ability tests. When African-Americans and Whites are compared on these tests, they found a d value of –0.83, indicating that the performance of African-Americans on these tests was lower. They also found d values of –0.55 and –0.64 for verbal ability and mathematical ability, respectively. The subgroup effect sizes were smaller for the comparison of Hispanic and White groups, as well as between male and female groups. For Hispanic-Americans, Schmitt, Clause and Pulakos found d values ranging from –0.45 to –0.58. For the male–female comparison they found a d value of –0.09 for GMA and cognitive ability tests, with females showing lower performance. However, in the case of mathematical ability females showed a higher performance than males ($d \approx 0.27$).

Roth, Bevier, Bobko, Witzer and Tyler's (2001) meta-analysis found that overall the standardized difference (d) in GMA between Whites and African-Americans was 1.10 and 0.72 for the comparison between Whites and Hispanics. However, they found that job complexity was an important moderator of group differences. The comparison of Whites and African-Americans in GMA showed d values of 0.86, 0.72 and 0.63 for jobs of low, medium and high complexity, respectively. They also found larger differences for GMA than for verbal and numerical abilities. Overall, d values of 0.83 and 0.74 were found for verbal and numerical abilities in the comparison between Whites and African-Americans, and 0.40 and 0.28 in the comparison between Whites and Hispanics. Unfortunately, it is not possible to calculate the differences in these abilities across the job complexity level due to the scarcity in the literature (Roth et al., 2001).

Hough, Oswald and Ployhart (2001) reviewed the evidence on subgroup (ethnic, age and gender) differences for GMA and specific abilities. Comparing Whites with African-Americans, Hispanics and East Asians, they found d values of 1.0, 0 .5 and –0.2 in GMA, respectively. The magnitude of the differences was smaller for verbal and quantitative abilities. An important conclusion found in Hough, Oswald and Ployhart (2001), Roth and colleagues (2001) and Bobko and Roth (2013) was that the construct level (GMA vs. specific abilities), the design (within job vs. between jobs), the sample (applicant vs. incumbents) and job complexity were significant moderators of the size of the differences between groups.

Studies on ethnic group differences were also carried out in European countries. In The Netherlands, te Nijenhuis and van der Flier (1997) compared a large group of immigrant applicants with a majority group on the GATB. The immigrant group included four sub-groups from Surinam, the Dutch Antilles, North Africa and Turkey. te Nijenhuis and van der Flier (1997) found large d values in verbal, numerical and spatial abilities, but no differences in attention. The d values in cognitive abilities ranged from 0.4 to 1.06 for the Surinamese group, 0.52 to 1.32 for the Antilleans, 0.87 to 2.87 for the heterogeneous North African group and from 0.53 to 1.96 for the Turkish group. Unfortunately, this study did not distinguish between first-generation and second-generation immigrants. This limitation was overcome in a study comparing both first- and second-generation immigrants from the same four ethnic groups with a majority group of a sample of police applicants (De Meijer, Born, Terlouw & van der Molen, 2006). Globally, the results show there were large differences between first-generation immigrants and the majority group of applicants, but smaller differences for second-generation immigrants. Moreover, large

Table 7.9 Ethnic differences (*d* values) between first- and second-generation immigrants versus the majority group in The Netherlands.

Ability	C	M	S	T
Majority vs. First Generation				
Verbal	1.27	0.98	1.00	1.18
Inductive	0.90	1.03	1.00	0.96
Numerical	0.66	1.08	0.79	0.67
Word fluency	1.03	1.15	0.88	1.12
Spatial	0.69	1.06	0.79	0.87
Picture arrangement	0.90	0.98	0.98	1.11
Average	*0.91*	*1.09*	*0.91*	*0.98*
Majority vs. Second Generation				
Verbal	0.33	0.48	0.41	0.82
Inductive	0.17	0.62	0.51	0.68
Numerical	0.43	0.56	0.58	0.43
Word fluency	0.28	0.60	0.48	0.71
Spatial	0.06	0.63	0.33	0.55
Picture arrangement	0.16	0.47	0.50	0.74
Average	*0.24*	*0.56*	*0.47*	*0.65*
Second Generation vs. First Generation				
Verbal	0.90	0.44	0.53	0.29
Inductive	0.64	0.60	0.44	0.25
Numerical	0.26	0.61	0.25	0.26
Word Fluency	0.81	0.60	0.44	0.46
Spatial	0.49	0.37	0.42	0.31
Picture arrangement	0.61	0.45	0.40	0.34
Average	*0.62*	*0.51*	*0.41*	*0.32*

C = Caribbean; M = Morocco; S = Surinam; T = Turkey
Source: Adapted from De Meijer et al. (2006).

differences were found in the comparison between first- and second-generation immigrants in the four ethnic groups (De Meijer et al., 2006). Consequently, about two-thirds of the differences between the majority group and the Caribbean, Moroccan and Surinamese group were explained by this factor (primarily, socio-educational), and about a third in the case of the Turkish group. Table 7.9 presents a summary of these findings.

In Sweden, Kvist and Gustafsson (2008) compared a large group of immigrants who applied for vocational training, with a majority group using a battery of 15 cognitive tests. Using their data (Kvist & Gustafsson, 2008, Table 2), the standardized differences between the majority group and two groups of immigrants (Europeans and non-Europeans) were computed. The Swedish group outperformed both European and non-European immigrant groups in all tests. The average *d* was 0.52 for the European immigrants and 0.90 for the non-Europeans. Classifying the tests in four cognitive abilities (fluid, crystallized, visual and speed), the size of the standardized differences was small for fluid, visual and speed abilities with *d* values ranging from 0.26 to 0.35 for the European immigrants and large for the non-Europeans with *d* values ranging from 0.52 to 0.90. However, the standard differences were very large for crystallized ability in both groups (1.27 and 1.42 for the European and non-European immigrants, respectively). It is worth noting that the sample consisted of the unemployed or those at risk of becoming unemployed. The results are shown in Table 7.10.

Table 7.10 Comparison between immigrants and a majority group in Sweden.

Test	1-order Ability	2-order Ability	d S-EU	d S-non-EU
Raven	Reasoning	Fluid	0.32	0.65
Aros number series	Numerical	Fluid	0.05	0.39
USTM number series	Numerical	Fluid	0.52	0.67
WIT numbers	Numerical	Fluid	−0.10	0.17
R16A mathematical	Numerical	Fluid	0.51	0.84
Instructions	V+N+S	Crystallized	1.42	2.14
SP2A spatial	Mechanical	Crystallized	1.34	2.10
DLS reading	Verbal	Crystallized	1.26	1.43
WIT antonyms	Verbal	Crystallized	1.08	1.90
WIT puzzle	Spatial	Visual	0.51	1.04
Aros metal folding	Spatial	Visual	0.49	1.16
Wire	Spatial	Visual-Psychomotor	−0.04	0.14
Stockholm box	Spatial	Visual	0.37	0.58
Crawford pins	Spatial	Visual-Psychomotor	0.05	0.16
P-numbers (perceptual)	Perceptual	Speed	0.36	0.65
P-words (perceptual)	Perceptual	Speed	0.28	0.62
P-figures (perceptual)	Perceptual	Speed	0.42	0.68
GMA (average of 17 tests)			0.52	0.90
Fluid			0.26	0.52
Crystallized			1.27	1.42
Visual			0.33	0.73
Visual without psychomotor tests			0.46	0.93
Speed			0.35	0.65

Note: D values calculated with data from Kvist & Gustafsson, (2008), Table 2.

An examination of ethnic differences was also performed in other countries. In recent years, South African psychologists have made important contributions to this topic. The significance of these studies is that they run counter to what is common in studies on ethnic differences as in South Africa the disadvantaged group is the majority one for political and historical reasons (i.e., the apartheid era). In South Africa prior to 1994, standardization measures were used only for Whites (Forbes, 2006; Kriek & Dowdeswell, 2010). However, after apartheid was abolished, a number of studies on ethnic group differences on psychological assessment were carried out on various ethnic groups. Kriek and Dowdeswell's (2009) study, consisting of a sample of 12,383 Black and 1,872 White South African clerical applicants to a financial institution, found $d=0.87$ in an online verbal ability test, and $d=0.55$ in an online numerical ability test, with White South Africans scoring higher. The authors also found that d values remained fairly constant over a five-year period (2002–2006). In a second study, with a sample of 104 employees from business advisory services (47 Black, 57 White), Kriek and Dowdeswell (2009) reported an average d of 1.10 for cognitive ability. In both studies White South Africans scored higher than Black South Africans. In another study, Strachan (2008) examined ethnic group differences in three cognitive tests using a large South African sample ($N=2,877$), consisting of 1,168 Blacks, 127 Coloured, 630 Indians and 952 Whites. He found differences across the four ethnic groups for the three cognitive tests. On average, Whites scored higher, followed by Indians, Coloureds and Blacks. Stracham also found that Indians outperformed Coloureds, who in turn outperformed Blacks in the three tests.

Ethnic group differences were also examined in New Zealand by comparing a group of 109 Maori applicants with a group of 55 European-heritage applicants in a verbal ability test (Guenole, Englert & Taylor, 2003). The study found $d=0.55$, with Europeans scoring higher. They also found an average $d=0.70$ ($N=75$) in two numerical ability tests, with Europeans again scoring higher.

In short, ethnic group differences were found across different countries, but despite these differences, researchers suggest that such differences were not due to any bias in the tests as predictors of job performance (Hunter, Schmidt & Hunter, 1979; Schmidt, Ones & Hunter, 1992; Schmitt, 2014). These authors claim the empirical findings have corroborated that GMA tests are predictively fair for minorities and that the validity coefficients are comparable. In other words, there is no test bias. Test bias means that systematic differences are found between groups (e.g., women and men; ethnic group members in comparison to a majority group), not only in mean test scores but also in how tests predict job performance ratings. For example, there is bias when an ethnic group scores lower in the test, but performs the job as effectively as the majority group. The usual conclusion has been that there was some small overprediction of minority performance based on intercept differences found in regressions of performance outcomes on test scores, minority status and their interaction. This method of analysis and the empirical research have been suggested by both AERA (1999) and SIOP (2003). Much research was undertaken in the 1970s, 1980s and 1990s, and there seems to be a broad consensus that cognitive tests have not resulted in biased predictions for women and minorities. The most common finding is that cognitive tests produce some small overprediction of performance scores of minority groups as there are intercept differences in regressions of performance outcomes on test scores, minority status and their interaction (Schmitt, 2014). These results have been found in US samples, and for example in The Netherlands and South Africa.

Since 2010, a series of scientific papers have empirically re-examined the issues of differential validity and differential prediction (Aguinis, Culpepper & Pierce, 2010; Berry, Clark & McClure, 2011; Berry, Cullen & Meyer, 2014; Berry & Zhao, 2015; Roth et al., 2014; Mattern & Patterson, 2013). Differential validity analyses focus on subgroup differences in the correlation between a test and a criterion (e.g., job performance) as evidence of subgroup differences in test criterion relationships. Differential prediction analyses focus on subgroup differences in test criterion unstandardized regression equations as evidence regarding subgroup differences in test criterion relationships.

With regard to the first issue, Berry and colleagues (2011) meta-analytically examined the validity of cognitive ability tests across Black, White, Hispanic and Asian subgroups in the US. They found that the average observed validity was smaller for Hispanics and African-American groups (0.33 for White and Asians vs. 0.30 and 0.24 for Hispanics and African-Americans). They also found that the magnitude of the differences was larger in military contexts than in civilian ones. Roth and colleagues (2014) suggest that Berry and colleagues' (2011) findings may be due to the effects of range restriction and measurement error. Using simulation, Roth and colleagues (2014) demonstrated that range restriction artificially increased the size of observed differential validity. Therefore, they claim that the concept of differential validity may be basically artifactual. However, this conclusion has been rejected by Berry and colleagues (2014), who conducted a study in which they controlled for range restriction. The results again show evidence of a small degree of differential validity in line with their earlier study.

According to the *Principles for Validation and Use of Personnel Selection Procedures* (SIOP, 2003, p. 32), 'predictive bias is found when for a given subgroup, consistent nonzero errors of prediction are made for the subgroup'. In connection with the issue of differential prediction, Aguinis and colleagues (2010) posited that the intercept differences test typically carried out in differential prediction analyses was biased in such a way that it overestimates the size of subgroup intercept differences. A second problem of the differential validity studies conducted in the past is that they all used observed validities. Consequently, according to Aguinis and colleagues (2010), the established conclusion of over-prediction of minority performance should be re-examined. This has been achieved in Mattern and Patterson's (2013), and Berry and Zhao's (2015) meta-analytic studies. Mattern and Patterson's (2013) research consisted of 348 SAT validity studies, with a total sample in excess of 475,000 individuals. In order to avoid the methodological problems raised by Aguinis and colleagues (2010), Mattern and Patterson (2013) corrected validities for range restriction and criterion reliability and used regression plots instead of the intercept differences test. They found that the grades of African-American and Hispanic students would be overpredicted.

More specifically in the personnel selection context, Berry and Zhao (2015) applied the appropriate corrections for indirect range restriction (i.e., there were three variables: X, Y and Z) and for criterion reliability to the observed validities of the GATB dataset. In indirect range restriction, selection is based on variables other than the predictor itself (Hunter, Schmidt & Le, 2006). In other words, for indirect selection scores on the test are not used in decision making. Berry and Zhao (2015) found that cognitive ability generally over-predicts, with under-prediction occurring only in unusual circumstances, for instance when the selection variable z is uncorrelated with job performance or exhibits no mean difference between African-Americans and Whites. Considering Mattern and Patterson's (2013) results and their own, Berry and Zhao (2014, pp. 14–15) concluded that:

> These studies are in agreement that, even when the biased intercept test is not used and analyses are carried out at the level of operational validity, cognitive ability tests generally still overpredict African American job and academic performance. Despite the excellent points made by Aguinis et al., the field still has a strong basis for concluding that cognitive ability test scores are not predictively biased against African Americans in employment or college admissions settings.

Applicant Reactions

In 1984, De Wolff and Van der Bosch pointed out that the perspective of applicants had not been taken into account in previous research on the validity of personnel selection procedures, and considered that such a perspective was of great importance for personnel selection as applicants also make hiring decisions, not only the organization. They suggested that applicant perceptions and reactions may be crucial for the success of personnel selection decisions and called for research into this issue. Apparently, their call was heard, and over the last 20 years a plethora of studies on the applicants' reactions and their perceptions of fairness were undertaken, many of them following seminal work by Steiner and Gilliland (1996). These researchers compared the perceptions of and reactions to 10 selection procedures in France and the US. Specifically for cognitive ability tests, Steiner and Gilliland (1996) found that cognitive tests were between the best rated procedures in both France and the US. Using the same or very similar questionnaires, studies were devoted to examining the perceptions and reactions of applicants in a large number of countries, including the US (Bauer et al., 1998; Steiner & Gilliland, 1996), France

Table 7.11 Applicant perceptions regarding favourability to cognitive ability tests in 18 countries.

Country	Sample Size	Favourability
Belgium	235	3.50
France	117	4.21
Greece	279	4.29
Iceland	235	4.80
India	93	4.92
Ireland	73	4.16
Italy	139	4.43
Lithuania	193	4.51
Morocco	52	4.30
Portugal	104	4.13
Romania	235	5.68
Singapore	158	4.56
Spain	125	4.15
South Africa	286	4.75
Sweden	90	4.02
The Netherlands	167	4.15
United States	472	4.30
Vietnam	225	4.87
Total:	4,092 Weighted average:	4.60

(Steiner & Gilliland, 1996), Germany (Marcus, 2003), the UK, Ireland (Scroggins, Benson, Cross & Gilbreath, 2008), Iceland (Jónsdóttir & Hafsteinson, 2008), Spain (Moscoso & Salgado, 2004), Portugal (Moscoso & Salgado, 2004), Morocco (Scroggins et al., 2008), Greece (Nikolau & Judge, 2006), Belgium (Stinglhamber, Vandenberghe & Brancart, 2009), Israel (Gamliel & Peer, 2009), Italy (Bertolino & Steiner, 2007), Lithuania (Sidaviciute, 2008), The Netherlands (Anderson & Witvliet, 2008), Romania (Ispas, Ilie, Iliescu, Johnson & Harris, 2010), Singapore (Chan, Schmitt, Jennings, Clause & Delbridge, 1998; Phillips & Gully, 2002), India (Snyder & Shahani-Denning, 2012), South Africa (De Jong, 2000), Sweden (Sidaviciute, 2008) and Turkey (Bilgic & Acarlar, 2010). The results of these studies were meta-analysed by Anderson, Salgado and Hülsherger (2010). Overall, they found that cognitive tests were the most favourably scored methods (mean $N = 4.59, 95\%CI = 3.89–5.30$). The main conclusions of Anderson, Salgado and Hülsherger's (2010) findings were that cognitive tests overall were: 1) rated positively; 2) perceived as the most scientifically valid method for personnel selection; 3) showed respect for privacy, and 4) provided applicants with an opportunity to perform. The main drawback of cognitive tests was that they were regarded as interpersonally cold. Several more studies have been carried out since this meta-analysis, but the picture remains much the same. Table 7.11 summarizes the favourability ratings of cognitive tests in 18 countries.

The main conclusion of this research was that applicants' perceptions of fairness influenced their reactions to the selection process and the organization's attractiveness (Gilliland & Steiner, 2012). Thus, Bauer and colleagues (2012) examined research on fairness perceptions and proposed a series of recommendations to elicit positive candidate reactions, some of them directly applicable to the use of cognitive tests (e.g., content appropriateness, explanations about the selection procedure).

Future Research

A chapter like this is not complete without suggesting some avenues for future research and mentioning some issues that are still unexplored. As for fresh avenues, I concur with Schmitt (2014; Schmitt & Frandre, 2008) that new studies on the validity of GMA and specific cognitive abilities should be undertaken given that, in general, the databases used in meta-analyses included in primary studies were undertaken 25 years or more ago. In addition, conceptions of job performance have changed and are now envisaged in multi-dimensional terms, but many of the early primary studies did not include criterion measures to capture performance subdimensions. Although some research on the relationship between cognitive ability and performance has been undertaken recently, this contrasts with the scarcity of primary studies in the past two decades. Thus, further studies are required to examine new aspects of organizational behaviour. The following list is a brief overview of some unexplored areas, which deserve some attention:

1 Additional cross-cultural research should be done on the relationship between GMA and specific cognitive abilities with job performance and other organizational criteria in Latin American, African and Asian-Pacific countries.

2 Studies on the relationships between cognitive abilities and CBW are also needed. As Gonzalez-Mulé and colleagues (2014) have pointed out, their meta-analyses contained only 35 primary studies, which clearly contrast with the number of primary studies included in the meta-analyses of cognitive ability–performance relations, many of which analysed hundreds of studies (e.g., Hartigan & Wigdor, 1989; Hunter & Hunter, 1984; Salgado et al, 2003b). Furthermore, the relationship between cognitive ability and CWB should be examined to determine if it is moderated by the nature of CWB itself (e.g., organizational CWB vs. interpersonal CWB).

3 New models of cognitive abilities and re-examination of older models (e.g. Thomson's) pose the question whether specific abilities are more valid predictors than GMA and whether they show incremental validity beyond GMA. The studies based on Spearman (e.g., Ree & Earles, 1991; Ree et al., 1994) showed that specific cognitive abilities did not increase validity over GMA. However, this is not necessarily the case with nested models of cognitive abilities and some studies have suggested a new way for exploring this area (e.g., Lang et al., 2009), or with the *Gf–Gc* model (Nisbett et al, 2012; Postlethwaite, 2011), and the studies by Campbell and Cattano (2004) and Mount et al. (2008) for perceptual speed ability.

4 Studies are required on differential validity and differential prediction, taking into account the methodological shortcomings underscored by Aguinis and colleagues (2010).

5 Further research on the relationship between cognitive ability and well-being in organizations should expand the number the criteria and add important organizational behaviours. The relationships between GMA and job satisfaction, happiness, burnout, abusive supervision, mobbing and subjective well-being should be analysed. Such studies will make relevant contributions to the study of abilities at work.

6 New studies should be conducted to explore the relationship between GMA and the Big Five personality factors as measured by quasi-ipsative forced-choice (QI-FC) personality inventories. Since 2014, meta-analyses have demonstrated that QI-FC personality inventories are more valid for predicting job performance than standard, single-stimulus (SS) personality inventories (Salgado, Anderson & Tauriz, 2015; Salgado & Tauriz, 2014). Several researchers have suggested that the cognitive strategies used to respond to SS and FC personality measures are different, with the first being less cognitively demanding than the second (e.g., Brown & Maydeu, 2013; Meade,

2004; Vasilopoulus, Cucina, Dyomina, Morewitz & Reilly, 2006). Consequently, QI measures may show a higher correlation with GMA than SS measures.

7   Another important area for future research is the potential relevance of group intelligence for predicting team performance and interpersonal performance. Woolley, Chabris, Pentland, Hasmi and Malone (2010) have shown that collective intelligence can be a valid predictor of team performance. This fresh area extends the number of criteria, adding to others such as group cohesion, team climate, team socialization, leadership effectiveness.

8   Finally, an interesting area for future research is the variability within groups in cognitive abilities and its potential effects on performance and differential prediction.

Conclusion

In *The Nature of Intelligence*, Thurstone (1924, p. xiv) wrote: 'there is considerable difference of opinion as to what intelligence really is, but, even if we do not know just what intelligence is, we can still use the test as long as they are demonstrably satisfactory for definite practical ends.' Ninety years later, we can conclude that intelligence and cognitive tests have demonstrated they are excellent procedures for the practical purposes of personnel selection and that, although opinions differ on what intelligence is persist, important advances on the theoretical account of cognitive ability have been made. There is no consensus about the nature and existence of a general factor of intelligence, but the vast majority of researchers now agree that a general factor can be found when a large battery of cognitive tests is factor analysed, and the majority of the psychometric models of cognitive abilities include a general factor (Horn's model is the exception). There is less agreement regarding the number of levels in the hierarchy and the number and type of medium and narrower abilities.

Though survey data show that GMA tests are frequently used in personnel selection across the world, this is not a sufficiently good reason for using the procedure for decision making. For example, graphology is very popular in some countries (e.g., Brazil, France and Israel), but the empirical evidence shows that its validity for predicting job proficiency is zero. In other words, if the validity of a procedure is zero, it would be the same as using a table of random numbers to choose an applicant. The empirical evidence cited in previous sections suggests that, in a rapidly changing world of work, GMA is the best predictor of the future adaptability to new tasks and functions.

Succinctly, the state-of-art suggests that: 1) the validity of cognitive ability tests are generalizable across occupations and situations, and moderated by job complexity, so that operational validity is 0.40 or higher; 2) the relationship between GMA and task performance is linear and its effects are primarily indirect thorough job knowledge; 3) GMA predicts moderately OCB, but not CWB; 4) there are ethnic and group differences in both GMA and the specific cognitive abilities, and the standardized differences are greater for lower job complexity levels and for crystallized ability; 5) although there is some evidence of differential validity, there is no differential prediction (bias) for African-Americans.

Finally, the findings underscore that cognitive ability tests may be valuable, cost-saving instruments for companies by ensuring high standards of individual job performance, which in turn raise productivity (Scherbaum et al., 2012).

References

Ackerman, P. L., & Heggestad, E.D. (1997). Intelligence, personality and interests: Evidence for overlapping traits. *Psychological Bulletin, 121*, 219– 245.

Aguinis, H., Culpepper, S. A., & Pierce, C. A. (2010). Revival of test bias research in preemployment testing. *Journal of Applied Psychology, 95*, 648–680. doi: 10.1037/a0018714.

Alfonso, V. C., Flanagan, D. P., & Radwan, S. (2007). The impact of the Cattell–Horn–Carroll theory on test development and interpretation of cognitive and academic abilities. *In* D. P. Flanagan & P. L. Harrison (Eds.), *Contemporary Intellectual Assessment, Theories, Tests, and Issues* (2nd ed., pp. 185–202). New York: Guilford Press.

Alonso, P., Moscoso, S., & Cuadrado, D. (2015). Personnel selection procedures in Spanish small and medium size organizations. *Revista de Psicología del Trabajo y de las Organizaciones, 31*, 79–89.

Ali, O., Gamer, I., & Magadley, W. (2009). An investigation of the relationship among personality, cognitive ability, emotional intelligence, and counterproductive workplace behaviors: Results from UAE Police. 8th Industrial and Organisational Psychology Conference, 25–28 June, Sydney, Australia.

American Educational Research Association (AERA). (1999). *Standards for Educational and Psychological Testing.* Washington, DC: American Psychological Association.

Anderson, N., Salgado, J. F., & Hülsheger, U. R. (2010). Applicant reactions in selection: Comprehensive meta-analysis into reaction generalization versus situational specificity. *International Journal of Selection and Assessment, 18*, 291–304.

Anderson, N., & Witvliet, C. (2008). Fairness reactions to personnel selection methods: An international comparison between The Netherlands, the United States, France, Spain, Portugal, and Singapore. *International Journal of Selection and Assessment, 16*, 1–13.

Barros, E., Kausel, E. E., Cuadra, F., & Díaz, D. A. (2014). Using general mental ability and personality traits to predict job performance in three Chilean organizations. *International Journal of Selection and Assessment, 22*, 432–438.

Bartholomew, D. J., Deary, I. J., & Lawn, M. (2009). A new lease of life for Thomson's bonds model of intelligence. *Psychological Review, 116*, 567–579.

Bartram, D., & Baxter, P. (1996). Validation of the Cathay Pacific Airways pilot selection program. *International Journal of Aviation Psychology, 6*, 149–169.

Bauer, T. N., Maertz, C. P., Dolen, M. R., & Campion, M. A. (1998). Longitudinal assessment of applicant reactions to employment testing and test outcome feedback. *Journal of Applied Psychology, 83*, 892–903.

Bauer, T. N., McCarthy, J., Anderson, N., Truxillo, D. M., & Salgado, J. F. (2012). *What We Know About Applicant Reactions To Selection: Research Summary and Best Practices.* SIOP White Paper Series. Bowling Green, OH: Society for Industrial and Organizational Psychology.

Baumgartl, V. O., & Primi, R. (2011). Evidencias de validade da Bateria de provas de raciocionio (BPR-5) para a selecçao de pessoal. *Psicologia: Reflexao e Critica, 19*, 246–251.

Beauducel, A., & Kersting, M. (2002).Fluid and crystallized intelligence and the Berlin Model of Intelligence structure (BIS). *European Journal of Psychological Assessment, 18*, 97–112.

Bennett, G. K., Seashore, H. G., & Wesman, A. G. (1982). *Differential Aptitude Tests.* New York: Psychological Corporation.

Berry, C. M., Clark, M. A., & McClure, T. K. (2011). Racial/ethnic differences in the criterion-related validity of cognitive ability tests: A qualitative and quantitative review. *Journal of Applied Psychology, 96*, 881–906.

Berry, C. M., Cullen, M. J., & Meyer, J. M. (2014). Racial/ethnic subgroup differences in cognitive ability test range restriction: Implications for differential validity. *Journal of Applied Psychology, 99*, 21–37.

Berry, C. M., & Zhao, P. (2015). Addressing criticism of existing predictive bias research: Cognitive ability test scores still overpredict African Americans' job performance. *Journal of Applied Psychology, 110*, 162–179.

Bertolino, M., & Steiner, D. D. (2007). Fairness reactions to selection methods: An Italian study. *International Journal of Selection and Assessment, 15*, 107–205.

Bertua, C., Anderson, N., & Salgado, J. F. (2005). The predictive validity of cognitive ability tests: A UK meta-analysis. *Journal of Occupational and Organizational Psychology, 78*, 387–409.

Bilgic, R., & Acarlar, G. (2010). Fairness perceptions of selection instruments used in Turkey. Paper presented at the XIIth Congress of the Turkish Psychological Association, Istanbul, Turkey. *Journal of Psychology, 30*, 17–24.

Black, J. (2000). Personality testing and police selection: Utility of the 'Big Five'. *New Zealand Journal of Psychology, 29*, 2–9.

Bobko, P., & Roth, P. L. (2013). Reviewing, categorizing, and analyzing the literature on Black–White mean differences for predictors of job performance: Verifying some perceptions and updating/correcting others. *Personnel Psychology, 66*, 91–126.

Burt, C. (1909). Experimental tests of general intelligence. *British Psychological Psychology, 3,* 94–177.

Campbell, S., & Cattano, V. M. (2004). Using measures of specific abilities to predict training performance in Canadian Forces operator occupations. *Military Psychology, 16,* 183–201.

Carroll, J. B. (1993). *Human Cognitive Abilities: A Survey of Factor-Analytic Studies.* New York: Cambridge University Press.

Castro-Solano, A., & Casullo, M. M. (2005). Estilos de personalidad, afrontamiento e inteligencia como predictores de las trayectorias académicas de cadetes en una institución militar. *Anales de Psicología, 36,* 197–210.

Cattell, R. B. (1963). Theory of fluid and crystallized intelligence: A critical experiment. *Journal of Educational Psychology, 54,* 1–22. doi: 10.1037/h0046743.

Cattell, R. B. (1971). *Abilities: Their Structure, Growth, and Action.* Boston, MA: Houghton Mifflin.

Cattell, R. B. (1987). *Intelligence: Its Structure, Growth, and Action.* New York: North Holland.

Cattell, R. B., & Horn, J. L. (1978). A check of the theory of fluid and crystallized intelligence with description of new subtest design. *Journal of Educational Measurement, 15,* 139–164.

Chan, D., & Schmitt, N. (2002). Situational judgment and job performance. *Human Performance, 15,* 233–254.

Chan, D., Schmitt, N., Jennings, D., Clause, C. S., & Delbridge, K. (1998). Applicant perceptions of test fairness: Integrating justice and self-serving bias perspectives. *International Journal of Selection and Assessment, 6,* 232–239.

Chartered Institute of Personnel and Development (2007). *2007 Recruitment, Retention, and Turnover Survey.* London: Chartered Institute of Personnel and Development.

Cobêro, C., Primi, R., & Muniz, M. (2006). Intêligencia emocional e desempenho no trabalho: Un estudo com MSCEIT, BPR-5, e 16PF. *Paidéia, 16,* 337–348.

Cuadra-Peralta, A. (1990). Un modelo matemático de selección basado en validez concurrente. *Revista de Psicología del Trabajo y de las Organizaciones, 6.*

Dale, G. J. (2010). Predicting learner performance in the clothing industry. Unpublished master's thesis. Cape Peninsula University of Technology, Cape Town, South Africa.

Dany, F., & Torchy, V. (1994). Recruitment and selection in Europe: Policies, practices and methods. *In* C. Brewster & A. Hegewisch (Eds.), *Policy and Practice in European Human Resource Management: The Price Waterhouse Cranfield Survey.* London: Routledge.

Deary, I. J. (2012). Intelligence. *Annual Review of Psychology, 63,* 453–482.

De Jong, A. V. D. (2000). Black and White employees' fairness perceptions of personnel selection techniques. *South African Journal of Psychology, 30,* 17–24.

De Kock, F., & Schlechter, A. (2009). Fluid intelligence and spatial reasoning as predictors of pilot training performance. *South African Journal of Industrial Psychology, 35,* 1–8.

De Meijer, L. A. L., Born, M. P., Terlouw, G., & van der Molen, H. T. (2010). Applicant and method factors related to ethnic score differences in personnel selection: A study at the Dutch police. *Human Performance, 19,* 219–251.

De Wolff, C., & Van der Bosch, G. (1984) Personnel selection. *In* P. D. Drenth, H. Thierry, P. J. Willems & C. J. de Wolff (Eds.), *European Handbook Of Work and Organizational Psychology* (pp. 33–58). Chichester: Wiley.

Di Milia, L., Smith, P. A., & Brown, D. F. (1994). Management selection in Australia: A comparison with British and French findings. *International Journal of Selection and Assessment, 2,* 80–90.

Fertig, S. (2009). The incremental validity of a situational judgment test (SJT) relative to personality and cognitive ability to predict managerial performance. Unpublished master's thesis, Stellenboch University, South Africa.

Flanagan, D. P., McGrew, K. S., & Ortiz, S. (2000). *The Wechsler Intelligence Scales and Gf–Gc theory: A Contemporary Approach and Interpretation.* Needham Heights, MA: Allyn & Bacon.

Forbes, A. (2006). The predictive validity of the Occupational Personality Questionnaire (OPQ 32i) in assessing competence in the workplace. Unpublished master's thesis. University of Cape Town, South Africa.

Gamliel, E., & Peer, E. (2009). Effect of framing on applicants' reactions to personnel selection methods. *International Journal of Selection and Assessment, 17,* 282–289.

Ghiselli, E. E. (1966). *The Validity of Occupational Aptitude Tests.* New York: Wiley.

Ghiselli, E. E. (1973). The validity of aptitude tests in personnel selection. *Personnel Psychology, 26,* 461–477.

Gilliland, S. W., & Steiner, D. I. (2012). Applicant reactions to testing and selection. *In* N. Schmitt (Ed.), *Personnel Assessment and Selection* (pp. 629–668). New York: Oxford University Press.

Goldstein, H. W., Scherbaum, C. A., & Yusko, K. P. (2010). Revisiting *g*: Intelligence, adverse impact, and personnel selection. *In* J. L. Outz (Ed.), *Adverse Impact. Implications for Organizational Staffing and High Stakes Selection* (pp. 95–134). New York. Routledge.

Gonzalez-Mulé, E., Mount, M. K., & Oh, I-S. (2014). A meta-analysis of the relationship between general mental ability and nontask performance. *Journal of Applied Psychology, 99*, 1222–1243.

Gowing, M. K., & Slivinski, L. W. (1994). A review of North American selection procedures: Canada and United States of America. *International Journal of Selection and Assessment, 2*, 103–114.

Green, T., & Macqueen, P. (2008). Cognitive ability. How important? Unpublished manuscript. Queensland, Australia: Compass Consulting.

Guenole, N., Englert, P., & Taylor, P. J. (2003). Ethnic group differences in cognitive ability test scores within a New Zealand applicant sample. *New Zealand Journal of Psychology, 32*, 49–54.

Guion, R. M. (1998). *Assessment, Measurement, and Prediction for Personnel Decisions.* Mahwah, NJ: Lawrence Erlbaum.

Gustafsson, J.-E. (1988). Hierarchical models of individual differences in cognitive abilities. *In* R. J. Sternberg (Ed.), *Advances in the Psychology of Human Intelligence* (Vol. 4, pp. 35–71). Hillsdale, NJ: Lawrence Erlbaum.

Gustafsson, J.-E. (1992). The 'Spearman hypothesis' is false. *Multivariate Behavioral Research, 27*, 265–267.

Harman, H. H. (1976). *Modern Factor Analysis* (3rd ed.). Chicago, Il: University of Chicago Press.

Hartigan, J. A., & Wigdor, A. K. (Eds.) (1989). *Fairness in Employment Testing: Validity Generalization, Minority Issues, and The General Aptitude Test Battery.* Washington, DC: National Academy Press.

Heylighen, F. (1999). Collective intelligence and its implementation on the web: Algorithms to develop a collective mental map. *Computational & Mathematical Organization Theory, 5*, 253–280.

Hirsh, H. R., Northrop, L. C., & Schmidt, F. L. (1986). Validity generalization results for law enforcement occupations. *Personnel Psychology, 39*, 399–420.

Holzinger, K., & Swineford, F. (1937).The bi-factor method. *Psychometrika, 2*, 41–54.

Horn, J. L. (1965). *Fluid and crystallized intelligence: A factor analytic study of the structure among primary mental abilities.* Ph.D. Thesis: University of Illinois.

Horn, J. (1989). Models of intelligence. *In* R. L. Linn (Ed.), *Intelligence: Measurement, Theory, and Public Policy* (pp. 29–73). Urbana, IL: Illinois University Press.

Hough, L. M., Oswald, F. L., & Ployhart, R. E. (2001). Determinants, detection, and amelioration of adverse impact in personnel selection procedures: issues, evidence and lessons learned. *International Journal of Selection and Assessment, 9*, 152–194.

Hülsheger, U. R., Maier, G. W., & Stumpp, T. (2007). Validity of general mental ability for the prediction of job performance and training success in Germany: A meta-analysis. *International Journal of Selection and Assessment, 15*, 3–18.

Humphreys, L. G. (1983).The hierarchical model and general intelligence. *In* N. Hirschberg & L. G. Humphreys (Eds.), *Multivariate Applications in the Social Sciences* (pp. 223–239). Hillsdale, NJ: Lawrence Erlbaum.

Hunt, E. A. (2011). *Human Intelligence.* New York: Cambridge University Press.

Hunter, J. E. (1983). *Test Validation for 12,000 jobs: An Application of Job Classification and Validity Generalization Analysis to the General Aptitude Test Battery (GATB).* Washington, DC: US Department of Labor, US Employment Service.

Hunter, J. E. (1986). Cognitive ability, cognitive aptitudes, job knowledge, and job performance. *Journal of Vocational Behavior, 29*, 340–362.

Hunter, J. E., & Hirsh, H. R. (1987). Applications of meta-analysis. *International Review of Industrial and Organizational Psychology* (Vol. 2, pp. 321–357). Chichester: John Wiley & Sons.

Hunter, J. E., & Hunter, R. F. (1984). Validity and utility of alternate predictors of job performance. *Psychological Bulletin, 96*, 72–98.

Hunter, J. E., & Schmidt, F. L. (2000). Racial and gender bias in ability and achievement tests: resolving the apparent paradox. *Psychology, Public Policy and Law, 6*, 151.

Hunter, J. E., Schmidt, F. L., & Hunter, R. (1979). Differential validity of employment tests by race: A comprehensive review and analysis. *Psychological Bulletin, 86*, 721–735.

Hunter, J. E., Schmidt, F. L., & Le, H. (2006). Implications of direct and indirect range restriction for meta-analysis methods and findings. *Journal of Applied Psychology, 91*, 594–612. doi: 10.1037/0021-9010.91.3.594

Ispas, D., Ilie, A., Iliescu, D., Johnson, R. E., & Harris, M. M. (2010). Fairness reactions to selection methods: A Romanian study. *International Journal of Selection and Assessment, 18*, 102–110.

Jäger, A. O. (1967). *Dimensionen der Intelligenz* [Dimensions of Intelligence]. Gottinge, Germany: Hogrefe.

Jäger, A. O. (1982). *Mehrmodale Klassification von intelligenzleistungen: Experimentell kontrollierte weiterentwicklung eines deskriptiven intelligenzstrukturmodells. [Multimodal classification of intelligence tests: Experimentally controlled development of a descriptive model of intelligence structure].* Gottingen: Hogrefe.

Jäger, A. O. (1984). Intelligenzstruktur fortschung: Konkurriende modelle, neue entwicklungen, perspektiven [Research on intelligence structure: Competing models, new developments, perspectives]. *Psychologische Rundau, 35*, 21–35.

Jenrich, R. I., & Bentler, P. M. (2011). Exploratory bi-factor analysis. *Psychometrika, 76*, 537–549.

Jensen, A. R. (1998). *The g Factor: The Science of Mental Ability*. Wesport, CT: Praeger.

Johnson, J. W., & LeBreton, J. M. (2004). History and use of relative importance indices in organizational research. *Organizational Research Methods, 7*, 258–282.

Johnson, W., & Bouchard, T. J. (2005a).The structure of human intelligence: It is verbal, perceptual and image rotation (VPR), not fluid and crystallized. *Intelligence, 33*, 393–416.

Johnson, W., & Bouchard, T. J. (2005b).Constructive replication of the visual–perceptual image rotation model of Thurstone's (1941) battery of 60 tests of mental ability. *Intelligence, 33*, 417–430.

Johnson, W., & Bouchard, T. J. (2007). Sex differences in mental abilities: *g* masks the dimensions on which they lie. *Intelligence, 35*, 23–39.

Johnson, W., & Bouchard, T. J. (2011). The MISTRA data: Forty-two mental ability tests in three batteries. *Intelligence, 39*, 82–88.

Johnson, W., Bouchard, T. J., Krueger, R. F., McGue, M., & Gottesman, I. I. (2004). Just one *g*: Consistent results from three test batteries. *Intelligence, 32*, 95–107.

Johnson, W., te Nijenhuis, J., & Bouchard, T. J. (2008). Still just 1 *g*: Consistent results from five test batteries. *Intelligence, 36*, 81–95.

Jónsdóttir, J. H., & Hafsteinson, L. G. (2008). Sanngimi átta aðferða sem notaðar eru við starfsmannaval: Viðbrögð Íslendinga [Fairness reactions to personnel selection methods in Iceland]. *Sálfræðiritð, 13*, 109–125.

Krantowitz, T. M. (2014). *2014 Global Assessment Trends Report*. Surrey: CEB-SHL.

Kriek, H., & Dowdeswell, K. (2009). Adverse impact & validity evidence in South Africa: 12 years of data trends. Unpublished manuscript. SHL, South Africa.

Kriek, H., & Dowdeswell, K. (2010). Adverse impact in South Africa. *In* J. L. Outz (Ed.), *Adverse Impact. Implications for Organizational Staffing and High Stakes Selection* (pp. 375–399). New York: Routledge.

Kvist, V., & Gustafsson, J.-E. (2008). The relation between fluid intelligence and the general as a function of cultural background: A test of Cattell's investment theory. *Intelligence, 36*, 422–436.

Lang, J. W. B., Kersting, M., Hülsheger, U. T., & Lang, J. (2010). General mental ability, narrower cognitive abilities, and job performance: The perspective of the nested-factors model of cognitive abilities. *Personnel Psychology, 63*, 595–640.

Lee, S. (2005). Cross-cultural validity of personality for predicting job performance of Korean engineers. Unpublished doctoral dissertation, Ohio State University.

Levine, E. L., Spector, P. E., Menon, P. E., Narayanon, L., & Cannon-Bowers, J. (1996). Validity generalization for cognitive, psychomotor, and perceptual tests for craft jobs in the utility industry. *Human Performance, 9*, 1–22.

Mann, C. (2011). Cognitive ability and job performance in a New Zealand service organization. Unpublished master's thesis. Massey University, New Zealand.

Marcus, B. (2003). Attitudes towards personnel selection methods: A partial replication and extension in a German sample. *Applied Psychology: An International Review, 52*, 515–532.

Marsden, P. V. (1994). Selection methods in US establishments. *Acta Sociologica, 37*, 287–301.

Mattern, K. D., & Patterson, B. F. (2013). Test of slope and intercept bias in college admissions: A response to Aguinis, Culpepper, and Pierce (2010). *Journal of Applied Psychology, 98*, 134–147.

McGrew, K. S. (1997). Analysis of the major intelligence batteries according to a proposed comprehensive Gf–Gc framework. *In* D. P. Flanagan, J. L. Genshaft & P. L. Harrison (Eds.), *Contemporary Intellectual Assessment: Theories, Tests, and Issues* (pp. 151–180). New York: Guilford Press.

McHenry, J. J., Hough, L. M., Toquam, J. L., Hanson, M. L., & Ashworth, S. (1990). Project A validity results: the relationship between predictor and criterion domains. *Personnel Psychology, 43*, 335–354.

Meade, A. W. (2004). Psychometric problems and issues involved with creating and using ipsative measures for selection. *Journal of Occupational and Organizational Psychology, 77*, 531–552.

Moreno-García, H. E. (2011). Identificarlas variables psicométricas críticas para la selección de candidatos al puesto de ejecutivo de servicio telefónico, en una empresa del sector financiero. Unpublished master's thesis, Universidad Autónoma de Nuevo León, México.

Moscoso, S., & Salgado, J. F. (2004). Fairness reactions to personnel selection techniques in Spain and Portugal. *International Journal of Selection and Assessment, 12*, 187–196.

Mount, M. K., Oh, I.-S., & Burns, M. (2008). Incremental validity of perceptual speed and accuracy over general mental ability. *Personnel Psychology, 61*, 113–139.

Muller, J., & Schepers, J. (2003). The predictive validity of the selection battery used for junior leader training within the South African National Defense Force. *South African Journal of Industrial Psychology, 29*, 87–98.

Murphy, K. R. (2002). Can conflicting perspectives on the role of *g* in personnel selection be resolved? *Human Performance, 15*, 173–186.

Myors, B., Livenes, F., Schollaert, E., van Hoye, G., ... & Sackett, P. R. (2008). International perspectives on the legal environment for selection. *Industrial and Organizational Psychology: Perspectives on Science and Practice, 1*, 206–246.

Nicholls, M., Viviers, A. M., & Visser, D. (2009). Validation of a test battery for the selection of call centre operators in a communications company. *South African Journal of Psychology, 39*, 19–31.

Nikolaou, I., & Judge, T. A. (2007). Fairness reactions to personnel selection techniques in Greece. *International Journal of Selection and Assessment, 15*, 206–219.

Nimura, H., Ishashiro, S., & Naito, J. (2000). A meta-analysis and validity generalization study of a personnel test and a general cognitive test for measuring managerial aptitude. *Japanese Journal of Administrative Science, 13*, 159–167.

Nisbett, R. E., Aronson, J., Blair, C., Dickens, W., Flynn, J., Halpern, D. F., & Turkheimer, E. (2012). Intelligence: New findings and theoretical developments. *American Psychologist, 67*, 130–159.

Oh, I.-S. (2010). The five-factor model of personality and job performance in East Asia: A cross-cultural validity generalization study. *International Personnel Assessment Council, Assessment Council News*, 10–19.

Oh, I.-S., Schmidt, F. L., Shaffer, J. A., & Le, H. (2008). The Graduate Management Admission Test (GMAT) is even more valid than we thought: A new development in meta-analysis. *Academy of Management Learning & Education, 7*, 563–570.

Olea, M. M., & Ree, M. J. (1994). Predicting pilot and navigator criteria: Not much more than *g*. *Journal of Applied Psychology, 79*, 845–851.

Ones, D. S., Dilchert, S., & Viswesvaran, C. (2012). Cognitive abilities. *In* N. Schmitt (Ed.). *Handbook of Personnel Assessment and Selection* (pp. 179–224). Oxford: Oxford University Press.

Ones, D. S., Dilchert, S., Viswesvaran, C., & Salgado, J. F. (2010). Cognitive abilities. *In* N. Tippins & J. Farr (Eds.), *Handbook of Employee Selection* (pp. 255–275). New York: Routledge.

Pearlman, K., Schmidt, F. L., & Hunter, J. E. (1980). Validity generalization results for test used to predict job proficiency and training success in clerical occupations. *Journal of Applied Psychology, 65*, 569–607.

Pelser, M., Berg, Z. C., & Visser, D. (2005). The concurrent validity of learning potential and psychomotor ability measures for the selection of haul truck operators in an open-pit mine. *South African Journal of Industrial Psychology*, *31*, 58–70.

Pereira, F. M., Primi, R., & Cobêro, C. (2003). Validade de testes utilizados em seleçao de pessoal segundo recrutadores. *Psicologia: teoria e Prática*, *5*, 83–98.

Phillips, J. M., & Gully S. M. (2002). Fairness reactions to personnel selection techniques in Singapore and the United States. *International Journal of Human Resource Management*, *13*, 1186–1205.

Posthlethwite, B. E. (2011). Fluid ability, crystallized ability, and performance across multiple domains: A meta-analysis. Unpublished doctoral dissertation, University of Iowa, Iowa City.

Ree, M. J., & Carretta, T. R. (1998). General cognitive ability and occupational performance. *In* C. L. Cooper & I. T. Robertson (Eds.), *International Review of Industrial and Organizational Psychology* (Vol. *13*, pp. 159–184). London: Wiley.

Ree, M. J., & Earles, J. A. (1991). Predicting training success: Not much more than *g*. *Personnel Psychology*, *44*, 321–332.

Ree, M. J., Earles, J. A., & Teachout, M. (1994). Predicting job performance: Not much more than *g*. *Journal Applied Psychology*, *79*, 518–524.

Reeve, C. L., & Hackel, M. D. (2002). Asking the right questions about *g*. *Human Performance*, *15*, 47–74.

Reise, S. P., Moore, T. M., & Haviland, M. G. (2010). Bi-factor models and rotations: Exploring the extent to which multidimensional data yield univocal scale scores. *Journal of Personality Assessment*, *92*, 544–559.

Roberts, B. W., Harms, P.D., Caspi, A., & Moffit, T. E. (2005). Predicting the counterproductive employee in a child-to-adult prospective study. *Journal of Applied Psychology*, *92*, 1427–1436.

Rosales-Lopez, P. P. (2012). Uso del test de aptitudes mecánicas de MacQuarrie en la selección de personal para mejorar la productividad. Unpublished master's thesis, Universidad Nacional Mayor de San Marcos, Lima, Peru.

Roth, P. L., Bevier, C. A., Bobko, P., Witzer III, F. S., & Tyler, P. (2001). Ethnic group differences in cognitive ability in employment and educational settings: A meta-analysis. *Personnel Psychology*, *54*, 297–330.

Roth, P. L., Le, H., Oh, I.-S, Van Iddekinge, C. H., Buster, M. A., Robbins, S. B., & Campion, M. A. (2014). Differential validity for cognitive ability tests in employment and educational settings: Not much more than range restriction. *Journal of Applied Psychology*, *99*, 1–21.

Rothstein, H. R. (1990). Interrater reliability of job performance ratings: Growth to asymptote level with increasing opportunity to observe. *Journal of Applied Psychology*, *75*, 322–327.

Ryan, A. M., McFarland, L., Baron, H., & Page, R. (1999). An international look at selection practices: Nation and culture as explanations for variability in practice. *Personnel Psychology*, *52*, 359–391.

Sackett, P. R., Borneman, M. J., & Connelly, B. S. (2008). High stakes testing in higher education and employment: Appraising the evidence for validity and fairness. *American Psychologist*, *63*, 215–227.

Salgado, J. F. (1999). Personnel selection methods. *In* C. L. Cooper & I. T. Robertson (Eds.), *International Review of Industrial and Organizational Psychology*, *1999* (Vol. *14*, pp. 1–54). Chichester: Wiley.

Salgado, J. F. (2001). Some landmarks of 100 years of scientific personnel selection at the beginning of the new century. *International Journal of Selection and Assessment*, *9*, 3–8.

Salgado, J. F., & Anderson, N. (2002). Cognitive and GMA testing in the European Community: Issues and evidence. *Human Performance*, *15*, 75–96.

Salgado, J. F., & Anderson, N. (2003a). Validity generalization of GMA tests across countries in the European Community. *European Journal of Work and Organizational Psychology*, *12*, 1–17.

Salgado, J. F., & Anderson, N. A. (2003b). Homogeneity in diversity: GMA validity across countries in the European Community. *In* H. K. Sinangil, F. Avalone & A. Caetano (Eds.), *Homogeneity in Diversity*. London: Psychology Press.

Salgado, J. F., Anderson, N., & Hülsheger, U. R. (2010). Employee selection in Europe: Psychotechnics and the forgotten history of modern scientific employee selection. *In* N. Tippins & J. L. Farr (Eds.), *Handbook of Employee Selection* (pp. 921–941). New York: Routledge.

Salgado, J. F., Anderson, N., Moscoso, S., Bertua, C., & De Fruyt, F. (2003a). International validity generalization of GMA and cognitive abilities: A European Community meta-analysis. *Personnel Psychology*, *56*, 573–605.

Salgado, J. F., Anderson, N., Moscoso, S., Bertua, C., De Fruyt, F., & Rolland, J. P. (2003b). A meta-analytic study of general mental ability validity for different occupations in the European Community. *Journal of Applied Psychology, 88*, 1068–1081.

Salgado, J. F., Anderson, N., & Tauriz, G. (2015). The validity of ipsative and quasi-ipsative forced-choice personality inventories for different occupational groups: A comprehensive meta-analysis. *Journal of Occupational and Organizational Psychology, 88*, 797–834.

Salgado, J. F., & Moscoso, S. (1996). Meta-analysis of the interrater reliability of job performance ratings in validity studies of personnel selection. *Perceptual and Motor Skills, 83*, 1195–1201.

Salgado, J. F., Moscoso, S., & Berges, A. (2013). Conscientiousness, its facets, and the prediction of job performance ratings: Evidence against the narrow measures. *International Journal of Selection and Assessment, 21*, 74–84.

Salgado, J. F., Moscoso, S., Sanchez, J. I., Alonso, P., Choragwicka, B., & Berges, A. (2015). Validity of the five-factor model and their facets: The impact of performance measure and facet residualization on the bandwidth-fidelity debate. *European Journal of Work and Organizational Psychology, 24*, 1–25.

Salgado, J. F., Ones, D. S., & Viswesvaran, C. (2001). A new look at the predictors in personnel selection. In N. Anderson, D. S. Ones, H. K. Sinangil & C. Viswesvaran (Eds.), *International Handbook of Work and Organizational Psychology* (Vol. 1). London: Sage.

Salgado, J. F., & Tauriz, G. (2014). The five-factor model, forced-choice personality inventories and performance: A comprehensive meta-analysis of academic and occupational validity studies. *European Journal of Work and Organizational Psychology, 23*, 3–30.

Scherbaum, C. A., Goldstein, H. W., Yusko, K. P., Ryan, R., & Hanges, P. J. (2012). Intelligence 2.0: Reestablishing a research program on *g* in I-O psychology. *Industrial and Organizational Psychology: Perspectives on Science and Practice, 5*, 128–148.

Schmidt, F. L., & Hunter, J. E. (1977). Development of a general solution to the problem of validity generalization, *Journal of Applied Psychology, 62*, 529–540.

Schmidt, F. L., & Hunter, J. E. (1998). The validity and utility of selection methods in personnel psychology: Practical and theoretical implications of 85 years of research findings. *Psychological Bulletin, 124*, 262–274.

Schmidt, F. L., Hunter, J. E., & Caplan, J. R. (1981). Validity generalization results for two job groups in the petroleum industry. *Journal of Applied Psychology, 66*, 261–273.

Schmidt, F. L., Ones, D. S., & Hunter, J. E. (1992). Personnel selection. *Annual Review of Psychology, 43*, 671–710.

Schmitt, N. (2014). Personality and cognitive ability as predictors of effective performance at work. *Annual Review of Organizational Psychology and Organizational Behavior, 1*, 45–65.

Schmitt, N., Clause, C., & Pulakos, E. (1996). Subgroup differences associated with different measures of some common job relevant constructs. In C. L. Cooper & I. T. Robertson (Eds.), *International Review of Industrial and Organizational Psychology* (Vol. 11, pp. 115–140). Chichester: Wiley.

Schmitt, N., & Fandre, J. (2008). Validity of selection procedures. In S. Cartwright & C. L. Cooper (Eds.), *The Oxford Handbook of Personnel Psychology* (pp. 163–192). Oxford: Oxford University Press.

Schmitt, N., Gooding, R. Z., Noe, R. A., & Kirsch, M. (1984). Meta-analyses of validity studies published between 1964 and 1982 and the investigation of study characteristics. *Personnel Psychology, 37*, 407–422.

Scroggins, W. A., Benson, P. G., Cross, C., & Gilbreath, B. (2008). Reactions to selection methods: An international comparison. *International Journal of Management, 25*, 203–216.

Shackleton, V., & Newell, S. (1994). European management selection methods: A comparison of five countries. *International Journal of Selection and Assessment, 2*, 91–104.

Sidaviciute, S. (2008). Attitudes toward personnel selection methods in Lithuanian and Swedish samples. Unpublished master's thesis. Växjö University, Lithuania.

Snyder, C., & Shahani-Denning, C. (2012). Fairness reactions to personnel selection methods: A look at professionals in Mumbai. *International Journal of Selection and Assessment, 20*, 297–307.

Society for Industrial and Organizational Psychology (2003). *Principles for Validation and Use of Personnel Selection Procedures*. Bowling Green, OH: SIOP.

Spearman, C. (1904). General intelligence, objectively determined and measured. *American Journal of Psychology, 15*, 201–293.

Spearman, C. (1927). *The Abilities of Man. Their Nature and Measurement*. London: Macmillan.

Steiner, D. I., & Gilliland, S. W. (1996). Fairness reactions to personnel selection techniques in France and the United States. *Journal of Applied Psychology, 81*, 124–141.

Stern, W. (1912). *Die Psychologischenmethoden der Inteligezprüfung*. Berlin, Germany [in English: *The Psychological Methods of Testing Intelligence*. Trans. G. M. Whipple. Baltimore, MD: Warwick, 1914].

Sternberg, R. J., & Detterman, D. K. (1986). *What is Intelligence? Contemporary Viewpoints on its Nature and Definition*. New York: Abblex Publishing.

Stinglhamber, F., Vandenberghe, C., & Brancart, S. (1999). Les réactions des candidats envers les techniques de selection du personnel: Une étude dans un contexte francophone [Reactions of job applicants to personnel selection techniques: An investigation in a French-speaking context]. *Le Travail Humain, 62*, 347–361.

Strachan, E. J. (2008). APIL-SV as a predictor of job performance in a South African financial consulting firm. Unpublished master's thesis. University of Cape Town, South Africa.

Swineford, F. (1949). General, verbal, and spatial bi-factors after three years. *Journal of Educational Psychology, 40*, 353–360.

Taylor, P., Keelty, Y., & McDonnell, B. (2002). Evolving personnel selection practices in New Zealand organisations and recruitment firms. *New Zealand Journal of Psychology, 31*, 8–18.

Taylor, P. J., Mills, A., & O'Driscoll, M. P. (1993). Personnel selection methods used by New Zealand organizations and personnel consulting firms. *New Zealand Journal of Psychology, 22*, 19–31.

te Nijenhuis, J., & van der Flier, H. (1997). Comparability of GATB scores for immigrants and majority group members: Some Dutch findings. *Journal of Applied Psychology, 82*, 675–687.

Thadeu, S. H., & Ferreira, M. C. (2013). The validity of psychological assessment in a selection process in the area of public safety. *Revista Iberoamericana de Diagnóstico y Evaluación*, 117–145.

Thomson, G. H. (1916). A hierarchy without a general factor. *British Journal of Psychology, 8*, 271–281.

Thomson, G. H. (1919). On the cause of hierarchical order among the correlation coefficients of a number of variates taken in pairs. *Proceedings of the Royal Society of London A, 95*, 400–408.

Thomson, G. H. (1951). *The Factorial Analysis of Human Ability* (3rd ed.). London: University of London Press.

Thurstone, L. L. (1924). *The Nature of Intelligence*. New York: Harcourt Brace.

Thurstone, L. L. (1938). *Primary Mental Abilities*. Chicago: University of Chicago Press.

Thurstone, L. L., & Thurstone, T. G. (1941). *Factorial Studies of Intelligence*. Chicago: University of Chicago Press.

Tonindandel, S., & LeBreton, J. M. (2011). Relative importance analysis: A useful supplement to regression analysis. *Journal of Business and Psychology, 26*, 1–9.

van der Maas, H. L. J., Dolan, C. V., Grasman, R. P. P. P., Wilcherts, J. M., Huizenga, H. M., & Raajmakers, M. E. J. (2006). A dynamical model of general intelligence: The positive manifold of intelligence by mutualism. *Psychological Review, 13*, 842–860.

Vasilopoulos, N. L., Cucina, J. M., Dyomina, N. V., Morewitz, C. L., & Reilly, R. R. (2006). Forced-choice personality tests: A measure of personality and cognitive ability? *Human Performance, 19*, 175–199.

Vernon, P. E. (1957). *The Structure of Human Abilities*. New York: Wiley.

Vernon, P. E. (1971). *The Structure of Human Abilities* (3rd ed.). New York: Wiley.

Vinchur, A. J., & Koppes, L. L. (2011). A historical survey of research and practice in industrial and organizational psychology. In S. Zedeck (Ed.), *APA Handbook of Industrial and Organizational Psychology. Building and Developing the Organization* (Vol. 1, pp. 3–36). Washington, DC: American Psychological Association.

Vinchur, A. K., & Koppes-Bryan, L. L. (2012). A history of personnel selection and assessment. *In* N. Schmitt (Ed.), *Personnel Assessment and Selection* (pp. 9–30). New York: Oxford University Press.

Viswesvaran, C., Ones, D. S., & Schmidt, F. L. (1996). Comparative analysis of the reliability of job performance ratings. *Journal of Applied Psychology, 81*, 557–574. doi: 10.1037/0021-9010.81.4.557.

Woolley, A. W., Chabris, C. F., Pentland, A., Hasmi, N., & Malone, T. W. (2010). Evidence for a collective intelligence factor in the performance of human groups. *Science, 330*, 686–688.

8

Using Personality Questionnaires for Selection

David J. Hughes and Mark Batey

Introduction

Employee selection is the process of choosing which member(s) of an applicant pool is (are) most likely to behave in a manner that will achieve or surpass organizationally defined metrics of success, such as selling products direct to consumers, preventing crime, building and nurturing business-to-business relationships, caring for the sick and educating or inspiring others to perform to the best of their ability. The definition of successful job performance varies greatly across roles and organizations. Thus, while some elements of behaviour are important for all jobs (e.g., exertion of effort), it is likely that many other behavioural patterns will be suited to performance in some roles but not others. This straightforward observation has led to a broad consensus from industry and academia that personality testing, which as we discuss below is the fundamental descriptor of human behaviour, should be useful during selection programmes. However, whether and to what extent personality is useful remains a contested issue (see Morgeson, Campion, Dipboye, Hollenbeck, Murphy & Schmitt, 2007a; Ones, Dilchert, Viswesvaran & Judge, 2007). In this chapter we critically consider the evidence regarding the use of personality assessments in selection.

We begin by setting the scene of personality test use in selection before defining personality, considering why it should be of value in selection and briefly considering how we arrived at the current state of knowledge in personality research generally. We then examine the predictive validity evidence for personality in selection, considering personality as a single predictor of job performance and as a part of a broader selection programme. We then explore debates regarding what level of the personality hierarchy (broad factors vs. narrow traits) is more useful during selection, whether universal job performance exists or whether different jobs require different behaviours and thus nuanced personality assessment, and we consider the potential utility of 'other ratings' of personality. We then move on from predictive validity and discuss how and when personality measures might be

The Wiley Blackwell Handbook of the Psychology of Recruitment, Selection and Employee Retention,
First Edition. Edited by Harold W. Goldstein, Elaine D. Pulakos, Jonathan Passmore and Carla Semedo.
© 2017 John Wiley & Sons Ltd. Published 2020 by John Wiley & Sons Ltd.

used within a selection programme. Finally, we suggest areas of research that offer great promise for improving our understanding, and subsequently evidence-based practice within selection.

Setting the Scene

There are three key stakeholders in the personality–selection domain: academia, organizations and test publishers. In principle, these three stakeholders share one objective: to produce and use assessments that are reliable and valid. However, each constituency possesses potentially conflicting drives and foci, which have led to some disarray in the development and use of personality assessments in selection.

Academics have a primary interest in understanding the nature, theory and structure of personality. A focus on considering what personality is and what it is not, how it is structured, the processes underlying personality observations and the nomological net that informs our understanding of how different aspects of personality and other individual difference constructs relate. Organizations have a primary interest in using personality assessments to deliver a return on investment. A focus is what predicts both productive and counterproductive behaviour and performance in organizational contexts. Finally, test publishers hold a primary interest in commercializing personality assessments thereby making money from personality measures – a focus on what is marketable and useable by those willing to pay for their assessments.

The result is a marketplace where the tools that organizations use are often at odds with the theoretical foundations prized by academics. Further, in an effort to present what appears to be either a unique or similar product, test publishers produce tools that possess the same trait labels, but measure different constructs, or tools with different trait labels that measure the same constructs. This is often referred to as the 'Jingle Jangle Fallacy' (Kelley, 1927; Thorndike, 1904). Ultimately, these trends stifle scientific progress and lead to confusion for practitioners and organizations, neither knowing which personality measures, if any, to use. What we have in the case of personality in selection is a classic example of a scientist/practitioner divide and often a lack of evidence-based practice (Rynes, Gyluk & Brown, 2007). The most theoretically and empirically valid measures are often passed over for less-grounded counterparts, with many test publishers failing to publish their validity studies and others simply not conducting them. These issues muddy the waters when we attempt to assess the utility of personality measures in selection. It is far beyond the scope of this chapter to put an end to this confusion, but we can at least start to address some of the important issues regarding how useful personality testing really is and, perhaps most importantly, what we can do to maximize its utility.

What is Personality?

Before discussing personality in selection we must first clarify what we mean by personality. Personality has been variously defined as: 'One's habits and usual style' (Cronbach, 1984, p. 6); 'a dynamic organization, inside the person, of psychophysical systems that create the person's characteristic patterns of behaviours, thoughts and feelings' (Allport, 1961, p. 11); 'a person's unique pattern of traits' (Guildford, 1959, p. 5); and 'relatively stable, internal factors, which produce consistent individual differences at the emotional and motivational level' (Pervin & John, 2001, p. 4).

A single definition would never satisfy all stakeholders. However, a review of definitions reveals that certain features are agreed. Personality is seen as a relatively stable and consistent set of traits that interact with environmental factors to produce emotional, cognitive and behavioural responses. Such theoretical views are supported by empirical evidence that shows that there are numerous identifiable personality traits (Cattell, 1954) with some cross-situation stability (Funder & Ozer, 1983; Mischel, 1968), and develop through maturation (e.g., conscientiousness and emotional stability increase with age), while demonstrating relative and rank-order consistency in adulthood (Roberts & DelVecchio, 2000; Roberts & Mroczek, 2008). Importantly, measures of personality traits can be used to explain and predict a wide range of behaviours and outcomes both cross-sectionally (Roberts, Kuncel, Shiner, Caspi & Goldberg, 2007) and longitudinally (Chamorro-Premuzic & Furnham, 2003).

For the purposes of this chapter we suggest that personality be defined as a collection of traits that influence a person's typical thought patterns (e.g., how deeply one considers the elements of a task), feelings (e.g., how anxious one is when faced with deadlines) and behaviour (e.g., how organized one is). There are three main assumptions with regard to the nature of personality traits that we adopt: 1) they are relatively stable (we discuss this further below); 2) each individual has a unique constellation of traits; and 3) they drive behaviour. Each of these assumptions is vital if personality is to predict behaviour at work.

Why should personality be relevant at work?

Given the broad agreement that personality is in part responsible for emotional, cognitive and behavioural responses, it must be relevant for the prediction of conduct at work. Workplace behaviour is not only defined in terms of what we *can* do (ability) but also *how* (style) we do it. Some people work systematically, others more haphazardly; some communicate empathetically, others in an authoritarian style; some are resilient under pressure, others appear less so. Is it possible to achieve the same level of performance regardless of these differences in style? Perhaps. Nevertheless, the manner in which tasks are conducted is undoubtedly important at work.

No employee or organization can operate in a vacuum. From a single person start-up, through to a multinational corporation, people must interact with others. Personality has a notable role in determining the quality and utility of these interactions. Indeed, 'personality clashes' are an often-cited cause of workplace conflict and finding like-minded colleagues is an often-cited contributor to job satisfaction.

Personality relates to the degree of enjoyment we take from certain elements of work and thus how much motivation we have to carry out certain tasks (Ackerman, 2000). For example, if employees are socially anxious and fearful of a negative evaluation, they will be less motivated to speak publicly. If they are particularly anxious, it might even reduce the quality of the communication and thus influence their job performance. Even if they are able to manage anxiety within the presentation effectively, the emotional labour and additional effects of the task on energy levels, well-being and subsequent performance could be considerable. If, however, an employee enjoys being in the limelight and finds performing a presentation is a fun opportunity to relish, it is likely that job satisfaction and performance will be higher.

In sum, personality influences how we approach a task, how we interact with others and how natural or enjoyable we find a task or environment. Different approaches to these aspects of working life may well influence job performance, yet even if they do not, variations in these three areas are still pivotal to a wide range of other organizational variables (organizational commitment, citizenship behaviour, tenure, employee relations, etc.).

Trait, State or Type?

Above, we assumed that personality is the product of a constellation of traits, yet a number of personality models and measures conceptualize personality through 'types' (e.g., Myers-Briggs type indicator; Myers, 1978). Personality types posit people as members of distinct and discontinuous categories (Carver & Scheier, 1996); for example, a person is either an extravert or an introvert. Typologies are suggested to have useful features, most notably that they are relatively simple to grasp, which can be beneficial when discussing personality with non-expert individuals, as we often do within organizations. Type approaches are often contrasted with the trait view of personality, which suggests that an individual can fall on a continuum for each trait, so that positioning towards either extreme of the continuum is indicative of a stronger tendency to think, feel or behave in that manner. A person is not simply extraverted or introverted, but rather is positioned somewhere along a scale ranging between the two extremes. A simple consideration of human personality and behaviour favours a continuum approach over a type approach: people do differ in their level of extraversion (or indeed any other trait) and are not simply one type or another. For this reason alone, we can say that trait theories are more valid than typologies. Typologies come under further scrutiny when we consider the measures designed to assess them. For example, the MBTI, despite being widely used, lacks internal consistency, test–retest reliability and predictive validity (Pittenger, 2005). Thus, due to poor reliability and questionable validity, the current authors recommend that regardless (or perhaps because) of their simplicity, typologies be treated with caution in all organizational contexts, and under no circumstances should be used for selection. That this point still needs to be raised is testament to the gulf between science and practice we raised in the introduction to this chapter.

A similarly contested yet more nuanced debate of real relevance to the personality in selection discussion relates to personality stability and the influence of situational variables. The extreme explanations that all behaviour is a product of the environment (if this were true no cross-situational consistency would exist) or that traits alone explain everything (if this were true any cross-situational variability would not exist) are inadequate. Indeed, both situational variables and traits can be of equal relevance to explaining any single behaviour. Often, traits share only modest correlations (0.3) with behaviour (Mischel, 1968), as do situational variables (Funder & Ozer, 1983).

Thus, behaviour is not simply the product of either traits or the environment. Rather, most behaviour is the product of complex trait × state interactions, whereby the influence of the trait tends to be greater than that of the state in circumstances where situational pressures are weak, and vice versa (e.g., Carver & Scheier, 1996; Judge & Zapata, 2015; Monson, Hesley & Chernick, 1982). Thus, the influence of personality traits differs across scenarios. Despite the role of situational variables, what we can conclude is that traits do predict behavioural patterns across situations and time (e.g., Feist & Barron, 2003); those who score high on measures of anxiety tend to be more anxious than those who score low on anxiety across situations. Such consistency is essential; without it, personality would not be a relevant construct to consider in a selection equation.

Identifying and organizing personality traits

Models of personality as they stand today are largely the result of work in two parallel traditions: the lexical and psychometric. The lexical hypothesis (Galton, 1869) suggests that if a trait is important in influencing how we think, feel and act, it will be enshrined in language; the more important the trait, the more likely that it will be encoded in language in a single adjective. Thus, researchers scoured dictionaries and psychological theories and compiled lists of adjectives that describe personality (see Allport & Odbert, 1936; Baumgarten, 1933; Cattell, 1943; Galton, 1869). This iterative work eventually culminated in the development of Cattell's bipolar personality–descriptor scales. These scales represent the foundations of many currently held trait measures of personality and served to generate, through numerous factor analyses, Cattell's 16PF, which is today widely used in selection.

Early attempts to replicate Cattell's work were not wholly successful, with numerous researchers finding that five broad personality traits consistently emerged from factor analyses of personality ratings (Borgatta, 1964; Fiske, 1949; Norman, 1963; Tupes & Christal, 1961). Further work in the area of personality structure continued to point towards five broad factors and as a result led to the general consensus that 'analyses of any reasonably large sample of English trait adjectives in either self- or peer descriptions will elicit a variant of the Big-Five structure' (Goldberg, 1990, p. 1223).

Today there are two main variants of these five traits: the lexical Big Five and the psychometric five-factor model (FFM). The five factors are neuroticism, extraversion, openness-to-experience (intellect in the lexical Big Five), agreeableness and conscientiousness (Costa & McCrae, 1992; for a historical description of the emergence of the five factors, see Digman, 1990). Despite some rather substantial differences in item content and structural relations between the two models (e.g., the trait warmth is considered a facet of extraversion in the FFM but a facet of agreeableness in the Big Five), researchers and practitioners often conflate the two and use them interchangeably (Pace & Brannick, 2010). These differences are often given only cursory discussion but are potentially critical in a selection environment. For example, if evidence from a job analysis or research literature suggests warmth is one of the most important behavioural characteristics of a care worker, how much emphasis is placed on extraversion or agreeableness in the selection equation should depend on which inventory is being used. This example also draws on another important debate that we will note here and consider in detail later. The bandwidth fidelity argument concerns the question of whether narrower personality traits (e.g., warmth) or broader factors (e.g., agreeableness) are more useful in predicting behaviour. Ultimately, this debate contrasts the measurement specificity one can gain using narrow traits versus the superior reliability one can get from a broader trait. Equally, it is suggested that predictors and outcomes should be matched in specificity, so when predicting complex and aggregate outcome variables such as job performance, complex and aggregate personality variables would be best.

Despite the differences between the two five-factor approaches, there is a considerable amount of evidence in favour of the broad five factors. In particular, the psychometric FFM, which is argued to be 'exhaustive of the personality sphere' (McCrae & Costa, 1985, p. 558), is the most dominant measurement framework in research. The widespread adoption of the FFM has undoubtedly benefited personality research. The FFM provides a parsimonious model to guide the accumulation of research findings, allowing for cross-study comparison and accelerating knowledge production. The ability to empirically aggregate research findings has ultimately resulted in the generation of meta-analytically derived estimates of magnitude of prediction (e.g., Barrick & Mount, 1991, 1996; Barrick, Mount & Judge, 2001; Judge & Ilies, 2002). Meta-analyses of the personality–job performance relationship are very important in understanding the role personality can play in selection.

Despite the popularity of the FFM, the adequacy of the model and even the fundamental notion that five broad orthogonal factors top the personality hierarchy, is frequently contested. Briefly, there are valid concerns of both a theoretical and methodological nature with regard to the development of the five-factor measures (e.g., Block, 1995, 2001, 2010). Further, research has been inconsistent in returning five factors from structural analyses (Booth & Hughes, 2014), and where five factors have been identified there has been debate as to whether or not these five factors are consistent (Pace & Brannick, 2010). In addition, the FFM does not fit in confirmatory factor analyses (Vassend & Skrondal, 2011) or less restrictive exploratory structural equation models (Booth & Hughes, 2014; Marsh, Lüdtke, Muthén, Asparouhov, Morin, Trautwein & Nagengast, 2010), suggesting that the models are in need of some revision. These concerns may seem like excessive academic navel-gazing, but quite simply if the measures do not offer optimal measurement, they are unlikely to produce optimal prediction. As a result, concerns of a structural nature are of utmost importance to personality in the selection debate.

A further consideration relates to claims of the exhaustive nature of the FFM. This is simply not the case. Many investigations have focused on traits that fall outside the FFM (Ashton, Lee & Son, 2000; Jackson, Ashton & Tomes, 1996; Jackson, Paunonen, Fraboni & Goffin, 1996; Lee & Ashton, 2004; Lee, Ashton, Hong & Park, 2000). Some of this research has led to the development of the HEXACO model, a six-factor model with more facets than the FFM. There is also ample evidence of narrow, facet-level personality traits being omitted. For example, Paunonen and Jackson (2000) noted that traits of conventionality, egotistical, integrity, femininity, seductiveness, manipulativeness, humour, thriftiness and religiosity were missing. From a cursory perspective, one can see that these traits might be of value in explaining some workplace behaviours. Further, these traits offered incremental predictive validity over and above the FFM in relation to 19 criteria across samples from Canada, England, Germany and Finland (Paunonen, Haddock, Forsterling & Keinonen, 2003).

There are three main concerns to be recapped here. First, the FFM was not developed in a theoretically or methodologically optimal manner. Second, FFM measures often provide suboptimal measurement. Third, the FFM is not exhaustive and the traits it excludes might be of value in selection. These limitations do not preclude the use of the FFM in selection, but we must keep them in mind when evaluating the evidence pertaining to the predictive validity of personality in selection. It is also important to note that these concerns are not exclusive to the FFM. Many other broad personality measures offer poor measurement and miss (or incorrectly model) important aspects of personality.

What Does the Evidence Say about the Utility of Personality within Selection?

When considering the role of personality in selection one question is of utmost importance: is the tool a valid predictor of relevant work-related criteria? Usually, the focus is on job performance, but it can also span other important related criteria (e.g., training performance, counterproductive work behaviour, citizenship behaviour). This section addresses the vexed question: what does empirical research say about the use of personality measures during personnel selection?

In 2007 a series of well-respected organizational researchers considered the use of personality in selection and concluded that 'Due to the low validity and content of some items, many published self-report personality tests should probably not be used for personnel selection' (Morgeson et al., 2007a, p. 720). In direct response, Ones and colleagues (2007, p. 1020) argued, 'Any selection decision that does not take the key personality characteristics of job applicants into account would be deficient.' Clearly, the jury on the utility of personality measures is still out.

The use of personality measures in selection remains a contested subject and the literature has been reviewed, in compelling fashion, to support both sides of the debate. There is evidence to suggest that personality measures can be useful, but the same evidence tends to suggest that their utility is limited. The current authors believe that the evidence shows personality can add value to selection decisions, but only if used appropriately. In this section, we discuss the evidence for and against the predictive validity of personality in selection, but we also address the perhaps most compelling aspect of this discussion: how can we maximize the utility of personality measures?

Predictive validity: Meta-analyses

The interpretation of meta-analytic correlations between personality ratings and job performance, often assessed by supervisor ratings, is central to the debate regarding the use of personality during selection. Before we look at some of those relationships, we must note that there are two main estimates of the correlation between personality and job performance: a raw correlation and a corrected correlation. Within a meta-analysis it is common practice to adjust or correct correlation coefficients based on estimates of unreliability. Often, there is an acknowledgement that the criterion variables (e.g., job performance metrics) and sometimes the predictor variables (in this case personality) lack reliability, and as a result attenuate the estimated relationship. Corrections increase the accuracy of population-level estimates of correlations and are well supported both theoretically and statistically (Hunter & Schmidt, 2004; Schmidt, Shaffer & Oh, 2008).

When addressing arguments or building theories and models, the more accurate our empirical estimates are the better. Nevertheless, despite the well-accepted practice of correcting correlations in meta-analyses, practitioners generally do not correct estimates in selection decisions (Morgeson et al., 2007a). Thus, there is a good argument for considering the magnitude and pattern of relationships of both the uncorrected and corrected estimates. In this chapter, we present both estimates where applicable.

In 1991, Barrick and Mount published a seminal paper describing the meta-analysis of 117 American and Canadian studies (undertaken between 1952 and 1988; $N=23,994$). Conscientiousness proved a reliable and valid correlate of job performance across occupations ($r=0.13$, corrected $r=0.23$). The remaining traits (extraversion, neuroticism, agreeableness and openness to experience) were unrelated to job performance *en masse*. Barrick and Mount (1991) examined the correlations between the Big Five and a composite variable of job performance, training performance and personnel data (e.g., salary, tenure) in the whole sample, but also provided estimates for different job roles. Once again, conscientiousness proved a valid and reliable predictor across all roles ($r=0.09–0.13$, corrected $r=0.20–0.23$). Extraversion was found to be relevant for those in sales ($r=0.09$, corrected $r=0.15$) or managerial roles ($r=0.11$, corrected $r=0.18$), while the other traits were generally unrelated. In a European equivalent, Salgado (1997) convergently found conscientiousness to be a valid and generalized predictor across occupations and performance criteria with a very similar magnitude of correlation coefficients. Divergently, Salgado reported a role for neuroticism ($r=-0.08$, corrected $r=-0.12$) across all occupational groups, which corresponds with other meta-analyses (Hough, Eaton, Dunnette, Kamp & McCloy, 1990). Again, in line with Barrick and Mount (1991), Salgado found that the other personality traits were not relevant to job performance but were relevant to some other important organizational criteria (e.g., training performance) in specific occupational groups.

The most compelling study examining the relationship between the Big Five traits and job performance was a meta-analysis of meta-analyses conducted by Barrick, Mount and Judge (2001). Conscientiousness was found to be important across occupational groups in terms of job performance (objective rating: $r=0.10$, corrected $r=0.23$; supervisor rating: $r=0.15$, corrected $r=0.31$) and all other job-relevant criteria examined. Neuroticism was also shown to be a generalizable predictor of supervisor-rated job performance ($r=-0.07$, corrected $r=-0.13$) but was lower in magnitude than conscientiousness and less consistent across the other criteria examined. Thus, a relatively firm conclusion can be made that conscientiousness is important for performance in all roles, and that in most instances lower levels of neuroticism are also related to improved performance. The three remaining traits, while not relevant to job performance across occupations, can be relevant in certain roles, for example management (extraversion: $r=0.10$, corrected $r=0.21$), and are related to specific work-related behaviours such as training performance (openness to experience: $r=0.14$, corrected $r=0.33$) and team working (agreeableness: $r=0.17$, corrected $r=0.34$).

Thus, decades of meta-analyses have now shown that working in an organized, responsible and industrious manner (conscientiousness), while maintaining a degree of emotional stability (neuroticism), is related to successful job performance across the board. Some researchers (and indeed practitioners) have argued that while evidence of some generally stable patterns of association between personality traits and job performance are informative, the magnitude of the relationships raises some serious questions (Guion & Gottier, 1965; Morgeson et al., 2007a). Indeed, with uncorrected rs of -0.10–0.15 and even corrected rs of -0.20 -0.30 the predictive validity of personality measures is roughly equivalent to many selection methods broadly considered unusable within selection (e.g., unstructured interviews, Schmidt & Hunter, 1998).

At a cursory level, we have to agree with Morgeson and colleagues (2007a). These results do pose serious questions about the utility of personality within selection. The current authors would certainly feel uncomfortable being selected, or not, based on our conscientiousness and neuroticism alone. However, we must travel beyond a cursory level and consider a number of important and substantial nuances within the personality–selection debate before we reach any firm conclusions. The remainder of this section focuses on five important nuances within this debate. First, when considering the personality of potential employees we rarely, if ever, focus on a single trait. Thus, we must look at the combined explanatory power of multiple personality traits not just univariate correlations. Second, selection by personality alone (or indeed any single selection method) would be indefensible. Thus, we must consider the relative and incremental explanatory power of personality when considered alongside other valid selection tools. Third, broad factors of personality, such as the FFM/Big Five, currently dominate personality assessment; we consider whether they offer superior levels of prediction compared to their constituent lower-order facets. Fourth, we contest the very premise of universal job performance: that successful job performance across occupational roles should or would require the same degree and combination of behaviours seems an odd assumption, one that has perhaps masked the true potential of personality in the prediction of job performance. Fifth, we consider long-standing concerns about the measurement error produced by response distortions during personality assessment with a special focus on the potential utility of partially ipsative measures and 'other ratings'.

Personality is multidimensional

Behaviour is complex. In seeking to explain complex behaviours at work (or anywhere else), we rarely expect a single trait to be sufficient. Rather, we identify multiple traits that might contribute and examine their combined ability to explain the behaviour of interest. Thus, univariate relationships between individual personality traits and job performance may underestimate the value that personality has to offer. In the same way we would not calculate the predictive validity of a structured interview or cognitive ability test based on their constituent parts, we should not judge personality based on single trait associations.

This line of argument has been most convincingly put forward by Ones and colleagues (2007), who re-examined the meta-analytic correlations presented by Barrick and colleagues (2001; discussed above) and computed the multiple correlations for all of the Big Five and job performance. The results show that personality predicts objective job performance with a multiple r of 0.27 (uncorrected $r=0.23$) and a composite overall job performance variable of $r=0.23$ (uncorrected $r=0.20$). Ones and colleagues (2007) also demonstrated that personality variables measured at the Big Five level are even more predictive of other important elements of workplace behaviour. For example, counter-productive work behaviours ($r=0.44$ and 0.45 for avoiding interpersonal and organizational deviance, respectively), organizational citizenship behaviours ($r=0.31$), leadership ($r=0.45$), teamwork ($r=0.37$) and training performance ($r=0.40$).

There is no doubt that Ones and colleagues' (2007) evidence provides a much more optimistic view of the role of personality in understanding workplace behaviour. Notably, however, and despite increases from the univariate estimates, the multivariate estimates relating to job performance – the crucial criterion for selection decisions – are still less than impressive. Indeed, the multivariate estimate is only slightly greater than that reported for conscientiousness alone (Barrick et al., 2001) and collectively the Big Five account for around 5–7% of variance in job performance measures. Thus, some have argued that these results still provide underwhelming support for the use of personality in selection (Morgeson et al., 2007b). Again, we generally agree, explaining the same amount of variance in job performance as unreliable selection methods such as unstructured interviews is hardly compelling. However, we do not believe that this means that personality tests are not or cannot be useful. Below, we continue to consider the ways in which personality assessments can be used effectively within selection.

Incremental predictive validity of personality measures

Selection decisions are never made based on personality assessments alone and nor should they be. Given that personality assessments are used as a part of a selection programme, the practical value of any validity debate pertains to the incremental predictive validity that personality assessments offer over and above other selection methods. Personality tends to be weakly correlated with other selection tools, and in particular other individual difference variables such as cognitive ability. For example, in their meta-analysis, Judge, Jackson, Shaw, Scott and Rich (2007) show that the correlations between general mental ability and the Big Five are small, with the largest correlation being just 0.22 with openness. Thus, personality and cognitive ability measures capture different information about an employee and thus personality measures may offer unique predictive validity beyond that obtained from cognitive ability measures.

Schmidt and Hunter (1998) estimated the incremental predictive validity of 18 selection methods beyond general mental ability using data from previous meta-analyses. Their analyses suggested that, when combined with general mental ability, the personality measures of integrity (a compound trait consisting of specific traits selected due to their likely relevance, e.g., conscientiousness, dependability, honesty) and conscientiousness offered 27% (multiple $r=0.65$) and 18% (multiple $r=0.60$) increases in prediction respectively. The only other methods to offer similar levels of incremental predictive validity were structured interviews and work samples (both multiple $r=0.63$), which are typically more expensive and time-consuming to construct and administer than personality assessments.

Given the positivity of these results, it surprising that little additional empirical study has followed. In 2006, Rothstein and Goffin, when reviewing personality and selection, found only two studies examining this question, one demonstrating that personality assessments offer incremental predictive validity over an assessment centre when predicting managerial potential (Goffin, Rothstein & Johnston, 1996) and the second showing personality supplements biodata in predicting job performance (McManus & Kelly, 1999).

In the years following Rothstein and Goffin's (2006) review a number of researchers have addressed this issue. In 2014, Oh and colleagues examined the incremental predictive validity of the Big Five and honesty–humility over and above cognitive ability when predicting task-based performance and also contextual performance (the extent to which employees support non-performance-related organizational and psychosocial aspects of work) of 217 military officer candidates. In relation to task-based performance, both cognitive ability ($\beta = 0.25$), and conscientiousness ($\beta = 0.34$) were significant predictors, with personality accounting for a 0.22 increase in the multiple correlation. When considering contextual performance, cognitive ability was not a significant predictor but the personality traits of conscientiousness ($\beta = 0.32$), extraversion ($\beta = 0.16$), and honesty-humility ($\beta = 0.13$) were, and collectively produced a multiple r of 0.37. (The figures presented here are the uncorrected estimates; the corrected estimates provided by Oh and colleagues (2014) show no deviation from this pattern but are generally increased in magnitude by around 0.1–0.15.) Similar results were reported by Colodro, Garcés-de-los-Fayos, López-García and Colodro-Conde (2015), who showed that personality traits (assessed using the Spanish 16PF) accounted for incremental predictive validity beyond cognitive ability, with personality explaining three times as much variance in performance.

Despite the positive trend in the incremental validity literature, a recent advance in meta-analytic corrections suggests that the increment offered might only be, on average, in the region of 5% variance explained (Schmidt, Shaffer & Oh, 2008). Nevertheless, personality does offer somewhere in the region of a 5–30% increase in predictive validity. Whether the validity is towards the upper of lower estimates will depend on the characteristics of the role and the quality and job relevance of the personality measurement.

Clearly, personality offers novel and useful information that can improve selection decisions regardless of whether assessments focus on task performance or broader definitions of performance. The incremental predictive validity offered by personality measures is particularly valuable to organizations because, in comparison to work samples, role-plays or structured interviews, personality scales can be purchased and administered in a time- and cost-effective manner.

Broad factors or narrow traits

Personality models generally build from large item pools, through facets to higher-order factors. For example, each of the Big Five factors as measured by the NEO-PI-R subsumes six narrower facets/traits, each measured by eight items. It has been suggested that there is little added value in measuring narrow facets, when the five broad factors account for much of the variance in their lower-order constituents. For instance, Ones and Viswesvaran (1996) have argued that the direct measurement of broad personality factors alone is sufficient, and in the case where the outcome variable is itself broad or complex (e.g., job performance), preferable, as they suggest predictor and outcome variables of similar bandwidth give optimal prediction.

However, this approach is also the subject of debate, with suggestions that regardless of the bandwidth of the outcome, narrow traits still offer important insights. Lower-order facets and the broad factors supposed to subsume them are not perfectly correlated; facet measures possess specific and reliable (non-random) variance that might offer increased predictive validity (Paunonen et al., 2003), which is lost when using broad factors.

A number of studies have empirically assessed the predictive validity offered by broad factors and narrow facets. The conclusion is that narrow facets consistently offer better and/or incremental predictive validity regardless of the complexity of the behavioural outcomes (Ashton, Jackson, Paunonen, Helmes & Rothstein, 1995; Jenkins & Griffith, 2004; Lounsbury, Sundstrom, Loveland & Gibson, 2003; Paunonen & Ashton, 2001; Rothstein, Paunonen, Rush & King, 1994; Tett, Steele & Beauregard, 2003; Timmerman, 2006).

Perhaps the most compelling evidence for the superiority of narrow facets when predicting job performance comes from Judge, Rodell, Klinger, Simon and Crawford's (2013) meta-analysis of 1,176 studies derived from 410 independent samples. Judge and colleagues examined the relationships between three hierarchical levels of personality and task performance, contextual performance and an overall composite performance variable. At the highest level of the trait hierarchy were the Big Five factors. At the next level, each factor split into two mid-level factors consistent with the framework derived by DeYoung, Quilty and Peterson (2007). At the lowest level of the hierarchy, each factor split into the six facets defined by FFM framework (Costa & McCrae, 1992).

Judge and colleagues' (2013) meta-analysis reveals that optimally weighted composites of facets resulted in greater criterion-related validity for predicting all performance outcomes than did the Big Five factors, often accounting for 3 or 4 times more variance in performance. With the exception of conscientiousness, which showed similar predictive validity at all three levels, there was a clear pattern of facets outperforming the De Young factors, which were in turn better than the Big Five, so providing clear evidence that the broader the factor the weaker the prediction. A summary of the correlations is shown in Table 8.1.

The muddying effect of aggregating personality facets into broad factors is detrimental to predictive validity. For example, when considering task-based performance, neuroticism at the Big Five level and facet level accounted for 0.7% and 6.4% of variance, respectively. One might conclude that 6.4% is not particularly impressive, but as an incremental addition to other personality traits and other selection methods such as cognitive ability it might prove very useful. Another stark example of the obscuring effect of broad factors is observed in the extraversion to contextual performance link where the facets accounted for 24.1% of variance compared to just 5.4% for the DeYoung factors and 4.8% for the Big Five factor.

Table 8.1 Correlations between personality at three levels of aggregation and overall, task, and contextual job performance.

| | Correlations with Job Performance | | | | | | | | |
| | Overall | | | Task | | | Contextual | | |
Trait	Facet	Mid	Broad	Facet	Mid	Broad	Facet	Mid	Broad
Emotional stability	0.23	0.12	0.10	0.25	0.10	0.08	0.30	0.21	0.16
Extraversion	0.40	0.21	0.19	0.18	0.14	0.12	0.49	0.23	0.21
Openness	0.30	0.10	0.08	0.17	0.13	0.12	0.18	0.06	0.03
Agreeableness	0.19	0.17	0.17	0.24	0.11	0.10	0.33	0.18	0.18
Conscientiousness	0.26	0.27	0.26	0.24	0.25	0.25	0.33	0.32	0.32

Facet = 6 NEO facets, Mid = DeYoung et al. (2007) factors, Broad = FFM
Source: Judge et al. (2013).

We noted earlier that conscientiousness did not as obviously follow this pattern and that the differences across the three levels are so marginal that they would have little practical significance. Thus, there seems to be something unique about conscientiousness in the selection context.

Each of the conscientiousness facets – achievement striving, competence, deliberation, dutifulness, orderliness – is positively related to job performance in the range of 0.11 to 0.28. This is not surprising given that the aspects of personality assessed by the items (e.g., pays attention to detail, follows a schedule, always prepared, determined to succeed) are clearly of importance for performance in a range of jobs. Thus, the common variance between these facets represented by broad conscientiousness is generally useful in every aspect of work. However, even some conscientiousness facets are unrelated or even negatively related to some aspects of job performance in certain roles (e.g., Bunce & West, 1995; Driskell, Hogan, Salas & Hoskin, 1994; Tett, Jackson, Rothstein & Reddon, 1999). In such cases, it is likely that facets would outperform aggregated factors. The same is true but more common and extreme for facets of the other factors, which more often show differential and even opposite relationships.

Further, from a measurement perspective the conscientiousness factor tends to fit well relative to the other four factors in structural examinations, suggesting that the broad factor accounts for a good proportion of the facet-level variance (Vassend & Skrondal, 2011). The other factors often do not fit as well in structural examinations (Vassend & Skrondal, 2011), suggesting that the facets are less closely related, which is also evident in the differential relationships displayed with performance criteria.

Given that organizations want to maximize predictive validity, narrow facets rather than broad factors – which lead to underestimates and/or distorted estimates of relationships – are evidently of greater value (even in some cases for conscientiousness). However, it is often not practically feasible or sensible to administer tests of all known personality traits. Thus, a process of identifying the specific traits to assess is needed.

Job analysis and the selection of relevant traits

So far we have reviewed evidence pertaining to the predictive validity of personality in predicting job performance *en masse*, whether that be for police officers, managers in an investment bank, managers in an ethical bank, nurses, teachers, or military personnel. Yet we contest the very premise of universal job performance and argue that it is not at all surprising to find that personality is not a simple universal predictor (Tett & Burnett, 2003; Tett et al., 1999). Cognitive ability is a linear predictor of performance, so the quicker you can acquire and utilize information the better, regardless of the job. Yet even for cognitive ability there are quite marked differences in the magnitude of predictive validity coefficients across roles. Typically, cognitive ability is most valid in cognitively demanding roles, with corrected correlations ranging from 0.3 for clerical workers and drivers to 0.7 for professionals and engineers (Bertua, Anderson & Salgado, 2005).

We suggest that most personality traits are differentially related to performance across job roles and that the Big Five level of aggregation is not specific enough to maximize prediction. The diversity of the narrow facets subsumed by the Big Five – warmth and excitement seeking in extraversion or impulsiveness and depression in neuroticism, for example – is such that knowing exactly why one of the Big Five should or should not correlate with performance is rather difficult. A ski instructor would probably benefit from scoring high on both warmth and excitement seeking; a nurse would probably benefit most from warmth but less so from excitement seeking (excitement seeking might even be detrimental if the nurse works on a rehabilitation ward where novelty is low); while a soldier would probably benefit most from excitement seeking but less from warmth. So, is extraversion relevant for ski instructors, nurses and soldiers? Some aspects are and some are not; some might even be negatively related (Tett, Jackson & Rothstein, 1991). Put another way, one would not ask the same structured interview questions or use the same assessment centre tasks when selecting a ski instructor, nurse or soldier. Nor should we use and weight personality assessments generically.

So, how do we choose which traits to measure during a selection programme? The answer is not particularly novel: job analysis. For years, recruiters have undergone a process of describing the characteristics of jobs in order to identify the knowledge, skills and abilities that are relevant for performance (Brannick & Levine, 2002). Often, such job analyses will reveal that broad sociability is important, thus a measure of extraversion is used. We suggest that job analysis should go one step further and identify which aspects of extraversion; is it warmth, excitement seeking, or both? By considering the role in such detail, recruiters can then choose facet-level measures with greater predictive validity than the Big Five and which ones are probably more time-efficient to administer.

Numerous authors have discussed personality-oriented job analysis methods (e.g., Costa, McCrae & Kay, 1995; Goffin, Rothstein, Rieder, Poole, Krajewski, Powell & Mestdagh, 2011; Jenkins & Griffith, 2004; Raymark, Schmit & Guion, 1997; Tett, Jackson, Rothstein & Reddon, 1999) and this area is now receiving more attention in both academia and practice. If organizational researchers and practitioners measure narrow facets that are theoretically and empirically demonstrated (through job analyses and existing research) to be relevant to performance in a specific role, we can begin to increase the predictive validity offered by personality within selection. Empirical support for this confirmatory approach to personality selection is provided by Tett and colleagues (1991, 1999), who showed that confirmatory strategies (i.e., those based on job analyses) yield predictive validity coefficients double in magnitude (uncorrected $r = 0.20$, corrected $r = 0.30$) compared to those derived using exploratory strategies (uncorrected $r = 0.10$, corrected $r = 0.16$). Further evidence is reported in a meta-analysis by Hogan and Holland (2003), who show corrected correlations between theoretically-related facets and performance-based criteria ranging from 0.3 to 0.4 (uncorrected 0.1–0.3).

The use of personality-oriented job analysis yields more detailed and precise hypotheses regarding the associations between personality and job performance. For example, one might find that being an effective team player is crucial to job performance. The literature might suggest that gregariousness and assertiveness (facets of extraversion) predict team functioning in similar industries. One can then begin to model personality appropriately as X (gregariousness, assertiveness) → M (team effectiveness) → Y (job performance). We know from years of mediation research that it is possible that X is modestly related to Y but strongly related to M, while in turn M is strongly related to Y. Such process models of personality more accurately approximate the real world and as a result are more informative and predictive (Hampson, 2012; Hughes, 2014). In order to evaluate such models one would also need robust measures of job performance that include ratings of the M variables. Such measures would not be particularly difficult to generate as these variables will be identified during job analysis. Presumably, managers would be interested in these facets of performance as well as an overall composite. Equally, one could adopt existing, multifaceted measures of job performance, such as the Universal Competency Framework (Bartram, 2005; Rojon, McDowall & Saunders, 2015).

Before closing this section, it is worth noting that there is likely one large hurdle to overcome before targeted, facet-level programmes are widely adopted in research and practice, namely, identifying a satisfactory list of facets that prove as marketable as the Big Five. One initial reaction might be simply to use the facets of the five-factor model.

This is certainly not a bad starting point. However, as we discussed earlier, neither the NEO-PI-R facet list nor a facet list from any popular omnibus measure is exhaustive of the personality sphere. Thus, one major goal has to be to develop such a list.

The first author of this chapter and colleagues (Booth, Irwing & Hughes, in preparation; Irwing & Booth, 2013) are in the process of building on the work of Booth (2011), who semantically sorted and then factor-analysed 1,772 personality items. The items were drawn from seven major omnibus personality inventories (NEO-PI-R, CPI, 16PF, MPQ, JPI-R, HEXACO, 6PFQ) and four specifically chosen narrow inventories with several specific measures (social dominance orientation, right-wing authoritarianism, Machiavellianism, need for cognition). In total, this analysis identified 78 seemingly unique personality facets, though it is evident that some important traits appear to be missing from this list and further validation work is ongoing (for details contact david.hughes@mbs.ac.uk). Should this research produce a final list of 100 or so reliable and valid traits, it can serve as a personality trait dictionary to be utilized to measure the important aspects of personality identified during a job analysis in a manner that reduces the general problems of the Jingle Jangle Fallacy discussed in the introduction to this chapter.

In the meantime, regardless of whether a universal list of personality facets is available, researchers and practitioners alike can adopt the targeted facet approach within whichever personality framework they deem most suitable. All personality measures have facets, which can be used to measure personality traits closely aligned with crucial aspects of job performance.

Response Distortions

The final predictive validity discussion concerns the persistent problem of response distortions. Personality items are designed to measure respondents' characteristic patterns of thinking, feeling and behaving. The utility of any measure corresponds to its reliability and validity, both of which are attenuated by measurement error (i.e., measuring things other than the intended target). Self-report questionnaire items are susceptible to a wide variety of measurement errors, from differences in item and response scale interpretations to systematic differences in response styles (e.g., acquiescence; extreme responding; Furnham, 1986). Many of these sources of measurement error are well known. However, of more interest in the selection literature is measurement error arising from response distortions due to low self-awareness and deliberate faking.

There is a number of excellent discussions of faking in the literature, covering areas such as how much people fake, how successful people are at faking and how faking influences reliability and validity (see Birkeland, Manson, Kisamore, Brannick & Smith, 2006; Morgeson et al., 2007a; Mueller-Hanson, Heggestad & Thornton, 2003; Ones & Viswesvaran, 1998; Tett & Christiansen, 2007), and we do not intend to reproduce these discussions here.

For the current authors, the bottom line is that response distortions such as faking almost certainly occur and that some individuals fake more than others, which is of course problematic from measurement, validity and ethical perspectives (Birkeland et al., 2006). Nevertheless, personality measures retain predictive validity, as discussed above, regardless of response distortions (Ones & Viswesvaran, 1998). Thus, personality measures are still useful in a world where response distortions are quite common. This does not mean, however, that we should ignore response distortion or, as some have suggested, see it as a desirable social skill (Morgeson et al., 2007a). Rather, we should aim to measure, model and prevent it. If we can reduce response distortions, then we may be able to improve the predictive validity of personality tests further and certainly reduce the associated ethical issues.

Numerous solutions to combat response distortions have been suggested. Solutions such as social desirability scales (Feeney & Goffin, 2015), forced-choice or ipsative measures (presenting candidates with multiple trait statements that are matched for social desirability and allowing them only to indicate one that is most like them; Heggestad, Morrison, Reeve & McCloy, 2006; Johnson, Wood & Blinkhorn, 1988; Meade, 2004), and imposing time limits for candidates (Holden, Wood & Tomashewski, 2001; Komar, Komar, Robie & Taggar, 2010). While each of these methods shows some promise, none has shown any genuinely compelling empirical support.

That forced-choice personality measures have little influence over social desirability ratings, despite appearing to be more difficult to fake, is surprising (Heggestad et al., 2006). It is also the prevailing view in the organizational psychology community that compared to Likert-type formats, ipsative measures produce lower predictive validity. Recent studies, however, provide evidence to the contrary (Bartram, 2007; Salgado, Anderson & Tauriz, 2014; Salgado & Tauriz, 2014).

Forced-choice measures come in two broadly different formats: fully ipsative (e.g., rank order four items/traits beginning with the one most like you) and partially ipsative, which contain a forced-choice element while retaining some flexibility (e.g., choose from a list of four the item/trait least and most like you; see Hicks, 1970). A recent meta-analysis by Salgado and colleagues (2014) suggests that fully ipsative measures perform poorly with regard to predictive validity, but that partially ipsative measures produce impressive levels of predictive validity (Salgado et al., 2014). Compared to validity estimates derived predominantly from Likert-type measures (Barrick et al., 2001), partially ipsative assessments of emotional stability, openness and conscientiousness are considerably larger, while measures of extraversion and agreeableness are equivalent across formats (See Table 8.2).

Salgado and colleagues (2014) also examined associations within eight job roles: clerical, customer service, health, managerial, military, sales, skilled and supervisory. The primary study numbers ($k = 2-11$) and sample sizes ($N = 171-3,007$) are small and vary markedly across job roles. Equally, estimates for each of the Big Five were not available across all roles (e.g. emotional stability not reported in customer service roles). We suggest that these notable limitations preclude firm conclusions regarding which traits best predict which role, however, the pattern of the results remains very interesting. Particularly striking is the range of validities reported, which in raw correlations vary from 0 to 0.4 and in corrected validates vary from 0 to 0.7. Table 8.3 includes the highest and lowest predictive validity reported for each of the Big Five. The difference in variance explained between the mean and largest validity estimates is substantial, with the largest estimates between 4 and 10 times as large as the mean.

The variation in predictive validity provides compelling support for the arguments put forward in the 'Job analysis and the selection of relevant traits' section, specifically, that universal job performance does not exist and that the nature of the role moderates the correlations between personality and job performance. Further research using job-relevant, partially ipsative personality measures identified through personality-oriented job analysis or theoretical frameworks appears warranted.

The results from partially ipsative measures appear compelling. However, self-report distortions remain resilient. One potential avenue for mitigating the problems with self-ratings altogether is not to rely on them but instead have 'others' rate candidates' personality. Two meta-analyses indicate that other ratings of personality might offer improved predictive validity over self-ratings. Connelly and Ones (2010) conducted a meta-analysis of 44,178 targeted individuals rated across 263 independent samples. Each target participant had at least one set of other ratings for the Big Five. Similarly, Oh, Wang and Mount (2011)

Table 8.2 Mean, lowest and highest predictive validities of partially ipsative measures of the Big Five.

	Correlations with Job Performance					
	Partially Ipsative			Likert-type		
Trait	$\bar{r}$	$r1$	r^2	$\bar{r}$	$r1$	r^2
Emotional stability						
Highest: Supervisory	0.37	0.68	460.2			
Lowest: Managerial	−0.01	−0.02	00.0			
Mean	0.11	0.20	40.0	0.09	0.10	10.0
Extraversion						
Highest: Managerial	0.21	0.34	110.6			
Lowest: Sales	0.05	0.08	00.6			
Mean	0.07	0.12	10.4	0.06	0.13	10.7
Openness						
Highest: Clerical	−0.27	−0.44	190.4			
Lowest: Sales	0.11	0.17	20.9			
Mean	0.14	0.22	40.8	0.02	0.03	00.0
Agreeableness						
Highest: Skilled	0.28	0.42	170.6			
Lowest: Managerial	−0.04	−0.07	00.5			
Mean	0.10	0.16	20.6	0.07	0.17	20.9
Conscientiousness						
Highest: Skilled	0.43	0.71	500.4			
Lowest: Supervisory	0.09	0.18	30.2			
Mean	0.22	0.38	140.4	0.10	0.23	50.3

Likert-type estimates taken from Barrick et al. (2001); $\bar{r}$ = uncorrected correlation; $r1$ = corrected for unreliability in criterion only and indirect range restriction in the predictor; r^2 = percentage of variance explained.

conducted a meta-analysis of some 2,000 target individuals from 18 independent samples. Table 8.3 displays a summary of the main findings of these meta-analyses.

The predictive validities of other ratings were substantially higher than for self-ratings, regardless of whether or what type of correction was utilized. In many instances the predictive validity of other ratings are 2, 3 or 4 times the magnitude of self-ratings. In the case of openness, the other ratings are 6 times the magnitude of self-ratings. The magnitudes of these relationships are impressive. If we use the estimates provided by Schmidt and Hunter (1998) as a guide, the univariate validities are equivalent to some of our most valid selection methods, the multivariate validity would no doubt surpass many of these other methods and the potential incremental predictive validity over and above other methods is substantial.

Oh and colleagues' (2011) meta-analysis provides two more particularly interesting findings for the selection domain. First, it appears that combining self-ratings with other ratings is of little value as self-reports offer little incremental predictive validity over other reports. Second, while predictive validity increases in line with the number of other ratings, the increment is generally small. Specifically, the increase from 1 to 3 other ratings ranges from 0.04 to 0.06 (uncorrected) and 0.05 to 0.09 (corrected), suggesting that while multiple other ratings are optimal, the value of a single other rating is still substantial (Oh et al., 2011).

Table 8.3 Correlations between job performance and personality as assessed by self-ratings and other ratings.

| Trait and rating type | Correlations with Job Performance | | | | |
| | Connelly and Ones (2010) | | | Oh et al. (2011) | |
	$\bar{r}$	r1	r2	$\bar{r}$	r3
Emotional Stability					
Other rating	0.14	0.17	0.37	0.17	0.24
Self-rating	0.06	0.11	0.12	0.09	0.14
Extraversion					
Other rating	0.08	0.11	0.18	0.21	0.29
Self-rating	0.06	0.11	0.12	0.06	0.09
Openness					
Other rating	0.18	0.22	0.45	0.20	0.29
Self-rating	0.03	0.04	0.05	0.03	0.05
Agreeableness					
Other rating	0.13	0.17	0.31	0.23	0.34
Self-rating	0.06	0.11	0.13	0.07	0.10
Conscientiousness					
Other rating	0.23	0.29	0.55	0.31	0.41
Self-rating	0.12	0.20	0.23	0.15	0.22

$\bar{r}$ = uncorrected correlation; r1 = corrected for unreliability in criterion only; r2 = corrected for unreliability in the predictor and criterion; r3 = corrected for unreliability in the criterion measure and range restriction in the predictor; Other ratings for Oh et al. (2011) refer to the mean predictive validity taken from three observers.

Clearly, other ratings offer a marked improvement over self-ratings in predicting job performance. One likely contribution to the increase is that other ratings mitigate the response distortions commonly associated with self-ratings, which is highly desirable. Perhaps less desirable is the possibility that observer ratings and job performance ratings are highly correlated due to an element of common method bias. It is plausible that other ratings of personality are assessing reputation and likeability, which is arguably what supervisor ratings of overall job performance are assessing. Whether this shared variance is a good or bad thing remains to be debated. Nevertheless, the results from studies of other ratings are highly promising.

Predictive validity: Conclusion

Self-ratings of higher-order factors of personality modestly relate to supervisor and objective ratings of overall job performance. The magnitude of the correlations (or corrected operational validities) typically ranges from 0.0 to 0.3 and this is true whether personality factors are examined in univariate (single-factor correlations) or multivariate (as a group of five factors) fashion. With the exception of conscientiousness, many broad personality factors appear to be generally unrelated to ratings of overall job performance. However, broad personality factors do offer much greater levels of prediction of other crucial elements of workplace performance, such as counterproductive behaviours, leadership and teamwork.

At this point, some might conclude that personality is generally not fit for purpose in the selection context (e.g., Morgeson et al., 2007a). However, that personality measures as a stand-alone do not offer particularly grand levels of predictive validity does not mean that they are useless. Rather, personality measures offer significant and cost-effective (in terms of time and money) incremental predictive validity over other selection methods. Notably, the combination of cognitive ability and personality is among the most powerful combinations of selection methods. Thus, we can endorse the use of personality as a component of a rigorous selection programme (Schmidt & Hunter, 1998; Schmidt et al., 2008).

Further, when we step away from meta-analytic correlations of the Big Five the picture is much more interesting. Narrow, lower-order facets offer much greater predictive validity (with the exception of conscientiousness, between 2 and 6 times more) than do their broad composite factors. While facet-level analyses are clearly superior to broad factor analyses, it is also likely that our current estimates of this superiority represent underestimates. Currently, the data we have lack nuance as they pertain to job performance *en masse* across numerous industries, organizations and roles. However, as we suggest, personality is not a universal predictor: different roles require the utilization of different levels and combinations of behaviours. In addition, no single facet list from popular measures of personality is exhaustive, and thus omits potentially important personality traits (e.g., the dark triad) and further underestimating the predictive validity of personality.

In spite of the current limitations on our estimates, it is clear that matching a few narrow traits on the basis of existing empirical evidence and theory leads to increased predictive validity (Judge et al., 2013; Paunonen & Ashton, 2001). Personality-oriented job analysis offers an avenue to identify the narrow facets of relevance and, if utilized appropriately, can further increase the predictive validity of self-ratings of personality. We know of no studies that have examined the incremental predictive validity of facet-level personality ratings, based on job analysis, over and above cognitive ability. We suggest that such a study is of great importance in furthering this debate.

One of the likely limiting factors in the validity of personality measures is their susceptibility to response distortions (e.g. low self-awareness, faking). The evidence reviewed here suggests that replacing self-ratings with other ratings might mitigate self-report response distortions and offer substantially increased predictive validity. An intriguing question remains just how much predictive validity increases by the simultaneous use of job analysis to identify relevant narrow facets, which are rated by others and used in a multivariate manner to predict nuanced measures of job performance. The evidence reviewed in this chapter suggests that this approach could yield substantial gains in predictive validity and ultimately improve our selection practices.

Equally, recent research suggests that partially ipsative personality measures have improved predictive validities compared to traditional, Likert-type measures. The utility of partially ipsative measures is even more pronounced when the moderating effects of job role are taken into account, with univariate relationships with performance within specific roles ranging from 0.3 to 0.7. In addition, recent advances in the scoring and modelling of ipsative items (Brown & Maydeu-Olivares, 2013, in press) make the measures more appealing and practically useful.

In sum, we believe that the predictive validity evidence suggests that personality traits are valuable during selection. Even a simple measure of conscientiousness offers incremental predictive validity in most selection scenarios. However, more nuanced use of personality measures leads to even greater levels of predictive validity which, in our view, make personality an important component of the selection toolbox.

How and When to Use Personality Assessments in Selection

The previous sections have examined the question of whether or not personality assessments are useful for selection. Having concluded that they can be, we now provide a slightly more practitioner-focused discussion of the questions *how* and *when* personality assessments can be useful.

Employees are often the single largest cost and most complex 'resource' to manage; they are also the source of the knowledge, skills and abilities needed for organizations to thrive. Therefore, effective employee selection is a crucial component of organizational functioning and there is an indisputable need for organizations to ensure that they manage the flow of talented people within their organizations. The activities and processes often identified as vital for talent management include recruitment, selection, development, reward, performance management and succession planning. Personality data can be useful in all these areas. Equally, selection does not refer exclusively to the selection of new employees. Personality data can be useful for the selection of redeployed staff, short-term secondments, expatriate workers and future talent.

In order to elucidate how and when personality assessment can be useful in selection and talent management more broadly, a selection paradigm is presented in Figure 8.1. There is no established framework for the selection paradigm, but authors have agreed on some key elements (Guion & Highhouse, 2006; Smith & Smith, 2005), which range from identifying the needs of the organization through to the evaluation of the selected candidate(s). As discussed above, personality-oriented job analysis offers a very useful framework but rather than repeat this discussion, in this section we focus on considerations when choosing selection methods (beyond predictive validity), administering selection methods (initial and additional) and how to use personality data after the initial selection decision is made.

Choosing selection methods

Selection methods should be chosen based on consideration of seven key criteria in four main areas: 1) reliability and predictive validity; 2) legality and fairness; 3) cost and practicality; and 4) candidate reactions. Personality assessments generally perform well against these key criteria (Hough, Oswald & Ployhart, 2001; Mount & Barrick, 1995).

The first and most important consideration, and the main focus of this chapter, is reliability and predictive validity. Put simply, if the method does not predict job performance, then it is of no interest in a selection context. It is important to note here that the reliability and predictive validity of each personality assessment will vary, and often free research scales perform better than for-pay scales (e.g. Hamby, Taylor, Snowden & Peterson, 2016; Salgado, 2003). Given the detailed exploration of predictive validity discussed above, little remains to say beyond check the research evidence pertaining to reliability and validity and choose the measure with the best predictive validity. There are, however, four caveats. First, make sure the test measures traits shown to be of relevance during the job analysis. Second, ensure the measure has been tested and validated on an appropriate sample that approximates the likely candidate pool. Third, be wary of wild claims about predictive validity – if a self-report measure of a construct closely approximating conscientiousness claims predictive validities much greater than 0.3, carefully examine this evidence. Fourth, gains in predictive validity should be considered alongside testing time and format. Choosing a more complex, demanding, lengthy or expensive measure for a marginal increase in validity (e.g., 0.33 vs. 0.35) makes little sense.

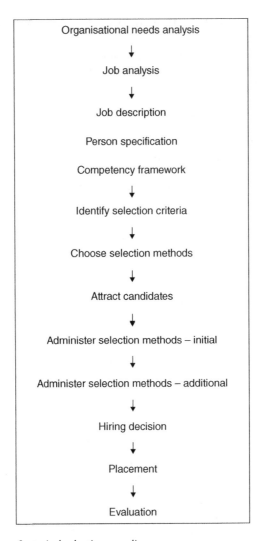

Figure 8.1 Overview of a typical selection paradigm.

Once predictive validity has been assessed, selection method choice moves on to concerns of fairness and practicality. Turning to legality, there is a requirement to check the relevant legislation in each geographical area of usage. That said, if a valid personality assessment was chosen based on a thorough job analysis and the measures are appropriate (e.g., are not clinical in nature), administered and interpreted by qualified personnel and are used as part of a fuller selection programme, then there is little to suggest that using them will be indefensible. This claim is further supported by the comprehensive body of evidence that shows personality assessments to be less prone to adverse impact than many other selection methods such as interviews, assessment centres or references (Hough et al., 2001; Sackett & Lievens, 2008). In general, there are minimal racial group and age group differences observed in personality assessments, and certainly these are much smaller than those observed in measures of cognitive ability and situational judgement tests.

However, there are some notable differences between men and women on personality measures, which may not be a result of measurement error but reflections of actual group differences (Costa, Terracciano & McCrae, 2001; Del Giudice, Booth & Irwing, 2012). These should be considered during selection (Hough et al., 2001). It is also currently unknown whether partially ipsative measures and other ratings of personality influence adverse impact. Nevertheless, we can conclude that self-ratings of personality perform relatively well in terms of fairness and legality.

The next considerations when choosing selection methods (or perhaps first in practice) are cost and practicality. Personality assessments are an extremely cost-effective selection method. They are largely inexpensive to procure and can be administered digitally without any negative effects on response patterns (Ployhart, Weekley, Holtz & Kemp, 2003), allowing time- and cost-efficient assessment of many candidates in multiple geographic locations. Personality measures are among the best selection methods when considering cost and practicality.

The final consideration is candidate reactions. Organizations do not want new employees' first interaction with the company to be unpleasant. Equally, organizations do not want talented but unsuccessful applicants to be deterred from applying for future vacancies. So it is important to consider how the candidate might feel during the selection process (however, this is much less important than predictive validity and fairness). Despite some concerns regarding intrusiveness and a lack of perceived job relevance (Rosse, Miller & Stecher, 1994), personality assessments are 'favourably evaluated' by selection candidates (Anderson, Salgado & Hülsheger, 2010, p. 291), but less so than interviews, work samples and cognitive ability tests (Anderson et al., 2010). Nevertheless, personality assessments are a 'scientific method of selection' (Steiner & Gilliland, 1996) and, when used, as we suggest throughout this chapter, in conjunction with cognitive ability, they receive positive candidate reactions (Anderson et al., 2010; Rosse et al., 1994). Indeed, organizations that employ rigorous selection procedures and use scientific selection methods are deemed to be more attractive to potential employees (Steiner & Gilliland, 1996), which is hugely important in recruiting a larger applicant pool. This is of course important, as selection will be poor, regardless of the quality of the selection methods employed, if the candidate pool does not consist of individuals with the knowledge, skills and abilities necessary to perform well.

Administering selection methods – Initial

An early stage of the selection process often involves the filtration of potential applicants (Cook, 2009). Traditionally, this first sift or filter is achieved through a number of methods which may include examination of application forms or curricula vitae, situational judgement tests, job knowledge or skills, minimum experience or qualifications, criminal record check or cognitive ability assessments. Personality assessment, if based on a job analysis and used in conjunction with other selection methods (e.g. cognitive ability), can be used to sift the initial candidate pool. This approach allows more expensive and labour-intensive methods to be applied to a reduced candidate pool. In general, initial assessments can be conducted online and thus, as discussed above, become very time- and cost-effective without any reduction in response quality and an improvement in candidate reactions (Salgado & Moscoso, 2003).

A recent trend concerns the 'selecting out' (removing from the candidate pool) of candidates with specific traits. Identifying the personality traits of the 'dark triad' – psychopathy, Machiavellianism and narcissism (Paulhus & Williams, 2002) – is popular in this area given their negative influence in the workplace (e.g., Moscoso & Salgado, 2004;

O'Boyle, Forsyth, Banks & McDaniel, 2012). However, further research is needed regarding selecting out in general and the potential adverse impact such a practice might induce in the selection process before any firm practitioner points can be made. For example, some research examining the dark triad suggests that higher scores are not universal indicators of poor performance or delinquency (Hogan, 2007).

Administering selection methods – Additional

Following initial sifting, most organizations employ additional selection methods before making a final selection decision. Personality assessments can be used at this stage to improve the efficacy of the selection process. First, as we have discussed throughout this chapter, personality assessments can be used to identify the extent to which candidates may possess the characteristics that will help them excel against competences or duties essential for the role. Second, the analysis of candidates' personality profiles can be used to identify specific interview questions which can be used alongside traditional structured interview questions (e.g., Morgeson et al., 2007a; Schmitt & Kunce, 2002). For example, candidates who report an extreme tendency to be introverted might be asked to explain how they tend to collaborate, while candidates who report an extreme tendency towards extraversion might be asked how they work independently. Third, personality assessments can be used to identify values and motives in order to ascertain potential cultural fit between the candidate and the recruiting organization (Blackman, 2002).

Using personality assessment data post-selection

Selection processes can be expensive and the data gathered can be of use beyond a final selection decision. The re-utilization of personality data after selection makes for a better return on investment and ensures that the data collected has continuing benefits. If personality data are to be used after selection, it is important that candidates be informed of this prior to completing the measures. If this is done, we see personality data as useful in four ways after selection.

First, when selecting multiple candidates, personality data can inform initial placement by matching the candidates with mentors (Wanberg, Kammeyer-Mueller & Marchese, 2006), teams (Morgeson, Reider & Campion, 2005) or leaders (Monzani, Ripoll & Peiró, 2015). In this approach, the personality profiles of the selected employee will be compared with those of existing team members or managers. It is important to note that this does not represent the 'cloning' of existing team members or leaders, which is generally to be avoided, but ensuring a complementary fit of typical tendencies for thinking, feeling and behaving.

Second, personality assessment data can inform initial employee coaching and development (Batey, Walker & Hughes, 2012). Here, the new employee can discuss their likely strengths and development areas on starting in their new role, and the same information can be shared with team colleagues as part of the induction process.

Third, the personality data might indicate that new employees possess managerial potential (Goffin et al., 1996) and are well suited to leadership positions (Judge, Bono, Illies & Gerhardt, 2002) or expatriate roles (Caligiuri, 2000) and thus they could be considered for 'high potential' or 'rising talent' programmes (Silzer & Church, 2010).

Fourth, if the role, team or department that new employees have joined is subsequently subject to redesign, restructuring or redeployment, the personality data could partially inform what new roles they could perform.

The key issue stressed here is that personality data collected during selection can be effectively used later, provided the candidate is informed of these potential uses during the selection process. Using selection data to inform placement and development offers other advantages. Framing personality assessment during selection as the first step in a developmental trajectory and explaining to candidates how the data are to be used increases the face validity and job relevance of the measure, thus improving candidate reactions during selection. It is also possible, though at this point speculative, that candidates may be more engaged in the selection process and 'fake' less if they understand that the personality assessment will influence with whom they will work and the training they will receive.

One final note is that while self-ratings are useful, other reports appear to offer greater predictive validity. Thus, we suggest that once a candidate has been in role for a year or so, the company ceases to use self-ratings and instead uses other ratings gleaned from colleagues, managers and subordinates as part of ongoing 360-degree development (Batey et al., 2012).

Future Research

To our mind, the study of personality is deeply fascinating. That we can measure the very essence of human character is marvellous. That those measurements predict workplace behaviour is hugely useful. The focused review and analysis in this chapter demonstrate that research regarding personality and selection has made incredible progress over the past 30 years and that the area remains vibrant with novel studies frequently challenging assumptions, improving knowledge and creating a very solid platform for evidence-based practice. In keeping with the dynamic nature of the personality–selection field, we finish this chapter by presenting a number of exciting avenues that are ripe for future research. Throughout the chapter, we have noted areas of research with promising findings that need further exploration. We will briefly recapitulate these and discuss some other areas we believe deserve research attention.

Our first suggestion for future research – the further development of personality measures – is unlikely to prove universally popular. Many researchers and practitioners have a preferred tool to which they are strongly committed. However, as discussed in the early sections of this chapter, there are limitations with currently popular measures based on the Big Five (e.g., NEO-PI-R, HEXACO, HPI). Specifically, the models were developed without a guiding theoretical framework and use suboptimal psychometric procedures, meaning that debate remains regarding how many factors exist at each level of the personality hierarchy and most omnibus personality measures have less than spectacular psychometric properties (Block, 2010; Booth & Hughes, 2014). In addition, and of great importance to the selection domain, all omnibus personality measures omit a large number of potentially important traits (Booth, 2011; Paunonen & Jackson, 2000). Further research that improves personality theory and measurement along these lines is very welcome.

We believe it is time to move away from producing meta-analyses of correlations between broad personality factors and broad measures of performance. Instead, we wish to see more theory-driven model testing approaches to personality–job performance research. Particularly, process models examining the effects of mediators (e.g., teamwork, communication, motivation) and moderators (e.g., organizational culture, team composition, leader behaviour) within the personality–job performance link appear to be a fruitful avenue of exploration.

In line with the argument that universal job performance does not exist and that job roles moderate predictive validity, we call for researchers to begin building a picture of role-specific associations (e.g., leadership roles, clerical roles, sales roles, policing, teaching). Within this call, we see a crucial role for personality-oriented job analysis and narrow facets of personality. In order to facilitate such research we believe that the production of a single, exhaustive list of narrow facets would reduce the common Jingle Jangle Fallacy problem and allow for the systematic exploration of the relations between narrow traits and job performance. It is also important within this research that we move away from unidimensional measures of performance and towards more realistic multidimensional models such as that proposed by Bartram (2005). Such research would be much more theory-laden and have great practical value. In time, we will be able to aggregate these studies to provide meta-analytic estimates while retaining useful, role-specific information. Similar efforts have been successful in cognitive ability research (e.g., Bertua et al., 2005).

Traits do not exist or act in isolation; as discussed above, personality is multidimensional. Currently, most multidimensional personality research adopts a simple, cumulative regression or aggregation approach. However, we believe that the value of traits is not simply additive. Rather, traits interact to drive motivation and behaviour. A number of studies show that trait interactions are of value in understanding performance at work (e.g., Blickle et al., 2013; Judge & Erez, 2007; Oh, Lee, Ashton & De Vries, 2011). Accordingly, we call for further research in this promising area.

Similarly, the relationship between personality and job performance in some roles might be curvilinear. It is possible that too much conscientiousness or too much extraversion will be counterproductive in some roles (e.g., Bunce & West, 1995; Driskell et al., 1994; Tett et al., 1999). Examinations of curvilinear relationships might increase understanding regarding when and where traits are most relevant and potentially indicate optimal trait levels for specific workplace tasks. Studies have been undertaken examining curvilinear effects, but to date the results are generally inconclusive (e.g., Le, Oh, Robbins, Ilies, Holland & Westrick, 2011).

One area of work we have not discussed in any detail is teamwork. People often work in teams, at least to some degree, with truly solitary work virtually unheard of in most roles. Despite the fact that workplace interdependence is the norm, we measure only individual traits and individual performance. While conscientiousness is the single most important predictor for individual task performance, it is possible that other traits are very important because they have an impact on the performance and well-being of others. Examining how personality enhances or suppresses group performance is a much-needed avenue of exploration.

Response distortions remain a problem for self-ratings of personality. Further research is required to understand these distortions and generate useful methods to overcome them. Forced-choice measures have generally offered limited utility in combating social desirability. However, recent research suggests that some of this underwhelming performance might be the result of suboptimal test construction, variable scoring and analytical procedures (Brown & Maydeu-Olivares, 2013, in press; Meade, 2004). Regardless of effects on social desirability, partially ipsative forced-choice measures offer impressive levels of predictive validity and outperform those achieved using Likert-type measures. Further examinations of the predictive validity of partially ipsative measures are warranted, as are explorations of how these rating formats influence adverse impact.

In related fashion, the results from other ratings are so promising that we must continue to examine them as a plausible measurement approach. Research must consider how other ratings perform when using facet measures and compare these to broad measures. If the increment in predictive validity offered by narrow traits in self-ratings applies equally to other ratings, then other ratings become even more attractive. We also need to explore more thoroughly how other ratings differ from self-ratings: do other ratings still perform fairly across different groups (e.g., are there sex or racial differences in ratings), does the rank order of applicants change from self-ratings and other ratings and to what extent does common method bias account for the increased correlations with job performance metrics? Equally, pragmatic research regarding how to source other ratings reliably is required.

Finally, we call for a tighter integration between academia, selection practitioners and test publishers. Practitioners have the ability to accelerate progress by adopting some of the approaches outlined in this chapter and collecting real-life, real-time data which can only serve to enhance our understanding of the personality–job performance link. Bridging the science–practitioner divide discussed in the introduction is paramount to the fruitfulness of our field.

Conclusion

In this chapter, we have reviewed the evidence for the utility of personality trait assessments within selection. We conclude that personality assessments can be a very useful component of the selection toolbox. We have also considered that the latest evidence suggests that the use of narrow facets based on theoretical and empirical reasoning offers superior predictive validity to broad factors and currently represent the most effective method of utilizing self-ratings of personality within selection. In addition, we discussed the potential of partially ipsative measures and other ratings to bypass response distortions and greatly increase predictive validity. Further, we have outlined a defensible and robust paradigm for integrating personality assessments into the selection process.

What we believe this review demonstrates for practitioners is this. The utilization of personality assessments in selection must operate concurrently with a broader selection programme involving cognitive ability or similar selection tools. Further, if personality is used in an off-the-shelf and uncritical fashion it will almost certainly yield modest values (correlations with job performance in the region of 0.1–0.3). In fact, using personality measures in this way is questionable given that trait measures are not linked to job performance. However, practitioners prepared to employ more nuanced job analyses and trait selections, within a rigorous selection paradigm, will maximize the value of personality assessment, thus increasing the likelihood that the chosen candidate(s) will think, feel and behave in a manner that will contribute to organizationally defined metrics of success.

References

Ackerman, P. L. (2000). Domain-specific knowledge as the 'dark matter' of adult intelligence: *gf/gc*, personality and interest correlates. *Journal of Gerontology: Psychological Sciences, 55B*(2), 69–84.

Allport, G. W. (1961). *Pattern and Growth in Personality*. New York: Holt, Rinehart & Wilson.

Allport, G.W., & Odbert, H. S. (1936). Trait-names: A psycho-lexical study. *Psychological Monographs, 47*(1, Whole No. 211).

Anderson, N., Salgado, J. F., & Hülsheger, U. R. (2010). Applicant reactions in selection: Comprehensive meta-analysis into reaction generalization versus situational specificity. *International Journal of Selection and Assessment, 18*(3), 291–304.

Ashton, M. C., Jackson, D. N., Paunonen, S. V., Helmes, E., & Rothstein, M. G. (1995). The criterion validity of broad factor scales versus specific facet scales. *Journal of Research in Personality, 29*, 432–442.

Ashton, M. C., Lee, K., & Son, C. (2000). Honesty as the sixth factor of personality: Correlations with Machiavellianism, primary psychopathy, and social adroitness. *European Journal of Personality, 14*, 359–368.

Barrick, M. R., & Mount, M. K. (1991). The Big Five personality dimensions and job performance: A meta-analysis. *Personnel Psychology, 44,* 1–26.

Barrick, M. R., & Mount, M. K. (1996). Effects of impression management and self-deception on the predictive validity of personality constructs. *Journal of Applied Psychology, 81*(3), 261–272.

Barrick, M. R., Mount, M. K., & Judge, T. A. (2001). The FFM personality dimensions and job performance: Meta-analysis of meta-analyses. *International Journal of Selection and Assessment, 9*(1–2), 9–30.

Bartram, D. (2005). The Great Eight competencies: a criterion-centric approach to validation. *Journal of Applied Psychology, 90*(6), 1185–1203.

Bartram, D. (2007). Increasing validity with forced-choice criterion measurement formats. *International Journal of Selection and Assessment, 15,* 263–272.

Batey, M., Walker, A., & Hughes, D. J. (2012). Psychometric tools in development – Do they work and how? *In* J. Passmore (Ed.), *Psychometrics in Coaching. Using Psychological and Psychometric Tools for Development* (pp. 49–58). London: Kogan Page.

Baumgarten, F. (1933). Die Charaktereigenschaften [The character traits]. *Beiträge zur Charakter- und Persönlichkeitsforschung* (Whole No. 1). Bern, Switzerland: A. Francke.

Bertua, C., Anderson, N., & Salgado, J. F. (2005). The predictive validity of cognitive ability tests: A UK meta-analysis. *Journal of Occupational and Organizational Psychology, 78*(3), 387–409.

Birkeland, S. A., Manson, T. M., Kisamore, J. L., Brannick, M. T., & Smith, M. A. (2006). A meta-analytic investigation of job applicant faking on personality measures. *International Journal of Selection and Assessment, 14*(4), 317–335.

Blackman, M. C. (2002). Personality judgment and the utility of the unstructured employment interview. *Basic and Applied Social Psychology, 24*(3), 241–250.

Blickle, G., Meurs, J. A., Wihler, A., Ewen, C., Plies, A., & Günther, S. (2013). The interactive effects of conscientiousness, openness to experience, and political skill on job performance in complex jobs: The importance of context. *Journal of Organizational Behavior, 34*(8), 1145–1164.

Block, J. (1995). A contrarian view of the five-factor approach to personality description. *Psychological Bulletin, 117,* 187–215.

Block, J. (2001). Millennial contrarianism: The five-factor approach to personality description 5 years later. *Journal of Research in Personality, 35,* 98–107.

Block, J. (2010). The five-factor framing of personality and beyond: Some ruminations. *Psychological Inquiry, 21,* 2–25.

Booth, T. (2011). A review of the structure of normal range personality. Unpublished doctoral thesis. University of Manchester, UK.

Booth, T., Irwing, P., & Hughes, D. J. (in preparation). The 11+ factor model: A structural analysis of 1,176 personality items.

Booth, T., & Hughes, D. J. (2014). Exploratory structural equation modeling of personality data. *Assessment, 21*(3), 260–271.

Borgatta, E. F. (1964). The structure of personality characteristics. *Behavioral Science, 9,* 8–17.

Brannick, M. T., & Levine, E. L. (2002). *Job Analysis: Methods, Research and Applications for Human Resource Management in the New Millennium.* Thousand Oaks, CA: Sage.

Brown, A., & Maydeu-Olivares, A. (2013). How IRT can solve problems of ipsative data in forced-choice questionnaires. *Psychological Methods, 18,* 36–52.

Brown, A., & Maydeu-Olivares, A. (in press). Modelling forced-choice response formats. *In* P. Irwing, T. Booth, & D. J. Hughes (Eds.), *The Wiley–Blackwell Handbook of Psychometric Testing.* Oxford: Wiley–Blackwell.

Bunce, D., & West, M. A. (1995). Self-perceptions and perceptions of group climate as predictors of individual innovation at work. *Applied Psychology, 44*(3), 199–215.

Caligiuri, P. M. (2000). The Big-Five personality characteristics as predictors of expatriates' desire to terminate the assignment and supervisor-rated performance. *Personnel Psychology, 53,* 67–88.

Carver, C. S., & Scheier, M. F. (1996). *Perspectives on Personality* (3rd ed.). Needham Heights, MA: Allyn & Bacon.

Cattell, R. B. (1943). The description of personality: I. Foundations of trait measurement. *Psychological Review, 50,* 559–594.

Cattell, R. B. (1954). The personality and motivation of the research scientist. *Wennergren Prize Essay*. New York Academy of Science.

Chamorro-Premuzic, T., & Furnham, A. (2003). Personality predicts academic performance: Evidence from two longitudinal university samples. *Journal of Research in Personality, 37*(4), 319–338.

Colodro, J., Garcés-de-los-Fayos, E. J., López-García, J. J., & Colodro-Conde, L. (2015). Incremental validity of personality measures in predicting underwater performance and adaptation. *Spanish Journal of Psychology, 18*, E15, 1–10.

Connelly, B. S., & Ones, D. S. (2010). An other perspective on personality: Meta-analytic integration of observers' accuracy and predictive validity. *Psychological Bulletin, 136*(6), 1092–1122.

Cook, M. (2009). *Personnel Selection: Adding Value through People* (5th ed.). Chichester: John Wiley & Sons.

Costa, P. T., & McCrae, R. R. (1992). *Revised NEO Personality Inventory (NEO-PI-R) and NEO Five-Factor Inventory (NEO-FFI) Professional Manual*. Odessa, FL: Psychological Assessment Resources.

Costa, P. T., McCrae, R. R., & Kay, G. G. (1995). Persons, places, and personality: Career assessment using the Revised NEO Personality Inventory. *Journal of Career Assessment, 3*(2), 123–139.

Costa, P. T., Terracciano, A., & McCrae, R. R. (2001). Gender differences in personality traits across cultures: Robust and surprising findings. *Journal of Personality and Social Psychology, 81*, 322–331.

Cronbach, L. J. (1984). *Essentials of Psychological Testing* (4th ed.). New York: Harper & Row.

Del Giudice, M., Booth, T., & Irwing, P. (2012). The distance between Mars and Venus: Measuring global sex differences in personality. *PloS One, 7*, e29265.

DeYoung, C. G., Quilty, L. C., & Peterson, J. B. (2007). Between facets and domains: 10 aspects of the Big Five. *Journal of Personality and Social Psychology, 93*(5), 880–896.

Digman, J. M. (1990). Personality structure: Emergence of the five-factor model. *Annual Review of Psychology, 41*, 417–440.

Driskell, J. E., Hogan, J., Salas, E., & Hoskin, B. (1994). Cognitive and personality predictors of training performance. *Military Psychology, 6*(1), 31–46.

Feeney, J. R., & Goffin, R. D. (2015). The overclaiming questionnaire: A good way to measure faking? *Personality and Individual Differences, 82*, 248–252.

Feist, G. J., & Barron, F. X. (2003). Predicting creativity from early to late adulthood: Intellect, potential, and personality. *Journal of Research in Personality, 37*(2), 62–88.

Fiske, D. W. (1949). Consistency of the factorial structures of personality ratings from different sources. *Journal of Abnormal and Social Psychology, 44*, 329–344.

Funder, D. C., & Ozer, D. J. (1983). Behavior as a function of the situation. *Journal of Personality and Social Psychology, 44*, 107–112.

Furnham, A. (1986). Response bias, social desirability and dissimulation. *Personality and Individual Differences, 7*, 385–400.

Galton, F. (1869). *Hereditary Genius*. London: Macmillan.

Goffin, R. D., Rothstein, M. G., & Johnston, N. G. (1996). Personality testing and the assessment center: Incremental validity for managerial selection. *Journal of Applied Psychology, 81*, 746–756.

Goffin, R. D., Rothstein, M. G., Rieder, M. J., Poole, A., Krajewski, H. T., Powell, D. M., & Mestdagh, T. (2011). Choosing job-related personality traits: Developing valid personality-oriented job analysis. *Personality and Individual Differences, 51*(5), 646–651.

Goldberg, L. R. (1990). An alternative 'description of personality': The Big Five factor structure. *Journal of Personality and Social Psychology, 59*, 1216–1229.

Guildford, J. P. (1959). *Personality*. New York: McGraw-Hill.

Guion, R. M., & Gottier, R. F. (1965). Validity of personality measures in personnel selection. *Personnel Psychology, 18*(2), 135–164.

Guion, R. M., & Highhouse, S. (2006). *Essentials of Personnel Selection: Personnel Assessment and Selection*. Mahwah, NJ: Lawrence Erlbaum.

Hamby, T., Taylor, W., Snowden, A. K., & Peterson, R. A. (2016). A meta-analysis of the reliability of free and for-pay Big Five scales. *The Journal of Psychology: Interdisciplinary and Applied, 150*(4), 422–430.

Hampson, S. E. (2012). Personality processes: Mechanisms by which personality traits 'get outside the skin'. *Annual Review of Psychology, 63*, 315–339.

Heggestad, E. D., Morrison, M., Reeve, C. L., & McCloy, R. A. (2006). Forced-choice assessments of personality for selection: Evaluating issues of normative assessment and faking resistance. *Journal of Applied Psychology, 91*(1), 9–24.

Hicks, L. E. (1970). Some properties of ipsative, normative, and forced-choice normative measures. *Psychological Bulletin, 74*(3), 167–184.

Hogan, J., & Holland, B. (2003). Using theory to evaluate personality and job–performance relations: A socioanalytic perspective. *Journal of Applied Psychology, 88*, 100–112.

Hogan, R. (2007). *Personality and the Fate of Organizations*. Mahwah, NJ: Lawrence Erlbaum.

Holden, R. R., Wood, L. L., & Tomashewski, L. (2001). Do response time limitations counteract the effect of faking on personality inventory validity?. *Journal of Personality and Social Psychology, 81*(1), 160–169.

Hough, L. M., Eaton, N. K., Dunnette, M. D., Kamp, J. D., & McCloy, R. A. (1990). Criterion-related validities of personality constructs and the effect of response distortion on those validities. *Journal of Applied Psychology, 75*(5), 581.

Hough, L. M., Oswald, F. L., & Ployhart, R. E. (2001). Determinants, detection and amelioration of adverse impact in personnel selection procedures: Issues, evidence and lessons learned. *International Journal of Selection and Assessment, 9*(1–2), 152–194.

Hughes, D. J. (2014). Accounting for individual differences in financial behaviour: The role of personality in insurance claims and credit behaviour. Unpublished doctoral thesis. University of Manchester, UK.

Hunter, J. E., & Schmidt, F. L. (2004). *Methods of Meta-Analysis: Correcting Error and Bias in Research Findings*. Thousand Oaks, CA: Sage.

Irwing, P., & Booth, T. (2013). An item level exploratory factor analysis of the sphere of personality: An eleven-factor model. *Paper presented at the 1st World Conference on Personality*, Stellenbosch, South Africa.

Jackson, D. N., Ashton, M. C., & Tomes, J. L. (1996). The six-factor model of personality: Facets from the Big Five. *Personality and Individual Differences, 21*, 391–402.

Jackson, D. N., Paunonen, S. V., Fraboni, M., & Goffin, R. G. (1996). A five-factor versus six-factor model of personality structure. *Personality and Individual Differences, 20*, 33–45.

Jenkins, M., & Griffith, R. (2004). Using personality constructs to predict performance: Narrow or broad bandwidth. *Journal of Business and Psychology, 19*(2), 255–269.

Johnson, C. E., Wood, R., & Blinkhorn, S. F. (1988). Spuriouser and spuriouser: The use of ipsative personality tests. *Journal of Occupational Psychology, 61*(2), 153–162.

Judge, T. A., Bono, J. E., Ilies, R., & Gerhardt, M. W. (2002). Personality and leadership: A qualitative and quantitative review. *Journal of Applied Psychology, 87*, 765–780.

Judge, T. A., & Erez, A. (2007). Interaction and intersection: The constellation of emotional stability and extraversion in predicting performance. *Personnel Psychology, 60*(3), 573–596.

Judge, T. A., & Ilies, R. (2002). Relationship of personality to performance motivation: A meta-analytic review. *Journal of Applied Psychology, 87*, 797–807.

Judge, T. A., Jackson, C. L., Shaw, J. C., Scott, B. A., & Rich, B. L. (2007). Self-efficacy and work-related performance: The integral role of individual differences. *Journal of Applied Psychology, 92*(1), 107–127.

Judge, T. A., Rodell, J. B., Klinger, R. L., Simon, L. S., & Crawford, E. R. (2013). Hierarchical representations of the five-factor model of personality in predicting job performance: Integrating three organizing frameworks with two theoretical perspectives. *Journal of Applied Psychology, 98*(6), 875–925.

Judge, T. A., & Zapata, C. P. (2015). The person–situation debate revisited: Effect of situation strength and trait activation on the validity of the Big Five traits in predicting job performance. *Academy of Management Journal, 58*, 1–31.

Kelley, T. L. (1927). *Interpretation of Educational Measurements*. Yonkers, NY: World Book.

Komar, S., Komar, J. A., Robie, C., & Taggar, S. (2010). Speeding personality measures to reduce faking. A self-regulatory model. *Journal of Personnel Psychology, 9*(3), 126–137.

Le, H., Oh, I. S., Robbins, S. B., Ilies, R., Holland, E., & Westrick, P. (2011). Too much of a good thing: Curvilinear relationships between personality traits and job performance. *Journal of Applied Psychology, 96*(1), 113–133.

Lee, K., & Ashton, M. C. (2004). Psychometric properties of the HEXACO Personality Inventory. *Multivariate Behavioral Research, 39,* 329–358.

Lee, K., Ashton, M. C., Hong, S., & Park, K. B. (2000). Psychometric properties of the Nonverbal Personality Questionnaire in Korea. *Educational and Psychological Measurement, 60,* 131–141.

Lounsbury, J. W., Sundstrom, E., Loveland, J. L., & Gibson, L. W. (2003). Broad versus narrow personality traits in predicting academic performance of adolescents. *Learning and Individual Differences, 14*(1), 65–75.

Marsh, H. W., Lüdtke, O., Muthén, B., Asparouhov, T., Morin, A. J. S., Trautwein, U., & Nagengast, B. (2010). A new look at the Big Five factor structure through exploratory structural equation modeling. *Psychological Assessment, 22,* 471–491.

McCrae, R. R., & Costa, P. T. (1985). Updating Norman's 'Adequate Taxonomy': Intelligence and personality dimensions in natural language and in questionnaires. *Journal of Personality and Social Psychology, 49,* 710–721.

McManus, M. A., & Kelly, M. L. (1999). Personality measures and biodata: Evidence regarding their incremental predictive value in the life insurance industry. *Personnel Psychology, 52,* 137–148.

Meade, A. W. (2004). Psychometric problems and issues involved with creating and using ipsative measures for selection. *Journal of Occupational and Organizational Psychology, 77,* 531–551.

Mischel, W. (1968). *Personality and Assessment.* New York: John Wiley & Sons.

Monson, T. C., Hesley, J. W., & Chernick, L. (1982). Specifying when personality traits can and cannot predict behavior: An alternative to abandoning the attempt to predict single act criteria. *Journal of Personality and Social Psychology, 43,* 385–399.

Monzani, L., Ripoll, P., & Peiró, J. M. (2015). The moderator role of followers' personality traits in the relations between leadership styles, two types of task performance and work result satisfaction. *European Journal of Work and Organizational Psychology, 24*(3), 444–461.

Morgeson, F. P., Campion, M. A., Dipboye, R. L., Hollenbeck, J. R., Murphy, K., & Schmitt, N. (2007a). Reconsidering the use of personality tests in personnel selection contexts. *Personnel Psychology, 60*(3), 683–729.

Morgeson, F. P., Campion, M. A., Dipboye, R. L., Hollenbeck, J. R., Murphy, K., & Schmitt, N. (2007b). Are we getting fooled again? Coming to terms with limitations in the use of personality tests for personnel selection. *Personnel Psychology, 60*(4), 1029–1049.

Morgeson, F. P., Reider, M. H., & Campion, M. A. (2005). Selecting individuals in team settings: The importance of social skills, personality characteristics, and teamwork knowledge. *Personnel Psychology, 58*(3), 583–611.

Moscoso, S., & Salgado, J. F. (2004). 'Dark side' personality styles as predictors of task, contextual, and job performance. *International Journal of Selection and Assessment, 12,* 356–362.

Mount, M. K., & Barrick, M. R. (1995). The Big Five personality dimensions: Implications for research and practice in human resources management. *Research in Personnel and Human Resources Management, 13*(3), 153–200.

Mueller-Hanson, R., Heggestad, E. D., & Thornton III, G. C. (2003). Faking and selection: Considering the use of personality from select-in and select-out perspectives. *Journal of Applied Psychology, 88*(2), 348–355.

Myers, I. (1978). *Myers–Briggs Type Indicator.* Palo Alto, CA: Consulting Psychologists Press.

Norman, W. T. (1963). Toward an adequate taxonomy of personality attributes: Replicated factor structure in peer nomination personality ratings. *The Journal of Abnormal and Social Psychology, 66,* 574–583.

O'Boyle, E. H., Forsyth, D. R., Banks, G. C., & McDaniel, M. A. (2012). A meta-analysis of the dark triad and work behavior: A social exchange perspective. *Journal of Applied Psychology, 97*(3), 557–579.

Oh, I. S., Lee, K., Ashton, M. C., & De Vries, R. E. (2011). Are dishonest extraverts more harmful than dishonest introverts? The interaction effects of honesty–humility and extraversion in predicting workplace deviance. *Applied Psychology, 60*(3), 496–516.

Oh, I. S., Le, H., Whitman, D. S., Kim, K., Yoo, T. Y., Hwang, J. O., & Kim, C.-S. (2014). The incremental validity of honesty–humility over cognitive ability and the Big Five personality traits. *Human Performance, 27,* 206–224.

Oh, I. S., Wang, G., & Mount, M. K. (2011). Validity of observer ratings of the five-factor model of personality traits: A meta-analysis. *Journal of Applied Psychology, 96*(4), 762.

Ones, D. S., Dilchert, S., Viswesvaran, C., & Judge, T. A. (2007). In support of personality assessment in organizational settings. *Personnel Psychology, 60*(4), 995–1027.

Ones, D. S., & Viswesvaran, C. (1996). Bandwidth-fidelity dilemma in personality measurement for personnel selection. *Journal of Organizational Behavior, 17,* 609–626.

Ones, D. S., & Viswesvaran, C. (1998). The effects of social desirability and faking on personality and integrity assessment for personnel selection. *Human Performance, 11*(2–3), 245–269.

Pace, V. L., & Brannick, M. T. (2010). How similar are personality scales of the 'same' construct? A meta-analytic investigation. *Personality and Individual Differences, 49,* 669–676.

Paulhus, D. L., & Williams, K. M. (2002). The dark triad of personality: Narcissism, Machiavellianism, and psychopathy. *Journal of Research in Personality, 36,* 556–563.

Paunonen, S. V., & Ashton, M. C. (2001). Big Five factors and facets and the prediction of behavior. *Journal of Personality and Social Psychology, 81,* 524–539.

Paunonen, S. V., Haddock, G., Forsterling, F., & Keinonen, M. (2003). Broad versus narrow personality measures and the prediction of behaviour across cultures. *European Journal of Personality, 17,* 413–33.

Paunonen, S. V., & Jackson, D. N. (2000). What is beyond the Big Five? Plenty! *Journal of Personality, 68,* 821–835.

Pervin, L., & John, O. P. (Eds). (2001). *Handbook of Personality: Theory and Research* (2nd ed.). New York: Guilford Press.

Pittenger, D. J. (2005). Cautionary comments regarding the Myers–Briggs type indicator. *Consulting Psychology Journal: Practice and Research, 57*(3), 210–221.

Ployhart, R. E., Weekley, J. A., Holtz, B. C., & Kemp, C. (2003). Web-based and paper-and-pencil testing of applicants in a proctored setting: Are personality, biodata, and situational judgment tests comparable? *Personnel Psychology, 56*(3), 733–752.

Raymark, P. H., Schmit, M. J., & Guion, R. M. (1997). Identifying potentially useful personality constructs for employee selection. *Personnel Psychology, 50*(3), 723–736.

Roberts, B. W., & DelVecchio, W. F. (2000). The rank-order consistency of personality from childhood to old age: A quantitative review of longitudinal studies. *Psychology Bulletin, 126,* 3–25.

Roberts, B. W., Kuncel, N. R., Shiner, R. L., Caspi, A., & Goldberg, L. R. (2007). The power of personality: The comparative validity of personality traits, socioeconomic status, and cognitive ability for predicting important life outcomes. *Perspectives on Psychological Science, 2,* 313–345.

Roberts, B. W., & Mroczek, D. (2008). Personality trait change in adulthood. *Current Directions in Psychological Science, 17,* 31–35.

Rojon, C., McDowall, A., & Saunders, M. N. (2015). The relationships between traditional selection assessments and workplace performance criteria specificity: A comparative meta-analysis. *Human Performance, 28*(1), 1–25.

Rosse, J. G., Miller, J. L., & Stecher, M. D. (1994). A field study of job applicants' reactions to personality and cognitive ability testing. *Journal of Applied Psychology, 79,* 987–992.

Rothstein, M. G., & Goffin, R. D. (2006). The use of personality measures in personnel selection: What does current research support? *Human Resource Management Review, 16*(2), 155–180.

Rothstein, M., Paunonen, S., Rush, J., & King, G. (1994). Personality and cognitive ability predictors of performance in graduate business school. *Journal of Educational Psychology, 86,* 516–530.

Rynes, S., Gyluk, T., & Brown, K. (2007). The very separate worlds of academic and practitioner periodicals in human resource management: Implications for evidence-based management. *Academy of Management Journal, 50,* 987–1008.

Sackett, P. R., & Lievens, F. (2008). Personnel selection. *Annual Review of Psychology, 59,* 419–450.

Salgado, J. F. (1997). The five factor model of personality and job performance in the European Community. *Journal of Applied Psychology, 82*(1), 30–43.

Salgado J. F. (2003). Predicting job performance using FFM and non-FFM personality measures. *Journal of Occupational and Organizational Psychology, 76,* 323–346.

Salgado, J. F., & Moscoso, S. (2003). Internet-based personality testing: Equivalence of measures and assessors' perceptions and reactions. *International Journal of Selection and Assessment, 11,* 194–205.

Salgado, J. F., Anderson, N., & Tauriz, G. (2014). The validity of ipsative and quasi-ipsative forced-choice personality inventories for different occupational groups: A comprehensive meta-analysis. *Journal of Occupational and Organizational Psychology, 88*(4), 797–834.

Salgado, J. F., & Tauriz, G. (2014). The five-factor model, forced-choice personality inventories and performance: A comprehensive meta-analysis of academic and occupational validity studies. *European Journal of Work and Organizational Psychology, 23,* 3–30.

Schmidt, F. L., & Hunter, J. E. (1998). The validity and utility of selection methods in personnel psychology: Practical and theoretical implications of 85 years of research findings. *Psychological Bulletin, 124*(2), 262–274.

Schmidt, F. L., Shaffer, J. A., & Oh, I. S. (2008). Increased accuracy for range restriction corrections: Implications for the role of personality and general mental ability in job and training performance. *Personnel Psychology, 61,* 827–868.

Schmitt, N., & Kunce, C. (2002). The effects of required elaboration of answers to biodata questions. *Personnel Psychology, 55*(3), 569–587.

Silzer, R. F., & Church, A. H. (2010). Identifying and assessing high potential talent: Current organizational practices. *In* R. F. Silzer & B. E. Dowell (Eds.), *Strategy-Driven Talent Management: A Leadership Imperative* (pp. 213–280). Chichester: Wiley.

Smith, J. M., & Smith, P. (2005). *Testing People at Work.* London: Blackwell.

Steiner, D. D., & Gilliland, S. W. (1996). Fairness reactions to personnel selection techniques in France and the United States. *Journal of Applied Psychology, 81*(2), 134–141.

Tett, R. P., & Burnett, D. D. (2003). A personality trait-based interactionist model of job performance. *Journal of Applied Psychology, 88* (3), 500–517.

Tett, R. P., & Christiansen, N. D. (2007). Personality tests at the crossroads: A response to Morgeson, Campion, Dipboye, Hollenbeck, Murphy, and Schmitt (2007). *Personnel Psychology, 60*(4), 967–993.

Tett, R. P., Jackson, D. N., & Rothstein, M. (1991). Personality measures as predictors of job performance: A meta-analytic review. *Personnel Psychology, 44*(4), 703–742.

Tett, R. P., Jackson, D. N., Rothstein, M., & Reddon, J. R. (1999). Meta-analysis of bidirectional relations in personality–job performance research. *Human Performance, 12*(1), 1–29.

Tett, R. P., Steele, J. R., & Beauregard, R. S. (2003). Broad and narrow measures on both sides of the personality–job performance relationship. *Journal of Organizational Behavior, 24*(3), 335–356.

Timmerman, M. E. (2006). Multilevel component analysis. *British Journal of Mathematical and Statistical Psychology, 59*(2), 301–320.

Thorndike, E. L. (1904). *An Introduction to the Theory of Mental and Social Measurements.* Oxford: Science Press.

Tupes, E. C., & Christal, R. E. (1961). Recurrent personality factors based on trait ratings. Technical Report No. *ASD-TR-61-97.* Lackland Air Force Base, TX: U.S. Air Force.

Vassend, O., & Skrondal, A. (2011). The NEO personality inventory revised (NEO-PI-R): Exploring the measurement structure and variants of the five-factor model. *Personality and Individual Differences, 50,* 1300–1304.

Wanberg, C. R., Kammeyer-Mueller, J., & Marchese, M. (2006). Mentor and protégé predictors and outcomes of mentoring in a formal mentoring program. *Journal of Vocational Behavior, 69*(3), 410–423.

9

Using Interviewing in Selection

Melinda Blackman

Introduction

Numerous tools and processes are available to help organizations narrow the range of candidates for a job and hone in on those who are most qualified and well suited for a given job opening. These include a variety of formal assessments, which range from high-fidelity assessment centres that provide a work sample for various ability, skill, knowledge and personality measures. In spite of the abundance of rigorous assessment measures, the employment interview remains the most commonly used selection instrument, either alone or in combination with complementary selection measures. Since its conception in the early 1920s, the employment interview has evolved considerably and, if developed and implemented properly, can be a reliable and valid selection tool. Thomas Edison was one of the first credited with implementing a selection interview on a regular basis (Dennis, 1984). Finding himself with hundreds of college graduates who wanted to work in his laboratory, Edison developed 150 selection questions that tapped a variety of subjects (e.g., geography, mathematics, manufacturing, history and trivia). His goal was to narrow the applicant pool, based on applicants' having comparable knowledge and intellect to his own, which would be a good match for the level of work that he was conducting.

Early uses of the selection interview took a similar approach, whereby specific questions were used, which interviewers thought would be relevant to their hiring decisions. Interviews were informal, with candidates being asked selected questions interspersed with small-talk and diversions. It is unlikely that any type of rating form or structured evaluation was used to assess candidates in relation to understood job requirements. Instead, like many continue to do today, interviewers relied primarily on their gut instinct to make selection decisions and then rationalized what went wrong if the chosen candidate failed to perform to par after being hired. Although the selection interview has evolved tremendously since its early days, many employers are still unaware of how to use it to their

The Wiley Blackwell Handbook of the Psychology of Recruitment, Selection and Employee Retention,
First Edition. Edited by Harold W. Goldstein, Elaine D. Pulakos, Jonathan Passmore and Carla Semedo.
© 2017 John Wiley & Sons Ltd. Published 2020 by John Wiley & Sons Ltd.

maximum advantage and the ability of the interview, used effectively, to rival the predictive accuracy of formal assessments.

Traditionally, the selection interview focused on predicting a candidate's technical skills relevant to the job in question (Campion, Palmer & Campion, 1997; Conway, Jako & Goodman, 1995; Cronshaw & Wiesner, 1989). However, by asking the right questions, it is possible to ascertain a wide variety of criteria during the interview. These include the applicant's personality, interests, motivation, person–job fit, organizational citizenship behaviour and integrity, among others (Blackman, 2002a; Blackman & Funder, 2002; Ones, Viswesvaran & Schmidt, 1993; Organ, 1988; Podsakoff, Whiting, Podsakoff & Mishra, 2011). In addition to predicting multiple criteria, the interview can be administered in different formats for a variety of purposes, ranging from a two-person interaction with standard questions to a multifaceted, multi-person encounter. Moreover, depending on how the interview is administered, what the interview is looking to predict and other factors (e.g., the extent of interviewer training, use of standard evaluation criteria, etc.), its reliability and validity can rival or even surpass standardized assessment measures (Hamdani, Valcea & Buckley, 2014; Huffcutt, Culbertson & Weyhrauch, 2013; Townsend, Bacigalupi & Blackman, 2007). This chapter will critically review research, theory and practice relevant to the employment interview and discuss how to use this selection measure to optimize hiring decisions.

Structured versus Unstructured Interview Questions

One prominent factor that can affect the reliability and predictive validity of an employment interview is the structure of the interview questions the candidate is asked. The most basic distinguishing attribute for interview question types is whether the questions are structured or unstructured. Structured questions are pre-planned questions that the interviewer asks of all applicants in a specific order with little or no follow-up questions on the part of the interviewer (Conway & Peneno, 1999). These questions are frequently based on job analyses or critical incidents. Unstructured questions are questions that usually develop spontaneously during the interview and at times are comparable to small-talk (Campion, Palmer & Campion, 1997; Dana, Dawes & Peterson, 2013). Typically, there is considerable follow-up to the applicant's responses. These questions are not based on a job analysis or critical incidents. One prominent disadvantage to unstructured interview questions is the higher likelihood of biases being unintentionally introduced. For instance, an interviewer who asks an unstructured question may develop the 'similar to me' error with the applicant, which ultimately can impact a protected group (Carson, Carson, Fontenot & Burdin, 2005). As most unstructured questions develop spontaneously during the interview they are more susceptible to bias or may even stereotype the applicants. These biases have the potential to leave an organization open to litigation (Carson, Carson, Fontenot & Burdin, 2005). Another disadvantage is that the applicant's responses are not directly comparable to other applicants' responses as the questions and depth of follow-up vary from interview to interview. Ultimately, the validity and reliability of the interviewer's ratings can be significantly compromised. However, research has shown that particular constructs (e.g., applicant integrity and personality characteristics) can be very accurately assessed through unstructured questions (Blackman & Funder, 2008). In a similar vein, Dana, Dawes and Peterson (2013) point out that extreme applicant personality traits (i.e., those at either end of the spectrum) can be easily identified with a screening interview by using unstructured questions. This topic is discussed in more detail in a later section.

Types of structured question

Over the years three basic types of structured interview questions have ben formulated in response to the demand for more reliable and valid interview questions. The three types are: situational, experience-based (referred to by Janz, 1989, as patterned behavioural description questions) and general structured questions. Situational questions are based on critical incidents and measure the candidate's future intentions and thus their future behaviour (Latham, 1989). Typically, these questions are preceded by 'What would you do if...?' A psychometric advantage of this type of question is that it can be directly compared to other applicants' responses, thus helping to enhance the reliability of the interviewer's rating. Another advantage to the situational interview question is that, if applicants have not had direct experience with the job at hand, they are still able to provide an answer by hypothesizing what they would do in the situation. Validity estimates for the situational interview question format in terms of predicting future job performance average about 0.27 (McDaniel, Whetzel, Schmidt & Maurer, 1994).

The second format, the experience-based interview question, is targeted at assessing the candidate's past job performance behaviour. These questions frequently begin with the prompt, 'What did you do when...?' A disadvantage of the experience-based question is that applicants use different examples of past behaviour in their responses which are not directly comparable for the raters, limiting the reliability and validity of the ratings. The validity estimates for experience-based interview questions have been found to average 0.55 (Motowidlo, Carter, Vaughn, Dunnette, Tippins, Werner & Burnett, 1992)

As a side note, Motowidlo and colleagues developed a hybrid variation of the situational and experience-based interview which they term 'structured behavioural interview' (Motowidlo, Carter & Vaughan et al., 1992). This format not only incorporates both past and future-oriented structured questioning, but stipulates using structured rating methods such as behaviourally anchored rating scales as well as explicit interviewer training.

Conway and Peneno (1999) measured the construct validity of the situational format versus the experience-based format. They found that the situational interview questions and the experience-based questions were highly correlated. More specifically, the situational questions tapped into job knowledge and the experience-based questions reflected previous job experience. Experience-based interview questions produced the highest validity coefficients in comparison to situational interview questions and predicted job performance for participants' current job. The researchers concluded that the two interview question formats each measured different content domains and that the different question types supplemented each other. In particular, the experience-based interview question format was found to measure intelligence, emotional intelligence and citizenship behaviour (Carson et al., 2005). Pulakos and Schmitt (1995) extended this research and found that both formats were equally predictive of subgroups, such as race (White, Hispanic, Black) and gender.

Conway and Peneno's (1995) study then evaluated general structured interview questions and concluded that they tend to reflect personality and general understanding of the job at hand. Interestingly, they found that general questions were preferred by the applicants in comparison to other formats.

Interview Formats

Today the employment interview has evolved and is now found in several versions or formats, each with its own optimal predictive criteria. The primary distinction with regard to interview formats is whether they are structured or unstructured. Structured interviews consist of standardized questions based on a job analysis and asked of all candidates in the same order with little to no follow-up questioning (Campion, Palmer & Campion, 1997). Also, with the structured format, interviewer training through the rating of videotaped candidates with feedback is encouraged so that all interviewers reach a similar level of reliability in their ratings. Note-taking during the interview is also encouraged so that the interviewers will recall details more accurately. In addition, the interviewer(s) then use a detailed rating form to evaluate the candidate's responses. The unstructured interview, on the other hand, consists of small-talk, perhaps some standardized questions and several spontaneous questions initiated by the interviewer as well as follow-up questioning to the candidate's responses (Campion, Pursell & Brown, 1988). Prior to the 1970s, employers entered the selection process with the single criterion of performance prediction in mind (Ulrich & Trumbo, 1965). Employers would choose what they thought was a 'structured interview', but in reality was unstructured in format. These early interviews consisted of pre-planned questions, however on closer inspection, the interviewers did not consistently adhere to a script but asked supplementary questions spontaneously, thus characterizing the format as more unstructured than structured (Campion, Palmer & Campion, 1997; Campion, Pursell & Brown, 1988; Levashina, Christopher, Morgeson & Campion, 2014; Schmidt & Hunter, 1998). Research, theory and practice served as the impetus that spotlighted the need for strict standardization of the structured interview to obtain good levels of predictive validity.

Predicting the job candidate's skill set, however, was not enough for practitioners as they were still plagued with the long-term problem of employee turnover. As a result it was realized that the structured interview was not able to predict the fit of the candidate to the organization. Researchers then started to examine other contributory factors of turnover, such as constructs of the candidate's personality, which had previously been overlooked (Blackman, 2002a, 2006). Researchers then started asking 'Does the candidate have the personality traits that optimally fit the job description and ultimately the climate of the organization?' Realizing also that counterproductive behaviour is another personality-related factor that contributes to turnover, researchers knew that accurately assessing traits like dependability and conscientious that are directly linked to counterproductive behaviour was crucial (Ones, Viswesvaran & Schmidt, 1993; Townsend, Bacigalupi & Blackman, 2007). It was soon apparent that the lack of these two prominent traits could potentially lead to chronic absenteeism, tardiness, volatile behaviour and even lack of attention to detail on the part of emploees (Taylor & Small, 2002). No doubt, in jobs where fatalities are a risk (e.g., Emergency Services dispatchers, firefighters, air traffic controllers and offshore oil and gas workers) accurately assessing these traits in a job candidate is essential.

The first priority for researchers was to ask, 'How accurate are lay interviewers in assessing job-relevant personality traits during the selection interview?' If an organization was relying on personality inventories to select candidates, this question was not relevant, but for those organizations that used the interview as their principal selection method it was crucial. Blackman's (2002a, 2000b) research pointed to the type of interview format used to answer this question. Blackman (2000a) examined the accuracy of personality judgements made by lay judges who used either a structured interview format or an unstructured format in an experimental setting. Her study found that college student interviewers who used the unstructured format produced significantly more accurate personality judgements of job candidates who were applying for a student clerical position when self-interviewer and peer-interviewer agreement was used as the criteria for accuracy. It is interesting to note in this study that the structured interview contained significantly more personality-related interview questions than did the unstructured format, yet the unstructured format still prevailed with regard to superior accurate personality judgements. Blackman found that the unstructured format elicita small-talk and many diversions in conversation which allows candidates to drop their guard. When this occurs, the applicants' true persona emerges. The relaxed job candidate might even see the interviewer as a friend and admit to relevant knowledge about their shortcomings. This allows the interviewer to glean information about the candidate's personality as well as their integrity. As candidates feel very comfortable with this format much more of their nonverbal behaviour is revealed, with references to past or future behaviour (Townsend, Bacigalupi & Blackman, 2007). Taking candidates out for coffee or lunch, or giving them a tour of the organization, are prime venues for an unstructured interview. Research reveals that candidates participating in an unstructured interview elaborate more in their responses, display significantly more nonverbal behaviours and have longer interviews than candidates in structured interviews (Blackman, 2002a). The inherent nature of this format lends itself to accurately predicting multiple criteria. Specifically, job-related personality characteristics and constructs such as conscientiousness, agreeableness, dependability, organizational citizenship, integrity and person–job fit can be more accurately predicted from an unstructured interview compared to other formats and even matching the accuracy of standardized personality and integrity tests (Blackman, 2008; Townsend, Bacigalupi & Blackman, 2007). Townsend and colleagues administered an integrity test very similar in content to the Reid Report (Reid London House, 2007) to job candidates in an experimental study. Then peers who knew the applicants well provided assessments of the job candidates using the integrity inventory, thus giving an additional perspective. The job applicants then participated in a structured, face-to-face interview. After the interview, the interviewer completed the integrity survey on the candidate. Self–interviewer agreement on the integrity inventory was very high, yet it was not significantly different from the high levels of peer–interviewer agreement that was obtained. It should be reassuring to interviewers to know that their integrity assessment made during an interview is just as accurate as that made by a well-acquainted peer of the job candidate and that of the applicant himself. Blackman (2008), however, urges that the interviewer still use the structured interview format to predict the candidate's skill set and then follow up with promising candidates by using an unstructured format to screen for personality and integrity-relevant traits.

Interviewers have been turning their attention to other formats in their search for greater predictive validity and efficiency. The structured, unstructured, panel, multiple-applicant, telephone and video-conference are among the many formats that the interviewer can choose from. The multiple-applicant interview (two or more candidates are interviewed simultaneously by one interviewer) is another format that can be deployed as an alternative for interviewers who are hiring seasonal help or need to interview a large pool of applicants (Tran & Blackman, 2006). An example is the case of Wynn Casino and Resort in Las Vegas, which needed to hire 3,000 employees in a three-week period leading up to its opening. A one-on-one, structured interview would not be efficient, but the multiple-applicant interview would be ideally suited for this purpose. The evidence suggests that interviewers who implement this format should use it only to predict job performance and not personality factors (Tran & Blackman, 2006). The cognitive load and multi-tasking that the multiple-applicant interview requires was found to compromise the interviewer's overall judgement. Tran and Blackman (2006) found that the one-on-one interview format was far superior in predicting the candidate's personality-relevant traits to the multiple-applicant format, although after reducing the applicant pool by employing the multiple-applicant format, a more intimate, one-on-one, unstructured format could be employed to determine personality factors and the integrity of employees if necessary.

Some employers find that the panel interview, in which two or more interviewers interview the candidate, suit their needs best. This format has been found not only to predict job performance and personality factors (if used in an unstructured format) but also to improve the accuracy of the assessment (Dipboye, Gaugler & Hayes, 1997; Prusha, 2014). When several interviewers pool their ratings of a factor, the increase in accurate ratings is substantial. Another merit of this technique is that biases and self-fulfilling prophecies that a single interviewer might hold can be minimized. A final benefit found with this format is that it is perceived as a fairer method by candidates than a simple, one-on-one format as the candidate may fail to develop a relationship with a single interviewer and thus perceive the process as unfair if not selected (Dipboye, Macan & Shahani-Denning, 2012; Farago, Zide & Shahani-Denning, 2013; Kuo & Chang, 2011). This perception of fairness leads to good public relations for the organization, especially if three or more interviewers are involved. Interviewers sometimes forget the social process involved in the interview, where both the organization and the candidate seek to project themselves in the most favourable light. The candidate's perception of the fairness of the interview and the questions asked will in turn determine the applicant's opinion of the organization regardless of what they had held prior to the interview (Dipboye, Macan & Shahani-Denning, 2012).

For travel and efficiency sake, telephone and video-conference interviews have become increasingly popular in some countries, such as the US, facilitated by the development of communications technology, but these perceived benefits come at a price (Chapman & Rowe, 2002; Sear, Zhang, Wiesner, Hackett & Yuan, 2013; Straus, Miles & Levesque, 2001). Evidence suggests that interviewers should use this format only with the predictive criterion of job performance as their goal. When employing the formats the interviewer will find that the candidate's responses via the telephone or video-conference monitor are briefer and have less informative details than one typically finds during a face-to-face format (Blackman, 2002b). The telephone conference call is efficient, but the accuracy of relevant personality factors is sacrificed. Nevertheless, these formats are useful for making broad cuts in the selection process before following up with in-person interviews with promising candidates.

It is important to remember that the selection interview should not be conceptualized as a one-time event. Instead, the effective interview should be conceptualized as a series of multifaceted interviews with different sources of judgement. Judgements from a variety of viewpoints create a fuller portrait of the candidate's persona and skills from which to make an informed hiring decision. Using not only the main interviewer, but the incumbent, potential subordinates, potential peers and long-standing clients in the interview process can also add to the accuracy of judgements (Blackman, 2008; Funder & Colvin, 1988). Funder and colleagues took peer assessment of personality further in their research. They solicited judgements from the participants' parents and friends. These sources from different aspects of the target participant's life provided reassurance that in general people's behaviour is cross-situationally consistent, that they display similar personality and behaviour patterns during the selection interview process at home or at school (Funder & Colvin, 1991). Funder and Colvin have also suggested that peers and lay interviewers are fairly accurate judges of personality when self–interviewer and peer–interviewer agreement is used as the criterion of accuracy. In addition, with multiple interviewer sources, any caveats about the candidate can be cross-referenced through this multifaceted approach. The multifaceted interview process parallels Campbell and Fiske's (1959) multi-trait, multi-method philosophy with the long-term goal of obtaining convergent validity about the candidate's job-related skills, personality traits and job fit.

The evidence suggests the need to prepare fully for the process, with interviewers thinking about what kind of criteria they wish to predict (e.g., integrity, personality, job performance). The fit between the criteria and interview format is crucial, as is the type of interview questions asked (see Table 9.1). The choice of interview questions is another important step that the interviewer should not take lightly. For the unstructured interview, in predicting personality any small-talk over a period of time has been shown to be highly predictive of the candidate's personality (Blackman, 2002a). But for assessing job performance, behaviourally/situationally-oriented scenario questioning is optimal (Taylor & Small, 2002). Asking the candidate to remember a time when they 'had to deal with a difficult customer. What was the problem and how did they resolve it?' these behaviourally cued questions allow the employer to ascertain candidates' potential to think on their feet and their aptitude within a matter of minutes.

Criteria for Evaluating Interview Responses

Every interviewer would like to be as accurate as possible about the potential of the candidate in question, so employing multiple criteria to evaluate interview responses should be high on the interviewer's list of priorities. One of several techniques that can facilitate the accurate evaluation of a candidate's responses is understanding the interview context within the framework of the Realistic Accuracy Model (RAM) (Funder, 1995). RAM advocates that there are four moderator variables that facilitate accurate interpersonal judgements of others. The first is judgemental ability (also known as the good judge). The RAM model has shown that some individuals are simply better judges of personality than others due to their ability to perceive and use cues from the target correctly. Past research (Akert & Panter, 1988) and theory (Funder, 1995) suggest that the good judge has an extraverted personality and wide experience in social settings (Christiansen, Wolcott-Burnam & Janovics, 2005; McLarney, 2003). Such experience undoubtedly gives the judge more knowledge about how personality is revealed in specific behaviours. Organizations should consider carefully before choosing an interviewer as the accuracy of the interview is largely dependent on that person. The most senior individual in the organization may not be the best interviewer (Funder, 1995). However, interviewers can become better judges by training and rating videotaped targets, thus increasing the accuracy of their judgements and decreasing biases or errors (Wexley, Sanders & Yukel, 1973).

A second moderator of interpersonal judgement according to RAM is termed the 'good trait'. Research shows that properties of the trait being judged also affect the degree to which an accurate interpersonal judgement is likely (Funder & Dobroth, 1987). RAM posits that some attributes are difficult to judge, while others are relatively easy (Funder, 1995). An attribute such as 'is socially at ease around others', which is revealed by frequent positive social interactions, is easier to judge than a quality such as 'daydreams or ruminates frequently'. For this trait the interviewer must infer its presence from verbal statements from the target or, even more difficult, from distracted responses. Funder and Dobroth (1987) revealed that the more visible the trait or cues of the trait, the higher the levels of inter-judge and self–other agreement. With this knowledge in hand, interviewers can be confident in the accuracy of their ratings for highly visible traits such as the degree to which the individual is conscientious, agreeable or even dependable. And for those hard-to-judge qualities or traits, such as the candidate's potential to sabotage others' work, the interviewer should focus on going beyond the interview (e.g. reading letters of recommendation, utilizing assessment centres) to increase the quality and quantity of information on which to base the judgement.

Table 9.1 The optimal usage of various interview formats.

Interview Format	Description	Predictive Criteria	Optimal Use	Research
Structured	Standardized questions, no follow-up questions, ratings forms	Skill sets, future job performance	To facilitate reliable comparisons between candidates	Campion, Palmer & Campion, 1997; Levashina, Christopher, Morgeson & Campion, 2014 Blackman, 2002a
Unstructured	Spontaneous questions, small-talk, informal format, follow-up questions	Personality characteristics, integrity, counterproductive behaviour, organizational citizenship	Assessing the candidate's potential for engaging in counterproductive behaviour and person–organization fit	
Panel	Multiple interviewers and one applicant	Skill sets	Reduces interviewer bias, perceived by applicants as a fair interview	Prusha, 2014; Dipboye, Gaugler & Hayes, 1997 Tran & Blackman, 2006
Group Interview/ Multiple Applicant Interview	Multiple applicants with a single interviewer	Skill sets, future job performance	Efficient pre-screening device to make broad cuts in applicant pool	
Telephone/ Conference Call	Interview over the phone or via a video-conference monitor	Skill sets, future job performance	Efficient pre-screening device to make broad cuts in applicant pool	Chapman & Rowe, 2002; Sear, Zhang, Wiesner, Hackett & Yuan, 2013; Straus, Miles & Levesque, 2001; Blackman, 2002b

The third moderator variable is termed 'good information'. This variable refers to the quantity and quality of information available to the judge of personality. At a basic level, the longer you have known or have experience with targets the more accurate you will be in assessing their traits and qualities (Funder & Colvin, 1988). More specifically, in an experimental setting, Blackman and Funder (1998) showed that self–other agreement steadily increases as acquaintanceship with a target subject via videotaped, 5-minute episodes increases. Other studies support this finding (Cloyd 1977; Colvin & Funder 1991; Funder & Colvin 1988; Paulhus & Bruce 1992; Paunonen & Jackson, 1988).

The quality of information likewise plays a role in the assessment process. Blackman and Funder's (1998) research specifically supports the utility of this moderator variable. When comparing the accuracy of ratings made by interviewers who conducted a structured interview with who those used an unstructured format, the interviewers using the unstructured format were significantly more accurate in assessing the job candidate's personality and job-relevant traits. This research indicates that the unstructured interview, in which the candidate's behaviour is spontaneous, is generally more informative about personality than meeting the candidate in a very structured format where personality is less likely to vary (Blackman, 2002a).

The implications for interviewers are that part of the interview should be unstructured when the candidate's behaviour is free to vary, thus producing high quality information on which they can base their judgements. The unstructured format will increase the likelihood that the interviewer will make an accurate judgement about the candidate job-related qualities. Evidence suggests, however, that interviewers should refrain from using interview techniques that yield poor quality information, such as the telephone conference or, in some cases, the multiple-applicant interview with more than four candidates participating (Blackman, 2002a; Chapman & Rowe, 2002; Straus, Miles & Levesque, 2001; Tran & Blackman 2006).

The final moderator variable in RAM is coined 'the good target'. Colvin's (1993a, 1993b) research found that some individuals are easier to judge than others. This ultimately increases the likelihood that candidates will be judged accurately. 'Judgable people' are those Colvin found to be consistent in their actions, cognitions, words and deeds in different situations. For this reason, their future behaviour is easy to predict and the judge of personality more likely to be accurate in the assessment.

Blackman and others have identified the challenge of candidate behavioural inconsistency. This behaviour may be an indication that the individual is trying to conceal a negative aspect of their personality or work-related traits (Funder, 1995; Blackman, 2008). Follow-up interviews are an ideal way to observe a candidate's behavioural patterns, while eliciting more information from which to make an accurate assessment (Blackman, 2008).

Interviewers who are able to increase the accuracy of their assessment of the candidate during the interview process are doing a lot more than hiring the most qualified candidate. Accurate interview assessments are also a preventative measure that an organization is taking to reduce the number of employees who might engage in counterproductive behaviour, such as absenteeism, weight, volatile behaviour and workplace violence (Blackman, 2008; Ones, Viswesvaran & Schmidt, 1993).

When interviewers incorporate into the interview process their knowledge of the four moderator variables that curb accurate interpersonal judgement they increase their likelihood of hiring the best candidate. Regrettably, due to the complexity of the characters involved and the interaction between them, there is no single way to accurately predict a job candidate's standing on every job-relevant attribute during an interview. But if the duration of the interview is increased, a larger breadth or quantity of information becomes available on which to base a judgement. Even when conducting a panel interview, if one interviewer misses a candidate-prompted indicative behavioural cue, another interviewer may spot it. With multiple judges, a more accurate picture of the candidate can be made (Prusha, 2014).

Once knowledge of how to increase the accuracy of one's interpersonal judgements has been achieved, interviewers should supplement this knowledge with structured response rating scales, such as the Behaviorally Anchored Ratings Scales (BARS). BARS were developed by Smith and Kendall (1963) as a superior appraisal method to subjective graphic rating scales. BARS focus on identifying important employee behaviours that are relevant to successfully completing a particular job, rated on a numerical scale. Standard graphic rating scales, on the other hand, do not focus on the specific behaviours, but on personality characteristics and subjectively determined work habits. An example is: 'Employee answers telephone within three rings.' A standard rating scale might state it more loosely: 'Employee answers telephone promptly and efficiently.'

Behavioural anchors are typically developed using a critical incident technique or task analysis. BARS have been to shown to be more accurate and reliable than mixed standard scales when evaluating job applicants (Benson, Buckley & Hall, 1988). The method has been shown to reduce the adverse impact of various ethnic groups in a college admission study (Sinha, Oswald, Imus & Schmitt, 2011). An advantage of BARS is that applicants and employees view the rating process as fairer than trait-rated scales (Latham & Seijts, 1997). In addition, this method is more legally defensible when evaluating employee performance than other graphic rating scales (Benson, Buckley & Hall, 1988). And if the interviewer plays a role in the development of the BARS, convergent validity has been shown to increase while errors or biases such as the halo decrease (Friedman & Cornelius, 1976). However, a disadvantage of BARS is that administrators need to update the behavioural anchors as the job requirements change or the work context evolves.

Biases in the Interview Process

It is essential to understand that the interview process is a bi-directional process (Dipboye, Macan & Shahani-Denning, 2012; DeGroot & Motowidlo, 1999; McFarland, Ryan & Kriska, 2002). The interviewer's qualities can influence the candidate's responses; equally, the qualities of the candidate can influence the interviewer's assessment at any given moment (Purkiss, Perrewé, Gillespie, Mayes & Ferris, 2006). Interviewers need to be educated and trained in the processes that can occur during the interview and affect the impartiality and integrity of the process. Once this education has occurred certain safeguards can be implemented (e.g., standardized questions, interviewer training, note-taking, BARS) to reduce the likelihood of biases prejudicing the interview process.

Something that can occur during the interview process is self-fulfilling behaviours or opinions about the candidate on the part of the interviewer (Dipboye, 1982; Dipboye, Macan & Shahani-Denning, 2012). Simply by reading a candidate's name or application file prior to the interview can cause the interviewer to conjure up a profile and supposed responses and behaviours, which the interviewer might unintentionally elicit from the candidate. Keep in mind that these responses and behaviours may be desirable or undesirable according to the interviewer's preconceived ideas. For instance, on seeing that the candidate attended the same undergraduate institution as the interviewer, the interviewer may assume that the candidate will share their work ethic, personality characteristics and motivation (Gilfford, Ng & Wilkinson, 1985; Rand & Wexley, 1975). It might even be as simple as the candidate's name that the interviewer develops preconceived ideas about and unconsciously confirms these ideas through questioning or nonverbal behaviour.

Ultimately, interviewers and applicants come to the interview with pre-interview information and impressions from many sources, ranging from the media to their personal networks. These impressions can include goals for the interview and expectations that affect how the interviewer perceives the candidate during the interview. During the interview itself, the behavioural, cognitive and affective reactions of the two have reciprocal effects. These reactions result in demographic stereotyping and the interviewer's potential to distort information to confirm expectations about the candidate. This section addresses bi-directional factors we often do not consider, but which can affect the selection interview. These are specifically the candidate's physical attributes (e.g. stigmas, weight, non-native accent, physical attractiveness) the candidate's diversity (e.g., disability, sexual orientation), the uniqueness of the candidate's responses, the interviewer's warmth, the candidate's perceptions of interview fairness, as well as the interviewer's level of training. Implications for these factors biasing the interviewer and candidate's perceptions are discussed next.

Job candidate-prompted biases

Physical attributes   The candidate's appearance and nonverbal behaviour provide an array of visual cues that can trigger a self-fulfilling prophecy (Hollandsworth, 1979; Hosoda, Stone-Romero & Coats, 2003; Nordstrom, Huffaker & Williams, 1998; Wade & Kinicki, 1997). In many Western cultures, piercings and tattoos have become more commonplace. In spite of this, interviewers may see piercings and tattoos as stigmas and hold negative opinions about the personality characteristics, work ethic and citizenship behaviour of individuals who have them. Research shows that individuals who have any type of bodily stigma often face discrimination in an employment interview (Breecher, Bragger & Kutcher, 2006; Dipboye, Gaugler & Hayes, 1997; Madera, 2008). Madera (2008) investigated the ways in which a stigma (birthmark, scar, piercing, tattoo) on the face affects interview outcomes. The study revealed that participants who faced an applicant with a stigma divided their attention between looking at the stigma and the interview process in comparison to participants looking at applicants without a stigma. Additionally, participants who looked at an applicant with a stigma rated that applicant lower than participants who viewed an applicant without a stigma.

Another physical appearance issue that can affect judgement is the job candidate's weight (O'Brien et al., 2008; Roehling, 1999). Regardless of whether the candidate is thin or obese, a self-fulfilling prophecy can occur. When interviewers were shown videotapes of average-weight candidates and overweight candidates, they rated the overweight candidates significantly poorer than the average-weight candidate (Kutcher & Bragger, 2004; Pingitore, Dugoni, Tindale & Spring, 1994). The results suggested that bias against hiring overweight applicants does exist, especially for female applicants. Bias was most evident when applicants were rated by participants who were satisfied with their own body size. The decision not to hire an obese applicant was, however, only partly mediated by personality attributes (Kutcher & Bragger, 2004). Keep in mind that the cited studies were conducted in the United States, New Zealand and Australia, so the results may not be generalizable to all societies. There may be poor societies in which obesity is an indicator of good health and wealth, so that slender applicants may be perceived as impoverished and in poor health.

The physical attractiveness of the job applicant can cloud the objectiveness of the interview (Berscheid & Walster, 1974; Gilmore, Beehr & Love, 1986). Interviewers (like people in general) link attributes such as physical attractiveness to other socially desirable traits and successful job outcomes. Dipboye and colleagues (1977) found that the perceived attractiveness of the candidates affected hiring decisions made by student and professional raters. Interestingly though, the interaction between applicants' sex and physical attractiveness have produced mixed results, which researchers posit is due to the perceived relevance of physical attractiveness for job performance (Cash, Gillen & Burns, 1977; Gilmore, Beehr & Love, 1986). But what the studies do point to is that physical attractiveness is an advantage in the interview process (Cash, Gillen & Burns, 1977; Dipboye et al., 1977; Gilmore, Beehr & Love, 1986). The idea that 'what (or who) is beautiful is good' in both the workplace and in general has been found to be a cross-cultural phenomenon using samples of French and Chinese participants (McColl & Truong, 2013; Zhang, Kong, Zhong & Kou, 2014).

With an increasingly global and diverse workplace, interviewers will be faced with applicants who are non-natives to the country and have ethnic accents, as well as class or regional accents. In the UK an accent is an indication of upbringing and education (Coupland & Bishop, 2007). An accent can result in unintentional bias in an interviewer's ratings. A study by Purkiss and colleagues (2006) conducted in the US examined two implicit sources of bias in the selection interview: accent and name. As hypothesized, an interaction existed between the applicant's name and accent which affected participants' positive judgements of the applicant's characteristics. Specifically, an applicant with an ethnic name and speaking with a foreign accent was rated less positively by interviewers than an ethnic-named applicant without a foreign accent and non-ethnic-named applicants with and without an accent. Another American study (Deprez-Sims & Morris, 2013) replicated these results. In this second study participants were asked to evaluate an applicant with one of three accents (Midwestern US, French, Mexican) at two levels (low and high). The interviewers were played audio versions of the applicants' voices. The results revealed that the applicant with the Midwestern accent was viewed as more hirable than the applicant with the difficult to understand French accent. The researchers' path model showed that the accent condition – the hiring recommendation relationship – was mediated by similarity, interpersonal attraction and understandability. Cross-cultural studies support these assertions. Hansen, Rakić and Steffens (2014) conducted a study in Germany with standard-accent job candidates and nonstandard Turkish accent job applicants. The researchers found that the interviewers discriminated against the Turkish accent applicants and perceived them as less competent. Interviewers should definitely be versed in the potential biases that can occur when interviewing a non-native speaker. It is imperative that safeguards be integrated into the interview process, such as standardized response rating scales and interview training to mitigate potential interview bias.

Diversity features   Almost every country, including many developing countries, have legislation that prohibits discrimination in the workplace, based on factors such as race, gender, disability, age and sexual orientation (O'Cinneide, 2011). But even with legislation in place, it has been documented that diversity factors (race, disability and sexual orientation; Baumle, 2013; Sacco, Scheu, Ryan & Schmitt, 2003; Tews, Stafford & Shu, 2009) can bias evaluations during employment interviews. Though blatant discrimination is generally declining, more subtle forms of discrimination, which the perpetrator is often unaware of committing, occur (Dipboye & Colella, 2005). Sexual orientation is a non-observable form of diversity and research about it is scarce (Van Hoye & Lievens, 2003). Most research on sexual orientation discrimination during the selection interview is qualitative and based on self-reports with small sample sizes (Crosteau, 1996). However, a Belgium study by Van Hoye & Lievens (2003) used an experimental approach with professional recruiters to determine if applicants' sexual orientation affected their hirability. The researchers, after examining paper applicants in which their sexual orientation was revealed, found that the recruiters were just as likely to hire qualified gay applicants as heterosexual applicants. Though this is just one study from one country, the results are encouraging with regard to how some interviewers are managing diversity during the interview process. One should bear in mind though that numerous countries still have legislation that criminalizes homosexuality (2013 Report from the International Lesbian, Gay, Bisexual and Trans and Intersex Association).

As with sexual orientation, research on the effect of applicant disability in the interview process is scant (Hayes & Macan, 1997; Miceli, 1997). Miceli (1997) found that applicants who revealed a disability reduced the favourable impact they had made during the interview and decreased their chance of being hired.

Unique responses   In addition to the physical and diverse features of the applicants, the uniqueness of their interview response can potentially bias the interviewer's rating. Research has explored the methods applicants use to 'stand out from other applicants'. Rouline, Bangerter and Yerly (2011) tested how an applicant providing a unique answer was evaluated relative to applicants providing qualitatively equivalent but non-unique answers. Applicants providing unique answers received higher evaluations and increased their chances of a job offer. The study indicates that interviewers can be influenced by the uniqueness of applicants' answers, regardless of applicants' true abilities to perform on the job. The researchers believe that a contrast effect can come into play when the previous job candidate gives competent, but non-unique answers, and is then followed by a candidate who supplies unique answers to the interview questions, regardless of the content. Ultimately, unique answers can give these candidates an advantage over their rivals (Rouline et al., 2011). The study also showed how applicants giving unique answers to interview questions received better ratings on knowledge, skills, abilities and other characteristics in comparison to candidates who supplied non-unique answers.

Interviewer-prompted biases

Warmth of the interviewer   In this subsection we focus on the interviewer's persona and actions as sources of bias in the selection interview. A potentially biasing facet is the affectivity of the interviewer, in particular, warmth. Based on their US studies, Farago, Zide and Shahani-Denning (2013) advocate that all interviewers should be trained in 'warmth' and should be screened for warmth when they are undergoing the selection process. Warm behaviours include eye contact, nodding, smiling and hand-shaking. Farago and colleagues also believe that interviewers should learn to establish common ground by incorporating small-talk (an aspect of unstructured interviews) before and after the structured interview questions. Interviewers should remember that they are representatives of the organization, so it is in everyone's interest to ensure that applicants feel at ease during the interview. Further, adding warmth to the interview process can be easily incorporated, so the benefits of such training is likely to outweigh the costs, such as the job candidate not accepting the job offer or denigrating the organization to peers (Chen, Yang & Lin, 2010).

Fairness and structure of the interview

Other studies take into account the applicant's perceptions of the interview process and how they affect job acceptance offers. A field study by Kuo and Chang (2011) conducted in the manufacturing industry in Taiwan set out to examine applicant reactions to the structure of the interview they had participated in. The study implemented organizational justice theory and examined the applicants' reactions (organizational attraction, intention to accept the job, self-efficacy, self-perceived performance) to the interview structure (job-relatedness, standardization) and investigated the bases for these reactions in terms of the perceived procedural justice. The researchers found that the interview structure had a significant predictability for perceived procedural justice. Compared to job-relatedness, the effects of standardization on perceived procedural justice were larger. It suggests that standardization has more influence on the applicants' perception of procedural justice than the influence of job-relatedness. In addition, perceived procedural justice had significant predictability for the applicants' post-interview reactions, such as organizational attraction, intention to accept the job, self-efficacy and self-perceived performance under the condition of controlling the applicants' demographic variables and pre-interview perception of the organization, intention to accept the job and self-efficacy. It shows that applicants rely on the interview structure to gain information and make evaluations about the recruiting firms and jobs. Therefore, in order to enhance the applicants' positive perception and reactions in organizational settings, practitioners should provide as much information as possible about the employment interview during the selection process. Ultimately, the researchers found that perceived procedural justice mediates the relationship between standardization and applicant reactions. The researchers believe that the quality of the interview as an assessment tool depends on taking into consideration both the interviewer's and the applicant's perspectives.

In the same vein, a study conducted by Campion, Palmer and Campion (1997) in the US identified elements of the interview structure and made predictions of how applicants and interviewers might react to these elements. The interview structure was described by four dimensions: questioning consistency; evaluation standardization; question sophistication; and rapport building. It was found that interviewers with formal training and those with a selection rather than recruiting focus employed higher levels of interview structure. In addition, reactions to increased structure were mixed. Both higher structure (question sophistication) and lower structure (rapport building) were positively related to interviewer reactions. It was found that applicants reacted negatively to the increased perceived difficulty of structured interviews, but perceptions of procedural justice were not affected by the interview structure. These results point to the importance of the interview structure, as it can directly affect applicants' perceptions and ultimately their decision whether or not to accept a job offer.

Interviewer Training

Despite the general use of employment interviews in personnel selection, we know very little about how interviewers are trained and whether interviewer training influences the way interviews are conducted (Campion, Palmer & Campion, 1997; Cogger, 1982; Palmer, Campion & Green, 1999). Interview practitioners and researchers agree that formal interviewer training is crucial to successful recruiting and selection practices. Researchers believe that formal training can be used to improve a variety of interviewer tasks, including establishing valid criteria for job analysis, evaluating candidates more effectively (Day & Sulsky, 1995) and improving rapport (Gatewood, Lahiff, Deter & Hargrove, 1989) and the recruiting function of the interview (Chapman & Rowe, 2002; Rynes, 1989).

Despite agreement on the need for interviewer training, the extent to which interviewers receive training and whether this training is effective remain overlooked topics in the research literature (Palmer et al., 1999). Surprisingly, studies have been mixed regarding the efficacy of training in increasing interview rater effectiveness (Palmer et al., 1999). Rynes (1989) discussed the duality of the employment interview as both a selection device and a recruiting tool. Rynes hypothesized that there might be differences in the extent to which interviewers focus on the selection function of the interview or the recruiting function. Researchers believe that these roles may conflict with each other in that a greater focus on selection has the potential to reduce the attractiveness of the organization, while a greater focus on recruiting can reduce the validity of the selection decision (Chapman & Rowe, 2002). Barber, Hollenbeck, Tower and Phillips (1994) manipulated the interview focus so that applicants received either a recruitment interview or an interview that combined recruitment and selection elements. The study found that student applicants for a part-time research assistant position reacted more positively to a combined recruitment and selection interview than those who received only a recruitment interview. These results suggest the importance of interviewer training and how direction of focus can potentially be a liability for the interviewer and the organization as a whole.

Future Research

The selection interview is now widely used in candidate selection. However, interviewers and professional practitioners are often ignorant of the wealth of research that can be used to inform practice and thus optimize recruitment decisions. This is one area where psychologists working in I-O psychology could focus more attention on communicating research findings in ways that are more accessible to practitioners. When it comes to setting up a selection process many lay interviewers are uncertain where to begin. It should be our charge to develop a learning process, perhaps in the form a matrix listing various predictive criteria (e.g., integrity, job performance, personality) and the optimal interview formats to utilize. The matrix would offer optional selection devices for specific criteria (e.g., in-basket task, inventories) to complement the interview. The matrix could serve as a quick reference for interviewers who are embarking on the initial phases of their selection process.

There are several gaps in the selection interview literature to which we might well aim our future research. One of these areas is finding methods to mitigate the effects of interviewer bias. As discussed, interviewers can be biased against candidates who have certain qualities, ranging from a non-native accent to conspicuous physical stigmas. Safeguards to mitigate these biases (e.g., standardized rating forms, training of interviewers, note-taking) can reduce these biases to some extent, but more foolproof techniques are needed and shown to significantly reduce bias.

Another research area to explore is utilizing applied samples of professional recruiters and job applicants. Samples of convenience that frequently utilize college students in simulated employment interviews seem to be the norm for the majority of selection interview research. However, researchers are encouraged to take it to the next level and network with practitioners in the field and solicit applied samples. Though these relationships can be difficult to form for legal reasons, the wealth of knowledge that is obtained from these samples will undoubtedly advance our knowledge base considerably.

Equally important is targeting multicultural populations. Cross-cultural research in the selection interview is very limited and could be greatly expanded. With our ever-expanding global workforce, interviewers must be well versed in cultural differences in interview procedures, biases and phrasing of interview questions. The generalizability of selection interview theory is limited due to the lack of cross-cultural studies.

Conclusion

Integrity tests, personality inventories and in-basket tasks are just a few devices that can be used in the selection process. These methods can be both complex and expensive. Selection interviews, however, can offer a low-cost method that can achieve similar ends when the process is well designed and well implemented. Practitioners who opt for a multifaceted interview approach with varied interview formats and multiple judges should ultimately feel confident that improved recruitment decisions can be achieved.

References

Akert, R. M., & Panter, A. T. (1988). Extraversion and the ability to decode nonverbal communication. *Personality and Individual Differences, 9*, 965–972.

Barber, A. E., Hollenbeck, J. R., Tower, S. L., & Phillips, J. M. (1994). The effects of interview focus on recruitment effectiveness: A field experiment. *Journal of Applied Psychology, 79*, 886–896.

Baumle, A. K. (2013). The demography of sexuality and the labor market. In A. K. Baumle (Ed.), *International Handbook on the Demography of Sexuality* (pp. 243–256). New York: Springer Science & Business Media.

Benson P., Buckley M., & Hall S. (1988). The impact of rating scale format on rater accuracy: An evaluation of the mixed standard scale. *Journal of Management, 14*(3), 415–423.

Berscheid, E., & Walster, E. H. (1974). Physical attractiveness. In L. Berkowitz (Ed.), *Advances in Experimental Social Psychology* (Vol. 7). New York: Academic Press.

Blackman, M. C. (2002a). Personality judgment and the utility of the unstructured employment interview. *Basic and Applied Social Psychology, 24*(3), 240–249.

Blackman, M. C. (2002b). The employment interview via the telephone: Are we sacrificing accurate personality judgments for cost efficiency? *Journal of Research in Personality, 36*(3), 208–223.

Blackman, M. C. (2006). Using what we know about personality to hire the ideal colleague. *The Industrial-Organizational Psychologist, 43*, 27–31.

Blackman, M. C. (2008). The effective interview. In S. Cartwright & C. L. Cooper (Eds.), *The Oxford Handbook of Personnel Psychology*. Oxford: Oxford University Press.

Blackman, M. C., & Funder, D. C. (1998). The effect of information on the accuracy and consensus of personality judgments. *Journal of Experimental Social Psychology. 34*, 164–181.

Blackman, M. C., & Funder, D. C. (2002). Effective Interview practices for accurately assessing counterproductive traits. *International Journal of Selection and Assessment, 10*(1–2), 109–116.

Breecher, E., Bragger, J., & Kutcher, E. (2006). The structured interview: Reducing biases toward job applicants with physical disabilities. *Employee Responsibilities and Rights Journal, 18*, 155–170.

Campbell, D. T., & Fiske, D. W. (1959). Convergent and discriminant validation by the multitrait–multimethod matrix. *Psychological Bulletin, 56*, 81–105.

Campion, M., Palmer, D., & Campion, J. (1997). A review of structure in the selection interview. *Personnel Psychology, 50*, 655–702.

Campion, M., Pursell, E., & Brown, B. (1988). Structured interviewing: Raising the psychometric properties of the employment interview. *Personnel Psychology, 41*, 25–42.

Carson, K. D., Carson, P. P., Fontenot, G., & Burdin, J. J. (2005). Structured interview questions for selecting productive, emotionally mature, and helpful employees. *The Health Care Manager, 24*(3), 209–215.

Cash, T. F., Gillen, B., & Burns, B. S. (1977). Sexism and 'beautyism' in personnel consultant decision making. *Journal of Applied Psychology, 62*, 301–310.

Chapman, D. S., & Rowe, P. M. (2002). The influence of videoconferencing technology and interview structure on the recruiting function of the employment interview a field experiment. *International Journal of Selection and Assessment, 10*, 185–197.

Chen, C. C., Yang, I. W., & Lin, W. (2010). Applicant impression management in job interview: The moderating role of interviewer affectivity. *Journal of Occupational and Organizational Psychology, 83*(3), 739–757.

Christiansen, N. D., Wolcott-Burnam, S., & Janovics, J. E. (2005). The good judge revisited: Individual differences in the accuracy of personality judgments. *Human Performance, 18,* 123–149.

Cloyd, L. (1977). Effect of acquaintanceship on accuracy of person perception. *Perceptual and Motor Skills, 44,* 819–826.

Cogger, J. W. (1982). Are you a skilled interviewer? *Personnel Journal, 61,* 840–843.

Colvin, C. R. (1993a). Childhood antecedents of young-adult judgability. *Journal of Personality, 61,* 611–635.

Colvin, C. R. (1993b). Judgable people: Personality, behavior, and competing explanations, *Journal of Personality and Social Psychology, 64,* 861–873.

Colvin, C. R., & Funder, D. C. (1991). Predicting personality and behavior: A boundary on the acquaintanceship effect. *Journal of Personality and Social Psychology, 60,* 884–894.

Conway, J., Jako, R., & Goodman D. (1995). A meta-analysis of interrater and internal consistency reliability of selection interviews. *Journal of Applied Psychology, 80,* 565–579.

Conway, J. M., & Peneno, G. M. (1999). Comparing structured interview question types: Construct validity and applicant reactions. *Journal of Business and Psychology, 13*(4), 485–506.

Coupland N., & Bishop, H. (2007). Ideologised values for British accents. *Journal of Sociolinguistics, 11*(1), 74–93.

Cronshaw, S. F., & Wiesner, W. H. (1989). The validity of the employment interview: Models from research and practice. *In* R.W. Eder & G. R. Ferris (Eds.), *The Employment Interview: Theory, Research, and Practice.* Newbury Park, CA: Sage.

Crosteau, J. M. (1996). Research on the work experience of lesbian, gay and bisexual people: An integrative review of methodology and findings. *Journal of Vocational Behavior, 48,* 195–209.

Dana, J., Dawes, R., & Peterson, N. (2013). Belief in the unstructured interview: The persistence of an illusion. *Judgment and Decision Making, 8*(5), 512–520.

Day, D. V., & Sulsky, L. M. (1995). Effects of frame-of-reference training and information configuration on memory organization and rating accuracy. *Journal of Applied Psychology, 80,* 158–167.

DeGroot, T., & Motowidlo, S. J. (1999). Why visual and vocal cues can affect interviewers' judgments and predict job performance. *Journal of Applied Psychology, 84*(6), 986–993.

Dennis, P. M. (1984). The Edison test. *Journal of the History of the Behavioral Sciences, 20*(1), 23–37.

Deprez-Sims, A., & Morris, S. B. (2013). The effect of non-native accents on the evaluation of applicants during an employment interview: The development of a path model. *International Journal of Selection and Assessment, 21*(4), 355–367.

Dipboye, R. L. (1982). Self-fulfilling prophecies in the selection-recruitment interview. *Academy of Management Review, 7*(4), 579–586.

Dipboye, R. L., Avery, R. D., & Terprestra, D. E. (1977). Sex and physical attractiveness of raters and applicants as determinants of résumé evaluations. *Journal of Applied Psychology, 62,* 288–294.

Dipboye, R. L., & Colella, A. (2005). The dilemmas of workplace discrimination. *In* R. L. Dipboye & A. Colella (Eds.), *Discrimination at Work: The Psychological and Organizational Bases* (pp. 17–43). Mahwah, NJ: Lawrence Erlbaum.

Dipboye, R. L., Gaugler, B. B., & Hayes, T. L. (1997). The validity of unstructured panel interviews: More than meets the eye? *Journal of Business and Psychology, 16,* 35–49.

Dipboye, R. L., Macan, T., & Shahani-Denning, C. (2012). The selection interview from the interviewer and applicant perspectives: Can't have one without the other. *In* N. Schmitt (Ed.), *The Oxford Handbook of Personnel Assessment and Selection* (pp. 323–352). New York: Oxford University Press.

Farago, B. E., Zide, J. S., & Shahani-Denning, C. (2013). Selection interviews: Role of interviewer warmth, interview structure, and interview outcome in applicants' perceptions of organizations. *Consulting Psychology Journal: Practice and Research, 65*(3), 224–239.

Friedman, B., & Cornelius, E. (1976). Effect of rater participation in scale construction on the psychometric characteristics of two rating scale formats. *Journal of Applied Psychology, 1*(2), 210–216.

Funder, D. C. (1995). On the accuracy of personality judgment: A realistic approach. *Psychological Review 102*(4), 652–670.

Funder, D. C., & Colvin, C. R. (1988). Friends and strangers: Acquaintanceship, agreement, and the accuracy of personality judgment. *Journal of Personality and Social Psychology, 55,* 149–158.

Funder, D. C., & Colvin, C. R. (1991). Explorations in behavioral consistency: Properties of persons, situations and behaviors. *Journal of Personality and Social Psychology, 60,* 773–794.

Funder, D. C., & Dobroth, K. M. (1987). Differences between traits: Properties associated with interjudge agreement. *Journal of Personality and Social Psychology, 52*(2), 409–418.

Gatewood, G. L., Lahiff, J., Deter, R., & Hargrove, L. (1989). The effects of training on the behaviors of the selection interview. *Journal of Business Communication, 21*(6), 17–31.

Gilfford, R., Ng, C. F., & Wilkinson, M. (1985). Nonverbal cues in the employment interview: Links between applicant qualities and interview judgments. *Journal of Applied Psychology, 70*(4), 729–736.

Gilmore D., Beehr T., & Love, K. (1986) Effects of applicant sex, applicant physical attractiveness, type of rater and type of job on interview decisions. *Journal of Occupational Psychology, 59*(2), 103–109.

Hamdani, M. R., Valcea, S., & Buckley, M. R. (2014). The relentless pursuit of construct validity in the design of employment interviews. *Human Resource Management Review, 24*(2), 160–176.

Hansen, K., Rakić, T., & Steffens, M. (2014). When actions speak louder than words: Preventing discrimination of nonstandard speakers. *Journal of Language and Social Psychology, 33*(1), 68–77.

Hayes, T., & Macan, T. (1997). Comparison of the factors influencing interviewer hiring decisions for applicants with and those without disabilities. *Journal of Business and Psychology, 11*(3), 357–371.

Hollandsworth, Jr., J. G. (1979). Relative contributions of verbal, articulate, and nonverbal communication to employment decisions in the job interview setting. *Personnel Psychology, 32,* 359–367.

Hosoda, M., Stone-Romero, E. F., & Coats, G. (2003). The effects of physical attractiveness on job-related outcomes: A meta-analysis of experimental studies. *Personnel Psychology, 56*(2), 431–462.

Huffcutt, A. I., Culbertson, S. S., & Weyhrauch, W. S. (2013). Employment interview reliability: New meta-analytic estimates by structure and format. *International Journal of Selection and Assessment, 21*(3), 264–276.

Janz, T. (1989). The patterned behavior description interview: The best prophet of the future is the past. *In* R.W. Eder & G.R. Ferris (Eds.), *The Employment Interview: Theory Research and Practice* (pp. 158–168). Newbury Park, CA: Sage.

Kuo, C., & Chang, S. (2011). The employment interview structure: A field study of perceived procedural justice and applicant reactions. *Chinese Journal of Psychology, 53*(1), 97–114.

Kutcher, E. J., & Bragger, J. (2004). Selection interviews of overweight job applicants: Can structure reduce the bias? *Journal of Applied Social Psychology, 34*(10), 1993–2022.

Latham, G. P. (1989). The reliability, validity and practicality of the situational interview. *In* R. W. Eder & G. R. Ferris (Eds.), *The Employment Interview: Theory Research and Practice* (pp. 169–182). Newbury Park, CA: Sage.

Latham, G., & Seijts, G. (1997). The effect of appraisal instrument on managerial perceptions of fairness and satisfaction with appraisals from their peers. *Canadian Journal of Behavioural Science/Revue Canadienne Des Sciences Du Comportement, 29*(4), 275–282.

Levashina, J. H., Christopher, J., Morgeson, F. P., & Campion, M. A. (2014). The structured employment interview. Narrative and quantitative: Review of the research literature. *Personnel Psychology, 67,* 241–293.

Madera, J. M. (2008). Reactions to stigmas in the employment interview: An eye tracking investigation. *Dissertation Abstracts International: Section B: The Sciences and Engineering, 69*(4–B), p. 2662.

McColl, R., & Truong, Y. (2013). The effects of facial attractiveness and gender on customer evaluations during a web–video sales encounter. *Journal of Personal Selling & Sales Management, 33*(1), 117–128.

McDaniel, M. A., Whetzel, D. L., Schmidt, F. L., & Mauer, S. (1994). The validity of employment interviews: A comprehensive review and meta-analysis. *Journal of Applied Psychology, 79*, 599–616.

McFarland, L. A., Ryan, A. M., & Kriska, S. D. (2002). Field study investigation of applicant use of influence tactics in a selection interview. *The Journal of Psychology: Interdisciplinary and Applied, 136*(4), 383–398.

McLarney, A. R. (2003). Trait predictors of the good judge: Three proposed underlying mediators. Dissertation. *Abstracts International: Section B: The Sciences and Engineering, 64*(3-B), 1552.

Miceli, N. (1997). An investigation of bias toward persons with disabilities in employment selection decisions. *Dissertation. Abstracts International Section A: Humanities and Social Sciences, 57*(8-A), 3580.

Motowidlo, S., Carter, G., Vaughan, M., Dunnette, M. D., Tippins, N., Werner, S., & Burnett, J. R. (1992). Studies of the structured behavioral interview. *Journal of Applied Psychology, 77*(5), 571–587.

Nordstrom, C. R., Huffaker, B. J., & Williams, K. B. (1998). When physical disabilities are not liabilities: The role of applicant and interviewer characteristics on employment interview outcomes. *Journal of Applied Social Psychology, 28*, 283–306.

O'Brien K., Latner J., Halberstad J., Hunter J., Anderson J., & Caputi P. (2008). Do antifat attitudes predict antifat behaviors? *Obesity, 16*(12), 87–92.

O'Cinneide, C. (2011). The uncertain foundations of contemporary anti-discrimination law. *International Journal of Discrimination and the Law, 11*(1–2), 7–28.

Ones, D. S., Viswesvaran, C., & Schmidt, F. (1993). Comprehensive meta-analysis of integrity test validities; Findings and implications for personnel selection and theories of job performance. *Journal of Applied Psychology, 78*, 679–703.

Organ, D. W. (1988). *Organizational Citizenship Behavior*. Lexington, MA: D. C. Heath.

Palmer, D. K., Campion, M. A., & Green, P. C. (1999). Interviewer training for both interviewer and applicant. *In* R. W. Eder & M. M. Harris (Eds.), *The Employment Interview Handbook*, Thousand Oaks, CA: Sage.

Paulhus, D. B., & Bruce, M. N. (1992). The effect of acquaintanceship on the validity of personality impressions: A longitudinal study. *Journal of Personality and Social Psychology, 63*, 816–824.

Paunonen, S. V., & Jackson, D. N. (1988). Accuracy of interviewers and students in identifying the personality characteristics of personnel managers and computer programmers. *Journal of Vocational Behavior, 31*, 26–36.

Pingitore, R., Dugoni, B. L., Tindale, R. S., & Spring, B. (1994). Bias against overweight job applicants in a simulated employment interview. *Journal of Applied Psychology, 79*(6), 909–917.

Podsakoff, N. P., Whiting, S. W., Podsakoff, P. M., & Mishra, P. (2011). Effects of organizational citizenship behaviors on selection decisions in employment interviews. *Journal of Applied Psychology, 96*(2), 310–326.

Prusha, C. (2014). Effectiveness of panel and individual interviews in detection of counterproductive behavior. Master's thesis, California State University, Fullerton.

Pulakos, E. D., & Schmitt, N. (1995). Experience-based and situational interview questions: Studies of validity. *Personnel Psychology, 48*(2), 289–308.

Purkiss, S. L. S., Perrewé, P. L., Gillespie, T. L., Mayes, B. T., & Ferris, G. R. (2006). Implicit sources of bias in employment interview judgments and decisions. *Organizational Behavior and Human Decision Processes, 101*, 152–167.

Rand, T. M., & Wexley, K. N. (1975). Demonstration of the effect 'similar to me' in simulated employment interviews. *Psychological Reports, 36*, 535–544.

Reid, London House. (2007). *Abbreviated Reid Report*. Minneapolis, MN: NCS Pearson.

Report from the International Lesbian, Gay, Bisexual, Trans and Intersex Association (2013). IGLA.org.

Roehling, M. V. (1999). Weight-based discrimination in employment: Psychological and legal aspects. *Personnel Psychology, 52*, 969–1016.

Rouline, N., Bangerter, A. & Yerly, E. (2011). The uniqueness effect in selection interviews. *Journal of Personnel Psychology, 10*(1), pp. 43–47.

Rynes, S. L. (1989). The employment interview as a recruitment device. *In* R. Eder & G. Ferris, (Eds.), *The Employment Interview: Theory, Research and Practice*. Newbury Park, CA: Sage.

Sacco, J. M., Scheu, C. R., Ryan, A. M., & Schmitt, N. (2003). An investigation of race and sex similarity effects in interviews: A multilevel approach to relational demography. *Journal of Applied Psychology, 88*(5), 852–865.

Schmidt, F. L., & Hunter, J. E. (1998). The validity and utility of selection methods in personnel psychology: Practical and theoretical implications of 85 years of research findings. *Psychological Bulletin, 124*, 262–274.

Sear, G. J., Zhang, H., Wiesner, W. H., Hackett, R. D., & Yuan, Y. (2013). A comparative assessment of video-conference and face-to-face employment interviews. *Management Decision, 51*(8), 1733–1752.

Sinha, R., Oswald, F., Imus, A., & Schmitt N. (2011). Criterion-focused approach to reducing adverse impact in college admissions. *Applied Measurement In Education, 24*(2), 137–161.

Smith, P. C., & Kendall, L. M. (1963). Retranslation of expectations: An approach to the construction of unambiguous anchors to rating scales. *Journal of Applied Psychology, 47*, 149–155.

Straus, S. G., Miles, J. A., & Levesque, L. L. (2001). The effects of videoconference, telephone, and face-to-face media on interviewer and applicant judgments in employment interviews. *Journal of Management, 27*, 363–381.

Taylor, P. J., & Small, B. (2002). Asking applicants what they would do versus what they did do: A meta-analytic comparison of situational and past behavior employment interview questions. *Journal of Occupational and Organizational Psychology, 75*, 277–294.

Tews, M. J., Stafford, K., & Shu, J. (2009). Beauty revisited: The impact of attractiveness, ability and personality in the assessment of employment suitability. *International Journal of Selection and Assessment, 17*, 92–100.

Townsend, R. J., Bacigalupi, S. C., & Blackman, M. C. (2007). The accuracy of lay integrity assessments in simulated employment interviews. *Journal of Research in Personality, 41*, 540–557.

Tran, T., & Blackman, M. C. (2006). The dynamics and validity of the group selection interview. *Journal of Social Psychology, 146*(2), 183–201.

Ulrich, L., & Trumbo, D. (1965). The selection interview since 1949. *Psychological Bulletin, 63*, 100–116.

Van Hoye, G., & Lievens, F. (2003). The effects of sexual orientation on hirability ratings: An experimental study. *Journal of Business and Psychology, 18*(1), 15–30.

Wade, K. J., & Kinicki, A. J. (1997). Subjective applicant qualifications and interpersonal attraction as mediators within a process model of interview selection decisions. *Journal of Vocational Behavior, 50*, 23–40.

Wexley, K., Sanders, R., & Yukel, G. (1973). Training interviewers to eliminate contrast effects in employment interviews. *Journal of Applied Psychology, 57*(3), 233–236.

Zhang Y., Kong F., Zhong Y., & Kou, H. (2014). Personality manipulations: Do they modulate facial attractiveness ratings? *Personality and Individual Differences, 70*, 80–84.

10

The Contribution of Others' Methods in Recruitment and Selection
Biodata, References, Résumés and CVs

Adrian Furnham

Introduction

Those wishing to select and recruit people know what a difficult task they face. People are complex and capricious, difficult both to predict and understand. Most attempt to find methods that help them gather data to be able to assess the ability, motivation and personality of an individual. Some become desperate and turn to methods such as graphology which has long since been discredited, though it remains widely used in France (Cook, 2009). This is discussed in a later section.

The questions for assessors and selectors are essentially what to assess, how to assess these characteristics, who is best suited to do it and when and why it should be done in a particular way.

To some extent the 'what' can neatly be divided into three areas:

- *What a person can do.* This refers to their ability. It is about their capacity to do various tasks efficiently given that they have the desire to do so. It also refers to their ability to learn new tasks. Assessing what a person can do is often measured by cognitive ability (intelligence) and skills tests.
- *What a person will do.* This refers to people's motivation or what they will to do when asked or instructed so to do. Motivation refers to values and drives. It is the extent to which people are energized and focused on achieving a particular goal or set of goals. Everyone can be persuaded to do things as a function of rewards and punishments, but this refers to what a person will do on an everyday basis without strong rewards or punishments shaping behaviour.
- *What a person wants to do.* This refers to preferences for certain activities over others. It is about what a person likes to do and will do freely with any form of cohesion. It is about values, personality and motivation, which push in one direction or another.

The Wiley Blackwell Handbook of the Psychology of Recruitment, Selection and Employee Retention,
First Edition. Edited by Harold W. Goldstein, Elaine D. Pulakos, Jonathan Passmore and Carla Semedo.
© 2017 John Wiley & Sons Ltd. Published 2020 by John Wiley & Sons Ltd.

Assessors need to know all three things about the job applicant they are assessing and recruiting.

It is generally accepted that it is reasonably easy to assess individuals' ability accurately. It is also not difficult to assess their normal and abnormal personality. It is, however, much more difficult to assess motivation, in part because people are often unable and unwilling to say what really motivates them.

There are, in essence, five methods to collect data on people: self-report, observational data, biographical data, test data and physiological data. In this chapter three of these are considered: self-report data, observational data and personal history. We also briefly discuss methods such as graphology, which have become popular in some countries, but lack any evidence to support their use as a selection tool.

Self-Report Data

This is essentially what people say about themselves in interviews (both structured and unstructured), personality and other preference tests, and CVs, personal statements or application forms. These are very common ways of assessing people. Most want and expect an interview when they can answer questions and talk about themselves. Further, most people now have a skilfully crafted CV, indeed multiple versions, which are available electronically to send to various potential employers.

There are, however, two major problems with self-reports. The first is referred to under various names – dissimulation, faking or lying. It concerns people giving false or embellished information about themselves. This behaviour has been broken down by psychologists into two further types. The first is called 'impression management': this is when the person attempts to create a good impression by leaving out information, adding untrue information (errors of omission and commission), as well as giving answers that are not strictly correct but, they hope, will create a good impression. This is done consciously and is very common (Cook, 2009; Furnham, 2008). Indeed, it is expected in the answer to some questions, but it can be very serious when, for instance, people claim to have qualifications or experiences they have not had, or leave out important information (e.g., about their health, criminal past).

The second is 'self-deception'. This occurs when individuals in their own view answer honestly, but what they say is untrue because they lack self-awareness. Thus they might honestly believe that they are a 'good listener' whereas evidence from reliable sources is that this is not the case. This can occur for both good qualities (cognitive and emotional intelligence) and weaknesses (impulsivity, depression). People with low self-awareness often self-deceive. The way personality and other preference tests attempt to deal with this is to use lie scales in the test. There are many of these and they go under various names. They are generally known as measures of response bias.

The third is self-insight. This is primarily concerned with what people cannot say about themselves even if they wanted to. This is best seen with such issues as motivation where people cannot, rather than will not, give honest answers about the extent to which they are motivated by power or security. Indeed, motivation is one of the most difficult topics to assess accurately, yet business people think of it as among the most important.

This chapter examines the curriculum vitae (CV), which is a presentational document that people construct to give a résumé of their education, experience, education, and so on. Although many organizations still ask people to complete an application form, it is common for applicants to have a prepared CV (also called a résumé), which allows them to choose what information to give others.

Observation Data

This is what other people say about an individual in references and testimonials, as well as 360-degree ratings (multi-source feedback), appraisal and other performance management data.

Most organizations attempt to obtain reliable reports from people who know the candidate they are assessing. Many application processes ask candidates to list individuals who know them well in a relevant situation and may be contacted. There are, however, problems with such data. The first is the observer's 'data bank'. This is the information the observer has about the candidate. Thus a manager will have a different dataset from a colleague or subordinate. A school teacher or university lecturer will have a different dataset from an employer. The question is what they know: the quality and quantity of data on a person's ability, motivation, work style.

The second issue is the extent to which referees are willing to be truthful about an individual. Some organizations ban staff from offering references because of the risk of litigation. They can be sued for what they did or did not say and this has led many organizations to provide references that are limited to factual statements such as 'X worked here from date A to date B'.

Next, people choose referees who, they hope, will be very positive about them. There seems to be an etiquette with respect to what people write or rate on references. Many know the power of negative information and resist providing any. It is therefore rare to obtain useful data on a person's weaknesses or challenges from references.

Biography

This is a person's personal history – where they were born and educated, their birth family and present family, and their current address. Some information is thought to be very important: the parents' social class; whether the applicant comes from a minority race or religious group; how many siblings they have and their place in the birth order; their schooling and how academically successful they were. This is called biodata. It aims to determine, empirically, the biographical markers of success in particular jobs. Its limitations will be discussed later.

Invalid Methods

Many studies have demonstrated that certain selection methods clearly lack validity. Ben-Shaktar, Bar-Hellel, Bilu, Ben-Abba, and Flug (1986) conducted a major and well-controlled study, and concluded that if a correspondence were to be empirically found between graphological features and such traits, it would be a major theoretical challenge to account for it. Further, they argued that, unless the graphologist makes a firm commitment to the nature of the correspondence between handwriting and personality, one can find ad hoc corroboration for any claim. They also note that handwriting is paradoxically not a robust and stable form of expressive behaviour. It may be extremely sensitive to extraneous influences that have nothing to do with personality (e.g., whether the script is copied or not, or the paper is lined or not, the condition under which the writing takes place, who reads the script).

In another review, Neter and Ben-Shaktar (1989) asked 63 graphologists and 51 non-graphologists to rate 1,223 scripts. They found that psychologists with no knowledge of graphology outperformed the graphologists on all dimensions, and they suggested that the limited validity of handwriting analysis is usually based on the script's content rather than its style.

King and Koehler (2002) demonstrated that an illusory correlation phenomenon may be a contribution to the persistence of graphology's use to detect personality traits. They found that a semantic association between the words used to describe handwriting features (e.g., bold) and personality traits was the source of the perceived correlation which, in part, 'may partially account for continued use of graphology despite overwhelming evidence against its predictive validity' (2000, p. 336).

Dean (1992) examined statistical effect sizes in this literature. Dean also attempted to explain why, if the empirical research literature is almost uniformly negative, it has not shaken graphologists' or lay people's faith in this type of analysis. He found over 60 reliability and 140 effect size study results for his analysis. The effect size is defined as the mean correlation (weighted by number of scripts) between personality as predicted from the handwriting by graphologist or others and personality determined by tests or ratings. After looking at 1,519 correlations, Dean concluded that effect sizes are too low to be useful and that non-graphologists are generally as good at handwriting analysis as graphologists. He admitted that there *is* an effect, but suggests that at least some is due to content, not the handwriting, and that graphology is not valid or reliable enough to be useful.

Dean, Kelly, Saklofske and Furnham (1992) attempted to explain why, if all the evidence suggests that graphology is barely related to any personality variable, clients of graphologists attest to its accuracy. They list 26 reasons why clients are convinced that graphology works, none of which requires that it is true. Interestingly, this may account for some graphologists' unshakeable belief in their 'art'. For various placebo-type reasons clients believe that graphology does work, which increases the graphologists' belief in their own skill. Hence each reinforces the other, despite the possibility that there is no validity in graphological analysis. Thus people are convinced that handwriting is linked to personality, yet nearly all the evidence suggests this is not true. As Driver, Buckley and Frink (1996, p. 78) concluded:

> While a few articles have proposed that graphology is a valid and useful selection technique, the overwhelming results of well-controlled empirical studies have been that the technique has not demonstrated acceptable validity. A review of relevant literature regarding both theory and research indicates that, while the procedure may have an intuitive appeal, graphology should not be used in a selection context.

Biodata

Biographical data, or biodata, include information about a person's background and life history (e.g., civil status, education and previous employment), ranging from objectively determined dates – date of first job, time in last job, years of higher education – to subjective preferences, though some rule that out as invalid biodata. Some, however, suggest that all biodata must be objective and verifiable. The diversity of constructs assessed (explicitly or implicitly) by biodata is such that there is no common definition. Indeed, 'biodata scales have been shown to measure numerous constructs, such as temperament, assessment of work conditions, values, skills, aptitudes, and abilities' (Mount, Witt & Barrick, 2000, p. 300). Some have argued that biodata represent a more valid predictor of occupational success than traditional personality tests (Mumford, Costanza, Connelly & Johnson, 1996) and reduce any aversive impact in comparison to cognitive ability or intelligence tests (Stokes, Mumford & Owens, 1994).

Biodata enthusiasts argue that the 'best predictor of future performance is past performance' (Wernimont & Campbell, 1968, p. 372), and that it is one of the best routes for understanding and improving the prediction of work performance. It is the link between individuals' life history and their performance at work (Fleishman, 1988).

Biodata are typically obtained from an application form. These are used extensively in most Western countries. In biodata terms they become weighted application blanks. The aim is to design an application form that collects only data known and shown to predict specific work-related performance. The form collects biographical information that has previously been correlated with desirable work criteria (notably job performance). Further it incorporates 'weighted scoring', by which questions are coded and treated as individual predictors of relevant work criteria.

Scoring of biodata

It is the scoring of biodata that sets it apart from the more informal use of application forms, references or CVs, from which employers simply eliminate candidates on the basis of scanning these documents. There are three different but related ways of scoring data, which have been compared by Cucina, Caputo, Thibodeaux and Maclane (2012).

One rigorous and effective approach is the empirical keying method (Devlin, Abrahams & Edwards, 1992), which codes each item or question as yes = 1 or no = 0 and weights them according to their correlations with the criterion (as derived from previous samples or a subset of the current sample). Item scores are totalled for each candidate. It has been reported that empirical keying shows incremental validity in the prediction of occupational success over and above personality scales and cognitive ability measures (Mount et al., 2000). Empirical keying makes biodata markedly different from standard personality inventories, which are scored in terms of reliability or internal consistencies but not on the basis of their association with the criteria they are used to predict. In that sense, personality measures are internally constructed whereas biodata items are externally constructed (Goldberg, 1972).

Biodata can also be scored by factorial keying, which identifies higher-order domains or common themes underlying groups of items, in the way that personality scales group questions on the basis of specific traits. Mumford and Owens (1987) identified adjustment, academic performance, extraversion and leadership in over 20 studies. Others have scored biodata items in terms of family and social orientation (Carlson, Scullen, Schmidt, Rothstein & Erwin, 1999) and money management (Stokes & Searcy, 1999). Other than that, factorial-keyed biodata are 'indistinguishable from personality items in content, response format, and scoring. Personality tests typically contain items regarding values and attitudes and biodata items generally focus on past achievements of behaviours, but even this distinction is not obvious in many biodata applications today' (Schmitt & Kunce, 2002, p. 570).

Third, rational keying is used to design biodata inventories that are based on the specific job requirements or characteristics. Fine and Cronshaw (1994) proposed that a thorough job analysis informs the selection of biodata items. Rational keying refers to the construction rather than analysis or scoring phase of biodata and there is no reason why it cannot be combined with factorial keying. Drakeley, Herriot and Jones (1988) found rational keying to be more valid than empirical keying, though more recent and robust investigations estimated the methods to have comparable validities (Stokes & Searcy, 1999).

Each method has its advantages and disadvantages: empirical keying is advantageous in that it makes biodata 'invisible' and hard to fake, as many predictors of occupational success are bound to be counterintuitive and identified purely on an empirical basis.

At the same time, however, this makes the inclusion of certain items hard to justify. Additional problems with empirical keying are that it does not generalize well to other samples and does not advance our theoretical understanding of the reasons for which items predict occupational success (Mount et al., 2000).

Rational keying may be easy to justify from a theoretical point of view and provides an opportunity for excluding items with an adverse impact. No wonder, then, that rational keying has been used extensively in recent years (Hough & Paullin, 1994; Schmitt, Jennings & Toney, 1999). However, the advantages of rational keying may come at the expense of making 'correct responses' too obvious for respondents and increasing the likelihood of faking (Lautenschlager, 1994).

Factorial keying, whether applied in conjunction with rational keying or not, makes biodata identical to personality inventories, especially if attitudinal or subjective items are included. It has been argued that even experts fail to distinguish between personality scales and factorial-keyed biodata (Robertson & Smith, 2001). Moreover, personality scales have some advantages over biodata: they are more 'theory-driven', assess higher-order and more stable dispositions, and generalize quite easily across settings and criteria.

There are other methods such as coding free responses to specific questions. This has been shown to reduce faking and measure verbal ability rather well (Levashina, Morgeson & Campion, 2012). Indeed, web technology means that organizations are analysing individuals' Facebook pages to find out about their true values and lifestyle.

Verifiability of biodata and faking

A main difference between personality and biodata inventories is that the latter include a larger number of verifiable or 'hard' items, such as basic demographic or background information. These items are uncontrollable (there is nothing one can do to alter one's place of birth or ethnicity) and intrusive compared to the 'soft', more controllable, unverifiable items assessing attitudes and behaviours, such as 'What are your views on recycling?' '[How often do you go to the gym?' 'Do you think people should drink less alcohol?' 'Do you like country & western music?' It has, however, been suggested that unverifiable items increase the probability of faking (Becker & Colquitt, 1992). Indeed, although some degree of inflation does exist for verifiable items, early studies reported inter-correlations in the region of 0.95 between responses given to different employers (Keating, Paterson & Stone, 1950), showing that verifiable items yield very consistent responses even across different jobs. Yet a review of the literature concluded that faking affects both verifiable and non-verifiable items and that attempts to control it have been largely unsuccessful, though empirical keying prevents faking more than other keying types (Lautenschlager, 1994).

One study compared the validity of verifiable and non-verifiable biodata items in call centre employees and applicants (Harold, McFarland & Weekley, 2006). Results show that although applicants did not score significantly higher on overall biodata items than their incumbent counterparts, non-verifiable items had lower validities in the applicant sample. Harold, McFarland and Weekley concluded that 'the good news is that a biodata inventory comprised of all verifiable items was equally valid across incumbent and applicant samples regardless of the criterion examined ... [T]he bad news, however, is that the validity of non-verifiable items shrank in the applicant sample' (2006, p. 343).

Regardless of these results, today jobs such as services and team work (Hough, 1998) call for attitudinal and interpersonal constructs to be assessed in order to predict occupational success. Thus, non-verifiable, soft, subjective items will inevitably be incorporated in contemporary biodata scales.

Schmitt and colleagues (2003) proposed that in order to reduce faking and social desirability respondents should be asked to elaborate on their answers – a method previously used in 'accomplishment records', for example, 'Give three examples of situations where you worked well under pressure' or 'Can you recall past experiences where you showed strength and leadership?' (Hough, 1984). Results indicated that respondents tended to score lower (be more modest) on items that required elaboration (Schmitt & Kunce, 2002); indeed, scores on elaborative items were 0.6 SD lower, which is approximately the difference found between participants instructed to respond honestly and those asked to 'fake good' in laboratory studies (Ellingson, Sackett & Hough, 1999; Ones, Visvesvarian & Reiss, 1996). A subsequent study showed that the validities of elaborative items were in line with standard biodata items and in some cases even higher (Schmitt et al., 2003). In addition, validities (predicting self-ratings, self-deception, impression management, GPA and attendance) were unaffected by elaboration instructions even though lower means were found for the elaborative items.

Other methods for reducing the likelihood of faking include warnings (Schrader & Osburn, 1977), such as 'Any inaccuracies or fake information provided will be checked and result in your no longer being considered for this job', to the more creative use of bogus (fake) items that may trick respondents into faking well (Paunonen, 1984), for example, 'How many years have you been using the HYU-P2 software?' However, including bogus items is widely thought of as unethical.

Validity of biodata

Just how valid are biodata? Early empirical evidence on the validity of biodata was provided by England (1961), who reported an average correlation of 0.40 between weighted application blanks and turnover. Wernimont (1962) identified three main variables that predicted length of service in female officers between 1954 and 1959 with similar accuracy, namely: high proficiency at shorthand, whether they left their previous jobs because of pregnancy, marriage, sickness or domestic problems, and whether they were willing to start their new job within the next week.

Meta-analyses are particularly important in biodata research because of the heterogeneity of different biodata studies and the importance of testing whether validities generalize from one sample to another. Unsurprisingly, validities for biodata vary significantly, from the low to mid-0.20s (Hunter & Hunter, 1984; Schmitt, Gooding, Noe & Kirsch, 1984) up to the 0.50s (Reilly & Chao, 1982). Although even the lower-bound validity estimates are higher than the validities reported for most personality scales (see this volume, chapter 8), and Schmidt and Hunter's (1998) seminal meta-analysis of 85 years of validity studies estimated a validity of 0.35 for biodata, it is important to provide an accurate estimate of the validity of biodata, which requires identification of the factors that moderate the impact of biodata predictors on occupational criteria.

Bliesener (1996) meta-analysed previously reported meta-analyses, paying careful attention to methodological differences among different validity studies. Over 100 samples of 106,302 participants were examined, yielding an estimated (uncorrected) validity of 0.38 (SD = 0.19). However, when correcting for methodological artefacts and statistical errors, the overall validity for biodata inventories dropped to 0.22 (usually, corrected estimates tend to yield higher rather than lower validities), which still meets the criteria for utility and incremental validity (Barthel & Schuler, 1989). Bliesener's results showed that biodata were a more valid predictor of occupational success for women (0.51) than for men (0.27). Larger than average (0.35) validities were found for studies that concurrently administered all measures. Bliesener concluded that 'Biographical data are a valid predictor of an applicant's suitability. This, combined with their high economy, their universal applicability, and the ease of combining them with other predictive procedures, makes them a valuable instrument in personnel selection' (1996, p. 118).

Turning to the generalizability of biodata, Carlson, Scullen, Schmidt, Rothstein and Erwin (1999) constructed a five-factor biodata inventory, which they found to correlate at 0.52 with occupational success in one organization. They then administered the same inventory to 24 organizations (including 7,334 employees) and found an overall validity of 0.48, indicating that biodata scales do indeed generalize to different organizations. That said, validities for biodata scales have been found to vary according to job type. Biodata have been found to be consistently more valid for clerical jobs, followed by managerial jobs. Sales jobs have yielded more mixed results, and military jobs have produced consistently lower validities.

Studies have also provided evidence for the incremental validity of biodata over established personality and cognitive ability measures. These studies are important because of the known overlap between these measures and biodata and show that even if personality and intelligence are measured and taken into account, biodata scales provide additional useful information about the predicted outcome. Incremental validity of biodata over cognitive ability tests has been demonstrated in samples of Army recruits (Mael & Ashforth, 1995), and air traffic controllers (Dean, Russell & Muchinsky, 1999; see also Karas & West, 1999).

Another study found that people's capacity to cope with change, self-efficacy for change and past experiences, as assessed from biodata items, predicted occupational success over cognitive ability, though cognitive ability was a more powerful predictor (Allworth & Hesketh, 2000). With regard to personality, studies have shown biodata scales to predict performance outcomes incrementally in U.S. Army cadets (Mael & Hirsch, 1993; for a replication, see McManus & Kelly, 1999). Moreover, Mount and colleagues' study simultaneously controlled for the Big Five personality traits and general cognitive ability and found that biodata still explained unique variance in four occupational criteria (Mount et al., 2000). They noted that biodata explained 2% of unique variance in problem-solving (even this incremental validity was significant, albeit marginally), 5% of unique variance in quantity and quality of work, 7% of additional variance in interpersonal relationships and 17% of extra variance in retention probability.

Structure of biodata

Mumford, Stokes and Owens' (1990) ecology model postulated that biodata can be organized in terms of core knowledge, skill, ability, value and expectancy variables. These explain how people develop their characteristic patterns of adaptation at work and elsewhere. These constructs 'facilitate the attainment of desired outcomes while conditioning future situational choice by increasing the likelihood of reward in certain kinds of situations' (p. 81).

Dean and Russell (2005) replicated these constructs using 142 biodata items and over 6,000 newly hired air traffic controllers. Part of the success of this study can be attributed to the fact that the authors combined rationally designed items, based on Mumford and Owens' (1987) approach, with traditional empirical data. Correlations between the various biodata scales, cognitive ability scores and a composite performance criterion can be found in this study. Overall, biodata correlated with job performance almost as well as cognitive ability. Furthermore, Dean and Russell corrected restriction of range in cognitive ability (the uncorrected correlation between cognitive ability and the criterion was 0.16, and the corrected correlation for biodata and the criterion was 0.43).

Although the wider literature has provided compelling evidence that cognitive ability tests, particularly general mental ability scores, are the best single predictor of work performance. Dean and Russell's results provide robust evidence in support of the validity of coherently constructed and scored biodata scales, not least because they organized their items according to established constructs (interpersonal skills, personality and values). Among the different scales or aspects of biodata, intellectual resources predicted job performance best, followed by choice processes and social and personality resources; filter processes were only weakly related to job performance.

Studies have also shown that using purpose-built biodata that include a defined structure (different scales) can be used successfully to predict performance in college, even when entry exam scores (SATs) and personality factors are taken into account (Oswald, Schmitt, Kim, Ramsay & Gillespie, 2004). Oswald and colleagues looked at 115 items of biodata in a sample of 654 college students and identified 12 major dimensions. These included knowledge ('Think about the last several times you have had to learn new facts or concepts about something. How much did you tend to learn?'), citizenship ('How often have you signed a petition for something you believe in?'), leadership ('How many times in the past year have you tried to get someone to join an activity in which you were involved or leading?'), and ethics ('If you were leaving a concert and noticed that someone had left their purse behind with no identification, what would you do?'), which they used to predict final academic grades. Most α's were higher than 0.6, with the exception of adaptability, career and interpersonal, which had lower internal consistencies. On the other hand, all factors except ethics correlated only modestly with impression management.

Oswald and colleagues (2004) also tested the extent to which their 12 biodata factors predicted GPA, absenteeism and peer ratings while controlling for SATs and personality scores. Their results showed that six facets were still significantly linked to these outcomes even when previous academic performance and psychometrically derived trait scores were included in the regression model. Leadership and health were linked to GPA, citizenship, interpersonal and learning predicted peer ratings, and absenteeism was predicted by health and ethics.

Manley, Benavidez and Dunn (2007) compared the predictive power of two self-reported measures of personality (locus of control and conscientiousness) with biodata measures of the same constructs. Results revealed that the biodata versions of these two constructs predicted ethical decision making better than the self-reported (personality-style) measures did.

In summary

Biodata in personnel selection is based on the premise that the best predictor of future performance is past performance. It continues to attract a good deal of attention (Becton, Matthews, Hartley & Whitaker, 2009; Sisco & Reilly, 2007) as well as significant reviews on the past and future of biodata research (Breaugh, 2009).

Although biodata vary widely in their structure, form and how they are collected and scored, they include both objective (hard and verifiable) and subjective (soft and unverifiable) items. The latter are more easily faked – and are influenced by socially desirable responding and impression management – than the former, though faking can potentially affect any form of biodata. One way to reduce faking appears to be to request respondents to elaborate on their answers.

The most important conclusion is no doubt that biodata represent a valid approach for predicting occupational success in its various forms. Indeed, meta-analytic estimates provided validities for biodata in the region of 0.25, and this is probably a conservative estimate.

This means that biodata are as valid as the best personality scales, though the fact that biodata scales overlap with both personality and cognitive ability measures limits their appeal. Incremental validity studies have shown that even when established personality and intelligence measures are taken into account, biodata still accurately predict job performance.

To some biodata research is a quaint research backwater for selection researchers, yet it cannot be readily dismissed and seems to be attracting more and better research (Breaugh, 2009).

CVs and Résumés

Application forms require individuals to provide specific information about themselves, such as their educational qualifications and job experience. Changes in the law and various other practices have resulted in new practices over the years: thus in some countries age discrimination legislation has meant that date of birth is no longer asked for, as well as place of birth. The practice of asking for a photograph has also been discouraged lest candidates are selected on their physical appearance more than their ability, motivation or experience. Yet most applicants now provide many of these details in their own CV or résumé voluntarily.

There is not a large academic literature on résumés, though helping individuals write them has become a serious business (this is now changing). There are self-styled consultants who claim to help people write a CV to increase their chances of getting a job interview and the job itself. They aim to help with both style and content. It is in essence an impression management exercise aimed to present information with a particular impact. Thus some information is omitted which may be thought of as unflattering (class of degree, time spent unemployed) while other information is presented to maximize impact but which may be misleading, such as the size of a budget controlled by a team not just the candidate. Further, there appear to be fashions in the way CVs are written and presented as well as cultural, cohort and sector differences. One study looked at erroneous claims about publications in doctors but found relatively little evidence of 'wilful misrepresentation' (Boyd, Hook & King, 1996). Weinstein (2012) identified three types of résumés: chronological, functional (organized by skills) and behaviourally focused, which are better and most useful.

Chen, Huang and Lee (2011), in a Taiwanese study, suggested that recruiters are interested in 'detecting' a number of very specific characteristics from the typical information on a CV; these include academic qualifications, work experience, extracurricular activities and the 'aetherics' of a résumé. Chen and colleagues showed that recruiters tried to elicit an indication of the candidate's job-related knowledge, interpersonal skills, intelligence and conscientiousness from the CV in order to make a hiring decision. A similar American study showed that it was recruiters' perception of the applicants' academic qualifications, work experience and extracurricular activities that were critical in determining their decisions. Yet comparatively little research has been undertaken on this topic. Elgin and Clapham (2004) examined whether there would be a difference between how people evaluated electronic versus paper résumés. They found that people on a paper résumé were rated as more friendly but those based on an electronic résumé were rated as better qualified and more intelligent, as well as more technically advanced. Another study, by Hiemstra and colleagues (2012) showed clear and predicted ethnic differences in résumé content. Indeed, the risk of discrimination resulting from résumé screening has attracted research (Derous, Ryan & Nguyen, 2011).

Because most people now have a least one CV which they use for various purposes these have begun to attract research, though the non-standard nature of the form and content of CVs makes this difficult. It thus remains a very under-researched area, which is surprising given the role of CVs in selection decision making.

References and Letters of Recommendation

Another widely used method in personnel selection is the reference report or letter of recommendation, simply known as the reference (Chamorro-Premuzis & Furnham, 2010). Referees are often former employers, teacher or colleagues who are asked to provide a description of a candidate or job applicant. They have usually been used to check for prior disciplinary problems, confirm details on an application form or gain new and salient information about a possible employee (Aamodt, Nagy & Thompson, 1998). Thus referees are expected to have sufficient knowledge of the applicant's previous work experience and suitability for the job. However it is widely known that these letters often exaggerate the candidates' ability (Nicklin & Roch, 2008).

Nevertheless, references are used almost as widely in personnel selection as the interview. Yet there is a dearth of research on the reliability and validity of the reference letter, and an' assessment of the evidence suggests that the reference is a poor indicator of candidates' potential. Thus Judge and Higgins (1998) concluded that 'despite widespread use, reference reports also appear to rank among the least valid selection measures' (1998, p. 207).

References are essentially observational data, that is, statements or ratings by employers or peers, and are therefore subjective. There is an extensive literature on multi-source or 360-degree feedback – the process whereby peers, subordinates and supra-ordinates provide ratings – aimed at assessing the reliability of self- and other ratings. Early research attempted to do a content analysis of letters to pick up certain traits and competencies such as dependability (Peres & Garcia, 1962).

Structured versus unstructured references

Like the employment interview, references can be classified on the basis of how structured or standardized they are, ranging from completely unstructured ('What do you think of X?') to totally structured (e.g., standardized multiple-choice questions, checklists and ratings). The latter require referees to address predefined areas and are often merely tickboxes. One of the most well-known structured references is the US Employment Recommendation Questionnaire (ERQ), developed for the civil service and investigated in many psychological studies. The ERQ covers five core areas referring to the candidate's competence or ability, reputation or character, qualifications relevant to the job, employability by the referee, and prior record of any problems at work. McCarthy and Goffin (2001) tested three rating items (rating on multi-item scales or making global trait ratings) and found the relative percentile method the best: that is where people rate an individual compared to the peer group. They gave a rating (percentage) that refers to the percentage of people in the applicant's peer group who would score lower than the applicant did.

Reliability of references

Early research on the reliability of the employment reference produced pessimistic results (Muchinsky, 1979). For example, a study examining letters of recommendation in the US civil service found that different ratings from different referees correlated only at 0.40

(Mosel & Goheen, 1959). This is somewhat lower than but still comparable to that obtained in multi-source or 360-degree feedback settings, where the inter-rater reliability can approach 0.60 (Murphy & Cleveland, 1995). This is to be expected as people may show different aspects of themselves to different people. As Murphy and Cleveland (1995) argue, there would be little point in using multiple sources if we expected them to provide the same information. This is a well-known contradiction in academic grading where exams are frequently double-marked by faculty only to agree similar marks in the end (Baird, Greatorex & Bell, 2004; Dracup, 1997). However, inter-rater agreements of 0.60 are low and mean that only 36% of the variance in candidates' attributes is accounted for, leaving a substantial percentage of variance unexplained.

This low reliability has been explained in terms of evaluative biases (Feldman, 1981) attributable to the personality characteristics of the referee. Referees' mood states when writing the reference will influence whether the reference is more or less positive (Judge & Higgins, 1998). This is in line with Fiske's well-known finding that emotional labels, notably extreme ones, are used to categorize factual information about others (Fiske, 1980). Thus when referees retrieve information about candidates their judgement is already clouded by emotional information (often as simple and general as 'good' or 'bad'). Some of the sources of such mood states are dispositional (e.g., emotionally stable and extraverted individuals more frequently experience positive affect states, whereas the opposite applies to neurotic, introverted people), and personality characteristics can have other (non-affective) effects on evaluations, too. Thus the ability, personality and values of the referee shape the unstructured reference so much that they have more to do with compatibility between the referee and candidate than the candidate's suitability for the job. It is, however, noteworthy that little research has been conducted in this area, so these hypotheses are speculative.

More reliable information from reference letters can be obtained if different raters base their ratings and conclusions on the same information. For instance, as early as the 1940s the UK Civil Service Selection Board (CSSB) examined multiple references for the same candidates (e.g., from school, university, the armed forces and previous employment), written by different referees. Results showed that inter-reliabilities for a panel of five or six people can be as high as 0.73 (Wilson, 1948). However, few employers can afford to examine such detailed information. Furthermore, even if internal consistencies such as inter-rater reliabilities are adequate, that does not mean that employment references will be valid predictors of job-related outcomes. Indeed, the validity of references has been an equally important topic of concern when assessing the utility of this method in personnel selection.

Validity of references

How valid are letters of recommendation in predicting relevant job outcomes? Again, research into the validity of references has been scant, especially in comparison to the frequent use of references in personnel selection. This is no doubt partly because it is unclear what the criterion variable is. Most of this research has focused on structured references, not least because it is easier to quantify the validity of these references (particularly compared to the highly variable and, by definition, hard to standardize, unstructured letters of recommendation). For example, studies on the ERQ showed that reference checks correlated in the range of 0.00 and 0.30 with subsequent performance. In a meta-analysis, Reilly and Chao (1982) reported a mean correlation of 0.18 with supervisory ratings, 0.08 with turnover and 0.14 with a global criterion. A more generous estimate of 0.26 (corrected for unreliability and restriction of range) was provided by Hunter and Hunter's (1984) meta-analysis, and one of the largest validities was (again, corrected) 0.36 for head teachers' references and training success in the Navy (Jones & Harrison, 1982). Jones and Harrison (1982) pointed out that teachers' (or, for that matter, professors') references tend to be more accurate because they are more motivated than former employers to maintain credibility as they are likely to write more references in the future.

It would be incongruent to expect higher validities from the reference letter if it is not reliable in the first place. Yet there are several other converging factors that threaten the validity of this assessment and selection method. References tend to be very lenient, which produces highly skewed data. This effect, often referred to as the Pollyanna effect, reduces the true variance between candidates (producing more heterogeneous outcomes than predictors) and means that 'most applicants are characterised as somewhat desirable' (Paunonen, Jackson & Oberman, 1987, p. 97). This is hardly surprising since referees are nominated by the candidates themselves and referees' 'primary interest is not with the organization but with the applicant' (Colarelli, Hechanova-Alampay & Canali, 2002, p. 316). Recent research shows that even in academic settings (e.g., for grant proposals) applicant-nominated assessors provide biased and inflated reviews of the candidates (Marsh, Bond & Jayasinghe, 2007). Clearly, referees who are asked to provide a reference have no incentives to be harsh and may indeed fear being too harsh as they may be sued by the candidates. Moreover, given that harsh comments are rare and seen as a 'kiss of death' (typically, negative points are given more weight than positive ones) referees are even more sensitive about making them, though research suggests that when both negative and positive comments are included references are perceived as more genuine and the result may consequently be a positive hiring decisions (Knouse, 1983). It is also likely that referees abstain from providing a reference if they cannot be positive about the applicant, which would explain the poor response rates found (Schneider & Schmitt, 1986).

Referees tend to write similar references for all candidates. In fact, it has been pointed out that references – particularly unstructured ones – provide more information about the referee than the candidate (Baxter, Brock, Hill & Rozelle, 1981). Moreover, dispositional traits (personality factors) and affective states (mood) distort references significantly (Judge & Higgins, 1998). This leads not only to low reliability but also to lower criterion-related validities.

Referees (often acting in benefit of their own organization) may wish to retain good employees and know that a positive reference may have the opposite effect. Moreover, for the same reasons they may choose to write very positive references for staff they are eager to see off. These 'hidden agendas' are hard to evidence but indicate that employers' motivations can have a profound effect on the type of reference provided.

There are now many serious legal issues associated with references, so much so that some organizations refuse to give them. People are directed only to say that the candidate was employed for the specified time they worked there and nothing else. Litigation has followed where a person has been hired partly on the basis of a reference only to discover the person was extremely poor at the job. In this instance it appears references have been unrealistically positive to get rid of the employee. However, what has more recently occurred is that people and organizations have been sued if they refuse to give a reference knowing the candidate is in some sense problematic (e.g., has criminal or anti-social tendencies). In this sense some employers claim with respect to references you are 'damned if you do and damned if you don't'.

Ways to improve the validity of references

In light of the literature, it is clear that the extent to which employers use and rely on references is unjustified and not supported by research evidence. However, research in this area provides some useful guidelines to improve the validity of recommendation letters.

First, it has long been suggested that forced-choice items (e.g. 'Does X like working in a team or working alone?') reduce the effects of overall leniency and can increase accuracy (Carroll & Nash, 1972). Yet forced-choice items must be carefully selected, and even then candidates could be described by either extreme as items are rarely mutually exclusive.

Second, employers should count key words (e.g., able, creative, reliable), previously determined on the basis of job analysis. This technique provides some order to unstructured references, though it is certainly not immune to the referee's style. Peres and Garcia (1962) scrutinized over 600 references and identified five key areas that can be used to organize the key word count: cooperation, intelligence, extraversion ('urbanity'), vigour and conscientiousness ('dependability'). Three decades later Aamodt, Bryan and Whitcomb (1993) analysed students' references and found support for these categories. Although it is questionable whether these categories truly represent the best way to organize and classify the content of references – notably because established personality taxonomies, such as the Big Five, and cognitive ability models (see chapters 7 and 6, respectively) have a stronger and more generalizable theoretical basis – it is clear that having a taxonomy or framework to assess unstructured references does help.

Third, the predictive validity of references tends to increase when referees are asked to use relative percentiles (comparative rankings of how well the candidate does in any given area relative to the group the referee uses as a frame of reference). Although percentiles are not normally distributed and inflated (80th percentiles being the average; McCarthy & Goffin, 2001), they still force referees to distinguish between candidates.

Fourth, it has been argued that if the anonymity of the referees were preserved, references would be less lenient, more varied and more accurate and valid (Ceci & Peters, 1984).

Research also indicates that using concrete examples to back up statements about the candidate's attributes and including both positive *and* negative information about the candidate leads to better references. This was Knouse's (1983) conclusion. The worst-case scenario, on the other hand, was for references that had no examples and included some negative information.

Popularity of references: An evolutionary perspective

Given the unreliability and poor validity of references, it is hard to understand why this method of assessment is used so widely. One reason may be that employers are unaware of the problems associated with it (Terpstra & Rozell, 1997), though in so far as references are requested by business and psychology schools, where employers have access to this literature and are aware of the low validity and reliability of recommendation letters, there may be other reasons. Colarelli and colleagues (2002) explain the widespread use of references in terms of what evolutionary theory calls reciprocal altruism (tit-for-tat), which is the basis of cooperation among non-kin (Buss, 1995). They applied the principle of reciprocal altruism to the relationship between the applicant and candidate, specifically how closeness between them determines the favourability of the references. They argue that 'a recommender will be inclined to write favourably if the applicant is perceived as a valuable resource or if there has been a history of mutually beneficial social exchange. An evolutionary psychological perspective suggests that cooperation, status competition and mating interests should affect the tone of letters of recommendation' (2002, p. 325).

A second hypothesis derived from evolutionary theory is that men's preference for younger females should be reflected in more favourable references. Specifically, Colarelli and colleagues explain that 'males typically desire attractive, younger females as mating partners because youth and beauty are cues of health and fertility. As such, males are likely to be most solicitous towards younger females and regard them in a positive way. This positive regard, in turn, is likely to be reflected in letters of recommendation' (2002, p. 328).

In summary

The frequency with which employers use references is unmatched by the predictive power of references, which have only modest validity, especially if they are not structured. This has led many employers to ask for references only after candidates have been offered the job simply as a standard legal requirement but without taking into account any evaluative judgements made about the candidates.

Why are references not more valid? 1) Because referees have no interest in helping the prospective employers by providing accurate information about the candidate. In fact, if the candidate is worth retaining, the current employer may be less motivated to write a positive reference; but if the candidate is not worth retaining, that may be an incentive to persuade a prospective employer to hire the applicant. 2) Because referees are biased. 3) Because candidates provide names of referees who they believe will comment positively about them. Finally, 4) because all too often the same is said about all candidates requesting a reference (bright, hard-working, reliable, talented, etc.).

The validity of references can be improved by using standardized forms, multiple referees, comparative ranking scales and preserving the anonymity of the referee. Still, the question remains whether in that case referees can provide any additional information to, say, psychometric tests, interviews and biodata.

Strengths and Weaknesses of Each Assessment Method

There are three sorts of data to investigate the strengths and weaknesses of each assessment method. The first is evaluation by academic experts. They are interested primarily in validity, but other factors too. There is no consensus, but clear trends can be seen. What these reviews lead one to conclude from the two criteria sets are the following. First, assessment centres and peer ratings are arguably the best selection methods. The former is expensive and the latter low cost. Second, many well-known methods (interviews, references) are of very limited validity. Third, surprisingly little is known about the potential bias of these tests. Fourth, despite the fact that this table was published over 15 years ago, few would disagree with the overall trends.

Schmitt (1989) argued for the validity of, but also fairness in, employment selection. Subgroup means refers to the fact that these tests show results for different groups of people (male vs. female, Black vs. White, old vs. young). This is an important area of bias (see Table 10.1). The larger the subgroup means, the more the potential bias in these tests which differentiate between various groups based on gender, age, race, etc.

Anderson and Cunningham-Snell (2000) make an interesting and important distinction between validity (i.e. predictive accuracy; see Table 10.2) and popularity (see Table 10.3).

Cook (2009, pp. 283–287) lists six criteria for judging selection tests:

1   Validity is the most important criterion. Unless a test can predict productivity, there is little point in using it.
2   Cost tends to be accorded far too much weight. Cost is not an important consideration if the test has validity. A valid test, even the most elaborate and expensive, is almost always worth using.

Table 10.1 Level of validity and subgroup mean difference for various predictors.

Predictor	Validity	Subgroup Mean Difference
Cognitive ability and special aptitude	Moderate	Moderate
Personality	Low	Small
Interest	Low	?[a]
Physical ability	Moderate-high	Large[b]
Biographical information	Moderate	?
Interviews	Low	Small (?)
Work samples	High	Small
Seniority	Low	Large (?)
Peer evaluations	High	?
Reference checks	Low	?
Academic performance	Low	?
Self-assessments	Moderate	Small
Assessment centres	High	Small

a = a lack of data or inconsistent data; b = mean differences largely between male and female subgroups.

Table 10.2 Predictive accuracy.

Predictive Accuracy	Range 0–1
Perfect prediction	1
Assessment centres – promotion	0.68
Work samples	0.54
Ability tests	0.54
Structured interviews	0.44
Integrity tests	0.41
Assessment centres – performance	0.41
Biodata	0.37
Personality tests	0.38
Unstructured interviews	0.33
Self-assessment	0.15
Reference	0.13
Astrology	0
Graphology	0

Table 10.3 Popularity of assessment methods.

Popularity	
Interviews	97%
References	96%
Application forms	93%
Ability tests	91%
Personality tests	80%
Assessment centres	59%
Biodata	19%
Graphology	2.6%
Astrology	0%

Table 10.4 Summary of 12 selection tests by six criteria.

Selection Test	VAL	COST	PRAC	GEN	ACC	LEGAL
Interview	Low	Medium/Low	High	High	High	Uncertain
Structured interview	High	High	?Limited	High	Untested	No problems
References	Moderate	Very low	High	High	Medium	Some doubts
Peer rating	High	Very low	Very limited	Very limited	Low	Untested
Biodata	High	High/Low	High	High	Low	Some doubts
Ability	High	Low	High	High	Low	Major problems
Psychomotor test	High	Low	Moderate	Limited	Untested	Untested
Job Knowledge	High	Low	High	Limited	Untested	Some doubts
Personality	Variable	Low	High	High	Low	Some doubts
Assessment	High	Very high	Fair	Fair	High	No problems
Work sample	High	High	Limited	Limited	High	No problems
Education	Moderate	Nil	High	High	Untested	Major doubts

VAL = validity, COST = cost, PRAC = practicality, GEN = generality, ACC = acceptability, LEGAL = legality.
Source: Adapted from Cook (2009, p. 386).

3   Practicality is a negative criterion – a reason for not using a test.
4   Generality simply means how many types of employees the test can be used for.
5   Acceptability on the part of candidates is important, especially in periods of full employment.
6   Legality is a negative criterion – a reason for not using something. It is often hard to evaluate, as the legal position on many tests is obscure or confused.

This implies that many organizations have to make a trade-off – cost for validity, practicality for generality. Second, while some methods perform well at some criteria and poorly at others, very few succeed at all criteria. Assessment centres are probably the most successful (see Table 10.4).

The six criteria provide some interesting issues for those using these methods to consider. A key criterion is cost. Cook notes that interview costs are generally graded as low to medium because interviews vary widely and because the costs are taken for granted as part of the process. In contrast, structured interview costs are high because the system has to be tailor-made and requires a full job analysis. Biodata costs are viewed as low or high, as their categorization depends on how they are used – the cost is high if the inventory has to be specially written for the employer, but it be might be low if 'ready-made' consortium biodata could be used. The cost of using educational qualifications is given as zero because the information is routinely collected from application forms, and limited analysis is used, save to confirm the data supplied matches the requirements of the role. A further check of qualification certificates may be made at the interview or on appointment, but even with this additional administration the costs remain low.

A second criterion is practicality. This means that the test is not difficult to introduce because it fits easily into the selection process. Ability and personality tests are very practical because they can be given when candidates come for interview, and they generally permit group testing. References are very practical because everyone is used to giving them. Employers may consider assessment centres as only fairly practical, because they need detailed organizing and do not fit into the conventional timetable of selection procedures.

Peer assessments are highly impractical because they require applicants to spend a long time with each other and may require briefings or pre-training to explain the process. Structured interviews may be seen as having limited practicality because managers may resist the loss of autonomy, preferring to use their own questions and questioning style. Finally, work-sample and psychomotor tests are seen as being of limited practicality because candidates have to be tested individually, rather than in groups.

The third criterion is generality. Most selection tests can be used for any category of worker, but Cook notes that true work samples and job knowledge tests can only be used where there is a specific body of knowledge or skill to test. This means they are restricted to skilled manual work. He notes that psychomotor tests are only useful for jobs that require dexterity or good motor control. Peer ratings can probably be used in uniformed disciplined services, due to issues of attendance, and the possible need for training or at least an understanding of the competences required. Assessment centres too tend to be restricted to managers, probably on grounds of cost, although they have been used for more junior posts.

The fourth criterion reviewed is legalization. While this varies between countries or states, much of the legislation has common origins relating to a desire to prevent discrimination on the grounds of gender, colour or ethnicity. Assessment centres, work samples and structured interviews do not usually cause legal problems, but educational qualifications and mental ability tests most certainly do. Cooked notes that in some areas, such as biodata, the position remains uncertain.

Cook notes that;

> Taking validity as the overriding consideration, there are seven classes of test with high validity, namely peer ratings, biodata, structured interviews, ability tests, assessment centres, work-sample tests and job-knowledge tests. Three of tests have very unlimited generality, which leaves biodata, structured interviews, ability tests and assessment centres.

- Biodata do not achieve such good validity as ability tests and are not as transportable, which makes them more expensive.
- Structured interviews have excellent validity but limited transportability, and are expensive to set up.
- Ability tests have excellent validity, can be used for all types of jobs, are readily transportable and are cheap and easy to use, but fall foul of the law in the US.
- Assessment centres have excellent validity, can be used for most grades of staff and are legally fairly safe, but are difficult to install and are expensive.
- Work samples have excellent validity, are easy to use and are generally quite safe legally, but are expensive, because they are specific to the job.
- Job-knowledge tests have good validity, are easy to use and are inexpensive because they are commercially available, but they are more likely to give rise to legal problems because they are usually paper-and-pencil tests.
- Personality inventories achieve poor validity for predicting job proficiency, but can prove more useful for predicting how well the individual will conform to the job's norms and rules.
- References have only moderate validity, but are cheap to use. However, legal cautions are tending to limit their value (Cook, 2009, pp. 386–387).

Arnold, Silvester, Pattersin, Robertson, Cooper and Burnes (2005) provided a similar analysis of the literature. This is summarized in Table 10.5.

What stands out from Tables 10.1–10.5 is their similarity despite the fact that they may be based on a different database. Occasionally, an individual technique, such as a structured interview, is judged as fair to average (in terms of validity) by one, as good to excellent by another

Table 10.5 A summary of studies on the validity of selection procedures.

Selection Method	Evidence for Criterion-Related Validity	Applicant Reactions	Extent of Use
Structured interviews	High	Moderate to positive	High
Cognitive ability	High	Negative to moderate	Moderate
Personality tests	Moderate	Negative to moderate	Moderate
Biodata	Can be high	Moderate	Moderate
Work sample tests	High	Positive	Low
Assessment centres	Can be high	Positive	Moderate
Handwriting	Low	Negative to moderate	Low
References	Low	Positive	High

but overall the results are robust. Assessment centres, work-sample tests and cognitive ability tests are usually judged most valid in all reviews. This is not surprising as many base their assessments on the same data. What we can say, therefore, is that among academic reviewers there remains good consensus as to the efficacy of different assessment methods.

Future Research

This is clearly not only an interesting but also an important area of research. However, as selection methods change so research has to catch up. A great deal of selection is now web-based, which brings its own set of challenges and opportunities for both professional and researchers. It is now possible to gather a great deal of information about candidates via social media which, though interesting, may conflict with what they report to potential employers. In this sense unobtrusive methods can be used to evaluate people.

There are also important developments in the biological and neurosciences which suggest that using physiological methods for selecting in, and out, may prove very important. However, both developments pose ethical issues, which practitioners and researchers will have to face.

Conclusion

This chapter has looked at three types of data that recruiters and selectors often have access to, to help them make better decisions. Without doubt most of the work in this area has concerned biodata, that is the analysis of how the biography of an individual can be used to predict their behaviour at work. There is much less work on references and CVs because it is recognized that there is considerable bias in these documents. This area is often diffi-cult to research and is not usually theoretically driven. Nevertheless, the very frequency with which application forms, résumés and letters of reference are used in assessment and selection suggests it is an area which merits more and better research.

Acknowledgement

Parts of this chapter have appeared in edited forms in other chapters and papers written by the current author and colleagues. I am particularly grateful to Tomas Chamorro-Premuzic for his help on this chapter.

References

Aamodt, M. G., Bryan, D. A., & Whitcomb, A. J. (1993). Predicting performance with letters of recommendation. *Public Personnel Management, 22*(1), 81–90.

Aamodt, M. G., Nagy, M. S., & Thompson, N. (1998). Employment references: Who are we talking about? Paper presented at the annual meeting of the International Management Association Assessment Council, 22 June, Chicago, IL.

Allworth, E., & Hesketh, B. (2000). Job requirements biodata as a predictor of performance in customer service roles. *International Journal of Selection and Assessment, 8*(3), 137–147.

Anderson, N., & Cunningham-Snell, N. (2000) Personnel selection. *In* N. Chmiel (Ed.), *Introduction to Work and Organisational Psychology* (pp. 69–99). Oxford: Blackwell.

Arnold, J., Silvester, J., Pattersin, F., Robertson, I., Cooper, C., & Burnes, B. (2005). *Work Psychology.* Harlow: Prentice-Hall.

Baird, J.-A., Greatorex, J., & Bell, J. F. (2004). What makes marking reliable? Experiments with UK examinations. *Assessment in Education: Principles, Policy & Practice, 11*(3), 331–348.

Barthel, E., & Schuler, H. (1989). Nutzenkalkulation eignungsdiagnostischer Verfahren am Beispiel eines biographischen Fragebogens [Utility calculation of personnel selection methods using the example of a biographical questionnaire]. *Zeitschrift für Arbeits- und Organisationspsychologie, 33*(2), 73–83.

Baxter, J. C., Brock, B., Hill, P. C., & Rozelle, R. M. (1981). Letters of recommendation: A question of value. *Journal of Applied Psychology, 66*(3), 296–301.

Becker, T. E., & Colquitt, A. L. (1992). Potential versus actual faking of a biodata form: An analysis along several dimensions of item type. *Personnel Psychology, 45*(2), 389–406.

Becton, J. B., Matthews, M. C., Hartley, D. L., & Whitaker, D. H. (2009). Using biodata to predict turnover, organizational commitment, and job performance in healthcare. *International Journal of Selection and Assessment, 17.*

Ben-Shakhar, G., Bar-Hillel, M., Bilu, Y., Ben-Abba, E., & Flug, A. (1986) Can graphology predict occupational success? *Journal of Applied Psychology, 71*, 645–653.

Bliesener, T. (1996). Methodological moderators in validating biographical data in personnel selection. *Journal of Occupational and Organizational Psychology, 69*(1), 107–120.

Boyd, A. S., Hook, M., & King Jr., & L. E. (1996). An evaluation of the accuracy of residency applicants' curricula vitae: Are the claims of publications erroneous? *Journal of the American Academy of Dermatology, 35*, 606–608.

Breaugh, J. A. (2009). The use of biodata for employee selection: Past research and future directions. *Human Resource Management Review, 19*, 219–231.

Buss, D. M. (1995). Evolutionary psychology: A new paradigm for psychological science. *Psychological Inquiry, 6*(1), 1–30.

Carlson, K. D., Scullen, S. E., Schmidt, F. L., Rothstein, H., & Erwin, F. (1999). Generalizable biographical data validity can be achieved without multi-organizational development and keying. *Personnel Psychology, 52*(3), 731–755.

Carroll, S. J., & Nash, A. N. (1972). Effectiveness of a forced-choice reference check. *Personnel Administration. 35*(2), 42–46.

Ceci, S. J., & Peters, D. (1984). Letters of reference: A naturalistic study of the effects of confidentiality. *American Psychologist, 39*(1), 29–31.

Chamorro-Premuzic, T., & Furnham, A. (2010). *The Psychology of Personnel Selection.* Cambridge: Cambridge University Press.

Chen, C.-C., Huang, Y.-M., & Lee, M.-I. (2011). Test of a model linking applicant resume information and hiring recommendations. *International Journal of Selection and Assessment, 19*, 374–387.

Colarelli, S. M., Hechanova-Alampay, R., & Canali, K. G. (2002). Letters of recommendation: An evolutionary perspective. *Human Relations, 55*, 315–344.

Cole, M. S., Feild, H. S., Giles, W. F., & Harris, S. G. (2004). Job type and recruiters' inferences of applicant personality drawn from résumé biodata: Their relationships with hiring recommendations. *International Journal of Selection and Assessment, 12*(4), 363–367.

Cook, M. (2009). *Personnel Selection*. Chichester: Wiley.

Cucina, J. M., Caputo, P. M., Thibodeaux, H. F., & Maclane, C. N. (2012). Unlocking the key to biodata scoring: A comparison of empirical, rational, and hybrid approaches at different sample sizes. *Personnel Psychology, 65*, 385–428.

Dean, G. (1992). The bottom line and effect size. *In* B. L. Betyerstein & D. F. Beyerstein (Eds.), *The Write Stuff* (pp. 269–341). Buffalo, NY: Prometheus Books.

Dean, G., Kelly. I., Saklofske, D., & Furnham, A. (1992). Graphology and human judgement. *In* B. L. Betyerstein & D. F. Beyerstein (Eds.), *The Write Stuff* (pp. 342–395). Buffalo, NY: Prometheus Books.

Dean, M. A., & Russell, C. J. (2005). An examination of biodata theory-based constructs in a field context. *International Journal of Selection and Assessment, 13*(2), 139–149.

Dean, M. A., Russell, C. J., & Muchinsky, P. M. (1999). Life experiences and performance prediction: Toward a theory of biodata. *Personnel and Human Resources Management, 17*, 245–281.

Derous, E., Ryan, A. M., & Nguyen, H.-H. D. (2011). Multiple categorization in résumé screening: Examining effects on hiring discrimination against Arab applicants in field and lab settings. *Journal of Organizational Behavior, 33*, 544–570.

Devlin, S. E., Abrahams, N. M., & Edwards, J. E. (1992). Empirical keying of biographical data: Cross-validity as a function of scaling procedure and sample size. *Military Psychology, 4*(3), 119–136.

Dracup, C. (1997). The reliability of marking on a psychology degree. *British Journal of Psychology, 88*(4), 691–708.

Drakeley, R. J., Herriot, P., & Jones, A. (1988). Biographical data, training success and turnover. *Journal of Occupational Psychology, 61*(2), 145–152.

Driver, R., Buckley, M., & Frink, D. (1996). Should we write off graphology? *International Journal of Selection and Assessment, 4*, 78–86.

Elgin, P. D., & Clapham, M. M. (2004). Attributes Associated with the Submission of Electronic versus Paper Résumés. *Computers in Human Behavior, 20*(4), 535–549.

Ellingson, J. E., Sackett, P. R., & Hough, L. M. (1999). Social desirability corrections in personality measurement: Issues of applicant comparison and construct validity. *Journal of Applied Psychology, 84*(2), 155–166.

England, G. W. (1961). *Development and Use of Weighted Application Banks*. Dubuque, IO: Wm. C. Brown.

Feldman, J. M. (1981). Beyond attribution theory: Cognitive processes in performance appraisal. *Journal of Applied Psychology, 66*(2), 127–148.

Fine, S. A., & Cronshaw, S. (1994). The role of job analysis in establishing the validity of biodata. *In* G. Stokes, M. D. Mumford & W. A. Owens (Eds.), *Biodata Handbook: Theory, Research and Use of Biographical Information in Selection and Performance Prediction* (pp. 39–64). Palo Alto, CA: Consulting Psychologists Press.

Fiske, S. T. (1980). Attention and weight in person perception: The impact of negative and extreme behavior. *Journal of Personality and Social Psychology, 38*(6), 889–906.

Fleishman, E. A. (1988). Some new frontiers in personnel selection research. *Personnel Psychology, 41*(4), 679–701.

Goldberg, L. R. (1972). Parameters of personality inventory construction and utilization: A comparison of prediction strategies and tactics. *Multivariate Behavioral Research Monographs*. No, 59.

Harold, C. M., McFarland, L. A., & Weekley, J. A. (2006). The validity of verifiable and non-verifiable biodata items: An examination across applicants and incumbents. *International Journal of Selection and Assessment, 14*(4), 336–346.

Hiemstra, A. M. F., Derous, E., Serlie, A. W., & Born, M. P. (2012). Ethnicity effects in graduates' résumé content. *Applied Psychology: An International Review*, 1–27.

Hough, L. M. (1984). Development and evaluation of the 'accomplishment record' method of selecting and promoting professionals. *Journal of Applied Psychology, 69*(1), 135–146.

Hough, L. M. (1998). Effects of intentional distortion in personality measurement and evaluation of suggested palliatives. *Human Performance, 11*(2–3), 209–244.

Hough, L., & Paullin, C. (1994). Construct-oriented scale construction: The rational approach. *In* G. S. Stokes, M. D. Mumford & W. A. Owens (Eds.), *Biodata Handbook: Theory, Research and Use of Biographical Information in Selection and Performance Prediction* (pp. 39–64). Palo Alto, CA: Consulting Psychologists Press.

Hunter, J. E., & Hunter, R. F. (1984). Validity and utility of alternate predictors of job performance. *Psychological Bulletin, 96,* 72–98.

Jones, A., & Harrison, E. (1982). Prediction of performance in initial officer training using reference reports. *Journal of Occupational Psychology, 55*(1), 35–42.

Judge, T. A., & Higgins, C. A. (1998). Affective disposition and the letter of reference. *Organizational Behavior and Human Decision Processes, 75*(3), 207–221.

Karas, M., & West, J. (1999). Construct-oriented biodata development for selection to a differentiated performance domain. *International Journal of Selection and Assessment. Special Issue: Background Data and Autobiographical Memory, 7*(2), 86–96.

Keating, E., Paterson, D. G., & Stone, C. H. (1950). Validity of work histories obtained by interview. *Journal of Applied Psychology, 34*(1), 6–11.

King, R., & Koehler, D. (2002). Illusory correlations in graphological analysis. *Journal of Experimental Psychology, 30,* 189–203.

Knouse, S. B. (1983). The letter of recommendation: Specificity and favorability of information. *Personnel Psychology, 36*(2), 331–341.

Lautenschlager, G. J. (1994). Accuracy and faking of background data. *In* G. S. Stokes, M. D. Mumford & W. A. Owens (Eds.), *Biodata Handbook: Theory, Research and Use of Biographical Information in Selection and Performance Prediction* (pp. 39–64). Palo Alto, CA: Consulting Psychologists Press.

Levashina, J., Morgeson, F. P., & Campion, M. A. (2012). Tell me some more: Exploring how verbal ability and item verifiability influence responses to biodata questions in a high-stakes selection context. *Personnel Psychology, 65,* 359–383.

Mael, F. A., & Ashforth, B. E. (1995). Loyal from day one: Biodata, organizational identification, and turnover among newcomers. *Personnel Psychology, 48*(2), 309–333.

Mael, F. A., & Hirsch, A. C. (1993). Rainforest empiricism and quasi-rationality: Two approaches to objective biodata. *Personnel Psychology, 46*(4), 719–738.

Manley, G. G., Benavidez, J., & Dunn, K. (2007). Development of a personality biodata measure to predict ethical decision making. *Journal of Managerial Psychology, 22*(7), 664–682.

Marsh, H. W., Bond, N. W., & Jayasinghe, U. W. (2007). Peer review process: Assessments by applicant-nominated referees are biased, inflated, unreliable and invalid. *Australian Psychologist, 42*(1), 33–38.

McCarthy, J. M., & Goffin, R. D. (2001). Improving the validity of letters of recommendation: An investigation of three standardized reference forms. *Military Psychology, 13*(4), 199–222.

McManus, M. A., & Kelly, M. L. (1999). Personality measures and biodata: Evidence regarding their incremental predictive value in the life insurance industry. *Personnel Psychology, 52*(1), 137–148.

Mosel, J. N., & Goheen, H. W. (1959). The employment recommendation questionnaire: III. Validity of different types of references. *Personnel Psychology, 12,* 469–477.

Mount, M. K., Witt, L. A., & Barrick, M. R. (2000). Incremental validity of empirically keyed biodata scales over GMA and the five factor personality constructs. *Personnel Psychology, 53*(2), 299–323.

Muchinsky, P. M. (1979). The use of reference reports in personnel selection: A review and evaluation. *Journal of Occupational Psychology, 52*(4), 287–297.

Mumford, M. D., Costanza, D. P., Connelly, M. S., & Johnson, J. F. (1996). Item generation procedures and background data scales: Implications for construct and criterion-related validity. *Personnel Psychology, 49*(2), 361–398.

Mumford, M. D., & Owens, W. A. (1987). Methodology review: Principles, procedures, and findings in the application of background data measures. *Applied Psychological Measurement, 11*(1), 1–31.

Mumford, M. D., Stokes, G. S., & Owens, W. A. (1990). Patterns of life history: The ecology of human individuality. *Series in Applied Psychology.* Hillsdale, NJ & Hove: Lawrence Erlbaum.

Murphy, K. R., & Cleveland, J. N. (1995). *Understanding Performance Appraisal: Social, Organizational, and Goal-Based Perspectives.* Thousand Oaks, CA: Sage.

Neter, E., & Ben-Shakhar, G. (1989). The predictive validity of graphological inferences. *Personality and Individual Differences, 10,* 737–745.

Nicklin, J. M., & Roch, S. G. (2008). Biases influencing recommendation letter contents: Physical attractiveness and gender. *Journal of Applied Social Psychology, 38,* 3053–3074.

Ones, D. S., Visvesvarian, C., & Reiss, A. D. (1996). Role of social desirability in personality testing for personnel selection: The red herring. *Journal of Applied Psychology, 81,* 660–679.

Oswald, F. L., Schmitt, N., Kim, B. H., Ramsay, L. J., & Gillespie, M. A. (2004). Developing a biodata measure and situational judgment inventory as predictors of college student performance. *Journal of Applied Psychology, 89*(2), 187–207.

Paunonen, S. V. (1984). Optimizing the validity of personality assessments: The importance of aggregation and item content. *Journal of Research in Personality, 18*(4), 411–431.

Paunonen, S. V., Jackson, D. N., & Oberman, S. M. (1987). Personnel selection decisions: Effects of applicant personality and the letter of reference. *Organizational Behavior and Human Decision Processes, 40*(1), 96–114.

Peres, S. H., & Garcia, J. R. (1962). Validity and dimensions of descriptive adjectives used in reference letters for engineering applicants. *Personnel Psychology, 15*(3), 279–286.

Reilly, R. R., & Chao, G. R. (1982). Validity and fairness of some alternative employee selection procedures. *Personnel Psychology, 35*(1), 1–62.

Robertson, I. T., & Smith, M. (2001). Personnel selection. *Journal of Occupational and Organizational Psychology, 74*(4), 441–472.

Schmitt, N. (1989). Fairness in employment selection. *In* M. Smith & I. Robertson (Eds.), *Advances in Selection and Assessment* (pp. 131–153). Chichester: Wiley.

Schmidt, F. L., & Hunter, J. E. (1998). The validity and utility of selection methods in personnel psychology: Practical and theoretical implications of 85 years of research findings. *Psychological Bulletin, 124,* 262–274.

Schmitt, N., Gooding, R. Z., Noe, R. A., & Kirsch, M. (1984). Meta-analyses of validity studies published between 1964 and 1982 and the investigation of study characteristics. *Personnel Psychology, 37,* 407–422.

Schmitt, N., Jennings, D., & Toney, R. (1999). Can we develop measures of hypothetical constructs? *Human Resource Management Review, 9*(2), 169–183.

Schmitt, N., & Kunce, C. (2002). The effects of required elaboration of answers to biodata questions. *Personnel Psychology, 55*(3), 569–587.

Schmitt, N., Oswald, F. L., Kim, B. H., Gillespie, M. A., Ramsay, L. J., & Yoo, T.-Y. (2003). Impact of elaboration on socially desirable responding and the validity of biodata measures. *Journal of Applied Psychology, 88*(6), 979–988.

Schneider, B., & Schmitt, N. (1986). *Staffing Organizations* (2nd ed.). Glenview, IL: Scott Freeman.

Schrader, A. D., & Osburn, H. G. (1977). Biodata faking: Effects of induced subtlety and position specificity. *Personnel Psychology, 30*(3), 395–404.

Sisco, H., & Reilly, R. R. (2007). Development and validation of a biodata Inventory as an alternative method to measurement of the five factor model of personality. *Social Science Journal, 44*(2), 383–389.

Stokes, G. S., Mumford, M. D., & Owens, W. A. (1994). *Biodata Handbook: Theory, Research, and Use of Biographical Information in Selection and Performance Prediction.* Palo Alto, CA: Consulting Psychologist Press.

Stokes, G. S., & Searcy, C. A. (1999). Specification of scales in biodata form development: Rational vs. empirical and global vs. specific. *International Journal of Selection and Assessment. Special Issue: Background Data and Autobiographical Memory, 7*(2), 72–85.

Terpstra, D. E., & Rozell, E. J. (1997). Why some potentially effective staffing practices are seldom used. *Public Personnel Management, 26*(4), 483–495.

Weinstein, D. (2012). The psychology of behaviorally-focused résumés on applicant selection: Are your hiring managers really hiring the 'right' people for the 'right' jobs? *Business Horizons, 55,* 53–63.

Wernimont, P. F. (1962). Reevaluation of a weighted application blank for office personnel. *Journal of Applied Psychology, 46*(6), 417–419.

Wernimont, P. F., & Campbell, J. P. (1968). Signs, samples, and criteria. *Journal of Applied Psychology, 52*(5), 372–376.

Wilson, N. A. B. (1948). The work of the Civil Service Selection Board. *Occupational Psychology, 22,* 204–212.

11

Situational Judgement Tests
for Selection

Jan Corstjens, Filip Lievens and Stefan Krumm

Introduction

When situational judgement tests (SJTs) began to regain popularity among the scientific community in the 1990s, there was an implicit notion that they captured context-dependent knowledge. In fact, the term 'situational judgement' carries the connotation of test-takers' responses being more effective when they consider the specifics of the situation. In recent years another perspective has emerged, which views SJTs as capturing relatively context-independent knowledge (or general domain knowledge; Motowidlo, Crook, Kell & Naemi, 2009; Motowidlo, Hooper & Jackson, 2006a). Although SJTs and their items will often fall somewhere between these two perspectives, we posit in this chapter that it might be useful to distinguish between them. So far, there has been no review of the SJT literature in terms of these two approaches. This is understandable, as over the years the two perspectives have emerged alongside each other. Therefore, the aim of this chapter is to review SJT research according to these two approaches.

The chapter is structured as follows. We start by presenting the traditional contextualized perspective underlying SJTs. We review the underlying theory, the developmental stages and the research evidence regarding this perspective (e.g., reliability, criterion-related validity, construct-related validity, subgroup differences, applicant reactions). We end our discussion of the contextualized perspective by homing in on new trends. Next, we present the general domain knowledge perspective, thereby following exactly the same structure as for the contextualized perspective. We end this chapter by presenting directions for future research and by giving recommendations for HR practices.

The Wiley Blackwell Handbook of the Psychology of Recruitment, Selection and Employee Retention,
First Edition. Edited by Harold W. Goldstein, Elaine D. Pulakos, Jonathan Passmore and Carla Semedo.
© 2017 John Wiley & Sons Ltd. Published 2020 by John Wiley & Sons Ltd.

Contextualized SJTs

The underlying rationale and theory

Simulations represent contextualized selection procedures that psychologically and/or physically mimic key aspects of the job (Lievens & De Soete, 2012). In accordance with this definition, contextualized SJTs aim to confront applicants with a set of situations similar to those they might encounter on the job and elicit their procedural knowledge about how to respond to these stimuli. Like other simulations such as assessment centre exercises or work samples, context-specific SJTs rest on the notions of point-to-point correspondence with the criterion (future job situations) and behavioural consistency (Bruk-Lee, Drew & Hawkes, 2014; Lievens & De Soete, 2012). Behavioural consistency denotes that candidates' performance on a selection test will be consistent with their future job performance (Schmitt & Ostroff, 1986; Wernimont & Campbell, 1968). To this end, simulations should ideally be constructed in such a way that there is a high degree of correspondence between the conditions in the simulation and those in the actual job context and tasks. Assessment centre exercises, for example, mimic actual job situations and generate behavioural samples and hence are referred to as high-fidelity simulations (Thornton & Rupp, 2006). Fidelity refers to the degree to which the simulation authentically reflects the targeted job in terms of both stimuli and responses (Motowidlo, Dunnette & Carter, 1990). To reduce development and administration costs of such simulations, most SJTs adopt a low-fidelity format in simulating the situations and responses. That is, SJTs typically present written (or video-based) descriptions of job-related situations and require a response to them by opting for an alternative from a list of multiple-choice responses (McDaniel, Hartman, Whetzel & Grubb, 2007; Weekley, Ployhart & Holtz, 2006).

Notably, situation descriptions are key to SJTs when viewed from the contextualized perspective because they simulate job contexts, guide candidates' situation perception and subsequent response selection and render responses more or less effective. Thus, the situation descriptions in SJTs aim to provide sufficient contextualization so that candidates can imagine the situation and make well-thought-out judgements about how they would or should behave according to the situational demands depicted (Richman-Hirsch, Olson-Buchanan & Drasgow, 2000). So, this view assumes that test-takers' behavioural response selection is contingent on how they perceive and construe the stimuli (job-related situations), which aligns well with interactionist theories that consider behaviour to be a function of both the person's traits and the person's perception of the situation (Campion & Ployhart, 2013; Mischel & Shoda, 1995). Each situation conveys specific cues, which are interpreted by each test-taker. The person's interpretation of the cues is guided by previous experiences in similar situations and determines the response selection believed to be appropriate. Without this context, it is assumed the test-taker is left in the dark as to what the appropriate response should be and might lack sufficient information to solve the item.

Developmental stages

The typical steps involved in developing contextualized SJTs are threefold (Lievens, Peeters & Schollaert, 2008; Motowidlo et al., 1990). The first stage concerns the development of item stems or situations to be presented in the SJT. The second stage involves the collection of response options from subject matter experts (SMEs), the choice of response instructions and of the response format. The third and final stage targets the development of the scoring key.

Stage 1: Item stems To gather the item stems or situations presented in the SJT, a job analysis is usually conducted. During this job analysis, SMEs are asked to generate critical incidents (Flanagan, 1954), which means that they are asked to recall examples of situations in which exceptionally good or exceptionally poor performance was demonstrated. The test developer often prompts the SMEs with the goal of collecting information about all the content domains and constructs deemed to be important for the job. The selected SMEs are typically incumbents, supervisors, managers or a mix of these sources of information. Alternatively, archival sources and even customers might serve as a source of information (Weekley et al., 2006). The critical incidents obtained are then sorted and checked for redundancy and level of specificity. The surviving incidents then serve to write item stems or descriptions of job-related situations. As an alternative to this inductive method of gathering critical incidents, a deductive method can be followed. In this strategy, the item stem content is derived from theoretical models (e.g., a model of conflict management).

Stage 2: Response options, response instructions, and response format After developing the situation descriptions, another group of SMEs is asked to generate response options they believe to be (in-)effective reactions to the situations. To obtain a wider range of response options with different levels of effectiveness, the test developer might also ask inexperienced workers to generate responses. The test developer then decides which options to retain, usually by choosing a mix of response options that are differentially effective in each situation. There are no general rules regarding the number of response options to retain. The majority of SJT items include 4 or 5 response options, even though SJT items with up to 10 response options also exist (e.g., the Tacit Knowledge Inventory; Wagner & Sternberg, 1991).

In the next stage, the test developer decides on the response instructions. This is not a trivial choice because the response instruction format affects the construct saturation of the SJT (McDaniel et al., 2007). One of two formats of response instructions is usually chosen: behavioural tendency instructions or knowledge instructions (McDaniel & Nguyen, 2001). Behavioural tendency instructions ask respondents what they would do in the given situation, whereas knowledge instructions ask respondents what they should do in the situation; in other words, they ask respondents to identify the best response to a given situation.

Test developers also make a choice about the response format to be employed. Generally, three response formats can be distinguished. Respondents are asked to select the best/worst response options, rank the response options from most to least effective or rate the response options on Likert-type scales. Arthur, Glaze, Jarrett, White, Schurig and Taylor (2014) comparatively evaluated these three common response formats by varying them while keeping the rest of the SJT design and content constant. The rate response format evidenced higher construct-related validity, lower levels of subgroup differences and increased reliability over the other two. A drawback of the rate response format, however, was its higher susceptibility to response distortion.

Stage 3: Scoring key After situations, response options, response format and instructions have been developed, the test requires a scoring key. Here, four different methods can be delineated. The rational method involves asking a group of SMEs to score the response options on (in-)effectiveness. Scores with acceptable inter-rater agreement (e.g., ≥ 0.60) are retained for the test. The second is the empirical method which involves quantifying endorsements of correct response options gathered from a large sample of lay people instead of SMEs. For instance, options that are chosen to be correct by over 25% of the sample are retained for the test. Although notably different in approach, researchers have found no differences between these two scoring keys in terms of validity (e.g., Weekley & Jones, 1999). Combining the rational and empirical method is a third approach that can be followed. An example of this hybrid approach is retaining an empirical key only after SMEs have agreed on it. The final and least frequently followed method involves the development of a scoring key with answer options that reflect effective performance according to a chosen theoretical framework (e.g., leadership theories) scored as correct (Weekley et al., 2006).

In Figure 11.1 we present an example of a contextualized SJT item that was taken from the Tacit Knowledge Inventory for Managers (Wagner & Sternberg, 1991). Although not strictly called an SJT by the developers, the test is similar to the format and content of a typical SJT (McDaniel, Morgeson, Finnegan, Campion & Braverman, 2001).

You are the director of sales for a consumer research firm. Your sales growth has kept pace with the marketplace but because you installed state-of-the-art web survey software you expected to be doing much better. Due to the costs associated with the new software you are likely to make less profit this year unless you can improve sales of additional services to your clients.

After discussions with several of your best clients you learned that the reports which accompanied the data you collect for your customers were generally thrown away or extensively rewritten by your clients. Some even hired freelance researchers to edit the reports after your company sent them. It is clear to you that if you can improve the quality of your research reports it will be easier to sell your customers additional services.

Therefore, since the busiest season of your year is fast approaching, you decide to distribute a list of "best practices" for business report writing.

Rate the quality of the following advice about business writing you are considering including in your talk (scored on a Likert-type 7-point scale ranging from 1= *below average* to 7= *above average*):

  a) Write reports so that the main points will be understood by a reader who only has time to skim the report.
  b) Explain, in the first few paragraphs, how a report is organized.
  c) Use everyday language and avoid all business jargon.
  d) Work hard to convey your message in the fewest number of words.
  e) Consider carefully for whom you are writing.
  f) Write carefully the first time around to avoid having to rewrite.
  g) Avoid visual aids, such as figures, charts, and diagrams, because they often oversimplify the message.
  h) Be formal rather than informal in your style.
  i) Use the passive rather than the active voice (e.g., write "30 managers were interviewed" rather than "we interviewed 30 managers").
  j) Avoid using the first person (e.g., write "it is recommended" rather than "I recommend").

Figure 11.1 Example of a contextualized SJT item. *Source*: Wagner & Sternberg (1991). Reproduced with permission of Robert J. Sternberg.

Overview of Prior Research

Research on SJTs has mushroomed following their reintroduction in the academic literature by Motowidlo and colleagues (1990). The vast majority of research evidence on SJTs pertains to the contextualized view as the traditional perspective on SJTs. In this section, we review such research evidence concerning reliability, criterion-related and incremental validity, construct-related validity, subgroup differences, applicant reactions, faking, retest and coaching effects. Whenever meta-analytic findings are available, we refer to them.

Reliability

Several meta-analyses have integrated internal consistency reliability coefficients that have been reported in the SJT literature. The mean α values reported in these meta-analyses ranged from 0.46 to 0.68 (Campion, Ployhart & MacKenzie, 2014; Catano, Brochu & Lamerson, 2012; Kasten & Freund, 2015). The reason for the moderate internal consistency reliability coefficients is the fact that SJTs are created on the basis of job situations that require the expression of a combination of different constructs, which results in heterogeneous test items *and* response options. Evidence for item heterogeneity comes from factor analytic investigations of SJTs that reveal no clear factor structure in the items (Schmitt & Chan, 2006).

As internal consistency is not a suitable reliability estimate for a measurement method that has heterogeneous items (Osburn, 2000), other types of reliability estimates, such as test–retest reliability and alternative form reliability, have been proposed in the literature (Lievens et al., 2008; Whetzel & McDaniel, 2009). Studies examining test–retest reliability are scarce but they tend to report considerably higher estimates. For instance, Catano and colleagues (2012) reported two SJT test–retest coefficients of $r = 0.82$ and $r = 0.66$, respectively. Studies examining alternative form reliability coefficients are even scarcer because of the difficulty in developing alternative form SJTs that capture the same constructs when these constructs are often not clearly distinguishable to begin with. Notwithstanding this, Clause, Mullins, Nee, Pulakos and Schmitt (1998) reported alternative test reliability estimates ranging from $r = 0.70$ to $r = 0.77$ when they adopted a rigorous item cloning method for constructing alternative SJT forms (see also Lievens & Sackett, 2007). So, SJTs have generally been found to be sufficiently reliable measurement instruments, provided that appropriate reliability estimates are used.

Criterion-related and incremental validity

Much data have accumulated over the years supporting the relation between SJTs and job performance. McDaniel and colleagues conducted two meta-analyses (McDaniel et al., 2001, 2007) and reported corrected estimated population correlations of 0.26 and 0.34, respectively (uncorrected correlations 0.20 and 0.26). The more recent analysis included data on over 24,000 respondents. The criterion used in most studies is a composite score of job performance ratings. However, as evidenced by Christian and colleagues' meta-analytic findings, criterion-related validity can increase when predictor and criterion are more carefully matched (Christian, Edwards & Bradley, 2010). These authors divided the job performance criterion into three facets: task performance (i.e., job-specific skills), contextual performance (i.e., soft skills and job dedication), and managerial performance (i.e., management skills). SJTs were then sorted into a typology of construct domains. The authors hypothesized that criterion-related validity would increase if particular criterion facets were closely matched with the content domains of the SJTs (e.g., contextual performance predicted by SJTs from the domains of interpersonal and teamwork skills). Overall, the authors found support for their content-based matching approach: relatively homogeneous SJTs saturated with a particular construct domain evidenced higher criterion-related validity with the criterion component they were designed to predict than heterogeneous composite SJTs.

In addition to moderation by criterion facet (a content-based moderator), the criterion-related validity of an SJT can be influenced by method-based moderators. We highlight three moderators identified in the literature relating to 1) test development procedure, 2) item stem format and 3) test delivery format. Meta-analytic evidence established that SJTs yield higher validities (r =0.38 vs. r = 0.29) when they are based on a careful job analysis than when they are based on intuition or theory (McDaniel et al., 2001). A second moderator is the level of detail in the item stem; less detailed questions show a slightly larger validity than highly detailed questions (r = 0.35 vs. r = 0.33). This runs somewhat counter to the premise of contextualized SJTs that context and level of detail increase the criterion-related validity of the test scores. Third, the test delivery format has been found to differentially affect validity, with video-based SJTs showing higher levels of criterion-related validity for predicting interpersonal skills than the traditional paper-and-pencil format, with a corrected population correlation of 0.36 for video-based SJTs and 0.25 for paper-and-pencil formats (Christian et al., 2010). This finding supports the contextualized perspective of SJTs because contextual information (e.g., about environmental cues, nonverbal behaviour) seems to be necessary to adequately apply interpersonal skills.

An interesting strand of research concerns investigating the incremental validity of SJTs as compared to other predictors of performance. McDaniel and colleagues (2007) found that SJTs explained 6–7% additional variance above the Big Five personality factors and 3–5% additional variance above cognitive ability, depending on the type of response instruction (knowledge instructions vs. behavioural tendency instructions). Further, SJTs explained 1–2% of variance above both cognitive ability and the Big Five factor scores. More recently, SJTs as low-fidelity simulations have been contrasted with assessment centre exercises in a high-stakes selection context. Lievens and Patterson (2011) found that criterion-related validity was similar for both the SJT and assessment centre exercises. Subsequent incremental validity analyses revealed that the assessment centre exercises explained 3% additional variance in the criterion job performance over the SJT. However, subsequent path analysis showed that assessment centre performance only partially mediated the effect of procedural knowledge as measured by the SJT on job performance, indicating that scores obtained from these two types of simulations should not be viewed as redundant.

In sum, contextualized SJTs predict variance in job-related criteria to an extent that is comparable to other frequently used selection tools (see Schmidt & Hunter, 1998). Importantly, contextualized SJTs contribute incrementally above and beyond Big Five personality factors and general mental ability.

Construct-related validity For the same reason that makes it difficult to estimate internal consistency reliability of SJT scores, item heterogeneity makes it challenging to delineate which construct(s) are being measured by the SJT. Next to decisions pertaining to the actual test content, the method of measurement can also influence which constructs are being measured by SJTs. Concerning measurement method, McDaniel and colleagues (2007) obtained a differential pattern of construct-related validity coefficients when SJTs with knowledge instructions ('What should you do in a given situation?') were compared to SJTs with behavioural tendency instructions ('What would you do in a given situation?'). Correlations between SJTs with behavioural tendency instructions and three Big Five personality factors were higher than for SJTs with knowledge instructions (agreeableness 0.37 vs. 0.19, conscientiousness 0.34 vs. 0.24, and emotional stability 0.35 vs. 0.12, respectively). Conversely, SJTs with knowledge instructions correlated at a higher rate with measures of cognitive ability than SJTs with behavioural tendency instructions (0.35 vs. 0.19, respectively).

Subgroup differences Although SJTs generally result in smaller subgroup differences than cognitive ability tests, they are not absent in SJTs (Lievens et al., 2008). Whetzel, McDaniel and Nguyen (2008) meta-analytically investigated race and gender as two demographic variables that can lead to subgroup differences in SJT scores. Regarding gender, females in general performed slightly better than males ($d = 0.11$). Concerning race, they found that Whites performed better than Blacks ($d = 0.38$), Hispanics ($d = 0.24$) and Asians ($d = 0.29$). Subgroup differences were not invariant across all SJTs because several moderators have been found to influence the relation with SJT performance. Racial differences, for example, could be explained by the cognitive loading of the SJT. That is, SJTs that were more correlated with general mental ability resulted in larger racial differences than SJTs that were more correlated with personality constructs (Whetzel et al., 2008). Reduced racial differences were also observed when behavioural tendency instructions were used instead of knowledge instructions (differences between Whites and Blacks of $d = 0.39$ for knowledge instructions and $d = 0.34$ for behavioural tendency instructions; Whetzel et al., 2008), and when video-based SJTs were used ($d = 0.21$ compared to a paper-and-pencil SJT, Chan & Schmitt, 1997). In contrast to racial differences, gender differences seemed to increase only when the personality loading of the SJT increased, thereby favouring women ($d = -0.37$ and -0.49 as compared to men for conscientiousness and for agreeableness, respectively) and remained invariant when the cognitive loading increased (Whetzel et al., 2008).

Other than the cognitive loading of SJTs, McDaniel and colleagues (2011) suggested that more extreme response tendencies might also explain Black–White subgroup differences in SJT scores and proposed controlling for these response tendencies in SJT scoring. They administered SJTs with Likert-type scales in two concurrent designs and subsequently adjusted the scale scores for elevation and scatter (i.e., respondents' item means and deviations). Their strategies resulted in a reduction of Black–White mean score differences across the two measurement occasions, with effect sizes dropping from around half an *SD* ($d = 0.43$–0.56) to about a third of an *SD* ($d = 0.29$–0.36) for the standardized scores to less than a fifth of an *SD* for the dichotomous scoring ($d = 0.12$–0.18). Roth, Bobko and Buster (2013) highlighted a caveat in this subgroup differences SJT research, namely that the studies have nearly always been conducted with concurrent designs (i.e., samples consisting of job incumbents and not applicants). A sole focus on concurrent designs could lead to range restriction attenuating the obtained effect sizes and thus to an underestimation of effect sizes in the population (see also Bobko & Roth, 2013). These authors argue that in order to reduce the potential issue of range restriction, subgroup differences should also be studied in samples of applicants who are assessed with the SJT at the earliest possible selection stage (and before any other measures have been deployed). In such applicant samples findings pointed towards Black–White differences of $d = 0.63$ for SJTs that were mainly saturated with cognitive ability, $d = 0.29$ for SJTs saturated with job knowledge and $d = 0.21$ for SJTs that mainly tapped interpersonal skills. These results further confirm previous findings of racial differences increasing with the cognitive loading of the SJT.

Applicant reactions In general, research has demonstrated that applicants prefer selection tools they perceive as job-related, that provide opportunities to show their capabilities and that are interactive (e.g., face-to-face interviews) (Hausknecht, Day & Thomas, 2004;

Lievens & De Soete, 2012; Potosky, 2008). High-fidelity simulations typically contain many of these aspects. Several studies have shown that applicant reactions to low-fidelity SJTs also tend to be favourable, and even more so when fidelity is increased and interactivity is added. Chan and Schmitt (1997) showed that a video-based SJT received higher face validity ratings than a written SJT. Richman-Hirsch and colleagues (2000) found that interactive video-based formats were preferred to computerized and paper-and-pencil formats. In an interactive (branched or nonlinear) SJT, the test-taker's previous answer is taken into account and determines the way the situation develops. Kanning, Grewe, Hollenberg and Hadouch (2006) went a step further and varied not only stimulus fidelity (situation depicted in a video vs. written format), but also response fidelity (response options shown in a video vs. written format) and interactivity of SJTs. In line with the previously mentioned studies, applicants reacted more favourably towards interactive video-based formats, and in this case towards both the stimulus and the response format.

Faking, retesting and coaching   Hooper, Cullen and Sackett (2006) compiled the research findings on faking and discovered that there was a lot of variation concerning the relation between faking and SJT performance: effect sizes ranged from $d = 0.08$ to 0.89 suggesting the presence of moderators. One such moderator proposed by the authors is the cognitive or g loading of the items. Although based on just a handful of studies, the trend is that SJTs with higher cognitive loadings are less easy to fake (Hooper et al., 2006; Peeters & Lievens, 2005). Similarly, the degree of faking can vary depending on the response instructions, with knowledge instructions being less easy to fake than behavioural tendency instructions (Nguyen, Biderman & McDaniel, 2005).

As SJTs are often part of large-scale, high-stakes selection programmes, it is also important to examine whether retest and coaching effects influence test scores and their psychometric properties. Concerning retest or practice effects, Lievens, Buyse and Sackett (2005) reported effects of $d = 0.29$ (0.49 after controlling for measurement error). A similar result was found by Dunlop, Morrison and Cordery (2011), who found an effect size of $d = 0.20$. Importantly, in both studies retest effects were found to be smaller for SJTs in comparison to cognitive ability tests. Dunlop and colleagues further noticed that practice effects decreased at a third measurement occasion for both the SJT and the cognitive ability tests. As far as coaching is concerned, only two studies have tackled this issue to date. Cullen, Sackett and Lievens (2006) investigated the coachability of two college admission SJTs and found that coaching increased the scores on one of the SJTs ($d = 0.24$) but not on the other. In contrast to Cullen and colleagues' study which took place in a laboratory setting, Lievens, Buyse, Sackett and Connelly (2012) investigated coaching on SJT scores in a high-stakes setting. Moreover, the latter study included pretest and propensity score covariates to control for self-selection in order to reduce the non-equivalence of the groups. Using this more sophisticated analysis, they found that coaching raised SJT scores with 0.53 SDs. Finally, a recent study (Stemig, Sackett & Lievens, 2015) found that organizationally endorsed coaching (i.e., coaching provided by the organization rather than commercial coaching) also enabled people to raise their SJT scores, but did not reduce the criterion-related validities of the SJT scores.

In sum, contextualized SJTs seem to be less prone to faking and retest effects than other selection methods. Such effects may be further reduced by using knowledge-based response instructions and developing SJTs with higher g loadings. Coaching effects can be reduced by enabling all candidates to practice on SJTs in advance of high-stakes assessments.

Contextualized SJTs: Implications and Trends

The contextualized perspective of SJTs has important implications for SJT design as it encourages test developers to increase the SJT situations' level of contextualization and fidelity. Over the years, various innovations have been proposed as alternatives to classic paper-and-pencil SJTs. These innovations have focused on increasing the realism of the situation depicted (i.e., stimulus fidelity) or the realism of the manner in which applicants are able to respond (i.e., response fidelity).

A well-known example of increasing stimulus fidelity consists of using video-based or multimedia formats instead of written scenarios. Recently, advances in terms of both 3D animation and motion-capture techniques have been employed by SJT developers as a way to increase stimulus fidelity (Weekley, Hawkes, Guenole & Ployhart, 2015). Companies that make use of technologically advanced selection tests also look more appealing to the contemporary, tech-savvy generation of gamers and internet users (Fetzer & Tuzinski, 2014). The use of 3D animation has several advantages over video-based SJTs. First, the costs involved in hiring actors and film crews are reduced since only voice actors and software programmers are required. Second, 3D animation can be more flexible than video-based SJTs because in the latter some situations cannot be filmed due to cost concerns and consequently have to be excluded (e.g., a factory fire). Third, 3D animations allow customization in different contexts and cultures. For example, with a little bit of programming one can change the gender and ethnic background of the characters depicted (Fetzer, Tuzinski & Freeman, 2010).

Motion-capture techniques are another recent development. They make use of live actors whose movements and facial expressions are registered by markers placed on the body and face. The computer registers the signals sent from these markers and the actors' movements and expressions are then digitally converted into the software environment. Motion-capture techniques make programming of movements themselves redundant and therefore require less time and effort from programmers (Fetzer et al., 2010). Although these technologies are intuitively appealing, research has not been able to catch up with these fast-paced developments and comparative research with more traditional SJTs has been lacking up to this point.

Another way to increase realism is to enhance the response fidelity of an SJT. Instead of giving applicants descriptions of possible behavioural response options, the test can be constructed to capture candidates' actual behavioural responses to the situations (e.g., via a webcam; see Oostrom, Born, Serlie & van der Molen, 2010). In this case, SJT responses resemble the behavioural responses typically demonstrated in assessment centre exercises and allow the measurement of (non-)verbal and paralingual communication and expressions of emotions. In occupations where communication skills are important, assessment of such responses might increase the SJT's point-to-point correspondence with the criterion and result in higher validity for predicting job performance than responses captured via multiple-choice formats. Lievens, De Corte and Westerveld (2015) compared two multimedia SJTs (one with written constructed responses, one with webcam-captured responses) for predicting police officer job performance. They found evidence of significant incremental validity (2.8–8.3% of additional explained variance) and higher media richness perceptions for the open-ended format that captured candidates' behaviour via webcam. Investing in response-gathering technologies such as webcam SJTs therefore seems warranted because research shows increases in validity (Oostrom et al., 2010), positive candidate reactions (Bruk-Lee et al., 2014) and decreases in test score subgroup differences because of their lower cognitive loading (e.g., De Soete, Lievens, Oostrom & Westerveld, 2013).

Although increasing the fidelity of the situation and the response format of SJTs undeniably makes the test more realistic, SJTs still proceed through situations in linear fashion. In other words, once a response option has been adopted or expressed, the tests proceed to the next situation. Another way to make SJTs more realistic and contextualized is then to present situations that depict the consequences of the choices that were made in the initial situation and assess how the candidate responds to these new developments. This can be achieved through item branching where subordinate situation stems are activated depending on the response that has been chosen or made in the 'mother' stem (Weekley et al., 2015). Technological advances in the gaming industry have inspired some selection test developers to create virtual sandbox environments that allow the implementation of such item branching. These adaptive simulations or serious games could very well become the future of SJTs and selection tests in general. However, the more these environments become unscripted and unstructured, the harder it becomes to accurately assess constructs and/or traits deemed to be important for the job (Fetzer & Tuzinski, 2014).

General Domain Knowledge SJTs

Underlying rationale and theory

In the past few years, an alternative paradigm has emerged which views SJTs as measures of general domain knowledge that is seen as more context-independent. In a series of papers, Motowidlo and colleagues (Motowidlo & Beier, 2010; Motowidlo, Hooper & Jackson, 2006a,b) provided the conceptual foundation for this perspective. According to these researchers, general domain knowledge pertains to general rules about the utility of behavioural acts across a wide range of situations in a specific domain. The more general this knowledge is, the more it is context-independent and the more it is broadly applicable across a wide range of situations. Importantly, general domain knowledge is not acquired from specific job experiences. Rather, general domain knowledge reflects fundamental socialization processes (parents, schooling, etc.) and personal dispositions. That is why this general domain knowledge is also referred to as implicit trait policies (ITPs; Motowidlo & Beier, 2010; Motowidlo et al., 2006b), which are inherent beliefs about the general effectiveness of actions that express traits to varying degrees. In addition, people might have learned exceptions in situations where their inherent trait expressions were not as effective and as a result had to update and modify their ITPs (Motowidlo & Beier, 2010; Motowidlo et al., 2006a). Motowidlo and Beier (2010) further refined their theory of knowledge determinants underlying SJT performance by distinguishing more explicitly between general domain knowledge and specific job knowledge as the two components making up procedural knowledge as captured by an SJT. They first demonstrated that their SJT from 1990 (which was taken to be a contextualized measure) mainly captures general domain knowledge because two scoring keys with effectiveness ratings obtained from both novices and experts largely overlapped and both were significantly related to job performance. Second, the expert key showed incremental variance (5.2%) over the novice key, indicating that while for the most part the SJT captured general domain knowledge, there was still a component of procedural knowledge that could not be solved on the basis of general domain knowledge alone. According to the authors, these expert residual scores reflect specific job knowledge, which is mostly acquired in the job or family of jobs that the SJT is targeting. Cognitive ability and personality are posited as antecedents to these two forms of procedural knowledge as captured by the SJT. The relationship between ability and procedural knowledge is based on the mechanism of one's capacity to learn. Conversely, the relationship between personality traits and ITPs is grounded by the mechanism of dispositional fit. That is, personality traits interact with traits expressed by the different actions put forward in the SJT items in such a way that people who possess high levels of the trait expressed by the action believe that their action is truly more effective than people who have a lower standing on the trait. For instance, when judging the effectiveness of behaviours described in the response options of an SJT, individuals high on the trait of agreeableness will favour those response options that express higher levels of agreeableness more than individuals low in agreeableness (Motowidlo et al., 2006b).

Developmental stages

As is the case for contextualized SJTs, the development process of general domain knowledge SJTs can be categorized into three main steps. However, as compared to contextualized SJTs, each of these steps differs when applied to the measurement of general domain knowledge.

Step 1: Item stems According to the general domain knowledge perspective, each stem needs to be designed in such a way that the stem activates the constructs reflected in the response options, thereby allowing people to show their varying levels of procedural knowledge about these targeted constructs. This means that the test designer should adopt a strategy to develop item situations (item stems) on the basis of theoretical frameworks or taxonomies so that these situations can activate specific behaviour related to the targeted traits or compound traits (or competences; Motowidlo et al., 2006a; Patterson, Ferguson, Norfolk & Lane, 2005). In other words, under the domain-general design scheme, the development of item stems mainly follows a deductive approach rather than an inductive approach. However, to guarantee the job-relatedness of the situations, it is sometimes important (though not absolutely necessary) to 'beef up' these situations with information from critical incident interviews or workshops. In any case, test developers are advised to keep the situation descriptions quite generic. An SJT measuring general domain knowledge requires just enough job-specific contextualization to make the SJT face valid and job-related.

Step 2: Response options, response instructions, and response format Collecting response options for general domain knowledge SJTs does not require a group of experienced SMEs with considerable job-specific knowledge about the domains to be tapped by the SJT, because the response options are intended to tap expressions of general domain knowledge. For instance, a sample of novices or industrial and organizational psychology students (because they have knowledge of traits and trait expressions) can be instructed to generate response options by asking them what they think would be the best way to handle the situation presented in each item stem (Motowidlo et al., 2006a). The test developer then edits these responses. A sample of 5–10 response options are then typically retained per item stem, with an equal number of response options that express high levels of the trait and low levels of the trait (effective vs. ineffective options).

To assess general domain knowledge, a knowledge-based response instruction format ('What should you do?') seems to be most appropriate. Applicants should be instructed to give effectiveness ratings for each option. In that case, the response format is typically a Likert-type scale rating format, although pick best/worst and rank order formats are also possible.

You are in charge of a meeting with six people from other departments. One of them has a very blunt way of announcing that something that was just said is stupid or that somebody's idea just won't work. By the time that the meeting is half over, he has done this twice in connection with remarks made by two different participants. You should...

a) During a break or after the meeting, explain to him that you appreciate his point of view, but that his comments are hurting the other coworkers (high).
b) During the meeting, tell him to keep his rude comments to himself or he won't have a job any more (low).
c) During a break or after the meeting, tell him that is comments were hurting group participation, and ask him to phrase his criticisms differently (high).
d) During the meeting, ask him to leave the meeting (low).
e) During a break or after the meeting, tell him that you don't want to hear any more comments from him unless they are positive (low).
f) Address the group as a whole and state that it is important to keep comments constructive (high).

Figure 11.2 Example of general domain knowledge SJT item (related to agreeableness). *Source*: Motowidlo, Hooper & Jackson (2006a).

Step 3: Scoring key   SMEs with extensive knowledge about the varying personality trait expressions in the response options are required to develop the scoring key. For the measurement of the personality trait conscientiousness, for example, personality psychologists or doctoral students in the domain of personality psychology could be approached to rate the response options. To this end, Likert-type scales can be used with verbal labels indicating the level of the trait expressed by the response option (e.g., 1 = very introverted to 7 = very extraverted; see Motowidlo & Beier, 2010). Agreement levels should be computed by comparing the ratings across judges and by comparing the ratings with a priori trait levels that the response options were designed to express.

In Figure 11.2, we present an example of a general domain knowledge SJT item that was taken from Motowidlo and colleagues (2006a). Contrary to contextualized SJTs (see Figure 11.1), the description of the situation is more generic and more widely applicable across many job situations and is specifically intended to serve as a framework for the measurement of a particular construct (in this case the personality trait agreeableness). Another difference is that the response options were specifically written to measure agreeableness. Whether the response options are indicative of high or low levels of agreeableness is mentioned in parentheses. People who rate those options that express high levels of the personality trait positively and those options that express low levels of the personality trait negatively are believed to be in high possession of the trait and have general domain knowledge about how to express this trait effectively in work situations.

Overview of prior research

Understandably, so far there has been less research on general domain knowledge SJTs. In the next subsection, we follow the same structure as with context-specific SJTs. That is, we review the research evidence to date on reliability, criterion-related and incremental validity, construct-related validity, subgroup differences, applicant reactions, faking, retest and coaching effects.

Reliability   The internal consistency reliability for domain-general SJT scores is not superior to context-specific SJT scores because it can be argued that domain-general SJTs also have a multidimensional nature. Although domain-general SJTs are designed to tap single personality traits, an expression of a trait like agreeableness, for example, could show some overlap with extraversion because extraversion could also be required to express agreeableness effectively in a particular situation (see also further below; Motowidlo et al., 2006a). Motowidlo and Beier (2010) reported internal consistency reliability estimates for a domain-general SJT tapping the personality dimensions of agreeableness, extraversion and conscientiousness ranging from 0.40 to 0.65, which is comparable to domain-specific SJTs. Motowidlo and colleagues (2009) further reported reliability estimates for their single-response SJT in the range of 0.21 to 0.55. Only one study so far has shown that, as with contextualized SJTs, alternative form reliability of domain-general SJT item scores tends to be higher ($r = 0.71$) than internal consistency reliability estimates (Motowidlo et al., 2006a).

Criterion-related and incremental validity   As stated above, the theory of knowledge determinants underlying SJT performance builds on the premise that knowledge predicts actual behaviour in both simulated and actual workplace settings. Recent studies (Lievens & Patterson, 2011; Lievens & Sackett, 2012) provide empirical support for the conceptual link between knowledge and behaviour. In these studies, the relation between procedural knowledge as measured by an SJT and future job performance was mediated by either internship behaviour or, in the case of the second study, assessment centre performance (see also Crook et al., 2011; Kell, Motowidlo, Martin, Stotts & Moreno, 2014; Motowidlo, Martin & Crook, 2013). Importantly, domain-general SJTs also show correlations with job performance of a similar magnitude to traditional SJTs. Motowidlo and Beier (2010) reported correlations from 0.21 to 0.29 for ITP scoring keys with supervisory ratings of job performance. Recently, Motowidlo and colleagues (2013) found evidence indicating that knowledge about effective and ineffective behaviour predicted role-play simulation performance in handling service encounters and work effort performance over and above the personality traits of extraversion, conscientiousness, emotional stability and openness. Crook and colleagues (2011) found similar results: knowledge remained an important predictor of job performance after personality was accounted for.

Construct-related validity   Research found that people's ratings on SJT response options that express high levels of the personality trait of conscientiousness or agreeableness show substantial correlations in the range of 0.40 to 0.50 with their corresponding personality trait scores as measured by self-reports (Motowidlo & Beier, 2010). For other personality dimensions, the evidence was less convincing. Extraversion, for example, correlated only 0.12–0.21 with the personality trait extraversion as measured by a self-report personality inventory. As suggested before, domain-general SJTs do not seem to solve the multidimensionality problems that characterize their contextualized counterparts. That is, behavioural content for one personality trait is potentially confounded by behavioural content expressing another personality trait (Motowidlo et al., 2006a). Consider the SJT example in Figure 11.2, and more specifically response option f), 'Address the group as a whole and state that it is important to keep comments constructive'. This option (especially the second half of the sentence) might represent high levels of agreeableness. However, one might interpret this response option (especially the first half of the sentence) as equally an expression of extraversion. So, even though general-domain knowledge SJTs can be specifically designed to measure a single trait (and a retranslation procedure with SMEs can be performed to verify this), the response options seem still saturated with more than one trait because of the well-known correlations among personality traits.

Subgroup differences   No studies to date have tackled the question of whether there are subgroup differences in domain-general SJT scores and whether these are lower than those found with traditional SJTs. It can be expected that domain-general SJT scores reduce subgroup differences in comparison with contextualized SJTs because they mainly tap test-takers' ITPs and require little if any specific job experience. Domain-general SJTs are also presumed to be less cognitively saturated, which is the main driver behind subgroup differences in selection test scores. So, racial differences might be reduced in applicant pools that take a generic SJT. Gender differences, on the other hand, might increase when generic SJTs are used to specifically tap the personality traits conscientiousness and agreeableness, thereby giving women an advantage over men (Whetzel et al., 2008).

Applicant reactions   Little is known about how applicants react to general domain knowledge SJTs. Given their generic nature, a key question for future research is to investigate if they are seen as sufficiently face-valid and job-related. We do not have empirical answers to these questions yet and therefore they remain to be answered in future research. Important moderators seem to be the sample (inexperienced vs. experienced applicants) and the SJT purpose (e.g., entry-level admission vs. advanced level testing). For instance, whereas inexperienced candidates may view generic SJT items as sufficiently face-valid, more experienced candidates may expect more contextualized information to apply to their fine-grained knowledge. Advanced level selection might also require more contextualization for the same reason.

Faking, retest and coaching effects   Theoretically, general domain knowledge SJTs that tap ITPs are supposedly less prone to faking than more explicit measures of personality since they cannot be subjected to response distortion and social desirability as easily as self-report personality questionnaires (Motowidlo et al., 2006b). However, no published research evidence attesting to this argument has been found thus far. In addition, we are not aware of studies comparing the fakability of SJTs measuring ITPs to contextualized SJTs.

As indicated earlier, the theory of knowledge determinants underlying SJT performance states that SJTs measure procedural knowledge acquired when people are exposed to situations that provide opportunities for learning (Motowidlo et al., 2006b). So, the theory implies that performance on SJTs that capture this general domain knowledge might be trainable since people can develop their knowledge about the costs and benefits of expressing certain traits in particular (job-related) situations and this knowledge can then supplement or even override their inherent trait expressions. Some initial research has tested these assumptions. In particular, a recent study of medical students in India reported that their procedural knowledge scores reflecting ITP expressions increased throughout the medical curriculum (Ghosh, Motowidlo & Nath, 2014).

General Domain Knowledge SJTs: Implications and Trends

The conceptualization of SJTs as measures of relatively context-independent knowledge has fundamental implications for SJT design. If SJTs aim to tap into general domain knowledge, it seems to make less sense to invest in elaborate, contextualized situation descriptions. Instead, this perspective conceptually guides research efforts to streamline SJTs. This can be done in at least two ways. One approach is to make use of single-response SJTs in which test-takers are asked to rate the effectiveness of a single critical action (Crook et al., 2011). As described above, traditional contextualized SJT items usually have multiple-response options. Test developers have to gather a large number of response options from SMEs in the test construction phase. Next, response options have to be investigated and checked for redundancy and SME agreement, before ending up with a pool of suitable response options for the final SJT. Single-response SJTs are proposed to reduce this laborious and time-intensive process because the edited critical incidents (i.e., retaining only the situation description and a single critical action) can directly serve as the response options, thereby rendering the need for generating large amounts of response options superfluous. SMEs also simply rate the effectiveness of edited critical incidents. When applicants complete the SJT, they have to provide an effectiveness rating for each item, which is compared to the one generated by the SME for scoring purposes. Thus, each item of a single-response SJT consists of a couple of sentences describing one critical brief incident, with candidates being asked to rate the effectiveness of this incident. Crook and colleagues (2011) created such single-response SJTs (see also Motowidlo et al., 2009; Motowidlo et al., 2013). In two studies, Crook et al. (2011) found single-response SJTs to be significantly correlated with performance ($r = 0.22$–0.33), and showed that job knowledge as measured by one of their SJTs showed 4% incremental variance on SJT scores above personality. These preliminary findings are in line with McDaniel and colleagues' (2007) meta-analytic evidence of traditional SJTs, suggesting that single-response SJTs do not appear to pay a 'predictive power reduction price' for their streamlined development.

A similar approach would be to eliminate the situation stem altogether and ask test-takers to rate the effectiveness of several courses of action from a multiple-choice response option set (Kell, Martin & Motowidlo, 2011) Kell et al. (2014) devised such a test consisting of 40 brief descriptions of courses of action – in this case physicians interacting with patients. An example of one such (effective) description is: 'When a 10 year old with a broken arm needed surgery, the anesthetist introduced herself to the parents and then knelt down to the child's eye level to introduce herself to the child'. The statements were developed from critical incidents. Test-takers have to score each item's effectiveness. Thus, their test is similar in format to single-response SJTs (with the exception that only the actions were retained and the situations were dropped from the items) and was designed to measure prosocial knowledge (i.e., helping behaviour). Prosocial knowledge as measured with this instrument correlated 0.20 with clinical skill on a standardized patient examination (SPE). Furthermore, prosocial knowledge scores were positively associated with students' clinical performance scores from their primary care rotations ($r = 0.22$), but non-significantly correlated to students' clinical performance scores in the specialties ($r = -0.04$). So, this study suggests that general-domain knowledge seems to be more important in the early phases of one's career before specialization takes place, and declines in importance in the later phases when specialized skills become more and more essential.

Suggestions for Future Research and Recommendations for Practice

After outlining two SJT perspectives (context-dependent vs. general domain knowledge), we end this chapter by highlighting some important avenues for future research. In the preceding sections, we briefly touched on some of those future research directions.

A first vital issue is to gain a better understanding of the circumstances in which each perspective produces the best criterion-related and construct-related validity evidence. For example, when designing an SJT for entry-level admission purposes, evidence accumulated throughout this chapter is unsupportive of contextualizing such an SJT and instead supports streamlining the SJT, thereby making it more context-independent (e.g., Kell et al., 2014). Interestingly, development costs are reduced while at the same time the test's criterion-related and construct-related validity are not jeopardized. As a potential disadvantage, however, applicants might perceive the generic SJT to be less job-related because the relation to the job becomes somewhat less obvious (as manifested in the more generic wording of the item stems and response options). Similarly, at this time we do not know how contextualized and domain-general SJTs compare to one another in terms of fakability, subgroup differences and coachability. In such comparative evaluations, it is important to take the method–construct distinction into account (Arthur & Villado, 2008). That is, when tests are compared on their content, the test format should be kept constant. By directly contrasting contextualized with domain-general SJTs, it becomes possible to provide HR practice with the empirical evidence it needs to confirm the legitimacy of these issues. Krumm and colleagues (2015) carried out an example of such a study. They distinguished between two conditions: one in which a traditional SJT was used and another condition in which the situation description was removed from the items of the same SJT. So, respondents received only the item options in that condition. These conditions were implemented across three SJTs: a teamwork SJT, an integrity SJT and an aviation SJT. The results showed that the provision of context had less impact than expected. That is, it did not matter for about 50–70% of the items whether situation descriptions were included in terms of the number of correct solutions per item. In addition, respondents' expertise level, item length, item difficulty and response instruction did not moderate the results.

A second area of research deals with examining the effectiveness of the different SJTs for specific practical purposes. As a backdrop to this, we recommend using domain-general SJT items for entry-level selection. Conversely, context-specific SJTs seem particularly useful when applicants have already acquired the requisite fine-grained procedural (general) and declarative (job-specific) knowledge. Contextualized SJT items can then home in on such context-dependent knowledge. These items are particularly useful for advanced-level selection and certification applications. When selecting for specialized functions, declarative knowledge is an essential component in addition to procedural knowledge for effective job performance. Initial research is supportive of these recommendations because in advanced-level selection, administering a contextualized SJT was found to capture both procedural and declarative knowledge (Lievens & Patterson, 2011). Future studies should focus on further elucidating the additional value of increasing the contextualization of SJTs in advanced-level selection as compared to domain-general SJTs.

Training applications represents another SJT purpose that is relevant to our distinction and in urgent need of research. For training purposes, we also recommend using contextualized SJTs. SJTs might be specifically adapted to use as tools in training needs analysis (assessment of pre-training knowledge), as actual training content materials or as a training outcome assessment instrument. In particular, contextualized SJTs might be useful as training content materials in scenario-based training in which scripted work situations allow trainees to practice critical job-related skills in a safe environment (Fritzsche, Stagl, Salas & Burke, 2006). So far, virtually no research is available on the efficacy of using SJTs in training. Therefore, we need studies that explore to what extent increasing the response and/or stimulus fidelity of SJTs improves the training's effectiveness.

Fourth, future research might benefit from making a clearer distinction between these two SJT types. Many existing SJTs contain both generic and contextualized items

(Krumm et al., 2015). This might impact construct measurement. In particular, keeping the contextualization of SJT items at the same level (as required by the criterion specificity to be predicted) might lead to a better measurement model underlying SJTs as some of the item heterogeneity that has been posited to lead to poor factor analytical results in SJTs is removed. Generally, we believe that SJT research should not receive a 'free pass' on the construct measurement issue and should continue to undertake efforts to improve construct measurement in SJTs.

Efforts on a clearer distinction between these two SJT types might also address when and how test-takers make use of the context provided. That is, we should also be concerned with the underlying thought processes when solving SJTs. Leeds (2012) suggests that solving an SJT is a two-step process in which test-takers first scrutinize response alternatives in an absolute ('How effective is this option?' 'Does it make sense?') as well as in a relative sense ('Is this option better than that one?'). In a second process, test-takers take the contextual information as presented in the situation description into account. So, one may assume that even contextualized SJTs are only 'used' for context-specific judgements if test-takers' primary perusal of response options is inconclusive as to how to respond. Interestingly, Rockstuhl, Ang, Ng, Lievens and van Dyne (2015) revealed that the judgements made by test-takers on the basis of the situation descriptions (i.e., their construal of the situation) were equally or even more predictive of job-related criteria in an international context as compared with the judgements made on the basis of response alternatives alone. Thus, how test-takers construe and use the context provided could also be an important part of the information captured with SJTs. An avenue for future research may be to comparatively examine the cognitive underpinnings described by Leeds (2012) and Rockstuhl and colleagues (2015) (e.g., through eye-tracking or verbal protocol analysis) and also to assess their relevance in contextualized and generic SJT items.

A final interesting aspect of context-independent SJTs that deserves more research deals with their claim that they can be used cross-culturally. This assumption is based on the notion that such SJTs were designed to measure general procedural knowledge of the costs and benefits of engaging in specific trait-relevant behaviour. Conversely, contextualized SJTs are more dependent on the context and culture for which they were developed, and therefore cross-cultural transportability might be a problem (Lievens, 2006). Like cognitive ability and personality tests, general domain knowledge SJTs are developed to have generalizability across a wide variety of situations. Therefore, they could potentially be implemented more easily across different cultures. That said, we also caution that ITPs might be valued differently across cultures. For example, individualistic cultures might value expressions of extraversion in a specific situation, whereas collectivistic cultures might value these expressions less in that same situation and instead value expressions of other traits such as agreeableness more. Accordingly, empirical evidence is needed to determine the extent to which domain-general SJTs can be successfully implemented across different cultures.

Conclusion

This chapter delineates two perspectives about the determinants of SJT performance: the contextualized perspective views SJTs as measures of job-specific knowledge, whereas the other perspective views SJTs as measures of general domain knowledge. Many current SJTs are situated somewhere between the two. Both perspectives are useful but have different SJT design implications. One perspective suggests further investing in more realistic stimulus and response formats. Conversely, the other perspective suggests streamlining SJTs. An important practical implication of the first perspective is the promise of improved predictive power involved in more realistic SJTs, while the second perspective posits that criterion- and construct-related validity would not suffer and indeed could benefit from designing more generic SJTs allowing broader predictions. This might especially hold for entry-level selection purposes because contextualization appears to be of higher importance for advanced-level selection. In the future, it seems beneficial that a clearer demarcation is used between these two perspectives. We also provide recommendations for practice and a research agenda for more comparative research between these two SJT perspectives in terms of key selection variables.

References

Arthur, W. J., Glaze, R. M., Jarrett, S. M., White, C. D., Schurig, I., & Taylor, J. E. (2014). Comparative evaluation of three situational judgement test response formats in terms of construct-related validity, subgroup differences, and susceptibility to response distortion. *Journal of Applied Psychology*, 99, 535–545. doi: 10.1037/a0035788.

Arthur, W. J., & Villado, A. J. (2008). The importance of distinguishing between constructs and methods when comparing predictors in personnel selection research and practice. *Journal of Applied Psychology*, 93, 435–442. doi: 10.1037/0021-9010.93.2.435.

Bobko, P., & Roth, P. L. (2013). Reviewing, categorizing, and analyzing the literature on Black–White mean differences for predictors of job performance: Verifying some perceptions and updating/correcting others. *Personnel Psychology*, 66, 91–126. doi:10.1111/Peps.12007

Bruk-Lee, V., Drew, E. N., & Hawkes, B. (2014). Candidate reactions to simulations and media-rich assessments in personnel selection. *In* M. S. Fetzer & K. Tuzinski (Eds.), *Simulations for Personnel Selection* (pp. 43–60). New York: Springer.

Campion, M. C., & Ployhart, R. E. (2013). Assessing personality with situational judgement measures: Interactionist psychology operationalized. *In* N. D. Christiansen & R. P. Tett (Eds.), *Handbook of Personality at Work* (pp. 439–456). New York: Routledge.

Campion, M. C., Ployhart, R. E., & MacKenzie, W. (2014). The state of research on situational judgement tests: A content analysis and directions for future research. *Human Performance*, 27, 283–310. doi.org/10.1080/08959285.2014.929693.

Catano, V. M., Brochu, A., & Lamerson, C. D. (2012). Assessing the reliability of situational judgement tests used in high-stakes situations. *International Journal of Selection and Assessment*, 20, 333–346. doi: 10.1111/j.1468-2389.2012.00604.x.

Chan, D., & Schmitt, N. (1997). Video-based versus paper-and-pencil method of assessment in situational judgement tests: Subgroup differences in test performance and face validity perceptions. *Journal of Applied Psychology*, 82, 143–159. doi: 10.1037/0021-9010.82.1.143.

Christian, M. S., Edwards, B. D., & Bradley, J. C. (2010). Situational judgement tests: Constructs assessed and a meta-analysis of their criterion-related validities. *Personnel Psychology*, 63, 83–117. doi: 10.1111/j.1744-6570.2009.01163.x.

Clause, C. S., Mullins, M. E., Nee, M. T., Pulakos, E., & Schmitt, N. (1998). Parallel test form development: A procedure for alternate predictors and an example. *Personnel Psychology*, 51, 193–208. doi: 10.1111/j.1744-6570.1998.tb00722.x.

Crook, A. E., Beier, M. E., Cox, C. B., Kell, H. J., Hanks, A. R., & Motowidlo, S. J. (2011). Measuring relationships between personality, knowledge, and performance using single-response situational judgement tests. *International Journal of Selection and Assessment*, 19, 363–373. doi: 10.1111/j.1468-2389.2011.00565.x.

Cullen, M. J., Sackett, P. R., & Lievens, F. (2006). Threats to the operational use of situational judgement tests in the college admission process. *International Journal of Selection and Assessment*, 14, 142–155. doi: 10.1111/j.1468-2389.2006.00340.x.

De Soete, B., Lievens, F., Oostrom, J. K., & Westerveld, L. (2013). Alternative predictors for dealing with the diversity-validity dilemma in personnel selection: The constructed response multimedia test. *International Journal of Selection and Assessment*, 21, 239–250. doi: 10.1111/ijsa.12034.

Dunlop, P. D., Morrison, D. L., & Cordery, J. L. (2011). Investigating retesting effects in a personnel selection context. *International Journal of Selection and Assessment, 19*, 217–221. doi: 10.1111/j.1468-2389.2011.00549.x.

Fetzer, M. S., & Tuzinski, K. (2014). *Simulations for Personnel Selection*. New York: Springer.

Fetzer, M. S., Tuzinski, K., & Freeman, M. (2010). 3D animation, motion capture, and SJTs: I-O is finally catching up with it. Paper presented at the 25th Annual Conference of Industrial and Organizational Psychology, April. Atlanta, GA.

Flanagan, J. C. (1954). The critical incident technique. *Psychological Bulletin, 51*, 327–358. doi: 10.1037/h0061470.

Fritzsche, B. A., Stagl, K. C., Salas, E., & Burke, C. S. (2006). Enhancing the design, delivery, and evaluation of scenario-based training: Can situational judgement tests contribute? *In* J. A. Weekley & R. E. Ployhart (Eds.), *Situational Judgement Tests: Theory, Measurement, and Application* (pp. 301–318). Mahwah, NJ: Lawrence Erlbaum.

Ghosh, K., Motowidlo, S. J., & Nath, S. (2014). Effects of prosocial and technical knowledge on students' clinical performance. Paper presented at the 29th Annual Conference of the Society for Industrial and Organizational Psychology, May, Honolulu, Hawaii.

Hausknecht, J. P., Day, D. V., & Thomas, S. C. (2004). Applicant reactions to selection procedures: An updated model and meta-analysis. *Personnel Psychology, 57*, 639–683. doi: 10.1111/j.1744-6570.2004.00003.x.

Hooper, A. C., Cullen, M. C., & Sackett, P. R. (2006). Operational threats to the use of SJTs: Faking, coaching, and retesting issues. *In* J. A. Weekley & R. E. Ployhart (Eds.), *Situational Judgement Tests: Theory, Measurement, and Application* (pp. 205–232). Mahwah, NJ: Lawrence Erlbaum.

Kanning, U. P., Grewe, K., Hollenberg, S., & Hadouch, M. (2006). From the subjects' point of view: Reactions to different types of situational judgement items. *European Journal of Psychological Assessment, 22*, 168–176. doi: 10.1027/1015-5759.22.3.168.

Kasten, N., & Freund, P. A. (2015). A meta-analytical multilevel reliability generalization of situational judgement tests (SJTs). *European Journal of Psychological Assessment*. doi: 10.1027/1015-5759/a000250.

Kell, H. J., Martin, M. P., & Motowidlo, S. J. (2011). Medical students' knowledge about medical professionalism predicts their professionalism performance. Poster presented at the 26th Annual meeting of the Society for Industrial and Organizational Psychology, April, Chicago, IL.

Kell, H. J., Motowidlo, S. J., Martin, M. P., Stotts, A. L., & Moreno, C. A. (2014). Testing for independent effects of prosocial knowledge and technical knowledge on skill and performance. *Human Performance, 27*, 311–327.

Krumm, S., Lievens, F., Hüffmeier, J., Lipnevich, A. A., Bendels, H., & Hertel, G. (2015). How 'situational' is judgement in situational judgement tests? *Journal of Applied Psychology, 100*, 399–416. doi: 10.1037/a0037674.

Leeds, J. P. (2012). The theory of cognitive acuity: Extending psychophysics to the measurement of situational judgement. *Journal of Neuroscience, Psychology, and Economics, 5*, 166–181. doi: 10.1037/a0027294.

Lievens, F. (2006). International situational judgement tests. *In* J. A. Weekley & R. E. Ployhart (Eds.), *Situational Judgement Tests: Theory, Measurement, and Application* (pp. 279–300). Mahwah, NJ: Lawrence Erlbaum.

Lievens, F., Buyse, T., & Sackett, P. R. (2005). Retest effects in operational selection settings: Development and test of a framework. *Personnel Psychology, 58*, 981–1007. doi: 10.1111/j.1744-6570.2005.00713.x.

Lievens, F., Buyse, T., Sackett, P. R., & Connelly, B. S. (2012). The effects of coaching on situational judgement tests in high-stakes selection. *International Journal of Selection and Assessment, 20*, 272–282. doi: 10.1111/j.1468-2389.2012.00599.x.

Lievens, F., De Corte, W., & Westerveld, L. (2015). Understanding the building blocks of selection procedures: Effects of response fidelity on performance and validity. *Journal of Management, 41*(6), 1604–1627. doi: 10.1177/0149206312463941.

Lievens, F., & De Soete, B. (2012). Simulations. *In* N. Schmitt (Ed.), *The Oxford Handbook of Personnel Assessment and Selection* (pp. 383–410). Oxford: Oxford University Press.

Lievens, F., & Patterson, F. (2011). The validity and incremental validity of knowledge tests, low-fidelity simulations, and high-fidelity simulations for predicting job performance in advanced-level high-stakes selection. *Journal of Applied Psychology, 96*, 927–940. doi: 10.1037/A0023496

Lievens, F., Peeters, H., & Schollaert, E. (2008). Situational judgement tests: A review of recent research. *Personnel Review, 37*, 426–441. doi: 10.1108/00483480810877598.

Lievens, F., & Sackett, P. R. (2007). Situational judgement tests in high-stakes settings: Issues and strategies with generating alternate forms. *Journal of Applied Psychology, 92*, 1043–1055. doi: 10.1037/0021-9010.92.4.1043.

Lievens, F., & Sackett, P. R. (2012). The validity of interpersonal skills assessment via situational judgement tests for predicting academic success and job performance. *Journal of Applied Psychology, 97*, 460–468. doi: 10.1037/A0025741.

McDaniel, M. A., Hartman, N. S., Whetzel, D. L., & Grubb, W. L. (2007). Situational judgement tests, response instructions, and validity: A meta-analysis. *Personnel Psychology, 60*, 63–91. doi: 10.1111/j.1744-6570.2007.00065.x.

McDaniel, M. A., Morgeson, F. P., Finnegan, E. B., Campion, M. A., & Braverman, E. P. (2001). Use of situational judgement tests to predict job performance: A clarification of the literature. *Journal of Applied Psychology, 86*, 730–740. doi: 10.1037//0021-9010.86.4.730.

McDaniel, M. A., & Nguyen, N. T. (2001). Situational judgement tests: A review of practice and constructs assessed. *International Journal of Selection and Assessment, 9*, 103–113. doi: 10.1111/1468-2389.00167.

McDaniel, M. A., Psotka, J., Legree, P. J., Yost, A. P., & Week, J. A. (2011). Toward an understanding of situational judgement item validity and group differences. *Journal of Applied Psychology, 96*, 327–336. doi: 10.1037/a0021983.

Mischel, W., & Shoda, Y. (1995). A cognitive-affective system-theory of personality: Reconceptualizing situations, dispositions, dynamics, and invariance in personality structure. *Psychological Review, 102*, 246–268. doi: 10.1037/0033-295x.102.2.246.

Motowidlo, S. J., & Beier, M. E. (2010). Differentiating specific job knowledge from implicit trait policies in procedural knowledge measured by a situational judgement test. *Journal of Applied Psychology, 95*, 321–333. doi: 10.1037/A0017975.

Motowidlo, S. J., Crook, A. E., Kell, H. J., & Naemi, B. (2009). Measuring procedural knowledge more simply with a single-response situational judgement test. *Journal of Business and Psychology, 24*, 281–288. doi: 10.1007/s10869-009-9106-4.

Motowidlo, S. J., Dunnette, M. D., & Carter, G. W. (1990). An alternative selection procedure: The low-fidelity simulation. *Journal of Applied Psychology, 75*, 640–647. doi: 10.1037/0021-9010.75.6.640.

Motowidlo, S. J., Hooper, A. C., & Jackson, H. L. (2006a). Implicit policies about relations between personality traits and behavioural effectiveness in situational judgement items. *Journal of Applied Psychology, 91*, 749–761. doi: 10.1037/0021-9010.91.4.749.

Motowidlo, S. J., Hooper, A. C., & Jackson, H. L. (2006b). A theoretical basis for situational judgement tests. *In* J. A. Weekley & R. E. Ployhart (Eds.), *Situational Judgement Tests: Theory, Measurement, and Application* (pp. 57–82). Mahwah, NJ: Lawrence Erlbaum.

Motowidlo, S. J., Martin, M. P., & Crook, A. E. (2013). Relations between personality, knowledge, and behaviour in professional service encounters. *Journal of Applied Social Psychology, 43*, 1851–1861. doi: 10.1111/jasp.12137.

Nguyen, N. T., Biderman, M. D., & McDaniel, M. A. (2005). Effects of response instructions on faking a situational judgement test. *International Journal of Selection and Assessment, 13*, 250–260. doi: 10.1111/j.1468-2389.2005.00322.x.

Oostrom, J. K., Born, M. P., Serlie, A. W., & van der Molen, H. T. (2010). Webcam testing: Validation of an innovative open-ended multimedia test. *European Journal of Work and Organizational Psychology, 19*, 532–550. doi: 10.1080/13594320903000005.

Osburn, H. G. (2000). Coefficient alpha and related internal consistency reliability coefficients. *Psychological Methods, 5*, 343–355. doi: 10.1037//1082-989x.5.3.343.

Patterson, F., Ferguson, E., Norfolk, T., & Lane, P. (2005). A new selection system to recruit general practice registrars: Preliminary findings from a validation study. *British Medical Journal, 330*, 711–714. doi: 10.1136/bmj.330.7493.711.

Peeters, H., & Lievens, F. (2005). Situational judgement tests and their predictiveness of college students' success: The influence of faking. *Educational and Psychological Measurement, 65,* 70–89. doi: 10.1177/0013164404268672.

Potosky, D. (2008). A conceptual framework for the role of the administration medium in the personnel assessment process. *Academy of Management Review, 33,* 629–648. doi: 10.5465/AMR.2008.32465704.

Richman-Hirsch, W. L., Olson-Buchanan, J. B., & Drasgow, F. (2000). Examining the impact of administration medium on examinee perceptions and attitudes. *Journal of Applied Psychology, 85,* 880–887. doi: 10.1037//0021-9010.85.6.880.

Rockstuhl, T., Ang, S., Ng, K. Y., Lievens, F., & Van Dyne, L. (2015). Putting judging situations into situational judgement tests: Evidence from intercultural multimedia SJTs. *Journal of Applied Psychology, 100,* 464–480. doi: 10.1037/a0038098.

Roth, P. L., Bobko, P., & Buster, M. A. (2013). Situational judgement tests: The influence and importance of applicant status and targeted constructs on estimates of Black–White subgroup differences. *Journal of Occupational and Organizational Psychology, 86,* 394–409. doi: 10.1111/Joop.12013.

Schmidt, F. L., & Hunter, J. E. (1998). The validity and utility of selection methods in personnel psychology: Practical and theoretical implications of 85 years of research findings. *Psychological Bulletin, 124,* 262–274. doi: 10.1037//0033-2909.124.2.262.

Schmitt, N., & Chan, D. (2006). Situational judgement tests: Method or construct? *In* J. A. Weekley & R. E. Ployhart (Eds.), *Situational Judgement Tests: Theory, Measurement, and Application* (pp. 135–155). Mahwah, NJ: Lawrence Erlbaum.

Schmitt, N., & Ostroff, C. (1986). Operationalizing the behavioural consistency approach: Selection test development based on a content-oriented strategy. *Personnel Psychology, 39,* 91– 108. doi: 10.1111/j.1744-6570.1986.tb00576.x.

Stemig, M., Sackett, P. R., & Lievens, F. (2015). Effects of organizationally-endorsed coaching on performance and validity of situational judgement tests. *International Journal of Selection of Assessment, 23,* 175–182.

Thornton, G. C., & Rupp, D. E. (2006). *Assessment Centres in Human Resource Management: Strategies for Prediction, Diagnosis, and Development.* Mahwah, NJ: Lawrence Erlbaum.

Wagner, R. K., & Sternberg, R. J. (1991). *Tacit Knowledge Inventory for Managers (TKIM).* New York: Psychological Corporation.

Weekley, J. A., Hawkes, B., Guenole, N., & Ployhart, R. E. (2015). Low-fidelity simulations. *Annual Review of Organizational Psychology and Organizational Behaviour, 2,* 295–322. doi: 10.1146/annurev-orgpsych-032414-111304.

Weekley, J. A., & Jones, C. (1999). Further studies of situational tests. *Personnel Psychology, 52,* 679–700. doi: 10.1111/j.1744-6570.1999.tb00176.x.

Weekley, J. A., Ployhart, R. E., & Holtz, B. C. (2006). On the development of situational judgement tests: Issues in item development, scaling, and scoring. *In* J. A. Weekley & R. E. Ployhart (Eds.), *Situational Judgement Tests: Theory, Measurement, and Application* (pp. 157–182). Mahwah, NJ: Lawrence Erlbaum.

Wernimont, P. F., & Campbell, J. P. (1968). Signs, samples and criteria. *Journal of Applied Psychology, 52,* 372–376. doi: 10.1037/H0026244.

Whetzel, D. L., & McDaniel, M. A. (2009). Situational judgement tests: An overview of current research. *Human Resource Management Review, 19,* 188–202. doi: 10.1016/j.hrmr.2009.03.007.

Whetzel, D. L., McDaniel, M. A., & Nguyen, N. T. (2008). Subgroup differences in situational judgement test performance: A meta-analysis. *Human Performance, 21,* 291–309. doi: 10.1080/08959280802137820.

12

The Role of Simulation Exercises in Selection

Ryan S. O'Leary, Jacob W. Forsman
and Joshua A. Isaacson

Introduction

Simulation exercises are a group of assessment methods that measure applicants' work-relevant performance while performing tasks, interacting with others or using equipment or technology (Callinan & Robertson, 2000; Ployhart, Schneider, & Schmitt, 2006). This includes a range of assessment procedures, all of which closely resemble actual parts of the focal job for which the applicant is being assessed, including situational judgement tests, assessment centre exercises and work-sample and performance tests. Across assessment types, simulations can be designed to measure a wide range of constructs such as hard and soft skills, personality, task performance, job knowledge and cognitive ability (Tuzinski, 2013). They have been used in selection systems for a full range of jobs and positions.

Unlike traditional assessment approaches which rely on indirect evidence of applicants' skill and ability to perform, simulations rely on direct evidence. The underlying premise of simulations is the idea of point-to-point correspondence (Asher & Sciarrino, 1974); that is, prediction is improved to the extent that the assessment mirrors the criterion domain for a given job, focusing on some or all of the behaviours required for successful overall performance. This approach is different from that used by measures such as assessments of personality and cognitive ability, which focus on applicants' pre-dispositions to behave. Simulations rely on samples of behaviours to predict subsequent job performance. Selection decisions are most accurate when based on behavioural consistency, the notion that the best predictor of future behaviour is past behaviour in the same or similar contexts. Simulations maximize the prediction of job performance by evaluating behavioural samples that match job performance requirements rather than signs (Wernimont & Campbell, 1968).

Simulations have a long history of use across the human capital lifecycle including personnel selection, certification and training programmes, as well as in a number of educational contexts. In personnel selection, the use of simulations dates back to their use

The Wiley Blackwell Handbook of the Psychology of Recruitment, Selection and Employee Retention,
First Edition. Edited by Harold W. Goldstein, Elaine D. Pulakos, Jonathan Passmore and Carla Semedo.
© 2017 John Wiley & Sons Ltd. Published 2020 by John Wiley & Sons Ltd.

in the military in the 1940s and the start of widespread organizational use with managerial assessment centres at AT&T in the 1950s (Bray, Campbell & Grant, 1979). Advances in technology are leading to increases in simulation sophistication, realism and fidelity and have made development and administration more economical. The once static and paper-based simulations of years past now include multimedia and leverage technology for administration and scoring. This has provided endless possibilities for development and measurement.

Today, simulations feature prominently in many selection systems across industry sectors in private and public organizations around the world. According to an international study conducted by the Corporate Executive Board (CEB) (Fallaw & Kantrowitz, 2013) on assessment trends, 67% of the companies surveyed use some form of simulations as part of their hiring process. Of these, 42% were from China, 13% were from South Africa, 11% were from the United Kingdom, 8% were from Australia, 8% were from the United States and Canada, and 18% were from other countries. This trend is likely to increase because of the number of benefits simulations provide over traditional approaches for predicting job performance, including practicality, criterion-related and incremental validity, potential for smaller subgroup mean differences and less adverse impact, and positive applicant reactions and engagement. Simulations remain the only assessment type that can simultaneously measure the interaction of constructs required for job performance.

The value of simulations is well understood and based in sound science. However, as technology advances our ability to develop simulations at an accelerated pace, a gap between research and practice has started to open. In this chapter we review the current research and trends related to the use of simulations in personnel selection. We begin by providing a taxonomy of simulation types, followed by a discussion of simulation fidelity and its impact. Next, we review the psychometric evidence supporting their use to include validity and subgroup mean differences and discuss issues related to construct measurement. This is followed by a discussion of applicant reactions, cross-cultural considerations and the important role simulations can play in recruitment and organizational branding. We conclude with a discussion of topics in need of consideration by simulation developers and users and we project the future of simulations for selection.

Taxonomy of Simulation Types

Organizational frameworks for classifying simulations are largely lacking. This has led to inconsistencies in the definition of simulations and standards for development, validation and scoring. Simulations represent a range of assessments with large variability in terms of format and function. It is not a single method or procedure, but an approach for assessment. For this reason simulations are often classified as measurement methods. Simulations for personnel selection can be grouped into four major assessment types: situational judgement tests (SJTs), work-sample and performance tests, assessment centre exercises and job try-outs (Tuzinski, 2013; U.S. Merit Systems Protection Board, 2009). Below, we present a brief summary of these groupings. The discussion is not comprehensive, but rather establishes a foundational understanding. Within each group, technology can play more or less of a role in delivery. Nor are the groups mutually exclusive, for example, it is common for a computer-based managerial in-basket to include multiple-choice SJT-type response options.

- *Situational judgement tests.* Situational judgement tests (SJTs) present applicants with a series of situations or scenarios similar to those they will encounter on the job and viable options for handling these situations. Depending on the approach, applicants are asked to select the most effective, or most and least effective, ways of handling the situation from the response alternatives. SJT stimuli can be presented in text-based format or can leverage multimedia.

- *Work-sample and performance tests.* Work-sample and performance tests consist of tasks or work activities that are physically or psychologically similar to the tasks and duties employees are required to perform on the job. Applicants' skills are evaluated by asking them to perform the tasks under the same conditions as those required on the job. For example, a hands-on work sample for an electrician may ask applicants to troubleshoot a circuit, inspect electronics for defects and conduct an electronics test. Increasingly, these are being delivered online. For example, software developers may be asked to debug sequences of code and plant operators may be required to monitor pressure in online gauges.
- *Assessment centre exercise.* When work samples are used for the selection of professionals, supervisors and managers, they are often referred to as assessment centre exercises. Exercises frequently include in-baskets, role-plays, analytic exercises and group discussions; these are typically scored by trained assessors. Technology has changed the means by which assessment centre exercises are delivered and scored. For example, in-baskets now mimic desktop applications and can employ the use of multiple-choice formats. Role-plays and performance counselling exercises are now using video- or avatar-based item presentations and complex, automated branching algorithms, removing the need for human role players and assessors.
- *Job tryouts.* Job tryouts are the most extreme form of simulations. In a job tryout, applicants are hired following an initial screening. Once on the job, they enter a probationary period when they are assessed to ensure satisfactory performance. Because these simulations are not developed and validated in a traditional sense, they are not a focus of this chapter.

Fidelity

Fidelity is the degree or precision to which something is reproduced. In the context of assessment, it is the degree to which a measure represents or replicates actual features of the focal job. While simulations vary in their level of fidelity, as a group one of their major benefits is their ability to achieve greater fidelity than other assessments types. Giving applicants an assessment with tasks that closely resemble actual features of the jobs for which they are being considered is not possible with more traditional assessment types. Fidelity can be considered a continuum, running from low to high. Traditional personality and intelligence tests typically fall at the low end of the continuum as these are usually not job-specific and do not typically measure constructs in the same manner in which they are needed on the job. At the other end of the continuum are more specific work-sample and performance tests, such as those used for air traffic controllers to simulate real work environments (e.g., monitor radar, interact with pilots, use real equipment) which immerse applicants in the job.

Psychological and physical fidelity

Researchers often distinguish between the psychological and physical fidelity of the assessment (Binning & Barrett, 1989; Goldstein, Zedeck & Schneider, 1993). Psychological fidelity refers to the extent to which an assessment requires test-takers to utilize the knowledge, skills and abilities during the assessment that they will use on the job.

Physical fidelity refers to the extent to which an assessment replicates actual tasks performed on the job. For an assessment to be valid it must have psychological fidelity. In addition, in most cases, as the level of physical fidelity increases, so does psychological fidelity. Many simulations, such as SJTs, only exhibit psychological fidelity. These simulations do not require a hands-on performance as applicants are presented with hypothetical scenarios to which they respond verbally or in writing. At the other end of the continuum are simulations such as call centre assessments where applicants take calls and enter information into programs or databases, and computer skills assessments where applicants are asked to perform tasks using real software packages. These assessments are hands-on and the tasks performed closely replicate the real-world setting. Between these extremes there is a range of simulations, such as managerial in-baskets with computer-based assessments that mirror the applicant's desktop, exhibiting a higher fidelity than paper-based in-baskets.

Stimuli and response fidelity

Assessment fidelity can also be discussed in terms of the stimuli presented and the modality of responses required. Stimulus fidelity refers to how closely the mode of delivery of the assessment content mirrors the job. Response fidelity refers to the way in which the candidate responds to the assessment stimuli (e.g., behavioural, verbal, written) and the extent to which the assessment affords the opportunity to exhibit the behaviours as they would on the job. Holding psychological fidelity constant, this concept is not unrelated to the idea of physical fidelity: the higher the level of stimulus and response fidelity, the higher the level of physical fidelity.

Simulations such as an automotive production assessment in which applicants must follow detailed instructions to select parts, perform drilling operations and monitor and inspect quality would be at the high end of the stimulus and response fidelity continua. SJTs which present scenarios in a text-based format and require multiple-choice responding would be low on both stimulus and response fidelity. Between these extremes there is a range of simulations that vary in stimulus and response fidelity. For example, a computer-based in-basket that requires written responses to emails for later scoring by human raters would be high on both stimulus and response fidelity, while a computer-based in-basket that presents multiple-choice options would be high on stimulus fidelity and low on response fidelity. A computer-based role-play that presents video-based scenarios and multiple-choice questions for branching would be low to moderate on stimulus fidelity and low on response fidelity. Finally, a money-counting exercise for banking and retail positions that presents applicants with an online, interactive money drawer and asks them to count out a specific amount of money by clicking on the appropriate combination of bank notes and coins could be considered moderate on both stimulus and response fidelity.

Impact of fidelity on validity

While a more detailed discussion of simulation validity will be presented later in this chapter, the impact of fidelity on validity is worth mentioning here. Under the assumption of point-to-point correspondence, one would assume that higher levels of fidelity would translate into higher observed validities. However, it is not always the case that correspondence between the predictor and criterion results in an assessment that is more job-related, and in practice the level of correspondence needed is not always straightforward (Callinan & Robertson, 2000). Interestingly, simulations across the fidelity continuum have exhibited similar levels of validity in individual studies, suggesting that moving to low-fidelity simulations may not always impact validity (Lievens & Patterson, 2011). This has led some to argue that, based on the current and limited understanding of fidelity and validity, the time and resources required to develop high-fidelity simulations may not be justified.

In their review of the validity of simulations ranging from low to high fidelity, Boyce, Corbet and Adler (2013) correctly assert that while various simulation types generally have exhibited comparable levels of validity across individual studies, same-sample studies directly comparing simulations ranging in fidelity are lacking. It is frequently argued that the impact of fidelity on validity needs to be examined in the context of both stimulus and response fidelity. For example, Lievens, De Corte and Westerveld (2012) examined how response fidelity impacted job performance. They found that for police trainees, only an actual behavioural response led to significant predictions of future job performance. Funke and Schuler (1998) found that increasing SJT stimulus fidelity had no impact on validity, while increases in response fidelity (multiple-choice, written, oral) were associated with greater validity.

Despite these studies, research examining the impact of fidelity on simulation validity is needed before definitive conclusions can be made. This is particularly true as advances in technology are continuing to accelerate our ability to vary stimulus and response fidelity. To date, no clear guidance has been provided on the level of fidelity required to achieve desired levels of validity, and this is a clear area of need when considering costs and utility. As research accumulates, frameworks can be developed that will guide simulation development. What makes researching fidelity difficult, beyond the distinction between stimulus and response fidelity, is the fact that fidelity's importance is likely to vary according to job.

Psychometric Characteristics

Research studies have repeatedly found that group simulations are one of the best predictors of job performance. These results have held across a range of positions and industries. There is a number of reasons to expect that simulations should be valid predictors of job performance. First, they are built on the premise of point-to-point correspondence, which suggests that prediction is improved to the extent that predictors mirror the criterion (Asher & Sciarrino, 1974). Second, unlike many predictors (other than tests of cognitive ability) simulations are 'show me' and not 'tell me' measures. That is, we do not ask the applicant to tell us how good they are at dealing with a problem or scenario; we given them one to solve. This provides two benefits: mitigating inflation and response distortion as applicants cannot fake proficiency and requiring a behavioural response that yields a more accurate measure of actual ability (Gatewood, Field & Barrick, 2008). In this section, we summarize the current state of the literature on simulation validity and discuss subgroup mean differences.

Validity

Meta-analytic studies have found simulations to be valid predictors of job performance. In perhaps one of the most influential studies examining criterion-related validity evidence for a variety of predictor measures, Schmidt and Hunter (1998) in a meta-analysis found work samples and assessment centres to have corrected validity coefficients for the prediction of job performance of 0.54 and 0.37, respectively. Interestingly, the corrected validity coefficient for tests of general mental ability was 0.51, suggesting that work samples are some of the best predictors available. A meta-analysis of performance tests conducted by Roth, Bobko and McFarland (2005) found a corrected validity coefficient of 0.33. McDaniel, Hartman, Whetzel and Grubb (2007) examined the validity of SJTs. Their meta-analysis found an overall corrected validity coefficient of 0.26. Finally, in meta-analyses of assessment centre validity, Gaugler, Rosenthal, Thornton and Bentson (1987) found a corrected validity coefficient of 0.36 for overall ratings, and Arthur, Day, McNelly, and Edens (2003) found corrected validity coefficients ranging from 0.25 to 0.39 for dimension ratings. It is important to note that simulations are frequently developed to assess multiple constructs and their level of observed validity will vary according to what is measured.

In addition to excellent criterion-related validity, simulations have been found to provide incremental validity beyond measures of cognitive ability. For example, Roth and colleagues (2005) found that performance tests added to the prediction of job performance when cognitive ability was also used as a predictor. Clevenger, Pereira, Wiechmann, Schmitt and Harvey (2001) found incremental validity for SJTs even when included in a selection battery consisting of measures of mental ability, conscientiousness, job experience and job knowledge. Schmidt and Hunter (1998) found assessment centres have modest incremental validity when used with a test of general mental ability.

To date, there is a substantial number of meta-analytic studies supporting the validity of traditional simulations. However, technology has changed the very nature of simulations and the ever-increasing rate of change has meant that science has not been able to keep pace. For example, few research studies have examined the validity of computer-based in-baskets or branching role-plays (Olson-Buchanan et al., 1998; McNelly, Ruggeberg & Hall, 2011; Mueller-Hanson et al., 2009). Additional studies and meta-analytic research are needed before stable estimates of validity can be achieved.

Subgroup mean differences, adverse impact and legal defensibility

Practitioners developing assessments for employee selection strive to balance the often competing goals of maximizing validity and reducing subgroup mean differences (e.g., minority–White, over 40–under 40) and adverse impact. To the extent that an assessment exhibits subgroup mean differences (d), there is the potential for adverse impact and legal scrutiny. Early studies examining subgroup differences led to the popular conclusion that simulations are valid assessments that do not yield score differences against ethnic groups. For example, Clevenger and colleagues (2001) found standardized mean difference between White and Black applicants of 0.37 across multiple samples. This is compared to a mean difference of approximately 1.0 commonly observed for cognitive ability tests (Hunter & Hunter, 1984). Schmidt, Greenthal, Hunter, Berner and Seaton (1997) examined mean score differences and passing rates between White and Black test-takers on a performance test and found no differences.

While these results are promising, many of the studies, particularly when examining performance tests, used job incumbent samples and are subject to range restriction from prior selection. In such samples, one would expect mean differences to be small as incumbents have been on, and have familiarity with, the job for which they are being assessed. Bobko, Roth and Buster (2005) examined the scores of White and Black applicants on a work-sample exercise in two studies using applicant samples. The mean differences observed approached what are commonly observed for cognitive ability tests ($d = 0.72$). In an examination of assessment centres, Schmitt and Mills (2001) found mean difference on assessment centre ratings ($d = 0.30$) that were about half the size of those observed for paper-and-pencil tests ($d = 0.61$) in the same study.

Several recent meta-analyses have examined subgroup mean differences across various types of simulations. Whetzel and colleagues (2008) examined mean differences for SJTs and found White–Black and White–Hispanic *d*s of 0.38 and 0.24, respectively. Roth, Bobko, McFarland and Buster (2008) examined mean differences for work-sample tests and found a White–Black *d* of 0.73. Dean, Roth and Bobko (2008) examined mean differences for assessment centre ratings and found a White–Black *d* of 0.52 in an applicant sample. The White–Black *d* in the incumbent sample was 0.32. Some of the *d*s observed in these studies are larger than many researchers had previously assumed, especially for work samples and assessment centres. Based on the research evidence to date, simulations appear to exhibit non-trivial racial mean differences.

It should be noted that simulations can range in the extent to which they tap cognitive constructs. The extent to which a simulation is cognitively loaded impacts the level of subgroup mean differences observed. For example, Goldstein, Yusko, Braverman, Smith and Chung (1998) found that the size of the mean differences observed varied by assessment centre exercise type and exercise types varied in their level of cognitive load. In Whetzel, McDaniel and Nguyen's (2008) meta-analysis, the cognitive and personality loadings of SJTs were found to be moderators of mean score differences in SJT performance. Similarly, Roth and colleagues' (2008) meta-analysis found that assessment centre exercises measuring cognitive constructs exhibited White–Black *d*s of around 0.80, while exercises measuring non-cognitive constructs exhibited *d*s of around 0.27. This research suggests, as others have stated, that decreasing the cognitive load of the simulation may be a viable method for mitigating adverse impact (Ployhart & Holtz, 2008; Ryan & Tippins, 2004). For example, one might consider verbal responses to in-basket items as opposed to written responses (Whetzel, McDaniel & Pollack, 2012). However, it should be cautioned that developing simulations that decrease the cognitive load may also reduce their observed validity.

Relatively little US case law exists as it relates to modern simulations used for employee selection. However, when soundly developed and validated, assessment centres have been supported by the courts and the US Equal Employment Opportunity Commission in cases of alleged discrimination (Gatewood et al., 2008). Additionally, Terpstra, Mohamed and Kethley (1999) and Terpstra and Kethley (2002) found support for work samples and assessment centres in US federal courts. While there were few cases to review, both work samples and assessment centres were significantly less likely to be challenged in court (when taking usage into account) and their use was successfully defended more frequently than other assessments. In fact, some employers are turning to simulations because they are less likely to be challenged (Whetzel et al., 2012). This movement is supported by applicant reactions research (discussed in more detail below), which has found litigation intentions may be lower when simulations are used (Hausknecht, Day & Thomas, 2004).

Construct Measurement

Simulations, when coupled with technology, present new opportunities to significantly expand the domain of constructs assessed in a selection context. Advances in selection science, such as measuring response latencies in an effort to enhance the measurement of personality (Ranger & Khun, 2013), and the collection of other micro-behaviours (such as click patterns and mouse over times which are being explored as possible predictors of workplace behaviour) (Reynolds & Dickter, 2010), are enriching the evidence used to make inferences about the constructs being measured and expanding construct representation.

However, we contend that simulations offer the most promise for expanding the domain of constructs assessed as they are uniquely able to model complex interactions among the traits required for job performance that might otherwise be difficult to capture (Aguinis, Henle & Beaty, 2001).

As one example, current research and theory suggest that, now more than ever, leaders need to be agile learners and that this ability differentiates successful from unsuccessful leaders (Charan, Drotter & Noel, 2000; Goldsmith, 2007; McCall, 1998). Learning agility is defined as the willingness and ability to learn from experience and subsequently apply that learning to perform successfully under novel or first-time conditions (De Meuse, Dai & Hallenbeck, 2010; Lombardo & Eichinger, 2000). It is important to note that true learning agility is indeed a twofold attribute: individuals must be both willing *and* able to learn from experience. At its core, learning agility is founded on a compilation of cognitive, personality and motivational factors and is about extracting key lessons from one situation and applying them later to a different situation. When assessing learning agility, practitioners have typically assessed the personality and motivational factors (the willingness) and the underlying cognitive ability required, leaving the true ability to learn and use new information unmeasured. Simulations allow for refined measurement of the ability component of the construct. They add benefit because they can require applicants to absorb, integrate and interpret information in a real-time, simulated environment and to model, explore and attempt different strategies when using new information: this is particularly important as these behaviours reflect the very essence of learning agility (Malka et al., 2012).

Simulations may simultaneously measure an array of constructs. It has often been difficult to assess their internal consistency, reliability and construct validity, and this has led to some controversy over their use in a selection context (Whetzel et al., 2012). What simulations measure and why they are predictive of job performance is in most cases not well understood (Callinan & Robertson, 2000). This is particularly true the further one moves away from direct point-to-point correspondence between the predictor and the criterion space. When there is a direct overlap between the assessment and the work performed on the job, we move away from a traditional focus on construct or trait-based assessment to a focus on what people are expected to do on the job (Guion, 2010). But a direct overlap is not always possible for a variety of reasons. As simulations are built and used in selection contexts, it is important to have a solid understanding of what is actually being measured.

To the extent that simulations are not high in stimulus and response fidelity, there is the potential to introduce construct irrelevant variance. As simulations are built, and technology is continually leveraged for their delivery, this concept needs to be explored. When engaged in a computer-based simulation, for example, applicants depend on their ability to operate computers or hardware. With a highly complex branching simulation or game, being able to navigate the environment itself may be a confounding variable – one not actually related to constructs required for job performance (e.g., Zenisky & Sireci, 2002). Such variance may attenuate test-takers' performance in a way that is unrelated to their true standing on the targeted constructs of interest and consequently undermine the validity of the selection outcomes. The use of technology for simulation delivery may be most appropriate for jobs where technology use is a fundamental job requirement. Similarly, it has been mentioned that video-based SJTs might give irrelevant contextual information and unintentionally insert more error into SJTs (Weekley & Jones, 1997). It may be the case that these irrelevant constructs may have different effects on test performance across different subgroups (Yongwei, Sireci & Hayes, 2013).

Applicant Reactions

In addition to psychometric considerations, it is important to evaluate applicant reactions to the assessments used in the selection process. This includes evaluating applicant preferences for various types of assessment, as well as the extent to which they see them as job-relevant and fair. Meta-analytic studies examining a range of assessment types have found that simulations yield among the most positive applicant reactions (Hausknecht et al., 2004). In this section we examine applicant reactions to simulations from a justice perspective and discuss the impact of fidelity and multimedia on applicant reactions.

Justice and reactions

Applicant reactions are typically evaluated using frameworks derived in organizational justice theory, most often Gilliland's (1993) model. Three key dimensions have been found to form the basis of applicants' fairness reactions to a selection process: 1) perceived job-relatedness, 2) opportunity to perform and 3) interpersonal treatment. The more job-related an assessment appears, the fairer it will be perceived (Gilliland & Cherry, 2000). Simulations present tasks and implicitly have higher face validity because they look like the job. Research has shown that applicants see simulations as job-relevant and therefore fair when compared to other assessment types (Huffcutt, 1990; Robertson & Kandola, 1982). These results have held across countries, including Belgium, France, Netherlands, Portugal, Singapore, Spain and South Africa (Anderson & Witvliet, 2008; Steiner & Gilliland, 1996, 2001). However, additional research is needed beyond countries with a shared European heritage.

Opportunity to perform is defined as having an adequate opportunity to demonstrate knowledge, skills and abilities in the testing situation. Schleicher, Venkataramani, Moregson and Campion (2006) suggest opportunity to perform is one of the most important procedural justice rules because applicants who feel they were able to demonstrate their skills and abilities can then justify a poor or favourable outcome. Conversely, if applicants do not feel they have had an opportunity, they may believe an unfavourable outcome was due to that perceived lack of opportunity. Simulations have a direct overlap to the target position making it explicit how performance on the exercise is related to performance on the job (Boyce et al., 2013) and leads to the belief that they represent a fair opportunity to demonstrate ability (Robertson & Kandola, 1982; Smith, 1991).

Simulations are typically just one assessment used in the selection process. They are frequently combined with other assessments such as measures of cognitive ability or personality which tend have more negative applicant reactions. Smither, Reilly, Millsap, Pearlman and Stoffey (1993) proposed that positive (or negative) reactions to one assessment can impact reactions to other assessments and the selection process as a whole. As such, the use of a simulation in an assessment battery may help to improve the perceptions of the entire process. Drew, Lamer, Burk-Lee, LeVine and Wrenn (2012) found that applicant reactions to personality and cognitive ability assessments were more positive when followed by an animated SJT than by a text-based SJT. However, research specifically examining the impact of simulations on applicant reactions to other tests and the overall hiring process is lacking.

Impact of fidelity and multimedia

In the same way that research examining the impact of changes in stimulus and response fidelity on validity is in its infancy, so too is research examining its impact on applicant reactions (Bauer et al., 2011). Much of the work in this area has focused on the impact of technology and the use of multimedia in simulations and has been in unpublished research literature. As summarized by Bruk-Lee, Drew and Hawkes (2013), innovative assessment items provide a more engaging experience and are perceived favourably by applicants. Additionally, innovative response option formats have been found to be more job-related and engaging compared to multiple-choice formats. Research related to the inclusion of multimedia in simulations has yielded generally positive applicant reactions and has been found to increase perceptions of job-relatedness. For example, audio- and video-based content presentation has been found to have higher perceptions of face validity than text-based presentation of the same content as have avatar-based SJTs compared to text-based SJTs presenting the same content (Bruk-Lee et al., 2013). Research examining the impact of technology and multimedia on the opportunity to perform is lacking and substantive conclusions cannot be drawn.

Cross-cultural Application

The globalization of the economy has necessitated the development of selection procedures that can be used across countries and cultures, while simultaneously recognizing and allowing for local differences and cultural norms. Applications include using an assessment developed for a job in one country to select for that job in other countries where the organization operates or using an assessment to select individuals from a host country who will work as an expatriate in another country. Surprisingly, internationally-oriented research has only emerged since 2005 (Lievens, 2008). This lack of research is particularly true for simulations.

Research has found differences in the extent to which a range of assessment types are used across countries (e.g., Newell & Tansley, 2001) and that contextual factors (e.g., cultural, national, political, legal, economical, technological) may in part drive those differences and impact the extent to which assessments and features generalize across cultures (e.g., Ryan, McFarland, Baron & Page, 1999). In the specific context of simulations, the impact of these factors has mostly been explored for assessments centres, which are used extensively in the industrialized countries (Lievens & Thorton, 2005). For example, Krause and Thorton (2008) explored cross-cultural differences in the use of assessment centres related to such variables as dimensions assessed, types of exercise used and the extent to which technology is employed. Lievens, Harris, Van Keer and Bisqueret (2003) found that a group discussion assessment centre exercises was predictive of success in a training programme for European managers in Japan, but a group presentation exercise was not. The authors hypothesized that the group discussion exercises reflected the team-based culture inherent in the country where the work was to be conducted. For SJTs, Lievens (2005) suggests that cultural differences may impact the applicability of the situations used, response options presented and the effectiveness of the response option. For example, cultures high in collectivism may be more likely to identify response options that promote 'group harmony' as effective when compared to cultures high on individualism.

Simulations are often highly contextualized, making them prone to cultural differences. This is particularly true if the skills and attitudes being assessed are culturally bound. The key to the validity of simulations is point-to-point correspondence and validity is compromised when the predictor and criterion domains do not overlap. Cultural differences in what constitutes an effective response have the potential to limit the generalizability of simulations across cultures. It is crucial that the simulation matches the definition of performance adopted by the country or culture where it is used

(Hough & Oswald, 2000; Lievens, 2008). When using simulations, users will have to make choices about what assessment features and specific practices to include, what needs to be adapted in consideration of the impact of cultural differences and the extent to which the features of those practices will generalize to other cultures. Simulation-specific research is needed to examine the value of modifying assessment processes to accommodate localization versus the costs and the value of being able to compare assessment results across locations.

One key issue is the extent to which assessment validity can generalize from one culture to another. That is, do criterion-related validities of simulations differ across countries? US-based meta-analyses are often used to support the validity of assessments in other countries. However, for the reasons previously discussed, these meta-analytic findings may not be transferable (Herriot & Anderson, 1997). To date, research in the area of cross-cultural validity has largely focused on cognitive ability and personality. For example, Salagado, Anderson, Moscoso, Bertua and De Fruyt (2003) found support for the generalizability of cognitive ability across seven European countries with validity coefficients similar to those found in US meta-analyses. Similar results support the generalizability of personality measures in European meta-analyses (Salgado, 1997).

Much of the simulation criterion-related validation studies have been done in the US. However, similar levels of criterion-related validity have been found in other countries. For example, a meta-analysis of work-sample validities conducted by Robertson and Downs (1989) focusing on British studies found observed validities of 0.41, 0.48, and 0.21 for training ratings, errors and job performance criteria, respectively. Chan and Schmitt (2002), Livens, Buyse and Sackett (2005) and Funke and Schuler (1998) demonstrated that SJTs developed in Singapore, Belgium and Germany for the prediction of job performance in those countries, respectively, had validities similar to SJTs developed in the US. For assessment centres, Becker, Hoft, Holzenkamp and Spinath (2011) found a mean corrected validity of 0.40 in German-speaking regions. While these results as a whole are promising, research is needed beyond countries with a shared European heritage, such as Africa, Asia, and Central and South America.

An important distinction needs to be made between within-country and across-country applications of selection measurers (Lievens, 2005, 2008). Much of the research has focused on within-country application – the development and validation of the assessment in one country for the prediction of job performance in that country. Little research has focused on the validity of simulations developed in one country and used for the prediction of job performance in another. For example, Such and Schmidt (2004) developed an SJT for use across countries based on the results of a cross-cultural job analysis. The assessment was found to be valid in the UK and Australia, but not in Mexico. Lievens and colleagues' (2003) study previously discussed is the only research that could be found looking at the validity of the across-country application of assessment centres. More research in this area is clearly needed to explore across-country application of simulations and the variables that allow for the generalization of results in order to guide development and use.

Finally, the use of simulations across cultures has inherent costs. First, when used globally, assessment content must be translated. These costs may be higher than for other assessments types as not only must assessment content be translated, but so too must interfaces and other features that attempt to replicate the job. There is also a need to establish translation equivalence. Additionally, to the extent that the validity of a simulation can or cannot generalize, costs for development and use may be more or less. The user must weigh the costs and benefits of using universal versus cultural-specific assessments.

Recruitment and Branding

An organization's selection process is necessarily linked to its recruitment strategy and approach. Both recruitment and selection are about placing people in jobs. A good recruitment strategy not only focuses on attracting people to the organization (and who will subsequently be assessed), but also increases the probability that applicants will accept job offers when made (Chapman, Uggerslev, Carroll, Piasentin & Jones, 2005). A selection process must necessarily support both the attraction and acceptance elements of an organization's recruitment strategy. In much the same way as recruitment factors, such as prompt follow-up and reactions to site visits, are positively related to whether the applicant stays in the recruitment pool and ultimately decides to accept a job offer, the specific assessments used in the process can have a large impact. It is here that simulations can play a significant role compared to traditional assessments.

Realistic job previews

Realistic job previews (RJPs) have long been an important part of many recruitment strategies (Wanous, 1992). In an RJP, the applicant is provided with information about both the positive and negative aspects of an organization and the specific position or role. The underlying idea is that by providing the applicant with a comprehensive picture of the job the dissonance that can occur as a result of differences between the applicant's expectations and the actual job once employed is mitigated. For example, it is important that an applicant for an airline manufacturing position not only sees how the work results in a completed airline at the cutting edge of the aerospace industry, but also that the successful applicant will be required to climb into tight and confined fuel cells as a regular part of the job. RJPs have been shown to have some impact on important bottom-line organizational metrics, such as reductions in turnover and increases in job satisfaction, but the size of these effects is usually only small to moderate (Earnest, Allen & Landis, 2011; Meglino, Ravlin & DeNisi, 2000; Phillips, 1998; Wanous, Poland, Premack & Davis, 1992). Despite these results, it is largely accepted that it is important to provide applicants with a realistic picture of the job (Breaugh, 2008; Buckley, Fedor, Carraher, Frink & Marvin, 1997) and that this preview provides applicants with the information they need to make an informed decision to self-select into (or out of) the job opportunity, based on a real or perceived match of skills, abilities, interests and preferences.

There is an increasing understanding that RJPs should be included throughout the recruitment process rather than at one point in time, such as in a recruitment video (Rynes & Cable, 2003). This includes the assessments used to evaluate applicants for positions. In comparison to other selection methods (e.g., measures of cognitive ability and personality), simulations have the unique ability to contribute to the RJP, allow for self-selection and self-suitability assessment, and result in a better job fit (Downs, Farr & Colbeck, 1978; U.S. Merit Systems Protection Board, 2009). They offer the applicant the opportunity to engage in job activities, either behaviourally or verbally, that present real-life activities and challenges that may be encountered on the job. At the high end of the fidelity spectrum, simulations can be seen as job tryouts under structured testing conditions. Regardless of their fidelity, simulations present a unique opportunity for applicants to learn about the position, assess the person–job fit and better determine if they are well suited to the position because they mimic job requirements. Additionally, organizations are increasingly embedding traditional RJP content, such as videos about organizational values or employee testimonials, as part of the actual assessment process.

Attraction and job acceptance

Simulations can also play an important role in attracting applicants to an organization and can increase the likelihood that applicants will accept job offers. At early stages in the recruitment and selection process, applicants' interest in an organization is influenced by perception of, and familiarity with, the organization (Gatewood et al., 2008). In these early stages, applicants have very limited information about the job and as such often make a choice about where to apply based on that limited information and perception. At later stages in the process, any additional information provided has an impact on which organizations they will pursue and where they will accept job offers (Rynes & Cable, 2003). Given that qualified applicants may well have multiple job offers, it is important to manage the organization's image throughout the recruitment and selection process.

Research has shown that applicants make inferences about an organization based on the information they are provided in the selection process and those inferences may impact their desire to pursue employment with an organization (French, 1987). In addition, they transfer those inferences to multiple organizational and job characteristics (Barber & Roehling, 1993). The assessments used as part of the selection process are another piece of information applicants use to form impressions. Applicant reactions to the selection process impact their attraction to, and views of, an organization (Chapman et al., 2005; Hausknecht et al., 2004). To the extent that applicants are impressed by the assessments used in the selection process, they are more likely to develop a favourable impression of the organization and will be more likely to stay in the recruitment pool and accept job offers when made. Meta-analytic studies have found simulations to be among the most favourably perceived by applicants (Hausknecht et al., 2004) due in large part to their face validity and the opportunity to perform that they provide. As such, unlike traditional assessments, simulations have the greatest potential to attract applicants to organizations and lead to offer acceptance because they provide insight into the job and its requirements.

Branding

Organizations are increasingly using assessments as an opportunity to promote their brand because they have the potential to influence perceptions (Yu & Cable, 2012). In addition, there is a growing understanding that applicants are often also customers (Boyce et al., 2013). As a result, not only is it important that those applicants/customers be treated fairly in the assessment process but also that the assessments present the organization in the most favourable light possible and leave applicants and customers with a positive impression. As previously mentioned, applicant impressions are related to job pursuit intentions. It is fundamental for the business (from direct-to-consumer, online retailers to large international hotel chains) that applicants (selected and not selected) view the organization favourably and remain customers. In a social media-rich world it is increasingly likely that candidates will share their impression of the organization and its brand with others and in turn impact others' impressions and intentions. It is not uncommon, for example, when watching an organization's recruitment videos on YouTube or other media players to find equally disparaging videos posted by disgruntled or indifferent applicants in the recommended video section. Simulations represent a unique opportunity to use assessments not only as a way to evaluate applicants' knowledge, skills and abilities, but also as a method for recruiting and branding. Engaging assessments can reinforce the organization's brand and can be used to share information as a source of competitive advantage.

Additional Considerations

In addition to investigating and understanding traditional assessment issues such as psychometric properties (i.e., validity and subgroup differences), construct measurement, cross-cultural considerations and applicant reactions related to simulations used for personnel selection, there is a range of other considerations that must be taken into account when considering the use of simulations. What follows is a brief summary of further topics in need of consideration.

Maximum versus typical performance and validity degradation

The changing nature of the predictor–criterion relationship has long been a focus of investigation (Ghiselli, 1956; Humphreys, 1960). A consistent finding of that work has been that the correlation between predictor and criterion measures decays over time (e.g., Alvares & Hulin, 1972; Hulin, Henry & Noon, 1990). Multiple models have been proposed to explain validity degradation (e.g., changing-person model, changing-task model, task consistency, skill acquisition models, dynamic criteria). A number of studies have been conducted to test these models with varying results, demonstrating the complexity of these relationships (e.g., Deadrick & Madigan, 1990; Keil & Cortina, 2001). These studies have mostly focused on cognitive and other ability measures (e.g., psychomotor ability, perceptual speed).

Relatively few studies have specifically examined the relationship between simulation measures and performance over time. While simulations have exhibited high criterion-related validities and have been found to be among the best predictors of job performance available, they likely maximize prediction at the point of selection. As a result, when used alone they may be deficient. Simulations are maximum as opposed to typical performance measure and assess 'can do' and not 'will do' performance over time (Borman, Bryant & Dorio, 2010; Callinan & Robertson, 2000). As such, they may have limited value for predicting long-term performance, which is a desired part of a selection system for most jobs. The few studies that have been conducted have found that, to a greater extent than other measures such as cognitive ability, the validity of simulations attenuate over time (Robertson & Downs, 1989; Robertson & Kandola, 1982; Siegel & Bergman, 1975).

The potential for validity degradation and its causes when using simulations merits additional investigation, especially in comparison to other measures which may cost less to develop and administer or lead to more or less adverse impact. Much in the same way that multiple models have been proposed to explain validity degradation for cognitive ability, similar research is needed that focuses on simulations. For example, the attenuation may be related to the specificity of skills that are sometimes measured (Callinan & Robertson, 2000). Alternatively, job performance models have described the interaction among personality, motivation and ability, as well as their importance for the prediction of job performance over time (Helmerich, Swain & Carsrud, 1986; Hollenbeck & Whitemer, 1988; Kanfer & Ackerman, 1989). Goldstein, Zedeck and Goldstein (2002) found that non-cognitive predictors become more important when the criterion data are collected later. The extent to which a simulation is cognitively loaded or correlated with personality variables may impact these relationships and the attenuation of validity. Cognitive ability may be more important than the competences assessed by a simulation at various points in the lifecycle of the job, such as during transitional stages when additional learning is required (e.g., when the job is new, when major duties or responsibilities change, when past experience cannot be relied on for performance) (Murphy, 1989). To the extent that the lifespan utility of a predictor can be estimated, a better understanding of its initial utility can be acquired (Keil & Cortina, 2001) and more informed decisions can be made about what predictors to use for specific hiring goals and their potential organizational return on investment.

Applicant experience and prior knowledge

Many simulations assume that applicants already have the experience, knowledge, skills and abilities required for performance. As a result, simulations may not be appropriate for entry-level jobs or more generalist positions, especially if post-hire training is to be provided (U.S. Merit Systems Protection Board, 2009; Whetzel et al., 2012).

Cost

While the use of technology has reduced administration costs in some cases, simulations can be more expensive to build and maintain than other assessment types. Because of their specificity, they require significant input from subject matter experts and test development professionals. When not delivered online, the equipment required may be expensive, as are the costs of assessment proctoring. In addition, as jobs change, simulations will need to be revised more frequently than other assessment types. This is of particular concern given the rapidly changing nature of work.

Costs are also directly related to the level of fidelity desired. Increasing fidelity means increasing costs, though the cost of increasing fidelity across different simulation types is not equal (Walsh & Jaye, 2012). For example, low-fidelity simulations can leverage automated scoring, while higher-fidelity simulations often rely on expensive human rating (Boyce et al., 2013). Similarly, the use of multimedia in a low-fidelity simulation such as a branching role-play may increase development costs compared to their in-person counterparts, but may be more cost-effective to administer over time when the resources required to administer and score an in-person assessment are taken into consideration. When considering the use of simulations, practitioners are advised to examine the range of cost factors and consider utility. This is particularly true given the research on fidelity and validity in selection contexts is not definitive. Taking an example from an educational context, Lapkin and Levett-Jones (2011) used a cost-utility analysis and found medium-fidelity simulations for nurse education were more cost-effective than the high-fidelity simulations, as the medium-fidelity simulation was one-fifth the cost and resulted in the same level of knowledge acquired and same level of student satisfaction.

Bandwidth

Bandwidth is the extent to which the job performance domain is covered by an assessment. Ideally, all job tasks are included in a simulation, but that is a practical impossibility, particularly for complex and multifaceted jobs (Felker, Curtin & Rose, 2007). This leaves open the possibility that the simulation will be job-related but deficient in that it is not sufficiently comprehensive to reflect the range of behaviours required for the job or role, and subsequently can attenuate criterion-related validity (Callinan & Robertson, 2000). In constructing simulations for selection, care must be taken to ensure the inclusion of a representative sample of job tasks or activities or inclusion of those that are the most critical to job performance (Campbell et al., 1990; Gatewood et al., 2008; Green & Wigdor, 1991). When simulations are used with other assessments, it is advisable to identify the critical job elements not assessed or not well measured and to target the simulation to those areas.

Specificity and generalizability

When developing simulations, practitioners must consider the level of specificity needed as it relates to the level of generalizability required. The more contextualized the simulation, the higher its fidelity and the more situation- and job-specific it becomes (Callinan & Robertson, 2000). For example, a hands-on performance test may be required to assess a set of specific tasks or technical skills needed for a given job. Alternatively, assessment centres can target behaviours required across jobs. There is a tradeoff between the fidelity of simulation and what is assessed and the generalizability of assessment outcomes (Reynolds & Dickter, 2010; Zenisky & Sireci, 2002). High-fidelity simulations are less generalizable across jobs. However, there may be situations where sacrifices in fidelity are justified to achieve generalizability (Boyce et al., 2013). The research suggests that, in some cases, this sacrifice may not be detrimental, at least not in terms of criterion-related validity. A meta-analysis by Whetzel, Rotenberry and McDaniel (2014) examined the level of specificity of in-basket content (generic vs. job-specific) and found that specificity had little impact. Generic and job-specific in-baskets exhibited equivalent operational validity estimates, suggesting no meaningful difference exists between the validity of the two types of assessment.

Use of technology

Advances in technology have undoubtedly accelerated the use of simulations for selection, improved their measurement properties, increased applicant reactions and changed the way they are administered and scored. This trend will continue and we are likely to see increases in simulation use and the development of novel assessment types. However, because of the speed of technology development, research has not been able to keep pace. There is a lack of research related to advanced simulations (Handler, 2013). In addition to the areas previously noted in this chapter (e.g., the impact of fidelity on validity, the potential for construct irrelevant variance, construct validity), this presents an exciting and unprecedented opportunity for research to expand our understanding of simulations in a number of areas. For example, continued research is needed on generational differences. Millennials who grew up relying on technology and social networking may react more favourably to a multimedia simulation. In fact, there is evidence indicating younger workers preferred the use of 3D media over other formats (Tuzinski, Drew, Bruk-Lee & Fetzer, 2012). Similarly, generational research is needed that examines how preferences and performance are related to the technology used for simulation delivery. As this field expands, it will be important for research to try to stay in stride with application.

The Future of Simulations for Selection

In just a few decades, technology has significantly changed the nature of personnel selection (Tippins & Adler, 2011). What was once unimaginable is now possible. For example, computers can be used to score free-text essays using state-of-the-art and psychometrically sound latent semantic analysis scoring engines that utilize machine learning models of human understanding of text. Over many validation studies with a variety of topics and test-takers, computer-generated scores have been found to correlate with human raters as well as scores provided by human raters correlate with each other. In the context of simulations, we are now able to replicate call centre, service, manufacturing and managerial environments with a high degree of realism, which has led to improved accuracy of measurement (see Fetzer & Tuzinski, 2013). In the next decade, simulations will most likely look and feel nothing like they do today.

To date, the simulations developed for personnel selection have been limited to jobs that are easy to replicate and have been largely linear in nature. Even when assessment stimuli are presented in a non-sequential manner, such as in computer-based in-baskets that use emails, voicemails and instant messaging, the simulations remain largely linear where responses at one point in time do not impact subsequent simulation stages (Fetzer, 2013; Handler, 2013). Branching and adaptive simulations (such as branching role-plays) are only starting to emerge. As jobs change and become more complex, simulations of the future will leverage technology to match that complexity and deliver assessments that more closely match the target job and its complex technology- and human-based interactions (Fetzer, 2013; Handler, 2013).

Even the most state-of-the-art simulations have been limited to constrained and scripted interactions. While our ability to make inferences about applicant ability from unstructured situations does not exist, they are a reality in modern work environments. Simulations of the future will leverage gaming technology to replicate those work environments and make this possible (see this volume, chapter 14 for a summary of gaming techniques applied to personnel selection and other human capital domains). Serious games leverage technology from the entertainment industry and have been employed in military and training contexts. For example, virtual worlds have been used to simulate operating theatres (Gerald & Antonacci, 2009). In addition, they have the potential to significantly increase applicant engagement. As stated by Handler (2013, p. viii), 'The Holy Grail of simulations is the ability to make inferences based on wide open and unstructured interactions within complex simulated work environments of all types'. Fetzer (2013, p. 262) expands on this lofty goal by suggesting the Holy Grail 'is to achieve a threshold of engagement where the candidate forgets he/she is being assessed, thus exhibiting true behaviour'. Technology may very well allow us to achieve the Holy Grail – the modelling of an infinite number of interactions in an engaging, virtual environment.

Future Research

Extensive research literature exists in support of the use and value of simulations as part of the selection system. However, a number of important areas are in need of more research. We highlight some of the emerging research needs below. Because of the rapidly changing nature of this area of work, this list can be expected to grow quickly. It will be important to do all we can to ensure research keeps pace and that the same rigorous standards that have guided the development and use of other predictors (e.g., cognitive ability and personality) must be applied to simulations.

First, additional research is needed that examines the cost and utility of various simulation features in order to guide development and use. For example, it is unclear what level of fidelity is required to achieve the benefits simulations provide, such as improved applicant reactions and validity. To date, no same sample studies have been conducted which examine the impact of fidelity on important organizational outcomes. The field would also benefit from cost-utility analyses similar to those that have been conducted for simulations used in training. As fidelity increases, so do the costs and resources required for development and administration. This is particularly true as organizations scale for cross-national administration. As organizations continue to seek ways to cut costs in resource-constrained environments, it will be important to understand the minimum level of fidelity required to achieve desired outcomes. In the same vein, additional research is needed to further understand the level of simulation specificity required, especially as it relates to the generalizability of assessment results. For example, how specific does a simulation need to be to achieve desired levels of validity, improve applicant reactions or be used as an RJP? It may be possible to leverage technology to package generic items with a job-specific skin that improves the user experience and achieve the same level of validity and applicant reactions as more job-specific simulations at a reduced cost.

Second, issues related to the cross-cultural application of simulations are not well understood. It is not enough simply to explore the frequency of use in different cultures. Rather, research examining the specific features of simulations as they relate to contextual factors that may drive their acceptance across cultures is needed, as is work examining the generalizability of validity findings. Where the research has been undertaken, it has largely focused on cultures with a shared European heritage, thus neglecting many emerging markets such as South America. Particular attention will need to be paid to across-country applications and the utility tradeoff between localization and the need to compare assessment results across locations.

Third, as technology is leveraged, psychometric research will be needed on emerging methodologies and new item types. For example, research allowing for stable estimates of validity has yet to be accumulated for computer-based in-baskets that present items in a non-linear fashion or for branching role-plays. It will be important to amass the studies needed from which meta-analytic validity estimates can be made to support the use of new and emerging simulations in the same way that has been done for more traditional simulations and selection assessments (e.g., cognitive ability). It will be interesting to understand the incremental validity provided by new simulations compared to more traditional simulation types. Additionally, questions about the construct validity and the potential for the introduction of construct irrelevant variance remain. These are questions that have led to some controversy over the use of simulations in the past (Whetzel at al., 2012). It will be important to explore these issues so that the reasons why simulations are predictive of job performance are well understood. As well, the potential for subgroup mean differences and adverse impact needs to be explored as the impact of irrelevant constructs on the performance of different subgroups are not known.

Finally, more applicant reaction research will be needed. While it has been shown that simulations result in positive application reactions through the lenses of justice models, it will be important to understand the specific features of simulations that drive those applicant reactions. Is it merely an engaging look and feel, or is it the items that showcase the job that drive the positive results observed? What features are most important from a recruiting and branding perspective? This will have important cost and utility implications. For example, it is unclear whether applicants will have similar positive reactions when simulations are presented as serious games. The literature suggests that perceived job relevance and opportunity to perform are important drivers of applicant reactions, yet it is not known if applicants in an immersive game will implicitly make those connections. From a branding perspective, it is possible that an applicant who is immersed and engaged but does not see a direct link to the job will become quite upset if not offered a job because of a 'game'. An in-depth understanding of technology-based simulations as it relates to these issues is needed, but the complex interactions will be difficult to tease apart. For example, we are only now beginning to explore the impact of the use of mobile devices on testing. Fursman and Tuzinski (2015) found that applicants have less trust in mobile delivery compared to personal computer use.

Conclusion

Simulations, a group of assessment methods that evaluate applicants' performance on tasks that are physically or psychologically similar to the tasks required on the job, are increasingly being used as part of selection systems around the globe. They are built on the premise of point-to-point correspondence, the idea that prediction is improved to the extent that there is overlap between the predictor measure and criterion domain. As a group, their value is well understood. Simulations have been found to be among the best predictors of job performance to date and they have been shown to provide incremental validity beyond measures of cognitive ability. Further, they have the potential to exhibit smaller subgroup mean differences than other assessments, to lead to positive applicant reactions and engagement, and can be used as an effective tool for recruitment and branding.

Advances in technology have made simulations easier and more cost-effective to develop, improved their fidelity and prediction, expanded construct measurement and enhanced applicant reactions. The cutting-edge simulations of today will rapidly become outdated and replaced by fully immersive serious games. With the rapid proliferation in use, a gap between research and practice has started to open up. For example, questions related to the potential for the introduction of construct irrelevant variance, the optimal balance between fidelity and utility and cross-cultural validity generalization needs to be addressed. Despite these gaps, simulations represent the only assessment that can simultaneously measure the complex interaction of traits required for job performance and offer perhaps the most potential for improving and expanding the science of measurement and selection. As the types and uses of simulations expand, it will be important to bridge these research gaps and ensure that the science keeps pace with practice.

References

Aguinis, H., Henle, C. A., & Beaty Jr., J. C. (2001). Virtual reality technology: A new tool for personnel selection. *International Journal of Selection and Assessment, 9*(1–2), 70–83.

Alvares, K. M., & Hulin, C. L. (1972). Two explanations of temporal changes in ability–skill relationships: A literature review and theoretical analysis. *Human Factors, 14*(4), 295–308.

Anderson, N. R., & Witvliet, C. (2008). Fairness reactions to personnel selection methods: An international comparison between The Netherlands, the United States, France, Spain, Portugal, and Singapore. *International Journal of Selection and Assessment, 16*(1), 2–13.

Arthur, W., Day, E. A., McNelly, T. L., & Edens, P. S. (2003). A meta-analysis of the criterion-related validity of assessment centre dimensions. *Personnel Psychology, 56*(1), 125–153.

Asher, J. J., & Sciarrino, J. A. (1974). Realistic work sample tests: A review. *Personnel Psychology, 27*(4), 519–533.

Barber, A. E., & Roehling, M. V. (1993). Job postings and the decision to interview: A verbal protocol analysis. *Journal of Applied Psychology, 78*(5), 845–865.

Bauer, T. N., Truxillo, D. M., Mack, K., & Costa, A. B. (2011). Applicant reactions to technology based selection: What we know so far. In N. T. Tippins & S. Adler (Eds.), *Technology Enhanced Assessment of Talent* (pp. 190–223). San Francisco: Jossey-Bass.

Becker, N., Hoft, S., Holzenkamp, M., & Spinath, F. M. (2011). The predictive validity of assessment centres in German-speaking regions: A meta-analysis. *Journal of Personnel Psychology, 10*(2), 61–69.

Binning, J. F., & Barrett, G. V. (1989). Validity of personnel decisions: A conceptual analysis of the inferential and evidence bases. *Journal of Applied Psychology, 74*(3), 478–494.

Bobko, P., Roth, P. L., & Buster, M. A. (2005). Work sample selection tests and expected reduction in adverse impact: A cautionary note. *International Journal of Selection and Assessment, 13*(1), 1–10.

Borman, W. C., Bryant, R. H., & Dorio, J. (2010). The measurement of task performance as criteria in selection research. *In* J. L. Farr & N. T. Tippins (Eds.), *Handbook of Employee Selection* (pp. 439–461). New York: Routledge.

Boyce, A. S., Corbet, C. E., & Adler, S. (2013). Simulations in the selection context: Considerations, challenges, and opportunities. *In* M. Fetzer & K. Tuzinski (Eds.), *Simulations for Personnel Selection* (pp. 17–41). New York: Springer.

Bray, D. W., Campbell, R. J., & Grant, D. L. (1979). *Formative Years in Business: A Long-Term AT&T Study of Managerial Lives*. Huntington, NY: R. E. Krieger Publishing.

Breaugh, J. A. (2008). Employee recruitment: Current knowledge and important areas for future research. *Human Resources Management Review, 18*, 102–118.

Bruk-Lee, V., Drew, E. N., & Hawkes, B. (2013). Candidate reactions to simulations and media-rich assessments in personnel selection. *In* M. Fetzer & K. Tuzinski (Eds.), *Simulations for Personnel Selection* (pp. 43–60). New York: Springer.

Buckley, M. R., Fedor, D. B., Carraher, S. M., Frink, D. D., & Marvin, D. (1997). The ethical imperative to provide recruits realistic job previews. *Journal of Managerial Issues, 9*(4), 468–484.

Callinan, M., & Robertson, I. T. (2000). Work sample testing. *International Journal of Selection and Assessment, 8*(4), 248–260.

Campbell, C. H., Ford, P., Rumsey, M. G., Pulakos, E. D., Borman, W. C., Felker, D. B., De Vera, M. V., & Riegelhaupt, B. J. (1990). Development of multiple job performance measures in a representative sample of jobs. *Personnel Psychology, 43*(2), 277–300.

Chan, D., & Schmitt, N. (2002). Situational judgement tests and job performance. *Human Performance, 15*(3), 233–254.

Chapman, D. S., Uggerslev, K. L., Carroll, S. A., Piasentin, K. A., & Jones, D. A. (2005). Applicant attraction to organizations and job choice: A meta-analytic review of the correlates of recruiting outcomes. *Journal of Applied Psychology, 90*(5), 928–944.

Charan, R., Drotter, S., & Noel, J. (2000). *The Leadership Pipeline: How to Build the Leadership Powered Company*. San Francisco: Jossey-Bass.

Clevenger, J., Pereira, G. M., Wiechmann, D., Schmitt, N., & Harvey, V. S. (2001). Incremental validity of situational judgement tests. *Journal of Applied Psychology, 86*(3), 410–417.

De Meuse, K. P., Dai, G., & Hallenbeck, G. S. (2010). Learning agility: A construct whose time has come. *Consulting Psychology Journal: Practice and Research, 62*(2), 119–130.

Deadrick, D. L., & Madigan, R. M. (1990). Dynamic criteria revisited: A longitudinal study of performance stability and predictive validity. *Personnel Psychology, 43*(4), 717–744.

Dean, M. A., Roth, P. L., & Bobko, P. (2008). Ethnic and gender subgroup differences in assessment centre ratings: A meta-analysis. *Journal of Applied Psychology, 93*(3), 685–691.

Downs, S., Farr, R. M., & Colbeck, L. (1978). Self appraisal: A convergence of selection and guidance. *Journal of Occupational Psychology, 51*(3), 271–278.

Drew, E. N., Lamer, J. J., Burk-Lee, V., LeVine, P. J., & Wrenn, K. A. (2012). Keeping up with the Joneses: Applicant reactions to multimedia SJTs. Paper presented at the annual meeting of the Society for Industrial and Organzational Psychology, San Diego, CA.

Earnest, D. R., Allen, D. G., & Landis, R. S. (2011). Mechanisms linking realistic job previews with turnover: A meta-analytic path analysis. *Personnel Psychology, 64*(4), 865–897.

Fallaw, S., & Kantrowitz, T. (2013). *2013 Global Assessment Trends Report*. Alpharetta, GA: SHL/CEB.

Felker, D. B., Curtin, P. J., & Rose, A. M. (2007). Tests of job performance. *In* D. L. Whetzel & G. R. Wheaton (Eds.), *Applied Measurement: Industrial Psychology in Human Resources Management* (pp. 319–348). Mahwah, NJ: Lawrence Erlbaum.

Fetzer, M. (2013). Future directions. *In* M. Fetzer & K. Tuzinski (Eds.), *Simulations for Personnel Selection* (pp. 259–264). New York: Springer.

Fetzer, M., & Tuzinski, K. (2013). *Simulations for Personnel Selection*. New York: Springer.

French, W. L. (1987). *Personnel Management Process: Human Resources Administration and Development*. Boston, MA: Houghton Mifflin.

Funke, U., & Schuler, H. (1998). Validity of stimulus and response components in video tests of social competence. *International Journal of Selection and Assessment, 6*(2), 115–123.

Fursman, P. M., & Tuzinski, K. A. (2015). Reactions to mobile testing from the perspective of job applicants. Paper presented at the annual conference of the Society for Industrial and Organizational Psychology, Philadelphia, PA.

Gatewood, R. D., Feild, H. S., & Barrick, M. (2008). *Human Resources Selection*. Mason, OH: Thompson.

Gaugler, B. B., Rosenthal, D. B., Thornton, G. C., & Bentson, C. (1987). Meta-analysis of assessment centre validity. *Journal of Applied Psychology, 72*(3), 493–511.

Gerald, S., & Antonacci, D. M. (2009). Virtual world learning spaces: Developing a Second Life operating room simulation. *EDUCASE Quarterly, 32*(1). www.educause.edu/ero/article/virtual-world-learning-spaces-developing-second-life-operating-room-simulation.

Ghiselli, E. E. (1956). Dimensional problems of criteria. *Journal of Applied Psychology, 40*(1), 1–4.

Gilliland, S. (1993). The perceived fairness of selection systems: An organizational justice perspective. *Academy of Management Review, 18*(4), 694–734.

Gilliland, S. W., & Cherry, B. (2000). Managing customer selection. In J. F. Kehoe (Ed.), *Managing Selection in Changing Organizations* (pp. 158–196). San Francisco: Jossey-Bass.

Goldsmith, M. (2007). *What Got You Here Won't Get You There: How Successful People Become Even More Successful*. New York: Hyperion.

Goldstein, H. W., Yusko, K. P., Braverman, E. P., Smith, D. B., & Chung, B. (1998). The role of cognitive ability in the subgroup differences and incremental validity of assessment centre exercises. *Personnel Psychology, 51*(2), 357–374.

Goldstein, H. W., Zedeck, S., & Goldstein, I. L. (2002). *g*: Is this your final answer? *Human Performance, 15*, 123–142.

Goldstein, I. L., Zedeck, S., & Schneider, B. (1993). An exploration of the job-analysis – content validity process. In N. Schmitt & W. Borman (Eds.), *Personnel Selection in Organizations* (pp. 2–34). San Francisco: Jossey-Bass.

Green, B. F., & Wigdor, A. K. (1991). Measuring job competencies. In A. K. Wigdor & B. F. Green (Eds.), *Performance Assessment for the Workplace* (pp. 53–74). Washington, DC: National Academy Press.

Guion, R. M. (2010). Employee selection: Musings about its past present, and future. In J. L. Farr & N. T. Tippins (Eds.), *Handbook of Employee Selection* (pp. 943–957). New York: Routledge.

Handler, C. (2013). Foreword. In M. Fetzer & K. Tuzinski (Eds.), *Simulations for Personnel Selection* (pp. v–ix). New York: Springer.

Hausknecht, J., Day, D. V., & Thomas, S. C. (2004). Applicant reactions to selection procedures: An updated model and meta-analysis. *Personnel Psychology, 57*(3), 639–683.

Helmerich, R. L., Swain, L. L., & Carsrud, A. L. (1986). The honeymoon effect in job performance. Temporal increases in the predictive power of achievement motivation. *Journal of Applied Psychology, 71*(2), 185–188.

Herriot, P., & Anderson, N. (1997). Selecting for change: How will personnel and selection psychology survive? In N. R. Anderson & P. Herriot (Eds.), *International Handbook of Selection and Assessment* (pp. 1–34). London: Wiley.

Hollenbeck, J. R., & Whitemer, E. M. (1988). Reclaiming personality traits for personnel selection: Self-esteem as an illustrative case. *Journal of Management, 14*(1), 81–91.

Hough, L. M., & Oswald, F. L. (2000). Personnel selection: Looking toward the future, remembering the past. *Annual Review of Psychology, 51*, 631–664.

Huffcutt, A. (1990). Intelligence is not a panacea in personnel selection. *The Industrial and Organizational Psychologist, 27*, 66–67.

Hulin, C. L., Henry, R. A., & Noon, S. L. (1990). Adding a dimension: Time as a factor in the generalizability of predictive relationships. *Psychological Bulletin, 107*(3), 328–340.

Humphreys, L. G. (1960). Investigations of the simplex. *Psychometrika, 25*(4), 313–323.

Hunter, J. E., & Hunter, R. F. (1984). Validity and utility of alternative predictors of job performance. *Psychological Bulletin, 96*(1), 72–98.

Kanfer, R., & Ackerman, P.L. (1989). Motivation and cognitive abilities: An integrative/aptitude-treatment interaction approach to skill acquisition. *Journal of Applied Psychology, 74*(4), 657–690.

Keil, C. T., & Cortina, J. M. (2001). Degradation of validity over time: A test and extension of Ackerman's model. *Psychological Bulletin, 127*(5), 673–697.

Krause, D. E., & Thornton, G. C. (2008). A cross-cultural look at assessment center practices: Survey results from Western Europe and North America. *Applied Psychology, 58*(4), 557–585.

Lapkin, S., & Levett-Jones, T. (2011). A cost-utility analysis of medium- vs. high-fidelity human patient simulation manikins in nursing education. *Journal of Clinical Nursing, 20*(23–24), 3543–3552.

Lievens, F. (2005). International situational judgement tests. In J. A. Weekly & R. E. Ployhart (Eds.), *Situational Judgement Tests: Theory, Measurement, and Application* (pp. 279–300). Mahwah, NJ: Lawrence Erlbaum.

Lievens, F. (2008). Research on selection in an international context: Current status and future directions. In M. M. Harris (Ed.), *Handbook of Research in International Human Resources Management* (pp. 107–124). New York: Lawrence Erlbaum.

Lievens, F., Buyse, T., & Sackett, P. R. (2005). The operational validity of a video-based situational judgement test for medical college admission: Illustrating the importance of matching predictor and criterion construct domains. *Journal of Applied Psychology, 90*(3), 442–452.

Lievens, F., De Corte, W., & Westerveld, L. (2012). Understanding the building blocks of selection procedures: Effects of response fidelity on performance and utility. *Journal of Management.* doi: 10.1177/0149206312463941.

Lievens, F., Harris, M. M., Van Keer, E., & Bisqueret, C. (2003). Predicting cross-cultural training performance: The validity of personality, cognitive ability, and dimensions measured by an assessment centre and a behaviour description interview. *Journal of Applied Psychology, 88*(3), 476–489.

Lievens, F., & Patterson, F. (2011). The validity and incremental validity of knowledge tests, low-fidelity simulations, and high-fidelity simulations for prediction job performance in advanced-level high-stakes selection. *Journal of Applied Psychology, 96*(5), 927–940.

Lievens, F., & Thorton, G. C. (2005). Assessment centers: Recent developments in practice and research. In A. Evers, O. Smit-Voskuijl, & N. Anderson (Eds.), *Handbook of Selection* (pp. 243–264). Malden, MA: Blackwell.

Lombardo, M. M., & Eichinger, R. W. (2000). High potentials as high learners. *Human Resources Management, 39*(4), 321–330.

Malka, A., Kubisiak, C., Thornbury, E., Stewart, R., Yankelevich, M., Grossman, M., Moye, N., & Ungemah, J. (2012, December). *Department of Veterans Affairs: Design and Development of Learning Agility Assessments* (Technical Report 773). Arlington, VA: PDRI, an SHL Company.

McCall, M. W. (1998). *High Flyers: Developing the Next Generation of Leaders.* Boston, MA: Harvard Business School Press.

McDaniel, M. A., Hartman, N. S., Whetzel, D. L., & Grubb, W. (2007). Situational judgement tests, response instructions, and validity: A meta-analysis. *Personnel Psychology, 60*(1), 63–91.

McNelly, T., Ruggeberg, B. J., & Hall, C. R. Jr. (2011). Web-based management simulations: Technology-enhanced assessment for executive-level selection and development. In N. T. Tippins & S. Adler (Eds.), *Technology-Enhanced Assessment of Talent* (pp. 251–266). San Francisco: Jossey-Bass.

Meglino, B. M., Ravlin, E. C., & DeNisi, A. S. (2000). A meta-analytic investigation of realistic job preview effectiveness: A test of three counterintuitive propositions. *Human Resources Management Review, 10*(4), 407–434.

Mueller-Hanson, R. A., Swartout, E. C., Nelson, J. K., Parish, C., Martin, C., & McGonigle, T. (2009). *Social Awareness and Leader Influence: Development of Classroom and Web-Based Learning Interventions* (Technical Report 1258). Arlington, VA: PDRI, an SHL Company.

Murphy, K. R. (1989). Is the relationship between cognitive ability and job performance stable over time? *Human Performance, 2*(3), 183–200.

Newell, S., & Tansley, C. (2001). International uses of selection methods. In C. L. Cooper & I. T. Robertson (Eds.), *International Review of Industrial and Organizational Psychology* (pp. 195–213). Chichester: Wiley.

Olson-Buchanan, J. B., Drasgow, F., Moberg, P. J., Mead, A. D., Keenan, P. A., & Donovan, M. A. (1998). Interactive video assessment of conflict resolution skills. *Personnel Psychology, 51*(1), 1–24.

Phillips, J. M. (1998). Effects of realistic job previews on multiple organizational outcomes: A meta-analysis. *Academy of Management Journal, 41*(6), 673–690.

Ployhart, R. E., & Holtz, B. C. (2008). The diversity–validity dilemma: Strategies for reducing racioethnic and sex subgroup differences and adverse impact in selection. *Personnel Psychology*, *61*(1), 153–172.

Ployhart, R. E., Schneider, B., & Schmitt, N., (2006). *Staffing Organizations: Contemporary Practice and Theory* (3rd ed.). Mahwah, NJ: Lawrence Erlbaum.

Ranger, J., & Khun, J. (2013). Analyzing response times with rank correlation approaches. *Journal of Educational and Behavioural Statistics*, *38*(1), 61–80.

Reynolds, D. H., & Dickter, D. N. (2010). Technology and employee selection. *In* J. L. Farr & N. T. Tippins (Eds.), *Handbook of Employee Selection* (pp. 171–194). New York: Routledge.

Robertson, I. T., & Downs, S. (1989). Work sample tests of trainability: A meta-analysis. *Journal of Applied Psychology*, *74*(3), 402–410.

Robertson, I. T., & Kandola, R. S. (1982). Work sample tests: Validity, adverse impact and applicant reaction. *Journal of Occupational Psychology*, *55*(3), 171–183.

Roth, P. L., Bobko, P., & McFarland, L. A. (2005). A meta-analysis of work sample test validity: Updating and integrating some classic literature. *Personnel Psychology*, *58*(4), 1009–1037.

Roth, P. L., Bobko, P., McFarland, L. A., & Buster, M. (2008). Work sample test in personnel selection: A meta-analysis of Black–White differences in overall and exercise scores. *Personnel Psychology*, *61*(3), 637–661.

Ryan, A. M., McFarland, L., Baron, H., & Page, R. (1999). An international look at selection practices: Nation and culture as explanations for variability in practice. *Personnel Psychology*, *52*(2), 359–391.

Ryan, A. M., & Tippins, N. T. (2004). Attracting and selecting: What psychological research tells us. *Human Resources Management*, *43*(4), 305–318.

Rynes, S. L., & Cable, D. M. (2003). Recruitment research in the twenty-first century. *In* I. B. Weiner (Ed.), *Handbook of Psychology* (pp. 55–76). Hoboken, NJ: Wiley.

Salagado, J. F. (1997). The five-factor model of personality and job performance in the European Community: Issues and evidence. *Journal of Applied Psychology*, *82*(1), 30–43.

Salagado, J. F., Anderson, N., Moscoso, S., Bertua, C., & De Fruyt, F. (2003). International validity generalization of GMA and cognitive abilities: A European Community meta-analysis. *Personnel Psychology*, *56*(3), 573–605.

Schleichner, D. J., Venkataramani, Y., Morgeson, F. P., & Campion, M. A. (2006). So you didn't get the job. Now what do you think? Examining opportunity-to-perform fairness perceptions. *Personnel Psychology*, *59*, 559–590.

Schmidt, F. L., Greenthal, A. L., Hunter, J. E., Berner, J. G., & Seaton, F. W. (1997). Job sample vs. paper-and-pencil trades and technical tests: Adverse impact and examinee attitudes. *Personnel Psychology*, *30*(2), 187–197.

Schmidt, F. L., & Hunter, J. E. (1998). The validity and utility of selection methods in personnel psychology: Practical and theoretical and practical implications of 85 years of research. *Journal of Applied Psychology*, *124*(2), 262–274.

Schmitt, N., & Mills, A. E. (2001). Traditional tests and job simulations: Minority and majority performance and test validities. *Journal of Applied Psychology*, *86*(3), 451–458.

Siegel, A. I., & Bergman, B. A. (1975). A job learning approach to performance prediction. *Personnel Psychology*, *28*(3), 325–339.

Smith, F. (1991). Work sample testing. *In* A. K. Wigdor & B. F. Green (Eds.). *Performance Assessment for the Workplace*. Washington, DC: National Academy Press.

Smither, J. W., Reilly, R. R., Millsap, R. E., Pearlman, K., & Stoffey, R. W. (1993). Applicant reactions to selection procedures. *Personnel Psychology*, *46*(1), 49–76.

Steiner, D. S., & Gilliland, S.W. (1996). Fairness reactions to personnel selection techniques in France and the United States. *Journal of Applied Psychology*, *81*(2), 134–141.

Steiner, D. S., & Gilliland, S. W. (2001). Procedural justice in personnel selection: International and cross-cultural perspectives. *International Journal of Selection and Assessment*, *9*(1–2), 124–137.

Such, M. J., & Schmidt, D. B. (2004). Examining the effectiveness of empirical keying: A cross-cultural perspective. Paper presented at the annual meeting of the Society for Industrial and Organizational Psychology, Chicago, IL.

Terpstra, D. E., & Kethley, R. K. (2002). Organizations' relative degree of exposure to selection discrimination litigation. *Public Personnel Management, 31*(3), 277–292.

Terpstra, D. E., Mohamed, A. A., & Kethley, R. B. (1999). An analysis of federal court cases involving nine selection devices. *International Journal of Selection and Assessment, 7*(1), 26–34.

Tippins, N. T., & Adler, S. (2011). *Technology-Enhanced Assessment of Talent*. San Francisco: Jossey-Bass.

Tuzinski, T. (2013). Simulations for personnel selection: An introduction. *In* M. Fetzer & K. Tuzinski (Eds.), *Simulations for Personnel Selection* (pp. 1–13). New York: Springer.

Tuzinski, K., Drew, E. N., Bruk-Lee, V., & Fetzer, M. (2012). Applicant perceptions of multimedia situational judgement tests. Paper presented at the annual meeting of the Society for Industrial and Organizational Psychology, April. San Diego, CA.

U.S. Merit Systems Protection Board. (2009). *Job Simulations: Trying out for a Federal Job*. Washington, DC.

Walsh, K., & Jaye, P. (2012). The relationship between fidelity and cost in simulation. *Medical Education, 46*, 1226–1228.

Wanous, J. P. (1992). *Organizational Entry: Recruitment, Selection, Orientation, and Socialization of Newcomers* (2nd ed.). Reading, MA: Addison-Wesley.

Wanous, J. P., Poland, T. D., Premack, S. L., & Davis, K. S. (1992). The effects of met expectations on newcomer attitudes and behaviors: A review and meta-analysis. *Journal of Applied Psychology, 77*(3), 288–297.

Weekley, J. A., & Jones, C. (1997). Video-based situational testing. *Personnel Psychology, 50*(1), 25–49.

Wernimont, P. F., & Campbell, J. P. (1968). Sign, samples, and criteria. *Journal of Applied Psychology, 52*(5), 372–376.

Whetzel, D. L., McDaniel, M. A., & Nguyen, N. T. (2008). Subgroup differences in situational judgement test performance: A meta-analysis. *Human Performance, 21*(3), 291–309.

Whetzel, D. L., McDaniel, M. A., & Pollack, J. M. (2012). Work simulations. *In* M. A. Wilson, W. Bennett, S. G. Gibson, & G. M. Alliger (Eds.), *The Handbook of Work Analysis* (pp. 401–418). New York: Routledge.

Whetzel, D. L. Rotenberry, P. F., & McDaniel, M. A. (2014). In-basket validity: A systematic review. *International Journal of Selection and Assessment, 22*(1), 62–79.

Yongwei, Y., Sirici, S. G., & Hayes, T. L. (2013). Assessments (truly) enhanced by technology: Rationale, validity, and value. Paper presented in T. L. Hayes (Chair), *Technology Enhanced Assessments, A Measurement Odyssey*, at the annual meeting of the Society for Industrial and Organizational Psychology, San Diego, CA.

Yu, K. Y. T., & Cable, D. M. (2012). Recruitment and competitive advantage: A brand equity perspective. *In* S. W. J. Kozlowiski (Ed.), *The Oxford Handbook of Organizational Psychology.* (Vol. 1, pp. 197–220). New York: Oxford University Press.

Zenisky, A. L., & Sireci, S. G. (2002). Technological innovations in large-scale assessment. *Applied Measurement in Education, 15*(4), 337–362.

13

The Potential of Online Selection

Dave Bartram and Nancy Tippins

Introduction

As technology continues to evolve rapidly it has been applied to a multitude of functions in organizations, including staffing. Many organizations have turned to online selection systems to help determine which candidates possess the knowledge, skills, abilities and other characteristics (KSAOs) necessary to perform the job because of the convenience to applicants and organizations, as well as the cost savings. While these online selection systems are efficient in many respects, they must still be effective and meet professional standards and legal requirements where they apply.

This chapter focuses on three important topics related to the use of online selection systems: 1) the globalization of selection systems that are enabled by online tools; 2) the security and cheating issues created by the use of online selection tools; and 3) the validity of online tools in light of the globalization of the instruments, the problems with security and the opportunity for cheating. Although technology has enabled a number of innovations in testing, including audio- and video-based assessments, gamification, the use of data from social media as well as 'big data' sets, there are too many variations in concerns about globalization, security, cheating and validity to address them all. Thus, the focus here is limited to online testing. The chapter concludes with a discussion of a future research agenda.

Background

Recent years have seen rapid growth in the use of technology-enhanced assessment tools used for selection purposes. Beginning in the 1980s, employers and consultants alike experimented with computer-based tests to measure specific skills, such as typing, data entry and computer programming. By the 1990s, testing professionals were exploring the

The Wiley Blackwell Handbook of the Psychology of Recruitment, Selection and Employee Retention,
First Edition. Edited by Harold W. Goldstein, Elaine D. Pulakos, Jonathan Passmore and Carla Semedo.
© 2017 John Wiley & Sons Ltd. Published 2020 by John Wiley & Sons Ltd.

possibilities of large-scale, computer-based testing in business and industry. For example, in 1991, Bell Atlantic (a precursor to the company that is now Verizon) implemented its Universal Test Battery, which was designed to evaluate foundational knowledge, skills, abilities and other characteristics of candidates for all non-management jobs using a computer-administered battery of 10 tests. At the time of implementation, almost 100,000 candidates were tested each year. The US Department of Defense (DoD) also was interested in converting its military enlistment test (the Armed Services Vocational Aptitude Battery – ASVAB) from paper-and-pencil to a computer adaptive testing (CAT) mode. (ASVAB is a cognitive abilities test that measures verbal, mathematical and technical skills.) After years of research to equate the paper-and-pencil ASVAB with the CAT version, DoD implemented the computer adaptive ASVAB in 1993 in 65 military entrance processing stations across the country. At that time, more than 500,000 young men and women took the CAT-ASVAB to determine their enlistment eligibility and occupational qualifications (Sellman, 1991; Waters, 1997; Wise, Curran & McBride, 1997). By the late 1990s, many large test publishers were offering a variety of tests via the internet (Bartram, 2000; Lievens & Harris, 2003).

Early challenges to the successful implementation of online testing included the costs and accessibility of the equipment, reliable internet connections and the effects of different kinds of equipment (e.g., font size, speed of processing) on the testing experience (Tippins, 1992). While access to equipment and the internet remains a concern in some parts of the world with some types of equipment (e.g., desktop computers, mobile devices) for some segments of the population, many if not most job candidates in the first world can access computer equipment that allows them to take a test online and visit testing sites through the internet. Similarly, the concerns about equivalence across equipment have greatly diminished. While some differences in speed of processing remain, the speed of today's computers makes most of the differences imperceptible to the user in test administration applications and irrelevant to test performance. Differences in the look and feel of the test are largely controlled by the test administration software.

In many respects, the differences between early computer-administered tests and their paper-and-pencil counterparts were minimal. The computerized test administration platform served as a test administrator, page-turner, storage device, test scorer and report generator, delegating many of the more onerous tasks associated with employment testing to the computer instead of human administrators. Often, these tests were given in the same testing environment as the paper-and-pencil forms had been. Proctors administered the test and monitored the test-taker's behaviour throughout the testing session.

As technology has become more ubiquitous, powerful, portable and affordable, two other important developments have emerged that have profoundly affected employment testing. First, more sophisticated technology has enabled more complex tests, such as complex simulations, technology-enhanced situational judgement tests (SJTs), algorithms for the use of social media and gamification. Second, developments in testing theory have moved beyond classic testing theory alone to include item-response theory (IRT) and CAT. The availability of more powerful and affordable technology has made applications of IRT and CAT feasible for employment testing programs. In combination, progress in these three areas – development of technology, applications of technology and testing theory – has facilitated the rapid growth of online testing in many forms, including unproctored internet testing (UIT) and mobile testing, as well as the use of data collected from settings not typically considered to be a test (e.g., social media and games).

While technology has rapidly evolved and been applied to a multitude of common daily chores, at the same time many businesses have become more global. Enabled by technology and driven by economic concerns, many large organizations have expanded their businesses by entering global markets. Customers exist around the world, and in response, many organizations have placed manufacturing centres and sales organizations in closer proximity to them. Cost structures in developed countries have driven manufacturing to places with lower costs. Competition for specialized labour requires many organizations not only to place work where workers are found but to recruit workers into expatriate positions and ask them to go where the work is. Consequently, many modern organizations are aligning their selection programs with the needs of the business. In some cases, this expansion of testing programs means that companies, especially those that are sensitive to costs, must develop selection programs that can be used anywhere in the world the company does business in. In other situations, it means designing programs that identify those with the skills to work in countries other than their native country.

The confluence of technology enhancements and the demand for global selection systems have created both opportunities and challenges for testing professionals. There are numerous advantages of using technology in testing. Most argue that substantial savings in costs can be achieved by substituting computers for human administrators and paper test forms. Although the costs of the hardware and software for most online tests are not insignificant, they are generally believed to be substantially less than the costs associated with labour to administer and score paper-and-pencil tests, generate reports and record scores. Similarly, the costs of printing and distributing paper forms, particularly, when the test is used globally, are usually higher than tests that are presented and distributed by computer. Certainly, the speed of delivery of a test by computer is faster than that of paper forms, which are often sent via a mail service. In addition, virtually all testing professionals who have administered large-scale testing programs agree that the accuracy of computers in the administration and scoring of tests is superior to that of humans.

Many testing and staffing professionals promote the improved availability of testing that UIT provides. Not only is the timeframe during which a test is available increased, but also the number of places where one can take a test is increased. Because candidates are not limited to office hours when UIT is used, it enables them to take a test at a time and place of their choice. Although there are few if any published studies comparing the characteristics of the applicant pools when proctored testing is used and when UIT is used, many believe that capabilities increase when UIT is used because the most qualified candidates are usually employed and will be reluctant to absent themselves from work to seek another employment opportunity.

Another advantage of the use of technology in employment testing is its role in attracting candidates to the organization. In addition to the convenience of testing at any time, anywhere, computer-based testing usually connotes objectivity in the staffing process, at least in the testing phase, by eliminating human scorers and interpreters. The realism of technology-enhanced assessments (e.g., video-based situational judgement inventories) also provides meaningful information about the organization and the job. In other situations, the 'fun' associated with instruments involving gamification conveys the idea that the company would be a pleasurable place at which to work. For others, the company image as an organization that is up-to-date with respect to technology is highly appealing.

Despite the advantages of online testing, there are challenges to its use. Regardless of the benefits, testing professionals must always ensure the instruments they use are valid for the purposes of the tests. In other words, no matter how fancy or glitzy the technology-enabled test used for employee selection is, it must predict a job-related outcome, such as job performance, training success, absenteeism or turnover, that is meaningful to the employer. Despite the obligation to demonstrate that pre-employment tests meet professional standards and in some countries legal guidelines, many test users appear more concerned with the technology of online testing than its validity and reliability.

In addition, online testing has made UIT commonplace, and with UIT come concerns about malfeasant behaviours, especially those related to the security of test materials and cheating. The globalization of testing programs highlights differences in attitudes to security and cheating and can make the prevention of theft or cheating considerably more difficult.

While some argue that applicants will find computer-based testing convenient and appealing, others argue that the 'hands-off' approach is a deterrent. Some applicants may fear that the low-touch treatment presages indifference to employee needs and prefer an employer that is more engaged with candidates in the recruiting and selection process. Others are not convinced that computer scoring is accurate and objective, and still others are sceptical of organizations that use selection procedures that appear to tolerate cheating and so may be reluctant to pursue employment.

Globalization

The Global Assessment Trends Report (Kantrowitz, 2014) is an annual online survey. The 2014 survey was conducted in early 2014 and completed by 1,406 human resources (HR) professionals from companies headquartered throughout the world. In summarizing the trends, the author concludes:

> Our findings indicate heightened interest in technology-based hiring tools and technology-enabled assessment, although their use is often characterised by inconsistent or inappropriate justification or processes, or without demonstrable job relevance. (Kantrowitz, 2014, p. 48)

The respondents indicated they were increasingly turning to social media as a hiring tool, though most HR professionals were unclear about the criticality or relevance of such information for hiring and few had formal processes in place to advise hiring managers on its use. At the time of the survey, interest in administering tests on mobile devices was modest, with some interest coming from candidates. However, the growth of mobile testing is a trend that has seen more recent significant increases in volume.

Historically, test producers and publishers worked on a national basis and developed tests for country-specific markets. Globalization has changed that. Not only are there increasing numbers of global or multinational organizations that use assessments, but there are providers of assessments that also operate on a multinational basis. Bartram (2000), in an early look at the impact of globalization on internet recruitment and selection, put forward the following scenario:

> An Italian job applicant is assessed at a test centre in France using an English language test. The test was developed in Australia by an international test developer and publisher, but is running from an ISP located in Germany. The testing is being carried out for a Dutch-based subsidiary of a US multi-national. The position the person is applying for is as a manager in the Dutch company's Tokyo office. The report on the test results, which are held on the multi-national's Intranet server in the US, are sent to the applicant's potential line-manager in Japan having first been interpreted by the company's out-sourced HR consultancy in Belgium. (Bartram, 2000, p. 272)

Bartram listed a number of questions that this scenario raises, including where the legal responsibility lies, who the 'user' of the test is, how the various countries' standards and regulations regarding testing apply, and so on. In particular, one issue that has come to the fore since this was written is the question of what norms should be used in comparing this Italian job applicant with other applicants.

It used to be standard practice to base test norms on a country-wide sampling approach. Aggregating data across countries was thought inappropriate despite the fact that country boundaries are often relatively arbitrary and countries contain a complex amalgam of culturally and linguistically diverse groups. In many countries, this mix is becoming increasingly diverse as cross-border employment continues to expand alongside the growth of multinational companies.

Increasingly, organizations are using assessment in an international context and need to compare the results of people who have completed an assessment using different languages. The development of online testing has made this possible as administration can be centrally controlled and then globally distributed. This testing environment raises the question of whether the results from two candidates applying for the same position who have completed different language versions of the same instrument should be compared using a common (i.e., multilingual) norm or each person's 'country-based' language norms. Bartram (2008a) has set out guidelines for making this decision. Essentially, the answer lies in establishing what level of equivalence exists between scores from the two countries. If evidence suggests that it is reasonable to conclude that a given raw scores on a test represents the same level of the same trait in both countries, then international norms should be used. However, establishing equivalence is not simple. Clearly, there is no point in developing common norms if an instrument does not measure the same characteristic across all groups.

If an instrument is administered in different cultures, it is necessary to check that test scores have the same psychological meaning in those cultures (Van de Vijver & Leung, 1997). An item or test is biased if scores do not have the same meaning across these groups (Poortinga, 1989). Differences in meaning can derive from three sources: in the constructs that are being measured; in the effects of the method being used to measure the constructs; or in issues arising from the content of specific items. If the construct being measured is not universal (i.e., does not have the same meaning across geographic and cultural groups), then the scores obtained from one group may indicate something different from those of other groups. Method biases can arise from different groups' susceptibilities to bias relating to response formats. For example, individuals from East Asian cultures tend to avoid extreme points on Likert response scales, whereas individuals from Central and Latin America are more likely to use the extremes (He & Van de Vijver, 2013; Hui & Triandis, 1989). Content-related bias is the most often observed source of non-equivalence and can arise from poor translation on the one hand or unnecessarily cultural-specific content in the source material on the other.

Equivalence, or freedom from bias, can be assessed both qualitatively and quantitatively. The most convincing evidence is provided by quantitative analyses. In the past decade or so, consensus has emerged on the need to consider three hierarchical levels of equivalence:

1 *Construct equivalence*: relates to the evidence that the instrument assesses the same underlying constructs in each group.
2 *Metric or measurement unit equivalence*: relates to the evidence that the instrument assesses the same underlying constructs, using the same metric of the response scale.
3 *Scalar or score equivalence*: relates to the evidence that the instrument assesses the same underlying constructs, using response scales that use the same metric and having the origin of the scales and the measurement units that are the same for each group.

Scalar equivalence is the most difficult to establish, but it is necessary if raw scores are to be compared across groups. Whenever we put two or more people together and use them as a reference or norm for making comparisons between people, we are assuming scalar equivalence, that the constructs we are measuring are the same for all the people in the group and that any differences in raw scores reflect comparable differences in levels or amounts of the construct. As discussed earlier, the process of aggregating people with varying demographics into a norm group has typically been carried out within countries rather than across countries without analysing the equivalence of demographic subgroups within the norm group. The introduction of online testing and its easy deployment across national boundaries has spurred interest in equivalence between groups and raised the issue of when it is appropriate to combine people across countries to form international norm groups.

Establishing equivalence involves accumulating evidence. No single study 'proves' equivalence at all levels. Techniques include the study of bilinguals, differential item functioning (DIF) analyses and the use of multilevel designs to identity sources of between-group differences. Bartram (2013a, 2013b), for example, has shown how multilevel analysis can be used to examine scale score variance between countries to determine how much can be accounted for by independent country variables. Personality scale scores aggregated to country level are correlated with country measures of culture, quality of life and global competitiveness. To the extent that we can account for country variance in personality in terms of these other country measures, we can support claims for scalar equivalence. In short, if we can show that the difference between two groups is a difference that predicts other independently assessed variables, then the difference is real and not bias attributable to non-equivalence.

Security

The past two decades have seen rapid growth in the deployment of employment tests via the internet, together with the increasing use of unproctored administration (Bartram, 2008b). This practice has raised concerns about the security of cognitive ability tests in particular, and more generally about the validity of scores from all types of tests administered in UIT conditions (Tippins et al., 2006). The early discussion of whether this should happen has moved on to an acceptance of this mode of administration. Now the focus is on how best to ensure it is safe, secure and valid (Bartram & Burke, 2013; Burke, 2006, 2009; Burke, Mahoney-Phillips, Bowler & Downey, 2011; Lievens & Burke, 2011; Tippins, 2008).

Cheating occurs and always has (Cizek, 1999). What concerns us here is whether cheating is more of an issue for technology-based testing or whether the technology provides a means of mitigating some of the risks associated with testing. Tate and Hughes (2007) reported results from a survey of the perceptions of UIT of 319 university undergraduates and postgraduates in 51 British universities. The majority (76%) had taken tests at home, with the next most frequently used testing location being a university computer room (27%). Taking a test at home was the preferred location (selected by 81% of undergraduates). Respondents were asked to report the frequency of different actions. Thirty-seven (12%) reported actions that could be considered to be cheating, and of these 15 reported colluding with friends, 15 reported obtaining the questions in advance and 6 reported circumventing the technology in some way. This survey indicates that the administration of traditional tests under UIT conditions may be subject to a degree of cheating. The challenge is how to counter this while retaining the logistical advantages of UIT.

We can divide instruments used in employment testing into two types: measures of maximum performance and measures of typical performance. The former, which include cognitive ability tests, have a right answer to each question. In this respect, they are similar to knowledge tests and other achievement-related measures in the way they are scored and normed. Typical performance measures, on the other hand, focus on how candidates typically behave in work settings. These are largely self-report measures (e.g., personality questionnaires), which do not have 'right' answers.

These two types of measure, maximum and typical performance, entail very different issues for ensuring the quality and validity of the data obtained. Measures of maximum performance are potentially open to various forms of cheating as candidates may find a way to obtain access to the correct answers or take the test with the assistance of another. Measures of typical performance are open to more subtle forms of distortion, such 'faking good'.

It is natural for applicants to attempt to create a good impression when applying for a job, but a line should be drawn between putting forward a positive but honest view of oneself and pretending to be something one is not. Faking on self-report measures not only reduces the construct validity of the test (Tett, Anderson, Ho, Yang, Huang & Hanvongse, 2006) but also skews the rank ordering of applicants, which in turn can cause false-positive errors in selection decisions (Griffith, Chmielowski & Yoshita, 2007). The same concerns arise with ability tests; inflated false-positive rates can occur when a candidate's responses to a test represent either unfair access to the correct answers, a proxy sitting the test on behalf of the candidate or a candidate colluding to obtain a score that is higher than his or her true level of ability.

Controlling cheating often depends on making it difficult for candidates to obtain access to the questions and checking that the candidate's score was obtained from the candidate in question rather than someone else and that the score was achieved without assistance. These two issues are often dealt with by item banking and verification testing.

Item banking provides the means to construct tests 'on the fly' that differ for each candidate using item-response theory as the basis for test construction. Tests may either be fixed-length fixed-difficulty linear on-the-fly testing (LOFT) or computer-adaptive, where the selection of the next question is based on the current estimate of the candidate's ability level determined from responses on the previous items. In either case, the candidate will not know which items will be presented or in the order in which they are presented. It is important to have a large item bank and to control item exposure levels to maintain security (Davey & Nering, 2002). Over time, test producers should monitor the questions in the item bank to check for changes in their parameters that might indicate they have been compromised through over-exposure or theft. They can also 'patrol' the internet to search for sites that offer illicit access to items from the bank and take action to close them down.

Verification testing involves the administration of a proctored test to shortlisted candidates who have previously been screened using an UIT. Scores on the UIT and the verification test can be compared to identify people with inconsistent scores. There are various ways of doing this. In one example – CEB's Verify 2 – CAT is used to provide an ability estimate in UIT and then, if the candidate passes the selection sift, this estimate is used as the starting value for the CAT verification test. If the final ability level estimate falls below the original cut-score, the candidate can be rejected.

In addition, it is now possible to use remote proctoring. This involves the use of technology such as webcams to monitor and record the test-taker during the test. In addition, behaviour is recorded in terms of response times, typing patterns and other measures. Data forensics software (Maynes, 2009) can alert a proctor to atypical behaviour and then the video record can be checked. Proctors can remotely stop a test or issue a warning (Foster, 2013; Foster, Mattoon & Shearer, 2009).

Faking on self-report measures is different from cheating on an ability test. Faking cannot be observed by a test proctor and few people ask a colleague to complete a personality inventory or other self-description inventory. However, if people differ in the degree to which they bias their scores by faking, this may confer an unfair advantage to those who fake more. Most of the research on 'faking good' (see Griffith & Peterson, 2006, for a comprehensive review) has been laboratory-based, with students being asked to role-play applicants in 'faking-good' conditions or non-applicants in so-called 'honest' conditions. In such situations, we find that people *can* fake on self-report inventories. In a laboratory setting, people are not only willing to adopt false roles but are indeed instructed to do so. There are no negative consequences associated with them lying about themselves. Indeed, the demand characteristics of the situation encourage people to 'fake' as much as they can with no real adverse consequences.

If, and to what extent, job applicants 'fake good' in real situations is a much more complex issue, and the research on faking in real selection situations is far more ambiguous than that for laboratory studies (Levashina, Morgeson & Campion, 2009). Many have challenged the view that because people can fake in simulated settings, they will fake in real ones when the demand characteristics of the situation are very different (Arthur, Woehr & Graziano, 2000; Hough & Schneider, 1996; Ones & Viswesveran, 1998; Viswesveran & Ones, 1999).

There are several ways to control 'faking good' behaviour. Some evidence suggests that lie scales, warnings and honour statements, among others, deter candidates from inflating their self-ratings. A common way to control faking is by making it difficult to do. Students in simulated selection situations can typically raise their scores by around 1 SD on instruments using Likert single stimulus item format response scales. However, they raise them by only around a third of that when forced-choice item format instruments are used (Christiansen, Burns & Montgomery, 2005; Jackson, Wroblewski & Ashton, 2000; Martin, Bowen & Hunt, 2002; Vasilopoulos et al., 2006). Most of the studies with forced-choice item formats have used forced-choice item pairs. Those with high ability are able to raise their scores more than others (Levashina et al., 2009). However, faking becomes increasingly difficult as the number of alternatives increases.

The challenge in constructing forced-choice items used to be in the process of matching statements in pairs (or triples or quads, depending on the format used) such that they provided good information about each of the scales involved and were equally desirable options. There was also an issue of ipsativity associated with how forced-choice format instruments were scored. Traditional methods of scoring forced-choice items result in the sum of the points given to the various scales being a constant. This means that if you know the scores obtained on all but one of the scales, the score on the last scale is determined. Ipsative items pose problems for a range of psychometric analyses and impose a constraint on the central location of score profiles (see Baron, 1996; Bartram, 1996). Recent developments have provided solutions to both problems. IRT scoring models have been developed (Brown & Bartram, 2009; McCloy, Heggestad & Reeve, 2005) and can be applied to forced-choice item data to recover the latent trait scores that determined the pattern of choice. These recovered scores are not ipsative. The IRT parameters of the items also provide a basis for assembling them into sets for forced-choice format use (Brown & Maydeu-Olivares, 2011).

Bartram and Burke (2013) argue that the degree to which people might cheat or 'fake good' depends on a combination of five factors;

1   People have to perceive a need to fake, which is determined by the level of the candidate's investment in the outcome of the process. The higher the personal consequences of 'failure' on a test, the more someone might be driven to find a way to avoid failure that involves some degree of dishonesty. If the stakes are low or if the situation is not one in which one can either 'pass' or 'fail', then the motivation to cheat or fake will be

low. We can identify this aspect of the situation as being 'the perceived cost of failure'. The higher the stakes, the higher the perceived cost of failure and the more likely someone is to fake.

2 People differ in their willingness to fake or cheat, which relates to the strength of an individual's moral or ethical stance on cheating or faking. Some are more willing to be dishonest in a given set of circumstances than others. Others may perceive collusion or cheating as fair play and believe that they are only doing what everyone else does.

3 People differ in their ability to cheat or fake. It is argued that 30–50% of applicants may inflate their scores (Griffith & McDaniel, 2006) by faking. Applicants can buy books such as *Ace the Corporate Personality Test* (Hoffman, 2000), and there is lots of advice on the internet on how to fake personality questionnaires. While we should not ignore the assistance that is available, the fact that people try to 'ace the test' does not imply necessarily that they will be successful. Applicants do not always get it right when they fake: as many as 20% of those who attempt to fake do so in the wrong direction (Griffith & McDaniel, 2006).

4 Test-takers have to believe that the benefits of cheating outweigh the risks associated with being caught. Although candidates might be willing and able to cheat in a laboratory study, in a real-life selection setting they might regard the situation as one in which the risks of being caught are too high.

5 Most important of all is the opportunity to fake or cheat, which the test designer can control. However, it is impossible to control the willingness or ability to behave dishonestly as these are attributes of the candidate.

Candidate can only cheat on a test if they have access to the answer or assistance, or use a proxy of higher ability. The opportunity to fake or cheat can be managed in several ways. Methods of test construction, including use of forced-choice item formats and test administration procedures (e.g., verification testing or remote proctoring) can mitigate the risks of cheating. The use of LOFT and CAT with verification testing limits foreknowledge of items and indicates who may have used a proxy or received some form illicit assistance. Multiple test forms were a key recommendation made by Tippins and colleagues (2006), and Hollinger and Lanza-Kaduce (1996) report a study in which 80% of students surveyed stated that the 'scrambling' of items was the most effective anti-cheating strategy of those included in this study. In addition, faking will become increasingly difficult as the complexity of what one is trying to fake increases.

Faking on a personality instrument is an invisible process that requires no prior knowledge of the content. A single-scale instrument (e.g., a conscientiousness scale or an extraversion scale) will be much easier to fake than a profile on a multi-scale instrument. It is fairly easy to role-play a given persona in terms of the Big Five, but role-playing a person defined by the 30 facets of the NEO-PI-R or the 32 scales of the OPQ32r is much more demanding. The use of multi-scale instruments with detailed levels of measurement not only makes faking harder, it also optimizes validity. The validity of personality instruments increases if relatively narrow bandwidth criterion-focused scales are aligned with specific criteria (Bartram, Warr & Brown, 2010; Ones & Viswesveran, 2001; Warr, Bartram & Martin, 2005).

Optimal test security puts in place multiple layers of control so that cheating the system becomes too complicated, too risky and too costly for the candidate. For self-report measures, measuring relatively large numbers of scales and using forced-choice item formats and non-transparent scoring algorithms and scale combination rules can curtail cheating. Systems of checks and balances can detect people whose results from one method of assessment at one stage of the process are inconsistent with those from another method at a later stage.

Finally, cheating can be deterred by informing candidates that they are expected to respond honestly and openly, and that there are consequence if they are found not to have done so. In many testing programs (e.g., CEB's), tests are introduced with a simple honesty contract which states that the candidate will undertake the test honestly and in the spirit of fairness to all candidates; this also serves as a reminder that the content of the tests are protected by copyright and covered by law. Ariely (2008) cites studies showing that subjects will cheat if given the opportunity to do so. However, when participants were asked to sign a simple honesty statement, the level of cheating dropped substantially. Honesty contracts have been shown to have a positive impact on the quality of information obtained from biographical questionnaires (Stokes, Mumford & Owens, 1994). Reminding candidates that they are expected to be honest is an easy way to make the 'rules of the game' clear to them.

Detailed guidelines on how to ensure test security and good practice in technology-based testing are contained in the International Test Commission's *Guidelines on Computer-based and Internet Delivered Testing* (International Test Commission, 2006) and *Guidelines on the Security of Tests, Examinations and Other Assessments* (International Test Commission, 2014).

Validity

Professional standards, legal guidelines and the ethical obligations of psychologists (see Table 13.1) require that employment tests are valid (i.e., are accurate predictors of important job outcomes). Moreover, employers who are cost-sensitive or need capable employees want selection programs that identify both 'good' and 'bad' candidates (i.e., those who are likely to perform well and those who are not, those who are likely to turnover and those who are not, those who are likely to be successful in training and those who are not).

Despite the importance of ensuring validity, online testing raises a number of issues related to establishing the validity of a testing procedure. Perhaps the greatest threat to the validity of UIT is the reliability of the score. Because some form of cheating is possible,

Table 13.1 Examples of professional requirements, legal guidelines, and ethical standards related to testing.

Professional Guidelines

AERA, APA, & NCME. (2014). *Standards for Educational and Psychological Testing.*

SIOP. (2003). *Principles for the Use and Validation of Personnel Selection Procedures.*

European Federation of Psychologists' Associations. (2013). *EFPA Review Model for the Description and Evaluation of Psychological and Educational Tests Version 4.2.6.*

ISO. (2011). *ISO-10667-2 Assessment Service Delivery – Procedures and Methods to Assess People in Work and Organizational Settings.*

International Test Commission. (2001). *International Guidelines for Test Use.*

International Test Commission. (2005). *International Guidelines on Test Adaptation.*

Legal Guidelines

EEOC. (1978). *Uniform Guidelines on Employee Selection Standards.*

Ethical Guidelines

American Psychological Association. (2010). *APA Ethical Principles of Psychologists and Code of Conduct.*

International Task Force on Assessment Center Guidelines. (2009). *Guidelines and Ethical Considerations for Assessment Center Operations.*

---

test users do not know how reliable any specific score is. To the extent that reliability is compromised, validity too is limited. Yet, UIT is not the only testing process related to technology that generates concerns regarding validity. When a test user switches from one form of technology (e.g., desktop computers to mobile devices), the test user cannot assume that the validity of the test is unchanged. Similarly, the assumption that validity exists regardless of where the test is used or which language is used for administration may not always be the case. In addition, when a test user implements a selection procedure that does not resemble a traditional test (e.g., games, credit checks, data from social media), the test user is still responsible for accumulating evidence to support the use of the procedure for a particular population in the organization.

Unproctored testing

Few research studies have been conducted to compare the validity of a cognitive ability test used in a proctored environment and that of the same test used in an unproctored environment. Kaminsky and Hemingway (2009) found comparable validities for the same test administered in proctored and unproctored conditions. Beaty and colleagues' (2011) meta-analysis also showed that the validities of the proctored and unproctored tests were similar. Despite the lack of many comparative studies, the validity of the unproctored test is typically assumed to be less than that of the proctored tests because of cheating. Nevertheless, when tests administered in unproctored environments are validated, their validity is usually at an acceptable level for use in pre-employment selection programmes.

Because of the challenges of collecting criterion data to conduct a validity study, another approach to comparing validities of proctored and unproctored testing is to evaluate the extent of cheating and impute lower validity when cheating occurs. The underlying assumption is that the more that cheating occurs, the lower the validity of the unproctored test is likely to be. When researchers compare scores of individuals who took a test under proctored conditions to those who took the same test in an unproctored setting, higher scores in the unproctored setting are presumed to indicate that some form of cheating has occurred and thus some negative impact on the validity of the test has also occurred.

Despite the opportunity to cheat, the incidence of higher scores in the unproctored setting compared to the proctored setting is relatively low. Arthur and colleagues (2009) compared test scores of individuals who took a speeded cognitive ability test in proctored and unproctored conditions and estimated an upper limit of 7.7% of test-takers cheating. In a slight twist of the typical research protocol, Lievens and Burke (2011) compared test scores on a timed cognitive ability test consisting of both numerical and verbal items obtained in an unproctored setting to those obtained in a verification testing session. They corrected for regression to the mean and found small d scores across four levels of jobs. At the individual test score level, fewer than 2.2% of those who passed the unproctored test and were invited to take the proctored test exhibited a negative score change, and some proctored scores were actually higher than unproctored scores. In a similar study, Kantrowitz and Dainis (2014) compared unproctored scores on a cognitive test to the proctored cognitive test scores of those who passed the battery of which the cognitive ability test was a part. Again, the incidence of significant score differences was very low (259 of 4,026 at the 0.05 level and 78 at the 0.01 level). Caution in extending the results of both these studies to the entire distribution of test scores is warranted because only people at the top of the score distribution from the unproctored test were invited to take the proctored test. An unanswered question is whether the rate of cheating is consistent at all score levels.

Several factors are particularly relevant to the degree of difference between proctored and unproctored test scores. Researchers use various statistical indicators of a difference. Some correct for regression to the mean. Few seem to correct for a practice effect but do acknowledge the potential to attenuate scores in the second administration. Lievens and Burke (2011) identify differences in test administration conditions other than the degree of proctoring and note that those who were asked to take a verification test under proctored conditions might be more motivated to concentrate on the test because they had passed the earlier hurdle of the unproctored test.

Based on limited research studies, work simulations appear to show similar response patterns in proctored and unproctored environments to cognitive ability tests. For example, Hense and colleagues (2009) reported an effect size of 0.32 between scores on a proctored and an unproctored job simulation.

In contrast to cognitive ability tests that have right and wrong answers, most researchers find that scores on other types of test have similar score distributions regardless of the environment in which the test is given. Nye and colleagues (2008) found no differences in scores from unproctored and proctored internet versions of a speeded perceptual accuracy test.

Personality tests in particular seem to show little or no score differences across administration conditions. Arthur and colleagues (2009) found little evidence of response distortions when they compared the mean scores from a low-stakes, speeded personality test and from high-stakes administrations of personality measures in the literature. Arthur and colleagues estimated the percentage of individual test-takers with elevated scores was estimated to be 30–50%. Although response distortions are common in high-stakes testing, there appears to be little difference in the extent of distortion in proctored and unproctored settings.

In summary, there are few research studies comparing the validity of proctored and unproctored tests; however, in the published studies, the low rates of cheating on different measures (cognitive ability tests, perceptual accuracy tests, simulations) suggest there is little impact on the tests' validity.

Global testing

Because globalization typically requires translations and adaptations of test materials, the deployment of tests internationally poses problems for establishing their validity. Although many organizations assume that a test that has sufficient validity for selection purposes in one country also has sufficient validity when translated and used in other countries, the assumption may not be true if test-takers are not familiar with the test format or content, or when the translation and adaption processes modify the construct being measured.

The problems with translation alone are well known. Translations and back-translations often significantly distort the original meaning of test content and are likely to create significant problems for test users. This is particularly apparent when personality tests are involved. Professional standards (e.g., AERA et al., 2014; ITC, 2005) emphasize the importance of using both effective translation and adaptation procedures. Although often technically infeasible, establishing the equivalence of various versions of a test supports the notion that validity extends across these test versions.

The familiarity of different populations with different item types and content can affect the validity of a test in certain cultures, even when the test-takers possess the skill being measured. For example, analogies seem to be more familiar to American applicants than to other foreign nationals. Items that involve calculations using the metric system may be more valid in one country than in another simply because of the applicants' familiarity with it.

Although the translations and adaptations of tests using unfamiliar item types or content may be adequate, the item itself may work to the advantage of those who are more familiar.

Testing with different devices

Another assumption employers sometimes make which may prove to be false is the idea that a test that is valid for a particular purpose when administered on one device remains valid (and equivalent) when administered on another device. For example, a test that was validated for a particular job in paper form may not be valid when administered on a computer, and a test validated on a desktop or laptop may or may not be valid when administered on a smart phone. Several studies comparing paper administration to computer administration and computer administration to mobile devices have been conducted.

Although there is some research on score differences and equivalence, there is little research on the validity of the same tests administered in different formats (e.g., paper and online versions) or on different devices. There are probably many reasons why such research is not conducted and published; however, a likely answer is the difficulty of acquiring an appropriate and reliable criterion to conduct a criterion-related validity study. Instead of validity studies, many researchers have turned to studies of the measurement invariance of scores across devices. Lack of invariance would suggest that the researcher should be concerned about the possibility that validities across different forms or devices are not equivalent. Research results indicate inconsistent patterns of equivalence across media. In addition, some researchers have established equivalence but noted higher scores or greater variance in one situation than in another. Consequently, some researchers (e.g., Buchanan & Smith, 1999; Lievens & Harris, 2003) emphasize that equivalence must be established for each new set of conditions because equivalence found under one set of conditions does not necessarily extend to another set of conditions.

Studies of the measurement equivalence of paper and computer-administered personality test have had mixed results. Some studies have concluded that the medium for administration has no effect on equivalence; others have reached the opposite conclusion. Several studies have compared scores from paper-based and computer-based tests. Although small differences in scores are sometimes found, most authors conclude that computer administration neither increases nor decreases socially desirable responding (Dwight & Fiegelson, 2000; Lautenschlager & Flaherty, 1990; Martin & Nagao, 1989; Potosky & Bobko, 1997; Richman et al., 1999).

Using item-response theory analyses, factor analysis, criterion-related validity and mean score differences, Chuah and colleagues (2006) looked at the equivalence of scores on a personality test administered on paper and online, and concluded that scores on neuroticism, extraversion, agreeableness and conscientiousness scales were equivalent. Salgado and Moscoso (2003) reached a similar conclusion regarding scores on a five-factor personality measure. They observed similar scores, factor structures and reliability estimates across the two formats, but noted greater variance in the computer-administered version of the test.

Morelli, Illingsworth, Scott and Lance (2012) evaluated the measurement equivalence and psychometric properties (configural, metric, scalar, measurement error, construct variance, and construct means) of a non-cognitive personality measure of conscientiousness, customer service, integrity, interpersonal, stress tolerance and teamwork given on mobile and non-mobile devices. They found scores from both types of device to be invariant, except for construct means. In addition, distributions, reliabilities, inter-correlations and descriptive statistics were similar. Illingsworth, Morelli, Scott and Boyd (2015) produced similar results. Using multi-group factor analysis, they demonstrated equivalence across mobile and non-mobile devices at the configural, metric, scalar and latent mean levels and the absence of meaningful practical score differences. Arthur and colleagues (2014) found a similar pattern: equivalence between the non-cognitive measures administered on mobile and non-mobile devices and no meaningful score differences.

Ployhart and colleagues (2003) and Mead and colleagues (2007) reached opposite conclusions. Looking at scores from a personality measure of conscientiousness, agreeableness and emotional stability, a biodata form and a situational judgement test administered in paper-and-pencil form and online, Ployhart and colleagues found the variance–covariance matrices were not equivalent, suggesting some sources of nonequivalence, and the online version had better distributional properties, lower means, more variance, higher internal consistency reliability and stronger correlations.

Mead and colleagues (2007) found equivalence on some measures (e.g., conscientiousness) but not all personality constructs when tests were administered using a paper-and-pencil form and an online form. When the study participants had a choice of format, metric invariance was present across formats; however, when participants had no choice, measurement invariance was not present.

Several researchers have found measurement equivalence between scores from tests administered on computers and those from tests administered on mobile devices; however, lower scores from tests administered on the mobile device appear to be consistent. Arthur and colleagues (2014) found measurement invariance when they compared scores on cognitive measures from tests taken on mobile and non-mobile devices and score differences with scores from tests taken on mobile devices to be significantly lower than those from tests taken on non-mobile devices. They also noted greater differences between scores on the verbal component of the test and scores on the numerical component.

Morelli and colleagues (2014) used multi-group confirmatory factor analysis to evaluate the measurement invariability of a cognitive ability test, multimedia work simulation, text-based SJI and a biodata measure of conscientiousness and customer service given on mobile and non-mobile devices. They concluded that the mobile and non-mobile versions of these tests were equivalent. They noted no score differences, except that the mean score for the SJI on mobile devices was lower than the non-mobile mean.

Several authors (e.g., Arthur et al., 2014; Hawkes, 2013; Mitchell & Blair, 2013) have hypothesized various reasons for the differences in scores from computer-based tests and mobile devices, among them the instability of the internet connection, the unavailability of a mobile application for the test, increased scrolling time, more difficulty manipulating the interface, more time required to read the small screen size, content incompatibility with the mobile device and higher-ability applicants' preference for the non-mobile device. This suggests that caution should be used when interpreting the research on mobile devices as portable devices range in size and ease of manipulation. For example, a small smart phone creates a different user experience from a tablet which in turn is different from a laptop, all of which are mobile devices.

Validity across cultures

Few researchers have systematically studied differences in validity across different cultures. In one such study, Baron, Martin, Proud, Weston and Elshaw (2003) compared cognitive ability scores and found consistent differences in scores among countries. In general, the scores from poorer countries with fewer educational opportunities were lower than those from wealthier countries with more educational opportunities. Baron and colleagues concluded that the validities (i.e., the relationships between test scores and job performance, training performance and educational opportunities) were consistent across countries.

Validity of non-traditional selection procedures

Validity studies of non-traditional selection procedures are scant in the literature. Credit checks are increasingly being used as a pre-hire selection device; however, work to systematically establish their job-relatedness or their relationship to job performance or other criteria of interest is lacking. Unlike credit ratings, which are objectively derived, information from social media is often used subjectively. The inferences made from these social media data have generally not been validated either. Similarly, many games used as selection devices do not result in a single score but rather give ratings based on the candidate's behaviour and made on behaviourally anchored rating scales. Validity studies for such tests are lacking in the published literature.

Future Research

In many respects, online testing is in its infancy and researchers and practitioners are only beginning to understand the opportunities that online testing programs offer, as well as the problems they present. One of the greatest challenges is the lack of information about online testing used globally. Another is the methodology to answer research questions that is appropriate for small sample sizes which are typically found in applicants from some countries in global testing programs. Ongoing research into online testing is required for testing professionals to use these tools effectively.

Tippins (2009a, 2009b, 2015) has compiled a list of research questions related to online testing, particularly when used in an unproctored environment, as well as other technology-enhanced assessments. Topics include questions about the extent to which cheating takes place, the effect of UIT on the validity and reliability of the tests, the impact of UIT on the individual and the organization, and applicant reactions. In addition, questions related to the implications of online testing for ethical practice, legal practice and professional guidelines are given. Although the list is long, it is neither complete nor unchanging. As research is conducted, some questions are answered, but new ones are raised. As the use of online testing continues, particularly in global programs, research needs to address the open questions practitioners face. This chapter concludes with a brief discussion of the future research that is needed in the three topics discussed above: 1) the globalization of selection systems that are enabled by online tools; 2) the security and cheating issues created by the use of online selection tools; and 3) the validity of online tools in light of the globalization of the instruments, the problems with security and the opportunity to cheat. Examples of research questions are provided followed by a brief discussion.

Research questions related to global online testing

- What are the best practices in developing tests that can be used cross-culturally?
- What are the best practices in evaluating test translations and adaptations?
- How can tests be shown to be equivalent across cultures when the sample size for some groups is small?
- Are applicant reactions to online testing the same across cultures?
- What are the factors that shape applicant reactions in each culture?

- Is the incidence of cheating stable across cultures?
- Are deterrents to malfeasant behaviour equally effective across cultures?
- How do cultural differences affect the validity of a test? Does differential validity exist across cultures, countries or linguistic groups?

One central question that often remains unanswered is the equivalence of tests across geographic and linguistic boundaries. Although best practices are well documented in standards such as ITC's *Guidelines for Test Adaptation*, procedures for developing equivalent tests and appropriately translating and adapting them are not guaranteed to produce a test that measures the same construct in every version. In addition, while there are multiple methods for establishing equivalence, many require large sample sizes that are not available to all test users for all sectors of the tested population. Thus, it is not always possible to establish equivalence across all the linguistic and/or cultural forms of the test. (It is worth noting that the problem of equivalence is further exacerbated when other variables, such as multiple device types, must also be included in the equivalence study.)

Another set of research questions deals with the responses to online testing in different cultures. For example, should testing professionals assume that the rates of cheating are similar regardless of culture or that the deterrents to cheating are equally effective regardless of where they are used? Similarly, applicants' reactions to technology-enhanced assessments may depend in part on their familiarity with the technology, which may in turn be predicated on where the individuals live. The level of acceptance of UIT may be dependent on individuals' experience with other UIT applications, expectations for appropriate testing conditions, the competition for jobs in the location, individuals' own definitions of malfeasant behaviours, as well as other factors.

Another important set of questions deals with the relationship between test scores and job performance or other criteria of interest (e.g., turnover, absenteeism, safe and dysfunctional working behaviours). Few studies have been undertaken that compare the validity of a single test used in different countries and languages. Even when such studies have been done, the results are often ambiguous. It is not clear if differences in validity are the result of the quality of the translation, cultural differences, characteristics of the sample or problems with the criterion measure.

Research questions related to security and cheating issues created by the use of online selection tools

- What kinds of cheating (e.g., assistance from a person or resources that are not allowed, use of a proxy) take place?
- How should cheating be defined operationally?
- What are the characteristics of those who are most likely to cheat in terms of demographics and test score?
- To what extent does cheating affect a test score?
- How is cheating detected?
- How effective are deterrents to cheating, such as warnings, honour statements and verification testing?
- Should an attempt be made to detect cheating on UIT?
- To what extent do external factors, such as the job level, the desirability of the job or the availability of other job opportunities, affect the incidence of cheating?

The open questions about cheating and test security are frequently discussed; however, definitive research that answers many of these questions is incomplete. Many of the questions deal with defining what cheating is and how frequently it occurs. Many studies put all forms of cheating into one category of malfeasant behaviour, which includes all acts related to testing that are not permitted. It is not clear if some groups defined by demographics or by ethnicity are more or less likely to cheat. Nor is it apparent that cheating occurs at the same rate across the entire range of test scores. Almost everyone agrees that cheating can occur when UIT is used, but there is disagreement on the operational definition of cheating. Similarly, there are multiple ways to detect cheating, but many of the statistical methods cannot be used until a large group has been tested, which is not always feasible in employment programs when applicants are continuously tested and hired. Other processes require verification testing, which adds to costs.

Several researchers have noted that deterrents to cheating, such as warnings and honour statements, decrease the frequency of cheating. It is not clear to what extent the threat of verification in contrast to the act of verification testing actually diminishes cheating.

Research questions related to the validity of online tools

- Which factors related to online testing lead to decreased validity? Does validity decrease because of cheating or because of interactions between characteristics of the test and features of the device on which the test is taken?
- What are the tradeoffs between the costs and benefits of online testing?
- What is the validity of non-traditional forms of testing, such as credit checks and information from social media?

Most researchers agree that online tests, even those given in unproctored conditions, have some validity. Many of the open research questions, however, deal with the relative validities of tests given via different media (e.g., computer vs. mobile device) or conditions (e.g., proctored vs. unproctored). The device and the nature of the test seem to affect the validity. Devices that are difficult to manipulate or to read may reduce the validity of test scores on cognitive ability tests. A related set of questions deals with the ethical obligations and legal requirements in some countries to use tests with higher validities. From a practical standpoint, several important questions explore the tradeoffs between increased validity and practical benefits, such as cost reductions and increased applicant pools.

As noted above, non-traditional forms of testing such as credit checks and data from social media are being used for hiring purposes; however, there are few data supporting the validity of such tools. Some argue for the job-relatedness of credit checks, assuming that success in one's personal finances carries over to responsibility in the workplace. Others argue that many events, some of which are beyond a person's control, e.g., extraordinary medical expenses can weaken a credit rating but do not suggest personal irresponsibility or carelessness.

In some respects, credit checks are a better predictor because credit ratings are typically quantified and based on objective data. In contrast, information derived from social media is rarely quantified and must be interpreted often against ill-defined standards. Again, there is little evidence that behaviours exhibited in one context will necessarily surface in a work setting at a later stage. In summary, much research remains to be conducted and put in the public domain so that it is accessible and can inform the decisions test users make. Those who use online testing must understand the tradeoffs between cheating and validity. In addition, research needs to guide the development of tests that measure the same constructs regardless of culture and national boundary in a manner that is valid.

Conclusion

In this chapter we have reviewed the growing use of online testing, reflecting the increase of internet usage and candidates' acceptance of this form of organizational engagement. While research in this area remains relatively sparse in comparison to other areas of organizational psychology, an increasing number of papers published since 2000 have helped deepen our understanding of the application and impact of this method as a potential tool to be used in the recruiters' armoury. In the previous section of this chapter we set out some of the gaps in our knowledge and how research studies may help continue to develop our knowledge in the coming years.

References

American Educational Research Association, American Psychological Association and National Council on Measurement in Education. (2014). *Standards for Educational and Psychological Testing.* Washington, DC: AERA.

American Psychological Association. (2010). *Ethical Principles of Psychologists and Code of Conduct.* www.apa.org/ethics/code/principles.pdf. Last accessed 17 June 2015.

Ariely, D. (2008). *Predictably Irrational: The Hidden Forces That Shape Our Decisions.* New York: HarperCollins.

Arthur, W., Jr., Glaze, R. M., Jarrett, S. M., White, C. D., Schurig, I., & Taylor, J. E. (2014). Comparative evaluation of three situational judgment test response formats in terms of construct-related validity, subgroup differences, and susceptibility to response distortion. *Journal of Applied Psychology,* 535–545.

Arthur, W. A. R. M., Villado, A. J., & Taylor, J. E. (2009). Unproctored internet-based tests of cognitive ability and personality: Magnitude of cheating and distortion. *Journal of Industrial and Organizational Psychology, 2,* 39–45.

Arthur, W., Woehr, D. J., & Graziano, W. G. (2000). Personality testing in employment settings: Problems and issues in the application of typical selection practices. *Personnel Review, 30,* 657–676.

Baron, H. (1996). Strengths and limitations of ipsative instruments. *Journal of Occupational and Organizational Psychology, 69,* 49–56.

Baron, H., Martin, T., Proud, A., Weston, K., & Elshaw, C. (2003). Ethnic group differences and measuring cognitive ability. *International Review of Industrial and Organizational Psychology, 18,* 191–238.

Bartram, D. (1996). The relationship between ipsatized and normative measures of personality. *British Journal of Occupational and Organizational Psychology, 69,* 25–39.

Bartram, D. (2000). Internet recruitment and selection: Kissing frogs to find princes. *International Journal of Selection and Assessment, 8,* 261–274.

Bartram, D. (2008a). Global norms? Towards some guidelines for aggregating personality norms across countries. *International Journal of Testing, 8*(4), 315–333.

Bartram, D. (2008b). The advantages and disadvantages of on-line testing. *In* S. Cartwright & C. Cooper (Eds.), *The Oxford Handbook of Personnel Psychology.* Oxford: Oxford University Press.

Bartram, D. (2013a). Scalar equivalence of OPQ32: Big Five profiles of 31 countries. *Journal of Cross-Cultural Psychology, 44*(1), 61–83.

Bartram, D. (2013b). A cross-validation of between country differences in personality using the OPQ32. *International Journal of Quantitative Research in Education, 1,* 182–211.

Bartram, D., & Burke, E. (2013). Industrial/organizational testing case studies. *In* J. A. Wollack & J. J. Fremer (Eds.), *Handbook of Test Security* (pp. 313–332). New York: Routledge.

Bartram, D., Warr, P., & Brown, A. (2010). Let's focus on two-stage alignment not just on overall performance. *Industrial and Organizational Psychology, 3,* 335–339.

Beaty, J. C., Nye, C., Borneman, M., Kantrowitz, T. M., Drasgow, F., & Grauer, E. (2011). Proctored versus unproctored internet tests: Are unproctored tests as predictive of job performance? *International Journal of Selection and Assessment, 19*, 1–10.

Brown, A., & Bartram, D. (2009). Doing less but getting more: Improving forced-choice measures with IRT. Paper presented at the 24th Annual Conference of the Society for Industrial and Organizational Psychology, 2–4 April, New Orleans, LA.

Brown, A., & Maydeu-Olivares, A. (2011). Item response modelling of forced-choice question-naires. *Educational and Psychological Measurement, 71*, 460–502.

Buchanan. T., & Smith J. L. (1999). Using the internet for psychological research: Personality testing on the world wide web. *British Journal of Psychology, 90*(1), 125–144.

Burke, E. (2006). *Better Practice for Online Assessment*. Thames Ditton, UK: SHL. www.shl.com/SHL/en-int/Thought_Leadership/White_Papers/White–Papers.aspx. Last accessed 28 July 2008.

Burke, E. (2009). Preserving the integrity of online testing. *Industrial and Organizational Psychology, 2*, 35–38.

Burke, E., Mahoney-Phillips, Bowler, W., & Downey, K. (2011). Going online with assessment: Putting the science of assessment to the test of client need and 21st-century technologies. *In* N. T. Tippins & S. Adler (Eds.), *Technology-enhanced Assessment of Talent*. San Francisco: Jossey-Bass.

Chuah, S. C., Drasgow, F., & Roberts, B. W. (2006). Personality assessment: Does the medium matter? No. *Journal of Research in Personality, 40*, 359–376.

Cizek, G. J. (1999). *Cheating on Tests: How To Do It, Detect It, and Prevent It*. Mahwah, NJ: Lawrence Erlbaum.

Christiansen, N. D., Burns, G. N., & Montgomery, G. E. (2005). Reconsidering the use of forced-choice formats for applicant personality assessment. *Human Performance, 18*, 267–307.

Davey, T., & Nering, M. (2002). Controlling item exposure & maintaining item security. *In* C. G. Mills, M. T. Potenza, J. J. Fremer & Ward, W. C. (Eds.), *Computer-based Testing: Building The Foundation for Future Assessments*. Mahwah, NJ: Lawrence Erlbaum.

Dwight, S. A., & Fiegelson, M. E. (2000). A quantitative review of the effect computerized testing on measurement of social desirability. *Educational and Psychological Measurement, 60*, 340–360.

Equal Employment Opportunity Commission, Civil Service Commission, Department of Labor, and Department of. (1978). *Uniform Guidelines on Employee Selection Procedures*. Federal Register.

European Federation of Psychologists' Associations. (2013). *EFPA Review Model for the Description and Evaluation of Psychological and Educational Tests Version 4.2.6*. www.efpa.eu/professional-development/assessment. Last accessed 17 June 2015.

Foster, D. F. (2013). Security issues in technology-based testing. *In* J. A. Wollack & J. J. Fremer (Eds.), *Handbook of Test Security* (pp. 39–84). New York: Routledge.

Foster, D. F., Mattoon, N., & Shearer, R. (2009). Using multiple online security measures to deliver secure course exams to distance education students: A white paper. kryteriononline.com/de_dl.htm.

Griffith, R. L., Chmielowski, T., & Yoshita, Y. (2007). Do applicants fake? An examination of the frequency of applicant faking behavior. *Personnel Review, 36*, 341–355.

Griffith, R. L., & McDaniel, M. (2006). The nature of deception and applicant faking behavior. *In* R. L. Griffith & M. H. Peterson (Eds.), *A Closer Examination of Applicant Faking Behavior* (pp. 1–19). Greenwich, CT: Information Age Publishing.

Griffith, R. L., & Peterson, M. H. (Eds.) (2006). *A Closer Examination of Faking Behavior*. Greenwich, CT: Information Age Publishing.

Hawkes, B. (2013). Developing evidence-based guidelines for testing on mobile devices. *In* C. Hedricks (Chair), *Goin' Mobile: Employers, Applicants, and Their References*. Practitioner forum conducted at the 28th Annual Conference of the Society of Industrial and Organizational Psychology, Houston, TX.

He, J., & van de Vijver, F. J. R. (2013). A general response style factor: Evidence from a multi-ethnic study in The Netherlands. *Personality and Individual Differences, 55*, 794–800.

Hense, R., Golden, J., & Burnett, J. (2009). Making the case for unproctored internet testing: Do the rewards outweigh the risks? *Industrial and Organizational Psychology: Perspectives on Science and Practice, 2*, 20–23.

Hoffman, E. (2000). *Ace the Corporate Personality Test*. New York: McGraw-Hill.

Hollinger R., & Lanza-Kaduce, L. (1996). Academic dishonesty and the perceived effectiveness of countermeasures. *NASPA Journal, 33*, 292–306.

Hough, L. M., & Schneider, R. J. (1996). Personality traits taxonomies and applications in organizations. *In* K. R. Murphy (Ed.), *Individual Differences and Behavior in Organizations* (pp. 31–88). San Francisco: Jossey-Bass.

Hui, C. H., & Triandis, H. C. (1989). Effects of culture and response format on extreme response style. *Journal of Cross-Cultural Psychology, 20*, 296–309.

Illingsworth, A. J., Morelli, N. A., Scott, J. C., & Boyd, S. L. (2015). Internet-based, unproctored assessments on mobile and non-mobile devices: Usage, measurement equivalence, and outcomes. *Journal of Business Psychology, 30*, 325–343.

International Standards Organization. (2011). *ISO-10667-2 Assessment service delivery – Procedures and Methods to Assess People in Work and Organizational Settings*. www.iso.org/iso/iso_catalogue/catalogue_tc/catalogue_detail.htm?csnumber=56436. Last accessed 7 June 2015.

International Task Force on Assessment Center Guidelines. (2009). Guidelines and ethical considerations for assessment center operations. *International Journal of Selection and Assessment, 17*, 243–253.

International Test Commission. (2001). International guidelines for test use, *International Journal of Testing, 1*, 93–114.

International Test Commission. (2005). *ITC Guidelines for Translating and Adapting Tests*. www.intestcom.org/upload/sitefiles/40.pdf. Last accessed 19 January 2015.

International Test Commission. (2006). International guidelines on computer-based and Internet delivered testing. *International Journal of Testing, 6*, 143–172.

International Test Commission. (2014). International guidelines on the security of tests, examinations and other assessments. Document reference ITC-G-TS-20140706. www.intestcom.org/Guidelines/Test+Security.php.

Jackson, D. N., Wroblewski, V. R., & Ashton, M. C. (2000). The impact of faking on employment tests: Does forced-choice offer a solution? *Human Performance, 13*(4), 371–388.

Kaminski, K. A., & Hemingway, M. A. (2009). To proctor or not to proctor? Balancing business needs with validity in online assessment. *Industrial and Organizational Psychology; Perspectives on Science and Practice, 2*, 24–26.

Kantrowitz, T. (2014). *2014 Global Assessment Trends Report*. Thames Ditton, UK: CEB SHL.

Kantrowitz, T. M., & Dainis, A. M. (2014). How secure are unproctored pre-employment tests? Analysis of inconsistent test scores. *Journal of Business and Psychology, 29*, 605–616.

Lautenschlager, G. J., & Flaherty, V. L. (1990). Computer administration of questions: More desirable or more social desirability? *Journal of Applied Psychology, 75*, 310–314.

Levashina, J., Morgeson, F. P., & Campion, M. A. (2009). They don't do it often, but they do it well: Exploring the relationship between applicant mental abilities and faking. *International Journal of Selection and Assessment, 17*, 271–281.

Lievens, F., & Burke, E. (2011). Dealing with the threats inherent in unproctored internet testing of cognitive ability: Results from a large-scale operational test program. *Journal of Occupational and Organizational Psychology, 84*, 817–824.

Lievens, F., & Harris, M. M. (2003). Research on internet recruiting and testing: Current status and future directions. *International Review of Industrial and Organizational Psychology, 18*, 131–163.

Martin, B. A., Bowen, C. C., & Hunt, S. T. (2002). How effective are people at faking on personality questionnaires? *Personality and Individual Differences, 32*, 247–256.

Martin, C. L., & Nagao, D. H. (1989). Some effects of computerized interviewing on job applicant responses. *Journal of Applied Psychology, 74*, 72–80.

Maynes, D. (2009). Combining statistical evidence for increased power in detecting cheating. caveon.com/articles/Combining_Statistical_Evidence_for_Increased_Power_in_Detecting_Cheating_2009_Apr_04.pdf.

McCloy, R., Heggestad, E., & Reeve, C. (2005). A silk purse from the sow's ear: Retrieving normative information from multidimensional forced-choice items. *Organizational Research Methods, 8*, 222–248.

Mead, A. W., Michels, L. C., & Lautenschlager, G. J. (2007). Are internet and paper-and-pencil personality tests truly comparable? An experimental design measurement invariance study. *Organizational Research Methods, 10,* 322–345.

Mitchel, D., & Blair, M. (2013). Goin' mobile. A mobile provider's foray into mobile assessments. *In* C. Hedricks (Chair), *Goin' mobile: Employers, Applicants, and Their References.* Practitioner forum presented at the 28th Annual Conference of the Society of Industrial and Organizational Psychology, Houston, TX.

Morelli, N. A., Illingworth, A. J., Scott, J. C., & Lance, C. E. (2012). Are internet-based, unproctored assessments on mobile and non-mobile devices equivalent? *In* J. C. Scott (Chair), *Chasing the Tortoise: Zeno's Paradox in Technology-based Assessment.* Symposium presented at the 27th Annual Conference of the Society for Industrial and Organizational Psychology, San Diego, CA.

Morelli, N. A., Mahan, R. P., & Illingworth, A. J. (2014). Establishing the measurement equivalence of online selection assessments delivered on mobile versus nonmobile devices. *International Journal of Selection and Assessment, 22,* 124–138.

Nye, C. D., Do, B., Drasgow, F., & Fine, S. (2008). Two-step testing in employee selection: Is score inflation a problem? *International Journal of Selection and Assessment, 16,* 112–120.

Ones, D. S., & Viswesveran, C. (1998). The effects of social desirability and faking on personality and integrity assessment for personnel selection. *Human Performance, 11,* 245–269.

Ones, D. S., & Viswesveran, C. (2001). Integrity tests and other criterion-focused occupational personality scales (COPS) used in personnel selection. *International Journal of Selection and Assessment, 9,* 31–39.

Ployhart, R. E., Weekley, J. A., Holtz, B. C., & Kemp, C. (2003). Web-based and paper-and-pencil testing of applicants in a proctored setting: Are personality, biodata, and situational judgment tests comparable? *Personnel Psychology, 56,* 733–752.

Poortinga, Y. H. (1989). Equivalence of cross-cultural data: An overview of basic issues. *International Journal of Psychology, 24,* 737–756.

Potosky, D., & Bobko, P. (1997). Computer versus paper-and-pencil mode and response distortion in noncognitive selection tests. *Journal of Applied Psychology, 82,* 293–299.

Richman, W. L., Kiesler, S., Weisband, S., & Drasgow, F. (1999). A meta-analytic study of social desirability distortion in computer-administered questionnaires, traditional questionnaires, and interviews. *Journal of Applied Psychology, 84,* 754–777.

Salgado, J. F., & Moscoso, S. (2003). Internet-based personality testing: Equivalence of measures and assessees' perceptions and reactions. *International Journal of Selection and Assessment, 11,* 194–205.

Sellman, W. S. (1991). Computer adaptive testing: Psychometrics, economics, and politics. Keynote address presented to the Workshop on Computer-Based Assessment of Military Personnel, April. NATO Defence Research Group, Brussels, Belgium.

Society for Industrial and Organizational Psychology. (2003). *Principles for the Validation and Use of Personnel Selection Procedures* (4th ed.). Bowling Green, OH: SIOP.

Stokes, G. S., Mumford, M. D., & Owens, M. A. (1994). *Biodata Handbook: Theory, Research, and Use of Biographical Information in Selection and Performance Prediction.* Palo Alto, CA: Consulting Psychologists Press.

Tate, L., & Hughes, D. (2007). To cheat or not to cheat: Candidates' perceptions and experiences of unsupervised computer-based testing. Paper presented at the annual conference of the Division of Occupational Psychology of the British Psychological Society, January, Bristol.

Tett, R. P., Anderson, M. G., Ho, C., Yang, T. S., Huang, L., & Hanvongse, A. (2006). Seven nested questions about faking on personality tests: An overview and interactionist model of item-level response distortion. *In* R. Griffith & M. H. Peterson (Eds.), *A Closer Examination of Applicant Faking Behavior.* Greenwich, CT: Information Age Publishing.

Tippins, N. T. (1992). Realizing cost savings through more efficient selection testing. Paper presented at the Society for Industrial and Organizational Psychology, May. Montreal.

Tippins, N. T. (2008). *Internet Testing: Current Issues, Research Solutions, Guidelines, and Concerns.* Symposium presented at the annual conference of the Society for Industrial and Organizational Psychology, April. San Francisco.

Tippins, N. T. (2009a). Internet alternatives to traditional proctored testing: Where are we now? *Industrial and Organizational Psychology; Perspectives on Science and Practice, 2,* 2–10.

Tippins, N. T. (2009b). Where is the unproctored internet testing train headed now? *Industrial and Organizational Psychology: Perspectives on Science and Practice, 2,* 69–76.

Tippins, N. T. (2015). Technology and assessment in selection. *Annual Review of Organizational Psychology and Organizational Behavior, 2,* 5.1–5.32.

Tippins, N. T., Beatty, J., Dragsow, F., Gibson, W. M., Pearlman, K., Segall, D. O., & Shepherd, W. (2006). Unproctored internet testing in employment settings. *Personnel Psychology, 59,* 189–225.

van de Vijver, F. J. R., & Leung, K. (1997). *Methods and Data Analysis of Comparative Research.* Thousand Oaks, CA: Sage.

Vasilopoulos, N. L., Cucina, J. M., Dyomina, N. V., Morewitz, C. L., & Reilly, R. R. (2006). Forced-choice personality tests: A measure of personality or cognitive ability? *Human Performance, 19,* 175–199.

Viswesveran, C., & Ones, D. S. (1999). Meta-analysis of fakeability estimates: Implications for personality measurement. *Educational and Psychological Measurement, 59,* 197–210.

Warr, P., Bartram, D., & Martin, T. (2005). Personality and sales performance: Situational variation and interactions between traits. *International Journal of Selection and Assessment, 13,* 87–91.

Waters, B. K. (1997). Army alpha to CAT-ASVAB: Four score years of military selection and classification testing. *In* R. F. Dillion (Ed.), *Handbook on Testing* (pp. 164–186). Westport, CT: Greenwood Press.

Wise, L. L., Curran, L. T., & McBride, J. R. (1997). CAT-ASVAB cost and benefit analyses. *In* W. A. Sands, B. K. Waters & J. R. McBride (Eds.), *Computerized Adaptive Testing: From Inquiry to Operation* (pp. 227–236). Washington, DC: American Psychological Association.

14

Gamification, Serious Games and Personnel Selection

Michael Fetzer, Jennifer McNamara and Jennifer L. Geimer

Introduction

The use of gamification and serious games has become a viable method for achieving key business objectives, with innovative applications in a diverse range of organizational initiatives. Customer attraction and retention programmes, employee recruitment and training strategies, marketing, performance management and talent measurement, to name a few, are increasingly leveraging gamification and/or serious games (DuVernet & Popp, 2014; Laumer, Eckhardt & Weitzel, 2012; Rodrigues, Costa & Oliveira, 2014). In fact, analysts estimate that the global serious games market will reach $10.96 billion by 2022 (Stratistics MRC, 2015). In addition, several surveys have indicated that the use of serious games and gamification will become more widespread in the next five years (e.g., Anderson & Rainie, 2012; Roberts, 2014). If these forecasts materialize, they could revolutionize the way organizations approach traditional business challenges.

The primary purpose of gamification and serious games is to enhance the level of engagement of the target audience. This increased level of engagement is predicted to lead to subsequent gains in important business outcomes, such as employee knowledge retention, market penetration, product awareness, employee performance enhancement and talent measurement. It is the potential for these gains and associated impacts on business growth and financial performance that has driven increasing interest and research in the use of these approaches in various business practices and processes.

In this chapter, we briefly consider definitions and the boundaries between gamification and serious games. We then primarily concentrate on serious games, recognizing that this covers gamification in general and the common challenges and potential benefits. In the next section, we cover current uses of serious games. We then discuss the rationale for using gaming techniques for personnel selection and offer practical guidelines for leveraging this methodology in a selection context. Finally, future directions in research and application of gamification and serious games are discussed.

The Wiley Blackwell Handbook of the Psychology of Recruitment, Selection and Employee Retention,
First Edition. Edited by Harold W. Goldstein, Elaine D. Pulakos, Jonathan Passmore and Carla Semedo.
© 2017 John Wiley & Sons Ltd. Published 2020 by John Wiley & Sons Ltd.

Understanding Gamification and Serious Games

The terms 'gamification' and 'serious games' are often used interchangeably. At a high level, gamification is the process of incorporating one or more game elements into a non-game context, whereas a serious game utilizes a number of game elements to create a game that will be used for purposes other than pure entertainment. The reason the two terms are used interchangeably is primarily due to the fact that there is no universally agreed number or even type of game elements required to cross the threshold from gamification to serious game (e.g., Susi, Johannesson & Backlund, 2007). Resolving this debate is beyond the scope of this chapter, so we have drawn on several sources (Bedwell, Pavlas, Heyne, Lazzara & Salas, 2012; Shute & Ke, 2012) to provide the reader with an overview of the elements typically employed in gamification and serious games (see Table 14.1). Certain attributes that might be expected when describing a game (e.g., engaging, fun) are not included due to their subjective nature; rather the focus is on objective characteristics.

Table 14.1 provides the reader with a solid foundation of typical elements currently used in gamification and serious game initiatives. This area continues to evolve, and new elements may be leveraged in future design and delivery.

Current uses of serious games

The number of ways serious games can be used is increasing and expanding beyond the areas where serious games have initially proved successful. According to one collaborative online database of serious games (serious.gameclassification.com), over 3,000 games have been classified according to their purpose (e.g., training, marketing), market (e.g., corporate, government, military, education) and target audience (e.g., general public, professionals, students), alongside user-contributed keywords. Although the database is extensive, it is probably an underestimate of the use of games for various purposes, because the database does not include many custom or proprietary games.

Today, serious games are used in healthcare, education, government, military and corporate environments. In healthcare, serious games have been used in such diverse areas as physical fitness, patient education, rehabilitation, clinical training, diagnosis of mental disorders, improvement of cognitive functioning and biofeedback control (Michael & Chen, 2006; Ricciardi & De Paolis, 2014; Susi, Johannesson & Backlund, 2007). In education, games have been used at all levels (pre-nursery through to postgraduate) to enhance learning and skill development across a wide number of subjects (Vogel, Vogel, Cannon-Bowers, Bowers, Muse & Wright, 2006; Wouters, van Nimwegen, van Oostendorp & van der Spek, 2013). These days, it would be rare to find a student in most developed countries that has not played at least one serious game during the course of their education (Michael & Chen, 2006).

The US government has utilized serious games across municipal, state and federal levels mainly for training employees in areas such as pandemics, biohazards, disaster management, city planning, police and firefighter training, ethics and policy training, and even defensive driving (Michael & Chen, 2006; Squire & Jenkins, 2003). The military is by far the largest developer and consumer of serious games (Susi, Johannesson & Backlund, 2007). Primarily used for training purposes, serious games offer the military a means to train its members on complex and/or dangerous situations that would otherwise be cost-prohibitive or too risky to accomplish in a real-world situation.

Although not primarily designed for training purposes, many consider the U.S. Army's release of the video game *America's Army* (www.americasarmy.com) to be the start of

Table 14.1 Game elements.

Game Element	Description
Interactive Problem Solving	This element usually involves solving a series of problems or completing a series of tasks, but can take other forms, such as responding to in-game characters, choosing appropriate paths (literal or figurative) to reach the goal, or collecting items or pieces of information that impact the outcome.
Specific Goal(s)	Every game should have one or more goals the player must accomplish. This may simply be gaining as many 'points' as possible or successfully completing the game. Some games are designed with competing goals in order to enhance the level of challenge (e.g., achieve the right balance between earning money and keeping the business running). Goals in games may be implicit or explicit.
Rules	Without some rules, a game would essentially be pointless. Rules may take the form of limiting certain actions or movements, requiring certain items to be obtained before being able to accomplish certain tasks or completing a series of tasks successfully in order to advance to the next level. A good game contains enough rules to make the game challenging, but not have too many rules that it leads to player frustration.
Adaptive or Branching Game Play	Games incorporate some form of adaptive or branching process to allow for multiple outcomes and/or game experiences. Some extremely complex games can give the impression that they a form of artificial intelligence built into them (although this has yet to be fully achieved), whereas other games leverage branching methods to increase the number of potential outcomes within a finite number of possible paths. Allowing multiple players to participate can greatly enhance this characteristic, as long as the actions of the other players can influence the experience/outcome.
Control	Players need to be able to influence the game play to some extent. Having total control would detract from the challenging aspect(s) of the game, but having no control would result in frustration or boredom. Games should encourage players to explore alternative paths to achieve the goal(s) by manipulating the game environment, characters or objects within the game, or the sequence in which they complete certain tasks or activities.
Ongoing Feedback	Feedback on a player's performance during the game provides the player with information on the success (or failure) of their actions in order to direct them towards achieving a positive or desired outcome. Feedback can be explicit or implicit. Explicit feedback can take the form of points displayed on screen, noting achievement of certain objectives, audio/visual cues when certain actions are taken or progression on to subsequent levels. Explicit feedback can also include comparison and/or competition with other players (e.g., ranks, badges, leader boards). Implicit feedback can be expressed by characters within the game or other subtle cues in the game environment.
Uncertainty	Similar to the characteristic of adaptive or branching game play, the use of uncertainty in a game evokes suspense and increases player engagement. The right move/action/decision should not be transparent, otherwise the game would be too easy and players would quickly lose interest. There does, however, need to be some rationale behind the uncertainty, so that players will understand the reason for the outcome once the move/action/decision has been made.
Sensory Stimuli	Sensory stimuli can refer to graphics (static or animated), video, sounds and/or storylines used to excite the senses and increase immersion in the game. Stimuli should be used in the right amount, as too much will overwhelm the player, but not enough could result in decreased engagement.
Technology-enabled	Given the increasing penetration of technology into daily life, most games incorporate some form of technology. This can take the form of multimedia (video or animation), computer/online delivery, smart phone apps or even popular gaming consoles.

today's serious gaming era. Towards the end of the 1990s, recruitment numbers were dwindling, and the Army needed a new tool to attract and engage its target demographic of 18–25-year-old males. Given the popularity of 'first person shooter' console video games such as *Halo* and *Call of Duty*, the Army hoped to capitalize on the potential to increase their recruitment numbers through a serious games approach (Gudmundsen, 2006). *America's Army* was and continues to be an extremely effective recruitment tool, enabling potential recruits to try their hand at various specialities and gain a quasi-firsthand experience of what it is like to be a soldier by playing a game that is very similar to popular entertainment games (Grossman, 2005).

In the corporate world, the use of serious games has increased exponentially over the past decade, and new applications are currently being developed (e.g., Dale, 2014). Like the military, the most prevalent use of serious games in corporate environments is for training. These cover teamwork, leadership, time and project management, communication skills, strategic planning, customer service, sales, on-boarding and, of course, job-specific skill development (Greco, Baldissin & Nonino, 2013; Lopes, Fialho, Cunha & Niveiros, 2013; Michael & Chen, 2006). In addition to training, serious games have been used to attract and retain customers, launch new products, enhance job performance and attract potential job candidates (Donovan, 2012). One promising new area for serious games in the corporate arena involves the use of serious games for personnel selection. This is discussed in the next section.

Rationale for Using Gaming Techniques in Selection

Given the wide range of tools and methods available for evaluating job candidates, and taking into consideration the years of research that support these approaches (e.g., Schmidt & Hunter, 1998), one may question the need for using gaming techniques in a selection context. However, as organizations continue to experience significant growth and profitability expectations, their ability to identify and attract the best talent efficiently will remain a critical business need. It is hypothesized that the use of gaming techniques has the potential to increase the predictive validity of assessment processes beyond what can be achieved with traditional methods as well as to yield engagement outcomes that are not possible with traditional methods.

Research has shown that high-fidelity work-sample assessments are valid predictors of job performance (Roth, Bobko & McFarland, 2005; Thornton & Kedharnath, 2013). This occurs because work-sample assessments reduce the inferential leaps that are required between candidates' scores on the assessment and their performance on the job. With most traditional selection tools (e.g., personality inventories and cognitive ability tests), the focus is on measuring competences or traits using multiple-choice items. Two inferential leaps are made: the first is between candidates' scores on the multiple-choice measurement tool and the degree to which they possess that competency or trait, and the second is between the competence or trait and how candidates will actually perform on the job. More robust predictions are achieved through the use of simulation assessments that require less inference. By putting candidates in situations that are similar to those they will encounter on the job, the goal of simulation is to elicit and measure behaviours similar to those that are required to perform the job. All else being equal, the closer a simulation comes to recreating the work environment and eliciting the full range of critical behaviours that are required for performance (U.S. Merit Systems Protection Board, 2009), the better the assessment will predict subsequent job performance.

Simulations and multimedia-based assessments are currently used to determine candidate suitability and measure knowledge, skills, abilities and other characteristics (KSAOS) that are critical for managers, customer service and sales representatives, clerical and administrative personnel, contact centre and collections agents, bank tellers, cashiers, manufacturing workers, professional staff and many others (for a comprehensive review, see Fetzer & Tuzinski, 2013). These are not only highly predictive of job performance (e.g., Lievens & De Soete, 2012; Schmidt & Hunter, 1998), but can potentially result in enabling organizations to augment their brand awareness, engage candidates and enhance positive perceptions of the company due to being at the cutting edge of technology, providing competitive advantage in the battle for talent.

The same rationale can be applied to support the use of gaming techniques. To the extent that these techniques are used to elicit in-game actions that mirror on-the-job behaviours, they will be more predictive of job performance than inferential measurement of traits or competences, all else being equal. Furthermore, gaming technology has the potential to increase the use of job-relevant behavioural assessments by increasing their scalability and cost-effectiveness. However, the greatest potential value of gaming techniques in a selection context arguably lies in a concept known as *stealth assessment*, which refers to embedding assessments in a game-like environment (Shute, 2011; Shute & Ventura, 2013; Shute, Ventura, Bauer & Zapata-Rivera, 2009). When players are engaged in playing the game, attentiveness to the fact they are being assessed is reduced and/or eliminated, due in part to a level of engagement not unlike Csikszentmihalyi's concept of flow (Csikszentmihalyi, 1990). This is the point at which candidates may become so immersed in the game that their true behaviours emerge, increasing the accuracy of the assessment, rather than being constrained or changed by social desirability and the propensity of candidates to second-guess their actions during employment assessment.

Development and Implementation of Serious Games for Selection Purposes

Developing and implementing serious games for personnel selection requires adherence to the same psychometric and legal considerations as any other selection tool, but there are some unique aspects that also need to be considered. We have grouped these into the following categories: objectives, design and utilization. Each aspect is discussed in turn.

Objectives

In order to design a game that is successful, game designers must first define what success looks like. The key objective that typically defines the success of any selection tool is how well it matches the needs of job performance criteria. More specifically, the stronger the correlation between candidates' scores and job performance measures, the more successful the tool. There are other ways to validate selection tools (i.e., content and construct validity methods), but a criterion-related approach provides evidence of the utility of the tool with regards to its ability to predict job performance.

Complete coverage of methods for analysing the domain of job performance and determining which criteria are most critical is beyond the scope of this chapter, but we will highlight the main ideas in order to provide a basis for the sections that follow. In simple terms, the first step in the process is to identify what aspects of job performance should correlate with scores produced by the game. These aspects can either be subjective criteria (e.g., supervisory ratings, customer satisfaction scores) or objective criteria (e.g., sales revenue, quality indices, production output). Once identified, these criteria need to be examined to determine which behaviours lead to successful job performance.

Once the behaviours have been determined, the game concept begins to take form. The behaviours form the basis for how the game is structured, specifically how these behaviours will be demonstrated during game play. The behaviours may be interpersonal (e.g., customer interaction, leadership, teamwork) or involve interacting with data or things (e.g., decision making, assembling parts, monitoring systems, safety procedures). It is important to understand not only which behaviours lead to successful job performance, but also which lead to poor performance.

Once the target performance criteria and related job behaviours have been identified, the next objective is to determine the measurement model. Will certain in-game behaviours lead to higher scores while others lead to lower scores? Will in-game behaviours lead to one overall score, or will sub-scores be produced? If the latter, how many sub-scores are needed? Will the sub-scores be rolled up into an overall score and if so, how will each sub-score be weighted? How will the scores be reported and what conclusions or interpretations should be made based on the results? Will a cut-score be required and if so, how will this be determined?

As with any other tool developed for use in personnel selection, a thorough job analysis is the foundation for answering these questions. Defining the job requirements in terms of type and level of KSAOs will inform the measurement model, which will in turn determine the scoring and reporting protocol. The validation and measurement objectives are the most critical elements of a successful game and serve to drive many aspects of design and utilization (see below). Much of the work involved in developing a game for selection purposes occurs before any coding begins and is time well spent once the game is operational. The technologies may be new and innovative, but adherence to sound psychometric principles and established procedures will lay the appropriate foundation to ensure the game provides a substantial return on the investment.

Design

In the design category, there are multiple elements that need to be considered. Aspects such as target audience, length, genre, multimedia style, scoring protocol, linear versus non-linear game play, branding and candidate feedback (in-game) should be addressed before development of the actual game begins. These elements will serve as a blueprint for building the game and will determine how the game is built and deployed. Each of these elements is detailed below.

Target audience   In a selection context, this element is always challenging from a game design perspective. There is probably a target audience that represents the majority of potential applicants, but in most cases the game should be designed for all potential applicants. This is primarily due to legal and fairness requirements, although these often lead to finding the most qualified applicants regardless of age, gender, and so on. In other words, the objective is to evaluate candidates on the skills and/or competences that lead to more successful job performance, and the game design should not lead to an advantage (or disadvantage) for any subset of candidates that are grouped based on characteristics that are not related to job performance.

The two most frequent demographic characteristics that are commonly associated with potential issues in using games for selection purposes are age and gender. Specifically, it is assumed that young males will have an unfair advantage over older generations and women because video games are associated with teenaged boys. That may have held true 10 years ago, but the demographics of so-called gamers are changing rapidly. In fact, the most recent report from the Entertainment Software Association (ESA) indicated the average game player in the US is 35 years old, with 44% of gamers aged 36 years or older, and females represent almost half (44%) of the US game-playing population (ESA, 2015).

Although the traditional lines dividing game play among certain demographic groups are blurring, it is still important to minimize potential demographic differences in selection scores when games are used. There are various ways to achieve this, with most focusing on the lack of complexity when it comes to the game structure and interface. By reducing complexity, the potential impact of prior gaming experience will be reduced and the less likely differences across demographic groups will be an issue. This does not mean the game itself should be easy; rather, it means it should be easy to learn how to *play* the game.

Length   Certain entertainment games can be played for hours or days on end. Despite the entertainment factor of serious games, length of game play is important. Most candidates will be applying for more than one job and in different companies, so if the selection process for one company is too great a time investment, candidate pools may start to shrink. Unfortunately, there is no simple answer to how long a selection game should be, but there are a few guidelines to consider.

First, the game should strike a balance between the time it takes to measure the target competences reliably and the amount of time spent in non-measurement sections of the game. These include the introduction and instructions, transitions between levels or scenarios, storyline sequences and any other part of the game that is not directly involved with soliciting player input. Second, candidates for higher-level jobs are more likely to invest time in the selection process than are candidates for lower-level jobs. A 3-hour game for a job that pays the minimum wage is not likely to be met with much acceptance. Third, at what stage the game is used in the selection process may have an impact on candidate retention. If the game is to be introduced in the later stages of the process, longer games may be more acceptable to candidates since they may perceive a greater chance of being hired and thus will be more willing to spend time completing the game. If the game is to be used early in the process, shorter games may be more appropriate. Fourth, every KSAO related to job performance does not *have* to be measured through the game. If there are shorter, more efficient assessments for certain KSAOs that would be difficult to measure in a game, these should be considered as part of the assessment process. Finally, current conventions related to candidate assessment time for traditional testing methods should be challenged, as time spent playing a game may be perceived as less arduous. In other words, an engaging, well-designed, 45-minute game may be less likely to see candidates drop out than a traditional test of similar length.

Genre   Genre refers to the structure, interaction and challenges of a game, and is a method for categorizing games. In the entertainment gaming space, there are many types of genres and even more subgenres. Those that are most relevant to today's serious games are described in Table 14.2. The examples provided are entertainment games, as it is anticipated that the reader will be more familiar with these.

In a selection context, the KSAOs to be assessed will be a major factor in determining the most appropriate genre. Interpersonal skills are typically best evaluated in adventure, RPG or simulation games. Critical thinking and decision making are a good fit for strategy games. Technical KSAOs lend themselves to action, simulation or even casual/mini-game genres. If multiple KSAOs are to be evaluated, combinations or hybrids of genres can be leveraged (i.e., action–adventure, RPG with embedded mini-games).

Table 14.2 Serious game genres.

Genre	Description	Entertainment Examples
Action	One of the broadest game genres, action games typically require players to respond quickly and accurately to game challenges.	Pong, PacMan, Mortal Kombat, MarioKart, Call of Duty, Grand Theft Auto, Halo
Adventure	Requires players to interact with in-game avatars, props and other elements of the environment in order to advance.	Myst, Portal, The Longest Journey
Role-playing (RPGs)	The player controls the actions of one or more characters through a series of quests while immersed in a fantasy world. Characters typically gain power and abilities as quests are completed.	Final Fantasy, Mass Effect, World of Warcraft
Simulation	Games that simulate the aspects of certain realistic (or semi-realistic) environments.	SimCity, Flight Simulator, The Sims, Formula 1
Strategy	Requires players to execute skilful, long-term planning, typically with regard to large numbers of characters and numerous resources across a large environment.	Age of Empires, Command and Conquer, Civilization
Casual (Mini-)	Games that are designed to be short, visually appealing distractions from day-to-day activities. These games are fairly simple, but offer frequent rewards and almost unlimited achievements. Casual games are most frequently played on mobile devices.	Angry Birds, Candy Crush, Peggle, Subway Surfers, Cake Mania, Plants vs. Zombies,

One topic that typically surfaces in discussions involving games for selection purposes is the difference between a serious game and a simulation. In fact, there is no difference, as simulations are a serious games genre. What distinguishes a simulation game from other game genres is essentially the degree of fidelity, or realism, represented throughout the entire experience. The more direct the link between actions or behaviours elicited during the game, the more critical it is to simulate the actual work environment. For example, evaluating pilots on their ability to fly a Boeing 767 would require a highly realistic simulation game as opposed to one that evaluated general piloting skills using a Second World War bomber game.

Game genres are useful tools to help guide the development process by providing a foundation for the game design. They are not meant to be absolute or mutually exclusive, but rather allow developers to draw on the existing knowledge base and best practices for creating an engaging game experience. A word of caution is appropriate here: resist the temptation to imitate the current 'game sensation' as it will probably have waned in popularity by the time your game development project is complete.

Multimedia style   The vast majority of both serious and entertainment games use computer generated (CG) animation. CG animation comes in two distinct forms: two-dimensional (2D) and three-dimensional (3D). 2D animation is characterized by 'flat' avatars, characters, environments and other elements that move in two-dimensional space. 3D is characterized by avatars, environments and other elements that appear to have depth. There are multiple varieties of 2D and 3D animation, some that are more realistic and some that are more stylized (see Figure 14.1 for examples).

In addition to CG animation, serious games make use of real people and environments through still images and/or video. This style of multimedia can be useful when conveying

Figure 14.1 Examples of 2D and 3D animation styles.

realistic emotions and actions is critical to the game objectives. New techniques in both photography and video can provide more immersive multimedia which can be manipulated by the player (think 'virtual/360-degree tour') during game play.

The choice of multimedia style can be driven by a number of factors, among them cost, time, branding, target audience and game genre. In general, video is more expensive than 3D, and 3D is more expensive than 2D. On the other hand, video is often faster to produce than 2D, which is faster to produce than 3D. Company branding may play a role in the choice of multimedia style depending on what style is currently being used in other areas of the organization. In terms of target audience, video may be more appropriate if your demographic is predominantly aged over 50, but the increasing use of CG animation in films and commercials makes it more appealing for older generations. Game genres are not tied to any particular multimedia style, although images and/or video may not be the best choice for casual or mini-games.

Scoring   How the game is scored, and what scores are reported, are key aspects of game design. In most cases, the scores produced will be related to the KSAOs measured during game play, either as indications of the specific KSAOs or as performance-based scores. These scores can be reported individually or as composites. As mentioned above, full coverage of the psychometric methods that lead to reliable and valid scores are beyond the scope of this chapter, and personnel with the appropriate training and experience in these areas should be key members of the game development project team.

Another consideration related to scoring is whether path- or outcome-based scoring is used. Path-based scoring is a cumulative approach, where the player is scored based on the paths chosen during game play. The number of paths that can be scored can be as few as two or three, or as many as the total number of possible combinations of all actions during game play. Outcome-based scoring involves evaluating the end-result of a player's actions during game play. In other words, how the player arrived at the particular outcome is not important, but rather which outcome was achieved at the end of the game. Outcome-based scoring is used primarily with strategy games, but can be applied to other genres if and when appropriate.

At a more granular level, one of the biggest elements of scoring in a serious game is what exactly is to be scored. Will it be limited to awarding points based on specific choices or actions during the game, or will it be more comprehensive and evaluate every action taken, or not taken, during the game? Should certain combinations or sequences of actions be scored higher than others? What other inputs could be scored? Should game time be scored? If so, is it overall time or time spent during different parts of the game? The answers to all questions related to scoring should be driven by sound scientific assessment principles, ensuring that scored elements are reliable and valid (e.g., related to the job requirements) and not just scored 'because we can'.

Linear versus non-linear   Related to scoring is the concept of linear versus non-linear game play. Linear refers to games where all candidates have essentially the same experience, regardless of their actions during the game. Linear games can result in sufficient score variance among candidates, but candidate actions do not change the game. Linear games are similar to most text-based assessments. That is, candidates can achieve different scores, but their response to each question does not alter the test.

In non-linear game play candidates' actions at specific points during the game influence their game experience after that point. In its simplest form, branching is a form of non-linear game play. For example, if the candidate chooses one of two possible actions, that decision will lead to two possible actions, which would be different from the possible actions presented if the candidate had chosen the other action in the first step. Despite its simplicity, branching game play can be quite complex from a game design and development perspective, depending on the number of branches possible during game play.

More complex versions of non-linear game play include adaptive designs (where the game challenges adapt to the level of the player), random events designs (where different challenges are presented randomly) and even designs that incorporate some degree of artificial intelligence (AI). These versions require much more effort and investment than linear or branching designs, so ensuring the added complexity will provide ROI in terms of validity should be a key consideration.

Branding In a selection context, an organization may want to take advantage of any branding opportunities available within the game. This is especially relevant if the game is to be more realistic and represent the work environment in some detail. Aspects such as colour values, logo placement, employee uniforms, signage, visual design, and so on should be determined in conjunction with the organization's marketing department. More often than not, organizations have a set of branding guidelines that are extremely useful to game developers.

Candidate feedback (in-game) In a selection context, this aspect of game design has been the subject of much debate, given the potential impact on test security. As noted above, ongoing feedback is a characteristic of serious games and usually takes the form of a score that is displayed continuously or at fixed intervals during the game. In most serious games designed for training and development purposes, this is done to enhance motivation and encourage repeated play in order to reinforce the learning objectives. When used for selection purposes, games that provide candidates with any sort of displayed score could result in the game being compromised and rendered ineffective. In addition, it would be rare to have candidates play the game more than once, as any practice effects would give repeat players an advantage.

Unfortunately, not providing any form of feedback in-game could reduce engagement and potentially increase the number of candidates who do not complete the game. Research on the amount and type of feedback is sparse, but initial studies offer some guidance (e.g., Geimer, Sanderson & Popp, 2015). At this point, the best proposed resolution to this issue is to provide fairly subtle, implicit feedback. This can take the form of a positive reaction from a game avatar if a certain action is chosen, a pleasant auditory stimuli (e.g., soft bell, chime) when the candidate successfully completes a certain activity or through advancement to subsequent levels. Of course, this could also aid those with malicious intent to reverse-engineer the game, but it would make it more difficult and less accurate than if a numerical score were displayed.

There is one final point to make here, especially when it comes to games that are designed to represent a realistic job environment (e.g., simulation games). In reality, our environments are filled with continuous feedback, some subtle and some not so subtle. This drives our subsequent actions, and a loop is formed until a particular interaction is completed. This is especially relevant when it comes to dealing with people. In a simulation game, a certain level of feedback is necessary to convey realism, as any absence of feedback would be perceived as unnatural and may influence game play.

More importantly, a key ability for most employees is to adapt their behaviour to the situation in order to be successful. Thus, most types of game need to incorporate some sort of continuous feedback in order to represent a true work environment, whether it is through branching or some other non-linear design. Not to evaluate candidates' ability to adapt to the situation and modify their behaviour would be a missed measurement opportunity and fail to utilize gaming methodology to increase validity.

In summary, there are a number of elements that need to be finalized before any actual programming is undertaken. For the most part, these are the key determinants of game success (or failure) and should not be taken lightly. As this chapter is intended as an overview of games in selection contexts, those who choose to embark on a project of this nature are advised to seek expert guidance on all of the areas outlined above.

Utilization

The elements covered in this subsection need to be addressed during the design stage too, but for the purposes of discussion have been grouped here. In other words, do not wait until the game has been developed before considering these elements, as doing so will usually require significant redesign. Conceptually, this subsection covers how the game is to be used and potential issues related to using a game for selection purposes. Like the preceding subsections, this is a fairly broad overview of areas and requires far more detail in an actual game development project, and so needs qualified experts to address them effectively.

Platforms and devices   One of the first elements to address is whether or not the game can be played on a mobile device. In most cases, games designed to be played on a PC or laptop are very different from those designed to be played on a mobile device, primarily because of the difference in screen size. Simply put, more information can be displayed on a PC or laptop screen than on a mobile device, and this leads to important decisions regarding the game interface and actual game play.

If the game is designed exclusively for PC or laptop use, there are still several areas to consider. How will the game be accessed? Does it have to be available via the internet, corporate intranet or only on designated local computers? If it is to be accessed via the internet, which browsers (and versions of browsers) need to be supported? Is a plan in place to support newer browser versions? What minimum resolution (screen size) does the game require? Will candidates need speakers or headphones in order to hear the game sounds? How fast should a candidate's internet connection be? What happens if the candidate is disconnected? Which operating systems (e.g., Windows, iOS, Linux) will be supported? Will a plug-in be required in order to play the game?

More questions need to be addressed if the game also needs to be playable on a mobile device (including a tablet). Does the game need to be playable on Android, iOS and Windows devices? Which mobile devices need to be supported? Is there a plan in place to update the game when new versions of these devices and/or operating systems are released? What is the minimum screen size needed to play the game? Will the game experience be the same on a mobile device as it is for those playing on a PC or laptop? Is a wireless internet (wifi) connection required, or can the game be played over the mobile network? What happens if the candidate drops the connection?

Determining whether the game should be mobile-enabled (i.e., playable on a mobile device but accessed through the internet) or developed as a mobile application (app) is another key decision. As a general recommendation, games for selection purposes should be mobile-enabled and not an app. First, it enhances security because the scoring protocol cannot be downloaded. Second, most candidates will be unwilling to download and install an app that they will play only once. Third, creating an app and making it available via the various app stores (e.g., iTunes, Google Play) adds time and cost to the project. Finally, data collection and retrieval are more efficient and reliable with mobile-enabled games.

Localization   Culturally adapting and translating a game for use outside the country or region it was originally designed for is known as localization. This involves translating the text and dialogue as well as ensuring all elements of the game have been adapted to cultural norms in order to ensure the equivalence of the KSAOs that are being measured. If possible, deciding in advance (i.e., before game design starts) which regions/languages will need to be supported is highly recommended, as this will provide useful input to how the game is designed in order to minimize the cost and time required to localize it.

If it is not possible to determine specific localization requirements in advance, even deciding whether or not the game will need to be localized at all is recommended.

A full explanation of the process and best practices of localization are beyond the scope of this chapter, but a few key questions follow to aid understanding of the importance of localization considerations. Will the game be accepted in the target culture as a selection tool? Is there anything in the original game that could be perceived as culturally inappropriate or even offensive? Are there any technical challenges to deploying the game in a different region? Are the KSAOs assessed during the game also important for job performance in the target culture? If so, how will measurement equivalence be determined? Will the game need to be validated in the target culture?

Depending on the game design, localization can be a fairly lengthy and expensive process or it can be short and inexpensive, so it is important to identify any localization requirements at the outset of the project. If the target languages or regions are known in advance, it is highly recommended to have translation or cross-cultural subject matter experts (SMEs) involved in the early stages of game design. If the languages are not known in advance but it is anticipated that there will be a need to localize in the future, then identifying a few of the principal languages that may be necessary will also help the SMEs advise on the design process. Of course, it is still possible to localize a game if it was initially built for only one language or region, but it will take longer and cost more than if localization considerations are known in advance.

Legal issues In the US, Canada, UK, Australia, South Africa, New Zealand, Israel, France, Germany, Chile, Japan, Belgium and elsewhere any form of assessment (including a game) used for selection purposes must meet certain legal criteria. In the US, the game must show evidence that it is valid for its intended use (American Educational Research Association, American Psychological Association, & National Council on Measurement in Education, 1999; Equal Employment Opportunity Commission, 1978; Society for Industrial and Organizational Psychology, 2003). In other words, research is required to show the job-relatedness of the score(s) produced by the game that are to be used for making employment decisions. Evidence is also required to show that the game is a reliable (i.e., consistently accurate) measure of whatever KSAO(s) it claims to measure. In addition, games used for selection should not result in an adverse impact for protected classes (racial/ethnic, gender and age groups). However, if the validation evidence clearly supports the use of the game, then the concern for adverse impact is mitigated from a legal perspective.

Although the bases for legal protections in the other countries noted above vary widely, all have some form of protection for members of specific groups. These protections outline requirements for many employment practices and nearly all have requirements specific to selection procedures. For a comprehensive overview of the legal environments for personnel selection in 22 countries, we highly recommend more detailed reviews (Myors et al., 2008; Sackett et al., 2010). Of course, a specific understanding of the legal requirements for each country is necessary for those who plan to utilize these methods in practice.

Single versus repeated play As opposed to games used in training environments, selection games are usually played only once. Since the purpose is to evaluate candidates' current skills, there is a strong need to avoid contaminating the scores obtained with practice. In other words, candidates should not be given the opportunity to play the game multiple times, as doing so will enable them to inflate their scores. The only exception to this is when playing the game multiple times does not impact the score.

Security As with all pre-employment assessments, there is a greater need for security when it comes to serious games used for selection purposes. In a training environment players who cheat (e.g., by attempting to get the 'right' answers from others) are only cheating themselves out of a learning opportunity, so the risk of cheating is small. In a hiring situation, especially one that is high-stakes, more players may attempt to 'game the game'.

Security considerations should not be taken lightly as serious games are developed and implemented in a personnel selection context. Care should be exercised in the development and implementation of the game to protect it from being compromised. The use of adaptive or branching methods is one way to increase a game's security, as is limiting access and allowing candidates to play the game once only. Other characteristics of serious games (e.g., uncertainty, non-linear design, game play rules) should be maximized in order to reduce the potential for cheating. In addition, ongoing monitoring is recommended to detect suspicious data trends and/or outright content breaches.

Future Research

Given the relative infancy of gamification and serious games as selection tools, there is a pressing need for research to further explore and better understand the many areas covered in this chapter. At this point, the following three categories are the most critical: validity, scoring methods and adverse impact. Aside from simulations, there is very little evidence regarding the validity of serious games when used for selection purposes. Criterion-related validity studies, especially those examining incremental validity compared to other (traditional) predictors of job performance, have yet to be published. Beyond that, comparative validity studies examining different game elements, genres, job performance criteria, multimedia styles and other characteristics would lead to further advancements.

Serious games also represent an opportunity to develop and refine new forms of scoring methods beyond the traditional question-and-answer approaches. Even in a relatively short game, hundreds or even thousands of potentially 'scoreable' events can be captured. Like consumers of other forms of 'big data', the challenge lies not in capturing the data, but rather in making sense of all the data that are available. Of course, from a theoretical standpoint, the question of which data should be captured and scored in the first place is paramount. However, there are certain to be advocates for the merits of 'dustbowl empiricism' (i.e., if the data correlate, they should be used even if the reason is not known) when the practicalities of traditional approaches are stretched to their limits.

Despite the shrinking gaps among gamer demographic groups, little is known about relative game performance across these groups. More importantly, which types of game have more (or less) adverse impact? What game characteristics can be modified in order to reduce adverse impact? Are there expected differences based on KSAOs measured? Or, better yet, do games result in little to no adverse impact in general, given their engaging and immersive nature?

On a broader level, leveraging ongoing research in other fields (e.g., education, training and development) is highly recommended to the extent it is relevant in a selection context. As the use of serious games for selection becomes more common, future research needs will become broader and deeper, assuming the relatively fundamental directions noted above are covered appropriately. Finally, as gaming technology advances, new research opportunities will evolve.

Conclusion

The use of serious games is becoming more common as a beneficial and effective method for accomplishing many different objectives across a wide variety of fields. Increasing engagement through the use of game design techniques has resulted in benefits that cannot be achieved using non-game approaches. As the use of serious games continues to expand, in terms of purpose and application, the use of games for selection purposes is somewhat inevitable. However, several factors deserve special consideration, including game objectives, design and utilization. Once addressed, serious games may have a marked impact on the field of personnel selection.

References

American Educational Research Association, American Psychological Association, & National Council on Measurement in Education. (1999). *Standards for Educational and Psychological Testing*. Washington, DC: American Psychological Association.

Anderson, J., & Rainie, L. (2012). The future of gamification. *Pew Research Center*. www.pewinternet. org/2012/05/18/the-future-of-gamification.

Bedwell, W. L., Pavlas, D., Heyne, K., Lazzara, E. H., & Salas, E. (2012). Toward a taxonomy linking game attributes to learning: An empirical study. *Simulation and Gaming, 43*, 729–760.

Csikszentmihalyi, M. (1990). *Flow: The Psychology of Optimal Experience*. New York: Harper & Row.

Dale, S. (2014). Gamification: Making work fun, or making fun of work? *Business Information Review, 31*, 82–90.

Donovan, L. (2012). *The Use of Serious Games in the Corporate Sector*. www.learnovatecentre.org/ wp-content/uploads/2013/06/Use_of_Serious_Games_in_the_Corporate_Sector_PRINT_ FINAL.pdf.

DuVernet, A. M., & Popp, E. (2014). Gamification of workplace practices, *The Industrial-Organizational Psychologist, 52*(1), 39–44.

Equal Employment Opportunity Commission. (1978). Uniform guidelines on employee selection procedures. *Federal Register, 43*(166), 38295–38309.

Entertainment Software Association. (2015). Essential facts about the computer and video game industry. www.theesa.com/wp-content/uploads/2015/04/ESA-Essential-Facts-2015.pdf.

Fetzer, M., & Tuzinski, K. (Eds.). (2013). *Simulations for Personnel Selection*. New York: Springer.

Geimer, J. L., Sanderson, K., & Popp, E. (2015). Effects of gamification on test performance and test taker reactions. Symposium presentation at the 30th annual conference of the Society for Industrial and Organizational Psychology, April. Philadelphia, PA.

Greco, M., Baldissin, N., & Nonino, F. (2013). An exploratory taxonomy of business games. *Simulation & Gaming, 44*, 645–682.

Grossman, L. (2005). The Army's killer app. *Time, 165*(9), 43–44.

Gudmundson, J. (2006). Movement aims to get serious about games. *USA Today*, 19 May.

Laumer, S., Eckhardt, A., & Weitzel, T. (2012). Electronic human resource management: Transformation of HRM? *Zeitschrift für Personalforschung*. Jahrg. 26, H. 3, 218–240.

Lievens, F., & De Soete, B. (2012). Simulations. *In* N. Schmitt (Ed.), *The Oxford Handbook of Personnel Assessment and Selection* (pp. 383–410). New York: Oxford University Press.

Lopes, M. C., Fialho, F. A. P., Cunha, C. J. C. A., & Niveiros, S. I. (2013). Business games for leadership development: A systematic review. *Simulation & Gaming, 44*, 523–543.

Michael, D., & Chen, S. (2006). *Serious Games: Games That Educate, Train, and Inform*. Boston, MA: Thomson Course Technology.

Myors, B., Lievens, F., Schollaert, E., Van Hoye, G., Cronshaw, S. F., Mladinic, A., et al. (2008). International perspectives on the legal environment for selection. *Industrial and Organizational Psychology: Perspectives on Science and Practice, 1*, 206–256.

Ricciardi, F., & De Paolis, L. T. (2014). A comprehensive review of serious games in health professions. *International Journal of Computer Games Technology*. dx.doi.org/10.1155/2014/787968.

Roberts, B. (2014). Gamification: Win, lose or draw for HR? *Society for Human Resource Management*. www.shrm.org/publications/hrmagazine/editorialcontent/2014/0514/pages/0514-gamification.aspx.

Rodrigues, L. F., Costa, C. J., & Oliveira, A. (2014). How gamification can influence the web design and the customer to use the e-banking systems. *Proceedings of the International Conference on Information Systems and Design of Communication*, 35–44. doi: 10.1145/2618168.2618174.

Roth, P. L., Bobko, P., & McFarland, L. A. (2005). A meta-analysis of work sample test validity: Updating and integrating some classic literature. *Personnel Psychology, 58*, 1009–1037.

Sackett, P., Myors, B., Lievens, F., Schollaert, E., Van Hoye, G., Cronshaw, S. F., Mladinic, A., et al. (2010). Perspectives from twenty-two countries on the legal environment for selection. *In* J. L. Farr & N. T. Tippins (Eds.), *Handbook of Employee Selection* (pp. 651–675). New York: Routledge/Taylor & Francis Group.

Schmidt, F. L., & Hunter, J. E. (1998). The validity and utility of selection methods in personnel psychology: Practical and theoretical implications of 85 years of research findings. *Psychological Bulletin, 124*(2), 262–274.

Schute, V. J. (2011). Stealth assessment in computer-based games to support learning. *In* S. Tobias & J. D Fletcher (Eds.), *Computer Games and Instruction* (pp. 503–523). Charlotte, NC: Information Age Publishing.

Schute, V. J., & Ventura, M. I. (2013). *Stealth Assessment: Measuring and Supporting Learning in Video Games*. Cambridge, MA: MIT Press.

Schute, V. J., Ventura, M., Bauer, M. I., & Zapata-Rivera, D. (2009). Melding the power of serious games and embedded assessment to monitor and foster learning: Flow and grow. *In* U. Ritterfeld, M. Cody, & P. Vorderer (Eds.), *Serious Games: Mechanisms and Effects* (pp. 295–321). Mahwah, NJ: Routledge, Taylor & Francis

Shute, V. J., & Ke, F. (2012). Games, learning, and assessment. *In* D. Ifenthaler, D. Eseryel, & X. Ge (Eds.), *Assessment in game-based learning: Foundations, innovations, and perspectives* (pp. 43–58). New York, NY: Springer.

Society for Industrial and Organizational Psychology. (2003). *Principles for the Validation and Use of Personnel Selection Procedures* (4th ed.). Bowling Green, OH: SIOP.

Squire, K., & Jenkins, H. (2003). Harnessing the power of games in education. *Insight, 3*(1), 5–33.

Stratistics MRC. (2015). *Serious Game Global Market Outlook – Trends, Forecast, and Opportunity Assessment (2014–2022), October*. Gaithersburg, MD: Market Research Consulting. www.reportbuyer.com/product/3326444/serious-game-global-market-outlook-trends-forecast-and-opportunity-assessment-2014-2022.html.

Susi, T., Johannesson, M., & Backlund, P. (2007). *Serious Games – An Overview*. Technical report. University of Skövde, Sweden.

Thornton, G. C., & Kedharnath, U. (2013). Work sample tests. *In* K. F. Geisinger (Ed.), *APA Handbook of Testing and Assessment in Psychology. Vol. 1, Test Theory and Testing and Assessment in Industrial And Organizational Psychology* (pp. 533–550). Washington, DC: American Psychological Association.

U.S. Merit Systems Protection Board. (2009). *Job Simulations: Trying out for a Federal Job*. Washington, DC: U.S. Merit Systems Protection Board. www.mspb.gov/netsearch/viewdocs.aspx?docnumber=452039&version=453207&application=ACROBAT.

Vogel, J. J., Vogel, D.S., Cannon-Bowers J., Bowers C.A., Muse K., & Wright, M. (2006). Computer gaming and interactive simulations for learning: A meta-analysis. *Journal of Educational Computing Research, 34,* 229–243.

Wouters, P., van Nimwegen, C., van Oostendorp, H., & van der Spek, E. D. (2013). A meta-analysis of the cognitive and motivational effects of serious games. *Journal of Educational Psychology, 105,* 249–265.

15

Team Assessment and Selection

Mengqiao Liu, Jason L. Huang and Marcus W. Dickson

Introduction

Teams have increasingly become the centre of organizational life, and decades of research have concluded that team effectiveness is the result of a combination of individual behaviour, interaction among team members, team characteristics, team process and team contextual influences. Highlighting team members as the key component of team effectiveness, the Input-Process-Output framework (McGrath, 1964) proposed and described a model in which team members' attributes, combined with other team-level contextual factors, drive team performance via team processes. Although considerable knowledge has been gained about the nature of teams and the contributing factors of team effectiveness, more remains to be learned on team staffing.

The purpose of this chapter is to provide a comprehensive, up-to-date literature review on how to assess and select individuals for teams in order to optimize team performance and effectiveness. In determining the scope of this chapter, we focus on the literature published since 2007, while incorporating findings highlighted in previous reviews on teams (Cohen & Bailey, 1997; Guzzo & Dickson, 1996; Mathieu, Maynard, Rapp & Gilson, 2008).

The chapter is organized into three main themes: the nature of teams (team type, team tasks and team task analysis, team contextual factors); the knowledge, skills, abilities and other personal characteristics (KSAOs) for effective teamwork; and assessment tools for team member candidates. In closing the chapter, we highlight several promising avenues for future research on team assessment and selection. By providing a synthetic review of the current literature on team assessment and selection, we hope to inform team researchers of the latest updates in the literature and foster more cutting-edge research in the near future.

The Wiley Blackwell Handbook of the Psychology of Recruitment, Selection and Employee Retention, First Edition. Edited by Harold W. Goldstein, Elaine D. Pulakos, Jonathan Passmore and Carla Semedo.

The Nature of Teams

An important distinction between individual selection and team selection lies in the need for the latter to determine how individuals with certain KSAOs will fit in a team. Therefore, prior to deriving the KSAOs needed for effective teamwork, a good understanding of the team, including team type, team tasks and team contextual factors, is in order.

Team type

Team type is a key element to understanding the determinants of team success. Whether it is a top management team (TMT) of a multinational company that operates on a long-term basis or a project team that convenes to tackle a single project for a short duration, the implications for selection can vary drastically.

Although there is no single, universally accepted taxonomy of teams, many researchers have attempted to categorize and summarize the types of team typically seen in research and practice (e.g., Cohen & Bailey, 1997; Devine, 2002; Hollenbeck, Beersma & Schouten, 2012; Klimoski & Jones, 1995; Sundstrom, McIntyre, Halfhill & Richards, 2000). A simple classification of teams was proposed by Devine (2002), which includes physical work teams (e.g., medical, military, production, service) and knowledge work teams (e.g., design, management, negotiation). Cohen and Bailey (1997) summarized four types: 1) work teams, 2) parallel teams, 3) project teams and 4) management teams. Using three dimensions underlying the type of teams (i.e., skill differentiation, authority differentiation, temporal stability), Hollenbeck and colleagues (2012) provided a comprehensive summary of 42 different team types identified in the organizational sciences. Based on team competence requirements, Cannon-Bowers and Bowers (2011) proposed four categorizations: 1) team-contingent, 2) task-contingent, 3) context-driven and 4) transportable.

Empirical evidence stemming from meta-analyses supports the importance of analysing team types. Bell, Villado, Lukasik, Belau and Briggs (2011) found that the relationship between functional background variety diversity and team performance was stronger for creativity and innovation teams and design/cross-functional teams than other types of teams (e.g., efficiency teams, TMT), indicating that the type of team (e.g., design or cross-functional teams) might serve as a situational cue to heighten team members' awareness of their functional backgrounds. Chiocchio and Essiembre (2009) argued that outcome performance is more salient in project teams compared to production or service teams, and that project teams rely more on a high level of team cohesion to plan, manage and complete projects interdependently compared to other types of teams. As expected, they found that team type significantly moderated the cohesion– performance relationship, such that cohesion contributed more to team performance in project teams when compared to production teams and service teams.

Team tasks and team task analysis

Multiple perspectives have been taken to describe team task demands, and many of them place interdependence at the core of understanding the nature of team tasks. On this notion, Cannon-Bowers and Bowers (2011) proposed four categories of team tasks based on interdependence: 1) pooled interdependence (group output is the sum of individual output; e.g., sales teams), 2) sequential interdependence (group output is a sequence of individual output; e.g., assembly lines), 3) reciprocal interdependence (group output is an interaction between two team members; e.g., command-and-control teams) and 4) team interdependence (group output is an interaction among all team members; e.g., self-managed work teams). The importance of task interdependence is highlighted in a meta-analysis by Gully, Devine and Whitney (2002), who found that task interdependence moderated the cohesion–performance relationship such that the relationship was stronger when task interdependence was high.

The goal of a team task analysis (TTA) is to identify KSAOs that can optimize the completion of team tasks. While job analysis conducted for team assessment and selection may in many ways resemble its counterpart for individual-based selection, team-based job analysis requires consideration of a variety of factors that contribute to both effective task performance and effective teamwork. Similar to individual-based selection, team task analysis is crucial to the success of team selection, yet research pertaining to TTA has only recently emerged (see Arthur, Villado & Bennett, 2012; Cannon-Bowers & Bowers, 2011; Mohammed, Cannon-Bowers & Foo, 2010). Most research on team job analysis has either been part of a larger study on team selection or an application of TTA in specific team interventions (Zaccaro & DiRosa, 2012). Due to the lack of research dedicated to validating TTA techniques, typical TTA has employed methods from individual-based task analysis, which often ignores the important contextual factors and multilevel principles entailed in a TTA (Mohammed et al., 2010).

As jobs performed in a team do not necessarily require team interdependence, team-based job analysis should employ specific strategies to uncover and differentiate individual- and team-based tasks via the level of coordination and interdependence (i.e., the extent to which successful performance of the job relies on team members working together). Research has shown that team relatedness and team workflow can be used as effective metrics for interdependence (Arthur, Edwards, Bell, Villado & Bennett, 2005; see also Arthur et al., 2012).

Pertaining to the procedures of TTA, Burke (2004) proposed seven steps: 1) conducting a requirements analysis, 2) identifying the job tasks, 3) identifying a taxonomy of teamwork, 4) conducting a coordination analysis, 5) determining relevant task work and teamwork tasks, 6) deriving KSAs from tasks and 7) linking KSAs to team tasks. Emphasizing the role of team interdependence (i.e., team-relatedness and team workflow), Arthur and colleagues (2012) proposed a model for identifying team-based tasks in a sequence of three steps: 1) generating a comprehensive list of tasks that constitute a job, 2) identifying job tasks that are team-based and 3) employing a detailed task analysis for tasks identified in the second step. Taking a contingency and multilevel perspective of TTA, Mohammed and colleagues (2010) proposed a conceptual framework for team selection, where a team's task demands (e.g., interdependence, coordination demands, behavioural discretion, role specialization, structure and level of autonomy) should be thoroughly examined before individual- and team-level KSAOs are derived. Some research has also been done to explore TTA techniques for tasks in particular types of teams (e.g., crime scene investigation teams, Smith, Baber, Hunter & Butler, 2008; military teams, van Berlo, Lowyck & Schaafstal, 2007; close air support teams, Zobarich, Lamoureux & Martin, 2007).

Team contextual factors

Teams function in contexts that may promote or hinder their effectiveness. Therefore, it is necessary to develop a solid understanding of the contextual factors affecting team effectiveness. Positioning teams as the primary level of analysis, teams are embedded in organizations, which are nested within larger societal and cultural environment. Earlier reviews (Guzzo & Dickson, 1996; Mathieu et al., 2008) provided two broad categories of team contextual factors, including the organizational context (e.g., organizational culture reward system, supervision) and the broader environmental context (e.g., culture, industry, market). In the following subsections, we discuss the latest research on organizational contextual influences (i.e., contextual factors on the organizational level) and environmental contextual factors (i.e., contextual factors that are outside of the organization).

Organizational contextual influences Organizational contextual factors have been shown to exert direct and moderating effects on team effectiveness (Mathieu et al., 2008). Using data from two field studies, Liu, Chen and Yao (2011) demonstrated organizational-level autonomy support had a direct positive impact on harmonious passion (i.e., 'autonomous internalization of an activity, making it part of one's identity and thus creating a sense of personal enjoyment and free choice about pursuing the activity', p. 294), which in turn led to increased individual creativity. The authors further demonstrated that organizational-level autonomy support had compensating effects for individual autonomy orientation (i.e., 'to be self-regulating and to orient toward the interest value of the environment and contextual supports for self-initiation', Baard, Deci & Ryan, 2004, pp. 2048–2049), such that the joint contribution of organizational-level autonomy support and individual autonomy orientation on harmonious passion was stronger for employees with lower levels of autonomy orientation. Similarly, the compensating effect of organizational-level autonomy support was shown for team-level autonomy support, such that teams with lower levels of autonomy support benefited more from a high level of organizational-level autonomy support. Their findings suggest that the benefit of unit-level autonomy support is more salient among individual team members who lack autonomy orientation as well as among teams with low levels of autonomy support.

Focusing on team bureaucratic practices (centralization and formalization), Hirst, van Knippenberg, Chen and Sacramento (2011) argued that team centralization and formalization would hinder individuals' abilities to explore and develop creative ideas, and would thus moderate the relationship between individual goal orientation and creativity. In a sample of 95 teams at the Taiwan Customs Bureau, Hirst and colleagues found that individual learning goal orientation (i.e., an intrinsic interest in learning and mastery of the task; Dweck, 1986) had a stronger positive relationship with individual creativity in teams with low centralization, whereas individual performance-avoid goal orientation (i.e., an extrinsic interest in the demonstration of competence by avoiding unfavourable judgements; VandeWalle, 1997) showed a stronger negative effect on individual creativity when teams were highly centralized. In addition, team formalization interacted with individual performance-proved goal orientation (i.e., an extrinsic interest in the demonstration of competence by gaining favourable judgements; VandeWalle, 1997) and performance-avoid goal orientation to influence individual creativity.

Environmental contextual influences In recent years, research has been conducted to investigate the direct and moderating effects of culture and its values on team functioning and effectiveness. Using Hofstede's (1980) cultural value dimensions, Taras, Kirkman and Steel (2010) examined the correlations between country-level cultural values and organizational outcomes. The results of their meta-analysis showed that innovation was positively related to individualism and negatively related to uncertainty avoidance, while conformity was positively associated with power distance and negatively associated with individualism. In addition, individualism was shown to be negatively related to satisfaction with the supervisor. Although cultural values were not directly linked to team-level outcomes, these findings certainly provide insight into the potential impact of culture on team functioning and performance.

Despite the long-theorized influence of micro- and macro-contexts on team functioning, little progress has been made to systematically examine such relationships. One exception is Project GLOBE (Global Leadership and Organizational Behavior Effectiveness; House et al., 2004), a 62-nation, cross-cultural leadership study. In particular, GLOBE identified nine cultural dimensions (performance orientation, future orientation, gender egalitarianism, assertiveness, institutional collectivism, in-group collectivism, power distance, humane orientation and uncertainty avoidance) that can be studied at the organizational and national levels. It was found that team members holding different cultural values prefer different leadership styles. This framework can also be applied to cross-cultural team research to identify the cultural contingencies to the relationships between team member attributes and team effectiveness.

KSAOs for Team Effectiveness

Interdependence among team members makes it necessary to consider the composition of team KSAOs as a whole, with the assumption that members' KSAOs may jointly influence team effectiveness. Therefore, the identification of KSAOs for team effectiveness warrants an examination of individual- (i.e., KSAOs at the individual level) and team-level KSAOs (i.e., team compositions of individual KSAOs), as well as the dynamic interplay between individual- and team-level KSAOs, and their joint influence on team effectiveness.

Individual-level KSAOs

The literature on individual-level KSAOs in team performance is extensive (see Table 15.1 for a summary of relevant individual-level and team-level KSAOs; Cannon-Bowers & Bowers, 2011; Mohammed et al., 2010). Researchers have exerted considerable effort into investigating moderators and mediators that further specify the boundaries, conditions and mechanisms underlying the effects of these KSAOs. Given that most of the studies revolve around the individual dispositional traits of team members, we group our discussion into dispositional traits and other individual attributes (skills, abilities, values and attitudes).

Dispositional traits   Using the five-factor model (FFM) of personality (McCrae & Costa, 1985), researchers have continued linking personality to team effectiveness. In a sample of MBA student teams, conscientiousness and emotional stability predicted both individual work performance and team performance, and a composite of these two personality traits with leadership and interpersonal skills provided incremental validity above and beyond general mental ability (Zimmerman, Triana & Barrick, 2010). Jung, Lee and Karsten (2012) discovered that, although extraverted individuals outperformed introverts in idea generation (measured by the number of unique ideas and the number of diverse ideas) in computer-mediated groups (CMGs), this advantage was only evident when cognitive stimulation was at a moderate or high level, but not in low or extremely high levels. Jung and colleagues' findings suggest that although extraverts might be more suited in teams with stimulating environments (e.g., CMGs), too little or too much cognitive stimulation might be ineffective or cognitively taxing. Focusing on voice behaviour (i.e., speaking up) in teams, Lee, Diefendorff, Kim and Bian (2014) found that agreeableness and extraversion positively related to supervisor-rated voice behaviours, and the linkage between agreeableness and voice behaviours was amplified by team participative climate.

Table 15.1 Individual- and team-level KSAOs for team assessment and selection.

Attribute	Individual-Level	Team-Level
Knowledge	Knowledge of teamwork skills	Team shared knowledge of teamwork skills
	Knowledge of team roles	Team shared knowledge of team roles
Skills	Performance monitoring	Team mutual performance monitoring
	Interpersonal skills	Team interpersonal skills
	Team management/leadership	Team self-leadership
	Communication skills	Team quality of communication
	Cross-boundary skills	Team of cross-boundary skills
Abilities	Adaptability	Team adaptability
	General mental ability	Team general mental ability (GMA)
	Emotional intelligence	Team emotional intelligence profile
	Metacognition	Team metacognition
Personality	Conscientiousness	Team conscientiousness
	Agreeableness	Team agreeableness
	Openness to experience	Team openness to experience
	Emotional stability	Team emotional stability
	Extraversion	Team extraversion
	Positive affect	Team positive affect
	Psychopathy	Team psychopathy
	Implicit aggression	Team implicit aggression
Values and Attitudes	Preference for teamwork	Team shared preference for teamwork
	Collectivism	Team collectivism
	Uncertainty avoidance	Team uncertainty avoidance
	Power distance	Team power distance
	Masculinity	Team masculinity
	Autonomy orientation	Team autonomy orientation
	Goal orientation	Team goal orientation
	Collectivism	Team collectivism
	Self-efficacy	Team collective efficacy or team potency
	Need for achievement	Team need for achievement
	Need for affiliation	Team need for affiliation
	Need for power	Team need for power
Demographics	Age	Age diversity
	Gender	Gender diversity
	Race/ethnicity	Race/ethnicity diversity
	Education	Education diversity
	Work experience	Work experience diversity
	Nationality	Nationality diversity

Besides the Big Five traits, proactive personality and its role in teams has received increasing attention in recent years. In addition to demonstrating a direct link between proactive personality and individual organizational citizenship behaviours (OCB), Li, Liang and Crant (2010) found that this relationship is mediated by a high-quality leader–member exchange (LMX) and strengthened by the work team's procedural justice climate. In 95 research and development (R&D) teams across 33 Chinese companies, Chen, Farh, Campbell-Bush, Wu and Wu (2013) demonstrated that the effect of proactive personality on individual innovative performance in teams was mediated by individual motivational states (i.e., role-breadth self-efficacy and intrinsic motivation). Findings from Li and colleagues and Chen and colleagues suggest that the effect of proactive personality on team performance was channelled through its positive impact on employees' exchange relationships with their supervisors as well as on their motivational states.

Emerging research has focused on individual dispositions that capture how team members perceive and evaluate their abilities and self-worth, such as core self-evaluations (CSE; a higher-order trait underlying individuals' fundamental, subconscious evaluations about themselves, which encompasses self-esteem, emotional stability, generalized self-efficacy and internal locus of control; Judge, Locke & Durham, 1997) and specific self-efficacy. Linking creative self-efficacy to individual creativity in teams, Richter, Hirst, van Knippenberg and Baer (2012) proposed that team informational resources serve as boundary conditions for the impact of CSE on individual creativity. As expected, they found a three-way interaction between creative self-efficacy and two types of team informational resources (shared 'knowledge of who knows what' (KWKW) and functional background diversity) in 34 R&D teams in four countries. In particular, the positive impact of creative self-efficacy on individual creativity was amplified in teams with higher levels of shared KWKW, and this interaction existed only in teams with high functional background diversity. Also interested in team innovation, Keller (2012) demonstrated that internal locus of control, self-esteem and innovative orientation each led to better job performance and innovativeness in project teams, and such effects were even stronger when the tasks at hand were non-routine, allowing more scope for individual characteristics to exert impact on performance and innovativeness.

Focusing on individual orientation, Hirst and colleagues (2011) argued that individuals with a high performance-avoid goal orientation will focus on performing the required tasks and avoid challenges that may give rise to creativity. Results supported their expectation and showed that performance-avoid goal orientation was negatively related to creativity. Liu, Zhang, Wang and Lee (2011) demonstrated that individuals with a high autonomy orientation tended to perceive a higher level of psychological empowerment, which subsequently led to lower voluntary turnover. While team leaders' and peers' autonomy support had an overall positive influence on members' psychological empowerment, this positive link was even stronger when team members perceived a large differentiation (i.e., varying levels) in autonomy support from leaders or peers. The authors further demonstrated that psychological empowerment mediated the interactive effect of autonomy support (from team leaders and peers) and its differentiation on individual voluntary turnover.

Other attributes   There are a few studies that examine individual knowledge, skills and abilities relating to team performance. Shi, Johnson, Liu and Wang (2013) found that individuals with higher political skill were viewed more positively (i.e., reward recommendation) by their supervisors in construction management teams, potentially because of better networking abilities and adaptability. To further explain the mechanism underlying this relationship, Shi and colleagues proposed and demonstrated that the positive link between political skill and supervisor evaluations was mediated by the frequency of interaction between team members and supervisors, and the positive effect of members' political skill on interaction frequency with supervisors was further moderated by supervisors' political behaviour. Based on trait activation theory (Tett & Burnett, 2003), Farh, Seo and Tesluk (2012) found that emotional intelligence (EI) was more positively related to teamwork effectiveness when the team had higher managerial work demands with more salient, emotion-based cues. In a simulation-based team training context, Ellington and Dierdorff (2014) applied a self-regulation theory framework (Kanfer & Kanfer, 1991) and demonstrated a positive relationship between metacognition (i.e., self-monitoring of learning) and a team member's declarative and procedural knowledge of training content, which was fully mediated by self-efficacy and heightened by team context (i.e., team overall performance and quality of cooperation). Findings from Ellington and Dierdorff highlight the importance of viewing individual- and team-level learning processes interactively rather than independently.

Values refer to relatively enduring 'beliefs about desirable behaviors that transcend specific situations, guide the evaluation of behavior, and are ordered in an individual in terms of relative importance' (Bell, 2007, p. 597). In a sample of 135 class project teams, Arthaud-Day, Rode and Turnley (2012) demonstrated that individual values of benevolence (loyalty, honesty, helpfulness and responsibility), achievement (ambition, influence, capability and success), self-direction (creativity, independence and curiosity) and conformity (politeness, self-discipline and obedience) predicted OCBs. Given a heightened interest in cross-cultural and global issues in the workplace, more and more research has been done to examine cultural values and their impact on team effectiveness. Although not directly linking cultural values to team performance, in a 2010 meta-analysis, Taras and colleagues (2010) pointed out several important cultural value dimensions that can be crucial to team functioning and effectiveness. Using Hofstede's cultural value dimensions (1980), Taras and colleagues found that individuals with high levels of uncertainty avoidance tended to harbour higher team commitment but also showed less innovation. In addition, team members holding different cultural values prefer different types of leadership style (see also House et al., 2004). Overall, cultural values have higher predictive validity for team-related attitudes compared to personality traits and demographics. In another study using MBA teams, Glew (2009) demonstrated that individuals who value sense of accomplishment received more *negative* evaluations from peers. This surprising result, as the author conjectured, was possibly due to peers' perception that such individuals prioritize personal goals over group goals, something that may not be viewed positively by other team members.

Team-level KSAOs

Research pertaining to compositions of KSAOs in teams has progressed significantly in the last decade (see Table 15.2 for a summary of meta-analytic results on team-level KSAOs and team performance). As a result, group composition (i.e., the configuration of group member attributes) has become one of the most commonly studied variables in the team literature (Guzzo & Dickson, 1996; Hollenbeck, DeRue & Guzzo, 2004), and different configurations of KSAOs have been used to predict a variety of team-related outcomes, such as team performance (Bell, 2007), collective turnover (Hausknecht & Trevor, 2011), OCB (Arthaud-Day et al., 2012) and CWB (Schmidt, Ogunfowora & Bourdage, 2012).

Although many of the individual-level KSAOs discussed above can be applied at the team level, team composition can be far more complex than merely totalling individual attributes (see Chan, 1998; Kozlowski & Klein, 2000). The most popular type of aggregation method has been mean aggregation, followed by diversity (e.g., dispersion, homogeneity) and extreme scores (maximum and minimum), and the results concerning the same type of team-level predictors can vary drastically depending on the type of aggregation method used.

In order to determine the appropriate type of aggregation for team research, Steiner (1972) proposed a task typology for aggregation method which has been considered helpful (Bell, 2007; Cannon-Bowers & Bowers, 2011; Mohammed et al., 2010). According to Steiner's typology, the mean or sum of individual scores is most appropriate where additive or compensatory tasks (i.e., team performance is the sum of individual performance) are

Table 15.2 Summary of recent meta-analyses on team attributes and team performance.

Attribute	*Validity Estimates from Meta-analyses*	*Citation*
Abilities		
General mental ability (GMA)	0.27 (k = 42, n = 2,995)	Bell (2007)
Emotional intelligence	0.18 (k = 6, n = 304)	Bell (2007)
Personality		
Conscientiousness	0.11 (k = 39, n = 2205)	Bell (2007)
Agreeableness	0.12 (k = 29, n = 1692)	Bell (2007)
Extraversion	0.09 (k = 38, n = 2243)	Bell (2007)
Emotional stability	0.04 (k = 22, n = 1439)	Bell (2007)
Openness to experience	0.05 (k = 25, n = 1697)	Bell (2007)
Values and Attitudes		
Collectivism	0.25 (k = 14, n = 1299)	Bell (2007)
Preference for teamwork	0.18 (k = 10, n = 490)	Bell (2007)
Collective efficacy	0.38 (s = 64, k = 78, n = 3738, N = 16009)	Stajkovic, Lee, and Nyberg (2009)
Group potency	0.34 (s = 29, k = 32, n = 1613, N = 9699)	Stajkovic et al. (2009)
Diversity		
Task-related diversity	0.13 (k = 15, N = 1209) for quality of team performance	Horwitz and Horwitz (2007)
	0.07 (k = 9, N = 704) for quantity of team performance	Horwitz and Horwitz (2007)
Bio-demographic diversity	−0.01 (k = 14, N = 1093) for quality of team performance	Horwitz and Horwitz (2007)
	−0.02 (k = 3, N = 182) for quantity of team performance	Horwitz and Horwitz (2007)
Functional background variety	0.10 (k = 31, n = 3726)	Bell, Villado, Lukasik, Belau, and Briggs (2011)
	−0.45 (s = 11, n = 3062)	Thatcher and Patel (2011)
Educational background variety	0.01 (k = 13, n = 2629)	Bell et al. (2011)
Education level diversity	−0.01 (k = 14, n = 3914)	Bell et al. (2011)
	−0.46 (s = 8, n = 1859)	Thatcher and Patel (2011)
Organizational tenure diversity	0.04 (k = 24, n = 4259)	Bell et al. (2011)
Team tenure diversity	−0.04 (k = 12, n = 2124)	Bell et al. (2011)
	−0.41 (s = 8, n = 980)	Thatcher and Patel (2011)
Race diversity	−0.11 (k = 31, n = 5298)	Bell et al. (2011)
	−0.35 (s = 23, n = 1890)	Thatcher and Patel (2011)
Sex diversity	−0.06 (k = 38, n = 6186)	Bell et al. (2011)
	−0.47 (s = 19, n = 1620)	Thatcher and Patel (2011)
Age diversity	−0.03 (k = 40, n = 10953)	Bell et al. (2011)
	−0.35 (s = 22, n = 1584)	Thatcher and Patel (2011)
Cultural diversity	−0.02 (k = 42, n = 7184)	Stahl, Maznevsi, Voigt, and Jonsen (2010)

(Continued)

Table 15.2 (Continued)

Attribute	Validity Estimates from Meta-analyses	Citation
Others		
Team cohesion	0.32 ($s=16$, $n=1460$)	Thatcher and Patel (2011)
Social cohesion	0.20 ($k=4$, $n=206$) for outcome performance	Chiocchio and Essiembre (2009)
Task cohesion	0.35 ($k=4$, $n=206$) for outcome performance	Chiocchio and Essiembre (2009)
Task conflict	–0.18 ($s=16$, $n=1832$)	Thatcher and Patel (2011)
Relationship conflict	–0.18 ($s=16$, $n=2021$)	Thatcher and Patel (2011)

$s=$ number of studies; $k=$ number of correlations; $n=$ number of teams; $N=$ total sample size.

concerned. As for extreme scores, the team's minimum score is best when the team is performing conjunctive tasks (weakest individual performance determines team performance), whereas maximum score is the most useful aggregation strategy when disjunctive tasks (strongest individual performance determines team performance) are the criterion. However, empirical evidence from meta-analyses suggests that the validity of aggregation method depends not only on the criterion but also the type of predictor (e.g., Bell, 2007). Given that most of the studies on team-level KSAOs were devoted to dispositional traits, we first discuss research findings regarding the team composition of dispositional traits, followed by other attributes (knowledge, abilities, values and needs).

Team composition of dispositional traits   Since 2000 there has been an increasing research focus on team-level KSAOs which has been devoted to examining the composition of personality traits in teams. Meta-analytic results from Bell (2007) highlight the importance of team personality operationalization (e.g., average, dispersion, minimum, maximum) in understanding team composition. Based on the FFM of personality (McCrae & Costa, 1985), Bell found that team minimum and average levels of agreeableness were the strongest predictors of team performance in field studies. Although team average conscientiousness, openness to experience, emotional stability and extraversion were shown to be positive predictors of team effectiveness in field studies, the extreme levels of these four personality traits contribute little to team performance.

On a similar note, Peeters, Van Tuijl Rutte and Reymen (2006) found that team average conscientiousness was positively related to team performance in student design teams. On the other hand, team average agreeableness, variability in agreeableness and variability in conscientiousness did not predict team performance. Using helping-norm emergence as the criterion, Raver, Ehrhart and Chadwick (2012) found that the maximum and minimum levels of agreeableness in student project teams were associated with team helping behaviour. Raver and colleagues' finding was in line with the 'sucker aversion' effect (Chen & Bachrach, 2003; Jackson & Harkins, 1985; Schroeder et al., 2003), which arises when team members experience a sense of inequity when one disagreeable person refuses to help others. The positive effect of team agreeableness was also found in project teams, where team average agreeableness was shown to be related to better team communication and cohesion and subsequently performance over time, though this relationship was evident only when team members were interacting face-to-face as opposed to virtually (Bradley, Baur, Banford & Postlethwaite, 2013). In the context of top management teams (TMTs), Colbert, Barrick and Bradley (2014) demonstrated a positive relationship between team average conscientiousness and organizational performance. Turning to dark personality traits, Baysinger, Scherer and LeBreton (2014) found that team average levels of psychopathy and implicit aggression were positively linked to both dysfunctional interactions and negative perceptions of the group, and these links were mediated by task participation and negative socioemotional behaviours.

At the team level, team self-efficacy can be broken down into collective efficacy (i.e., shared beliefs in the collective capabilities to perform *specific* tasks; Bandura, 1997, p. 447) and team potency (i.e., shared beliefs in the collective capabilities to perform a *wide range* of tasks across situations; Gully, Incalcaterra, Joshi & Beaubien, 2002; Guzzo, Yost, Campbell & Shea, 1993; Zaccaro, Blair, Peterson & Zazanis, 1995). Collectively, a group's belief that it is capable of performing tasks can promote the initiation of actions and boost the collective effort towards a common goal. Stajkovic, Lee and Nyberg (2009) showed a positive relationship between collective efficacy and team performance and between group potency and team performance. In addition, collective efficacy was found to fully mediate the effect of group potency on team performance. In a longitudinal study, Goncalo, Polman and Maslach (2010) demonstrated the different effects of team efficacy in the early versus late stages of team functioning. In particular, a high level of team efficacy in the early stages was associated with fewer perceived process conflicts but not with overall performance, whereas teams experiencing more process conflicts early on had higher team efficacy during later stages and better overall performance. Taking a unique approach of viewing team efficacy as either physical efficacy or mental efficacy, Hirschfeld and Bernerth (2008) showed team size increased both types of team efficacy; more team members might offer greater resources for task accomplishments (note that a curvilinear relationship between team size and team efficacy could not be tested due to restriction on team size, which ranged from 12 to 15 members per team). Team mental efficacy also predicted team internal social cohesion, problem solving and teamwork effectiveness, whereas team physical efficacy predicted team cohesion only.

In addition to personality traits and team self-efficacy, team collective motivational traits, such as collective learning and performance orientation, can influence team adaptability and performance, both independently and interactively (Porter, Webb & Gogus, 2010). Relating a team's affective makeup to team effectiveness, Kaplan, Laport and Waller (2013) uncovered a positive effect of team homogeneity in positive affect (PA), but not average PA, on team effectiveness in nuclear power plant crews during crises, and this effect was carried through by a reduction in negative emotions. Despite the positive links shown between individual-level CSE and team effectiveness, research has shown that CSE does provide incremental validity above and beyond the Big Five in predicting team performance (Haynie, 2012). In addition, the positive relationship between team CSE and team performance was only evident when the team also exhibited a high level of LMX.

Team composition of other attributes Focusing on team knowledge, Wildman and colleagues (2012) suggested that team average level of knowledge is positively linked to team processes and outcomes. Shamsie and Mannor (2013) demonstrated a positive link between tacit knowledge, a form of organizational resource, and sports team performance in a sample of Major League Baseball teams. In terms of team-level abilities, meta-analyses have demonstrated a strong association between general mental ability (GMA) and team performance (Bell, 2007; Devine & Phillips, 2001; Stewart, 2006). Randall, Resick and DeChurch (2011) demonstrated that teams with higher mean levels of cognitive ability were more likely to develop adaptive strategies in decision-making tasks. In addition, a high degree of team-level EI has been shown to be beneficial in teams, but this effect seems to be more robust in laboratory settings than in field settings (Bell, 2007).

Team shared values can function as key motivational components to team functioning. Research has shown that teams that value equality had higher team performance and importance placed on the value of equality played a bigger role in predicting team performance than past performance (Glew, 2009). Interest in the role values and beliefs play in helping norm emergence in teams, Raver and colleagues (2012) found that a team's minimum, but not maximum, levels of other-oriented values and personal helping beliefs were positively related to the emergence of a helping norm.

Focusing on cultural values and team-related phenomena, a meta-analysis by Taras and colleagues (2010) showed that cooperation in groups was positively associated with team-level power distance and uncertainty avoidance, as well as negatively related to individualism and masculinity. Similarly, Bell's (2007) meta-analytic evidence demonstrated a positive link between team average collectivism and team performance, and between team average preference for teamwork and team performance in field studies. Research has shown that the positive effect of team average psychological collectivism on team effectiveness was mediated by its influence on information-sharing (Randall et al., 2011). To further examine the different facets of team psychological collectivism (preference, reliance, concern, norm acceptance and goal priority), Dierdorff, Bell and Belohlav (2011) demonstrated that the relationship between team psychological collectivism facets and performance was moderated by performance stage and LMX.

In the context of multicultural teams, Cheng, Chua, Morris and Lee (2012) investigated the relationship between team composition of cultural values and performance in self-managing teams over time. Results from a sample of MBA student teams suggested that cultural value makeup has a differential impact on team performance at various stages of team formation: although teams with a low mean level and a moderate dispersion level in uncertainty avoidance had better performance early on, teams with a high mean level of leadership orientation as well as a moderate dispersion of relationship orientation worked better in the long run.

Shifting the focus from 'what people believe in' to 'what people want', researchers have investigated the influence of team composition of members' psychological needs on team effectiveness. Chun and Choi (2014) found that members' need for achievement was positively linked to task conflict when operationalized as the group mean and negatively related to task conflict when operationalized as dispersion. In addition, the team mean need for affiliation was shown to correlate negatively with relationship conflict, whereas the team mean and dispersion of need for power were positively and negatively related to status conflict, respectively.

Interaction between individual- and team-level KSAOs In addition to studying individual- and team-level KSAOs independently, some researchers have started to examine the joint effects of individual- and team-level constructs in predicting team effectiveness and performance. Building on the main effects of individual conscientiousness and extraversion on team outcomes, Schmidt and colleagues (2012) showed that team compositions of conscientiousness and extraversion, as well as core group evaluations (i.e., a group-level construct that represents 'fundamental assessments that individuals make about their worth, competence, and capability'; Kacmar, Collins, Harris & Judge, 2009, p. 1572), moderated the effects of individual-level traits on performance and counterproductive behaviours in university football teams. Similarly, team collective efficacy has been shown to moderate some of the positive effects individual-level traits (i.e., CSE, conscientiousness and agreeableness) had on teamwork behaviours (i.e., interpersonal teamwork behaviour and performance management teamwork behaviours; Tasa, Sears & Schat, 2011).

In an attempt to tease out the process of team collective efficacy formation, Tasa, Taggar and Seijts (2007) tested a longitudinal, multilevel model and found that individual teamwork self-efficacy, individual task-relevant knowledge and team collective efficacy each predicted individual teamwork behaviour. In turn, team-level teamwork behaviour (aggregated from individual teamwork behaviour) was positively related to subsequent collective efficacy, which then predicted final team performance.

Taking individual and team efficacy into a global virtual team context, Hardin, Fuller and Davison (2007) examined virtual and generalized team efficacy beliefs in a sample of computer-mediated teams from the US and Hong Kong and found that virtuality negatively affected team members' perceptions of team efficacy. However, this effect was buffered by individualism, such that team members from the US, an individualistic culture, perceived higher levels of group self-efficacy and virtual team self-efficacy compared to those from Hong Kong, a collectivistic culture. Given that team generalized and virtual efficacy was linked to team outcomes (satisfaction and performance), this research highlights the importance of understanding efficacy beliefs and cultural values in virtual teams.

Linking dispositional goal orientations to self-regulated learning in simulation-based team training, Dierdorff and Ellington (2012) uncovered the interaction between individual- and group-level learning and performance goal orientations in predicting leaning outcomes. In addition, Maynard, Mathieu, Marsh and Ruddy (2007) found that both individual-level and team-level resistance to empowerment climate negatively predicted individual job satisfaction, and the effect of team resistance to empowerment climate on individual job dissatisfaction was partly due to its influence on team interpersonal processes (e.g., conflict and affect management).

Using Schwartz's (1992, 1994) values theory, Arthaud-Day and colleagues (2012) tested and demonstrated the interactive effect of individual- and group-level power and self-direction on OCB. In particular, group mean power weakened the association between individual power and OCB-I and OCB-O, whereas group mean self-direction strengthened the positive effect of self-direction on OCB-I.

Person–group fit　Person–group (P-G) or person–team fit is a type of person–environment (P-E) fit that describes the degree of compatibility between individuals and their teams (Edwards, 1991; Kristof-Brown, Zimmerman & Johnson, 2005). This notion of matching individuals with teams is aligned with Schneider's (1987) attraction–selection–attrition (ASA) framework, which suggests that individuals are more likely to be attracted to, be selected into and remain in teams that are compatible with their own attributes (Dickson, Resick & Goldstein, 2008). Applying the two most commonly adopted conceptualizations of P-E fit, P-G fit can also be categorized into complementary fit (i.e., individual attributes compensate the weaknesses or the needs of the team, and vice versa) and supplementary fit (i.e., individuals' attributes replicate the strengths or characteristics possessed by the team; Muchinsky & Monahan, 1987).

Oh and colleagues (2014), in a meta-analysis, showed that P-G fit is positively related to organizational commitment, job satisfaction and job performance, and negatively related to intent to quit in both North America and East Asia. The effects of P-G fit on outcomes were stronger in East Asia than in North America. Results from other analyses suggest that these differential relationships can be explained by cultural values (i.e., collectivism and power distance), which influence how individuals view and value their compatibility with teams. Focusing on P-G fit along the trait of efficacy, Litrico and Choi (2013) demonstrated that individuals who perceived congruence between their self-efficacy, reflected efficacy (i.e., efficacy as perceived by team members) and team efficacy had higher levels of work collaboration engagement. In a sample of manufacturing teams in

Korea, Seong and Kristof-Brown (2012) discovered that distinct dimensions of P-G fit had differential impact on individual behaviour. In particular, KSA-based fit was positively related to knowledge-sharing, personality-based fit positively predicted voice behaviours and values-based fit was positively associated with team commitment. In addition, each dimension of P-G fit was positively linked to performance in the team.

Team diversity Due to the changing nature of the workforce, team researchers have paid increasing attention to the topic of team diversity and its impact on team effectiveness. Overall, results from this area of research have remained largely inconclusive, suggesting that team diversity might be a doubled-edged sword.

The most popular typologies of diversity differentiate between bio-demographic diversity (i.e., team heterogeneity in age, gender and race/ethnicity) that is more observable and less job-relevant, and job-relevant diversity (i.e., team heterogeneity in function, education, knowledge and skills; van Knippenberg & Schippers, 2007). It has, however, been suggested that the effect of bio-demographic diversity diminishes over time as a result of increased interactions among team members, whereas the effect of deep-level diversity amplifies over time (Bell et al., 2011; Korsgaard, Jeong, Mahony & Pitariu, 2008). On the one hand, meta-analytic results have not demonstrated a significant relationship between bio-demographic diversity and team effectiveness, whether the criterion concerns team innovation (Hülsheger, Anderson & Salgado, 2009) or team performance (Horwitz & Horwitz, 2007). On the other hand, job-relevant diversity has been shown to benefit team creativity and innovation (Bell et al., 2011; Hülsheger et al., 2009) and team performance (Horwitz & Horwitz, 2007). Although it seems reasonable to believe that job-relatedness might explain the differential effects of diversity on team performance, an extensive review of team diversity suggests otherwise (van Knippenberg & Schippers, 2007). In order to illuminate the inconsistent findings regarding team diversity, researchers have started to explore and investigate moderators in the team diversity–performance relationship. In a sample of 68 teams from China, Shin, Kim, Lee and Bian (2012) demonstrated the moderating effects of member creative self-efficacy and transformational leadership, such that cognitive team diversity benefited individual creativity only when members of the team had high creative self-efficacy or perceived their leaders as transformational.

Viewing diversity dimensions as interactive, some researchers have studied the relationship between team diversity, demographic fault-lines (i.e., 'hypothetical dividing lines that split a team into subgroups based on one or more attributes'; Lau & Murnighan, 1998, p. 328) and team effectiveness. Meta-analytic results showed that demographic diversity (age, race, sex, tenure, functional background and education) is significantly related to demographic fault-line strength, which in turn relates to decreased team cohesion, team performance and team satisfaction, as well as increased conflict (Thatcher & Patel, 2011).

In the context of cross-cultural teams, cultural diversity has also been linked to team performance. Results from two experimental studies showed that cultural diversity had a negative main effect on dyadic performance (i.e., joint task performance by a group of two individuals working as a team) even after controlling for team average cultural intelligence, English proficiency and other types of diversity (age, gender and function; Nouri et al., 2013). But more importantly, task structure and task type moderated the relationship between cultural diversity and performance, such that the negative influence of heterogeneity in members' cultural background diminished when the dyads performed convergent tasks (i.e., tasks that require cooperation and interdependence) with high levels of task specificity and divergent tasks (i.e., tasks that do not require high levels of cooperation or interdependence) with low levels of task specificity. In a meta-analysis, Stahl, Maznevski, Voigt and Jonsen (2010) did not find a direct link between cultural diversity and team performance in multi-cultural teams. However, cultural diversity negatively predicted social integration and positively predicted creativity, conflict and satisfaction, and these effects were moderated by team tenure, dispersion, size and task complexity. In another field study, the effect of cultural diversity on team performance was also found to be moderated by team members' goal orientation (Pieterse, van Knippenberg & van Dierendonck, 2012).

In the context of virtual teams, bio-demographic diversity, particularly diversity in age and nationality, was shown to interact with process conflict and technical experience in predicting team creativity (Martins & Shalley, 2011). In addition, nationality diversity also negatively predicted team creativity, whereas diversity in sex and race was not associated with team creativity.

In sum, we have discussed the major research findings regarding team member individual and team compositions of KSAOs that facilitate or hinder team effectiveness. The vast literature suggests that team selection should strike a balance between seeking the best individuals and the best combination of individuals with regard to their KSAOs. In the next section, we consider assessment of team member candidates based on the KSAOs discussed above.

Team Assessment

Many of the widely adopted assessments for individual-based personnel selection, such as those for cognitive ability and personality traits, can be used to select individuals for teams. However, assessments pertaining to team-based KSAOs (e.g., teamwork skills) may not be directly adapted from individual selection tools and thus need to be developed and validated in a team context.

Situational judgement tests (SJTs) have been widely applied as a measurement tool to assess team-related KSAs. Overall, meta-analytic evidence has shown that SJTs assessing team role knowledge and teamwork skills have criterion-related validity in predicting performance across various job performance facets (i.e., contextual performance and task performance; Christian, Edwards & Bradley, 2010). Using SJTs, a population measurement tool for individual teamwork capabilities is the Teamwork Knowledge, Skills, and Abilities (KSA) test (Stevens & Campion, 1999). Based on Stevens and Campion's (1999) taxonomy of teamwork capacities, the Teamwork KSA test consists of 35 SJT items that assess interpersonal KSAs (i.e., conflict resolution, collaborative problem solving and communication) and self-management KSAs (goal-setting and performance management, and planning and coordination). Scores on the sub-dimensions of the Teamwork KSA test are then aggregated to produce a single score representing overall teamwork KSAs for team selection purpose. A series of validation studies have demonstrated criterion-related validity of the Teamwork KSA test across performance facets (e.g., teamwork performance, task performance and contextual performance) and organizational settings (organizational and military samples; e.g., McClough & Rogelberg, 2003; Mohammed et al., 2010; but see O'Neill, Goffin & Gellatly, 2012). This test can be paired with structured interviews and personality inventories to assess additional social skills and personality traits (Morgeson, Reider, & Campion, 2005).

Focusing on the role team members play, Mumford, Van Iddekinge, Morgeson and Campion (2008) developed and validated a team role knowledge situational judgement test. Based on Mumford, Campion and Morgeson's (2006) team role typology, the purpose of this team role test (TRT) is to assess team members' declarative and procedural knowledge of team roles as well as the situational contingencies underlying each role and use it to predict individual role performance. Notably, the TRT presents 9 scenarios (for 9 team roles) and 10 items (behavioural descriptions) for each scenario, and the test-takers are asked to rate the effectiveness of each item. Results from two field studies showed that scores on the TRT predicted team member role performance in academic (student project teams) and applied (production and maintenance teams) settings, as well as providing incremental validity above and beyond mental ability and the Big Five traits in the student sample and team tenure in the employee sample.

Given the positive relationship between EI and team performance (e.g., Farh et al., 2012), researchers have developed measures to capture a team's emotional intelligence profile. The Workgroup Emotional Intelligence Profile (WEIP; Jordan, Ashkanasy, Hartel & Hooper, 2002; Jordan & Lawrence, 2009) was developed and validated as a self-reported assessment of team contextualized individual EI and predicts positive team behaviours and team performance (e.g., Jordan et al., 2002; Sue-Chan & Latham, 2004).

Taking a different approach from self-report, McCormack, Duchon, Geyer and Orvis (2009) used data from mining and network analyses to derive team task requirements and team-related KSAOs from archival data. The relevant KSAOs needed for teamwork were obtained from biodata (e.g., résumés) and past performance data (e.g., team roles and individual performance), communication data (e.g., responsiveness to emails) to form a set of assessments for task requirements, task work and teamwork skills, and relationship quality. Macormack and colleagues' approach offers an alternative way of conceptualizing and developing team assessment that can be used in research and practice.

Future Research

Expanding the understanding of teams

'What is a team?' In today's world, new types of team are emerging at a rapid pace. The changing nature of teams raises a series of questions regarding team membership (e.g., frequently changing membership), task and relational interdependence (e.g., ambiguity in task interdependence) and team effectiveness (e.g., performance standards by multiple shareholders; Wageman, Gardner & Mortensen, 2012), all of which are essential to team assessment and selection. In order to support evidence-based practice, team researchers can adopt different definitional elements of team components (e.g., team members, leaders, stakeholders) and explore the validity of KSAOs in different types of collaborations.

TTA

TTA plays a crucial role in team assessment and selection, yet there are many unanswered questions regarding the validity of different TTA approaches. Organizational researchers and practitioners have commonly adopted individual-based task analyses that might be inappropriate for team selection, which heightens the need to further develop and validate more team-based TTA that encompasses contextual factors and multilevel principles. Despite the existence of many commonly endorsed TTA approaches, the field lacks a single taxonomy to organize and explain various approaches of TTA to provide a common guideline for conducting TTA across time and situation (Bennett, Alliger, Wilson & Gibson, 2012). Gaps in the literature call for the development of a comprehensive guideline for conducting individual- and team-based TTA. In addition, efforts are needed to validate existing types of team-based TTA that have yet to be tested and develop new tools and methods for conducting TTA.

Team composition

Given the complexity and relatively short history of research, team composition remains a promising avenue for future research (Mohammed et al., 2010). Results from meta-analyses (Bell, 2007) suggest that mean aggregation has been the most popular method of team composition, whereas other operationalizations for team composition variables are less well studied. Depending on the composition variable and the context of the team, researchers should consider combining multiple operationalizations of team compositions instead of relying on a single operationalization. In addition to the commonly studied operationalizations of team composition (e.g., mean, variance, maximum and minimum), alternative operationalizations, such as the proportion of individuals high or low on certain attributes (e.g., star performers; see Aguinis & O'Boyle, 2014) or performance distribution among team core and non-core role-holders (e.g., Humphrey, Morgeson & Mannor, 2009) can be used to study team effectiveness. In addition, most research on team composition thus far has relied on cross-sectional data, which fails to capture the temporal dynamics of team composition. A future direction of research is to explore the potential evolution of team composition in the life of a task or team as team members or their attributes evolve.

Diversity

Given the mixed results and heated debate over team diversity and its impact on team effectiveness, there are challenges and opportunities for researchers to continue making progress in this area. First, team researchers need to look beyond demographic and functional diversity and explore other typologies (e.g., diversity in attitudes and values, shared cognition). Second, diversity impacts team effectiveness via team processes (information-sharing and decision making). Although a few studies have used longitudinal data to capture the differential impact of team diversity at various stages of a task or team cycle (e.g., Bell et al., 2011; Cheng et al., 2012; Korsgaard et al., 2008), a better understanding of these mediating mechanisms requires research designs and methodologies (e.g., experimental study, experience sampling technique, social network analysis) that capture the interactions among group members and the contextual influence in this process. Third, viewing diversity dimensions as interactive in nature, demographic fault-lines and fault-line strength present a promising avenue for future research. Fourth, there is room to continue exploring factors that moderate the diversity–team effective relationship, as well as the mediating mechanisms underlying such a relationship.

Team assessment

While research on assessment of team members' individual dispositional attributes has generated a large body of validity evidence, future research should focus more on testing the predictive validity of member team-based attributes (e.g., task work skills and team-work skills; Zaccaro & DiRosa, 2012). In addition, team assessment can advance beyond paper-and-pencil tests and incorporate more advanced strategies, such as team-based assessment centres (Klimoski & Zukin, 1999) and intelligent video-based systems (e.g., Cannon-Bowers, Bowers & Sanchez, 2008).

Conclusion

Since Mathieu and colleagues' (2008) review, numerous research studies have contributed to the knowledge base on the contributing factors of team effectiveness. Although there have been previous reviews of the team effectiveness literature (e.g., Kozlowski & Bell, 2013), a review specifically devoted to team assessment and selection is lacking. In this chapter, we have summarized research findings over the past few years that offer insight for team assessment and selection. In particular, we organized our discussion into job analysis pertaining to teams, individual- and team-level KSAOs for effective teamwork and assessment for team member candidates. Although considerable progress has been made in exploring and investigating individual- and team-level KSAOs, different conceptualizations and operationalizations of team composition offer promising avenues for future research. In addition, much research is needed to develop a comprehensive taxonomy for TTA and to further validate team-based assessment tools.

References

Aguinis, H., & O'Boyle, E. J. (2014). Star performers in twenty-first century organizations. *Personnel Psychology, 67,* 313–350. doi: 10.1111/peps.12054.

Arthaud-Day, M. L., Rode, J. C., & Turnley, W. H. (2012). Direct and contextual effects of individual values on organizational citizenship behavior in teams. *Journal of Applied Psychology, 97,* 792–807. doi: 10.1037/a0027352.

Arthur, W. J., Edwards, B. D., Bell, S. T., Villado, A. J., & Bennett, W. J. (2005). Team Task Analysis: Identifying Tasks and Jobs That Are Team Based. *Human Factors, 47,* 654–669. doi:10.1518/001872005774860087.

Arthur, W. J., Villado, A. J., & Bennett, W. J. (2012). *Innovations in team task analysis: Identifying team-based task elements, tasks, of Work Analysis: Methods, Systems, Applications and Science of Work Measurement in Organizations* (pp. 641–661). New York: Routledge/Taylor & Francis Group.

Baard, P. P., Deci, E. L., & Ryan, R. M. (2004). Intrinsic Need Satisfaction: A Motivational Basis of Performance and Well-Being in Two Work Settings. *Journal of Applied Social Psychology, 34,* 2045–2068. doi:10.1111/j.1559-1816.2004.tb02690.x.

Bandura, A. (1997). Collective efficacy. *In* A. Bandura (Ed.), *Self-efficacy: The Exercise of Control* (pp. 477–525). New York: Freeman.

Baysinger, M. A., Scherer, K. T., & LeBreton, J. M. (2014). Exploring the disruptive effects of psychopathy and aggression on group processes and group effectiveness. *Journal of Applied Psychology, 99,* 48–65. doi: 10.1037/a0034317.

Bell, S. T. (2007). Deep-level composition variables as predictors of team performance: A meta-analysis. *Journal of Applied Psychology, 92,* 595–615.

Bell, S. T., Villado, A. J., Lukasik, M. A., Belau, L., & Briggs, A. L. (2011). Getting specific about demographic diversity variable and team performance relationships: A meta-analysis. *Journal of Management, 37,* 709–743. doi: 10.1177/0149206310365001.

Bennett, W. J., Alliger, G. M., Wilson, M. A., & Gibson, S. G. (2012). Concluding thoughts: Challenges and opportunities in work analysis. *In* M. A. Wilson, W. J. Bennett, S. G. Gibson & G. M. Alliger (Eds.), *The Handbook of Work Analysis: Methods, Systems, Applications and Science of Work Measurement In Organizations* (pp. 741–747). New York: Routledge/Taylor & Francis Group.

Bradley, B. H., Baur, J. E., Banford, C. G., & Postlethwaite, B. E. (2013). Team players and collective performance: How agreeableness affects team performance over time. *Small Group Research, 44,* 680–711. doi: 10.1177/1046496413507609.

Burke, C. S. (2004). Team task analysis. *In* N. A. Stanton, A. Hedge, K. Brookuis, E. Salas & H. Hendricks (Eds.), *Handbook of Human Factors and Ergonomic Methods* (pp. 365–423). Boca Raton, FL: CRC Press.

Cannon-Bowers, J. A., & Bowers, C. (2011). Team development and functioning. *In* S. Zedeck (Ed.), *APA Handbook of Industrial and Organizational Psychology, Vol. 1: Building and Developing the Organization* (pp. 597–650). Washington, DC: American Psychological Association. doi: 10.1037/12169-019.

Cannon-Bowers, J. A., Bowers, C. A., & Sanchez, A. (2008). Using synthetic learning environments to train teams. *In* V. I. Sessa & M. London (Eds.), *Work Group Learning: Understanding, Improving and Assessing How Groups Learn in Organizations* (pp. 315–346). New York: Taylor & Francis Group/Lawrence Erlbaum.

Chan, D. (1998). Functional relations among constructs in the same content domain at different levels of analysis: A typology of composition models. *Journal of Applied Psychology, 83*, 234–246.

Chen, X., & Bachrach, D. G. (2003). Tolerance of free-riding: The effects of defection size, defection pattern, and social orientation in a repeated public goods dilemma. *Organizational Behavior & Human Decision Processes, 90*, 139–147. doi: 10.1016/S0749-5978(02)00511-3.

Chen, G., Farh, J., Campbell-Bush, E. M., Wu, Z., & Wu, X. (2013). Teams as innovative systems: Multilevel motivational antecedents of innovation in R&D teams. *Journal of Applied Psychology, 98*, 1018–1027. doi: 10.1037/a0032663.

Cheng, C., Chua, R. J., Morris, M. W., & Lee, L. (2012). Finding the right mix: How the composition of self-managing multicultural teams' cultural value orientation influences performance over time. *Journal of Organizational Behavior, 33*, 389–411. doi: 10.1002/job.1777.

Chiocchio, F., & Essiembre, H. (2009). Cohesion and performance: A meta-analytic review of disparities between project teams, production teams, and service teams. *Small Group Research, 40*, 382–420. doi: 10.1177/1046496409335103.

Christian, M. S., Edwards, B. D., & Bradley, J. C. (2010). Situational judgment tests: Constructs assessed and a meta-analysis of their criterion-related validities. *Personnel Psychology, 63*, 83–117. doi: 10.1111/j.1744-6570.2009.01163.x.

Chun, J. S., & Choi, J. N. (2014). Members' needs, intragroup conflict, and group performance. *Journal of Applied Psychology, 99*, 437–450. doi: 10.1037/a0036363.

Cohen, S. G., & Bailey, D. E. (1997). What makes teams work: Group effectiveness research from the shop floor to the executive suite. *Journal of Management, 23*, 239–290.

Colbert, A. E., Barrick, M. R., & Bradley, B. H. (2014). Personality and leadership composition in top management teams: Implications for organizational effectiveness. *Personnel Psychology, 67*, 351–387. doi: 10.1111/peps.12036.

Devine, D. J. (2002). A review and integration of classification systems relevant to teams in organizations. *Group Dynamics: Theory, Research, and Practice, 6*, 291–310.

Devine, D. J., & Philips, J. L. (2001). Do smarter teams do better? A meta-analysis of cognitive ability and team performance. *Small Group Research, 32*, 507–532. doi: 10.1177/104649640103200501.

Dickson, M. W., Resick, C. J., & Goldstein, H. (2008). Seeking explanations in people not in the results of their behavior: Twenty-plus years of the Attraction–Selection–Attrition Model. *In* D. B. Smith (Ed.), *The People Make the Place* (pp. 5–36). New York: Lawrence Erlbaum.

Dierdorff, E. C., Bell, S. T., & Belohlav, J. A. (2011). The power of 'we': Effects of psychological collectivism on team performance over time. *Journal of Applied Psychology, 96*, 247–262. doi: 10.1037/a0020929.

Dierdorff, E. C., & Ellington, J. K. (2012). Members matter in team training: Multilevel and longitudinal relationships between goal orientation, self-regulation, and team outcomes. *Personnel Psychology, 65*, 661–703. doi: 10.1111/j.1744-6570.2012.01255.x.

Dweck, C. S. (1986). Motivational processes affecting learning. *American Psychologist, 41*, 1040–1048.

Edwards, J. R. (1991). Person–job fit: A conceptual integration, literature review, and methodological critique. *In* C. L. Cooper & I. T. Robertson (Eds.), *International Review of Industrial and Organizational Psychology* (Vol. 6, pp. 283–357). Oxford: John Wiley & Sons.

Ellington, J. K., & Dierdorff, E. C. (2014). Individual learning in team training: Self-regulation and team context effects. *Small Group Research, 45*, 37–67. doi: 10.1177/1046496413511670.

Farh, C. C., Seo, M., & Tesluk, P. E. (2012). Emotional intelligence, teamwork effectiveness, and job performance: The moderating role of job context. *Journal of Applied Psychology, 97*, 890–900. doi: 10.1037/a0027377.

Glew, D. J. (2009). Personal values and performance in teams: An individual and team-level analysis. *Small Group Research, 40*, 670–693. doi: 10.1177/1046496409346577.

Goncalo, J. A., Polman, E., & Maslach, C. (2010). Can confidence come too soon? Collective efficacy, conflict and group performance over time. *Organizational Behavior & Human Decision Processes, 113*, 13–24. doi: 10.1016/j.obhdp.2010.05.001.

Gully, S. M., Devine, D. J., & Whitney, D. J. (1995). A meta-analysis of cohesion and performance: Effects of levels of analysis and task interdependence. *Small Group Research, 26*, 497–520. doi: 10.1177/1046496495264003.

Gully, S. M., Incalcaterra, K. A., Joshi, A., & Beaubien, J. M. (2002). A meta-analysis of team-efficacy, potency, and performance: Interdependence and level of analysis as moderators of observed relationships. *Journal of Applied Psychology, 87*, 819–832. doi: 10.1037/0021-9010.87.5.819

Guzzo, R. A., & Dickson, M. W. (1996). Teams in organizations: Recent research on performance and effectiveness. *Annual Review of Psychology, 47*, 307–338.

Guzzo, R. A., Yost, P. R., Campbell, R. J., & Shea, G. P. (1993). Potency in groups: Articulating a construct. *British Journal of Social Psychology, 32*, 87–106. doi: 10.1111/j.2044-8309.1993.tb00987.x.

Hardin, A. M., Fuller, M. A., & Davison, R. M. (2007). I know I can, but can we? Culture and efficacy beliefs in global virtual teams. *Small Group Research, 38*, 130–155. doi: 10.1177/1046496406297041.

Hausknecht, J. P., & Trevor, C. O. (2011). Collective turnover at the group, unit, and organizational levels: Evidence, issues, and implications. *Journal of Management, 37*, 352–388. doi: 10.1177/0149206310383910.

Haynie, J. J. (2012). Core-self evaluations and team performance: The role of team–member exchange. *Small Group Research, 43*, 315–329. doi: 10.1177/1046496411428357

Hirschfeld, R. R., & Bernerth, J. B. (2008). Mental efficacy and physical efficacy at the team level: Inputs and outcomes among newly formed action teams. *Journal of Applied Psychology, 93*, 1429–1437. doi: 10.1037/a0012574.

Hirst, G., Van Knippenberg, D., Chen, C., & Sacramento, C. A. (2011). How does bureaucracy impact individual creativity? A cross-level investigation of team contextual influences on goal orientation–creativity relationships. *Academy of Management Journal, 54*, 624–641. doi: 10.5465/AMJ.2011.61968124.

Hofstede, G. (1980). *Culture's Consequences: International Differences in Work-Related Values.* Beverly Hills, CA: Sage.

Hollenbeck, J. R., Beersma, B., & Schouten, M. E. (2012). Beyond team types and taxonomies: A dimensional scaling conceptualization for team description. *Academy of Management Review, 37*, 82–106.

Hollenbeck, J. R., DeRue, D. S., & Guzzo, R. A. (2004). Bridging the gap between I/O research and HR practice: Improving team composition, team training, and team task design. *Human Resource Management, 43*, 353–366.

Horwitz, S. K., & Horwitz, I. B. (2007). The effects of team diversity on team outcomes: A meta-analytic review of team demography. *Journal of Management, 33*, 987–1015. doi: 10.1177/0149206307308587.

House, R. J., Hanges, P. J., Javidan, M., Dorfman, P. W., & Gupta, V. (2004). *Culture, Leadership, and Organizations: The GLOBE Study of 62 Societies.* Thousand Oaks, CA: Sage.

Hülsheger, U. R., Anderson, N., & Salgado, J. F. (2009). Team-level predictors of innovation at work: A comprehensive meta-analysis spanning three decades of research. *Journal of Applied Psychology, 94*, 1128–1145. doi: 10.1037/a0015978.

Humphrey, S. E., Morgeson, F. P., & Mannor, M. J. (2009). Developing a theory of the strategic core of teams: A role composition model of team performance. *Journal of Applied Psychology, 94*, 48–61. doi: 10.1037/a0012997.

Jackson, J. M., & Harkins, S. G. (1985). Equity in effort: An explanation of the social loafing effect. *Journal of Personality and Social Psychology, 49*, 1199–1206. doi: 10.1037/0022-3514.49.5.1199

Jordan, P. J., Ashkanasy, N. M., Härtel, C. J., & Hooper, G. S. (2002). Workgroup emotional intelligence: Scale development and relationship to team process effectiveness and goal focus. *Human Resource Management Review*, *12*, 195–214. doi: 10.1016/S1053-4822(02)00046-3.

Jordan, P. J., & Lawrence, S. A. (2009). Emotional intelligence in teams: Development and initial validation of the short version of the Workgroup Emotional Intelligence Profile (WEIP-S). *Journal of Management and Organization*, *15*, 452–469.

Judge, T. A., Locke, E. A., & Durham, C. C. (1997). The dispositional causes of job satisfaction: A core evaluation approach. *Research in Organizational Behavior*, *19*, 151–188.

Jung, J. H., Lee, Y., & Karsten, R. (2012). The moderating effect of extraversion–introversion differences on group idea generation performance. *Small Group Research*, *43*, 30–49. doi: 10.1177/1046496411422130.

Kacmar, K. M., Collins, B. J., Harris, K. J., & Judge, T. A. (2009). Core self-evaluations and job performance: The role of perceived work environment. *Journal of Applied Psychology*, *94*, 1572–1580. doi: 10.1037/a0017498.

Kanfer, R., & Kanfer, F. H. (1991). Goals and self-regulation: Applications of theory to work settings. *In* M. Maehr & P. Pintrich (Eds.), *Advances in Motivation and Achievement* (pp. 287–326). Greenwich, CT: JAI Press.

Kaplan, S., LaPort, K., & Waller, M. J. (2013). The role of positive affectivity in team effectiveness during crises. *Journal of Organizational Behavior*, *34*, 473–491. doi: 10.1002/job.1817.

Keller, R. T. (2012). Predicting the performance and innovativeness of scientists and engineers. *Journal of Applied Psychology*, *97*, 225–233. doi: 10.1037/a0025332.

Klimoski, R., & Jones, R. G. (1995). Staffing for effective group decision making: Key issues in matching people and task. *In* R. A. Guzzo & E. Salas (Eds.), *Team Effectiveness and Decision Making in Organizations* (pp. 292–332). San Francisco: Jossey-Bass.

Klimoski, R. J., & Zukin, L. B. (1999). Selection and staffing for team effectiveness. *In* E. Sundstrom (Ed.), *Supporting work team effectiveness: Best management practices for fostering high performance* (pp. 63–91). San Francisco: Jossey-Bass.

Korsgaard, M. A., Jeong, S. S., Mahony, D. M., & Pitariu, A. H. (2008). A multilevel view of intragroup conflict. *Journal of Management*, *34*, 1222–1252. doi: 10.1177/0149206308325124.

Kozlowski, S. W. J., & Bell, B. S. (2013). Work groups and teams in organizations. *In* N. W. Schmitt, S. Highhouse, & I. B. Weiner (Eds.), *Handbook of Psychology, Vol. 12: Industrial and Organizational Psychology* (2nd ed., pp. 412–469). Hoboken, NJ: John Wiley & Sons.

Kozlowski, S. W. J., & Klein, K. J. (2000). A multilevel approach to theory and research in organizations: Contextual, temporal, and emergent processes. *In* K. J. Klein & S. W. J. Kozlowski (Eds.), *Multilevel Theory, Research, and Methods in Organizations: Foundations, Extensions, and New Directions* (pp. 3–90). London: Wiley.

Kristof-Brown, A. L., Zimmerman, R. D., & Johnson, E. C. (2005). Consequences of individuals' fit at work: A meta-analysis of person–job, person–organization, person–group, and person–supervisor fit. *Personnel Psychology*, *58*, 281–342.

Lau, D. C., & Murnighan, J. K. (1998). Demographic diversity and fault-lines: The compositional dynamics of organizational groups. *Academy of Management Review*, *23*, 325–340. doi: 10.5465/AMR.1998.533229.

Lee, G. L., Diefendorff, J. M., Kim, T., & Bian, L. (2014). Personality and participative climate: Antecedents of distinct voice behaviors. *Human Performance*, *27*, 25–43. doi: 10.1080/08959285.2013.854363.

Li, N., Liang, J., & Crant, J. M. (2010). The role of proactive personality in job satisfaction and organizational citizenship behavior: A relational perspective. *Journal of Applied Psychology*, *95*, 395–404. doi: 10.1037/a0018079.

Litrico, J., & Choi, J. N. (2013). A look in the mirror: Reflected efficacy beliefs in groups. *Small Group Research*, *44*, 658–679. doi: 10.1177/1046496413506943.

Liu, D., Chen, X., & Yao, X. (2011). From autonomy to creativity: A multilevel investigation of the mediating role of harmonious passion. *Journal of Applied Psychology*, *96*, 294–309. doi: 10.1037/a0021294

Liu, D., Zhang, S., Wang, L., & Lee, T. W. (2011). The effects of autonomy and empowerment on employee turnover: Test of a multilevel model in teams. *Journal of Applied Psychology, 96,* 1305–1316. doi: 10.1037/a0024518.

Martins, L. L., & Shalley, C. E. (2011). Creativity in virtual work: Effects of demographic differences. *Small Group Research, 42,* 536–561. doi: 10.1177/1046496410397382.

Mathieu, J., Maynard, M. T., Rapp, T., & Gilson, L. (2008). Team effectiveness 1997–2007: A review of recent advancements and a glimpse into the future. *Journal of Management, 34,* 410–476.

Maynard, M. T., Mathieu, J. E., Marsh, W. M., & Ruddy, T. M. (2007). A multilevel investigation of the influences of employees' resistance to empowerment. *Human Performance, 20,* 147–171. doi: 10.1080/08959280701332885.

McClough, A. C., & Rogelberg, S. G. (2003). Selection in teams: An exploration of the Teamwork Knowledge, Skills, and Ability test. *International Journal of Selection and Assessment, 11,* 56–66. doi: 10.1111/1468-2389.00226.

McCormack, R. K., Duchon, A., Geyer, A., & Orvis, K. (2009). A case study in data mining for automated building of teams. *In* E. Eyob (Ed.), *Social Implications of Data Mining and Information Privacy: Interdisciplinary Frameworks and Solutions* (pp. 247–265). Hershey, PA: IGI-Global.

McCrae, R. R., & Costa, P. T., Jr. (1985). Updating Norman's 'adequacy taxonomy': Intelligence and personality dimensions in natural language and in questionnaires. *Journal of Personality and Social Psychology, 49,* 710–721.

McGrath, J. E. (1964). *Social Psychology: A Brief Introduction.* New York: Holt, Rinehart & Winston.

Mohammed, S., Cannon-Bowers, J., & Foo, S. C. (2010). Selection for team membership: A contingency and multilevel perspective. *In* J. L. Farr & N. T. Tippins (Eds.), *Handbook of Employee Selection* (pp. 801–822). New York: Routledge/Taylor & Francis Group.

Morgeson, F. P., Reider, M. H., & Campion, M. A. (2005). Selecting individuals in team settings: The importance of social skills, personality characteristics, and teamwork knowledge. *Personnel Psychology, 58,* 583–611. doi: 10.1111/j.1744-6570.2005.655.x.

Muchinsky, P. M., Monahan, C. J. (1987). What is person–environment congruence? Supplementary versus complementary models of fit. *Journal of Vocational Behavior, 31,* 268–277.

Mumford, T. V., Campion, M. A., & Morgeson, F. P. (2006). Situational Judgement in Work Teams: A Team Role Typology. *In* J. A. Weekley, R. E. Ployhart, J. A. Weekley, R. E. Ployhart (Eds.), *Situational judgment tests: Theory, measurement, and application* (pp. 319–343). Mahwah, NJ, US: Lawrence Erlbaum Associates Publishers.

Mumford, T. V., Van Iddekinge, C. H., Morgeson, F. P., & Campion, M. A. (2008). The team role test: Development and validation of a team role knowledge situational judgment test. *Journal of Applied Psychology, 93,* 250–267. doi: 10.1037/0021-9010.93.2.250.

Nouri, R., Erez, M., Rockstuhl, T., Ang, S., Leshem-Calif, L., & Rafaeli, A. (2013). Taking the bite out of culture: The impact of task structure and task type on overcoming impediments to cross-cultural team performance. *Journal of Organizational Behavior, 34,* 739–763. doi: 10.1002/job.1871.

O'Neill, T. A., Goffin, R. D., & Gellatly, I. R. (2012). The knowledge, skill, and ability requirements for teamwork: Revisiting the teamwork-KSA test's validity. *International Journal of Selection and Assessment, 20,* 36–52. doi: 10.1111/j.1468-2389.2012.00578.x.

Oh, I., Guay, R. P., Kim, K., Harold, C. M., Lee, J., Heo, C., & Shin, K. (2014). Fit happens globally: A meta-analytic comparison of the relationships of person–environment fit dimensions with work attitudes and performance across East Asia, Europe, and North America. *Personnel Psychology, 67,* 99–152. doi: 10.1111/peps.12026.

Peeters, M. G., Van Tuijl, H. M., Rutte, C. G., & Reymen, I. J. (2006). Personality and team performance: A meta-analysis. *European Journal of Personality, 20,* 377–396. doi: 10.1002/per.588.

Pieterse, A. N., van Knippenberg, D., & van Dierendonck, D. (2013). Cultural diversity and team performance: The role of team member goal orientation. *Academy of Management Journal, 56,* 782–804. doi: 10.5465/amj.2010.0992.

Porter, C. H., Webb, J. W., & Gogus, C. I. (2010). When goal orientations collide: Effects of learning and performance orientation on team adaptability in response to workload imbalance. *Journal of Applied Psychology, 95,* 935–943. doi: 10.1037/a0019637.

Randall, K. R., Resick, C. J., & DeChurch, L. A. (2011). Building team adaptive capacity: The roles of sense giving and team composition. *Journal of Applied Psychology, 96*, 525–540. doi: 10.1037/a0022622.

Raver, J. L., Ehrhart, M. G., & Chadwick, I. C. (2012). The emergence of team helping norms: Foundations within members' attributes and behavior. *Journal of Organizational Behavior, 33*, 616–637. doi: 10.1002/job.772.

Richter, A. W., Hirst, G., van Knippenberg, D., & Baer, M. (2012). Creative self-efficacy and individual creativity in team contexts: Cross-level interactions with team informational resources. *Journal Of Applied Psychology, 97*, 1282–1290. doi: 10.1037/a0029359.

Schmidt, J. A., Ogunfowora, B., & Bourdage, J. S. (2012). No person is an island: The effects of group characteristics on individual trait expression. *Journal of Organizational Behavior, 33*, 925–945. doi: 10.1002/job.781.

Schneider, B. (1987). The people make the place. *Personnel Psychology, 40*, 437–454.

Schroeder, D. A., Steel, J. E., Woodell, A. J., & Bembenek, A. F. (2003). Justice within social dilemmas. *Personality and Social Psychology Review, 7*, 374–387.

Schwartz, S. H. (1992). Universals in the content and structure of values: Theoretical advances and empirical tests in 20 countries. *Advances in Experimental Social Psychology, 25*, 1–65. doi: 10.1016/S0065-2601(08)60281-6.

Schwartz, S. H. (1994). Are there universal aspects in the structure and contents of human values? *Journal of Social Issues, 50*, 19–45. doi: 10.1111/j.1540-4560.1994.tb01196.x.

Seong, J. Y., & Kristof-Brown, A. L. (2012). Testing multidimensional models of person–group fit. *Journal of Managerial Psychology, 27*, 536–556.

Shamsie, J., & Mannor, M. J. (2013). Looking inside the dream team: Probing into the contributions of tacit knowledge as an organizational resource. *Organization Science, 24*, 513–529.

Shi, J., Johnson, R. E., Liu, Y., & Wang, M. (2013). Linking subordinate political skill to supervisor dependence and reward recommendations: A moderated mediation model. *Journal of Applied Psychology, 98*, 374–384. doi: 10.1037/a0031129.

Shin, S. J., Kim, T., Lee, J., & Bian, L. (2012). Cognitive team diversity and individual team member creativity: A cross-level interaction. *Academy of Management Journal, 55*, 197–212. doi: 10.5465/amj.2010.0270.

Smith, P. A., Baber, C., Hunter, J., & Butler, M. (2008). Measuring team skills in crime scene investigation: Exploring ad hoc teams. *Ergonomics, 51*, 1463–1488. doi: 10.1080/00140130802248076.

Stahl, G. K., Maznevski, M. L., Voigt, A., & Jonsen, K. (2010). Unraveling the effects of cultural diversity in teams: A meta-analysis of research on multicultural work groups. *Journal of International Business Studies, 41*, 690–709. doi: 10.1057/jihs.2009.85.

Stajkovic, A. D., Lee, D., & Nyberg, A. J. (2009). Collective efficacy, group potency, and group performance: Meta-analyses of their relationships, and test of a mediation model. *Journal of Applied Psychology, 94*, 814–828. doi: 10.1037/a0015659.

Steiner, I. D. (1972). *Group Processes and Productivity.* New York: Academic Press.

Stevens, M. J., & Campion, M. A. (1999). Staffing work teams: Development and validation of a selection test for teamwork settings. *Journal of Management, 25*, 207–228. doi: 10.1016/S0149-2063(99)80010-5.

Stewart, G. L. (2006). A meta-analytic review of relationships between team design features and team performance. *Journal of Management, 32*, 29–55.

Sue-Chan, C., & Latham, G. P. (2004). The situational interview as a predictor of academic and team performance: A study of the mediating effects of cognitive ability and emotional intelligence. *International Journal of Selection snd Assessment, 12*, 312–320. doi: 10.1111/j.0965-075X.2004.00286.x.

Sundstrom, E., McIntyre, M., Halfhill, T., & Richards, H. (2000). Work groups: From the Hawthorne studies to work teams of the 1990s and beyond. *Group Dynamics: Theory, Research, and Practice, 4*, 44–67.

Taras, V., Kirkman, B. L., & Steel, P. (2010). Examining the impact of culture's consequences: A three-decade, multilevel, meta-analytic review of Hofstede's cultural value dimensions. *Journal of Applied Psychology, 95*, 405–439. doi: 10.1037/a0020939.

Tasa, K., Sears, G. J., & Schat, A. H. (2011). Personality and teamwork behavior in context: The cross-level moderating role of collective efficacy. *Journal of Organizational Behavior*, 32, 65–85. doi: 10.1002/job.680.

Tasa, K., Taggar, S., & Seijts, G. H. (2007). The development of collective efficacy in teams: A multilevel and longitudinal perspective. *Journal of Applied Psychology*, 92, 17–27. doi: 10.1037/0021-9010.92.1.17.

Tett, R. P., & Burnett, D. D. (2003). A personality trait-based interactionist model of job performance. *Journal of Applied Psychology*, 88, 500–517. doi: 10.1037/0021-9010.88.3.500

Thatcher, S. B., & Patel, P. C. (2011). Demographic faultlines: A meta-analysis of the literature. *Journal of Applied Psychology*, 96, 1119–1139. doi: 10.1037/a0024167.

van Berlo, M. W., Lowyck, J., & Schaafstal, A. (2007). Supporting the instructional design process for team training. *Computers in Human Behavior*, 23, 1145–1161. doi: 10.1016/j.chb.2006.10.007.

van Knippenberg, D., & Schippers, M. C. (2007). Work group diversity. *Annual Review of Psychology*, 58, 515–541. doi: 10.1146/annurev.psych.58.110405.085546.

VandeWalle, D. (1997). Development and validation of a work domain goal orientation instrument. *Educational and Psychological Measurement*, 57, 995–1015.

Wageman, R., Gardner, H., & Mortensen, M. (2012). The changing ecology of teams: New directions for teams research. *Journal of Organizational Behavior*, 33, 301–315. doi: 10.1002/job.1775

Wildman, J. L., Thayer, A. L., Pavlas, D., Salas, E., Stewart, J. E., & Howse, W. R. (2012). Team knowledge research: Emerging trends and critical needs. *Human Factors*, 54, 84–111.

Zaccaro, S. J., Blair, U., Peterson, C., & Zazanis, M. (1995). Collective efficacy. *In* J. E. Maddux (Ed.), *Self-Efficacy, Adaptation, and Adjustment* (pp. 305–328). New York: Plenum.

Zaccaro, S. J., & DiRosa, G. A. (2012). The processes of team staffing: A review of relevant studies. *In* G. P. Hodgkinson & J. K. Ford (Eds.), *International Review of Industrial and Organizational Psychology 2012* (Vol. 27, pp. 197–229). Chichester: Wiley-Blackwell.

Zimmerman, R. D., Triana, M. C., & Barrick, M. R. (2010). Predictive criterion-related validity of observer ratings of personality and job-related competencies using multiple raters and multiple performance criteria. *Human Performance*, 23, 361–378. doi: 10.1080/08959285.2010.501049.

Zobarich, R. M., Lamoureux, T. M., & Martin, L. E. (2007). *Forward air controller: Task analysis and development of team training measures for close air support (DRDC CR 2007-156)*. Toronto: Defense R&D Canada.

16

Selection for Virtual Teams

Geeta D'Souza, Matthew S. Prewett and Stephen M. Colarelli

Introduction

Due to the increased globalization of business and rapid improvements in communication technologies, virtual teams have become a popular and effective means of conducting work. Their widespread use stems from the fact that they help overcome some of the limitations and constraints faced by conventional teams and work structures. Virtual teams transcend spatial and temporal boundaries, eliminate the expense and inconvenience of travel, increase the speed and efficiency with which knowledge and resources are shared and integrated, and facilitate collaboration among experts from different functions, fields, locations and cultures. Their increasing use in organizations has also led to a burgeoning body of research examining their attributes, composition, processes and outcomes.

A major advantage of virtual teams over that of traditional teams is that organizations may select talent with few restraints placed on the locations of prospective team members. Thus, organizations can focus on members' qualifications when staffing virtual teams, often to a greater extent than when staffing traditional teams. Yet, selection for virtual teams also poses a new challenge: to what extent does this relatively new work arrangement change the meaning and importance of the selection processes used for traditional teams? In just about every arena of organizational life, people have been selecting individuals for face-to-face teams and they have been doing so for millennia. From ancestral hunting groups and war parties to modern sports and work teams, our species has ample experience in selecting face-to-face team members. One could argue that, simply given the test of time, our baseline competence for selecting team members are reasonably high (Adams, Elacqua & Colarelli, 1994). However, virtual team selection is an altogether different matter. The virtual world is a relatively new experience, and as a result selection for virtual teams is likely to be a complex matter. Successful efforts to achieve virtual team selection require answers to several questions: What is a virtual team?

The Wiley Blackwell Handbook of the Psychology of Recruitment, Selection and Employee Retention,
First Edition. Edited by Harold W. Goldstein, Elaine D. Pulakos, Jonathan Passmore and Carla Semedo.
© 2017 John Wiley & Sons Ltd. Published 2020 by John Wiley & Sons Ltd.

What are the characteristics of virtual teams? Are the characteristics that make someone a good virtual team member the same as those that make someone a good face-to-face team member?

Despite the vast amount of research on virtual team characteristics and work processes, there is relatively little research on the selection and placement of individuals in these teams. The aim of this chapter is to examine research in the area of selection for virtual teams, identify gaps in our knowledge of virtual team selection and suggest directions for future research. To accomplish this objective, we first describe the context of virtual teams, followed by a discussion of knowledge, skills, abilities and other qualifications (KSAOs) that are theoretically relevant to virtual teamwork. We then review a variety of selection tools that may be useful when staffing virtual teams, noting strengths and limitations from the available validity evidence. We conclude with a discussion of research needed to advance our understanding of virtual team selection.

Definition

Virtual teams have been defined in various ways in the literature. While early definitions described virtual teams as distinctly separate from face-to-face teams, current definitions characterize virtual teams along several continuous dimensions of virtuality, in which teams become more or less 'virtual' based on where they fall on these dimensions (Bell & Kozlowski, 2002; Gibson & Gibbs, 2006; Griffith & Neale, 2001; Kirkman & Mathieu, 2005; Martins, Gilson & Maynard, 2004). One reason for the shift in definition from a dichotomous description to a continuous construct could be that the workplace has been undergoing continual changes to meet the growing demands of globalization and technological advances. To remain competitive in such an environment, organizations have been adopting more sophisticated communication media, more flexible work forms and structures, greater complexity in tasks and processes, and a more diversified workforce. As a result, for some work structures such as teams, there has been a merging of traditional and virtual ways of working. For example, teams may use face-to-face and technology-mediated communication to varying degrees, have some co-located and some dispersed team members, and use real-time as well as asynchronous means of communication depending on the nature of the task. In such a situation, a continuum-based distinction between face-to-face and virtual teams would be more fitting. Purely face-to-face teams would lie at one end of the scale, while teams that fall closer to the virtual end of the scale would rely more on electronic media for interaction, have more asynchronous communication and would evidence greater physical and cultural dispersion of members. This suggests that as the virtuality of a team increases, the context in which the team operates changes. This needs to be taken into account when considering the selection and placement of individuals in a virtual team.

Contextual Factors

Contextual work factors can influence the KSAOs required for workers to successfully perform their tasks. We draw attention to several contextual factors that exert a considerable influence on virtual team processes and outcomes. These factors are broadly classified as: the degree of team virtuality; the geographic, temporal and cultural boundaries spanned; the team's life span (whether ad hoc or long-term); the nature of the task and team leadership; and the types of outcome or criteria desired from the virtual team.

The degree of team virtuality

Kirkman and Mathieu proposed three important dimensions to define team virtuality: 'the extent to which team members use virtual tools to coordinate and execute team processes, the amount of informational value provided by such tools, and the synchronicity of team member virtual interaction' (2005, p. 702). Each of these dimensions can be used to determine the degree of virtuality a team possesses. The first dimension, technology reliance, suggests that virtuality increases as the reliance on technological devices increases. Some teams may work in close physical proximity and primarily communicate face-to-face, while others rely mainly on technological devices such as email, video-conferencing, mobile phones and groupware (software applications that facilitate group work) for communication and information exchange. Most teams, however, fall between the two extremes, using a mix of face-to-face and virtual means to interact and communicate.

Informational value, the second dimension, is closely linked to the technologies the team is using. The medium used differs in the amount of information richness each medium can carry (Daft & Lengel, 1986). Face-to-face interaction, with its ability to convey information by simultaneously using verbal expression, para-verbal and non-verbal cues, facilitates effective communication and provides information that is rich in meaning. Technological media that come close to imitating face-to-face interaction would therefore be less virtual. Kirkman and Mathieu (2005) argue, however, that in addition to direct communication, technological media can be used to transmit data in a way that increases the informational value of the exchange, thereby reducing virtuality. Therefore, instead of richness, they suggest the broader term 'informational value' to determine virtuality. The greater the informational value provided by the media, the lower the virtuality.

The third dimension is the synchronicity of communication. When media such as face-to-face communication and video-conferencing are used, messages are sent and received instantly and information exchange takes place in real time. In email communication, on the other hand, there is a time-lag between sending and receiving messages. This could be disadvantageous if feedback is required immediately, but could also prove advantageous if the exchange requires a more thought-out and reasoned response (Rasters, Vissers & Dankbaar, 2002).

The above three dimensions can be used to categorize teams based on low, moderate or high virtuality. At one extreme, teams with low virtuality rely less on virtual tools and have higher informational value and more synchronous informational exchange, while teams with high virtuality have greater reliance on virtual tools, lower informational value and more asynchronous informational exchange. Researchers have examined the impact of high virtuality in terms of issues such as anonymity (Sassenberg & Boos, 2003), personality characteristics (Lee-Kelley, 2006; Staples & Webster, 2007; Straus, 1996), communication patterns (Bhappu, Griffith, & Northcraft, 1997; Hightower & Sayeed, 1996; Hiltz, Johnson & Turoff, 1986; Jonassen & Kwon, 2001; Siegel, Dubrovsky, Kiesler & McGuire, 1986), cohesion (Chidambaram, 1996; Lind, 1999; van der Kleij, Paashuis & Schraagen, 2005; Warkentin, Sayeed & Hightower, 1997), trust (Jarvenpaa & Leidner, 1999; Wilson, Straus & McEvily, 2006), participation (Siegel et al., 1986), decision making (Adams, Roch & Ayman, 2005; Hollingshead, 1996; Siegel et al., 1986; Straus & McGrath, 1994), team performance (Andres, 2002; van der Kleij et al., 2005) and member satisfaction (Adams et al., 2005; Andres, 2002; Chidambaram, 1996; Jonassen & Kwon, 1996; van der Kleij et al., 2005; Warkentin et al., 2006). Although results have not been consistent, virtual teams are believed to be more task-focused, less personal, more uninhibited, prone to greater status equalization and participation among members, and take longer to build relational links and trust.

Geographic, temporal and cultural boundaries

A common reason for virtual collaboration is the different boundaries that can separate team members. O'Leary and Cummings (2007) describe team dispersion in terms of three dimensions: spatial, temporal and configurational. The spatial dimension involves distance, where team members are geographically separated from one another; the temporal dimension refers to the time differences in team member interaction; and the configural dimension describes how team members are clustered in their locations (e.g., two members may be placed together, while a third is separated). The greater the spread in terms of distance, time and configuration, the greater the need for virtual communications among team members.

Given the challenges posed by member dispersion, virtual team members may require competences for managing boundaries and member diversity that are less emphasized in traditional teams. Geographically dispersed teams will have a more heterogeneous organizational and cultural background, have little history of working together before and may bring different expectations to the team (Bosch-Sijtsema, 2007). Researchers have examined geographically dispersed teams in terms of their individualistic–collectivistic orientation (Hardin, Fuller & Davison, 2007; Oyserman, Coon & Kemmelmeier, 2002), communication (Cramton & Weber, 2005), innovation (Gibson & Gibbs, 2006) and status closure (Metiu, 2006). As teams become more geographically distant, time zone differences can be expected to play a role in team effectiveness. People working at different optimum circadian cycles are likely to find it difficult to work together optimally, as these temporal differences create scheduling conflicts and inhibit synchronous communication. Other negative outcomes of geographical dispersion involve expectation mismatches (e.g., about task, role and process) between team members, which negatively impact motivation and satisfaction, less communication, coordination and innovation, and reduced intragroup cooperation (Bosch-Sijtsema, 2007; Cramton & Webber, 2005; Gibson & Gibbs, 2006; Metiu, 2006).

The team's life span

Most research on virtual teams, and especially those comparing virtual teams with face-to-face teams, has used ad hoc teams. Research on group cohesion (Chidambaram, 1996; Dennis & Garfield, 2003) and group identity (Bouas & Arrow, 1996) has shown that groups using computer-mediated communication are slow to establish cohesion and group identity compared to face-to-face groups. Over time, however, computer-mediated communication groups catch up with face-to-face groups in establishing relational links between members (Walther & Burgoon, 1992).

A general concern many researchers express is the lack of studies using longitudinal designs and examining stages of team development. The few studies to date report that development in virtual teams tends to be non-linear, with bursts of regular and intense face-to-face interactions followed by periods of less intense interaction (Maznevski & Chudoba, 2000; Ratcheva & Vyakarnam, 2001). Membership in virtual teams also tends to be more dynamic than face-to-face teams (Gibson & Gibbs, 2006). These findings suggest that member adaptability or flexibility may be more relevant in virtual teams than in face-to-face teams due to the differences in the life span and membership boundaries of the virtual team.

The nature of tasks and leadership

Virtual teams can be used for a wide variety of tasks and in a wide variety of domains. Virtual teams, for example, have been used in university projects (Aubert & Kelsey, 2003), data entry tasks (Aiello & Kolb, 1995), engineering and construction (Forester, Thomas & Pinto, 2007), information technology (Belanger & Watson-Manheim, 2006; Morris, Marshall & Rainer, 2002), customer service (Froehle, 2006), product development (Geber, 1995) and many other domains. In virtual teams, as in traditional teams, the nature of the tasks being performed can greatly affect virtual team processes and outcomes. In particular, task complexity can dictate the communication patterns and the extent of virtuality in virtual teams (Bell & Kozlowski, 2002). Task complexity can be understood in terms of Thompson's (1967) pattern of workflow model or Van de Ven, Delbecq and Koenig's (1976) taxonomy. A key feature of the low–high complexity distinction is interdependence. Highly complex tasks involve a high degree of interdependence, which makes them more difficult to perform virtually. Thus, as tasks become more complex, interaction between team members tends to become less virtual. By implication, KSAOs related to interpersonal interactions should attain greater importance as team interdependence increases.

The complexity of the task will also impact the nature of leadership of the team. The ability of leaders to monitor performance and implement work solutions will be impacted not only by the nature of the task but also by the extent of the team's virtuality. Highly complex tasks and highly virtual teams tend to have members with vast expertise and competence. In such situations, leaders will be more effective if they delegate important functions to the team and encourage self-regulation within the team. Studies on leadership research have shown that transformational leadership is related to team creativity (Sosik, Avolio & Kahai, 1998), that shared leadership has better outcomes for virtual teams than a single emergent leader (Johnson, Suriya, Yoon, Berrett & La Fleur, 2002) and that virtual teams with shared leadership are more successful if emergent leaders focus on keeping track of group work (Carte, Chidambaram & Becker, 2006).

Criteria for virtual teams

An important consideration that needs to be taken into account in any selection system is how success is defined in a team environment. Success can be examined at the individual-level and/or at the team-level of analysis. At the individual level, researchers have looked at criteria such as member satisfaction, creativity and customer service (Jessup & Tansik, 1991; Ocker, 2005; Weisband & Atwater, 1999). Studies have shown mixed results with regard to satisfaction. The size of the team appears to have an impact as members of smaller virtual teams express greater satisfaction than members of larger teams (Bradner, Mark & Hertel, 2005). Also, higher levels of trust and project structure increase member satisfaction (Edwards & Sridhar, 2005). With regard to idea generation, groups relying on electronic brainstorming had better outcomes in terms of number of ideas, production blocking and evaluation apprehension (Gallupe et al., 1992). Brainstorming in virtual teams where members are anonymous was also found to be more successful than brainstorming in teams where members could be identified (Mejias, 2007). Gibson and Gibbs (2006) found that diversity and geographic dispersion affected team innovation negatively.

Several studies have looked at outputs at the team level of analysis. The introduction of appropriate virtual tools appears to increase team efficiency, sales volume and flexibility, and reduce time and cost (May & Carter, 2001). Efficient team processes and good member relations also affect team performance positively (Lurey & Raisinghani, 2001). Studies also show that greater geographic dispersion leads to lower performance, increased costs and reduced earnings (Boh, Ren, Kiesler & Bussjaegar, 2007; Cramton & Weber, 2005; McDonough, Kahn & Barczak, 2001). However, shared leadership and responsibility among team members, development of effective work patterns, appropriate training and active management can increase the chances of success for global virtual teams (James & Ward, 2001).

We have thus far reviewed the dynamic nature of virtual teams and the many contextual factors that affect their success, including the boundaries separating team members, the team's life span, task complexity, leadership structure and the criteria for virtual team success. Careful consideration of these factors is necessary when designing a selection system for staffing virtual teams. Context not only affects virtual team performance and member satisfaction, but also influences the KSAOs required in virtual team members.

Job Analysis and KSAOs for Virtual Team Selection

Before any selection system can be developed, a thorough job analysis is needed to ensure that relevant KSAOs are identified and weighted appropriately in selection. Job analyses can also highlight which outcomes and processes are most relevant when evaluating team performance, which is important to the validation of a selection system. Given the variety of previously discussed contextual variables that can affect virtual teamwork, we strongly recommend a local job analysis to guide the development and/or choice of KSAO assessments. Local job analyses should account for the multiple levels of performance in virtual teams, including the individual-within-the-team (Ostroff, 2002), the team itself and the broader organizational context. Though selection typically occurs at the individual level, a selection system for virtual teams is unlikely to be successful if team-level phenomena are not considered in the job analysis (Ployhart & Schneider, 2002). A team-level job analysis, such as Brannick, Levine and Morgeson's (2007) Multiphase Analysis of Performance (MAP) method, allows for a detailed assessment of team tasks and the subsequent inference of team-level KSAOs. At the individual level, an analysis of team member roles and tasks provides information for planning the distribution of KSAOs among team members (Morgeson, Humphrey & Reeder, 2012). In addition to the functional task roles, it is important to analyse team roles, defined as behavioural sets performed by team members that promote effective teamwork (for a complete review, see Mumford, Campion & Morgeson, 2006). For example, the specific leadership functions or roles for a project leader should be noted in order to guide the generation of KSAOs for this position. To summarize, a job analysis of virtual teams will consist of four steps: 1) an analysis of team tasks and functions in the broader organizational context, 2) the generation of team-level KSAOs, 3) an analysis of functional and team member roles, including the relative importance and the desired distribution of these roles, and 4) the generation of KSAOs for specific team members based on desired team KSAOs and member roles.

The tasks and KSAOs for virtual teamwork will differ between members and organizations. However, several taxonomies of traditional and virtual teamwork can provide guidelines regarding the typical KSAOs for virtual teams. We next review past research in these domains to provide some insight into the KSAOs for effective virtual team performance.

KSAOs in traditional teams

Traditional teams are distinguished from virtual teams by having regular opportunities to meet and work face-to-face. These teams have been the focus in much of the applied psychology and management literature. Several researchers have provided KSAO taxonomies for traditional teamwork, with a focus extending beyond core task competences (e.g., Cannon-Bowers, Tannenbaum, Salas & Volpe, 1995; Hoegl & Gemuenden, 2001; Stevens & Campion, 1994). Stevens and Campion (1994) organized teamwork KSAOs into two broad domains: interpersonal and self-management. Interpersonal KSAOs include competences for conflict resolution, collaborative problem solving and communication. These KSAOs refer to a member's competence to interact appropriately and adaptively with others. Self-management KSAOs are premised on the assumption that teams are empowered to make decisions and manage members' activities. As such, these KSAOs define competences that assist team coordination, goal-setting and performance monitoring. Other taxonomies of teamwork KSAOs echo those proposed by Stevens and Campion (1994), though they have several other dimensions (e.g., Cannon-Bowers et al., 1995; Hoegl & Gemuenden, 2001; Loughry, Ohland & Morre, 2007). Cannon-Bowers and colleagues (1995), for example, proposed additional KSAOs for situational awareness and adaptability in team members. Beyond the initial planning and successful adaptation depends on members' awareness potential problems (situational awareness) and the thoughtful adjustment of their actions to respond to such problems.

Although the teamwork competences provided by these frameworks are highly intuitive, they lack empirical scrutiny (Krumm & Hertel, 2013). Because the taxonomies were generated with inferential methods, potentially useful KSAOs could be missing. In addition, the broad range of tasks performed by teams is likely to alter the relative importance of teamwork KSAOs. As Cannon-Bowers and colleagues (1995) note, KSAOs may be task-generic (i.e., highly relevant to all team tasks) or task-specific (i.e., highly relevant only to certain tasks). For example, some teams perform routine tasks in a stable environment, which reduces the importance of situation awareness and adaptability relative to other KSAOs. The unique nature of virtual teams should create task demands that may not be adequately addressed by the general competence models of traditional teams.

KSAOs in virtual teams

The shift from traditional teams to virtual teams may affect the importance of several KSAOs, based on many of the contextual factors described earlier in this chapter. Virtual team members are infrequently monitored and typically receive less feedback, which places greater demands on self-management (Harvey, Novicevic & Garrison, 2004; Krumm & Hertel, 2013). Virtual team members experience greater barriers to developing team trust and cohesion due to their physical isolation, which in turn may demand greater communication and interpersonal KSAOs (e.g., Duarte & Snyder, 2001; Jarvenpaa & Leidner, 1999). Written communication KSAOs may be particularly relevant if most virtual team communication is in a written format, such as an email or chat platform. To the degree that virtual team members represent multiple cultures and/or nationalities, intercultural competences should be highly valued in team members (Ellingson & Wiethoff, 2002). For readers interested in intercultural competences (which may also apply to some traditional teams), we refer to Krumm, Terweil and Hertel (2013). Of relevance to the current chapter, these authors found that intercultural competences were generally similar in traditional and virtual teams that were culturally diverse (Krumm et al., 2013). Finally, Krumm and Hertel (2013) noted that virtual teams are often less stable than traditional teams, which gives added importance to member traits such as flexibility and tolerance for ambiguity.

In pulling these concepts together, Hertel, Konradt and Voss (2006) created a formal taxonomy of virtual team member competences and organized them into three domains: task work-related KSAOs; teamwork-related KSAOs; and tele-cooperation KSAOs. The first two dimensions generally refer to KSAOs that are relevant to teamwork in general: task work KSAOs refer to conscientiousness, integrity and loyalty, whereas teamwork-related KSAOs are defined by cooperation and communication skills. These two dimensions generally correspond to the two domains posited by Stevens and Campion (1994) for traditional teamwork. The third dimension, tele-cooperation KSAOs, refer to KSAOs theorized to have greater importance in virtual team settings. These KSAOs include persistence, creativity, independence and interpersonal trust. The KSAOs proposed by Hertel and colleagues (2006) were subsequently reorganized by Krumm and Hertel (2013) into three of the 'Great Eight' competence dimensions: supporting and cooperating; organizing and executing; and creating and conceptualizing (Bartram, 2005). The supporting and cooperating dimension includes communication, trust-building and mutual support KSAOs. The organizing and executing dimension refers to KSAOs for conscientiousness, loyalty and integrity. Finally, the creating and conceptualizing dimension includes KSAOs for a learning orientation, independence and creativity.

Whereas Krumm and Hertel's (2013) framework is of specific competences for virtual teamwork, Orvis and Zaccaro (2008) provided a more general approach which describes a process for identifying and distributing competences across a virtual team. Using Cannon-Bowers and colleagues' (1995) taxonomy, they first emphasized the importance of maximizing generic task and team competences in team members, as these competences apply to all teams, virtual included. With regard to generic task work KSAOs, all team members should possess an appropriate level of technical skill relevant to their job or profession. As an example, all members of a software development team should have a minimum level of competence in computer coding. Generic teamwork skills are similar to the domains proposed by Stevens and Campion (1994), referring to KSAOs for collaboration, communication, dependability and generic leadership expertise. Once the generic competences are identified, then task- and team-specific competences should be identified and weighted to create the right mix of competences in the team (Orvis & Zaccaro, 2008). In other words, Orvis and Zaccaro (2008) argued that generic competences provide a supplementary fit among team members, whereas specific competences provide a complementary fit among team members. Specific task work skills refer to the technical competences needed to perform a specific functional role, such as a training design team which requires both a content specialist and a computer programmer in order to create a completed product. Specific teamwork skills indicate competences required for working with a specific set of team members, such as knowledge of the preferences and skills of other team members (Orvis & Zaccaro, 2008).

The validity of virtual team KSAOs   Much of the empirical evidence for the validity of virtual team KSAOs has been indirect. For example, comparisons of virtual and face-to-face teams have vindicated the assumption that virtual groups experience greater barriers to the development of trust (e.g., Wilson, Straus & McEvily, 2006). By implication, KSAOs that facilitate the development of team trust should be highly valued. This implication is supported by research showing that non-task communication occurs more frequently in productive virtual teams than in unproductive virtual teams (Hofner Saphiere, 1996). Further, team processes such as coordination and mutual support become more relevant as the dispersion of the team increases (Hoegl, Ernst & Proserpio, 2007). As team members become more disconnected they experience greater social instability (Siebdraht, Hoegl, & Ernst, 2009) and require greater effort to achieve the development and maintenance of team cohesion. Finally, asynchronous communications between team members appear to demand more proactivity in team members in the form of requesting the information they need (Munzer & Holmer, 2009). Generally speaking, these KSAOs are important in traditional teams, but researchers have suggested that they have greater importance in virtual teams.

However, validation studies on virtual team member KSAOs are few. In one of the rare direct assessments of virtual teamwork KSAOs, Hertel and colleagues developed a self-assessment inventory, the Virtual Team Competency Inventory (VTCI), to validate the competences they propose (Hertel et al., 2006). They found that member reports of loyalty and cooperativeness were robust predictors of manager ratings of member performance, but other KSAOs yielded only modest effects. When correlating aggregated (team-level) competence scores with team-level performance, however, the authors found stronger relationships. Most notably, evidence for supplementary fit was provided by conscientiousness, cooperativeness and creativity (Hertel et al., 2006). That is, minimum and average team scores positively correlated with team performance, whereas within-team variance in these competences were negatively associated with performance. These findings are similar to those found in traditional teams, as meta-analytic evidence also indicates that conscientiousness and agreeableness operate as supplementary traits within teams (e.g., Prewett, Walvoord, Stilson, Rossi & Brannick, 2009). Indeed, a primary conclusion from the authors of the VCTI is that traditional task work and teamwork KSAOs, such as those proposed by Stevens and Campion (1994), appear to be most relevant to virtual team member performance. However, Hertel and colleagues' findings (2006) also support the assertion that creativity is demanded more commonly in virtual teams than in traditional teams.

A weakness of the VCTI is its reliance on self-reports of KSAOs. Perhaps alternative assessment methods (e.g., judgements from work samples, interviews or prior training and experiences) would provide a more accurate measurement of the proposed virtual team KSAOs. One must not only consider which KSAOs are relevant to the job, but also which assessment methods will best capture them. Thus, in the next section we turn to different assessment options for virtual team KSAOs.

Assessment of KSAOs for virtual team selection and staffing

The KSAOs for virtual teams present a variety of assessment options, with varying advantages and disadvantages. However, there is a paucity of validation studies specific to a virtual team context, so research is required to verify the efficacy of different assessment methods for virtual teams. In particular, the unique context and demands of virtual teamwork may necessitate alternative assessments to the traditional selection measures covered in most textbooks. Taking these issues into consideration, we review some of the assessment methods used for traditional teams and suggest ways they might be adapted to better represent the job context of virtual collaboration.

Non-cognitive tests　　Many of the virtual team KSAOs described by Hertel and colleagues (2006) refer to personality traits that can be easily assessed using a personality inventory. Indeed, a review of the VCTI items suggests that they are very similar to self-report measures of personality in both form and function. Previous research has supported the notion that teams benefit when all members are conscientious and agreeable (Bell, 2007), but the effects are quite modest unless teams are highly interdependent or evaluated according to behavioural criteria (Prewett et al., 2009). Research on extraversion and team performance, on the other hand, has yielded disappointing results, as both mean and variance estimates of team extraversion have shown weak relationships with performance, although there is a strong relationship between extraversion and leadership effectiveness in face-to-face teams (Judge, Bono, Ilies & Gerhardt, 2002).

Another useful non-cognitive measure is an integrity test. Personality-based and overt integrity tests provide valid prediction of counterproductive work behaviours, although their relationship with job performance is disputed (Sackett & Schmitt, 2012). It is likely that the criterion-related validity of integrity tests, much like personality testing in general, is influenced by the work context. Within a virtual team context, integrity tests may show greater validity due to the lower levels of control and oversight associated with remote collaboration. For example, Hertel and colleagues (2006) suggested that loyalty and dependability were more important in virtual teams than in traditional teams.

There is limited research examining the criterion-related validity of personality testing in virtual teams specifically. Hertel and colleagues (2006) found positive relationships for self-reported traits of conscientiousness, cooperativeness, and creativity. Other research has found that conscientiousness and agreeableness relate to the task and social dimensions of virtual team leadership, respectively (Cogliser, Gardner, Gavin & Broberg, 2012). Extraversion did not relate to emergent leadership (Cogliser et al., 2012). This finding runs counter to most face-to-face research on leadership emergence (e.g., Ensari, Riggio, Julie & Carslaw, 2011). However, leadership in virtual teams may be associated with a different set of personal characteristics from those in face-to-face teams. In virtual teams, dispositions associated with social dominance are probably less relevant to assuming and maintaining leadership roles because virtual teams involve little physical social interaction, influence and intimidation. This may be why women (who are on average less socially dominant than men) are more likely to emerge as leaders in virtual than in face-to-face groups (Colarelli, Spranger & Hechanova, 2006).

Laboratory research on command-and-control teams has indicated that higher levels of openness to experience positively contribute to team adaptation beyond cognitive ability (LePine, 2003). Interestingly, the same study found opposing effects for different dimensions of conscientiousness, whereby achievement orientation positively related to team adaptation but dependability showed a negative relationship with adaptation. These results suggest that some qualification might be warranted with regard to the beneficial effects of team conscientiousness, in which specific facets of conscientiousness must be weighed in conjunction with task demands for adaptation.

From this research, we can draw some preliminary conclusions. Assessment of agreeableness and conscientiousness should be considered for all prospective virtual team members. The assessment of openness to experience may also prove useful because many virtual team tasks require innovation, creativity and/or adaptability. However, research on personality and virtual team effectiveness remains in its infancy and additional research, particularly with field samples, is needed before drawing firm conclusions about its practical benefit in selection.

Situational judgement tests Whereas personality and integrity tests tend to focus on a candidate's propensity to perform job-relevant behaviours, situational judgement tests (SJTs) focus on a candidate's knowledge and recognition of effective behaviours. Stevens and Campion (1999), for example, developed and validated an SJT to assess knowledge of the different teamwork skills listed in their 1994 taxonomy. Mumford, Van Iddekinge, Morgeson and Campion (2008) developed an SJT assessing knowledge of team roles and used it to successfully predict team role performance. In a meta-analysis examining SJTs, Christian, Edwards and Bradley (2010) found generally high criterion-related validities for tests of teamwork, with uncorrected coefficients ranging from 0.27 for contextual performance ratings to 0.39 for task performance.

Despite the promise that SJTs hold for the assessment of teamwork KSAOs, several issues remain when considering their use in virtual teams. First, published validation studies of teamwork SJTs have largely focused on traditional team contexts (e.g., Stevens & Campion, 1999; Mumford et al., 2008), with item scenarios that may be less applicable to virtual teams (e.g., scenarios depicting production processes, face-to-face meetings). Although previous research suggests that traditional teamwork KSAOs remain relevant to virtual team performance, it remains to be seen whether SJTs developed for traditional teamwork can generalize to virtual team contexts. This issue relates to whether SJTs measure context-dependent knowledge, which is the traditional view, or general knowledge, which applies across situations (see this volume, chapter 11). If it can be inferred that an SJT developed for traditional teams captures more general knowledge of effective teamwork, then these SJTs are more likely to generalize to virtual teams. Second, because SJT questions tap into multiple teamwork and job constructs, SJT composite scores typically suffer from lower reliabilities than other forms of assessment (Catano, Brochu & Cheryl, 2012). This issue might be addressed by using parallel forms or alternative indices of reliability (e.g., Lievens & Sackett, 2007), but measurement error still warrants additional consideration in SJTs. Third, supporting evidence for the validity of teamwork SJTs rests on a limited number of studies (Christian et al., 2010). That is, we still have much to learn about the validity of SJTs for traditional teams, and more so for virtual teams.

Interviews The employment interview is the most common assessment method for selection and can be used to assess a wide variety of KSAOs. When structured appropriately, interviews provide a valid assessment of candidate KSAOs (Schmidt & Hunter, 1998). Interviews typically assess personality traits and applied social skills (Huffcut, Conway, Roth & Stone, 2001), KSAOs that are frequently mentioned in relation to virtual teams. However, the traditional interview assesses these KSAOs in face-to-face interactions between the interviewer and the candidate, and these interactions are largely infrequent in a virtual team context. Thus, a remote interview format, such as telephone and web-based interviews, may provide a more accurate context for the assessment of virtual interaction KSAOs.

An examination of remote interviews suggests several potential issues when using this format. The first concerns interviewer accuracy. Silvester, Anderson, Haddleton, Cunningham-Snell and Gibb (2000) found that telephone interviewers were less accurate in assessing interviewees' personality traits. One explanation for this is the lack of direct and physical context in the interaction from which the interviewer can draw. Individuals frequently modify their behaviour and interactional style when they cannot see the person they are communicating with (Rutter, 1987; Stephenson, Ayling & Rutter, 1970). Yet, this research also speaks to the need for assessing candidate interaction styles when communication is remote, as is often the case in virtual teams.

Adding a visual presence appears to mitigate some of the issues that arise with telephone interviews. Straus, Miles and Levesque (2001) found that distance interviews via video-conference elicited no differences from face-to-face interviews in interviewers' ratings of applicants. However, Blackman (2002) found that candidate responses were briefer and less detailed in remote interviews. In addition, interviewers have been rated as less likable by applicants in the video-conference condition than their face-to-face and telephone counterparts (Straus et al., 2001). Synchrony (the extent to which both parties communicate in a coherent, uninterrupted manner) is lower in video-conference interviews, which negatively affects the applicant's perception of the interview interaction.

This highlights a second issue with remote interviews: negative applicant perceptions of the interviewer and/or organization. Currently, the remote interview is recommended as an initial hurdle for applicants in order to reduce the size of the applicant pool (see Blackman, 2017, this volume, chapter 9).

A limitation with much of the research on remote interviews is that they were used to select for job positions that did not emphasize virtual work. A theoretical advantage of using the remote interview for virtual team selection is that it allows for a more accurate assessment of the virtual interaction competences of the candidate. Unfortunately, research has yet to address the link between the interview and job contexts; much of the remote interview literature has been conducted as screening measures for traditional jobs. However, organizations interested in assessing competences for virtual interaction may be well served if they structure their interviews to allow for such interaction. At the very least, organizations may benefit from making separate evaluations for remote interactions and in-person interactions.

Work samples and simulations Work-related exercises or simulations, like those conducted in an assessment centre, rely on direct observation of behaviours to infer competences. They have demonstrated acceptable criterion-related validity in selection and promotion (Arthur, Day, McNelly & Edens, 2003; Schmidt & Hunter, 1998). Although selection in assessment centres traditionally uses KSAO scores obtained from observations across multiple exercises, the use of exercise scores has also been suggested because they tend to demonstrate better construct validity than competence scores (Lance, Foster, Gentry & Thoreson, 2004). Thus, some initial decisions for using work simulations for virtual team selection is whether to use KSAO scores or exercise (task) scores for prediction, as well as specific dimension ratings or overall assessor ratings (OAR).

Regardless of the approach one takes, a major challenge in the use of work simulations for virtual teams resides in the issue of fidelity, or the extent that the simulation mirrors the psychological, physical and/or behavioural elements of a job. To illustrate this challenge, we summarize some critical points from O'Leary, Forsman and Isaacson (this volume, chapter 12). Although research has found that simulations exhibit similar criterion-related validities between low- and high-fidelity simulations (Boyce, Corbet & Adler, 2013), studies that directly compare different simulation fidelities have found significant differences in results. In particular, research has found that response fidelity (the degree to which the simulation requires participants to respond or behave in a way that is required on the job) has a much greater impact on criterion-related validity than other types of fidelity manipulation (e.g., Funke & Schuler, 1998; Lievens, De Corte & Westerveld, 2015).

Given these findings, a simulation for virtual team selection could be more useful for selection if it requires computer-mediated collaboration with others. Experimental research has highlighted a number of differences in group communication and decision making when comparing face-to-face and computer-mediated groups (Coovert & Thompson, 2001). Thus, it is reasonable to suspect that the use of computer-mediated exercises may affect the expression and evaluation of teamwork KSAOs. For virtual teams, exercises designed to tap the skills for interpersonal interactions, conflict management and managing others should strive to simulate virtual interactions. For example, if a virtual team will meet via video- or teleconference, then a leaderless group discussion exercise may yield more useful evaluations as a teleconference than a face-to-face meeting. One study has found that the use of interactive computerized exercises demonstrated validity beyond cognitive ability (Lievens, Van Keer & Volckaert, 2010), but direct comparisons between computer-mediated and face-to-face simulations have not been made.

Unfortunately, the use of such advanced and tailored simulations is not without disadvantages. The published research on technology-enhanced work simulations is still an emerging field and many of the exercises that have been studied (e.g., in-basket exercises) are not designed to measure competences for tele-cooperation. Thus, further research is needed to verify the efficacy of technology-enhanced exercises that are appropriate to virtual teams. In addition, virtual teamwork simulations may present significant financial and logistical obstacles an organization will need to overcome.

Training and experience evaluations   The final method discussed here for assessing virtual team competences is the evaluation of relevant training and experiences. Training in traditional teams generally shows a positive impact on subsequent team performance (Salas et al., 2008). Although training is typically considered an alternative to selection, some organizations require employees to complete a training programme before selecting them to work in a virtual team (Rosen, Furst & Blackburn, 2006), with the presumption that participation in the training programme will ensure the employee has the requisite tele-cooperation competences. Evidence from research on virtual team training is equivocal. In a survey of HR managers from organizations using virtual teams, Rosen and colleagues (Kirkman, Rosen, Tesluk & Gibson, 2006) found that over 70% of respondents viewed training as either ineffective or only 'slightly' effective. Another study found no significant main effect of training proficiency on team customer satisfaction, but the authors did find a positive effect of training when teams had higher levels of technology support, leader experience and team trust. More targeted training programmes, such as those focused on specific team processes, have positively affected virtual team effectiveness as well (Rice, Davidson, Dannenhoffer & Gay, 2007).

Taken together, the findings from training research suggest that those who participate in training are more likely to perform well than those who do not. Yet, mere participation in a training programme should not be viewed as equivalent to having the necessary KSAOs for virtual teamwork. This is especially true given the variations in the design, delivery, evaluation and organizational support for different training programmes (Kirkpatrick, 1976). Although training may improve virtual team KSAOs, explicit assessment of the KSAOs embedded in the training should be conducted to verify that participants have the minimum level of competences needed for the virtual team.

Assessments of prior virtual team experiences may also provide valuable information when staffing a virtual team, an approach called 'benchmarking' (Filgo, Hines & Hamilton, 2008). Although benchmarking is viewed positively by practitioners, there is little if any published research on the validity of benchmarking assessments for virtual team selection. Virtual teams are now common and many people have some experience of working in them. Therefore, as a practical matter, some type of explicit assessment of virtual team experience may be the most efficient, simple and acceptable way to estimate how well an individual will perform in a virtual team. Assessment of virtual team experience may be at least as valid as reference checks or letters of recommendation, which have passable validities (Schmidt & Hunter, 1998).

Future Research

The field of virtual teamwork is relatively new and presents a multitude of needs and opportunities for future research. This is particularly true in the area of selection and assessment. We previously discussed some frameworks for virtual team member KSAOs (Krumm & Hertel, 2013; Orvis & Zaccaro, 2008), but these taxonomies have received little empirical attention. Thus, the effect that virtual collaboration has on teamwork KSAOs is largely unknown. We also noted that many of the traditional assessment tools have not been adapted to a work context appropriate for virtual teams. Teamwork SJTs, employment interviews and work simulations have typically focused on traditional teamwork and competences for face-to-face interactions. It is unclear whether these methods require adaptation more suitable to a virtual team context, though there is at least a theoretical argument that such an adaptation would be beneficial.

Alternative assessments and experiences may also emerge that can uniquely inform virtual teamwork competences. For example, experience evaluations could be improved by moving beyond the traditional work environment and assessing virtual interaction competences in social network or gaming domains. Those skilled at building relationships via social networks may also excel at building relationships in a virtual team. Similarly, leaders of an online videogame group can be expected to have developed some leadership skills that generalize to a work context. As the twenty-first century progresses, organizations may increasingly find valuable information on worker competences in unfamiliar places.

Conclusion

Virtual teams are part of the working environment in the internet age. They are ubiquitous and have enabled teams to form and work together despite geographical boundaries. By bringing people together virtually, they have increased the diversity of teams and team members in organizations. This has undoubtedly increased the cross-fertilization of ideas, work styles, cultures and perspectives. This, in conjunction with the features of the virtual environment, presents unique challenges when building teams that will work together electronically. In this chapter, we have taken stock of theory, research, and practice for virtual teams, identifying gaps and suggesting directions for future research.

Selection for face-to-face teams is daunting in itself. Adding the complexities of the virtual environment to teams increases not only the difficulty of selecting team members, but also the importance of doing so. The internet and working in a virtual landscape are huge changes in work and society, on the same scale as the printing press, assembly line, service economy and globalization. These changes require major shifts in the way people work together, the skills required to work effectively and how organizations identify and select people. We hope this chapter will help industrial and organizational psychologists as they face the challenge of crafting teams and sustaining teamwork in an increasingly virtual workplace.

References

Adams, G. A., Elacqua, T. C., & Colarelli, S. M. (1994). The employment interview as a sociometric selection technique. *Journal of Psychotherapy, Psychodrama and Sociometry, 47,* 99–113.

Adams, S. J., Roch, S. G., & Ayman, R. (2005). Communication medium and member familiarity: The effects on decision time, accuracy, and satisfaction. *Small Group Research, 36,* 321–353.

Aiello, J. R., & Kolb, K. J. (1995). Electronic performance monitoring and social context: Impact on productivity and stress. *Journal of Applied Psychology, 80,* 339–353.

Andres, H. P. (2002). A comparison of face-to-face and virtual software development teams. *Team Performance Management, 8,* 39–48.

Arthur, W., Day, E. A., McNelly, T. L., & Edens, P. S. (2003). A meta-analysis of the criterion-related validity of assessment center dimensions. *Personnel Psychology, 56*(1), 125–153.

Aubert, B. A., & Kelsey, B. L. (2003). Further understanding of trust and performance in virtual teams. *Small Group Research, 34,* 575–618.

Bartram, D. (2005). The great eight competencies: A criterion-centric approach to validation. *Journal of Applied Psychology, 90,* 1185–1203.

Belanger, F., & Watson-Manheim, M. B. (2006). Virtual teams and multiple media: Structuring media use to attain strategic goals. *Group Decision and Negotiation, 15,* 299–321.

Bell, S. T. (2007). Deep-level composition variables as predictors of team performance: A meta-analysis. *Journal of Applied Psychology, 92,* 595–615.

Bell, B. S., & Kozlowski, S. W. J. (2002). A typology of virtual teams: Implications for effective leadership. *Group & Organization Management, 27,* 14–49.

Bhappu, A. D., Griffith, T. L., & Northcraft, G. B. (1997). Media effects and communication bias in diverse groups. *Organizational Behavior and Human Decision Processes, 70,* 199–205.

Blackman, M. C. (2002). The employment interview via the telephone: Are we sacrificing accurate personality judgments for cost efficiency? *Journal of Research in Personality, 36*(3), 208–223.

Boh, W. F., Ren, Y., Kiesler, S., & Bussjaeger, R. (2007). Expertise and collaboration in the geographically dispersed organization. *Organization Science, 18*(4), 595–612.

Bosch-Sijtsema, P. (2007). The impact of individual expectations and expectation conflict on virtual teams. *Group & Organization Management, 32,* 358–388.

Bouas, K. S., & Arrow, H. (1996). The development of group identity in computer and face-to-face groups with membership change. *Computer Supported Cooperative Work, 4,* 153–178.

Boyce, A. S., Corbet, C. E., & Adler, S. (2013). Simulations in the selection context: Considerations, challenges, and opportunities. *In* M. Fetzer & K. Tuzinski (Eds.), *Simulations for Personnel Selection* (pp. 17–41). New York: Springer.

Bradner, E., Mark, G., & Hertel, T. D. (2005). Team size and technology fit: Participation, awareness, and rapport in distributed teams. *IEEE Transactions on Professional Communication, 48*(1), 68–77.

Brannick, M. T., & Levine, E. L., & Morgeson, F. P. (2007). *Job and Work Analysis: Methods, Research, and Applications for Human Resource Management* (2nd ed.). Thousand Oaks, CA: Sage.

Cannon-Bowers, J., Tannenbaum, S., Salas, E., & Volpe, C. (1995). Defining team competencies and establishing team training requirements. *In* R. Guzzo & E. Salas (Eds.), *Team Effectiveness and Decision Making in Organizations* (pp. 333–380). San Francisco: Jossey-Bass,

Carte, T. A., Chidambaram, L., & Becker, A. (2006). Emergent leadership in self-managed virtual teams. *Group Decision and Negotiation, 15,* 323–343.

Catano, V. M., Brochu, A., & Lamerson, C. D. (2012). Assessing the reliability of situational judgment tests used in high-stakes situations. *International Journal of Selection and Assessment, 20,* 333–346.

Chidambaram, L. (1996). Relational development in computer-supported groups. *MIS Quarterly, 20,* 143–165.

Christian, M. S., Edwards, B. D., & Bradley, J. C. (2010). Situational judgment tests: Constructs assessed and a meta-analysis of their criterion-related validities. *Personnel Psychology, 63,* 83–117. doi: 10.1111/j.1744-6570.2009.01163.x.

Cogliser, C. C., Gardner, W. L., Gavin, M. B., & Broberg, J. C. (2012). Big Five personality factors and leader emergence in virtual teams: Relationships with team trustworthiness, member performance contributions, and team performance. *Group & Organization Management, 37*(6), 752–784.

Colarelli, S. M., Spranger, J. L., & Hechanova, M. R. (2006). Women, power, and sex composition in small groups: An evolutionary perspective. *Journal of Organizational Behavior, 27,* 163–184.

Coovert, M. D., & Thompson, L. F. (2001). *Computer-supported Cooperative Work: Issues and Implications for Workers, Organizations, and Human Resource Management.* Thousand Oaks, CA: Sage.

Cramton, C. D., & Weber, S. S. (2005). Relationships among geographic dispersion, team processes, and effectiveness in software development work teams. *Journal of Business Research, 58,* 758–765.

Daft, R. L., & Lengel, R. H. (1986). Organizational information requirement, media richness and structural determinants. *Management Science, 32,* 554–571.

Dennis, A. R., & Garfield, M. J. (2003). The adoption and use of GSS in project teams: Toward more participative processes and outcomes. *MIS Quarterly, 27,* 289–323.

Duarte, D. L., & Snyder, N. T. (2001). *Mastering Virtual Teams.* San Francisco: Jossey-Bass.

Edwards, H. K., & Sridhar, V. (2005). Analysis of software requirements engineering exercises in a global virtual team Setup 1. *Journal of Global Information Management, 13*(2), 21–41.

Ellingson, J. E., & Wiethoff, C. (2002). From traditional to virtual: Staffing the organization of the future today. *In* R. Heneman & D. G. (Eds.), *Human Resource Management in Virtual Organizations* (pp. 141–177). Charlotte, NC: Information Age Publishing.

Ensari, N., Riggio, R. E., Christian, J., & Carslaw, G. (2011). Who emerges as a leader? Meta-analyses of individual differences as predictors of leadership emergence. *Personality and Individual Differences, 51*(4), 532–536.

Filgo, S. K., Hines, S., & Hamilton, S. (2008). Using assessments to predict successful virtual team collaboration performance. *In* J. Nemiro, M. M. Beyerlein, L. Bradley & S. Beyerlein (Eds.), *The Handbook of High-Performance Virtual Teams: A Toolkit for Collaborating Across Boundaries* (pp. 533–551). San Francisco: Jossey-Bass.

Forester, G. L., Thomas, P., & Pinto, J. K. (2007). Importance of goal setting in virtual project teams. *Psychological Reports, 100*, 270–274.

Froehle, C. M. (2006). Service personnel, technology, and their interaction in influencing customer satisfaction. *Decision Sciences, 37*, 5–38.

Funke, U., & Schuler, H. (1998). Validity of stimulus and response components in video tests of social competence. *International Journal of Selection and Assessment, 6(2)*, 115–123.

Gallupe, R. B., Dennis, A. R., Cooper, W. H., Valacich, J. S., Bastianutti, L. M., & Nunamaker, Jr., J. F. (1992). Electronic brainstorming and group size. *Academy of Management Journal, 35*, 350–369.

Geber, B. (1995). Virtual teams. *Training, 32*, 36–40.

Gibson, C. B., & Gibbs, J. L. (2006). Unpacking the concept of virtuality: The effects of geographic dispersion, electronic dependence, dynamic structure, and national diversity on team innovation. *Administrative Science Quarterly, 51*, 451–495.

Griffith, T. L., & Neale, M. A. (2001). Information processing in traditional, hybrid, and virtual teams: From nascent knowledge to transactive memory. *In* B. M. Staw & R. I. Sutton (Eds.), *Research in Organizational Behavior* (Vol. 23, pp. 379–421). Greenwich, CT: JAI Press.

Hardin, A. M., Fuller, M. A., & Davison, R. M. (2007). I know I can, but can we? Culture and efficacy beliefs in global virtual teams. *Small Group Research, 38*, 130–155.

Harvey, M., Novicevic, M. M., & Garrison, G. (2004). Challenges to staffing global virtual teams. *Human Resource Management Review, 14*(3), 275–294.

Hertel, G., Konradt, U., & Voss, K. (2006). Competencies for virtual teamwork: Development and validation of a web-based selection tool for members of distributed teams. *European Journal of Work and Organizational Psychology, 15*, 477–505.

Hightower, R., & Sayeed, L. (1996). Effects of communication mode and prediscussion information distribution characteristics on information exchange in groups. *Information Systems Research, 7*, 451–465.

Hiltz, S. R., Johnson, K., & Turoff, M. (1986). Experiments in group decision making. *Human Communication Research, 13*, 225–252.

Hoegl, M., Ernst, H., & Proserpio, L. (2007). How teamwork matters more as team member dispersion increases. *Journal of Productive Management, 24*, 156–165.

Hoegl, M., & Gemuenden, H. G. (2001). Teamwork quality and the success of innovative projects: A theoretical concept and empirical evidence. *Organization Science, 12*, 435–449.

Hofner Saphiere, D. M. (1996). Productive behaviors of global business teams. *International Journal of Intercultural Relations, 20*, 227–259.

Hollingshead, A. B. (1996). The rank-order effect in group decision making. *Organizational Behavior and Human Decision Processes, 68*, 181–193.

Huffcutt, A. I., Conway, J. M., Roth, P. L., & Stone, N. J. (2001). Identification and meta-analytic assessment of psychological constructs measured in employment interviews. *Journal of Applied Psychology, 86*, 897–913.

James, M., & Ward, K. (2001). Leading a multinational team of change agents of Glaxo Wellcome (now Glaxo SmithKline). *Journal of Change Management, 2*, 148–159.

Jarvenpaa, S. L. & Leidner, D. E. (1999). Communication and trust in global virtual teams. *Organization Science, 10*, 791–815.

Jessup, L. M., & Tansik, D. A. (1991). Decision making in an automated environment: The effects of anonymity and proximity with a group decision support system. *Decision Sciences, 22*(2), 266.

Johnson, S. D., Suriya, C., Yoon, S. W., Berrett, & J. V., & La Fleur, J. (2002). Team development and group processes of virtual learning teams. *Computers & Education, 39*, 379–393.

Jonassen, D. H., & Kwon, H. I. (2001). Communication patterns in computer mediated versus face-to-face group problem solving. *Educational Technology Research and Development, 49*, 35–51.

Judge, T. A., Bono, J. E., Ilies, R., & Gerhardt, M. (2002). Personality and leadership: A qualitative and quantitative review. *Journal of Applied Psychology, 87*, 765–780.

Kirkman, B. L., & Mathieu, J. E. (2005). The dimensions and antecedents of team virtuality. *Journal of Management, 31*, 700–718.

Kirkman, B. L., Rosen, B., Tesluk, P. E., & Gibson, C. B. (2006). Enhancing the transfer of computer-assisted training proficiency in geographically distributed teams. *Journal of Applied Psychology, 91*, 706–716.

Kirkpatrick, D. L. (1976). Evaluation of training. *In* R. L. Craig (Ed.), *Training and Development Handbook: A Guide to Human Resources Development* (pp. 18.1–18.27). New York: McGraw-Hill.

Krumm, S., & Hertel, G. (2013). Knowledge, skills, abilities, and other characteristics (KSAOs) for virtual teamwork. *In* D. Bakker (Ed.) *The Psychology of Digital Media and Work* (pp. 80–99). Hove: Psychology Press.

Krumm, S., Terwiel, K., & Hertel, G. (2013). Challenges in norm formation and adherence: The knowledge, skills, and ability requirements of virtual and traditional cross–cultural teams. *Journal of Personnel Psychology, 12*(1), 33–44.

Lance, C. E., Foster, M. R., Gentry, W. A., & Thoresen, J. D. (2004). Assessor cognitive processes in an operational assessment center. *Journal of Applied Psychology, 89*(1), 22–35.

Lee-Kelley, L. (2006). Locus of control and attitudes to working in virtual teams. *International Journal of Project Management, 24*, 234–243.

LePine, J. A. (2003). Team adaptation and post-change performance: Effects of team composition in terms of members' cognitive ability and personality. *Journal of Applied Psychology, 88*, 27–39.

Lievens, F., De Corte, W., & Westerveld, L. (2015). Understanding the building blocks of selection procedures: Effects of response fidelity on performance and utility. *Journal of Management, 41*, 1604–1627. doi: 10.1177/0149206312463941.

Lievens, F., & Sackett, P. R. (2007). Situational judgment tests in high-stakes settings: Issues and strategies with generating alternate forms. *Journal of Applied Psychology, 92*(4), 1043.

Lievens, F., Van Keer, E., & Volckaert, E. (2010). Gathering behavioral samples through a computerized and standardized assessment center exercise: Yes, it is possible. *Journal of Personnel Psychology, 9*(2), 94–98.

Lind, M. R. (1999). The gender impact of temporary virtual work groups. *IEEE Transactions on Professional Communication, 42*, 276–285.

Loughry, M. L., Ohland, M. W., & Morre, D. D. (2007). Development of a theory-based assessment of team member effectiveness. *Educational and Psychological Measurement, 67*, 505–524.

Lurey, J. S., & Raisinghani, M. S. (2001). An empirical study of best practices in virtual teams. *Information & Management, 38*(8), 523–544.

Martins, L. L., Gilson, L. L., & Maynard, M. T. (2004). Virtual teams: What do we know and where do we go from here? *Journal of Management, 30*, 805–835.

May, A., & Carter, C. (2001). A case study of virtual teams working in the European automotive industry. *International Journal of Industrial Ergonomics, 27*, 171–186.

Maznevski, M. L., & Chudoba, K. M. (2000). Bridging space over time: Global virtual team dynamics and effectiveness. *Organization Science, 11*, 473–492.

McDonough III, E. F., Kahn, K. B., & Barczak, G. (2001). An investigation of the use of global, virtual, and colocated new product development teams. *The Journal of Product Innovation Management, 18*, 110–120.

Mejias, R. J. (2007). The interaction of process losses, process gains, and meeting satisfaction within technology-supported environments. *Small Group Research, 38*, 156–194.

Metiu, A. (2006). Owning the code: Status closure in distributed groups. *Organization Science, 17*, 418–435.

Morgeson, F. P., Humphrey, S. E., & Reeder, M. C. (2012). Team selection. *In* N. Schmitt (Ed.), *The Oxford Handbook of Personnel Assessment and Selection* (pp. 832–848). New York: Oxford University Press.

Morris, S. A., Marshall, T. E., & Rainer, R. K., Jr. (2002). Impact of user satisfaction and trust on virtual team members. *Information Resources Management Journal, 15,* 22–30.

Mumford, T. V., Campion, M. A., & Morgeson, F. P. (2006). *Situational] in Work Teams: A Team Role Typology* (pp. 319–343). Mahwah, NJ: Lawrence Erlbaum.

Mumford, T. V., Van Iddekinge, C. H., Morgeson, F. P., & Campion, M. A. (2008). The team role test: Development and validation of a team role knowledge situational judgment test. *Journal of Applied Psychology, 93,* 250–267.

Munzer, S., & Holmer, T. (2009). Bridging the gap between media synchronicity and task performance: Effects of media characteristics on process variables and task performance indicators in an information pooling task. *Communication Research, 36,* 76–103.

Ocker, R. J. (2005). Influences on creativity in asynchronous virtual teams: A qualitative analysis of experimental teams. *IEEE Transactions on Professional Communication, 48,* 22–39.

O'Leary, M. B., & Cummings, J. N. (2007). The spatial, temporal, and configurational characteristics of geographic dispersion in teams. *MIS Quarterly, 31,* 433–452.

Orvis, K. L., & Zaccaro, S. J. (2008). Team composition and member selection: Optimizing teams for virtual collaboration. *In* J. Nemiro, M. M. Beyerlein, L. Bradley & S. Beyerlein (Eds.), *The Handbook Of High-Performance Virtual Teams: A Toolkit for Collaborating Across Boundaries* (pp. 243–262). San Francisco: Jossey-Bass.

Ostroff, C. (2002). Leveling the selection field. *In* F. J. Yammarino & F. Dansereau (Eds.), *The Many Faces of Multi-Level Issues* (pp. 141–154). Amsterdam: Elsevier Science/JAI Press.

Oyserman, D., Coon, H. M., & Kemmelmeier, M. (2002). Rethinking individualism and collectivism: Evaluation of theoretical assumptions and meta-analysis. *Psychological Bulletin, 128,* 3–72.

Ployhart, R. E., & Schneider, B. (2002). A multi-level perspective on personnel selection: When will practice catch up? *In* F. J. Yammarino & F. Dansereau (Eds.), *The Many Faces of Multi-Level Issues* (pp. 165–175). Amsterdam: Elsevier Science/JAI Press.

Prewett, M. S., Walvoord, A. G., Stilson, F. R. B., Rossi, M. E., & Brannick, M. D. (2009). The team personality–team performance relationship revisited: The impact of criterion choice, pattern of workflow, and method of aggregation. *Human Performance, 22,* 273–296.

Rasters, G., Vissers, G., & Dankbaar, B. (2002). An inside look: Rich communication through lean media in a virtual research team. *Small Group Research, 33,* 718–754.

Ratcheva, V., & Vyakarnam, S. (2001). Exploring team formation processes in virtual partnerships. *Integrated Manufacturing Systems, 12,* 512–523.

Rice, D. J., Davidson, B. D., Dannenhoffer, J. F., & Gay, G. K. (2007). Improving the effectiveness of virtual teams by adapting team processes. *Computer Supported Cooperative Work (CSCW), 16*(6), 567–594.

Rosen, B., Furst, S., & Blackburn, R. (2006). Training for virtual teams: An investigation of current practices and future needs. *Human Resource Management, 45*(2), 229–247.

Rutter, D. R. (1987). *Communicating by Telephone.* Oxford: Pergamon Press.

Sackett, P. R., & Schmitt, N. (2012). On reconciling conflicting meta-analytic findings regarding integrity test validity. *Journal of Applied Psychology, 97*(3), 550–556.

Salas, E., DiazGranados, D., Klein, C., Burke, C. S., Stagl, K. C., Goodwin, G. F., & Halpin, S. M. (2008). Does team training improve team performance? A meta-analysis. *Human Factors, 50*(6), 903–933.

Sassenberg, K., & Boos, M. (2003). Attitude change in computer-mediated communication: Effects of anonymity and category norms. *Group Process & Intergroup Relations, 6,* 405–422.

Schmidt, F. L., & Hunter, J. E. (1998). The validity and utility of selection methods in personnel psychology: Practical and theoretical and practical implications of 85 years of research. *Journal of Applied Psychology, 124*(2), 262–274.

Siebdraht, F., Hoegl, M., & Ernst, H. (2009). How to manage virtual teams. *MIT Sloan Management Review, 50,* 63–68.

Siegel, J., Dubrovsky, V., Kiesler, S., & McGuire, T. W. (1986). Group processes in computer-mediated communication. *Organizational Behavior and Human Decision Processes, 37,* 157–187.

Silvester, J., Anderson, N., Haddleton, E., Cunningham-Snell, N., & Gibb, A. (2000). A cross-model comparison of telephone and face-to-face interviews in graduate recruitment. *International Journal of Selection and Assessment, 8,* 16–21.

Sosik, J. J., Avolio, B. J., & Kahai, S. S. (1998). Inspiring group creativity: Comparing anonymous and identified electronic brainstorming. *Small Group Research, 29,* 3–31.

Staples, D. S., & Webster, J. (2007). Exploring traditional and virtual team members' 'best practices': A social cognitive theory perspective. *Small Group Research, 38,* 60–97.

Stevens, M. J., & Campion, M. A. (1994). The knowledge, skill, and ability requirements for teamwork: Implications for human resource management. *Journal of Management, 20,* 503–530.

Stevens, M. J., & Campion, M. A. (1999). Staffing work teams: Development and validation of a selection test for teamwork settings. *Journal of Management, 25*(2), 207–228.

Stephenson, G. M., Ayling, K., & Rutter, D. R. (1970). Eye-contact, distance, and affiliation: A re-evaluation. *British Journal of Social and Clinical Psychology, 15,* 113–120.

Straus, S. G. (1996). Getting a clue: The effects of communication media and information distribution on participation and performance in computer-mediated and face-to-face groups. *Small Group Research, 27,* 115–142.

Straus, S. G., & McGrath, J. E. (1994). Does the medium matter? The interaction of task type and technology on group performance and member reactions. *Journal of Applied Psychology, 79,* 87–97.

Straus, S. G., Miles, J. A., & Levesque, L. L. (2001). The effects of videoconference, telephone, and face-to-face media on interviewer and applicant judgments in employment interviews. *Journal of Management, 27,* 363–381.

Thompson, J. D. (1967). *Organizations in Action: Social Science Bases of Administrative Theory.* New York: McGraw-Hill.

van der Kleij, R., Paashuis, R., & Schraagen, J. M. (2005). On the passage of time: Temporal differences in video-mediated and face-to-face interaction. *International Journal of Human-Computer Studies, 62,* 521–542.

Van de Ven, A. H., Delbecq, A. L., & Koenig, R., Jr. (1976). Determinants of coordination modes within organizations. *American Sociological Review, 41,* 322–338.

Walther, J. B., & Burgoon, J. K. (1992). Relational communication in computer-mediated interaction. *Human Communication Research, 19,* 50–88.

Warkentin, M., Sayeed, L., & Hightower, R. (1997). Virtual teams versus face-to-face teams: An exploratory study of a web-based conference system. *Decision Sciences, 28,* 241–262.

Weisband, S., & Atwater, L. (1999). Evaluating self and others in electronic and face-to-face groups. *Journal of Applied Psychology, 84*(4), 632–639.

Wilson, J. M., Straus, S. G., & McEvily, B. (2006). All in due time: The development of trust in computer-mediated and face-to-face teams. *Organizational Behavior and Human Decision Processes, 99,* 16–33.

17

Assessment for Leader Development

Neta Moye, Rose Mueller-Hanson and Claus Langfred

Introduction

A significant body of research recognizes that leaders matter to the success of organizations and that there are tremendous costs to hiring the wrong leader (Hogan, Hogan & Kaiser, 2010). Since the early 1970s, the statistics regarding leader derailment have been consistently worrying. Depending on the study, the reported percentage of leaders who 'derail' (where derailment denotes being fired, demoted or plateaued below their projected level of attainment) ranges between 30% and 67% (Hollenbeck, 2009) despite the growing use of assessments for selection and the development of current leaders as well as those being groomed to be the next generation of leaders (Church & Rotolo, 2013). This suggests that there may be room for improvement in how assessments are being used for leader selection and development.

How to develop leaders has been covered in great depth (Day, Fleenor, Atwater, Sturm & McKee, 2014; Dongen, 2014; O'Connell, 2014) and several chapters have focused on the use of assessments for leader selection (Howard, 2001; Howard & Thomas, 2010; Thornton, Hollenbeck & Johnson, 2010). While assessments are being used principally for development (Church & Rotolo, 2013; for an exception, see Wall & Knights, 2013), how to use assessments for leader development has received less focused attention. For that reason, this chapter focuses solely on the use of assessment for leader development purposes.

For this reason, we review research and best practices relevant to assessment system design in the context of leader development. In particular, using the London, Smither and Diamante (2007) framework for assessment system design, we focus on three key design decisions: Why? – Clearly define the purpose assessments are intended to serve. Which? – Determine which attributes to assess. And how? – Decide what type of assessment instrument to use. We explore what makes these decisions particularly challenging in a leader development context, share what research and/or best practice has to offer to help

The Wiley Blackwell Handbook of the Psychology of Recruitment, Selection and Employee Retention,
First Edition. Edited by Harold W. Goldstein, Elaine D. Pulakos, Jonathan Passmore and Carla Semedo.
© 2017 John Wiley & Sons Ltd. Published 2020 by John Wiley & Sons Ltd.

guide each decision and highlight critical questions that remain unanswered. We conclude by highlighting future research directions that could help practitioners continue to hone their practice and improve the organizational impact of assessments used for leader development.

Why? The Purpose of the Assessment

When using assessments for selection, the purpose is fairly clear: to maximize prediction. Numerous studies have demonstrated that using high-quality assessments to inform selection decisions results in higher employee performance, reduced turnover and a host of other benefits (CEB, 2013). However, when using assessments for development, the value proposition is less clear. For example, a 2014 survey of HR leaders found that while 76% use assessments for external hiring, only 56% use them for leadership development (Kantrowitz, 2014). Moreover, only 37% of organizations indicated that they collect metrics to determine how assessments add value to development programmes. The same study found that assessment use increased the higher the job level being assessed. Similarly, Church and Rotolo (2013) found that 90% of organizations use assessments for executive development, but only 47% use them for first-line supervisor development.

One reason why assessments are not used more often for development may be ignorance of how assessments contribute to development. 'Best practice' summaries of leadership development frequently highlight individual components of development programmes (e.g., 360-degree feedback, action learning) but do not address how each component relates to others or to a systematic learning process (Day & Halpin, 2001). Organizations tend to select learning activities and developmental assessments based on their popularity or familiarity (i.e., leadership programme staff choose the assessments with which they have personal experience) without careful thought as to how these assessments will support the development process, resulting in missed opportunities, cynical participants and wasted time and money. Therefore, the first step in choosing the right assessment is to consider the purpose. Why is the assessment being used, how will it support development and what outcomes does the organization hope to achieve? A clearly defined purpose is the first step in improving the fit between what to measure and how to measure it, and improving the effectiveness of assessments. In this section, we explore the various ways that assessments can contribute in a systematic leader development process.

How assessments contribute to development

We define development as the acquisition of new beliefs, knowledge, skills and/or behaviour that expands an employee's capacity to contribute to the organization. Therefore, assessments used for development must contribute to improving an employee's capacity to contribute to the organization's strategic objectives. With this definition in mind, Figure 17.1 organizes the existing research into a framework that illustrates how assessments can contribute to development.

Identifying leader development needs to begin with a clear understanding of the organization's strategic objectives and priorities. In order to have leaders ready to execute strategy, the key drivers of the business strategy must first be identified (CCL, 2009). Starting with the strategy and the key business drivers allows a clear alignment between leader development and business outcomes. The value of assessments for development becomes more apparent when the purpose of the overall leadership development process is linked to critical business needs.

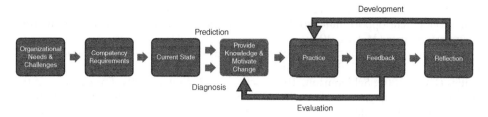

Figure 17.1 Framework for how assessments can contribute to development.

The next step is to translate the key business drivers into leader talent implications (CCL, 2009). The questions raised at this stage are these: based on the key drivers, what will leaders need to be able to do well? For example, a key driver of strategy may be expansion into new markets, rapid development of new products or increasing operational efficiency. Each of these key drivers has different implications for the talent that is necessary to support them.

Many organizations have expressed serious concerns about the quality and availability of leader talent necessary to support their business goals (Hollenbeck, 2009). Understanding these challenges and the potential impact on the business is essential for defining what development is needed, and from there, how assessments can support this development. Next we explore some commonly cited challenges.

Leadership quality needs improvement Hogan and colleagues (2010) note that estimates of the percentage of managers who fail in their roles ranges from 30 to 67%, costing organizations vast sums of money in turnover and lost productivity. In organizations where survey or business results indicate that leadership needs to be improved, assessments can be useful for raising collective awareness among leaders about their strengths and development needs. Feedback from assessments is often an important catalyst for change, as leaders gain direct feedback about the gap between their current skills and requirements for success.

An inadequate leadership pipeline Many organizations lack the internal candidates necessary to fill projected vacancies. Adler and Mills (2008) noted that 56% of organizations do not have adequate leadership talent and 31% expect this shortage to hamper their performance. Assessments can provide a systematic process for identifying leadership potential and help organizations avoid a common misperception about employees' readiness for higher-level jobs: that past performance is the best predictor of future performance. Effective performance is necessary but not sufficient for predicting future success. In addition to performance, an individual's potential to operate effectively at the next level must be considered. Leadership assessments, which can provide valuable insight for evaluating potential, are more objective and provide better predictive validity than managers' judgements alone. Identifying individuals with the most potential to succeed at a higher level will help ensure that the right people are selected and developed, fostering a stronger leadership bench.

Increased demands without increased resources Given the pace of change and increased complexity in the current work environment (CEB, 2012), there is more pressure than ever for leaders to continuously learn and perform at higher levels (O'Connell, 2014). In a time of reduced resources, learning investments must be precisely targeted. Rather than implement one-size-fits-all development programmes, assessments can identify strengths and development opportunities so that leaders receive the training they need to improve their performance (McCall, 2010).

Once the organization has defined clear strategic drivers and specific leader talent challenges, it can identify the individual attributes leaders need to contribute to these priorities (CCL, 2009; Schippmann, 1999; Schneider & Konz, 1989). For example, if the organization has determined that increased innovation is the key to competitive advantage in the future, then leaders will need to be able to create a climate in their teams that allows innovation to thrive. Specific attributes that leaders may need to do this well include behaviours such as encouraging new ideas, skills related to divergent thinking and traits such as openness to experience.

Once the leader attributes required for success are identified, it is useful to assess the current state of leader talent to determine how it compares with the desired future state (CCL, 2009). If used at this point, the purpose of assessment is to identify the gap between leader talent needs and leader talent availability. The results from these assessments can be used for two purposes: prediction and diagnosis. Prediction is used to identify individuals who are most likely to succeed at a more senior level and who are ready to take on more responsibility. This has great organizational benefit as it facilitates decisions about whom to select for a leadership role or for a high-profile development opportunity. When development programmes have limited space or are time- and resource-intensive, assessments help organizations identify where to invest their scarce development resources (i.e., differential investment), which it is hoped will improve the return on investment of those resources. Church and Rotolo (2013) found that 50% of organizations they surveyed used assessments to identify potential.

As Howard and Thomas (2010) note, while prediction is used to determine in whom to invest, diagnosis is used to identify learning needs. At the individual level, diagnosis can inform development planning. Moreover, becoming aware of the gap between one's current and desired level of competencies can provide motivation to engage in development. At the organizational level, aggregate assessment results can be used to diagnose learning needs at the organizational level and inform decisions about the types of programme that need to be developed.

Once individuals whom the organization chooses to invest development resources in are selected and their individual strengths and development needs have been evaluated, assessments can aid in the learning process itself. First, assessments facilitate development by raising self-awareness of strengths and development needs (Byham, Smith & Paese, 2002; Day, Harrison & Halpin, 2009). This self-awareness goes beyond identifying skill gaps to include a deeper understanding of the psychological drivers of behaviour, such as personality attributes, motives and attitudes, as well as specific behaviours and their impact on others, as typically assessed in 360-degree feedback. However, assessments that are done only for the purpose of raising self-awareness may not be sufficient to change behaviour. Smither, London and Reilly (2005) conducted a meta-analysis of the effectiveness of multi-source feedback for behaviour change in managers. The effect sizes were relatively small (corrected mean $d = 0.12$ for measures by direct reports and mean $d = 0.15$ for measures by supervisors), suggesting that most managers do not change their behaviour significantly after receiving feedback. Therefore, feedback by itself is usually insufficient for development. Smither and colleagues (2005) proposed a model that highlights the importance of goal-setting and developmental action as mediators between feedback and actual behaviour change.

Some assessments, especially simulations, can provide a learning experience in and of themselves beyond self-awareness by offering a medium for practice, feedback and reflection

(Thornton & Rupp, 2006). For example, assessment centres and other simulations provide participants with a complex set of leadership challenges that mirror a real-world environment. Working through each scenario exposes the participant to a broad range of situations in which to engage in deliberate practice. When feedback is offered during or at the end of the assessment, additional learning occurs. This type of assessment is particularly powerful when multiple simulations are used so that participants can obtain feedback between each round of practice (Rupp et al., 2006).

Finally, assessments can be used to evaluate the impact of development. According to Church and Rotolo (2013), 25% of organizations use assessments to confirm skill acquisition or capability. Assessments for evaluation purposes can be used to determine whether participants have learned and whether they can apply new knowledge and skills acquired through development programmes to improving performance on the job. By measuring changes in important knowledge, skills and behaviours, these assessments can indicate a leadership programme's value to the organization.

Early in the design of the assessment solution, which of these purposes assessments will be asked to fulfil should be discussed and even prioritized. From an assessment design point of view, each of these potential purposes will yield a different answer in terms of what needs to be assessed and how. For example, if the most important purpose of assessments is to identify who has the greatest potential to grow into higher-level leader roles in the future, then assessments that measure stable traits such as motivation to lead or intelligence, where feedback to individuals may not be necessary, may be a good fit (Silzer & Church, 2009). Alternatively, if the most important purpose that assessments will fulfil is diagnosing individual talent gaps in a current leader role to help individuals decide development targets, then an assessment that measures current behaviours and has detailed feedback with developmental advice may be best suited. Because the purposes of assessments within a leader development process are many, and purpose has important implications for the choices of both what and how to assess, the assessment purpose must be clearly specified before moving on to decisions regarding what to assess and how.

Starting with a clear purpose in mind can improve the fit and effectiveness of assessments in the context of leader development. Once this purpose has been defined, the next question to consider is what needs to be assessed.

What? The Attributes to Assess

Just as the existing research literature can inform the purpose of leader assessment, it can also provide considerable insight into which particular individual attributes are the most important and how those attributes are operationally defined (Thornton et al., 2010). There are many examples of such attributes in the research literature and a clear success profile of a leader in a given role in a given organization, with the requisite level of detail to match the purpose(s) of assessment, must be defined (Byham et al., 2002; Shippmann et al., 2000).

As noted earlier, for assessments to have the maximum impact on leader development, there must be a strong connection between what is being assessed and what determines leader success in an organization (Schippmann, 1999). As Howard (2001, p. 414) notes, 'the assessment design process requires an understanding of the talent implications of the organization's strategic and cultural priorities'. This cannot be achieved unless two issues are addressed: 1) how an organization's strategic and cultural priorities translate into leader role requirements; and 2) how those role requirements translate into a list of attributes required for success (Schneider & Konz, 1989).

While understanding the requirements of a role and converting these into a list of operationally defined individual attributes required for success is a challenge common to assessment design for any occupation, it is particularly challenging in the context of leaders and leadership development, for several reasons. Leadership development focuses on preparing individuals for broad roles that are contextual to a given organization. Despite a focus on broad roles, there is a need for specificity of attributes across the full range of descriptors – behaviours, knowledge, traits – depending on assessment purpose. Finally, criterion-validated knowledge about which leader attributes lead to success is hard to come by (Howard & Thomas, 2010). Given these challenges, both the role requirements of leaders in a given organizational context and the attributes that best enable success in carrying out these roles across situations could be better understood (Dierdorff, Rubin & Morgeson, 2009).

With these challenges in mind, we share what research has to offer for improving our understanding of leader role requirements and attributes that best enable success in enacting them. In particular, we review the process of choice for translating organizational strategy into leader role requirements – competency modelling – and the debates regarding its usefulness. We also review literature on leader effectiveness and consider themes within this vast research that may contribute to understanding which individual leader attributes, or categories of leader attributes, best enable leader role enactment.

Determining leader role requirements

The traditional method for understanding role requirements is through analysis of job duties and tasks via a job analysis (Harvey, 1991; Sanchez & Levine, 2012). While traditional job analysis is commonly used to build detailed success profiles in most assessment contexts, it is not particularly well suited to the leader development context (Campion et al., 2011; Dierdorff et al., 2009) for two reasons. First, leader roles are ambiguous, complex and dynamic, and cannot easily be converted into detailed task lists (Thornton et al., 2010). Second, the focus of leader development efforts are to prepare individuals for broad leader roles, not a specific job or position (Hollenbeck, McCall & Silzer, 2006). Therefore, the narrowly defined task lists that are the level of analysis for traditional job analysis are less likely to represent the nature of a leader's work. Broad role expectations and how that role contributes to organizational strategic success, now and in the future, is more reflective of the work of leaders (Howard & Thomas, 2010; Schneider & Konz, 1989) and the intent of leader development.

As a result, competency modelling emerged as an alternative to job analysis for understanding the role requirements and related attributes for leader roles (Hollenbeck et al., 2006). Although the definition varies, generally speaking competencies are clusters of knowledge, skills, abilities, behaviours and attitudes that differentiate success from failure in a given role (Spencer, McClelland & Spencer, 1994). There are a number of key differences between competency modelling and job analysis (Stone, Webster & Schoonover, 2013). For example, competency modelling can be described as more deductive (i.e., the process starts with the outcomes a leader needs to accomplish and then determines the role requirements, tasks, behaviours and KSAOs that enable the accomplishment these outcomes), whereas traditional job analysis is more like an inductive approach, starting with job tasks and KSAOs then building up to the job. Furthermore, competency models often describe how competencies may vary depending on the level of the employee and are typically linked to the organizational strategy or overall business objectives, whereas job analysis focuses very directly on the specific tasks an individual performs.

There are numerous advantages to using competency modelling in the context of leadership development. With a top-down approach, competency modelling helps to translate the strategic priorities of an organization into leader role requirements, as reflected by competencies. Also, as a person-centred approach (as opposed to the job-centred approach of traditional job analysis), competency modelling also fits the purpose of leader development context better; preparing individuals for the broad roles involved in leadership, and not limited to specific jobs.

On the other hand, there are some possible disadvantages to using competency modelling in the context of leadership development. Despite its widespread use and popularity, debate continues about the suitability of competency modelling (Hollenbeck et al., 2006; Sanchez & Levine, 2012; Shippmann et al., 2000; Stone et al., 2013). The debate centres on how competency modelling is being conducted, as well as on broader concerns about the usefulness of competencies themselves to understanding either leader role requirements or the attributes that enable leaders to perform those roles. One of the most common complaints is that of implementation; the competency modelling process lacks rigour and validation (Shippmann et al., 2000; Stone et al., 2013). On a more conceptual basis, there are also concerns that competency models are too general and therefore not precise enough for such uses as determining what to assess (Campion et al., 2011). There are also complaints that competency models are too simplistic and miss the contextual complexity of leader behaviour in micro-contextual situations (Hollenbeck, 2009). In other words, while single sets of behaviours on a production line can produce a quality set of results, the linkage between traits, behaviours and results becomes much less clear as we progress through the ranks. In senior leadership positions success can come in seemingly infinite guises. The underlying suggestion is that competency modelling may not be ideal for understanding the attributes that lead to leader success and that behaviour may ultimately be the wrong focus for leader roles.

Beyond the question of whether competency modelling is superior to job analysis in the context of assessing leadership development, it may also be worth considering a combination of the two, or even alternative approaches. Schippmann and colleagues (2000) suggest that a merger of competency modelling and job analysis may be the most effective solution. There are other possible alternatives, among them strategic job modelling (Schippmann, 1999), role-based work analysis (Dierdorff et al., 2009) and a more rigorous approach to competency modelling as described by Campion and colleagues (2011).

All these approaches may be helpful in translating role requirements for leadership development into relevant attributes. However, an understanding of the leadership literature and various theories and frameworks can also be very informative in helping to determine attributes that enable leaders to perform their required roles. In the next subsection we provide a brief overview of a number of relevant perspectives from the leadership literature that may be particularly helpful towards this end.

A brief overview of perspectives on leadership and leadership development

There is a long and rich history of research related to leader effectiveness (DeRue & Myers, 2014; Yukl, 2012). Theoretical models regarding leader effectiveness have evolved over time, beginning with the perspective of understanding what traits make leaders different. This is referred to as the 'great man' approach (Carlyle, 1907). The focus eventually shifted away from traits and towards behaviour, including theoretical models that describe how effectiveness of a given leader behaviour depends on the situation or context, as represented by situational or contingency leadership models (Hersey & Johnson, 1997;

Leister, Borden & Fiedler, 1977). Interest expanded to the study of more enduring leader styles, such as charismatic leadership (Conger & Kanungo, 1998) and the broader transformational leader style. The perspective shifted again when leadership was seen as a process of social exchange, including attention to the dyadic relationships that emerge from leader interactions with followers (Graen & Uhl-Bien, 1995) and most recently to complexity models (Uhl-Bien & Marion, 2008) that envisage leadership as a complex, iterative process of behavioural exchange between leader and followers.

Each of these approaches to leadership analysis has contributed to our understanding of leader effectiveness in some way (for a comprehensive review, see Bass & Bass, 2008). For each, there are different implications for which attributes may lead to success. Unfortunately, the list is seemingly endless. There is evidence that a large variety of attributes may influence leader effectiveness. These can include (but are not limited to) stable traits such as conscientiousness, drive and intelligence (Blair, Gorman, Helland & Delise, 2014; Judge, Bono, Ilies & Gerhardt, 2002; Kirkpatrick & Locke, 1991), styles like charisma and transformational leadership (Conger, Kanungo & Menon, 2000), various skills, including interpersonal and information processing (Mumford, Campion & Morgeson, 2007; Riggio & Tan, 2014), and a long list of narrowly defined behaviours, such as providing coaching, teaching and assigning tasks (Borman & Brush, 1993; Tett, Guterman, Bleier & Murphy, 2000; Yukl, 2012; Yukl, Gordon & Taber, 2002).

The cross-cultural applicability of some of these theories and related individual attributes has been examined (Chhokar, Brodbeck, House, 2013). As part of the GLOBE research project, an etic approach (using an existing theory from outside the cultures being studied) to develop a new universal model of leader effectiveness was then tested in 62 countries (House et al., 2004) to explore how cultural context influences the relationship between individual attributes and leader effectiveness. Beyond the cross-cultural applicability of the various leadership perspectives, new individual attributes are being proposed for leaders operating in a global context (Holt & Seki, 2012). As with the general leadership models, the challenge is that there are myriad perspectives and frameworks regarding how to incorporate global demands into models of leader effectiveness (Holt & Seki, 2012; Inceoglu & Bartram, 2012).

While studied less commonly than leader effectiveness, factors that influence individual effectiveness at developing leadership skills (Day et al., 2009; Derue & Wellman, 2009; Dragoni, Tesluk, Russell & Oh, 2009) are also relevant to the question of what to assess when using assessments for development. Theoretical perspectives from three research domains outside leader effectiveness are most relevant: general models of learning and expert skill acquisition (Ericsson, 1993; Goldstein, 2006); constructive leader development models related to adult development theories (McCauley et al., 2006); and identity (Avolio, 2007; Burnette, O'Boyle, VanEpps, Pollack & Finkel, 2013). From these theoretical models, various meta-cognitive skills and motivations related to learning and behavioural flexibility have been identified as important to leader development effectiveness. These include goal orientation (DeGeest & Brown, 2011; Dweck, 1986), learning agility (DeRue, Ashford & Myers, 2012), adaptability (Pulakos, Arad, Donovan & Plamondon, 2000), and self-regulation (Burnette et al., 2013).

The model that best integrates these varying perspectives and is specific to leader development is Avolio's developmental readiness model (Avolio, 2007) which includes learning goal orientation (engage in task to learn and grow), developmental efficacy (level of confidence in ability to develop), self-concept clarity (self-awareness), complexity of a leader's self-construct (leader mental model elaboration) and meta-cognitive skill (skill at thinking about thinking). These attributes are often important to assess when the purpose of assessment is prediction of potential and whom to invest organizational resources in (Silzer & Church, 2009).

Overall, each theoretical perspective and framework contributes a unique facet to our overall understanding of what makes a leader effective in current or future roles. Meta-analyses have supported the basic premises of some of these models (DeGroot, Kiker & Cross, 2000; Ilies, Nahrgang & Morgeson, 2007; Judge et al., 2002; Judge, Colbert & Ilies, 2004; Judge, Piccolo & Ilies, 2004; Rockstuhl, Dulebohn, Ang & Shore, 2012), and are summarized in Table 17.1. The challenge remains to integrate these perspectives to help decide which individual attributes should be assessed.

Integrating perspectives and attributes

While the overview provides a wealth of information that is potentially useful to help determine relevant attributes for assessment in the context of leader development, it also creates a 'bewildering variety' (Yukl, 2012, p. 66) of different individual attributes that seem difficult to integrate. In order to manage this complexity, researchers have grouped attribute types and created taxonomies that categorize attributes into larger themes.

There is general agreement that there are three types of attribute that enable leader success. Perhaps the best known of these is the U.S. Army's longstanding model of leader effectiveness, the 'Be-Know-Do' model (U. S. Department of the Army, 1999), where 'Be' represents motives, values and character (traits); 'Know' represents four categories of knowledge and skill – the interpersonal, conceptual, technical and tactical; and 'Do' represents actions leaders engage in, including influencing, operating and improving (behaviours). Zaccarco (2007) extended this idea by incorporating them into a three-part causal model with categories representing distal attributes (traits), which influence more proximal attributes (knowledge and skills), which in turn lead to leader processes (behaviours). Figure 17.2 illustrates these factors by showing how traits, skills and knowledge, and behaviours are important leadership attributes, and are connected.

A different approach, also illustrated in Figure 17.2, is the creation of taxonomies of attributes, based on categorizing them into larger themes (Bartram, 2005; Borman & Brush, 1993; Tett et al., 2000). Although different taxonomies may focus on different types of analysis or different types of attribute, there is an underlying connection between categories in different taxonomies that can help identify groups or clusters of relevant attributes. As one illustrative example, Mumford, Zaccaro, Harding, Jacobs and Fleishman (2000) developed a taxonomy of leader skills using the categories of creative problem solving (identifying problems and generating solutions), judgement skills (refinement of solutions and implementation plans) and social skills (to motivate and direct others). Similarly, Yukl (2012) created a taxonomy focused on leader behaviours instead of skills, categorized across four meta-categories, including the task-oriented (e.g., clarifying, planning, problem solving), relations-oriented (e.g., supporting, empowering), change-oriented (e.g., advocating change, encouraging innovation), and external (e.g., networking; external monitoring). Although these taxonomies are clearly different – one focusing on skills and the other on behaviours – the larger picture (illustrated in Figure 17.1) is that categories across the taxonomies are conceptually linked. For instance, the change-oriented behaviours in the category that Yukl (2012) conceptualized are aligned with the creative problem-solving skills that Mumford and colleagues (2000, 2007) categorized, and the latter are necessary for the former. In the same way, we can see how skills and behaviours align on other dimensions and even align with the leader role requirements categorizations created by Drath and colleagues (2008).

Table 17.1 Meta-analytic findings on leadership research.

Study	Focus of meta-analysis	Findings
DeGroot, Kiker & Cross, 2000	Relationship between charismatic leadership style and leadership effectiveness, subordinate performance, subordinate satisfaction, subordinate effort and subordinate commitment.	• The relationship between leader charisma and leader effectiveness is much weaker than reported. • Charismatic leadership is more effective at increasing group performance than at increasing individual performance.
Ilies, Nahrgang & Morgeson, 2007	Relationship between the quality of leader–member exchanges (LMX) and citizenship behaviours performed by employees.	• Moderately strong, positive relationship between LMX and citizenship behaviours. • Moderating role of the target of the citizenship behaviours on the magnitude of the LMX–citizenship behaviour relationship.
Judge, Bono, Ilies & Gerhardt, 2002	Trait perspective in leadership research.	• The relations of neuroticism, extraversion, openness to experience and conscientiousness with leadership generalized in that more than 90% of the individual correlations were greater than 0. • Extraversion was the most consistent correlate of leadership.
Judge, Colbert & Ilies, 2004	The relationship between intelligence and leadership.	• The corrected correlation between intelligence and leadership is 0.21 (uncorrected for range restriction) and 0.27 (corrected for range restriction). • Leader's stress level and directiveness moderated the intelligence–leadership relationship.
Judge, Piccolo & Ilies, 2004	The relationship of the Ohio State leadership behaviours – Consideration and Initiating Structure – with leadership.	• Both consideration (0.48) and initiating structure (0.29) have moderately strong relations with leadership outcomes.
Rockstuhl, Dulebohn, Ang & Shore, 2012	The role of national culture in moderating relationships between LMX and its correlates.	• Relationships of LMX with organizational citizenship behaviour, justice perceptions, job satisfaction, turnover intentions and leader trust are stronger in horizontal-individualistic (e.g., Western) contexts than in vertical-collectivistic (e.g., Asian) contexts. • National culture does not affect relationships of LMX with task performance, organizational commitment and transformational leadership.

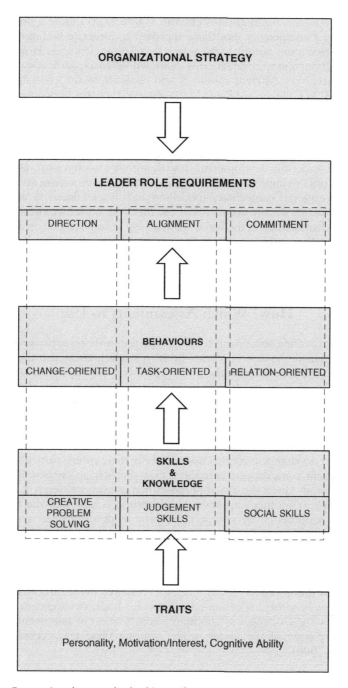

Figure 17.2 Connections between leadership attributes.

This general conceptualization (illustrated in Figure 17.2) can be a powerful tool to help those using a competency modelling approach to integrate findings from the vast leadership literature more easily into the search for relevant attributes. However, as noted above, it is important also to consider cross-cultural differences, particularly how different attributes can have very different meanings and implications for leadership in different cultural contexts. As Caligiuri and Paul (2010) observe, there has been limited research on cross-cultural issues in selection and assessment, even though local norms have been found to be very important (Bartram, 2008).

In this section, we have discussed best practice for translating organizational contexts into leader role requirements, and how those requirements can lead to the specific attributes to assess for leadership development. In so doing, we explored what research and best practice have to offer to improve understanding of leader role requirements and attributes. Specifically, we explored competency modelling and its usefulness, as well as possible alternative approaches. Finally, we reviewed the literature on leader effectiveness, as the vast accumulated knowledge in the literature may help inform relevant attributes.

So far we have discussed what the purposes of assessments are in the context of leader development and how to identify the attributes we need to assess. The next topic we need to address is the crucial question of how best to assess the relevant attributes.

How? Which Assessments to Use

Once the purpose of using assessments (the why) and the attributes to be assessed (the what) have been determined, the next important decision is which assessment tools will be used to measure the attributes selected (the how). There is a wide variety of assessment tools from which to choose, from widely available, off-the-shelf inventories to highly customized situational judgement tests (Ryan & Ployhart, 2014). For assessments to best contribute to the ultimate goal of increasing the pool of leaders ready to take the organization into the future, careful consideration should be given to the choice of assessment.

While a standard set of criteria is often recommended for choosing assessments (Howard, 2001), the leader development context makes three of these criteria particularly important. As in all assessment contexts, one criterion is how precisely an assessment measures the attributes of interest. Given the varied purposes that assessments serve in the context of leader development, another important consideration is how well the feedback from the assessment supports either selection decisions or developmental goals. The third consideration is how acceptable the assessment experience will be to the specific demands of the audience (Howard & Thomas, 2010).

In this section, we review research and best practice in two key areas to help guide decisions of which assessments are most appropriate. First, we review the common types of measures, how they relate to the attribute types reviewed in the earlier section, and best practice regarding how they are commonly used in the leader development context. Then we briefly review the challenges of choosing a combination of assessments to provide a comprehensive picture of the leader, while ensuring these are acceptable to leaders (Bell & Arthur, 2008).

Assessment types

Many assessments are available (Church & Rotolo, 2013; Howard & Thomas, 2010; Thornton et al., 2010) and can be categorized and classified in a number of ways. The most common distinction is in terms of how distal or proximal the assessment is to actual behaviour (Wernimont & Campbell, 1968). These can range from assessments that provide inferences about behaviour, such as personality and cognitive tests, to assessments that describe behaviour, such as interviews or past performance, to actual demonstrations of behaviour, such as simulations (Howard & Thomas, 2010). In this section, we briefly discuss a variety of assessment types, highlighting the attributes measured and the purposes for which they are typically used. Table 17.2 highlights the general advantages and disadvantages of each type. It is important to note that, in an increasingly globalized world with organizations that often operate in numerous countries and have employees from many cultures, globalization of selection systems is a key concern (Ryan & Ployhart, 2014), yet there has been little research on globalizing selection systems (Caligiuri & Pail, 2010; Carey, Herst & Chan, 2010).

Personality Personality tests are self-reported and measure behavioural dispositions (traits). Some assessments measure traits based on the five-factor model (FFM), which is commonly used in selection (Barrick & Mount, 2012); others use more specific sub-scales. It has been found that specific personality tests can be more predictive than a more general FFM (Pulakos, Borman & Hough, 1988). Another interesting set of scales in the leader development context is derailers, or the dark side of traits (Gaddis & Foster, 2015; Judge, Piccolo & Kosalka, 2009). In recent years, the use of personality tests in the context of leader development has increased substantially. Whereas Hogan and colleagues (2010) noted that it was rarely used to select executives and Howard, Erker and Bruce (2007) reported that 65% of organizations did not use it for selection, a more recent study reports that 57% of organizations now use it for the assessment of senior executives and 66% use it for the assessment of high-potential employees (Church & Rotolo, 2013).

Cognitive ability These tend to be written tests that measure general mental ability or specific mental abilities (e.g., reading, verbal or maths). They often include multiple-choice or right/wrong answers, and may include images or patterns as a component of reasoning or logic questions. In general, cognitive ability tests have a high correlation with performance among leaders (Judge, Colbert et al., 2004), and are relatively common in the selection of senior leader positions (Thornton et al., 2010). Church and Rotolo (2013) found that around 40% of organizations use them to assess high-potential employees and senior executives, and Howard and colleagues (2007) reported that about half of organizations use them for senior leaders.

Motivation and interests These represent self-reported tests designed to assess the aspirations or desire of individuals to attain a leadership position in the organization, or individuals' general likes and dislikes compared to opportunities provided by the position (i.e., the fit). One criticism of these tests is that they may not be specific enough to predict how a leader will fit into a particular role or culture in an organization (Howard & Thomas, 2010). The use of such tests is not common, with Church and Rotolo (2013) reporting that only about 20% of organizations use them to assess high-potential employees and executives.

Biographical data This is the use of data about past experiences and accomplishments as a way to infer KSAs and try to use past accomplishments to predict future potential. It has traditionally been used as a screen or criterion for selection or promotion in organizations at all levels due to considerable evidence that biographical experience can be a strong predictor of job performance (Stokes & Cooper, 1994). The use of biographical data can be an important component of executive assessment (Howard, 2006). Howard, Erker and Bruce (2007)

Table 17.2 Advantages and disadvantages of leadership assessment tools.

Assessment Type	Advantages	Disadvantages
Personality Self-report. Typically presented as statements with forced-choice or Likert scales (e.g., level of agreement with each statement).	• Inexpensive. • Quick and easy to administer. • Minimal or no adverse impact.	• Self-report, potential for faking. • Candidates sometimes object when tests do not appear directly relevant to the job.
Cognitive Ability General intelligence or reasoning tests. Typically multiple-choice items with right/wrong answers; questions may be presented verbally or as images such as patterns.	• Modest prediction of future job success. • Usually inexpensive. • Quick and easy to administer. • Objective and consistent. • Good predictors of future job success across a variety of roles.	• Tends to result in adverse impact for minorities. • Candidates sometimes object when tests do not appear directly relevant to the job.
Motivation/Interests Self-report. Typically presented as statements with forced-choice or Likert scales (e.g., how much do you agree with each statement?).	• Inexpensive. • Quick and easy to administer. • Minimal or no adverse impact.	• Self-report, potential for faking. • May not predict future success – link between aspirations and role needs to be established before using for selection.
Biographical Data Past experiences and accomplishments such as work experience, academic achievement and specific work roles (including leadership roles). Typically gleaned from résumés or background checks.	• Very useful to verify needed KSAs or experience.	• Often too general or simplistic for high-level positions or leader development purposes. • Sometimes require additional data (or interview) in order to fully interpret.
Leadership Style Typically presented as statements with forced-choice or Likert scales (e.g., how much do you agree with each statement?).	• Provides unique information from typical personality assessments. • Because styles can be changed, participants can use feedback as basis for development modified through training.	• Self-report, potential for faking. • Many people adapt their styles to fit different situations, and the assessment may not be sensitive enough to detect the ability to shift styles. • Weak link between assessment results and job performance.
Situational Judgement Tests (SJTs) and Simulation Realistic, scenario-based measures, generally in a multiple-choice format that ask the respondent to choose from a list of alternative actions; scenarios may be presented as text only, text with pictures, video or other media. Can simulate the job environment by providing complex situations that call for a complex set of behavioural responses; exercises typically include role-plays, in-baskets, case analyses, etc.	• Appears job-relevant and therefore more acceptable to test-takers. • Can measure a variety of competencies. • Can be used as a learning tool, when detailed feedback is provided on incorrect responses.	• Some potential for adverse impact when reading requirements are high. • Multiple-choice versions limit complexity of possible responses. • Measures judgement only, not actual behaviour. • Expensive and time-consuming to develop and administer.

Structured Interviews

Consistent questions structured scoring guidelines applied to all participants to enable direct comparisons among individuals.

- Minimal adverse impact.
- Can be tailored to each job as needed.
- More valid and fair than unstructured interviews.

- Some managers resist using structured interviews, preferring to go with their 'gut'.
- Time-consuming to develop questions and scoring guidelines.

360-degree feedback

Supervisor, peers, direct reports and others are asked to score a leader on several critical leadership behaviours or competencies; these multiple ratings are designed to capture multiple viewpoints about the leader's skills.

- Honest feedback due to multiple sources.
- Helpful for leader development.
- Increases self-awareness.

- Time-consuming to administer.
- Some raters may be biased (e.g., peers who compete with each other for promotion).

Assessment Centres

Multiple exercises combined in an intensive format to measure candidates' aptitude and ability on a variety of job-related measures. Candidates are typically taken to an off-site location where exercises are facilitated by external consultants. Exercises typically include leaderless group discussions, in-basket exercises and others.

- Can measure many skills.
- High-fidelity exercises that can be applied directly to the job.
- Can identity strengths and areas for development.

- Expensive to facilitate.
- Time-consuming.
- Typically used for leader development, not candidate selection.

reported that 60% of organizations used some form of application requiring biographical data, and 23% used a specific biographical data form. Church and Rotolo (2013) found that 43% of organizations used biographical data in some form to assess high-potential employees and senior executives.

Leadership styles   This type of test is designed to determine an individual's preferred leadership style (e.g., transformational, empowering). An underlying assumption is that style can be flexible and modified through leadership training, and that the tests determine the way an individual is most likely to lead. In the context of leader and executive selection, there are many variants of leadership questionnaires. Some focus on personality; others focus on behaviours (Thornton et al., 2010). The use of leadership questionnaires and tests of leadership styles, however, are not particularly common or widespread in the selection of executives or high-potential employees (Church & Rotolo, 2013).

Situational judgements and simulations   These represent realistic and scenario-based measures or simulations that require judgements or decisions related to a variety of topics, such as strategic planning, decision making and job roles (Rockstuhl, Ang, Ng, Lievens & Van Dyne, 2015). Decision making on job-specific tasks can provide an indication of KSAs, as well as of experience. There is considerable variation within this category, as simulations can range from the simple and role-specific – perhaps a short vignette and question – to the very complex and broad, which may involve multiple rounds of rich simulation of complex business problems with multiple options and an evolving situation. The use of simulations in organizations ranges from 23% to 41%, depending on the type of simulation and type of assessment (Church & Rotolo, 2013), but it is used more often for high-potential employees than for executives. Howard and Thomas (2010) note that simulations can be very useful for executive assessment and have a number of advantages over other methods, but also point out that complex simulations can be expensive and labour-intensive.

Structured interviews   These represent a specific set of questions asked in a predetermined order, given to all candidates to enable direct comparisons between individuals. Interviewers are given a list of questions to assess specific skills and competencies and are required to follow the script as it is written. They are designed to assess motives and interests, as well as KSAs and experience. Although interviews of varying levels of structure are widely used, Howard and Thomas (2010) note that they are not a very efficient selection method for executives and leaders because they require a lot of time and coordination to administer. Furthermore, structured interviews run the risk of various biases. However, Hollenbeck (2009) notes that interviews in general are an important component of executive selection if they are implemented effectively.

360-degree feedback   Sometimes also referred to as multisource feedback, this is a process by which supervisors, peers, direct reports and others (e.g., clients or customers) are asked to score a leader on several critical leadership behaviours or competencies (Dalessio, 1998). These ratings are designed to capture multiple viewpoints about the leader's skills and assess on-the-job behaviours. They have become increasingly popular for leadership and executive positions over the past few decades (Dalton, 1996; Markham, Smith, Markham & Braekkan, 2014; Thornton et al., 2010), and are often considered one of the principal components of executive assessment (Hollenbeck, 2009). Church and Rotolo (2013) found that 60% of organizations used them for the assessment of senior executives and 66% used them for high-potential employees.

Assessment centres   These consist of multiple exercises combined in an intensive format to measure candidate aptitude and ability on a variety of job-related measures. Candidates are typically taken to an off-site location where exercises are facilitated by external consultants; virtually administered assessment centres have recently also been developed (Byham et al., 2002). Exercises, particularly for leader and executive selection, typically include simulations, leaderless group discussions, in-basket exercises and others tasks (Thornton, Byham & Warr, 2013; Thornton & Rupp, 2006). The key feature of assessment centres is the combination of multiple forms of assessments, which can include cognitive ability tests, personality inventories, 360-degree feedback, interviews and simulations. Thornton and Krause (2009) note that a variety of surveys indicates widespread use of assessment centres in organizations for selecting executives and high-potential employees, and assessment centres are generally considered an effective tool for executive assessment (Hollenbeck, 2009; Howard & Thomas, 2010). In contrast, Church and Rotolo (2013) found that only 30% of organizations used them for assessing executives and high-potential employees. A possible reason for this discrepancy may be that assessment centres can take many forms and organizations may define them differently. While traditionally used primarily for selection, assessment centres are now often used for the dual purpose of assessment and development (Rupp et al., 2006).

Other considerations

Given the criterion of assessment precision, an approach using multiple methods is recommended (Nunnally, 1978). One common solution is a multi-trait, multi-method (MTMM) approach, where different attributes are measured using multiple methods, typically organized in a matrix (Campbell & Fiske, 1959). The key assumption is that each assessment method will contain some error or bias and by combining multiple methods, a more precise and reliable overall measure will be generated (Church & Rotolo, 2013). This begs the question of how to combine data from different methods in order to inform selection decisions or development planning (Ryan & Ployhart, 2014), which is a topic under discussion and evolution in the area of assessment and measurement.

Balanced against the need for a precise and rigorous measure is the consideration of how acceptable the assessment experience will be to the leader audience. Especially for leaders in the organization, as opposed to a candidate for an entry-level position, the effect of the assessment is important. Not only are leaders often very busy – and typically ambitious and successful – but they may also wield substantial power in the organization. This can result in considerable resistance on their part to the time required to complete an extensive series of assessments on multiple attributes (Howard & Thomas, 2010). As a result, it is important to be cognizant of face validity (i.e., the individual should be able easily to see and understand the relevance of the assessments to their role as a leader). It is equally important that relevant and useful feedback is provided, which is seen as and easily translatable into action.

As part of our section on how to determine which assessments to use, we have discussed the importance of specific criteria for leadership development, have reviewed a number of relatively common assessment types and have discussed the importance of using multiple methods and combining data – all with the underlying goal of assessing the appropriate attributes in the most acceptable way possible. When deciding which assessments to use, it is vital that the decision is based on an understanding of the assessment purpose and what specific attributes need to be assessed. Beyond that, there is the consideration of how to maximize precision while balancing acceptability to the unique demands of the leader audience.

Future Research

This chapter suggests many possible directions for future research. One of the crucial unanswered questions for leadership development is 'what is the criterion of interest?' In other words, what measurement would allow us to conclude that a leader has improved or substantially developed their capacity to lead? In part this is a question of which level of Kirkpatrick's training evaluation framework should be used (Kirkpatrick 1975, 1994). Is it a matter of what new skills have been learned, what new behaviours are demonstrated or old behaviours improved, or a measure of improved organizational performance? Should the criterion include leader emergence, follower satisfaction or behavioural flexibility or adaptability? These are important questions that remain to be answered.

We have discussed a number of suggestions for how the traditional competency modelling approach can be modified or improved with the incorporation of a hybrid approach taking advantage of other models. A further question is whether or not we might be able to systematically incorporate attributes that the leadership literature can point us towards. The competency modelling approach, despite its strengths, remains an internally focused approach in which the attributes are generated from the internal perspective of the organization and its context alone. However, it seems likely that the perspective of a century of leadership research may also provide a valuable source of relevant attributes (especially from leadership models that incorporate context), and that this external perspective might be combined with an approach rooted in competency modelling. By combining the two more systematically not only would a bridge between research and practice be built, but the recursive feedback loop could enrich both. The underlying research question is whether we can develop a standardized taxonomy that delineates common leader roles (Drath et al., 2008) and the attributes that enable enactment of those roles (e.g. behaviours, KSAs, traits).

Another challenge is the question of how to present feedback, especially in the context of leadership development. Obviously, the purpose of development is to help people improve their capabilities, or work on weaknesses, but that implies that a gap exists and that they need to change. Unfortunately, such feedback can easily trigger defensiveness and rejection, especially if the audience is an ambitious one accustomed to success. Thus, finding a way to create feedback that motivates change and action, but does not reject the feedback process, is an important challenge for leader assessment and development that future research may inform.

A particular challenge for leader development also is that the underlying purpose of leader development is not merely to develop and improve specific competencies or skills, but also to change the leader's underlying self-concept and identity (Day et al., 2009). Currently, none of our assessment tools and feedback procedures directly measures that, and a fascinating question is whether or not we need different tools or if we need to use existing tools and feedback techniques in ways that are more consciously related to the individual's self-concept and identity as a leader.

Conclusion

Our purpose in this chapter has been to improve the practice of assessment use in leader development, by reviewing research and best practices relevant to assessment system design in this context. We discussed the why, what and how of assessment system design. In so doing, we raised a number of important questions and possible avenues for future research. With continued refinement of our existing knowledge and practice, we can improve the impact of leader development processes and, it is hoped, reduce the prevalence of leader derailment.

References

Adler, S., & Mills, A. (2008). *Controlling Leadership Talent Risk: An Enterprise Imperative*. London: Aon Consulting.

Avolio, B. J. (2007). Promoting more integrative strategies for leadership theory-building. *American Psychologist, 62*(1), 25–33 (discussion at 23–27).

Barrick, M. R., & Mount, M. K. (2012). Nature and use of personality in selection. *In* N. Schmitt (Ed.), *The Oxford Handbook of Personnel Assessment and Selection*. New York: Oxford University Press.

Bartram, D. (2005). The Great Eight competencies: A criterion-centric approach to validation. *Journal of Applied Psychology, 90*(6), 1185–1203.

Bartram, D. (2008). Global norms: Towards some guidelines for aggregating personality norms across countries. *International Journal of Testing, 8*(4), 315–333.

Bass, B. M., & Bass, R. (2008). *Handbook of Leadership: Theory, Research, and Application*. New York & Toronto: Free Press.

Bell, S. T., & Arthur, W. (2008). Feedback acceptance in developmental assessment centers: The role of feedback message, participant personality, and affective response to the feedback session. *Journal of Organizational Behavior, 29*(5), 681–703.

Blair, C. A., Gorman, C. A., Helland, K., & Delise, L. (2014). The smart leader: Examining the relationship between intelligence and leader development behavior. *Leadership and Organization Development Journal, 35*(3), 241–258.

Borman, W. C., & Brush, D. H. (1993). More progress toward a taxonomy of managerial performance requirements. *Human Performance, 6*(1), 1–21.

Burnette, J. L., O'Boyle, E. H., VanEpps, E. M., Pollack, J. M., & Finkel, E. J. (2013). Mind-sets matter: A meta-analytic review of implicit theories and self-regulation. *Psychological Bulletin, 139*(3), 655–701.

Byham, W. C., Smith, A. B., & Paese, M. J. (2002). *Grow Your Own Leaders: How to Identify, Develop, and Retain Leadership Talent*. Upper Saddle River, NJ: Prentice-Hall.

Caligiuri, P., & Paul, K. B. (2010). Selection in multinational organizations. *In* J. L. Farr & N. P. Tippins (Eds.), *Handbook of Employee Selection* (pp. 781–799). New York & London: Taylor & Francis Group.

Campbell, D. T., & Fiske, D. W. (1959). Convergent and discriminant validation by the multitrait–multimethod matrix. *Psychological Bulletin, 56*(2), 81–105.

Campion, M. A., Fink, A. A., Ruggeberg, B. J., Carr, L., Phillips, G. M., & Odman, R. B. (2011). Doing competencies well: best practices in competency modeling. *Personnel Psychology, 64*(1), 225–262.

Carey, T., Herst, D., & Chan, W. (2010). Global selection: Selection in international contexts. *Going global: Practical Applications and Recommendations for HR and OD Professionals in the Global Workplace*. San Francisco: Jossey-Bass.

Carlyle, T. (1907). *On Heroes, Hero-Worship, and The Heroic in History*. Boston, MA: Houghton Mifflin.

CCL. (2009). Developing a leadership strategy. *Global Organizational Leadership Development White Paper Series*. Greensboro, NC: Center for Creative Leadership.

CEB. (2012). *Driving Breakthrough Performance in the New Work Environment*. Arlington, VA.

CEB. (2013). *Business outcomes study report*. ceb.shl.com/assets/BOS-092013-USeng-US.pdf.

Chhokar, J. S., Brodbeck, F. C., & House, R. J. (Eds.). (2013). *Culture and Leadership across the World: The GLOBE Book of In-Depth Studies of 25 Societies*. New York: Routledge.

Church, A. H., & Rotolo, C. T. (2013). How are top companies assessing their high-potentials and senior executives? A talent management benchmark study. *Consulting Psychology Journal: Practice and Research, 65*(3), 199–223.

Conger, J. A., & Kanungo, R. N. (1998). *Charismatic Leadership in Organizations*. Thousand Oaks, CA: Sage.

Conger, J. A., Kanungo, R. N., & Menon, S. T. (2000). Charismatic leadership and follower effects. *Journal of Organizational Behavior*, 21(7), 747–767.

Dalessio, A. T. (1998). Using multi-source feedback for employee development and personnel decisions. *In* J. W. Smither (Ed.), *Performance Appraisals: State-of-the-Art in Practice*. San Francisco: Jossey-Bass.

Dalton, M. (1996). Multirater feedback and conditions for change. *Consulting Psychology Journal: Practice and Research*, 48(1), 12–16.

Day, D. V., Fleenor, J. W., Atwater, L. E., Sturm, R. E., & McKee, R. A. (2014). Advances in leader and leadership development: A review of 25 years of research and theory. *The Leadership Quarterly*, 25(1), 63–82.

Day, D. V., & Halpin, S. M. (2001). *Leadership Development: A Review of Industry Best Practices*. Alexandria, VA: U.S. Army Research Institute for the Behavioral and Social Sciences.

Day, D. V., Harrison, M. M., & Halpin, S. M. (2009). *An Integrative Approach to Leader Development: Connecting Adult Development, Identity, and Expertise*. New York: Psychology Press.

DeGeest, D., & Brown, K. G. (2011). The role of goal orientation in leadership development. *Human Resource Development Quarterly*, 22(2), 157–175.

DeGroot, T., Kiker, D. S., & Cross, T. C. (2000). A meta-analysis to review organizational outcomes related to charismatic leadership. *Canadian Journal of Administrative Sciences/Revue Canadienne des Sciences de l'Administration*, 17(4), 356–372.

DeRue, D. S., Ashford, S. J., & Myers, C. G. (2012). Learning agility: In search of conceptual clarity and theoretical grounding. *Industrial and Organizational Psychology*, 5(3), 258–279.

DeRue, D. S., & Myers, C. G. (2014). Leadership development: A review and agenda for future research. *In* D. Day (Ed.), *Oxford Handbook Of Leadership and Organizations* (pp. 829–852). New York: Oxford University Press.

DeRue, D. S., & Wellman, N. (2009). Developing leaders via experience: The role of developmental challenge, learning orientation, and feedback availability. *Journal of Applied Psychology*, 94(4), 859–875.

Dierdorff, E. C., Rubin, R. S., & Morgeson, F. P. (2009). The milieu of managerial work: An integrative framework linking work context to role requirements. *Journal of Applied Psychology*, 94(4), 972–988.

Dongen, M. A. D. (2014). Toward a standardized model for leadership development in international organizations. *Global Business and Organizational Excellence*, 33(4), 6–17.

Dragoni, L., Tesluk, P. E., Russell, J. E. A., & Oh, I. S. (2009). Understanding managerial development: Integrating developmental assignments, learning orientation, and access to developmental opportunities in predicting managerial competencies. *Academy of Management Journal*, 52(4), 731–743.

Drath, W. H., McCauley, C. D., Palus, C. J., Van Velsor, E., O'Connor, P. M. G., McGuire, J. B., & Yearly Review of Leadership (2008). Direction, alignment, commitment: Toward a more integrative ontology of leadership. *The Leadership Quarterly*, 19(6), 635–653.

Dweck, C. S. (1986). Motivational processes affecting learning. *American Psychologist*, 41(10), 1040–1048.

Ericsson, K. A. (1993). The role of deliberate practice in the acquisition of expert performance. *Psychological Review*, 100(3), 363–406.

Gaddis, B. H., & Foster, J. L. (2015). Meta-analysis of dark side personality characteristics and critical work behaviors among leaders across the globe: Findings and implications for leadership development and executive coaching. *Applied Psychology*, 64(1), 25–54.

Goldstein, I. L. (2006). *Training and Development in Organizations* (2nd ed.). Ann Arbor, MI: Universit of Michigan.

Graen, G. B., & Uhl-Bien, M. (1995). Relationship-based approach to leadership: Development of leader–member exchange (LMX) theory of leadership over 25 years: Applying a multi-level multi-domain perspective. *The Leadership Quarterly*, 6(2), 219–247.

Harvey, R. (1991). Job analysis. *In* M. Dunnette & L. Hough (Eds.), *Handbook of Industrial and Organizational Psychology* (2nd ed., Vol. 2). Palo Alto, CA: Consultant Psychologists Press.

Hersey, P., & Johnson, D. E. (1997). Situational leadership in the multicultural organization. *In* F. Hesselbein, M. Goldsmith & R. Beckard (Eds.), *The Organization of the Future* (pp. 265–274). San Francisco: Jossey-Bass.

Hogan, J., Hogan, R., & Kaiser, R. B. (2010). Management derailment: Personality assessment and mitigation. *In* S. Zedeck (Ed.), *American Psychological Association Handbook of Industrial and Organizational Psychology.* Washington, DC: American Psychological Association.

Hollenbeck, G. P. (2009). Executive selection: What's right and what's wrong. *Industrial and Organizational Psychology, 2*(2), 130–143.

Hollenbeck, G. P., McCall, M. W., & Silzer, R. F. (2006). Leadership competency models. *The Leadership Quarterly, 17*(4), 398–413.

Holt, K., & Seki, K. (2012). Global leadership: A developmental shift for everyone. *Industrial and Organizational Psychology, 5*(2), 196–215.

House, R. J., Hanges, P. J., Javidan, M., Dorfman, P. W., & Gupta, V. (Eds.). (2004). *Culture, Leadership, and Organizations: The GLOBE Study of 62 Societies.* Palo Alto, CA: Sage.

Howard, A. (2001). Identifying, assessing, and selecting senior leaders. *In* S. J. Zaccaro & R. J. Klimoski (Eds.), *The Nature of Organizational Leadership: Understanding the Performance Imperatives Confronting Today's Leaders* (pp. 305–346). San Francisco: Jossey-Bass.

Howard, A. (2006). Best practices in leader selection. *In* J. A. Conger & R. E. Riggio (Eds.), *The Practice of Leadership: Developing the Next Generation of Leaders* (pp. 11–40). San Francisco: Jossey-Bass.

Howard, A., Erker, S., & Bruce, N. (2007). *Selection Forecast 2006/2007.* Pittsburgh, PA: Development Dimensions International.

Howard, A., & Thomas, J. N. (2010). Executive and managerial assessment. *In* J. C. Scott & D. H. Reynolds (Eds.), *Handbook of Workplace Assessment: Evidence-based Practices for Selecting and Developing Organizational Talent.* San Francisco: Jossey-Bass.

Ilies, R., Nahrgang, J. D., & Morgeson, F. P. (2007). Leader–member exchange and citizenship behaviors: A meta-analysis. *Journal of Applied Psychology, 92*(1), 269–277.

Inceoglu, I., & Bartram, D. (2012). Global leadership: The myth of multicultural competency. *Industrial and Organizational Psychology, 5*(2), 216–218.

Judge, T. A., Bono, J. E., Ilies, R., & Gerhardt, M. W. (2002). Personality and leadership: A qualitative and quantitative review. *Journal of Applied Psychology, 87*(4), 765–780.

Judge, T. A., Colbert, A. E., & Ilies, R. (2004). Intelligence and leadership: A quantitative review and test of theoretical propositions. *Journal of Applied Psychology, 89*(3), 542–552.

Judge, T. A., Piccolo, R. F., & Ilies, R. (2004). The forgotten ones? The validity of consideration and initiating structure in leadership research. *Journal of Applied Psychology, 89*(1), 36–51.

Judge, T. A., Piccolo, R. F., & Kosalka, T. (2009). The bright and dark sides of leader traits: A review and theoretical extension of the leader trait paradigm. *The Leadership Quarterly, 20*(6), 855–875.

Kantrowitz, T. (2014). *Global Assessment Trends 2014.* ceb.shl.com/assets/GATR-122014-UKeng.pdf.

Kirkpatrick, D. L. (1975). Techniques for evaluating training programs. *In* D. L. Kirkpatrick (Ed.). *Evaluating Training Programs.* Alexandria, VA: ASTD.

Kirkpatrick, D. L. (1994). *Evaluating Training Programs* (2nd ed.). San Francisco: Berrett-Koehler.

Kirkpatrick, S. A., & Locke, E. A. (1991). Leadership: Do traits matter? *The Executive, 5*(2), 48–60.

Leister, A., Borden, D., & Fiedler, F. E. (1977). Validation of contingency model leadership training: Leader match. *The Academy of Management Journal, 20*(3), 464–470.

London, M., Smither, J. W., & Diamante, T. (2007). Best practices in leadership assessment. *In* J. A. Conger & R. E. Riggio (Eds.), *The Practice of Leadership.* San Francisco: Jossey-Bass.

Markham, S. E., Smith, J. W., Markham, I. S., & Braekkan, K. F. (2014). A new approach to analyzing the Achilles' heel of multisource feedback programs: Can we really trust ratings of leaders at the group level of analysis? *The Leadership Quarterly, 25*(6), 1120–1142.

McCall, M. W. (2010). Recasting leadership development. *Industrial and Organizational Psychology, 3*(1), 3–19.

McCauley, C. D., Drath, W. H., Palus, C. J., O'Connor, P. M. G., Baker, B. A., & The Leadership Quarterly Yearly Review of Leadership. (2006). The use of constructive-developmental theory to advance the understanding of leadership. *The Leadership Quarterly, 17*(6), 634–653.

Mumford, M. D., Zaccaro, S. J., Harding, F. D., Jacobs, T. O., & Fleishman, E. A. (2000). Leadership skills for a changing world: Solving complex social problems. *Leadership Quarterly, 11*(1), 11.

Mumford, T. V., Campion, M. A., & Morgeson, F. P. (2007). The leadership skills strataplex: Leadership skill requirements across organizational levels. *The Leadership Quarterly, 18*(2), 154–166.

Nunnally, J. C. (1978). *Psychometric Theory*. New York: McGraw-Hill.

O'Connell, P. K. (2014). A simplified framework for 21st century leader development. *The Leadership Quarterly, 25*(2), 183–203.

Pulakos, E. D., Arad, S., Donovan, M. A., & Plamondon, K. E. (2000). Adaptability in the workplace: Development of a taxonomy of adaptive performance. *Journal of Applied Psychology, 85*(4), 612–624.

Pulakos, E. D., Borman, W. C., & Hough, L. M. (1988). Test validation for scientific understanding: Two demonstrations of an approach to studying predictor–criterion linkages. *Personnel Psychology, 41*(4), 703–716.

Riggio, R. E., & Tan, S. J. (2013). *Leader Interpersonal and Influence Skills: The Soft Skills of Leadership*. New York: Routledge.

Rockstuhl, T., Ang, S., Ng, K. Y., Lievens, F., & Van Dyne, L. (2015). Putting judging situations into situational judgment tests: Evidence from intercultural multimedia SJTs. *Journal of Applied Psychology, 100*(2), 464–480.

Rockstuhl, T., Dulebohn, J. H., Ang, S., & Shore, L. M. (2012). Leader–member exchange (LMX) and culture: A meta-analysis of correlates of LMX across 23 countries. *Journal of Applied Psychology, 97*(6), 1097–1130.

Rupp, D. E., Mitchell Gibbons, A., Baldwin, A. M., Snyder, L. A., Spain, S. M., Eun Woo, S., & Kim, M. (2006). An initial validation of developmental assessment centers as accurate assessments and effective training interventions. *The Psychologist-Manager Journal, 9*(2), 171–200.

Ryan, A. M., & Ployhart, R. E. (2014). A century of selection. *Annual Review of Psychology, 65*(1), 693–717.

Sanchez, J. I., & Levine, E. L. (2012). The rise and fall of job analysis and the future of work analysis. *Annual Review of Psychology, 63*(1), 397–425.

Schippmann, J. S. (1999). *Strategic Job Modeling: Working at the Core of Integrated Human Resources*. Mahwah, NJ: Lawrence Erlbaum.

Schippmann, J. S., Ash, R. A., Batjtsta, M., Carr, L., Eyde, L. D., Hesketh, B., & Sanchez, J. I. (2000). The practice of competency modeling. *Personnel Psychology, 53*(3), 703–740.

Schneider, B., & Konz, A. M. (1989). Strategic job analysis. *Human Resource Management, 28*(1), 51–63.

Silzer, R. O. B., & Church, A. H. (2009). The pearls and perils of identifying potential. *Industrial and Organizational Psychology, 2*(4), 377–412.

Smither, J. W., London, M., & Reilly, R. R. (2005). Does performance improve following multisource feedback? A theoretical model, meta-analysis, and review of empirical findings. *Personnel Psychology, 58*, 33–66.

Spencer, L. M., McClelland, D. C., & Spencer, S. M. (1994). *Competency Assessment Methods: History and State of the Art*. Boston, MA: Hay-McBer Research Press.

Stokes, G. S., & Cooper, L. A. (1994). Selection using biodata: Old notions revisited. *In* G. S. Stokes, M. D. Mumford & W. A. Owens (Eds.), *Biodata Handbook: Theory, Research, and Use of Biographical Information in Selection and Performance Prediction*. Palo Alto, CA: CPP Books.

Stone, T. H., Webster, B. D., & Schoonover, S. (2013). What do we know about competency modeling? *International Journal of Selection and Assessment, 21*(3), 334–338.

Tett, R. P., Guterman, H. A., Bleier, A., & Murphy, P. J. (2000). Development and content validation of a 'hyperdimensional' taxonomy of managerial competence. *Human Performance, 13*(3), 205–251.

Thornton, G. C., Byham, W. C., & Warr, P. (2013). *Assessment Centers and Managerial Performance*. Cambridge, MA: Academic Press.

Thornton, G. C., Hollenbeck, G. P., & Johnson, S. K. (2010). Selecting leaders: Executives and high potentials. *In* J. L. Farr & N. T. Tippins (Eds.), *Handbook of Employee Selection*. New York: Routledge.

Thornton, G. C., & Krause, D. E. (2009). Selection versus development assessment centers: An international survey of design, execution, and evaluation. *The International Journal of Human Resource Management, 20*(2), 478–498.

Thornton, G. C., & Rupp, D. E. (2006). *Assessment Centers in Human Resource Management: Strategies for Prediction, Diagnosis, and Development.* Mahwah, NJ: Lawrence Erlbaum.

Uhl-Bien, M., & Marion, R. (2008). *Complexity Leadership.* Charlotte, NC: IAP, Information Age Publishers.

U.S. Department of the Army. (1999). *Army Leadership: Be, Know, Do-FM 22-100.* Arlington, VA: U.S. Department of the Army.

Wall, T., & Knights, J. (Eds.). (2013). *Leadership Assessment for Talent Development.* London: Kogan Page.

Wernimont, P. F., & Campbell, J. P. (1968). Signs, samples, and criteria. *Journal of Applied Psychology, 52*(5), 372–376.

Yukl, G. (2012). Effective leadership behavior: What we know and what questions need more attention. *Academy of Management Perspectives, 26*(4), 66–85.

Yukl, G., Gordon, A., & Taber, T. (2002). A hierarchical taxonomy of leadership behavior: integrating a half century of behavior research. *Journal of Leadership & Organizational Studies, 9*(1), 15–32.

Zaccaro, S. J. (2007). Trait-based perspectives of leadership. *American Psychologist, 62*(1), 6–16.

18

Talent Management in a Gender-Diverse Workforce

Jeanette N. Cleveland, Jaclyn Menendez and Lauren Wallace

Introduction

Women and men do not differ substantially in terms of their overall levels of performance or effectiveness at work (Landy, Shankster & Kohler, 1994; Wexley & Pulakos, 1982); if anything, women show slightly higher levels of job performance (Roth, Purvis & Bobko, 2012). Furthermore, women and men do not differ substantially in job-related abilities or in the individual determinants of job performance. For example, there are few differences in the general cognitive abilities of men and women (Halpern, Benbow, Geary, Gur, Hyde & Gernsbacher, 2007; Hyde, 2005; Hyde, Fennema & Lamon, 1990; Hyde & Linn, 1988). Similarly, there are few general differences in overall levels of work motivation, although women report motivation levels lower in environments that are characterized by strong sex role segregation or by stereotypically masculine traits (e.g., an emphasis on competitiveness; for reviews, see Eagly, Karau, Miner & Johnson, 1994; Gneezy, Niederle & Rustichini, 2003; Hyde & Kling, 2001; Kalkowski & Fritz, 2004). Despite their many similarities, though, the experiences of men and women with work and with the rewards associated with work differ in important ways. Further, women and men manage their work lives in a larger societal context, which can influence what occurs within organizations.

The goal of this chapter is to provide a targeted review of the literature on gender and human resource management practices that influence women's and men's experiences at work. This chapter examines the role of the processes that organizations use to attract, select and retain job candidates in understanding the experiences of women and men in the workplace. We begin with a brief review of the historical assumptions underlying women entering the workplace in large numbers during the last 60 years. In the sections that follow, we review key research findings for the respective areas of recruitment, selection and retention. Finally, we discuss at least four factors that shape the expectations, assumptions and even our criteria of success within the larger workplace environment:

The Wiley Blackwell Handbook of the Psychology of Recruitment, Selection and Employee Retention,
First Edition. Edited by Harold W. Goldstein, Elaine D. Pulakos, Jonathan Passmore and Carla Semedo.
© 2017 John Wiley & Sons Ltd. Published 2020 by John Wiley & Sons Ltd.

1) occupational sex segregation of jobs; 2) persistent limiting beliefs held by both women and men; 3) the uneven playing field for women outside the workplace; and 4) the narrow criteria for success and the dysfunctional behaviour associated with it.

Historical Background

Women have always worked. Single women and Black women have always had high rates of paid workforce participation (Costello & Stone, 2001). Further, the growth in the number of working married women with children has been dramatic, moving from 44% in 1978 to 65% by 1998 (Costello & Stone, 2001). Globally, women are increasing their participation in the workforce, with 64% of women in China and 61% of women in Norway engaged in paid employment in 2013, according to the World Bank. Yet women continue to lag behind men in terms of pay, limited occupational mobility (e.g., sex segregation of occupations) and access to top management positions.

Persistent differences in pay continued through 2012 in the United States, with the median weekly earnings for full-time waged and salaried females at $691 compared to males at $854. Women, therefore, made about 81% of the median earnings of men. Women's earnings are highest between the ages of 35 and 64, and those earnings tend to remain somewhat stable ($747 at their lowest, $766 at their highest; US Bureau of Labor Statistics, 2013). These differences are found in many other developed economies.

Education continues to have a strong influence on both men's and women's earnings, although the growth in earnings has a stronger effect on women. However, women continue to be paid less than similarly employed men in management, business and financial operations. As recently as 2014, the female-to-male wage ratios in a number of countries continued to show wage gaps, including Australia, Germany, South Africa, China and the US (World Economic Forum, 2014).

Second, men and women continue to be concentrated in different occupations. Specifically, relatively few women work in construction, production or transportation, and women are far more concentrated in administrative support jobs (US Bureau of Labor Statistics, 2013). In addition, women are more likely than men to work in professionally-related occupations, yet the proportion of women employed in the higher-paying job groups is much smaller than the proportion of men employed in them, with 9% of women employed in the relatively high-paying computer and engineering fields, compared with 45% percent of men in this field. Even within professional fields, women are concentrated in education and healthcare (68% women vs. 30% men), in which the pay is generally lower than that for computer and engineering jobs. (We discuss occupational sex segregation in more detail later in the chapter.)

Although women have made inroads into the workforce, they continue to be concentrated in lower-skilled jobs and have lower pay and a restricted range of occupational types. Historically, work was categorized by paid and unpaid work, with women's roles primarily considered part of the private, unpaid work domain, while men's work reflected the public, paid domain. When women performed paid work outside the home, they were perceived as qualified for a narrow range of jobs reflecting lower wages. The rationalization for this was based on the assumption that women possessed lower ability, skills and appropriate work temperament. However, despite the influx of women who worked and performed well during the two world wars in the US and Europe (and increasingly in the 1960s and beyond), women continued to be denied access to higher-skilled, higher-paying jobs. This was in part due to negative gender stereotypes depicting women as incompetent and 'too nurturing' for managerial and leadership roles. Career counsellors and organizational gatekeepers also routinely guided female applicants to female-dominated, low-paid, low-impact occupations. Indeed, throughout the first half of the twentieth century women who sought more education or employment in more traditionally male jobs were often perceived to be aberrant or to possess unsuitable temperaments (Eagly & Johnson, 1990).

During the 1960s, this pattern was repeated. As women acquired greater education and skilled jobs became more plentiful, they slowly entered more traditionally masculine areas of work. Initially, women encountered discrimination based on the belief that they did not have the skill levels of their male counterparts to perform these jobs. However, research on gender differences in job-related skills, especially interpersonal and leadership skills (Eagly & Johnson, 1990), did not support the belief that men were better qualified than women; further, women appear to demonstrate greater effectiveness than men in using productive leader skills. Since women and men did not differ in terms of job-related skills, gender research focused on the assumption that women and men had different motivations. Such differences were cited as the rationale underlying women's lack of upward mobility at the top of organizations, in critical organizational decision roles and in power and influence. However, there is little evidence to support the claim of significant variations in work motivation between men and women (Eagly & Johnson, 1990).

In sum, research shows few significant gender variations in work-related knowledge, skill and abilities or motivation. However, women and men may face differences in how they experience the workplace. Women may encounter both subtle discrimination and challenges when interacting with HR practices, including recruitment and selection. Further, the antecedents or causes of these variations range from differences in the socialization of men and women (Cocoran & Courant, 1987; Perry, David-Blake & Kulik, 1994; Terborg, 1977; Weisman, Morlock, Sack & Levine, 1976) to outright discrimination (Bobbitt-Zeher, 2011).

Recruitment

Recruitment can be described as 'those practices and activities carried out by the organization with the primary purpose of identifying and attracting potential employees' (Barber, 1998, p. 5). Recruitment experts make a distinction between external and internal recruitment, the first of which involves bringing people into the organization, while the latter involves attracting candidates for vertical or lateral moves within an organization.

Ten years after the implementation of Title VII of the Civil Rights Act of 1964, studies were still showing clear evidence of discrimination against women in recruitment interviews for jobs that were non-traditional or had 'male-oriented' aspects (Cohen & Bunker, 1975). It is likely that differences in the way men and women are treated in the recruitment process still have an impact, but there is relatively little research on the way recruitment might contribute to gendered differences in hiring (Bygren & Kumlin, 2005). Studies to date have produced inconsistent results in terms of the effect of the applicant's sex on recruiter evaluations, though results generally tend to demonstrate men receiving more favourable ratings and higher starting salaries when all else is held equivalent (Powell, 1987). Unfortunately, there are few field studies of the effects of gender on recruitment (Elliott, 1981 and Graves & Powell, 1988 are exceptions). The vast majority of existing recruitment and gender studies use hypothetical résumés that are evaluated by college students in laboratory settings, and the lack of external validity in these studies casts doubt on the findings of these studies (e.g., Cohen & Bunker, 1975; Dipboye, Arvey & Terpstra, 1977; Dipboye, Fromkin & Wiback, 1975). However, some conclusions can be drawn from the meagre body of relevant research. Tosi and Einbender (1985) concluded that lack of information about applicants was the primary culprit that led to biased judgements, and when job-relevant information levels are high, there is little to no favouritism shown towards men during the recruitment phase.

Résumés have been, and continue to be, an initial screening tool, in part because they are a fast and inexpensive way to assess basic qualifications and fit before investing in the applicant (Cole, Feild & Giles, 2004). This is especially true for large organizations and entry-level jobs where large numbers of applications are often received. Because résumés are often the recruiters' first impression of the applicants, they represent an important part of the recruitment and selection process. In theory, it would be possible to minimize the role of gender in résumé evaluation by removing information from résumés that identifies the gender of the applicant (Futoran & Wyer, 1986), but this is not a common practice.

Recruitment processes can be formal, especially those conducted using public and private employment agencies, trade unions, school or college placement bureaux and advertisements, or informal, such as recruitment based on referrals and walk-ins (Granovetter, 1995). Informal sources, such as referrals, are generally believed to produce superior applicants (Breaugh, 1981; Decker & Cornelius, 1979; Gannon, 1971; Kirnan, Farley & Geisinger, 1989), yet informal recruitment is also more likely to lead to a homogeneous workplace (Pfeffer, 1977). This may be explained by the pre-screening hypothesis, which states that anyone who gets a referral from an existing employee has already been mentally screened for fit by that employee (Ullman, 1966), and few employees are willing to risk their reputation on a questionable referral applicant.

The difference in recruitment that is based on applicant gender is an important issue, because the sex composition of workgroups has been shown to affect many aspects of an organization's efficiency and process. The integration, effectiveness of communication and levels of conflict among workgroup members are influenced by the group's gender composition (Williams & O'Reilly, 1998). This composition has consequences for subjective outcomes, such as job satisfaction, motivation, organizational attachment and turnover (Allmendinger & Hackman, 1995; Tsui, Egan & O'Reilly, 1992; Wharton & Baron, 1987). Furthermore, an organization's gender composition can lead to men and women having different experiences within the same organization or group in terms of job mobility (Tolbert, Simons, Andrews & Rhee, 1995). There is a positive correlation between the number of women present in an organization and an individual woman's chance of promotion (Cohen, Broschak & Haveman, 1998), indicating the effects of social isolation and sexist stereotyping (Konrad, Winter & Gutek, 1992).

In a meta-analysis on recruitment, Chapman, Uggerslev, Carroll, Piasentin and Jones (2005) found that women and men do not differ in their reactions to recruiter characteristics, including gender. However, other reviews on gender recruiter characteristics are inconclusive. Graves and Powell (1988) found that although there were no gender differences in recruiter evaluations, they did find a 'similar to me' bias such that when viewed as similar, applicants were rated more positively. In a separate study, female recruiters viewed male applicants as more similar and more qualified than female applicants (Graves & Powell, 1995). Once again this finding may vary depending on the gender typing of the occupation (Wood, 2008).

Theories/framework

The most prevalent theoretical focus in research on recruitment and gender involves gender stereotypes. Gender stereotypes are generalizations that remain stable over time and focus on the differences, real or perceived, between men and women (Cole, Feild & Giles, 2004). For example, there are widespread beliefs regarding 'masculine' and 'feminine' traits. A study conducted in the US identified masculine traits as typically including 'dominance, independence, and competitiveness' (Cole, Feild & Giles, 2004, p. 598) and feminine traits encompassing 'dependence, nurturance, and communality' (Cole, Feild & Giles, 2004, p. 598). These traits are reflected internationally. Moghandam (2004) found that in the Middle East and North Africa, women's roles were concentrated in the home and with the children. Though the Western perspective views these roles as restrictive, women in the Middle East did not view their role of caregiver as oppressive but rather as an important responsibility, for which they are relieved of the burden of work outside the home (Moghandam, 2004). Oppenheimer (1968) coined the phrase 'women's work' or 'men's work' to describe this kind of stereotyped labelling in the workplace. These beliefs are not limited to men; men and women have similar perceptions of traits that are viewed as masculine or feminine (Powell, 1987). Gender stereotypes do not necessarily reflect actual differences between men and women, but they remain equally powerful as perceptions. In particular, gender stereotypes are likely to influence recruitment decisions when the nature of a job is categorized as male- or female-oriented, which can often occur implicitly if not explicitly (Powell, 1987).

These gender stereotypes can be prescriptive or descriptive. Prescriptive stereotypes can be understood as beliefs about how a certain gender *should* behave, while descriptive stereotypes reflect beliefs about how men and women *actually* behave, which in a work context can have a strong impact on assessments of fitness for or ability to perform a certain job (Cole, Feild & Giles, 2004). Recruiters and leaders can rely on one or both of these stereotype processes. One common outcome of this type of stereotyping is that females are often evaluated as less suitable than males for managerial positions or for positions described as demanding (Cohen & Bunker, 1975).

Gender stereotypes are a problem because gender often has little to do with actual performance in or fitness for most occupations, and any focus on gender is likely to distract attention from accurate perceptions of ability or capability (Cole, Feild & Giles, 2004). When recruiters have little information about applicants, they are more likely to rely on gender stereotypes when deciding whether to recruit a man or a woman (Gardner & Berger, 1980; Heilman, 1984). This is one reason why applicant demographics explain variance in hiring decisions beyond what can be explained by applicant qualifications (Powell & Butterfield, 2002). Olian, Schwab and Haberfeld (1988) suggested that gender explains at least 4% of the variability in recruitment and selection outcomes above and beyond the effects of actual qualifications, though this number has varied (Cole, Feild & Giles, 2004). Sex and gender not only influence recruiters' responses to applicants, they also influence applicants' responses to recruiters and to the organization (Powell, 1984). These responses include attitudes, perceptions, expectations and behaviours (Schmitt, 1976).

Numerous contextual factors play a role in shaping the relationship between gender and recruitment. Sex structuring theory provides a useful framework for understanding gender differences in recruiting. Sex differences in socialization and roles outside the workplace (e.g., caretaker roles) are linked to power differentials in the workplace, or a 'sex structuring' at work. This leads to selective recruitment of women into roles that require more passive behaviour, as well as into situations that keep them in these roles rather than advancing in the organization (Acker & Van Houton, 1974; Bartol, 1978). Sex structuring occurs at different stages of the career and can have a significant effect on entry into the organization (Powell, 1987).

Jobs can be categorized as male-dominated, female-dominated or sex-ratio balanced. These categories can determine the success of job-seeking applicants. Cohen and Bunker (1975) found that job recruiters were more likely to recommend female applicants for female-dominated jobs and more likely to recommend male applicants for male-dominated jobs.

Davison and Burke (2000) show more recent meta-analytic findings supporting Cohen and Bunker's original study that applicants receive lower ratings when applying for the opposite-sex type job.

Organizational size also appears to play a role in explaining the relationship between gender and recruitment. Smaller organizations are likely to be more homogeneous, while large and/or expanding organizations need to be less selective in whom they recruit, thus introducing more potential variety into the demographics of the organization (Bygren & Kumlin, 2005). Large organizations are also more likely to institute formal recruitment processes, which may result in more diverse recruitment and hiring practices. They are also more vulnerable to lawsuits, so they are likely to be more cognizant of diversity when recruiting and hiring candidates.

The competitiveness of the field also provides some explanation for recruitment differences as a function of gender. The more competitive the market, the more heterogeneous organizations tend to be. This observation is often explained in terms of neoclassical economic theory (Becker, 1962), which states that a competitive market will alter what seems important in an applicant: where sex might have been a deciding factor in a low competition market, hard-headed competitors just want the best worker regardless of gender (Bygren & Kumlin, 2005).

Ultimately, the demographics of an organization are the result of who is recruited, who is hired, who is retained, who quits and who is fired (Bygren & Kumlin, 2005). Schneider's (1987) Attraction–Selection–Attrition (ASA) framework provides a particularly useful model for understanding the interplay between the processes organizations use to attract and select applicants and the decisions job incumbents make about staying with or leaving organizations (see also Schneider, Goldstein & Smith, 1995). This model suggests that organizations tend to look for and select applicants who are similar to current organization members in terms of values, preferences, ideas and demographic characteristics. Individuals who join the organization but find they are not a good fit will be motivated to leave, especially if there are opportunities to join organizations that they find more compatible. As a result, organizations tend to become increasingly homogeneous over time, and if gender is one of the dimensions that is important in defining the organization, they may become less and less able to attract and retain a gender-balanced workforce.

Selection

Once a group of applicants has been selected, organizations must make decisions about which applicants to hire and which to reject. Hough, Oswald and Ployhart (2001) reviewed a variety of commonly used selection tools and explored gender differences for each one. Consistent with research cited earlier, they concluded that men and women do not significantly differ in mean scores on measures of general cognitive ability (g). However, the distribution for male scores has a larger standard deviation, indicating that more men score in the high and low extremes than women. Though the mean scores on measures of g are similar for men and women, there are mean differences for men and women in different factors of cognitive ability. For example, women tend to score higher in verbal ability (Hyde & Linn, 1988) and men tend to score higher in spatial ability (Greary, Saults, Liu & Hoard, 2000).

Hough and colleagues (2001) examined gender differences in scores on situational judgement tests and physical ability tests. Women tend to score higher on both paper-and-pencil and video-based situational judgement tests. However, men consistently outperform women in physical ability tests. The difference is largest in tests of muscular strength, with smaller group differences in cardiovascular endurance and movement quality. Additionally, the authors note that women are more anxious about test-taking and tend to evaluate the test as more difficult than men do.

Personality tests are generally thought of as appropriate for selection due to the general stability of personality over time, as well as its relative lack of mean subgroup differences (Goldberg, Sweeny, Merenda & Hughes, 1998). However, the literature shows mixed findings on whether mean group differences between men and women exist. For example, Hough and colleagues (2001) report small differences, with women being slightly more agreeable and dependable (a facet of conscientiousness) and scoring higher on facets of extraversion affiliation and lower on surgency (a trait aspect of emotional reactivity in which a person tends towards high levels of positive affect) than men. Saad and Sackett (2002) examined three employment-oriented personality measures used by the military: adjustment, dependability and achievement orientation, and suggested small differences (favouring males) on all three measures. However, other studies show no group differences based on gender. Ones and Anderson (2002) examined three commonly used pre-employment personality inventories: the Hogan Personality Inventory, the Occupational Personality questionnaire and the Business Personality Indicator. They concluded that there are no large subgroup differences between men and women.

Many selection tools are moving to online platforms as technology advances. This could have implications for gender, especially when age is considered. The idea that technology is a male domain is fading, as adoption and use of technology among younger generations is equal for both men and women. However, for older workers this stereotype may persist, making the adoption and use of technology less common, especially among women (Morris, Venkatesh & Ackerman, 2005). Therefore, older female workers may be less comfortable than other groups taking selection assessments on a computer.

Subjective selection methods

Tests play an important role in selection decisions, but these decisions also often incorporate a range of more subjective measures, including interviews and ratings of various types. Selection methods that involve subjective judgements are thought to be especially vulnerable to discrimination on the basis of demographic characteristics (Cesare, 1996). Rudman and Glick (2001) found that female applicants for a managerial job who demonstrated confidence, ambition and competitiveness were perceived as highly qualified. However, they were less likely to receive a hiring recommendation because they were more disliked than males. Other research suggests that when women demonstrate traits that violate implicit gender stereotyping (e.g., confidence), they are penalized in the workplace (Eagly & Karau, 2002; Heilman, Wallen, Fuchs & Tamkins, 2004). Heilman's lack of fit model suggests that the effects of gender on subjective judgements will be especially strong when there is a mismatch between the gender of the applicant and the gender stereotype of the job (e.g., a female applying for the position of truck driver; Heilman, 2012; Lyness & Heilman, 2006). Interviews might also allow irrelevant criteria to influence decisions. For example, marital status influences perceptions of female applicants. Nadler and Kufahl (2014) found that married heterosexual women received higher ratings in interviews than single heterosexual women.

The use of structured interviews (which often involve a standard set of job-related questions, clear standards for evaluation and multiple interviewers) appears to minimize the effects of gender on interview outcomes (Macan, 2009). In a series of studies examining promotions to high-level government positions, Powell and Butterfield (2002) reported encouraging results for women working in the government. Their 1994 US-based study showed that women were favoured in panel evaluations and referral decisions. However, there was no significant effect of gender on the final hiring decision. They reported that female applicants benefited when the review panel and selecting officials are diverse in both race and gender.

There is promising research to support that discrimination and prejudicial thinking are reduced or even penalized in certain organizational circumstances. For example, in the selection and evaluation stages of employment, women and men receive similar ratings on their competence and ability when more information about their background or educational attainment is provided. In other words, reliance on inaccurate stereotypes is more likely to occur if the applicant's gender is the only thing known about them. This is particularly true if the employee's gender is salient due to attractiveness, pregnancy or token status (Fuegen, Biernat, Haines & Deaux, 2004; Kanter, 1976). Organizations can therefore take steps to reduce gender discrimination, such as leaving the demographic section to the end of an application or providing evaluative raters with quality information on which to base their decisions (Davison & Burke, 2000; Terborg, 1977).

Justice/diversity programmes

Many organizations have made an effort to hire diverse applicants. A diverse workforce can be seen as a competitive advantage because organizations that feature a representative workforce are often viewed positively by consumers (Richard & Kirby, 1998). To achieve this goal, some organizations have implemented diversity programmes to influence both hiring and promoting procedures. While these programmes can be beneficial in expanding diversity of employees in organizations, endorsing diversity for the sake of appearances can backfire. The justice literature can inform the success or failure of programmes such as these. Diversity programmes not only should have distributive justice components, but also should address procedural justice. Applicants react poorly to diversity programmes when there is no explanation for why the organization has implemented the programme. Richard and Kirby (1998) found that without procedural justice, manifesting in this study as a reason for the diversity programme, applicants have negative attitudes about the decision to hire them, their abilities and the diversity programme itself. They will also believe that co-workers perceive them as less competent when the diversity programme lacks procedural justice. Providing a reason for the diversity programme, thereby increasing procedural justice, should be an essential component of diversity programmes used in hiring and promotion decisions.

Gender discrimination and the bottom line

At the larger organizational level there is evidence that discriminatory hiring and promotion practices ultimately harm the organization by making it less competitive (Weber & Zulehner, 2014). In their study of archival data (1977–2006) from Austria, Weber & Zulehner compared the proportion of female employees in start-up firms to the industry average. Using the Austrian Social Security database, they found firms with median and high levels of female employees were more likely to survive. Specifically, firms with the least number of female employees relative to the industry standard failed on average 18 months before firms with an average number of female employees relative to the industry standard (Weber & Zulehner, 2014).

Retention

Recruitment and selection concern the process of bringing men and women into organizations. Organizations have numerous experiences, practices, policies and characteristics that can influence the decision of male and female employees to remain in or leave organizations. One factor in the decision to stay or leave has to do with the consistency between the demands and the nature of the job and the structure and climate of the organization, and the values, preferences and characteristics of employees. In this section, we start by examining how the design and nature of jobs and organizations might affect the retention of male and female employees. We then consider the way men and women are led and the way they lead, the way they are evaluated and rewarded, and the way they are helped or hampered by the organization, boss and co-workers in balancing the demands of their work and non-work domains. All these factors are likely to have a bearing on the ability of organizations to retain employees they have recruited and selected.

Gendered organizations and organizational culture

One of the major challenges in retaining a diverse workforce is that organizations are largely structured around a set of assumptions and preferences that might have characterized the workforce in the past but that no longer fully apply today. For example, work organizations often place substantial and unpredictable demands on employees' time and focus, placing a high value on face time and on putting the interests of the organization first. Some organizations encourage competition among employees and reward employees who maximize their own success, even at the expense of their colleagues. Organizations that follow these principles are likely to be uncomfortable environments for workers who do not share values that centre on competition and putting the organization first. Even workers who do share these values may find it difficult to practise them without the support systems that only a subset of workers have access to, such as a non-working partner or the ability to delegate non-work responsibilities to a partner. One of the earliest barriers to women in organizations is that the structure and culture of these organizations is built around a set of values, preferences and experiences that is male-oriented. To succeed in these workplaces, female employees might need to adapt to, or at least endure, this particular orientation.

Organizational culture is a pattern of basic assumptions that are developed by a group as a way to function in and understand their environment. These assumptions must be successful enough to be considered valid, and in turn they are passed on to new members as the appropriate way to think, act and behave in the work environment (Schein, 1990). An organization's culture often sets the tone for its climate, or the observable policies and practices that individuals reinforce on a daily basis by (James, 1982).

Potential conflicts between the male-centric culture of many organizations and the values, preferences and life experiences of female employees often first emerge during the 'onboarding' process, when new employees are socialized to become members of the organization. After accepting a job offer or promotion, all employees need to 'learn the ropes' and become familiar with a new environment. Ideally, socialization consists of interactions or events that clearly reflect the new environment as a whole. The socialization process can look different for every organization, though there are established tactics and approaches to take that will result in known socialization outcomes (Van Maanen & Schein, 1979). Effective socialization is linked to higher levels of employee job satisfaction, performance and commitment, and less turnover (Ashford & Black, 1996).

Regardless of socialization tactics, female employees have historically been at risk of being viewed as different or token, particularly in non-traditional occupations or male-dominated organizations (Terborg, 1977). Employees that have limited experience working with females are more likely to rely on sex role stereotypes as well as sex characteristic stereotypes, both of which carry connotations of the woman being an ineffective or relatively weak worker. This viewpoint, which isolates the female employee from the rest of the group, does not bode well for a successful socialization process.

Historically, the majority of organizational cultures have been male-oriented, categorized by features such as top-down communication, strict hierarchies and autocratic leadership (Hofstede, 1980). This entrenched cultural type has been a persistent obstacle for females in organizations, particularly as women continue to enter the workforce and pursue positions in leadership and management (Bajdo & Dickson, 2001). In order to fully understand the role of gender in the workplace, the organization's culture must be understood and incorporated.

Early research on gender and organizational culture suggested that men and women valued fundamentally different components of their job (Herzberg, Mausner & Capwell 1957; Taveggia & Ziemba, 1978). Extrinsic factors, such as social atmosphere, were believed to be more important for women. Men were seen as prioritizing the intrinsic aspects of a job, such as personal fulfilment and the opportunity to use their skills. Later studies questioned the label 'extrinsic/intrinsic factors', and a more generalized interpretation of these differences emerged with men valuing power, prestige and pay compared to women's valuing of personal relationships (Miller, 1980; Neil & Snizek, 1987).

One reason for these differences may be due to historical differences in each gender's organizational structure experience rather than to an innate gender difference (Kanter, 1976). Employees with positions that are low in status, pay or mobility are likely to place value on job aspects that are more relevant to their situation, such as the social climate or job security (Neil & Snizek, 1987). Women have historically occupied these positions, giving the appearance that these values are a function of the gender rather than of the job itself.

While some past studies have found support for this theory (Brief, Rose & Aldag, 1977), other research has found that differences in values exist even after controlling for job type (Bartol & Butterfield, 1976; Neil & Snizek, 1987; Schuler, 1975). These inconsistent findings point to a complicated issue, in which gender differences in organizational values may be due to the nature of the job, but can also be explained by the sex of the worker. Context appears to be the key determinant, as gender differences may explain more variance when gender stereotypes are salient within an organization or if the organization has a culture of strong norms based on gender (Neil & Snizek, 1987).

It is now generally accepted that organizational culture and gender impact each other (Mills, 1988). The culture of an organization can shape, change and redefine the gender identities of its employees. While both genders can be affected by an organization's culture and values, it is more typical for males to have favourable outcomes related to these cultures and for women to experience unfavourable or discriminatory issues (Mills, 1988).

Conflict resolution, rewards and the gender composition of the workplace

Support for gender differences has been found in studies of conflict resolution. Men and women in similar managerial positions are likely to employ different strategies when dealing with conflict (Holt & DeVore, 2005). Males tend to use direct and more aggressive resolution tactics, while women prefer indirect or communication-dominant tactics (Ting-Toomey, 1986). A recent meta-analysis by Holt and DeVore (2005) also found that women are more likely to compromise in a conflict than their male counterparts. Though these findings are not universal, and some studies have found evidence to suggest opposite relationships in certain contexts (Muir, 1991; Rahim, 1983), gender does appear to explain some inherent differences in how men and women behave in an organization's culture and value system.

One of the most salient ways in which an organization can interact with gender is based on values and rewards systems. It is common for traditionally male behaviours and characteristics (e.g., competitiveness, long working hours) to be rewarded in organizations (Morgan, 1986). Women that possess traditionally feminine characteristics are then less likely to be viewed as capable or competitive leaders and attempts to embrace 'masculine' characteristics may backfire (Mills, 1988).

Organizations can also shift the identity of its employees through socialization tactics. Starting at the recruitment stage, organizations may have embedded expectations for employees to act in stereotypical or traditional ways (Barron & Norris, 1976). Gender then becomes a defining characteristic and accomplishments or failures are viewed through the lens of employees' masculinity or femininity. These gender-based values can lead to discrimination against females in the workplace, as males have typically been viewed as the prototypical worker.

In order for culture to have a positive or advantageous effect on women, many researchers have suggested that organizations should embrace more 'feminine' or non-traditional values. Bajdo and Dickson (2001) examined organizational culture and the advancement of women in organizations. They found that, controlling for national culture, organizational cultures and climates that were high in humane orientation, gender equity and performance orientation were related to women's advancement in an organization. Organizations that were low in power distance (i.e., had a culture of shared power and collaboration) were likely to provide more opportunities for women's advancement. Bajdo and Dickson (2001) also found that the strongest predictor of a woman's advancement was the number of other women who already held managerial positions. This suggests that social norms regarding gender equity in the workplace may be the biggest cultural obstacle to overcome. Organizations still struggle to increase their female management demographic and create a culture of gender equity, and many face the risk of inadvertently creating a culture that views female executives as simply filling a quota or as unqualified for the role (Ragins, 1995).

Research has also examined men's reaction to women in male-dominated workplaces. Kvande and Rasmussen (1994) identified four categories of responses to female workers in male-dominated industries: those higher up in the organization who do not see women as competition; those at the same level in the organization who see women as potential competitors in promotion opportunities; those who are lower in the organization and do not currently see the need to compete with women; and those who see their success as dependent on what they do rather than whom they must compete with. These authors also suggest that there are two types of structure and culture, static hierarchy and dynamic networks, which set the context for female workers climbing up the career ladder. Unlike static hierarchies, dynamic structures allow the flexibility for young employees, both men and women, to take on more responsibilities and opportunities to develop, which allows them to move up in the organization.

Leadership

Research shows that female leaders can be just as or more effective than male leaders (Eagly & Carli, 2003; Eagly, Johannesen-Schmidt & Van Engen, 2003; Eagly & Johnson, 1990; Powell, Butterfield & Bartrol, 2008; Yoder, 2001). Further, there is evidence that gender diversity in top management teams is related to positive organizational performance (Krishnan & Park, 2005). Yet the evidence shows that female leaders are often *perceived* as less effective leaders. Appelbaum, Audet and Miller (2003) claim that this perception is based on how we are socialized rather than on leader performance.

Perceptions of gender differences in leadership effectiveness may say more about *how* women lead than about *how well* they lead. Some studies of leadership measures (e.g., Bass and Avolio's (1997) multifactor leadership questionnaire) suggest strong similarities in basic leadership strategies (Antonakis, Avolio & Sivasubramaniam, 2003). Other studies suggest differences in how men and women exercise leadership. Eagly and Johnson's (1990) meta-analysis showed that women tend to have a more participative and democratic leadership style than men, and that this tendency is seen in both laboratory and field studies. A later meta-analysis showed that women tend to engage in more transformational leadership behaviours, while men engage in more transactional and laissez-faire leadership behaviours (Eagly, Johannesen-Schmidt & Van Engen, 2003).

Women appear to be less likely than men to use strategies that fit the stereotype of a strong, highly directive leader and that might contribute to the perception that women are not effective leaders. This is ironic, since transformational leadership behaviours are more effective than behaviours associated with other leadership styles (Lowe & Kroeck, 1996). Undoubtedly, leadership styles are not set in stone; both men and women can learn techniques to be more effective leaders and adopt new leadership styles (Appelbaum et al., 2003). However, the belief that women are ineffective as leaders may be a function of the widely held stereotype that leadership requires top-down direction (an activity consistent with masculine stereotypes) rather than collaboration (an activity consistent with feminine stereotypes).

The sex-type of an industry or job can also influence leadership styles of men and women. Leadership styles did not differ between men and women in male-type industries, however, in female-type industries women showed a more interpersonal leadership style (Gardiner & Tiggemann, 1999). Women in all industries perceive more discrimination in the workplace than men, but women in male-type jobs report even more discrimination. Gardiner and Tiggemann (1999) found that in male-dominated industries, female leaders' mental health suffered when applying interpersonal strategies, whereas male leaders' mental health improved when they used the same strategies. These findings might be explained by role congruity theory, which proposes that when an individual holds a stereotype about a certain group that is incompatible with the role that group member has taken, the group member will be perceived as less effective in that role by the individual. When applied to gender and leadership, the theory states that employees may show prejudice against female leaders because of the incongruity of the female role and the leadership role (Eagly & Karau, 2002). When this happens, employees perceive female leaders as less effective, leaving the employee with a negative attitude to the female leader or potential leader, making it more difficult for female leaders to advance in the organization.

Performance expectations, evaluations and pay expectations

There is a substantial body of theory and research suggesting that the performance of men and women may be evaluated differently. Across organizations and fields, women are still largely viewed as unfit for numerous roles, particularly those in upper management or leadership (Heilman, 2012). This is attributed to the longstanding stereotype that a successful manager must possess 'male' traits, coupled with the entrenched belief that women are unable to embody these traits or effectively lead without them (Schein, 2001).

Therefore, a woman leader may be caught in a Catch-22 in which she is seen as either too feminine to be taken seriously or too masculine to be accepted (Costrich, Feinstein, Kidder, Marecek & Pascale, 1975).

This perceived lack of fit can distort the information-processing of raters during performance appraisals and evaluations. Their attention to detail, the details that are recalled and their interpretation can all be affected by the gender and role of the employee (Heilman, 2012). For example, a male manager's actions may be interpreted as 'assertive', while the same actions in a female manager may be viewed as 'nagging'.

These differences in performance expectations and evaluations, to the extent that they actually exist, can cause permanent harm to the career and self-perception of female employees. The negative outcomes range from obstacles during the hiring process to a reduced likelihood of being selected for training programmes or promotions (Heilman, 2012). This perceived lack of fit can also affect women's perception of their own abilities, causing them to rate themselves and each other negatively (Hentschel, Heilman & Peus, 2013).

In our discussion of recruitment research, we noted that much of the literature that suggests that there are differences in the recruitment of men and women is based on laboratory studies using naïve raters and minimally informative stimuli. This also applies to much of the research suggesting that men and women who perform similarly will be evaluated differently. Field research that examines whether men and women actually do receive different evaluations for the work they perform paints a somewhat different picture. On the whole, however, there is little unequivocal evidence that men and women receive different evaluations when studies are based on actual performance appraisals conducted by supervisors in organizations (Bowen, Swim & Jacobs, 2000; Landy et al., 1994; Roth, Purvis & Bobko, 2012; Wexley & Pulakos, 1982). There is, however, some evidence of lower ratings for women if all the supervisors are male (Bowen et al., 2000).

Although there might not be large differences in the average ratings men and women receive, the meaning and interpretation of these ratings miay differ between the two genders. For example, supervisors are less likely to attribute the success of their female subordinates in managerial positions to merit than they are to attribute this success to male managers (Greenhaus & Parasuraman, 1993). It is widely assumed that women and men are successful in their careers for different reasons. Melamed (1995) proposed that there should be separate models for men and women due to these differences. This suggests that women succeed at work due to their merit and limited domestic responsibilities, while men's success is more influenced by their career choices and personality. Women who are successful in male-oriented jobs are less well liked, and this can affect their career outcomes (Heilman et al., 2004).

Not only are women evaluated more negatively in their own performance evaluations, but women in supervisory roles are perceived differently from men when they perform an appraisal and give feedback. When disciplining employees, female managers are perceived as less effective and less fair (Atwater, Cary & Waldman, 2001). In particular, men react less favourably to negative feedback from women (Atwater et al., 2001). The authors hypothesize that this could be a rejection of women being influential in the workplace or a result of the negative evaluations men typically give female managers. This effect could also be due to women being more tentative than men, leading to a lack of confidence in being perceived as a lack of competence.

Similar levels of performance do not guarantee similar levels of rewards. Research shows there is a wage gap that favours men, even in female-oriented professions (Ostroff & Atwater, 2003). In management positions where the field is dominated by women, pay is lower

(Ostroff & Atwater, 2003). In merit-pay systems, studies show that even with equal scores on performance evaluations, women are compensated less than men (Castilla & Benard, 2010). A possible factor in the wage gap could that women have lower pay expectations, are less likely to negotiate and report fewer opportunities for legitimate negotiations for pay (Kaman & Hartel, 1994). This research shows that women tend to have lower perceived pay entitlement. Women have lower positions in organizations, lower salaries when controlled for position and perceive their possible peak position as lower than men's (Hind & Baruch, 1997). To explore this further, Desmarais and Curtis (1997) examined the salience of recent pay when applicants evaluate how much money should be allocated to their salary. When the most recent pay experience is not salient, women allocate significantly less for their pay than do men. However, when previous pay is made salient, the difference between men and women in allocated self-pay is non-significant, as women pay themselves more and men pay themselves less than when previous pay is not salient.

Traditionally, pay and opportunities for promotion have been viewed as important factors in employee motivation and willingness to remain in an organization. Evidence regarding promotion through the lower and mid-levels of organizations is mixed, but there is clear evidence that women are less likely than men to reach the higher levels of many organizations. The 'glass ceiling' paradigm describes the difficulty women have reaching the top of the corporate ladder (Federal Glass Ceiling Commission, 1995). The glass ceiling is often attributed to stereotypes and the subjectivity involved in promotion decisions (Weyer, 2007). Whatever its cause, the lack of diversity in the top management of most organizations suggests that women are, at least at some point in their careers, less likely to receive rewards that are highly valued by many members of the organization.

Work and non-work

Although men and women often possess similar abilities to perform the tasks their jobs entail, they have different responsibilities and orientations towards the non-work sphere. Women are still more likely than men to assume responsibility for their family (both child rearing and elder care) and other aspects of maintaining the non-work side of their life and the life of their partner, and balancing the demands of work and non-work spheres can place burdens on female employees that are different from males'. The literature on gender differences in work–life balance shows mixed findings. Some studies have shown that women experience greater work–life conflict than men (Lundberg, Mardberg & Frankenhaeuser, 1994), while others show men and women experience similar levels of work–life conflict (Emslie, Hunt & Macintyre, 2004).

Bekker, Croon and Bressers (2005) reported that women have greater childcare obligations and activities than men. Taking care of children leads to sickness absence, but only in part due to emotional exhaustion. The authors suggest that sickness absence for childcare investment could be due to limited flexibility in scheduling work rather than emotional exhaustion. The number of working hours to which men devote more time was found to influence emotional exhaustion. Emslie and Hunt (2009) used qualitative techniques to investigate work–life balance in adults aged 50–52. They found that women, though no longer with young children in the home, continue to attempt to balance more conflict, including caring for adult children and ageing parents, while men generally spoke of conflict that had occurred in the past.

Organizations can use a variety of policies or procedures to reduce work–life conflict for its employees, such as flexible work hours or telework. Policies for flexible working hours are typically linked to female workers, especially those who have children. These policies have been shown to be effective in reducing work–life conflict, especially for women (Beauregard & Henry, 2009). As long as employees perceive the policies to be viable, they can lead to increases in organizational commitment and job satisfaction (Scandura & Lankau, 1997).

Hilbrecht, Shaw, Johnson and Andrey (2008) conducted in-depth interviews with teleworking women with young children. The participants had a positive attitude to telework, saying it allowed them to combine their work and family roles more success-fully. They reported a better work–life balance and a higher perceived quality of life. Smithson and Stokoe (2005) interviewed focus groups about organizational policies phrased to be gender-neutral. The authors found that even when using gender-neutral language policies, employees assumed that these policies would be primarily used by women rather than by men. Even when men and women take advantage of these same policies, they may have very different reasons for doing so. Loscocco (1997) found that men view flexible scheduling as being in control while women view it as a resource for handling work–life conflict.

An organization's human resource practices involving work design can influence the success of female employees. There is a wide variety of ways an organization can redesign the work, including flexible schedules, work–family-friendly policies, telework opportunities and justice policies. Work design practices predict employees' perceived control in managing work and family demands (Batt & Valcour, 2001). According to this research, men say they have more control over managing work and family demands, while women say they have more work–family conflict. Supportive supervisors can reduce perceptions of work–family conflict for women, but not for men. To further explore how family dynamics are affected, these researchers examined whether the employment conditions of one partner influenced work–family conflict outcomes for the other and found no significant cross-over effects (Batt & Valcour, 2001).

Flexible work policies are important for all employees, but especially for female employees. When female employees perceive their organization as having flexible work hours, they are more committed to the organization and more satisfied with their job. These policies are also beneficial to men with family responsibilities (Scandura & Lankau, 1997). Flexible work policies have been shown to have positive effects across cultures and countries, although European organizations have traditionally been ahead of other Western cultures in adapting these policies, with the Nordic countries being at the fore-front of the movement (Stavrou & Kilaniotis, 2010). For example, in Norway flexible work arrangements are a right in law accorded to all workers (Eiken, 2008). The positive effects of these longer-established policies have been reflected in consistently low turnover, high productivity and a satisfied workforce in Finland and Norway (Brewster, Mayrhofer & Morley, 2004).

Work–family conflict can lead to more than dissatisfaction with work. Women can feel torn by the competing roles of work and family. Research shows that working mothers who take advantage of their organization's telework policy reported less depression than mothers who did not telework (Kossek, Lautsch & Eaton, 2006). The authors hypothesize that telework allows mothers to be more involved in their work and family roles.

As technology continues to give organizations a greater global reach, it is imperative to develop a keener sense of how culture and gender interact. Research shows that the effect of gender in American organizational culture can be different from that in other countries. Those in American organizations tend to view modesty as favourable in women but not in men, while a Polish sample viewed modesty as equally favourable in the two sexes (Wosinska, Dabul, Whetstone-Dion & Cialdini, 1996). As the GLOBE studies illustrate, many national cultures exist and each cluster contains unique perceptions and expectations (House, Javidan & Dorfman, 2001).

The Social Context of Recruitment, Selection and Retention, and Gender

On the whole, our review suggests that for most of the twentieth century there were noticeable differences in the patterns of recruitment of men and women into different types of jobs and occupations. Women were less likely than men to be selected for many jobs, especially those in male-dominated occupations, but these differences are slowly fading. A more complex picture emerges when considering retention, with many barriers still existing to retaining women in jobs that pay well and involve significant responsibility. We believe that four factors can explain these differences: 1) occupational segregation, 2) the lack of a level playing field, 3) differences in the willingness to engage in behaviours that are viewed as important for high-pay, high-responsibility positions and 4) the male-centric culture at the top of most organizations.

Sex segregation of occupations shapes and defines the choices women and men make about their careers, including whom they work with, as well as the continuing wage gap (Jacobs, 1999). Women continue to be concentrated in low-status jobs and under-represented in high-status jobs and occupations (Jacobs, 1999). This crowding of women into specific occupations reduces their opportunities and limits their earning potential (Bergmann, 1986; Parcel & Mueller, 1989) due to excess supply and lower demand in these jobs.

In terms of a level playing field, women's time spent on housework is related to paid work involvement (Bianchi, Milkie, Sayer & Robinson, 2000). The popular press and recent publications such as *Lean In* (Sandberg, 2013) have highlighted continued gender gaps at work and home in spite of the narrowed gap between men and women in labour force participation rates. Gender equality theorists argue that these differences undergird inequality, placing women at a distinct disadvantage at home and at work (Budig & Folbre, 2004). Even though women and men both report that they want to spend more time with their children, women are the ones who are more likely in practice to scale back on their work time to prioritize their family (Becker & Moen, 1999).

Differences in behaviour are also key, and failure to rise in a company is not necessarily due to a lack of desire or motivation to advance. A 2004 Catalyst survey of senior male and female leaders in Fortune 1000 companies found comparable aspirations to reach the CEO level. Among those in line and staff positions, more women than men aspired to the CEO level (Catalyst, 2004). However, men and women, particularly in jobs or occupations that require heavy and unpredictable investments of time, differed substantially in their ability and willingness to engage in the behaviours that are often required to make it to the top, especially if these represent stereotypically masculine behaviour patterns.

Last, male-centric work cultures at the top of most organizations can explain some of these gender differences. Work organizations can dominate the lives of their members, particularly those at the top of the organization, and there are good reasons to believe that women find this type of work life less attractive and less manageable than do men. In jobs that combine high pay with high levels of responsibility, the tendency to put work first and non-work (family, leisure time) second is especially pronounced. Yet, devotion to the workplace above all else can take a substantial toll. For example, there is evidence that executives are more likely to be divorced and to experience family conflicts than individuals in less time-intensive occupations (Burke, 2006).

Future Research

Talent management continues to be paramount to organizational and employee success. The future of research in this field is likely to target several specific themes, which we highlight in this section.

The development of cross-cultural studies will advance our understanding of several key research questions, such as how employment policies impact retention rates. As organizations become increasingly global, research on recruitment, selection and retention will be critical if we are to understand how to dismantle language and culture barriers, how to integrate different leadership styles across countries and how to respect and appreciate every country's talent management needs while presenting a unified organizational front.

Paired with global outreach, technology will continue to impact talent management practices in yet unseen capacities. Top organizations, such as GoPros and Google Glass, are already embracing new technology in order to attract and recruit millennial applicants (Godfrey, 2015). Organizations will need to streamline their efforts at recruitment, selection and retention in ways that capitalize on the immediacy and convenience of the internet and social media.

Finally, diversity in general will continue to be a key topic in talent management research. Beyond the collaboration of research across countries and cultures, it will be crucial to understand the demographics of modern teams and departments. A few years ago the US Bureau of Labor Statistics predicted that, by 2016, over 50% of new job applicants would be female and 43% non-White (Arnold, 2011). In these circumstances, we can expect that the changing makeup of organizations will also change our approach to recruitment, selection and retention policies.

Conclusion

Organizations that succeed in attracting, selecting and retaining the best employees enjoy a distinct competitive advantage. But this can be undermined by a lack of fit between the methods used to attract, select and retain employees and the realities of the current workforce. Historically, the talent management process has been built by and for a narrow segment of the workforce – usually male, usually White, usually involved in family arrangements that are supportive of a stereotypically masculine work culture that features long work hours, high levels of commitment to the organization and a low likelihood that the non-work life sphere will interfere with work. Stereotypes about women, men and occupations may influence the recruitment, retention and selection of employees. Once men and women enter organizations, they may find large differences in the degree to which the culture and the demands of organizations fit their needs, values, preferences and constraints. These factors are likely to combine in ways that will continue to make it difficult for organizations to attract, select and retain a diverse workforce.

Recruitment, selection and retention historically reinforced gender stereotypes and served as gatekeepers for women's upward mobility. In the past, women were not recruited or selected for entire categories of jobs. Today, however, recruitment, selection and even to some degree retention, play a critical role as HR practices in promoting the entrance of skilled women and men into organizations are based on equivalent skills, knowledge and abilities. Rather than limiting opportunities for women at work, both recruitment and selection have become instrumental in narrowing the gender gap in leadership, pay, responsibilities and work experiences. Future research must focus on the practices of retention in organizations in order to maximize the work experiences of both women and men.

References

Acker, J., & Van Houten, D. R. (1974). Differential recruitment and control: The sex structuring of organizations. *Administrative Science Quarterly*, 152–163.

Allmendinger, J., & Hackman, J. R. (1995). The more, the better? A four-nation study of the inclusion of women in symphony orchestras. *Social Forces*, 74(2), 423–460.

Antonakis, J., Avolio, B. J., & Sivasubramaniam, N. (2003). Context and leadership: An examination of the nine-factor full-range leadership theory using the multifactor leadership questionnaire. *The Leadership Quarterly*, 14, 261–295.

Appelbaum, S. H., Audet, L., & Miller, J. C. (2003). Gender and leadership? Leadership and gender? A journey through the landscape of theories. *Leadership & Organization Development Journal*, 24(1), 43–51.

Arnold, P. (2011). The role of diversity management in the global talent retention race. www.diversityjournal.com/4530-the-role-of-diversity-management-in-the-global-talent-retention-race. Last accessed 29 January 2016.

Ashford, S. J., & Black, J. S. (1996). Proactivity during organizational entry: The role of desire for control. *Journal of Applied Psychology*, 81, 199–214.

Atwater, L. E., Carey, J. A., & Waldman, D. A. (2001). Gender and discipline in the workplace: Wait until your father gets home. *Journal of Management*, 27(5), 537–561.

Bajdo, L. M., & Dickson, M. W. (2001). Perceptions of organizational culture and women's advancement in organizations: A cross-cultural examination. *Sex Roles*, 45(5–6), 399–414.

Barber, A. E. (1998). *Recruiting Employees: Individual and Organizational Perspectives* (Vol. 8). Palo Alto, CA: Sage.

Barron, R. D., & Norris, G. M. (1976). Sexual divisions and the dual labour market. *In* D. Barker & S. Allen (Eds.), *Dependence and Exploitation in Work and Marriage* (pp. 47–69). Upper Saddle River, NJ: Prentice Hall.

Bartol, K. M. (1978). The sex structuring of organizations: A search for possible causes. *Academy of Management Review*, 3(4), 805–815.

Bartol, K. M., & Butterfield, D. A. (1976). Sex effects in evaluating leaders. *Journal of Applied Psychology*, 61(4), 446.

Bass, B. M., & Avolio, B. J. (1997). *Full Range Leadership Development: Manual for the Multifactor Leadership Questionnaire*. Palo Alto, CA: Mind Garden.

Batt, R., & Valcour, P. M. (2001). Human resources practices as predictors of work–family outcomes and employee turnover. *Industrial Relations: A Journal of Economy and Society*, 42(2), 189–220.

Beauregard, T. A., & Henry, L. C. (2009). Making the link between work–life balance practices and organizational performance. *Human Resource Management Review*, 19, 9–22.

Becker, G. S. (1962). Irrational behavior and economic theory. *The Journal of Political Economy*, 1–13.

Becker, P. E., & Moen, P. (1999). Scaling back: Dual-earner couples' work–family strategies. *Journal of Marriage and the Family*, 995–1007.

Bekker, M. H., Croon, M. A., & Bressers, B. (2005). Childcare involvement, job characteristics, gender and work attitudes as predictors of emotional exhaustion and sickness absence. *Work & Stress*, 19(3), 221–237.

Bergmann, B. (1986). *The Economic Emergence of Women*. New York: Basic Books.

Bianchi, S. M., Milkie, M. A., Sayer, L. C., & Robinson, J. P. (2000). Is anyone doing the housework? Trends in the gender division of household labor. *Social Forces*, 79(1), 191–228.

Bobbitt-Zeher, S. (2011). Gender discrimination at work: Connecting gender stereotypes, institutional policies, and gender composition of the workplace. *Gender and Society*, 25, 764–786.

Bowen, C. C., Swim, J. K., & Jacobs, R. R. (2000). Evaluating gender biases on actual job performance of real people: A meta-analysis. *Journal of Applied Social Psychology*, 30(10), 2194–2215.

Breaugh, J. A. (1981). Relationships between recruiting sources and employee performance, absenteeism, and work attitudes. *Academy of Management Journal*, 24(1), 142–147.

Brewster, C., Mayrhofer, W., & Morley, M. (2004). *Human Resource Management in Europe: Evidence of Convergence?* New York: Routledge.

Brief, A. P., Rose, G. L., & Aldag, R. J. (1977). Sex differences in preferences for job attributes revisited. *Journal of Applied Psychology, 62*(5), 645–646.

Budig, M., & Folbre, N. (2004). Activity, proximity, or responsibility? Measuring parental childcare time. *In* N. Folbre & M. Bittman (Eds.), *Family Time: The Social Organization of Care* (pp. 51–68). New York: Routledge.

Bureau of Labor Statistics. (2013a). *Current Population Survey*, Table 3: Employment status of the civilian non-institutional population by age, sex, and race, annual averages 2012. Washington, DC: Bureau of Labor Statistics.

Bureau of Labor Statistics. (2013b). *Current Population Survey*, Table 11: Employed persons by detailed occupation, sex, race, and Hispanic or Latino ethnicity, annual averages 2012. Washington, DC: Bureau of Labor Statistics.

Burke, R. J. (2006). *Research Companion to Working Time and Work Addiction.* Northampton, MA: Edward Elgar.

Bygren, M., & Kumlin, J. (2005). Mechanisms of organizational sex segregation organizational characteristics and the sex of newly recruited employees. *Work and Occupations, 32*(1), 39–65.

Castilla, E. J., & Benard, S. (2010). The paradox of meritocracy in organizations. *Administrative Science Quarterly, 55*(4), 543–676.

Cesare, S. J. (1996). Subjective judgment and the selection interview: A methodological review. *Public Personnel Management, 25*, 291–306.

Chapman, D. S., Uggerslev, K. L., Carroll, S. A., Piasentin, K. A., & Jones, D. A. (2005). Applicant attraction to organizations and job choice: A meta-analytic review of the correlates of recruiting outcomes. *Journal of Applied Psychology, 90*(5), 928.

Cocoran, M. E., & Courant, P. N. (1987). Sex-role socialization and occupational segregation: An exploratory investigation. *Journal of Post-Keynesian Economics, 9*, 330–346.

Cohen, L. E., Broschak, J. P., & Haveman, H. A. (1998). And then there were more? The effect of organizational sex composition on the hiring and promotion of managers. *American Sociological Review*, 711–727.

Cohen, S. L., & Bunker, K. A. (1975). Subtle effects of sex role stereotypes on recruiters' hiring decisions. *Journal of Applied Psychology, 60*(5), 566.

Cole, M. S., Feild, H. S., & Giles, W. F. (2004). Interaction of recruiter and applicant gender in résumé evaluation: A field study. *Sex Roles, 51*(9–10), 597–608.

Connecting Corporate Performance and Gender Diversity. (2004). Retrieved June 1, 2015, from www.catalyst.org/system/files/The_Bottom_Line_Connecting_Corporate_Performance_and_Gender_Diversity.pdf

Costello, C. B., & Stone, A. J. (2001). *The American Woman, 2001–2002: Getting to the Top.* New York: W.W. Norton.

Costrich, N., Feinstein, J., Kidder, L., Marecek, J., & Pascale, L. (1975). When stereotypes hurt: Three studies of penalties for sex-role reversals. *Journal of Experimental Social Psychology, 11*(6), 520–530.

Davison, H. K., & Burke, M. J. (2000). Sex discrimination in simulated employment contexts: A meta-analytic investigation. *Journal of Vocational Behavior, 56*, 225–248.

Decker, P. J., & Cornelius, E. T. (1979). A note on recruiting sources and job survival rates. *Journal of Applied Psychology, 64*(4), 463.

Desmarais, S., & Curtis, J. (1997). Gender and perceived pay entitlement: Testing for effects of experience with income. *Journal of Personality and Social Psychology, 72*(1), 141.

Dipboye, R. L., Arvey, R. D., & Terpstra, D. E. (1977). Sex and physical attractiveness of raters and applicants as determinants of résumé evaluations. *Journal of Applied Psychology, 62*(3), 288.

Dipboye, R. L., Fromkin, H. L., & Wiback, K. (1975). Relative importance of applicant sex, attractiveness, and scholastic standing in evaluation of job applicant resumes. *Journal of Applied Psychology, 60*(1), 39.

Eagly, A. H., & Carli, L. L. (2003). The female leadership advantage: An evaluation of the evidence. *The Leadership Quarterly, 14*(6), 807–834.

Eagly, A. H., Johannesen-Schmidt, M. C., & Van Engen, M. L. (2003). Transformational, transactional, and laissez-faire leadership styles: a meta-analysis comparing women and men. *Psychological Bulletin, 129*(4), 569.

Eagly, A. H., & Johnson, B. T. (1990). Gender and leadership style: A meta-analysis. *Psychological Bulletin, 108*(2), 233–256.

Eagly, A. H., & Karau, S. J. (2002). Role congruity theory of prejudice toward female leaders. *Psychological Review, 109*(3), 573–598.

Eagly, A. H., Karau, S. J., Miner, J. B., & Johnson, B. T. (1994). Gender and motivation to manage in hierarchic organizations: A meta-analysis. *Leadership Quarterly, 5*, 135–159.

Eiken, T. (2008). *Flexible Working Hours Can Hinder Work–Life Balance.* Oslo: European Foundation for the Improvement of Living and Working Conditions, National Institute of Occupational Health.

Elliott, A. G. P. (1981). Sex and decision making in the selection interview: A real-life study. *Journal of Occupational Psychology, 54*(4), 265–273.

Emslie, C., & Hunt, K. (2009). Live to work or work to live? A qualitative study of gender and work–life balance among men and women in mid-life. *Gender, Work & Organization, 16*(1), 151–172.

Emslie, C., Hunt, K., & Macintyre, S. (2004). Gender, work–home conflict and morbidity amongst white-collar bank employees in the UK. *International Journal of Behavioral Medicine, 11*(3), 127–134.

Federal Glass Ceiling Commission. (1995). Solid investments: Making full use of the nation's human capital. www.dol.gov/oasam/programs/history/reich/reports/ceiling2.pdf.

Fuegen, K., Biernat, M., Haines, E., & Deaux, K. (2004). Mothers and fathers in the workplace: How gender and parental status influence judgments of job-related competence. *Journal of Social Issues, 60*(4), 737–754.

Futoran, G. C., & Wyer, R. S. (1986). The effects of traits and gender stereotypes on occupational suitability judgments and the recall of judgment-relevant information. *Journal of Experimental Social Psychology, 22*, 475–503.

Gannon, M. J. (1971). Sources of referral and employee turnover. *Journal of Applied Psychology, 55*(3), 226.

Gardner, D. G., & Berger, C. J. (1980). *The Effects of Sex Stereotypes, Amount of Relevant Information, and Awareness of Organizational Selection Practices on Sex Discrimination for a Managerial Position.* West Lafayette, IN: Institute for Research in the Behavioral, Economic, and Management Sciences, Krannert Graduate School of Management, Purdue University.

Gardiner, M., & Tiggemann, M. (1999). Gender differences in leadership style, job stress and mental health in male- and female-dominated industries. *Journal of Occupational and Organizational Psychology, 72*, 301–315.

Gneezy, U., Niederle, M., & Rustichini, A. (2003). Performance in competitive environments: Gender differences. *Quarterly Journal of Economics, 118*, 1049–1074.

Godfrey, C. (2015). General Mills using virtual technology to attract, recruit millennials. Fox News. www.fox9.com/news/20321929-story.

Goldberg, L. R., Sweeny, D., Merenda, P. F. & Hughes, J. E. (1998). Demographic variables and personality: The effects of gender, age, education, ethnic/racial status on self-descriptions of personality attributes. *Personality and Individual Differences, 24*, 393–403.

Granovetter, M. (1995). *Getting a Job: A Study of Contacts And Careers.* Chicago, IL: University of Chicago Press.

Graves, L. M., & Powell, G. N. (1988). An investigation of sex discrimination in recruiters' evaluations of actual applicants. *Journal of Applied Psychology, 73*(1), 20.

Graves, L. M., & Powell, G. N. (1995). The effect of sex similarity on recruiters' evaluations of actual applicants: A test of the similarity-attraction paradigm. *Personnel Psychology, 48*(1), 85–98.

Greary, D. C., Saults, S. J., Liu, F., & Hoard, M. K. (2000). Sex differences in spatial cognition, computational fluency, and arithmetical reasoning. *Journal of Experimental Child Psychology, 77*, 337–353.

Greenhaus, J. H., & Parasuraman, S. (1993). Job performance attributions and career advancement prospects: An examination of gender and race effects. *Organizational Behavior and Human Decision Processes, 55*(2), 273–297.

Halpern, D. F., Benbow, C. P., Geary, D. C., Gur, R. C., Hyde, J. S., & Gernsbacher, M. A. (2007). The science of sex differences in science and mathematics. *Psychological Science in the Public Interest, 8*, 1–51.

Heilman, M. E. (1984). Information as a deterrent against sex discrimination: The effects of applicant sex and information type on preliminary employment decisions. *Organizational Behavior and Human Performance, 33*(2), 174–186.

Heilman, M. E. (2012). Gender stereotypes and workplace bias. *Research in Organizational Behavior, 32*, 113–135.

Heilman, M. E., Wallen, A. S., Fuchs, D., & Tamkins, M. M. (2004). Penalties for success: Reactions to women who succeed at male gender-typed tasks. *Journal of Applied Psychology, 89*(3), 416.

Hentschel, T., Heilman, M. E., & Peus, C. (2013). Have perceptions of women and men changed? Gender stereotypes and self-ratings of men and women. Presentation at the annual conference of Society of Personality and Social Psychology, New Orleans, LA.

Herzberg, F., Mausner, R., & Capwell, D. (1957). *Job Attitudes: Review of Research and Opinion.* Pittsburgh, PN: Psychological Service of Pittsburgh.

Hilbrecht, M., Shaw, S. M, Johnson, L. C., & Andrey, J. (2008). 'I'm home for the kids': Contradictory implications for work–life balance of teleworking mothers. *Gender, Work and Organization, 15*(5), 454–476.

Hind, P., & Baruch, Y. (1997). Gender variations in perceptions of performance appraisal. *Women in Management Review, 12*(7), 276–289.

Hofstede, G. (1980). Motivation, leadership, and organization: Do American theories apply abroad? *Organizational Dynamics, 9*(1), 42–63.

Holt, J. L., & DeVore, C. J. (2005). Culture, gender, organizational role, and styles of conflict resolution: A meta-analysis. *International Journal of Intercultural Relations, 29*(2), 165–196.

Hough, L. M., Oswald, F. L., & Ployhart, R. E. (2001). Determinants, detection and amelioration of adverse impact in personnel selection procedures: Issues, evidence and lessons learned. *International Journal of Selection and Assessment, 9*(1–2), 152–194.

House, R., Javidan, M., & Dorfman, P. (2001). Project GLOBE: An introduction. *Applied Psychology, 50*(4), 489–505.

Hyde, J. S. (2005). The gender similarities hypothesis. *American Psychologist, 60*(6), 581–592.

Hyde, J. S., Fennema, E., & Lamon, S. (1990). Gender differences in mathematics performance: A meta-analysis. *Psychological Bulletin, 107*(2), 139–155.

Hyde, J. S., & Kling, K. C. (2001). Women, motivation, and achievement. *Psychology of Women Quarterly, 25*(4), 364–378.

Hyde, J. S., & Linn, M. C. (1988). Gender differences in verbal ability: A meta-analysis. *Psychological Bulletin, 104*(1), 53–69.

Jacobs, J. A. (1999). The sex segregation of occupations: Prospects for the 21st century. *In* G. Powell (Ed.), *Handbook of Gender and Work* (pp. 125–144). Thousand Oaks, CA: Sage.

James, L. R. (1982). Aggregation bias in estimates of perceptual agreement. *Journal of Applied Psychology, 67*(2), 219.

Kalkowski, K. L., & Fritz, S. M. (2004). A survey of gender-related motivation studies: Subordinate status, roles and stereotypes. *Journal of Leadership Education, 3*(2), 19–34.

Kaman, V. S., & Hartel, C. E. (1994). Gender differences in anticipated pay negotiation strategies and outcomes. *Journal of Business and Psychology, 9*(2), 183–197.

Kanter, R. M. (1976). The impact of hierarchical structures on the work behavior of women and men. *Social Problems, 23*(4), 415–430.

Kirnan, J. P., Farley, J. A., & Geisinger, K. F. (1989). The relationship between recruiting source, applicant quality, and hire performance: An analysis by sex, ethnicity, and age. *Personnel Psychology, 42*(2), 293–308.

Konrad, A. M., Winter, S., & Gutek, B. A. (1992). Diversity in work group sex composition: Implications for majority and minority members. *Research in the Sociology of Organizations, 10*(1), 15–140.

Kossek, E. E., Lautsch, B. A., & Eaton, S. C. (2006). Telecommuting, control, and boundary management: Correlates of policy use and practice, job control, and work–family effectiveness. *Journal of Vocational Behavior, 68*(2), 347–367.

Krishnan, H. A., & Park, D. (2005). A few good women on top management teams. *Journal of Business Research, 58*(12), 1712–1720.

Kvande, E., & Rasmussen, B. (1994). Men in male-dominated organizations and their encounter with women intruders. *Scandinavian Journal of Management, 10*(2), 163–173.

Landy, F. J., Shankster, L. J., & Kohler, S. S. (1994). Personnel selection and placement. *Annual Review of Psychology, 45*, 261–296.

Loscocco, K. A. (1997). Work–family linkages among self-employed women and men. *Journal of Vocational Behavior, 50*(2), 204–226.

Lowe, K. B., & Kroeck, K. G. (1996). Effectiveness correlated of transformational and transactional leadership: A meta-analysis of the MLQ literature. *The Leadership Quarterly, 7*(3), 385–415.

Lundberg, U., Mardberg, B., & Frankenhaeuser, M. (1994). The total workload of male and female white-collar workers as related to age, occupational level, and number of children. *Scandinavian Journal of Psychology, 35*(4), 315–327.

Lyness, K. S., & Heilman, M. E. (2006). When fit is fundamental: Performance evaluations and promotions of upper-level female and male managers. *Journal of Applied Psychology, 91*(4), 777–785.

Macan, T. (2009). The employment interview: A review of current studies and directions for future research. *Human Resource Management Review, 19*(2), 203–218.

Melamed, T. (1995). Barriers to women's career success: Human capital, career choices, structural determinants, or simply sex discrimination. *Applied Psychology, 44*(4), 295–314.

Miller, J. (1980). Individual and occupational determinants of job satisfaction: A focus on gender differences. *Sociology of Work and Occupations, 7*(1), 337–366.

Mills, A. J. (1988). Organization, gender and culture. *Organization Studies, 9*(3), 351–369.

Moghadam, V. M. (2004). Patriarchy in transition: Women and the changing family in the Middle East. *Journal of Comparative Family Studies, 35*(2), 137–162.

Morgan, G. (1986.) *Images of Organization*. Thousand Oaks, CA: Sage.

Morris, M. G., Venkatesh, V., & Ackerman, P. L. (2005). Gender and age differences in employee decisions about new technology: An extension to the theory of planned behavior. *Engineering Management, IEEE Transactions on Engineering Management, 52*(1), 69–84.

Muir, B. O. (1991). Managerial conflict resolution as a function of role status and gender. PhD dissertation. Long Beach, CA: California State University.

Nadler, J. T., & Kufahl, K. M. (2014). Marital status, gender, and sexual orientation: Implications for employment hiring decisions. *Psychology of Sexual Orientation and Gender Diversity, 1*(3), 270–278.

Neil, C. C., & Snizek, W. E. (1987). Work values, job characteristics, and gender. *Sociological Perspectives, 30*(3), 245–265.

Olian, J. D., Schwab, D. P., & Haberfeld, Y. (1988). The impact of applicant gender compared to qualifications on hiring recommendations: A meta-analysis of experimental studies. *Organizational Behavior and Human Decision Processes, 41*(2), 180–195.

Ones, D. S., & Anderson, N. (2002). Gender and ethnic group differences on personality scales in selection: Some British data. *Journal of Occupational and Organizational Psychology, 75*(3), 255–276.

Oppenheimer, V. K. (1968). The sex labeling of jobs. *Industrial Relations: A Journal of Economy and Society, 7*(3), 219–234.

Ostroff, C., & Atwater, L. E. (2003). Does whom you work with matter? Effects of referent group gender and age composition on managers' compensation. *Journal of Applied Psychology, 88*(4), 725.

Parcel, T. L., & Mueller, C. W. (1989). Temporal change in occupational earnings attainment, 1970–1980. *American Sociological Review, 54*(4), 622–634.

Perry, E. L., David-Blake, A., & Kulik, C. L. (1994). Explaining gender-based selection decisions: A synthesis of contextual and cognitive approaches. *Academy of Management Review, 19*(4), 786–820.

Pfeffer, J. (1977). The ambiguity of leadership. *Academy of Management Review, 2*(1), 104–112.

Powell, G. N. (1984). Effects of job attributes and recruiting practices on applicant decisions: A comparison 1. *Personnel Psychology, 37*(4), 721–732.

Powell, G. N. (1987). The effects of sex and gender on recruitment. *Academy of Management Review, 12*(4), 731–743.

Powell, G. N., & Butterfield, D. A. (1994). Investigating the 'glass ceiling' phenomenon: An empirical study of actual promotions to top management. *Academy of Management Journal, 37*(1), 68–86.

Powell, G. N., & Butterfield, D. A. (2002). Exploring the influence of decision makers' race and gender on actual promotions to tip management. *Personnel Psychology, 55*(2), 397.

Powell, G. N., Butterfield, D. A., & Bartol, K. M. (2008). Leader evaluations: A new female advantage? *Gender in Management: An International Journal, 23*(3), 156–174.

Ragins, B. R. (1995). Diversity, power, and mentorship in organizations: A cultural, structural, and behavioral perspective. *In* M. Chemers, S. Oskamp & M. Constanzo (Eds.), *Diversity in Organizations: New Perspectives for a Changing Workplace.* Thousand Oaks, CA: Sage.

Rahim, M. A. (1983). A measure of styles of handling interpersonal conflict. *Academy of Management Journal, 26*(2), 368–376.

Richard, O. C., & Kirby, S. L. (1998). Women recruits' perceptions of workforce diversity program selection decisions: A procedural justice examination. *Journal of Applied Social Psychology, 28*(2), 183–188.

Roth, P. L., Purvis, K. L., & Bobko, P. (2012). A meta-analysis of gender group differences for measures of job performance in field studies. *Journal of Management, 38*(2), 719–739.

Rudman, L. A., & Glick, P. (2001). Prescriptive gender stereotypes and backlash toward agentic women. *Journal of Social Issues, 57*(4), 743–762.

Saad, S., & Sackett, P. R. (2002). Investigating differential prediction by gender in employment-oriented personality measures. *Journal of Applied Psychology, 87*(4), 667.

Sandberg, S. (2013). *Lean in: Women, Work, and the Will to Lead.* New York: Knopf.

Scandura, T. A., & Lankau, M. J. (1997). Relationships of gender, family responsibility and flexible work hours to organizational commitment and job satisfaction. *Journal of Organizational Behavior, 18*(4), 377–391.

Schein, V. E. (2001). A global look at psychological barriers to women's progress in management. *Journal of Social Issues, 57,* 675–688.

Schein, E. H. (1990). Organizational culture. *American Psychologist, 45*(2), 109–119.

Schmitt, N. (1976). Social and situational determinants of interview decisions: Implications for the employment interview. *Personnel Psychology, 29*(1), 79–101.

Schneider, B. (1987). The people make the place. *Personnel Psychology, 40*(3), 437–453.

Schneider, B., Goldstein, H. W. & Smith, D. B. (1995). The ASA framework: An update. *Personnel Psychology, 48*(4), 747–779.

Schuler, R. S. (1975). Sex, organizational level, and outcome importance: Where the differences are. *Personnel Psychology, 28*(3), 365–375.

Smithson, J., & Stokoe, E. H. (2005). Discourses of work–life balance: Negotiating 'genderblind' terms in organizations. *Gender, Work & Organization, 12*(2), 147–168.

Stavrou, E., & Kilaniotis, C. (2010). Flexible work and turnover: An empirical investigation across cultures. *British Journal of Management, 21*(2), 541–554.

Taveggia, T., & Ziemba, T. (1978). Linkages to work: A study of the 'central life interests' and 'work attachments' of male and female workers. *Journal of Vocational Behavior, 12*(1), 305–320.

Terborg, J. R. (1977). Women in management: A research review. *Journal of Applied Psychology, 62*(6), 647.

Ting-Toomey, S. (1986). Conflict communication styles in Black and White subjective cultures. *Current Research in Interethnic Communication, 10,* 75–89.

Tolbert, P. S., Simons, T., Andrews, A., & Rhee, J. (1995). The effects of gender composition in academic departments on faculty turnover. *Industrial & Labor Relations Review, 48*(3), 562–579.

Tosi, H. L., & Einbender, S. W. (1985). The effects of the type and amount of information in sex discrimination research: A meta-analysis. *Academy of Management Journal, 28*(3), 712–723.

Tsui, A. S., Egan, T. D., & O'Reilly III, C. A. (1992). Being different: Relational demography and organizational attachment. *Administrative Science Quarterly, 37*(4), 549–579.

Ullman, J. C. (1966). Employee referrals: Prime tool for recruiting workers. *Personnel, 43*(3), 30–35.

US Bureau of Labor Statistics. (2013). *Highlights of Women's Earnings in 2012.* http://www.bls. gov/cps/cpswom2012.pdf.

Van Maanen, J., & Schein, E. H. (1979). Toward a theory of organizational socialization. *Research in Organizational Behavior, 1,* 209–264.

Weber, A., & Zulehner, C. (2014). Competition and gender prejudice: Are discriminatory employers doomed to fail? *Journal of the European Economic Association, 12*(2), 492–521.

Weisman, C. S., Morlock, L. L., Sack, D. G., & Levine, D. M. (1976). Sex differences in response to a blocked career pathway among unaccepted medical school applicants. *Sociology of Work and Occupations, 3,* 187–208.

Wexley, K. N., & Pulakos, E. D. (1982). Sex effects on performance ratings on manager– subordinate dyads: A field study. *Journal of Applied Psychology, 67,* 433–439.

Weyer, B. (2007). Twenty years later: Examining the persistence of the glass ceiling for women leaders. *Women in Management Review, 22,* 482–496.

Wharton, A. S., & Baron, J. N. (1987). So happy together? The impact of gender segregation on men at work. *American Sociological Review, 52*(5), 574–587.

Williams, K. Y., & O'Reilly, C. A. (1998). Demography and diversity in organizations: A review of 40 years of research. *Research in Organizational Behavior, 20,* 77–140.

Wood, G. (2008). Gender stereotypical attitudes: past, present and future influences on women's career advancement. *Equal Opportunities International, 27*(7), 613–628.

World Economic Forum (2014). *The Global Gender Gap Report.* Geneva: World Economic Forum.

Wosinska, W., Dabul, A. J., Whetstone-Dion, R., & Cialdini, R. B. (1996). Self-presentational responses to success in the organization: The costs and benefits of modesty. *Basic and Applied Social Psychology, 18*(2), 229–242.

Yoder, J. D. (2001). Making leadership work more effectively for women. *Journal of Social Issues, 57,* 815–828.

19

Race and Cultural Differences in Predictors Commonly Used in Employee Selection and Assessment

Charles A. Scherbaum, Michael M. DeNunzio, Justina Oliveira and Mary Ignagni

Introduction

The aim of this chapter is to summarize current research on differences between racial or ethnic groups and national cultural groups on predictors that are frequently used in employee selection. The chapter is organized around three questions: 1) What are the observed group mean score differences on commonly used predictors? 2) What are the possible explanations for those differences? 3) Where should future research exploring score differences be directed? Although summarizing differences between racial/ethic groups is well-trodden territory (Bobko & Roth, 2013; Hough, Oswald & Ployhart, 2001; Ployhart & Holtz, 2008; Roth, Bevier, Bobko, Switzer & Tyler, 2001; Schmitt, Clause & Pulakos, 1996), a considerable body of recent research has proposed further possible explanations for score differences that merit consideration alongside the explanations that have traditionally been offered (Scherbaum, Goldstein, Ryan, Agnello, Yusko & Hanges, 2015). These more recent explanations challenge the long-standing positions advocated by some researchers that the differences between group are inevitable and intractable. Additionally, little work has been devoted to systematically summarizing the emerging literature on score differences between different cultural groups (e.g., immigrants and non-immigrants; Scherbaum et al., 2015). Current research finds that mean score differences for immigrant and non-immigrant groups within a given country can, for example, be as large as those typically observed between White and African-Americans in the United States (te Nijenhuis & van der Flier, 1997, 1999, 2001, 2003, 2005). Given the increasing trends in globalization and immigration, exploring these differences is important for both science and practice (Ryan & Tippins, 2009). In this chapter we review the research on score differences for African-American, US Hispanic/Latinos and Whites, as well as national culture groups, examine the various explanations for those differences and propose directions for future research aimed at further understanding score differences between groups.

The Wiley Blackwell Handbook of the Psychology of Recruitment, Selection and Employee Retention, First Edition. Edited by Harold W. Goldstein, Elaine D. Pulakos, Jonathan Passmore and Carla Semedo. © 2017 John Wiley & Sons Ltd. Published 2020 by John Wiley & Sons Ltd.

What are the Observed Differences
in Commonly Used Predictors?

This review includes differences in the most commonly used predictors (e.g., cognitive ability tests, personality inventories, interviews, biodata, assessment centres, simulations and situational judgement tests) between Whites and African-Americans and Whites and US Hispanics/Latinos as well as for different national culture groups (e.g., immigrants and non-immigrants). Before investigating the research on observed score differences, it is important to highlight the scope of the predictors we cover and the difference between constructs and methods in the predictors commonly used in personnel selection (Arthur & Villado, 2008). Psychological constructs include the personal attributes used to describe candidates and employees, such as cognitive ability, personality dimensions and job knowledge. These are the theoretical predictors – knowledge, skills, abilities and other characteristics (KSAOs) – used in personnel selection and, along with the criterion constructs (e.g., task performance, organizational citizenship behaviours), should be the focus of theory-building and hypothesis-testing in the design and implementation of a selection system (Binning & Barrett, 1989; Landy, 1986). Methods, on the other hand, are the vehicles by which theoretically-relevant constructs are assessed. Methods include biodata, work samples, situational judgement tests, assessment centres, as well as others. These can be used to measure just one construct or multiple constructs (e.g., an assessment centre with exercises measuring decision making, communication and supervisory skills). When discussing group mean score differences in methods it must be understood that these are not constructs, and that score differences need to be interpreted through the lens of the constructs that the methods assess.

It is also important to highlight that much of the research and observed score differences between racial and ethnic groups that has been quantitatively reviewed using meta-analytic methods comes from the United States. This focus is largely the result of the unique social, historical and legal factors found in the US, as well as how these factors interact with the nature of the labour market and the widespread use of employment testing. Thus, generalizing these findings to other contexts with different social, historical and legal environments should be done with great thought. Although the patterns may generalize to other contexts, the effect sizes may be appreciably different.

Observed Score Differences between Whites
and African-Americans

According to the U.S. Census Bureau (2014), African-Americans comprise about 13.2% of the US population, making them the third largest racial-ethnic group in the country after Whites and Hispanics/Latinos (until recently, they were the second largest racial-ethnic group). This group has historically been at the centre of the discussion on mean score differences in high-stakes assessment contexts (e.g., Bobko & Roth, 2013; Cottrell, Newman & Roisman, 2015; Herrnstein & Murray, 1994; Hough et al., 2001; Jensen, 1985, 2000; Neisser et al., 1996; Nisbett et al., 2012; Ployhart & Holtz, 2008; Roth et al., 2001). There are several reasons for the distinct focus on this group. For example, African-Americans played a central role in the Civil Rights Movement, the subsequent passing of the Civil Rights Act 1964 and Title VII, and various landmark Supreme Court cases such as *Griggs v. Duke Power Co.* (1971), which was heard after this critical piece of legislation was enacted (Aiken, Salmon & Hanges, 2013). Moreover, this group is typically the most disadvantaged relative to other groups in the US in terms of the magnitude of standardized group mean score differences with Whites (Bobko & Roth, 2013; Hough et al., 2001; Roth et al., 2001). A host of primary studies has been conducted to explore, quantify and understand these differences. Given the abundance of primary studies, we focus on the most recent meta-analyses and narrative reviews in the following subsections.

Cognitive ability

African-American and White group mean score differences on measures of cognitive ability have historically been the most researched topic in the literature on group differences in personnel selection. Two highly influential papers examining African-American–White group mean score differences on cognitive ability tests used in high-stakes assessment (e.g., personnel selection) are Hough and colleagues' (2001) narrative review and Roth and colleagues' (2001) meta-analysis. Hough and colleagues provided a summary and synthesis of earlier literature on the determinants, detection and mitigation of adverse impact in personnel selection, covering various constructs, methods and groups. With regard to cognitive ability, they reviewed the research looking at differences on global measures of cognitive ability, as well as measures assessing more specific facets of cognitive ability, such as verbal and quantitative ability. Given extant findings (e.g., Herrnstein & Murray, 1994; Hunter & Hunter, 1984), they estimated the effect size for the standardized means difference (i.e., Cohen's d) to be about 1.0 in favour of Whites. Estimated differences in more specific facets of cognitive ability tended to be appreciably smaller, though they were still substantial. Specifically, they reported the following effect sizes, with all favouring Whites: verbal ability $d = 0.6$, quantitative ability $d = 0.7$, science achievement $d = 1.0$, spatial ability $d = 0.7$, memory $d = 0.5$ and mental processing speed $d = 0.3$. It is important to note that the size of the difference in these tests tends to vary with the degree to which the test is capturing cognitive domains that rely on acquired knowledge versus basic cognitive operations. Tests of basic operations show smaller differences than those relying on acquired knowledge.

To this point, the literature – including Hough and colleagues' (2001) narrative review – suggested a generally accepted African-American and White d for cognitive ability tests of about 1.0. Roth and colleagues (2001) sought to provide more precise estimates of these differences by meta-analysing the empirical research in this domain. In addition to harnessing the benefits of meta-analysis in terms of obtaining more accurate quantitative estimates of the score differences, they were able to use this method to expand our understanding of the issue by also exploring the effects of important moderators, including range restriction and job complexity. For the overall African-American and White comparison on global measures of cognitive ability, which included educational and military samples, they estimated a d of 1.10 ($k = 105$; $N = 6,246,729$). However, when isolating industrial samples from the dataset, they obtained an estimate of $d = 0.99$ ($k = 34$; $N = 464,201$), a value almost identical to the commonly accepted value for d.

Roth and colleagues (2001) identified important changes in d when taking range restriction into account. Across all studies, estimated ds for applicants (not restricted) and incumbents (restricted) were 1.00 ($k = 11$; $N = 375,307$) and 0.90 ($k = 13$; $N = 50,799$), respectively, demonstrating that the type of sample has an appreciable impact on the magnitude of the difference. When removing large samples that included data from the Wonderlic and GATB tests, the applicant sample d decreased marginally to 0.99 ($k = 8$; $N = 6,169$), and the incumbent sample d decreased substantially to 0.41 ($k = 11$; $N = 3,315$). As will be subsequently discussed, findings such as these showing that the effect size varies with the type of test points to the role that measurement of the construct may play in the observed differences.

Personality

Including personality measures in selection systems along with cognitive ability measures is commonly seen as a potential way to reduce African-American and White score differences (Ployhart & Holtz, 2008). This is because effect sizes for personality measures tend to be much smaller (close to zero) and in some cases favour African-Americans. Score differences have been explored for a number of personality variables, predominantly the Big Five personality dimensions: extraversion, emotional stability, conscientiousness, agreeableness and openness to experience.

Hough and colleagues' (2001) narrative review summarized the research exploring Black–White group mean score differences on the Big Five personality factors. They also reported effect sizes for measures of the facet-level personality constructs of affiliation (i.e., sociability) and surgency (i.e., potency, dominance) for extraversion, and achievement and dependability for conscientiousness. In general, all ds were modest or close to zero, with a few exceptions. For extraversion, Hough and colleagues reported a d of 0.10 favouring Whites. However, at the facet level, ds were appreciably different, with $d = 0.31$ for affiliation favouring Whites and $d = 0.12$ for surgency favouring African-Americans. Thus, composite measures of extraversion may mask underlying differences. For conscientiousness $d = 0.06$, again favouring Whites. At the facet level, ds were much closer to that of the composite as compared with the extraversion findings: $d = 0.01$ for achievement and $d = 0.11$ for dependability, both favouring Whites. The Big Five personality factor of adjustment (i.e., emotional stability or reverse-scored neuroticism) and agreeableness demonstrated effect sizes close to zero with respective ds of 0.04 (favouring African-Americans) and 0.02 (favouring Whites). In contrast, the remaining Big Five personality – dimension of openness to experience – demonstrated the largest effect size with $d = 0.21$ favouring Whites.

In a meta-analysis, Foldes, Duehr and Ones (2008) provided updated estimates of Black–White group mean score differences on personality measures. This meta-analysis included data on additional personality facets, including facets for emotional stability and additional facets for conscientiousness. They also included separate estimates for global measures of the constructs that assess the trait at a broad level, with the composite measures of each construct comprised of the global- and facet-level measures together. The results are as follows (unless otherwise noted, differences favour Whites): For emotional stability, $d = 0.09$ with respective global measure, self-esteem facet measure, low anxiety facet measure and even-tempered facet measure ds of 0.12, 0.17 (favouring African-Americans), 0.23 and 0.06 (favouring African-Americans); for extraversion, $d = 0.16$ with respective global measure, dominance facet measure and sociability facet measure ds of 0.21, 0.03 and 0.39; for openness to experience, $d = 0.10$; for agreeableness, $d = 0.03$; for conscientiousness, $d = 0.07$ (favouring African-Americans) with respective global measure, achievement facet measure, dependability facet measure, cautiousness facet measure and order facet measure ds of 0.17 (favouring African-Americans), 0.03, 0.05, 0.15 (favouring African-Americans) and 0.01. Here again, while composite-level effect sizes are generally rather small and often close to zero, appreciable facet-level effect sizes emerge. Notable are the ds reported for the low anxiety facet of emotional stability (0.23), global measures of extraversion (0.21) and especially the sociability facet of extraversion (0.39). Of these updated effect sizes, only the openness to experience estimate was considerably different (lower) from that reported by Hough and colleagues (2001; 0.10 vs. 0.21). Overall, while Big Five measures generally demonstrate much lower Black–White group mean score differences than do measures of cognitive ability, there is considerable variation in the size of these differences depending on the construct and whether one is looking at facet versus global measures.

Integrity is another commonly studied personality-like construct in the personnel selection literature, and a fair amount of research has explored Black–White group mean score differences on this construct. Measures of integrity are quite heterogeneous and include elements of various constructs such as conscientiousness, agreeableness and emotional stability, and honesty/humility (Berry, Sackett & Wiemann, 2007; Ones & Viswesvaran, 1998). In their narrative review, Hough and colleagues (2001) also looked at differences in mean integrity scores. They reported a very modest d of 0.04 favouring Whites. van Iddekinge, Taylor and Eidson (2005) further explored this question in their meta-analysis by examining group mean score differences at the facet level, although it should be noted that these researchers limited their meta-analysis to studies using the Honesty Scale of the Personnel Selection Inventory– Customer Service (London House, 1995). The authors identified eight facets of integrity based on this measure and estimated ds for each in addition to the overall measure. For the overall measure, d=0.12, which is somewhat higher than the estimate reported by Hough and colleagues. In terms of the facets, the differences were as follows (favouring Whites unless otherwise noted): admissions of dishonesty (0.21), honesty image (0.28), norms of counterproductive work behaviours (0.34), norms of general dishonesty (0.36), norms of serious dishonesty (0.77), punishment of dishonesty (0.06, favouring African-Americans), thief loyalty (0.08 favouring African-Americans) and dishonest thoughts and temptations (0.03). They included significance tests for these effect sizes and found only the differences for norms of general dishonesty and of serious dishonesty to be statistically significant. Overall, as with the Big Five personality variables, composite-level integrity differences are modest, but when focusing on facets, differences are wide-ranging and in some cases quite large.

Job knowledge

Studies examining job knowledge often combine job knowledge tests with work-sample tests and situational judgement tests (Roth, Bobko, McFarland & Buster, 2008). Thus, it is often difficult to isolate differences on job knowledge. For example, Schmitt and colleagues (1996) reported a Black–White d of 0.38 in their meta-analysis (k=37, N=15,738), based on a combination of work-sample, job knowledge and situational judgement tests. One meta-analysis that did (in part) isolate job knowledge to estimate an effect size was that conducted by Roth and colleagues (2008). Although the study focused on work samples, these authors performed analyses in which they isolated constructs based on their saturation in work samples. They were able to estimate a d of 0.80 (corrected to 0.82 for measurement error in the work-sample tests/exercises; k=13, N=785) for work samples with a high saturation of cognitive and job knowledge. It should be noted that the authors combined these constructs because 'the two sets of constructs were so tightly related within work sample exercises' (p. 652). Thus, African-American and White group mean score differences on job knowledge appear to be high, but it is difficult to determine the degree to which the cognitive ability aspect biases this estimate.

Methods

In the following sections, we review previous findings regarding African-American and White group mean score differences on the methods of interviews, biodata, assessment centres, simulations and situational judgement tests. It should be noted that racial-ethnic group mean score differences on each method largely depend on the saturation of various constructs, most notably cognitive ability (Bobko & Roth, 2013). Thus, while estimates of the Black–White ds exist for the various methods, these differences are ostensibly a function of the constructs that the methods aim to assess.

Interviews

Interviews, the most commonly used selection method, have been previously proffered as an alternative to cognitive ability tests due to supposed lower racial-ethnic group mean score differences. Huffcutt and Roth (1998) provided one of the first meta-analyses investigating these differences on employment interviews (see also Hough et al., 2001). These authors reported an overall mean d of 0.25 favouring Whites ($k = 31$, $N = 10,476$). However, they identified a number of moderators, including the level of structure, job complexity, cognitive ability saturation and minority representation in the sample (all ds favouring Whites unless otherwise noted). When interviews had more structure, the effect size tended to decrease. Interviews with lower structure demonstrated a d of 0.32 ($k = 10$, $N = 1,659$) as compared with a d of 0.23 ($k = 21$, $N = 8,817$) for interviews with a higher degree of structure. (Potosky, Bobko and Roth, 2005, later applied a statistical correction for range restriction to the high-structure d estimate of 0.23, increasing this estimate to $d = 0.31$.) Interviews for low-, medium- and high-complexity jobs demonstrated respective ds of 0.43 ($k = 12$, $N = 5,148$), 0.22 ($k = 13$, $N = 4,093$) and 0.09 (favouring African-Americans; $k = 5$, $N = 768$). Interviews with a lower saturation of cognitive ability demonstrated a smaller effect size than interviews with a higher saturation of cognitive ability, with d decreasing from 0.45 ($k = 7$, $N = 1,213$) to 0.26 ($k = 17$, $N = 6,118$). Finally, samples with a lower ratio of Black participants (<30%) demonstrated a lower d as compared with samples with a higher ratio of Black participants, with d decreasing from 0.41 ($k = 12$, $N = 4,797$) to 0.15 ($k = 19$, $N = 5,679$).

As indicated above, the effect sizes for interviews vary depending on the constructs measured (Huffcutt, Conway, Roth & Stone, 2001). Huffcutt and colleagues' meta-analysis provided a taxonomy of constructs for interviews that included cognitive constructs (e.g., general intelligence, job knowledge and skills), personality constructs (e.g., Big Five personality factors), social skills, occupational interests, organizational fit and physical attributes. Separate effect sizes were reported for all the identified constructs and by low versus high structure (though many estimates were obtained from a small number of studies and small sample sizes; e.g., $k = 1$ and $N = 103$ for interviews measuring job knowledge and skills). Effect sizes demonstrated a considerable variation depending on the construct and degree of structure. For example, the mean d for high-structure interviews measuring the organizational fit construct of 'values and moral standards' was 0.12 favouring African-Americans ($k = 3$, $N = 568$), while the mean d for low-structure interviews measuring the mental capability construct of 'general intelligence' was 0.58 favouring Whites ($k = 5$, $N = 1,564$). As another example, high-structure interviews assessing personality constructs tended to demonstrate more modest effect sizes as compared with low-structure interviews assessing the same traits. To demonstrate, Huffcutt and colleagues reported a d of 0.17 ($k = 7$, $N = 2,889$) for high-structured interviews measuring conscientiousness compared with $d = 0.41$ for low-structure interviews measuring conscientiousness ($k = 8$, $N = 2,554$).

Finally, Roth, van Iddekinge, Huffcutt, Eidson and Bobko (2002) highlighted that ds for interviews are likely larger than those reported in earlier studies due to range restriction (see also Potosky et al., 2005). For example, Huffcutt and Roth (1998) reported a mean d of 0.10 (favouring Whites) in their meta-analysis for high-structured interviews that were behavioural in nature ($k = 6$, $N = 1,614$). Roth and colleagues (2002) reported ds for two forms of a behavioural interview of 0.34 and 0.54, with corrected estimates increasing to 0.36 and 0.56, respectively. Note that this was a single primary study, and as Roth and colleagues (2002) highlighted in the limitations of their study, much more work needs to be done to understand how range restriction affects Black–White group differences in interviews, whether behavioural or otherwise. Overall, given the variability in the constructs measured, degree of structure and range restriction in studies using interviews, Bobko and Roth (2013) suggest a tentative range for *d* of 0.31–0.46.

Biodata

Black–White group mean score differences on biodata inventories have also been explored, albeit to a much lesser extent than interviews. According to Bobko and Roth (2013), initial estimates of *d* for biodata inventories were about 0.33 (e.g., Bobko, Roth & Potosky, 1999). These authors noted that updating this finding was difficult given the limited research in this area. However, two studies offer some guidance. Potosky and colleagues (2005) combined and corrected for range restriction the results of a few primary studies to *d*=0.57 (*k*=2, *N*=6,115). More recently, Becton, Matthews, Hartley and Whitaker (2009), in a large study exploring the predictive validity of a biodata inventory for a wide variety of healthcare jobs, reported a Black–White *d* of 0.31 (uncorrected; *N*=13,301). Combining these results, Bobko and Roth (2013) suggested an updated average *d* of about 0.39, noting that this estimate varies depending on construct saturation.

Assessment centres

Early in the literature it was thought that Black–White group mean score differences for assessment centres was small (Dean, Roth & Bobko, 2008), though the range reported by Bobko and Roth (2013) was quite wide (*d*=0.03 to 0.60, favouring Whites). In the only meta-analysis on this topic to date, Dean and colleagues (2008) estimated an overall *d* of 0.52 favouring Whites (*k*=17, *N*=8,210). They found range restriction to be an important moderator, with *d*=0.56 among job applicants (*k*=10, *N*=3,682) as compared with *d*=0.32 among job incumbents (*k*=6, *N*=1,689). As Bobko and Roth note, assessment centres can measure a wide range of constructs, and cognitive ability can increase estimates of *d*. Interpreting these differences is problematic, though, as assessment centres generally comprise multiple exercises (e.g., simulations such as role-plays and in-basket exercises, personality inventories, cognitive ability tests, interviews) that assess multiple constructs. Thus, it is unclear whether most of the variance in these effect sizes is a function of exercises, constructs or even formats.

Simulations

A simulation is a broad term that can refer to a number of different, more specific methods. The terms simulation, work sample and assessment centre are often confounded and the distinctions are not always clear. For example, an assessment centre can include a simulation such as a role-play or in-basket. Roth and colleagues (2008), in their meta-analysis of Black–White group mean score differences in work samples, suggest some differences between work samples and assessment centres, including 'the types of exercises they include (exclusively simulations vs. a variety of exercises including traditional paper-and-pencil tests)' (p. 638). Thus, this meta-analysis of work samples focused on simulations. Across all studies and samples they estimated a *d* of 0.36 for incumbents (*k*=19, *N*=5,611) and 0.73 for early-stage applicants (*k*=21, *N*=2,476). In terms of incumbents, the type of sample moderated this effect size. The *d* for military samples was close to zero at 0.03 (*k*=7, *N*=1,869), while non-military samples has a much larger *d* of 0.53 (*k*=12, *N*=3,742).

These effects were also moderated by exercise type and construct measured. For the early-stage applicant samples the effect sizes (corrected for measurement error in the exercises) varied considerably between exercises: in-basket exercise *d*=0.82 (*k*=8, *N*=1,508l, though one study with a fairly large sample size of $N=400$ had a d of 1.15; after removing this study from the analysis, the corrected in-basket d was reduced to 0.60), technical exercise $d=0.78$ ($k=11$, $N=659$), scheduling exercise $d=0.57$ ($k=6$, $N=201$), oral briefing exercise $d=0.24$ ($k=4$, $N=847$) and role-play exercise $d=0.24$ ($k=15$, $N=1,322$). Roth and colleagues' (2008) hypothesis that the oral briefing and role-play exercises would demonstrate smaller differences was supported. These authors argued that the substantial oral communication component involved in these types of exercise may account for this reduction.

Situational judgement tests

In their 2001 narrative review, Hough and colleagues estimated Black–White ds to be about 0.61 and 0.43 (both favouring Whites) for written- and video-based situational judgement tests, respectively. In 2008, Ployhart and Holtz reported lower estimates of about 0.40 and 0.31, respectively. Whetzel, McDaniel and Nguyen (2008), in one of the few meta-analyses exploring Black–White differences on situational judgement tests, reported a Black–White d of 0.38 ($k=62$, $N=42,178$). These authors also found minimal differences when comparing ds for knowledge-focused or behavioural tendency-focused situational judgement tests.

Bobko and Roth (2013) note that the previous research exploring Black–White differences on situational judgement tests are generally based on incumbent samples. They cautioned that Whetzel and colleagues' (2008) meta-analytically derived estimate of 0.38 is likely downwardly biased. Additionally, job level and construct saturation – in particular, cognitive ability – impact these estimates. Thus, it is currently unclear what the magnitude of the score differences actually is for situational judgements tests. Based on a summary of various primary studies using job applicants, Bobko and Roth provide the following examples based on construct saturation: $d=0.19$ for interpersonal skills, $d=0.65$ for cognitive ability and job knowledge and $d=1.02$ for leadership.

In summary, the size of the observed score differences between Whites and African-Americans has received considerable research attention. The research described in this chapter shows that the size of the differences and who is advantaged vary depending on what is measured. In general, non-cognitive constructs show near-zero differences and, when the differences are greater than zero, they advantage Whites or African-Americans depending on the specific facet of the construct. The observed score differences tend to be larger for cognitive constructs and more consistently favour Whites. However, the size of the difference tends to vary with the specific test or cognitive domain measured, a point we return to later in this chapter, with domains requiring acquired knowledge showing the largest differences. For the various measurement methods, the existence and size of the differences vary widely between the methods and appear to be an interaction between the method of measurement and the relative saturation of the construct that is measured by the method. Thus, contrary to what is often claimed that there are intractable differences between groups, it appears that the observed differences are far more complicated and non-uniform, and the measurement method may play a role.

Observed Score Differences between Whites and US Latinos/Hispanics

Latinos/Hispanics are the largest, most ethnically diverse and fastest-growing non-dominant group in the US. According to the U.S. Census Bureau (2014), Latinos/Hispanics comprise about 17.4% of the US population. The presence of Latinos/Hispanics in the

US is expected to increase due to higher immigration and fertility rates than other minority groups (Choi, Sakamoto & Powers, 2008). In fact, the Latino/Hispanic population grew by 43% between 2000 and 2010, four times the increase in the total population (Ennis, Rios-Vargas & Albert, 2011). With regard to the current US population of Latinos/Hispanics, based on the 2010 Census, 50.5 million (16%) self-identified as being of Latino or Hispanic origin (Ennis et al., 2011). This is an increase from the year 2000 when this population made up 13% of the total population. Utilizing data from the 2010 Census, it was reported that within the Latino/Hispanic population, people of Mexican origin were the largest Latino/Hispanic group, representing 63% of the total US Latino/Hispanic population (Ennis et al., 2011). Puerto Ricans were the second largest group, comprising 9% of the Latino/Hispanic population, while Cubans made up about 4% of the Latino/Hispanic population (Ennis et al., 2011). These three groups accounted for approximately three-quarters of the total US Latino/Hispanic population.

Despite the size of Latino/Hispanics groups in the US and the global workforce, as well as their rate of growth, research on score differences has focused primarily on African-Americans to the seeming exclusion of Latinos/Hispanics (Dean et al., 2008; Dovidio, Gluszek, John, Ditlmann & Lagunes, 2010; Reynolds, Willson & Ramsey, 1999; Verney, Granholm, Marshall, Malcarne & Saccuzzo, 2005). Our review of score differences between Whites and US Latinos/Hispanics focuses on current meta-analyses and narrative reviews, which are limited.

Cognitive ability

Roth and colleagues' meta-analysis (2001) found an overall d of 0.72 between Latinos/Hispanics and Whites in favour of Whites ($k=39$, $N=5,696,519$). However, when isolating industrial samples from the dataset, they obtained an estimate of $d=0.83$ ($k=14$, $N=313,635$), but the value decreases to 0.58 when Wonderlic samples were removed ($k=11$, $N=6,133$).

Hough and colleagues' (2001) narrative review found that Latino/Hispanic test-takers, on average, scored lower than White test-takers on cognitive ability tests ($d=0.50$). Hough and colleagues' estimates of differences on more specific facets of cognitive ability tended to be appreciably smaller, but were still substantial. Specifically, they reported the following effect sizes, with all favouring Whites: verbal ability $d=0.40$, quantitative ability $d=0.30$, science achievement $d=0.60$ and mental processing (i.e., cognitive speed and decision speed) $d=0.38$. As was the case with the White and African-American comparison, the effect sizes tend to be larger on tests requiring acquired knowledge.

Personality

Hough and colleagues' (2001) narrative review summarized the published research exploring Latino/Hispanic–White group mean score differences on the Big Five personality factors. They also reported effect sizes for measures of the facet-level personality constructs of surgency (i.e., potency, dominance) for extraversion and achievement and dependability for conscientiousness. In general, ds were modest (with a few exceptions). For conscientiousness, they report $d=0.04$ favouring Whites. On the facet of achievement, they report small differences that favour Latinos/Hispanics, $d=0.04$. However, on the facet of dependability there were larger differences favouring Whites, $d=0.11$.

For extraversion, the difference is near zero ($d=0.01$), favouring Latinos/Hispanics. At the facet level, the difference is near zero ($d=0.01$), again favouring Latinos/Hispanics. On the construct of adjustment (i.e., emotional stability or reverse-scored neuroticism) the difference is near zero ($d=0.01$), also favouring Latinos/Hispanics. However, the differences favoured Whites on the dimensions of agreeableness ($d=0.06$) and openness to experience ($d=0.10$).

Foldes and colleagues (2008) expanded their meta-analysis and reported the following differences (unless otherwise noted, differences favour Latinos/Hispanics). For emotional stability, $d=0.03$ with respective global measure, self-esteem facet measure, low anxiety facet measure and even-tempered facet measure ds of 0.04 (favouring Whites), 0.25, 0.25 and 0.09; for extraversion, $d=0.02$ (favouring Whites) with respective global measure, dominance facet measure and sociability facet measure ds of 0.12, 0.04 (favouring Whites) and 0.16 (favouring Whites); for openness to experience, $d=0.02$ (favouring Whites); for agreeableness, $d=0.05$ (favouring Whites); for conscientiousness, $d=0.08$ with respective global measure, achievement facet measure, dependability facet measure, cautiousness facet measure and order facet measure ds of 0.20, 0.10, 0.00 and 0.00. Again, while composite-level effect sizes are generally small and often close to zero, appreciable facet-level effect sizes emerge. Overall, while Big Five measures by and large demonstrate much lower Latino/Hispanic–White group mean score differences than do measures of cognitive ability, there is some variation in the size of these differences depending on the construct and whether one is looking at facet or global measures.

On measures of integrity, Hough and colleagues (2001) report that Latinos/Hispanics score higher than Whites ($d=0.14$). In addition, it was found that Latinos/Hispanics also score higher than Whites ($d=0.56$) on measures of social desirability. More recent primary research has confirmed this finding (e.g., Dudley, McFarland, Goodman, Hunt & Sydell, 2005).

Methods

In the following subsections, we review earlier findings regarding Latino/Hispanic–White group mean score differences on the methods of interviews, biodata, assessment centres, simulations and situational judgement tests. We repeat that racial-ethnic group mean score differences in each method largely depend on the saturation of various constructs, most notably cognitive ability (Bobko & Roth, 2013). Thus, while some limited estimates of the Latino/Hispanic–White ds exist for the various methods, these differences may be a function of the constructs that the methods aim to assess.

Interviews

Huffcutt and Roth's (1998) meta-analysis found a mean d of 0.25 favouring Whites ($k=15$, $N=4,902$). However, they identified the level of structure and job complexity as moderators (all ds favour Whites unless otherwise noted). Interviews with lower structure demonstrated a d of 0.71 ($k=3$, $N=667$) as compared with a d of 0.17 ($k=12$, $N=4,235$) for interviews with a higher degree of structure. Interviews for low-, medium- and high-complexity jobs demonstrated respective ds of 0.54 ($k=5$, $N=1,598$), 0.20 ($k=6$, $N=2,553$) and 0.23 (favouring Latinos/Hispanics; $k=3$, $N=545$).

Biodata

Some studies have examined group mean score differences between Latinos/Hispanics and Whites on biodata inventories. Schmitt and Kunce (2002) do not report the exact value or sample size, but indicate a difference of about $d=0.12$ favouring Whites. Becton and colleagues (2009) reported a Latino/Hispanic–White d of 0.07 favouring Whites (uncorrected; $N=8,512$), in a large, predictive validity study in the healthcare industry. However, the sample for Latinos/Hispanics was small ($N=350$). Gandy, Dye and MacLane (1994) reported a $d=0.08$ on a biodata inventory used in the US federal government.

Assessment centres

Dean and colleagues' (2008) meta-analysis obtained an overall d of 0.28 between Latinos/Hispanics and Whites, with Whites scoring higher ($k=9$, $N=40,591$). After removing one study ($N=36,613$), the difference increased to $d=0.40$ ($k=8$, $N=3,978$). Dean and colleagues did not report any tests for moderators in the Latino/Hispanic and White comparisons. As previously noted, interpreting these differences is difficult, as assessment centres generally comprise multiple exercises that assess multiple constructs. Thus, it is unclear whether the majority of the variance in these effect sizes is due to exercises, constructs or even formats.

Simulations

Summaries of the Latino/Hispanic–White differences on simulations are limited. Schmitt and colleagues (1996) reported that there was no difference between Latinos/Hispanics and Whites. Other studies have reported larger differences. Pulakos and colleagues (1996) found that on role-plays the difference is $d=0.37$. Thus, it appears that there are some differences, but the evidence is extremely limited.

Situational judgement tests

Hough and colleagues (2001) estimated Latino/Hispanic–White ds to be about 0.26 and 0.39 (both favouring Whites) for written- and video-based situational judgement tests, respectively. More recently, Whetzel and colleagues' (2008) meta-analysis reported a Latino/Hispanic–White d of 0.26 ($k=43$, $N=15,195$). These authors also found minimal differences when comparing ds for knowledge-focused and behavioural tendency-focused situational judgement tests. The cautionary note that Bobko and Roth (2013) sounded for Black–White differences on situational judgement tests may well apply to these comparisons as well. Job level and construct saturation – particularly cognitive ability – impacts these estimates. Thus, it is currently uncertain what the magnitude of the ds actually is between Lantos/Hispanics and Whites for situational judgements tests.

In summary, the size of the observed score differences between Whites and US Hispanic/Latinos has received far less research attention than the score differences between Whites and African-Americans. While the research shows smaller differences, a similar pattern emerges that the size of the differences and who is advantaged vary depending on what is measured. In general, non-cognitive constructs show near-zero differences and when the differences are greater than zero they advantage Whites or Hispanics/Latinos depending on the facet of the construct. The observed score differences tend to be larger for cognitive constructs and more consistently favour Whites. However, the size of the difference tends to vary with the specific test or cognitive domain measured. For the various measurement methods, there is much less research, so conclusions about the existence and size of the differences are more tentative. Research to date suggests that the magnitude of the effect sizes varies across measurement methods. Also, there may be an interaction between the method of measurement and the relative saturation of the construct that is measured by the method. As with the White and African-American comparisons, the observed differences are far more complicated and non-uniform, and the measurement method seems to play a role.

Observed Score Differences between National Culture Groups

Given the spread of globalization and increase in immigration in recent years, understanding the role of culture in selection systems has become imperative (Ryan & Tippins, 2009). Culture has been defined as the shared system of meaning or values among members of a group or community (Erez & Earley, 1993; Triandis, 1994). Similarly, the definition proposed by the Global Leadership and Organizational Behavior Effectiveness Research Program (GLOBE) project states that culture is the 'shared motives, values, beliefs, identities, and interpretations or meanings of significant events that result from common experiences of members of collectives that are transmitted across generations' (House & Javidan, 2004, p.15). Thus, culture can reasonably be expected to impact test scores on common predictors.

In much of the research on culture and common predictors, race and culture have been intertwined (Helms, 1992; Hough et al., 2001). For example, culture has been used to examine differences between Whites and African-Americans in the US and South Africa. Although there may be distinct cultures for the groups in these countries, they still have a national culture in common (e.g., Malda, van de Vijver & Temane, 2010). Other research, while often still intertwining race and culture, compares individuals from different national cultures (e.g., immigrants and non-immigrants, test scores from different countries). Our review focuses on research comparing immigrants and non-immigrants as this provides the best available examination of the impact of national culture on common predictors. Also, this research tends to focus on working-age populations whereas much of the cross-national differences research focuses on children (van de Vijver, 1997). In particular, this review focuses on cognitive ability as most comparisons of immigrants and non-immigrants focus on this predictor. In addition, we briefly consider the broader research on cross-cultural differences in personality. Currently, little research exists comparing methods of measurement for different national culture groups and thus are not reviewed here. Lastly, we consider the general research on the impact of cultural content embedded in tests and assessments on test performance.

Cognitive ability

Reviews and primary research focusing on group mean score differences between immigrant and native-born individuals on cognitive ability measures are based in Sweden and The Netherlands (see te Nijenhuis & van der Flier, 1999, for a review of Dutch studies). Early research in The Netherlands examining group score differences on cognitive ability tests within the context of selection demonstrated that length of time living in The Netherlands was positively correlated with scores on tests of verbal reasoning ($r = 0.30$) but not for nonverbal reasoning (van Leest & Bleichrodt, 1990). Additionally, on the General Aptitude Test Battery (GATB) vocabulary subtest, the non-immigrant majority group scored substantially higher than North African immigrants in The Netherlands ($d = 2.07$; te Nijenhuis & van der Flier, 1997). Te Nijenhuis and van der Flier (1999) identified a pattern where verbal-based cognitive ability tests tended to demonstrate score differences between immigrants and non-immigrants, but nonverbal tests did so to a much smaller extent overall, if at all. These studies, as well as those discussed below, imply that language proficiency may play a role in observed differences for natives compared to immigrants on some cognitive ability tests, especially tests with a high verbal load.

An additional review of studies examining cognitive ability test score differences of non-immigrants (ethnic Dutch) participants compared to immigrants (Turks, Moroccans, Surinamese, Netherlands Antilleans and Indonesians) reported that all but South-East Asian immigrants scored lower than the non-immigrant group (te Nijenhuis, de Jong, Evers & van der Flier, 2004). Indicating further evidence of potential language proficiency and acculturation effects, a comparison of first-generation immigrants to later generations found significant increases in cognitive ability scores. Te Nijenhuis and colleagues stated that 'it is clear that for certain groups the average IQ scores or test scores are underestimates of g due to low proficiency in the language of the test...' (p. 426).

Te Nijenhuis, Willigers, Dragt and van der Flier (2016) recently analysed a very large database of cognitive ability test data from Dutch samples. They concluded that group mean differences in cognitive ability test scores can be largely explained by subtests within cognitive test batteries. Specifically, native Dutch-speakers consistently outperformed those whose native language was not Dutch on subtests that were considered language-loaded (i.e., tests that require proficiency in the language used in the test). This results in an underestimation of immigrants' overall cognitive ability due to these verbally-loaded aspects of the test battery. Interestingly, te Nijenhuis and colleagues also found that, after taking language proficiency into account, there was little unaccounted variability that could be attributed to cultural bias. This may raise questions about the effect of cultural values and norms on group differences within these tests, but offers more clarity regarding the pattern that language proficiency may have on these differences.

Valentin Kvist and Gustafsson (2008) conducted a study in Sweden which demonstrated large group differences between immigrants and non-immigrants on crystallized intelligence and, to a smaller extent, on broad visual perception, with immigrants scoring lower than non-immigrants. In a follow-up study also conducted in Sweden, Valentin Kvist (2011) reported that European immigrants scored lower than native Swedes (approximate $d = 2.0$) while the difference was much larger for non-European immigrants (approximate $d = 3.0$). For visual perception, European ($d = 0.75$) and non-European immigrants ($d = 1.50$) scored lower than non-immigrant majority group. Furthermore, although the differences were less extreme, immigrants from European countries scored lower on measures of fluid intelligence ($d = 0.22$) as compared with non-immigrants. This finding is important as race is, to a degree, controlled in this comparison as the majority of the European immigrants were White. For non-European immigrants, the differences were larger ($d = 0.62$).

It is important to note the larger literature examining cross-national differences in cognitive ability test scores. As noted previously, much of this research has used samples of children. While these results may not fully generalize to working populations, the findings are nevertheless instructive. van de Vijver's (1997) meta-analysis of cross-national mean score differences on cognitive ability tests found that the mean effect size was close to zero, but the distribution of effect sizes was positively skewed and the median value demonstrated differences between national cultures. The magnitude of the effect size was moderated by a number of factors and the level of stimulus complexity, with larger effect sizes for more complex stimuli. The type of task was related to the effect size such that Western tasks produced larger differences than tasks developed in the local culture. Finally, the level of national wealth was related to the magnitude of the effect sizes such that effect sizes were larger in comparisons involving wealthier countries.

Personality

There is a large literature on cross-cultural and cross-national differences on personality measures (e.g., Triandis & Suh, 2002). While most of the literature shows that the strucutre of personality is similar across cultures (e.g., Hough et al., 2001; McCrae & Costa, 1997), there are few studies examining these differences in the context of the personality predictors used in employee selection contexts. Both te Nijenhuis, van der Flier and van Leeuwen (1997) and te Nijenhuis, van der Flier and van Leeuwen (2003) report that the basic taxonomy of commonly used personality factors (e.g., neuroticism and extraversion) can be generalized to immigrant groups in The Netherlands, even for first-generation immigrants, and that the items function similarly across groups. These studies also report that the score differences between immigrants and non-immigrants are small on measures of broad personality traits and more specific facets of personality.

Impact of cultural content

One area of relevant, general cross-cultural research has focused on the impact of culture-specific content on test performance (e.g., Freedle, 2003; Freedle & Kostin, 1997; Helms-Lorenz et al., 2003; Malda et al., 2010; van de Vijver, 1997, 2008). This line of research has found that test performance suffers when the cultural content embedded in a test is different from the cultural content with which the test-taker is familiar. For example, Malda and colleagues (2010) experimentally manipulated the cultural content embedded in measures of short-term memory, attention, working memory and figural and verbal fluid reasoning to be consistent with White South African culture or Black South African culture. In this study, Malda and colleagues created test items that were equivalent, but manipulated the cultural content so that it was more familiar for one culture than the other. They found test performance was better on the test versions that were consistent with the test-taker's culture. The cultural content of the test moderated the relationship between race and test performance.

Freedle and colleagues (Freedle, 2003; Freedle & Kostin, 1997) have found that cultural differences in the use and interpretation of common words can lead to differential item functioning and serves to disadvantage the cultural minority test-taker. Common to both these research studies is that the linguistic demands of tests may be confounded with the cultural content embedded in the tests (Ortiz, Ochoa & Dynda, 2012). As Helms-Lorenz and colleagues (2003) explain, 'differential mastery of the testing language by cultural groups creates a spurious correlation between g and intergroup performance differences, if complex tests require more linguistic skills than do simple tests' (p. 13).

In summary, the research comparing different culture groups on predictors commonly used in an employment context is limited and most of the research focuses on predictor constructs rather than predictor methods. Current research finds that minority cultural groups (e.g., immigrants) tend to score lower on cognitive tests than the majority cultural group (e.g., non-immigrants). However, the size of the differences varies, with tests relying on acquired knowledge and the dominant language of the culture showing the largest differences. Tests of basic cognitive operations tend to show much smaller differences. As with the other comparisons we have reviewed, non-cognitive constructs tend to show near-zero score differences. However, the degree to which cultural context is embedded in the measurement of the constructs can have a large impact on the nature of the differences observed. As was true for the research on score differences between race and ethnic groups, aspects of the measurement can play a role in differences observed.

What are the Explanations for The Observed Score Differences?

Many hypotheses have been proposed to explain why these differences occur. In general, these explanations can be classified according to genetics, social and cultural factors and the nature of the measurement of the predictor (e.g., Goldstein, Scherbaum & Yusko, 2009; Neisser et al., 1996; Verney et al., 2005). It is unlikely that any one factor can explain or account for all the differences observed, and the factors impacting scores will vary between groups. For example, language and cultural familiarity are likely to apply to a greater degree to immigrants and Latinos/Hispanics in the US than they would to African-Americans. We briefly consider each of these three classes of explanations for score differences.

Explanations based on genetics

One set of explanations is based on heritability and genetic aspects of individual differences (Herrnstein & Murray, 1994; Neisser et al., 1996). The basic idea here is that many individual differences (e.g., cognitive ability, personality) have a genetic basis and are passed from parent to offspring. Thus, the observed differences reflect real differences in the individual difference variable. This has been the most controversial when applied to cognitive abilities as the only conclusion is that people are born intelligent or unintelligent and there is nothing that can be done to change it. As Nisbett and colleagues (2012) argue, while the evidence suggests that genetics can play a role, the role is much smaller than the proponents of this approach claim, and the interactions between the genotypes and environment are too complex to pinpoint the precise impact of genes on individual differences. Moreover, the evidence does not show that the genetic component is intertwined with race and ethnicity. However, the arguments for this perspective on the differences in scores seems to assume that the research does show such an interrelationship.

Numerous explanations explicitly or implicitly build on the position that there are inherent differences in cognitive ability between race groups. One example is the Spearman hypothesis (Jensen, 1998; Spearman, 1927), which predicts that racial differences in test performance increase as the cognitive loading of a test increases. Essentially, this means that the better the test is at measuring cognitive ability (i.e., a higher g load), the greater the differences that will be observed between races. This hypothesis is premised on the assumption that the observed differences are true differences between groups.

Social and cultural factors

Another class of explanation also holds that the differences are real, but asserts that they are created by the environmental context. These explanations focus on the effect of educational opportunity, socio-economic status, culture, nutrition and child-rearing practices, among others (Nisbett et al., 2012), on individual differences. These explanations are psychological in nature and focus on the interaction between the individual and the environment. As is true of the genetic explanations, the interactions between the genotypes and environment are too complex to pinpoint the exact impact of the environment on individual differences.

One example of this approach is Cottrell and colleagues' (2015) model of the factors impacting score differences between African-Americans and Whites on cognitive ability tests.

Their model focuses on a sequential process over time and includes variables related to maternal education, household income, availability of learning materials in the home, parental style, birth order and the physical environment (e.g., overcrowding in the home, safety). In the first step, their model posits that race predicts a number of concepts under the umbrella of 'maternal advantage'. These include the socio-economic variables of income and maternal education level, as well as maternal verbal ability/ knowledge, due to historical factors such as housing, educational and occupational segregation. In turn, these maternal advantage variables predict a host of parenting factors, including maternal sensitivity to children, acceptance behaviours, the child's physical environment (e.g., access to healthcare, living in a safe neighbourhood), access to learning materials and birth order and weight (i.e., greater maternal education leads to smaller family size and heavier birth weight, which contribute to a child's cognitive ability). Finally, these parenting styles proximally predict cognitive ability test scores in the last step. These authors also posit distal relationships between race and parenting factors, and maternal advantage factors and cognitive ability scores. In a longitudinal study of children (five measurement points from age 54 months to 15 years), Cottrell and colleagues found support for their model as a whole and that the score differences between African-Americans and Whites is established by 54 months of age.

The nature of the measurement of the predictor

A third class of explanation focuses on the measurement of individual differences as a contributing factor to the size of the score differences. Many authors have argued that the way we measure the construct introduces construct-irrelevant variance to the assessment (e.g., Chen & Gardener, 2005). Construct-irrelevant variance refers to any extraneous variance captured by an assessment that is not due to the construct of interest, but to the assessment capturing additional constructs or to the assessment's methodology (Messick, 1995). Unlike random error, construct-irrelevant variance systematically impacts assessment scores for individuals or groups. Consequently, it compromises the construct validity of assessments and hence our ability to draw inferences from assessment scores (Binning & Barrett, 1989; Messick, 1995). Sources of construct-irrelevant variance in intelligence assessments include indeterminable items (Freedle, 2003), cultural content (Freedle, 2003; Freedle & Kostin, 1997; Helms-Lorenz et al., 2003; Malda et al., 2010; Scherbaum et al., 2015), differential prior knowledge and exposure (Agnello, Ryan & Yusko, 2015; Fagan & Holland, 2002, 2007; Ortiz et al., 2012; Scherbaum et al., 2015) and content not relevant to the intended domain (Helms-Lorenz et al., 2003; Malda et al., 2010; Scherbaum et al., 2015). For example, some research has examined the use of content requiring previously acquired knowledge that is not related to the test domain impacts test performance. Fagan and Holland (2002, 2007, 2009) have conducted a series of studies examining whether score differences between race groups on cognitive ability tests could be attributed to differences in the ability to process information (i.e., fluid intelligence) or differences in prior exposure to the acquired knowledge that test items use. They found no differences in test performance when knowledge required by the test items was unfamiliar to both groups and there was an equal opportunity to learn it. However, when the knowledge required by the test items was such that it was believed to be common and previously acquired by all test-takers, the typical Black–White score differences emerged. These findings are likely to have implications for understanding score differences for national culture groups.

Future Research

Although there are many avenues for future research, we focus here on three which we believe hold the potential to generate novel and far-reaching insights, or are examples of areas greatly in need of additional research – specifically, research on score differences for Latinos/Hispanics, research on score differences related to national culture and research on the role of the measurement on the observed score differences.

Research on score differences for Latinos/Hispanics

Given the size and growth of Latino/Hispanic populations in the workforce, the lack of research on score differences between Latinos/Hispanics and other groups in the US is a missed opportunity. Much of the research assumes that the findings from the research on Black–White comparisons will apply to Latino/Hispanic–White comparisons too. Given their unique histories and cultures, it is very unlikely that the results from Black–White comparison will generalize to Latinos/Hispanics (e.g., Alcoff, 2003). At the most basic level, research directed at understanding more nuanced aspects of the score differences is needed. For example, many of the moderators which have examined meta-analytic research on cognitive ability score group mean differences have not been examined for Latino/ Hispanic comparisons. Moreover, the meta-analytic estimates of the score differences for Latinos/Hispanics are often much less than the score differences for African-Americans. There is little theoretical work aimed at understanding why there are differences and why the differences are smaller for Latinos/Hispanics. At this point, the degree to which models and theories of score differences in Black–White comparisons (e.g., Cottrell et al., 2015) apply to Latinos/Hispanics is unclear.

Research on score differences related to national culture and measurement

Much more research is needed to explore the magnitude of score difference between national culture groups and immigrant and non-immigrant groups on a wider range of commonly used predictors. The work to date has primarily focused on differences in measures of cognitive ability and personality. Even this research has been limited to a handful of countries. Despite calls to increase our understanding of the role of culture in score differences (e.g., Helms-Lorenz et al., 2003), little research in the area of personnel assessment has heeded these calls. Future research and theoretical work are needed that explores the cultural factors responsible for these differences. Brouwers and van de Vijver (2015) provide one example of a direction this research could take. They argue that personnel assessment will not advance unless a contextualized view of assessing individual differences is taken. This is consistent with van de Vijver's (1997) conclusion that locally developed assessments (i.e., contextualized) tend to show smaller score differences than the typical Western-style assessment (i.e., decontextualized). They propose an assessment strategy that can take a more contextualized approach which explicitly allows culture into the process of measuring individual differences.

The cross-cultural and cross-national research reviewed here points to the need to understand the degree to which tests and assessments contain culturally-specific or non-domain-relevant content, particularly as it relates to linguistic content. The inclusion of this content considerably raises the likelihood of admitting a source of contamination into the measurement process. In the domain of personnel assessment this is particularly important given that tests may be used on a global scale and used with culturally diverse populations within a country. In these cases, a lack of familiarity with content that is not related to the construct of interest can create substantial problems for accurately assessing individuals and interpreting test scores. Although best practice recommendations cover many aspects of test content when applied to the development or adaptation of tests for use globally (e.g., Byrne et al., 2009; Ryan & Tippins, 2009), these same recommendations are much less frequently applied when tests are developed for domestic use with globally diverse populations.

Another area for future research is investigating the role that measurement plays in the observed score differences. This research has many possible avenues. One is further exploring how test content requiring previously acquired knowledge that is not related to the test domain impacts test performance. Although the initial work offers some insight (Fagan & Holland, 2002, 2007), more research is clearly needed. Another avenue for research is further examining ways to create test times that minimize cultural and non-domain-relevant content. One promising direction is research using items containing non-entrenched tasks (e.g., Sternberg, 1981a, 1981b, 1982a; Sternberg & Gastel, 1989; Tetewsky & Sternberg, 1986). Non-entrenched tasks are those that use novel or atypical stimuli or concepts to solve problems. The core feature of non-entrenched items is that they do not represent the natural state of problems or stimuli in everyday life (Sternberg, 1982b). For example, Sternberg (1981a) described a number of non-entrenched tasks including one for which individuals need to determine the physical state of an object (e.g., liquid or solid) and the object's fictional name (e.g., plin, kwef) as it moves from north to south or south to north on the fictional planet Kryon from a set of rules presented at the start of the task. Although the initial work suggests that the use of these items can reduce score differences (e.g., Sternberg, 2006), more work is needed to better understand how these items work and whether there are boundary conditions on their effectiveness.

More generally, research is needed to articulate the knowledge structures, cognitive process and cognitive strategies that are required to solve a test problem, as well as understand how these processes lead to items being more or less difficult for test-takers (Embretson, 1983). On a related note, theoretical work has also been devoted to understanding how stimulus features of items contribute to item difficulty and impact item performance (e.g., Irvine & Kyllonen, 2002; Lievens & Sackett, 2007).

Conclusion

Score difference between groups has been and will continue to be of great interest to researchers and practitioners working in the field of personnel assessment and selection (Goldstein et al., 2009; Hough, Oswald & Ployhart, 2001; Ployhart & Holtz, 2008). This chapter has summarized current research on differences between racial/ethnic groups and national cultural groups on predictors frequently used in employee selection. Current literature, while limited for all group comparisons except African-Americans and Whites, indicates that there are differences which vary as both a function and feature of the predictor. At this point, there are as many answered questions as unanswered questions. Additional empirical work documenting both the work and theoretical work explaining these differences are clearly needed.

References

Agnello, P., Ryan, R., & Yusko, K. P. (2015). Implications of modern intelligence research for assessing intelligence in the workplace. *Human Resource Management Review, 25*(1), 47–55.

Aiken, J. R., Salmon, E. D., & Hanges, P. J. (2013). The origins and legacy of the Civil Rights Act of 1964. *Journal of Business & Psychology, 28*(4), 383–399. doi: 10.1007/s10869-013-9291-z.

Alcoff, L. M. N. (2003). Latino/as, Asian Americans, and the Black–White binary. *The Journal of Ethics, 7*, 5–27.

Arthur, W., Jr., & Villado, A. J. (2008). The importance of distinguishing between constructs and methods when comparing predictors in personnel selection research and practice. *Journal of Applied Psychology, 93*(2), 435–442. doi: 10.1037/0021-9010.93.2.435.

Becton, B. J., Matthews, M. C., Hartley, D. L., & Whitaker, D. H. (2009). Using biodata to predict turnover, organizational commitment, and job performance in healthcare. *International Journal of Selection and Assessment, 17*(2), 189–202. doi: 10.1111/j.1468-2389.2009.00462.x.

Berry, C. M., Sackett, P. R., & Wiemann, S. (2007). A review of recent developments in integrity test research. *Personnel Psychology, 60*(2), 271–301. doi: 10.1111/j.1744-6570.2007.00074.x.

Binning, J. F., & Barrett, G. V. (1989). Validity of personnel decisions: A conceptual analysis of the inferential and evidential bases. *Journal of Applied Psychology, 74*(3), 478–494. doi: 10.1037/0021-9010.74.3.478.

Bobko, P., & Roth, P. L. (2013). Reviewing, categorizing, and analyzing the literature on Black–White mean differences for predictors of job performance: Verifying some perceptions and updating/correcting others. *Personnel Psychology, 66*(1), 91–126. doi: 10.1111/peps.12007.

Bobko, P., Roth, P. L., & Potosky, D. (1999). Derivation and implications of a meta-analytic matrix incorporating cognitive ability, alternative predictors, and job performance. *Personnel Psychology, 52*(3), 561–589. doi: 10.1111/j.1744-6570.1999.tb00172.x.

Brouwers, S. A., & van de Vijver, F. J. (2015). Contextualizing intelligence in assessment: The next step. *Human Resource Management Review, 25*(1), 38–46.

Byrne, B., Oakland, T., Leong, F., van de Vijver, F., Hambleton, R., Cheung, F. M., & Bartram, D. (2009). A critical analysis of cross-cultural research and testing practices: Implications for improved education and training in psychology. *Training and Education in Professional Psychology, 3*(2), 94–105.

Chen, J., & Gardner, H. (2005). Assessment based on multiple-intelligence theory. *In* D. P. Flanagan & P. L. Harrison (Eds.), *Contemporary Intellectual Assessment: Theories, Tests, and Issues* (2nd ed., pp. 77–102). New York: Guilford Press.

Choi, K. H., Sakamoto, A., & Powers, D. (2008). Who is Hispanic? Hispanic identity among African Americans, Asian Americans, others, and Whites. *Sociological Inquiry, 78*, 335–371.

Cottrell, J. M., Newman, D. A., & Roisman, G. I. (2015). Explaining the Black–White gap in cognitive test scores: Toward a theory of adverse impact. *Journal of Applied Psychology, 100*(6), 1713–1736. doi: 10.1037/apl0000020.

Dean, M. A., Roth, P. L., & Bobko, P. (2008). Ethnic and gender subgroup differences in assessment center ratings: A meta-analysis. *Journal of Applied Psychology, 93*(3), 685–691. doi: 10.1037/0021-9010.93.3.685.

Dudley, N. M., McFarland, L. A., Goodman, S. A., Hunt, S. T., & Sydell, E. J. (2005). Racial differences in socially desirable responding in selection contexts: Magnitude and consequences. *Journal of Personality Assessment, 85*, 50–64.

Dovidio, J. F., Gluszek, A., John, M.-S., Ditlmann, R., & Lagunes, P. (2010). Understanding bias toward Latinos: Discrimination, dimensions of difference, and experience of exclusion. *Journal of Social Issues, 66*, 59–78.

Embretson, S. (1983). Construct validity: Construct representation versus nomothetic span. *Psychological Bulletin, 93*, 179–197.

Ennis, S. R., Rios-Vargas, M., & Albert, N. G. (2011). *The Hispanic Population: 2010.* www.census.gov/grod/cen2010/briefs/c2010br-04.pdf.

Erez, M., & Earley, P. C. (1993). *Culture, Self-identity, and Work.* New York: Oxford University Press.

Fagan, J., & Holland, C. (2002). Equal opportunity and racial differences in IQ. *Intelligence, 30*(4), 361–387. doi: 10.1016/S0160-2896(02)00080-6.

Fagan, J., & Holland, C. (2007). Racial equality in intelligence: Predictions from a theory of intelligence as processing. *Intelligence, 35*(4), 319–334. doi: 10.1016/j.intell.2006.08.009.

Fagan, J. F., & Holland, C. R. (2009). Culture-fair prediction of academic achievement. *Intelligence, 37*(1), 62–67.

Foldes, H. J., Duehr, E. E., & Ones, D. S. (2008). Group differences in personality: Meta-analyses comparing five U.S. racial groups. *Personnel Psychology, 61*(3), 579–616. doi: 10.1111/j.1744-6570.2008.00123.x.

Freedle, R. (2003). Correcting the SAT's ethnic and social-class bias: A method for reestimating SAT scores. *Harvard Educational Review, 73*, 1–42.

Freedle, R., & Kostin, I. (1997). Predicting Black and White differential item functioning in verbal analogy performance. *Intelligence, 24*(3), 417–444. doi: 10.1016/S0160-2896(97)90058-1.

Goldstein, H. W., Scherbaum, C. A., & Yusko, K. (2009). Adverse impact and measuring cognitive ability. In J. Outtz (Ed.) *Adverse Impact: Implications for Organizational Staffing and High Stakes Testing* (pp. 95–134). New York: Psychology Press.

Gandy, J. A., Dye, D. A., & MacLane, C. N. (1994). Federal government selection: The individual achievement record.

Griggs v. Duke Power Co. 401 U.S. 424 (1971).

Helms, J. E. (1992). Why is there no study of cultural equivalence in standardized cognitive ability testing? *American Psychologist, 47*(9), 1083.

Helms-Lorenz, M., van de Vijver, F., & Poortinga, Y. (2003). Cross-cultural differences in cognitive performance and Spearman's hypothesis: *g* or *c? Intelligence, 31*, 9–29.

Herrnstein, R. J., & Murray, C. (1994). *The Bell Curve: Intelligence and Class Structure in American Life.* New York: Free Press.

Hough, L. M., Oswald, F. L., & Ployhart, R. E. (2001). Determinants, detection and amelioration of adverse impact in personnel selection procedures: Issues, evidence and lessons learned. *International Journal of Selection and Assessment, 9*(1–2), 152–194. doi: 10.1111/1468-2389.00171.

House, R. J., & Javidan, M. (2004). Overview of GLOBE. In R. J. House, P. J. Hanges, M. Javidan, P. W. Dorfman, & V. Gupta (Eds.), *Culture, Leadership, and Organizations: The GLOBE Study of 62 Societies* (pp. 9–26). Thousand Oaks, CA: Sage.

Huffcutt, A. I., & Roth, P. L. (1998). Racial group differences in employment interview evaluations. *Journal of Applied Psychology, 83*(2), 179–189. doi: 10.1037/0021-9010.83.2.179.

Huffcutt, A. I., Conway, J. M., Roth, P. L., & Stone, N. J. (2001). Identification and meta–analytic assessment of psychological constructs measured in employment interviews. *Journal of Applied Psychology, 86*(5), 897–913. doi: 10.1037/0021-9010.86.5.897.

Hunter, J. E., & Hunter, R. F. (1984). Validity and utility of alternative predictors of job performance. *Psychological Bulletin, 96*(1), 72–98. doi: 10.1037/0033-2909.96.1.72.

Irvine, S., & Kyllonen, P. (2002). *Generating Items from Cognitive Tests: Theory and Practice.* Mahwah, NJ: Lawrence Erlbaum.

Jensen, A. R. (1985). The nature of the Black–White difference on various psychometric tests: Spearman's hypothesis. *Behavioral and Brain Sciences, 8*(2), 193–263. doi: 10.1017/S0140525X00020392.

Jensen, A. R. (1998). The g factor: The science of mental ability.

Jensen, A. R. (2000). The dilemma of group differences. *Psychology, Public Policy, and Law, 6*(1), 121–127. doi: 10.1037//1076-8971.6.1.121.

Landy, F. J. (1986). Stamp collecting versus science: Validation as hypothesis testing. *American Psychologist, 41*(11), 1183–1192. doi: 10.1037/0003-066X.41.11.1183.

Lievens, F., & Sackett, P. (2007). Situational judgment in tests in high-stakes settings: Issues and strategies with generating alternate forms. *Journal of Applied Psychology, 92*, 1043–1055.

London House. (1995). *Personnel selection inventory: PSI-CS with math.* Rosemont, IL: McGraw-Hill/London House.

Malda, M., van de Vijver, F., & Temane, M. (2010). Rugby versus soccer in South Africa: Content familiarity explains most cross-cultural differences in cognitive test scores. *Intelligence, 38*, 582–595.

McCrae, R., & Costa, P. (1997). Personality trait structure as a human universal. *American Psychologist, 52*(5), 509–516. dx.doi.org/10.1037/0003-066X.52.5.509.

Messick, S. (1995). Validity of psychological assessment: validation of inferences from persons' responses and performances as scientific inquiry into score meaning. *American Psychologist, 50*(9), 741.

Neisser, U., Boodoo, G., Bouchard, T., Boykin, A., Brody, N., Ceci, S., Halpern, D., Loehlin, J. C., Perloff, R., Sternberg, R., & Urbina, S. (1996). Intelligence: Knowns and unknowns. *American Psychologist, 51*, 77–101.

Nisbett, R. E., Aronson, J., Blair, C., Dickens, W., Flynn, J., Halpern, D. F., & Turkheimer, E. (2012). Intelligence: New findings and theoretical developments. *American Psychologist, 67*(2), 120–159. doi: 10.1037/a0026699.

Ones, D. S., & Viswesvaran, C. (1998). Integrity testing in organzations. *In* R. W. Griffin, A. O'Leary-Kelly & J. M. Collins (Eds.), *Dysfuntional Behavior in Organizations: Vol. 2, Nonviolent Behaviors in Organizations.* Greenwich, CT: JAI Press.

Ortiz, S. O., Ochoa, S. H., & Dynda, A. M. (2012). Testing with culturally and linguistically diverse populations: Moving beyond the verbal–performance dichotomy into evidence-based practice. *In* D. P. Flanagan & P. L. Harrison (Eds.), *Contemporary Intellectual Assessment: Theories, Tests, and Issues* (3rd ed, pp. 526–552). New York: Guilford Press.

Ployhart, R. E., & Holtz, B. C. (2008). The diversity–validity dilemma: Strategies for reducing racio-ethnic and sex subgroup differences and adverse impact in selection. *Personnel Psychology, 61*(1), 153–172. doi: 10.1111/j.1744-6570.2008.00109.x.

Potosky, D., Bobko, P., & Roth, P. L. (2005). Forming composites of cognitive ability and alternative measures to predict job performance and reduce adverse impact: Corrected estimates and realistic expectations. *International Journal of Selection and Assessment, 13*(4), 304–315. doi: 10.1111/j.1468-2389.2005.00327.x.

Pulakos, E. D. & Schmitt, N. (1996). An evaluation of two strategies for reducing adverse impact and their effects on criterion-related validity. *Human Performance, 9*(3), 241–258.

Reynolds, C. R., Willson, V. L., & Ramsey, M. (1999). Intellectual differences among Mexican Americans, Papagos and Whites, independent of *g. Personality and Individual Differences, 27,* 1181–1187.

Roth, P. L., Bevier, C. A., Bobko, P., Switzer, F. S., & Tyler, P. (2001). Ethnic group differences in cognitive ability in employment and educational settings: A meta-analysis. *Personnel Psychology, 54*(2), 297–330. doi: 10.1111/j.1744-6570.2001.tb00094.x.

Roth, P. L., Bobko, P., McFarland, L., & Buster, M. (2008). Work sample tests in personnel selection: A meta-analysis of Black–White differences in overall and exercise scores. *Personnel Psychology, 61*(3), 637–662. doi: 10.1111/j.1744-6570.2008.00125.x.

Roth, P. L., van Iddekinge, C. H., Huffcutt, A. I., Eidson, C. E., Jr., & Bobko, P. (2002). Corrections for range restriction in structured interview ethnic group differences: The values may be larger than researchers thought. *Journal of Applied Psychology, 87*(2), 369–376. doi: 10.1037/0021-9010.87.2.369.

Ryan, A. M., & Tippins, N. (2009). *Designing and Implementing Global Selection Systems.* Malden, MA: Wiley-Blackwell.

Scherbaum, C. Goldstein, H., Ryan, R., Agnello, P., Yusko, K., & Hanges, P. (2015). New developments in intelligence theory and assessment: Implications for personnel selection. *In* J. Oostrom & I. Nikolaou (Eds.), *Employee Recruitment, Selection, and Assessment: Contemporary Issues for Theory and Practice.* Hove: Taylor & Francis and New York: Psychology Press.

Schmitt, N., Clause, C. S., & Pulakos, E. D. (1996). Subgroup differences associated with different measures of some common job relevant constructs. *In* C. L. Cooper & I. T. Robertson (Eds.), *International Review of Industrial and Organizational Psychology* (pp. 115–139). New York: Wiley.

Schmitt, N., & Kunce, C. (2002). The effects of required elaboration of answers to biodata questions. *Personnel Psychology, 55*(3), 569–587.

Spearman, C. (1927). *The Abilities of Man, Their Nature and Measurement.* New York: Macmillan.

Sternberg, R. (1981a). Intelligence and non-entrenchment. *Journal of Educational Psychology, 73,* 1–16.

Sternberg, R. (1981b). Testing and cognitive psychology. *American Psychologist, 36,* 1181–1189.

Sternberg, R. (1982a). Nonentrenchment in the assessment of intellectual giftedness. *Gifted Child Quarterly, 26,* 63–67.

Sternberg, R. (1982b). Natural, unnatural, and supernatural concepts. *Cognitive Psychology, 14,* 451–488.

Sternberg, R. (2006). The Rainbow Project: Enhancing the SAT through assessments of analytical, practical, and creative skills. *Intelligence, 34,* 321–350.

Sternberg, R., & Gastel, J. (1989). If dancers ate their shoes: Inductive reasoning with factual and counterfactual premises. *Memory and Cognition, 17,* 1–10.

te Nijenhuis, J., & van der Flier, H. (1997). Comparability of GATB scores for immigrants and majority group members: Some Dutch findings. *Journal of Applied Psychology, 82,* 675–687.

te Nijenhuis, J., & van der Flier, H. (1999). Bias research in the Netherlands: Review and implications. *European Journal of Psychological Assessments, 15*(2), 165–175.

te Nijenhuis, J., & van der Flier, H. (2001). Group differences in mean intelligence for the Dutch and third world immigrants. *Journal of Biosocial Science, 33*(3), 469–475.

te Nijenhuis, J., & van der Flier, H. (2003). Immigrant–majority group differences in cognitive performance: Jensen effects, cultural effects, or both? *Intelligence, 31,* 443–459.

te Nijenhuis, J., & van der Flier, H. (2005). Immigrant–majority group differences on work-related measures: The case for cognitive complexity. *Personality and Individual Differences, 38,* 1213–1221.

te Nijenhuis, J., de Jong, M. J., Evers, A., & van der Flier, H. (2004). Are cognitive differences between immigrant and majority groups diminishing? *European Journal of Personality, 18*(5), 405–434.

te Nijenhuis, J., van der Flier, H., & van Leeuwen, L. (1997). Comparability of personality test scores for immigrants and majority group members: Some Dutch findings. *Personality and Individual Differences, 23,* 849–859.

te Nijenhuis, J., van der Flier, H., & van Leeuwen, L. (2003). The use of a test of neuroticism, extraversion, and rigidity for Dutch immigrant job applicants. *Applied Psychology: An International Review, 52,* 630–647.

te Nijenhuis, J., Willigers, D., Dragt, J., & van der Flier, H. (2016). The effects of language bias and cultural bias estimated using the method of correlated vectors on a large database of IQ comparisons between native Dutch and ethnic minority immigrants from non-Western countries. *Intelligence, 54,* 117–135.

Tetewsky, S., & Sternberg, R. (1986). Conceptual and lexical determinants of nonentrenched thinking. *Journal of Memory and Language, 25,* 202–225.

Triandis, H. C. (1994). Cross-cultural industrial and organizational psychology. *In* H. C. Triandis, M. D. Dunnette, & L. M. Hough (Eds.), *Handbook of Industrial and Organizational Psychology* (vol. 4, pp. 103–172). Palto Alto, CA: Consulting Psychologists Press.

Triandis, H. C., & Suh, E. M. (2002). Cultural influences on personality. *Annual Review of Psychology, 53*(1), 133–160.

U.S. Census Bureau. (2014). QuickFacts. www.census.gov/quickfacts/table/PST045215/ 00#headnote–js-a. Last accessed 10 February 2016.

Valentin Kvist, A. (2011). Interpretation of cognitive test scores in relation to Swedish and immigrant groups. *Nordic Psychology, 63,* 51–71.

Valentin Kvist, A., & Gustafsson, J.-E. (2008). The relation between fluid intelligence and the general factor as a function of cultural background: A test of Cattell's investment theory. *Intelligence, 36,* 422–436.

van Iddekinge, C. H., Taylor, M. A., & Eidson, C. E., (2005). Broad versus narrow facets of integrity: Predictive validity and subgroup differences. *Human Performance, 18*(2), 151–177. doi: 10.1207/s15327043hup1802_3.

van Leest, P. F., & Bleichrodt, N. (1990). Testing of college graduates from ethnic minority groups. *In* N. Bleichrodt & P. J. D. Drenth (Eds.), *Contemporary Issues in Cross-Cultural Psychology: Selected Papers from a Regional Conference of the International Association of Cross-Cultural Psychology.* Amsterdam: The Netherlands.

van de Vijver, F. (1997). Meta-analysis of cross-cultural comparisons of cognitive test performance. *Journal of Cross-Cultural Psychology, 28,* 678–709.

van de Vijver, F. (2008). On the meaning of cross-cultural differences in simple cognitive measures. *Educational Research and Evaluation, 14*(3), 215–234.

Verney, S. P., Granholm, E., Marshall, S. P., Malcarne, V. L., & Saccuzzo, D. P. (2005). Culture-fair cognitive ability assessment: Information processing and psychophysiological approaches. *Assessment, 12,* 303–319.

Whetzel, D. L., McDaniel, M. A., & Nguyen, N. T. (2008). Subgroup differences in situational judgment test performance: A meta-analysis. *Human Performance, 21*(3), 291–309. doi: 10.1080/08959280802137820.

20

Legal and Fairness Considerations in Employee Selection

Kenneth P. Yusko, Brian L. Bellenger, Elliott C. Larson, Paul J. Hanges and Juliet R. Aiken

Introduction

Choosing which job applicants to hire constitutes one of the most important decisions organizations can make. It can also be among the most legally vulnerable. Indeed, the current legal situation has been described as the 'age of litigation' (Guion, 2011; Guion & Highouse, 2006). Litigation itself is not necessarily negative, as evolving case law and the threat of a legal challenge can motivate and guide organizations to improve their hiring procedures. However, the continual growth of regulations and increased debates regarding the relevance of past guidelines in the United States (for example, see King, Avery, & Sackett, 2013; McDaniel, Kepes, & Banks, 2011), more multinational organizations operating within the boundaries of multiple countries' hiring rules and regulations, and the general lack of clarity around best practices has resulted in an increasingly complex legal sphere in which employee selection is conducted. This complexity makes it difficult for managers and other employees, especially those working outside of legal and HR specialty areas, to navigate the challenges of identifying and bringing in talent without running undue legal risk. Coupled with the need to address multiple stakeholders' goals and perceptions, the selection process, particularly as it relates to diversity, has become a convoluted amalgam of legal, ethical, social and financial factors.

The goal of this chapter is to help professionals leverage current legal hiring requirements and standards in order to create and implement more effective and valid employee selection systems. To this end, we begin with a brief overview of key legal developments, including major legislation and case law over the past 50 years. Next, we review some of the professional standards in the field that help guide the development of legally defensible systems. This includes a discussion of both the legal and psychometric concepts that impact the development and implementation of selection systems. We then provide a brief overview of some of the legal events that are currently changing the landscape of selection. While our discussion mainly focuses on the legal environment in the US due to its historical

The Wiley Blackwell Handbook of the Psychology of Recruitment, Selection and Employee Retention,
First Edition. Edited by Harold W. Goldstein, Elaine D. Pulakos, Jonathan Passmore and Carla Semedo.
© 2017 John Wiley & Sons Ltd. Published 2020 by John Wiley & Sons Ltd.

focus on developing regulatory standards and oversight (e.g., Gutman, 2008; Myors et al., 2008a), we highlight relevant legal guidelines and practices in other countries where possible. In doing so we hope to provide a more global perspective of legal standards, which is increasingly important as organizations expand their operations overseas.

A Brief Historical Review of Employee Selection in the United States – Major Legislation and Case Law

The Civil Rights Act 1964

While many historical events have impacted employee selection procedures, arguably the largest paradigm shift in legislation came as a result of the Civil Rights Act 1964 (the Act). The Act was preceded by years of political and social movements that sought to reduce the racial and gender inequality in the US (for a detailed overview and commentary, see Aiken, Salmon & Hanges, 2013; Gutman, Koppes & Vadonovich, 2011). The Act proscribed the discrimination that was prevalent and sometimes even legally sanctioned in some states (Aiken et al., 2013) and paved the way for future legislation intended to eliminate discrimination for other groups (e.g., the American with Disabilities Act of 1990). As such, the impact of the Act on social policies related to equal rights cannot be understated. Specific to selection procedures, Title VII of the Act prohibits employers from discriminating in the employment process against people based on their race, colour, religion, sex or national origin. Title VII also provided the foundation for the Equal Employment Opportunity Commission (EEOC). The Commission began with limited authority, mainly restricted to investigating complaints and seeking voluntary compliance with Title VII, but its responsibilities and impact later expanded (Hanges, Salmon & Aiken, 2013).

Age Discrimination in Employment Act 1967

As the 1960s progressed, public policy continued to focus on addressing economic and social justice concerns by expanding legislation to other discriminated groups. The Age Discrimination in Employment Act (ADEA) 1967 was passed to limit the imposition of arbitrary age limits in employment decisions; now, decisions have to be based on ability and not age (Gutman et al., 2011; Rothenberg & Gardner, 2011). ADEA specifically prohibited private and public employers from discriminating against individuals over the age of 40 years on the basis of their age (Bellenger & Yusko, 2015).

Griggs v. Duke Power Company (1971)

The first real test of the Act came when the Supreme Court heard *Griggs v. Duke Power Company* in 1970 (Outtz, 2011). All the African-American employees at Duke Power Company were restricted to working in the labour department. After the passing of the Act, the company instituted new requirements for transfers and new hires. Those employees looking to transfer from the labour department to another department in Duke Power Company had to have a high school diploma. Employees without a diploma had to pass two aptitude tests in order to transfer. Furthermore, new employees who applied to work in a department outside of labour also had to pass the same two aptitude tests (Hanges et al., 2013; Outtz, 2011).

In their ruling in 1971, the Supreme Court concluded that African-Americans were discriminated against as a result of these new testing policies. Specifically, they determined that the manner in which an employment opportunity is offered to candidates must be usable on equal terms by individuals from all groups. This was a major victory for civil rights advocates. The lower courts had found the test requirements to be acceptable as there was no intent to discriminate against minorities. However, the Supreme Court's ruling demonstrated that the intent of the test is irrelevant. Rather, if the requirements for a job cannot be shown to be job-related and they negatively impact the hiring of minorities, the tests are not legal (Outtz, 2011).

The Supreme Court's decision suggested that there was a shifting burden of proof in discrimination cases. Based on this model, the plaintiffs must first offer evidence that some form of discrimination has occurred. If the court decides that the plaintiff has provided enough evidence for a prima facie case, the burden shifts to the defendant, who must show that the hiring practice in question is job-related.

The Equal Employment Opportunity Act 1972

While the ruling of the Supreme Court in *Griggs* signified the Supreme Court's support for the Act, a number of challenges limited the Act's impact. A large backlog of discrimination complaints, delays by the Justice Department in bringing Title VII suits and the overwhelming number of agencies attempting to enforce EEO law, with at times inconsistent regulations and guidelines, eventually led to the Equal Employment Opportunity Act of 1972 (Hanges et al., 2013). This Act extended the EEOC's coverage to include smaller businesses, as well as state and local governments, and granted the EEOC power to enforce Title VII (Aiken et al., 2013; Jones, 1977).

The Rehabilitation Act 1973

The Rehabilitation Act of 1973 was passed to prevent discrimination in the federal government against people with physical and mental disabilities. This Act was eventually expanded by the Americans with Disabilities Act of 1990 to include private employers (Bellenger & Yusko, 2015).

Albemarle Paper Co. v. Moody (1975)

Just a few months after the Supreme Court's decision in *Griggs v. Duke Power Company* in 1971, *Albemarle Paper Co. v. Moody* came before a district level court. The case revolved around Albemarle's employment practices, specifically focusing on two selection tests that the plaintiffs asserted were not related to job performance and led to a disproportionate number of African-Americans not being hired. The case focused primarily on the process for determining the tests' ability to predict performance in the jobs for which it was used (Gutman et al., 2011; Outtz, 2011). This process was conducted by a psychologist in less than a day immediately prior to the case going to trial. The psychologist did not conduct a job analysis. Further, each of the focal jobs had a small sample size, so the psychologist combined data across multiple jobs in order to conduct the analyses. The jobs in the same progression line were grouped together, as there was no job analysis data to group jobs more accurately (Outtz, 2011).

The district court level determined that the analyses conducted by the psychologist were sufficient to demonstrate the tests' ability to predict performance. Therefore, the court found that the tests were not in violation of Title VII. The case proceeded to the appeals court, where the original ruling was overturned. The appeals court leveraged the ruling from *Griggs* and the EEOC's guidelines to determine that the process for determining the employment test's relationship with job performance was defective. The case eventually made its way to the Supreme Court, where the appeals court decision was upheld.

This ruling helped clarify the standards for job-relatedness, with the Court placing the employer's process for determining job relatedness under close scrutiny. The Court found that, in this case, it could not be demonstrated or determined exactly what standards supervisors used to rank their subordinates. It also could not be determined that the same standards were being applied across supervisors. Furthermore, the employees who participated in the hastily conducted validation study were not sufficiently diverse and primarily worked in jobs towards the top of the progression line. Counter to the 1970 EEOC guidelines, these participants were not representative of the entry-level job candidate population. Finally, the study was found deficient in several other ways, including failing to explore or consider the possibility of differential validity between different racial groups (Gutman et al., 2011; Hanges et al., 2013; Outtz, 2011).

The Supreme Court's ruling also had important ramifications for expanding the shifting burden of proof. Specifically, the Court's majority opinion stated that it was the employer's burden to demonstrate the job-relatedness of any selection test. If a defendant can present evidence that a practice is job-related, the plaintiff has the opportunity to show the practice was nevertheless a pretext for discrimination. This can be achieved by demonstrating that there are alternative practices that are less discriminatory and would meet the business purposes of the employer (Hanges et al., 2013).

Civil Rights Reform Act 1978

In an attempt to consolidate the numerous EEO enforcement programmes established through various legislative Acts, the Civil Rights Reform Act of 1978 established the EEOC as the primary agency to enforce Title VII, the Equal Pay Act and the Age Discrimination in Employment Act, along with providing for equal employment opportunities for federal employees (Aiken et al., 2013; Hanges et al., 2013).

Wards Cove Packing Company v. Antonio (1989)

Wards Cove Packing Company operated salmon canneries in remote areas of Alaska. Owing to the nature of the work, Wards Cove would hire seasonal employees for the canneries. Seasonal jobs were generally classified into two broad groups: those involving unskilled work on the cannery lines and those considered skilled positions. The majority of the unskilled positions were filled by non-White employees, specifically Alaskan natives and Filipinos, whereas the skilled positions were mostly filled by Whites (Bryan, 1990; Gutman et al., 2011). The plaintiffs in this case argued that the employer's use of hiring and promotion practices, including subjective hiring criteria and nepotism, led to both systematic and individualized discrimination against non-White applicants to the skilled jobs (Bryan, 1990). At the district court level, many of the plaintiffs' allegations were found to be unsupported. Eventually, the case was heard by the Supreme Court, whose opinion stated that it was the plaintiffs' responsibility to demonstrate that selection discrimination was due to a particular employment practice. This decision signified a major shift in the type of evidence plaintiffs were required to provide. Furthermore, the Supreme Court determined that the defendant's burden of proof was to show the employment practice in question met the employer's employment goals, and the defendant did not have to demonstrate the more stringent requirement of the practice's job-relatedness (Hanges et al., 2013).

The Supreme Court then returned the case to the appeals court, where it was determined that the plaintiffs did not provide sufficient evidence of discrimination and ruled in favour of the defendants. This ruling dramatically changed the procedure and standards of evidence applied to discrimination cases by increasing the plaintiff's relative burden of proof (Hanges et al., 2013). As a result, it became the plaintiff's responsibility to demonstrate evidence of illegal discrimination, which might be accomplished through hiring experts in selection to review (Bellenger & Yusko, 2015).

The Civil Rights Act 1991

The Civil Rights Act of 1991, which amended Title VII of the Civil Rights Act 1964, was passed by Congress at least in part as a reaction to the decision made in *Wards Cove Packing Company*. This Act returned much of the burden of proof to the defendant and redefined the meaning of 'business necessity' for selection procedures. Specifically, the legislation restored both the shifting burden of proof and the legal definition of business necessity as decided in *Griggs v. Duke Power Company* (Bellenger & Yusko, 2015).

Furthermore, the Act enabled victims of intentional discrimination to sue for punitive damages in addition to previously sanctioned compensatory damages. In addition, employers were not allowed to create normed scores by adjusting test scores according to subgroups of job candidates (i.e., developing separate scores for groupings based on race, sex, colour, religion or national origin) or use different cut scores for these subgroups. This final provision was of particular importance as it addressed a practice many organizations had been following up to this point. In an attempt to promote diversity in their selection procedures, many organizations had used race norming by creating separate lists of candidates based on demographics and selecting the top candidates from those lists. This practice allowed organizations to select the desired number of candidates from each particular demographic, but did not ensure that the selection procedures being used did not have an adverse impact. As such, this provision addressed a major issue in perceptions of fairness by making race-norming illegal.

Professional Standards for Employment Testing

Throughout the years of civil rights legislation, legislators and experts in selection convened several times to draw up specific standards to guide employers and practitioners in creating fair, legal and valuable selection tools. While some of these standards can be traced back several decades, they remain relevant in guiding legal practices today (Hanges et al., 2013; see Jeanneret and Zedeck, 2010, for a rich discussion of professional standards).

Uniform Guidelines on Employee Selection Procedures (1978)

In combination with the Civil Service Commission (CSC), the Department of Labor (DOL) and the Department of Justice (DOJ), the EEOC published the *Uniform Guidelines on Employee Selection Procedures* (the *Uniform Guidelines*) in 1978. The *Uniform Guidelines* were intended to be a technical guide and resource for employers and court systems to ensure selection procedures adhered to Title VII. The *Uniform Guidelines* were particularly important at the time as they helped document the decisions made from prior Supreme Court decisions and acted as a cohesive expression of EEO policies and procedures (Hanges et al., 2013). The *Uniform Guidelines* focused on two general areas: the extent to which a personnel test results in differences between subgroups (i.e., fosters adverse impact); and the extent to which a personnel test enhances the organization's efficiency or safety. Many of the key concepts and definitions that appear in subsequent employee selection litigation derive from the *Uniform Guidelines*. The *Uniform Guidelines*, therefore, provide a foundation for understanding many of the EEO policies that are still relevant today. However, the *Uniform Guidelines* have not been updated since they were first published, which has led some to question their continuing utility (Hanges et al., 2013; see McDaniel et al., 2011).

Standards for Educational and Psychological Testing

The American Psychology Association (APA) developed its own set of standards which align with and extend the standards outlined in the *Uniform Guidelines* in order to outline best practices for 'test construction, evaluation, documentation (e.g., validity, reliability) and fairness in testing (e.g., language difficulties, disabilities) for all psychological and educational measurement' (Hanges et al., 2013, p. 696). This work was known as the *Standards for Educational and Psychological Testing* (frequently referred to as the *Standards*). Interestingly, the *Standards* were intended for a broad audience, informing test administrators and test-takers on the ethical use of testing procedures. Today, the *Standards* are revised in collaboration with the American Educational Research Association (AERA) and the National Council on Measurement in Education (NCME) (Hanges et al., 2013). The most recent edition was published in 2014 and includes updates on the use of tests in the workplace and the role of technology in testing.

Principles for the Validation and Use of Personnel Selection Procedures

The Society for Industrial-Organizational Psychology (SIOP), a division of the APA, drew up its own standards for employment testing; these are known as the *Principles for the Validation and Use of Personnel Selection Procedures* (known as the *Principles*; most recent edition, 2003). The main goal of the *Principles* is to offer insight from the field of I-O psychology on employment testing and assessment, particularly in relation to validation strategies (Hanges et al., 2013). The *Principles* are a useful guide for those overseeing or conducting a validation study and for those assessing the appropriateness and legal vulnerability of a selection process (Jeanneret & Zedeck, 2010).

While the *Uniform Guidelines* focus on legal regulations, the *Standards* and *Principles* are intended to offer more technical and professional support for those developing, implementing, and assessing selection procedures (Jeanneret & Zedeck, 2010). The three documents are different from each other in their specificity and intended audience, but each provides uniquely valuable information for the development of selection processes. However, it is important for test developers and administrators to understand that the documents should not be seen as an administrative checklist. Rather, they should be understood as providing professional benchmarks for legal selection procedures and must be applied on the basis of sound professional judgement. Both the *Standards* and *Principles* have been updated several times to incorporate advances made in research on employment test fairness and utility. While it is essential to understand the legal requirements governing selection, it is equally important to balance the regulatory requirements against current research and what an employer's selection process intends (Jeanneret & Zedeck, 2010).

It is important to recognize that I-O psychology is in its infancy in many countries outside the US; therefore, similar guidelines and professional standards are not always accessible in those countries. For example, while the Romanian government offers some training opportunities on employment discrimination legislation, there are no guidelines to ensure consistent application of the law (Cozma & Woehr, 2008). However, some countries have adopted principles similar to those established in the US. In South Africa, which has only recently begun to implement anti-discrimination laws, the Society of Industrial and Organizational Psychology of South Africa (SIOPSA) has adopted many of SIOP's *Principles* (Myors et al., 2008b). While the standards applied by any country must be consistent with its laws and practices, all countries, including the US, should look to best practices from beyond their borders.

Legacy of Civil Rights Legislation

It is impossible to refute the significance of civil rights legislation, nevertheless there are disparate viewpoints about its impact. King and colleagues (2013) identified three perspectives regarding the legacy of the Civil Rights Act and subsequent legislation. The first viewpoint suggests that the legislation, while not eliminating discrimination altogether, has been successful in at least reducing it and has essentially done what it was supposed to do. The second viewpoint is that despite trying to protect civil rights, civil rights legislation is inappropriate, misguided and itself discriminatory by favouring diversity over hiring those who will perform best in a job. The third viewpoint is that legislation has not gone far enough to address discrimination in selection. Proponents of this last perspective suggest that civil rights legislation and the bodies that enforce them are too narrowly tailored to traditional subgroups and, in any case, are not given the power necessary to impose the law effectively. In addition, this perspective holds that legislation has not progressed and therefore misses subtler forms of discrimination as the nature of prejudice and discrimination has changed over time. Offerman and colleagues (2014), for example, found that people who held more 'colour-blind' attitudes (i.e., who believe race does and/or should not matter) were less likely to perceive subtle forms of discrimination than those with less colour-blind attitudes. This is of particular importance as some have begun to argue for a colour-blind approach to selection to make procedures equally fair for all races. If colour-blindness is associated with overlooking discrimination, a colour-blind approach to selection could lead to more discrimination in hiring, the opposite of what its proponents suggest it should.

In reality, all three perspectives have some validity and therefore have a bearing on legislation for selection systems. While there is no consensus among selection experts on the three perspectives, in order to make progress in the civil rights arena it is important for their proponents to acknowledge opposing views and guide future attempts to address discrimination in hiring practices (King et al. 2013).

Legal Concepts Related to Discrimination

There have been some changes in the way scholars and practitioners discuss discrimination, but much of the language and processes used in legal proceedings around discrimination in selection processes still comes from the *Uniform Guidelines*, which identified two forms of discrimination: disparate treatment and adverse (disparate) impact.

Disparate treatment

Disparate treatment occurs when a job applicant from a protected class is treated differently from other applicants during the selection process. Specifically, when an applicant from a protected class applies and is qualified for a job, yet is rejected and the employer continues to look for a new hire without adjusting their qualifications, or hires someone else with the same or lower qualifications, there is evidence of disparate treatment. The key features of disparate treatment are that it can apply to a single person or a small group of people, and that it relates to an intentional difference in treatment because of membership in a protected class. Disparate treatment differs from the second form of discrimination.

Adverse (disparate) impact

Adverse impact (also referred to as disparate impact) pertains to situations where an organization treats all applicants equally (e.g., administers everyone the same tests in the same way) throughout the hiring process, but the process yields differential outcomes according to subgroup (e.g., racial, gender, religious). If this occurs, even if there is no intent to discriminate, the personnel procedure results in a disparate impact on a subgroup. If the subgroup constitutes a protected class, there may be important legal ramifications for the organization and affected class. Adverse impact provides prima facie evidence of discrimination.

Identifying adverse impact   Several techniques can be used to determine if the differences between subgroups are substantial enough to justify labelling them as adverse impact. Perhaps the best known is the four-fifths or 80% rule. The four-fifths rule has been codified in the *Uniform Guidelines* as a possible guideline for establishing adverse impact. Based on the rule, adverse impact is present when the selection ratio for a minority group is less than 80% of the selection ratio in the comparison majority group. For example, assume 10 White applicants take a selection test, and 5 Black applicants take the same test. All 10 of the White applicants pass and are offered a hire, compared to 3 of the Black applicants. Therefore, the hiring rate for White applicants (the majority group in this example) is 100%, whereas the hiring rate for Black applicants (the minority group in this example) is 60%. The minority/majority ratio hiring rates are 0.60/1.00, or 0.60. Since 0.60 is less than 0.80, adverse impact would be considered evident in this example under the four-fifths rule.

While Whites and/or males are often the majority group in these comparisons, they could in some circumstances be considered as the minority group. While there are protected classes of individuals under Title VII (e.g., race, gender), there are no specific subgroups (e.g., Blacks, women) that are considered as always favoured or discriminated against. Therefore, the majority and minority classification in adverse impact analyses vary and are based on the composition of the job, organization or industry (Hanges et al., 2013).

The four-fifths rule is frequently used to identify adverse impact and is easily understood, particularly by practitioners. However, there is evidence that it leads to false-positive indications of adverse impact (Roth, Bobko & Switzer, 2006). In addition, the four-fifths rule is strongly influenced by the way the test is used (e.g., how severe the cut score or fail point is).

Fortunately, there are other ways to identify adverse impact. The *Uniform Guidelines* reference using statistical tests to identify adverse impact, though the *Guidelines* also stress the need to have an adequate sample size. While many types of statistical analysis might be used to identify adverse impact, Fisher's exact test, the chi-square test and the Z test for difference in proportions are the most frequently implemented techniques (Hanges et al., 2013). Murphy and Jacobs (2012) also argue for the use of effect sizes, such as standardized difference and the percentage of variance explained, as indicators of adverse impact that do not rely on statistical significance testing to make this determination. This recommendation fits with best practices in academia as effect sizes help clarify the magnitude of an effect above and beyond its statistical significance.

Using more than one type of adverse impact test (e.g., using the four-fifths rule, an effect size estimate and a statistical significance test) can help reduce the number of false-positives and provide more context to the presence or absence of adverse impact. The rich information provided by multiple types of adverse impact tests is important for those making decisions in the legal process as it offers a more detailed understanding of the test and its potential effects on protected groups. Because these statistical tests do not overcome some of the problems that can also create challenges for the four-fifths rule, such as small sample sizes, they should not be seen as replacements for the four-fifths rule or other adverse impact tests, but rather as complementary to them.

These methods for identifying adverse impact are established by guidelines and enforcement agencies in the US, but other countries often do not specify how adverse impact should be demonstrated (Sackett et al., 2010). Within the European Union alone a number of member states allow for statistical tests as an indicator of adverse impact whereas others may perceive the same tests to be unacceptable or insufficient (Hanges & Feinberg, 2010).

Regardless of how adverse impact is measured, it is important to recognize that evidence of adverse impact is not a feature of the test, but a feature of how the test is being used in a given context. A test may cause adverse impact for one job in a specific context but not for other jobs or the same job in different contexts. Using a given test in combination with other selection tools or with cut scores will impact the percentage of people passing the test, which in turn will influence pass rates for different subgroups. Therefore, tests of adverse impact need to be understood in relation to both the features of the test itself and how it is being applied in a specific context (Hanges et al., 2013).

It is important to remember that establishing a prima facie case for adverse impact does not mean a test is discriminatory. As discussed above, in most countries there is a shifting burden of proof that must be addressed by plaintiffs and defendants in turn (Sackett et al., 2010). A plaintiff meets the burden of production requirement to show that discrimination may exist by presenting evidence of disparate treatment or adverse impact. It then falls to the defendant to demonstrate a burden of persuasion. That is, the defendant has to show that a qualified applicant was not hired for non-discriminatory reasons in a disparate treatment case or show that the selection tool that was used is job-related and meets the organization's business necessity in an adverse impact case (Hanges et al., 2013). Finally, if the defendant establishes the job-relatedness of the test in question, the burden of proof shifts back to the plaintiff. In this final step, the plaintiff must offer alternative selection procedures that show reduced adverse impact but equivalent job-relatedness.

In summary, the *Uniform Guidelines* outline two forms of discrimination – disparate treatment and disparate (adverse) impact – which may be seen in an employment context. Demonstrating disparate treatment requires showing that a member or members of a protected group were treated differently from other applicants in a way that disadvantaged them. Demonstrating adverse impact requires showing that the same personnel process applied consistently across applicants results in differential outcomes for individuals from different protected groups. Various measures can be used to assess adverse impact, including the four-fifths rule, statistical significance tests and effect size measures. Ideally, multiple measures are used to provide triangulation of adverse impact evidence. Finally, adverse impact cases rely on the shifting burden of proof model, where the plaintiff must first establish adverse impact, followed by the defendant establishing the job-relatedness of a personnel procedure and concluding with the plaintiff suggesting alternatives that show less adverse impact but serve the business's purpose. Next, we provide an overview of a key component of the defendants' arguments establishing job-relatedness: the psychometric properties of the test.

Psychometric Properties

In establishing the job-relatedness of a testing process, defendants must pay particular attention to the psychometric properties of their selection tools. There are several important factors that employers should focus on when demonstrating the job-relatedness of their tests, much of which is outlined in the various professional standards for employment testing.

Reliability

Reliability concerns the amount of random error variance in a set of test scores. In other words, observed test scores are in some part a 'true score' (what the test is designed to measure) and in some part an error (both systematic and random). Estimates of reliability specifically assess random error, with the expectation that the less variance in test scores can be attributed to random error, the more it can be attributed to true score. Thus, estimates of reliability concern the test's precision, or consistency, in producing results. This consistency in turn sets limits on the validity (or job-relatedness) of a test. Specifically, a test cannot be job-related (i.e., valid) if it is not first shown to be reliable. For employment tests, it is practically impossible to remove all random errors; there will always be some discrepancies between the assessment of a candidate's potential and the candidate's true potential.

Because selection tests cannot be entirely free of random errors, rank-ordered test scores are unlikely to produce a perfect rank order in the ability or knowledge a test is designed to measure. To accommodate for random error in measurement, researchers have proposed using test bands to determine groups of candidates who are expected to be interchangeable, or near- interchangeable, on their true scores (Cascio, Outtz, Zedeck & Goldstein, 1991). Test bands utilize a test's reliability to create a standard error of difference (SED). The SED is then used to specify bands such that all candidates within a band may overlap, and hence not differ, in their true potential.

Although candidates are first rank-ordered in order to establish bands, hiring in a banding approach is then conducted using a secondary criterion (e.g., randomly) within bands rather than starting with the top-ranked candidate. Thus, the banding approach is an alternative to simply hiring in a top-down fashion. Because of the potential imprecision in ranking one candidate over another if there is error in a test, test banding minimizes the potential negative effects of a test's 'unreliability'. This can be particularly valuable from a diversity standpoint. When using test bands, more minorities can be included in the top group for hiring and therefore have a greater chance of being hired. For example, if the top two-ranked candidates are both White, but the two candidates ranked directly below them are Black, a test band including all four candidates will result in an increased chance of the two Black candidates receiving initial offers.

As such, employers can improve diversity in their hiring without utilizing subgroup norming, which is prohibited by the Civil Rights Act of 1991. Test banding is a relatively recent development and remains a controversial strategy (for reviews, see Bobko & Roth, 2004; Campion et al., 2001). While test banding generally has been upheld in the courts for selection procedures when decisions were not based solely on race (e.g., *Chicago Fire-fighters v. City of Chicago*, 2001; *San Francisco Fire Fighters Local 798 v. San Francisco*, 2006), it has yet to be reviewed by the Supreme Court. Furthermore, test banding has been found to be improper in other contexts, such as promotions (*Massachusetts Association of Minority Law Enforcement Officers v. Gerald T. Abban and Others*, 2001). Therefore, its use and how decisions will be made within bands must be considered and reviewed carefully before implementation (Hanges et al., 2013).

Appropriateness of inferences: Test validity

In most countries the burden of persuasion for the defendant in an adverse impact case centres on the need to demonstrate the business necessity of a selection process. While the notion of providing evidence of the test's job-relatedness is consistent across most countries, the evidence is often not specified (Sackett et al., 2010). An exception is found in the US where an employer must establish validity, or the appropriateness of inferences resulting from their selection process, to demonstrate job-relatedness. Validation is important for any assessment – selection processes specifically – as it involves providing empirical data to demonstrate that the inferences made from a test are appropriate. In the selection context validation efforts might focus on demonstrating that a test is an accurate predictor of performance on a job. Much like adverse impact, validity is not a feature of a test, but refers to the use of a test in a particular context. A test's application may be more or less appropriate for assessing candidates depending on the goals of the testing process. For example, a test of computer programming may be a valid predictor of performance for a software engineer but will not be a valid predictor of performance for a kindergarten teacher. The very same test may not even be a good predictor of performance for software engineers in different organizations depending on the content of the job and the content of the test.

While there is often agreement between the *Uniform Guidelines, Standards* and *Principles*, in some situations these professional standards diverge, for example, in how the documents codify validity. The *Uniform Guidelines* have been interpreted as specifying three types of validity – criterion, construct and content – with each considered to be a different kind of validity requiring its own type of evidence, and with each seen as most appropriate only in certain situations. On the other hand, the *Principles* and the *Standards* consider validity to be a unitary construct with each of the three strategies supporting validity in a different way (see Landy, 1986). The three discrete validities of the *Guidelines* and the three strategies of the *Principles* and *Standards* are in fact the same, and therefore many of the principles for validation overlap across these documents. However, there are differences in how validity is treated in the documents given these different frames, and these have implications for employers and their validation processes. Here, our description of validity leans towards the *Guidelines*' interpretations, as they are the ones most frequently cited in court proceedings (see Jeanneret, 2005); however, we encourage readers to review the *Standards* and *Principles* for a more comprehensive understanding of validity issues.

Generalizing validity evidence

In addition to discussing the three types of validity described above, the *Guidelines* address the potential for a validity transportability procedure (Biddle & Nooren, 2006). In this process, evidence of validity in one employment context is 'imported' from another employment context. A caveat here is that the *Guidelines* describe transportability as utilizing the evidence of the same test in different contexts (Hanges et al., 2013). Several requirements must be met for transportability to be supported as appropriate. These requirements include: 1) job similarity in the two work contexts in relation to work behaviours, as demonstrated by a job analysis; 2) validity evidence for the test should meet the requirements outlined in the *Guidelines*; and 3) the test must demonstrate fairness for protected groups (Equal Employment Opportunity Commission, Civil Service Commission, Department of Labor & Department of Justice, 1978).

While the *Guidelines* speak directly to transportability, the *Standards* and *Principles* describe the broader concept of validity generalization. Validity generalization studies directly examine the robustness of validity inferences made from other contexts, including environments, jobs and even tests (Hanges et al., 2013). This process can be done through multiple techniques, including the use of meta-analysis and synthetic validity. A meta-analysis is a process in which the results of multiple studies are aggregated to examine the overall ability of a selection test to predict performance across contexts. As such, when a test has high average validity across contexts, there is no need to demonstrate the validity of the test in a specific context. Even when a meta-analysis supports the validity of a given test across contexts, there should still be evidence of the similarity in job requirements at the local level, as well as evidence of similarity in job requirements of those jobs involved in the meta-analysis (Schmitt & Sinha, 2011). Further complicating the issue of validity generalization, case law to date seems to both support and refute the use of validity generalization using meta-analysis. For that reason, Landy (2003) suggests supplementing the use of meta-analyses with transportability analyses and ensuring that a proper and detailed job analysis is conducted.

Similarly, synthetic validity (also referred to as job component validity) is a process for inferring the validity of a selection test or set of tests in a particular situation based on the elements of a job (Johnson et al., 2010). This process is most often used when an employer does not have enough incumbents to conduct a criterion validity study for a particular job or set of jobs. In this case, a group of jobs is analysed based on the key components of those jobs, including their tasks and work behaviours as determined by a job analysis. Tests are then selected that are expected to predict the key components of those jobs. Finally, the relationship between these job components and the predictor tests is estimated (Scherbaum, 2005). A test battery can then be built using the validity inferences of the job components and predictors.

Synthetic validity overcomes the issue of small incumbent sample sizes by aggregating the same job components across different jobs. While synthetic validity has many benefits, including providing stable validity estimates and enabling mass production of tests, there are still legal risks (Johnson et al., 2010). So far just two court cases have addressed synthetic validity and neither gave a direct endorsement of the procedure. However, the legal risks associated with synthetic validation are inherent in most types of validity generalization. Therefore, employers must examine the limitations they have for estimating validity coefficients and determine whether a validity generalization approach that uses best practices, as outlined in the *Principles* and *Standards*, is the best route for them.

Post-validation considerations

After demonstrating the job-relatedness of a selection process through validation procedures, and convincing the judge that the selection process is indeed job-related, the burden of proof shifts back to the plaintiff(s). At this point it is their responsibility to demonstrate that the employment practice is a pretext for discrimination. This can be done by providing evidence of other selection processes that are equally valid and result in less adverse impact (Hanges et al., 2013).

An International Perspective on Employment Discrimination

The US has a long and varied history of legislation and case law that addresses discrimination in selection processes. This has led to considerable detail in the regulations and oversight created to combat discrimination. However, some have referred to the US as an outlier in these laws and practices compared to the rest of the international community (Dunleavy, Cohen, Aamodt & Schaeffer, 2008). In fact, the legal environment is seen as having a substantial impact on employee selection practices in only a few other countries (e.g., Canada and South Africa; Sackett et al., 2010). In particular, the US and other countries differ in terms of who is considered a member of a protected group, the use of legislation for promoting preferential treatment and the enforcement of the laws. We therefore present a brief overview of some of the key trends in how other countries approach anti-discrimination legislation for selection practices.

To date, Sackett and colleagues (2010) have provided the most comprehensive review of the legal context in other countries. They demonstrate that most countries have some form of law or directive that explicitly prohibits discrimination, though these may be no more than general statements against discrimination and do not specifically address selection processes. Despite enacted legislation, there is a dearth of concrete guidelines on how to establish that discrimination has occurred and what kind of evidence is required to support a discrimination charge. Very few cases outside the US challenging the adverse impact or discriminatory nature of formal tests exist and therefore most countries rarely rely on validity evidence to refute discrimination. In fact, most countries do not even require evidence of validity (Sackett et al., 2010). In many places, the empirical validity of assessment instruments is implicitly assumed. To address a discrimination claim, organizations typically offer qualitative evidence of job-relatedness or bona fide occupational requirement. In any event, punishment following an adverse ruling can be rather light (Sackett et al., 2010).

While there is consistency in condemning discrimination, the groups that are protected differ greatly across countries. Often the protected groups of a nation are directly tied to its history and frequently address the disadvantages of indigenous people or immigrants (Sackett et al., 2010). For example, many EU member states have experienced an unbroken influx of migrants over the past several decades (e.g., Hanges & Feinberg, 2010; Laczko, 2001). In many of these countries, immigrants experience high unemployment rates and struggle to move beyond blue-collar positions (Myors et al., 2008b). Therefore, these countries need to address a much broader range of national and ethnic groups than legislation in the US does, increasing the complexity of case law and enforcement in those countries (Myors et al., 2008a).

Examples of disadvantaged groups include immigrants, First Nation people and Francophones in Canada; Indigenous Australians in Australia; Pacific peoples and Maori in New Zealand; Black people (who constitute a disadvantaged minority), mixed-race individuals and Indians in South Africa; Taiwanese aborigines in Taiwan; certain Hindu castes in India; and religious minorities and Kurds in Turkey.

In terms of specific protected classes, in the US these include race, sex, national/ethnic origin, colour, age, religion and disability. In addition to the classes, many countries include sexual orientation (e.g., France, Germany, South Africa), political opinion (e.g., New Zealand, Belgium, Israel), and marital or family status (e.g., Chile, Taiwan, the UK) (Sackett et al., 2010).

In their survey of 22 countries, Sackett and colleagues (2010) demonstrate that most of the countries they sampled afforded protections to 7–9 of these 10 categories. South Africa and New Zealand cover all 10, Canada covers all categories except religion and Kenya covers all categories except age, while Germany covers six of the categories but not colour, age, political opinion and family or marital status. In addition to some or all of the categories, many countries protect classes such as breastfeeding mothers, having an irrelevant criminal record and physical features (Australia), social status (Japan), lower castes (India), union membership (Chile), moral principles and genetic characteristics (France) and personal status and military service (Israel) (for a more complete list, see Sackett et al., 2010).

The US also differs from most other countries in its use of quotas and other preferential treatments. As set out in legislation, notably the Civil Rights Act of 1991, employers are not allowed to use quotas, within-group norming or separate cut scores for protected groups. However, there are numerous countries that not only promote preferential treatment but require it. Japan, France, Kenya and Korea have quotas for disabled employees, Taiwan requires a certain number of employees in an organization to be aborigines and South Africa promotes the use of racial quotas (Sackett et al., 2010). Beyond these practices, many countries have some form of preferential treatment, ranging from relaxing qualifying scores for protected groups to utilizing within-group cut-off scores (Sackett et al., 2010). Clearly, there is a fairly large divide between the use of preferential treatment in the US and other countries.

While many countries have passed legislation to protect people from discrimination, it is evident that without implementation its effectiveness is threatened. Even in the US the enforcement of selection legislation has been turbulent, with long periods of inactivity. However, some countries suffer difficulties in enforcing legislation due to the absence of case law and agencies like the EEOC to support their application. Praslova (2008) notes that while Russia has many protected classes, it lacks enforcement practices. This results in many recruitment advertisements not adhering to the country's laws regarding selection and hiring practices. Compounding this is the fact that most Russians do not believe it is possible to prove discrimination and that the courts are more likely to side with the employers. Similarly, in Romania the implementation of laws related to selection are seen as problematic as employment decisions are frequently based on organizational directives rather than the law (Cozma & Woehr, 2008). This speaks to the importance of not evaluating the progress of a country on its legislation alone, but on its enforcement of the law too.

The differences in how countries treat protected groups, legislation covering preferential treatment and the enforcement of those laws are influenced by a multitude of factors. Dunleavy and colleagues (2008) proposed a model in which a country's Zeitgeist, which includes its moral, intellectual and cultural climate, influences the legal protections, professional guidelines, enforcement and case law for selection procedures. Others have proposed that societal factors, such as cultural values (Hanges & Feinberg, 2010) and economic conditions (Myors et al., 2008a), may similarly influence a country's legal atmosphere for selection. Due to the large variation in these factors, it is important to acknowledge that no one system of laws and practices will fit all countries perfectly. While the US is often used as a reference point in the selection literature, it is important to understand how some practices do not exist in other countries and may even be detrimental in those contexts. Similarly, we should be aware that other countries may apply standards that the US should still strive for when the introduction of new laws is being considered.

Adverse impact in the US and EU

Hanges and Feinberg (2010) note that despite the substantive differences between the US and other countries in many facets of discrimination, understandings of its of adverse impact in the EU and US are similar (though one needs to bear in mind that member states of the EU may differ from each other on discrimination issues). This includes construing adverse impact as involving negative consequences or outcomes for minority groups and the use of statistical data to establish a claim. As in the US, when adverse impact is found the burden of proof is borne by the defendant, who must then demonstrate that the practice in question is valid (Hanges & Feinberg, 2010).

Differences include the EU countries tending to cover more protected groups and not setting out specific rules or guidelines to assess adverse impact (e.g., the four-fifths rule or statistical procedures establishing adverse impact) (Hanges & Feinberg, 2010).

Current Legal Issues in Employee Selection

Ricci v. DeStefano (2009)

Despite decades of litigation and federal regulatory efforts, employment discrimination cases are still commonplace. In this respect, *Ricci v. DeStefano* (2009) is one high-profile case that demonstrates this.

In this action, the New Haven Fire Department was administering a promotional test which no Black/African-American employee had passed. Even though there was no clear evidence of a technical issue or problem with the test, New Haven invalidated it on the basis of potential liability due to its disparate impact. The Supreme Court then ruled for the plaintiffs, a group of White and Hispanic candidates who passed the test but were not promoted, on the basis that there was demonstrated evidence of validity and that the city did not have a 'strong basis in evidence' that it would have created liability by promoting the White and Hispanic candidates.

Many selection practitioners were frustrated that the Supreme Court had failed to consider the use of alternative measures that would have been available to the department. While there was some evidence of validity for the existing test, there might have been equally valid measures that could have fostered greater diversity among the group that passed, and if diversity was valued by the Fire Department, they might have chosen one of those alternatives. Another interesting issue arising from this ruling was that the disparate impact due to race was apparently an insufficient reason to abandon the use of the test. This, along with other recent rulings by the Supreme Court regarding affirmative action programmes, suggests that a more colour-blind viewpoint is being adopted by the Court and that efforts designed to increase workplace representation are being viewed differently from those in previous decades (Bellenger & Yusko, 2015).

One outcome of the case was for many employers to reconsider test-weighting strategies. Prior to *Ricci*, employers sometimes considered multiple methods of weighting test items and exercises, then, given equal validities, selected the method that produced the most diversity among the pool of successful candidates. After the Supreme Court's ruling, some jurisdictions determined that they could no longer follow such a weighting procedure due to concerns about making a race-based decision *after* the test had been scored. Practitioners should monitor such rulings to ensure that they do not put their organization at risk (Bellenger & Yusko, 2015).

Some have argued that cases such as this represent a more colour-blind approach on the part of the courts or, more extremely, a general mindset among Whites that there is an anti-White bias. Consistent with this perspective, Norton and Sommers (2011) found that Whites perceive an anti-White bias more than they do an anti-Black bias. This may have important implications for EEO cases going forward. Specifically, there is the potential for greater conflict between affirmative action policies and anti-discrimination laws (Thompson & Morris, 2013).

Equal employment opportunities and lesbian, gay, bisexual and transgender rights

Lesbian, gay, bisexual and transgender (LGBT) rights have become an important and prominent movement in today's world. Over the past several decades there has been ever-more discussion about LGBT issues in employment. In Australia, Belgium, Korea and South Africa sexual orientation is already considered a protected class (Sackett et al., 2010). Currently, LGBT individuals in the US do not have explicit federal protection under Title VII, leaving them vulnerable in many employment situations. Legislation has been introduced to mitigate this. For example, the Employment Non-Discrimination Act is a long-gestating piece of legislation intended to prohibit discrimination in selection based on sexual orientation or gender identity by organizations that have at least 15 employees. However, the law has not yet passed both the House of Representatives and Senate since it was first introduced in 1994. Recently, many pro-LGBT groups have withdrawn their support for the bill as it has been amended to allow for broad religious exemptions. In April 2015, President Obama signed an executive order prohibiting discrimination by federal contractors based on sexual orientation or gender identity.

Recently, the EEOC has begun to file lawsuits and amicus curiae briefs in LGBT discrimination cases under Title VII by classifying them as sex-based discrimination. In these cases the argument has been made that employees targeted for their gender nonconformity or gender reassignment can be protected under Title VII. However, there are difficulties in making these arguments and providing adequate evidence of discrimination. As such, there is still a call for comprehensive legislation that protects LGBT employees much like Title VII protects other classes.

'Ban the box' initiatives

Much as sexual orientation has become a protected class in some countries, some countries, Australia and Korea, for example, have begun to protect applicants with irrelevant criminal records (Sackett et al., 2010). In the US, advocacy groups have been seeking additional protections for ex-offenders during the selection process. These groups have been calling for employers to delay asking candidates if they have a criminal history until later in the application process, often once a conditional offer has been made. Such campaigns are known as 'ban the box' initiatives (in reference to the check box on employment applications regarding a candidate's prior criminal history) and have gained ground in the last few years. The first ban the box initiative was passed in Hawaii in 1998 and it has been adopted in other states since then. At the time of writing, 15 states have passed such legislation, with several more pursuing similar bills. Furthermore, President Obama has called for similar legislation for federal employment.

Individual cities and employers, such as Target, have implemented similar policies. The intention of this initiative is to reduce the impact of potential biases against people with a criminal history by allowing employers to have more information about the applicant's skills and qualifications rather than focusing on their conviction status (D'Alessio, Stolzenberg & Flexon, 2015). This can have many benefits, among them successfully reintegrating ex-offenders into society and reducing the number of repeat offenders (D'Alessio et al., 2014). While this initiative helps all ex-offenders, there is evidence suggesting that Blacks with a criminal record struggle more than White ex-offenders to get a job interview (Pager, Western & Sugie, 2009), highlighting the initiative's importance for reducing detrimental selection procedures for minorities.

Educating those outside the I-O field

While it is not a uniquely contemporary issue for I-O, psychologists working in this field strive to educate others in best practices and recommendations for employment selection. Despite decades of outreach on their part, research-supported best practice remains under-utilized and underappreciated. Drew and Viswesvaran (2013) found that many of the best adverse impact reduction strategies according to research are seen as only moderately influential on legal outcomes. They call for I-O psychologists to communicate more with major stakeholders, including the EEOC, about their findings and recommendations. Furthermore, Arthur, Doverspike, Barrett and Miguel (2013) caution I-O psychologists against setting highly aggressive goals for organizations to reduce adverse impact. Specifically, it is important to keep goals realistic. It may not be possible to eliminate or even reduce adverse impact in an organization immediately. However, I-O psychologists can leverage extensive resources and research to develop valid and legally defensible selection tools over time. As such, and whether working internally or as consultants to an organization, I-O psychologists must draft agreements with employers that set out clear expectations about what can be done using the best practices and recommendations from the field.

Future Research

Differences in the legal context for selection across countries present challenges that future research can help address. First, employers of companies with locations in more than one country need to understand how the laws and regulations governing selection in each of the countries where staff are employed. At present the amount of systematic comparative information across individual countries' legal systems is scant. Additionally, if an employer staffs a location with both local and expatriate staff, from fairness, legal and business perspectives, the employer will need to manage differences in how those employees are treated and will need to be deeply attentive to the culture of the organization. If employees are hired using different systems according to their status, these differences may cultivate disparate organizational cultures. If employees are hired using the same selection system, the employer must ensure that the selection system is appropriate given all the laws, rules and regulations that pertain in each country. The impact of such approaches is at present poorly understood.

Other implications for research focus on differences in the legal context for selection across countries. First, as discussed in this chapter, some countries do not require that tests be validated (Sackett et al., 2010). How do the outcomes of tests that are not validated compare to the outcomes of those that are? Is adverse impact higher or lower for these tests? Does not requiring tests to be validated lead to differences in who is selected and so lead to differences not only in organizational performance, but also in organizational culture.

Considering selection in an international context also opens up the possibility of exploring questions the predominant Western viewpoint in I-O psychology has overlooked.

For example, when thinking about the outcomes of selection systems, research in the US typically focuses on performance outcomes. There may be other outcomes, or other ways of looking at performance, that might be desirable elsewhere. For example, in collectivistic cultures performance outcomes may be more relevant at the team or organizational level rather than at the individual level. Or perhaps issues of fit become a more important outcome depending on the cultural context. Finally, our understanding of validity and adverse impact for types of selection tests is largely grounded in Western research. Measures of personality, cognitive ability, biodata, and so on may have divergent validities in different countries. Research in other countries on outcomes of different kinds of selection measure may highlight marked differences across countries in the strategies that would result in the fairest and most appropriate selection systems.

Conclusion

Employment litigation can be a frustrating and painful process for all parties involved. Even when a good selection system is challenged, organizations may suffer serious distractions from their regular operations, bear heavy court costs and other litigation expenses, and be subjected to negative public opinion and image problems. When a poorly designed system is challenged the costs can be even greater, including missed opportunities to capitalize on the many advantages of a diverse and competent workforce, damage to the organization's culture, punitive penalties and redress expenses, as well as the personal costs to those against whom the organization may be discriminating.

Given the financial and organizational costs of employment litigation, it is simply good business practice to abide by the law and invest in high-quality selection processes. This chapter is designed to lay out a path for organizations so that they can avoid the pitfalls and landmines of employment litigation and put themselves in a better position to improve their hiring procedures and, ideally, escape avoidable litigation.

References

Aiken, J. R., Salmon, E. D., & Hanges, P. J. (2013). The origins and legacy of the Civil Rights Act of 1964. *Journal of Business and Psychology, 28*(4), 383–399.

Arthur Jr., W., Doverspike, D., Barrett, G. V., & Miguel, R. (2013). Chasing the Title VII Holy Grail: The pitfalls of guaranteeing adverse impact elimination. *Journal of Business and Psychology, 28*(4), 473–485.

Bellenger, B. L., & Yusko, K.P. (2015). Legal issues in employee selection: Negotiating the obstacles and avoiding the landmines. *In* R. R. Sims, W. J. Sauser, R. R. Sims & W. J. Sauser (Eds.), *Legal and Regulatory Issues in Human Resources Management* (pp. 117–135). Charlotte, NC: Information Age Publishing.

Biddle, D. A., & Nooren, P. M. (2006). Validity generalization vs. Title VII: Can employers successfully defend tests without conducting local validation studies? *Labor Law Journal, 57,* 216–237.

Bobko, P., & Roth, P. L. (2004). The four-fifths rule for assessing adverse impact: An arithmetic, intuitive, and logical analysis of the rule and implications for future research and practice. In J. Martocchio (Ed.), *Research in personnel and human resources management* (Vol. 23, pp. 177–198). New York: Elsevier.

Bridgeport Guardians, Inc. v. City of Bridgeport, 933 F. 2d 1140 (1991).

Bryan, J. S. (1990). Shifting the burdens in disparate impact cases: *Wards Cove Packing v. Atonio. Labor Lawyer,* 6233–6249.

Campion, M. A., Outtz, J. L., Zedeck, S., Schmidt, F. L., Kehoe, J. F., Murphy, K. R., & Guion, R. M. (2001). The controversy over score banding in personnel selection: Answers to 10 key questions. *Personnel Psychology, 54*, 149–185.

Cascio, W. F., Outtz, J., Zedeck, S., & Goldstein, I. L. (1991). Statistical implications of six methods of test score use in personnel selection. *Human Performance, 4*(4), 233.

Chicago Firefighters v. City of Chicago, 249 F. 3d 649 (2001).

Cozma, I., & Woehr, D. (2008). International perspectives on the legal environment for selection: Romania case. *Industrial and Organizational Psychology: Perspectives on Science and Practice, 1*(2), 260–263.

D'Alessio, S., Stolzenberg, L., & Flexon, J. (2015). The effect of Hawaii's ban the box law on repeat offending. *American Journal of Criminal Justice, 40*(2), 336–352.

Drew, E. N., & Viswesvaran, C. (2013). Lost in translation: Disparate impact reduction strategies and legal stakeholders. *Industrial & Organizational Psychology, 6*(4), 463–466.

Dunleavy, E. M., Cohen, D. B., Aamodt, M. G., & Schaeffer, P. (2008). A consideration of international differences in the legal context of selection. *Industrial and Organizational Psychology: Perspectives on Science and Practice, 1*(2), 247–254.

Equal Employment Opportunity Commission, Civil Service Commission, Department of Labor, & Department of Justice. (1978). Adoption by four agencies of *Uniform Guidelines* on employee selection procedures. *Federal Register, 43*, 38290–38315.

Guion, R. M. (2011). *Assessment, Measurement, and Prediction for Personnel Decisions*. Hove: Taylor & Francis.

Guion, R. M., & Highhouse, S. (2006). *Essentials of Personnel Assessment and Selection*. New York: Psychology Press.

Gutman, A. (2008). Legal environment for selection in the United States. *Industrial and Organizational Psychology: Perspectives on Science and Practice, 1*(2), 255–257.

Gutman, A., Koppes, L. L., & Vodanovich, S. J. (2011). *EEO Law and Personnel Practices* (3rd ed.). New York: Psychology Press.

Hanges, P. J., & Feinberg, E. G. (2010). International perspectives on adverse impact: Europe and beyond. *In* J. L. Outtz (Ed.), *Adverse Impact: Implications for Organizational Staffing and High Stakes Selection* (pp. 349–373). New York: Routledge/Taylor & Francis Group.

Hanges, P. J., Salmon, E. D., & Aiken, J. R. (2013). Legal issues in industrial testing and assessment. *In* K. F. Geisinger, B. A. Bracken, J. F. Carlson, J. C. Hansen, N. R. Kuncel, S. P. Reise, & M. C. Rodriguez (Eds.), *APA Handbook of Testing and Assessment in Psychology, Vol. 1: Test Theory and Testing and Assessment in Industrial and Organizational Psychology* (pp. 693–711). Washington, DC: American Psychological Association.

Jeanneret, A. (2005). Professional and technical authorities and guidelines. *In* F. J. Landy (Ed.), *Employment Discrimination Litigation: Behavioral, Quantitative, and Legal Perspectives* (pp. 47–100). San Francisco: Jossey-Bass.

Jeanneret, P. R., & Zedeck, S. (2010). Professional guidelines/standards. *In* J. L. Farr & N. T. Tippins, (Eds.), *Handbook of Employee Selection* (pp. 593–625). New York: Routledge/Taylor & Francis Group.

Johnson, J. W., Steel, P., Scherbaum, C. A., Hoffman, C. C., Jeanneret, P. R., & Foster, J. (2010). Validation is like motor oil: Synthetic is better. *Industrial & Organizational Psychology, 3*(3), 305–328.

Jones, J. E. (1977). The development of modern equal employment opportunity and affirmative action law: A brief chronological overview. *Harvard Law Journal, 20*, 74–99.

King, E. B., Avery, D. R., & Sackett, P. (2013). Editorial: Three perspectives of employment discrimination 50 years after the Civil Rights Act – A promise fulfilled? *Journal of Business and Psychology, 28*(4), 375–382.

Laczko, F. (2002). New directions in migration policy in Europe. *Philosophical Transactions: Biological Sciences, 357*(1420), 599–608.

Landy, F. J. (1986). Stamp collecting versus science: Validation as hypothesis testing. *American Psychologist, 41*, 1183–1192.

Landy, F. J. (2003). Validity generalization: Then and now. *In* K. R. Murphy (Ed.), *Validity Generalization: A Critical Review* (pp. 155–196). Mahwah, NJ: Lawrence Erlbaum.

Massachusetts Association of Minority Law Enforcement Officers v. Gerald T. Abban & others, 434 Mass. 256 (2001).

McDaniel, M., Kepes, S., & Banks, G. (2011). The *Uniform Guidelines* are a detriment to the field of personnel selection. *Industrial and Organizational Psychology*, *4*, 494–514.

Murphy, K. R., & Jacobs, R. R. (2012). Using effect size measures to reform the determination of adverse impact in equal employment litigation. *Psychology, Public Policy, and Law*, *18*(3), 477–499.

Myors, B., Mariani, M., Lievens, F., Schollaert, E., Van Hoye, G., Fraccaroli, F., & Bayazit, M. (2008a). Broadening international perspectives on the legal environment for personnel selection. *Industrial and Organizational Psychology: Perspectives on Science and Practice*, *1*(2), 266–270.

Myors, B., Fraccaroli, F., Lievens, F., Schollært, E., Van Hoye, G., Sekiguchi, T., & Sackett, P. R. (2008b). International perspectives on the legal environment for selection. *Industrial and Organizational Psychology: Perspectives on Science and Practice*, *1*(2), 206–246.

Norton, M. I., & Sommers, S. R. (2011). Whites see racism as a zero-sum game that they are now losing. *Perspectives on Psychological Science*, *6*(3), 215–218.

Offermann, L. R., Basford, T. E., Graebner, R., Jaffer, S., De Graaf, S. B., & Kaminsky, S. E. (2014). See no evil: Color blindness and perceptions of subtle racial discrimination in the workplace. *Cultural Diversity and Ethnic Minority Psychology*, *20*(4), 499–507.

Outtz, J. L. (2011). The unique origins of advancements in selection and personnel psychology. In S. Zedeck & S. Zedeck (Eds.), *APA Handbook of Industrial and Organizational Psychology, Vol 2: Selecting and Developing Members for the Organization* (pp. 445–465). Washington, DC: American Psychological Association.

Pager, D., Western, B., & Sugie, N. (2009). Sequencing disadvantage: Barriers to employment facing young Black and White men with criminal records. *Annals of the American Academy of Political and Social Science*, *623*(1), 195–213.

Praslova, L. (2008). The legal environment for selection in Russia. *Industrial and Organizational Psychology: Perspectives on Science and Practice*, *1*(2), 264–265.

Ricci v. DeStefano, 129 S. Ct. 2658 (2009).

Roth, P. L., Bobko, P., & Switzer, F. S. (2006). Modeling the behavior of the 4/5ths rule for determining adverse impact: reasons for caution. *Journal of Applied Psychology*, *91*(3), 507–522.

Rothenberg, J. Z., & Gardner, D. S. (2011). Protecting older workers: The failure of the Age Discrimination in Employment Act of 1967. *Journal of Sociology and Social Welfare*, *38*, 9–30.

San Francisco Fire Fighters Local 798 v. San Francisco, 38 Cal. 4th 653 (2006).

Sackett, P. R., Shen, W., Myors, B., Lievens, F., Schollaert, E., Van Hoye, G., & Aguinis, H. (2010). Perspectives from twenty-two countries on the legal environment for selection. In J. L. Farr, & N. T. Tippins (Eds.), *Handbook of Employee Selection* (pp. 651–676). New York: Routledge/Taylor & Francis Group.

Scherbaum, C. A. (2005). Synthetic validity: Past, present, and future. *Personnel Psychology*, *58*(2), 481–515.

Schmitt, N., & Sinha, R. (2011). Validation support for selection procedures. In S. Zedeck, & S. Zedeck (Eds.), *APA Handbook of Industrial and Organizational Psychology, Vol 2: Selecting and Developing Members for the Organization* (pp. 399–420). Washington, DC: American Psychological Association.

Thompson, J. L., & Morris, S. B. (2013). What factors influence judges' rulings about the legality of affirmative action plans? *Journal of Business & Psychology*, *28*(4), 411–424.

Section III
Retention

21

Employee Turnover and Strategies for Retention

Angela R. Grotto, Patrick K. Hyland, Anthony W. Caputo and Carla Semedo

Introduction

For decades, business leaders, human resource professionals and organizational researchers have sought to understand what causes employees to quit their jobs, and with good reason: turnover, whether functional or dysfunctional, can be expensive and disruptive. One recent study found that turnover costs (e.g., separation costs, replacement costs) range from 90% to 200% of the exiting employee's salary (Allen, Bryant & Vardaman, 2010). When turnover increases, the social fabric of an organization is disrupted (e.g., Batt & Colvin, 2011), intangible knowledge and skills are lost (Nyberg & Ployhart, 2013), operational effectiveness decreases (e.g., Ton & Huckman, 2008), accidents rates rise (e.g., Shaw, Gupta & Delery, 2005), customer service and quality suffer (e.g., Hancock, Allen, Bosco, McDaniel & Pierce, 2013) and customer satisfaction declines (Heavey, Holwerda & Hausknecht, 2013), which in turn can negatively impact a company's financial performance (e.g., Park & Shaw, 2013; Shaw, Duffy, Johnson & Lockhart, 2005). In light of such negative consequences, many organizations place great emphasis on identifying the factors that impact employee retention and turnover.

Over the past 50 years, a robust body of literature focused on employee retention and turnover has emerged. Starting with March and Simon's seminal work (1958), researchers have explored how a wide range of factors, including, attitudes, cognitions, experiences, events and economic conditions, affect an employee's decision to keep or quit a job. Considered together, these studies emphasize that turnover is a complex phenomenon influenced by a host of distal and proximal forces, contextual and individual difference variables, and on- and off-the-job experiences and events.

While an abundance of turnover and retention research exists, few recent integrative reviews have been published, making it challenging to understand what has been discovered to date. In this chapter, we seek to help researchers and practitioners develop a comprehensive understanding of turnover and retention by synthesizing the most prominent

The Wiley Blackwell Handbook of the Psychology of Recruitment, Selection and Employee Retention,
First Edition. Edited by Harold W. Goldstein, Elaine D. Pulakos, Jonathan Passmore and Carla Semedo.
© 2017 John Wiley & Sons Ltd. Published 2020 by John Wiley & Sons Ltd.

theories, studies and models that have emerged over the past 50 years. In the first section, we trace the evolution of turnover and retention research, showing how scholars have progressively expanded their focus over the past five decades. In the second section, we present a unifying framework of the dynamic process of turnover that integrates the major factors in an employee's decision to quit. In the third section we highlight evidence-based strategies for managing turnover and retention within organizations. Finally, we highlight directions for future research. Our hope is that this review will help integrate a broad set of findings, generate applicable insights and spur new research.

A Review of Turnover

Over the past half-century, the retention and turnover literature has grown exponentially, from just a handful of studies in the 1950s and 1960s to over 7,000 by 2014. The practitioner literature has also expanded: currently there are over 9,000 turnover and retention-related books. Keeping track of such a vast body of research can be daunting. But amid the thousands of studies, theories and recommendations, six influential turnover models stand out because of their notable impact on the field (Figure 21.1).

In this section, we trace the progression of turnover research by reviewing and evaluating these models. As we do, we highlight how turnover research has progressed through five important stages.

Turnover as a rational decision

The first formal model of turnover was developed by March and Simon in 1958. Based on the rational decision-making process of administrative theory, this model posits that turnover and retention can best be understood through a framework of organizational equilibrium. When an employee believes his or her contributions to the organization outweigh the rewards and benefits received, the employee–employer relationship becomes out of balance. This causes the employee to consider leaving the organization (i.e., perceived desirability of movement) and consider how easy it would be to move to another organization (i.e., perceived ease of movement). Mobley (1977) identified job satisfaction as an indicator of movement desirability, and Price (1977) and Price and Mueller (1981)

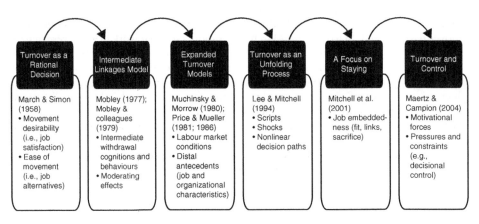

Figure 21.1   Themes and components of influential turnover models.

noted that job availability provides a good indication of perceived ease of movement. Therefore, the model predicts that job dissatisfaction (i.e., movement desirability) prompts a consideration of alternative job opportunities (i.e., ease of movement). If dissatisfaction is strong enough and other jobs are available, the model predicts an employee will quit. Extensive research has shown that both job dissatisfaction and job opportunities are related to turnover intentions and actual turnover (Blau, 1993; Griffeth, Steel, Allen & Bryan, 2005; Kopelman, Rovenpor & Millsap, 1992; Lee, Gerhart, Weller & Trevor, 2008; Podsakoff, LePine & LePine, 2007; Smith, Holtom & Mitchell, 2011; Swider & Zimmerman, 2010; Van Dick et al., 2004).

Mobley and colleagues (Mobley, 1977; Mobley, Griffeth, Hand & Meglino, 1979) expanded March and Simon's original model to explain how an employee will behave once job satisfaction starts to decline. Influenced by Fishbein and Ajzen's (1975) theory of reasoned action, they proposed an 'intermediate linkages model', which predicts that a sequence of cognitive and behavioural steps of withdrawal will occur between the initial experience of job dissatisfaction and the ultimate act of quitting.

Informed by this model, turnover researchers have explored a number of withdrawal cognitions and behaviours that emerge after employees become dissatisfied and before they leave an organization. Withdrawal cognitions (thoughts about quitting, the expected utility of leaving and psychological withdrawal from work) have all been linked to turnover (Hom & Kinicki, 2001; Hulin, 1991; Hulin, Roznowski & Hachiya, 1985). Researchers have investigated other emotional and cognitive states as consequences of job dissatisfaction and determinants of turnover. These include stress (Sheridan & Abelson, 1983), burnout (Swider & Zimmerman, 2010), perceived organizational support (Maertz, Griffeth, Campbell & Allen, 2007; Shore & Tetrick, 1991) and perceptions of justice (García-Chas, Neira-Fontela & Castro-Casal, 2014; Posthuma, Maertz & Dworkin, 2007; Spreitzer & Mishra, 2002).

In terms of withdrawal behaviours, job searching, the evaluation of job alternatives, lateness and absences, work withdrawal and job avoidance have all been linked with turnover (Griffeth, Hom & Gaertner, 2000; Harrison, Newman & Roth, 2006; Hom & Kinicki, 2001; Kammeyer-Mueller, Wanberg, Glomb & Ahlburg, 2005).

Mobley and colleagues (1979) also proposed a number of moderating effects on the relationship between withdrawal cognitions and actual turnover. For instance, personality traits related to impulsiveness (e.g., openness to experiences) were thought to be associated with turnover, and evidence supports this (e.g., Zimmerman, 2008).

The turnover process first defined by March and Simons and extended by Mobley and colleagues has given a comprehensive picture of the turnover process. The basic premise supporting this body of research is that employees are rational decision makers and continuously seek to maintain a balance between their efforts and what they receive from their organization. If this relationship becomes unbalanced, employees will engage in a series of withdrawal cognitions and behaviours that ultimately may lead to the employee leaving the organization.

Expanded turnover models

Beginning in the 1980s, researchers started to expand on the rational turnover model by exploring a wide range of job, organizational and environment factors as distal antecedents of turnover. Muchinsky and Morrow (1980), for example, proposed that the labour market would indirectly influence turnover through individual perceptions of job alternatives (Blau, 1993; Griffeth et al., 2005; Kopelman et al., 1992). When unemployment rates were high, it was expected that employees would assume that job alternatives were few, thus decreasing their thoughts of quitting. There is much empirical support to show that conditions in the relevant job market (e.g., high demand for a particular job) and labour market (e.g., the unemployment rate) influence perceived job alternatives (Gerhart, 1990; Kammeyer-Meuller et al., 2005; Steel, 1996; Steel & Lounsbury, 2009; Trevor, 2001).

Price and Mueller's (Price, 1977; Price & Mueller, 1981, 1986) comprehensive turnover model incorporated distal antecedents of turnover by proposing an array of job and organizational characteristics that shape employee attitudes. Also, organizational commitment was proposed as a mediator between job satisfaction and intention to leave. Empirical work shows that distal job and organizational factors do indeed impact turnover-related attitudes and behaviours. For example, positive perceptions of jobs (e.g., empowerment, high pay) and the work environment (e.g., organizational support) have been associated with higher levels of job satisfaction and organizational commitment (Allen, Shore & Griffeth, 2003; Gong, Law, Chang & Xin, 2009; Jiang, Liu, McKay, Lee & Mitchell, 2012; Rhoades, Eisenberger & Armeli, 2001; Spreitzer & Mishra, 2002) and reduced withdrawal intentions and behaviours (Allen et al., 2003; Bloom & Michel, 2002; Gong et al., 2009; Heavey et al., 2013; Messersmith, Guthrie, Ji & Lee, 2011). Organizational commitment also has been established as an antecedent of turnover (Culpepper, 2011; Ng & Butts, 2009; Stanley, Vandenberghe, Vandenberg & Bentein, 2013; Vandenberghe, Panaccio & Ayed, 2011) and a mediator of job satisfaction and intention to leave (Griffeth et al., 2000; Meyer, Allen & Smith, 1993; Price & Mueller, 1981, 1986).

The development of turnover models that incorporated job, organizational and environmental factors – along with the extensive empirical support for these models – greatly increased researchers' and practitioners' understanding of the turnover process. Yet these models continued to view turnover as a rational decision process that followed a linear path. According to attitude theory (Fishbein, 1967; Fishbein & Ajzen, 1975; Pratkanis, Breckler & Greenwald, 1989), employee attitudes and perceptions are thought to become more negative over time during an employee's tenure in response to gradual changes in the work environment and the employee–employer relationship. These negative attitudes and perceptions may lead to withdrawal cognitions and behaviours, and eventually result in turnover. This path from negative or disappointing experiences to deteriorating attitudes and turnover cognitions and behaviour does describe the process that many exiting employees take. But, as researchers started to notice, not everyone follows this path to quitting.

Turnover as an unfolding process

In the 1990s, a fundamentally different approach to understanding turnover emerged. Concerned about the inability to predict why certain employees were leaving, Lee and Mitchell (1994) developed an unfolding model of turnover that recognized that some employees are pushed to leave an organization while others are pulled out of their organization by market forces. Based on interview and survey data, Lee, Mitchell, Wise and Fireman (1996) discovered that individuals use different and distinct psychological processes when deciding to quit. As some of the processes were not consistent with turnover theories at the time, the unfolding model made a unique contribution to the turnover literature. This model moved away from the rational turnover models and conceptualized turnover as a dynamic, nonlinear process that unfolds over time in response to shocks, defined as jarring events 'that initiate the psychological decision processes involved in quitting a job' (Lee & Mitchell, 1994, p. 6). Based on image theory (Beach, 1990), when a shock occurs, the values and goals of the organization may change in a way that causes individuals to evaluate the fit of their values and goals with those of the organization. An image violation occurs when individuals' values and goals do not fit with those of the organization as a result of a shock. This violation prompts them to consider quitting.

Shocks come in many different forms. Work-related shocks include organizational changes (e.g., a merger, new policy), psychological contract breaches (e.g., a missed job opportunity) and the introduction of a new HR practice (e.g., a new compensation system). Non-work-related shocks include childbirth, a death in the family, elderly care, marriage and divorce.

The emotional value of a shock largely depends on how it is perceived by the employee experiencing it. What may be considered a positive event for one may be perceived as a negative for another (e.g., an overseas assignment, pregnancy). Events perceived as negative are likely to be appraised as hindrance stressors that constrain an individual's personal development and accomplishments (e.g., lay-offs, an abusive supervisor, missed job opportunities, demotion, relocation for spouse/partner, divorce). Hindrance stressors certainly negatively impact job satisfaction and turnover (Cavanaugh, Boswell, Roehling & Boudreau, 2000; Podsakoff et al., 2007). Conversely, some shocks may be appraised as challenge stressors, which promote personal growth and achievement (e.g., overseas assignments, promotions, childbirth, marriage). Challenge stressors tend to positively impact job satisfaction and thus lead to lower turnover (Podsakoff et al., 2007).

Empirical tests have established that not only do many quitters leave in response to a shock (Chin, & Hung, 2013; Holtom, Mitchell, Lee & Inderrieden, 2005; Morrell, Loan-Clarke & Wilkinson, 2004; Weller, Holtom, Matiaske & Mellewigt, 2009), they also follow different paths to their turnover decisions, depending on the type of shock (e.g., Lee et al., 2008; Lee, Mitchell, Holtom, McDaniel & Hill, 1999). Thus, the unfolding model has made a significant contribution to turnover research by acknowledging that the decision process can sometimes occur quite abruptly in response to a sudden personal or work-related shock. However, not everyone leaves when they experience a negative shock. Adding a layer of complexity to the unfolding model, Mitchell, Holtom, Lee, Sablynski and Erez (2001) introduced the notion of job embeddedness as a reason why people may choose to stay with an organization.

Staying

Mitchell and colleagues' (2001) work on job embeddedness highlights the role of context, which includes both the work environment and the larger community. The extent to which employees are enmeshed in these environments is considered to be a key factor that influences whether they will stay with an organization (Mitchell et al., 2001). A robust body of evidence supports the fact that embeddedness impacts turnover (Dawley & Andrews, 2012; Halbesleben & Wheeler, 2008; Heavey et al., 2013; Holtom & Inderrieden, 2006; Smith Holtom & Mitchell, 2011). In fact, research suggests that both on- and off-the-job embeddedness predict turnover beyond attitudinal variables (Crossley, Bennet, Jex & Burnfield, 2007; Jiang et al., 2012; Lee, Mitchell, Sablynski, Burton & Holtom, 2004; Mitchell et al., 2001). Job embeddedness is also indirectly related to turnover through job search behaviour, such that individuals who are more embedded in their jobs are less likely to engage in a job search and leave the organization (Holtom, Burton & Crossley, 2012; Swider, Boswell & Zimmerman, 2011).

Mitchell identifies three components of job embeddedness: links, fit and sacrifice. Links or relational ties are made to people in the individual's organization or community. Relational ties that may lead to lower turnover intentions and turnover include mentoring relationships (Friedman & Holtom, 2002; Payne & Huffman, 2005), social network ties (Friedman & Holtom, 2002; Mossholder, Settoon & Henagan, 2005), perceived co-worker support (Mossholder, et al., 2005), satisfaction with co-workers (Golden, 2007), perceived supervisor support (Maertz et al., 2007), high leader–member exchange (Ballinger, Lehman, & Schoorman, 2010; Bauer, Erdogan, Liden & Wayne, 2006; Han & Jekel, 2011; Harris, Kacmar & Witt, 2005), transformational leadership (Tse, Huang & Lam, 2013) and volunteer work (Haivas, Hofmans & Pepermans, 2013).

Sacrifice represents what an employee will have to give up on leaving the organization and includes on- and off-the-job benefits. For example, many high-performing organizations have high-commitment HR practices that enhance employee skills, motivation and opportunities (e.g., training, incentive programmes, opportunities for advancement, supervisor support). These practices increase job satisfaction and so motivate employees to stay. Many employees would not be willing to sacrifice rewards that they may not get elsewhere. Competitive compensation packages, opportunities for learning, high-involvement work practices and long-term investments in employee development have all been linked to lower turnover intentions and turnover (Batt & Colvin, 2011; Boroş & Curşeu, 2013; Chang, Wang & Huang, 2013; Ng & Butts, 2009; Shaw, Delery, Jenkins & Gupta, 1998), typically through increased job satisfaction (e.g., García-Chas et al., 2014).

By taking into account links, relationships and sacrifices, this job embeddedness model augments our ability to understand why people stay or leave their jobs. However, more recent research by Maertz (2001) and Maertz and Griffeth (2004) emphasize that turnover is a personal decision, and people stay or leave depending on the extent of control they have over their options and choices.

Turnover and control

Maertz and Griffeth's (2004) notion of decisional control marks a notable recent contribution to the turnover and retention literature. At the core of their model is the argument that, in addition to job embeddedness, motivational forces are expected to shape an individual's preference to stay or leave an organization and ultimately predict turnover (Hom, Mitchell, Lee & Griffeth, 2012; Maertz & Campion, 2004). They proposed a comprehensive set of six motivational forces that impact turnover. First, affective forces – positive or negative emotional responses to the organization – give rise to psychological comfort or discomfort with organizational membership: psychological comfort motivates staying while discomfort motivates leaving. Examples of affective forces that influence preferences to stay or leave are good or poor job fit, positive or negative job attitudes, and positive or negative workplace shocks. Second, calculative forces involve rational calculation of the probability of attaining important values and goals in the future through continued organizational membership. A favourable future state influences an individual to stay, while an unfavourable future state motivates quitting. Third, alternative forces are the magnitude and strength of self-efficacy beliefs about obtaining another job, the desirability of job alternatives and the certainty of obtaining a job alternative. Lower self-efficacy beliefs motivate staying while higher self-efficacy beliefs motivate leaving. Fourth, moral/ethical forces are desires to maintain consistency between behaviours and values regarding turnover, such as 'quitting is bad/persistence is a virtue' or 'changing jobs regularly is good/staying long results in stagnation'. Fifth, constituent forces refer to motivations to remain or quit depending on the employees' attachment to others within the organization or the wider community. Attachment to a constituent implies attachment to the organization which motivates staying. A lack of attachment or unhealthy relationships (e.g., bullying by co-workers, abusive supervisors) motivate leaving. If the constituent shows signs of leaving, this can lead to turnover contagion. Lastly, embedding HRM practices, such as workforce inducement investments, motivate staying, while poor HRM practices motivate leaving.

Regardless of the preference to stay or leave the organization, there are certain pressures and constraints that affect the control an individual has over the final decision (Hom et al., 2012; Maertz & Campion, 2004). Perceived decisional control depends on: 1) legal forces: employer pressure to leave, employment contracts, etc. that force staying; 2) normative forces: external or workplace pressure to stay or quit, assuming some motivation to comply with these expectations; 3) behavioural forces: desires to avoid the job, community and family sacrifices of quitting; higher costs pressure someone to stay while lower costs sway quitting; 4) alternative forces: few or undesirable job alternatives force someone to stay; 5) job protection systems: unionization and tenure/seniority protections compel individuals to stay; 6) performance enhancing HRMs: contingent rewards, performance monitoring, etc. compel staying; and 7) just termination practices result in voluntary quitting.

Based on preferences and decisional control, Hom and colleagues (2012) categorized stayers/leavers into four groups. Enthusiastic stayers prefer to stay and have control over the decision; thus they remain with the organization because they want to stay and do not feel pressure to stay or leave. Enthusiastic leavers prefer to leave the organization and have high control over the decision, so they want to and can leave. Reluctant leavers prefer to stay with the organization but have low control over the decision, and therefore leave because they must. Reluctant stayers prefer to leave but have little control over the decision; they stay because they feel they cannot leave even though they would prefer to do so.

Taking into account decisional control, this approach to turnover expands the criterion by acknowledging that voluntary turnover may sometimes be involuntary. What drives someone to leave involuntarily may be quite different from what drives someone to leave voluntarily (Hom et al., 2012). It is critical to make this distinction in order to understand all the factors impacting turnover.

Cross-Cultural Turnover Research

In our review of the cross-cultural research on employee turnover and retention we highlight two areas: the generalizability of turnover constructs and models to non-US countries; and the retention of international workers.

Understanding turnover in non-US countries

Much of the cross-cultural research on turnover focuses on whether turnover constructs that are deemed important in the turnover decisions of American employees are also relevant in the turnover decisions made by employees elsewhere (e.g., Morrell, Loan-Clarke, Arnold & Wilkinson, 2008). Cross-cultural studies have also tested whether turnover models developed and validated in the US can be corroborated in other countries. The cross-cultural literature on turnover posits that the environment perceived by employees determines whether, and to what extent, certain turnover constructs are important in the decision to leave an organization. Additionally, traditional turnover models may not apply in certain cultural contexts because of differences in employee values and perspectives. For instance, whether employees are working in an individualistic or collectivistic context may determine the extent to which community embeddedness is important to their decision to leave (Ramesh & Gelfand, 2010).

These cross-cultural studies typically test for generalizability in a single non-US sample (e.g., China, Mexico, India; Allen et al., 2009; Harman et al., 2009; Maertz et al., 2003; Morrell et al., 2008; Peltokorpi, 2013; Peltokorpi, Allen & Froese, 2015; Wocke & Heymann, 2012) or by comparing the results of a US sample to a non-US sample of employees (e.g., U.S. vs. India; Ramesh & Gelfand, 2010; Wang, Lawler, Walumbwa & Shi, 2004). Very rarely do these studies employ multinational samples, but there are some examples (e.g., Sturman et al., 2012).

The turnover models that have been tested in non-US cultural contexts include general models of turnover decisions which incorporate constructs such as perceived job alternatives, job search and the perceived cost of leaving (Maertz, Stevens & Campion, 2003), the performance–turnover curvilinear model (Sturman, Shao & Katz, 2012), the cognitive withdrawal model (Allen et al., 2009), the job embeddedness model (Harman, Blum, Stefani & Taho, 2009; Peltokorpi, 2013; Tanova & Holtom, 2008) and the unfolding model (Morrell et al., 2008).

Some studies have tested whether particular constructs are relevant in the turnover decisions of non-US employees. Kim, Lee and Lee (2013) tested the effects of supervisor and co-worker relationships on turnover intentions in China and South Korea. Yingyan (2010) examined demographics and facets of satisfaction as predictors of intentions to stay among Chinese employees. Wöcke and Heymann (2012) examined the role of shocks and demographics in the decision to leave among South African workers. Peltokorpi and colleagues (Peltokorpi, 2013; Peltokorpi et al., 2015) tested the effects of job embeddedness on turnover in Japanese samples. Lastly, Ramesh and Gelfand (2010) investigated the generalizability of various job embeddedness constructs (e.g., organizational links, community links, and family embeddedness) by comparing American and Indian employees.

Generally, research indicates that many of the turnover models developed in the US predict turnover in other contexts (e.g., Aladwan, Bhanugopan & Fish, 2013; Allen et al., 2003; Maertz et al., 2003; Ramesh & Gelfand, 2010; Sturman et al., 2012; Tanova & Holtom, 2008). However, some constructs emerge as more or less important in these other countries, and the details of some models change due to cultural and environmental factors. In one study that employed a multinational sample, Sturman and colleagues (2012) concluded that cultural factors across 24 countries affected the curvilinearity of the performance–turnover relationship. Regarding the decision to leave, Maertz and colleagues (2003) found that the influence of the family was quite pervasive in the turnover decisions of Mexican employees. Morrell and colleagues' (2008) findings challenged the generalizability of the unfolding model, as most leavers could not be classified using the model with a sample of nurses in the UK. The authors attributed this to variations in the labour market for nurses there.

Several cross-cultural studies have focused on staying by testing the job embeddedness model. Peltokorpi (2013) concluded that distinct cultural factors affected on- and off-the-job embeddedness among Japanese employees, such as in-group ties. Additionally, Peltokorpi and colleagues (2015) found that risk-aversion moderated the relationship between organizational embeddedness and turnover intentions in a Japanese sample. Ramesh and Gelfand's (2010) results showed that person–job fit predicted higher retention in the US (an individualistic culture), but person–organization fit, organizational links and community links predicted higher retention in India (a collectivistic culture). Harman and colleagues (2009) found that job embeddedness was not a predictor of turnover intentions over and above job satisfaction for Albanian employees, despite this relationship being quite robust in samples in the US. They concluded that the volatile employment situation in Albania (e.g., many new businesses moving in, many migrant workers moving to the cities) may be a factor.

In summary, although many of the turnover relationships and models that have been developed and validated in the US hold in other settings, there are nuances in these relationships that can be attributed to the cultural context and environmental influences. Future research should continue to examine the role of these situational factors in turnover decisions. More suggestions on research in this area are discussed in the section on future research.

Retaining international employees

For multinational organizations, the 'war for talent' has become global. When organizations face skill shortages they can draw on international workers as a source of human capital. Similarly, in-demand skilled workers are willing to work overseas where their competences are needed. Consequently, multinational organizations need to address the unique needs and circumstances of qualified immigrant workers and expatriates when developing employee retention strategies. The few studies that have been conducted in this area have focused on expatriates working in the US (Siers, 2007), US expatriates (Ren, Shaffer, Harrison, Fu & Fodchuk, 2014) and skilled migrant workers (Bahn, 2014; Halvorsen, Treuren & Kulik, 2015).

As discussed earlier, retention studies based on traditional employee samples have consistently shown the importance of various worker perceptions and attitudes, including perceived fit, equity, justice and support, as well as job satisfaction and organizational commitment. In addition to these critical perceptions and attitudes, studies conducted on expatriates suggest a few other factors necessary for the retention of international workers, most notably the extent to which they are able to adjust and embed themselves in a new organization, community and culture (Bahn, 2014; Halvorsen et al., 2015; Ren et al., 2014; Siers, 2007). Appropriate adjustment and a good fit tend to lead to greater organizational commitment and cognitive states of engagement, which ultimately enhance retention (e.g., Halvorsen et al., 2015; Ren et al., 2014).

The expatriate literature has predominantly viewed expatriates as having to react to and navigate the demands and pressures of an uncertain international assignment (e.g., learning a new language, becoming familiar with cultural novelty, managing differences in cultural values; e.g., Bhaskar-Shrinivas, Harrison, Shaffer & Luk, 2005; Black & Gregersen, 1991; Ren et al., 2014) in order to adjust appropriately to the new environment. If the expatriate does not respond well or properly adjust to the new environment, cognitive and behavioural withdrawal is expected. However, Ren and colleagues (2014) proposed that expatriates can also engage in proactive tactics to ease their transition to an unfamiliar environment and fully engage in the new organization, community and culture. Indeed, the proactive tactic of positive framing (e.g., casting circumstances in a favourable way) has been linked to more successful adjustment, and both positive framing and relationship-building (e.g., networking with host country colleagues) were linked with greater expatriate embeddedness (Ren et al., 2014). Furthermore, Ren and colleagues found that adequate adjustment and embeddedness were positively related to intentions both to stay on international assignments and renew their contracts.

These results indicate that organizational retention strategies should be adjusted for international workers. The traditional turnover models suggesting that perceived fit, equity, justice and organizational support are important to retention strategies certainly apply to international workers. However, there are other factors and nuances to consider for this employee group. Psychological adjustment to a new environment is critical, so organizations should equip their international employees not only to manage the demands and pressures of a new environment, but to proactively acclimatize themselves to it. Foremost, it is not only job fit and organizational fit that matter, but also embeddedness in a new community and culture. The research suggests that organizations employing international workers should provide them with opportunities for engaging socially with the local community and reducing cultural distance (Halvorsen, Treuren & Kulik, 2015).

Evaluating Turnover Literature

A review of the most prominent turnover theories reveals a holistic picture of the turnover process. This includes work and non-work antecedents of turnover, the mechanisms of turnover, the consequences of turnover and moderating effects (Steel & Lounsbury, 2009). Focusing on the antecedents of turnover, each model offers unique contributions, but the models converge on three key antecedents: job attitudes (e.g., job satisfaction), withdrawal cognitions (e.g., thoughts of quitting) and withdrawal behaviours (e.g., job avoidance). In an attempt to explain as much variance as possible in the turnover criterion, researchers have also examined a number of individual, job, organizational and environmental factors as distal antecedents. Furthermore, the notion of shocks introduced the idea that not all turnover decisions follow a systematic, linear process. Rather, some decisions are made in response to jarring events that prompt sudden changes in employee attitudes and behaviours and consequently lead to turnover. Lastly, to understand why some individuals stay and some leave even when they prefer not to, researchers have examined the role of job embeddedness, motivational forces and constraints in the turnover process. These models have been tested in both US and non-US contexts.

Figure 21.2 summarizes the antecedents of turnover reviewed in this section. The antecedents towards the centre of Figure 21.2 represent distal antecedents, while antecedents appearing towards the circumferences represent proximal antecedents. According to the reviewed literature, the antecedents are presented in order of their distance from the criterion: individual differences (e.g., personality, interests), environmental, organizational and job characteristics (e.g., organizational policies, job autonomy, unemployment rate), shocks (e.g., significant work and personal life-events), affect and attitudes (e.g., stress, job satisfaction), cognitive withdrawal states (e.g., thinking about quitting) and withdrawal intentions and behaviours (e.g., job searching). The analysed models also capture the boundary conditions of job embeddedness, motivational forces and constraints, which are thought to interact with withdrawal intentions, behaviours and decisions to stay or leave. As Figure 21.2 illustrates, researchers and practitioners now have an almost complete picture of the factors impacting turnover.

What is missing is the notion of time. Although the unfolding model recognizes that a turnover decision process unfolds over a period of time, the time sequences as an individual moves from one phase of the decision process to the next are not specified. Also, there is currently no model that is inclusive of the more gradual and rational turnover process based on March and Simon's work and the more sudden turnover decisions that occur in response to shocks. In the next section, and based on the literature, we integrate the key factors of the various dynamic models of turnover and summarize the two primary pathways to turnover, considering, moreover, the various time sequences that occur during the turnover process.

Integrating the Dynamic Models of Turnover

As this review of more than five decades of research emphasizes, turnover is a complex phenomenon. Theorists and researchers have searched for the affective, attitudinal and cognitive antecedents of turnover. They have proposed gradual and rapid pathways to

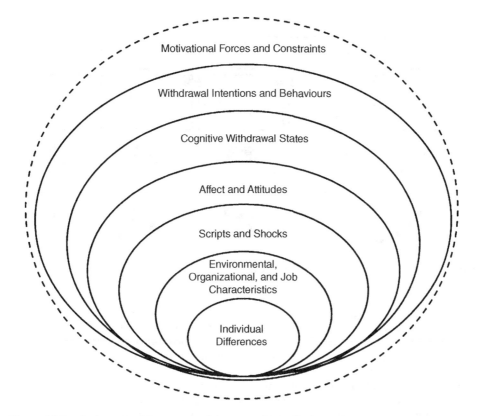

Figure 21.2 An integrated framework of the antecedents of turnover.

quitting. They have explored individual differences and context-specific factors that trigger turnover. And they have identified events inside and outside of work that can cause someone to leave an organization.

The models reviewed above provide key insights into various factors that promote retention and cause turnover. But this review raises an important question: which model is most accurate? Each model has received ample empirical support, so choosing one over another seems limiting and unjustifiable. Fortunately, making such a choice is not necessary because each model approaches turnover in a different way.

In this section we integrate the key factors of these different approaches in a unifying understanding of the dynamic nature of turnover, based on five common factors (see Figure 21.3), as well as the theory of planned behaviour (Ajzen & Fishbein, 1980), the unfolding model (Lee & Mitchell, 1994) and affective events theory (AET; Weiss & Cropanzano, 1996).

Factor 1: Fit – The foundation of retention

A critical element of employee retention is fit, a central component of the job embeddedness model (Mitchell et al., 2001). When employees join an organization, they each have a set of individual differences, including their demographic profile (e.g., gender, age and ethnicity), personality, economic and psychological needs, and personal interests and

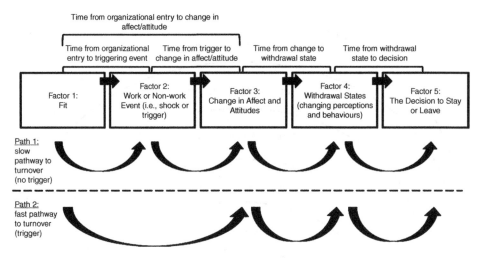

Figure 21.3 An integrated framework of the dynamic turnover process.

aspirations. By and large, employees accept jobs that fit with their individual differences (Shacklock, Brunetto & Nelson, 2009; Allen, Weeks & Moffitt, 2005). As new hires take up their roles and start to experience the organization, their individual differences interact with various aspects of the work environment, including the job (e.g., autonomy, complexity), the organization (e.g., policies, culture) and other individuals (supervisors, co-workers). The degree to which an employee's individual values, needs, interests and preferences match those of the job (person–job fit) and organization (person–organization fit) determines the extent and quality of the employee's work experience and the employee–employer relationship (Peterson, 2004). Employees' experiences at work shape their attitudes toward and perceptions of the workplace. Positive work experiences and good quality relationships are likely to lead to high levels of job satisfaction, engagement and organizational commitment. Negative experiences and poor quality relationships at work are likely to lead to low levels of job satisfaction, engagement and organizational commitment. These fit-related attitudes and perceptions are a critical first step in the turnover decision process, as low levels of job satisfaction and organizational commitment present a turnover risk (Carmeli & Weisberg, 2006; Hollenbeck & Williams, 1986; Hom & Kinicki, 2001). Figure 21.3 illustrates fit as the foundational element in turnover decisions. It is the first step in the dynamic turnover process, at the point of an employee's entry into an organization.

Factor 2: Triggering events – Fast and slow pathways to turnover

One of the more compelling findings that has emerged is that the decision to quit may develop over months or even years, or it may materialize in a matter of moments. First, for some employees, the decision to quit is a slow process that emerges over time in response to various changes in the work and non-work environment that create a sense of misfit. As March and Simon (1958) originally noted, a decline in employee attitudes, such as job satisfaction, can indeed lead to withdrawal cognitions and behaviours and eventually turnover. For other employees, the turnover process is more abrupt. According to the unfolding model of turnover, specific work or non-work events (i.e., shocks) can affect the employee–employer relationship and trigger a sudden shift in employee attitudes and perceptions, leading to withdrawal cognitions and behaviours and subsequently actual turnover (Lee et al., 1996, 1999). A trigger can be a significant work event (e.g., a negative performance evaluation) or personal life-event (e.g., childbirth). Moreover, the triggering event can be expected or unexpected as well as positive or negative, depending on how the individual perceives it (Lee & Mitchell, 1994; Maertz & Campion, 2004). Although both types of change process lead to turnover, they are independent paths, as critical events have predicted turnover in a manner distinct from the operation of attitudes and perceptions (Iverson & Pullman, 2000; Kammeyer-Mueller et al., 2005). Figure 21.3 depicts shocks and triggers as the second factor in the dynamic turnover process following fit, with slow and fast pathways to turnover depending on whether there is a triggering event.

Factor 3: Change in affect and attitudes

According to affective events theory (AET), an event can set off a chain reaction of emotional and attitudinal responses (Mignonac & Herrbach, 2004; Rupp & Spencer, 2006; Weiss & Cropanzano, 1996). The event and the responses can develop into behavioural reactions, according to planned behaviour theory (Ajzen & Fishbein, 1980). Thus, affect is a proximal consequence of a triggering event and mediates the relationship between the event and attitudinal change, the distal consequence of the trigger (Zhao, Wayne, Glibkowski & Bravo, 2007). Together, AET and the theory of planned behaviour suggest that when a negative shock occurs (e.g., a breach in the psychological contract) an employee may have a negative emotional reaction, such as feeling violated (Morrison & Robinson, 1997; Zhao et al., 2007). These negative feelings may deflate critical work attitudes, such as job satisfaction (Zhao et al., 2007). Conversely, a positive shock, such as a promotion, typically elicits positive feelings (e.g., attachment to the organization), which may evolve into positive attitudes (e.g., engagement) towards one's job and organization. Thus, triggering events set the stage for a fast pathway to turnover (see Figure 21.3), as shocks result in somewhat sudden changes in affect and attitude.

Even if a shock is not experienced, employee affect and attitudes may still change (March & Simon, 1958); this is depicted as the slow pathway to turnover in Figure 21.3. Over time an individual may become aware of a sense of misfit with the job or organization, not because of a particular event but perhaps because of progressive changes in identity, interests, preferences or needs as the individual moves through life-stages (Rothuasen, Henderson, Arnold & Malshe, 2015; Skinner, Elton, Auer & Pocock, 2014). As discussed earlier, a sense of misfit can generate a slow decline in positive affect towards the job or organization and a gradual decline in positive work attitudes, such as job satisfaction.

Factor 4: Withdrawal states – Changing perceptions and behaviours

The shift in work attitudes and perceptions, whether it follows a significant work or non-work event or takes place gradually over time, is a critical component of the turnover process, as work attitudes (e.g., organizational commitment) typically lead to a cognitive state of intention – the intention to withdraw or engage in the job/organization (Hom et al., 2012; see Figure 21.3). Cognitive states of withdrawal include preferences to leave, thoughts of quitting and intentions to leave. Withdrawal behaviours may take the form of interruptions at work, lateness and/or absences. For example, employees who perceive conflict between their different life domains (e.g., work and family) may show signs of withdrawal by allowing the family to interrupt their work time (Hammer, Brauer & Grandey, 2003).

The reasoned action approach (Ajzen & Fishbein, 1980) to behaviour posits that people's behaviours follow on reasonably from their beliefs, attitudes and intentions. Therefore, cognitive states of withdrawal or engagement are thought to translate into behavioural reactions that vary for stayers and leavers (Hom et al., 2012). A cognitive state of withdrawal is likely to result in negative work behaviours, including withdrawal (e.g., absences), job searching and/or counterproductive work behaviours. For instance, the employee who has negative perceptions of leadership (Holtz & Harold, 2013), organizational justice or ethical climate (Chernyak-Hai & Tziner, 2014) may engage in counterproductive work behaviours. Conversely, a cognitive state of engagement is likely to result in positive workplace behaviours, such as organizational citizenship behaviours (Dalal, Baysinger, Brummel & LeBreton, 2012). Withdrawal states and behaviours are represented as factor 4 in Figure 21.3.

Factor 5: The decision to stay or leave

Figure 21.3 illustrates how cognitive states lead to the final factor in the turnover process – the decision to stay or leave. An individual in a cognitive state of withdrawal who is engaging in negative work behaviours, such as job searching, will eventually leave the organization (Hom & Kinicki, 2001; Kammeyer-Mueller et al., 2005; Somers, 1999; Vandenberghe et al., 2011). On the other hand, an individual in a state of engagement who is engaged in positive workplace behaviours is likely to stay with the organization (Haivas et al., 2013; Halbesleben & Wheeler, 2008). However, various sources of pressure and environmental constraints may affect how much control an individual has over the final decision to stay or leave (Hom et al., 2012; Maertz & Campion, 2004), for example, undesirable job alternatives may force employees to stay even when they prefer to leave (Holtom, Mitchell, Lee & Eberly, 2008).

A summary of the dynamic models of turnover

In sum, common across the dynamic models of turnover are five critical factors and two main pathways to turnover. First, there are the employee's pre-existing conditions (e.g., individual differences, employee attitudes, affect and perceptions) and workplace conditions (e.g., job and organizational characteristics) that determine how well an individual fits with the job and organization. As conditions change over time during an employee's tenure, the extent to which an individual fits in the work environment will also change. If an employee begins to feel a sense of misfit, a gradual change in affect or attitudes towards the job and/or organization may occur. This is the slow pathway to turnover and does not involve a specific triggering event. Alternatively, a significant work or non-work event may trigger a change in affect or attitude, which is the fast pathway to turnover. Depending on whether attitudes shift in a positive or negative direction, an individual will fall into a cognitive state of engagement or withdrawal and then enact behaviours indicative of a decision to stay or leave the organization. This is the withdrawal phase of the model. The process ends with an actual decision to stay or leave. There are boundary conditions to this, including motivational forces and environmental constraints.

The decision to stay or leave an organization can be affected by many things. Thus, the time-lag in each path will vary with each individual. First, the timing of shocks will vary according to individual features (e.g., length of tenure, gender, career stage) and the type of shock (e.g., performance evaluations typically occur once a year, while promotions are less frequent). Second, the speed of responding to a shock will vary depending on the characteristics of the shock (e.g., the extent to which it is unexpected), individual factors (e.g., current levels of job satisfaction) and contextual factors (e.g., whether previous shocks have been experienced). The length of time between the reaction and the withdrawal state will typically vary for the same reasons. The time gap between the withdrawal state and the actual decision will vary for individuals, depending on personality (e.g., decisiveness), extent of job embeddedness, availability of job alternatives and other constraints. Furthermore, the timing of each phase will vary for each individual, depending on personal factors (e.g., life-stage, personality), the type of shock experienced and contextual factors (e.g., job embeddedness). Taking into consideration existing turnover models, it emerges from the literature that turnover is a time-driven process, which involves five major decision factors and takes place along either a slow or fast pathway.

Organizational Responses: Employee Retention

The turnover literature identifies various ways to increase employee retention. In this section, we highlight four research insights for reducing unwanted turnover: 1) create a positive work environment, 2) promote fit, 3) encourage leaders to behave in supportive ways and 4) help employees manage shocks.

Create a positive work climate

Researchers have found that one of the best ways to prevent turnover is to cultivate a positive work environment (e.g., Ramsay, 2006; Vance, 2006). Work climate is how employees perceive their work environment, which is based on the cultural values and beliefs the organization holds. To enhance employee retention, a work climate must have a set of positive company values and beliefs as its foundation. High-retention companies tend to have a strong and engaging organizational culture that is based on integrity, respect, equality, teamwork and worker involvement (Holtom, Mitchell, Lee & Eberly, 2008; Richman, Civian, Shannon, Jeffrey & Brennan, 2008). These positive values can help create a work climate that employees perceive as rewarding, supportive and equitable. It is the leaders of organizations who are largely responsible for cultivating a positive culture not only by establishing positive work values for the organization, but also in their daily actions and decisions enacting the company's beliefs (Breevaart, Bakker, Hetland, Demerouti, Olsen & Espevik, 2014; Campbell, Perry, Maertz, Allen & Griffeth, 2013).

Earlier studies have demonstrated the importance of work climate for turnover and retention. For instance, perceptions of supervisor support, organizational support and procedural justice have all been linked with lower turnover intentions, mainly by increasing employee commitment and reducing burnout (Campbell et al., 2013; Maertz et al., 2007; Posthuma, Maertz & Dworkin, 2007). Conversely, perceptions of inequity, such as a psychological contract breach, can increase turnover intentions (Chin & Hung, 2013). Thus, the research implies that companies must create positive work experiences for employees in order to increase satisfaction and commitment and thereby increase intentions to stay (Allen et al., 2010; Boroş & Curşeu, 2013; Chang et al., 2013). To do so, it is critical that HR and leaders continually assess whether organizational policies (e.g., reward systems) are fair and competitive and whether managerial actions (e.g., pay and promotion decisions) are supportive and just.

Promote fit

According to the job embeddedness literature and the organizational model of employee persistence, integrating employees into various organizational systems (e.g., the social, career and performance systems) can help embed employees in the organization and thereby increase retention (Mitchell et al., 2001; Peterson, 2004). Researchers have found that a high level of fit contributes to job satisfaction, organizational commitment and intentions to stay (Allen, 2006; Kammeyer-Mueller & Wanberg, 2003; Mossholder et al., 2005; Payne & Huffman, 2005).

There are numerous ways to promote this deep level of integration and fit, which extend across various stages of the employee experience. First, during the recruitment process, realistic job previews help prevent psychological contract breaches and foster fit with the job and organization (Allen et al., 2010; Breaugh & Starke, 2000; Zhao, et al., 2007). During the application process, selecting certain personality traits (e.g., conscientiousness and agreeableness) may improve retention (Zimmerman, 2008). Ensuring that individual knowledge, skills and abilities fit the job well and that the individual's values match the organization's can also help improve retention (Allen et al., 2010; Griffeth & Hom, 2001; Kristof-Brown, Zimmerman & Johnson, 2005). When on-boarding and socializing employees, research suggests that it may help to ensure that employees are adjusting well (i.e., they are adequately learning how to do their jobs and function in the social and cultural environment; Allen et al., 2010; Peterson, 2004). Also, managers who foster positive relationships between employees and supervisors (e.g., high leader–member exchanges) can help integrate employees. Positive interactions with members of the organization can help create a sense of belonging, connectedness and person–environment fit (Peterson, 2004).

Encourage leaders to behave in supportive ways

It has been said that employees do not leave jobs, they leave managers. Research shows that leaders do in fact impact employee retention and turnover. In a study of 225 social services workers, Maertz and colleagues (2007) found that employee perceptions of supervisor support was an important predictor of turnover behaviour and that employees' relationship with their managers can directly impact turnover decisions. In fact, their results suggest that a high level of perceived supervisor support can compensate for a low level of perceived organizational support and prevent employees from quitting. Likewise, Han and Jekel (2011) found that when employees find their manager is supportive, they are more satisfied with various aspects of their job, which in turn reduces intentions to quit. Research by McClean, Burris and Detert (2013) suggests that managerial responsiveness to employee feedback is a critical determinant of turnover. In this study of employees working in 136 restaurants, McClean and colleagues found that when managers were willing and able to engage in change, vocal employees – those frequently demanding improvements – were less likely to quit. Tse, Huang and Lam (2013) found that transformational leadership behaviours increase employees' affective commitment to the organization, thereby reducing intention to leave and turnover behaviour. Together, these studies emphasize that when leaders behave in supportive, responsive and inspiring ways, they are more likely to engage their employees, increase their job satisfaction and reduce turnover.

Help employees manage shocks

Change, at both the individual and organizational levels, is increasingly common in today's work environment. Research shows that organizations can help employees manage change, and thereby prevent attrition, if they provide appropriate opportunities and support. For example, support can be provided when employees experience job shocks that may cause them to leave, such as a missed promotion, a poor performance review or changes to their job (Allen et al., 2010; Griffeth & Hom, 2001; Heneman & Judge, 2006). Additionally, Allen and colleagues (2010) found that when growth opportunities, such as coaching, mentoring, training, career planning and development, were provided throughout employees' tenure, employees were more likely to stay with their organizations through challenging times (Allen et al., 2010).

Peterson's (2004) organizational model of employee persistence provides a road map for developing responsive strategies to attrition causing events at the organizational level. Peterson argues that when organizational events change the employee–employer relationship, organizations have the opportunity to manage the negative emotional and attitudinal reactions that employees may have to those changes. Organizational changes and work events can be operational (e.g., new leadership, strategic redirection, mergers, restructuring, introduction of new systems, processes, products or services) or people-related (e.g., implementation of new HR policies or programmes, psychological contract breaches).

According to Peterson's (2004) model, leaders and managers should provide emotional and instrumental support following these organizational changes to maintain a balanced relationship and prevent employee turnover. If the change event is anticipated, the organization can provide support by preparing employees, gaining support for the changes and providing guidance during the transition period. Managers play an especially important role during organizational changes and events, as they have direct and frequent contact with employees. Essentially, they have the responsibility to monitor reactions to work-related and personal shocks and help employees cope; this could prevent employees from leaving (Zhao et al., 2007). They can do so by providing instrumental and emotional support and making accommodations for employees following a shock.

Future Research

Over the past five decades or so, researchers have learned a great deal about the factors that influence employees' decision to stay or leave. But there is still much we do not understand about the causes of turnover. Here we present seven areas of opportunity for future research that could shed new light on the turnover process.

Life-stage

March and Simon (1958) suggested that the compatibility of the work role with other life roles was an important component of the turnover process. Indeed, an employee's stage in various areas of personal life and professional life may affect the turnover decision-making process and the speed of transition from one phase to the next. Professionally, there are different stages in a job, career and organization. Personally, there are different stages in friendships, marriage, parenthood and other relationships.

Stages in various life roles may influence not only what occurs during each phase of the dynamic turnover process but also how quickly an individual moves between the phases. For instance, the degree to which an employee's values, needs, interests and preferences match those of the job and the organization will change depending on where an individual is in various life roles. Also, the type, timing and frequency of shocks experienced will vary depending on life-stages, and where an individual is in life may influence the final decision to stay or leave.

Earlier research explored constructs related to life-stage. For instance, role conflict between work and non-work roles can create negative reactions that lead to withdrawal cognitions (Hom & Kinicki, 2001) and turnover (Huffman, Casper & Payne, 2014). Additionally, the extent to which organizational policies meet the diverse needs of workers at different life-stages has been linked with turnover intentions (e.g., Skinner et al., 2014). But most research on life-stages has been cross-sectional or retrospective, preventing researchers from truly understanding how life-stages affect the turnover process. Future research needs to evaluate where employees are in their personal life roles, job roles, tenure in an organization and careers.

In line with prior authors' calls, researchers need to continue utilizing repeated measures and longitudinal designs that follow employees as they move through the stages of their personal and professional roles, as this will allow researchers to determine whether the turnover process unfolds differently for employees at different life-stages. Researchers could measure the relative importance of different decision inputs over time by asking employees at various life-stages what is salient to them in their turnover decisions (Holtom et al., 2008; Russell, 2013).

Individual decision modelling

In addition to between-subject differences in the decision to quit, how a single employee decides to quit can vary greatly depending on a number of variables (e.g., life-stage, extent of job embeddedness). To examine within-subject differences in the turnover decision process, we concur with Russell's (2013) call to make more use of decision simulation exercises. Focusing more on how employees decide to quit can help researchers estimate individual models that map idiosyncratic decisions to stay or leave an organization.

Stayers

The long-standing presumption that staying and leaving are related behaviours (Harman, Lee, Mitchell, Felps & Owens, 2007; Mitchell et al., 2001; Steel, Griffeth & Hom, 2002) has led to the false assumption that the factors contributing to turnover are related to retention. Because staying and leaving are psychologically distinct constructs, the decision processes and antecedents for each may differ, making it important to examine them independently. Indeed, Steel and colleagues (2002) argued that different motives may be salient for stayers (e.g., a strong relationship with a supervisor) and leaving (e.g., career advancement). Many organizations do indeed conduct 'stay' interviews. Future research should continue to explore why people stay in their organizations; results could be used to bolster retention efforts.

Newcomers

Turnover often occurs early in an employee's tenure (Hom & Griffeth, 1995), yet this employee population has been ignored (Holtom et al., 2008). Early turnover can be costly, as investments in employees are not typically realized until they have been with an organization for at least six months. As a preventative measure, scholars have suggested identifying applicants with turnover propensities prior to organizational entry (Barrick & Zimmerman, 2005). For instance, applicants have pre-existing attitudes and intentions that are indicative of turnover (Hom & Griffeth, 1995), such as desire for the position and advanced quitting plans (Hom & Griffeth, 1995; Lee & Mitchell, 1994; Maertz & Campion, 2004). Future research should explore both individual differences and contextual factors that cause newcomers to leave soon after joining an organization.

Boomerang employees

Employees who leave their organizations and return at a later date – so-called boomerang employees – are a unique population. This group has received very little attention in the turnover literature, despite the prevalence of this hiring strategy (Shipp, Furst-Holloway, Harris & Rosen, 2014) and evidence suggesting that boomerangs tend to stay on the job longer and perform well on return, particularly those who initiated their own departure and performed well before leaving the organization (Sertoglu & Berkowitch, 2002; Swider, Liu, Harris & Gardner, 2015). A focus on this population can help organizations understand not only what drives employees to leave, but what compels them to return. For instance, Shipp and colleagues' (2014) examination of re-hires revealed that when these individuals decided to leave they had more often formed a plan for what to do after leaving the job (e.g., pregnancy, going to graduate school, pursuing a specific career goal) than those who quit and never returned. These findings imply that when employees leave for planned personal reasons, rather than because of negative work experiences, employers may be able to influence them to stay. Future research on boomerangs could reveal whether such strategies are effective.

Turnover destinations

To date, little is known about where employees go after leaving their organizations. Studies of turnover destinations could provide much insight into what drives employees to leave (Hom et al., 2012). Exit interviews typically include questions about the leaver's new job and organization. This information could be used to determine whether predictors of turnover differ depending on destination. For example, the motivational forces that cause a high-skilled worker to go to a competitor are likely to differ from the motivational forces that compel a stagnant worker to move on to a new occupation.

Multinational samples

Many turnover studies have been conducted on non-US samples, as discussed earlier (Harman, Blum, Stefani & Taho, 2009; Robinson, Griffeth, Allen & Lee, 2012), with the majority of non-US studies conducted in Australia (e.g., Smith, Oczkowski & Smith, 2011), the UK (e.g., Morrell, Loan-Clarke, Arnold & Wilkinson, 2008), China (e.g., Hom & Xiao, 2011) and India (e.g., Guchait & Cho, 2010). The purpose of these studies has mainly been to replicate US findings (e.g., Allen et al., 2009) and determine whether relationships vary by culture and national content (Gelfand, Erez & Aycan, 2007). The research suggests that certain variables that are highly predictive of turnover in the US, such as job embeddedness, may have differential effects cross-culturally (Harman et al., 2009; Ramesh & Gelfand, 2010). For instance, off-the-job embeddedness may be more important in collectivistic culture than in individualistic cultures (Jiang et al., 2012). Although some cross-cultural research has gone beyond examining just one nationality by making comparisons between US and non-US employees (e.g., Bingham, Boswell & Boudreau, 2005; Wang, Lawler, Walumbwa & Shi, 2004), this crash approach (i.e., comparing just one country's results with the rest of the world) is still quite limited. Other cross-cultural studies have compared multiple countries within a region, such as Europe (Tanova & Holtom, 2008; Zheng & Lamond, 2010). But to truly understand how antecedents, consequences and turnover decisions differ across regions, future research needs to be conducted with large cross-national samples.

In summary, there are many emerging areas in turnover research that can serve as the foundation for future research over the following decades. We have highlighted just a few in this section. Future research on employee life-stages and individual decision modelling can build on the critical notion of time in the turnover process. Further research on stayers, newcomers, boomerang employees and turnover destinations can greatly expand our understanding of the factors impacting employee turnover and retention. Lastly, large multinational samples can expand existing turnover models and provide further insight into the role of cultural values and context in turnover decisions.

Conclusion

We are in the human capital era (Burke & Cooper, 2008; Fitz-enz, 2000). A growing body of research shows that in today's business environment, where technology and global economies can level the playing field, employees represent one of the few unique competitive advantages that companies have (Pfeffer, 1994, 1998; Ulrich & Brockbank, 2005; Ulrich & Smallwood, 2003). With this in mind, many organizations are doing everything they can to attract, engage and retain their employees.

Over the past five decades or more, we have learned much about why employees quit their jobs. For some, the decision is based on a considered analysis of inputs and outputs. For others, it comes after months of disengaging and disappointing experiences. Some employees leave because sudden changes at work cause them to re-evaluate their jobs and careers. Others experience events outside of work – the birth of a child, the onset of an illness – that pull them away.

Based on this body of research, we now have a much better understanding of the various ways that turnover decisions are made. While the turnover process is complex and multiple pathways exist, there are evidence-based strategies that leaders and managers can utilize to increase retention. By building and sustaining a positive work environment, organizations can proactively create a culture that prevents turnover. By socializing employees, fostering relationships and creating a good job fit, managers can help employees fully embed in the organization. Through supportive, fair and rewarding behaviours and actions, leaders and managers can increase employees' job satisfaction and organizational commitment. Finally, during periods of change, leaders and managers can respond to employees' concerns and develop adaptive strategies that discourage top talent from quitting. Through exit interviews and retention-specific linkage studies, HR analysts can identify turnover trends, concerns and root causes within their own organization.

Despite decades of progress, there is still more to learn about employee retention and turnover. We hope this chapter encourages researchers and practitioners to continue exploring new ways to prevent dysfunctional turnover and create work environments that are productive, rewarding and engaging for employees.

References

Ajzen, I., & Fishbein, M. (1980). *Understanding Attitudes and Predicting Social Behavior*. Englewood Cliffs, NJ: Prentice-Hall.

Aladwan, K., Bhanugopan, R., & Fish, A. (2013). Why do employees jump ship? Examining intent to quit employment in a non-western cultural context. *Employee Relations, 35*, 408–422. doi:10.1108/ER-03-2012-0027.

Allen, D. G. (2006). Do organizational socialization tactics influence newcomer embeddedness and turnover? *Journal of Management, 32*, 237–256. doi: 10.1177/0149206305280103.

Allen, D. G., Bryant, P. C., & Vardaman, J. M. (2010). Retaining talent: Replacing misconceptions with evidence-based strategies. *Academy of Management Perspectives, 24*, 48–64. doi: 10.5465/AMP.2010.51827775.

Allen, D. G., Griffeth, R. W., Vardaman, J. M., Aquino, K., Gaertner, S., & Lee, M. (2009). Structural validity and generalisability of a referent cognitions model of turnover intentions. *Applied Psychology: An International Review, 58*, 709–728. doi: 10.1111/j.1464-0597.2008.00374.x.

Allen, D. G., Shore, L. M., & Griffeth, R. W. (2003). The role of perceived organizational support and supportive human resource practices in the turnover process. *Journal of Management, 29*, 99–118. doi: 10.1177/014920630302900107.

Allen, D. G., Weeks, K. P., & Moffitt, K. R. (2005). Turnover intentions and voluntary turnover: The moderating roles of self-monitoring, locus of control, proactive personality, and risk aversion. *Journal of Applied Psychology, 90*, 980–990. doi: 10.1037/0021-9010.90.5.980.

Bahn, S. (2014). Managing the well-being of temporary skilled migrants. *The International Journal of Human Resource Management* (ahead of print), 1–19. doi: 10.1080/09585192.2014.971849.

Ballinger, G. A., Lehman, D. W., & Schoorman, F. D. (2010). Leader–member exchange and turnover before and after succession events. *Organizational Behavior and Human Decision Processes, 113*, 25–36. doi: 10.1016/j.obhdp.2010.04.003.

Barrick, M. R., & Zimmerman, R. D. (2005). Reducing voluntary, avoidable turnover through selection. *Journal of Applied Psychology, 90*, 159–166. doi: 10.1037/0021-9010.90.1.159.

Batt, R., & Colvin, A. J. (2011). An employment systems approach to turnover: Human resources practices, quits, dismissals, and performance. *Academy of Management Journal, 54*, 695–717. doi: 10.5465/AMJ.2011.64869448.

Bauer, T. N., Erdogan, B., Liden, R. C., & Wayne, S. J. (2006). A longitudinal study of the moderating role of extraversion: Leader–member exchange, performance, and turnover during new executive development. *Journal of Applied Psychology, 91*, 298–310. doi: 10.1037/0021-9010.91.2.298.

Beach, L. R. (1990). *Image Theory: Decision Making in Personal and Organizational Contexts.* Chichester: Wiley.

Bhaskar-Shrinivas, P., Harrison, D. A., Shaffer, M. A., & Luk, D. M. (2005). Input-based and time-based models of international adjustment: Meta-analytic evidence and theoretical extensions. *Academy of Management Journal, 48*, 257–281. doi:10.5465/AMJ.2005.16928400.

Bingham, J. B., Boswell, W. R., & Boudreau, J. W. (2005). Job demands and job search among high-level managers in the United States and Europe. *Group & Organization Management, 30*, 653–681. doi: 10.1177/1059601104269527.

Black, J. S., & Gregersen, H. B. (1991). Antecedents to cross-cultural adjustment for expatriates in Pacific Rim assignments. *Human Relations, 44*, 497–515. doi: 10.1177/001872679104400505.

Blau, G. (1993). Further exploring the relationship between job search and voluntary individual turnover. *Personnel Psychology, 46*, 313–330. doi: 10.1111/j.1744-6570.1993.tb00876.x.

Bloom, M., & Michel, J. G. (2002). The relationships among organizational context, pay dispersion, and managerial turnover. *Academy of Management Journal, 45*, 33–42. doi: 10.2307/3069283.

Boroş, S., & Curşeu, P. L. (2013). Is it here where I belong? An integrative model of turnover intentions. *Journal of Applied Social Psychology, 43*, 1553–1562. doi: 10.1111/jasp.12104.

Breaugh, J. A., & Starke, M. (2000). Research on employee recruitment: So many studies, so many remaining questions. *Journal of Management, 26*, 405–434. doi:10.1177/014920630002600303.

Breevaart, K., Bakker, A., Hetland, J., Demerouti, E., Olsen, O. K., & Espevik, R. (2014). Daily transactional and transformational leadership and daily employee engagement. *Journal of Occupational & Organizational Psychology, 87*, 138–157. doi:10.1111/joop.12041.

Burke, R. J., & Cooper, C. L. (2008). *Building More Effective Organizations.* Cambridge: Cambridge University Press.

Campbell, N. S., Perry, S. J., Maertz, C. P., Allen, D. G., & Griffeth, R. W. (2013). All you need is … resources: The effects of justice and support on burnout and turnover. *Human Relations, 66*, 759–782. doi: 10.1177/0018726712462614.

Carmeli, A., & Weisberg, J. (2006). Exploring turnover intentions among three professional groups of employees. *Human Resource Development International, 9,* 191–206. doi: 10.1080/13678860600616305.

Cavanaugh, M. A., Boswell, W. R., Roehling, M. V., & Boudreau, J. W. (2000). An empirical examination of self-reported work stress among U.S. managers. *Journal of Applied Psychology, 85,* 65–74. doi: 10.1037/0021-9010.85.1.65.

Chang, W. J., Wang, Y. S., & Huang, T. C. (2013). Work design-related antecedents of turnover intention: A multilevel approach. *Human Resource Management, 52,* 1–26. doi: 10.1002/hrm.21515.

Chernyak-Hai, L., & Tziner, A. (2014). Relations between counterproductive work behavior, perceived justice and climate, occupational status and leader–member exchange. *Journal of Work and Organizational Psychology, 30,* 1–12. doi:10.5093/tr2014a.

Chin, P.L., & Hung, M. L. (2013). Psychological contract breach and turnover intention: The moderating roles of adversity quotient and gender. *Social Behavior and Personality, 41,* 843–860. doi: 10.2224/sbp.2013.41.5.843.

Crossley, C. D., Bennett, R. J., Jex, S. M., & Burnfield, J. L. (2007). Development of a global measure of job embeddedness and integration into a traditional model of voluntary turnover. *Journal of Applied Psychology, 92,* 1031–1042. doi: 10.1037/0021-9010.92.4.1031.

Culpepper, R. A. (2011). Three-component commitment and turnover: An examination of temporal aspects. *Journal of Vocational Behavior, 79,* 517–527. doi: 10.1016/j.jvb.2011.03.004.

Dalal, R., Baysinger, M., Brummel, B., & LeBreton, J. (2012). The relative importance of employee engagement, other job attitudes, and trait affect as predictors of job performance. *Journal of Applied Social Psychology, 42,* 295–325. doi: 10.1111/j.1559-1816.2012.01017.x.

Dawley, D. D., & Andrews, M. C. (2012). Staying put: Off-the-job embeddedness as a moderator of the relationship between on-the-job embeddedness and turnover intentions. *Journal of Leadership & Organizational Studies, 19,* 477–485. doi: 10.1177/1548051812448822.

Fishbein, M. (1967). *Readings in Attitude Theory and Measurement.* Oxford: Wiley.

Fishbein, M., & Ajzen, I. (1975). *Belief, Attitude, Intention and Behavior: An Introduction to Theory snd Research.* Reading, MA: Addison-Wesley.

Fitz-enz, J. (2000). *The ROI of Human Capital: Measuring the Economic Value of Employee Performance.* New York: American Management Association.

Friedman, R. A., & Holtom, B. (2002). The effects of network groups on minority employee turnover intentions. *Human Resource Management, 41,* 405. doi: 10.1002/hrm.10051.

García-Chas, R., Neira-Fontela, E., & Castro-Casal, C. (2014). High-performance work system and intention to leave: A mediation model. *The International Journal of Human Resource Management, 25,* 367–389. doi: 10.1080/09585192.2013.789441.

Gelfand, M. J., Erez, M., & Aycan, Z. (2007). Cross-cultural organizational behavior. *Annual Review of Psychology, 58,* 479–514. doi: 10.1146/annurev.psych.58.110405.085559.

Gerhart, B. (1990). Voluntary turnover and alternative job opportunities. *Journal of Applied Psychology, 75,* 467–476. doi: 10.1037/0021-9010.75.5.467.

Golden, T. (2007). Co-workers who telework and the impact on those in the office: Understanding the implications of virtual work for co-worker satisfaction and turnover intentions. *Human Relations, 60,* 1641–1667. doi: 10.1177/0018726707084303.

Gong, Y., Law, K. S., Chang, S., & Xin, K. R. (2009). Human resources management and firm performance: The differential role of managerial affective and continuance commitment. *Journal of Applied Psychology, 94,* 263–275. doi: 10.1037/a0013116.

Griffeth, R. W., & Hom, P. W. (2001). *Retaining Valued Employees.* Thousand Oaks, CA: Sage.

Griffeth, R. W., Hom, P. W., & Gaertner, S. (2000). A meta-analysis of antecedents and correlates of employee turnover: Update, moderator tests, and research implications for the next millennium. *Journal of Management, 26,* 463–488. doi: 10.1177/014920630002600305.

Griffeth, R. W., Steel, R. P., Allen, D. G., & Bryan, N. (2005). The development of a multidimensional measure of job market cognitions: The employment opportunity index (EOI). *Journal of Applied Psychology, 90,* 335–349. doi: 10.1037/0021-9010.90.2.335.

Guchait, P., & Cho, S. (2010). The impact of human resource management practices on intention to leave of employees in the service industry in India: The mediating role of organizational commitment. *International Journal of Human Resource Management, 21*, 1228–1247. doi: 10.1080/09585192.2010.483845.

Haivas, S., Hofmans, J., & Pepermans, R. (2013). Volunteer engagement and intention to quit from a self-determination theory perspective. *Journal of Applied Social Psychology, 43*, 1869–1880. doi: 10.1111/jasp.12149.

Halbesleben, J. R., & Wheeler, A. R. (2008). The relative roles of engagement and embeddedness in predicting job performance and intention to leave. *Work & Stress, 22*, 242–256. doi: 10.1080/02678370802383962.

Halvorsen, B., Treuren, G. J., & Kulik, C. T. (2015). Job embeddedness among migrants: Fit and links without sacrifice. *International Journal of Human Resource Management, 26*, 1298–1317. doi:10.1080/09585192.2014.990399.

Hammer, L., Bauer, T., & Grandey, A. (2003). Work–family conflict and work-related withdrawal behaviors. *Journal of Business and Psychology, 17*, 419–436. doi: 10.1023/A:1022820609967.

Han, G., & Jekel, M. (2011). The mediating role of job satisfaction between leader–member exchange and turnover intentions. *Journal of Nursing Management, 19*, 41–49. doi: 10.1111/j.1365-2834.2010.01184.x.

Hancock, J. I., Allen, D. G., Bosco, F. A., McDaniel, K. R., & Pierce, C. A. (2013). Meta-analytic review of employee turnover as a predictor of firm performance. *Journal of Management, 39*, 573–603. doi: 10.1177/0149206311424943.

Harman, W. S., Blum, M., Stefani, J., & Taho, A. (2009). Albanian turnover: Is the job embeddedness construct predictive in an Albanian context? *Journal of Behavioral & Applied Management, 10*, 192–205.

Harman, W. S., Lee, T. W., Mitchell, T. R., Felps, W., & Owens, B. P. (2007). The psychology of voluntary employee turnover. *Current Directions in Psychological Science, 16*, 51–54. doi: 10.1111/j.1467-8721.2007.00474.x.

Harris, K. J., Kacmar, K. M., & Witt, L. A. (2005). An examination of the curvilinear relationship between leader–member exchange and intent to turnover. *Journal of Organizational Behavior, 26*, 363–378. doi: 10.1002/job.314.

Harrison, D. A., Newman, D. A., & Roth, P. L. (2006). How important are job attitudes? Meta-analytic comparisons of integrative behavioral outcomes and time sequences. *Academy of Management Journal, 49*, 305–325. doi: 10.5465/AMJ.2006.20786077.

Heavey, A. L., Holwerda, J. A., & Hausknecht, J. P. (2013). Causes and consequences of collective turnover: A meta-analytic review. *Journal of Applied Psychology, 98*, 412–453. doi: 10.1037/a0032380.

Heneman, H. G., & Judge, T. A. (2006). *Staffing Organization*. Middleton, WI: Mendota House.

Hollenbeck, J. R., & Williams, C. R. (1986). Turnover functionality versus turnover frequency: A note on work attitudes and organizational effectiveness. *Journal of Applied Psychology, 71*, 606–611. doi: 10.1037/0021-9010.71.4.606.

Holtom, B. C., & Inderrieden, E. J. (2006). Integrating the unfolding model and job embeddedness model to better understand voluntary turnover. *Journal of Managerial Issues, 18*, 435–452.

Holtom, B. C., Burton, J. P., & Crossley, C. D. (2012). How negative affectivity moderates the relationship between shocks, embeddedness and worker behaviors. *Journal of Vocational Behavior, 80*(2), 434–443. doi: 10.1016/j.jvb.2011.12.006.

Holtom, B. C., Mitchell, T. R., Lee, T. W., & Eberly, M. B. (2008). Turnover and retention research: A glance at the past, a closer review of the present, and a venture into the future. *The Academy of Management Annals, 2*, 231–274. doi: 10.1080/19416520802211552.

Holtom, B. C., Mitchell, T. R., Lee, T. W., & Inderrieden, E. J. (2005). Shocks as causes of turnover: What they are and how organizations can manage them. *Human Resource Management, 44*, 337–352. doi: 10.1002/hrm.20074.

Holtz, B., & Harold, C. (2013). Effects of leadership consideration and structure on employee perceptions of justice and counterproductive work behavior. *Journal of Organizational Behavior, 34*, 492–519. doi: 10.1002/job.1825.

Hom, P. W., & Griffeth, R. W. (1995). *Employee Turnover*. Mason, OH: South-Western Publishing.

Hom, P. W., & Kinicki, A. J. (2001). Toward a greater understanding of how dissatisfaction drives employee turnover. *Academy of Management Journal, 44*, 975–987. doi: 10.2307/3069441.

Hom, P. W., Mitchell, T. R., Lee, P. W., & Griffeth, R. W. (2012). Reviewing employee turnover: Focusing on proximal withdrawal states and an expanded criterion. *Psychological Bulletin, 138,* 831–858. doi: 10.1037/a0027983.

Hom, P. W., & Xiao, Z. (2011). Embedding social networks: How guanxi ties reinforce Chinese employees' retention. *Organizational Behavior and Human Decision Processes, 116,* 188–202. doi: 10.1016/j.obhdp.2011.06.001.

Huffman, A. H., Casper, W. J., & Payne, S. C. (2014). How does spouse career support relate to employee turnover? Work interfering with family and job satisfaction as mediators. *Journal of Organizational Behavior, 35,* 194–212. doi: 10.1002/job.1862.

Hulin, C. (1991). Adaptation, persistence, and commitment in organizations. *In* M. D. Dunnette, & L. M. Hough (Eds.), *Handbook of Industrial and Organizational Psychology* (2nd ed., Vol. 2, pp. 445–505). Palo Alto, CA: Consulting Psychologists Press.

Hulin, C. L., Roznowski, M., & Hachiya, D. (1985). Alternative opportunities and withdrawal decisions: Empirical and theoretical discrepancies and an integration. *Psychological Bulletin, 97,* 233–250. doi: 10.1037/0033-2909.97.2.233.

Iverson, R. D., & Pullman, J. A. (2000). Determinants of voluntary turnover and layoffs in an environment of repeated downsizing following a merger: An event history analysis. *Journal of Management, 26,* 977–1003. doi: 10.1177/014920630002600510.

Jiang, K., Liu, D., McKay, P. F., Lee, T. W., & Mitchell, T. R. (2012). When and how is job embeddedness predictive of turnover? A meta-analytic investigation. *Journal of Applied Psychology, 97,* 1077–1096. doi: 10.1037/a0028610.

Kammeyer-Mueller, J. D., & Wanberg, C. R. (2003). Unwrapping the organizational entry process: Disentangling multiple antecedents and their pathways to adjustment. *Journal of Applied Psychology, 88,* 779–794. doi: 10.1037/0021-9010.88.5.779.

Kammeyer-Mueller, J. D., Wanberg, C. R., Glomb, T. M., & Ahlburg, D. (2005). The role of temporal shifts in turnover processes: It's about time. *Journal of Applied Psychology, 90,* 644–658. doi: 10.1037/0021-9010.90.4.644.

Kim, T. G., Lee, J. K., & Lee, J. H. (2013). Do interpersonal relationships still matter for turnover intention? A comparison of South Korea and China. *International Journal of Human Resource Management, 24,* 966–984. doi:10.1080/09585192.2012.743472.

Kopelman, R. E., Rovenpor, J. L., & Millsap, R. E. (1992). Rationale and construct validity evidence for the job search behavior index: Because intentions (and New Year's resolutions) often come to naught. *Journal of Vocational Behavior, 40,* 269–287. doi: 10.1016/0001-8791(92)90051-Z.

Kristof-Brown, A. L., Zimmerman, R. D., & Johnson, E. C. (2005). Consequences of individuals' fit at work: A meta-analysis of person–job, person–organization, person–group, and person–supervisor fit. *Personnel Psychology, 58,* 281–342. doi: 10.1111/j.1744-6570.2005.00672.x.

Lee, T. H., Gerhart, B., Weller, I., & Trevor, C. O. (2008). Understanding voluntary turnover: Path-specific job satisfaction effects and the importance of unsolicited job offers. *Academy of Management Journal, 51,* 651–671. doi: 10.5465/AMR.2008.33665124.

Lee, T. W., & Mitchell, T. R. (1994). An alternative approach: The unfolding model of voluntary employee turnover. *Academy of Management Review, 19,* 51–89. doi: 10.5465/AMR.1994.9410122008.

Lee, T. W., Mitchell, T. R., Holtom, B. C., McDaniel, L. S., & Hill, J. W. (1999). The unfolding model of voluntary turnover: A replication and extension. *Academy of Management Journal, 42,* 450–462. doi: 10.2307/257015.

Lee, T. W., Mitchell, T. R., Sablynski, C. J., Burton, J. P., & Holtom, B. C. (2004). The effects of job embeddedness on organizational citizenship, job performance, volitional absences, and voluntary turnover. *Academy of Management Journal, 47,* 711–722. doi: 10.2307/20159613.

Lee, T. W., Mitchell, T. R., Wise, L., & Fireman, S. (1996). An unfolding model of voluntary employee turnover. *Academy of Management Journal, 39,* 5–36. doi: 10.2307/256629.

Maertz, C. P. (2001). Why employees stay with or quit an organization. Paper presented at the 61st annual meeting of the Academy of Management. Washington, DC.

Maertz, C. P., & Campion, M. A. (2004). Profiles in quitting: Integrating process and content turnover theory. *Academy of Management Journal, 47,* 566–582. doi: 10.2307/20159602.

Maertz, C. P., & Griffeth, R. W. (2004). Eight motivational forces and voluntary turnover: A theoretical synthesis with implications for research. *Journal of Management, 30,* 667–683. doi: 10.1016/j.jm.2004.04.001.

Maertz, C. P., Griffeth, R. W., Campbell, N. S., & Allen, D. G. (2007). The effects of perceived organizational support and perceived supervisor support on employee turnover. *Journal of Organizational Behavior, 28,* 1059–1075. doi: 10.1002/job.472.

Maertz, C. P., Stevens, M. J., & Campion, M. A. (2003). A turnover model for the Mexican *maquiladoras. Journal of Vocational Behavior, 63,* 111–135. doi:10.1016/S0001-8791(02)00023-4.

March, J. G., & Simon, H. (1958). *Organizations.* Oxford: Wiley.

McClean, E. J., Burris, E. R., & Detert, J. R. (2013). When does voice lead to exit? It depends on leadership. *Academy of Management Journal, 56,* 525–548. doi: 10.5465/amj.2011.0041.

Messersmith, J. G., Guthrie, J. P., Ji, Y. Y., & Lee, J.–Y. (2011). Executive turnover: The influence of dispersion and other pay system characteristics. *Journal of Applied Psychology, 96,* 457–469. doi: 10.1037/a0021654.

Meyer, J. P., Allen, N. J., & Smith, C. A. (1993). Commitment to organizations and occupations: Extension and test of a three-component conceptualization. *Journal of Applied Psychology, 78,* 538–551. doi: 10.1037/0021-9010.78.4.538.

Mignonac, K., & Herrbach, O. (2004). Linking work events, affective states, and attitudes: An empirical study of managers' emotions. *Journal of Business & Psychology, 19,* 221–240. doi: 10.1007/s10869-004-0549-3.

Mitchell, T. R., Holtom, B. C., Lee, T. W., Sablynski, C. J., & Erez, M. (2001). Why people stay: Using job embeddedness to predict voluntary turnover. *Academy of Management Journal, 44,* 1102–1121. doi: 10.2307/3069391.

Mobley, W. H. (1977). Intermediate linkages in the relationship between job satisfaction and employee turnover. *Journal of Applied Psychology, 62,* 237–240. doi: 10.1037/0021-9010.62.2.237.

Mobley, W. H., Griffeth, R. W., Hand, H. H., & Meglino, B. M. (1979). Review and conceptual analysis of the employee turnover process. *Psychological Bulletin, 86,* 493–522. doi: 10.1037/0033-2909.86.3.493.

Morrell, K. M., Loan-Clarke, J., & Wilkinson, A. J. (2004). Organisational change and employee turnover. *Personnel Review, 33,* 161–173. doi: 10.1108/00483480410518022.

Morrell, K., Loan-Clarke, J., Arnold, J., & Wilkinson, A. (2008). Mapping the decision to quit: A refinement and test of the unfolding model of voluntary turnover. *Applied Psychology: An International Review, 57,* 128–150. doi: 10.1111/j.1464-0597.2007.00286.x.

Morrison, E. W., & Robinson, S. L. (1997). When employees feel betrayed: A model of how psychological contract violation develops. *Academy of Management Review, 22,* 226–256. doi: 10.5465/AMR.1997.9707180265.

Mossholder, K. W., Settoon, R. P., & Henagan, S. C. (2005). A relational perspective on turnover: Examining structural, attitudinal, and behavioral predictors. *Academy of Management Journal, 48,* 607–618. doi: 10.5465/AMJ.2005.17843941.

Muchinsky, P. M., & Morrow, P. C. (1980). Multidisciplinary model of voluntary employee turnover. *Journal of Vocational Behavior, 17,* 263–290. doi: 10.1016/0001-8791(80)90022-6.

Ng, T. W., & Butts, M. M. (2009). Effectiveness of organizational efforts to lower turnover intentions: The moderating role of employee locus of control. *Human Resource Management, 48,* 289–310. doi: 10.1002/hrm.20280.

Nyberg, A. J., & Ployhart, R. E. (2013). Context-emergent turnover (CET) theory: A theory of collective turnover. *Academy of Management Review, 38,* 109–131. doi: 10.5465/amr.2011.0201.

Park, T. Y., & Shaw, J. D. (2013). Turnover rates and organizational performance: A meta-analysis. *Journal of Applied Psychology, 98,* 268–309. doi: 10.1037/a0030723.

Payne, S. C., & Huffman, A. H. (2005). A longitudinal examination of the influence of mentoring on organizational commitment and turnover. *Academy of Management Journal, 48,* 158–168. doi: 10.5465/AMJ.2005.15993166.

Peltokorpi, V. (2013). Job embeddedness in Japanese organizations. *International Journal of Human Resource Management, 24*(8), 1551–1569. doi:10.1080/09585192.2012.723636.

Peltokorpi, V., Allen, D. G., & Froese, F. (2015). Organizational embeddedness, turnover intentions, and voluntary turnover: The moderating effects of employee demographic characteristics and value orientations. *Journal of Organizational Behavior, 36*, 292–312. doi:10.1002/job.1981.

Peterson, S. L. (2004). Toward a theoretical model of employee turnover: A human resource development perspective. *Human Resource Development Review, 3*, 209–227. doi: 10.1177/1534484304267832.

Pfeffer, J. (1994). *Competitive Advantage Through People: Unleashing the Power of the Work Force*. Boston, MA: Harvard Business School Press.

Pfeffer, J. (1998). *The Human Equation: Building Profits by Putting People First*. Boston, MA: Harvard Business School Press.

Podsakoff, N. P., LePine, J. A., & LePine, M. A. (2007). Differential challenge stressor–hindrance stressor relationships with job attitudes, turnover intentions, turnover, and withdrawal behavior: A meta-analysis. *Journal of Applied Psychology, 92*, 438–454. doi: 10.1037/0021-9010.92.2.438.

Posthuma, R. A., Maertz, C. P., & Dworkin, J. B. (2007). Procedural justice's relationship with turnover: Explaining past inconsistent findings. *Journal of Organizational Behavior, 28*, 381–398. doi: 10.1002/job.427.

Pratkanis, A. R., Breckler, S. J., & Greenwald, A. G. (1989). *Attitude Structure and Function*. Hillsdale, NJ: Lawrence Erlbaum.

Price, J. L. (1977). *The Study of Turnover*. Ames, IO: Iowa State University Press.

Price, J. L., & Mueller, C. W. (1981). *Professional Turnover: The Case of Nurses*. Bridgeport, CT: Luce.

Price, J. L., & Mueller, C. W. (1986). *Absenteeism and Turnover of Hospital Employees*. Greenwich, CT: JAI Press.

Ramesh, A., & Gelfand, M. (2010). Will they stay or will they go? The role of job embeddedness in predicting turnover in individualistic and collectivistic cultures. *Journal of Applied Psychology, 95*, 807–823. doi:10.1037/a0019464.

Ramsay, C. S. (2006). Engagement at Intuit: It's the people. Symposium conducted at the Society for Industrial and Organizational Psychology 21st annual conference. Dallas, TX.

Ren, H., Shaffer, M. A., Harrison, D. A., Fu, C., & Fodchuk, K. M. (2014). Reactive adjustment or proactive embedding? Multistudy, multiwave evidence for dual pathways to expatriate retention. *Personnel Psychology, 67*, 203–239. doi:10.1111/peps.12034.

Rhoades, L., Eisenberger, R., & Armeli, S. (2001). Affective commitment to the organization: The contribution of perceived organizational support. *Journal of Applied Psychology, 86*, 825–836. doi: 10.1037/0021-9010.86.5.825.

Richman, A. L., Civian, J. T., Shannon, L. L., Jeffrey, H. E., & Brennan, R. T. (2008). The relationship of perceived flexibility, supportive work–life policies, and use of formal flexible arrangements and occasional flexibility to employee engagement and expected retention. *Community, Work & Family, 11*, 183–197. doi: 10.1080/13668800802050350.

Robinson, S. D., Griffeth, R. W., Allen, D. G., & Lee, M. B. (2012). Comparing operationalizations of dual commitment and their relationships with turnover intentions. *The International Journal of Human Resource Management, 23*, 1342–1359. doi: 10.1080/09585192.2011.579917.

Rothausen, T. J., Henderson, K. E., Arnold, J. K., & Malshe, A. (2015). Should I stay or should I go? Identity and well-being in sensemaking about retention and turnover. *Journal of Management*. Online publication. doi:10.1177/0149206315569312.

Rupp, D. E., & Spencer, S. (2006). When customers lash out: The effects of customer interactional injustice on emotional labor and the mediating role of discrete emotions. *Journal of Applied Psychology, 91*, 971–978. doi: 10.1037/0021-9010.91.4.971.

Russell, C. J. (2013), Is it time to voluntarily turn over theories of voluntary turnover? *Industrial & Organizational Psychology, 6*, 156–173. doi: 10.1111/iops.12028.

Sertoglu, C., & Berkowitch, A. (2002). Cultivating ex-employees. *Harvard Business Review, 80*, 20–21.

Shacklock, K., Brunetto, Y., & Nelson, S. (2009). The different variables that affect older males' and females' intentions to continue working. *Asia Pacific Journal of Human Resources, 47*, 79–101. doi: 10.1177/1038411108099291.

Shaw, J. D., Delery, J. E., Jenkins, G. D., & Gupta, N. (1998). An organization-level analysis of voluntary and involuntary turnover. *Academy of Management Journal, 41*, 511–525. doi: 10.2307/256939.

Shaw, J. D., Duffy, M. K., Johnson, J. L., & Lockhart, D. E. (2005). Turnover, social capital losses, and performance. *Academy of Management Journal, 48,* 594–606. doi: 10.5465/AMJ.2005.17843940.

Shaw, J. D., Gupta, N., & Delery, J. E. (2005). Alternative conceptualizations of the relationship between voluntary turnover and organizational performance. *Academy of Management Journal, 48,* 50–68. doi: 10.5465/AMJ.2005.15993112.

Sheridan, J. E., & Abelson, M. A. (1983). Cusp catastrophe model of employee turnover. *Academy of Management Journal, 26,* 418–436. doi: 10.2307/256254.

Shipp, A. J., Furst-Holloway, S., Harris, T. B., & Rosen, B. (2014). Gone today but here tomorrow: Extending the unfolding model of turnover to consider boomerang employees. *Personnel Psychology, 67,* 421–462. doi: 10.1111/peps.12039.

Shore, L. M., & Tetrick, L. E. (1991). A construct validity study of the survey of perceived organizational support. *Journal of Applied Psychology, 76,* 637–643. doi: 10.1037/0021-9010.76.5.637.

Siers, B. (2007). Relationships among organisational justice perceptions, adjustment, and turnover of United States-based expatriates. *Applied Psychology: An International Review, 56,* 437–459. doi:10.1111/j.1464-0597.2007.00269.x.

Skinner, N., Elton, J., Auer, J., & Pocock, B. (2014). Understanding and managing work–life interaction across the life course: A qualitative study. *Asia Pacific Journal of Human Resources, 52,* 93–109. doi:10.1111/1744-7941.12013.

Smith, A., Oczkowski, E., & Smith, C. S. (2011). To have and to hold: Modelling the drivers of employee turnover and skill retention in Australian organisations. *The International Journal of Human Resource Management, 22,* 395–416. doi: 10.1080/09585192.2011.540162.

Smith, D. R., Holtom, B. C., & Mitchell, T. R. (2011). Enhancing precision in the prediction of voluntary turnover and retirement. *Journal of Vocational Behavior, 79,* 290–302. doi: 10.1016/j.jvb.2010.11.003.

Somers, M. J. (1999). Application of two neural network paradigms to the study of voluntary employee turnover. *Journal of Applied Psychology, 84,* 177–185. doi: 10.1037/0021-9010.84.2.177.

Spreitzer, G. M., & Mishra, A. K. (2002). To stay or to go: Voluntary survivor turnover following an organizational downsizing. *Journal of Organizational Behavior, 23,* 707–729. doi: 10.1002/job.166.

Stanley, L., Vandenberghe, C., Vandenberg, R., & Bentein, K. (2013). Commitment profiles and employee turnover. *Journal of Vocational Behavior, 82,* 176–187. doi: 10.1016/j.jvb.2013.01.011.

Steel, R. (1996). Labor market dimensions as predictors of the reenlistment decisions of military personnel. *Journal of Applied Psychology, 81,* 421–428. doi: 10.1037/0021-9010.81.4.421.

Steel, R. P., Griffeth, R. W., & Hom, P. W. (2002). Practical retention policy for the practical manager. *Academy of Management Executive, 16,* 149–162. doi: 10.5465/AME.2002.7173588.

Steel, R. P., & Lounsbury, J. W. (2009). Turnover process models: Review and synthesis of a conceptual literature. *Human Resource Management Review, 19,* 271–282. doi:/10.1016/j.hrmr.2009.04.002.

Sturman, M. C., Shao, L., & Katz, J. H. (2012). The effect of culture on the curvilinear relationship between performance and turnover. *Journal Of Applied Psychology, 97,* 46–62. doi:10.1037/a0024868.

Swider, B. W., Boswell, W. R., & Zimmerman, R. D. (2011). Examining the job search–turnover relationship: The role of embeddedness, job satisfaction, and available alternatives. *Journal of Applied Psychology, 96,* 432–441. doi: 10.1037/a0021676.

Swider, B. W., Liu, J. T., Harris, T. B., & Gardner, R. G. (2015). Employees on the rebound: Toward a framework for boomerang employee performance. Paper presented at the 75th annual meeting of the Academy of Management, Vancouver, BC.

Swider, B. W., & Zimmerman, R. D. (2010). Born to burnout: A meta-analytic path model of personality, job burnout, and work outcomes. *Journal of Vocational Behavior, 76,* 487–506. doi: 10.1016/j.jvb.2010.01.003.

Tanova, C., & Holtom, B. C. (2008). Using job embeddedness factors to explain voluntary turnover in four European countries. *International Journal of Human Resource Management, 19,* 1553–1568. doi: 10.1080/09585190802294820.

Ton, Z., & Huckman, R. S. (2008). Managing the impact of employee turnover on performance: The role of process conformance. *Organization Science, 19,* 56–68. doi: 10.1287/orsc.1070.0294.

Trevor, C. O. (2001). Interactions among actual ease-of-movement determinants and job satisfaction in the prediction of voluntary turnover. *Academy of Management Journal, 44,* 621–638. doi: 10.2307/3069407.

Tse, H. H., Huang, X., & Lam, W. (2013). Why does transformational leadership matter for employee turnover? A multi-foci social exchange perspective. *The Leadership Quarterly, 24,* 763–776. doi: 10.1016/j.leaqua.2013.07.005.

Ulrich, D., & Brockbank, W. (2005). *The HR Value Proposition.*Boston, MA: Harvard Business Press.

Ulrich, D., & Smallwood, N. (2003). *Why the Bottom Line Isn't! How to Build Value Through People and Organizations.* New York: Wiley.

Van Dick, R., Christ, O., Stellmacher, J., Wagner, U., Ahlswede, O., Grubba, C., & Tissington, P. A. (2004). Should I stay or should I go? Explaining turnover intentions with organizational identification and job satisfaction. *British Journal of Management, 15,* 351–360. doi: 10.1111/j.1467-8551.2004.00424.x.

Vance, R. J. (2006). *Employee Engagement and Commitment: A Guide to Understanding, Measuring and Increasing Engagement in Your Organization.* Alexandria, VA: SHRM Foundation.

Vandenberghe, C., Panaccio, A., & Ayed, A. K. (2011). Continuance commitment and turnover: Examining the moderating role of negative affectivity and risk aversion. *Journal of Occupational & Organizational Psychology, 84,* 403–424. doi: 10.1348/096317910X491848.

Wang, P., Lawler, J. J., Walumbwa, F. O., & Shi, K. (2004). Work–family conflict and job withdrawal intentions: The moderating effect of cultural differences. *International Journal of Stress Management, 11,* 392–412. doi: 10.1037/1072-5245.11.4.392.

Weiss, H. M., & Cropanzano, R. (1996). Affective events theory: A theoretical discussion of the structure, causes and consequences of affective experiences at work. *Research in Organizational Behavior, 18,* 74.

Weller, I., Holtom, B. C., Matiaske, W., & Mellewigt, T. (2009). Level and time effects of recruitment sources on early voluntary turnover. *Journal of Applied Psychology, 94,* 1146–1162. doi: 10.1037/a0015924.

Wöcke, A., & Heymann, M. (2012). Impact of demographic variables on voluntary labour turnover in South Africa. *International Journal of Human Resource Management, 23,* 3479–3494. doi:10.1080/09585192.2011.639028.

Yingyan, W. (2010). Intention to stay in Chinese foreign-invested companies: Previous experiences, initial expectations and current satisfactions. *International Journal of Human Resource Management, 21,* 1996–2012. doi:10.1080/09585192.2010.505100.

Zhao, H., Wayne, S. J., Glibkowski, B. C., & Bravo, J. (2007). The impact of psychological contract breach on work-related outcomes: A meta-analysis. *Personnel Psychology, 60,* 647–680. doi: 10.1111/j.1744-6570.2007.00087.x.

Zheng, C., & Lamond, D. (2010). Organisational determinants of employee turnover for multinational companies in Asia. *Asia Pacific Journal of Management, 27,* 423–443. doi: 10.1007/s10490-009-9159-y.

Zimmerman, R. D. (2008). Understanding the impact of personality traits on individuals' turnover decisions: A meta-analytic path model. *Personnel Psychology, 61,* 309–348. doi: 10.1111/j.1744-6570.2008.00115.x.

22

Talent Management and Retention

Crystal Zhang and Jim Stewart

Introduction

Talent management and retention have become widely acknowledged as among the most important factors for organizational success since the McKinsey Report coined the term 'the war for talent' in 1997 (Collings & Mellahi, 2009). Given its popularity and strategic importance in the corporate world (Collings, Scullion & Vaiman, 2011; Festing & Schafer, 2014; PricewaterhouseCooper [PWC], 2013), the discourse and the practice have been principally driven by business and consulting firms (Al Ariss, Cascio & Paauwe, 2014), particularly under the notion of talent shortage. For example, the Economist Intelligence Unit in 2006 reported that 7 in 10 leaders spent more than 20% of their time on talent management activities. However, talent management has also become the most important challenge for HR directors in Europe and a 'headache' for CEOs (PWC, 2013), with only 30% of them saying they have the talent they need to fulfil their future growth ambitions. According to the Manpower Talent Shortage Survey (2015), different countries or regions have different demands on talents. In the Americas (Argentina, Brazil, Canada, Colombia, Costa Rica, Guatemala, Mexico, Panama, Peru and the United States), skilled trade workers, technicians and sales representatives are the three most difficult positions to fill, while in Asia-Pacific (Australia, China, Hong Kong, India, Japan, New Zealand, Singapore and Taiwan) sales representatives, engineers and technicians are the top three positions. In Europe, Middle East and Africa (Austria, Belgium, Bulgaria, Czech Republic, France, Germany, Greece, Hungary, Ireland, Israel, Italy, The Netherlands, Norway, Poland, Romania, Slovakia, Slovenia, South Africa, Spain, Sweden, Switzerland, Turkey and the UK), skilled trade workers, engineers and sales representatives are in high demand.

While organizations are waging this talent war with each other, it would appear that it is talent itself that has won (Bersin, 2013). Indeed, while unemployment rates remain high, those with skills critical to organizations continue to be in demand. Furthermore, the effect of the global village has enabled the workforce to be more mobile and eager to

The Wiley Blackwell Handbook of the Psychology of Recruitment, Selection and Employee Retention,
First Edition. Edited by Harold W. Goldstein, Elaine D. Pulakos, Jonathan Passmore and Carla Semedo.
© 2017 John Wiley & Sons Ltd. Published 2020 by John Wiley & Sons Ltd.

seek out and move to better organizations and labour markets (PWC, 2013). So, how do organizations attract talent and, crucially, how do they retain talent? This review first outlines the emerging literature on talent and talent management and then focuses on different types of retention strategy: employer branding, organizational attractiveness, talent engagement (the impact of leadership style, human resource development opportunity, rewards, benefits, on-boarding and organizational culture and identity), and their impact on talent retention. Finally, the future of talent retention research and strategy is discussed.

What is Talent Management?

Much has been written and discussed about the diverse definitions of talent and talent management, especially in the last six years, for example, when six special issues on talent management were published in the *Journal of World Business* (Al Ariss et al., 2014; Collings, Scullion & Vaiman, 2015; Dries, 2013; Glaister, Tatoglu & Demirbag, 2016; McDonnell, Collings & Burgess, 2012; Scullion, Collings & Caligiuri, 2010; Vaiman & Collings, 2013). From the practitioners' side, the UK Chartered Institute for Personnel Development (CIPD) has produced its own Learning and Talent Development annual report since 2011 (www.cipd.co.uk/research/learning-talent-development). Around the world, other societies such as the Society of Human Resource Management (SHRM) and the Association of Talent Development (previously American Society of Training and Development) in the US, and the Australian Human Resource Institute have also published reports and white papers on global talent management and global trends in talent development (Tarique & Schuler, 2012; www.td.org; www.ahri.com.au). Similarly, global consultancy companies (e.g., McKinsey, PricewaterhouseCoopers, Hay Group, Towers Watson, Manpower Group and Boston Consulting Group) regularly release updates on their global survey of talent management. However, given the increase of popularity of this topic and the importance of its role for organizations, little consensus on its definition has been achieved (Dries, 2013). McKinsey, which started the trend, produced a comprehensive definition of talent as 'the sum of a person's abilities ... intrinsic gifts, skills, knowledge, experience, intelligence, judgement, attitude, character and drive' (Michaels, Handfield-Jones & Axelrod, 2001). It also includes that talent has the ability to learn and grow. In the academic field, Gallardo-Gallardo, Dries and Gonzales-Cruz (2013) synthesized the various definitions and constructed a framework to understand talent (Figure 22.1). Thus, talent is a characteristic of either a person (an object) or a whole person (a subject).

In our review, we take this forward and consider talent as a fluid concept which is very dependent on circumstances (e.g., sector, size of organization, culture). Talent is valuable only to the organization; thus, a talent is identified only if there is a need for such skills in the organization. Talent management is therefore not just about attracting and retaining the talent, but also about reviewing the organizational needs and letting unrequired talent leave. In this review, we focus on selected retention strategies practised by high-retention companies.

Retention Strategies

Retention of valuable employees has been of serious concern to managers in the face of the ever-increasing high rate of employee turnover (Hay Group, 2014). A recent industry-wide survey of 618 organizations revealed that the majority of all attrition (52%) occurs, on

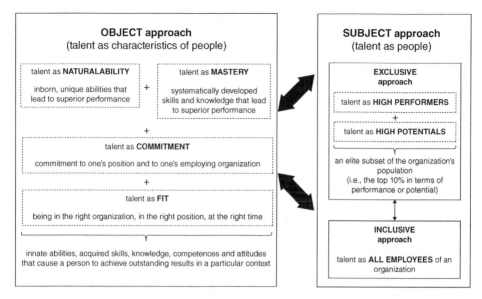

Figure 22.1   Gallardo-Gallardo's framework for conceptualization of talent within the world of work. *Source*: Gallardo-Gallardo et al. (2013). Reproduced with permission of Elsevier.

average, in the first year of employment, dropping to 27% thereafter (Talent Keepers, 2013). Why do people leave? Turnover is a complex phenomenon which is dependent on many variables. Griffeth and Hom (2001) described turnover according to three parameters: voluntary/involuntary, functional/dysfunctional and avoidable/unavoidable. Ineffective selection and on-boarding processes contribute to this early attrition spike. Poor fit based on the skills required (37%) and unfulfilled expectations of job duties and work schedules (30%) are the main reasons why people leave early (Talent Keepers, 2013). We discuss here some of the crucial factors affecting talent attraction and subsequently talent retention.

Employer branding

The term 'employer branding' describes how an organization markets what it has to offer to potential and existing employees (CIPD, 2009; Mandhanya & Shah, 2010). It characterizes the package of functional, economic and psychological benefits provided by employment and identified with the employing organization (Ambler & Barrow, 1996) as a means to differentiate itself in the competitive labour market highlighted by the 1997 McKinsey Report (Collings & Mellahi, 2009). Employer branding is borrowed from the field of marketing, where branding helps to attract customers (talent recruitment in our case), communicate with them effectively (talent engagement) and maintain their loyalty (talent retention). Organizations are increasingly looking to capitalize on their brand equity to successfully attract and retain talent, applying branding principles to people management (Backhaus & Tickoo, 2004). For example, the status of 'best employer' or 'employer of choice' is something that more and more organizations are striving for (Berthon, Ewing & Hah, 2005).

What factors underlie employer branding? Backhaus and Tickoo (2004) suggested several dimensions which can be grouped into corporate social responsibility, customer orientation and satisfaction, organizational climate, workers' non-work-related responsibilities, work–life balance and stakeholders' responsibility. Research into employer branding and its impact on talent retention is sparse, but many of the dimensions identified by Backhaus and Tickoo (2004) impact employee retention. Thus Botha, Bussin and De Swardt (2011) constructed a model which linked branding to talent attraction and retention. Indeed, attitudes to branding are different from attraction to retention (Ito, Brotheridge & McFarland, 2013). Sokro's (2012) study of the banking sector in Ghana revealed that 70% of surveyed bank employees valued their company image as an incentive to stay, closely followed by job security (71%) and opportunities for growth (74%). Similarly, a significant relationship was found between employer branding and employee retention in a survey of academics in Indian management institutes (Mehta & Sharma, 2013). Much academic focus has been on employer branding and its ability to attract talent, with the assumption that recruits attracted by a company's brand equity will more likely stay with the organization (Supornpraditchai, Miller, Lings & Jonmundsson, 2007). Thus several studies have shown that employer branding and the brand equity of an organization impact to some extent the attractiveness of the organization as a place of employment (e.g., Jiang & Iles, 2011; Moroko & Uncles, 2009; Priyadarshi, 2011; Shahzad, Gul, Khan & Zafar, 2011; Wilden, Gudergan & Lings, 2010). However, employees differ in their responses to employer branding and brand equity. Jiang and Iles (2011) found that national and cultural differences exist for rating the brand equity of organizations. Likewise, differences exist between the age and gender of employees (Alniacik & Alniacik, 2012). The benefits of brand equity include both internal and external organizational attractiveness (Jiang & Iles, 2011), which will be discussed in the following sections.

Organizational attractiveness

There has been a proliferation of assessments of organizational attractiveness (Auger, Devinney, Dowling, Eckert & Lin, 2013; Berthon et al., 2005; Ito et al., 2013). For example, consistent ranking in the 'Best Employer Survey' can influence choice in seeking organizations for employment (Berthon et al., 2005; Ito et al., 2013). It is sometimes assumed that attracting and retaining talent are similar processes (e.g. Botha et al., 2011). However, a global workforce survey by Towers Watson (2012) reveals that there are clear differences in priorities between organizational attractiveness and retention (see Table 22.1).

Talent engagement

Talent engagement can be summarized as the rational or emotional commitment to something or someone in the organization, how hard they work as a result of this commitment and how long they intend to stay (Macey & Schneider, 2008; Welch, 2011). Employees who are engaged are considered to be more productive, content and more likely to be loyal (Grumana & Saksb, 2011; Halbesleben & Wheeler, 2008;

Table 22.1 Priorities in talent attraction and retention.

Priority	Attraction	Retention
1	Base salary	Base salary
2	Job security	Career advancement opportunities
3	Career advancement opportunities	Relationship with manager
4	Convenient work location	Trust/confidence in leadership
5	Learning and development opportunities	Ability to manage/limit work-related stress

Source: Towers Watson (2012).

Markos & Sridevi, 2010; Rich, Lepine & Crawford, 2010). The growing importance of talent engagement to the organization can be seen in the increased cost of engaging employees: a survey from the HR consultancy Bersin by Deloitte revealed that $720 million was spent in the US, which was forecast to grow to about $1.5 billion (Kowske, 2012). Importantly for our discussion, a 2004 survey of 50,000 employees in 27 countries by the Corporate Leadership Council (2004) revealed a link between engagement and retention. Similar results were found in later global surveys (Towers Perrin, 2007; Towers Watson, 2012) and in academic research on talent engagement and retention in organizations ranging from business processing outsourcing (Arora, 2012; Bhatnagar, 2007; Tymon, Stumpf & Doh, 2010) and healthcare (Spence Laschinger, Leiter, Day & Gilin, 2009; Tillot, Walsh & Moxham, 2013) to hospitality (Hughes & Rog, 2008; Tews, Stafford & Michel, 2014a; Yang, Wan & Fu, 2012).

A workplace survey of 142 countries revealed that only 13% of the global workforce *is* engaged and 20% of the employees surveyed are reported to be actively disengaged, creating a negative atmosphere in the workplace (Gallup, 2013). What can be done to increase engagement? Much is being spent (Kowske, 2012), but are the large resources earmarked for talent engagement used effectively? The Corporate Leadership Council (2004) examined more than 300 potential factors affecting employee engagement and classified them into several overarching themes: management and leadership; financial rewards; benefits; on-boarding; learning and development opportunities; and organizational culture.

The Impact of Management and Leadership Style

Once hired, most of the responsibility for talent engagement and retention shifts to the line manager. Although the HR department and the senior management team may feel it is their responsibility to manage talent retention, it is crucial to include the direct managers to direct, guide and evaluate employees. Buckingham and Coffman's (1999) seminal analysis of the Gallup studies on workplace engagement, which includes interviews with 1 million employees and 80,000 managers across 142 countries, reveals that people leave managers not companies. Thus academic research has focused on understanding and improving management and leadership styles (Anthony et al., 2005; Duffield, Roche, Blay & Stasa, 2011; Taunton, Boyle, Woods, Hansen & Bott, 1997; Waldman, Carter & Hom, 2012; Wallis & Kennedy, 2013).

We focus our discussion on the healthcare sector, which provides an ideal research setting for investigating the role of leadership and retention. It has been proposed that nurse managers form a bridge between the senior executive team and frontline bedside nurses, and that nurse retention is one of the many responsibilities that characterize nurse managers' work (Andrews & Dziegielewski, 2005). Nursing staff turnover is high, with about 17.5% of newly licensed registered nurses leaving their first job within a year and 33.5% leaving within two years (Hayes et al., 2012). However, nurses do not leave the hospital; rather, they leave their managers (Ribelin, 2003) and thus they can provide further information regarding their reasons for leaving. This has also been observed across professions, with a survey reporting that 42% of employees leave because they dislike their manager (People Management CIPD, 2015). A study of leadership styles of nurse managers revealed that transformational style, in which the leader motivates followers to move beyond self-interest and work for the collective good, was significantly associated with lower staff turnover (Blake, Leach, Robbins, Pike & Needleman, 2013; Cowden, Cummings & Profetto-McGrath, 2011; Raup, 2008), whereas transactional leadership, in which the leader clarifies expectations and rewards followers for fulfilling these, was found to be a deterrent to retention (Kleinman, 2010). Similarly, research on leadership and retention in other sectors, such as the information technology, business process outsourcing (Resmi, Gemini, Silvian & Kannan, 2014; Thirulogasundaram & Kumar, 2012) and hospitality industries (Baytok, Kurt & Zorlu, 2014; Dai, Dai, Chen & Wu, 2013; Whitelaw, 2013), showed that transformational leadership positively affects organizational commitment through distributive justice and trust, leading to lower turnover.

If employees are viewed as drones working simply to fulfil work expectations, motivation and intention to stay can be low. However, if employees are treated as valuable members and motivated to perform, they are more likely to stay and work beyond expectations (Wang, Oh, Courtright & Colbert, 2011). The transformational leader will usually act as a mentor, coaching subordinates individually on their career path and providing the right work environment to draw on their talents and strengths, such as setting challenging job assignments and opportunities to contribute and make a difference, and allocating appropriate salary increases based on job performance (Tse, Huang & Lam, 2013).

In addition to appropriate leadership style, Kaye and Jordan-Evans (2000) suggested that a good manager should be able and empowered to choose the right talent to join the team, as this greatly increases the chances for strong group dynamics and reduces the risk of turnover. Thus research shows that a poor team climate is associated with a greater turnover rate in healthcare (Goh, Eccles & Steen, 2009; Kivimäki et al., 2007) and the hospitality industry (Tews, Michel & Allen, 2014b). When managers develop and utilize these key behaviours with high-potential individuals, they increase the overall likelihood for that high potential to remain with the organization.

The Impact of Financial Rewards

A Towers Watson survey (2012) placed salary as the top priority for both talent recruitment and retention. Referring to Maslow's hierarchy of needs (1943), the first level of needs is associated with the physiological needs that must be met for survival. Thus income represents the basic financial need to be fulfilled before other levels are considered. Furthermore, higher financial rewards make alternative employment unattractive. However, it is important to consider that the value of money is dependent on the profile of the talent, with age, gender, number of dependants, stage of career and professional background all influential factors. For example, money is important for the principal wage earner in the low-wage sector or in resource-poor countries (Dill, Morgan & Marshall, 2013), whereas those in higher-paid work or high-income countries will be more interested in work quality and career opportunities, for example (Ahmed et al., 2012). A Corporate Leadership Council's survey (2004) reveals that some employees will be more motivated by financial rewards than others, such as those in sales, where pay is more commonly related to performance. Indeed, tying compensation to performance was found to be a powerful lever of discretionary effort (Fang & Gerhart, 2012). As a precautionary note, it is important to remember that public sentiment about large annual bonuses for performance was negative following the financial crisis and bailouts of banks during the 2008–2009 economic crisis (DeSantis, 2008). Furthermore, pay for performance, when structured badly, is believed to provide an incentive for distorted behaviours to maximize short-run performance of the kinds that led to the implosion of organizations such of Enron and WorldCom (Rappaport, 2005).

To retain the most valuable people, it has become common practice to give employees retention bonuses, especially following a merger (Kohers & Ang, 2000;

Cosack, Guthridge & Lawson, 2010). However, retention cannot be accomplished through financial incentives alone (e.g., performance-based cash bonuses, increases in basic pay and stock) as evidence shows that for people with good salaries, some non-financial motivators (praise from line manager, attention from leaders and opportunities to lead projects or taskforces) are more effective in building long-term talent engagement in most sectors, job functions and business context (Dewhurst, Guthridge & Mohr, 2009). Furthermore, offeirng more pay for work can lead to a transactional leadership style which has been shown to increase turnover, as discussed earlier. In the aftermath of the economic recession, remuneration costs were cut by 15% or more (Dewhurst et al., 2009) leading some to comment on the relative importance of financial rewards for retention (Cosack et al., 2010; Giancola, 2012; Heskett, 2009). These rewards are estimated to be at least 5–8% of an employee's salary (Withers, 2001). Yet other types of non-financial, 'soft' benefits were found to be less expensive (about 4% of salary) and just as effective as a financial reward, if not more so.

The Impact of Benefits

In addition to medical and dental insurance, pension contributions and annual leave, organizations are offering more attractive 'soft' benefits (Hannay & Northam, 2000), such as medical insurance covering the employee's family, more annual leave based on seniority, a generous housing subsidy or a car loan (Chew, 2005). In addition, the provision of easy-access or on-site childcare facilities and flexible working hours has been shown to increase the retention of female employees in healthcare at all levels, from managers (Abbot, De Cieri & Iverson, 1998) to frontline nurses (Klemm & Scbreiber, 1992), especially for those returning after taking maternity leave (Nowak, Naude & Thomas, 2013).

The impact of non-financial benefits has also been investigated in retaining talent in developing areas, to counter the so-called brain drain (Willis-Shattuck et al., 2008, Taylor et al., 2011). This talent loss is associated with emigration from poor to developed countries, and, in the absence of financial benefits, retention initiatives have focused on housing subsidies, continuing education and hot meals (Gow et al., 2013; Taylor, Hwenda, Larsen & Daulaire, 2011; Willis-Shattuck et al., 2008). Interestingly, similar initiatives are also found in developed countries: healthcare workers are given housing benefits to prevent them from leaving hospitals in expensive locations (e.g., London), and also to prevent them from leaving undesirable locations (Baumann, Yan, Degelder & Malikov, 2006).

The Impact of On-boarding

Many organizations have realized that talent retention starts at the hiring process, and the window of opportunity to impact and impress new recruits comes within the first six months of employment (Gilmore & Turner, 2010; Lundberg & Young, 1997; Verlander & Evans, 2007). According to one HR consultancy, the Wynhurst Group, new employees decide whether they feel at home or not in the first three weeks on the job, 4% of new employees leave after a disastrous first day and 22% of staff turnovers occur within the first 45 days (cited in Caela, 2007). Thus, more and more companies have established formal on-boarding programmes and here there are areas which can be developed to maximize its effectiveness. Importantly, on-boarding is not simply the orientation tour given during the first or second day on the job, but a more comprehensive and strategic programme of integrating new recruits into the organization and providing them with the resources and information needed to integrate and succeed (Friedman, 2006; Lavigna, 2009). Communication is key to a successful on-boarding (Serbin & Jensen, 2013). This section describes strategies to make on-boarding effective.

Define and explain the formal and informal organization

New recruits will already have knowledge of the organization they are joining. The first day on the job is commonly their introduction to the actual work environment and introduction to the company culture. The indoctrination process attempts to show the newcomers 'how things are done around here' at both the formal and informal levels. Ross and colleagues (2014) propose assigning three levels of communication channels: 1) an orientation navigator who manages the day-to-day challenges of work and requires paperwork to be completed; 2) a 'work buddy' and mentor of equal standing in the organization who will provide moral support and information on how to get things done; and 3) a transition mentor to serve as a coach and 'sounding board' to promote growth, development and success in the organization. Mentors are an important asset for new staff training and retention, and poor mentoring is cited as a reason for staff turnover in many industries (Hayes et al., 2012; Sengupta & Gupta, 2012; Waterman & He, 2011; Yang et al., 2012). It is no wonder then that much effort has been spent in improving the selection of mentors (Haggard, Dougherty, Turban & Wilbanks, 2011). Thus it is important to consider the influence of the mentor's sex (Gray & Goregaokar, 2010) and learning styles (Armstrong, Allinson & Hayes, 2002) when selecting mentors to maximize the mentorship success (Ensher & Murphy, 2011).

Specify the role and responsibilities

According to the HR consultancy Novations, almost half of the staff leaving said that their departure was hastened by unrealistic expectations of the job and the organization (reported in Amble, 2007). The concept of a realistic job preview (RJP) has been introduced to provide job applicants with a clear idea of what the job really entails, so that, in theory, the potential new recruit is able to make an informed acceptance decision (Landis, Earnest & Allen, 2013). RJPs are defined as programmes, materials and/or presentations that provide applicants with accurate information and should objectively show both the positive and negative aspects of the job and the organizational environment (Wanous, 1989). After recruitment, the roles and responsibilities are confirmed during the on-boarding process. In the absence of RJPs, there is a risk of mismatch between expectations and reality, resulting in an increased intention to leave (Earnest et al., 2011). Some studies, though, have shown that RJPs have only a modest effect on turnover (e.g., McEvoy & Cascio, 1985; Premack & Wanous, 1985), but the low cost of implementing RJPs makes them a very cost-effective tool to manage turnover, especially when they are customized to particular talent targeted for recruitment (Earnest, Allen & Landis, 2011).

Performance management

All new employees want to know how they will be assessed and rewarded. The more an employee can see a direct link between effort and reward, the greater the probability (although not the certainty) of satisfaction and retention. Setting goals using the SMART process can increase positive feelings for retention; if expectations are too high or different from the original realistic job preview, the employee will experience mismatch, stress and negative feelings towards the organization (Latham, 2004). The SMART goals, according to Doran (1981), are:

- Specific – target a specific area.
- Measurable – quantify, or at least suggest, an indicator of progress.
- Assignable – specify who will do it.
- Realistic – state what results can realistically be achieved, given available resources.
- Time-related – specify when the result(s) can be achieved.

Research on performance and turnover has been inconsistent in its findings. A significant body of data exists establishing that, as performance decreases, employees are most likely considering to leave (McEvoy & Cascio, 1987; Voight & Hirst, 2014; Williams & Livingstone, 1994). High performers, who are rewarded for their superior work, will remain with an organization that values their performance and thus will be less likely to leave voluntarily. Should low performers be allowed or encouraged to leave? While there is a valid argument for this, Google, for example, believes that all employees are talented and should be retained, and that poor performance is most likely due to a mismatch with the job or poor management (Davenport, Harris & Shapiro, 2010). On the other side of the spectrum, some research has shown that high performers also leave (Nyberg, 2010; Park & Shaw, 2013; Salamin & Hom, 2005; Trevor, Gerhart & Boudreau, 1997). The argument for this turnover is that higher-performing employees, who are more desirable to rival companies as a result of their superior work product, will have more external job opportunities and will, consequently, be more likely than their lower-performing colleagues to leave voluntarily. Longitudinal studies confirm that pay and the unemployment rate can affect the impact of the performance–turnover relationship (Nyberg, 2010; Trevor et al., 1997).

Accentuate professional and career development

While most organizations provide some opportunities for training and development, what most employees are concerned with is a lack of guidance offered by their supervisors for career development. Here the role of the transition coach who serves as a mentor for career development is crucial to retaining talent. Studies in various industries replicate these findings: employees with lower turnover intentions receive more career development support from their mentor, and this mentor is someone more senior in the organization (Bhatnagar, 2007; Chang, Chou & Cheng, 2007; Chen, Chang & Yeh, 2004; Joiner, Garreffa & Bartram, 2004; Payne & Huffman, 2005; Scandura & Viator, 1994). An important caveat lies in enhancing the employees' career opportunities: too many employable skills might facilitate their exit from the organization. Benson (2006) indicated that on-the-job training to obtain specific skills increases retention while tuition-reimbursed classes on topics chosen by employees to add to their skills increased intention to leave. The conclusion is that this can be countered by integrating employee development programmes with a clear career path in the organization.

Foster socialization

Socialization is broadly defined as 'a process in which an individual acquires the attitudes, behaviours and knowledge needed to successfully participate as an organizational member' (van Maanen & Schein, 1977). Through socialization, new employees learn to adapt, form work relationships and find their place in the organization. A happy and caring work environment can improve organizational commitment and decrease the intention to leave (Allen & Shanock, 2013; Rink, Kane, Ellemers & Van der Vegt, 2013). Indeed, supervisor and co-worker incivilities, such as poor acceptance of the newcomer and reluctance to share knowledge, have been correlated with turnover intent (Allen & Shanock, 2013; Ghosh, Reio & Bang, 2013; Kammeyer-Mueller, Wanberg, Rubenstein & Song 2013; Lundberg & Young, 1997). This can be minimized by effective leadership behaviours (Taormina, 2008).

The Impact of Learning and Development Opportunities

It is often argued that employers increasingly expect individuals to take responsibility for managing their own careers (Sturges, Conway, Guest & Liefooghe, 2005). Career needs are defined by Chen and colleagues (2004) as personal needs for goals (e.g., a career landmark achieved), tasks (opportunities to develop in order to achieve the career goal) and challenges (future career needs arising from career developmental opportunities). In so far as career needs are highly dependent on many factors, among them individual needs, the stage employees have reached in their career, their level in the organization, career planning and management must be broad and diverse (Baruch, 2006). Opportunities for further educational and career development are important for talent retention. Neglecting to provide adequate career development programmes that satisfy the employees' career needs can lead to a decline in job satisfaction, job performance and morale, and an increased turnover intention (Chang et al., 2007; Chen et al., 2004; Hayes et al., 2012; Schmidt, 2007). However, even if programmes are in place for further training and development, it is important to realize that these opportunities are not perceived equally at all levels and with all types of employee. For example, some employees find that the opportunities offered are inadequate or that there is insufficient organizational support to pursue their development, leading to reduced engagement and increased turnover intentions (Shuck, Twyford, Reio & Shuck, 2014). Here, the good manager, coach and mentor should identify early signs of a lacuna between opportunities and needs. At the organizational level, by understanding the career needs of individual employees, it is possible to determine the gap and design career development programmes to address the deficiencies (Chang et al., 2006; Cleary, Horsfall, Muthulakshmi, Happell & Hunt, 2013).

The Impact of Organizational Culture and Organizational Identification

Talent is valuable only if the organization needs their skills and expertise. Similarly, if the talent does not match the organization, there is a high chance of turnover. Here we explore some of the factors affecting turnover.

Leader–member exchanges

The common saying is that 'people quit managers, not jobs.' Given that the direct representative of the organization is the line manager, we start by looking at the quality of the relationship between supervisor and subordinate using leader–member exchange (LMX) theory, which has been shown to correlate with turnover intention across several sectors (Brunetto et al., 2013; DeConink, 2011; Harris, Li & Kirkman, 2014;

Portoghese, Galletta, Battistelli & Leiter, 2014). LMX is different from person–supervisor fit in that it refers to the exchange between supervisor and subordinate. For example, employees who have a poor relationship with their manager will be assigned disliked tasks, leading to turnover intention. Conversely, a positive relationship with the manager can benefit the employee through an easier promotional climb and more rewarding work assignments (Brunetto et al., 2013). Several LMX models have been proposed, with the following key factors influencing the exchange: expectation of positive outcomes; affection for each other; loyalty to each other; perceptions of their contribution to the common goal; and professional respect (Dulebohn, Bommer, Liden, Brouer & Ferris, 2012; Liden & Maslyn, 1998). Furthermore, at the early stage of employment, Liden, Wayne & Stilwell, (1993) survey of supervisor–subordinate relationships shows that it is possible to predict the quality of the future LMX and thus whether the newcomer will stay or leave based on job expectations, the perception of similarity between supervisor and subordinate and the initial sense of rapport. Therefore, it is crucial to recruit the correct talent and assign that talent to an appropriate supervisor in order to ensure a good relationship.

Organization–person fit

Identification with the organization is closely related to turnover intentions (Smith, Amiot, Callan, Terry & Smith, 2012; van Dick et al., 2004). Alignment of the employee with the organization's culture, identity and values and having participative goal-setting can add to the organization–person fit (O'Reilly, Chatman & Caldwell, 1991; Vandenberghe, 1999). Smith and colleagues (2012) proposed and validated a model in which supervisor validation (an aspect of LMX), team validation and perception of organizational justice (fair treatment) result in increased organizational self-investment and reduced turnover intention. Indeed, organizational justice has also been associated with an improved leader–member relationship (Lee, Murrmann, Murrmann & Kim, 2010).

When discussing organizational culture, it is important to consider national culture too. Abrams and colleagues (1998) compared the individualistic culture of the UK with the collectivist culture of Japan. They showed that while organizational membership was through social identification for both cultures, the collectivist culture was a psychological anchor that made the employee more committed to the organization and discouraged turnover intention. The individualistic culture made employees less concerned about the problems the organization would have should they leave. These findings resonate with the work of Besser (1993) on Toyota employees in Japan and in the US, and were later expanded to multiple cultures including a European-wide study (Vandenberghe, Stinglhamber, Bentein & Delhaise, 2001). Thus, commitment to the organization is also dependent on the national culture of both the organization and the talent. In fact, national culture has been shown to impact on most if not all the factors leading to turnover (Shao, Rupp, Skarlicki & Jones, 2013; Sturman, Shao & Katz, 2012; Taras, Kirkman & Steel, 2010).

The Future of Talent Management

Talent analytics

While other departments (marketing, finance and supply chain management) have embraced data-driven methodologies for generating business-critical strategic decisions, HR management (and, by proxy, talent management) has lagged behind (Harris et al., 2011).

In the era of big data, talent management has finally become the subject of mathematical modelling, which requires a large body of credible data in order to function (Ashton & Morton, 2005; Davenport et al., 2010; Lawler, Levenson & Boudreau, 2004). Indeed, the HR department usually holds a record of all personnel from the date potential candidates apply for positions in the organization, through to their promotion and development until they leave employment. This longitudinal dataset is ideal for data mining and modelling, and there are now software applications on the market which attempt to manage talent within the organization (e.g., Oracle Embedded Analytics Solution and SAP Success Factors Workforce Analytics). This analytics software trawls through HR data and compiles a list of the causes and effects of employee turnover. Thus, they can forecast which personnel are at risk of leaving by correlating the different factors discussed in this chapter and offer solutions for talent retention. For example, factors such as a salary, career development opportunities, commute distance and relationship with the manager are assigned weightings in risk level such that if the total risk reaches a certain level, the software will trigger an at-risk alarm so that HR and senior management can consider remedies for retention (Harris & Craig, 2011). More sophisticated modelling can analyse effective and ineffective career paths (i.e., those that will retain talent and those that will cause them to leave; Davenport et al., 2010). To date uptake for talent analytics applications has been taken by relatively few organizations (e.g., Google, Convergys and AC Milan; Harris et al., 2011) but it is expected that more organizations will be using their personnel data more productively and effectively to obtain predictive insight for talent management in the future (Bersin, 2013; Corsello, 2012). It is important to note that since talent analytics is a model of the potential factors affecting the lifetime of an employee and relies on large datasets to run correlations and look for causality, the onus is on providing reliable data – as the jargon goes, 'garbage in, garbage out'. Updating the dataset with newer external data can make the analysis richer and predictions more accurate, leading perhaps to the creation of a new type of talent management consultant: the talent modeller.

Workforce planning

The retirement of baby boomers is now a reality and an ageing workforce presents challenges to organizations as valuable talent leave (Armstrong-Stassen & Ursel, 2009; Calo, 2008; O'Brien-Pallas, Duffield & Alksnis, 2004; Paullin & Whetzel, 2012; Rappaport et al., 2003). Is it simply a case for increasing the legal retirement age (O'Brien-Pallas et al., 2004) or does it require a more focused approach to retaining talent while planning for replacement (Calo, 2008; Paullin & Whetzel, 2012; Towers Perrin, 2005)? In the same vein, in order to design programmes for retention, it is important to understand what motivates the older generation to work. A Towers Perrin survey (2005) revealed that a growing number of companies do indeed analyse their workforce demographics and implement targeted strategies and programmes to recruit and retain age 50+ talent and, most importantly, capture the knowledge of workers approaching retirement. Retention here is part of a phased retirement programme designed for smooth workforce planning (Calo, 2008). A flexible retention strategy can focus on the older employee's ability to physically and cognitively perform required meaningful work and perception of financial and health security (Paullin & Whetzel, 2012). A generational empathy environment serves to decrease the potential of perceived ageism which can reduce engagement (Armstrong-Stassen & Ursel, 2009; Rappaport, Bancroft & Okum, 2003), while intergenerational mentoring can facilitate skills retention for succession planning following retirement (Calo, 2008; Paullin & Whetzel, 2012).

Future Research

There are many areas of research that can expand our understanding of talent management. In broad terms, it is probably the case that theoretical development of the concept has outweighed empirical investigation to date. Thus, there is a need for greater attention to fieldwork to provide insight into talent management through examples of practice. As part of this, a broader set of methodologies and methods needs to be adopted. Much of our knowledge and understanding of practice comes from surveys and broad-brush case studies conducted by both academics and consultancy firms. They can provide interesting but limited understanding of the lived experience of those undertaking talent management and those engaged as participants in talent management programmes. Therefore, as a wider agenda for future research, we would argue for the need for in-depth approaches which can provide a deeper understanding of the day-to-day and lived experience of talent management in practice.

As part of these general principles, we see a need for specific foci for future research. One of these is talent management in small and medium-sized organizations. As with much business and management research, large enterprises tend to be the focus. It is likely that talent management will imply something different in this context and approaches will be more variable. But it is arguable at a conceptual level that small organizations engage in processes and activities which, in other contexts, would be identified as talent management. Little is known though about how that is manifested in small organizations. A similar claim could be made about talent management in developing countries. Much, perhaps most, research into the practice of talent management has been and continues to be undertaken in Western countries (obvious exceptions are China and India). Whole continents such as Africa and South America have a dearth of research and so provide opportunities for much needed knowledge on practice in those geographic and cultural contexts, as well as opportunities for comparative studies. Furthermore, there have been issues regarding the brain drain from developing to developed countries, leading us to propose that talent retention should also be investigated at the macro-level (countries and regions).

This point suggests an additional field of future research. Talent management often occurs in a cross-cultural context (e.g., in multinational corporations). There is a whole area of research with such a focus within, for example, international business, leadership competences and leadership development. The connections between these areas are not generally articulated. These opportunities suggest a need for more inter- and multi-disciplinary research to examine the relationship between talent management and other aspects of business management, especially where talent management takes place across national borders.

Conclusion

The war for talent, which started as a 'corporate credo' (Dries, 2013), has now become arguably the hottest topic for consultants, researchers and managers. Regardless of the diverging definitions for talent and talent management, it is important to remember that talent is valuable for organizational success, and that the process of attracting, managing, developing and retaining talent depends on the organization's needs.

Indeed, as organizations evolve, what is currently held as talent may not remain talent in the future. Hence we propose that the concept of talent is fluid. It can become exclusive, inclusive or even untalented, depending on the organization's needs. For example, a researcher in a pharmaceutical company with specific skills is recruited to join an R&D

team. Here the newcomer would be an inclusive talent, in a pool of talented researchers. Assuming that the researcher acquires unique skills in operating a specific instrument, the researcher will become an exclusive talent. However, if the research directions of the pharmaceutical company change and there is no longer a need for such an instrument operator, the exclusive talent will return to the pool of inclusive talent. Furthermore, if there is no requirement for an R&D team at all, the once talented employee will no longer needed and will be made redundant (Subbaraman, 2011). Hence talent retention is only implemented if there is a need in the organization. During restructuring, mergers or other strategic changes, talent management becomes crucial in deciding who should be retained and who should not. Thus the war for talent could also be a war to remain and be retained as a talent.

References

Abbott, J., De Cieri, H., & Iverson, R. D. (1998). Costing turnover: Implications of work/family conflict at management level. *Asia Pacific Journal of Human Resources, 36*(1), 25–43.

Abrams, D., Ando, K., & Hinkle, S. (1998). Psychological attachment to the group: Cross-cultural differences in organizational identification and subjective norms as predictors of workers' turnover intentions. *Personality & Social Psychology Bulletin, 24*(10), 1027–1040.

Ahmed, N., Conn, L. G., Chiu, M., Korabi, B., Qureshi, A., Nathens, A. B., & Kitto, S. (2012). Career satisfaction among general surgeons in Canada: A qualitative study of enablers and barriers to improve recruitment and retention in general surgery. *Academic Medicine, 87*(11), 1616–1621.

Al Ariss, A., Cascio, W. F., & Paauwe, J. (2014). Talent management: Current theories and future research directions., *49*, 173–179.

Allen, D. G., & Shanock, L. R. (2013). Perceived organizational support and embeddedness as key mechanisms connecting socialization tactics to commitment and turnover among new employees. *Journal of Organizational Behavior, 34*(3), 350–369.

Alniacik, E., & Alniacik, U. (2012). Identifying dimensions of attractiveness in employer branding: Effects of age, gender and current employment status. *Procedia – Social and Behavioral Sciences, 58*, 1336–1343.

Amble, B. (2007). New hires seek a quick divorce. www.management-issues.com/news/4009/new-hires-seek-a-quick-divorce.

Ambler, T., & Barrow, S. (1996). The employer brand. *Journal of Brand Management, 4*(3), 185–206.

Andrews, D. R., & Dziegielewski, S. F. (2005). The nurse manager: Job satisfaction, the nursing shortage and retention. *Journal of Nursing Management, 13*(4), 286–295.

Anthony, M. K., Standing, T. S., Glick, J., Duffy, M., Paschall, F., Sauer, M. R., Sweeney, T. S., Modic, M. B., & Dumpe, M. L. (2005). Leadership and nurse retention: The pivotal role of nurse managers. *Journal of Nursing Administration, 35*(3), 146–155.

Armstrong, S. J., Allinson, C. W., & Hayes, J. (2002). Formal mentoring systems: An examination of the effects of mentor/protégé cognitive styles on the mentoring process. *Journal of Management Studies, 39*(8), 1111–1137.

Armstrong-Stassen, M., & Ursel, N. D. (2009). Perceived organizational support, career satisfaction, and the retention of older workers. *Journal of Occupational and Organizational Psychology, 82*(1), 201–220.

Arora, R. (2012). A research study of factors influencing talent retention in BPO industry. *Journal of Strategic Human Resource Management, 1*(2), 54–62.

Ashton, C., & Morton, L. (2005). Managing talent for competitive advantage: Taking a systemic approach to talent management. *Strategic HR Review, 4*(5), 28–31.

Auger, P., Devinney, T. M., Dowling, G. R., Eckert, C., & Lin, D. (2013). How much does a company's reputation matter in recruiting? *MIT Sloan Management Review*.

Backhaus, K., & Tikoo, S. (2004). Conceptualising and researching employer branding. *Career Development International*, 95(5), 501–517.

Baruch, Y. (2006). Career development in organizations and beyond: Balancing traditional and contemporary viewpoints. *Human Resource Management Review*, 16(2), 125–138.

Baumann, A., Yan, J., Degelder, J., & Malikov, K. (2006). Retention strategies for nursing: A profile of four countries. *Human Health Resource*, No. 5.

Baytok, A., Kurt, M., & Zorlu, Ö. Ö. (2014). The role of transformational leader on knowledge sharing practices: A study about international hotel chains. *European Journal of Business and Management*, 6(7), 46–61.

Benson, G. S. (2006). Employee development, commitment and intention to turnover: A test of 'employability' policies in action. *Human Resource Management Journal*, 16(2), 173–192.

Bersin, J. (2013). *Predictions for 2014.* London: Deloitte Development.

Berthon, P., Ewing M. J., & Hah L. L. (2005). Captivating company: Dimensions of attractiveness in employer branding. *International Journal of Advertising*, 24(2), 151–172.

Besser, T. L. (1993). The commitment of Japanese workers and U.S. workers: A reassessment of the literature. *American Sociological Review*, 58 (Dec), 873–881.

Bhatnagar, J. (2007). Talent management strategy of employee engagement in Indian ITES employees: Key to retention. *Employee Relations*, 29(6), 640–663.

Blake, N., Leach, L.S., Robbins, W., Pike, N., & Needleman, J. (2013). Healthy work environments and staff nurse retention: The relationship between communication, collaboration, and leadership in the pediatric intensive care unit. *Nursing Administration Quarterly*, 37(4), 356–370.

Botha, A., Bussin, M., & De Swardt, L. (2011). An employer brand predictive model for talent attraction and retention: Original research. *SA Journal of Human Resource Management*, 9(1), 1–12.

Brunetto, Y., Shriberg, A., Farr-Wharton, R., Shacklock, K., Newman, S., & Dienger, J. (2013). The importance of supervisor–nurse relationships, teamwork, wellbeing, affective commitment and retention of North American nurses. *Journal of Nursing Management*, 21(6), 827–837.

Buckingham, M., & Coffman, C. (1999). *First, Break All the Rules.* New York: Simon & Schuster.

Caela, F. (2007). Help new hires succeed. Beat the statistics. www.hr.com/en/app/blog/2007/05/help-new-hires-succeed-beat-the-statistics_f24qxvt5.html.

Calo, T. J. (2008). Talent management in the era of the aging workforce: The critical role of knowledge transfer. *Public Personnel Management*, 37(4), 403–416.

Chang, P. L., Chou, Y. C., & Cheng, F. C. (2006). Designing career development programs through understanding of nurses' career needs. *Journal for Nurses in Professional Development*, 22(5), 246–253.

Chang, P. L., Chou, Y. C., & Cheng, F. C. (2007). Career needs, career development programmes, organizational commitment and turnover intention of nurses in Taiwan. *Journal of Nursing Management*, 15(8), 801–810.

Chen, T. Y., Chang, P. L., & Yeh, C. W. (2004). A study of career needs, career development programs, job satisfaction and the turnover intentions of R&D personnel. *Career Development International*, 9(4), 424–437.

Chew, Y. T. (2005). Achieving organizational prosperity through employee motivation and retention: A comparative study of strategic HRM practices in Malaysian institutions. *Research and Practice in Human Resource Management*, 13(2), 87–104.

CIPD. (2009). *Employer Brand.* London: Chartered Institute of Personnel and Development.

Cleary, M., Horsfall, J., Muthulakshmi, P., Happell, B., & Hunt, G. E. (2013). Career development: Graduate nurse views. *Journal of Clinical Nursing*, 22(17–18), 2605–2613.

Collings, D. G., & Mellahi, K. (2009). Strategic talent management: A review and research agenda. *Human Resource Management Review*, 19(4), 304–313.

Collings, D. G., Scullion, H., & Vaiman, V. (2011). European perspectives on talent management. *European Journal of International Management*, 5(5), 453–462.

Collings, D. G., Scullion, H., & Vaiman, H. (2015). Talent management: Progress and Prospects. *Human Resource Management Review*.

Corporate Leadership Council. (2004). *Driving performance and retention through employee engagement.* Washington, DC: Corporate Executive Board.

Corsello, J. (2012). Managing talent in the cloud. *Training Journal*, 20–23.

Cosack, S., Guthridge, M., & Lawson, E. (2010). Retaining key employees in times of change. *McKinsey Quarterly*, *3*, 135–139.

Cowden, T., Cummings, G., & Profetto-McGrath, J. (2011). Leadership practices and staff nurses' intent to stay: A systematic review. *Journal of Nursing Management*, *19*(4), 461–477.

Dai, Y. D., Dai, Y. Y., Chen, K. Y., & Wu, H. C. (2013). Transformational vs. transactional leadership: Which is better? A study on employees of international tourist hotels in Taipei City. *International Journal of Contemporary Hospitality Management*, *25*(5), 760–778.

Davenport, T. H., Harris, J., & Shapiro, J. (2010). Competing on talent analytics. *Harvard Business Review*, *88*(10), 52–58.

DeConinck, J. B. (2011). The effects of leader–member exchange and organizational identification on performance and turnover among salespeople. *Journal of Personal Selling & Sales Management*, *31*(1), 21–34.

DeSantis, J. (2008). 'Dear A.I.G., I quit!' *New York Times*, 25 March, A25. www.nytimes.com/2009/03/25/opinion/25desantis.html?scp=1&sq=Dear%20A.I.G.,%20I%20Quit!&st=cse&_r=0.

Dewhurst, M., Guthridge, M., & Mohr, E. (2009). Motivating people: Getting beyond money. *McKinsey Quarterly*, *1*(4), 12–15.

Dill, J. S., Morgan, J. C., & Marshall, V. W. (2013). Contingency, employment intentions, and retention of vulnerable low-wage workers: An examination of nursing assistants in nursing homes. *The Gerontologist*, *53*(2), 222–234.

Doran, G. T. (1981). There's a S.M.A.R.T. way to write management's goals and objectives. *Management Review (AMA FORUM)*, *70*(11), 35–36.

Dries, N. (2013). The psychology of talent management: A review and research agenda. *Human Resource Management Review*, *23*(4), 272–285.

Duffield, C. M., Roche, M. A., Blay, N., & Stasa, H. (2011). Nursing unit managers, staff retention and the work environment. *Journal of Clinical Nursing*, *20*(1–2), 23–33.

Dulebohn, J. H., Bommer, W. H., Liden, R. C., Brouer, R. L., & Ferris, G. R. (2012). A meta-analysis of antecedents and consequences of leader–member exchange: Integrating the past with an eye toward the future. *Journal of Management*, *38*(6), 1715–1759.

Earnest, D. R., Allen, D. G., & Landis, R. S. (2011). Mechanisms linking realistic job previews with turnover: A meta-analytic path analysis. *Personnel Psychology*, *64*(4), 865–897.

Ensher, E. A., & Murphy, S. E. (2011). *Power Mentoring: How Successful Mentors and Protégés Get the Most out of Their Relationships*. Chichester: John Wiley & Sons.

Fang, M., & Gerhart, B. (2012). Does pay for performance diminish intrinsic interest? *The International Journal of Human Resource Management*, *23*(6), 1176–1196.

Festing, M., & Schafer, L. (2014). Generational challenges to talent management: A framework for talent retention based on the psychological-contract perspective. *Journal of World Business*, *49*, 262–271.

Friedman, L. (2006). Are you losing potential new hires at hello? *T+D*, *60*(11), 25–27.

Gallardo-Gallardo, E., Dries, N., & Gonzales-Cruz, T. F. (2015). Towards an understanding of talent management as a phenomenon-driven field using bibliometric and content analysis. *Human Resource Management Review*, *25*(3), 264–279.

Gallup. (2013). *State of the Global Workplace: Employee Engagement Insights for Business Leaders Worldwide*. Washington, DC.

Giancola, F. L. (2012). The uncertain importance of pay: The need for better answers. *Compensation & Benefits Review*, *44*(1), 50–58.

Ghosh, R., Reio Jr, T. G., & Bang, H. (2013). Reducing turnover intent: Supervisor and co-worker incivility and socialization-related learning. *Human Resource Development International*, *16*(2), 169–185.

Gilmore, D. C., & Turner, M. (2010). Improving executive recruitment and retention. *The Psychologist-Manager Journal*, *13*(2), 125–128.

Glaister, A., Tatoglu, E., & Demirbag, M. (2016). Talent management motives and practices in an emerging market: A comparison between MNEs and local firms. *Journal of World Business*, *51*(2), 278–293.

Goh, T. T., Eccles, M. P., & Steen, N. (2009). Factors predicting team climate, and its relationship with quality of care in general practice. *BMC Health Services Research*, *9*(1), 138.

Gow, J., George, G., Mwamba, S., Ingombe, L., & Mutinta, G. (2013). An evaluation of the effectiveness of the Zambian Health Worker Retention Scheme (ZHWRS) for rural areas. *African Health Sciences, 13*(3), 800.

Gray, D. E., & Goregaokar, H. (2010). Choosing an executive coach: The influence of gender on the coach–coachee matching process. *Management Learning, 41*(5), 525–544.

Griffeth, R. W., & Hom, P. W. (2001). Retaining valued employees. Thousand Oaks, CA: Sage.

Grumana, J. A., & Saksb, A. M. (2011). Performance management and employee engagement. *Human Resource Management Review, 21*(2), 123–136.

Haggard, D. L., Dougherty, T. W., Turban, D. B., & Wilbanks, J. E. (2011). Who is a mentor? A review of evolving definitions and implications for research. *Journal of management, 37*(1), 280–304.

Halbesleben, J. R. B., & Wheeler, A. R. (2008). The relative roles of engagement and embeddedness in predicting job performance and intention to leave. *Work and Stress, 22*(3), 242–256.

Hannay, M., & Northam, M. (2000). Low-cost strategies for employee retention. *Compensation & Benefits Review, 32*(4), 65–72.

Harris, J. G., Craig, E., & Light, D. A. (2011). Talent and analytics: New approaches, higher ROI. *Journal of Business Strategy, 32*(6), 4–13.

Harris, J. G., & Craig, E. (2011). Developing analytical leadership. *Strategic HR Review, 11*(1), 25–30.

Harris, T. B., Li, N., & Kirkman, B. L. (2014). Leader–member exchange (LMX) in context: How LMX differentiation and LMX relational separation attenuate LMX's influence on OCB and turnover intention, *The Leadership Quarterly, 25*(2), 314–328.

Hay Group. (2014). UK talent exodus on the horizon as economic outlook improves. atrium. haygroup.com/uk/your-challenges/misc.aspx?id=3878.

Hayes, L. J., O'Brien-Pallas, L., Duffield, C., Shamian, J., Buchan, J., Hughes, F., Spence Laschinger, H. K., & North, N. (2012). Nurse turnover: A literature review – An update. *International Journal of Nursing Studies, 49*(7), 887–905.

Heskett, J. (2009). Are retention bonuses worth the investment? *Harvard Business School Working Knowledge.* hbswk.hbs.edu/item/6246.html.

Hughes, J. C., & Rog, E. (2008). Talent management: A strategy for improving employee recruitment, retention and engagement within hospitality organizations. *International Journal of Contemporary Hospitality Management, 20*(7), 743–757.

Ito, K. J., Brotheridge, M. C., & McFarland, K. (2013). Examining how preferences for employer branding attributes differ from entry to exit and how they relate to commitment, satisfaction, and retention. *Career Development International, 18*(7), 732–752.

Jiang, T. T., & Iles, P. (2011). Employer-brand equity, organizational attractiveness and talent management in the Zhejiang private sector, China. *Journal of Technology Management, 6*(1), 97–110.

Joiner, T., Garreffa, T., & Bartram, T. (2004). The effects of mentoring on perceived career success, commitment and turnover intentions. *Journal of American Academy of Business, Cambridge, 5*(1–2), 164–170.

Kammeyer-Mueller, J., Wanberg, C., Rubenstein, A., & Song, Z. (2013). Support, undermining, and newcomer socialization: Fitting in during the first 90 days. *Academy of Management Journal, 56*(4), 1104–1124.

Kaye, B., & Jordan-Evans, S. (2000). Retention: Tag, you're it! *Training and Development-Alexandria-American Society for Training and Development, 54*(4), 29–39.

Kivimäki, M., Vanhala, A., Pentti, J., Länsisalmi, H., Virtanen, M., Elovainio, M., & Vahtera, J. (2007). Team climate, intention to leave and turnover among hospital employees: Prospective cohort study. *BMC Health Services Research, 7*(1), 170.

Kleinman, C. (2004). The relationship between managerial leadership behaviors and staff nurse retention. *Hospital Topics, 82*(4), 2–9.

Klemm, R., & Scbreiber, E. J. (1992). Paid and unpaid benefits: Strategies for nurse recruitment and retention. *Journal of Nursing Administration, 22*(3), 52–56.

Kohers, N., & Ang, J. (2000). Earnouts in mergers: Agreeing to disagree and agreeing to stay. *The Journal of Business, 73*(3), 445–476.

Kowske, B. (2012). Employee engagement: Market review. *Buyer's Guide and Provider Profiles*. Washington, DC: Bersin and Associates.

Latham, G. P. (2004). The motivational benefits of goal-setting. *The Academy of Management Executive, 18*(4), 126–129.

Landis, R. S., Earnest, D. R., & Allen, D. G. (2013). Realistic job previews: Past, present. *The Oxford Handbook of Recruitment* (p. 423). New York: Oxford University Press.

Lavigna, B. (2009). Getting on board: Integrating and engaging new employees. *Government Finance Review, 25*(3), 65–70.

Lawler III, E. E., Levenson, A., & Boudreau, J. W. (2004). HR metrics and analytics – Uses and impacts. *Human Resource Planning Journal, 27*(4), 27–35.

Lee, H.-R., Murrmann, S. K., Murrmann, K. F., & Kim, K. (2010). Organizational justice as a mediator of the relationships between leader–member exchange and employees' turnover intentions. *Journal of Hospitality, Management and Marketing, 19*(2), 97–114.

Liden, R. C., & Maslyn, J. M. (1998). Multidimensionafity of leader–member exchange: An empirical assessment through scale development. *Journal of Management, 24*(1), 43–72.

Liden, R. C., Wayne, S. J., & Stilwell, D. (1993). A longitudinal study of the early development of leader-member exchanges. *Journal of Applied Psychology, 78*(4), 662–674.

Lundberg, C. C., & Young, C. A. (1997). Newcomer socialization: Critical incidents in hospitality organizations. *Journal of Hospitality & Tourism Research, 21*(2), 58–74.

Macey, W. H., & Schneider, B. (2008). The meaning of employee engagement. *Industrial and Organizational Psychology, 1*(1), 3–30.

Mandhanya, Y., & Shah, M. (2010). Employer branding – A tool for talent management. *Global Management Review, 4*(2), 43–48.

Manpower Group Talent Shortage Survey. (2015). us.manpower.com/us/en/multimedia/2015-Talent-Shortage-Survey.pdf.

Markos, S., & Sridevi, M. S. (2010). Employee engagement: The key to improving performance. *International Journal of Business and Management, 5*(12), 89–96.

Maslow, A. H. (1943). A theory of human motivation. *Psychological Review, 50*, 370–396.

McDonnell, A., Collings, D. G., & Burgess, J. (2012). Asia Pacific perspectives on talent management. *Asia Pacific Journal of Human Resources, 50*, 4, 391–98.

McEvoy, G. M., & Cascio, W. F. (1985). Strategies for reducing employee turnover: A meta-analysis. *Journal of Applied Psychology. 70*(2), 342–353.

McEvoy, G. M., & Cascio, W. F. (1987). Do good or poor performers leave? A meta-analysis of the relationship between performance and turnover. *Academy of Management Journal, 30*(4), 744–762.

Mehta, P., & Sharma, K. (2013). Impact of employer branding on retention of employees of management institutes. *Abhinav, 2* (2), 59–71.

Michaels, E., Handfield-Jones, H., & Axelrod, B. (2001). *The War for Talent*. Cambridge, MA: Harvard Business Press.

Moroko, L., & Uncles, M. D. (2009). Employer branding and market segmentation. *Journal of Brand Management, 17*(3), 181–196.

Nowak, M. J., Naude, M., & Thomas, G. (2013). Returning to work after maternity leave: Childcare and workplace flexibility. *Journal of Industrial Relations, 55*(1), 118–135.

Nyberg, A. (2010). Retaining your high performers: Moderators of the performance–job satisfaction – Voluntary turnover relationship. *Journal of Applied Psychology, 95*(3), 440–453.

O'Brien-Pallas, L., Duffield, C., & Alksnis, C. (2004). Who will be there to nurse? Retention of nurses nearing retirement. *Journal of Nursing Administration, 34*(6), 298–302.

O'Reilly, C. A., Chatman, J., & Caldwell, D. F. (1991). People and organizational culture: A profile comparison approach to assessing person–organization fit. *Academy of Management Journal, 34*(3), 487–516.

Park, T. Y., & Shaw, J. D. (2013). Turnover rates and organizational performance: A meta-analysis. *Journal of Applied Psychology, 98*(2), 268–309.

Paullin, C., & Whetzel, D. L. (2012). Retention strategies and older workers. *The Oxford Handbook of Work and Aging* (pp. 392–418). New York: Oxford University Press.

Payne, S. C., & Huffman, A. H. (2005). A longitudinal examination of the influence of mentoring on organizational commitment and turnover. *Academy of Management Journal, 48*(1), 158–168.

People Management CIPD. (2015). Almost half of workers have left a job because of a bad boss, survey finds. www.cipd.co.uk/pm/peoplemanagement/b/weblog/archive/2015/08/25/almost-half-of-workers-have-left-a-job-because-of-a-bad-boss-survey-finds.aspx. Last accessed 11 November 2015.

Portoghese, I., Galletta, M., Battistelli, A., & Leiter, M. P. (2014). A multilevel investigation on nursing turnover intention: The cross-level role of leader–member exchange. *Journal of Nursing Management*. doi: 10.1111/jonm.12205.

Premack, S. L., & Wanous, J. P. (1985). A meta-analysis of realistic job preview experiments. *Journal of Applied Psychology*, *70*(4), 706–719.

Priyadarshi, P. (2011). Employer brand image as predictor of employee satisfaction, affective commitment & turnover. *The Indian Journal of Industrial Relations*, *46*(3), 510–522.

PWC (PricewaterhouseCoopers). (2013). Talent mobility 2020 and beyond: *The Next Generation of International Assignments*. www.pwc.com/en_GX/gx/managing-tomorrows-people/future-of-work/pdf/pwc-talent-mobility-2020.pdf. Last accessed September 2014.

Rappaport, A. (2005). The economics of short-term performance obsession. *Financial Analysts Journal*, 65–79.

Rappaport, A., Bancroft, E., & Okum, L. (2003). The aging workforce raises new talent management issues for employers. *Journal of Organizational Excellence*, *23*(1), 55–66.

Raup, G. H. (2008). The impact of ED nurse manager leadership style on staff nurse turnover and patient satisfaction in academic health center hospitals. *Journal of Emergency Nursing*, *34*(5), 403–409.

Resmi, A. T., Gemini, V. J., Silvian, P., & Kannan, K. (2014). Leadership, commitment, culture and employee turnover – A deeper examination. *International Journal of Enterprise Network Management*, *6*(1), 1–13.

Ribelin, P. J. (2003). Retention reflects leadership style. *Nursing Management*, *34*(8), 18–19.

Rich, B. L., Lepine, J. A., & Crawford, E. R. (2010). Job engagement: Antecedents and effects on job performance. *Academy of Management Journal*, *53*(3), 617–635.

Rink, F., Kane, A. A., Ellemers, N., & Van der Vegt, G. (2013). Team receptivity to newcomers: Five decades of evidence and future research themes. *The Academy of Management Annals*, *7*(1), 247–293.

Ross, W. E., Huang, K. H., & Jones, G. H. (2014). Executive onboarding: Ensuring the Success of the newly hired department chair. *Academic Medicine*, *89*(5), 728–733.

Salamin, A., & Hom, P. W. (2005). In search of the elusive U-shaped performance–turnover relationship: Are high performing Swiss bankers more liable to quit? *Journal of Applied Psychology*, *90*(6), 1204.

Scandura, T. A., & Viator, R. E. (1994). Mentoring in public accounting firms: An analysis of mentor–protégé relationships, mentorship functions, and protégé turnover intentions. *Accounting, Organizations and Society*, *19*(8), 717–734.

Schmidt, S. W. (2007). The relationship between satisfaction with workplace training and overall job satisfaction. *Human Resource Development Quarterly*, *18*(4), 481–498.

Scullion, H., Collings, D. G., and Caligiuri, P. (2010). Global talent management. *Journal of World Business*, *45*(2), 105–8.

Sengupta, S., & Gupta, A. (2012). Exploring the dimensions of attrition in Indian BPOs. *The International Journal of Human Resource Management*, *23*(6), 1259–1288.

Serbin, K. M., & Jensen, S. (2013). Recruiting, hiring, and onboarding case managers: Communication and setting expectations are keys to success. *Professional Case Management*, *18*(2), 95–97.

Shahzad, K., Gul, A. Khan, K., & Zafar, R. (2011). Relationship between perceived employer branding and intention to apply: Evidence from Pakistan. *European Journal of Social Sciences*, *18*(3), 462–467.

Shao, R., Rupp, D. E., Skarlicki, D. P., & Jones, K. S. (2013). Employee justice across cultures: A meta-analytic review. *Journal of Management*, *39*(1), 263–301.

Shuck, B., Twyford, D., Reio, T. G., & Shuck, A. (2014). Human resource development practices and employee engagement: Examining the connection with employee turnover intentions. *Human Resource Development Quarterly*, *25*(2), 239–270.

Smith, L. G., Amiot, C. E., Callan, V. J., Terry, D. J., & Smith, J. R. (2012). Getting new staff to stay: The mediating role of organizational identification. *British Journal of Management*, *23*(1), 45–64.

Sokro, E. (2012). Impact of employer branding on employee attraction and retention. *European Journal of Business and Management, 4*(18), 164–173.

Spence Laschinger, H. K., Leiter, M., Day, A., & Gilin, D. (2009). Workplace empowerment, incivility, and burnout: Impact on staff nurse recruitment and retention outcomes. *Journal of Nursing Management, 17*(3), 302–311.

Sturges, J., Conway, N., Guest, D., & Liefooghe, A. (2005). Managing the career deal: The psychological contract as a framework for understanding career management, organizational commitment and work behavior. *Journal of Organizational Behavior, 26*(7), 821–838.

Sturman, M. C., Shao, L., & Katz, J. H. (2012). The effect of culture on the curvilinear relationship between performance and turnover. *Journal of Applied Psychology, 97*(1), 46.

Subbaraman, N. (2011). Researchers cut loose as Pfizer and Merck shutter European sites. *Nature Biotechnology, 29*(4), 299–300.

Supornpraditchai, T., Miller, K., Lings, I. N., & Jonmundsson, B. (2007). Employee-based brand equity: Antecedents and consequences. Proceedings of the Australia–New Zealand Marketing Academy Conference, Dunedin, New Zealand.

Talent Keepers. (2013). *Engagement and Retention in 2013: Moving from Strategy to Execution.* Annual survey. UK: Talent Keepers.

Taormina, R. J. (2008). Interrelating leadership behaviors, organizational socialization, and organizational culture. *Leadership & Organization Development Journal, 29*(1), 85–102.

Taras, V., Kirkman, B. L., & Steel, P. (2010). Examining the impact of culture's consequences: A three-decade, multilevel, meta-analytic review of Hofstede's cultural value dimensions. *Journal of Applied Psychology, 95*(3), 405.

Tarique, I., & Schuler, R. S. (2012). Global talent management: Theoretical perspectives, systems, and challenges. *In* G. Stahl, I. Bjorkman, & S. Morris (Eds.), *Handbook of Research in International Human Resource Management* (pp. 205–219). Cheltenham, UK: Edward Elgar.

Taunton, R. L., Boyle, D. K., Woods, C. Q., Hansen, H. E., & Bott, M. J. (1997). Manager leadership and retention of hospital staff nurses. *Western Journal of Nursing Research, 19*(2), 205–226.

Taylor, A. L., Hwenda, L., Larsen, B. I., & Daulaire, N. (2011). Stemming the brain drain – A WHO global code of practice on international recruitment of health personnel. *New England Journal of Medicine, 365*(25), 2348–2351.

Tews, M. J., Stafford, K., & Michel, J. W. (2014a). Life happens and people matter: Critical events, constituent attachment, and turnover among part-time hospitality employees. *International Journal of Hospitality Management, 38*, 99–105.

Tews, M. J., Michel, J. W., & Allen, D. G. (2014b). Fun and friends: The impact of workplace fun and constituent attachment on turnover in a hospitality context. *Human Relations.* 0018726713508143.

Thirulogasundaram, V. P., & Kumar, S. S. (2012). The correlation between leadership approach and employees turnover intention in software industry at Bangalore City, India. *International Journal of Innovative Research and Development, 1*(9), 600–615.

Tillott, S., Walsh, K., & Moxham, L. (2013). Encouraging engagement at work to improve retention: Sarah Tillott and colleagues explore how a social interaction tool can help managers recruit and retain staff, and boost patient care. *Nursing Management, 19*(10), 27–31.

Towers Perrin. (2005). The business case for workers age 50+: Planning for tomorrow's talent needs in today's competitive environment. Stamford, CT: Towers Perrin.

Towers Perrin. (2007). Closing the engagement gap: A road map for driving superior business performance. *Towers Perrin Global Workforce Study 2007–2008.* Stamford, CT: Towers Perrin.

Towers Watson. (2012). Engagement at risk: Driving strong performance in a volatile global environment. *Towers Watson Global Workforce Study 2012.* Bristol: Towers Watson.

Trevor, C. O., Gerhart, B., & Boudreau, J. W. (1997). Voluntary turnover and job performance: Curvilinearity and the moderating influences of salary growth and promotions. *Journal of Applied Psychology, 82*(1), 44–61.

Tse, H. H., Huang, X., & Lam, W. (2013). Why does transformational leadership matter for employee turnover? A multi-foci social exchange perspective. *The Leadership Quarterly, 24*(5), 763–776.

Tymon Jr, W. G., Stumpf, S. A., & Doh, J. P. (2010). Exploring talent management in India: The neglected role of intrinsic rewards. *Journal of World Business*, 45(2), 109–121.

Vaiman, V. & Collings, D.G. (2013). Talent management: Advancing the field. *International Journal of Human Resource Management*, 24(9), 1737–1743.

van Dick, R., Christ, O., Stellmacher, J., Wagner, U., Ahlswede, O., Grubba, C., Hauptmeier, M., Hoehfeld, C., Moltzen K., & Tissington, P. A. (2004). Should I stay or should I go? Explaining turnover intentions with organizational identification and job satisfaction. *British Journal of Management.*, 15(4), 351–360.

van Maanen, J. E., & Schein, E. H. (1977). Toward a theory of organizational socialization. *Sloan School of Management Working Paper*, 960–977.

Vandenberghe, C. (1999). Organizational culture, person–culture fit and turnover: A replication in the healthcare industry. *Journal of Organizational Behavior*, 20, 113–149.

Vandenberghe, C., Stinglhamber, F., Bentein, K., & Delhaise, T. (2001). An examination of the cross-cultural validity of a multidimensional model of commitment in Europe. *Journal of Cross-Cultural Psychology*, 32(3), 322–347.

Verlander, E. G. & Evans, M. R. (2007). Strategies for improving employee retention. *Clinical Leadership & Management Review*, 21(2), E4.

Voigt, E. & Hirst, G. (2014). High and low performers' intention to leave: Examining the relationship with motivation and commitment. *The International Journal of Human Resource Management*, 26(5), 574–588.

Waldman, D. A., Carter, M. Z., & Hom, P. W. (2012). A multilevel investigation of leadership and turnover behavior. *Journal of Management.* 0149206312460679.

Wallis, A., & Kennedy, K. I. (2013). Leadership training to improve nurse retention. *Journal of Nursing Management*, 21(4), 624–632.

Wang, G., Oh, I. S., Courtright, S. H., & Colbert, A. E. (2011). Transformational leadership and performance across criteria and levels: A meta-analytic review of 25 years of research. *Group & Organization Management*, 36(2), 223–270.

Wanous, J. P. (1989). Installing a realistic job preview: ten tough choices. *Personnel Psycholog*, 42, 117–134.

Waterman, S., & He, Y. (2011). Effects of mentoring programs on new teacher retention: A literature review. *Mentoring & Tutoring: Partnership in Learning*, 19(2), 139–156.

Welch, M. (2011). The evolution of the employee engagement concept: Communication implications. *Corporate Communications: An International Journal*, 16(4), 328–346.

Whitelaw, P. A. (2013). Leadership up the ladder: The construction of leadership styles in the hospitality industry. *Journal of Contemporary Issues in Business and Government*, 19(1), 65.

Wilden, R., Gudergan, S., & Lings, I. (2010). Employer branding: Strategic implications for staff recruitment. *Journal of Marketing Management*, 26(1), 56–73.

Williams, C. R., & Livingstone, L. P. (1994). Another look at the relationship between performance and voluntary turnover. *Academy of Management Journal*, 37(2). 269–298.

Willis-Shattuck, M., Bidwell, P., Thomas, S., Wyness, L., Blaauw, D., & Ditlopo, P. (2008). Motivation and retention of health workers in developing countries: a systematic review. *BMC Health Services Research*, 8(1), 247.

Withers, P. (2001). Retention strategies that respond to worker values. *Workforce*, 80(7), 36–41.

Yang, J. T., Wan, C. S., & Fu, Y. J. (2012). Qualitative examination of employee turnover and retention strategies in international tourist hotels in Taiwan. *International Journal of Hospitality Management*, 31(3), 837–848.

23

The Impact of Organizational Climate and Culture on Employee Turnover

Mark G. Ehrhart and Maribeth Kuenzi

Introduction

This chapter addresses the impact that organizational culture and climate have on employee turnover. Organizational culture and climate capture the meaning employees derive from cues in their work environment as well as the salience of these cues. The interaction between individuals and their work environment has important implications for employees' attitudes and behaviours (Johns, 2006), which in turn have direct effects on employee turnover (Griffeth, Hom & Haertner, 2000; Heavey, Holwerda & Hausknecht, 2013). In light of the substantial tangible and intangible costs of turnover (Hancock, Allen, Bosco, McDaniel & Pierce, 2013; Hausknecht & Trevor, 2011; Park & Shaw, 2013), it is critical that we understand the role that contextual factors such as organizational culture and climate have in employee turnover.

We begin by providing an overview of the topics of organizational culture and climate, including the key similarities and differences between the constructs. We then review the literature on the relationship between each of these concepts and employee turnover. For organizational culture, we examine three perspectives: that some cultures may be more desirable to employees and thus have lower turnover; that the fit between employee values and the organization's values are a primary predictor of turnover; and that some organizations may have a culture of turnover. For organizational climate, we examine the general effects of the molar climate (the overall organizational environment) on turnover, as well as the relationships found between a variety of specific, focused climates and turnover. We end the chapter with a number of future directions for research on organizational culture, climate and turnover.

The Wiley Blackwell Handbook of the Psychology of Recruitment, Selection and Employee Retention,
First Edition. Edited by Harold W. Goldstein, Elaine D. Pulakos, Jonathan Passmore and Carla Semedo.
© 2017 John Wiley & Sons Ltd. Published 2020 by John Wiley & Sons Ltd.

Organizational Culture and Climate

The constructs of organizational culture and climate both have long research histories, and although the two constructs capture critical aspects of the internal environment in organizations, their literatures have remained relatively independent. Before addressing how organizational culture and climate are related to turnover, we first give a brief overview of how culture and climate have been conceptualized and studied.

Organizational culture has been defined as 'a pattern of shared basic assumptions learned by [an organization] as it solved its problems of external adaptation and internal integration, which has worked well enough to be considered valid and, therefore, to be taught to new members as the correct way to perceive, think, and feel in relation to those problems' (Schein, 2010, p. 18). Perhaps the primary distinction in the organizational culture literature is between those who study culture as something organizations *are* versus those who study culture as something organizations *have* (Smircich, 1983). In the first perspective, the focus is typically on the symbolic meaning of employee experiences in their organizations, and almost anything that occurs within the organization could be considered to have some sort of cultural component. In the second perspective, culture is one of many relevant variables that affects and is affected by other variables, and is studied to help us understand organizational effectiveness. In general, research from the 'organizations are cultures' perspective tends to use qualitative methods, while research from the 'organizations have cultures' perspective tends to use quantitative methods (although there are exceptions). One of the critical ideas in organizational culture research as a whole is that organizational cultures have levels or layers. The most common conceptualization of the levels of culture comes from Schein (2010), who proposed three levels: artifacts (the outer layer of readily accessible cultural information, like language, architecture, dress and rituals), espoused values (management's statements about the mission or values of the organization) and underlying assumptions (the deepest level of culture that captures the taken-for-granted assumptions that guide day-to-day life in organizations).

Organizational climate has been defined as 'the shared meaning organizational members attach to the events, policies, practices, and procedures they experience and the behaviors they see being rewarded, supported, and expected' (Ehrhart, Schneider & Macey, 2014, p. 69). Although climate is measured in terms of individuals' perceptions, it is an aggregate property of the unit (e.g., team, department, organization). There are several important distinctions that can be made among the approaches to studying organizational climate (Ehrhart et al., 2014). One is the distinction between studying climate at the unit level (organizational climate) and at the individual level (psychological climate; James & Jones, 1974). Even though we view climate as a shared construct that exists as a characteristics of organizational units (i.e., organizational climate), there is relatively little research on organizational climate and turnover, and thus we include research on psychological climate as well. Another key distinction is between molar climate and focused climate. Molar climate measures seek to capture all relevant aspects of the organizational environment and thus include a broad range of generic dimensions that can be used to describe organizations or their subunits. In contrast, research on focused climate, originating from the work of Schneider (1975), captures those aspects of the organizational environment that are most relevant for the achievement of a specific goal or strategic imperative. The focused climate approach has been applied to a wide variety of issues in organizations, including an organization's strategic outcomes (strategic climates, such as service or safety climates) and its internal processes (process climates, such as justice, ethical or diversity climates). As we review the literature on climate and turnover below, we will attempt to be clear about its level (psychological vs. organizational climate) and its focus (molar vs. focused climate).

Although there are many similarities between the concepts of organizational culture and organizational climate, there are also some key differences. It is beyond the scope of this chapter to describe these issues in depth, therefore, we summarize here the key points from Ehrhart and colleagues (2014). First, with regard to similarities, Ehrhart and colleagues describe how both constructs 1) take a macro- (i.e., gestalt) perspective, 2) focus on the influence of the overall context rather than how individuals experience it, 3) emphasize those experiences that are shared by individuals within the organization, 4) emphasize meaning, 5) describe the central role of leaders, 6) discuss issues of strength and alignment, and 7) are concerned with organizational effectiveness. In terms of differences, Ehrhart and colleagues highlight that organizational culture and climate differ in 1) their theoretical roots and often in their methodology, 2) the breadth of constructs included, 3) the extent to which employees are aware of their existence, 4) how malleable or changeable they are, and 5) the extent to which they have a strategic focus. In sum, we view culture and climate as overlapping, but distinct constructs.

Organizational Culture and Employee Turnover

The role of organizational culture in employee turnover has been studied from several angles; we describe three of the primary ones in this section. We begin with the straightforward idea that some cultures are more desirable to employees and thus are associated with higher retention rates. Of course, the opposite is true as well. We next address the idea of fit and how cultures may vary in their desirability depending on the fit between the employees' values and the values embedded in the organization's culture. Finally, we turn to the idea of a 'turnover culture', including how that term has been used and what aspects of organizational culture it captures.

The effects of culture on employee turnover

Although studies of actual turnover are few, there is some evidence to suggest an organization's culture influences turnover rates. For example, using survival analysis to study the relationship between culture and voluntary turnover in a sample of working professionals at large international accounting firms, Sheridan (1992) found that participants in a culture that valued tasks had a much higher rate of voluntary turnover than those in a culture that valued interpersonal relationships, such that employees stayed on average 14 months longer in a culture that valued interpersonal relationships compared to a culture that valued tasks. Furthermore, Sheridan showed that the difference in turnover rates was consistent across individual levels of performance, such that the difference in turnover rates applied equally across high and low performers. In a sample of private manufacturing organizations in Japan, Jung and Takeuchi (2010) found that although community culture did not have a significant effect on turnover rate, there was evidence for indirect effects through the supportive leadership of top management. Based on data from East Coast retail stores and organizations from Chicago's metropolitan area, Cooke and Szumal (1993) found evidence for the relationship between the normative beliefs of culture and supervisor-reported annual turnover rates. Across the two samples, three dimensions of passive-defensive culture (approval, dependent, conventional) and one dimension of aggressive-defensive culture (oppositional) were positively related to annual turnover rates, whereas one dimension of constructive culture (achievement) was negatively related to annual turnover rates. In another example, Aarons and Sawitzky (2006) examined the cross-level link between culture and turnover among clinical and case management service providers working in mental health programmes. They found that a constructive culture was positively related to work attitudes (job satisfaction and organizational commitment) and a defensive culture was negatively related to work attitudes; work attitudes were then significantly negatively related to staff turnover. In a similar study of child welfare and juvenile justice services case managers, Glisson and James (2002) found that team-level constructive culture was negatively associated with individual-level turnover after controlling for a variety of individual-level and team-level covariates. As a final example, Shim (2014) found a significant difference in organizational culture when comparing low-turnover and high-turnover public child welfare agencies, such that low-turnover agencies had a more positive culture than high-turnover agencies. Of the three dimensions of organizational culture Shim studied, only the emphasis on rewards was significantly different between the high- and low-turnover agencies, with low-turnover agencies placing a stronger emphasis on rewards than high-turnover agencies.

Some studies have failed to find support for a relationship between organizational culture and turnover, however. For instance, Glisson, Schoenwald, Kelleher, Landsverk, Hoagwood, Mayberg and Green (2008) examined culture profiles (worst, average and best as measured by the dimensions of rigidity, proficiency and resistance in the organization) in a nationwide study of mental health clinics. They found that the differences in culture profiles were not significantly related to turnover rates. Similarly, in Williams and Glisson's (2013) study of child welfare agencies, the authors found proficiency culture was not significantly related to the annual turnover rate for caseworkers working in those agencies. Finally, although Glisson and James (2002) found that team-level constructive culture was negatively associated with individual-level turnover (as described above), they did not find a significant relationship between passive-defensive culture and individual-level turnover among their sample of caseworkers.

Although there are mixed findings for the relationship between organizational culture and actual turnover, studies of turnover *intentions* (individual reports that employees are likely to leave the organization in the near future) generally add support to the notion that culture plays a critical role in employee turnover and provide insight into the potential complexity in the relationship between culture and turnover. The weakness of studies of turnover intentions is that they are often focused on individual-level perceptions of culture rather than cross-level relationships of aggregate culture perceptions or relationships. Nevertheless, there is evidence that a variety of culture dimensions or types are related to turnover intentions, including the dimensions of support, aggression and teamwork (Sharoni, Tziner, Fein, Shultz, Shaul & Zilberman, 2012), employability culture (Nauta, van Vianen, van der Heijden, van Dam & Willemsen, 2009), passive-defensive, aggressive-defensive and constructive cultural norms (Balthazard, Cooke & Potter, 2006) and work–family culture (Mauno, Kiuru & Kinnunen, 2011). Qualitative studies also support this relationship; Mulcahy and Betts (2005), for instance, reported on an organizational change effort aimed at improving organizational culture that was associated with decreases in the turnover intentions of neonatal nurses. Beyond the direct relationship between culture and turnover intentions, this literature also suggests that job satisfaction may play a mediating role in the relationship between culture and turnover intentions (Egan, Yang & Bartlett, 2004) and that the strength of the relationship between culture and turnover may vary due to moderator variables. Chenot, Benton and Kim (2009) found that passive-defensive culture was negatively related to turnover intentions for early career child welfare workers, but not for mid- or late career workers.

In summary, although there is some evidence that organizational culture is directly related to turnover and turnover intentions, the relationship between organizational culture and turnover may be more complex than simple direct relationships. Indeed, there is evidence to suggest that organizational culture may be indirectly related to employee turnover through mediators or may be affected by moderators. More work is needed to identify factors that affect the relationship between organizational culture and turnover and the mechanisms through which culture affects turnover. Another issue to explore further is how the relationship between organizational culture and turnover is affected by the way culture is operationalized and measured. For instance, culture has been studied across multiple levels of organizations; it is likely that some levels of culture may be more related to employee turnover than others. Finally, although certain organizational cultures may be more or less desirable to employees, the relative importance of different dimensions of culture across employees may also be salient. We explore this possibility next.

Cultural fit and employee turnover

In contrast to the research in the previous section, which generally implies a direct effect of organizational culture on turnover, research on person–culture fit, or person–organization fit, suggests that it is the alignment between the values of the individual and those of the organization that drives turnover in organizations. Note that the terms person–culture fit and person–organization fit are both used in the literature, seemingly interchangeably, which is appropriate because both are focused on alignment between individuals' values and the organization's values. Thus, we will also use both terms, although person–culture fit is more aligned with the focus in this chapter on organizational culture.

Highly relevant to the discussion of fit and turnover is the attraction–selection–attrition (ASA) cycle as first described by Schneider (1987). Schneider proposed that individuals will be differentially attracted to occupations and organizations, that selection systems will result in individuals being hired who are more similar to those currently in the organization relative to those not hired, and finally that individuals who do not fit the organization will be more likely to leave than those who do fit. Empirical research has offered support for this model (e.g., Bradley-Geist & Landis, 2012; Ployhart, Weekley & Baughman, 2006; Schaubroeck, Ganster & Jones, 1998; Schneider, Smith, Taylor & Fleenor, 1998), although the focus is typically on personality rather than other individual difference variables (e.g., values). The last piece of the ASA cycle focusing on attrition is most germane to this chapter. Applied to organizational culture, the argument is that those individuals whose values do not align well with the values embedded in the organization's culture will be more likely to turnover, whereas those individuals with similar values will be more likely to stay. Over time this process strengthens the organization's culture and results in an increasingly homogeneous set of employees (Schneider, 1987).

Before discussing specific studies of fit, it is important to note that fit can be assessed in several ways (Kristof, 1996). Subjective fit is assessed when individuals are directly asked how they perceive their fit with the organization. Perceived fit is assessed when individuals are asked to describe their own characteristics or values and then to report the organization's values; these are used to calculate a fit score. Finally, objective fit is assessed similarly to perceived fit, except current employees' ratings are used to measure the characteristics (or culture) of the organization, which are then used with the individual's self-ratings to calculate fit.

Although there are several empirical studies finding evidence that person–culture fit is related to turnover rates, one of the most notable ones is O'Reilly, Chatman and Caldwell (1991). These researchers provided some of the earliest and most compelling evidence that person–organization fit was related to turnover in a sample of accountants from eight large American public accounting firms. They showed that objective person–organization fit was significantly correlated with turnover intentions one year later ($r=-0.37$), and using survival analysis, demonstrated that person–organization fit was significantly related to actual turnover two years after the initial measurement of fit. Others providing evidence that fit is related to turnover rates include Chatman (1991) and Vandenberghe (1999).

Perhaps the most useful evidence for the relationship between fit and turnover comes from meta-analyses that have been conducted on the relationship between person–organization fit and turnover intentions and turnover. With regard to turnover intentions, Verquer, Beehr and Wagner (2003) reported an overall corrected correlation of –0.21, although the strength of this effect was moderated by a number of factors, including the type of fit, with the strongest relationships for subjective fit, followed by perceived fit and objective fit. Kristof-Brown, Zimmerman and Johnson (2005) reported stronger results for turnover intentions, with a corrected correlation of –0.35 (–0.47 after removing Vancouver & Schmitt's 1991 study which had a particularly large sample size). With regard to actual turnover, Kristof-Brown and colleagues (2005) reported a corrected correlation with person–organization fit of –0.14 across all the studies they included. The results were slightly stronger when distinguishing between indirect measures of fit (perceived fit or objective fit; $r = -0.12$) and direct subjective measures ($r = -0.16$).

In summary, although there is solid evidence that certain cultures are more or less desirable in general to employees, research suggests that organizational cultures may also vary in their desirability among employees depending on the fit between each employee's values and the values embedded in the organization's culture. Despite the evidence that person–culture fit matters, more work is needed. For instance, organizations can have many different values; thus, it would be helpful to identify whether an employee has to fit well with all organizational values or just some of them, and, relatedly, whether fit with certain values is more important than fit with others. Research is also needed to understand whether strong cues in the work environment can change or shape an employee's work values. Such research should help organizations identify strategies for attracting, selecting and retaining desirable employees. Finally, other types of fit, such as the fit between individuals' ideal cultures and their perceived current culture (Harris & Mossholder, 1996), should be examined relative to other measures of person–culture fit to understand their relative contributions to turnover.

Turnover culture

The final theme we identified in the literature on organizational culture and turnover is turnover culture. Rather than focusing on how culture or its fit with employees' values impacts turnover, research and writing on the construct of turnover culture focuses on the extent to which turnover can become a normative part of organizational life and ingrained in the organization's culture. Turnover culture has been defined as 'the systematic pattern of shared cognitions by organizational or subunit incumbents that influence decisions regarding job movement' (Abelson, 1993, p. 388). In such a culture, turnover in the organization is accepted as a norm and viewed as an appropriate or expected occurrence (Moore & Burke, 2002). Employees perceive the organization as one step in their career and assume that they will not remain there (Vardaman, 2013). Turnover in such an organization can be thought of as an artifact of its culture. A turnover culture develops when those artifacts 'are interpreted by and influence organizational members...these artifacts ultimately transform into basic assumptions and mutual cognitive schema regarding turnover perceptions, intentions, and behaviors' (Moore & Burke, 2002, p. 74). Thus, research on turnover culture addresses the artifacts and stories found in the organization, how individuals interpret these artifacts and how shared cognitions and assumptions about the organization evolve from these shared interpretations (Abelson, 1993).

A number of factors contribute to the development of a turnover culture. Abelson (1993) explained that leaders have a decisive role in shaping turnover culture. The leader's behaviours and management style influence 'how others perceive organizational events. It is this perception of organizational events through organizational incumbents' interpretation of artifacts that affects turnover decisions' (p. 346). Along with leaders, organizational issues and HRM practices can influence the turnover culture by impacting how people view the organization's values. For instance, socialization processes shape how employees perceive organizational norms; those who do not fit into the values may feel alienated and leave. HRM practices of recruitment, promotion, reward and appraisal can also reinforce organizational values that relate to turnover (e.g., valuing internal vs. external promotion; Abelson, 1993). Environmental factors such as the economy, job availability and competition can also shape the turnover culture within an organization. The literature on turnover cultures has focused particularly on the culture in certain industries or occupations. For example, there may be a high turnover culture in IT occupations because many IT organizations employ college graduates, who leave after only a few years (Moore & Burke, 2002). They can do so because there is a high demand for IT professionals and those who leave are often treated as 'heroes' (Moore & Burke, 2002). North, Leung, Ashton, Rasmussen, Hughes and Finlayson (2013) also reported evidence of a turnover culture in nursing, noting that 'nurse managers displayed an indifference to turnover, conveying an acceptance and tolerance of high turnover rates' (p. 24).

The hospitality industry has perhaps received the most attention in terms of the presence of a turnover culture. Davidson, Timo and Wang (2010) argue that a turnover culture is found in the hospitality industry because of the low-paid work that requires little skill, unsocial working hours and little opportunity for advancement. Furthermore, because turnover is viewed as the norm in the hotel industry, people enter it with the belief that it will be a short-term position offering little scope for advancement. In a quantitative study of turnover culture in five-star hotels, Iverson and Deery (1997) found that a turnover culture was positively associated with intention to leave, routinization, role ambiguity, role conflict, work overload, resource inadequacy, negative affectivity and job opportunity, and it was negatively associated with job satisfaction, organizational commitment, co-worker support, supervisor support, distributive justice, job security, promotional opportunity and career development. They did not find differences between permanent workers and casual or part-time workers, suggesting that a turnover culture in the hospitality industry was not attributable to the disproportionate number of part-time workers, but instead is a more basic assumption that pervades the entire industry. In a final example of research on turnover culture in hospitality, Deery and Shaw (1997) performed an exploratory cluster analysis of questionnaire items covering a broad variety of constructs related to morale and organizational culture to better understand the content of the turnover culture. The analysis distinguished two forms of turnover culture: positive and negative. Employees viewed a positive turnover culture when quitting meant there was a better job available to them or when the demands of the organization were high. A negative turnover culture occurred when employees quit because they disliked their job and not because they had a better job opportunity elsewhere. Deery and Shaw suggested that employees perceiving a negative turnover culture may also have a hostile attitude to the job, even though managers may exhibit behaviours encouraging long-term commitment. This discrepancy in manager and employee perspectives, Deery and Shaw noted, may mean that a negative turnover culture is more often a subculture than the organization's overarching culture.

In summary, although the literature on turnover culture is fairly limited, such an approach holds promise in understanding how employees think about, react to and communicate about turnover. Previous research by Harrison and Carroll (1991) suggested that, in general, the culture of an organization was robust to turnover rates; however, the research on turnover culture suggests that high turnover rates can be an artifact that can become embedded in the deeper layers of culture until it becomes an underlying assumption. More research is needed to demonstrate how turnover cultures manifest across the various levels of organizational culture (artifacts, espoused values and underlying assumptions; Schein, 1985), what the causal relationship is between turnover culture and turnover rates, and whether turnover cultures can be changed, particularly in the long term. Such research should help create a more holistic picture of turnover and aid in identifying more effective strategies for managing turnover (Abelson, 1993).

Organizational Climate and Employee Turnover

In this section, we turn to the topic of organizational climate and its relationship with employee turnover. As described above, the organizational climate literature can be divided into two categories: molar climate (capturing the broad environment of the organization) and focused climate (related to a specific goal or strategic imperative). We organize this section in line with these two categories, considering molar climate first and then focused climate.

Molar climate and employee turnover

Molar climate research considers the breadth of the organizational environment by capturing any possible dimensions that may be used to describe the work environment as a whole, including such dimensions as role stress and lack of harmony; job challenge and autonomy; leadership support and facilitation; and work group cooperation, friendliness and warmth (James & James, 1989). There is empirical support for the relationship between molar climate and turnover. For example, in a sample of multinational firms located in Hong Kong, Ngo, Foley and Loi (2009) found a significant negative relationship between molar climate as reported by the HR managers and the firms' overall turnover rate. Glisson and colleagues (2008) looked at how climate may affect therapist turnover in mental health clinics. Climate profiles were created for organizations based on engagement, functionality and stress in the organization. They found that turnover was higher (22%) in clinics with the worst organizational climate profiles as compared to clinics with the average (13%) and best (10%) climate profiles. Shim's (2014) comparison of low-turnover and high-turnover public child welfare agencies revealed that low-turnover agencies tended to have more positive climates, particularly with regard to the dimension of workload such that low-turnover agencies tended to have less overwhelming and more manageable workloads. Other research has examined the effects of molar climate on turnover as mediated by alternative variables. Aarons, Sommerfeld and Willging (2011) studied climate and turnover during a statewide behavioural health reform and found that an empowering climate was negatively associated with turnover intentions and a demoralizing climate was positively associated with turnover intentions; turnover intentions were then positively associated with actual turnover. Similarly, Aarons and Sawitzky's (2006) study of mental health providers showed that molar climate's cross-level relationship with turnover was mediated by work attitudes.

Some studies have failed to find a significant effect of molar climate on turnover, however. For instance, Glisson and James's (2002) study of case managers in child welfare found no significant relationship between climate and turnover. Sheidow, Schoenwald, Wagner, Allred and Burns (2007) showed some support for molar climate's relationship with turnover when examining climate variables at the individual level (i.e., psychological climate), but none of the aggregate measures of climate was significantly related to turnover. Such findings suggest the possibility of moderators, although we found little research examining such a possibility. In one exception, Terbog and Lee (1984) studied climate and turnover rates in retail stores and found some evidence for the relationship between climate and turnover for managers, but no relationship for salespersons after accounting for demographic variables. Thus, level in the organization or the job type may play a role in whether molar climate is associated with turnover.

In summary, although there is some evidence supporting the relationship between molar organizational climate and employee turnover, such evidence is relatively limited. The mixed results of the few studies we were able to find indicate that the relationship between organizational climate and turnover is complicated and thus there is a need to examine both the moderators and mediators of this relationship. Early organizational climate work suggested that climate affects outcomes by motivating individuals (Litwin & Stringer, 1968). This may be a place to start when looking for the mechanisms through which climate is related to turnover. Climate research in other areas has found that the strength of a climate affects its impact on outcomes (see Ehrhart et al., 2014; Kuenzi & Schminke, 2009); we return to this later in the chapter in our directions for future research. Finally, there are measurement issues to consider as the lack of consistency in operationalizing and measuring molar organizational climate may have contributed to the variability in support for its relationship with turnover. More fine-tuned theorizing on the relevance of specific dimensions of molar climate may add needed specificity to research examining the outcome of turnover. Moreover, examining the role of climate profiles or configurations (Schulte, Ostroff, Shmulyian & Kinicki, 2009) could offer insight into how the various dimensions of molar climate come together to impact issues related to employee turnover.

Focused climate and employee turnover

Focused climates address those aspects of the work environment that are most relevant to the accomplishment of a specific goal or strategic imperative, including service, safety, justice and diversity (Ehrhart et al., 2014). In general, there are few studies examining the relationship between focused climates and actual turnover. Nevertheless, there are some exceptions. In a sample of nurse managers, Sellgren, Ekvall and Tomson (2007) investigated how different aspects of creative climate, which included 10 dimensions – challenge, freedom, idea support, trust, dynamism, playfulness, debates, conflicts, risk-taking and idea time – related to turnover. They found that two aspects of creative climate – challenge and debate – were negatively related to turnover, and one aspect – playfulness – was positively related to turnover. In a study of justice climate in hotels, Simons and Roberson (2003) showed that both interpersonal and procedural justice perceptions indirectly predicted turnover rate through multiple mediators, including employee commitment, satisfaction with supervisor and turnover intentions. In a case study of the implementation of a safety-based programme in intensive care units, Timmel, Kent, Holzmueller, Paine, Schulick and Pronovost (2010) found that perceptions of the safety climate improved and turnover decreased during the implementation, leading them to suggest a relationship between the two variables. Finally, in a study of automotive services stores, Sowinski, Fortmann and Lezotte (2008) studied the relationship of service climate level (the average score in the store) and strength (the variability of employees' climate scores within the stores) with store turnover rates. They found that one relationship between the climate strength for the dimension of means emphasis (capturing an emphasis on improving service knowledge and skills through training) approached statistical significance ($p = 0.055$), suggesting that not only climate level but climate strength may contribute to turnover.

As with the research on culture, there is more evidence for the relationship between focused climates and turnover intentions than actual turnover. This relationship has been investigated most frequently in the literatures on diversity climate and ethical climate. One example of research on diversity climate is Boehm, Kunze and Bruch's (2014) study of age-diversity climate in German small and medium-sized companies. They found that age-diversity climate was negatively correlated with collective turnover intentions. In addition, age-diversity climate, along with collective perceptions of social exchange, mediated the relationship between age-inclusive HR practices and collective turnover intentions. Specifically, HR practices that were age-inclusive were positively related to age-diversity climate, which in turn was directly positively related to collective perceptions of social exchange (i.e., relationships in which both parties reciprocally work towards the benefit of the other party over time; Wayne, Shore & Liden, 1997). Finally, collective perceptions of social exchange were negatively related to collective turnover intentions, forming a three-path mediation model. Most other examples of research on diversity climate and turnover intentions have focused on individual perceptions of climate. Examples include Stewart, Volpone, Avery and McKay's (2011) study showing that individual-level perceptions of diversity climate interacted with individual perceptions of ethical climate to predict turnover intentions, McKay, Avery, Tonidandel, Morris, Hernandez and Hebl's (2007) study showing evidence that race moderated the relationship between individual-level perceptions of diversity climate and turnover intentions, and Singh and Selvarajan's (2013) study showing that the relationship between individual-level diversity climate and turnover intentions was moderated by individual perceptions of the community diversity climate.

Although there is a fairly substantial literature on the relationship between ethical climate and turnover intentions, that research is almost exclusively at the individual level. A number of studies have shown evidence for a direct correlation between individual-level ethical climate perceptions and turnover intentions (Fournier, Tanner, Chonko & Manolis, 2010; Hart, 2005; Jaramillo, Mulki & Boles, 2013; Jaramillo, Mulki, & Solomon, 2006; Mulki, Jaramillo & Locander, 2008; Schminke, Ambrose & Neubaum, 2005; Schwepker, 2001; Stewart et al., 2011). Other studies have found evidence for mediators in the relationship between perceptions of ethical climate and turnover intentions, such as organizational commitment in Schwepker's (2001) study of sales workers or role stress, interpersonal conflict, emotional exhaustion, trust in supervisor and job satisfaction in Mulki and colleagues' (2008) study on healthcare workers. Still other studies have looked at interactions of ethical climate perceptions with other variables to predict turnover intentions, including with diversity climate (Stewart et al., 2011) and individual performance (Fournier et al., 2010).

Some research on ethical climate and turnover has taken a fit perspective in line with what we previously described in the organizational culture section with regard to person–culture fit. One approach to studying fit and ethical climate has been to analyse differences between preferred ethical climate and actual ethical climate at the individual level (e.g., Sims & Kroeck, 1994). In a sample of hospital workers, Sims and Kroeck found that preferred–actual fit for the independence ethical climate (a climate that emphasizes following personal beliefs in making ethical decisions) was significantly related to turnover intentions. Ambrose, Arnaud and Schminke (2008) also analysed fit as it pertains to ethical climate and individual moral development. In their study, ethical climate was measured by taking the average score in the participating companies; thus this approach was in line with the objective fit approach described above. They found that two of the three fit variables (conventional moral development–caring ethical climate fit and post-conventional moral development–independence ethical climate fit) were significantly negatively related to turnover intentions, but the third (pre-conventional moral development–instrumental ethical climate fit) was not significant. They concluded that at pre-conventional moral development, which is the lowest stage of moral development, participants may not find ethical values as important, and thus ethical value congruence would not be relevant.

There are other examples of research on focused climate and turnover intentions outside of the literatures on diversity climate and ethical climate. In a study of retail apparel stores, Hunter, Neubert, Perry, Witt, Penney and Weinberger (2013) found that store-level service climate was negatively related to individual-level turnover intentions and that store-level service climate fully mediated the negative relationship between store servant leadership and turnover intentions. O'Neill, Harrison, Cleveland, Almeida, Stawski and Crouter (2009) studied three dimensions of work–family climate in the hotel industry: organizational time expectations, career consequences and managerial support. They found in their analyses of within-hotel variability in turnover intentions (and thus addressing psychological climate) that all three dimensions were significant predictors, and in their between-hotel analyses (addressing organizational climate) that only managerial support predicted turnover intentions. Although there is research on other focused climates and turnover intentions (including justice climate, Ansari, Kee & Aafaqi, 2007; and innovation climate, Campbell, Im & Jeong, 2014), much of that literature focuses only on individual-level perceptions of climate.

In summary, there is evidence that focused climates are related to employee turnover. However, as with our examination of the molar climate literature, there are mixed results, suggesting the need to examine potential moderators of the relationship between focused climate and employee turnover as well as to understand the mechanisms through which climate affects turnover. It is notable that studies rarely examine more than one climate at a time, yet we know that multiple climates can exist simultaneously in organizations. It would be interesting to see if there is a profile of focused climates that is related to employee turnover. Relatedly, it is possible that one type of focused climate could mitigate the negative impact of another type of focused climate. So, for instance, the negative impact of a low-service climate may be less severe if there are high levels of a climate for diversity or fairness. Further, we need to understand better the relationship between molar and focused climate. It may be that certain climates are tied directly to employee turnover while other climates moderate those relationships. For instance, the relationship between molar climate and employee turnover may be moderated by diversity climate and/or ethical climate. Another possibility is that focused climates may be more relevant for fit issues. For strategic climates such as service or safety, for example, the employee's personal values for providing high-quality customer service or working safely may need to fit the strategic climate of the organization; if they do not, the employee will be inclined to leave. For process climate such as ethics, justice and diversity, the fit between the climate and the salience of those issues for employees' self-concepts may be relevant to their effects on turnover.

Future Research

In addition to the gaps in the literature outlined above, we highlight three major directions for future research in this final section: 1) the integration of organizational culture and climate in understanding turnover; 2) the role of culture strength and climate strength in understanding turnover; and 3) the interrelationships among culture, climate and turnover.

The integration of organizational culture and climate

Research on organizational culture and climate has existed relatively independently for several decades. However, since 2010 there has been some effort to integrate these two concepts. Ehrhart and colleagues (2014) discussed three models integrating culture and climate. First, Zohar and Hofmann's (2012) model used Schein's (2010) layers of culture (artifacts, espoused values and basic assumptions) as a basis, adding climate as a representation of the enacted values of the organization that employees infer from the overall pattern of artifacts in the organization and that can be contrasted with the organization's espoused values to gain insight into the organization's underlying basic assumptions. A second model comes from Ostroff, Kinicki and Muhammad (2012), who emphasized organizational culture as the foundation for its structure and processes, which form the building blocks of organizational climate. Climate, then, is the proximal predictor of collective attitudes and behaviour, which subsequently impact organizational outcomes. Finally, Schneider, Ehrhart and Macey's (2011) 'climcult' model contrasts organizational culture with strategic climates, with more positive cultures resulting in higher levels of attraction and retention, and strategic climate leading to higher strategic success, which then combine to impact the organization's overall effectiveness.

Although a handful of studies in our review (all of which were in child welfare or mental health settings) included both organizational culture and climate in predicting turnover, most did not integrate culture and climate in the ways described above. Instead, the more typical approach was to examine culture and climate as simultaneous predictors of outcomes (see Glisson & James, 2002; Glisson et al., 2008; Shim, 2014). One exception was Aarons and Sawitzky's (2006) study, which showed that a demoralizing climate partially mediated the cross-level effects of constructive and defensive culture on work attitudes, which then predicted turnover. Their model is in line Ostroff and colleagues' (2012) proposed model, such that the deeper-level culture values manifest themselves in the climate, which then affects employee outcomes.

More research is needed that integrates organizational culture and climate in understanding turnover. For instance, research on organizational culture primarily focuses on its intermediate or outer layers, but perhaps Zohar and Hofmann's (2012) model can be applied, such that climate can be used to understand how employees experience the enacted values of the organization. By contrasting the enacted values in the climate with the espoused values of the culture, insight can be gained into the organization's deeper cultural assumptions, particularly with regard to turnover. Another possibility would be to pursue the framework proposed by Schneider and colleagues (2011). They suggested that a positive organizational culture that supports employees' well-being is most critical for outcomes related to attracting and retaining talent, and a strategic climate is most critical for achieving the organization's goals and competing with other firms in the marketplace. Although some research has examined both culture and molar climate as described above, the role of strategic climates, and particularly how they can be integrated with research on the main effects of culture and person–culture fit, merits further investigation.

The role of organizational culture and climate strength

Our review of the literature related to turnover has revealed very little discussion of issues related to culture or climate strength. There are two exceptions: one theoretical paper by DelCampo (2006) on culture strength, and one empirical paper by Sowinski and colleagues (2008) on service climate level and strength.

DelCampo (2006) proposed that strong cultures will have higher turnover rates than weak cultures. The basis of his argument is that it is easier to identify the important shared assumptions in a strong culture, and thus individuals new to the culture can quickly identify whether their personal values are a fit or not. If not, these individuals will leave. However, in a weak culture it is more challenging for new workers to understand the core values and assumptions, and they may believe they can even change the organization to fit their own values. In this case, individuals who do not fit the culture will be less likely to leave. An alternative perspective is that strong cultures develop because of the organization's success; in other words, the reason the values become deeply accepted and embedded in the organization is because they have been reinforced over time by the positive results with which they are associated (Schein, 2010). In general, such cultures are expected to be positive. There are certainly exceptions. Cooke and Szumal (2000) described two mechanisms through which this can occur: the defensive misattribution of success ('organizations that enjoy strong franchises, munificent environments, extensive patents and copyrights, and/or massive financial resources are likely to perform quite adequately, at least in the short term', even if they have negative cultures', p. 160) and the culture bypass (organizations can create operational systems that minimize the effect of culture on outcomes, such as in fast-food restaurants). However, these are expected to be the exception rather than the rule. If strong cultures have tended to be successful in the past, and if successful cultures are more likely to be positive, then it would be expected for turnover to be lower in strong cultures than in weak cultures. Weak cultures, by contrast, are not internally aligned. Employees are more likely to receive conflicting messages from various sources or have different experiences of the organization's culture from their co-workers'. The resulting stress associated with role conflict and/or ambiguity is likely to result in higher turnover (Beehr & Glazer, 2005; Firth & Britton, 1989; Griffeth et al., 2000; Podsakoff, LePine & LePine, 2007).

The evidence from the climate literature is more in line with this argument. Specifically, Sowinski and colleagues (2008) found that stores with weak climates on the means emphasis sub-dimension of service climate had higher turnover rates (although just outside the commonly accepted cutoff for statistical significance at $p=0.055$). They explained their results:

> when there are no clearly defined guidelines about what behaviours and practices are encouraged and rewarded in an organization, individuals may become frustrated and experience stress as a result of interpersonal friction, conflict, and process loss (Lindell & Brandt, 2000), or experience reduced psychological well-being (Bliese & Halverson, 1998). Any of these experiences would most likely have a negative impact on resulting employee behaviours, including voluntary turnover. (Sowinski et al., 2008, pp. 85–86)

As opposed to examining main effects, climate strength may moderate the relationship between climate level and turnover. This approach conforms to the way climate strength is typically studied (e.g., Colquitt, Noe & Jackson, 2002; González-Romá, Peiró & Tordera, 2002; Schneider, Salvaggio & Subirats, 2002), and suggests that the negative effects of climate level on turnover are even more negative when employees tend to agree that the climate is negative (vs. when there is less agreement).

More research is needed to understand the role of culture and climate strength in predicting turnover. When cultures or climates are generally positive, it seems that strength should be associated with lower turnover. When the culture or climate is generally negative, however, it seems that strength should be associated with higher turnover. When the aspect of culture or climate under investigation (e.g., the focused climate) is neutral, then perhaps fit becomes the stronger determinant of turnover. Moreover, this discussion has treated culture and climate as equivalent, but in line with the previous section, the distinction between culture and climate is important. Along those lines, research on the unique roles of culture strength versus climate strength is also needed.

Alternative models of the interrelationships among culture, climate and turnover

In general, the research reviewed in this chapter has viewed organizational culture and climate as predictors of turnover, either directly or indirectly, or through their alignment with personal characteristics, as in the fit literature. We next describe two other possibilities: turnover as a predictor of climate or culture and the moderating role of culture and climate on the outcome of turnover.

The view that turnover can be a predictor of culture or climate is perhaps most closely aligned with the idea of turnover cultures described earlier. In that case, the high levels of turnover, management's strategies for managing the turnover and organizational members' norms for dealing with the continuous loss of their co-workers all contribute to the development of the organization's culture. In addition, as discussed previously, the organization's turnover culture is affected by the culture of the industry or occupation. Thus if the organization's management applies the industry's or occupation's assumptions about turnover to a newer organization, acceptance of turnover may be instilled in the organization even before it directly experiences high turnover itself, thus perpetuating the turnover culture. Research on the ASA model also suggests that turnover can influence culture and/or climate. According to the core idea of the ASA model that people make the place (Schneider, 1987), if an organization experiences enough turnover, the infusion of new ideas, values and personalities may well have an impact on the organization's culture and climate. Dlugosz, Ehrhart and Aarons (2012) showed in a sample of mental health provider teams that higher turnover levels were associated with higher levels of innovation climate, which they attributed to the fresh ideas and approaches that the new team members introduced. They did not find an effect on innovation climate strength, although such a relationship would be expected, particularly if the new members varied significantly from those already employed in the organization. More research on how turnover can impact the culture and climate of the organization is needed.

The second way of thinking about how culture and climate are related to turnover is that they may act as moderators of the outcomes of turnover. We identified two examples of research which examined this hypothesis, both on organizational culture. In a study of nurses in outpatient medical centres, Mohr, Young and Burgess (2012) found that the centre's group-oriented culture (which emphasizes a sense of belonging, participation and encouragement) moderated the relationship between turnover and customer service. When the group-oriented culture was high, turnover did not have an effect on customer service, but when the group-oriented culture was low, more turnover resulted in lower customer service. They explained these results in terms of social capital and knowledge-sharing, such that centres with a high group-oriented culture are more likely to have high levels of trust and to share knowledge. Thus, when members leave, the centre is better able to recover and minimize their loss. In a study by Williams and Glisson (2013), a proficient organizational culture was found to moderate the relationship between caseworker turnover and youth outcomes. Specifically, lower turnover was associated with improved outcomes only when the agency had high levels of proficient culture. Research along these lines demonstrates that the organizational context, as indicated by its culture, plays an important role in the consequences of turnover for organizations.

Future research could consider contexts that may result in positive outcomes for turnover, as well as whether climate can play a similar moderating role.

Conclusion

Although substantial literatures have developed over time on how organizational culture and climate are related to turnover, the overlap between the culture and climate literatures leaves something to be desired. There are a number of areas where research is still needed to better understand the interrelationships among culture, climate and turnover. One area that comes to the fore is examining more complex models. This could include studying the effects of culture and climate together, as well as studying multiple climates simultaneously. It could also include exploring the mechanisms and boundary conditions of culture and climate on turnover. Another area that could use additional work involves fit and turnover. Little work has been done on organizational climate and fit, but even the work on culture and fit could be expanded to clarify the areas of culture where fit is more important or to incorporate different types of fit by considering ideal versus preferred cultures and climates in order to add to our understanding of turnover. Finally, most of the research we examined focuses on how culture and climate impact whether employees leave the organization or not. We found little evidence, if any, of research that takes into account the different reasons employees leave. For instance, the culture and climate predictors of turnover may be different for employees who leave for better career opportunities from those who leave because they are unhappy with their current organization. We hope this chapter stimulates research in these areas and look forward to seeing the findings of such research.

References

Aarons, G. A., & Sawitzky, A. C. (2006). Organizational climate partially mediates the effect of culture on work attitudes and staff turnover in mental health services. *Administration and Policy in Mental Health and Mental Health Services Research, 33*(3), 289–301. doi: 10.1007/s10488-006-0039-1.

Aarons, G. A., Sommerfeld, D. H., & Willging, C. E. (2011). The soft underbelly of system change: The role of leadership and organizational climate in turnover during statewide behavioral health reform. *Psychological Services, 8*(4), 269–281.

Abelson, M. A. (1993). Turnover cultures. *Research in Personnel and Human Resources Management, 11*, 339–376.

Ambrose, M., Arnaud, A., & Schminke, M. (2008). Individual moral development and ethical climate: The influence of person–organization fit on job attitudes. *Journal of Business Ethics, 77*(3), 323–333. doi: 10.1007/s10551-007-9352-1.

Ansari, M., Kee, D., & Aafaqi, R. (2007). Leader–member exchange-subordinate outcomes relationship: role of voice and justice. *Leadership & Organization Development Journal, 28*(1).

Balthazard, P., Cooke, R., & Potter, R. (2006). Dysfunctional culture, dysfunctional organization. *Journal of Managerial Psychology, 21*(8), 709–732.

Beehr, T. A., & Glazer, S. (2005). Organizational role stress. *In* J. Barling, E. K. Kelloway & M. R. Frone (Eds.), *Handbook of Work Stress* (pp. 7–33). Thousand Oaks, CA: Sage.

Boehm, S. A., Kunze, F., & Bruch, H. (2014). Spotlight on age-diversity climate: The impact of age-inclusive HR practices on firm-level outcomes. *Personnel Psychology, 67*(3), 667–704.

Bradley-Geist, J. C., & Landis, R. S. (2012). Homogeneity of personality in occupations and organizations: A comparison of alternative statistical tests. *Journal of Business and Psychology, 27*(2), 149–159. doi: 10.1007/s10869-011-9233-6.

Campbell, J. W., Im, T., & Jeong, J. (2014). Internal efficiency and turnover intention: Evidence from local government in South Korea. *Public Personnel Management, 43*(2), 259–282. doi: 10.1177/0091026014524540.

Chatman, J. (1991). Matching people and organizations: Selection and socialization in public accounting firms. *Administrative Science Quarterly, 36*(3), 459–484.

Chenot, D., Benton, A. D., & Kim, H. (2009). The influence of supervisor support, peer support, and organizational culture among early career social workers in child welfare services. *Child Welfare: Journal of Policy, Practice, and Program, 88*(5), 129–147.

Colquitt, J., Noe, R., & Jackson, C. (2002). Justice in teams: Antecedents and consequences of procedural justice climate. *Personnel Psychology, 55*(1), 83–109.

Cooke, R., & Szumal, J. (1993). Measuring normative beliefs and shared behavioral expectations in organizations – The reliability and validity of the organizational culture inventory. *Psychological Reports, 72*(3), 1299–1330.

Cooke, R. A., & Szumal, J. L. (2000). Using the organizational culture inventory to understand the operating couture of organizations. *In* N. M. Ashkanasy, C. P. M. Wilderom & M. F. Peterson (Eds.), *Handbook of Organizational Culture and Climate* (pp. 147–162). Thousand Oaks, CA: Sage.

Davidson, M. G., Timo, N., & Wang, Y. (2010). How much does labour turnover cost? A case study of Australian four- and five-star hotels. *International Journal of Contemporary Hospitality Management, 22*(4), 451–466. doi: 10.1108/09596111011042686.

Deery, M. A., & Shaw, R. N. (1997). An exploratory analysis of turnover culture in the hotel industry in Australia. *International Journal of Hospitality Management, 16*(4), 375–392. doi: 10.1016/S0278-4319(97)00031-5.

DelCampo, R. G. (2006). The influence of culture strength on person–organization fit and turnover. *International Journal of Management, 23*(3). 465.

Dlugosz, L. R., Ehrhart, M. G., & Aarons, G. A. (2012). The effects of change on innovation climate level and strength. Poster presented at the 27th annual conference of the Society for Industrial and Organizational Psychology, April. San Diego, CA.

Egan, T. M., Yang, B., & Bartlett, K. R. (2004). The effects of organizational learning culture and job satisfaction on motivation to transfer learning and turnover intention. *Human Resource Development Quarterly, 15*(3), 279–301.

Ehrhart, M. G., Schneider, B., & Macey, W. H. (2014). *Organizational Climate and Culture: An Introduction to Theory, Research, and Practice*. New York: Routledge.

Firth, H., & Britton, P. (1989). 'Burnout', absence and turnover amongst British nursing staff. *Journal of Occupational Psychology, 62*(1), 55–59. doi: 10.1111/j.2044-8325.1989.tb00477.x.

Fournier, C., Tanner, J. F., Chonko, L. B., & Manolis, C. (2010). The moderating role of ethical climate on salesperson propensity to leave. *Journal of Personal Selling & Sales Management, 30*(1), 7–22.

Glisson, C., & James, L. R. (2002). The cross-level effects of culture and climate in human service teams. *Journal of Organizational Behavior, 23*(6), 767–794. doi: 10.1002/job.162.

Glisson, C., Schoenwald, S. K., Kelleher, K., Landsverk, J., Hoagwood, K., Mayberg, S., & Green, P. (2008). Therapist turnover and new program sustainability in mental health clinics as a function of organizational culture, climate, and service structure. *Administration and Policy in Mental Health and Mental Health Services Research, 35*(1–2), 124–133. doi: 10.1007/s10488-007-0152-9.

González-Romá, V., Peiró, J. M., & Tordera, N. (2002). An examination of the antecedents and moderator influences of climate strength. *Journal of Applied Psychology, 87*(3), 465–473. doi: 10.1037/0021-9010.87.3.465.

Griffeth, R. W., Hom, P. W., & Haertner, S. (2000). A meta-analysis of antecedents and correlates of employee turnover: Update, moderator tests, and research implications for the next millennium. *Journal of Management, 26*, 463–488.

Hancock, J. I., Allen, D. G., Bosco, F. A., McDaniel, K. R., & Pierce, C. A. (2013). Meta-analytic review of employee turnover as a predictor of firm performance. *Journal of Management, 39*(3), 573–603. doi: 10.1177/0149206311424943.

Harris, S. G., & Mossholder, K. W. (1996). The affective implications of perceived congruence with culture dimensions during organizational transformation. *Journal of Management, 22*(4), 527–547. doi: 10.1177/014920639602200401.

Harrison, J., & Carroll, G. R. (1991). Keeping the faith: A model of cultural transmission in formal organizations. *Administrative Science Quarterly, 36*(4), 552–582. doi: 10.2307/2393274.

Hart, S. E. (2005). Hospital ethical climates and registered nurses' turnover intentions. *Journal of Nursing Scholarship, 37*(2), 173–177.

Hausknecht, J. P., & Trevor, C. O. (2011). Collective turnover at the group, unit and organizational levels: Evidence, issues, and implications. *Journal of Management, 37*, 352–388.

Heavey, A. L., Holwerda, J. A., & Hausknecht, J. P. (2013). Causes and consequences of collective turnover: A meta-analytic review. *Journal of Applied Psychology, 98*(3), 412–453. doi: 10.1037/a0032380.

Hunter, E. M., Neubert, M. J., Perry, S. J., Witt, L. A., Penney, L. M., & Weinberger, E. (2013). Servant leaders inspire servant followers: Antecedents and outcomes for employees and the organization. *The Leadership Quarterly, 24*(2), 316–331. doi: 10.1016/j.leaqua.2012.12.001.

Iverson, R. D., & Deery, M. (1997). Turnover culture in the hospitality industry. *Human Resource Management Journal, 7*(4), 71–82.

James, L. A., & James, L. R. (1989). Integrating work environment perceptions: Explorations into the measurement of meaning. *Journal of Applied Psychology, 74*, 739–751.

James, L. R., & Jones, A. P. (1974). Organizational climate: A review of theory and research. *Psychological Bulletin, 81*(12), 1096.

Jaramillo, F., Mulki, J. P., & Boles, J. S. (2013). Bringing meaning to the sales job: The effect of ethical climate and customer demandingness. *Journal of Business Research, 66*(11), 2301–2307. doi: 10.1016/j.jbusres.2012.03.013.

Jaramillo, F., Mulki, J. P., & Solomon, P. (2006). The role of ethical climate on salesperson's role stress, job attitudes, turnover intention, and job performance. *Journal of Personal Selling & Sales Management, 26*(3), 271–282.

Johns, G. (2006). The essential impact of context on organizational behavior. *The Academy of Management Review, 31*(2), 386–408. doi: 10.2307/20159208.

Jung, Y., & Takeuchi, N. (2010). Performance implications for the relationships among top management leadership, organizational culture, and appraisal practice: Testing two theory-based models of organizational learning theory in Japan. *The International Journal of Human Resource Management, 21*(11), 1931–1950. doi: 10.1080/09585192.2010.505093.

Kristof, A. L. (1996) Person–organization fit: An integrative review of its conceptualizations, measurement, and implications. *Personnel Psychology, 49*, 1–49.

Kristof-Brown, A. L., Zimmerman, R. D., & Johnson, E. C. (2005). Consequences of individual's fit at work: A meta-analysis of person–job, person–organization, person–group, and person–supervisor fit. *Personnel Psychology, 58*(2), 281–342. doi: 10.1111/j.1744-6570.2005.00672.x.

Kuenzi, M., & Schminke, M. (2009). Assembling fragments into a lens: A review, critique, and proposed research agenda for organizational work climate literature. *Journal of Management, 35*, 634–717.

Litwin, G. H., & Stringer, R. A. (1968). *Motivation and Organizational Climate*. Boston, MA: Division of Research, Graduate School of Business Administration, Harvard University.

Mauno, S., Kiuru, N., & Kinnunen, U. (2011). Relationships between work–family culture and work attitudes at both the individual and the departmental level. *Work & Stress, 25*(2), 147–166. doi: 10.1080/02678373.2011.594291.

McKay, P. F., Avery, D. R., Tonidandel, S., Morris, M. A., Hernandez, M., & Hebl, M. R. (2007). Racial differences in employee retention: Are diversity climate perceptions the key? *Personnel Psychology, 60*(1), 35–62.

Mohr, D. C., Young, G. J., & Burgess, J. R. (2012). Employee turnover and operational performance: The moderating effect of group-oriented organisational culture. *Human Resource Management Journal, 22*(2), 216–233. doi: 10.1111/j.1748-8583.2010.00159.x.

Moore, J., & Burke, L. A. (2002). How to turn around 'turnover culture' in IT. *Communications of the ACM, 45*(2), 73–78.

Mulcahy, C., & Betts, L. (2005). Transforming culture: An exploration of unit culture and nursing retention within a neonatal unit. *Journal of Nursing Management, 13*(6), 519–523. doi: 10.1111/j.1365-2934.2005.00588.x.

Mulki, J. P., Jaramillo, J. F., & Locander, W. B. (2008). Effect of ethical climate on turnover intention: Linking attitudinal and stress theory. *Journal of Business Ethics*, *78*(4), 559–574.

Nauta, A., van Vianen, A., van der Heijden, B., van Dam, K., & Willemsen, M. (2009). Understanding the factors that promote employability orientation: The impact of employability culture, career satisfaction, and role breadth self-efficacy. *Journal of Occupational and Organizational Psychology*, *82*(2), 233–251. doi: 10.1348/096317908X320147.

Ngo, H., Foley, S., & Loi, R. (2009). Family-friendly work practices, organizational climate, and firm performance: A study of multinational corporations in Hong Kong. *Journal of Organizational Behavior*, *30*(5), 665–680.

North, N., Leung, W., Ashton, T., Rasmussen, E., Hughes, F., & Finlayson, M. (2013). Nurse turnover in New Zealand: Costs and relationships with staffing practices and patient outcomes. *Journal of Nursing Management*, *21*(3), 419–428.

O'Neill, J. W., Harrison, M. M., Cleveland, J., Almeida, D., Stawski, R., & Crouter, A. C. (2009). Work–family climate, organizational commitment, and turnover: Multilevel contagion effects of leaders. *Journal of Vocational Behavior*, *74*(1), 18–29.

O'Reilly, C. A., Chatman, J., & Caldwell, D. F. (1991). People and organizational culture: A profile comparison approach to assessing person–organization fit. *Academy of Management Journal*, *34*(3), 487–516. doi: 10.2307/256404.

Ostroff, C., Kinicki, A. J., & Muhammad, R. S. (2012). Organizational culture and climate. *In* N. W. Schmitt & S. Highhouse (Eds.), *Handbook of Psychology, Vol. 12: Industrial and Organizational Psychology* (2nd ed., pp. 643–676). Hoboken, NJ: Wiley.

Park, T., & Shaw, J. D. (2013). Turnover rates and organizational performance: A meta-analysis. *Journal of Applied Psychology*, *98*(2), 268–309. doi: 10.1037/a0030723.

Ployhart, R. E., Weekley, J. A., & Baughman, K. (2006). The structure and function of human capital emergence: A multilevel examination of the attraction–selection–attrition model. *Academy of Management Journal*, *49*(4), 661–677. doi: 10.5465/AMJ.2006.22083023.

Podsakoff, N. P., LePine, J. A., & LePine, M. A. (2007). Differential challenge stressor–hindrance stressor relationships with job attitudes, turnover intentions, turnover, and withdrawal behavior: A meta-analysis. *Journal of Applied Psychology*, *92*(2), 438–454. doi: 10.1037/0021-9010.92.2.438.

Schaubroeck, J., Ganster, D. C., & Jones, J. R. (1998). Organization and occupation influences in the attraction–selection–attrition process. *Journal of Applied Psychology*, *83*(6), 869–891. doi: 10.1037/0021-9010.83.6.869.

Schein, E. H. (1985). *Organizational Culture and Leadership*. San Francisco: Jossey-Bass.

Schein, E. H. (2010). *Organizational Culture and Leadership* (4th ed.). San Francisco: Jossey-Bass.

Schminke, M., Ambrose, M. L., & Neubaum, D. O. (2005). The effect of leader moral development on ethical climate and employee attitudes. *Organizational Behavior & Human Decision Processes*, *97*(2), 135–151. doi: 10.1016/j.obhdp.2005.03.006.

Schneider, B. (1975). Organizational climates: An essay. *Personnel Psychology*, *28*, 447–479.

Schneider, B. (1987). The people make the place. *Personnel Psychology*, *40*, 437–453.

Schneider, B., Ehrhart, M. G., & Macey, W. A. (2011). Perspectives on organizational climate and culture. *In* S. Zedeck (Ed.), *APA Handbook of Industrial and Organizational Psychology: Vol. 1. Building and Developing the Organization* (pp. 373–414). Washington, DC: American Psychological Association.

Schneider, B., Salvaggio, A., & Subirats, M. (2002). Climate strength: A new direction for climate research. *Journal of Applied Psychology*, *87*(2), 220–229.

Schneider, B., Smith, D. B., Taylor, S., & Fleenor, J. (1998). Personality and organizations: A test of the homogeneity of personality hypothesis. *Journal of Applied Psychology*, *83*(3), 462–470. doi: 10.1037/0021-9010.83.3.462.

Schulte, M., Ostroff, C., Shmulyian, S., & Kinicki, A. (2009). Organizational climate configurations: Relationships to collective attitudes, customer satisfaction, and financial performance. *Journal of Applied Psychology*, *94*, 618–634.

Schwepker Jr, C. H. (2001). Ethical climate's relationship to job satisfaction, organizational commitment, and turnover intention in the salesforce. *Journal of Business Research*, *54*(1), 39–52.

Sellgren, S., Ekvall, G., & Tomson, G. (2007). Nursing staff turnover: Does leadership matter? *Leadership in Health Services, 20*(3), 169–183.

Sharoni, G., Tziner, A., Fein, E. C., Shultz, T., Shaul, K., & Zilberman, L. (2012). Organizational citizenship behavior and turnover intentions: Do organizational culture and justice moderate their relationship? *Journal of Applied Social Psychology, 42*(Suppl 1), E267–E294. doi: 10.1111/j.1559-1816.2012.01015.x.

Sheidow, A. J., Schoenwald, S. K., Wagner, H. R., Allred, C. A., & Burns, B. J. (2007). Predictors of workforce turnover in a transported treatment program. *Administration and Policy in Mental Health and Mental Health Services Research, 34*(1), 45–56.

Sheridan, J. E. (1992). Organizational culture and employee retention. *Academy of Management Journal, 35*(5), 1036–1056. doi: 10.2307/256539.

Shim, M. (2014). Do organisational culture and climate really matter for employee turnover in child welfare agencies? *British Journal of Social Work, 44*(3), 542–558.

Simons, T., & Roberson, Q. (2003). Why managers should care about fairness: The effects of aggregate justice perceptions on organizational outcomes. *Journal of Applied Psychology, 88*(3), 432–443.

Sims, R. L., & Kroeck, K. (1994). The influence of ethical fit on employee satisfaction, commitment and turnover. *Journal of Business Ethics, 13*(12), 939–947.

Singh, B., & Selvarajan, T. T. (2013). Is it spillover or compensation? Effects of community and organizational diversity climates on race differentiated employee intent to stay. *Journal of Business Ethics, 115*(2), 259–269. doi: 10.1007/s10551-012-1392-5.

Smircich, L. (1983). Concepts of culture and organizational analysis. *Administrative Science Quarterly, 28*(3), 339–358. doi: 10.2307/2392246.

Sowinski, D. R., Fortmann, K. A., & Lezotte, D. V. (2008). Climate for service and the moderating effects of climate strength on customer satisfaction, voluntary turnover, and profitability. *European Journal of Work and Organizational Psychology, 17*(1), 73–88.

Stewart, R., Volpone, S. D., Avery, D. R., & McKay, P. (2011). You support diversity, but are you ethical? Examining the interactive effects of diversity and ethical climate perceptions on turnover intentions. *Journal of Business Ethics, 100*(4), 581–593.

Terborg, J., & Lee, T. (1984). A predictive study of organizational turnover rates. *The Academy of Management Journal, 27*(4), 793–810.

Timmel, J., Kent, P. S., Holzmueller, C. G., Paine, L., Schulick, R. D., & Pronovost, P. J. (2010). Impact of the Comprehensive Unit-based Safety Program (CUSP) on safety culture in a surgical inpatient unit. *Joint Commission Journal on Quality and Patient Safety, 36*(6), 252–260.

Vancouver, J. B., & Schmitt, N. (1991). An exploratory examination of person–organization fit: Organizational goal congruence. *Personnel Psychology. 44*, 333–352.

Vandenberghe, C. (1999). Organizational culture, person–culture fit, and turnover: A replication in the health care industry. *Journal of Organizational Behavior, 20*(2), 175–184. doi: 10.1002/(SICI)1099-1379(199903)20:2<175::AID-JOB882>3.0.CO;2-E.

Vardaman, J. (2013). Turnover. *In* V. Smith (Ed.), *Sociology of Work: An Encyclopedia* (pp. 891–894). Thousand Oaks, CA: Sage.

Verquer, M. L., Beehr, T. A., & Wagner, S. H. (2003). A meta-analysis of the relations between person–organization fit and work attitudes. *Journal of Vocational Behavior, 63*, 473–489.

Wayne, S. J., Shore, L. M., & Liden, R. C. (1997). Perceived organizational support and leader–member exchange: A social exchange perspective. *Academy of Management Journal, 40*, 82–111.

Williams, N. J., & Glisson, C. (2013). Reducing turnover is not enough: The need for proficient organizational cultures to support positive youth outcomes in child welfare. *Children and Youth Services Review, 35*(11), 1871–1877. doi: 10.1016/j.childyouth.2013.09.002.

Zohar, D., & Hofmann, D. H. (2012). Organizational culture and climate. *In* S. W. J. Kozlowski (Ed.), *The Oxford Handbook of Industrial and Organizational Psychology* (pp. 643–666). Oxford: Oxford University Press.

24

The Impact of Work–Life Balance on Employee Retention

Kristen M. Shockley, Christine R. Smith
and Eric A. Knudsen

Introduction

Organizations now recognize the importance of attending to employees' work–life concerns. Doing so not only improves employee well-being (Amstad, Meirer, Fasel, Elfering & Semmer, 2011), but also has links to the organization's bottom line in terms of attracting and retaining top talent. Data suggest that a focus on work–life issues will continue to be imperative, as the youngest generation of workers (Generation Y or Millennials) cite work–life balance as a key work value (Society for Human Resource Management, 2004; Twenge, Campbell, Hoffman & Lance, 2010).

The focus of this chapter is to summarize research related to work–life issues and retention. We begin by defining work–life balance and associated terms researchers have used to study the concept. Next, we review research linking work–life balance to retention-related outcomes. We then move on to a discussion of the role of formal and informal work–family support policies in improving work–life outcomes as well as retention-related outcomes. The chapter closes with practical ideas for improving work–life culture and suggestions for future research.

Defining Work–Life Balance

The term work–life balance is commonly used to describe multiple role management; however, academic research has focused limited attention on the balance concept, instead focusing on related but distinct constructs, including work–life (or work–family) conflict and enrichment. The discrepancy between the popular terminology and the research operationalization stems, in part, from a lack of agreement on the definition itself of work–life balance (Greenhaus & Allen, 2011). As examples, the following are definitions offered by various researchers: balance occurs when conflict between roles is low and positive,

The Wiley Blackwell Handbook of the Psychology of Recruitment, Selection and Employee Retention,
First Edition. Edited by Harold W. Goldstein, Elaine D. Pulakos, Jonathan Passmore and Carla Semedo.
© 2017 John Wiley & Sons Ltd. Published 2020 by John Wiley & Sons Ltd.

enriching processes between roles are high (Frone, 2003); when personal resources are distributed across all life roles (Kirchmeyer, 2000); when an employee is fully engaged and attentive to all life roles (Marks & MacDermid, 1996); when an employee is equally satisfied and effective in various life domains (Greenhaus, Collins & Shaw, 2003; Kirchmeyer, 2000). Based on a comprehensive and critical review of these definitions, Greenhaus and Allen (2011) devised a new definition that allows for some idiosyncrasy: 'an overall appraisal of the extent to which an individual's effectiveness and satisfaction in work and family roles is consistent with their life values at a given point in time' (p. 174). Generally, the concept of work–life balance within research remains elusive, and as such lacks programmatic research.

On the other hand, there is a considerable amount of research devoted to work–life conflict and, to a lesser extent, work–life enrichment. Building on Kahn, Wolfe, Quinn, Snoek and Rosenthal's (1964) classic role theory, Greenhaus and Beutell (1985) were the first to formally define work–family conflict as 'a form of inter-role conflict in which the role pressures from the work and family domains are mutually incompatible in some respect. That is, participation in the work (family) role is made more difficult by virtue of participation in the family (work) role' (p. 77). Subsequent researchers (e.g., Boswell & Olson-Buchanan, 2007; Hill, Erickson, Holmes & Ferris, 2010; Reynolds, 2005; Siegel, Post, Brockner, Fishman & Garden, 2005) expanded this definition to focus on work conflicting with any type of extra-work role (i.e., 'life'), not necessarily limited to family. Examples of work–life conflict include situations such as working late and missing family dinners or being preoccupied while at work with a child's poor school performance.

Researchers have acknowledged that not all interactions between work and non-work result in incompatibility. Numerous concepts (e.g., work–family positive spillover, Crouter, 1984; work–family facilitation, Grzywacz, 2000; and work–family enrichment, Greenhaus & Powell, 2006) refer to the beneficial transfer of resources or experiences from one domain to another. This occurs, for example, in the form of skills learned at home such as multitasking that make one a better employee, or a positive mood from work transferring to positive interactions with family members. The differences between each construct are slight, namely that positive spillover involves only the process of gains being transferred from one domain to the other, and enrichment and facilitation involve some type of enhanced functioning occurring from this spillover. The enrichment construct focuses on improvements in individual functioning, whereas facilitation involves the functioning of the overall work–family system (see Wayne, 2009, for discussion of the nuanced difference between constructs). Because of the degree of overlap and for ease of interpretation, we use the term work–life enrichment to refer to this class of constructs. Similar to work–family conflict, although initial conceptualizations were specific to the family domain, researchers have also considered the broader concept of work–life enrichment (e.g., Haar, 2013; Pedersen & Jeppesen, 2012).

Both work–life conflict and work–life enrichment are considered bi-directional (Frone, 2003; Greenhaus & Beutell, 1985). That is, work can interfere with (or enrich) life and life can interfere with (or enrich) work. These constructs are empirically distinct and generally have unique patterns of correlates, particularly on the antecedent side, such that predictors of work-to-family conflict and enrichment tend to reside in the work domain (e.g., long work hours, work pressure, work support), whereas predictors of the family-to-work direction stem from the family (e.g., family demands, family stress) (Amstad et al., 2011; McNall, Nicklin & Masuda, 2010).

In the following sections we cover research that links work–life balance (where available), conflict and enrichment to retention-related concepts. The terms work–family, work–life and work–non-work will be used to describe the same general phenomena found in the literature. Our choice of nomenclature is based on the original terms researchers used when describing specific findings.

Empirical Association between Work–Life Conflict and Work–Life Enrichment and Retention-related Outcomes

In considering the impact of work–life balance on retention, we turn to research that examines the association between work–life conflict and enrichment and withdrawal attitudes and behaviours. The theoretical link between work–life conflict and withdrawal attitudes and behaviours lies in general stressor theories (e.g., Lazarus & Cohen, 1977). Work–life conflict is considered a psychosocial stressor, which can produce strain reactions. These reactions occur in many forms: poor physical health, diminished affect or withdrawal behaviours. Additionally, in the specific context of work–life conflict, work withdrawal behaviours may occur as a coping mechanism (i.e., quitting a job to alleviate constant work–life conflict). Furthermore, affective events theory (Weiss & Cropanzano, 1996) is relevant. This theory argues that work-related events impact emotional reactions, which in turn relate to attitudes and behaviours. Considering work–life conflict as a negative work-related event, negative emotional reactions may ultimately lead to dissatisfaction, withdrawal and other negative outcomes, such as production deviance (Ferguson, Carlson, Hunter & Whitten, 2012).

Empirical evidence supports the theoretical association between work–life conflict and withdrawal-related attitudes. Specifically, meta-analytic estimates suggest a small positive relationship between both work-to-life and life-to-work conflict and turnover intentions, and a small negative relationship between both directions of conflict and organizational commitment (Amstad et al., 2011; Meyer, Stanley, Herscovitch & Topolnytsky, 2002). Several researchers have also tested mediators of the work–life conflict/turnover intention association, including emotional exhaustion (Boles, Johnston & Hair, 1997; Hang-yue, Foley & Loi, 2005; Yavas, Babakus & Karatepe, 2008), job satisfaction (Boles et al., 1997; Hang-yue et al., 2005; Özbağ & Ceyhun, 2014; Rode, Rehg, Near & Underhill, 2007), life satisfaction (Rode et al., 2007), job stress (Chelariu & Stump, 2011), perceived organizational support (Liao, 2011) and leader–member exchange (Liao, 2011). Taken together, these mediation results suggest that work–life conflict leads to stress and negative attitudes towards the organization. This in turn prompts individuals to consider changing their job situation, presumably to reduce such conflict and negative outcomes.

Considerably less research has been conducted on turnover behaviours. Only five known peer-reviewed studies have examined actual turnover in five very different contexts: employees in a manufacturing and assembly plant (Carr, Boyar & Gregory 2008); full-time working mothers following the birth of a child (Carlson, Grzywacz, Ferguson, Hunter, Clinch & Arcury, 2011); U.S. Army officers (Huffman, Casper & Payne, 2013); department store retail managers (Good, Page & Young 1996); and public accountants (Greenhaus, Parasuraman & Collins, 2001). Both Carr and colleagues (2008) and Greenhaus and colleagues (2001) found a direct link between work-to-family conflict and turnover, whereas the authors of the other three studies found support models indirectly linking the variables through mental and physical health (Carlson et al., 2011), job satisfaction (Huffman et al., 2013), and job satisfaction, organizational commitment and intention to leave (Good et al., 1996). Only Greenhaus and colleagues (2001) included family-to-work conflict, finding a non-significant association with turnover.

Research on work–life enrichment and turnover intentions has produced less consistent findings. A meta-analysis (McNall et al., 2010) of four studies (Balmforth & Gardner, 2006; Boyar & Mosley, 2007; Gordon, Whelan-Berry & Hamilton, 2007; Wayne, Randel & Stevens, 2006) concluded that the association between both work-to-family enrichment and family-to-work enrichment with turnover intentions was significant ($r = 0.07$ and 0.02, respectively). Studies published subsequent to the meta-analyses are mixed, as some researchers found a significant association between work-to-family enrichment and turnover intentions (Russo & Buonocore, 2012) but not to family-to-work enrichment (Haar & Bardoel, 2008), while others found that no direction of enrichment significantly related to intent to turnover (Hammer, Kossek, Yragui, Boder & Hanson, 2009; Karatepe & Magaji, 2008). These inconsistent findings, along with the large credibility intervals cited in McNall and colleagues' (2010) meta-analysis, suggest the likely presence of moderators. Moreover, only one known study has examined enrichment in relation to actual turnover (Carlson et al., 2011), finding an indirect relationship between work-to-family enrichment and turnover as a result of physical health. Lastly, in contrast to research involving turnover intentions, studies linking work-to-family and family-to-work enrichment to organizational commitment have been fairly consistent, and one meta-analysis suggests a positive, fairly large association (McNall et al., 2010).

In summary, although there are some inconsistencies, research has generally found that experiencing work–life conflict elicits withdrawal attitudes and behaviours, and the experience of work–life enrichment results in favourable retention-related outcomes.

Moderators of Work–Life Conflict–Work–Life Enrichment and Retention-related Outcomes Relationships

Beyond simple associations, context often is important in the relationship between work–life interactions and employee retention outcomes. Several variables have been consistently examined as moderators, including gender, national culture, support, and domain centrality. The value of this research in the retention field lies primarily in the greater empirical understanding of the factors that can reinforce desirable employee outcomes (i.e., high retention) and/or mitigate undesirable ones (i.e., high turnover).

Gender is the most frequently investigated moderator of work–life and retention relationships. This most likely stems from an initial framing of work–life issues as primarily women's issues, resulting from the traditional division of labour within the household in many societies. As such, most studies hypothesize that the experience of work–life conflict will have a greater impact on women, resulting in turnover-related actions and intentions. However, empirical results have largely been mixed. Based on a Turkish sample, Yavas and colleagues (2008) found that the positive relationship between work-to-family conflict and employee turnover intentions was moderated by gender in this manner, such that the effect was stronger for female frontline employees relative to male employees. Other researchers have noted the absence of any significant interaction effect between work-to-family conflict and gender on actual or intended turnover (Greenhaus, Collins, Singh & Parasuraman, 1997; Huang & Cheng, 2012). With regard to family-to-work conflict, Huang and Cheng (2012) found the association with turnover intentions is stronger for women, whereas Karatepe (2009) found the opposite. Thus, there remains a lack of empirical consensus on the role of gender in work–life issues. One explanation is that the changing nature of gender roles now means that men and women experience similar levels of work–life conflict and that consequently the impact of such conflict has similar repercussions for them (Leslie & Manchester, 2011; Shockley, Shen, Denunzio, Arvan & Knudsen, 2014).

Another important moderator is national or societal culture. Spector and colleagues (2007), in a study of several thousand participants across multiple countries, found that the positive relationship between work-to-family conflict and turnover intentions is greater for employees in cultures that are broadly characterized as individualistic (e.g., Anglo countries) relative to those that are more collectivistic (e.g., Asian countries). Similarly, Wang, Lawler, Walumbwa and Shi (2004) found that the positive relationship between work-to-family conflict and job withdrawal intentions was stronger for individuals high in self-rated idiocentrism (individualism). Self-rated allocentrism (collectivism), however, had no significant moderating effect on this relationship. The authors also examined family-to-work conflict and found the opposite pattern; family-to-work conflict was most strongly related to job withdrawal intentions in individuals high in allocentrism or low in idiocentrism (Wang et al., 2004). These moderating effects of self-rated idiocentrism and allocentrism were independent of country of origin (i.e., whether the participants were from the US or China did not change the pattern of results).

The authors' explanations for these patterns in work-to-family conflict lie in the notion that individualists are more self-focused than are collectivists. This greater focus on personal needs initiates a greater affective response and inclination to change the situation when the needs are interfered with, as when work-to-family conflict occurs. Also, collectivists may be more inclined to turn to co-workers for support in coping with work-to-family conflict rather than respond by withdrawing from the job. Wang and colleagues (2004) also tested cultural values as a moderator of family-to-work and turnover relationships but did not offer any theoretical explanations for why the relationship is weaker for those who are higher in idiocentrism.

Although we explain organizational support for work–life issues in greater detail later in this chapter, it is worth mentioning here the specific moderating role support plays in work–life conflict and retention relationships. Nohe and Sonntag (2014) found a significant positive relationship between work-to-family (but not family-to-work) conflict and turnover intentions over a five-month period, but the effect was attenuated when leaders were perceived as being more supportive of work–life issues. Other research (Qiu, 2010) has documented comparable moderation effects. Interestingly, Nohe and Sonntag (2014) did not find that support from the family significantly moderated the work-to-family–turnover relationship. We speculate that this may be due to the fact that the family role boundaries tend to present more flexibility and permeability than work roles (e.g., Ashforth, Kreiner & Fugate, 2000), so leaders' support may be perceived as more effective in dealing with and ameliorating role conflict.

Not all the empirical work concurs with these positions. Haar (2004), while supporting the direct relationships between work-to-family as well as family-to-work conflict and turnover intentions, did not find any interaction effect between perceived work–family supportiveness and either form of conflict on turnover intentions. This study did, however, acknowledge that the use of a single-item measure of turnover (compared with the three-item measure Nohe and Sonntag, 2014, used) may have limited its construct validity. Despite some contrasting evidence, the core of the literature on supportiveness primarily indicates that the presence of family-focused support from organizational leadership is instrumental in shaping employees' perceptions of conflict experienced between the work and family environments. Thus, leaders in organizations looking to reduce turnover should be ever-mindful of the degree to which employees feel that they are adequately supported with regard to their non-work responsibilities.

Finally, work (family) centrality is defined as the relative importance of work (family) to individuals' lives, the amount of resources they devote to that role, and how highly identified they are with the role (Carr, Boyar & Gregory, 2008). Carr and colleagues (2008) provide evidence that employees with high family centrality (relative to work centrality) were more likely to leave their organization voluntarily when faced with work-to-family conflict. Interestingly, employees with high work centrality exhibited less voluntary turnover (relative to those with high family centrality) in response to work-to-family conflict. The authors' explanation for these moderating effects is that employees in the face of conflict attribute blame to the role they value less (e.g., an individual with high family centrality will blame the work role for conflict and consider leaving the organization as a consequence).

Greenhaus and colleagues (2001) provide a slightly different explanation for similar effects. Their empirical study showed that the strong positive relationship between work-to-family conflict and withdrawal intentions, as well as actual turnover, was magnified for employees with low versus high work involvement. These findings, which align with Carr and colleagues' (2008), were posited to be the result of differences in tolerance of conflict rather than attribution of blame. In other words, they suggested that employees high in work involvement were more likely than those low in work involvement to tolerate work–family conflict because their careers are more salient and highly valued (Greenhaus et al., 2001). In sum, these results suggest that understanding how these different employees are uniquely impacted by conflict across work–life domains can be valuable in maintaining low turnover in the organization.

The investigation of interaction effects for the relations between work-to-family and family-to-work conflict and retention outcomes (e.g., turnover intentions) is crucial in that it advances our understanding of the increase and reduction of turnover in the workplace. Many moderators have been studied in the empirical literature; while this review does not offer exhaustive coverage of every one, it highlights several moderators which have remained prominent features of the work–life literature and have been repeatedly studied by work–life academicians.

Organizational Work–Life Policies and Practices

Given the negative impact of work–life conflict on retention-related attitudes and behaviours, it is in an organization's best interest to implement policies, practices, benefits and procedures aimed at reducing employees' conflict experiences. Similarly, the positive association between work–life enrichment and retention highlights the importance of having programmes that foster enrichment. Data from the 2014 National Study of the Changing Workforce indicate that many US organizations do offer some form of work–family support and that the availability of such policies is generally increasing (Matos & Galinksy, 2014). This trend is similar in many Scandinavian and Western European countries (e.g., The Netherlands, Austria, Finland, France and the UK), although it remains notably lower in some East European and South European countries (e.g., Romania, Lithuania, Bulgaria, Cyprus, Malta) (Prag & Mills, 2014).

Work–life support policies can be divided into two broad categories: formal and informal benefits. These are discussed next.

Formal work–life support policies and work–life outcomes

Formal work–life support policies are those that provide tangible support to employees in the form of time, services or financial policies (Butts, Casper & Yang, 2013). They can be further divided into two types: flexibility-based policies and dependant care supports. Examples of flexibility-based policies include flextime, telecommuting, compressed work weeks, reduced hours, part-time work and job sharing. Dependant care support includes policies aimed specifically at assisting with the care of dependants, such as caregiving leave, childcare or eldercare referral services, dependant care assistant plans that help employees pay for childcare with before-tax money, and childcare vouchers or subsidies, on-site daycare, and emergency or sick care for children (Matos & Galinksy, 2014).

Flexibility-based policies, particularly flextime and telecommuting, are the most common formal support policies. Of the 1,051 US employers involved in the 2014 National Study of Employers, 81% offered occasional flexibility in the start and stop times of work and 67% allowed employees to telecommute on occasion. A further 41% of employers offered schedule flexibility on a daily basis, and 38% permitted regular telecommuting. Flexibility-based policies that involve reducing time at work are less common; 43% of employers allowed compressed work weeks, 29% of employers offered job-sharing arrangements and 18% offered part-time work to some of their employees.

Despite the fact that flexibility-based policies are often advocated as a panacea to employees' work–life struggles (Allen & Shockley, 2009; The White House, 2014), empirical research suggests that these policies, in terms of directly reducing work-to-family conflict and family-to-work conflict, may be overstated. Specifically, Allen, Johnson, Kiburz and Shockley (2013) meta-analytically explored the association between both directions of work–family conflict and telecommuting and flextime use. Only in the relationship between telecommuting and work-to-family conflict was significant, and the effect size was quite small, calling into question its practical significance. The relationship between work–life enrichment and flexibility has yet to be assessed meta-analytically, but a review of individual studies reveals that most found insignificant correlations (Beham, Drobnič & Präg, 2011; Carlson et al., 2011; Carlson, Grzywacz & Kacmar, 2010; Dikkers, Geurts, den Dulk, Peper, Taris & Kompier, 2007; Moen, Fan & Kelly, 2013; Pedersen, Minnotte, Kiger & Mannon, 2009), although a few others report larger positive correlations (Carlson et al., 2011; Kacmar, Crawford, Carlson, Ferguson & Whitten, 2014) and a qualitative study suggests a positive effect (Pedersen & Jeppesen, 2012).

The other forms of flexibility-based policies have been examined much less frequently. Some researchers found that part-time work is negatively associated with work-to-family conflict but is not significantly related to family-to-work conflict (Hill, Yang, Hawkins & Ferris, 2004; Oishi, Chan, Wang & Kim, 2014; van Rijswijk, Bekker, Rutte & Croon, 2004). Research on compressed work weeks generally shows that the policy favourably relates to work–life outcomes (e.g., work–family conflict, Dunham, Pierce & Castenada, 1987; work–family balance, Lingard, Brown, Bradley, Bailey & Townsend, 2007; management of personal activities, Vega & Gilbert, 1997). Job-sharing, probably due to its rarity, has not yet been empirically linked to work–life conflict or enrichment to our knowledge.

With regard to dependant care policies, Matos and Galinsky (2014) reported that, in the US, many large organizations have at least one dependant care policy, with the most common being flexible spending accounts for dependant care (61%) and childcare resources and referrals (37%). Much like flexibility-based policies, the empirical findings assessing the relationship between dependant care policies and work–life outcomes such as work–life conflict and work–life enrichment are mixed. In a meta-analysis of 20 studies, Butts and colleagues (2013) found that dependant care support availability and use were negatively related to work-to-family conflict ($r=-0.08$ and -0.18, respectively). It is important to note that Butts and colleagues (2013) included studies that involved a single dependant care policy and those that only reported results for bundles or composite measures of multiple policies. With regard to family-to-work conflict, research findings are mixed. Some studies found no significant associations between dependant care policy availability and family-to-work conflict (Mennino, Rubin & Brayfield, 2005; Thompson & Prottas, 2005), whereas others found a significant negative association (Breaugh & Frye, 2007; Premeaux, Adkins & Mossholder, 2007). Looking at the positive side of work–family interference, Thompson and Prottas (2005) found that dependant care policies were positively correlated to enrichment, which was measured as enrichment in either direction.

Whereas these studies focus on composites or bundles of dependant care policies, it is also important to consider the relationship between specific polices and work–life outcomes. This follows the concern raised by researchers that qualitative differences between dependant care policies are often ignored when using composite measures, despite the fact that there are distinct differences between individual policies (Butts et al., 2013; Glass & Finley, 2002). With regard to paid leave policies, research has found that the use and availability of such policies are negatively associated with work-to-family conflict (Breaugh & Frye, 2008; Dikkers et al., 2007; Voydanoff, 2004). One study found a positive association between availability of leave and work-to-family facilitation (Voydanoff, 2004), although another study reported a negative association when focusing on actual use (Dikkers et al., 2007).

Results are less clear with the family-to-work direction of conflict and enrichment. Counterintuitively, Dikkers and colleagues (2007) found that paid leave is positively associated with family-to-work conflict but not significantly associated with family-to-work enrichment. Pedersen and colleagues (2009) reported a similar null result with availability of leave and family-to-work enrichment. Examining access to parental leave at the national level, based on legislation, Allen, Johnson and colleagues (2014) found that greater access to leave was associated with less work-to-family conflict but not with family-to-work conflict. Overall, it seems that paid leave results in favourable outcomes in the work-to-family direction, but not the family-to-work direction. One explanation may lie in the nature of paid leave. When employees use paid leave, they are away from work and spending considerably more time at home. This may allow family demands to increase and have a greater potential to spill over into the work domain following return to work.

Research on other policies is scarcer. Using a composite measure of childcare support and subsidies, Aycan and Eskin (2005) found a significant negative relationship with work-to-family conflict but not family-to-work conflict for women. None of the variables was related for men. Similarly, Banjeree and Perrucci (2012) found no association between various childcare support and subsidies and work-to-family conflict in a nationally representative sample of men and women. Dikkers and colleagues (2007) examined only childcare subsidies in relation to conflict and enrichment. They found that they were negatively related to both work-to-family conflict and enrichment, positively related to family-to-work conflict but not to family-to-work facilitation. With regard to on-site childcare, Pedersen and colleagues (2009) reported no significant association between availability of on-site childcare and family-to-work enrichment, and Goff, Mount and Jamison (1990) and Fujimoto, Kotani and Suzuki (2008) found no association between availability and use, respectively, of on-site childcare and work–family conflict. Lastly, the only known study of elder care programmes in relation to work–family outcomes found that those who made use of the programme (which included referrals and information) reported that caregiving exacerbated interference with work compared to non-users of the programme (Wagner & Hunt, 1994).

In summary, the evidence linking work–life support policies to work–life outcomes is mixed, although it is worth noting that rarely do researchers find that such policies have negative effects on the work–life interface. Some researchers (e.g., Allen et al., 2013; Allen & Shockley, 2009; Shockley & Allen, 2007) have argued that the lack of consistent findings may be attributable to moderating variables. That is, there may be certain contexts where policies are more or less effective, and when these contexts are not taken into account or samples vary substantially, findings may appear artificially negative or vary considerably from sample to sample.

This notion has received little empirical attention, but there is evidence that family responsibility moderates the relationship, such that the link between flextime and telecommuting and work–family conflict is more negative for those with greater family responsibilities (Shockley & Allen, 2007). The authors argue that those who have little family responsibility do not have much to gain in terms of conflict reduction by using flexibility. The supportiveness of the organization for family issues was also tested as a moderator by Shockley and Allen (2007) but was found not to be significant.

There also is variation in the measurement of support policies. Some researchers assess whether policies are in place, whereas others assess actual use of these policies, and a few others assess amount of use (Allen & Shockley, 2009). These are unique variables in the sense that, although everyone who uses policies must have access to them, not everyone with access actually uses them. Further, availability and use are thought to influence outcomes via different processes (Allen et al., 2013). Use may influence outcomes through the benefits that using policies brings (e.g., increased flexibility to manage non-work needs, which in turns fosters the desire to stay in that work role). Alternatively, availability communicates the organization's concern for employees (Batt & Valcour, 2003) and may induce positive feelings of support, which can reduce conflict and enhance enrichment. Whatever is the case here, a clearer differentiation between availability and use in reporting results would aid in a nuanced understanding of these relationships. Overall, recognizing the contextual boundaries of work–life support policies is very important for organizations wishing to implement and evaluate such programmes. We urge future researchers to explore this area of inquiry further.

Formal work–life support policies and retention-related outcomes

Beyond work–family outcomes, researchers have evaluated the impact of formal policies on retention-specific outcomes, including turnover, intention to turnover and organizational commitment. Table 24.1 presents a comprehensive list of published studies that have examined formal, flexibility-based and dependant care policies in relation to these outcomes. Information about the sample size, relationship examined and nature of the association, as well as effect size, are included. Of note is that in one case – telecommuting use and turnover intentions – meta-analytic research previously aggregated studies that examine this relationship and estimated an overall effect; thus, for this category we review only studies that were not included in the meta-analysis. Additionally, although there is a meta-analysis on dependant care supports and turnover intentions and organizational commitment (Butts et al., 2013), because it combined bundles of policies with individual policies, we deemed it appropriate to include primary studies from the meta-analysis that reported results by individual policy in order to gain a better sense of specific relationships. Table 24.1 also distinguishes between studies that focus on the availability versus the use of formal work–life support policies. As noted above, this differentiation is important as use and access may influence outcomes through different processes.

To summarize Table 24.1, beginning with flexibility-based policies, overall bundles or a composite of flexible policies show favourable associations with turnover, turnover intentions and organizational commitment. In some cases, studies found no effects, but in no case were detrimental associations with retention-related variables observed. The pattern is generally consistent across both availability and use, although there is considerably more research on availability and proportionally fewer of these studies cite no results compared

Table 24.1 Association between formal work–family support policies and turnover, turnover intentions, and organizational commitment.

	N	Turnover		Turnover Intentions		Org. Commitment	
		Effect	Effect Size (d)	Effect	Effect Size (d)	Effect	Effect Size (d)
Flexible bundles or composites							
Use							
Allen (2001)	522	–	0.20			+	0.30
Casper & Harris (2008)	286			0		0	
de Janasz, Forret, Haack & Jonsen (2013)	560					0	
Moen, Kelly & Hill (2011)	775	–	NR				
Porter & Ayman (2010)	227			0			
Richman, Civian, Shannon, Hill & Brennan (2008)	57,231			–	NR		
Availability							
Allen (2001)	522			–	0.22	+	0.32
Batt & Valcour (2003)	557			0			
Bond & Galinsky (2006)	2,810			–	NR		
Casper & Harris (2008)	286			0		+	0.26
de Sivatte & Guadamillas (2013)	420			–	0.70	+	1.25
Eaton (2003)	463					0	
Hornung, Rousseau & Glaser (2008)	887					0	
McNall, Masuda & Nicklin (2009)	220			–	0.41		
Ngo & Tsang (1998)	746					+	0.58
Porter & Ayman (2010)	227			0			
Premeaux, Adkins & Mossholder (2007)	564					+	0.18
Richman, Civian, Shannon, Hill & Brennan (2008)	82,989			–	NR		
Stavrou (2005)[a]	2,811 firms	–	0.22				
Thompson & Prottas (2005)	3,504			–	0.32		
Vandenburg, Richardson & Eastman (1999)	3,570	–	016	0			
Wang, Lawler & Shi (2011)	615					+	0.22
Wang & Walumbwa (2007)	475					+	0.18
Flexible schedules/Flextime							
Use							
Dalton & Mesch (1990)	271	0					
Dunham, Pierce & Castenada (1987)	102			0			
Schneider, Trukeschitz, Muhlmann & Ponocny (2013)	902			+	NR		

	N						
Availability							
Barrah, Shultz, Baltes & Stolz (2004)	301			0			
Behson (2005)	3,551			0			
Giffords (2009)						0	
Glass & Estes (1996)	246	0		0			
Glass & Riley (1998)	288	0		0			
Hopp & Sommerstad (1977)	25,000	0		−			
Krausz, Sagie & Bidermann (2000)	1,122			−	0.45	+	0.56
Lu, Kao, Chang, Wu & Cooper (2011)	10,678					+	0.56
Lyness, Gornick, Stone & Grotto (2012)	1,211					+	NR
Masuda et al. (2012) – Latin American sample	1,211			0			
Masuda et al. (2012) – Asian sample	1,492			0			
Masuda et al. (2012) – Anglo sample	3,000			−	0.22		
Mueller & Cole (1977)	2,021	−	NR				
Pavalko & Henderson (2006)	138	−	NR				
Pierce & Newstrom (1983)	2,894			0			
Roehling, Roehling & Moen (2001)	306			0		+	0.39
Rosin & Korabik (1991)	460			0			
Rothbard, Phillips & Dumas (2005)	160			0		+	0.30
Scandura & Lankau (1997)	3,337 firms	−	0.22				
Stavrou & Kilaniotis (2010)[a]	954 firms	−	0.41 for males 0.52 for females				
Yanadori & Kato (2009)							
Telecommuting							
Use							
Caillier (2013)	263,475			−	0.06		
Gajendran & Harrison (2007)[b]	7,580			−	0.16		
Glass & Estes (1996)	246	−	NR				
Glass & Riley (1998)	288	−	NR				
Golden (2006) – extent of telecommuting	393					+	0.26
Golden, Veiga & Dino (2008) – extent of telecommuting	261			0			
Kelliher & Anderson (2010)	2,066					+	NR
Availability							
Hunton & Norman (2010)	160					+	NR
Masuda et al. (2012) – Latin American sample	1,211			0		+	NR

(Continued)

Table 24.1 (Continued)

	N	Turnover Effect	Turnover Effect Size (d)	Turnover Intentions Effect	Turnover Intentions Effect Size (d)	Org. Commitment Effect	Org. Commitment Effect Size (d)
Masuda et al. (2012) – Asian sample	1,211			+	0.14		
Masuda et al. (2012) – Anglo sample	1,492			0			
Stavrou (2005)[a]	2,811 firms	+	0.12				
No clear differentiation between availability and use							
Martin & MacDonnell (2012)[b]	3,114					+	0.20
Part-time							
Use							
Barnett, Gordon, Gareis & Morgan (2004)	178			0			
Bernhard-Oettel, De Cuyper, Berntson & Isaksson (2008)	716					0	
Clinebell & Clinebell (2007)	282					0	
Conway & Briner (2002)	357			0		−	0.18
Gakovic & Tetrick (2003)	601					0	NR
Kelliher & Anderson (2010)	2,066					+	
Marchese & Ryan (2001)	727					0	
Thorsteinson (2003)	15,426					0	
Wittmer & Martin (2011)	2,056			+	1.01	−	.18
Availability							
Stavrou & Kilaniotis (2010)[a]	3,337 firms	+	0.45				
Compressed work week							
Use							
Dunham, Pierce, & Castenada (1984)	84					0	
Availability							
Masuda et al. (2012) – Latin American sample	1,211			−	0.18		
Masuda et al. (2012) – Asian sample	1,211			0			
Masuda et al. (2012) – Anglo sample	1,492			−	0.14		
Bundles or composites of dependant care policies							
Availability							
Butts et al. (2013)[b]	8,394 or 14,562			−	0.24	+	0.26
Yamamoto (2011)	1,228			−	0.61		

	N				
Use					
Butts et al. (2013)	3174 or 2,253	−	0.16	+	0.18
Childcare assistance (on-site and off-site childcare; childcare vouchers)					
Availability					
Lyness, Thompson, Francesco & Judiesch (1999)	86	0		0	
Grover & Crooker (1995)	745	0		0	
Roehling, Roehling & Moen (2001)	2,894			+	0.20
Wang, Lawler & Shi (2011)	615			+	0.20
Wang & Walumbwa (2007)	475			+	0.28
Youngblood & Chambers-Cook (1984)	410	0		+	NR
Use					
Milkovich & Gomez (1976)	19	−	5.46		
Rothausen, Gonzalez, Clarke & O'Dell (1998)	271	0		0	
Parental leave (e.g., for childbirth, adoption, other family matters)					
Availability					
Giffords (2009)	214			+	NR
Grover & Crooker (1995)	745	−	0.45	+	0.22
Lyness, Thompson, Francesco & Judiesch (1999)	86			0	
Pavalko & Henderson (2006)	2021	0			
Yanadori & Kato (2009)[a]	954 firms	−	0.35 for females; 0.20 for males		
Use					
Glass & Riley (1998) (length of leave)	285	−	NR		

Note: Effect sizes are in the form of Cohen's *d*. Rules of thumb for interpretation are that 0.2 = a small effect, 0.5 = a medium effect, and 0.8 and greater = a large effect (Cohen, 1988). NR = the effect size was not reported and cannot be computed based on the statistics reported in the study.

[a] Study was conducted at the firm level rather than the individual level (i.e., comparison of policy availability across firm in comparison to turnover rates of those firms).

[b] Study is a meta-analysis and represents the results of several aggregated studies.

+ = a positive relationship.

− = a negative relationship.

0 = a nonsignificant relationship.

to studies focused on actual use. Results from research on flexible schedules exhibit a similar pattern, with generally either no or favourable associations with turnover, turnover intentions and organizational commitment. Notable is the lack of studies that focus on actual use of flexibility and the fact that most effect sizes were small or medium in size.

The association between telecommuting and turnover intentions has been assessed meta-analytically and research suggests a negative association, though the effect is small. Studies conducted after the meta-analysis, and therefore not included in that estimate, are not consistent with this, with most finding no association and one reporting a positive link. With regard to turnover, research in this area is scant, with reports from only three studies. One found a positive association, although it is important to bear in mind that this study was conducted at the organizational level rather than the individual level; thus, other organizational factors beyond telecommuting policies may have impacted the average turnover rate within each organization. Finally, the results with organizational commitment are consistent, suggesting that use and availability of telecommuting relates positively to commitment.

Synthesizing results from studies focused on part-time work and a compressed work week is less straightforward. We hesitate to draw conclusions about patterns or relationships based on the small number of studies in each category coupled with the inconsistencies across studies. One noticeable trend is that, compared to the other types of policies, the link between part-time work and commitment seems weaker, or absent, in most cases. This may be attributable to the fact that people working part-time are inherently less committed to the job because they spend fewer hours working or that the nature of jobs that offer part-time work, at least in the US, are less attractive than many full-time jobs. There is too a dearth of research linking part-time work or compressed work week policies to turnover. The only known study was again at the firm level and found a positive association between part-time work availability and turnover. Overall, our assessment is that the availability and use of flexibility-based policies seem to enhance organizational attitudes and turnover, although more studies are needed based on actual turnover to draw any firm conclusion.

For dependant care policies, Butts and colleagues' (2013) meta-analysis and the single identified study published subsequent to their data collection (Yamamoto, 2011) suggest that both use and availability of policies are negatively related to turnover intentions and positively related to organizational commitment. One relationship absent from these studies is that between these composite measures and actual turnover.

As for the specific dependant care policies, studies were divided according to whether they measured childcare assistance policies (e.g., on- and off-site childcare and childcare vouchers or referral services) or parental leave policies. For childcare assistance policies, only tentative conclusions can be made given the small number of studies measuring policy availability or use. There is a fairly consistent finding that the availability of childcare assistance policies is positively associated with organizational commitment; however, there is a lack of research on the relationship between the use of these policies and commitment. On the other hand, it is worth noting that, although limited, research has shown no findings for the relationship between childcare assistance policy availability and use as well as actual turnover and turnover intentions. Moreover, the single study that reports a negative association has a very small sample size (Milkovich & Gomez, 1976). Overall, these findings provide preliminary evidence that, although childcare assistance policies help in increasing employee commitment, they may not aid in the ultimate retention of employee.

Turning to parental leave, there appears to be a favourable pattern of findings, although the number of studies is small. There is more evidence, in comparison to childcare assistance polices, that both availability and use of parental leave policies are related to less actual turnover. In particular, Yanadori and Kato (2009) showed that availability of parental leave was associated with significantly less turnover for both men and women, which suggests the importance of these policies for employees regardless of their sex. In general, there is tentative evidence that parental leave policies may be beneficial to employee retention in terms of employee commitment and turnover. One caveat to interpreting these findings for both types of formal policy is that with a few exceptions (i.e., Dalton & Mesch, 1990; Dunham et al., 1987; Hunton & Norman, 2010; Milkovich & Gomez, 1976; Moen, Kelly & Hill, 2011; Mueller & Cole, 1977; Youngblood & Chambers-Cook, 1984), most research is based on correlational survey data. Thus, inferences of causality are not warranted. It is feasible that only those who are the highest performers and are already highly commited to the organization are those given access to certain policies. In that sense, commitment would be driving access to policies rather than the reverse relationship. Testing these relationships with experimental designs is an area ripe for future research and would contribute greatly to our understanding.

Contextual factors in formal policy and retention relationships

As noted above with work–life outcomes, one reason for the lack of consistency in studies examining family-friendly policies and retention-related outcomes is likely to be the presence of moderating variables. In this section, we discuss common variables that have been mentioned and examined as moderators of these relationships.

Gender has been most commonly studied as a moderating variable. One study reported no significant moderating effect of gender on the relationship between work flexibility and organizational commitment (Ngo & Tsang, 1998), but other researchers found that women whose organizations offered flexible schedules reported higher commitment than women whose organizations did not offer such policies. However, for men, commitment was not affected by the availability of flexibility (Scandura & Lankau, 1997). Moreover, adding another level of complexity by examining availability and use of schedule flexibility in tandem with gender, Casper and Harris (2008) reported a significant three-way interaction. For women, schedule flexibility was positively related to commitment regardless of use, but for men, schedule flexibility was positively associated with commitment only when use was high. A negative relationship was observed when use was low. The same relationships were tested for dependant care support, but no significant interactions were observed. Overall, it seems that for women availability of flexible policies alone communicates a positive message about organizational support, whereas men benefit in terms of commitment only when using these policies.

Other streams of research highlight indirect evidence for gender differences in the formal benefit–retention relationship. First, there is some evidence of differential access to flexible work arrangements based on the gender composition of the occupation in the US (Glauber, 2011). Specifically, a curvilinear relationship exists, such that the probability of a person's organization offering flexible scheduling is highest when occupations have a more even gender ratio (i.e., around 55% of workers in that occupation are female). When the proportion of females is low, the odds of flexibility being offered are also lower; the same trend (albeit with a weaker effect) is observed when the proportion of women is very high. Given that, by definition, men are more likely to be in occupations that are male-dominated, this finding suggests that men may have less access to flexibility. Clearly, without access to policies one cannot possibly reap their retention-related benefits. Of note is that these findings may not generalize outside the US, as there is considerable variation in the gap in gender differences in access to flexibility in Europe. Notably, in a comparison of 30 European countries, in all cases (except Greece and Malta) the gender differences were such that men had greater access to flexibility (Plantega & Remery, 2009).

In a qualitative study focused on employees' views about the implementation of a Results Only Work Environment (ROWE; an initiative aimed at reorienting employees and managers towards measurable results while playing down the need to be physically present at work for a set number of hours each day) at Best Buy corporation, Kelly, Ammons, Chermack and Moen (2010) reported that men and women differed in their reactions. Women, especially mothers, were very enthusiastic about working in a ROWE arrangement. Men, particularly those early in their careers, were more ambivalent, focusing on the potential negative career repercussions (e.g., being passed over for promotion) of using flexibility. Quantitative data from a study in Greece support this finding, as men reported greater concerns about career costs associated with using flexible work arrangements than did women (Giannikis & Mihail, 2011). It is unclear whether flexibility users do suffer penalties, as three studies (Cohen & Single, 2001; Glass, 2004; Judiesch & Lyness, 1999) found that flexible benefit use results in fewer promotions and pay increases for both men and women, whereas others found that users of flexible work practices earn higher wages (Leslie, Manchester, Park & Mehng, 2012; Weeden, 2005). Regardless, it appears that women seem more attracted to flexible work arrangements, perhaps because they focus more on the potential work–life benefits (Butler, Gasser & Smart, 2004; Sharpe, Hermsen & Billings, 2002; Sullivan & Smithson, 2007; Vandello, Hettinger, Bosson & Siddiqi, 2013).

Moving beyond gender, preference for role segmentation versus integration is mentioned frequently in discussions of use and efficacy of formal policies. According to boundary theory (Ashforth et al., 2000; Nippert-Eng, 1996), people create boundaries around different life roles to help manage them and simplify their complex environments, but there are individual differences in the extent to which people prefer and are able to keep boundaries permeable and flexible, which in turn influences the relative segmentation or integration of roles (Ashforth et al., 2000; Kossek, Lautsch & Eaton, 2006; Trefalt, 2013). Preference for segmentation versus integration lies along a continuum, with the most extreme preference for each serving as poles at each end. Thus, most individuals are not qualified as pure segmenters or integrators, but rather fall between the two extremes.

Researchers argue that many types of formal family-friendly policies alter the nature of the workplace in terms of the integration or segmentation that it allows (Rau & Hyland, 2002; Rothbard, Phillips & Dumas, 2005; Shockley & Allen, 2010). For example, because telecommuting typically involves working from home, the place where the family domain resides, it is likely to lead to role blurring, an undesirable state for those who prefer to segment their roles. A similar argument can be made for on-site daycare. On the other hand, whether or not flextime is an integrating or segmenting policy has been debated. Some argue that it allows for greater integration (Rau & Hyland, 2002; Shockley & Allen, 2010) by making boundaries less permeable, but others argue that it allows employees to alter their schedules so that role blurring does not have to occur, making it more of a segmenting policy (Rothbard et al., 2005). Empirical results support both positions, as segmentation preferences negatively relate to use of flextime (Shockley & Allen, 2010), but moderate the relationship between flextime use and organizational commitment, such that the association is positive for segmenters but negative for integrators. In other words, those who prefer to segment benefit from flextime in terms of greater organizational commitment, whereas the opposite trend is true for integrators, suggesting it may be a policy that is more conducive to segmentation. Whatever the case, this individual difference variable has important implications for work–life management and family-friendly policies, although the nature of these associations remains unclear (Allen, Cho & Meier, 2014).

With regard to the specific policy of telecommuting, a sense of professional and social isolation that may accompany being physically removed from the workplace is a matter of concern (Cooper & Kurland, 2002; Golden, Veiga & Dino, 2008; Greer & Payne, 2014). Although telecommuting may grant additional flexibility and ability to manage work and family demands, it can also easily lead to seclusion and loneliness, and may ultimately result in turnover. Arrangements that are not fully remote may offset this effect; in fact, research suggests that job satisfaction is maximized when an employee telecommutes around 15 hours a week (Golden, 2006; Golden & Veiga, 2005). This hypothesis has not been investigated with retention-specific outcomes, but given the association between job satisfaction and turnover (Podsakoff, LePine & LePine, 2007), a credible link exists. Additional research suggests that the association between professional isolation and turnover intentions among teleworkers is weaker when they have greater access to communication-enabling technologies, as this may work as a partial substitute for face-to-face interactions (Golden et al., 2008).

Finally, several researchers have discussed the role of the informal work environment. Specifically, when available, policies are not perceived to be usable when the culture is highly focused on face-time or the supervisor does not support policy use, so that even when policies are available, employees are less likely to use them (Allen, 2001; Breaugh & Frye, 2008; Eaton, 2003; Thompson, Beauvais & Lyness, 1999: Shockley & Allen, 2010). Additionally, when policies are used despite a non-supportive environment, any gains (i.e., better work–life management) may be offset by the stress that comes with taking advantage of the policy (Shockley & Allen, 2007). In general, if the organizational norms and values are not consistent with use of available policies, there is cause to suspect that their value will be greatly undermined (Kirby & Krone, 2002; Lobel & Kossek, 1996; Ryan & Kossek, 2008; Wallace & Young, 2008). We discuss the issue of informal support and colleagues next.

Informal work–life support policies and work–life outcomes

Although the research linking formal work–life support to work–life outcomes is mixed, research on informal support is considerably more consistent. Informal work–life support has been conceptualized in a variety of ways, most commonly as work–family culture (Thompson et al., 1999), family-supportive organizational perceptions (Allen, 2001) and family-supportive supervision (Hammer, Kossek, Zimmerman & Daniels, 2007). Regardless of the fine differences between each of these concepts, the core idea of informal support is that it represents beliefs about the extent to which the organization or supervisor values employees' contribution and is concerned about their well-being, specifically in relation to non-work matters. These beliefs may stem in part from the presence of formal policies, but are also unique and offer incremental variation in the prediction of outcomes (e.g., Allen, 2001). Additionally, as discussed below, having formal policies in place does not require perceptions of a supportive culture.

The earliest conceptualization of informal work–family support came from Thomas and Ganster (1995), who argued that family-supportive supervisors are an important component of a family-supportive work environment. They described such a supervisor as 'one who empathizes with the employee's desire to seek balance between work and family responsibilities' (p. 7). They listed various examples of behaviours that represent a supportive supervisor, such as allowing the employee to work flexibly in the absence of a formal policy, being tolerant of occasional family intrusions into work (phone calls, bringing a child in to work) or general emotional support in the face of family hardships.

Thompson and colleagues (1999) expanded on this concept, moving it beyond the immediate supervisor. They coined the term work–family culture, defined as 'the shared assumptions, beliefs, and values regarding the extent to which an organization supports and values the integration of employees' work and family lives' (p. 394) and set out three components of a work–family culture: organizational time demands that enforce the prioritization of work over family; perceived career consequences associated with using formal policies or devoting time to family; and – paralleling Thompson and Ganster (1995) – manager's support and sensitivity to employees' family responsibilities. Shortly afterwards, Allen (2001) coined a similar term – family-supportive organizational perceptions – defined as 'global perceptions that employees form regarding the extent the organization is family-supportive' (p. 416). This was intended to overcome some limitations in Thompson and colleagues' (1999) measure, namely that the referent shifts between the overall organization and supervisor; thus, it is not a pure assessment of overall culture.

Both Thompson and colleagues' (1999) and Allen's (2001) conceptualizations have been widely adopted in the literature and, to date, are the most common way researchers assess the notion of informal work–family support at the organizational level (Shockley, Thompson & Andreassi, 2013). Both work–family culture and family-supportive organizational perceptions are negatively related to work-to-family conflict and family-to-work conflict (Allen et al., 2013; Behson, 2002a, 2002b; Booth & Matthews, 2012; Dickson, 2008; Dikkers, Geurts, den Dulk, Peper & Kompier, 2004; Greenhaus, Zeigert & Allen, 2012; Lapierre et al., 2008; Lauzun, Major & Jones, 2012; Major, Fletcher, Davis & Germano, 2008; O'Driscoll et al., 2003; Premeaux, Adkins & Mossholder, 2007; Shockley & Allen, 2007), though effect sizes for family-to-work conflict are generally weaker. Additionally, work–family culture and family-supportive organizational perceptions account for unique variance in work–family conflict beyond access to formal policies (Allen, 2001; Thompson et al., 1999). Findings are also favourable for enrichment, as many researchers note a positive association between informal support and work-to-family (Taylor, Delcampo & Blancero, 2009; Voydanoff, 2004; Wayne, Casper, Matthews, & Allen 2013) and family-to-work enrichment (Baral & Bhargava, 2010; Dikkers et al., 2007; Tang, Siu & Cheung, 2014; Thompson & Prottas, 2005; Wayne et al., 2006).

The family supportiveness of the supervisor, one of the dimensions noted in Thompson and colleagues' (1999) work–family culture conceptualization, has received particular attention. Aiming to examine the joint influences of general supervisor support, supervisor support specific to work–family issues and perceptions of overall organizational support for work–family, Kossek, Pichler, Bodner and Hammer (2011) tested a meta-analytic path model involving all variables in relation to work–family conflict. They found that both types of support were related to lower levels of work–family conflict, but that the effect size was stronger for perceptions of organizational work–family support. Results are less clear for family–work conflict; some studies have found a work–family supportive supervisor relates negatively to family–work conflict (e.g., Aycan & Eskin, 2005; Fiksenbaum, 2014; Frye & Breaugh, 2004; Karatepe & Kilic, 2007; Lapiere & Allen, 2006; Odle-Dusseau, Britt & Greene-Shortridge, 2012; O'Driscoll et al., 2003; Thompson & Prottas, 2005), but others cite no significant association (e.g., Barrah, Schultz, Baltes & Stolz, 2004; Greenhaus et al., 2012; Hammer et al., 2009; Lu, Siu, Spector & Shi, 2009; Seiger & Weise, 2009; Smith & Gardner, 2007). Family-supportive supervision also relates positively to both directions of enrichment (Baral & Bhargava, 2010; Hammer, Kossek, Bodner & Crain, 2013; Lu et al., 2009; Odle-Dusseau et al., 2012; Thompson & Prottas, 2005; Voydanoff, 2004; Wayne et al., 2013). In summary, there is strong evidence to support the notion that the informal work–life environment relates favourably to work–life outcomes.

Informal work–life support policies and retention-related outcomes

As Table 24.1 demonstrates, the association between family-friendly policies and retention-related outcomes is somewhat ambiguous. However, almost all studies investigating work–family culture have found it to be positively associated with organizational commitment (Behson, 2002a; de Janasz, Behson, Jonsen & Lankau, 2013; de Janasz, Forret, Haack & Jonsen, 2013; Kopelman, Prottas, Thompson & Jahn, 2006; Lyness, Thompson, Francesco & Judiesch, 1999; Major, Morganson & Bolen, 2013; O'Neill, Harrison, Cleveland, Almeida, Stawski & Crouter, 2009; Premeaux et al., 2007; Prottas & Kopelman, 2009; Wayne et al., 2013) and negatively related to turnover intentions (Ahmad & Omar, 2013; Barrah et al., 2004; Dickson, 2008; Haar & Roche, 2010; Mauno, Kiuru & Kinnunen, 2011; O'Neill et al., 2009; Prottas & Kopelman, 2009; Thompson & Prottas, 2005). Similar patterns are observed for family-supportive supervision (turnover intentions: Aryee, Luk & Stone, 1998; Bagger & Li, 2014; Barrah et al., 2004; Behson, 2005; de Sivatte & Guadamillas, 2013; Hammer, Kossek, Anger, Bodner & Zimmerman, 2011; Hammer, Kossek, Bodner & Crain, 2013; Hammer et al., 2009; organizational commitment Aryee et al., 1998; de Sivatte & Guadamillas, 2013; Mills, Matthews, Henning & Woo, 2014). Studies of actual turnover are absent from this literature.

Furthermore, correlations between informal support and retention-related outcomes are often larger than those between formal policies and such outcomes (e.g., Allen, 2001; Barrah et al., 2004; Dickson, 2008; Lu et al., 2009; Lyness et al., 1999; Prottas & Kopelman, 2009). Relatedly, a few studies (Allen, 2001; Thompson et al., 1999) have found that work–family supportive culture accounts for incremental variance in organizational commitment and turnover intentions above and beyond the offering of formal policies. Taken together, these results highlight the importance of organizational culture in directly influencing work–life outcomes, retention outcomes and the efficacy of formal policies (Galinksy & Stein, 1990; Lobel & Kossek, 1996).

The informal support findings beg the question how, practically speaking, can an organization or manager foster work–life supportiveness? This question was addressed by Harrington and James (2006), who outlined several key components for creating a work–life supportive culture. These include ensuring that organizational leaders understand the importance of work–life issues and see it as key to the success of the business, ensuring that a work–life strategic plan is put in place that supports the overall vision and goals of the organization, adopting a systematic and proactive approach to work–life strategies, creating accountability between the employee and employer for work–life management, establishing a culture that is built on mutual respect among employees, clearly communicating work–life strategies and the availability of resources, and continuously measuring the effectiveness of work–life strategies and adjusting them according to the results. Harrington and James (2006) additionally offer practical proposals for the execution of each of these components.

Other practical advice can be gleaned from Hammer and colleagues' (2007, 2009) research aimed at understanding the specific behaviours that drive perceptions of a supervisor as family-supportive. Their research suggests four dimensions: emotional support (e.g., willingness to listen to subordinates' problems about balancing work and non-work), instrumental support (e.g., helping with scheduling conflicts), role modelling behaviours (e.g., the supervisor demonstrating effective work–life balance behaviours) and creative work–life management (e.g., creatively reorganizing work so that it benefits the employee and company alike). The benefit of isolating specific behaviours is that they are amenable to training. In fact, the research team has conducted several training sessions in different organizational settings with favourable results (Kossek, Hammer, Kelly & Moen, 2014).

Finally, a useful initiative is Perlow's (2012) predictability, teaming and open (PTO) communication. This initiative was developed for a consulting firm, where employees work very long and irregular hours. Using an experimental design, Perlow found that consulting teams that were practising PTO, which involves each member of the team disconnecting for one night a week and requires weekly team meetings to communicate processes, reported greater satisfaction with work–life balance than non-participating teams. Improvements were also seen in productivity and efficiency. Ultimately, the success of the experiment led to a cultural shift within the organization about time norms. Perlow's findings highlight the importance of gaining initial agreement from top management and using data to drive acceptance for change.

Future Research

Our first recommendation for future research is a call for studies that examine actual behavioural outcomes, namely turnover in relation to work–life policies. Very few studies have addressed this relationship, and many of those that have were undertaken some decades ago (e.g. Glass & Estes, 1996; Milkovich & Gomez, 1976; Mueller & Cole, 1977) or focused on the firm level (Stavrou, 2005; Yanadori & Kato, 2009). While the latter is informative in that it provides insight about the percentage of people using a work–life policy in relation to turnover at the firm, it does not allow conclusions to be drawn regarding individual use of policies and consequent turnover. Moreover, given the dearth of experimental or even quasi-experimental research in this area, studies that use experimental designs would be particularly useful in arriving at causal conclusions.

Relatedly, future researchers should focus on exploring the differences between policy availability and policy use in relation to employee retention. As stated earlier, Allen and colleagues (2013) suggested that there could be differences in the way policy availability and use influence outcomes. Of the studies we reviewed, only four (Allen, 2001; Casper & Harris, 2008; Porter & Ayman, 2010; Richman et al., 2008) provided findings on the impact of both policy availability and use. By not measuring availability and use of work–family polices or not clearly delineating which they are measuring, researchers limit a deeper understanding of how these processes relate to employee retention outcomes.

Greater understanding of context is also an important avenue for future research. While the extant work–life and retention literature contains some, mostly exploratory, cross-cultural work (e.g., Spector et al., 2007; Wang et al., 2004), it has largely neglected investigating in depth retention outcomes as a function of both work–life and cultural constructs, and has provided little in the way of theoretical underpinnings for observed relationships. We urge future researchers to replicate and extend established links between these variables, to seek new influential variables, and to back up all with established or novel theory. In order to do so, scholars should continue to move away from using country or geographic location as a proxy for culture and seek to understand how variance in specific cultural values (e.g., gender egalitarianism, humane orientation, power distance, etc.) impacts retention through work–life variables or how it moderates the work–life and retention link. Together, these suggestions should enable researchers to parse the universal and culture-specific factors influencing the work–life and retention interface.

Conclusion

At the start of this chapter we stated that organizations have begun to recognize the importance of work–life issues in the retention of top talent. As the research reviewed here suggests, there is some evidence to support the existence of this link. However, the relationship between work–life issues and employee retention is not necessarily a straightforward one but is shaped by moderators (e.g., culture, gender, work and family centrality) and by the type of formal or informal support policies the organization offers. Additionally, the impact of formal organizational policies appears to differentially relate to retention, according to whether policy availability or use is the focus of the study. Therefore, while work–life issues and practice appear to be important for retention, there is a need for further research on this relationship in order to better understand how organizations can minimize turnover and retain their top employees.

References

Ahmad, A., & Omar, Z. (2013). Informal workplace family support and turnover intention: Testing a mediation model. *Social Behavior and Personality, 41*, 555–556.

Allen, T. D. (2001). Family-supportive work environments: The role of organizational perceptions. *Journal of Vocational Behavior, 58*, 414–435.

Allen, T. D., Cho, E., & Meier, L. L. (2014). Work–family boundary dynamics. *Annual Review of Organizational Psychology and Organizational Behavior, 1*, 99–121.

Allen, T. D., Johnson, R. C., Kiburz, K., & Shockley, K. M. (2013).Work–family conflict and flexible work arrangements: Deconstructing flexibility. *Personnel Psychology, 66*(2), 345–376.

Allen, T. D., Lapierre, L. M., Spector, P. E., Poelmans, S. Y., O'Driscoll, M., Sanchez, J. I., & Woo, J. (2014). The link between national paid leave policy and work–family conflict among married working parents. *Applied Psychology: An International Review, 63*(1), 5–28. doi:10.1111/apps.12004

Allen, T. D., & Shockley, K. M. (2009). Flexible work arrangements: Help or hype? *In* D. R. Crane, & E. J. Hill (Eds.), *Handbook of Families and Work: Interdisciplinary Perspectives* (pp. 265–284). Lanham, MD: University Press of America.

Amstad, F. T., Meier, L. L., Fasel, U., Elfering, A., & Semmer, N. K. (2011). A meta-analysis of work–family conflict and various outcomes with a special emphasis on cross-domain versus matching-domain relations. *Journal of Occupational Health Psychology, 16*, 151–169.

Ashforth, B. E., Kreiner, G. E., & Fugate, M. (2000). All in a day's work: Boundaries and micro-role transitions. *Academy of Management Review, 25*, 472–491.

Aryee, S., Luk, V., & Stone, R. (1998). Family responsive variables and retention-relevant outcomes among employed parents. *Human Relations, 51*, 73–87.

Aycan, Z., & Eskin, M. (2005). Relative contributions of childcare, spousal support, and organizational support in reducing work–family conflict for men and women: The case of Turkey. *Sex Roles, 53*, 453–471.

Bagger, J., & Li, A. (2014). Being important matters: The impact of work and family centralities on family-to-work conflict–satisfaction relationship. *Human Relations, 65*, 473–500.

Balmforth, K., & Gardner, D. (2006). Conflict and facilitation between work and family: Realizing the outcomes for organizations. *New Zealand Journal of Psychology, 35*(2), 69–76.

Banjeree, D., & Perrucci, C. C. (2012). Employee benefits and policies: Do they make a difference for work/family conflict? *Journal of Sociological & Social Welfare, 39*, 131–147.

Baral, R., & Bhargava, S. (2010). Work–family enrichment as a mediator between organizational interventions for work–life balance and job outcomes. *Journal of Managerial Psychology, 25*, 274–300.

Barnett, R. C., Gordon, J. R., Gareis, K. C., & Morgan, C. (2004). Unintended consequences of job redesign: Psychological contract violations and turnover intentions among full-time and reduced-hours MDs and LPNs. *Community, Work, & Family, 7*, 227–246.

Barrah, J. L., Shultz, K. S., Baltes, B., & Stolz, H. E. (2004). Men's and women's eldercare-based work–family conflict: Antecedents and work-related outcomes. *Fathering, 2*, 305–330.

Batt, R., & Valcour, P. M. (2003). Human resources practices as predictors of work–family outcomes and employee turnover. *Industrial Relations, 42*, 189–220.

Beham, B., Drobnič, S., & Präg, P. (2011). Work demands and resources and the work–family interface: Testing a salience model on German service sector employees. *Journal of Vocational Behavior, 78*, 110–122.

Behson, S. J. (2002a). Coping with family-to-work conflict: The role of informal work accommodations to family. *Journal of Occupational Health Psychology, 7*, 324–341.

Behson, S. J. (2002b). Which dominates? The relative importance of work–family organizational support and general organizational context on employee outcomes. *Journal of Vocational Behavior, 61*, 53–71.

Behson, S. J. (2005). The relative contribution of formal and informal organizational work family support. *Journal of Vocational Behavior, 66*, 487–500.

Bernhard-Oettel, C., De Cuyper, N., Berntson, E., & Isaksson, K. (2008). Well-being and organizational attitudes in alternative employment: The role of contract and job preferences. *International Journal of Stress Management, 15*, 345–363.

Boles, J. S., Johnston, M. W., & Hair Jr, J. F. (1997). Role stress, work–family conflict and emotional exhaustion: Inter-relationships and effects on some work-related consequences. *Journal of Personal Selling & Sales Management, 17*(1), 17–28.

Bond, J. T., & Galinsky, E. (2006). *How Can Employers Increase the Productivity and Retention of Entry-Level, Hourly Employees?* (Issue Brief No. 2). New York: Families and Work Institute.

Booth, S. M., & Matthews, R. A. (2012). Family-supportive organization perceptions: Validation of an abbreviated measure and theory extension. *Journal of Occupational Health Psychology, 17*, 41–51.

Boswell, W. R., & Olson-Buchanan, J. B. (2007). The use of communication technologies after hours: The role of work attitudes and work–life conflict. *Journal of Management, 33*, 592–610.

Boyar, S. L., & Mosley Jr, D. C. (2007). The relationship between core self-evaluations and work and family satisfaction: The mediating role of work–family conflict and facilitation. *Journal of Vocational Behavior, 71*, 265–281.

Breaugh, J. A., & Frye, N. K. (2007). An examination of the antecedents and consequences of the use of family-friendly benefits. *Journal of Managerial Issues, 19*, 35–52.

Breaugh, J. A., & Frye, N. K. (2008). Work–family conflict: The importance of family-friendly employment practices and family supportive supervisors. *Journal of Business and Psychology, 22*, 345–353.

Butler, A., Gasser, M., & Smart, L. (2004). A social-cognitive perspective on using family-friendly benefits. *Journal of Vocational Behavior, 65*, 57–70.

Butts, M. M., Casper, W. J., & Yang, T. S. (2013). How important are work–family support policies? A meta-analytic investigation of their effects on employee outcomes. *Journal of Applied Psychology, 98*, 1–25.

Caillier, J. G. (2013). Are teleworkers less likely to report leave intentions in the United States federal government than non-teleworkers are? *The American Review of Public Administration, 43*, 72–88.

Carlson, D. S., Grzywacz, J. G., Ferguson, M., Hunter, E. M., Clinch, C. R., & Arcury, T. A. (2011). Health and turnover of working mothers after childbirth via the work–family interface: An analysis across time. *Journal of Applied Psychology, 96*, 1045–1054.

Carlson, D. S., Grzywacz, J. G., & Kacmar, K. (2010). The relationship of schedule flexibility and outcomes via the work–family interface. *Journal of Managerial Psychology, 25*(4), 330–355.

Carr, J. C., Boyar, S. L., & Gregory, B. T. (2008). The moderating effect of family centrality on work–family conflict, organisational attitudes, and turnover behaviour. *Journal of Management, 34*, 244–262.

Casper, W. J., & Harris, C. M. (2008). Work–life benefits and organizational attachment: Self-interest utility and signaling theory models. *Journal of Vocational Behavior, 72*, 95–109.

Chelariu, C., & Stump, R. (2011). A study of work–family conflict, family–work conflict and the contingent effect of self-efficacy of retail salespeople in a transitional economy. *European Journal of Marketing, 45*, 1660–1679.

Clinebell, S. K., & Clinebell, J. M. (2007). Differences between part-time and full-time employees in the financial services industry. *Journal of Leadership & Organizational Studies, 14,* 157–167.

Cohen, J. R., & Single, L. E. (2001). An examination of the perceived impact of flexible work arrangements on professional opportunities in public accounting. *Journal of Business Ethics, 32,* 317–328.

Conway, N., & Briner, R. B. (2002). Full-time versus part-time employees: Understanding the links between work status, the psychological contract, and attitudes. *Journal of Vocational Behavior, 61,* 279–301.

Cooper, C. D., & Kurland, N. B. (2002). Telecommuting, professional isolation, and employee development in public and private organizations. *Journal of Organizational Behavior, 23,* 511–532.

Crouter, A. C. (1984). Spillover from family to work: The neglected side of the work–family interface. *Human Relations, 37,* 425–441.

Dalton, D. R., & Mesch, D. J. (1990). The impact of flexible scheduling on employee attendance and turnover. *Administrative Science Quarterly, 35,* 370–387.

de Janasz, S., Behson, S.J., Jonsen, K., & Lankau, M. (2013). Dual sources of support for dual roles: How mentoring and work–family culture influence work–family conflict and job attitudes. *The International Journal of Human Resource Management, 24,* 1435–1453.

de Janasz, S., Forret, M., Haack, D., & Jonsen, K. (2013). Family status and work attitudes: An investigation in a professional services firm. *British Journal of Management, 24,* 191–210.

de Sivatte, I., & Guadamillas, F. (2013). Antecedents and outcomes of implementing flexibility policies in organizations. *The International Journal of Human Resource Management, 24,* 1327–1345.

Dickson, C. E. (2008). Antecedents and consequences of perceived family responsibilities discrimination in the workplace. *The Psychologist-Manager Journal, 11*(1), 113–140.

Dikkers, J. S. E., Geurts, S. A. E., den Dulk, L., Peper, B., & Kompier, M. (2004). Relations among work–home culture, the utilization of work–home arrangements, and work–home interference. *International Journal of Stress Management, 11,* 323–345.

Dikkers, J. E., Geurts, S. E., den Dulk, L., Peper, B., Taris, T. W., & Kompier, M. J. (2007). Dimensions of work–home culture and their relations with the use of work–home arrangements and work–home interaction. *Work & Stress, 21,* 155–172.

Dunham, R. B., Pierce, J. L., & Casteneda, M. B. (1987). Alternative work schedules: Two field quasi-experiments. *Personnel Psychology, 40,* 215–242.

Eaton, S. C. (2003). If you can use them: Flexibility policies, organizational commitment, and perceived performance. *Industrial Relations, 42,* 145–167.

Ferguson, M., Carlson, D., Hunter, E., & Whitten, D. (2012). A two-study examination of work–family conflict, production deviance and gender. *Journal of Vocational Behavior, 81,* 245–258.

Fiksenbaum, L. M. (2014). Supportive work–family environments: Implications for work–family conflict and well-being. *The International Journal of Human Resource Management, 25,* 653–672.

Frone, M. R. (2003). Work–family balance. *In* J. C. Quick & L. E. Tetrick (Eds.), *Handbook of Occupational Health Psychology* (pp. 143–162). Washington, DC: American Psychological Association.

Frye, N. K., & Breaugh, J. A. (2004). Family-friendly policies, supervisor support, work–family conflict, family–work conflict, and satisfaction: A test of a conceptual model. *Journal of Business and Psychology, 19,* 197–220.

Fujimoto, T., Kotani, S., & Suzuki, R. (2008). Work–family conflict of nurses in Japan. *Journal of Clinical Nursing, 17,* 3286–3295.

Gajendran, R. S., & Harrison, D. A. (2007). The good, the bad, and the unknown about telecommuting: Meta-analysis of psychological mediators and individual consequences. *Journal of Applied Psychology, 92,* 1524–1541.

Gakovic, A., & Tetrick, L. E. (2003). Perceived organizational support and work status: A comparison of the employment relationships of part-time and full-time employees attending university classes. *Journal of Organizational Behavior, 24,* 649–666.

Galinsky, E., & Stein, P. J. (1990). The impact of human resource policies on employees: Balancing work/family life. *Journal of Family Issues, 11,* 368–383.

Giannikis. S. K., & Mihail, D. M. (2011). Flexible work arrangements in Greece: A study of employee perceptions. *The International Journal of Human Resource Management, 22*, 417–432.

Giffords, E. E. (2009). An examination of organizational commitment and professional commitment and the relationship to work environment, demographic, and organizational factors. *Journal of Social Work, 9*, 386–404.

Glass, J. L. (2004). Blessing or curse? Work–family policies and mothers' wage growth over time. *Work and Occupations, 31*, 367–394.

Glass, J. L., & Estes, S. B. (1996). Workplace support, childcare, and turnover intentions among employed mothers of infants, *Journal of Family Issues, 17*, 317–335.

Glass, J. L., & Finley, A. (2002). Coverage and effectiveness of family-responsive workplace policies. *Human Resource Management Review, 12*, 313–337.

Glass, J. L., & Riley, L. (1998). Family responsive policies and employee retention following childbirth. *Social Forces, 76*, 1401–1435.

Glauber, R. (2011). Limited access: Gender, occupational, composition, and flexible work scheduling. *The Sociological Quarterly, 52*, 472–494.

Goff, S. J., Mount, M. M., & Jamison, R. L. (1990). Employer supported child care, work/family conflict, and absenteeism: A field study. *Personnel Psychology, 43*, 793–809.

Golden, T. D. (2006). Avoiding depletion in virtual work: Telework and the intervening impact of work exhaustion on commitment and turnover intentions. *Journal of Vocational Behavior, 69*, 176–187.

Golden, T. D., & Veiga, J. F. (2005). The impact of extent of telecommuting on job satisfaction: Resolving inconsistent findings. *Journal of Management, 31*, 301–318.

Golden, T. D., Veiga, J. F., & Dino, R. N. (2008). The impact of professional isolation on teleworker job performance and turnover intentions: Does time spent teleworking, interacting face-to-face, or having access to communication-enhancing technology matter? *Journal of Applied Psychology, 93*, 1412–1421.

Good, L. K., Page, T. J., & Young, C. E. (1996). Assessing hierarchical differences in job-related attitudes and turnover among retail managers. *Journal of the Academy of Marketing Science, 24*(2), 148–156.

Gordon, J. R., Whelan-Berry, K. S., & Hamilton, E. A. (2007). The relationship among work–family conflict and enhancement, organizational work–family culture, and work outcomes for older working women. *Journal of Occupational Health Psychology, 12*(4), 350–364. doi: 10.1037/1076-8998.12.4.350.

Greenhaus, J. H., & Allen, T. D. (2011). Work–family balance: A review and extension of the literature. In L. Tetrick & J. C. Quick (Eds.). *Handbook of Occupational Health Psychology* (2nd ed., pp. 165–183). Washington, DC: American Psychological Association.

Greenhaus, J. H., & Beutell, N. J. (1985). Sources and conflict between work and family roles. *Academy of Management Review, 10*, 76–88.

Greenhaus, J. H., Collins, K. M., & Shaw, J. D. (2003). The relation between work–family balance and quality of life. *Journal of Vocational Behavior, 63*(3), 510–531.

Greenhaus, J. H., Collins, K. M., Singh, R., & Parasuraman, S. (1997). Work and family influences on departure from public accounting. *Journal of Vocational Behavior, 50*(2), 249–270.

Greenhaus, J. H., Parasuraman, S., & Collins, K. M. (2001). Career involvement and family involvement as moderators of relationships between work–family conflict and withdrawal from a profession. *Journal of Occupational Health Psychology, 6*(2), 91.

Greenhaus, J. H., & Powell, G. N. (2006). When work and family are allies: A theory of work–family enrichment. *Academy of Management Review, 31*, 72–92.

Greenhaus, J. H., Zeigert, J.C., & Allen, T. D. (2012). When family-supportive supervision matters: Relations between multiple sources of support and work–family balance. *Journal of Vocational Behavior, 80*, 266–275.

Greer, T. W., & Payne, S. C. (2014). Overcoming telework challenges: Outcomes of successful telework strategies. *The Psychologist-Manager Journal, 17*, 87–111.

Grover, S. L., & Crooker, K. J. (1995). Who appreciates family-responsive human resource policies? The impact of family-friendly policies on the organizational attachment of parents and non-parents. *Personnel Psychology, 48*, 271–288.

Grzywacz, J. G. (2000). Work–family spillover and health during midlife: Is managing conflict everything? *American Journal of Health Promotion, 14,* 236–243.

Haar, J. (2004). Work–family conflict and turnover intention: Exploring the moderation effects of perceived work–family support. *New Zealand Journal of Psychology, 33,* 35–39.

Haar, J. M. (2013). Testing a new measure of work–life balance: A study of parent and non-parent employees from New Zealand. *The International Journal of Human Resource Management, 24,* 3305–3324.

Haar, J. M., & Bardoel, E. A. (2008). Positive spillover from the work–family interface: A study of Australian employees. *Asia Pacific Journal of Human Resources, 46,* 275–287.

Haar, J. M., & Roche, M. A. (2010). Family supportive organization perceptions and employee outcomes: The mediating effects of life satisfaction. *The International Journal of Human Resource Management, 21,* 999–1014.

Hammer, L. B., Kossek, E. E., Anger, W. K., Bodner, T. E., & Zimmerman, K. (2011). Clarifying work–family intervention processes: The roles of work–family conflict and family-supportive supervisor behaviours. *Journal of Applied Psychology, 96,* 134–150.

Hammer, L. B., Kossek, E. E., Bodner, T. E., & Crain, T. (2013). Measurement development and validation of the Family Supportive Supervisor Behaviour Short-Form (FSSB-SF). *Journal of Occupational Health Psychology, 18,* 285–296.

Hammer, L. B., Kossek, E. E., Yragui, N. L., Bodner, T. E., & Hanson, G. C. (2009). Development and validation of a multidimensional measure of family supportive supervisor behaviours (FSSB), *Journal of Management, 35*(4), 837–856.

Hammer, L. B., Kossek, E. E., Zimmerman, K., & Daniels, R. (2007). Clarifying the construct of family supportive supervisory behaviours: A multilevel perspective. *Research in Occupational Stress and Well-Being, 6,* 171–211.

Hang-yue, N., Foley, S., & Loi, R. (2005). Work role stressors and turnover intentions: A study of professional clergy in Hong Kong. *The International Journal of Human Resource Management, 16,* 2133–2146.

Harrington, B., & James, J. B. (2006). The standards of excellence in work–life integration: From changing policies to changing organizations. *In* M. Pitt-Catsouphes, E. Kossek & S. Sweet (Eds.), *The Work and Family Handbook: Multi-Disciplinary Perspectives, Methods, and Approaches* (pp. 665–683). Mahwah, NJ: Lawrence Erlbaum.

Hill, E., Erickson, J., Holmes, E. K., & Ferris, M. (2010). Workplace flexibility, work hours, and work–life conflict: Finding an extra day or two. *Journal of Family Psychology, 24,* 349–358.

Hill, E. J., Yang, C., Hawkins, A. J., & Ferris, M. (2004). A cross-cultural test of the work–family interface in 48 countries. *Journal of Marriage and Family, 66,* 1300–1316.

Hopp, M. A., & Sommerstad, C. R. (1977). Reaction at computer firm: More pluses than minuses. *Monthly Labor Review, 100,* 69–71.

Hornung, S., Rousseau, D., & Glaser, J. (2008). Creating flexible work arrangements through idiosyncratic deals. *Journal of Applied Psychology, 93,* 655–664.

Huang, M. H., & Cheng, Z. H. (2012). The effects of inter-role conflicts on turnover intention among frontline service providers: does gender matter? *The Service Industries Journal, 32,* 367–381.

Huffman, A. H., Casper, W. J., & Payne, S. C. (2013). How does spouse career support relate to employee turnover? Work interfering with family and job satisfaction as mediators. *Journal of Organizational Behavior, 35*(2), 194–212. doi: 10.1002/job.1862.

Hunton, J. E., & Norman, C. S. (2010). The impact of alternative telework arrangements on organizational commitment: Insights from a longitudinal field experiment. *Journal of Information Systems, 24,* 67–90.

Judiesch, M. K., & Lyness, K. S. (1999). Left behind? The impact of leaves of absence on managers' career success. *Academy of Management Journal, 42,* 641–651.

Kacmar, K., Crawford, W. S., Carlson, D. S., Ferguson, M., & Whitten, D. (2014). A short and valid measure of work–family enrichment. *Journal of Occupational Health Psychology, 19*(1), 32–45.

Kahn, R. L., Wolfe, D. M., Quinn, R. P., Snoek, J. D., & Rosenthal, R. A. (1964). *Organizational Stress: Studies in Role Conflict and Ambiguity.* New York: John Wiley & Sons.

Karatepe, O. M. (2009). An investigation of the joint effects of organisational tenure and supervisor support on work–family conflict and turnover intentions. *Journal of Hospitality and Tourism Management*, 16(01), 73–81.

Karatepe, O. M., & Kilic, H. (2007). Relationships of supervisor support and conflicts in the work–family interface with the selected job outcomes of frontline employees. *Tourism Management*, 28, 238–252.

Karatepe, O. M., & Magaji, A. B. (2008). Work–family conflict and facilitation in the hotel industry a study in Nigeria. *Cornell Hospitality Quarterly*, 49(4), 395–412.

Kelliher, C., & Anderson, D. (2010). Doing more with less? Flexible working practices and the intensification of work. *Human Relations*, 63, 83–106.

Kelly, E. L., Ammons, S. K., Chermack, K., & Moen, P. (2010). Gendered challenge, gendered response: Confronting the ideal worker norm in a white-collar organization. *Gender and Society*, 24, 281–303.

Kirby, E., & Krone, K. (2002). 'The policy exists but you can't really use it': Communication and the structuration of work–family policies. *Journal of Applied Communication Research*, 30, 50–77.

Kirchmeyer, C. (2000). Work–life initiatives: Greed or benevolence regarding workers' time? *In* C. L. Cooper & D. M. Rousseau (Eds.), *Trends in Organizational Behaviors* (Vol 7, pp. 79–93). Chichester: Wiley.

Kopelman, R. E., Prottas, D. J., Thompson, C. A., & Jahn, E. W. (2006). A multilevel examination of work–life practices: Is more always better? *Journal of Managerial Issues*, 18, 232–253.

Kossek, E., Hammer, L. B., Kelly, E. L., & Moen, P. (2014). Designing work, family & health organizational change initiatives. *Organizational Dynamics*, 43, 53–63.

Kossek, E. E., Lautsch, B. A., & Eaton, S. C. (2006). Telecommuting, control, and boundary management: Correlates of policy use and practice, job control, and work–family effectiveness. *Journal of Vocational Behavior*, 68, 347–367.

Kossek, E., Pichler, S., Bodner, T., & Hammer, L. B. (2011). Workplace social support and work–family conflict: A meta-analysis clarifying the influence of general and work–family-specific supervisor and organizational support. *Personnel Psychology*, 64, 289–313.

Krausz, M., Sagie, A., & Bidermann, Y. (2000). Actual and preferred work schedules and scheduling control as determinants of job-related attitudes. *Journal of Vocational Behavior*, 56, 1–11.

Lapiere, L. M., & Allen, T.D. (2006). Work-supportive family, family-supportive supervision, use of organizational benefits, and problem-focused coping: Implications for work–family conflict and employee well-being. *Journal of Occupational Health Psychology*, 11, 169–181.

Lapierre, L. M., Spector, P. E., Allen, T. D., Poelmans, S., Cooper, C. L., O'Driscoll, M. P., Sanchez, J. I., Brough, P., & Kinnunen, U. (2008). Family-supportive organization perceptions, multiple dimensions of work–family conflict, and employee satisfaction: A test of model across five samples. *Journal of Vocational Behavior*, 73, 92–106.

Lauzun, H. M., Major, D. A., & Jones, M. P. (2012). Employing a conservation of resources framework to examine the interactive effects of work domain support and economic impact on work–family conflict. *The Psychologist-Manager Journal*, 15, 25–36.

Lazarus, R. S., & Cohen, J. B. (1977). Environmental stress. *Human Behavior and Environment*, 2, 89–127.

Leslie, L., & Manchester, C. (2011). Work–family conflict is a social issue not a women's issue. *Industrial and Organizational Psychology: Perspectives on Science and Practice*, 4(3), 414–417.

Leslie, L. M., Manchester, C. F., Park, T., & Mehng, S. A. (2012). Flexible work practices: A source of career premiums or penalties? *Academy of Management Journal*, 55, 1407–1428.

Liao, P. Y. (2011). Linking work–family conflict to job attitudes: The mediating role of social exchange relationships. *The International Journal of Human Resource Management*, 22, 2965–2980.

Lingard, H., Brown, K., Bradley, L., Bailey, C., & Townsend, K. (2007). Improving employees' work–life balance in the construction industry: Project alliance case study. *Journal of Construction Engineering and Management*, 133, 807–815.

Lobel, S. A., & Kossek, E. E. (1996). Human resource strategies to support diversity in work and personal lifestyles: Beyond the 'family friendly' organization. *In* E. E. Kossek & S. A. Lobel

(Eds.), *Managing Diversity: Human Resource Strategies for Transforming the Workplace* (pp. 221–243). Cambridge, MA: Blackwell.

Lu, L., Kao, S., Chang, T., Wu, H., & Cooper, C. L. (2011). Work/family demands, work flexibility, work/family conflict, and their consequences at work: A national probability sample in Taiwan. *International Perspectives in Psychology: Research, Practice, Consultation, 1*(S), 68–81.

Lu, J., Siu, O., Spector, P. E., & Shi, K. (2009). Antecedents and outcomes of a fourfold taxonomy of work–family balance in Chinese employed parents. *Journal of Occupational Health Psychology, 14*, 182–192.

Lyness, K. S., Gornick, J. C., Stone, P., & Grotto, A. R. (2012). It's all about control: Worker control over schedule and hours in cross-national context. *American Sociological Review, 77*, 1023–1049.

Lyness, K. S., Thompson, C. A., Francesco, A. M., & Judiesch, M. K. (1999). Work and pregnancy: Individual and organizational factors influencing organizational commitment, timing of maternity leave, and return to work. *Sex Roles, 41*, 485–508.

Major, D. A., Fletcher, T. D., Davis, D. D., & Germano, L. M. (2008). The influence of work–family culture and workplace relationships on work interference with family: A multilevel model. *Journal of Organizational Behavior, 29*, 881–897.

Major, D. A., Morganson, V. J., & Bolen, H. M. (2013). Predictors of occupational and organizational commitment in information technology: Exploring gender differences and similarities. *Journal of Business and Psychology, 28*, 301–314.

Masuda, A. D., Poelmans, S. A., Allen, T. D., Spector, P. E., Lapierre, L. M., Cooper, C. L., Abarca, N., Brough, P., Ferreiro, P., Fraile, G., Lu, L., Lu, C.-Q., Siu, O. L., O'Driscoll, M. P., Simoni, A. S., Shima, S., Moreno- Velazquez, I., & Woo, J.-M. (2012). Flexible work arrangements availability and their relationship with work-to-family conflict, job satisfaction, and turnover intentions: A comparison of three country clusters. *Applied Psychology: An International Review, 61*, 1–29.

Marchese. M. C., & Ryan, J. (2001). Capitalizing on the benefits of utilizing part-time employees through job autonomy. *Journal of Business and Psychology, 15*, 549–560.

Marks, S. R., & MacDermid, S. M. (1996). Multiple roles and the self: A theory of role balance. *Journal of Marriage and the Family, 58*(2), 417–432.

Martin, B. H., & MacDonnell, R. (2012). Is telework effective for organizations? A meta-analysis of empirical research on perceptions of telework and organizational outcomes. *Management Research Review, 35*, 602–616.

Matos, K., & Galinsky, E. (2014). *2014 National Study of Employers.* Families and Work Institute. familiesandwork.org/downloads/2014NationalStudyOfEmployers.pdf.

Mauno, S., Kiuru, N., & Kinnunen, U. (2011). Relationships between work–family culture and work attitudes at both the individual and the departmental level. *Work & Stress, 25*, 147–166.

McNall, L. A., Masuda, A. D., & Nicklin, J. M. (2009). Flexible work arrangements, job satisfaction, and turnover intentions: The mediating role of work-to-family enrichment. *The Journal of Psychology: Interdisciplinary and Applied, 144*, 61–81.

McNall, L. A., Nicklin, J. M., & Masuda, A. D. (2010). A meta-analytic review of the consequences associated with work–family enrichment. *Journal of Business and Psychology, 25*(3), 381–396.

Mennino, S. F., Rubin, B. A., & Brayfield, A. (2005). Home-to-job and job-to-home spillover: The impact of company policies and workplace culture. *The Sociological Quarterly, 46*, 107–135.

Meyer, J. P., Stanley, D. J., Herscovitch, L., & Topolnytsky, L. (2002). Affective, continuance, and normative commitment to the organization: A meta-analysis of antecedents, correlates, and consequences. *Journal of Vocational Behavior, 61*, 20–52.

Milkovich, G. T., & Gomez, L. R. (1976). Research notes: Day care and selected employee work behaviors. *Academy of Management Journal, 19*, 111–115.

Mills, M. J., Matthews, R. A., Henning, J. B., & Woo, V. A. (2014). Family-supportive organizations and supervisors: How do they influence employee outcomes and for whom? *The International Journal of Human Resource Management, 25*, 1763–1785.

Moen, P., Fan, W., & Kelly, E. L. (2013). Team-level flexibility, work–home spillover, and health behaviour. *Social Science & Medicine, 84*, 69–79.

Moen, P., Kelly, E. L., & Hill, R. (2011). Does enhancing work-time control and flexibility reduce turnover? A naturally occurring experiment. *Social Problems, 58,* 69–98.

Mueller, O., & Cole, M. (1977). Concept wins converts at federal agency. *Monthly Labor Review, 100,* 71–74.

Ngo, H., & Tsang, A. (1998). Employment practices and organizational commitment: Differential effects for men and women? *The International Journal of Organizational Analysis, 6,* 251–266.

Nippert-Eng, C. (1996). Calendars and keys: The classification of 'home' and 'work'. *Sociological Forum, 11,* 563–581.

Nohe, C., & Sonntag, K. (2014). Work–family conflict, social support, and turnover intentions: A longitudinal study. *Journal of Vocational Behavior, 85,* 1–12.

Odle-Dusseau, H. N., Britt, T. W., & Greene-Shortridge, T. M. (2012). Organizational work–family resources as predictors of job performance and attitudes: The process of work–family conflict and enrichment. *Journal of Occupational Health Psychology, 17*(1), 28–40.

O'Driscoll, M. P., Poelmans, S., Spector, P. E., Kalliath, T., Allen, T. D., Cooper, C. L., & Sanchez, J. I. (2003). Family-responsive interventions, perceived organizational and supervisor support, work–family conflict, and psychological strain. *International Journal of Stress Management, 10,* 326–344.

Oishi, A., Chan, R. H., Wang, L., & Kim, J. (2014). Do part-time jobs mitigate workers' work–family conflict and enhance wellbeing? New evidence from four East-Asian societies. *Social Indicators Research.* doi: 10.1007/s11205-014-0624-8.

O'Neill, J. W., Harrison, M. M., Cleveland, J., Almeida, D., Stawski, R., & Crouter, A. C. (2009). Work–family climate, organizational commitment, and turnover: Multilevel contagion effects of leaders. *Journal of Vocational Behaviour, 74,* 18–29.

Özbağ, G. K., & Ceyhun, G. Ç. (2014). Does job satisfaction mediate the relationship between work–family conflict and turnover? A study of Turkish marine pilots. *Procedia-Social and Behavioral Sciences, 140,* 643–649.

Pavalko, E. K., & Henderson, K. A. (2006). Combining care work and paid work: Do workplace policies make a difference? *Research on Aging, 28,* 359–374.

Pedersen, V., & Jeppesen, H. (2012). Contagious flexibility? A study on whether schedule flexibility facilitates work–life enrichment. *Scandinavian Journal of Psychology, 53,* 347–359.

Pedersen, D. E., Minnotte, K., Kiger, G., & Mannon, S. E. (2009). Workplace policy and environment, family role quality, and positive family-to-work spillover. *Journal of Family and Economic Issues, 30*(1), 80–89.

Perlow, L. A. (2012). *Sleeping With Your Smartphone: How to Break the 24/7 Habit and Change The Way You Work.* Cambridge, MA: Harvard Business Review Press.

Pierce, J. L., & Newstrom, J. W. (1983). The design of flexible work schedules and employee responses: Relationships and process. *Journal of Occupational Behavior, 4,* 247–262.

Plantega, J., & Remery, C. (2009). *Flexible Working Time Arrangements and Gender Equality: A Comparative Review of 30 European Countries.* Brussels: European Commission. ec.europa.eu/social/BlobServlet?docId=6182&langId=en.

Podsakoff, N. P., LePine, J. A., & LePine, M. A. (2007). Differential challenge stressor-hindrance-stressor relationships with job attitudes, turnover intentions, turnover, and withdrawal behaviour: A meta-analysis. *Journal of Applied Psychology, 92,* 438–454.

Porter, S., & Ayman, R. (2010). Work flexibility as a mediator of the relationship between work–family conflict and intention to quit. *Journal of Management and Organization, 16,* 411–424.

Prag, P., & Mills, M. (2014). *Family-related Working Schedule Flexibility across Europe: Short Statistical Report No. 6.* Santa Monica, CA: The Rand Corporation. www.rand.org/content/dam/rand/pubs/research_reports/RR300/RR365/RAND_RR365.pdf.

Premeaux, S. F., Adkins, C. L., & Mossholder, K. W. (2007). Balancing work and family: A field study of multi-dimensional, multi-role work–family conflict. *Journal of Organizational Behavior, 28,* 705–727.

Prottas, D. J., & Kopelman, R. E. (2009). Comparative work–family practice availability and employee attitudes. *The Psychologist-Manager Journal, 12,* 79–96.

Qiu, L. (2010). A study on the moderating effects of supervisor support on the relationship between work–family conflict and turnover intention. *In Management and Service Science (MASS), 2010 International Conference on* (pp. 1–4). New York: IEEE.

Rau, B. L., & Hyland, M. A. (2002). Role conflict and flexible work arrangements: The effects on applicant attraction. *Personnel Psychology, 55,* 111–136.

Reynolds, J. (2005). In the face of conflict: Work–life conflict and desired work hour adjustments. *Journal of Marriage and Family, 67,* 1313–1331.

Richman, A. L., Civian, J. T., Shannon, L. L., Hill, E. J., & Brennan, R. T. (2008). The relationship of perceived flexibility, supportive work–life policies, and use of formal flexible arrangements and occasional flexibility to employee engagement and expected retention. *Community, Work, & Family, 11,* 183–197.

Rode, J. C., Rehg, M. T., Near, J. P., & Underhill, J. R. (2007). The effect of work/family conflict on intention to quit: The mediating roles of job and life satisfaction. *Applied Research in Quality of Life, 2*(2), 65–82.

Roehling, P. V., Roehling, M. V., & Moen, P. (2001). The relationship between work–life policies and practices and employee loyalty: A life course perspective. *Journal of Family and Economic Issues, 22,* 141–170.

Rosin, H. M. & Korabik, K. (1991). Workplace variables, affective responses, and intention to leave among women managers. *Journal of Occupational Psychology, 64,* 317–330.

Rothbard, N. P., Phillips, K. W., & Dumas, T. L. (2005). Managing multiple roles: Work–family policies and individuals' desires for segmentation. *Organization Science, 16,* 243–258.

Rothausen, T. J., Gonzalez, J. A., Clarke, N. E., & O'Dell, L. L. (1998). Family-friendly backlash – Fact or fiction? The case of organizations' on-site child care centers. *Personnel Psychology, 51,* 685–706.

Russo, M., & Buonocore, F. (2012). The relationship between work–family enrichment and nurse turnover. *Journal of Managerial Psychology, 27*(3), 216–236.

Ryan, A. M., & Kossek, E. E. (2008). Work–life policy implementation: Breaking down or creating barriers to inclusiveness? *Human Resource Management, 47,* 295–310.

Scandura, T. A., & Lankau, M. J. (1997). Relationships of gender, family, responsibility and flexible work hours to organizational commitment and job satisfaction. *Journal of Organizational Behavior, 18,* 377–391.

Schneider, U., Trukeschitz, B., Mühlmann, R., & Ponocny, I. (2013). 'Do I stay or do I go?' Job change and labor market exit intentions of employees providing informal care to older adults. *Health Economics, 22,* 1230–1249.

Seiger C. P., & Weise, B. S. (2009). Social support from work and family domains as an antecedent or moderator of work–family conflicts? *Journal of Vocational Behavior, 75,* 26–37.

Sharpe, D. L., Hermsen, J. M., & Billings, J. (2002). Factors associated with having flextime: A focus on married workers. *Journal of Family and Economic Issues, 23,* 51–72.

Shockley, K. M., & Allen, T. D. (2007). When flexibility helps: Another look at the availability of flexible work arrangements and work–family conflict. *Journal of Vocational Behavior, 71,* 479–493.

Shockley, K. M., & Allen, T. D. (2010). Investigating the missing link in flexible work arrangement utilization: An individual difference perspective. *Journal of Vocational Behavior, 76,* 131–142.

Shockley, K. M., Shen, W., Denunzio, M., Arvan, M., & Knudsen, E. (2014). Clarifying gender and work–family conflict: A meta-analytic approach. *In M. J. Mills (Chair), Work–Life Interface Meets Employee Gender: Challenge and Opportunity.* Symposium presented at the Work Family Researchers Network conference. New York.

Shockley, K. M., Thompson, C. A., & Andreassi, J. K. (2013). Workplace culture and work–life integration. *In D. Major & R. Burke (Eds.), Handbook of Work–Life Integration of Professionals: Challenges and Opportunities.* Cheltenham & Northampton, MA: Edward Elgar.

Siegel, P. A., Post, C., Brockner, J., Fishman, A. Y., & Garden, C. (2005). The moderating influence of procedural fairness on the relationship between work–life conflict and organizational commitment. *Journal of Applied Psychology, 90,* 13–24.

Smith, J., & Gardner, D. (2007). Factors affecting employee use of work–life balance initiatives. *New Zealand Journal of Psychology, 36*, 3–12.

Society of Human Research Management. (2004). *SHRM Generational Differences Survey Report: A Study by the Society for Human Resources Management*. Alexandria, VA: Author.

Spector, P. E., Allen, T. D., Poelmans, S. Y., Lapierre, L. M., Cooper, C. L., O'Driscoll, M., … Widerszal-Bazyl, M. (2007). Cross-national differences in relationships of work demands, job satisfaction, and turnover intentions with work–family conflict. *Personnel Psychology, 60*(4), 805–835.

Stavrou, E. T. (2005). Flexible work bundles and organizational competitiveness: A cross-national study of the European work context. *Journal of Organizational Behavior, 26*, 923–947.

Stavrou, E. T., & Kilaniotis, C. (2010). Flexible work and turnover: An empirical investigation across cultures. *British Journal of Management, 21*, 541–554.

Sullivan, C., & Smithson, J. (2007). Perspectives of homeworkers and their partners on working flexibility and gender equity. *International Journal of Human Resource Management, 18*, 448–461.

Tang, S., Siu, O., & Cheung, F. (2014). A study of work–family enrichment among Chinese employees: The mediating role between work support and job satisfaction. *Applied Psychology, 63*, 130–150.

Taylor, B. L., Delcampo, R. G., & Blancero, D. M. (2009). Work–family conflict/facilitation and the role of workplace supports for U.S. Hispanic professionals. *Journal of Organizational Behavior, 30*, 643–664.

The White House. (2014). *Continue the Conversation on Workplace Flexibility*. www.whitehouse. gov/work-flex-kit.

Thomas, L., & Ganster, D. C. (1995). Impact of family-supportive work variables on work–family conflict and strain: A control perspective. *Journal of Applied Psychology, 80*, 6–15.

Thompson, C. A., Beauvais, L. L., & Lyness, K. S. (1999). When work–family benefits are not enough: The influence of work–family culture on benefit utilization, organizational attachment, and work–family conflict. *Journal of Vocational Behavior, 54*, 392–415.

Thompson, C. A., & Prottas, D. J. (2005). Relationships among organizational family support, job autonomy, perceived control, and employee well-being. *Journal of Occupational Health Psychology, 11*, 100–118.

Thorsteinson, T. J. (2003). Job attitudes of part-time vs. full-time workers: A meta-analytic review. *Journal of Occupational and Organizational Psychology, 76*, 151–177.

Trefalt, Š. (2013). Between you and me: Setting work–nonwork boundaries in the context of workplace relationships. *Academy of Management Journal, 86*, 1802–1829.

Twenge, J. M., Campbell, S. M., Hoffman, B. J., & Lance, C. E. (2010). Generational differences in work values: Leisure and extrinsic values increasing, social and intrinsic values decreasing. *Journal of Management, 36*, 1117–1142.

van Rijswijk, K., Bekker, M. J., Rutte, C. G., & Croon, M. A. (2004). The relationships among part-time work, work–family interference, and well-being. *Journal of Occupational Health Psychology, 9*, 286–295.

Vandello, J. A., Hettinger, V. A., Bosson, J. K., & Siddiqi, J. (2013). When equal isn't really equal: The masculine dilemma of seeking work flexibility. *Journal of Social Issues, 69*, 303–321.

Vandenburg, R. J., Richardson, H. A., & Eastman, L. J. (1999). The impact of high involvement work processes on organizational effectiveness: A second-order latent variable approach. *Group & Organization Management, 24*, 300–339.

Vega, A., & Gilbert, M. J. (1997). Longer days, shorter weeks: Compressed work weeks in policing. *Public Personnel Management, 26*(3), 391–402.

Voydanoff, P. (2004). The effects of work demands and resources on work-to-family conflict and facilitation. *Journal of Marriage and Family, 66*, 398–412.

Wagner, D. L., & Hunt, G. G. (1994). The use of workplace eldercare programs by employed caregivers, *Research on Aging, 16*, 69–84.

Wallace, J. E., & Young, M. C. (2008). Parenthood and productivity: A study of demands, resources and family-friendly firms. *Journal of Vocational Behavior, 72*, 110–122.

Wang, P., Lawler, J. J., & Shi, K. (2011). Implementing family-friendly employment practices in banking industry: Evidence from some African and Asian countries. *Journal of Occupational and Organizational Psychology, 84,* 493–517.

Wang, P., Lawler, J. J., Walumbwa, F. O., & Shi, K. (2004). Work–family conflict and job withdrawal intentions: The moderating effect of cultural differences. *International Journal of Stress Management, 11*(4), 392.

Wang, P., & Walumbwa, F. O. (2007). Family-friendly programs, organizational commitment, and work withdrawal: The moderating role of transformational leadership. *Personnel Psychology, 60,* 397–427.

Wayne, J. H. (2009). Cleaning up the constructs on the positive side of the work–family interface. *In* D. R. Crane & E. J. Hill (Eds.), *Handbook of Families and Work: Interdisciplinary Perspectives.* Lanham, MD: University Press of America.

Wayne, J. H., Casper, W. J., Matthews, R. A., & Allen, T. D. (2013). Family-supportive organizational perceptions and organizational commitment: The mediating role of work–family conflict and enrichment and partner attitudes. *Journal of Applied Psychology, 98,* 606–622.

Wayne, J. H., Randel, A. E., & Stevens, J. (2006). The role of identity and work–family support in work–family enrichment and its work-related consequences. *Journal of Vocational Behavior, 69*(3), 445–461.

Weeden, K. A. (2005). Is there a flexiglass ceiling? Flexible work arrangements and wages in the United States. *Social Science Research, 34,* 454–482.

Weiss, H. M., & Cropanzano, R. (1996). Affective events theory: A theoretical discussion of the structure, causes and consequences of affective experiences at work. *In* B. M. Staw & L. L. Cummings (Eds.), *Research in Organizational Behavior* (Vol. 18, pp. 1–74). Greenwich, CT: JAI Press.

Wittmer, J. L., & Martin, J. E. (2011). Work and personal role involvement of part-time employees: Implications for attitudes and turnover intentions. *Journal of Organizational Behavior, 32,* 767–787.

Yamamoto, H. (2011). The relationship between employee benefit management and employee retention. *International Journal of Human Resource Management, 22,* 3550–3564.

Yanadori, Y., & Kato, T. (2009). Work and family practices in Japanese firms: Their scope, nature and impact on employee turnover. *The International Journal of Human Resource Management, 20,* 439–456.

Yavas, U., Babakus, E., & Karatepe, O. M. (2008). Attitudinal and behavioral consequences of work–family conflict and family–work conflict: Does gender matter? *International Journal of Service Industry Management, 19,* 7–31.

Youngblood, S., & Chambers-Cook, K. (1984). Childcare assistance can improve employee attitudes and behaviour. *Personnel Administrator, 29,* 45–46.

Index

Page numbers in **bold** indicate figures/tables.

The Wiley Blackwell Handbook of the Psychology of Recruitment, Selection and Employee Retention,
First Edition. Edited by Harold W. Goldstein, Elaine D. Pulakos, Jonathan Passmore and Carla Semedo.
© 2017 John Wiley & Sons Ltd. Published 2020 by John Wiley & Sons Ltd.

experience-based interview questions 184
'extended mutualism model', intelligence
    123–4
external recruitment 34–40
extraversion 154, **161**, 163, 165, **166**
extrinsic motivation 81

Facebook 104, 106
factorial keying, biodata 207
Fagan, J. 415, 417
fairness *see also* biases; discrimination; legal
        issues
    applicant reactions 58, 62, 63, 65
    cognitive ability tests 140
    equal employment opportunities 437
    ex-offender candidates/employees 437–8
    interviews 194–5
    selection 77, **79**
    testing process 431–4
faking
    biodata 207–8
    online tests 276–80, 286–7
    personality assessments 164, 173, 279
    self-report data 203
    situational judgement tests 233, 239
    tricking of respondents 208
Fallaw, S. 248
family connections, employees with 17
family-to-work conflict 516–18
feedback, leadership development 355, **367**,
        368, 370
Feinberg, E.G. 436
Felker, D.B. 261
females *see* gender; women in the workplace
feminine traits 380
Fernandez, R.M. 16
Fetzer, M.S. 234, 235, 263, 293–309
FFM *see* five-factor model of personality
Fine, S.A. 206
Finland 390
Fishbein, M. 448
Fisher, C.D. 73
Fiske, S.T. 213
fit, employee retention/turnover 455–6, 460
five-factor model (FFM) of personality 84–5,
        155–6, 314
flexible working 389–90, 519, 521–6, 527–8
Flier, H. van der 411, 413
fluid ability 132, **134**
focused climate, organizational environment
        495, 502–4
Fodchuk, K.M. **96**
Foldes, H.J. 403, 409
Folger, R. 58
Forde, C. 36, **97**, 98

Forsman, J.W. 247–70
Foster, D.F. 277
Freedle, R. 413
French, W.L. 259
Funder, D.C. 153, 187, 190
Funke, U. 345
Furnham, A. 71–90

Galinsky, E. 519
Gallardo-Gallardo, E. **475**
Galliland, S. 53–7, 59, 61, 62, 77, 139
Gallup 477
Galton, F. 154–5
gamification 273, 293–309
    3D animation 300–1
    computer generated animation 300–2
    definition 294
    development/implementation for selection
            297–306
        branding 303
        candidate in-game feedback **295**, 303
        criterion-related approach 297–8, 306
        design 298–303
        duration of game 299
        feedback in-game **295**, 303
        genres 299–300
        legal issues 305
        length of game 299
        linear versus non-linear game play 302–3
        localization 304–5
        measurement model 298
        mobile devices 304
        multimedia style 300–2
        objectives 297–8
        outcome-based scoring 302
        path-based scoring 302
        scoring 302, 306
        security 306
        single versus repeated play 305
        target audience 298–9
        utilization 304–6
    'dustbowl empiricism' 306
    elements of **295**
    future research 306
    knowledge, skills, abilities and other
            characteristics 299, 304, 305
    rationale for using in selection 293, 296–7
    stealth assessment 297
    validity of 306
Ganster, D.C. 529
Garcia, A.M. 53–70
Gardiner, M. 387
Gatewood, R.D. 251
Gaucher, D. 20
gay rights 437

Printed and bound by CPI Group (UK) Ltd, Croydon, CR0 4YY